Every Day, Just Write

Persons interested in the subject matter of this book are invited to correspond with our secretary, c/o GN Press, Inc., R.D. 1, Box 832, Port Royal, PA 17082

Printed in India

GN Press gratefully acknowledges the BBT for the use of verses and purports from Śrīla Prabhupāda's books.

Library of Congress Cataloging-in-Publication Data

Gosvāmī, Satsvarūpa Dāsa
Every day, just write: welcome home to the one big book of your life, Geaglum, Inis Rath, November 14–30, 1996/ Satsvarūpa Dāsa Goswami.
p. cm.
ISBN 0–911233–29–6
1. Gosvāmī, Satsvarūpa Dāsa, —Diaries. 2. International Society for Krishna Consiousness. I. Title.
BL1175.G628A324 1996
294.5'512—dc21 98–5108
CIP

Author's Note

In the autumn of 1996, while finishing one timed book and trying to decide on the form of the next, it occurred to me that everything I write is part of one big book. Although it is good for a writer to think in different genres, it can also be right to admit that he is essentially writing the same book each time he sets pen to paper. That is, a writer is writing his life. While he may express it in one genre or another, it is still his life that he is expressing. In my case, it is as Kerouac stated: "Uninterrupted and unrevised full confessions about what actually happened in life."

When this thought occurred to me about my own writing, I was traveling from Italy to Ireland. By the time I arrived, I had decided to begin a project without end. I would call it *Every Day, Just Write*, and title each segment thematically.

Although each volume of *Every Day, Just Write* was composed individually, due to economic concerns, Gītā-nāgarī Press has chosen to bind the first three volumes, and in future books, a subsequent two or three volumes, together. The very first title in the series, *Welcome Home to the One Big Book of Your Life*, seems particularly right to me. I welcome readers who would like to join me on an open-ended journey. The direction is to Kṛṣṇa, whom the *Vedas* accept as the Supreme Personality of Godhead. I cannot guarantee when I'll "arrive" (back home, back to Godhead), but by the grace of my spiritual master, Śrīla Prabhupāda, I know I won't give up.

Acknowledgments

I would like to thank the following disciples and friends who helped produce and print this book:

Baladeva Vidyābhūṣaṇa dāsa
Bhakta William Webb
Caitanya-dayā-devī dāsī
Guru-sevā-devī dāsī
Kaiśorī-devī dāsī
Keśīhanta dāsa
Kṛṣṇa-kṛpā dāsa
Lalitāmṛta-devī dāsī
Mādhava dāsa
Madhumaṅgala dāsa
Nārāyaṇa-kavaca dāsa
Prāṇadā-devī dāsī
Tulasī-prīyā-devī dāsī
Varuṇa dāsa

Special thanks to Mahā-mantra dāsa, Śāntā-devī dāsī, Prāṇadā-devī-dāsī and Linc Kinnicutt for their kind donations to print this book.

Welcome Home to the One Big Book of Your Life

Every Day, Just Write

Volume 1

Geaglum, Inis Rath
November 14–30, 1996

Satsvarūpa dāsa Goswami

GN Press, Inc.

Contents

November 14, 1996

12:40 A.M., ŚRĪLA PRABHUPĀDA'S DISAPPEARANCE DAY

I want to be real, and writing helps. One devotee wrote me, "Your clarity of service direction has *only* been achieved by deep reflective thought." Yes, that's true. Today is Śrīla Prabhupāda's disappearance day. I want to feel my personal relationship with him in separation. It can't be exactly the same as when Prabhupāda was here, but I shouldn't think that the relationship with him in separation is less than the relationship I had then. The guru-disciple relationship is based on absolute principles, yet it is also subjective and personal. It's also crucial for going back to Godhead. Therefore, I fight to remain on course in my life of writing and *sādhana.*

Ideas are tight-rolled balls. They can be easily relaxed in discussion, these tight buds ready to flower.

I want to live each moment of the day, simultaneously loving life in this world (with Kṛṣṇa conscious insight) and developing attachment and yearning for the spiritual world where the soul goes. Each day reveals this to one who searches, and writing helps create the attitude of discovery.

5 A.M.

Reading *Śrīla Prabhupāda-līlāmṛta* on Prabhupāda's disappearance. It is well written and contains plenty of quotes from those who were present. In those days I would never have dreamed of writing so freely and about myself as I do now. It's another symptom of "craziness" from being separated from him. We have nothing left to do but lament and push on, and we each do it in one way or another, while we all suffer from his lack of presence. Someone says, "Why lament? He's right here with you at all times." Others claim equally, "It's not the same without him." *The Nectar of Devotion* describes how Mother Yaśodā and Nanda Mahārāja had differing attitudes toward Kṛṣṇa's absence. Mother Yaśodā constantly reprimanded Nanda Mahārāja's calm appearance in Kṛṣṇa's absence. She wanted him to do something to bring Him back. Nanda Mahārāja asked, "Why are you acting crazy and disturbing my home? Can't you see that Kṛṣṇa is right here?" Both of them were right—He was there and He was not there.

We should feel something, recall the spiritual master, tell others about him. I'm hoping today that my health will hold up so that I can do just that—go over to the temple, get through the liturgy of songs and worship, and then be able to speak my piece. I will not give the world's greatest speech, I know, and the devotees who hear it will probably not change much. Each of them will still have to contend—the mothers with their children, the sick with their afflictions, the restless with their minds—with themselves. At least I will have made an attempt to glorify Śrīla Prabhupāda. I can feel that much. I too, after speaking, will have to return to my day and its lack of intensity of love in service. Still, I'm not going to write myself off as a non-lover or as an offender. Rather, I'll stay active and read about Prabhupāda, or read his book, then write as I know how.

In my talk I plan to mention that Prabhupāda departed in a perfect way. He was in the perfect place, Vṛndāvana, surrounded by devotees chanting the holy names. He taught the perfect lesson of how to die; he was inspiring and instructive up until his last breath. Even after his disappearance he remains with us in our service in separation. In that way, he is open to everyone.

It wasn't easy for him or for us in 1977. Now we talk about it in a philosophical way, but then it was real raw suffering and grief. Crying, crying, our best friend and guide was gone. Everyone felt it. Then the leaders moved in and to top positions, sincerely, but with some motive, no doubt. They were the chosen ones. I am bitter about it now, myself one of the leaders of those days. I'm gradually backing away from it so I don't commit more mistakes while sincerely trying to maintain and push on his movement. I am pushing on now with the pen and the typewriter, with "wild mind" and honest, unrehearsed feeling.

I want to find again what I actually think. I want to face doubts. This is the time to do these things because these are my last years. Be who you are and then improve. Hare Kṛṣṇa.

Face it: I don't love him, followed by I do love him. I don't believe in Kṛṣṇa, followed by I do believe in Kṛṣṇa. I don't like to read the *Bhāgavatam*, followed by I do like to read the *Bhāgavatam.*

I'm reading a book called *Nourishing Wisdom* about food and attitudes toward food. It teaches that we should not be slaves to any one diet or person insisting that we follow any one regimen. We have to find out what's best for us at each stage of our lives. I cannot apply this principle in the same way in my spiritual life. I follow a regimen and a person who is my spiritual master.

At the same time, the "question authority" attitude can be helpful even in spiritual life, but only up until that time when we find the actual authority. At that point, all that is helpful is surrender. Then in surrender, we strive to get beyond fear and duty to love.

How to discern our actual level of love? We start by admitting our worst. One way to acknowledge "the worst," however, is not open to me. That is, I cannot break the rules or promises I made to Prabhupāda in order to "liberate" myself from taboos. No. The author of the food book tells a story of how he was forbidden to eat bacon by his Jewish upbringing. One day, however, while suffering in many ways in material life, he almost unconsciously went into a cafeteria and ordered a bacon, lettuce, and tomato sandwich. He said it was a happy, liberating experience and that there was no bad aftertaste from it. Of course, he doesn't know that real aftertaste is karma.

11:45 A.M.

Don't wait, just write. Lecture over. I felt loud, strong-voiced, and made gestures, the audience spread left and right in the long room. They didn't *seem* so tuned in; the lecture didn't seem to click. I don't know what it is you feel when it's really good. Questions afterwards weren't to the heart of my lecture at all.

Then outside in the last rich-colored autumn trees and to the quay. Water in bottom of rowboat, and for the second time, I unconsciously dipped the end of my *dhotī* in it. Arjuna pushed off the rowboat and away we went.

It gets rough some mornings in the strait. I tense when the boat rocks.

Looked again at Robert Lax interviewed by Peter France on hermit life. Lax said he's not a hermit, but sought solitude to write.

Peter France asked, "Do you write to discover what you have in mind?"

Lax replied, "More to keep it from getting away. I think that, from moment to moment, I usually know what I have in mind and I also seem to know that five minutes from now I won't be able to rediscover it unless I've written it down. . . . I look back through my notebooks and remember the different things that have happened and read what I said about it at the time, and you won't be surprised to hear that I usually agree with it."

France asked him if there was an element of helping people in his poems and writings.

"Well, yes. I think, first of all, I have this confidence that if I ever manage to clear things up for myself I'll be helping clear them up for some other people, and if I put it in language that I can really understand and find simple enough to communicate to myself . . . then some other people too will be able to pick up on it."

Lax mentioned that he listens to the BBC News broadcasts. France asked if hearing the news made him feel a conflict of moral duty, "to be informed of all the disasters you can do nothing about."

Lax replied, "I just don't think we're ever in a position of being able to do nothing. Because—take an analogy from science—if a man is working on the discovery of penicillin, I think he's right to keep on with his work even if all the cities in the world are falling. He should keep to that work. We'll need some penicillin. I don't think you can rush off with a gun on your shoulder every time there's an alarm. I think if there is destruction and turmoil in the world, people need penicillin. They need any good thing you can produce." *(Hermits: The Insights of Solitude*, edited by Peter France, pp. 200–205)

In preparing for this morning's lecture I found a nice section in the *Līlāmṛta* describing the quiet *kīrtanas* in Prabhupāda's room:

"... Śrīla Prabhupāda would ask that the *kīrtanas* be continued, and he would become silent, as the devotees sang softly, hour after hour: Hare Kṛṣṇa Hare Kṛṣṇa, Kṛṣṇa Kṛṣṇa Hare Hare/ Hare Rāma Hare Rāma, Rāma Rāma Hare Hare. A very small pair of *karatālas*, the only instrument, produced a soft, pleasant ringing. The voices of the chanters were subdued, but their minds were firmly fixed in devotion to Śrīla Prabhupāda and the holy name, concerned that Prabhupāda could hear the *mahā-mantra* without interruption." (SPL, Vol. 6, p. 320)

I read that section during the lecture and added that Prabhupāda taught us the importance of chanting Hare Kṛṣṇa and reading from his books without speculation, and that Prabhupāda would always be with us in the future through this method. Then I described (without naming myself as the subject) an experience I actually felt while chanting in Prabhupāda's presence. I said that sometimes during this chanting, Prabhupāda communicated unspoken feelings to his disciples: "He might simply glance at one of the devotees, but that devotee would feel a surge of loving emotion and realization. Suddenly he would understand better how pure and compassionate Śrīla Prabhupāda was. And the devotee might recall how Śrīla Prabhupāda had come and saved him, bringing him to Kṛṣṇa consciousness." (SPL, Vol. 6, pp. 320–21)

It was good to remember that again. That's what I'm looking for here in Geaglum—I'm trying to recover fresh love for Prabhupāda. I realize, though, that I have to cut through a lot of falsity in myself and also whatever resistance has come into my mind and life, which is perhaps not always my fault, but is created by circumstances. More on that later. It was just nice to see and recall how by being near Prabhupāda, I felt indebtedness and loving exchange.

2:50 P.M., SHED

Black Kerry cows snort as I leave the house, warning me not to trespass on their bit of green turf. Surly ladies, I don't intend to trespass on your land, although I feel challenged by your leader's snorting. I'll walk past you. Head, hold out.

I walked through a wet meadow to get to this shed on the edge of the lake where I am free to write and draw. Ani has built a serviceable desk with both a central and right-hand surface to it. I place the art materials on the right side.

I read in *Nourishing Wisdom* about cravings and sweets. We all have an innate need for sweets, but by positive control, we can stop it from becoming an unwanted habit. The author recommends a "holding technique." If you don't want to yield to a habit, then sit there and experience all the physical and mental aspects of the urge without giving in to it.

The author asserts that a sweet craving is a yearning for "sweetness" (nectar) in one's life, and he thinks that can be fulfilled by listening to music. Nondevotional music is another forbidden sweet for a monk like me. Oh, gosh,

oh, bosh,
it ain't easy.
Boss, you ask me to
give up Henry Adams and
Bob Ribicoff and even Alan
Freed favorites and then Monk
and Miles and Coltrane and
Bach
if I want to find the sweetness in Kṛṣṇa
madhurām—sweeter than biscuits and applesauce
Kṛṣṇa Kṛṣṇa.

"The seven musical notes—*ṣa*, *ṛ*, *gā*, *ma*, *pa*, *dha* and *ni*—are used in musical instruments, but originally they come from the *Sāma Veda*. The great sage Nārada vibrates sounds describing the pastimes of the Supreme Lord. By such transcendental vibrations, such as Hare Kṛṣṇa Hare Kṛṣṇa, Kṛṣṇa Kṛṣṇa Hare

Hare/ Hare Rāma Hare Rāma, Rāma Rāma Hare Hare, he fixes his mind at the lotus feet of the Lord. Thus he directly perceives Hṛṣīkeśa, the master of the senses." (*Bhāg.* 6.5.22)

Nārada muni bājāya viṇā/ 'rādhikā ramaṇa'-nāme. He vibrates the strings, and the devotees sing in response, drowning in the ecstatic nectar.

O Kṛṣṇa, I'll write quickly as the sun goes down, those last rays descending like a desk lamp shining in over my right shoulder. White clouds, punched holes, yellow fret work, blue spaces, and the gray, angry clouds of Lord Śiva. Let it go, Casey.

Like a bucket, water
not ashes (sometimes),
barber shop memories, unconsc.
Slump in batting average.
Gil Hodges down to .250 and below.
Gil,
O God, priest prayed mid-
summer, "May first baseman
Gil resume batting upswing as
he fields with mitt and long
stretch and stride to catch ball."

Gil, good-natured. Tough and big, if need be, against rowdies.

Gil, good Gil should hit .260 at least, if not .275. And homers—30, 40. "Bless him," they prayed.

Purely material desires in summer Ebbets Field.

Purely material desires. O Kṛṣṇa, let Sats rise to the occasion and pour his heart out within the *sampradāya.* Don't break habits and rules, especially the four, and eat warm biscuits and sweet applesauce, sweet *prasāda.*

November 15

12:30 A.M.

Śrīla Prabhupāda outlives his disappearance day. 7:30 P.M. arrives, he "dies," then goes on living. He lives forever, and his followers live with him. He lives on in his *mūrti* and accepts biscuits and applesauce at 7:30 P.M. He's there the next morning to accept his dictaphone from me and to hear the results of the Prabhupāda book distribution marathon. And he lives in me; when I die, I don't die either. You see? Even my poor love, selfish, body-centered stuff, my concealed fear, is not really me. I'm within, beyond the modes of danger and pain.

Feeling restless this morning. A slight warning sign flickers in my head, and I'm afraid to concentrate on any one thing that requires effort. Instead, I write very little, read only two *Bhāgavatam* verses and purports, read a little in my new book, *Memories*, and then stop, forewarned. I proceed at risk. I don't want to go back to bed, but maybe I should.

Restless day after Prabhupāda's disappearance. What am I doing right or wrong?

Two things that came out yesterday while reading *Śrīla Prabhupāda-līlāmṛta*:

1. It's not true, as some harsh critics say, that the *Prabhupāda-līlāmṛta* treats Prabhupāda offensively as an ordinary human being. I consistently portray Prabhupāda as a liberated soul, but as one who manifested human traits to us. There is a good section on this in SPL where Prabhupāda's last months are described. I say that his "dying" was obviously a transcendental experience, yet he taught us ordinary persons by example how we may approach death. I felt reassured against the critics by hearing yesterday's readings.

2. *Śrīla Prabhupāda-līlāmṛta* is an official biography of Prabhupāda's life, and in that sense, it is not my most honest expression of how I feel about him. An example of this was when I described that the dealings with Prabhupāda in his very last days were the most intimate that he allowed us in his life. I said that the only thing that could compare to it was Prabhupāda's association with his first disciples in 1966, but that those who were present then and who were present at the end of Prabhupāda's life said that the later pastimes were the most intimate. I wrote that statement as a concession to the viewpoint expressed by those wonderful servants who were with him at the end, such as Tamāl Krishna Mahārāja, Bhavānanda, and others. It was their opinion that these later pastimes were more intimate than the 1966 ones, and they presented many reasons why this was true. Actually, however, those devotees were not present for the 1966 pastimes. Neither do I, who was there in 1966, concede that for me the later pastimes were more intimate. In fact, for me Prabhupāda

was aloof in the later pastimes, and I was not able to break through the barrier. It was the same barrier that Prabhupāda personally had to break for me in 1966 when he said, "If you love me, then I will love you."

Now I am able to write more freely how I actually feel. Thus my writing can be more honest than the official biography. Nowadays I can still recall memories and go over them in various ways, and I hope to always be doing so. Still, I must work with my immediate life in separation from Prabhupāda, how he is in my life, in my heart—even though in some ways I don't follow some of the externals as strictly as I did when he was here. Let's work at this lovingly and honestly.

2:25 P.M., SHED

Thinking of Bach and how he was given so much ability by Kṛṣṇa to create music. Imagine those times, dancers in garters and knickers, women wearing hourglass gowns and décolletages, and both men and women in powdered wigs. No electricity in those days—

like these days in this house.

Oh, happy day,

the Lord creates in me bubbles and waves of possibility. I can do many nice things in His service.

O my Lord, let me not
fall down.

I remember that Bach's suites often have a variety of movements in them, rondeaux and sarabands, fast dances and slow meditations. I like that image for my writing. A saraband might tell of sad events, a village wiped out by plague or war, or of a dying mother, a simple son betrayed, a candy bar lost, a collie dog who followed someone wherever he went just died (we *all* die), and pain. The story would be told in three or four minutes, the allotted time for sadness before the pace picked up.

You do the same
this pen and others each run out in due course and
you fill 'em up again to
tell the memory—
but forget to bring
a book of poems, a tape
a dictaphone
a bride and groom and
wedding cake and Woody
Allen joke
but Bach had a
harpsichord player and great
violinist to carry on
and finish the concert to the ghosts
in a German king's court who
said, "Old Bach has arrived." He died two hundred years ago and wet leaves now tell the story as they pile up and I speculate on the soul eternal. Bach's soul? Somewhere in a new body.

The Sunday school will tell us what to do. I beseech you, sir, please pray, undo this button.

Minuet, Kṛṣṇa, Kṛṣṇa. We dance the Lord's way—even elephants can prance on tiptoe under bright chandeliers.

Too many gnats in here to dance, and I forgot to bring my *Śrīmad-Bhāgavatam* out here, so I can't tell you how Dakṣa's second set of 1,000 sons were taken by Nārada, who made them saintly and renounced.

Renunciation is superior. Stick to your *āśrama* once and for all.

What? You need to meet your emotional needs? Can we help you meet them in some other way?

There's no joy in stepping down. But judge not and be not judged. Just keep dancing the minuet.

O Bach, you served Kṛṣṇa as "Gott" with fast beats and slow, violins, organs, served Him as a person or in His energy manifested in all things

holy God
who can lift Govardhana
no problem.
He doesn't need any hernia operations
like Madhu, and He has no
headaches but wants us all to return to Him
from this
darkening day of work.
Blow deep
you who are not an angel
old sense-gratifying monk
ask forgiveness for your discrepancies
while sitting near this calm lake.
Give me a verse and I'll lecture simple twice a week,
ridin' the track
a Kṛṣṇaite
I bow and scrape
tow and bow—
and move into the presto movement,
sweating and working and loving through the hollow emptiness of my body
made of flesh, bones, pain—
it all brings
Kṛṣṇa

I seek You, God, and pray to You. Please let me remember to bring the *Bhāgavatam* next time I'm out here and when returning to the house, *if* lights are on, I'll read (and if not, by candle!). Or chant *japa* and be at peace.

I am happiest when in line; pulling the traces of *bhakti*. I am a servant of the Lord, not of the senses and mind. In mantras find God!

November 16

12:45 A.M.

Thinking of a Godbrother who left his duties to satisfy his emotional needs, which he says he has neglected for many years. I don't judge him, but I fear following that path. I pray for protection from my own emotional needs. May they be fulfilled in a Kṛṣṇa conscious way without my having to relinquish duties. I have nothing left in life but to fulfill my obligations—to set a decent example as a *sannyāsī* and spiritual master. I accepted the posts; now I must live with them. I don't feel dissatisfied with the posts but with myself. May Kṛṣṇa protect me.

I want to write in a way that is suitable for ordinary days—usual and common, as an everyday occurrence.

There are everyday occurrences here:
rain,
weeds and rushes on the shore of Lough Erne,
breakfast (Śyāmānanda comes in complete dark and cold by rowboat to cook for me),
lunch.

Everyday wonders. In Zen they say to see wonder in the ordinary. Don't seek exotic twists but ordinary life, free from self-consciousness,
seen from this
everyday common body.

Fantasizing that Allen Ginsberg had a late awakening (in his seventies) that he should give up Buddhism and come to Kṛṣṇa conscious theism. Devotees direct him to me. I show him a poem written about him by Anne Waldman. Then we get down to business, and I see how willing he is, or how possible it is for him, to receive Kṛṣṇa conscious blessings. To do so he must become like a child and accept the authority of *brahma-śabda*.

Common, everyday prayer doesn't have to wait for inspiration or a special awareness of beauty. Do it in your night notes, your evensong,
and whenever you can on legs and feet,
in Wellies,
walking to the shed,
to the beat in your head
with the dictaphone,
measuring the pollen count,
in yesterday's cool and clear and today's spitting rain—
anytime is good.

In winter there are no pleasure boats,
in early summer I have felt more inspired
to write poems from my day's account,
or to draw the boathouse in the distance, the fence poles in the foreground. I can't fail because I believe in the "No-fail school." There is no worst or best in that school.

This rowboat has no leaks, but there's always a little water in the bottom of it. The devotees put a piece of cardboard down for passengers to sit on as they row across, back and forth, from the island to Geaglum Quay.

5:15 A.M.

My unconscious often floats into my conscious. Of course, that happens when I get sleepy sitting in a chair, trying to chant a few more rounds. I wonder if I have abused transference of states from unconscious to conscious through the free-writing. Does that account for my inability to control the mind in *japa* even when I'm awake? I don't usually blame it on the free-writing because it's already been going on. Free-writing looks into what is going on already and then tries wholeheartedly to bring one to a Kṛṣṇa conscious state. I hope for Kṛṣṇa conscious states flowing from the uncontrolled to the controlled. Prabhupāda says we are all innately Kṛṣṇa conscious.

I don't want my Kṛṣṇa consciousness to be simply a matter of reiterating what I just read. It should be more than that. At the same time, I don't mean to make light of what I get from reading. It is primary and called *śravaṇaṁ kīrtanam*.

The truth is eluding me,
the *satyaṁ param*, the *Bhāgavatam*.
Satyā, a girl who married an older man and
no longer writes me, although I'm the guru.
But I am not the guru of her heart. Just as well
because I am somewhat contaminated and we see
most of these Western so-called gurus sooner or
later give up trying and give in to
their psycho-physical natures.

Fortunately I do this in writing
and don't commit worse barbs. This is the worst.
I hope this is the worst. I don't even jog or binge
or pig-out on ice cream and bran muffins
like the nutrition Ph.D. who confessed it
and then told us how to kick such habits
by sitting through them, feeling all the feelings but
not giving in to actually eating
the homemade vanilla ice cream and bran muffins
or whatever it is that makes you cry and
yearn as you sit on your couch and
the fantasies roar over your *gāyatrīs*.
You think going to India would help?

WINTER

No winter here—or at least no snow. In snow you move indoors and slow down. Oxen draw carts over the frozen earth and Japanese haiku priests walk in blinding snow, but all hearts at the hearthside.

Icicles drop from the eaves, and Christmas approaches where people try to overlook bad feelings
in the world
while devotees run out on book distribution
marathon
in heavy coats, music,
Vivaldi's "Winter" playing
over the radio,
reminding people of heavy blankets, coats, a scholar's solitude,
the Lord of Heaven.

Vivaldi's second movement—yes, I remember ice skating with the tune in my head
hearty and healthy
swooning
swooning
then hot chocolate with puff of marshmallow cream
on top.

Icy slopes and fire, the world's music meant to dissuade us from suicide, to wile away our time otherwise,
warming-up, revving.
In winter people rub hands together in prayer, the monks in stone-cold monasteries warmed by the flames of love.

It's cold in Vraja—no heat available.
Cling only to beads and master's words,
Deities warm in blankets
and stylish quilts.

Allegro—rain on green and brown. Can't repent. I belong to the world but have retired until they draft me again and pull me out of solitude. Prabhupāda says that a preacher's life is not easy-going. He has to face obstacles and sometimes pain inflicted by *mūḍhas*.

Oh, I did that when I was younger. Give me days now to write to the Lords of the Boston Common and to the new, almost-born *bhaktas* and *bhaktins* who may wander to this island or get one of my books in the shadow of oaks near Pretoria or in Wisconsin or down some back street while sitting on a wooden back porch in Czech Republic or China or the streets of Tokyo. May I give them what my master gave me: love and *capātīs*, bread balls and chaunced *dāl*, and may they eat it with the whole self by the mercy of God as I both fail and succeed.

2:30 P.M., SHED

Ugly vision of Sharon Olds—sex and torture. It's the world, of course, and Ms. Olds is just seeing it eye-on, from the poet's mold, full of what she identifies as compassion (a big word—three syllables). She's a good woman, I'm sure, but faces life without God. Can't believe in God because He should have stopped the torture. She stops loving Him there and goes on into her own body and mind, striving to belong to, and love, the world incomprehensibly with the tough vision of what it is to belly and eye and

esophagus.

I don't judge her

but I hear my master say that those who don't believe in God, the scientists and other atheists, are the biggest sinners and rascals. That one failure, Rāvaṇa's failure, caused the golden city to lie in ruins and its families to die. Hanumān finished them off or

in this case,

Śiva or Yama.

November 17

12:30 A.M.

I'm a writer, but now I'm sacrificing products in favor of the diary expression. I hope to also go beyond the usual diary concerns of self into writing exercises and toward the deeper self, into life itself, into *śāstra* and the holy name. I don't seem capable now of a concentrated, sustained effort in reading or writing. This is partly due to health. We read of students writing their Ph.D. theses or a writer burning intensely as he creates his novel, etc. I do a little every day in this roomy form. It's also a form. Other things to do, like writing letters, also occupy me.

Just spent about twenty minutes with Cc., Lord Caitanya's expressing direct meaning of *Vedānta-sūtra* to Sārvabhauma.

Brahman means Supreme Brahman. Absolute Truth is both personal and impersonal, but personal is stronger. One must favor direct meaning of *śāstra (brahma-śabda)* over interpretations, inferences, etc. Lord Caitanya is convincing him.

Read it, little man,
and save your soul.

A disciple writes that she is overwhelmed with material misery. She has seen so much suffering and death in her life, and she wants to use the negative energy to push herself from all attachment and to attain the spiritual world. She wants me to instruct her how to make a dramatic leap forward. I don't think I can or I'd be leaping myself. I can only tell her to be patient. She doesn't think she'll make it back to Godhead in this lifetime and fears being reborn into yet another life filled with suffering. Yeah.

She says she's turning to *japa* and sometimes cries out, but at other times loses that feeling. She wants to come to me and pour out all her feelings. I'm no rock to sustain all storms. Neither do I know enough deep suffering experienced with the eye of Vedic wisdom to overcome it right on the battlefield of sorrow. Kṛṣṇa has spared me. I teach what I can, tossed in my own teacup by the slightest storms. Still, we have *śāstra*. We have what Nārada says, what Vyāsa says, and what Prabhupāda says. A wise man doesn't lament for the living or the dead.

We have to turn the ferry around in the water (white-capped waves) and head back in the other direction. Each day from morning to night, sing a little song of sorrow and tepid joy and restrained senses, and hang in there.

3:30 A.M.

Got plans today—if Kṛṣṇa will let me carry them out—to do the introductions for *Sketchbooks of Joy*. I plan to do it this afternoon in the shed if I get the chance. This morning will be taken up by going over to the island and trying to keep myself headache-free before that.

O word-spiller, you've got plenty to do. Flying wedge, lipstick—

no, I don't want to say any old word. Why say "lipstick"? I won't allow such words to influence me, you pit poets. I want to find that holy place above the rooftops, above the influence of this world.

Do you mean find yourself or lose yourself and just repeat scripture with no additions or subtractions? Is that writing at all?

Whatever I mean, just get the words out.

On the way here a few days ago through miles of construction work on the motorway, I jammed my last pages with travel data. Now we are settled in and there is nothing to report except that Abhaya dāsī's daughter has bad asthma and can't even use her inhaler, but breathes shallower with each breath. Her mother thought she would leave her body, but she kept on breathing.

As for me, I've been feeling much better, thank you. Haven't had a bad headache since the day before we left Spain. Maybe I'm getting better and maybe I'm just getting a few good days, but I'm doing what I can with the pain-free time. I still can't leap like Evel Knievel over a chasm in my hundred-mile-per-hour jet-propelled motorcycle (he crashed and broke his bones).

Yes, it's quiet here in Geaglum. We gather together each night at 5 to light candles and sing "*namāmīśvaraṁ sac-cid-ānanda-rūpam.*" After that we read a section of *Nāmāmṛta* and say a few words (we don't record it). The mail will be arriving soon. That's what's going on.

11:25 A.M.

I went strong in the lecture, forgetting my semi-invalid condition. In fact, I've forgotten it for almost a week now, and I'm not even interested in looking at the book *Healing the Body*

I fail, I succeed . . .

Brand him with yellow tilakas.

Heigh ho.

GAURA

To Love means
to Love
KRSNA

Betrayed: A Self-Paced, Self-Guide to Regaining Psychological Control of Your Chronic Illness. It was a Sunday morning Cc. reading with comment. After the half-hour lecture, the devotees' questions were so right to the point that it was enlivening, and I kept going for another fifteen or twenty minutes. Then we continued the mood of speaking *kṛṣṇa-kathā* as we walked from the temple down to the quay. Only when I got back to the house did I notice a tingling starting behind my right eye. I laid down for awhile and it hasn't built much. It's not going away, either—my old friend.

3 P.M.

By Kṛṣṇa's grace that headache went down. Opened the curtains and saw a bright sunny day out there. The trees are all dressed in rusts and reds and auburns and green this time of year. Each tree was carefully planted by rich men cultivating an island paradise in days gone by. Now the trees live in all their glory on this sunny November day.

Today I compiled rough drafts of introductions for the three sections of *Sketchbooks of Joy* and awakened in myself a desire to do more of that artwork with words. All glories to the creative flow that Kṛṣṇa allows us.

I'm dawdling. Madhu wants to talk and pin down the details of our India travels, but the sky is blue and the white outlined clouds rise up from the ground and the sea. The wonderful old trees. Shining sunlight on wet grass blades, the dead weeds. Plenty of gnats still banging around outside—their last days. Howling dogs from another island.

November 18

12:44 A.M.

I'd like to be serious and think of Kṛṣṇa the way a devotee does. Because that's what's needed to go back to Godhead. (Seems like a dwarf trying to catch the moon.) At the time of death—that could be at any moment! Don't waste time.

Living with a handicap. Headache returned yesterday, so I took rest at 6 P.M. Feel okay now, but I've canceled the *Bhāgavatam* lecture. It requires a big effort to speak like that, and it threatens the entire day. Better I move along in reading and writing and honor the day in a sincere output of words and drawings. Hare Kṛṣṇa.

3:50 A.M.

It seems I'll never forget the body as long as I'm living in it. And all the literary allusions and confessions, what I thought about during *japa* (and even in the bathroom), chewing on the same thought again and again. I let it come and told myself that we need safety valves sometimes to let off the pressure.

Prabhupāda said that his duty was to draw us to him in love. He lectured in Vṛndāvana and told us that in Vraja, all entities are individual but have one common purpose: to satisfy Kṛṣṇa. He said it dramatically, as an orator, in the outdoor *kīrtana* hall, until the bell rang nine. At the end, he said, "The guru should not cheat his disciples. *Gurur na sa syāt.*"

Later, I heard him lecturing on Ṛṣabhadeva entering a forest fire created by the wind. He said it was just like we sing each day in "*Gurvāṣṭakam,*" *saṁsāra-dāvānala*. As he lectured on that, I thought, "When I have to lecture, I can remember these techniques and ways to shift to vital topics regardless of the topic of the verse." He said he saw a fire high on a hill in some station in India. No one wanted it to start, and no one could put it out until the "mercy rainfall" came.

My words, my . . . firecrackers. Finger burnt off words that lose control. Now preach and lecture and tell us, dogmatic saint, what you really mean. I mean to be in favor of Kṛṣṇa consciousness and never against it, but we speak honestly and sometimes you may think I'm putting down ISKCON or worse, our master, when really, I can't do that. I'm only trying to dig under the official surface. Sometimes worms squeeze out or roaches escape, or even mice or rats have been known to . . . And I want to return to safety, singing, "*kṛṣṇa he . . . rakṣa mām, pāhi mām*"—please save me and protect me. Ten minutes per round, "Please accept me" is all we pray.

Again my words, not Zimmer's or Duncan's, or anybody's. Not my Daddy's, "My mind is in the sewer." Not my

Mommy's, "Oh Stevie, don't suck around. Ask straight for what you want."

I want a small billiard table like the kid next door has.

And what else?

A chocolate rabbit for Easter, and whatever else you can get, maybe from Jimmy Duncan. Get me a blue Schwinn tricycle with chain action so I can ride up and down 76th Street and dare (Romapāda Swami must have similar memories) to go to 77th Street—strange territory where they never saw this tow-haired kid racing on an expensive tricycle past their houses. They didn't catch me, I went so fast on three wheels. I circled and went around back to 76th Street where everyone knew me in knickers and straight blonde hair, a skinny kid with a father in the Pacific during World War II.

My word, not my sister's. "Stevie, you *are* a jerk."

No, she didn't say that. Or maybe she did. I don't remember. She said, "The truth hurts, doesn't it?" She harpooned, I recall, and cried sometimes, her sweet face.

There now, cuts on your fingers.

I am saying this to you. This is an old memory. Not my words but the words of the *Vedas* and how my spiritual master spoke them in N.Y.C. Yeah, I got that memory too. And bad ones I can't print.

Therefore, I had better sober up.

For looking at poets we fine you and curse you.

Make it tough.

No, make it your own expression of praise of God. If you don't, you'll be killed and smashed to pieces. Why don't you love the Supreme? Because you were contaminated in the past? Then why do you go back and plug into it again? That's what I'm asking. Why don't you do like the strict brothers claim to do and think only of Kṛṣṇa and ISKCON and stay on the computer and get faxes on how to manage this big movement and get the deviants in line and fight back and raise money? We've got enough to do without plugging into our pre-ISKCON past, don't we?

There is no angel, there is no devil, there is no myth. I hear and repeat what Ṛṣabhadeva said. He walked into a forest which burnt His own body to ashes. He did that of His own volition.

There is a spider sitting on the saffron painted wall. This is here and now. What about the spider? He has four legs on each side. Or rather some are both feelers and legs, and they encircle his body, the limbs coming out like rays or the points of the compass. He gets around and he distracts me. I was talking about Ṛṣabhadeva. You want varieties. I want the honest truth paved. Lay it down.

So Kṛṣṇa consciousness is like that. You can't keep your thoughts straight. All you can do is keep moving on.

Then how Kṛṣṇa conscious can you be?

It depends on your love. You have to receive mercy or you'll stay in the fire of matter. Unless you get at least a drop of the mercy, you cannot know God. The nondevotees would reject all this as mythological. You have to know by now that you will never be appealing to nondevotees. You are writing for devotees, but their number is increasing by the distribution of Prabhupāda's books and other preaching endeavors. You take advantage of it (as the spider takes advantage of the wall) and write for the audience who knows Kṛṣṇa. That's my virtue, that I stay within the Kṛṣṇa conscious context. I am a spider, a spiderman. I stay within the walls and have safety valves (new word and concept) to let me feel emotions without going outside the four rules. My emotions sometimes soar like blues horns and drums, and my pulse beats time. My life turns more to prayer, yes, prayer. Please accept me as I chant.

7 A.M.

Manu, on his way out to sell paintings for days at a time (in his car which appears to be falling apart), left me with a letter. He said, "I'm sure you know more than me how valuable these days are coming up to the end of the year again. It seems like a good opportunity for you to, with abandon, launch into your most important service to Kṛṣṇa, Śrīla Prabhupāda, the Vaiṣṇavas, and the greater community, and we need you fit and healthy for that. Today should be a good day, and I am praying you'll be healthy and ready. Please keep me informed on the conditions in the hut or in the room so I can respond."

I wrote him back that as yet I haven't been deeply into writing. But yes, the last days of the year are special.

8:13 A.M.

Shed windows completely iced over—can't see out. Ground covered in white frost, amazing red-pink clouds close to ground and going right up against blue and white sky background. Called Madhu to take a photo of it, but he wasn't in his room.

Read *Gītā*—what Kṛṣṇa says. Manu wrote to me regarding the place of women in society—they should be subordinate. I make no comment, say I agree. All I said last night was that if there's an aloud reading in the temple and a book is passed around, why can't women take a turn reading?

Cold
necklace
more words—

let's warm up by reading *Bhagavad-gītā* aloud and hear what Kṛṣṇa says while I write. Otherwise, what's the point? It's all crap and speculation—no good no matter how racy or whatever—human, how *human* it is.

Kṛṣṇa is great. He's the source of twenty-one patriarchs, seven sages, four Kumāras, and all the Manus.

Do I believe that? It sounds so much like Indian mythology. I thought He was a universal God. Do we have to insist on twenty-five patriarchs?

Yes, I'm afraid we do. They come from Garbhodakaśāyī Viṣṇu, and you can't deny Him or you'll end up denying Kṛṣṇa. Believe it, man, it's the *śāstra*. Don't think you can be an eclectic fool with your intelligence stolen by *māyā*.

Be Vedic all the way. Put it on your T-shirt: Kṛṣṇa is the source of all.

Church organ—I remember—and Win B. moving loafered feet across the wooden things to play, me beside him, sound emanating all around us in the Dutch Reformed Church. God, Lord of hosts, You are honored and praised directly we hope by this exercise of moving fingers up and down the keys.

This hut is clean and the floors are unvarnished. The desk has "merry eye" knots. I can't see out the frosted panes, but I know there's a sun out there to melt the ice and give us sight.

Kṛṣṇa plays His flute, and the demigods are amazed. He doesn't crash down the scale on a rolling organ solo,

crying pax

pax, but when I think of it, the bishops and cardinals, their thirteenth-century scepters—a different world.

I go alone to better follow.
Light of sun breaks frost prisms
into hundreds of white shards
with yellow and a hint of purple
soon to drip.

Your problem, sir, is that you want to be yourself, but you want to be Kṛṣṇa conscious, right? And Kṛṣṇa consciousness means to follow. Rohiṇīnandana asked, "Can you be an original thinker in Kṛṣṇa consciousness?" Yes and no. You can think originally how to present the old in the best way. For me the question is, "Can you be yourself and be a Kṛṣṇa conscious person?"

Do you want to dance?

No, not with a dame close and sexy. I want to dance in *kīrtana* in my own way, but I have a bad ankle.

The fact is, twenty-five patriarchs means you rule out all other cultural religious systems and say that they are at best shadows and offshoots of the original *Vedas*. Twenty-five or forty-five million years ago. Whatever it was it's still good.

I have to uphold this. Say I don't know everything about the universe. I don't know, but I accept *śāstra*. I'm a plain self. No other music or culture required. Okay.

11:25 A.M.

While massaging Prabhupāda I heard him lecturing in Vṛndāvana, November 30, 1976. His lecture had mostly been about the fire of repeated birth and death and how it can't be put out by an ordinary fire brigade. It takes Kṛṣṇa's mercy delivered through the spiritual master. At the end of his lecture he spoke about how envious persons are like snakes who bite even inoffensive creatures. Similarly, cruel persons attack even devotees who are faultless. The "very good example" is Jesus Christ, who was crucified although his only fault was that he was speaking of God. Lord Nityānanda continued to give mercy to Jagāi and Mādhāi even after they hit Him and drew blood. " . . . therefore a preacher devotee is so, I mean to say, favorite to Kṛṣṇa. They have to meet actually dangerous persons, *krūraḥ* persons. . . . It is not very sitting idly, comfortably, and discuss *Vedānta*. No. It is not like that. Preaching practically. Practically meeting dangerous position because sympathetic. . . . *Para-duḥkha-duḥkhī*. . . . He meets Jagāi-Mādhāi class and faces all kinds of danger. Therefore he is the powerful, authorized agent of Kṛṣṇa."

While I listened, at first it sounded ordinary—the same examples I've heard before. But by accumulation, when he got to the end of his lecture I asked myself, "What about me?" What preaching am I doing? And then I thought of my headaches and I wondered if someday I can be more active. I thought of those who are active now, especially the book distributors.

2:28 P.M., SHED

Do you not want to write? Sorry you're not a preacher? Not a Kṛṣṇaite alive with the flame of love? Just poking along (with hurting left ankle)? Missed the touch of gratitude, joy, etc.? Eat too much pasta?

Private thoughts to set into a private log.

M. says our plane to India is booked for January 3 from London; we leave here January 1. So there, I'm not sitting idly. Today I insisted that even though we don't have money, we must arrange to go to the Caribbean in early '97. So there, I am a moving preacher.

Ṛṣabhadeva sat in one place like a python; to keep inimical persons away, He smeared his body with His own stool. Śrīla Prabhupāda said that if people disturb us too much we can sit down in one place, but even then *yāre dekha, tāre kaha 'kṛṣṇa'-upadeśa*. People will come and we should preach to them. If I stay for some weeks at Inis Rath, the mail will find me and I will preach through my responses. Oh, and set an example—I won't fall down, I'll remain attracted to my *japa*, I'll read Prabhupāda's books. Many are counting on me to lead them, so I can't fall down. That's even more important than how many miles I travel and how many lectures I give, or how much I huff and puff.

And of course, my writing is preaching because it helps others. Although I write mostly for myself, when others read it, it helps them find their own truths in Kṛṣṇa consciousness. If I write what's important and meaningful to me, then others will relate it to what's important and meaningful to them. That's my faith.

The pied piper. Peter Pan collar. Mary Martin singing in this world, swinging back and forth on a cable, "I'm flying!" And I am looking to the other world, fighting for faith.

Rowboat makes its way across
I only see small silhouette
of person rowing.

Time about up. White paper, blue gloves—colors I see. Noise outside nearby. Sounds like a machine loading or pushing something in this place where I expect all to be quiet. A good day it's been so far despite the lull and the depression about my purpose. I heard Prabhupāda say the devotee-preacher is best as I poured warm, clear water on his bare body, my Prabhupāda.

Little concerns of my life here. "Oh, write with abandon," he suggested. On wood desk, with feet on floor, write.

Words slip away with the clock.

As I walked back from the shed I saw the Ireland *saṅkīrtana* van. It was parked right on the path where I walk. The doors were open and music poured out, "*saṁsāra dāvā . . .* " with electric bass and singing voices. Some men were inside cleaning it out and singing along with the tape. All the doors were open, but I walked by at such an angle so they wouldn't see me. I hesitated, thinking maybe I should play the friendly old senior devotee and go over and chat with them, but somehow I kept walking. Then I saw one of the *bhaktas* coming out from the warehouse with a big stack of books in his hands. We made friendly eye contact, but I kept walking, wishing a little I had stopped to talk so that a little of their energy could rub off on me. And to show that I was friendly, to get out of the hermit mood and somehow be able to say to myself, "I talked to some *saṅkīrtana* men. I'm not so bad." But as I kept walking toward Manu's house where I have my own room, it seemed I had done the right thing. I shouldn't be so dissatisfied with my own lot. They have their *saṅkīrtana* life as *brahmacārīs* distributing books and I have my life. They're both okay.

> I find it wholesome to be alone the greater part of the time. To be in company, even with the best, is soon wearisome and dissipating. I love to be alone. I never found the companion that was so companionable as solitude. We are for the most part more lonely when we go abroad among men than when we stay in our chambers.
>
> — "Solitude" from *Walden*, p. 135, H.D. Thoreau

November 19

12:30 A.M.

"By the mercy of the Lord, all truths were revealed to Sārvabhauma Bhaṭṭācārya, and he could understand the importance of chanting the holy name and distributing love of Godhead everywhere." (Cc. *Madhya* 6.205)

You might think a *bhakta* could write a more ecstatic diary than this one. He would be making discoveries in his inner life and becoming a changed man. He would be crying for Kṛṣṇa, realizing that Kṛṣṇa and His name are nondifferent—and record it all in his diary. Or he would record his preaching adventures. This diary is quieter, more "static," telling of my asking Aniruddha to build bookshelves for my room and to please put a lock on the shed door. Let me show the virtue of patiently accepting the life that has been given to me so generously by the Supreme Lord *(kāla)*. Or at least show that I am sorry I couldn't be better.

"Śrī Caitanya Mahāprabhu said, 'Today I have conquered the three worlds very easily. Today I have ascended to the spiritual world.'" (Cc. *Madhya* 6.230)

Please write here—the emptiness of heart. And this:

"But anyone who is specifically favored by the Supreme Lord, the Personality of Godhead, due to unalloyed surrender unto the service of the Lord, can overcome the insurmountable ocean of illusion and can understand the Lord. But those who are attached to this body, which is meant to be eaten at the end by dogs and jackals, cannot do so." (*Bhāg.* 2.7.42)

From the purport: " . . . and unless there is knowledge of God, all advancement of material civilization, however dazzling, should be considered a failure."

3:58 A.M.

I have a book here called *Rooms: American Writers Recall Rooms They Have Lived In.* This could be a spark for me to write about rooms—my memories of the places in and out of ISKCON in which I have lived for the past fifty years. A sequel to *Memories.* Why? Because a writer has to keep writing.

Which rooms *have* I lived in? I won't tell of that room I lived in for fourteen years from 1948 until I went into the Navy in 1962. I don't expect to live in any room in my whole life for as long as I lived in that attic boy's room, but it's a place of shame and lonely passions, of blindness when I didn't know self or spirit and gradually passed through innocent, dumb childhood to adolescence. I was a "rebel-without-a-cause" type stinking kid following whatever trends were prevalent and cowering in my dreams, hoping to become popular or at least not discovered for what I was. And what was that? I didn't know, but it frightened me nonetheless. Lived there for my P.S. 8 and Tottenville High School days (class 57–1), and even through my days at college.

That room still seeps through into my memories. I can't pretend that 26 Second Avenue is the only room in my life and that the room at 125 Katan Avenue counts for nothing. Still, when I went back to look at my old house, I felt dispossessed. Some other Staten Islanders live there now, and it's their home. The old Guarino was a stranger and unwelcome. I no longer counted there, not even if my hand is still imprinted in the cement walk from when they poured the concrete in 1952. It doesn't count. I have moved on, so move on.

Besides, what a strange creature I have become. A Hare Kṛṣṇa? No, you can't go back upstairs to look at your old bedroom. It's completely different now anyway, so just forget it. Your memories are dead. You won't even find them stuffed into the closet.

I don't seem able to write much right now—can't concentrate. Waiting for later when a topic jumps at me, something to talk about as the sun rises and I'm in the shed. Or maybe it will be just the same. Nothing. A few words and then I stop. I look at a book, think of something else, then assure myself, "This little bit was good. It doesn't have to be so much."

Is this the running down of the clock for me? Is it? Or just that I want to write of the best thing but cannot? Back to packing for India: earplugs, Kleenex, note pads (will you be able to write more there?), Post-its—I don't know what else. It's the mixture and too much hankering for a better form. Anyway, here is the morning black: outside wind rushing against the house like a football tackle and we are all right.

9:20 A.M.

My interest flared this morning with the plan to write memories of places where I have lived. "The whole world is home." After resting for half an hour after breakfast, however, the idea seemed less alive. So I've accepted it that way. If it wants to come and direct me, it will. Otherwise, I can wait until the end of December when Baladeva will visit and we will churn memories. Back to this diffuse diary where I sometimes bang against the wall and ask, "What's the use?" It's all right, though, most of the time. I'm not writing a structured book, so no one should expect that. That was part of the thrill of the "Everywhere Is Home" project. It would be a book (i.e., publishable), not a diary.

Rainy, windy day. White caps breaking like rolling waves in the strait between Geaglum and Inis Rath. Still the rowboat travels over the water when the devotees want to go back and forth. I thought I wouldn't go out to the shed because the weather was too rough, but if I start that habit, I'll *never* get out. I can expect frequent weather like this.

Little red spider, get off my page. Go walk on the desk. Me, write along. Pain. Don't stop regardless. I'd like to be serious, keep reading *śāstra*, and praying. I don't want to splay my energies. That may be another reason not to do the memories project. I didn't feel it for direct, prayerful Kṛṣṇa consciousness. Can't say the free-write diary is more so, but it's what it is. It doesn't lead the way; it follows.

There's a quail nest near the path. The large and small quails fly up at my approach. Kṛṣṇa, Kṛṣṇa.

Kṛṣṇa, I laid down in a hotel bed in New Delhi. I put my head under the faucet and relieved a headache. I saw a rat in the lobby late at night scurrying under chairs and sofas. I rode in a taxi. I rode in a devotee's van, heard what they were doing in Delhi, and asked, "What Swamis are in town?" And we planned to go to Vṛndāvana the next morning after giving the lecture, provided I felt well enough to travel.

Those are real memories and real places.

Kites and bombs in Delhi tenements. That rooftop room the temple president lets us use. The old lady who has the key but doesn't like to be wakened early. Yellow teeth people have (some have none).

That's Delhi and this is here. I see two swans managing to stay afloat on the rocking waters. The island trees are all a dark, greenish-gray by now, and they provide a skyline like a low-lying hill, rising up on both sides and forming a peak. Reminds me of Govardhana Hill. The four or five tallest trees on the island seem to be some kind of evergreen. They say there are redwoods there too. And deer, big hares, inbred. They try to keep the wild creatures out of the building.

From here I can also see the brown weeds blowing on Geaglum's shore and mats of green grass flattened by the rain. The brown weeds flutter like a flag. They think it's cold here, but it's nothing compared to America's winter.

Boat. Matter. Sense perception. Is that all? I dig with the pen and come up with—? Listen, what did you read? About *buddhi-yoga*. It's definitely true. *Bhagavad-gītā* 10.10–11 says the poor, less advanced devotee can get the Lord's direct mercy even if he fails to comprehend the knowledge given by guru and *śāstra*. That's what it says. But he must be pure and work for Kṛṣṇa in love.

My wrist strains too much with the skinny Pilot pen. Need my big pens out here, except they leak.

Oh, Sārva got happy and the Lord too. The Lord's already happy, but His bliss increased as He danced and touched the converted Sārva. "I was like an iron bar from reading too many books on logic, but You have melted me." Eat the *prasāda* with full faith in Jagannātha. Devotees laugh to see him so changed. The joke is on him, but he doesn't mind.

You were in Kansas? Yes, and Detroit. Govardhana dāsa, stained pillow, Deities in attic, rock song, "Where Rādhā-Kṛṣṇa Kiss." What happened to all those devotees? Rudra-sampradāya, magician, black arts. I know I'm not making sense. Mahābuddhi and me, the-*sannyāsī*-in-charge babysitter, Atreya said. Memories of rain streaking down windows.

10:45 A.M.

I say I want to break through. Maybe I can. M. said, "If you keep practicing at something, you can learn things." Is it not true of this searching from the little life what to say? *Keśava dhṛta-mīna-śarīra, jaya jagadīśa hare.* I play the typewriter while Prabhupāda sings *Daśāvatāra-stotra* and the waters lap roughly, rippling, while twigs and leaves shake on the trees. The wind is stormy, but the sky blue-gray. I ate a full bowl of *halavā* while the storm buffeted outside. Śyāmānanda rowed over and when I asked, "How did you manage it?" he laughed and said, "This is nothing. This is not a really bad storm. They are yet to come." Then while I ate he paced outside the house chanting *japa*.

The true, the naive artist, the dejected. He doesn't want to be comfortable for a month and a half but should produce something. Well, what? My head is on the platter. I mean, I get headaches. It's hard to be always peaceful. Some artists work feverishly for years and produce many brilliant paintings, then drop out all together. I want to be a better devotee and work for that production. I walked to the shed and that's all—a simple life.

"What does he do all day?"

"He's a writer."

"Oh? What's he writing? A novel? A collection of his memories in ISKCON?"

"No, he just goes out there and writes what he sees and feels. He knows that isn't much or even enough, but he feels it's what he should do and there is nothing else."

The rat carries Gaṇeśa; the bull, Śiva; Garuḍa, Kṛṣṇa; the swan, Brahmā. Kali-ghat artists are reviewed by the sophisticated Indian who considers all that mythology. What the hell *does* he believe? He thinks he's some kind of hot-shot critic. The British are gone and he wants the world to appreciate Indian culture, that's all. Culture, not religion, mind you. He doesn't know Kṛṣṇa consciousness. Well, I want to be a Kṛṣṇa conscious artist and depict Kṛṣṇa in some way.

My old “friend”.

Book distributors loading up.

Beginning of the December book distribution marathon.

Simple life.

Heaven is open and rain's pouring in.

If it fades, we'll pray on beads.

I talk of breaking through and here is the moment to do it. I don't bite my fingernails or do anything wrong. I just move through the day. M. will soon take my passport to the Indian embassy in Dublin to have it stamped for a visit to India. Right now, however, it's the dregs. I sit around and look at a book on art—pictures done by Kali-ghat artists and outsider art. And me? I'm an outsider too, or a half-insider to ISKCON.

I once sat in Great Kills station and smoked a cigarette for the first time (thirteen, fourteen years old). L&M and Marlboros were just coming out. Winstons, Chesterfields, and Kools were already popular. Then years later I sat and was identified as a devotee with the rest. I don't know what to tell you. I worked entirely on the things that had to be done and never on my inner life. Everything had to have an immediate purpose for the *saṅkīrtana* movement, for the temple preaching, or I wouldn't express it. In terms of writing, I was either editing for the Swami or writing for *Back to Godhead.* I wouldn't be caught dead writing an extensive diary (or even a single word) like this. What if my wife found it and called it *māyā*? "What would Prabhupāda say? What would your Godbrothers say? This is *māyā*! You are idle. You are speculating. You should do more active preaching. This is the mind. We are meant to do preaching like pure devotees. What if I told Prabhupāda you were doing this?" Thus I would be chastised.

Now I give into it, the urge to tell what I am, what I am doing. I have broken free from the mooring. I am lost in the wet, blowy air. I seek to find my bearings and to tie the boat to the right dock. This is what I mean to do.

Crying shame. He got his *dhotī* wet and dirty from walking in the air. Saffron sweat pants also got smudges on them. He was walking down the path, but there was a construction machine at work, and a devotee, so he backed away, looking for privacy. Busy little doings at Geaglum. He wanted his own world, so he walked in the opposite direction and came here to say this. Kṛṣṇa, Kṛṣṇa! He chanted loudly—loud and clear—and the rain beat against his eyeglasses. When it hurt, cold, he chanted at that time. Dear Lord, please allow me to serve my master. He is kind to me.

First sight of snow. It's driving horizontally due to the wind. I don't think it will stick on the green grass, though, but I can see it blowing across the fence posts with their two strands of barbed wire, in from the lake. From here I can see the boathouse where Abhaya dāsī's family lives. She's been away for several days now in the hospital with her asthmatic daughter.

Hearing cars come and go, I anticipate the delivery of the mail pack that went from U.S.A. to France and was re-routed (I hope) to reach us here.

I could go with M. to America and mix and preach in the temples, but I don't want that. Then face the quiet alone here. I think, "But how am I making my time worthwhile?" Improve it. Read more. Pray to Kṛṣṇa to reveal to you how to be.

Magpies in black and white
formal dinner suits, waiting
on lawn, snowflakes wetter.

Copper leaves still on tree by lake. Shore lined with tan, plume-headed weeds.

Kṛṣṇa Kāliya—see Him there?

2:40 P.M.

My dear Lord Kṛṣṇa, please let me cry to You for mercy. I read the purport aloud (Bg. 10.12–13) how You are the Supreme. It struck me, and I felt the dirty, unclear things in my heart move about. Let me write to reach You. Let me do everything I can to reach You. And to save myself. Prabhupāda says we must become *akiñcana*, free of all material desire for sense enjoyment. I have to earn the right—we have to earn the right—to cry for pure Kṛṣṇa consciousness by recognizing our lack of it.

Kṛṣṇa can be known only by devotional service. Let that information penetrate. Only then will we automatically want to distribute it, this secret of all secrets. When I go to the shed, I pray by reading-crying aloud from Kṛṣṇa's words, *Bhagavad-gītā*.

"Please tell me in detail of Your divine opulences by which You pervade all these worlds." (Bg. 10.16)

Then tell us of the lake chill, the water bucket, and give us words, and more words while Madhu backs the van into its winter shelter. Practice *bhajana* throughout the day and don't waste time. "O Kṛṣṇa, O supreme mystic, how shall I constantly think of You, and how shall I know You? In what various forms are You to be remembered, O Supreme Personality of Godhead?" (Bg. 10.17)

It's almost too dark to read, although it's only 3:05 P.M. Clouds are scudding by like big gray fleece blankets over the island. Reminds me of how quickly water moves on the Tuscarora after a spring rain.

Mail may not come, it could even be lost—all those people who wrote me. In any case, I can read the *Gītā* and finish that Cc. chapter where Sārva is happy and Gopīnātha Ācārya is happy and they are dancing and laughing and clapping, celebrating that Sārva has become a pure Vaiṣṇava. Yes, because of his relationship with Gopīnātha Ācārya, who is dear to Lord Caitanya, Sārvabhauma Bhaṭṭācārya has received drops of mercy from the ocean of love of God. He is ecstatic. *Vairāgya-vidyā-nija-bhakti-yoga*. Pray for that to happen to you.

NIGHT NOTES

Prabhupāda assures us that we can be with Kṛṣṇa and the spiritual master by sound. Don't stress exclusively seeing. Kṛṣṇa is with us in the chanting of Hare Kṛṣṇa and in His teachings in *Bhagavad-gītā*. I read this in *Nāmāmṛta* tonight to four devotees gathered for the Kārttika candle lighting. I was impressed to hear it. Suddenly I remembered how I heard Bill Clinton give his acceptance speech earlier this month. I was in Italy and picked it up on short-wave radio. In the same way, spiritually, we can be with Kṛṣṇa by the "radio" of our chanting and hearing. It's not just us chanting, but Kṛṣṇa is with us if we want Him. Serve by chanting.

I wrote earlier today that I wanted to break through. I meant breaking through to freer writing, more honest, or whatever. The breakthrough is to touch Kṛṣṇa, to write without any reason other than to please Him, to swim spontaneously in *kṛṣṇa-kathā.*

Reading more will help, and I will naturally want to write what I read. Not forced but spontaneously. Not forced . . . Hare Kṛṣṇa.

Lord Caitanya wanted to go on a tour of South India with just one *brāhmaṇa* assistant. He loves His devotees, but wants to spread Kṛṣṇa consciousness and deliver the people of the South. That was also part of His mission.

Kṛṣṇa, Kṛṣṇa, You dove into the Yamunā and displaced the water one hundred yards onto the banks as if something very heavy had fallen into the river. And indeed it had, because You are the source of all strength.

Hare Kṛṣṇa, Kṛṣṇa Kṛṣṇa. Let His pastimes become my reality. Hare Kṛṣṇa.

What about the desire to become a literary artist in His service? Kṛṣṇa can instantly make me the best artist. I don't have to learn art in some other way. He gives the ability and the memory and intelligence so that I can go to Him. What art do I want anyway but the art of serving and pleasing Him? I want to convey that to readers and know it myself—the art of pleasing Kṛṣṇa.

November 20

12:58 A.M.

Read of Lord Caitanya who is sometimes like a rose and sometimes like a thunderbolt. I am happy with the simple and quiet routine here although sometimes I feel it's lacking. I may want more outer excitement and action or feel guilty that I'm not "out there" preaching directly, but circumstances bring me here at the end of the year. Let me cherish the time and use it well. Now my "mantra" is to gradually increase my reading of Prabhupāda's books and to stay focused in Kṛṣṇa consciousness. Writing will follow this direction naturally. I also want to look for opportunities to pray and call out to Kṛṣṇa, to ask for His help, "Please accept me. Please engage me in Your service."

By His grace, my headaches haven't been coming for a week now. Rejoice in quiet way to use time productively. When you're not able to do that, accept the shutdown of activities and go on serving and praying in another way.

Please, Lord, I don't want to be splayed out in interests that aren't directly Kṛṣṇa conscious. I want to be a devotee who thinks only of Kṛṣṇa, studies the scripture, restrains the senses, thinks of the welfare of others, and distributes the holy names.

Can I write beyond myself and my diary? Yes. I was cold last night, or my body was. I put on a sweatshirt and some socks, then later woke up and took them off again. The hot water bottle placed in my bed for warmth wasn't warm enough, but then I felt too warm. Dreamt I was obliged to go for counseling. Long waits in office. No apparent benefit, yet I was considered handicapped. Dined with the woman who was my counselor, although she'd been on the job only three weeks. I went to the cashier but couldn't remember what I'd eaten. I began to cry and hoped they would see that I was absorbed in higher thoughts, and that's why I forgot what I'd ordered. Still, the incident proved I was in need of help. (The counselor had asked, "Are you feeling pain?" "No, not today.") After this I was told I'd be dropped off at the Philadelphia Airport. I looked forward to spending the night in the Mt. Airy ISKCON temple, even though it was snowing, snug in the family of devotees.

I've said I would go once a week to visit Rādhā-Govinda in the afternoon. Today is the disappearance day of Gaurakiśora dāsa Bābājī and tomorrow is Ekādaśī. I ought to go on one of these days and write notes while there.

Mundane poets—can they help? It seems to help me to read a poem and then springboard off it into writing one of my own, but lately I haven't had the interest to discipline myself into writing separate poems.

This started out with a question: "Can I write beyond myself?" Yes, I say, I can, but I know I told you about needing to put on a sweatshirt and socks. Now I'll tell you how I rankle in my prose and wonder what to do. I can think of Śrīla Gaurakiśora dāsa Bābājī, the spiritual master of Śrīla Bhaktisiddhānta Sarasvatī, but he's far, far beyond my comprehension. Therefore, I can only be simple and pray to him from my position not inclined to *tapasya* or devotion. From my position of wishful thinking.

Yes, I *can* go beyond my petty self. I can chant and be with Kṛṣṇa and realize the self as spirit soul.

Muffins, betoward,
pennants, cold days
winter comin' in.
Be here now—your body
can't last: Everyone dies.
Don't think you are
better than someone who has died.
We who are here now will be swept away by Time
like peas on a plate.
Kṛṣṇa! Kṛṣṇa! Please save me.

Kṛṣṇa, Kṛṣṇa. Chant nine rounds. Help yourself. Be your own best friend to body and soul and mind. What? You don't always know how to care for yourself? You are not able to do the right thing? You are not enough of a hero and can't reach out to heroically save others? Well, crawl along the earth then. Be kinder, nonviolent, and walk twice a day out to the shed or down the road to the quay where dirty-looking foam gathers in from the lake.

The lake—the cold, dark sheen on the water, moved only by the breeze. O my great God, You give us life. I shouldn't complain or rebel against You, but pray to You. Please, as I am reborn in my next life and can't remember this one, please don't let me forget You. I am forced to live in the now and I have a human body, which is precious. Please don't allow me to cultivate attachment to this world. Twice in recent lectures I heard Prabhupāda say that if we have even a pinch of material desire, we are not qualified to enter the spiritual world. I also read recently how pure devotees are not interested in going back to Godhead, but in serving Kṛṣṇa.

"Therefore, of the five types of liberation, the first four (*sālokya*, *sāmīpya*, *sārūpya* and *sārṣṭi)* are not so undesirable because they can be avenues of service to the Lord. Nonetheless, a pure devotee of Lord Kṛṣṇa rejects even these types of liberation; he only aspires to serve Kṛṣṇa birth after birth. He is not very interested in stopping the repetition of birth, for he simply desires to serve the Lord, even in hellish circumstances." (Cc. *Madhya* 6.268, purport)

3:40 A.M.

I don't like to disappoint readers by always complaining or by writing too much that I'm not able to write. It's just that gremlin trying to convince me that I'm no good. I'm sure it gives readers the impression that this writer is never able to write but is only able to talk about it. What can I do? I seem to have to say it again and again. At least I as a reader don't mind reading it provided it's real. I seem to be grieving for something. You can take it as spiritual, authorial bleeding. I mean, because I haven't chosen a more structured form, and because I think what I am writing can't be published, I have to question the purpose of it.

It comes down to having faith in the writing process both for purification and for preaching. I tend to think most of what I write won't be published, but that doesn't seem to be the case. Still, I'm always sorry I can't write something more ordered. I feel like I'm climbing a mountain. I can't change the shape of it, so I simply have to grip the rocks with my hobnailed boots and begin the ascent. By Kṛṣṇa's grace both writer and reader can be uplifted.

It's true that I too feel confined by the repetition in this writing. Yes, I'm still waiting for the mail to come; the weather (I'm not really tired of reporting that) is still blowy.

One devotee said that he wearied of me complaining of my lack of spiritual advancement and my lack of triumph. He went to another guru. Should I be afraid that readers won't stick with me? Those who do want to read what I have to say, they want me to open up from the heart. If, however, they demand what shape my heart takes and insist that I form it into a proper novel or essay, I won't be able to comply. Therefore, we both have to accept it in the form it comes.

8:29 A.M., SHED

Shed windows warming up but still frozen-sheeted. I'm in here cold but hope to warm up before I flee.

It's important to me to write without pretension and to discuss Kṛṣṇa consciousness. Is it possible to make a pretentious presentation of Kṛṣṇa consciousness? Yes, if you are trying to show off your learning (Vallabhācārya's pride) instead of glorifying Kṛṣṇa. Or if you speak Kṛṣṇa consciousness without full faith or impersonally or from way beyond your realization.

Can you understand why I like sentences describing things I perceive immediately with my senses? They can also be non-pretentious because they are what is, even if not absolutely. Kṛṣṇa tells of His manifestations in this world *(Bhagavad-gītā*, tenth chapter) so that the common man can know Him. Of course, He lists only the most prominent features; His opulences are unlimited. As Kṛṣṇa tells us, we can also appreciate, not separately from Him—the weather, the lake—but in remembrance of Him.

And of ourselves and our own experiences. We identify with the body, so "we" feel cold and the ache in our fingers. We have indigestion or feel sleepy. To mention it, not as if it's absolute truth, but as something touching us now for better or for worse, can be non-pretentious too.

Gaurakiśora dāsa Bābājī was against all pretension in the name of *bhakti*. He recognized the phonies among so many so-called *tapasvīs*. In his own mood he was tasting separation from Kṛṣṇa. He became blind and didn't care if he was dressed or not. He spent twenty years as a *gṛhastha*, thirty as a *paramahaṁsa* in Vṛndāvana, associated with leading Vaiṣṇavas, then lived the last years of his life in Navadvīpa, associated with Bhaktivinoda Ṭhākura there, and accepted Bhaktisiddhānta as his disciple.

He chanted the names of the *gopīs* in a deep voice and sometimes made sounds of disgust. He wore a tigerskin cap and had a basket filled with devotional items. He gave ropes to Bhaktivinoda Ṭhākura for chanting *nāma*. He fasted or ate earth from the bank of the Ganges. He reminded people of Raghunātha dāsa Gosvāmī's austerities.

From the dictionary:

"Pretentious: making claims, explicit or implicit, to some distinction, importance, dignity or excellence; too affectedly grand; ostentatious."

That's a tall claim, to be free of pretension. You may be dignified, you may actually be important, but you don't claim it. You don't blow your own horn, don't try to make it appear that you are a holy man, a serious writer, anything. You just be. Every day, just write. Every day, just read Prabhupāda's books. Every day, just practice Kṛṣṇa consciousness—without the claim that you are a great devotee, or even a good one, a faithful reader, and so on. There's no reason to be pretentious, factually, because even if you increase a little, you're still so low.

2:40 P.M.

Prabhupāda says a guru should chastise disciples, but when they turn sixteen, he should become their friend. If you try to chastise a grown-up son or disciple, he will break. Prabhupāda said he was an old man (1976) and for that reason, he could not chastise us. With folded hands he requested the men to shave their heads at least once a month on *pūrṇimā*. We are known all over the world as shaven-headed, not long-haired. I shaved my head this morning.

Sun over right shoulder, glancing off windows and my eyeglasses. It has warmed the air and I have had to unbundle myself. Reading, drawing (a Jagannātha today), and writing.

The Himalayas don't move, so they are greater than Mount Meru, which does. Take in what Prabhupāda says in his gruff voice in the last years due to cold or old age or transcendental anger. We listeners and disciples have to take it on our heads. No point finding fault. It's like calling the Ganges dirty during the rainy season. We simply bathe in the river, confident of its purity. I like the gruff voice. My soul rises to it. It's as if I've been dying. Adore the master's words. Kṛṣṇa is the Supreme Soul, and I pray for Him to carry me to the purport of *yasya deve parā bhaktir*. Kṛṣṇa, Kṛṣṇa, Kṛṣṇa.

Now in the pure light blue sky and sunshine, the island trees are predominately green. Picture postcard clarity. The brilliant water moving, rippling, but no white breakers for sure.

November 21

12:30 A.M.

Lord Caitanya embraced the leper Vāsudeva, who then became a beautiful man. To protect him from pride, Lord Caitanya told him to always chant the Hare Kṛṣṇa mantra. He also advised him to preach about Kṛṣṇa and to liberate *jīvas*. "As a result, Kṛṣṇa would very soon accept him as His devotee." (Cc. *Madhya* 7.148) Prabhupāda writes, "If one wants to be recognized as a devotee by Kṛṣṇa, he should take to preaching work, following the advice of Śrī Caitanya Mahāprabhu. Then one will undoubtedly attain the lotus feet of Śrī Kṛṣṇa Caitanya, Lord Kṛṣṇa Himself, without delay."

Earlier Lord Caitanya advised the Kūrma *brāhmaṇa* to stay at home and chant and teach Kṛṣṇa's *upadeśa* to whomever he met. Even when I'm not traveling or reaching out physically to large numbers of people, I may always chant (my sixteen rounds), speak in classes, and publish profusely (my disciples will print and distribute the books).

December is coming and many devotees in ISKCON will participate in active book distribution on a marathon scale. I'll be here, staying in this room and going out daily to the shed to read and write. I'll also speak in the temple once a week. I won't feel guilty about this. By reading and preaching I also participate. Others may criticize me, but I won't be disturbed by that, especially by imagining their criticisms. "He still gets headaches?" I'll do what I can.

Words. Do I no longer trust the process of free-writing? Do I not want to "sully" or ruin the pages of my quiet diary with silly talk and word experiments? Do I fear if I let go it will not look Kṛṣṇa conscious? Will it destroy an image I want to project of the simple saintly life? Consider it.

What's the difference between the sober control of mind (beat your mind a hundred times with shoe and broom) and a pretentious restraint? What's the line between right restraint and suppression which builds up and isn't really doing the job? Writing here to discover this by sometimes exploring, expressing so we can see, "Oh, this is excess." Don't always play it safe.

A tisket, a tasket. But old Ella Fitzgerald allusions come pouring in. It's like switching the tape recorder onto "radio" and riding the tuner dial, picking up sounds from the world. No profit in that, I say. Better to stay away from news reports and worldly music. Yes, stay on the Kṛṣṇa conscious wavelength that reaches you from *śāstra* and by listening carefully to the intelligence and the direction that comes from Supersoul. Prabhupāda is in his *nitya-līlā*, his *aprakaṭa* form. I have to tune in to him. *That's* the advantage of this quiet Geaglum life. At least that's what's possible. Writing can help.

M. put the van in the winter shed. The back tires skidded so a small group of men assembled and pushed it in. Now he's getting ready for his trip to America for his hernia operation. I wish him well and pray Kṛṣṇa will protect him.

We read about an hour in stories of Gaurakiśora dāsa Bābājī. Realized we can't specifically apply the teachings he gave over a hundred years ago in a different place and to his contemporaries. For that we turn to Prabhupāda. Still, Gaurakiśora dāsa Bābājī's emphasis remains with us—his absorption in genuine *bhajana*, austerity, and how that is required before we can speak of Rādhā-Kṛṣṇa. Many examples of his life and words. Hypocrites he exposed.

3:45 A.M.

Ṛṣabhadeva said that we shouldn't trust the mind, and Śrīla Prabhupāda lectures on the same point. Look at Lord Śiva, who chased after Mohinī. Okay, but how does this apply to my writing down what passes through my mind? And what about the writing instructions of Natalie Goldberg regarding the "wild mind"? She says a writer should trust the mind. She says it's all we have. We shouldn't think, shouldn't get "logical," etc. Somehow I accept what she says and don't see it as contradictory to what Prabhupāda says. My contention is that I have fully accepted Kṛṣṇa consciousness, or at least have accepted it as my foundation so that I notice when I am not Kṛṣṇa conscious, and I am willing to change and correct myself. At the same time, I have to fight the mechanical, merely official acceptance of Kṛṣṇa consciousness, as if it were only my "religion" or a dogma. Therefore, I want to know what is actually going on in my mind. A person might be so out of touch with himself that he assumes he's a first-class devotee. He assumes he has no errant thoughts or that they are not dangerous—or that they are too dangerous to even consider. He keeps a lid on the Pandora's box of his self. He suppresses it, but it will explode. I regularly let off steam by letting the mind babble. Often this produces significant data. You start by saying, "I want ice cream and a pretty girl," then you look at that and ask, "What's *this*?" You reason with it and find yourself turning toward Kṛṣṇa for shelter.

Letting the devil have his due for a while is something I do regularly as writing practice and as therapy. It is truthful too. I have to learn how to control it. It is part of the larger subject of controlling the mind. Controlling a horse, for example, is done not by always holding back on the reins but by sometimes allowing him freer rein. Sometimes you even spur him on. It's a process of letting go and pulling in. It's an art learned by practice. The mind can learn to cooperate with us, can be supple, flexible, and travel long distances under our control. At least that's the theory.

The distance we want to cover is the distance it takes us to get to Kṛṣṇa's lotus feet. Turn the mind to Kṛṣṇa. Always look at the Lord's lotus feet. Don't be in a hurry to see His face. In this way, use the mind in Kṛṣṇa's service. Chant Hare Kṛṣṇa. While chanting we often find ourselves conjuring, conjecturing, dozing, hallucinating, struggling with one illusion or another because of our lazy or passionate and uncontrolled natures. We witness the mind's insubordination and then beg to be allowed to bring it back under the control of the higher self, *especially* when we're chanting. When writing, I can easily insert, "Kṛṣṇa, Kṛṣṇa," and then while telling of my little life and of what I have read recently, express gratitude befitting a would-be *sādhaka*.

ABHAYA DĀSĪ

Abhaya dāsī's at the hospital with her
daughter turned blue and the hospital
authorities are concerned.
Abhaya is overwhelmed, thinking of the cats and dogs
she has seen chloroformed, some she did herself,
her three favorite aunts who died
in their 40s from cancer, her own
younger brother died from an "OD."

"If I were in a man's body," she said,
"I would come to you and beg to talk with you."
Please don't. I am only a teacup.
I don't know how to face oceans of misery.
I can quote like a *sādhu*, but are
you ready to hear from the scripture's statements
supporting that we should be callous toward the death
of even a close relative
and go on with our Kṛṣṇa conscious duties?

Are you ready to admit that lamentation is
in the mode of ignorance
and recall Kṛṣṇa's statement that the wise lament neither
for the living nor the dead?

Abhaya asks for instruction. She
wants to leap ahead so she won't
be reborn in this world of sorrow.
I don't know. If I did, I'd be leaping.
But instead I'm slow and steady.
I doubt I'll be going back to Godhead at the end
of this life. Is it faithless
she asked, if she doesn't expect
to go back to Godhead right away?
No, it's realistic, humble.
Even Mahārāja Parīkṣit prayed, "If I don't
make it to the spiritual world at the end,
let me be born with full devotion to Kṛṣṇa,
with friends who are devotees,
and compassion for all."

Her daughter's still in the hospital, soon to be released.
Then smoke will rise from her chimney and
life will go on in the cold and happy-sad
Gay-glum. The key to life
on the quay—hard work and don't complain
of cold, eat simply (not too much),

And you are doing good things, even
new tings with each day. It is
eventful, exciting in *its quiet way*.
Reading; drawing (a *French today*)
& writing

Ascension.

"Prabhu, sit down."

Every Day
Just
Right

row your own boat,
and get together with others to talk
out what's wrong, how to make money,
how to improve.

And where's that hermit?
He's gone to the shed.

I AM THE MAN

I am the man who lives in the house
and who treasures his own sayings.
He doesn't allow sarcasm
or bash himself or others.
He's got it figured out, those compassionate sayings
of saints. Looks at himself
under a glass darkly, can't
figure it out, the soul, the *śāstra*,
the soul in every atom—can't be cut or burnt—
looks at it by negative and positive definition.
He is a person who can play with Kṛṣṇa
but who can't surmise it yet.
He goes on walking and chanting and
neverminding until he ends.
Maybe just before that,
he sees what he lacks and what he should have done.

Muddy walk, cow's hoof impressions, crumbled buildings—walking the same brisk walk, but new ideas.

Walking in the city, the European birds—she doesn't know their names. Did they fly from Majorca, Spain? Are they Irish or British? Does it matter? Oh, yes.

The man walks, wearing three pairs of socks and ten layers of pants and coats. He leaves accuracy behind and moves under the misshapen moon, less than half full but still substantial. It won't be long now before we see the full moon at the end of Kārttika. There'll be plenty of sweets in the bazaars, although he's been eating sweets all along and didn't follow the *vratas* he promised at the beginning of the month. At least he lit candles almost every night. It has been good not to have so many headaches. Whatever Kṛṣṇa desires, he sees the good in it.

8:20 A.M., SHED

Shed windows frosted over. It's getting too cold here for a morning visit. Aniruddha said that he and Manu could arrange for a gas heater which would take the fumes out of the room. When Madhu is away (or when he's here), I thought this morning, I shouldn't demand too many things for myself. Ladies have to give up a morning to cook for me. I shouldn't ask for things I don't need. My hands are cold.

Oh man, I want to see Kṛṣṇa in Christmas, in wood knots, in men and women working hard to confront *karmīs* on the street, "Please take a book."

The end. Has he written his last? I don't believe it for a moment. He won't give up.

Here's a story he wrote:

Once there was a mouse and a monster. One was a devotee, the other was innocent. The mouse told the story that once a monster received a Kṛṣṇa conscious book and was going to eat it, but he decided to read a page of it first. The page was on the immortality of the soul. It opened his eyes, blew his mind. "I believe," he said. The monster decided to drop out of the Monster Flying Academy, but he couldn't because he had signed a contract.

The monster said, "I must always chant Hare Kṛṣṇa and eat vegetarian *prasādam*," and he began singing loudly. They thought of smacking him on both ears and jailing him, but decided to kick him out of the Academy. He joined a local temple whose devotees didn't like him being a monster.

"But I'm not this body. Don't think of me as a monster."

"Gee, you're right there," they said, but in their minds they retained their prejudice.

O monster, hang in there.
The Lord loves you.
Your soul is bright and pure and
you are the gentle servant
of the true monists who
love God. You'll soon get
awarded your *svarūpa* and
that will be lovely and joyful forever.

My God it's cold. *Mātrā-sparśās.*
Finger tips sting, the body chills.
Of rulers I am Yama
of Devarṣis, Nārada
of Daityas, saintly Prahlāda
of *yajña*, Hare Kṛṣṇa mantra *japa*.

9:50 A.M.

Don't get too ordered with your schedule, or too virtuous, about how many Kṛṣṇa conscious books you're going to read or even how much of Śrīla Prabhupāda's writing you'll cram in, in one day. I noticed you spaced out at 9:30 A.M., neither drawing nor reading nor writing. Minutes ticked by while you browsed through a few items. Is that wasting time? I prefer to call it "taking a breather," or "looking for sparks."

Adrienne Rich writes in her Introduction to *Best American Poetry of 1996:* (p. 17) "I was constantly struck by how many poems published in magazines today are personal to the point of suffocation. The columnar, anecdotal, domestic poem, often with a three-stress line, can be narrow in more than a formal sense." Hmm.

Back in the house, waiting for the mail (still). So many clear days in a row. How best to use them? What if someone asks me how I feel? Should I say I forget? I think I'm still weak? They might wonder why I didn't immediately sign up as a member of the board of directors for the nearest zone (who draw pistols faster than anyone), or emblazoned my slogan, "Have *daṇḍa*, will travel." How about that?

Oh, you're witty. Diana Witty. Remember her? John Young called her "Dim Witty." Such a cruel boy, that Juan Joven. Did she get him back? I doubt it. They already knew he was a failure with girls.

I made nine points in one intramural basketball game when our class (57–1) triumphed over another class. We lost the next game (or maybe we didn't even play one). O wonder-scorer, that was your afternoon when Kathy Swanson attended and saw you score those baskets. Wonderful.

These are the memories. A scared kid getting on Bus 103 on Hylan Boulevard, heading north from the southernmost tip of Staten Island. The dream can be repaired, the memories revised, if you fish them out and do something with them. But what?

And Navy ships. Don't let them get stuck in the sewer.

Okay, this has been fun, part of the relaxation, but now it's time to read.

Kṛṣṇadāsa Kavirāja Gosvāmī says near the end of Chapter Seven of *Madhya-līlā:* "One who hears these pastimes of Śrī Caitanya Mahāprabhu with great faith will surely very soon attain the lotus feet of Lord Śrī Caitanya Mahāprabhu." In his purport to the next verse, Prabhupāda writes that everyone should engage in preaching, following in the footsteps of Śrī Caitanya Mahāprabhu. Certainly Chapter Seven shows Lord Caitanya preaching mightily, empowering all kinds of people as He tours South India. Every person who met Him went and preached and influenced others to become devotees. "In this way one will be very much appreciated by Lord Kṛṣṇa and will quickly be recognized by Him. Actually a devotee of Śrī Caitanya Mahāprabhu must engage in preaching in order to increase the followers of the Lord. By thus preaching actual Vedic knowledge all over the world, one will benefit all mankind."

I again asked myself in an accusatory way, "Are you preaching?" I even wondered why Prabhupāda should mention preaching since Kṛṣṇadāsa Kavirāja didn't mention it in his verse. Thus I tortured myself. Yes, yes, I am preaching with the *bṛhat-mṛdaṅga*. For example, just the other day a devotee called from Japan and asked to use some of my drawings on the cover of the Japanese edition of *Śrīla Prabhupāda-līlāmṛta*. That's preaching, isn't it?

But perhaps Prabhupāda and the *ācāryas* want us to always feel bad. He says that unless we feel really unworthy, then we won't be able to improve. I know the psychologists say we ought to feel good, and that makes sense too, but there's a balance there somewhere.

Am I convinced that Kṛṣṇa consciousness is for the betterment of mankind? Yes, and I'm also convinced that a preacher has to keep striving to teach that. Out of the many persons to whom a preacher speaks, hardly one will become serious. Still, the preacher is determined to continue for Kṛṣṇa's pleasure.

NOON

Just a thought—in December I could chant thirty-two rounds a day, write another directed journal such as *Begging For the Nectar of the Holy Name*, and spend time reading.

2:30 P.M.

I'm so easily swayed in my resolution. I thought earlier about stopping *Every Day, Just Write* and starting a book about *japa*. I even glanced for a few moments at *Begging For the Nectar* and *Japa Reform Notebook*, and then I saw the good in *Every Day, Just Write*. The very fact that it has no focus is truthful. Is that a strange thing to say? It's saying the truth rather than what should be said in a book on chanting or anything else. The writing's as pure as I can get it. I mean, free from pretension.

Now I find myself swaying toward not increasing my *japa* but increasing my writing, so I talk to myself as an old friend.

Gently, gradually, I remind myself about the goal of life and my need to improve. Śrīla Prabhupāda said that his disciples were too grown-up for him to chastise. "I am an old man. I cannot chastise you."

I don't feel like chastising myself either. Neither do I want to whip myself into writing a certain book. I made a list of vows or restrictions on the first day of Kārttika, but I didn't follow any of them. Or rather, I followed the gist but not the letter. Despite my lack of rigidity, I now find myself without desire to do the things I decided to restrict myself against. I sense that they don't help me in my Kṛṣṇa consciousness. Maybe this is a better path for me, to do what I want not out of force. I'm too old to chastise. I prefer peace.

This has relevance to my decision about whether or not to increase my *japa* quota. Maybe I should take the same approach. Rather than making a bold announcement and forced start—thirty-two rounds to start on such and such a day, with such and such a book to keep me company—it's probably better to keep in mind that *harināma* is the only way and an increased quota may help (although whenever I try it, it usually returns to the same state later).

Better to do the free roll ease motion of writing with no topic.

Damn it, *I* like it

even though I don't always know what it is.

I suspect that writing another book like *Begging* would start to feel too structured for who I am right now. Is that because I'm living too much in ease these days? Would a *japa-vrata* tighten me up? Directed writing might work in the same way. If I'm not on book distribution, at least be chanting. "Then if anyone reads this diary, they will see I'm a serious devotee."

O pretense, begone.

At the same time, improve your chanting if you can.

4:20 P.M., TEMPLE ROOM

Rādhā-Govinda: dressed in red and white with designs in silver *jāri*. Rādhā's blouse has a high neck, and Her flouncy skirt is covered by a pinafore. Tulasī leaf on Her palm, blessing us. Lakṣmī-Nārāyaṇa worship they say, but They are Rādhā and Govinda.

Kṛṣṇa has a buffalo horn that curves in the same direction as His hip where it rests. His garland extends to His ankles; Hers is shorter.

Rādhā-Kṛṣṇa worship is topmost, but we can't jump to it artificially. Gaurakiśora dāsa Bābājī says we need to first practice austerity, give up all sense gratification, and practice *bhajana* for a long time before we will find ourselves free enough of lust and able to hear of Their pastimes. What to speak of serving Them directly—or Their *sakhīs*—in our own spiritual form.

Island paths, beautiful copper tones, leaves piled, clear air, calm and cold—the paths are darkening.

A prayer before I leave: Dear Lords, if You like, please keep me active reading Śrīla Prabhupāda's books and writing. Give me insight how to better serve You. O Harināma, please let me pay attention and *pray* the Hare Kṛṣṇa mantra.

I want to absorb Your beauty. You are the center of Inis Rath. Everything here is Yours and is done for Your pleasure. Even this writing done across the lake at Manu's house is for You. When I look at the lake and the island, the trees, please let me be aware that You are the jewel in this setting and the life of the devotees.

November 22

12:22 A.M.

I hesitate to write more openly because I am unworthy. Would I really outpour so many dirty things? Perhaps. If I could get past the vomiting of blood, as Kāliya did, and get to the offering of flowers and sincere prayers of surrender, if I could get past my brokenness into some kind of wholeness, then it would be worth the effort of living this life. I need to learn how to dance. "O son of Pṛthā, those who take shelter in Me, though they be of lower birth—women, *vaiśyas* [merchants], as well as *śūdras* [workers]—can attain the supreme destination." (Bg. 9.32)

"*Śrī-kṛṣṇa-caitanya prabhu doyā koro more*"—"My dear Lord, please be merciful to me, because who can be more merciful than Your Lordship within these three worlds? Your incarnation is just to reclaim the conditioned, fallen souls, but I assure You that You will not find a greater fallen soul than me." (Śrīla Narottama dāsa Ṭhākura, *Prārthanā*, song 39)

Rain beginning and pain in this body. The material body is a treasure house of miseries. Then use this time fully in the Lord's service. What other hope is there?

When I read, I pray to be deeply present. I notice the words going by as Lord Caitanya embraces Rāmānanda Rāya. Rāmānanda Rāya considered the Lord's embrace His mercy on a fallen soul; the Vedic injunctions forbid a *sannyāsī* to embrace a *śūdra*. Then they agreed to meet and speak *kṛṣṇa-kathā* in private. Prabhupāda comments in that section that topics of Kṛṣṇa and the *gopīs* should not be discussed in public.

Dreamt last night that Maṇḍaleśvara Prabhu and I were present at a meeting of top politicians. President Clinton was notable by his absence. Reagan was there instead—some kind of coup? Reagan announced that he meditated several times a week. This was a great opportunity for me or Maṇḍaleśvara to say something about Kṛṣṇa consciousness, but we didn't. That's all I remember, that we didn't preach. We were fortunate to be at such a meeting and fortunate that Reagan introduced the topic of meditation, but we could not capitalize on it.

When we returned to Geaglum last night from our Inis Rath visit, the sky's last light was turning the cows into silhouettes. Kāliya warned us not to come near. The sky was cold and beautiful. The collie greeted us, tail wagging, as we landed at the quay.

"Be careful, there is ice on the cement." I placed my hand on Śyāmānanda's back and stepped carefully out of the blue rowboat. I wanted to record that *while it was happening*, but I did not have the presence of mind to do it when I reached the house. I knew it was precious, but I couldn't convince myself it was worth recording. Later, I drew a picture of a man walking with a black cow in the background.

Was it a Kṛṣṇa conscious moment? Every moment is. Did I see Rādhā-Govinda in the sky? Maybe not, but I inserted Them in my mind. The collie greeted us and we walked. We were returning from *darśana*. Every moment is a Kṛṣṇa conscious moment.

PRAYER TO GURU AND KṚṢṆA

O Rādhā, O Kṛṣṇa,
outsiders cannot understand You.
They think God is Christ or
Christ's impersonal Father or
who knows what. They see
You only as a statue or cultural
expression of God. I enter
the sacred circle.

O master, Śrīla Prabhupāda,
you are my household deity.
O *mūrti* of mine,
my sentimental song becomes purified
when I sing it for you. Please rest
warmly and rise as you like
to write with dictaphone your *Śrīmad-Bhāgavatam*.
Then kindly chant *japa*
with me.

Lord of all, in my heart,
please grant me better chanting.

3:38 A.M.

Take a deep breath and let it out. Okay, a story. Once Nellie fell into despair, broke her wrist, and it wouldn't mend. She kept a secret diary of her intentions to go back to Godhead.

Her Christian friends told her how they offer their suffering to God, but she read in the monthly newsletter put out by her guru that this is not exactly the same as love of God. Offering suffering means . . .

She went on working in a shoe repair shop, a health sanatorium, in the highways and byways until she was sufficiently old. She was told that women don't take *sannyāsa*, so why not just chant Hare Kṛṣṇa, be simple, and read the books?

That didn't seem practical. There has to be more to fill out a life. She thought the advice was for liberated souls and not for her. She felt she needed human companionship and work, a sense of belonging to a cause. She also wanted to feel part of the *saṅkīrtana* effort, but she was limited in what she was able to do.

Or let's think of the manager. The intelligent preaching supervisor knows the limits of the preachers and assigns them duties which are not too hard for them. He himself spends most of his time telling others what to do and working to raise the money to carry on, talking on the phone, receiving faxes and e-mails, and going out to meet big Indian businessman to ask for donations. Then back to the streets where dogs and cats and men and women engage in endless sense gratification. Our hero eventually makes his way back to the temple where he hopes to find a plate of hot *prasādam* waiting. He knows he's not fulfilling his topmost spiritual ideals, and he thinks he cannot be considered a devotee because of it, but Kṛṣṇa favors him because he's trying to spread Kṛṣṇa consciousness. He knows that too.

I'm not writing—"O America" and "O Tokyo" like that girl. I'm not writing a Paul Zimmer poem. I would like to give a little poetic discourse on some aspect of the nine methods of devotional service instead, something from out of my life and that touches on yours. To touch base with Lord Caitanya and Haridāsa Ṭhākura.

Devotee 1: "Hey, whatcha reading?"

Devotee 2: "I've been reading this page in *Kṛṣṇa* book for the last thousand years. I am making a birthday cake for the eight hundredth anniversary . . . and the one hundredth, and my own thirtieth, and the third of when you were born, honey. (Honey is okay. You can offer it to Kṛṣṇa.)

Slobby Miskept, yeah, we know the type. He does the externals, sometimes, and acts like an *avadhūta*, talking about the *gopīs* despite his lack of qualification. Better to start from the beginning, Slobby, and follow the rules, chant the rounds, and follow the Swami. Don't be miskept *and* misled.

(Uh-oh, here comes the gremlin around the block. He sees me and starts his discourse. "Don't you know you should be working to pick up the pieces in that temple where the leader fell down and the other where that Christian New Age psychotherapist came and turned the devotees to a new openness in support of feelings?")

I can't, I just can't. I can't go there and tell them that everything they heard was *māyā* and that they should just do whatever their authorities say. I have ulcers and headaches and a bad ankle and athlete's foot and no money.

I will say this, however: It was no ordinary thing to meet Kṛṣṇa's pure devotee and be allowed to take direction from him. He is the master of our hearts, and we should follow him with faith. We have only a few more years left in these bodies. He left in 1977, and we will all be leaving soon after him. I hope to catch up to him and to be with him again.

Kṛṣṇa, this day is Yours. I was reading in a collection of writing sessions I did last summer one that discussed our faith in spreading Kṛṣṇa consciousness. I said that sometimes it gets depleted and smothered by rhetoric. Then I wrote this: "*That's why, more than anything, I seek to free my own language from rhetoric*. That's why writing sessions are important."

I'm feeling convinced that the more I write, the more the process will work to bring me to new discoveries of truth. And books will also come from it. To confirm this, I saw in these writing sessions I wrote last summer how *Memories* was gradually building and taking shape. It started with giving lectures about Vyāsa asking Nārada to speak about his life. I said that we all know a life into which we should inquire; that is, our own. In the writing session I wrote, "What I couldn't say, what was really on my mind and heart, is that we ought to tell our confession, our real story, we ought to know who we are and that it is part of Kṛṣṇa consciousness." That lecture was a harbinger for the *Memories* project, but no one in the audience—and not I myself either—could know that at the time. Let me have the faith and hope that right now I'm on a wave of good things to come. Even when it seems I'm not going anywhere, Kṛṣṇa sees. He's the ultimate mover behind the process.

8:31 A.M.

Mail due today. Tenth chapter of *Bhagavad-gītā* reading completed. There now. What's new in the world of the spirit soul? Haridāsa Ṭhākura said, when Lord Caitanya asked what's the news, "Whatever mercy You can bestow upon me." In other words, I have nothing. I await Kṛṣṇa's muse, Kṛṣṇa's direction.

Real free-writing means to admit to the blank and the struggle and to be left with the most external reportage on your own. Then to realize that you know nothing but Kṛṣṇa as your Lord and that He may handle you roughly in His embrace or make you brokenhearted by not being present before you. This is Śrīmatī Rādhārāṇī's mood, but all *jīvas* know an infinitesimal spark of that feeling, especially those who are treading the *bhakti-mārga*. Your mercy, Kṛṣṇa, is all I know.

They are putting the carrier on the roof of the car and going to Dublin for the day for ISKCON Ireland's National Council meeting. I plan to walk in the grass and confer with some grass blades and the sky and a pen on a blank page. I don't even discuss issues with managers. I just, just—mouth like a fish and don't pretend this is better or worse, this navel-gazing. I'll read a little too. Not as cold today.

O Kṛṣṇa, of secrets You are silence, and of feminine qualities *kṣamā*, (patience). You are the rod of chastisement for wrong-doers, and of birds You are Garuḍa. Of the Pāṇḍavas You are Arjuna, of months November–December, and of seasons, flower-bearing Spring. All these are just a tiny sample of Your qualities as they are manifest in the material world. There is no need to list them all. "Know that all opulent, beautiful and glorious creations spring from but a spark of My splendor." As the Supersoul, You are the life of all that lives.

Kṛṣṇa, Kṛṣṇa, Kṛṣṇa, where do we go from here?

I don't want to go back to what I was before just in order to live. But I do want to live, quietly. I know the external act is not enough. Therefore, remembering helps. Each *jīva* must work hard to survive in the material world. Best to work in *bhakti* and produce fruits, flowers, and trees that grow up to Goloka.

Thank You, Lord Kṛṣṇa, the origin of all, for giving me days of health and pain. Please let me fulfill my aspiration to become a better devotee. My life's not over yet; I could still improve by Your grace.

1:09 P.M.

We draw a blank sometimes in trying to understand where to go or how to move forward in spiritual life. We hear from *śāstra*, but it doesn't move us. When we get into that mood, it creates an emotion in which we question our entire identity and purpose as we have been living them out. At the same time, it's not that racing to make a change will bring relief. We have to face our lack of taste at certain times of the day because they seem to be almost physical cycles.

I can just see the lake through my window, and it's a perfect mirror today. Still cold, though. The lake will change. Will we? How long will we sit and measure time before we are forced to pray?

Those words: bored, dry, empty. We watch ourselves going through the motions and wonder why we don't chant more. It's something to do. We'd feel bored, empty, and dry no matter what we were doing sometimes, but that shouldn't stop our attempt to increase our surrender to *hari-nāma*. Chanting will take us where we want to go. And I know I've said this before, but I feel the same way about my writing service. The more I write, the more I will be able to forge ahead in the way I want to go. Simply chant (and for me, write). It doesn't have to be pretentious (there's that word again).

When I am alone, I like to try to sink into a *bhajana* mood. That means more chanting, actually vocalizing the cries of "Dry!" "Alone!" "Bored!" "Is this all there is?"—through the words of the Hare Kṛṣṇa mantra, and always looking for more.

It's funny when you chant more what goes through your mind. You might think you have some secret to convey to the devotees, but maybe you don't. Often, all you feel from increased chanting is the sheer increase itself. I mean, more moving of the abacus counter beads. That's all. Still, an undercurrent develops as you recite the holy name more and more. The Vaiṣṇava "ordeal" to chant as Lord Caitanya ordered. Our perfection will be found there. If we give our hearts.

Prabhupāda compared child marriage in Vedic culture to the practice of Deity worship. When the bride and groom are so young, there's really no question of love between them, but the custom is that the girl brings some food to the husband and does little services for him, and in this way they have various exchanges although they continue to live with their parents. By going through the motions of marriage, however, the husband and wife gradually become attached to each other until they fall so much in love that they would never leave one another. This gradual development of love is compared to *vaidhi-bhakti*. What is true of Deity worship is also true of chanting. Chant, chant, chant, without love, chant, chant, chant with offenses—but eventually . . .

November 23

12:08 A.M.

Devotees are always meant to be seeking a balance. I have a list of things I'd like to do all at once but can't. I'd like to

write structured books while remaining intensely focused on the moment;
be peaceful yet excited in life;
not get headaches but accept my pain;
read books to learn about health and coping with illness, yet avoid reading all non-Kṛṣṇa conscious books;
travel, but stay in one place;
chant extra, read extra, write extra, and so on.

The local courier company promised they would come out last night with the mail package. Madhu has their *home* phone

Last daylight turning cows into silhouettes.

pure devotees
KRSN

I want no pain but it
comes. go
BTG

Hare Krsna Pray to Krsna.

number. I took rest and expected to find the package outside my door at midnight, but it wasn't there. The hallway was cold and empty. I went back to reading Cc. and preparing a lecture for the disciples' meeting on the four suggestions Rāmānanda Rāya offered Lord Caitanya, and which He rejected. I have noted down a condensed phrase to describe each of the four suggestions: (1) *varṇāśrama*; (2) *kṛṣṇe karmārpaṇa;* (3) *svadharma-tyāga*; (4) *jñāna-miśrā bhakti*. The principle that was accepted by the Lord was *jñāna-śūnyā bhakti*, or hearing from self-realized devotees about Kṛṣṇa.

Thinking about my health and my resolve to increase my *japa* quota. I hope the increased *japa* will fill up a feeling I have of "something missing." At the same time, the increased endeavor will bring the risk of more headaches. Śamīka Ṛṣi dāsa wrote and suggested I follow these steps in dealing with my chronic illness: "Please take more slow, natural, positive steps when you take on any stressful situation. Do only what you feel you can handle in a relaxed way. Keep a positive attitude. If it still bothers you, step back and try some other time."

The "something missing" may be health, so I simply have to face my limits. Accepting it can increase the sweet awareness of Kṛṣṇa's mercy. I don't have to see it as something negative or void. At the same time, I don't want to live a life of under-endeavor either. It's a fact that thirty-two rounds a day would strain my daily life. It's also true that favorable stress is positive in meeting the challenge of life. Śrīla Prabhupāda states that Kṛṣṇa consciousness and an easy-going life go ill together. We must do what we can without getting stuck on what we can't do. I remember Saint Thérèse and even Saint Teresa of Avila saying that they couldn't perform certain devotional acts because of illness and because of the limits of being women (not being able to preach as the male missionaries were).

3:38 A.M.

When writing, you have to go off into thin air and what comes out may not always be so cogent. You allow words to come and never mind the looks from the folks who read them. You are your own first reader, so help yourself. That seems important to me this morning. If writing helps the writer, then it succeeds at least that far. Of course, I may not always know what helps or what I need immediately. I accept that I am Kṛṣṇa's servant and that I *need* to serve Him, need to work to please Him. Kṛṣṇa doesn't need my help, but He is willing and eager for us to offer our services—"I want to help Kṛṣṇa in His pastimes." At the same time, it is a rare soul who is qualified to assist Him, especially in *mādhurya-rasa.* To become qualified, we have to serve and satisfy our spiritual master in his mission to spread Kṛṣṇa consciousness all over the world. That is real self-help.

But . . . does it feel good? Does it help your health? Your peace of mind? Yes, and sometimes no. We used to say stridently, "To hell with peace of mind and physical health! Just work for Kṛṣṇa twenty-four hours a day!" But we couldn't. We weren't pure enough. And others have been hurt by our inexpert and contaminated preaching. Dear preacher-self, dear big disciple of your spiritual master, if you're going to take charge of body, mind, and soul, I want to know how you are you going to take care of me. Get the point?

Kṛṣṇa consciousness has to be realistic. It should deliver tangible results as well as the not so tangible spiritual results promised in the *śāstra*. No one should be acting blindly in spiritual life. We may not chart our illnesses because we know we're not this body. We may not imitate Proust in our expression because we don't believe in art for art's sake. We pull like horses in the traces, nodding our heads and treading over cobblestones, urged on by the master, but we shouldn't be pulling while forgetting who we are and why we are running. We have to run under the whip of transcendental realization.

THERAPY

Here is the therapist.
She-he says, "Move your
arm. Now relax your body foot by
foot. Now clear your mind of emotions.
Now just be yourself and like a good science student
examine the damage of your pain.
It's okay? All pain gone?
No? Well maybe you didn't do it right. Try again.
Keep practicing with this tape and buy some more tapes.
We also will sell a wristwatch that
denotes your rise in temperature as you meditate."

That's therapy. Now let's do
bhakti. Mad-gatenāntarātmanā.
Only by devotion. By even a slight
touch of impersonalism, devotion flees.
Faultfinding, especially blasphemy
against God and scripture and holy men
is bad. Read too many cynical poets
and you'll wind up in hell
(in which they don't believe).
They believe in their egos,
their jokes and publishing and especially
in sex, trees, favorite words,
friends and booze and writing discipline.
They all have editors and most of them work in colleges.

But devotion you learn from your spiritual master
and it's best you keep away from others because
that's the ninth offense—to teach the glories of the name
to the faithless. And don't teach the intimate pastimes.
Don't eat meat or have illicit sex.
Be calm and work for Kṛṣṇa.

After writing a poem, Henry knew from experience that he would get drowsy by sitting in the comfortable chair, fingering his beads. Today he was prepared to wash his face, even if it smeared his *tilaka*, to keep the drowsiness away.

8:28 A.M.

Feeling good on all fronts:
physical health steady like a rowboat crossing on a calm day;
mind cheerful;
spirit fixed on best path;
writing okay;
and happy to be here to give a class on the vital topics Lord Caitanya discussed with Rāmānanda Rāya.
The waves of hope raise me higher.
Is all this only to be dashed by a few ripples and harsh notes, a setback to body, mind, or spirit?
The sailor raises his paper sail, stands on deck, hand on mast, prays the Hare Kṛṣṇa mantra
and sets off.
He is prepared to live long
or short
to die
or not,
because either way it's the same—
the *bhakta's* position.

4:20 P.M.

Almost full moon rising over Inis Rath. The sky is pale blue, not night, so the moonlight illumines like a lantern. As I gaze at it, one of the black Kerry cows walks into the foreground of this picture and begins to graze. I see pasture, then plume-headed weeds on the shore, then the "drink" of the strait, then the forest island, and above it, the lantern moon.

The mail pack finally came and the mail is now strewn across my desk. I began reading and answering it, but then got the first sign of a headache behind my right eye. I had to stop. I also canceled our evening gathering to sing "Dāmodarāṣṭakam." I'll try to recover so I can answer the letters at midnight. I also hope to go to the temple in the morning.

Devotees express their lives in their letters, and they stay on my mind. One disciple straying, one Godbrother sending his encouragement, and dozens of others.

That moon has a face with an "O"-shaped mouth and deeply sunken eyes. I don't know whether he's happy or sad. He looks cool, this end of Kārttika moon.

November 24

NOON

Missed the earlier writing times because I wanted to answer the mail, and I also gave the morning lecture. Now I am back and trying to find the thread of where I left off.

In a few hours, Madhu will leave for two weeks. I look forward to being that much more alone, although it may also be lonely. I look forward to his safe return. We decided I couldn't go to Guyana next year, but Paramātmā dāsa wrote me that he's built a little house where I can stay. I think I will go, and disciples can visit me there.

Answered the mail. One theme running through a few letters is that ISKCON has ruined some devotees' lives and health. Another said the search for individual spiritual life is in conflict with the demands of the institution. Hearing this places a burden on me. One devotee who has left ISKCON even suggested I speak out against the whole GBC. He said I don't realize how powerful I am and how much I understand Prabhupāda's spirit. How can he say I know more than the whole GBC body combined? Maybe the movement *is* hollow and superficial; it's certainly full of faults. I don't believe, however, that real spirituality cannot be developed within the institution. It's just not true.

The snow began to fall seriously. It's sticking to the ground. I saw the lake's waves roughen, and snow lashed us in the face, soaking our coats and *dhotīs* and my gloves. Arjuna dāsa was rowing strong, but Abhaya dāsī, in a rowboat with her two kids, wasn't doing so well. Arjuna had to go back and tow her. She and her daughter and son wore lifejackets. I wouldn't have minded having a lifejacket myself, but Arjuna got us there safely. I tensed as we made our way across the strait. Then in the temple room, beholding Rādhā-Govinda and reading the Cc. for the Sunday morning class, I relaxed. Much of what I read was about the Deity and the *nitya-siddha* status of the two *brāhmaṇas* in the Sākṣi-Gopāla story. All glories to Śrīla Prabhupāda. I wish to find him in my own heart and life. There is no other way.

2:30 P.M.

Rainbow against the dark gray sky. Two swans at lake's edge. Snow almost all melted. Fear of material attachments. I don't want them. I want to be detached like a bow without a string, now and at the time of death.

Madhu's about to leave. Showed me how to use the phone. There are some things we should not say in order to protect others. Disciples should think we are happy. Be quiet about your pain. Don't complain (too much) and don't confess the worst if it may harm others. This is a lesson in my Godbrother's leaving. I don't judge him, but I have to face that I myself should not hurt others by my own act of self-expression or self-satisfaction.

The water has calmed.

"He writes with a pen, rises in the middle of the night, and his headaches start near his shoulder blade. He's got half of his work or less done so far"—this the psychic "saw."

Did she see the calm lake? Does God speak in my voice? Will I answer all my mail?

My hat is too tight.

No, I knew I wouldn't be able to swim in rough waters with a big coat and boots on, so I tensed my hold on the side of the boat and my gloves became soaked by the snow.

Madhu is showing me more things: how to use the heater, leaving my feelings open. Good-bye. Someone sent a page from the *Washington Post* showing the AIDS quilt on the lawn of the D.C. Mall—350,000 people in America have died of the disease, and it is "inter-knit into the U.S. psyche like no other disease." The devotee who sent it was among the crowd, selling Śrīla Prabhupāda's books.

Is this a form of notes or meant to be read as final work? How to judge it? I wrote *Svevo* first time free and Kowit said, "It's great," but he thought it was only notes, not the "finished" work. I'm finished as soon as I write.

To the spiritual world, go. When I speak upholding *paramparā*, often quoting what Śrīla Prabhupāda said, is that not also true? As true as this uncovering truth? Here I may say, "I don't feel that old innocent love for Prabhupāda. I have to fight for it. I don't care for the Italian-made, full-sized *mūrti* of Prabhupāda." On the *vyāsāsana* I wouldn't talk like that. I uphold *paramparā* and go light on confessions, on tear-down. They hear and benefit by that performance. Both are required.

"Thank you for coming to the island even in such bad weather."

That's okay, I like to come.

And I like to go home to write, to open the door to "my" room and feel the warm air (glasses fogging) and bow down to Prabhupāda thanking him for preserving me on the rough strait crossing.

Oh, little people. Rwanda rape victims give birth to thousands. What karma. I should not complain.

She was . . . there, there, calm down and be quiet to preserve the quiet of friends. Not all horrors need be recited. I called it a grocery list of horror and said it didn't have to be stated. You can cruise along.

How about reading?

> One cannot be honest even at the end of one's life, for no one is wholly alone. We are bound to those we love, or to those who love us, and to those who need us to be brave, or content, or even happy enough to allow them not to worry about us. So we must refrain from giving pain, as our last gift to our fellows. For love of humanity consume as much of your travail as you can. Not all, never that terrible muteness that drains away human warmth. But when we are almost free of life we must retain guile that those still caught in life may not suffer more. The old must often try to be silent, if it is within their power, since silence may be like space, the intensely alive something that contains all. The clear echo of what we refrained from saying, everything, from the first pause of understanding, to the quiet of comprehension."
>
> —*The Measure of My Days*,
> Florida Scott-Maxwell, p. 142–43

November 25

9:30 A.M.

Two irregular days in a row. Pain behind the right eye. The old-time favorite special. It makes me feel grateful for those days of quiet and ability which I fill up with a mixed bag of reading Śrīla Prabhupāda (even though I'm not so ecstatic), writing in my own way (although I have doubts), and extracurricular reading (such as books on health or whatever).

3:45 P.M.

Pain still there. Took a short walk in 3 P.M. sunshine, collie Tilaka walking close behind. She groaned or cried and I turned around to her. Her eyes are scabby and sore at the corners. I couldn't help her, but patted her head and under her neck. Is she groaning because she knows I have a headache or because Madhu's away? Now Jayānanda is coming out of the house and shooting arrows into the air. His sister and another girl join him. Back inside I lie down to relax and hope relief will come overnight. Today's rounds were all silent.

5:30 P.M.

Dark, I sit facing the window with the curtain open and see the full moon rising over the trees on Inis Rath. My headache is clearing. Celebrate with *japa*.

November 26

12:38 A.M.

In *dāsya-rasa*, the disciple fears the Lord (or the spiritual master). In *sakhya-prema*, friendship, the devotee considers himself equal with the Lord and knows that Kṛṣṇa will never be displeased with him. Thus *dāsya-rasa* is characterized by a lack of confidence and affection compared to *sakhya-rasa* (and *vātsalya* and *mādhurya*).

These points may seem disappointing because our relationship with our spiritual master is in *dāsya*. Lord Caitanya's devotees also approach Him in *dāsya*. Another point: through the *dāsya* relationship with the guru, we learn of higher *rasas* with Rādhā-Kṛṣṇa.

We cannot jump over. We are in a *dāsya* relationship with Prabhupāda eternally. We will never be his equals. Yet friendship can develop within this relationship, and through that friendship with the guru, we can learn of our relationship with Rādhā and Kṛṣṇa.

O Kṛṣṇa, love for You is never destroyed. *Nehābhikrama-nāśo 'sti:* even a little devotional service will not suffer loss or diminution and can save me from the greatest fear at death.

Thinking ahead to next Saturday and what I will say to the eight disciples here at Inis Rath. I could discuss *sādhu-saṅga*, but the practical application becomes a relative discussion of how to get along with one another. Too sticky. I could talk about the holy names, but it seems I ought to do so out of realization (which I lack?). Since I spoke last week of Lord Caitanya's talks with Rāmānanda Rāya, someone suggested I continue that, but that means talking about the conjugal *rasa*—how could I avoid it?—and that's not appropriate for me or them.

There's a difference between mechanical and spontaneous service . . . No, I can't think at present of what to speak. On our level, spontaneous service may mean doing what we like to do, what attracts us within the nine principles of *bhakti*. That is usually determined by our psycho-physical nature and not pure *rasa*. Pure *rasa* means wanting to serve Kṛṣṇa as a cowherd boy or as a servant *(kiṅkara, mañjarī)* of Rādhārāṇī. If we can't serve spontaneously (by *rasa*), then may we serve enthusiastically through one of the services available to us in ISKCON that attract us? Someone wants to be an academic scholar, someone else wants to sing in a rock band, he wants to teach children, she wants to mother them . . . or someone may want his cake and to eat it too by having the privileges of both *brahmacārī-* and *gṛhastha-āśramas*. Are we free to choose? Or is that only *karma-yoga*? Where is the freedom to find our spontaneity?

The whole truth and nothing but the truth so help me God.
The part truth—the bit-by-bit added parts.
He doesn't have much strength to read.

Gets knocked away (doubts, fears, pain, *something* . . . a loss of taste, over-familiarity, you know).

O Kṛṣṇa, I want to chant better *japa* today now that I'm not in pain. But I know

the mind won't listen
to the syllables of the mantra
and I can't drive hard and fast.

3:45 A.M.

Nāma ruci, vaiṣṇava sevā, jīva dayā—Lord Caitanya taught these three principles. One Godbrother told me that when people in ISKCON talk about drafting a mission statement, he thinks of these three principles. He also said he thought I was doing good service in these areas.

Taste for the name increasing, when will that day come? Service to disciples by writing books and traveling. Yes, I should extend myself a little further and go to Guyana, but I may not be able to go everywhere. That would be folly, especially not knowing what would happen with my health. I agreed we shouldn't go to Puerto Rico because it would require another plane or two and a long ride up that winding hill and then later down it again. I just can't do it, or I guess I can, but I'm holding back.

Get with it, man, and take care of the body. When you're feeling stress, do biofeedback relaxation. Then go out and exercise. And when you eat fruit, add a little cheese for carbohydrate so you don't get a sugar rush all of a sudden.

Oh, but the other guys say don't eat cheese because you can't digest it.

And then the other other guys say don't listen to any of the schools. Just tune in to your body and ask, "What does it want?"

And Śrīla Prabhupāda says don't be so body conscious. Even if you do everything right, it won't work unless the fifth factor is there, *daiva-netrena*, the will of God. He can kill you or save you. Serve Him and He will take care of you. Don't divert your mind to that other body stuff too much.

RĀGA RAGS

He said they have no right, the ISKCON
authorities, to chase me from
the streets. I was not collecting money
on the pretext of ISKCON begging.
I was there as a street musician singing *rāgas*.
"Well you can do it but then
don't come to our temple. You are a street musician
selling rags."

The TP got mad and sent a fax
to the Boston basement
where they found the street musician's guru.
"Your disciple is creating havoc
in Bulgaria. You better tell him
to stop and cooperate with us."
"Oh, yes," said the guru precisely, and
he sent a semaphore message to the street musician:
"Cool it."
And he did.

Now they live happily cooperating I hear.
He sings his *rāgas* in the temple and I don't
know what he does in the streets. What they
don't know won't hurt them either. Now let's look
and see what's coming in the mail.
It's the falldown
and farewell of the latest old-timer,
and rebuttal from headquarters informing us
how to think.

I'm still struggling with the poets, those who speak hard words and who face enemies and cower, who admit they are cowards, who work on poems, who say it will be wretched to get old (what to speak of dead). They rail against God and inhumanity and one young Japanese poet thinks Coltrane's a saint and then describes all the men she has slept with. I tell you, they are not my company. They are *asādhu*, *strī-saṅgī*, and *kṛṣṇa-abhakta*. I prefer to hear from my friends, the devotees, and acorns to the poets.

This morning I'll hear again how Rāmānanda Rāya responded to Lord Caitanya's questions about *rasa*. He says that all the *rasas* are good, but *mādhurya* is the best. It contains the qualities of all the others. Lord Caitanya didn't normally discuss this. He usually chanted Hare Kṛṣṇa and when there were competent persons with whom He could speak, He discussed philosophy. But *mādhurya parakīya* was for Rāmānanda Rāya and a very few others. Prabhupāda kept the same mood.

God can punish us if He likes. We can't dictate to Him, "God, You must be more responsive if You want us to accept Your ways. Don't expect us to love You if You don't conform to our latest social attachments. You shouldn't be against homosexuals or abortion. Don't be Republican but something we can accept, a groovy God without a body."

Śrīla Prabhupāda said that the materialists and impersonalists simply want to kill Kṛṣṇa. But they can't. All they can kill is the chance the innocent people have to accept Him with faith.

One correspondent wrote and said, "It's better to accept only the little bit that is real for you from Prabhupāda's teachings. Don't try to accept the whole thing." I decided not to write him back.

8:28 A.M.

Reading eleventh chapter—"O Arjuna, whatever you wish to see, behold at once in this body of Mine!"

Using heater in shed. Pieces of ice melt onto the floor, windows frozen but ice on them also melting into droplets. Sun ball rising but sunlight confined to one part of the sky, blazing up through the cold and clouds.

Lantern moon over Inis Rath.

Be good, be tough, be obedient, follow your master.

Gaura Prabhu
Gaura Prabhu
Ignorance defeated
IN KIRTAN

Nanda
Krsna
Bhaja
Bhakta
KRSNA

It's quiet. I have nothing much to say because my energy is low today after the headache yesterday. Anticipating travel with the new year. O Lord of lords, fierce of form, I don't know Your mission, Arjuna said.

Fierce of form—thighs, mouths, bellies, soldiers entering the mouths of Kṛṣṇa's *viśvarūpa.* The demigods see it and are afraid, offer prayers, cry out, "Peace!"

Peace, the sunrise
coming through frets of trees
pouring like colored music,
the sun-eye of God.

In cold November the atmosphere is miles high, those woolly, breaking apart, ever-changing clouds. They seem to influence the nature of the water, now cold and calm. The weeds on the shore are frozen stiff and frosted white.

I scratch this pen
with amends and
salutations,
ready to chant after hearing
that there is repetition in some of Arjuna's statements about the universal form. It's typical for someone in ecstasy to repeat himself: "Oh! Oh!"

2:22 P.M.

Pain control books recommend self-hypnosis (which never worked for me. They tell you to imagine the pain to be a red ball getting smaller and turning softer in color, a mellow pink) and relaxation. They say not to be negative and recommend other strategies, such as taking hot baths and listening to Brahms.

I feel the pain and look out the window at the ever-changing portrait of the lake and island and marsh. Today five rowers in five canoes and four swans all together.

I go by circadian body rhythms. Peak times and ebbs are individual. I do get tired around 4–6 A.M., after rising at midnight and doing my *bhajana,* then showering, etc. They also say that old people tend to sleep light and be restless at night—wake about five times during the night. Yeah, that's me. "Over fifty-five"—that's me too. I'm pure spirit soul and never grow old. That's me too.

Arjuna prays to the Lord. Kṛṣṇa is all things. As Time, He devours those *brāhmaṇas* and *kṣatriyas* instantly. They are already dead. *Kālo 'smi*, time I am, He says, and Arjuna stood in wonder.

STICK WITH IT

I say "Kṛṣṇa" and stand by it. I
am faithful sticking here to ISKCON
even though a guy says why
don't you leave if you are right
and the GBC is wrong. For what?
To join him down the block?
No thanks.

I'm here in December, World
Enlightenment Day. I'm here on
my birthday and Christ's and the
disappearance of BSS. I'm here until
the end of the year.

Blessings come down on those
who read in peace. I don't
seem to be getting better
at prayer, but maybe I
am. Don't say "maybe" or
"I guess" the pain management book
says. Assert yourself.

Okay, there's no pain, and I
breathe deep from the diaphragm and chase
the blues away. The pain
moves on, diminishing.

As I was walking back from the shed I heard a car start up and figured it was a Godbrother I heard was visiting. I was too close to it to walk the other way—I could see the exhaust fumes—so I kept walking and went right past him. My Godbrother and another devotee stayed in their car while I passed, then turned it around and prepared to drive away. I could have left it at that, but it seemed too unfriendly. Therefore, I stood on the side path and waited for them to drive past so at least I could wave, and they waved back and folded their hands in *praṇāmas*.

After they had pulled away, I kept walking and talking to myself, saying that I was glad I was left behind to write. Then I realized that I felt embarrassed. Embarrassed? About what? That this Godbrother may go and report that he saw me out here apparently not doing anything—not traveling to different continents like him or getting involved in the book distribution marathon, preaching, raising money? Never mind. I am who I am. Still, I wanted to admit it here: I was embarrassed. Better not to have been seen.

4:30 P.M.

I was speaking about spontaneity, but when I chant, I can see I'm not a spontaneous lover of Kṛṣṇa. I ground out two extra rounds with Prabhupāda's *japa* tape and imagined that I could be doing other things instead. To keep going I told myself, "What if this is the last evening of your life?" That didn't hit me so hard, but it was enough to hold on to the rounds.

Please, Lord, please. I can only become truly Kṛṣṇa conscious if You give me Your mercy. I can read endlessly but still not get Your mercy. You have to actually give it to me. There is nothing I can do to attain it. Please let me chant, and let me pray while I chant.

Madhu is not here, and therefore it's especially silent. The silence is so complete, it's hard to fill it up. My mind wanders to the fruit I will eat at 5:30—a sweet taste to substitute for the sweet taste of *bhakti-rasa*, which I don't possess. We each have to pray for that on our own. No one can do it for us. Not Thomas Merton or anyone. We are each alone with Kṛṣṇa.

November 27

12:30 A.M.

Hope against hope that I could improve in these last days of the year. Wouldn't it be wonderful to become firmly fixed *(niṣṭhā)* in mostly exclusive reading of Prabhupāda's books? And chanting?

Sometimes I read my own writings and I profit from them. At the same time, I have misgivings, fed by the criticisms of others, that my writings are simply mental life. By contrast, here is what Rāmānanda Rāya said about his speaking before Lord Caitanya:

> Śrī Rāmānanda Rāya replied, "I do not know what I am saying, but You have made me speak what I have spoken, be it good or bad. I am simply repeating that message.

> "Actually You are speaking through my mouth, and at the same time You are listening. This is very mysterious."
>
> —Cc. *Madhya* 8.198, 200

William Blake claimed a similar thing. He said, " . . . I am under the direction of Messengers from Heaven, Daily & Nightly." (from a letter to Thomas Butts, January 10, 1803, p. 88) His poetry was being written " . . . from immediate Dictation, twelve or sometimes twenty or thirty lines at a time, without Premeditation & even against my Will." *(The Essential Blake*, Ecco Press, from letter to Thomas Butts, April 25, 1803, p. 89)

When I write, I struggle to express what I want to say, and I don't feel God speaking through me. When I do repeat His words from scripture or what I've learned from His pure devotee, that's valid Kṛṣṇa consciousness, but it's also a student's regurgitation. Of course, everything is within Kṛṣṇa's energy, so whatever I write also comes from Him, but He allows me (and everyone) my free will. So many writers in this world are babbling and not pleasing to Him.

That is my constant question: am I pleasing Him by my attempts, and to what degree is He inspiring me? To what degree am I writing out of my tiny independence? I write uncertain of the answers to these questions, yet I feel enough conviction to continue.

Here are more statements by Rāmānanda Rāya describing his enviable position as he speaks before Lord Caitanya:

> Śrī Rāmānanda Rāya replied, "I do not know anything about this. I simply vibrate the sound You make me speak.
>
> "I simply repeat like a parrot whatever instructions You have given me. You are the Supreme Personality of Godhead Himself. Who can understand Your dramatic performances?"
>
> —Cc. *Madhya* 8.121–22

> Śrī Rāmānanda Rāya said, "I am just a dancing puppet, and You pull the strings. Whichever way You make me dance, I will dance.
>
> "My dear Lord, my tongue is just like a stringed instrument, and You are its player. Therefore I simply vibrate whatever arises in Your mind."
>
> —Cc. *Madhya* 8.132–133

Śrīla Prabhupāda explains the principle behind the words of a pure devotee:

> All intelligence emanates from the Supreme Personality of Godhead, the Supersoul within the heart of everyone. Nondevotees want to ask the Supreme Lord for sense gratification; therefore nondevotees come under the influence of *māyā*, the illusory energy. A devotee, however, is directed by the Supreme Personality of Godhead and comes under the influenced of *yogamāyā*. Consequently there is a gulf of difference between statements made by a devotee and those made by a nondevotee.
>
> —Cc. *Madhya* 8.200, purport

3:40 A.M.

This morning I was listening to a tape of Prabhupāda speaking in his room to devotees in Paris, 1974. He was talking about the guests he had been seeing and how they were not devotees. He said that he strongly believed in Kṛṣṇa's statement in *Bhagavad-gītā* that if one is not a devotee of the Lord, he's in one of the four categories of *duṣkṛtī: mūḍhā, narādhama, māyayāparhṛta-jñānā*, and *āsuraṁ bhāvam āśritāḥ*. Then Prabhupāda asked that this purport be read from his *Bhagavad-gītā*. "It is very interesting," he said. Then he said, "Where is Satsvarūpa?"

Someone said something, but I couldn't hear it on the tape. Maybe they said I was typing. I remember that I sometimes didn't attend Prabhupāda's meetings because I had so much typing to do. Also, I lacked sufficient interest to stay with him hour after hour hearing him say "the same things."

I want to make up for that shortcoming. Śrīla Prabhupāda, Satsvarūpa is listening to your purports from *Bhagavad-gītā*.

The truth is vibrant images. The truth is Prabhupāda saying people have made wine and women their masters. Rāya Rāma dāsa left because he said we do not allow the bare necessities of life. Oh, that's true. They laughed in the room. That one young devotee was talking so much, repeating Prabhupāda's instructions and his own opinion and much news about U.S. politics and sins, sins, sins of the nondevotees. I wonder where that devotee is now or who he was. I tend to put them all down and say I am the good one, the quiet one, the faithful one, but how can I make that claim? My actual place is different. Now I'm chronically ill and chronically unable to taste the nectar of the holy name, chronically a faultfinder, and chronically not found in the front ranks of the preachers.

The book on chronic illness says that one who has it must acknowledge he can't move with the fast-action crowd. He can do the best he can, but he has to admit that some days are slower than others. Maybe he cannot meet with people—I can't. The chronically ill should not try to forget that they are actually ill. One injured man said that for a long time he kept thinking he would be cured; one day he would wake up and everything would be all right. Now he moves within his actual limits. I know people often ask me, "Do you still have headaches?" They think it's going to go away. When I say that I still have them, I feel as if I'm prolonging something that should have been finished by now. There is a tinge of something inside me that thinks I'm making it up or why would they keep asking? The question seems to imply that my pain ought to have diminished by now, and it's unbelievable that headaches could last twenty years. Don't they know some things last for a lifetime? Perhaps we will each find out as we each enter old age and its accompanying diseases. I write this so that people who read it will understand me, and also to find self-acceptance. The fact is, I get at least one bad headache (lasting over twenty-four hours) a week, and if I push myself, I get headaches every day. Face it and move one step at a time. And I have to face the fact that the illness shapes how I read, how I chant, and especially how I write.

I imagine a greater hero than myself overcoming the pain or being able to ignore it and serve through it. I just can't do that anymore. Instead, I find myself moving slowly on the wooded path or staying in a room where it's quiet, not even going to the temple every morning. And so it goes.

This image came to mind: a lily has no thorns like the rose or horns like the ram. It is beautiful without giving others pain. Can I be like that? Give others the best? But I give them the pain of reality in my writing. At least let it be a sleek song and interesting and of ultimate value.

WHAT KIND OF A POET

What kind of Vaiṣṇava poet
is this who lives in North Ireland,
doesn't stay in Vraja, Uttar Pradesh?

What kind of blasphemer is this?
Throw him out, some say.
Others recognize my worth as
I ardently, silently walk in the woods.
I can live peacefully
chanting the holy names and
not see anyone and gain
a good reputation and
keep writing, keep reading,
sometimes with others,
from Prabhupāda's purport on four kinds of
men who don't surrender to God.
I can also listen and listen to *Caitanya-caritāmṛta*
regarding Rāmānanda Rāya's talks.
This is what you get
if you ask me for a poem.

"You are caustic and cynical in your humor," a disciple said, but he read me anyway. He said it was a wonder that a wise guy like me could also have complete faith in the *paramparā*. Was he implying that I didn't have faith?

Oh, Hare Kṛṣṇa, the urge to
be saintly, the urge to sin—
these two urges play upon his nerves.

Don't believe a word of it. He makes up a story about a person joining the Hare Kṛṣṇa temple, and it's fiction for sophisticated fools. He delivers an interreligious address and is applauded and writes it up in his diary where he also states that he will refrain from another day of sin but he thinks of himself as one in the universe. Hare Kṛṣṇa comes straight from Kṛṣṇaloka, but with chanting I have no connection. Day and night I am burning in the dark world without seeking to make the connection. Śrīla Prabhupāda noted that in Paris they drink on the street and the churches are empty, but the "Follies" attract thousands. Other cities are like that too.

9:40 A.M.

All morning I've been trying to come up with a new writing project. I even wrote a farewell to *Every Day, Just Write* and I attempted a Prologue to a new work. Then I returned to you, dear diary.

When I do a writing session, I'm saying I don't have to write exactly; just put down my thoughts as they come. When I step back and say I will choose a structure and a topic, then I have to face my poverty. It's anguish.

I mentioned earlier that my illness determines how I write. What I meant is that I have to maintain almost absolute peace as far as possible. Anguish is something I can't afford if I want to stay pain-free. Therefore, peace is a major theme in my diary. I write to get peace, not to excel in literary structure, and thus I only accept the discipline of writing what comes.

12:30 NOON

My headache is developing quickly into real pain behind the right eye. I'd like to not be afraid of it when it comes. I attribute the pain partly to the passion of trying to think up a new writing project. It really got me into high gear mentally.

2:30 P.M.

Process is better than product. Just write.

M. made it to America and will have his hernia operation at 9 P.M. our time tonight. I should be sleeping by then, and I guess he will too, under the anesthesia. May all be well.

Now, sir, you should be satisfied. Just glad to be alive. Calm and grateful. Don't go further right now to lament your lack of *kṛṣṇa-prema*. Just say, "Thanks for life." One chronically ill man said he coped by his love for life and his appreciation of little things—the two hours a day when the sun shone in a shaft onto his hospital bed and the sight of birds at the window.

Ringing in ears. Heat in the shed. Body, body, love the body, body betrayed, you can't be happy in the body—it's either pleasure, mixed pleasure and pain, or pain. Actually, it's all pain because it always ends in death.

The afternoon darkens even before 3 P.M. today because all the sky is covered with one gray mass. Little light to show off the copper leaves, just calm, foggy, not-so-cold, dampness.

"Please forgive me." Arjuna apologized for being the Supreme Lord's close friend now that he saw His splendors and fearful form. "Please forgive me," but he couldn't forget their friendship. Then he asked to see the four-armed form. I could only read a little at a time.

November 28

12:30 A.M.

Who has the most glorious reputation?
One reputed to be a devotee of Kṛṣṇa.
Who is the richest capitalist?
He who is richest in love for Rādhā and Kṛṣṇa.

Draw lines and loops and see what comes out. Accept it. Another face, stylized eyes and mouth and nose. And when you write is it similar?

Are you on the liberated platform and entitled to hear the loving pastimes of Rādhā and Kṛṣṇa? Is that disciple who has left me? Should we hear from someone other than Prabhupāda? No, I don't want to. ISKCON has declared it wrong and for good reason. "By practicing the regulative principles, one should rise to the platform of spontaneous attraction to Kṛṣṇa. Then and only then should one hear about *rādhā-kṛṣṇa-līlā*." (Cc. *Madhya* 8.255, purport)

Sometimes I fantasize that I may get strong health or some new, strong willpower and become an inspired preacher later in life. It doesn't seem likely though.

Healing the Body Betrayed gives examples of persons who were active and successful despite chronic pain. Mickey Mantle hit 536 home runs despite the intense pain he suffered from crippled knees and legs. Marcel Proust and Robert Louis Stevenson were mostly bed-ridden, yet they wrote their books. FDR conducted World War II and the American Presidency from his wheelchair after suffering from adult polio. JFK campaigned and conducted the American Presidency with intense back pain.

I can't lecture when I have a headache, but I can persist in traveling, and when the headache subsides, I can plan to lecture the following day.

It seems even more important that I write in process. If it gives me only one publishable book a year I will be satisfied.

Faith in practice. Faith in service.

Mini and Sal. Mini never became a devotee. She divorced Sal who became a devotee. But he too sprouted more material desires and decided to try for material fortune. He went to Manhattan to work and get the pot of gold. He read *śāstra* only fifteen minutes a day. Oh well, what can you expect? It's a full-time endeavor to work in the world. I'm thankful I'm away from it.

Śukadeva Gosvāmī invoked the blessings of the Supreme Lord before delivering the *Bhāgavatam* to Mahārāja Parīkṣit. The Supreme Lord originally inspired Lord Brahmā in the heart. He again appeared in the heart of Rāmānanda Rāya and manifested all knowledge of Rādhā and Kṛṣṇa to him. I pray to the Lord to please direct me in my heart and to allow me to write Vedic truths, bringing mango-like sweetness to the devotees of the Lord.

Writing in process. Remember Henry Miller's statement about writing?

> . . . I proved to my satisfaction that, like any other mortal, I too could write. But since I wasn't really meant to be a writer all that was permitted me to give expression to was this business of writing and being a writer; in short, my own private struggles with this problem. My grief, in other words. Out of the lack I made my song. Very much as if a warrior, challenged to mortal combat and having no weapons, must first forge them himself. And in the process, one that takes all his life, the purpose of his labors gets forgotten or sidetracked.
>
> —letter to Alfred Perlès, from *Art And Outrage*, p. 56

True of me? No stories or essays. Few poems.

Another struggle is the balance between implicit expression and explicit expression. I live to cultivate seeing Kṛṣṇa in all things. When I see a tree, I want to understand that it's the combination of Kṛṣṇa's material energy and a spirit soul. The combination of atoms is not separate from Kṛṣṇa; it all comes from Him. Okay, but I want to see Him even if I don't tag on the words: "Here in this tree, matter and spirit combine and come from the Supreme Source, the Supreme Person."

There are swans on the lake, there is the lake itself, and a beaten-down path leading to the shed, and the shed itself, and the cold air. The mother and her kids, the island, whatever I see or think—all coming from Him. O Kṛṣṇa, I know I am limited, but give me the vision I crave to see You everywhere. Sometimes I don't mention it, I just mention the moon or the weather. But You are there and I know it and remember You.

A letter from a disciple about reading: "I'm slowly but surely reading *Śrīmad-Bhāgavatam*, which I always find to be the answer to all questions. I'm up to the story about Durvāsā Muni and Mahārāja Ambarīṣa. It is so nice to hear these pastimes. In doing so it feels like the spiritual world is opening to me. I admit, too, at times, finding myself distracted from reading for different reasons (like my unsteadiness), but I quickly realize the implications of not keeping a good steady level of hearing and find there's nothing so satisfying as absorbing myself in *Śrīmad-Bhāgavatam* and your books when I really get down to it."

I wrote back with these quotes I found in the purports to Rāmānanda Rāya's talks with Lord Caitanya:

tasmāt sarvātmanā rājan
hariḥ sarvatra sarvadā
śrotavyaḥ kīrtitavyaś ca
smartavyo bhagavān nṛṇām

> The business of the living entity is to always remember the Supreme Personality of Godhead in every circumstance. The Lord should be heard about, glorified and remembered by all human beings.
>
> —*Bhāg.* 2.2.36, as quoted in Cc. *Madhya* 8.252

tasmād ekena manasā
bhagavān sātvatāṁ patiḥ
śrotavyaḥ kīrtitavyaś ca
dhyeyaḥ pūjyaś ca nityadā

> Everyone should very attentively listen to the pastimes of the Supreme Personality of Godhead. One should glorify His activities and meditate upon Him regularly.
>
> —*Bhāg.* 1.2.14, as quoted in Cc. *Madhya* 8.253

3:32 A.M.

Hearing Śrīla Prabhupāda speak in Paris. I was in the other room. One guy, very aggressive and unsubmissive, was speaking of "The Light." Probably a Guru Maharaj Ji follower. Prabhupāda said, "Go away! You're wasting my time. You know everything!" The devotees had to ask him to leave. He readily agreed, but I know that if he hadn't, the devotees would have thrown him out—Bhagavān, Puṣṭa Kṛṣṇa, and the others.

Prabhupāda was always exposing himself to such people as this guest. The night before that, he had spoken at La Salle Pleyel and a riot had almost broken out. Someone had even come with spray paint.

Śrīla Prabhupāda, please let me worship you unhindered by doubts such as, "Did you know that the Lord Buddha we speak of in the *Bhāgavatam* is not the Gautama Buddha who formed that world religion?" I plague myself with these things unnecessarily. When the guy asked you, "What do you think of the Hebraic Kabala?" you said, "I have not read it, nor do I know of it." That was the perfect reply for me. I do not need you to know everything. You need only know devotion to Kṛṣṇa, which gives you understanding of everything else. *Yasmin vijñāte sarvam evaṁ vijñātaṁ bhavati.*

I can spare myself the plague and the offense if I become simple and have full trust in you as I used to have. It's hard. So many Gaudiya Math teachers and gurus have come and taught a little differently than you, emphasizing something else. Some of your followers go to them for the "extra" or the difference. That's a strain sometimes. And of course there is the strain of the falldowns. I too am full of shortcomings. Just see how I write and don't know what to write.

I pray for guidance. I would like to write something straight from my heart in Kṛṣṇa consciousness. I don't want to be like that guy in Paris who said he felt the Light "right here" and "that's all I know." I want to surrender even though I fail to do so. Please keep me on course gently, as is my nature, and allow me to read your holy books with faith. Please excuse me

"I saw Satsver. He's walking around upright. I don't know what he's doing, but he looks okay."

Hare Nama
maha mantra

We want
Gosta

From the *bhakti* field of best flowers.

Sun ball rising, blazing up through cold and clouds of Geaglum life.

and make me more learned, more simple, more pure. Lord of my heart, I pray for this.

And give me faith in ISKCON. We talk of ISKCON's maladies and we quarrel with one another and the schisms hurt the unity of ISKCON. The lack of purity and inspirational leadership also hurts, and the lack of faith due to falldowns. But outside of this imperfect, too-institutional movement, the howling madness of violence and sex is a million times worse. Where else can we turn? We can't go there. Some say that devotees make it sound worse than it is. They say they have been "out there" and seen that it's not so bad. It's just the world, after all, and it is filled with many fine and spiritually minded people. Just as in ISKCON there are fine people and terrible people, so in the world it is the same. They say we ISKCON people are too insular and afraid and that we have cheated them by our too stark analysis of the outside world.

I don't feel I have to answer this challenge. I can only go my way with the faith that I have accumulated. When you read Cc. day after day, you see the mad, sex-obsessed poets for what they are, despite their ability to use language to express. It's true that ISKCON has some of that energy too—the madness, the falldown, the political intrigues. I avoid it *wherever* I see it. I'm looking to become more tough to it, but also more obedient to my master. He wants us each to fight on his behalf against infamy—*all* infamy. O Prabhupāda, please help me. I pray for your guidance and the strength you can give me to hear better the holy names and to make ever clearer presentations of Kṛṣṇa consciousness.

Prabhupāda, I don't know anything. You say we should give things in even numbers; an odd number means we are giving to an enemy.* Why? It's just the Vedic way. You say the stool of a cow and the bone of a conch are pure, whereas all other stool and bones are contaminated. If you touch stool,

* Conversation with George Harrison, July 26, 1976, London.

even your own, you have to wash. You say that sex is only for the procreation of good children to be raised in *bhakti-yoga*, that education should only be spiritual, that animals are living out karma but not accumulating new reactions, and that there are good animals and bad animals according to their previous deeds. You say the soul is an eternal spirit spark, that it has a shape, that we do not belong in this world and will have to leave eventually. O master, you know Kṛṣṇa, and you reveal Him in your purports to *Bhagavad-gītā* and other books.

Some devotees are reaching out beyond the institutional walls for help in managing the institution. They want to learn how men and women should behave and how to live in community. Learn this from the Jehovah's Witnesses, learn that from the Rama-Krishna Mission. See also their bad examples and avoid them. Ultimately, however, everyone looks to you to understand how to chant the holy name purely and how to honor *prasādam* with devotion. We gave up our sinful habits at your bidding, you had such power. The U.S. government was spending millions of dollars to help its youth overcome LSD abuse, but not one person could they save. Kṛṣṇa, Kṛṣṇa. Only you could really help.

8:20 A.M.

Dreamt my *dhotī* caught on fire and still I smell burnt cloth. O hippos, O worldly stuff—so much of it. I refrained from listening to anything at all, but sat in silence. A Benedictine monk in Germany told Prabhupāda that he chanted, "Jesus Christ, please have mercy on me." Prabhupāda approved. We chant Hare Kṛṣṇa Hare Rāma, the names of God and His energy. We pray, "Please engage me in Your service."

The Christians in Paris—arguing, arguing.

Layers of soft, white-pink—like a baby's clothes or a blanket—and baby blue, above the island. The trees' silhouettes familiar to me now. He said it takes an hour to cross the strait when it's frozen and they have to chop the ice. If that happens, I'll stay home.

The grass is half-frozen, but still wet and a bit soggy. No hard ridges or ruts. It will probably melt by this afternoon.

Hare Kṛṣṇa Hare Kṛṣṇa, Kṛṣṇa Kṛṣṇa Hare Hare.

This is the way it is. An ideal setting under a reddish horizon turning yellow-white-blue. The water is blue-gray and dark and cold, with surface ripples and a movement to it. Not like an old fishing pond.

2:32 P.M.

Last time I was out I saw a squirrel climb a tree. At first I was not even sure it was a squirrel because I couldn't see a bushy tail. He climbed to the top of a short tree and stared down at me. He was a pointy-eared, ugly pug of a beast, a rodent. Kept looking at me looking at him. As I walked away I thought it was good for me, a kind of training, to see that live rodent face again.

Now raining. I came out to the shed with an umbrella. Rain beats against the windows, but the heat makes it tolerable in here. Still reading of the universal form. Now Kṛṣṇa shows His *mānuṣaṁ-rūpa*, His original two-handed form for all to know that He is the source of the four-armed and universal forms. *Mūḍhas* can't believe it; they think the Absolute is impersonal and the universal form is more important than original Kṛṣṇa. But *Bhagavad-gītā* clearly states that Kṛṣṇa can only be known by unalloyed devotional service and as the two-handed Kṛṣṇa, He is the source of all *(īśvaraḥ paramaḥ kṛṣṇaḥ . . . sarva-kāraṇa-kāraṇam. Mattaḥ parataraṁ nānyat)*.

Read a poem by Al Young, who let his brother speak through him. O. O. Gabugah: "Draws strong folk poetry from the voice of a strident but vital revolutionary who attacks the Uncle Tom."

Where does that leave me?

Ofay Hare Kṛṣṇa

leave it

that's why I say, be here in shed and room and satisfied with regular music of pure Kṛṣṇa consciousness. You know mainstream black and white civilization puts down Hare Kṛṣṇa movement. You're in the solidly rejected cult. You're less than a minority. That's okay. I'll tune in to Lord Kṛṣṇa and Vyāsa (both "black") and Balarāma ("white") and Lord Caitanya and Rādhārāṇī ("golden").

Pure spirits
United Nations
let there be one religion—there *is*,
it's called *bhakti*.
"Yes, yes," nodded the Benedictine monk but didn't believe
the Swami. After all he's in
his orthodox Catholic monastery
and we are in one Hare Kṛṣṇa house,
schloss,
after another.

Leave it
as in spacecraft leaving earth
leave it
ascend
Kṛṣṇa, Kṛṣṇa, our culture and language.

If some old stuff clings to you from white Europe or black America, I say don't plug into it. You'll get more than you are expecting. You'll get a load of karma. We were right in the old days to take only ISKCON Kṛṣṇa consciousness day and night in the temple. Whatever else came we restrained and refrained because Kṛṣṇa consciousness is the truth.

November 29

12:20 A.M.

Woke up humming. Wrote a letter to Arjuna's brother, Bhakta Leo, telling him that I'm sorry I caused him sorrow by implying he shouldn't write me because I'm not initiating. That seemed urgent, to write him a letter first thing before he slips away.

Then I started reading of Lord Caitanya's travels to holy places in South India. My mind slips over the terrain and cannot pay attention. The people of South India were as strong as elephants, but they were in the clutches of the crocodiles of various philosophies such as Jainism, Buddhism, and Māyāvādī philosophy. My rascal mind says, "Is this an exaggeration? He saved all the people of South India by converting them into Vaiṣṇavas?" The Bengali text does not state which philosophies they belonged to, so why does Prabhupāda translate it as Jainism, Buddhism, and Māyāvādī philosophy?

O Kṛṣṇa, please don't let me read with doubts. Yes, Bhaktisiddhānta Sarasvatī Ṭhākura was right when he said we should beat our minds with shoes and brooms. Don't trust the mind. Trust authorities such as Kṛṣṇadāsa Kavirāja Gosvāmī and Śrīla Prabhupāda, and not with half-a-hen logic either. We have to accept *everything* they say. We may inquire into why they said the things they said, but only to inform ourselves, never to challenge. Thinking about this, I realized that it's not so much doubt in what is being said, but in *how* it could possibly be true according to my own limited experience and estimation. That means I underestimate the power of the holy name and the Vaiṣṇavas, and even the power—or existence—of the Supreme Lord.

Yes, *all* the people in *all* the villages the Lord visited became Vaiṣṇavas (Cc. *Madhya* 9.7–8). Śrīla Prabhupāda states that his disciples are spreading the holy names and becoming "almost as potent" as Lord Caitanya. "Indeed, everywhere people are very seriously chanting Hare Kṛṣṇa Hare Kṛṣṇa, Kṛṣṇa Kṛṣṇa Hare Hare/ Hare Rāma Hare Rāma, Rāma Rāma Hare Hare." How can I deny it? Therefore, I hereby declare my mind a faithless rascal for not believing that Lord Caitanya and the holy name could convert everyone to Vaiṣṇavism. I need to develop more faith in the potency of *hari-nāma*.

I do pray alone in *japa* and desire to see the world become Kṛṣṇa conscious, but I have a problem—and I doubt it's only my problem. That is, I need to see the *qualitative* spreading of Kṛṣṇa consciousness. Preaching doesn't mean just cheap taking up of Kṛṣṇa consciousness for awhile and then stopping. ISKCON—can it accommodate people who come to the institution for shelter and guidance? We see both ISKCON's so-called and real faults and doubt its capacity to actually care for millions of people. This adds to our doubts in the mission. If I, as one member, concentrate on improving myself and telling of this attempt, I see that as one aspect of Kṛṣṇa conscious preaching. It's not opposed to other types of preaching. *Āpani ācari, prabhu jīvere śikhāya.*

Doubt is a heavy thing. I see myself getting hung up on material details, such as how could the same *arcā-vigrahas* of Rāma and Sītā be worshiped for millions of years? Well, why not? Do I think stone can't last that long? Or if the Supreme likes, that He can't refurbish it, keep it "young" and in good repair? You fool! Even if He replaces the Deity, what's the harm?

"How old is this tree? Millions of years? I don't believe it. I don't believe Hanumān could jump so far or that a bridge could be made of floating stones."

I *don't* doubt all that. I know Kṛṣṇa has inconceivable potency. I'm not like Jamadagni dāsa challenging Prabhupāda to his face about the size of the Yadu dynasty in *Kṛṣṇa* book: "How could they have so many toilets in Dvārakā?" I'm not that bad, but I'm trying to look at what doubts there are.

Sometimes I fantasize about doing some really great work. This comes when I hear some well-composed music or see a good painting or hear about some tremendous Vaiṣṇava activities, such as Lord Caitanya's traveling all over India and converting people, or about the exploits of a Godbrother who is doing the same. Then I come down to earth and tell myself, "This is it, baby. Whatever you're doing."

Do you mean just this funny kind of writing and these limited travels to the Caribbean and the Northeast U.S.? Those little pilgrimages here and there?

Yes, that's what's happening. If Kṛṣṇa likes, He could expand what I'm doing, and I could also try to work up some new bravery or desire to do more. Regardless of that, I have to see what I'm doing and inject it with quality devotion. I can't see how I will suddenly expand into something else. I already have to pray for the nerve to do these activities. I just pray to remain enthusiastic until my last breath.

3:36 A.M.

Possible topics of a new book:

What it is to be a guru, how I feel about it.

Or a repeat: my relationship with Śrīla Prabhupāda tackled fresh each time in directed free-write sessions. I already wrote *My Relationship With Lord Kṛṣṇa*, and I've reviewed the books I have read in my life. At the end of the month Baladeva will come and I will give most of my time to discussing memories with him. I have three weeks in which to shift gears if I want to.

Whether or not I shift gears, the more important thing to me is to speak in my own voice. Sometimes I feel physically small (an Alice in Wonderland trick), and that's me too. Beyond me, however, there are the modes of nature, especially the mode of goodness, which is the gateway to the *śuddha-sattva*. That's me too, but I don't know it yet. Prabhupāda is leading me toward that identity—I'm eternally his *śiṣya*—and I could write a book on that.

Last night I told Śyāmānanda that surrender means to give up things unfavorable to *bhakti*, but also to use things—good things and talents—in the Lord's service. Like your own voice. That's my surrender.

Return to your own. I belong with the *śāstras*. I feel good that I'm regularly hearing Prabhupāda's lectures and inserting them into my diary so there'll be something good to read later. It's like cooking with the best ingredients. Prabhupāda spoke on the opening verses of the seventeenth chapter of *Bhagavad-gītā:* "This is very important, Arjuna's question about people who don't follow the *śāstras* or a bona fide guru but who have some faith." What about them? Prabhupāda said again, "This is very important." We listen more closely. We want it; we're interested in what Bhagavān Śrī Kṛṣṇa has to say. When He has something authoritative to say, Kṛṣṇa is described as Bhagavān because the rascals misunderstand Kṛṣṇa as an ordinary man.

8:24 A.M.

What is beyond me? Of course, I'm only a cipher. Almost everyone is more important than I am. I don't have money, influence, etc., except in a very limited way. But to myself I'm important, the center of existence. I ought to see Kṛṣṇa as the center of my life as well as center of all—*ahaṁ sarvasya prabhavo. Bhoktāraṁ yajña-tapasāṁ sarva-loka-maheśvaram*—but I see myself, my body, my mind, my little attachments for food and music and dreams and sex. Just dreamt a very old man was embracing a child of three or four. I was disgusted and tried to stop it. The old lecher was supposed to be giving medical or professional attention to the little girl, but he brought his face close to hers for lascivious kisses—and she was open to it. I tried to stop them but I was doing something dubious myself (can't recall what it was, but nothing like *that*). I'm absorbed in such small things—dreams and other life—and advising myself to become even more absorbed in it. I say it's the way to God and that it's required. We have to know ourselves, be honest, speak our truths, etc. A simpler devotee, however, might think it enough to be fixed in seeking out Kṛṣṇa's pleasure.

Sharon Olds writes in her poem "Little Things" about a tiny pool of maple syrup on the dinner table and, "My son's sunburn peels like insect wings, where I peeled his back." She says she remembers little things to love about her father, "Because of all the big things/ I could not love, no one could, it would be wrong to."

And these last lines:

"I am doing something I learned early to do, I am
paying attention to small beauties,
whatever I have—as if it were our duty to
find things to love, to bind ourselves to this world."

I coach myself to go after little things too, but not to bind myself to this world. I want to leave this world of rebirth and sorrow and pain. By attending to little things I find a connection to Kṛṣṇa and devotion, moment to moment.

Little things: waking up after a twenty-minute nap each morning after breakfast, the room still dark. I reach over from the bed and jerk the curtain aside and the first light of morning enters the room.

The key in the brass lock that opens the shed door. Copper-colored trees, the sound of rain on the shed roof, droplets melting on the window.

"The Supreme Godhead exchanges transcendental love in His original form of Kṛṣṇa." (Bg. 11.54, purport) Go to Kṛṣṇa for that, not vague concepts of God or specific lumps of attraction or pleasures flickering in this world. Kṛṣṇa in His original form and our transcendental relationship with Him—by His mercy and the mercy of His pure devotees.

We want to go to Kṛṣṇaloka. "He has full knowledge of that planet, and therefore he is not interested in any other." (Bg. 11.55, purport)

"He does not want to be transferred even to the highest planet, Goloka Vṛndāvana. His only objective is to serve Kṛṣṇa wherever he may be." (Bg. 11.55, purport)

Stay near these descriptions of Kṛṣṇa's form as essential and supreme. *Bhagavad-gītā As It Is* will give them to you. Carry that book wherever you go and read it.

Read it.

Then when you hit a wall you can turn to the *Gītā* phrases—or near phrases—already alive in your mind, such as, My devotee will never perish; he comes to Me; you are My dear friend, so I'm telling this most confidential knowledge; think of Me; become My devotee; come to Me when you leave your body by thinking of Me; engage in My devotional service.

Mean it and feel it.

And now it's done. Kṛṣṇa has stopped showing Arjuna (and the demigods and demons) the Viśvarūpa and has returned to revealing His original two-handed form. The next chapter addresses the topic of devotional service. Finally He says work for Me, worship Me, and then the chapter is over. I decide that's enough for me now, until the next time.

It has become warmer and the sky lighter. I'm not feeling so young that I could draw a picture of Rādha-Kṛṣṇa, and not so adventuresome either. Instead, I scribble lines and stay longer in the chaos before I "resolve" it with form—usually a squat, cartoony man walking, and in the poverty of my imagination, carrying the same beadbag (worn mistakenly on his left hand) and branded with yellow *tilaka*. His *śikhā* is messy and untied, like mine.

2:55 P.M.

I just began "Conversations With Śrīla Prabhupāda," a series of spoken prayers. I'm springboarding from St. Teresa's method of personal prayer as taught in a book called *Conversation With Christ*. It's interesting how prayer seeks to control the mind's wanderings while writing *allows* it. When I'm writing, the words take a trip of their own, but when speaking to Prabhupāda, I'm in the confessional, contrite, eyes shut, aspiring for the holy contact. He said it would depend on my purity whether I would be able to contact the spiritual master in the heart.

Today I introduced myself to Prabhupāda and mentioned my failings, but I also acknowledged that he is my link to Kṛṣṇa. I quoted the last two *ślokas* of "*Gurvāṣṭakam*". I made no petitions; I mainly wanted to make contact. I want to develop the habit of being able to pray to him always. It's quite simple.

Next to last day of November. Still awaiting word from Madhu on his hernia operation. Tomorrow I'll speak to disciples by having Śyāmānanda read from *The Wild Garden*. Then I'll comment. Chant a round with them too.

O Lord, it ain't easy?

O Lord, ain't it hard?

The rain came down even through the sunshine and I saw a rainbow. Then it rained some more. Little Jayānanda had to stay indoors, but as soon as it cleared he ran outdoors and shot his twig arrows high in the sky. He said, "There's an invisible demon up there. No one can see him but me."

4:30 P.M.

Manu gets back late tonight. His car looks like it's falling apart. He too is wearing thin at the edges from hard work. A good man. And Śyāmānanda dāsa will come over. He's got a kind, young heart and good intelligence to understand his spiritual master's books. Sees more in them than I do sometimes. Oh yeah, that's right, I'm not a goof-off, I'm a guru. Hey, what about the limp and rash and quirk and tremor on your left side when you read something? It happens.

A *mātājī* opens the outer door, and then I know they've put the *prasādam* on the trunk out there. I told you how it's done. Today there was one tiny piece of cookie on Śrīla Prabhupāda's plate and I got none. What was that about?

The heavens have opened and it's pouring rain. I assume that I'll be here in the morning to write again on the prayer project and that I'll be able to go to India in 1997 and then the millennium will come. I assume I'll get plenty of warning and things will go along as Clinton promised. That is, that America will keep winning while he's the president. I hope so. They bombed Iraq again, and the Iraqis would sure like to bomb New York City or Washington, D.C., but they can't. They don't have that much power in the skies. That's why they have to do things like plant bombs on airplanes. There are mastermind terrorists over there, and the FBI is constantly tracking them down. Yusef Ahald, the brain of Pakistan's back alleys, is researching how to make a bomb that can fit into a cigarette pack and not be detected, and the other side is researching how to brain them back, or smear them into the dust as any good, redneck American would like to see done with the whole Middle East. None of the above is ultimately possible without Kṛṣṇa's sanction, that we know, and the karma will rebound. We know that too. The scientists will call the reaction "black spring" or "winter fallout." But blow back on us all it will.

Meanwhile, North Ireland is peaceful—at least this part of it. I have to give credit to the young men loading up their trucks with Prabhupāda's books. That's what this world needs.

Graham crackers, slim crackers, people want peace. What if you've been recently diagnosed with a bad disease? If it's benign, okay. Live with it. If it's malignant? Read the chapter and see how Betty B. coped with it and went on skiing. Someone else wrote penpals later and sat by the pool jazzing, and still had sex despite broken legs and asthma. I said, "Geez, how can these people teach me anything?" You'll get misled. Be careful.

November 30

MIDNIGHT

Good news. Madhu's hernia operation was successful. He spoke with Śyāmānanda on the phone and said that he didn't even take any painkillers after the operation. "I'm a man," Madhu boasted. So that's happiness in the material world—your friend's hernia operation is a success!

Dear Śrīla Prabhupāda, I'm grateful to have received from you and the Supersoul the starting idea to pray and converse with you. I did the first "session" yesterday. I shouldn't analyze it to death, but just gratefully receive the gift and then turn to you and speak.

Yesterday it seemed auspicious to me when I desired to return to prayer. One reason is that prayer allows me to be entirely focused on Kṛṣṇa conscious means of expression. In conversing with Śrīla Prabhupāda, I'm not going to need to read modern poets, or for that matter, writers on Christian prayer.

It also made me face the challenge of why I look at modern poets. It seems like such a big *anartha*, exposed once again. Today I'm trying to look at it positively. My studies in modern writing by nondevotees still have a place in my service. I want to write in the very best way. I may have to learn how to do that from those who are dedicated to writing even though they are not devotees.

I want to be devoted to writing in Kṛṣṇa's service, and I could say that Kṛṣṇa will teach me everything I need through my heart, and that's true, but it's a stark truth that I can't work with now. I suppose I should just admit that I have some attachment to these nondevotee writers and their expression even though neither the attachment nor the writers are pure. I'm dovetailing.

Aside from that, however, I see my reading in poetry as part of the risks inherent in my service. Book distributors regularly risk contact with the unholy materialists when they go out on the streets to distribute books. Sometimes they fall on the battlefield because their attachments are reawakened. It's a risk that our spiritual master asked us to take for the greater good of distributing books. There is nothing to compare it with, and I certainly don't dare to compare myself to those brave soldiers. Nevertheless, the principle is that for service, we want to make the very best contribution for Kṛṣṇa. My daydream is to write works which will last and be appreciated in the future even by nondevotees or even those a little inclined toward devotional life. It would be helpful for me to know about prosody, and I don't mean from an academic point of view. I should have it float through my blood and be as expert as they are, to know how to write a good sentence and to be well practiced at it every day.

3:50 A.M.

I don't really need to read *lectio divina*—St. Teresa or St. John of the Cross or modern persons in that line—to learn how to speak in a prayerful way to Śrīla Prabhupāda. My reading of those works is more for general knowledge about prayer, not a need to learn direct application. Prayer comes from the heart naturally. I know what to do when I speak, and I have faith that the communication is valid because Prabhupāda is hearing me. It depends on my purity how deep this awareness is, so I'm trying to pray honestly and purely, openly confessing and praising.

In Cc. Lord Caitanya says that in Goloka Vṛndāvana, the Vrajavāsīs don't think of Kṛṣṇa as God. They don't care for His opulence, but they adore His sweetness. This made me wonder about my *aiśvarya* prayers to Prabhupāda and Kṛṣṇa. Of course, Prabhupāda encourages us to think of Kṛṣṇa as the all-great and inconceivable Lord. At the same time, he tells us to think of Kṛṣṇa as a bluish cowherd boy holding a flute, the lover of Rādhā. I'm trying to follow what he teaches in terms of praying to Kṛṣṇa.

In talking to Prabhupāda himself, however, I have been thinking more mystically that I'm not actually making an attempt to talk to him in order to receive an answer. I am trying to contact what I call my "inner Prabhupāda."

Feeling happy on waking at midnight (actually, eight minutes before). I made up the bed, tucked in the sheets and covers, washed my mouth and face with cold water, scraped my tongue, put on a sweater and sweatshirt, and gave Śrīla Prabhupāda his dictaphone. I then sat to work. I answered the mail that arrived last night before I took rest, then read—not much, but I was amazed at Lord Caitanya's wonderful teachings. He said that Lakṣmī-devī cannot enter the *rāsa* dance, but the personified *Upaniṣads* can. Lord Caitanya asked Vyeṅkaṭa Bhaṭṭa if he knew why this was so. Vyeṅkaṭa said, "I am

Bhagavad-gita
10.12–14
O KRSNA

This Truth

OM NAMAH
BHAKTI

We like you to flow with tears, blood, sweat, and ink.

Draupadī wants attention.

an ordinary human being. Since my intelligence is very much limited and I am easily agitated, my mind cannot enter within the deep ocean of the pastimes of the Lord. You are the Supreme Personality of Godhead Kṛṣṇa Himself. You know the purpose of Your activities, and the person whom You enlighten can also understand Your pastimes." (Cc. *Madhya* 9.125–26) Lord Caitanya told him that we need to follow the *gopīs'* path if we hope to enter *rāsa-līlā*. Lakṣmī-devī is unable to do that. There's no teaching like this in Christianity. Follow the path of Rādhā-Kṛṣṇa. It is inconceivably sweet beyond all *aiśvarya*.

Vivaldi please. One music piece, a religious one. The one he composed in honor of Rādhārāṇī in Vraja or the aria he wrote about the cowherd boys—the one he learned in *paramparā*. You don't have it? He's just a mundane Italian from long ago? Then how was he able to capture the mind so? Oh, that's *māyā*. But isn't it Kṛṣṇa too? Could you imagine it being played while devotees take *prasādam*?

No, we can only play rock-'n'-roll. It's the music to which we perform our duties—thump, thump, rocky and hoarse—but at least we chant Hare Kṛṣṇa and become transformed.

Oh ho, I wrote a snappy letter to a woman in America who wants to talk about issues. She thinks there is such a thing as soul mates, husbands and wives who meet in the spiritual world. What's your opinion on that, SDG? We regard you as an ecclesiastical authority, so please speak into the mike.

"Okay, I'll talk, but only on certain conditions. I don't want to be quoted or dragged into heated debates. I don't want to be introduced to your friends who support the schisms, and I definitely don't want to be reminded about the misdeeds we have seen in ISKCON. Those memories are just too painful. I'd rather be alone to pontificate humbly from my solitude via letters. If you want to hear from me, those are the rules, but if you don't like my restrictions, better you write to someone else. Anyway, it is hopeless to try to change things, ma'am. Don't you know there *is* no reform except of the self? We don't have to take the part of big reformers and drive all the homosexuals out.

2:54 P.M.

I just spoke to you, Śrīla Prabhupāda, and it felt good. You became present in the room. I awaken to you by vibrating my voice in this shed. The pen is silent, but the voice breaks through in a different way.

I am about to close out Volume One of this journal. I don't need anything but life, little life, life of *śāstra*, the fact of my service relationship with the Supreme Lord and His Divine Grace, Śrīla Prabhupāda.

I told the devotees today to be peaceful and yet berate their complacency. In that way, they will eventually find the balance. I said so many things, but who am I to speak? I don't know. I defend ISKCON and have faith that we are gradually becoming pure. I glorify Kṛṣṇa. I don't need to analyze that or attempt to measure Kṛṣṇa's mercy on me. I simply have to love Him and serve Him even when I'm dull or my head is in a vise.

The two swans on the lake remind me of the Supersoul and the individual soul. Kṛṣṇa, You remain with us always. The lake is this world, or the world of our hearts.

O Kṛṣṇa, please allow me to give out *Śrīmad-Bhāgavatam* truths through the gut, through the grinder, in words. As kids we used to mock, "Truer words were never spoken through falser teeth." As if a toothless person were the epitome of the despicable, the object of laughter. Well, now I have no teeth, and it hasn't budged me from my conviction to speak out in praise of guru and Kṛṣṇa.

Prabhupāda writes, "A pure devotee is constantly engaged. Sometimes he chants, sometimes he hears or reads books about Kṛṣṇa, or sometimes he cooks *prasādam* or goes to the marketplace to purchase something for Kṛṣṇa, or sometimes he washes the temple or the dishes—whatever he does, he does not let a single moment pass without devoting his activities to Kṛṣṇa. Such action is in full *samādhi*." (Bg. 12.2 purport) He makes it sound so easy. Just live in the temple, be a full-time devotee, and by virtue of your assignment you'll always be able to serve Kṛṣṇa. If you do it sincerely and mindfully, then you'll be in the "presence of God." Is it really "too simple"?

Thank You, Lord Kṛṣṇa, for giving us this easy process of *bhakti-yoga*. Maybe it doesn't always feel as easy as falling off a log, but it's certainly not as hard as the impersonal practice. "Often there is much penance involved before one fully surrenders to Him." Please let me do the needful.

Appendix

REPERTOIRE

These are some of the modes of expression that I used in this volume of *Every Day, Just Write* and which I hope to use in Volume Two. This is only a partial list.

LITTLE LIFE

Don't be ashamed to give the data, names, places, events. Don't fear repetition. Confess.

WRITING WHILE READING

Read one of Prabhupāda's books; it is essential to my daily routine. Write on it simply and straightforwardly and use it to springboard. Come back to it frequently as if answering the questions, "What did I just read? What struck me?"

FREE-WRITING

While all my writing may use this method, I will also take time for "pure" exercises of "keep the hand moving," etc.

POEMS

At least once a day write a poem with typewriter or pen. Read a poetry book, then break into one from your free-writing prose. Just force your way into the first lines even if they make no logical sense. After the triggering lines, you'll usually find a theme.

DREAMS

Capture them and do something with them.

PRAYER

This is the newly begun "Conversations with Śrīla Prabhupāda." I hope to continue it twice a day in the shed. It's a separate project from writing, but I can also write prayers in *Every Day, Just Write*.

DRAWINGS

With colors and Tombos, let hand move in chaos until you find a form (or forms) you want to express.

No failure here. Some will express themes and scenes in the writing or just immediate feelings. Try to give it some Kṛṣṇa conscious identification. The drawings are welcome!

Search for the Authentic Self

Every Day, Just Write

Volume 2

Geaglum, Inis Rath
December 1–29, 1996

Satsvarūpa dāsa Goswami

GN Press, Inc.

Contents

December 1, 1996

12:08 A.M.

Dreamt Madhu and I were living like bum wanderers, determined not to settle down and take ordinary jobs. Madhu kept a neatly drawn cartoon book of our amazing and often humorous adventures. For example, once two policemen came to arrest us when we were camping in the woods. They were confident we must be carrying marijuana, but they couldn't find any. There was nothing wrong with us. I told the policeman that my father was a fireman, so I knew something about a policeman's life, and I praised them for risking their lives to protect the citizens. Dream and wake, dream and wake, danger and rescue, all recorded in this cartoon book. What's it leading to, adding up to?

Took rest at 6 P.M. yesterday because of a viselike headache. I thought how nice it would be to wake up at midnight clear of pain, and here I am. My wish came true. Later, I'm supposed to give class in the temple, so I had better look at the Cc. for topics. We've been reading Cc. regularly. We're up to the pastime when Lord Nityānanda breaks Lord Caitanya's *daṇḍa*. Quick, want to comment on that? But the Lord's pastimes are grave, and only a pure devotee can understand them. Lord Caitanya wanted to observe the rules of *sannyāsa*, but Lord Nityānanda—anyway, that's already explained in the purport. I do appreciate, however, that we get glimpses of Lord Caitanya as a *person*. He's blackish Kṛṣṇa covered in the golden complexion of Śrīmatī Rādhārāṇī and tasting *vipralambha*. He is the most munificent person. A verse in *Mahābhārata* states that He took *sannyāsa* at a young age to save us all.

Every day, just write. It's good for me. In a segment of the same dream, I was wearing swimming trunks (ill-fitting ones) and working with two *karmīs*. I went aside from them and ate my only food of the day—two apples. My face and form immediately filled out and became healthy from eating the apples, but something told me I still needed more nutrients than that.

Is it cheese I need or just a laugh?

Laugh if you're chronically ill.

"Where is the *kṛṣṇa-prema*? Did you bring me any?" I asked Mahā-mantra on her return from Vṛndāvana. No, she didn't, but she did bring me some mixed hard raisins, nuts in the shell, and white granules you buy at the store there. I spoke foolishly on the "reality" of Vṛndāvana as non-ideal. The next time I speak I should correct what I say and be sure people know I am talking about my subjective "reality," not the actual Vṛndāvana.

TAKE TO IT

Another happy day in life,
take to it brother,
read some Cc. or
Bhagavad-gītā—He's the
sound in ether
you can breathe or
not be able to breathe—
due to some mercy of
God, Kṛṣṇa.

While you breathe and move
your hand and *see*—blessed
gift—praise Him who
knows all, creates all,
sustains all and destroys.
Praise your best friend.

O spiritual master, through you
I reach Kṛṣṇa and Kṛṣṇa
reaches me. Kindly give
me intelligence to serve you.
You are great and kind
to come to us and to
stay with us. You provide
the boat that carries us
across.

Yes, it's good to praise instead of always facing my own faults and failures. Give the reader (and writer) relief.

By reading *Caitanya-caritāmṛta*,
I see Lord Nityānanda throw the
broken *daṇḍa* in the
Bhārgīnadī River.

Now the Lord moves to
Nīlācala—He's six miles away but
every mile seems like eternity
in His yearning for Lord Jagannātha,
whom He sees
as Kṛṣṇa carrying the flute.

Move on that road,
spirit soul in
the wake of Lord Caitanya.

5:40 A.M.

Teresa speaks of the importance of walking in self-knowledge all the days of our life. The commentator writes, "An important point about Teresian self-knowledge is that it is not introspective or centered in the incomplete self; rather it is God- and Christ-centered." One Godbrother wrote me, "Don't think about yourself so much in your books. It's a drag to read it; we want to hear the glories of Kṛṣṇa. If you did that you'd be more saintly. Sure, we all have faults and we don't progress, but we don't want to keep hearing that you slopped up your *gāyatrīs* again."

Well, then what else can I say? All glories to the *gāyatrī-mantra*? Yes, I know it comes from Kṛṣṇa's flute and enters Lord Brahmā's eight ears, then comes out his mouth (I think) as the Sanskrit *ślokas* that we recite. The *gāyatrīs* are the *kāma-bīja* mantras for perfect persons. They have deep meanings. I *know* that. But I'm not just a religious academic who wants to repeat the facts. I want to discuss my experience and to overcome complacency.

I know my writing has a sharp edge of self-accusation, but I am too easy on myself. I'm a squirrel running a treadmill. Please help.

Last Sunday it snowed, but we went to the island anyway. It's warmer this Sunday. I have my margin pencil notes written into the Cc., and I'm ready to speak about Lord Caitanya as the ideal *sannyāsī*. Lord Caitanya didn't like to hear others call Him God, but Lord Nityānanda didn't like Him to be seen as ordinary. Sometimes a devotee's feelings are in conflict with the Lord's.

Do I have anything relevant to say? Maybe I can tell the mothers that taking care of their children is devotional service. What about the fact that everyone should take *sannyāsa*? And we should all love this person, Lord Caitanya. We can get close to Him by reading the Cc.

Pulling through rounds—it's hour after hour chanting. Madhu drives hour after hour in heavy traffic and I usually sit in the back hour after hour. Jet pilots fly hour after hour over the ocean on their way to the Middle East or India. I chant hour after hour, trying to face the name head-on.

Kṛṣṇa, please help us. There's still time.

8 A.M., IF I HAD TO GO TO WORK: A DREAM

I was observing workers in a supermarket. It would be hard if I had to work like *that*. I saw meat in a freezer and thought of having to work long hours, riding an elevator carrying things, waiting for the time to pass. One worker opened a can of soda and was drinking it during his break.

WATCHING THE KILLER

Then the dream imagery shifted. I was still watching rather than participating directly when I saw a mysterious character, a killer. He had a knife broken at the tip, and two women in gray sweaters in a nearby house were frightened of him. It was strange because he seemed to be standing half submerged in the earth. Above him a fire burned hotter and hotter. Suddenly I felt a pain in my right leg just above the knee. It woke me up. It occurred to me as I woke that I have been taking life too easy. Without doubt I will have to face such pain at the time of death.

And so?

And so it's almost time to go over to the island. We were worried that it would be too windy, but the wind has died down and the sky has become a beautiful pearl gray.

It's embarrassing that my dreams are not ready-made Kṛṣṇa conscious experiences. Neither are they dissertations on the philosophy or even me dancing in ecstasy before the Deities. They are filled with strange things I cannot understand. Still, I at least have some faith in the premise that some good part within myself, some benevolent director, is trying to give me messages I need to hear in order to make a reformation of myself.

Therefore, dear reader, if you see dreams in this volume, please accept this statement of faith as a disclaimer. Don't think of the dreams as frivolous or as simply mundane. I do think they have a purpose, although I haven't figured out what that purpose is. I assume it is to make me a better devotee.

2:45 P.M.

Pray to Prabhupāda. Saying his name again and again is the perfection (satisfaction) of vowels and consonants. Oh,

baby-talk spiritualist

you say "Fie on AG's cosmopolitan greeting."

Unless he chants Hare Kṛṣṇa once, what use is it? Only Hare Kṛṣṇa

can bring peace,

if the rascals would stop trying to prevent it.

A preacher's thankless task is to spread the name.

Came to Boston Pier 1965 and said to himself, "When I ask them, 'No meat, no illicit sex, etc.,' they will say, 'Go home (to India).'" That some Western boys and girls have come is proof of his power.

O sunlight after rain, I ask my little hand to write.

Naive artists need apply: submit 500 drawings in wax color all with *tilaka* of obsessed patience.

Oh, Kṛṣṇa Caitanya is the most munificent person.

Now I want to be pure..
But It's too late!
Flood

GURU on his birthday

Lough Erne *haṁsa*.

Gītā waits for me.

I love you
and you love me
Śrīla Prabhupāda said, and
in Trinidad they *say*
they love you. "That's a different thing"—whether we are sentimentalists and say we love you but don't act on your behalf.

You say that the first requirement is to be sinless, as in *yeṣāṁ tv anta-gataṁ pāpaṁ janānāṁ puṇya-karmaṇām.* (Bg. 7.28) Four rules. Or no initiation by him. Follow them—get his grace.

Māyā is strong, so don't give her a chance.

Kleśo 'dhikataras teṣām avyaktāsakta-cetasām. (Bg. 12.5)

The embodied soul . . . thinking of the times we used to cheat and steal for Kṛṣṇa. Embarrassing now. We could have been arrested. I won't name names, but "some devotees" used to put metal slugs in the public telephone instead of dimes, and then they devised a method of hitting people up in the airport. They dressed nicely, and in the rush of foot traffic they would turn suddenly to some person and say, "Excuse me, sir, but I've just lost my wallet and I have a ticket. I'm about to fly out but I just don't have any money. Could you lend me some money?" People would give them ten or twenty dollars, whatever they needed. Preying upon people's natural kindness to strangers. In one temple, they collected money like that to buy the chandeliers.

Better not to confess such stuff, huh? I remember when Prabhupāda's letters were published by the BBT in Mexico completely unedited. I felt they shouldn't have printed some of them. Prabhupāda says black market, white market money, it's all like that in this world.

Water dripping down the outside of this window. Do they fog over because my body is becoming dehydrated? My body is a little powerhouse emanating so many different things—odors and auras, mental vibrations. I can even invite mental beings and dragons and bugs and psychic entities from outer space, but I won't call them! I'll just call Kṛṣṇa, Hare Kṛṣṇa! Kṛṣṇa, Kṛṣṇa.

In the early days of ISKCON we were so filled with happiness in Prabhupāda's presence that we didn't need to keep crazy diaries—although that would have been nice too, "scribbled notes for yr own joy"—by devotees in Kṛṣṇa consciousness, spontaneous, not full of complaints against others, blaming, naming the perpetrator of wrongs, but joy over apple crumble with whipped cream! Yeah, we finally got it again, and veggies and soup. You finish it quickly . . . got to move along in schedule and get rid of dross collected in the form of outside influences.

4:15 P.M.

I too could do 244 choruses like "Mexico City Blues," only mine would be Kṛṣṇa conscious blues, *brahmacārī* blues by Hayagrīva gone. He asked me in his last months to visit him at his bedside in New Vrindaban, but I couldn't get through the wall of those days. But I wrote him a letter saying I loved him.

Now I could write 244 choruses, but the jazz man blowing image which Kerouac uses is something unbefitting a Kṛṣṇa conscious person. I could give 244 *Śrīmad-Bhāgavatam* lectures, but that would be too long.

I am to give out *gāyatrī-mantras* to a devotee today. Better to give them to myself too, those blessed mantras in conjugal *rasa* that I don't deserve to chant but that have been given to me anyway. The flute sound enters Lord Brahmā's ear and comes out as *kāma-gāyatrī*. I don't deserve it, so at least don't sully it.

I want to gain courage by hearing straight from guru, *śāstra*, and *sādhu*. I read one psychologist who said that all organized religion is invalid and that when the charismatic leaders leave, religion becomes a dry and cynical business; that's the history of organized religion. Maybe, but Francis of

Assisi and Teresa of Avila stayed within the fold, and Śrīla Prabhupāda too, and so will I.

Kṛṣṇa, Kṛṣṇa—chant an extra round. My body continues to eat and consume and assimilate and digest even while Kṛṣṇa dives into the Yamunā and out again. We have to tread the holy path carefully and soberly if we want to stay in touch with Kṛṣṇa's pastimes. Peace. God is a person, but not a generic one. Therefore, chant the holy names. Kerouac didn't know the holy names and never had the opportunity to meet Śrīla Prabhupāda. Ginsberg met him and that's to his credit, but he wasn't pious enough, or was too self-conscious, to give up the things you have to give up in order to chant. He thought Kṛṣṇa consciousness was dogmatic. He wanted something universal, but not a Kṛṣṇa conscious version of it. He missed it because he preferred to run free in lust and false ego and the kind of Buddhism that allows you to do what you want and still end up at zero.

5:05 P.M., NIGHT NOTES

There is only one small light on down at the boathouse. I could write many choruses too, rhyming and chiming. As Kerouac gives out his half-baked Buddhism, could I give out my baked twice KC? Kṛṣṇa consciousness is the pinnacle. Only devotees can understand it.

Just a small light on at the boathouse. I could say "Kṛṣṇa, Kṛṣṇa," and be proud I chanted an extra round. Oh, for the day when many poets and writers, many thousands of intelligentsia, politicians, and athletes will chant Hare Kṛṣṇa. When will that day come when we will spread out like a vast oak or banyan tree under the sky? *Kīrtana* played with the musical instruments of every country.

Of course, we wish for such a thing, but Sören Kierkegaard said that when Christianity became the state religion, it ceased to exist. He said that there was a day when the apostles made a huge number of converts and that that signaled doom to pure religion. Lord Caitanya doesn't say things like that. Bhaktivinoda Ṭhākura and Śrīla Prabhupāda don't say those things either. But it does seem to imply the risk of watering down as the movement grows and spreads. How will we keep our simple purity?

December 2

12:20 A.M.

Distraction while trying to read Cc. I recorded my dreams during the night, re-entered them, captured key words, etc. Then I thought, "We learn by hearing from authority, not from dreams." Our time is limited, and so is our mental attention and devotion. We cannot splay out our energy everywhere with equal effectiveness. What purpose does becoming a dabbler serve in our attempt to attain the highest goal?

I want to attain *samādhi*, so I again find myself regretting that I have come here thinking about a dream. I believe there is truth in dreams somewhere, and certainly they are compelling stories, but I have to ask my dream-self to please excuse me from paying him too close attention. He knows I would rather opt for serving my guides, guru, *śāstra*, and the sages. Please don't divert my attention. These December weeks I want a quiet, determined homestretch of the year to read and write, pray to Prabhupāda and learn. This is on my mind as I read Lord Caitanya's talks to Vyeṅkaṭa Bhaṭṭa. Now the Lord has left Śrī Raṅgam. Pray, savor slowly, ruminate, and milk each phrase for mercy. I wish the Lord would pick me up and into the narrative. Just see this *brāhmaṇa* devotee of Lord Rāmacandra, how he's in *samādhi* within the *Rāmāyaṇa* pastime. Lord Caitanya was attracted to his mood and wanted to help him understand and rejoice in the actual meaning of the *Rāmāyaṇa* (Sītā-devī was never kidnapped, only a false Sītā was taken by Rāvaṇa.)

Kṛṣṇa will give us *darśana* if we keep trying for it. Do we want dreams? O Lord in heart who directs things, I can't understand the many obscure and bizarre dreams I experience. If You would like to instruct me in dreams, please do so, but please know that I especially need strength to surrender. I need to be convinced of the *reality* of the spiritual world of the *Bhāgavatam* and *Caitanya-caritāmṛta.* Let me dream of *that*, or at least of how to approach it. Otherwise, I'll sleep and wake and return to reading and writing and chanting Hare Kṛṣṇa mantra and continue to live without success.

Reading a diary I kept in Jagannātha Purī, 1993. It traces my return to Śrīla Prabhupāda's exclusive shelter. Unfortunately, many pages are missing in the copy I'm reading, but I remember that time well. Writing it made me feel more appreciative of Śrīla Prabhupāda and more at home in his ISKCON movement. Even when I feel uneasy in a particular ISKCON temple, it's still my home and where I belong. Please allow me to contribute to ISKCON, to improve it, and to maintain it in any way I can.

I still have issues to face in returning to that exclusive shelter. One effect is that I had begun to think that Prabhupāda teaches only the basics and that we need to hear about *rāgānuga-bhakti* in large, regular doses. Besides that, if we want to assimilate the teachings about *rāgānuga-bhakti,* we need the mercy of a *rasika* Vaiṣṇava other than Śrīla Prabhupāda. I no longer agree with those ideas. Neither am I interested in constantly hearing about the amorous, joking pastimes of Rādhā and Kṛṣṇa or the technical science of *rāgānuga* terminology. I'm not qualified to hear the pastimes of Kṛṣṇa and the *gopīs* in the *kuñjas.* That's my simple position.

But neither am I satisfied always with basics at the expense of thinking of Vraja. I know theoretically that *gopī-bhāva* is the highest goal. Am I like a riven cloud between *vaidhi* and *rāgānuga,* between the early cantos of the *Bhāgavatam* and the Tenth Canto?

I've decided that since I am not qualified to hear of the *kuñja* pastimes, I can at least pray for *ruci.* I don't want to try rooting out every influence I received from studying the "*ujjvala*" books of Rūpa and Raghunātha Gosvāmīs. It's bona fide *bhakti* philosophy. Still, I'm rightly situated as Śrīla Prabhupāda's *śiṣya.*

9:47 A.M.

If you can't think of Kṛṣṇa with love, without deviation, then follow the rules and regs of *bhakti-yoga;* you'll develop love of God eventually.

O Kṛṣṇa, I am a tiny Prabhupādānuga; as my master writes at midnight, so do I. In this shed fighting to stay alert and awake (although I'm waning). Did fifteen minutes of spoken prayer and about ten minutes of reading verses in *Bhagavad-gītā.* Now time for writing but . . . feeling tired. Is it gas fumes? Open windows. Sun behind cloud—"stage lights" by nature's director. God's water rippling, golden weeds at shore edge, "like Caitanya, Gaura."

Did you write in A.M. two crazy verses? Yeah, my own verses. Go now and take a brisk walk. Preserve the body a little longer. *He* Kṛṣṇa! *He* Kāna! When Śrīmatī Rādhārāṇī heard that name, She became agitated in *pūrva-rāga.* Just hearing His name! And when young Kṛṣṇa heard the name Rādhā, He became bewildered and embarrassed in the company of the *gopas*. Madhumaṅgala and Paurṇamāsī noted it.

Snapshots of local guru in rowboat—smile.

3:02 P.M.

Bhagavad-gītā teaches both the direct method of surrender and the step-by-step approach. We should chant Hare Kṛṣṇa, serve Kṛṣṇa with body, mind, and words, and propagate Kṛṣṇa consciousness (or help those who are propagating it). Direct means offering food to Kṛṣṇa, thinking of Him, bowing down before Him in the temple, regularly hearing His teachings, and applying them in our lives. It also means inquiring from and serving His pure devotees, especially the spiritual masters.

Okay, but our lives are filled with dreams and schemes and poems and loans and thievery and sneaking in little bits of sense gratification. Does that mean we should try more honestly the step-by-step approach? Or are we going backwards? I feel like I am crawling forward, zigzagging in my imperfection, always seeking the goal. I'll have to make up for my mistakes and I have until death to attain perfection.

Prabhupāda's memorable phrase, "Kṛṣṇa consciousness is the sublime method for reviving our original consciousness," reverberates in my head. He thought Kṛṣṇa consciousness was for everyone, whether he be a scholar or a child. "Everyone can take part in this chanting. Even a child can take part. Even a *dog* can take part—and chant and dance in ecstasy."

Today a headache. Not much time to write.

December 3

12:37 A.M.

Do you remember how this writing goes? You put your left foot in, you take your left foot out, you put your left foot in and you shake it all about . . .

Oh yes. I do remember, and I remember Kṛṣṇa, the great master of the Yadu dynasty. I read, skimming philosophy, fortunate and unfortunate at the same time. I'm right and blessed to be in the right place, turning the pages of Cc. It will stick. Something will stick. My peers will appreciate that I am frequently in touch with *śāstra*, but aside from that, *śāstra* will live in my heart and mind. But still I am both fortunate and unfortunate. I am fortunate to touch the holy scripture and unfortunate because I don't read carefully. I pass over whole verses and even occasional purports without noticing what they are about.

I did read that Tukārāma was initiated by Śrī Caitanya Mahāprabhu. He worshiped Viṭṭhala, a form of Viṣṇu, at Pāṇḍarapura, where Lord Caitanya's brother Viśvarūpa (Śaṅkarāraṇya) achieved perfection and left the world. Lord Caitanya met Raṅga Gosvāmī there. Raṅga Gosvāmī remembered that he went with his guru, Mādhavendra Purī, to Navadvīpa, where they were warmly received at the home of Jagannātha Miśra. He remembered how Śacīmātā was affectionate to the *sannyāsīs*, and he even remembered an unprecedentedly excellent curry she served made with banana flowers.

O friend, you appear to have been listening to the Tenth Canto. (You appear distracted, unattached to the world as if you have been listening to the music of Kṛṣṇa's flute.)

If we just keep telling, we'll eventually find the heart of it. Give us the flow of tears, blood, sweat, and ink. Like an artesian well there's always more, and when it rains due to the downpour of the guru's mercy, the flow will become a torrent.

Watched BBC video of Uddhava, the IRA man who became a Hare Kṛṣṇa devotee. He looked as handsome as an actor. His wife is growing older, but she's a real person. They showed an intimate moment with her as she applied *tilaka* and looking radiant said, "I'm sure if I aborted a child in my womb I would become a fetus in my next life to be aborted by someone else." Praghoṣa said a Unionist would become a Republican next life.

"Hmph. That's his opinion," a devotee viewer here at Inis Rath said.

Uddhava and his wife stood on the hill above Belfast. He looked down and said that from a distance it all seems rather insignificant, but while he was living there, he was wrapped up in the activities like everyone else. He hoped there would be peace. Newsreel shots of the troubles—police fighting Irish Catholics.

Shot of peaceful Wicklow, a deer, a spider, Prabhupāda dāsa teaching children how to draw a leaf.

3:37 A.M.

We can use our energy in many ways. Contemplating our choices we think we can do all that we want and that whatever we do will be joyous, energetic, and productive. This is largely an illusion. Energy runs low, we feel pain, and those things stop us. But before they do, we try to run the crest of each brief wave thinking we will do so many things at once. We don't like to make what we consider lesser choices. If we can only do a few things, which few things will they be? Better to choose the chanting first and then see if there is energy left over for other things. The holy name is the only way to understand God in this age, and understanding God is the main point.

9 A.M.

Happy and strong-voiced, I sing in the shed. Six—count them—six swans bob on the rough strait water. Steady downpour of rain. I'm snug in here reading and praying to my Guru Mahārāja. I explained myself to him—felt good.

Strong voice awhile. Our limited senses. Pen scratches. *Dharma* art—an attitude of non-aggressive, unpretentious, honest self-observation painted in brilliant colors and bold lines with a meditative mind. What do I see? I see how truth ebbs and flows.

Think of the swan's way. There are no clouds because the sky is all one dark blanket. I have already chanted my sixteen rounds, but I could chant more. I lost an hour this morning because of headache pain. Had to retreat to bed around 4:15, but I'm okay now singing here in the rain.

Śyāmānanda tells me that Draupadī's bellowing is not out of rage or to scare us away from her sister cow. He says she just wants attention. When she was a baby, she got a lot of human attention, so now she demands it. He said when she bellows like that, he goes right up to her and pats her and she becomes silent and calm. I don't know. She looks pretty unfriendly to me. And I heard about the protecting-the-herd theory from a reliable source.

2:50 P.M.

Madhu phoned and talked with Śyāmānanda. He said the doctor told him he has a second hernia on the other side and maybe next year he ought to have another operation. Madhu said there's no way he wants to go through *that* again. I'm concerned for him and want him to be careful not to lift anything heavy. Also, I flashed on a dream I had today where my father complained of hernia pain. Why all these hernias?

I prayed to Prabhupāda today. He's in his books and tapes, but to hear and apply his advice is not always easy. Prayer seems to help. It puts me more in touch with him aside from the usual assurance I feel of his presence.

It's up to a disciple to serve and please the spiritual master. Our surrender is a deliberate act of free will, and we have to make that surrender day after day, hour after hour. It's an art and we can always improve it. The overall surrender and desire to obey the guru, to love him, will lead to using our intelligence in various situations. We have to ask ourselves, "Is this for me or is this for Śrīla Prabhupāda? Am I fulfilling his mission by this act?" We can always refine our understanding.

Manu sent me a note before he left to sell paintings for the week. He began reading *Pada-yātrā* and said he was impressed by it. It seems to be an evolution in my process, he said, in that I'm in control more *while* doing the free-writing. He said I was able to take larger breaths to sing the melodies. I take it that free-writing needs to be developed. It may appear to be folly, but if I persist in it, I'll get wise, get control, be more lucky to find those metaphors (serendipity) that can last for a whole book like the *Pada-yātrā*—writing is walking every day, or writing my memories.

Every Day, Just Write is different because I take only the assignment each day to write what comes. Since I allow myself freedom from the need to present a formal metaphor by which to present my writing, then at least I have to keep writing. That's the basic premise.

Life at Geaglum is smooth sailing. I'm in a bubble of peaceful days and nights, living on devotee-owned land. There are no alien sounds and no alien faces. It's a holy *dhāma*. In January I'll have to leave and meet the outside world. That doesn't mean I have to pop the bubble now and seek to tune in to the world of controversy and danger in and out of ISKCON. Stay absorbed.

The water in the strait is the roughest I've seen it in a long time. It looks like a rushing river. I don't think the water is actually flowing, but the top is being blown into white caps. It would be difficult to cross now in the rowboat, and I'm not going to attempt it. Rain, heavy all day. I see the collie wandering around, soaked. The cows too.

December 4

12:45 A.M.

I say the predictable. When reading, I also feel, "Oh, here it is, the same thing I read not long ago"—where King Pratāparudra inquired from Sārvabhauma about Lord Caitanya. Same old thing? I stop, sigh, pause, and then go forward with some effort—and awareness—that there is nectar here. I have to work at finding it. I certainly haven't milked Prabhupāda's books dry.

"In this age of Kali there are no genuine religious principles other than those established by Vaiṣṇava devotees and Vaiṣṇava scriptures. This is the sum and substance of everything.

"The pastimes of Śrī Caitanya Mahāprabhu are just like an unfathomable ocean. It is not possible for me to enter into them. Simply standing on the shore, I am but touching the water.

"The more one hears the pastimes of Śrī Caitanya Mahāprabhu with faith, analytically studying them, the more one attains the ecstatic riches of love of Godhead." (Cc. *Madhya* 9.362–64)

I complain, I read in cycles, I rejoice, I repeat, I do the loop-de-loop and pass through familiar country. It's my poverty, but also my richness.

It's like where I'm living nowadays. I'm not traveling, so every day I see the same shed, the same path, wet leaves, lake, and island. I don't grow tired of the view—especially at dawn—or the seasons (spring and early summer are especially nice). I know I can't live here forever, so whatever I see and repeat has to become an act of devotion. Whatever I read, familiar as it seems, also has to become an act of devotion because I won't be here forever. The reading experience can be transformed from restlessness to love of Kṛṣṇa by such an attempt.

3:30 A.M.

Śrīla Prabhupāda: "So this is all dream. . . . because this body is false, so whatever we are acting, it is just like dream. Just like in dream at night we also work. So this is gross dream and that is subtle dream. But real life is spiritual life." (Lecture by Śrīla Prabhupāda, *Bhāg.* 1.5.23, August 4, 1974)

A DREAM

In a dream I was in a classroom with a friendly teacher. He asked me to read aloud from the dictionary. I think the word was "I." I went to read it and then saw the word "who," but couldn't read what followed. Either the print was too small or the situation too stressful. A small group of girls began to laugh at me, but Madhu was there and told me not to be concerned because their attitude was simply pedantic.

When I awoke I thought, "It's true, people don't appreciate us. Still, we shouldn't become stressed or intimidated by that, or try to adjust ourselves to do everything their way."

That became obvious to me when reflecting on this dream. As Prabhupāda says, the dream and the activities of our conscious lives are all false. We simply have to remember Kṛṣṇa and learn how to please Him. Everything else is immaterial.

6 A.M.

Kṛṣṇa is *part* of my life. I usually don't admit that. I say He's my whole life, twenty-four hours a day—*anyābhilāṣitā-śūnyam*. The fact is, however, that I have other interests. I take a break, a holiday from Kṛṣṇa consciousness. It sounds awful, but maybe it does me good—I need it. My vacation doesn't include stopping my sixteen rounds or breaking the regulative principles. It's more like sleeping, eating, dreaming . . . In the dreams, the fact that my devotee identity is often vague and the actions mostly not spiritual—doesn't that say something about my stage of devotion? I could try to deny it, but it's true.

They say the body doesn't lie. My body is not always interested in Kṛṣṇa conscious pursuits. That's because "I'm not this body"—that truth—is still theoretical to me. I feel hurt when my body is hurt. I'm not detached.

Wise guy, you should be
booted in the ass. Don't you know you
can even get booted out of Kṛṣṇa consciousness and
into Army boot camp next life?
Then you'll be sorry!

8:50 A.M.

The sunrise: butter gold melting blaze. Jewel hot spiky rays. Shimmery melted. Searchlight by day. Fire in sky. Coming through the trees, essential life-giving light. Light of Brahman. The aura of denizens of sun planet. Sūrya's chariot.

Let yourself write. The topic is God. He is *all* things. Don't let non-God conscious people speak to your heart even if they seem to have valuable information. Turn to your old best

Swan's way.

Walk your way and pray to God in Hare Kṛṣṇa mantras.

Before day closes out with headache, get in a shed session.

Walk on earth and chant.

friends, starting with guru and the Supersoul, then onto the Vaiṣṇavas of ancient times up to right now.

Bump against shed—a bird? Pearl dewdrops barely frozen, globules clinging to the weeds. As the sun rises, they will melt.

Madhu will be back in a week. It hasn't been much different without him, and when he comes back he'll be forbidden to lift any weight. No more sliding under the van for a half-hour's work.

Then how will we do our European tours? We'll be two old men, not much different from the tourists you sometimes see. Somehow they dare to travel abroad, and with a little money, they manage to get someone to carry the luggage or to repair the car. We could hobble around like that as long as Madhu can drive. I think I'll lend him my book on chronic illness so he can see how to cope with reduced power. Or more power, but of an inner, less passionate kind. I liked having a sidekick who could carry and strain, but I'd rather have Madhu back than a younger, physically strong replacement. Rather have his brains—even if we can't travel in the old way.

December 5

1 A.M.

I want to be a pure devotee like Svarūpa Dāmodara Gosvāmī, who took *sannyāsa* in madness, stayed alone to practice *bhajana*, and didn't want to be disturbed by the formalities of *sannyāsa*. He surrendered to Lord Caitanya Mahāprabhu at Nīlācala.

Words pop up in my brain and I let them out onto the page, words like *viruddha* and *rasābhāsa*. Pure devotees don't accept *rasābhāsa* or any other imperfections in understanding. Svarūpa Dāmodara Gosvāmī wouldn't even allow such imperfect scholars to meet with Śrī Caitanya Mahāprabhu.

Oh. I should change.

Is it too late for me? Please, Lord, Vaiṣṇavas, accept me with my volumes of diaries. I too am mad and want to avoid the formalities of *sannyāsa*.

In this Cc. chapter, the devotees come to see Lord Caitanya Mahāprabhu on His return from South India like rivers flowing toward the ocean. I wish to be among them. I know that as time goes on, I will begin to diminish in my abilities to concentrate. I won't be able to write as many pages. If my wrist begins to hurt too much, I'll just have to learn to speak my prayers more.

I want to turn to Kṛṣṇa. Please, Lord, You are more real and infinitely greater than I am. You should be the center of this *jīva's* life. Why should I insist that my ego comes before Your desires? I am so foolish.

If rendering service to Kṛṣṇa is the goal of life, I should follow this formula and make everything I do service. Right now I'm writing this in a hurry to make up for lost time this morning. I'm hoping to have a good day—pain free.

Egyptian hieroglyphics don't contain Kṛṣṇa conscious messages. Śrīla Prabhupāda said that the Sphinx is sitting in a particular yoga *āsana* and that even frogs can do that—keeping the body alive for thousands of years. Ignorance of the soul and the real nature of immortality. Do we want real knowledge? Then become devoid of pride. Chant Hare Kṛṣṇa and become free.

3:35 A.M.

What is Kṛṣṇa consciousness? How do we know we are "it," whatever "it" is? When we are free from material desires? Yes, that's it. We can know when we hear Kṛṣṇa's name and we actually relish it. That's the real test of improvement. Another test is when we want to serve Kṛṣṇa's mission in this world. That means preaching. Never mind that this movement is thought to be a strange "Indian" cult by Westerners. Preach anyway and remove their misgivings with upright behavior. We're not crazy despite people's misunderstandings. It takes courage to be Kṛṣṇa conscious in this world and especially to preach. There are so many people who will never understand it. Therefore it also takes tolerance.

There was a time when we *liked* the fact that we were different. And people were attracted to us for that reason. Not people from the mainstream, but other people wanting to be more real or even just different. Where has that spirit gone? I wish it were being replaced by the ecstasy of deep compassion for the conditioned souls. Lacking that, I am a little stunted in my ability to do more. I just can't seem to do things based only on duty—at least not everything. I'm just not inspired enough, even if others quote Prabhupāda to me. Too much has "gone down" for the high spirit to remain in me. At least I have a spirit to write and to chant and to travel to the temples where they receive me as a devotee worth hearing from.

DHANURDHARA SWAMI INVITES ME TO LUNCH

Dhanurdhara Swami inside an apartment and me standing outside on the balcony. He gestures to me, but I don't understand at first. I thought I was waiting to take *prasādam* out on the balcony, but the *prasādam* has already been placed on plates inside on a low table. In a smiling, humble way, Dhanurdhara Swami gestures to me to come in. I catch his meaning and enter the room. (After this dream I thought I should write him a letter.)

8:58 A.M.

The Lord's abode is self-effulgent. We should be captivated to hear of it and desire to extricate ourselves from the material cycle and go back to Godhead. Each soul is a living spark of eternal spirit, eternally individual (fragmental). We are expansions of Kṛṣṇa. Wake up to it and return to Him.

My prayer talk. Keep going, slow pen, but slow down. Meditate on Kṛṣṇa's abode. The sun and the general universal idea of God—that's okay, but to be more specific in our meditation is better. See Kṛṣṇa—His name, form, and *līlā*. Want to go to that *cintāmaṇi-dhāma* and beg Kṛṣṇa, the beautiful cowherd boy, to take us. We are *jīva-loke—jīva-bhūtaḥ sanātanaḥ*.

We live between worlds. We are here and we want to be there and sometimes we *are* there. The person moves because the soul is in the heart with Kṛṣṇa. It stays long enough in one body and then moves onto another as long as it is not ready to resume its spiritual body. Praghoṣa explained that to the many BBC TV viewers in the interview I saw on tape. He spoke with his hands, trying to illustrate his point. "Reincarnation," he said, "it's simply this: the soul is eternal, the body is temporary. When the body dies, the soul has to get a new body. That's all."

Lake water

Quay joy

the key for shed shines chrome in my mitt.

I desire to write 340 songs at a stretch.

Willims and mittens

the owl and pussy cat rowed in a boat across the strait and sang by the light of the moon.

A *kīrtana* of beats

a feast for Kṛṣṇa, teach y'all how to cook for the Lord. Sneak a *bhajana* (*govinda jaya jaya—rādhā-ramaṇa hari*) up to number one pop hit but without mentioning it's Hare Kṛṣṇa—but they're finding out.

O angels of remorse

Corsican, Sicilian

Dīna, we're sorry we didn't get to talk with you and hear how you survived the crippling car accident, your side paralyzed by it. I heard you said you didn't much want to live and that you didn't attempt the painful physical therapy. Forgive us for not talking with you about it. We'll have another chance.

And

I'm sorry, Mom. I'm not waiting for you to die. Don't haunt me and don't curse me. Know that Kṛṣṇa protects me. When you die, I pray He'll remember you as my mom—that makes you a Hare Kṛṣṇa mom (like a Navy mom), even though you disown it. Say Jesus, say your prayers, and I wish you a safe and better passage.

Walking back from the shed I go into my private section of the woods for laps back and forth. Two days in a row a visiting German devotee has come by in his car. Hey, I thought this was my private forest. Then coming out of the woods, Draupadī leads the cows and bellows. She's behind a barbed-wire fence, so I think this is my chance to find out if she's really friendly. I go closer. She's roaring away, sticking out her gray tongue and foaming at the mouth. She looks mad enough, but I remember that Śyāmānanda said she just wants attention. I talk to her saying, "Don't be afraid of me and I won't be afraid of you." Then she looks up at me bashfully out of that big, black head with bulging eyes. I come closer and reach over the fence and pat her on the snoot, under the mouth, on top of the head. She quiets down and I go on talking, telling her different things. Then she starts up with a mild bellow again and I raise my voice and tell her not to roar, that she's all right. I see a stump of horn on her head—all that's left—and it makes me think of all the hardships she has been through. I start chanting to her: Hare Kṛṣṇa Hare Kṛṣṇa, Kṛṣṇa Kṛṣṇa Hare Hare. When I leave she's quiet. Of course, the other cows and the ox are always quiet. It's just her—she wants attention.

2:32 P.M.

This is my time for conversing with Śrīla Prabhupāda into the tape recorder, but instead I'm writing. It doesn't seem right to record my private thoughts like that. The making of prayers and the making of literature are often at odds.

O Kṛṣṇa, I am a spirit soul. I struggle in the world when I remain apart from You. I transmigrate according to the modes with which I associate; the subtle body chooses its next body throughout life and carries me there at death. Yes, again I will have suitable ears, suitable eyes—all senses perfectly arranged to fulfill my desires and to suffer out my karma. That's the science and for most of us, that's as much advanced knowledge as we should need to change and improve ourselves.

O Kṛṣṇa, I pray and pause and feel and think and ask for Your help. What else can I do?

6:40 P.M., NIGHT NOTES

Each evening Śyāmānanda has been reading a selection from one of my books and I have been commenting on it. Tonight he asked, "How do we know the difference between Kṛṣṇa testing us and an ordinary adverse condition?"

I said that everything is a test from Kṛṣṇa. Kṛṣṇa tests us to see how much we can use any situation in His service. I have my headaches and my solitude, and I have to prove that I can use my time well. As I spoke to Śyāmānanda, I felt guilty about whatever frivolities I pursue. Should I be doing more reading?

December 6

12:30 A.M.

Ekādaśī and my old birthday, December 6, 1939. Germany invades Poland.

Indigestion from the little dab of cream cheese with fruit or maybe just the fruit. Quit it. You'll feel lighter and better. Old men don't have to eat so much, do they? Head dizzy.

The king wanted to see the Lord. Prabhupāda comments on *ārādhanānāṁ sarveṣāṁ viṣṇor ārādhanaṁ param*. Usually this means that worship of Viṣṇu's devotees is even better than worship of Viṣṇu, but Prabhupāda takes it further in his purport: worship of devotees in *mādhurya-rasa* is best. Lord Caitanya came to teach this. "*Anarpita-carīṁ cirāt karuṇayā-vatīrṇaḥ kalau*—Śrī Caitanya Mahāprabhu appeared in this age of Kali to exhibit the superexcellence of *mādhurya-rasa*, a gift never previously bestowed by any *ācārya* or incarnation. . . . It is He only who distributed love of Kṛṣṇa while exhibiting the superexcellence of loving Kṛṣṇa in the conjugal *rasa*." (Cc. *Madhya* 11.31, purport)

8:18 A.M.

We would like to further our Kṛṣṇa consciousness, and it seems hard to work only out of duty. It just doesn't seem right to remain on that platform. Then we wonder, "Should I do what I love and find a way to offer it to Kṛṣṇa?" What if we feel like doing something that isn't totally Kṛṣṇa conscious? If we indulge in it, even in the name of service, we soon lose our taste. As the *śāstra* says, that happiness which is nectar in the beginning soon turns to poison. We taste the poison and feel the guilt for having been misled again.

Modern psychologists don't believe guilt is a healthy function of the psyche. They say it causes stress and stress isn't good for us. What we really need to do is to find spontaneous pleasure in *śāstra*, so much so that we don't care for anything else. Even eating and sleeping become unattractive. We become "lost" in the pleasure of transcendental ecstasy, of chanting and hearing.

Unfortunately, we haven't yet achieved that. We read a little and then stop. We chant and then interrupt our rounds for other things. And we live in fear that we are not pleasing guru and Kṛṣṇa.

Fear comes from rebelliousness. *Why* do we have to follow authority (God and guru)? Where is our full heart's commitment? Where is the joy?

Drawing a picture of it: a strange face and form. A body moving, a face growing older, strained but smiling so people don't feel disturbed to look at him. And I brand him with Vaiṣṇava *tilaka*.

This is my confession. Nevertheless, I submit to duty, acting for *śreyas* and in knowledge that in the long run, things have to get better.

In my attempt to improve my spiritual life, and when my mind drifts to creative pursuits, I think of these two obligations: (1) to be Kṛṣṇa conscious; (2) to find pleasure in my Kṛṣṇa consciousness, creatively. The two are sometimes in conflict or they don't pull the weight together, but I have to do both.

Gas heater not working. Out of gas? I'm writing, but it's frosty outside and will soon chill up in here. I'll run away. Farewell.

2:30 P.M.

The drink, the lake, the reservoir, the blue chill. Calm Lough Erne, passage for pleasure boats in spring and summer. None out now. Ice sheets on puddles. Smashed a few with my cane. Saw three deer on my way down here. Their big ears like antennae—they can't see so well—and their noses twitching to drink in the odor that will get them to leap away as I walk forward, holding what they must think is a gun-like stick. Three of them leaped into the next field, but at the far end they came against a high fence. I left them to figure it out.

The *Gītā* waits for me. I have a sense of my limited time. The purport says that the fallible soul appears to pass through six changes. I've already passed through birth and growth, and I'm in the process of maintenance and giving off by-products (writing books), and I'm beginning to dwindle, preparing to vanish. Will I vanish in the day or at night? "Let my air enter the totality of air," the devotee in the *Īśopaniṣad* prays. Let my soul go to You. Please let there be no hindrance.

Those are favorite prayers. When I was giving my six-day seminar on *Vandanam*, a couple of my Godbrothers walked in. I half froze, then kept speaking. I said that my favorite prayers included one made by Mādhavendra Purī. I found, however, that I couldn't speak my heart in front of those Godbrothers. What I wanted to say was that I must be myself even though others may criticize me. I will worship Govinda in my way without respect for rituals or even liturgy. I couldn't say it so publicly, of course.

Tomorrow night Baltimore time Madhu will fly overnight and arrive Sunday in England-Belfast. I miss him. We'll have to see what he's like with his new limitations. Get the news from him, and the mail.

Dreaming something . . . Now trying to see how it checks with reality. Will a swan try to touch me as in that twilight zone dream I had earlier? Or was the swan a symbol? For what? The *śāstra* will open by Kṛṣṇa's grace. The *Bhagavad-gītā* verse, *sarvasya cāhaṁ hṛdi sanniviṣṭo*, informs us that Kṛṣṇa helps us both in ordinary life and in spiritual life by giving us transcendental knowledge. Without Kṛṣṇa we can't remember what to do when we start a new life after transmigrating from one body to another. According to our karma, we're supposed to remember some things but forget others. Kṛṣṇa gives us the amount of remembrance and forgetfulness we deserve. Then if we're serious about God conscious, He gives us Vedic knowledge. O dear Lord, I don't think I was serious. I was serious in my way, but not about religion. Somehow you saved me and directed me to Śrīla Prabhupāda. You said in effect, "Go here. Go into that storefront. Hear from him and be respectful. He's your guru." I followed like a blind man, gave up my pretense, my persona of Lower East Side hippie before it was too late. Hare Kṛṣṇa.

December 7

12:40 A.M.

Reading . . . I read some Cc. this morning. Pray with it. First prayer is, "Please let me read nicely, with submission." You need to pray because as Lord Brahmā said:

athāpi te deva padāmbuja-dvaya-
prasāda-leśānugṛhīta eva hi
jānāti tattvaṁ bhagavan-mahimno
na cānya eko 'pi ciraṁ vicinvan

My Lord, if one is favored by even a slight trace of the mercy of Your lotus feet, he can understand the greatness of Your personality. But those who speculate to understand the

> Supreme Personality of Godhead are unable to know You, even though they continue to study the Vedas for many years.
>
> —*Bhāg.* 10.14.29, as quoted in Cc. *Madhya* 11.104

I pray for that by pausing as I read, quietly bowing my head and asking for it. I have the power to enter because I have brains to comprehend it, but more importantly, I already have Prabhupāda's mercy when he ordered me, "Whenever you get time, read my books." To pray and push out doubts takes practice. Finally, it requires direct mercy.

It's the same with writing. I have to write from a life filled with a devotional mood. Then it's worth something. Writing should express *bhāva,* even the emotion of emptiness. I wrote like this at Castlegregory. I went to the ocean and felt tiny and ordinary. That writing I called "Forgetting the Audience," and I think it was the first time I had written like that.

Writing isn't crazy or simply passion. I want to get something out. I'm not in the grip of the inner critic but I am learning to let go. Some nonsense may also come out, but I trust the process even though it doesn't always lead to instant success. At least I feel relieved. Life is short and soon we'll die. We have to do what Kṛṣṇa has allowed us to do before it's too late, and we have to do it free from the pressure others place upon us wittingly or unwittingly. We have to face ourselves and develop a quiet kind of urgency that permeates everything we do. I didn't resolve to discover God in the time I spent at Castlegregory. Rather, the last words written are a cry, "Where is *bhāva*?" I can almost hear the echo in waves crashing against the rocky shore as I read it again now.

Kṛṣṇa, Kṛṣṇa, Kṛṣṇa, I'm writing poems—"Songs of a Hare Kṛṣṇa Man." Keep them coming. Kerouac wrote Ginsberg, "You guys call yourselves poets, write little short lines. I'm a poet but I write lines, paragraphs and pages, many pages long." Poets blow off steam and contact emotions.

A gift-wrapped package of potatoes and apples arrived here. What more do I want? I'm contemplating my birthday. Let there be a six-foot high birthday cake like the one Clinton had, and Whoopi Goldberg narrating jokes at the *karmīs'* expense, poking fun at those who don't love me.

Re-elect me, please, as guru of the year.

One reason I don't let loose in free-writing is that it may seem irresponsible. I want to make a better record. I don't know. Cee-ripes.

This time keep the hammers felling their blows. "Keep the presses rolling—our family business"—slogan of "The Friends of GNP." Yeah, I permit their slick, somewhat organized, professional approach. Fill up the pen with a hundred thousand dollars so we can print freely. Cough up dough. We need your money. It will be sent to him on his birthday wherever he is in the world. The pennies trickle into the central fund headquarters.

Do a TV marathon and read from your works. Jerry Lewis' March of Dimes, "We just received a hundred dollars from a little old lady in Duluth, God bless her."

Trickles. My left fist is clinched and the clock reads 1. Next program for me is to chant in ecstasy or at least awake in the comfortable chair by the electric heater facing the altar illuminated by candle light, the pictures in their winter blankets. We'll be out of here on January 1st after a quiet New Year's Eve.

RARE CHANCE TO SERVE PRABHUPĀDA

I dreamt I was with Prabhupāda, although the presence of the person in the dream wasn't much like him. I went to a place where only a few people were gathered, then walked away thinking that Prabhupāda didn't want to be bothered. Then I said to myself, "This is a rare chance. You should go back and be with him." I went back and hung around, hoping to get some service to do for Prabhupāda. The dream had different incidents like this of "Prabhupāda" reciprocating with us, either being pleased or his not being served nicely by our activities.

Awake I think of groupie and superficial activities that sometimes surround the guru—socializing and even politicking among his disciples. How to cut through all that? Sometimes we just want to get away from it all. In the dream, however, I was told to tolerate and to at least chalk up some bona fide service so that the guru would recognize me. Now that I'm awake, I think that service can also be rendered in separation from the main crowd who travel with the guru from place to place. Still, it is very important that we are recognized by the spiritual master and that he gives us direction so that we don't serve in whimsical ways.

Fortunately I received a lot of direction during my life from Prabhupāda, and much of it has been recorded in letters as well as in my heart and memory. I can also read what Prabhupāda wrote in his books. We shouldn't think those instructions are only general. For example, today I read how Prabhupāda wants the devotees to go to Māyāpur and chant congregationally. We each have to think in our lives how we can fulfill at least some part of his order and dedicate our lives to his mission. We can't do everything he asked of us, but we can take some portion of it and make it our all in all. Viśvanātha Cakravartī advised this: make the order of the spiritual master your life and soul.

12:30 NOON

Disciples' meeting. Śyāmānanda reading selections from *Castlegregory* prose-poems. After awhile it began to feel too personal. I was describing my own way, my writing life. I suggested we chant a round of *japa* together and I tried to make things more generally applicable. Is it best for devotees to go off alone, sit by the ocean, and yearn for improved chanting? Maybe not for everyone. It's better to live in Rādhā-Govinda's temple at Inis Rath or wherever. I didn't feel saying that was untrue to what I had written in *Castlegregory*, but that was a personal expression and not necessarily the path for everyone. What's probably good for everyone is an occasional pilgrimage or retreating from the social scene to actually find solitude to chant. Not only should that be done occasionally, but every day we should find some alone time.

2:45 P.M.

Swan ducking. Me in bliss.

What about it?

What will I read after this Chapter Fifteen of *Bhagavad-gītā As It Is*? And when the well runs dry on the *Mexico City Blues* take-off, what will I write?

Oh, if nothing else, I'll revert to no poems and more little life.

And when life runs out?

Don't just write, "I did this at 9 A.M., I did that at 9:05 A.M."

Why not? If I were only always engaged in Kṛṣṇa's service, then the little life would be thrilling.

You could write *japa* with pen—Hare Kṛṣṇa mantras all over the page. No one would criticize that or make you stop chanting. Do you think you owe a debt to the Beat poets?

No, I owe a debt only to Govinda. That is truth.

I tell myself to cross out the bad words. My heart is one big cross-out. I go blank and can't think.

That's because prayer is hard. Why? Because the mind loops back to myself instead of remaining focused on Kṛṣṇa—to myself or to so many false concepts of me and the things I do, my fears, schemes, dreams, poems, homes, friends, and enemies. Therefore, how can I pray?

Anyway, what more is there to say but, "Please accept me"? Yes, that's all.

I was happy this morning. I felt my heart beating strongly and thought, "I could burst with happiness!" It's the ecstasy of service, of empowerment, or electricity flowing through

Dream of talking,
disembodied head

HARI
BOL

Avoiding
surveillance

Local guru in rowboat—smile.

Every day, just write.

the line. I am alive and protected in His service. That is real happiness.

I know it's not much. I have a long way to go before I can reach the *bhāva* in which I am trying only to please Kṛṣṇa and in which it is revealed that He is pleased with me. My cup runneth over, but it's still only a little cup. Take away my lunch, and my happiness may become tarnished. Give me a stubbed toe or a bruised shin and I lose my focus on the bliss.

December 8

12:45 A.M.

Overnight my sleep was broken many times. I dictated dreams into the tape recorder, thought of today's Cc. class, and came up with a subtitle for Volume One of *Every Day, Just Write: Welcome Home to the One Big Book of Your Life*.

I'm peaceful here at Geaglum with kind and gentle souls. One dream, however, reminded me of vicious people in the world:

CONFRONTATION WITH A TOUGH KID IN GREAT KILLS

I was stopped from going through a turnstile to a train because I didn't have the proper token. One man told me he would have to "phone Vancouver" to see whether the piece of cardboard I was attempting to use was acceptable. While I was waiting for this situation to resolve itself, I walked out onto the street and saw something that belonged to me. It was a *śuci* kit lying near the door leading to the trains. I went to pick it up, but a tough kid, about fourteen years old, came up to pick it up at the same time as I did. He wanted to fight me for it. I explained to him that it was mine and why it was mine. He listened and I showed him the contents of the bag. It was all kitchen stuff.

Suddenly two of his friends came by and I realized I was in the company of *very bad boys.* They could do anything. Although they were young, they were desperate bad kids without scruples, potential killers. I wanted to get away from them as soon as possible.

After I woke up, I remembered a scene I had witnessed when I lived in Allston, where some kids about the same age as the kids in the dream were terrorizing the owner of a small superette next to our temple storefront. We were similarly terrorized by the older kids in the neighborhood. I often think about the cruelty people face in this world and how I have not had to face anything so terrible.

I also thought about how dream teachers advise us to confront adversaries in dreams. Perhaps in this dream, I missed an opportunity for some kind of realization or resolution. The dream teachers claim that dream adversaries often turn out to be well-wishers in disguise, and we have to face them down in order to receive their messages. By hearing their messages, we may be able to become braver and more confident in waking life.

Following this train of thought, it occurred to me that a Kṛṣṇa conscious person really has nothing to fear. If a devotee met a vicious killer in this world, he would remain aware within himself of Kṛṣṇa's protection, would remember that he's not his body, and perhaps would try to give Kṛṣṇa consciousness to his attacker, just as Lord Nityānanda blessed Jagāi and Mādhāi despite their aggression.

I once read an essay on frightening confrontations in dreams by Strephon Kaplan-Williams. This is what he said:

> Many dreamers come to dream work scared of their adversaries. They have a nightmare and wake themselves instead of staying in the dream situation. So to take a journey means a commitment to dealing with whatever comes up, including that which would limit or destroy you . . . A commitment to dream work means a willingness to stay in the dream to face whatever the Dream Source presents us with . . . Thus the journey is not what you expect but what you get . . . so often in dreams we are presented with situations to resolve and not the resolution . . . the Dream Source evaluates our behavior and wants more from us than we presently express . . . Most dreams can be seen as challenges by the Dream Source to give up attempting to control, and instead serve the Self, the center within.
>
> —*The Elements of Dream Work*
> Strephon Kaplan-Williams

The last statement by Kaplan-Williams reminds me of surrender to Kṛṣṇa, the Supreme Self. Instead of being afraid and fleeing from a vicious kid in a dream, I could have remembered Kṛṣṇa and preached Kṛṣṇa consciousness. Even if I was attacked as a result, I would not have forgotten Kṛṣṇa. Of course, doing it in a dream is easier than facing similar situations in waking life, but dreams are a place to begin to build resolve and courage, I guess.

6 A.M.

Madhu must be in the air now, approaching England. He'll be here around 1:30 P.M. I had another dream about my father with a hernia.

In this morning's Cc. reading in the temple we'll discuss Lord Caitanya's ecstatic bodily symptoms when He entered the Jagannātha temple. It's significant that Sārvabhauma

Bhaṭṭācārya, although a Māyāvādī, was fully acquainted with the science of *prema*. According to the *Gaura-gaṇoddeśa-dīpikā*, Sārvabhauma Bhaṭṭācārya was formerly Bṛhaspati, the spiritual master of the demigods. Thus he was able to discern that Lord Caitanya was experiencing the highest stage of *mahā-bhāva*. The purport also demonstrates that Prabhupāda is certainly capable of discussing the technical terminology of *rāgānuga-bhakti*. Still, he doesn't dwell on it.

AVOIDING SURVEILLANCE: A DREAM

I was sitting with three people around a table. We were high school students. Two of the boys—they were my pals—hit each other while the teacher looked on. My back was to the teacher, and I was glad she hadn't caught me hitting anyone.

In a subsequent dream, I was talking to someone secretly, concealing myself from the authorities. I think we were hiding from the Nazis. The person with whom I was speaking came into a store where I was waiting and I played a tape recording of a phony conversation—"Hello, how are you? Good day. Nice weather." This was supposed to throw the authorities off our track so we could say what we actually had to say, but I don't remember what that was.

I want a private life, and I like to discourse with my friends not secretly but discreetly. Neither dream provided any resolution to these feelings or even hinted at ways in which such discretion could be carried out. Neither did they present a challenge to that mood. All I felt was that I had to escape surveillance.

12:26 P.M.

Ever since I gave class this morning (8:30–9:15) and walked cheerfully down to the quay with the devotees, I've been struggling to subdue head pressure. I tried a wet rag, aromatherapy, rest, a hot-cold shower, deep breathing, and relaxation exercises. Now it's lunch time and the pressure is still on the rise. Maybe the *bhakti*-filled lunch prepared by Śyāmānanda will do the trick.

Anyway, it proves I am still a delicate creature and can't run the mile marathon. Simply give a class and this is what comes of it.

O swan, I'd rather
be writing vigorous songs
but can't now. Like you, I
float on the cold lake and wait.
Hare Kṛṣṇa Hare Kṛṣṇa, Kṛṣṇa Kṛṣṇa Hare Hare.
Let mantras be heartbeats.

December 10

1:25 A.M.

Yesterday I was not able to write here because of an all-day headache. Does that mean I should change the title to *Almost Every Day, Just Write*?

It's not as easy as that. More questions and doubts about this writing come up on days when I am not able to actually get to the page. I'm still feeling shaky from yesterday, but I hope to clear the air and explain myself. However, the batch of mail has just arrived and must be tended to. It appears that my meditation of the last three weeks in which I was able to write and read undisturbed is broken. Still, that doesn't mean I should stop writing.

Here are some of the questions that arose yesterday:

How much of *Every Day* is written for therapy, coping, and how much with the hope to discover art or literature?

If it is entirely therapy, then should my attitude toward it be different? Should its form of expression change?

Some answers:

Art is also part of my therapy. I cope by writing. I practice writing.

The form and subject of *Every Day, Just Write* will change according to time and place. When I am traveling or when I'm busy lecturing, the writing will reflect that. One might say, "The writing will be more shallow and less concentrated when you can't work at it full time," but that's not necessarily so.

Doubts come to test how badly I want to write this book. It's a new project in that I have decided to write it one volume at a time. I'll use the umbrella title, *Every Day, Just Write*, and then subtitle each volume according to the mood in which it was written.

The real response I have to give is that I shouldn't write to make publishable literature. *Every Day, Just Write* can be a matrix from which other books can come. That's what the subtitle of the first volume means: "Coming Home to the One Big Book of Your Life."

STUDENT BEATEN TO DEATH: A DREAM

A student took an anti-war stance and refused to go into the war. This was legal at Harvard, where he was on campus, but still everyone mocked him and spat at him. I saw a bunch of guys grab him and throw him into a room where they each began to punch him. The student realized he was going to die and his assailants realized they were killing him.

The dream turned into moralizing as I dreamt on. Because the other students were mocking him even for majoring in English Literature and for sympathizing with the black students, I began to identify with him. I imagined what it would be like if I had to die in this way and how you would just endure it until you left your body.

When I awoke I was still enduring the pain of a headache. That is my "beating."

5 A.M.

Madhu was telling me about a disciple of mine who attended a meeting I was holding. This disciple confided to Madhu that at the beginning of the meeting he had some bad thoughts (which he called his "demonic" thoughts toward me), and it seemed that I looked at him and read his thoughts. He left the room and prayed to Lord Nṛsiṁha.

When Madhu related this to me, I said, "Sometimes that may happen. Śrīla Prabhupāda has no fault, but sometimes I may find fault in him." As I said that I felt good about it. I had sincerely stated that Prabhupāda has no fault. I spoke it as fact: the struggling with *anarthas*, by which I may see some fault in Prabhupāda, is *my* hang-up.

December 11

1 A.M.

Answered almost all the mail yesterday. This morning I answered a letter to a friend who was raising the question of how to balance traveling and preaching and concentration on chanting and reading. He read something I wrote in "Among Friends" where I referred to Prabhupāda saying that a *sannyāsī* need do nothing other than to chant Hare Kṛṣṇa. Prabhupāda has a particular way of balancing these two. He mostly seems to say that we should not go alone to chant in a solitary place, but should simultaneously chant Hare Kṛṣṇa and preach. He wanted us to be *goṣṭhyānandīs*. One verse seems to sum up the balance: "My dear child, continue dancing, chanting and performing *saṅkīrtana* in association with devotees. Furthermore, go out and preach the value of chanting *kṛṣṇa-nāma*, for by this process You will be able to deliver all fallen souls." (Cc. *Ādi* 7.92)

FIRING THE STOVES: A DREAM

I was with some devotees and we were all putting fuel into stoves. The heat became intense because the stoves were good quality and the heating system complicated. I was part of an award-winning team of men building these stoves.

Then one of my Godbrothers from the beginning days said, "Satsvarūpa, you used to fire these stoves long ago when it was a simple job. Now it's been built up and become complicated, but you're still here."

I went back to tending the fire, but thought, "I'm an old-timer in ISKCON. I was here in the days when we did everything simply." Often I think I can't keep pace nowadays and I'm not even that interested in making the change to how devotees do things now. In the dream I was there stoking the fire. Seems similar.

8:45 A.M.

Chant a little, cry, beg for mercy. Prabhupāda is merciful, has been merciful already. Now it is my turn to show mercy.

How to help myself on this page? Bolder strokes? I'm still recovering from the disruption of the last few days' headaches. First time in three days in the shed. Swans out on the lake, the lake cold, dark, gray at near nine.

Photo of Prabhupāda at the airport and we, his young disciples, looking up to him. Open adoration on our faces even though we are in public. The nondevotees can see our bliss. Good for them. He was an elderly saint, and we were young kids in those days.

I write these sentences with no oomph behind them, or clarity. My endurance is low right now. I write on anyway.

Someone told me that in Vṛndāvana it's going from bad to worse. She meant that devotees were leaving ISKCON and moving into the Gaudiya Math. The same in Australia. Some devotees are sad and disgusted and heartbroken over my Godbrother's departure. They're afraid they'll keep accepting one ISKCON guru after another only to hope that one won't fall down before they die. Therefore, they run to an Indian guru, someone older and proven and who will teach them of the higher topics. I think about this often and feel sorry.

This propaganda that other gurus are discussing more advanced topics and that we are missing out on something doesn't hurt my faith in Prabhupāda. I'm not concerned that much about objectivity in my following of Prabhupāda. I have decided that I want only to be nurtured by His Divine Grace A. C. Bhaktivedanta Swami Prabhupāda. Kṛṣṇa consciousness is ultimately subjective in that sense—who we give our faith to and our individual relationship with Kṛṣṇa.

We all want to be enlivened in spiritual life. Prabhupāda says we should preach if we want to taste *bhāva*. We will taste Lord Nityānanda's *bhāva*. That's what Prabhupāda said.

2:55 P.M.

Do what Kṛṣṇa says. His representative, the spiritual master, gives Kṛṣṇa's order and we shouldn't neglect it. Don't make whimsical offerings in the name of service. Don't try to act as the master and enjoyer of the world. Get it?

Yes.

What is Prabhupāda's order?

Follow initiation vows—four rules and sixteen rounds. Preach. Always hear about Kṛṣṇa in the *Śrīmad-Bhāgavatam* and *Bhagavad-gītā*. Live with devotees. Don't deviate. So many instructions. Among all the instructions, however, the practical details as to where in the world I'll live, what kind of preaching I'll develop for ISKCON, which devotees I'll work with, whether I'll manage affairs or lecture or write—and to what degree I'll "do everything"—that depends on my capacity as a person. And on other factors too. Some of those crucial factors have to be decided by the devotee himself by careful discrimination. Śrīla Prabhupāda didn't tell us what to do exactly in each and every circumstance in changing times, but he gave sufficient instruction so that we can carry them out no matter where we are and who we are.

Do you understand, Satsvarūpa?

Yes, I think I do, and I'm trying.

Swans duck their heads under the water. *Haṁsas*. That is mentioned in King Kulaśekhara's prayer. As the swan entangles its head in the network of the lotus's underwater roots, please allow me to entangle my mind in thoughts of Kṛṣṇa's holy name, pastimes, and form. Let me die now chanting while I'm able to utter the name well because at death my throat will be choked and I may not be able to speak *hari-nāma* or think clearly of Kṛṣṇa.

Do you hear that, Lough Erne *haṁsas*?

Yes, they know. Everyone knows.

December 12

12:40 A.M.

This is my reading time, but I'm praying here and noting it down. I attempted to incubate a dream last night. I wrote this down on an index card and put it under my pillow: "Please send me a dream to help inspire me to read Śrīla Prabhupāda's books in a fresh, worshipful way."

I'll tell you what dreams I had later, although they remain enigmatic. Here I am in the waking light of the desk lamp with the intention of rereading *Īśopaniṣad*, starting with Mantra Fourteen. I still feel a little haunted by hearing that we need more than Prabhupāda's books to go all the way back to Godhead. Therefore, I want to enter his books slowly and stop and pray on the way. That's harder than the usual way I read, but I think it's required. Prabhupāda has packed his purports with thoughtful statements, and I should read them carefully.

For example, the purport to Mantra Fourteen states that the advancement of material knowledge has not relieved us of the basic problems of birth, death, disease, and old age. Everything and everyone in the material world has to pass through six stages of transformation. "Therefore the entire material universe is called Martyaloka, the place of death."

Do we doubt it? I mean, the literal truth of Vedic knowledge? It contradicts *all* material knowledge, and it demands that we accept eternal spirit and the Supreme Person in the specific way presented in India's spiritual heritage. I contend with those ideas and go on reading. Determination helps.

Then another thought passed through my mind. I could turn to a Godbrother and find out how he reads, how he maintains fresh interest and faith. It wouldn't hurt, but ultimately no one else can do what's necessary for me to do. In that sense we are each alone with Prabhupāda and his books. That's good because if we became conscious of it, it would create a prayer of desperation and hope.

5:30 A.M.

Here's the dream that came from my attempt to incubate it:

I was observing the President's chauffeur. He was always on call, but he also had privileges and security clearance, and wherever he went people honored him.

What does this dream have to do with my question about reading Prabhupāda's books? Is it that I am privileged to be close to the great man?

8:40 A.M.

"The living entity gets what he deserves . . . " (Bg. 18.61, purport)

I'm leaning to this—Vedic study, truth, being situated in Kṛṣṇa consciousness. O master, please believe me.

I'm reading 18.64, 65, and 66 where there is mention of surrender, especially in 18.66. But it makes me wonder what surrender actually means. How do we do it?

Well, if you don't know by now . . . It means giving up material attachments and following the will of the Supreme, and following the principle of accepting the favorable and rejecting the unfavorable.

It's the high point conclusion of *Bhagavad-gītā*, but I'm subdued (fear of ache).

There go six low-flying swans. Only two remain in the drink. Another gray day, but lovely nonetheless. Faintest trace of pink "smoke" behind the overcast. The trees are winter brown and the evergreens cold and dark.

2:40 P.M.

Ah man, I tell you, this is the way it goes. The Rastaman sells ices and bananas. He holds no shiv or machete, but other fellas do. In these pics I drew in Guyana in '95, I get to go again. Will they laugh at me at the airport?

An older devotee is not necessarily better than a young one. It's sincerity that counts. Thus Prahlāda was asked to go forward and pacify Lord Nṛsiṁhadeva although it was like putting a child into a lion's cave. No one would do it . . .

So intense, Sharon Olds writing on the goodness of her daughter on her way to summer camp. Where is my intensity? I recall someone saying Robert Frost wasn't a great poet because he lacked intensity. Frost heard that remark and replied, "It depends what you mean by intensity."

As a pre-Kṛṣṇa conscious writer on the Lower East Side, I said I wanted vividness. Someone said I had it. I wanted intensity. I said someone else lacked it. Burning bright, my candle lit at both ends. Intense to find truth, to pose as an artist-truth seeker.

The person is moving because *jīva* soul is in his heart.

Notes, fragments of experience.

KRSNA
CONSC
CAITANYA
HARIBOL
These points may seem deceptively
Keep writing, the teachings, your feelings, whatever comes.

Dream of chanting with giant birds.

Dream I visit myself in hospital.

Intense temple president of Boston temple, intensely afraid of thugs and teenage ruffians, intense in mouthing *japa:* Hare Kṛṣṇa Hare Kṛṣṇa,

ah, you were intense but

don't fade, do not go gentle into that good night.

If to be intense I have to get angry, then no.

And intensity in pain provokes stress.

But what about the *gopīs*? Yes, they were intense. I fall short. I say, "Take it easy."

Nice 'n' easy
does it
every time.

Kṛṣṇa, Kṛṣṇa

spleen, pancreas, liver and all—this body of mine, the soul one ten-thousandth the tip of the hair—me, Kṛṣṇa's eternal servant. I am hereby ready to go back to the house, calm, burning.

December 13

12:45 A.M.

Hearing submissively, applying intelligence to understand the Supreme Lord in *śāstra*. Don't need to hear any emphasis other than Śrīla Prabhupāda's. Kṛṣṇa will help me if I sincerely want to approach Him. I am tiny and prone to doubt, prone to maintain contaminating association in this world. Nevertheless I pray to be uplifted and kept in devotional service. Any service is valid and pleasing if it's done with devotion. Prahlāda was able to please the Lord even when Brahmā and Lakṣmī-devī could not approach Him in His anger. Prahlāda acted as a simple boy and went forward when asked, "Lord Nṛsiṁha came to kill your father, so it's your duty, Prabhu, to calm Him now." All right, Prahlāda agreed. He was unafraid. How sweetly Śrīla Prabhupāda described it in his '76 Vṛndāvana lecture.

Steadily, slowly, I approach Prabhupāda, although he may be angry with me sometimes. If he is displeased with me I have to face him and accept the punishment or penance. That's how confession operates: you confess sins, feel the contrition, and accept the blessing. We are meant to live a life of service.

A GODBROTHER'S "MONKS" OUTRAGE A STRONG MAN IN CHINATOWN: A DREAM

Wandering through Chinatown, dragging behind me a luggage carrier. I am with a Godbrother and someone else. My Godbrother is in charge of our particular order of *sannyāsa*. We walk around like Japanese monks, going door to door to beg, under my Godbrother's order. One young, very strong man feels cheated by something we said. He comes to the *āśrama*, ready to fight. I sit in a corner hoping he won't hit me, then step out to reason with him. I say, "We are not a society of cheaters, although you may have been cheated by one of us."

Now the parts of the dream: who is the Godbrother and what does he represent to me? He's a strong person, and perhaps I am intimidated by him too. I needn't be afraid of him, however, even though in real life I don't always appreciate everything he says. He's often right, actually, and he sees it as his duty to protect ISKCON.

I was and am willing to face the giant, young man who was angry with us. He's a symbol for all the adverse reactions against Hare Kṛṣṇa devotees. Such persons exist. It would have been good to reason with him that ISKCON is not corrupt, although we have experienced corruption among some of its members. I would like to try to pacify that anger people sometimes feel toward the movement, but that anger is still too volatile and dangerous. Is that it? I fear violence and I fear the bad opinion others have of us. I also sometimes fear my own negative feelings toward ISKCON. Sometimes ISKCON's critics have dared me to stand up and speak honestly what I feel, but I never really do. I'm not the kind of man who rages against monks.

8:45 A.M.

I'm anxious about the spider. He came wonderfully into my view, lowering himself on an invisible thread, stepped onto the desk, and cavorted around. In order to avoid his crawling on my papers, I slipped a piece of paper under him and tried to lift him away, but it didn't happen so smoothly and he fell about a foot. I thought he'd be able to take it, but he remained contracted into a ball. I worried that he was unconscious or even dead. After some time I placed him back on the desk. Finally, he stuck out a leg. Minutes passed and he stuck out another leg. He's definitely alive. I'll have to be more careful how I handle Kṛṣṇa's creatures when they get in my way.

If I write past immediate concerns, I can get in touch with myself and then something good may happen. I may even be able to pray in words, meditate by pen. Dear Lord Kṛṣṇa, I can pray to You because You are everything. If I have the slightest grain of *bhakti*, or even a shadow of it, I can attempt to address the Supreme. He's hard to reach—He withholds Himself—yet He's easy too. The starting points of meditation are to taste Him in water, see Him in the light of the sun, hear Him in the sound of ether. Let me feel it to be so.

(I'll be relieved when that spider recuperates and starts walking. Don't want it held against me that I crippled him. Why is he so slow to move about? What can he be *thinking*?)

Kṛṣṇa, Kṛṣṇa.

Random items:

1. M. says he's wearing his blue winter coat (purchased in Boston, 1991) to India. He invites me to wear mine.

2. Tickets, tickets, he's struggling to get the tickets.

3. A devotee calls and asks M., "I heard there is going to be a little get-together" (on my birthday). He denies it but feels

bad later. I plan to stay out of it. Whoever comes here on that day, that's okay. I can't guarantee my participation. I could have a headache that day for all I know.

4. I moved books and items into my room today. My clerical nature was aroused as I sorted out drawing pads, writing pads, "notes to secretary" pads, pocket folders, labels, typing paper, books in categories of Śrīla Prabhupāda's, SDG's, health, Gauḍīya Vaiṣṇavism, etc. So?

5. Feeling good about *Every Day, Just Write*. Don't know how long it will last.

6. Dreams. If you want to take them seriously, you could get involved in them more. I don't. I'm just taking advantage of this period when I'm on my own schedule to record dreams and learn more about them for my own use in Kṛṣṇa consciousness.

7. Drawings are important in my life. Planning to carry sketch pads and color instruments to India and the Caribbean. Wherever I go. They go well with published writings.

8. Heigh-ho, your honor, your unconscious, your self who wants to express.

9. Not to make it a mere number nine on a list, yet say, "Last but not least"—I read my master's books. Let my body-earth enter the total earth and my life air enter the total air, and may the supreme beneficiary of all my acts, Lord Kṛṣṇa, please remember all that I have done for Him. Thoughts by a devotee at the time of death. He prays and I study it.

The spider is on a sit-down strike. I know he's not paralyzed, but he remains immobile. His front legs (there are two legs, but they divide half-way down so that he has a total of four front legs) and two rear legs are poised, and his body is one turtlelike lump in the middle. If he's going to walk, he will unfold more and start galumphing around. I could touch him to get him going, but I have meddled enough.

2:45 P.M.

In the shed and glad to say the spider is not where I left him, crumpled and inert. He's nowhere to be seen. I hope I learned my lesson not to meddle with or hurt creatures. I got away without having killed that one. He was handsome (God-made) in his spidery way.

Be Kṛṣṇa conscious. Chant Hare Kṛṣṇa.

Oh, there he is, walking around like a blind man with several canes. Started up the wall. Now he has drawn himself into a tight ball again, but I didn't cause it this time. His thinking is inscrutable to me.

December 14

MIDNIGHT, WORLD ENLIGHTENMENT DAY

Mantras Seventeen and Eighteen from *Īśopaniṣad* are wonderful. *All* the books are wonderful if we can just find the clarity and patience to read them. When I read alertly, I see how Prabhupāda addresses my immediate concerns.

In Mantra Seventeen, the devotee prays to enter the kingdom of God after death. What happens in the next life is determined by our thoughts at the time of death. "The devotees, however, develop a sense of love for Godhead by practicing devotional service to the Lord. Even if at the time of death a devotee does not remember his service to the Lord, the Lord does not forget him." The devotee also asks the Lord, "Please remember all my sacrifices." This sacrifice refers to, "denying the interest of the senses. One has to learn this art by employing the senses in the service of the Lord during one's lifetime."

Prabhupāda begins his purport to Mantra Eighteen: "By surrendering to the Lord and praying for His causeless mercy, the devotee can progress on the path of complete self-realization." It's nice to see Prabhupāda stating that prayer itself is an *act* of devotion. Then I should pray for the Lord's causeless mercy. That's like the Jesus prayer, "Jesus Christ, please have mercy on me, a sinner." Kṛṣṇa can respond to the person who is praying to Him and trying to surrender. "He can give directions to His sincere devotees by which they can attain the right path. Such directions are especially offered to the devotee, even if he desires something else."

Of course, we have to try to rectify ourselves, but Kṛṣṇa is powerful and He can cleanse our hearts from within. In the purport Prabhupāda quotes *Śrīmad-Bhāgavatam* 11.5.42:

"The Lord is so kind to the devotee who is fully surrendered to His lotus feet that even though the devotee sometimes falls into the entanglement of *vikarma*—acts against the Vedic directions—the Lord at once rectifies such mistakes from within his heart. This is because the devotees are very dear to the Lord." Prabhupāda goes on to say that it's human to make mistakes, and the only remedial measure against our perhaps unknown sins is to surrender to Kṛṣṇa in the heart so He can guide us. We're guided in two ways: by the saints, scriptures, and spiritual master, and by the Lord in the heart Himself.

8:30 A.M.

Manu noted tension in my writing, uncertainty whether this way is best. He compared it to the nerve-jangling courage and the insistence of an existentialist who thinks life has no meaning—as far as he can honestly see—yet who gives it meaning anyway. I am leaving a testimony, Manu said, of one who has applied American skepticism to Kṛṣṇa consciousness, never letting up on it for an easy ride, yet coming out faithful and convinced in the *bhakti-mārga* and Bhaktivedanta Swami Prabhupāda. What I write will be convincing to other Westerners. I am trying like that, even if not deliberately. I have no other choice.

Does it mean to be calm I need to remain on the surface? Swans do, but I notice they also duck underwater when they have to. Manu likes to see energy released and tension expressed. He says it makes for better reading. But it's calm here this December, and my schedule is quiet.

Calm and simple,
spare the spider,
pet the cow,
walk your way and
pray to God
Hare Kṛṣṇa mantra
sixteen rounds.

We have become afraid of excessive self-expression. We don't want to wind up like those who have left, saying that to be true to self is higher than any duty given by guru.

Draupadī (the cow) is growling, then moaning right outside this window. I could go out and pet her . . . She's a strange cow.

Be confident. Guy standing with hand on hip, right hand in beadbag. He's heroic in swell of chest, cock of head, happy and simple, but daring and active. Wearing *brahmacārī* dress. My attempt at an earnest portraiture.

2:30 P.M.

Manu and Īśānī have gone for the afternoon to distribute books. Uddhava and Patrī are going into Dublin today to distribute books, and then they'll come here for my class tomorrow morning. I'm going to play excerpts of Śrīla Prabhupāda speaking on a morning walk in Chicago. He praises the book distributors, asks Ghanaśyāma dāsa to increase his enthusiasm (it was already great) for distributing books. He says the preacher will be quickly recognized by Kṛṣṇa and, "once recognized by Kṛṣṇa, his going back to Godhead is guaranteed." Preachers don't have to follow all the regulations (such as chanting extra rounds and fasting on Ekādaśī). Preaching is so exalted.

Then why don't you do it?

I do, Sam. This is it.

What, this scribbling?

Yes, watch your language. Don't offend me. I's preaching by this word. Kṛṣṇa is the Supreme Personality of Godhead—that's preaching. To say it and mean it and get it out somehow on the airwaves or the printed form.

Ah, look at all those swans gliding in the overcast day on the rippled lake. It is a most aesthetic sight, like seeing ballerinas in *Swan Lake*. They glide by.

Open the door to the shed, feel time passing when soon it'll be my last time in and out of here. End of year? Yes, that too.

Parry and thrust. He's going to write every day. You mean until the gas bottle runs out?

In mail—letters from Bhaktin Sile of Dublin, Pradyumna of Portlaoise, an Irish sweater mailed by Patrī, and two tapes of poets reading their works.

O fallow, O Derry
O dew and blood and
rocks and fists by the
heart that ails you,
mortal men.

Believe in poet and jazzter. Don't forget you're supposed to be a devotee first and last. Muster, fall in for muster.

"Guarino!"

"Here! Yo!" and so it goes. The exact welfare route I go
down is bugged and booted to speak ISKCON message no mistaking it.

He says it sounds so predictable.

Be careful—our master talks that way. Yeah, but he's got surprises and authority and he did it, he spread the Kṛṣṇa consciousness movement all over with his words. It's different in your mouth.

I repeat. I thought that was the supreme virtue.

Yes, you should be true.

You *should* be. Take the chance to serve him under all conditions. Prabhupāda admitted the nondevotee enjoyers are not likely to take to Kṛṣṇa consciousness. "Don't bother us," they say. But the devotees keep plugging away at them.

Getting close to Friday night.

NIGHT NOTES, 6:10 P.M.

This is the way it ends. I drew a yin and yang circle to show Manu that I strive to write as much as possible, cutting through with free-writing to reveal my hidden truths, and with the other half relaxing and not striving to achieve, flowing with the little life as it occurs each day. In either case I try to let go of words, to write without premeditation. Touch Kṛṣṇa consciousness.

Tonight it's over; tomorrow, keep going.

December 15

12:08 A.M.

I have my agenda for the 9:30 A.M. meeting, and I hope I'll be well enough to speak. This excerpt from a purport praising preaching: "Now, we can imagine how merciful Kṛṣṇa is to those engaged in His service, risking everything for Him. Therefore it is certain that such persons must reach the supreme planet after leaving the body." (Bg. 11.55, purport)

In his purport to Bg. 12.2, Prabhupāda mentions the simple services we can render to please Kṛṣṇa. "Sometimes he chants, sometimes he hears or reads books about Kṛṣṇa, or sometimes he cooks *prasādam* or goes to the marketplace to purchase something for Kṛṣṇa, or sometimes he washes the temple or the dishes—whatever he does, he does not let a single moment pass without devoting his activities to Kṛṣṇa. Such action is in full *samādhi.*"

And this: Kṛṣṇa personally rescues His devotee from the ocean of birth and death.

Things to say: I'm taking the bluish sheets off the bed and giving them to Īśānī to wash.

The hallway is cluttered with the belongings we have stored in trunks. Madhu will have to sort them out.

Autobiography is supposed to be more than an annotation of a life. It should mean something to others; it should get things moving for them. Still, it gets things moving by speaking in a personal language, in one's own words, by being who one is.

Something else: I face the fact that I don't know a damn thing. But that's momentary emotion. Actually, I *do* know who I am—I am a gaunt-fat creature (but not a frog) who speaks a language that slides away and returns (although I no longer care who hears). I'm someone who would like to think that whatever I wrote was readable, or even better, helpful, that Prabhupāda was sanctioning it as useful for his preaching movement. But how can I claim a 1.000 batting average? The best don't hit more than .350. An impossible best would mean that one-fourth of my chances were successful hits.

Well, this isn't baseball. Even when a baseball champ strikes out, no one says he's worthless. They recognize his failure in the moment and wait for his next success. They chalk it up in his statistics. In devotional service there are no losses. You never strike out and you never lose anything.

What about if you commit an offense?

Oh yeah, that creates not a loss, but a strike-out. That is especially true of Vaiṣṇava *aparādha.* Your devotional creeper can be uprooted—it can need to be re-rooted. What you have already done, however, is never lost.

If Kṛṣṇa consciousness is to relieve the miseries of the world, we have to preach it. People are free to take to it or not, as they like. I like to preach to the devotees who have already pledged themselves to the practice. They too are free to hear or not, as they like. After all, we're asking for a lot—complete surrender—and even we who are preaching it have not always attained that ideal. Still we teach it, speak it, recite it from memory, repeat it again and again. To whatever degree we each surrender, to that degree we will become free of the material miseries. To that degree we give up hope of seeing improvement in this world. Seamus Heaney wrote poems touching on the violence in Northern Ireland. You see, he wants to make things better, but he doesn't know how. We "know" the answer but can't live in it enough to show the way completely or to cause a major shift in world consciousness. Our stories are still incomplete.

Poets. Writing poems about windy days, enchanting language. Do such words give us strength? Maybe. Poems are stories, and the words are carefully planted to create an effect. Why? Because life is inexplicable, and a poet is talking about life. It's not philosopher's talk or preacher's talk, yet he presumes to write his own "scripture." He *works* at it, is humble perhaps, or not, but he's a craftsman speaking as deep a truth as he can muster up in his own words.

There are jazz poets, nature poets, rural and sophisticated poets, inner and outer poets, academics, and Beat generation rappers. Well, why not devotee poets speaking in their own language?

My belongings can be taken by whoever needs them, he said. I, Father Sergius, will disappear into the peasantry. In Tolstoy's tale, Sergius leaves his famous monk's cave and wanders with a group of peasants going to Siberia. We get only a brief final scene where he is completely obscure, now salt of the earth. He gets harassed by a military officer demanding ID. He accepts it and he's holy. Holy of the earth. No more monk Sergius.

9:30 A.M.

I was talking with Madhu about next Friday, my birthday. We had to make definite plans. He said I shouldn't think of it as a day I was going to enjoy, but a day in which I would have to put out energy. I should think in terms of how much I could do. I said, "That's right. For me, an enjoyable day is quiet, and I can go to the shed."

I had been thinking perhaps that my birthday would be a day *for me*. Now I'm seeing it differently; it will be a disruption to my regular life and a real challenge. The main external challenge will be that after inviting people here, I may get a headache. Then what? We're going ahead anyway, planning and gambling on my health. The highlight for me will be the afternoon session in which I'll read selections of things I've written in 1996.

December 16

12:45 A.M.

Took rest at 5 P.M. with ache. Gradually it went down. Up at midnight doing editing work I missed yesterday. "Last days" feeling closing in. I'm getting trained to write under more difficult conditions. I'll try to arrange for more full-time writing, but I can't always have it. Don't get distressed at those times or think that writing is only superficial unless you're in a writing retreat. Go at it any minute you have. Give us a hasty note, like a kiss.

VISION OF CONFRONTING A SĀDHU AT A DISTANCE

I was half asleep, walking on a dirt path in India. It was dark—the sun wasn't up yet. Far ahead there was a *sādhu.* He had a child with him. He was startled to see me just as I was startled

KRSNA!

Christmas morn—don't hate it.

Christmas entertainment, Inis Rath.

to see him. We were both afraid to go forward, thinking that the other might be an attacker. I thought, "There's two of them. They're more threatening to me." I woke up with a vivid remembrance.

Because I remember this dream so vividly, I tend to think it had some importance. Maybe some day in the future, maybe on Vṛndāvana *parikrama*, I'll see in reality what I saw in the dream. But how will I take advantage of it? Why were we afraid of each other? It's as if we were half asleep and then suddenly startled to see each other. Such a dream would definitely have to be followed up to get more out of it. Maybe sometime when I'm in a similar "twilight" state of consciousness I will remember this and try to re-enter it.

8:45 A.M.

Saw a big hare on my way out to the shed. The four Kerry cows were sitting in the green meadow near the footpath. I passed close by, chanting quietly so as not to arouse Draupadī. I heard one cow breathing heavily. Now here . . . tired from the long stretch I've gone through and the one still ahead.

Reading random verses from the *Gītā*. *Kārpaṇya-doṣopahata . . . śiṣyas te 'haṁ śādhi māṁ tvāṁ prapannam*. (Bg. 2.7) Now I am feeling weak and can't do my duty . . . please accept me as Your disciple and instruct me.

I don't feel that way, desperate and lost. Should I? I claim, "Kṛṣṇa was there face to face with Arjuna, but my spiritual master has left." Prabhupāda is here, but it takes real cultivation to hear him now. He has given us our freedom in separation, so we have to show him clearly and repeatedly over a long time that we want to hear from him and that we're willing to follow him. Arjuna said, "Now I am Your disciple and a soul surrendered unto You."

What can we learn? Don't be a *kṛpana*, but a *brāhmaṇa*.
O black cow on wet earth
wet grass—not frozen today
this Monday in rural North Ireland,
we're people too.

December 17

12:30 A.M.

In preparing for Friday morning's talk, I've gathered quotes on the spiritual master and the disciple. I'll go over them with the devotees, not attempting to present a structured lecture, but to gain insights from each statement and tell them what they mean to me personally.

The first one that came to mind was a phrase in Prabhupāda's purport to Bg. 2.7: "He wants to stop friendly talks. Talks between the master and the disciple are serious, and now Arjuna wants to talk very seriously with the recognized spiritual master."

"Serious talks" means I must give my disciples what Prabhupāda and the *śāstras* teach. I'm aware that they've come to me to solve the perplexities of life.

One who falsely poses as a spiritual master is incriminated. An outstanding example of this is the verse and purport to *Bhāg.* 5.5.18 where it says that no one should become a spiritual master unless he can save the dependents from repeated birth and death. This statement is daunting. I become fearful whenever I hear it. When I examine the statement, I tend to think I can deliver my dependents if I stick to the process as Prabhupāda taught it and then share the knowledge I receive with disciples. (Whether or not they take it is a matter of their own free will.) In that sense, the *Bhāgavatam* verse doesn't describe something impossible for me to do, but it presents me with a grave responsibility. I'm committed to my disciples for life, and that in turn further commits me to the basic duties of *sannyāsa* and *sādhana*.

I seem to feel the need for assurance that I can function as a spiritual master. Prabhupāda has made many statements that indicate that it is not difficult to become a guru, but these liberal statements force me to pursue the highest standard possible. Here is one statement defining that standard from Cc. *Ādi* 1.46, purport: "The bona fide spiritual master always engages in unalloyed devotional service to the Supreme Personality of Godhead. By this test he is known to be a direct manifestation of the Lord and a genuine representative of Śrī Nityānanda Prabhu."

And another from the same purport: "A spiritual master is not an enjoyer of facilities offered by his disciples. He is like a parent. Without the attentive service of his parents, a child cannot grow to manhood; similarly, without the care of the spiritual master one cannot rise to the plane of transcendental service."

A statement to guide and shape the nature of the guru-disciple relationship: "The relationship of a disciple with his spiritual master is as good as his relationship with the Supreme Lord. A spiritual master always represents himself as the humblest servitor of the Personality of Godhead, but the disciple must look upon him as the manifested representation of Godhead." (Cc. *Ādi* 1.45, purport)

I don't have to pretend to hold an exalted status I don't have, yet I can play the role of God's representative, of Prabhupāda's son. In this way I can guide disciples to maintain their initiation vows and to develop their spiritual lives as much as possible.

How do I dare take a position of being honored by others? In his essay, "Humbler Than A Blade of Grass," Śrīla Bhaktisiddhānta Sarasvatī Ṭhākura speaks on this point eloquently and humorously. I will read his statement where he quotes Caitanya Mahāprabhu:

> By My command, become guru and deliver this land." Since it is Lord Caitanya's order, we have to do it and assume we will be protected from arrogance. He says, "As the saying goes, 'Having started on the dance, it is no use to draw close the veil.' I am doing the duty of the guru, but if I preach that no one should shout, 'Jaya,' that is to say, if I say in a roundabout way, 'Sing jaya to me,' it will be nothing short of duplicity . . . I have to serve God in the straightforward way . . . Especially as Śrī Gurudeva has directed me saying, 'On My command, being guru, save this land.' This command has my Gurudeva preached. My Gurudeva in his turn has conveyed the command to me. I will not be guilty of any insincerity in carrying out that command.

I also want to discuss the important topic of the spiritual master as a Prabhupādānuga in ISKCON. Prabhupāda is the founder-*ācārya* of our ISKCON *sampradāya*. My main qualification is that I'm Prabhupāda's disciple, and I present his teachings with the exact emphasis that he gave them.

3:36 A.M.

Seamus Heaney wrote a poem called "Exposure" while living in Wicklow and feeling anxious that he had escaped the violence of Northern Ireland. He wanted to know if that was the right thing to do to nurture the kind of poetry he wanted to write. He hoped he could write poetry that would be "adequate" to what he felt a poet should do. Poets want to speak of the times in which they're living. Poetry shouldn't be just pretty music for the ear.

Devotees are preaching poets, not just propagandists. A devotional poet wants to be Kṛṣṇa conscious, but not in a narrow-minded way. He wants to offer hope to others and prove that Kṛṣṇa consciousness is for everyone. He wants to explore his own moments of hesitation in spiritual life in case others also hesitate from time to time; he wants to tell you what he felt when he took a walk outdoors. He wants to give you his Kṛṣṇa.

I know Kṛṣṇa consciousness is demanding and requires total surrender, and I also know I'm not up to that standard. Perhaps because of that I want to offer solace or some sort of compensation to those who are fellow walkers on the same path. I don't want to be pretentious enough to assume that as a poet I have a big task in the movement, but I do like the sense of responsibility Heaney also expressed. He seems to feel in "Exposure" that he missed the chance to speak out when he left the dangerous North for the safer South.

The bounce I got from springboarding
Kerouac's *Mexico City Blues* I can't
find in the lines of British and Irish poets.
I can't turn it on unless
the Lord gives me that gift
to sing in modern idiom.
In the meantime I can appreciate,
like doing push-ups and stretches,
the loveless uninspired attempts
of imitative ruminating bellowing
pisswissing the exact count.
No, this morning I feel I want to be
in tune with straight Kṛṣṇa consciousness,
something like that.

I am afraid people won't accept Kṛṣṇa. Of *course* they won't. But I accept Him. If I speak with my own conviction, I should trust that a few will pull away from the masses and accept Him as the Supreme Personality of Godhead. The whole thing in preaching revolves on the preacher's conviction, which in turn provides him the ability and willingness to speak the truth. From the will to preach grows more personal conviction. The preacher is rescued from matter, and so are those who hear him with faith.

8:30 A.M.

Cold page
icy windows
warm blood and heart.

The Christmas rush, the Kṛṣṇa conscious rush. I want to say . . .

I want to be a better devotee, but what? At my price? If the Lord increases my powers, I'll suddenly notice I'm not interested in non-Kṛṣṇa conscious things. I'll find new lights and interests wherever I dip into Śrīla Prabhupāda's books. I'll sincerely want to help others in Kṛṣṇa consciousness. I'll have the strength to do this. Pure desires. Let me do what Kṛṣṇa wants, not what I want.

Can I expect such a windfall blessing? Oh, let me work for it, reading even when it's dry, preaching, chanting, doing my duty, waiting for joy, waiting to taste deeper faith, not living for the pleasure, but loving Kṛṣṇa.

But . . .

I'm just saying I need help. I can't do it on my own.

I'm just saying it's cold. The word "science" means "knowledge," and Sadāpūta Prabhu explains how scientists have tried to kill God because they consider Him unnecessary for the equation explaining nature's laws. Occam's razor.

Read *Gītā* verses. In *Show Me Your Face, Lord*, an Italian priest teaches *lectio divina*. American Hare Kṛṣṇa sees if he can swan something from it. Dreamt we were in the old Boston temple. Exploding up through the roof—gushing water up there. What?

Sleepy, wake up. Whatcha got? Arjuna's new used car parked with headlights on while he is inside the house. I walk past it and down toward the shed. Stop and see over shoulder first light of sky.

Now light yellow sunlight through ribs of bare tree and through the icy window pane. Into my eyeballs.

Lord, we've got these senses on loan from You and not for long.

2:30 P.M.

Lord Kṛṣṇa says, "Whoever renders service to Me is in Me, is a friend, and I am a friend to him." I wrote it on 3" × 5" index cards years ago. Bhāgavata Purāṇa dāsa wrote some of them out for me; he has neat handwriting. I used to sit on the rocks in the hills and read such verses aloud. Was I actually praying? Yes, when I *think* of what I was reciting and reading. When I feel it. That's a good state. That's what I should do with my time.

Śrīla Prabhupāda on the roof in Māyāpur, '76. You can hear him and the disciples walking over the boards on his morning walk. They were challenging him about science. I felt at ease, not intimidated. I didn't need to hear Śrīla Prabhupāda give a materially learned explanation of why the sun moves or doesn't move. It was a nice listening experience. But I couldn't tolerate his talk with the woman TV interviewer in Chicago. I had it on during lunch but said aloud, "It's too hard!" and turned it off to play later. That interviewer was just too hostile. I know what Śrīla Prabhupāda means when he says we approve of polygamy or that a woman is less intelligent, but I wince when I hear him speak those phrases to an American woman reporter. Her dislike was painful.

O Kṛṣṇa, this day You let me have good health and all I did was read and write a little. I give thanks to You. The ease also comes from You.

Kṛṣṇa says whatever you do, do as an offering to Him. When you eat, when you perform austerity, when you sit in this shed, make it an offering. Dear Lord Kṛṣṇa, I can know You only through my spiritual master, Śrīla Prabhupāda. This is right. He guides us. I pray to You, Lord, He who gives intelligence in the heart, *antaryāmī*, please guide me to worship my master's words. I will accept him as absolute because he is Your representative. I will carry out his orders.

Dear Lord Kṛṣṇa, when You speak *Bhagavad-gītā* and when my spiritual master explains it, that's *good.* He explains it in such a way that even if You are not directly speaking of *bhakti* and pure surrender, Śrīla Prabhupāda reminds us of the goal. Consciousness of You is the topmost yoga and meditation. All else is nonsense and all but devotees are rascals. Hare Kṛṣṇa.

A materialist thinks he's big. A devotee knows God is *vibhu* and he is "nothing." We know we are small when we compare ourselves to Kṛṣṇa's greatness. He's the source of all gods and the material and spiritual worlds. To disagree with this conclusion of *Bhagavad-gītā* is to leave yourself with only the words of speculators. Eclecticism is a lonely path, never surrendering to the teacher of Absolute Truth. You are left only with a little Rilke, a little short change, a little dream life, a little Jung and Freud and Gurdjieff and Kowit and Garibaldi—the list is endless and leaves me aching just to recall it.

4 P.M.

I walked back from the shed. It was sprinkling and the rain smeared across my eyeglasses. I heard noises from the old buildings. That's the place where Arjuna dāsa used to live, where Tribhuvanātha stays when he visits, and where I saw the *saṅkīrtana* party loading books. Are they here again? No,

I didn't see their van. We heard they're the leading book distribution party in all of the UK. Remarkable. I'd be shy if I saw them now. I could say, "You guys are champions!" They would compare me in their minds with their champion spiritual master, who inspires them to distribute Prabhupāda's books. Or would they? Well, it doesn't matter because they weren't here. Just a noise in the building. Maybe Aniruddha was looking for piping to fix the heating system in the temple. I walked on, the collie behind me.

I'm a Hare Kṛṣṇa boy. I've got no more songs for awhile. I've got no voice for awhile. Be *still* and let the Lord inside you make you the best musician or take away your voice. He can knock you down in the woods and you could die. I thought of that in passing. He could knock me down and I'd think, "At least I had time to finish two volumes of *Every Day, Just Write.*"

Is that what you'd think at the time of death?

Death takes you to your roots, so where are my roots? Are they on those 3" × 5" index cards with *Bhagavad-gītā* verses on them? Are they sunk into pop songs of the 1950s? Am I rooted in Prabhupāda-isms?

Oh, who will help me among the devotees? Will my master come to me or leave me to my own devices because I too often chose selfish comfort instead of his remembrance?

O Prabhupāda, I accept it all, the whole hog—polygamy, killing the murderer (it's good for him), the words about women, the demigods with a million heads, Lord Śiva and *dharma* and Gaṇeśa's rat carrier. I accept it all. And I give the rest up. No more New York City nightlife, no more *karmī* clothes, no more wife or striving to be a Kafkaesque writer, no more attachment to posthumous fame. I give it up. Talks between the spiritual master and the disciple are serious.

6 P.M.

Browsing through *The Spiritual Master and the Disciple*, I found a heading, "The spiritual master trains and engages a disciple according to his ability." Then this statement by Śrīla Prabhupāda:

> There are different departments of activity in Kṛṣṇa consciousness, and a spiritual master, knowing the particular ability of a particular man, trains him in such a way that by his tendency to act he becomes perfect. . . . Arjuna offered his service fully as a military man, and he became perfect. Similarly, an artist can attain perfection simply by performing artistic work under the direction of the spiritual master. If one is a literary man, he can write articles and poetry for the service of the Lord under the direction of the spiritual master. One has to receive the message of the spiritual master regarding how to act in one's capacity, for the spiritual master is expert in giving such instructions.
>
> —*Bhāg.* 3.22.7, purport

December 18

MIDNIGHT

My persona in my writings (whether it be titled *Every Day, Just Write* or something else) is a person whose mission is to survive in ISKCON and in spiritual life. He's not out to reform the world. Indeed, he often checks such reformer tendencies as presumptuous or "too controversial." He doesn't have that hope or desire to be a social or institutional leader. He feels the wrongs, alludes to them, but mostly talks of his own survival activities. You could say he is a survivalist, or more simply, a survivor.

Is this my actual self? Or is it yet another mask? Am I trying to portray the simple *brāhmaṇa* who remains free from management and doesn't want to make waves? I don't know.

Is it even desirable that I be a survivor, or should I become someone different or better? I don't know that either. All I know is that if I keep writing as truthfully as I can, I may eventually climb beneath the present "I" to find the real self. We are each carrying personas and masks, and we create characters from which to live out our lives. I have to keep writing to get beyond that.

And perhaps that's the beauty and facility of *Every Day, Just Write* as I originally conceived of it. It invites me to be inclusive of everything I am and want to be. It fulfills the advice to spend all when I write. Not only can I express my desires to survive, it doesn't bar me from artistic or preaching aims. I want to therefore be intense when I write, and to think of the writing life as a diamond: as you turn it this way or that, you can see all the facets.

4 A.M.

The spiritual master says what he says and the disciple should not criticize. The female TV interviewer didn't like what she heard. She got angry and left. A disciple, however, shouldn't become angry. We should allow the spiritual master to blast our scientific allegiance, our national allegiance, and anything else that is not śāstric or Kṛṣṇa conscious. We have to listen to him.

I said, "Prabhupāda, in Hong Kong you told the interviewer that Guru Maharaj Jī was a cheater. You couldn't help yourself."

"Yes," said Prabhupāda, "and it has been proven."

It has been proven. Therefore, I should be quiet. Sometimes it takes time for things to be proven or to be revealed, and I simply have to be patient. I should never think my spiritual master is wrong in what he has said. Śrīla Prabhupāda told us that he had once had a doubt in his Guru Mahārāja when he ordered that a snake be killed. Later, Prabhupāda found a *Bhāgavatam* verse that stated that even a saintly person is happy to see a snake killed.

9 A.M.

Unseasonably warm, foggy drizzle. The shed door is swollen shut. I can't pry it open. I look in the window (in case someone locked it from the inside) and see the cozy setup with desk, sketch pad, etc.—a nice place to work. Pause and pee outdoors, then try again to open the door. I look it over intelligently as Madhu might and as he will have to do once I tell him I'm locked out. I see the door is shut tightest at the bottom. I reach down there and find a pulling leverage underneath. Tug, tug, and it's open.

Now faced with a blank.

But I brought a list exercise with me: "Make a list of a hundred." It's all right if you repeat yourself. Use words and phrases. One hundred sources of stress.

(1) Anything.

(2) Stoves when they heat up too much.

(3) Aromatherapy when it makes the air too thick with oily odor.

(4) Lecturing.

(5) Complicated talks with Madhu.

(6) Lectures, meetings.

(7) The walk if it gets too brisk.

(8) Car travel, airplane travel.

(9) You name it—anything too much causes stress.

(10) Thinking of dangers that may befall.

(11) News from ISKCON that threatens me and my publishing, my freedom, my reputation, etc.

(12) Hate mail.

(13) Individual meetings face-to-face with someone who starts to speak at length.

(14) Trip to a bookstore.

(15) Too many loud noises.

(16) The thought of going somewhere and doing something.

(17) Trip to the doctor.

(18) Walks in the fields too long in some place where someone wants to show me something.

(19) Mathematical or accounting puzzles I'm asked to comprehend.

(20) Politics I'm drawn into.

(21) Long complicated situations I have to hear and sort out.

(22) Staying up instead of taking rest on time.

(23) Late meals.

(24) Any delay or disruption in my schedule.

(25) Missing sleep at night.

(26) Pain.

(27) Anxiety of possible impending legal implication.

(28) Telephone call I have to make.

(29) Anticipation of any group meeting—as the hours go by and I have to wait.

(30) Editing too many pages.

(31) Reading—paying attention.

(32) Attending a *Śrīmad-Bhāgavatam* lecture.

(33) Paying attention to Śrīla Prabhupāda's tape conversations when the people are hostile or he's heavy.

(34) Answering mail—making my reply.

(35) Reading a *karmī* magazine with cheap print and photos.

(36) Watching a video.

(37) Deciding what to write next.

(38) Worrying about what I'm writing now—if it's okay.

(39) Demands of dreamwork.

(You simply want peace and ease, but hardly know how to enjoy it. You push yourself to produce, produce. It would be nice to release strain and just walk in the woods or look out the window at the lake.)

(40) Writing for a quota.

(41) Guilt if I do anything that seems like sense gratification.

(42) From here on my list will be repetitious: car or plane travel and meetings head the list as triggers for headaches. To me, "stress" means triggers for headaches. A fully developed headache is the result I get several times a week when I feel any of this stress, and slighter versions of it every day.

Therefore, I avoid stress as much as possible. But even normal events are stressful for me and promote headaches.

(43) People not understanding my illness or my imagining or guessing that they don't sympathize.

(44) Queues for immigration, especially in the Caribbean.

(45) Waiting of any kind, especially in dealing with the outside world.

(46) Opinions of others, whether long distance, merely in my own head, or met with in letters or face-to-face.

(47) My envy—my faultfinding does it, I guess. At least I don't like it.

(48) "Life itself is stress for you," said TKG, claiming that he had hit on the actual cause of my headaches.

(49) Rodents (phobia).

(50) Vigorous *japa* (I know one becomes free of stress by chanting Hare Kṛṣṇa, but when it's vigorous it seems to cause headaches).

(51) Loud temple *kīrtanas*.

(52) Being kept awake by loud noises coming from the nearby apartment or street when trying to sleep during the day.

(53) Fears of criticism, bad press, or even the attacks of inimical people.

(54) Aging—the body finds it stressful to do anything much, such as physical exercise.

I better end this list. It's not a transcendental list. It does teach me that stress is all around and that I should live in such a way as not to aggravate it. It leads to headaches. Relax, relax, breathe deeply and easily. Or lie down and deep breathe.

Peace.

Oh man, you sure are a case.
If life is such stress then
do you want to die and
rest in peace?
Impossible. There's rebirth,
the biggest stress.
I need relief from *saṁsāra*.

12:05 NOON

"This folly," he said, "this folly."

What?

He said, "This folly, this folly."

Quicken the pulse, the life, the dance, the ache of a thumb pushing a pen as long as it can. Kṛṣṇa protects His devotees and rich men's sons don't work.

White foglike smoke low and horizontal over the lake. No boats.

It hurt
trying to open the shed door.
Kṛṣṇa, Kṛṣṇa,
our peons (I mean paeans)
raise praises to Kṛṣṇa:

All glories to the *saṅkīrtana* devotees!

All glories to each of the nine practices of *bhakti*!

All glories to each of the devotees who serve in each way or in several at the same time!

All glories to *Śrīmad-Bhāgavatam*!

All glories to the devotees of Lord Caitanya!

All glories to the *ācāryas* who wrote blissful and learned *bhakti*-filled commentaries!

All glories to Śrīla Prabhupāda, who stayed with us on walks, in lectures, in his orders, in his books!

All glories! All glories!

2:35 P.M.

Kathleen Adams's book, *Mightier Than the Sword*, contains a chapter called "Authenticity." She writes, "The discrepancy between image/ being, external/ internal, acculturated self/ authentic self—'the maintenance of the lie'—reverberates in the journals of men like an echo bouncing off canyon walls. The search for authenticity is a modern-day grail quest. It is the beating heart of many men's writings."

Alpha poems—thank you, Lord Kṛṣṇa.

Beam back to me, Mr. Moon.

Hare
Authentic Self

Haribol puppeteer.

At the end of the chapter she gives exercises.

"Complete these sentence stems:

'Authenticity is . . . '"

Here's what I wrote:

Authenticity is when I don't lie, when I let my actual voice speak. We say an authentic ranch, an authentic American Indian village, or, "It had the authentic sound of bop." For myself I'm authentic when I admit that I'm a Hare Kṛṣṇa man with all my flaws. I'd like to say I'm a *perfect* Hare Kṛṣṇa man, an authentically pure devotee, or an authentic spiritual master, an authentic *mahā-bhāgavata*, but authentic has to mean the truth. I can't make phony claims that sound śāstric but are not actually true for me. When a devotee speaks in the *Śrīmad-Bhāgavatam* class, we can immediately hear the authentic ring of truth. It's not enough that the quotes he offers are perfect.

"My authentic self . . . "

My authentic self comes out when I allow the different sides of myself to express themselves. That is, when I listen to more than one voice. Ultimately, however, I know my authentic self is close to the pure spirit soul. When I'm able to hit the ring of truth, that's when I'm Prabhupāda's disciple, when I can remember and *feel* my contact with him.

Now complete the sentence stem, "I am . . . "

I am that I am. I am an eternal, fragmented part and parcel of Kṛṣṇa. I am the disciple of my spiritual master. I am, like it or not, serving as spiritual master to hundreds of devotees. I am sitting in this shed, glad to be alone, peaceful, for at least a little while every day. I am witnessing what I see with my senses, and right now I see beautiful swans and the calm lake. Another bird has just arrived and is sitting on the shore, its long neck extended.

And, "I am not . . . "

I am not a GBC man anymore. I was one and I am glad I was (but that's an "I am" sentence). I am not a woman-chaser, a homosexual, an uptight priest, a musician, a toady. I am not a politician. I am not responsible for the management or income of any ISKCON temples. I am not trying to run away from ISKCON. I am not immortal in this body. I am not somebody's husband or boyfriend. I am not trying to enjoy myself at the expense of disciples. I am not able to write the truth as deeply as I'd like to or as well as I could.

"Something very few people know about me . . . "

Something very few people know about me is that my actual name is Popeye. Very few people know all the books I write. They only know the few that are published. Very few people know, therefore, all the sins and confessions that I've made. Few people know my inner feelings, my dreams, the dirtiness, and they don't know my real spiritual aspirations. That's all right. Privacy is part of my authenticity, and I preserve my confidential self even though others don't care or don't know what I'm about. That is, I am someone beyond my image. That's another meaning of authenticity. You just be yourself as best you can and serve your spiritual master according to your capacity and nature. You don't have to live up to others' expectations unnecessarily. Few people know that I'm just a little boy inside who's afraid of the sins he's committed. Although I keep telling people that I can't pay attention in chanting, few people know how difficult it is for me to maintain attention on the holy names. Nobody knows how I ride the little bubbles and waves of happiness each day. Few people in my life now know much about my pre-Kṛṣṇa conscious life and all the junk that it constitutes, although slowly and gradually I'm sharing little bits of it.

"Look back at your childhood joys and pleasures. What do you remember? Jot down words or phrases."

Lying on my back in the grass, exhausted from solitary play, throwing a rubber ball against the house or just running around. Smelling the grass, looking up at the sky. Picking blackberries. Eating breakfast, especially Nabisco's Shredded Wheat with milk, sugar, and blackberries. Reading the Sunday funnies, reading comic books with family or friends. Feeling secure in our house because of having a strong father.

I can think of plenty more, but they're too domestic to repeat—family outings and so on.

"Think of somebody who only knows the public you. See yourself through this person's eyes. How would he or she describe you?"

He's a thin *sannyāsī*, aging. He is one of Prabhupāda's first disciples. He tells Prabhupāda stories and teachings that he personally heard from Prabhupāda. He's humble, but he seems to have retired from active preaching. He used to be a GBC man and manage temples. I'm not sure what he does now. He writes a lot of books. His disciples are fond of him. He gets headaches. He travels a lot. He's faithful to Prabhupāda and repeats him in his lectures. He's into creative writing. I hope he's not another guru who falls down and disappoints us.

"Imagine yourself doing something you really, truly love. Now imagine that a private detective known for his brilliant powers of observation watches you. What does he write in his report?"

I followed Satsvarūpa out of the house around dawn in late springtime in County Kerry. He walked with a walking stick toward the beach. I could overhear him chanting Hare Kṛṣṇa on his beads. He had a brisk stride and seemed to be happy to be out walking. I became interested when he took a tape recorder out of his pocket and started talking into it—talking to himself or about himself, about how he felt. He seemed to be making a rough draft or composing poetry or something. And trying to pray out loud.

When he thought he was alone on the beach he sat on a rock and began making a speech as if to an audience. He seemed to really get off by doing that. I guess he was rehearsing for lectures he makes in his church. He started writing in his notebook. The real thing will be to find out what he writes in his notebook. Otherwise, he's a quiet person who keeps to himself and takes a solitary walk, talks out loud, and records it. I'm not exactly sure what he's up to or why he's accumulating all this evidence about his thoughts. I've watched him follow this routine for several days in a row—he regulates his day by his watch. On the way back from the walk I saw he was limping and he had lost the briskness in his pace.

One hundred ways I fake it:

(1) I take a persona in writing even when I try to be honest—the scribe, spiritual journalist, Beat poet for Kṛṣṇa, etc.

(2) I do what people whammy me to do.

(3) I imitate my spiritual master.

(4) I imitate a pure devotee, act humble.

(5) I bluff on the *vyāsāsana* in all sorts of ways, giving right answers, but a basic or subtle pose is always at work.

(6) I don't eat much, but I desire to eat more.

(7) I don't let on that I'm attracted to women.

(8) I may exaggerate my illness. No, I don't think I do; I fake myself.

(9) I appear to be a good student, always faithful to Śrīla Prabhupāda.

(10) I pretend to be interested in improving my *japa*—I give that impression.

(11) I pretend to be exclusively interested in Kṛṣṇa consciousness, but I read other books.

(12) I don't know *ślokas* accurately but fudge my way through the Sanskrit when lecturing.

(13) I sometimes allude to interest in *mādhurya-līlā* or a taste for it beyond what I actually have.

(14) I pretend that I don't or never had interests in *gopī-bhāva* literature or pursuits.

(15) I pretend to be an honest guy.

(16) I tell people I don't write much.

(17) I don't let on that I draw pictures every day.

(18) I fake it, I fake it—I am not a pure devotee.

(19) I don't tell how I stop after sixteen rounds.

(20) I don't let on how weak I feel when my head starts to ache while I'm lecturing. I fake it.

(21) I fake composure when I'm sometimes afraid.

(22) I fake compassion.

(23) I have fake teeth.

(24) I fake my prayers.

(25) I fake devotion to Śrīla Prabhupāda *mūrti*. By that I don't mean that I lack complete devotion, but I pretend to more than I actually have.

(26) I bow down with body, but not mind and heart. I make fake obeisances.

(27) Sometimes I fake that I'm a refined, quiet gentleman, when actually I'm a coarse New Yorker.

(28) Sometimes I fake aesthetic pleasures and aesthetic appreciation.

(29) I also fake it in poems, in writing them and in appreciating poems that I read. I'm in on the big fake of modern art.

(30) Sometimes I fake it when I talk about death. I don't really think about it deeply, but I sometimes give the impression that I do.

(31) I fake being serious and very much interested in Kṛṣṇa conscious topics. Actually, I'm usually more interested in light topics that touch upon Kṛṣṇa consciousness but that are not so heavy. Therefore, I basically fake it as a lecturer.

(32) I fake it if I say I have no ecstasy. I feel bursts of happiness every day and certainly it is due to Kṛṣṇa consciousness.

(33) I fake it if I say I don't have love for my spiritual master.

(34) Sometimes I fake it in admitting a fault which I don't really feel to be a fault. I basically think I'm doing the best I can, but because there's such a virtue in admitting faults, I bluff it and admit faults without actually believing I have them.

(35) If, when I appear in a temple room carrying a *daṇḍa* and give a lecture with enthusiasm, people get the impression

that I do this every day, then they're wrong. I'm faking it. Because of my weak health, I spend my life in another way. My appearance on any occasion in a temple room is faking it because I'm acting as if I have the strength of a normal person. I don't. Those who are taken in see only the thin veneer covering my tottering weakness.

Having admitted so often to my shortcomings, if I go on in any number of ways to give the impression that I'm a topmost devotee, that's faking it. Just as I said that I sometimes have to give the impression that I'm healthy in order to get through a lecture, and that's normal, so it seems inevitable that we have to fake our way through so many things. That's just part of life. We can't be utterly true to ourselves at every given moment, or even at many given moments, and we certainly can't be utterly true to others either.

It's not innocent or harmless to fake it as a spiritual master, but as they say, once you agree to dance you can't cover yourself with a veil. That would be another kind of faking it, another insincerity, as Śrīla Bhaktisiddhānta Sarasvatī calls it. We have to go forward and serve, confident of Lord Caitanya's support. We may hesitate as we go forward because we are rookie policemen. That is, we're afraid as we walk down the street and possibly encounter criminals. But what can we do? We *have* to fake the courage and confidence because we have to inspire confidence and courage in others. That is our bravery. And when it comes down to it, we have been given the pistol and the club; we have been given the charge to use them.

Yes, I have to do things that are not entirely harmonious with my inner self. For example, on Friday we'll celebrate Vyāsa-pūjā here. I'll sit on an exalted seat and receive the honor of my disciples. I'm asking them to be prepared to speak their homages and yes, I will listen to them. It's all less than authentic, but it's not that the inauthenticity is entirely rotten or hypocritical. We are all filled with imperfections and we are not one hundred percent true, but that doesn't mean we should give up trying to make what we do authentic. In the meantime, we have to fake our way through. Best to do so with a smile or a laugh or even by letting others know, "Hey, I'm faking it here."

Eventually, as we practice *sādhana*, the outer man will become harmonized with the inner man.

4:15 P.M.

Heaney said he read Dante with "intense gratitude." I believe him. He got so much out of poetry. I'd like to feel that gratitude as I read Vyāsadeva and Prabhupāda. Dante is intense with his grotesque descriptions of pain and suffering. Heaney sees these as parallel to the troubles in Northern Ireland. Vyāsadeva, however, gives descriptions that relieve us from the pain and suffering of birth and death.

December 19

4 A.M.

Heaney speaks of the joy of poetry, its prerogative as well as its responsibility. What about the joy of Kṛṣṇa consciousness and its prerogative and responsibilities? We have the joy of freedom from birth and death. Not that we have already achieved it, but this is our purpose; we already feel some of it. We are working for the highest cause. Surely the joy we feel is a shadow of *hlādinī-śakti*, the love of God Kṛṣṇa confers on His pure devotees.

We have the responsibility to preach Kṛṣṇa consciousness truthfully and to not let up. To preach effectively we must experience taste. I feel that way every day when I go to write. I can't bluff the readership. I have to say where I'm at and at the same time, give perfect teachings. The teachings are more perfect than *I* am capable of expressing, but still, my speaking them is proof that a Western student, a conditioned soul, can rise up and aspire to really practice Kṛṣṇa consciousness. It's also proof that conditioning creates difficulties on the path. Despite the difficulties, however, we stay with it and triumph. That's a joy in itself. Therefore, I am not a poet in the tradition of Dante or Joyce or Heaney, or any of those who don't have the joy, prerogative, or responsibility of Kṛṣṇa consciousness.

8:35 A.M.

A LIST OF FEARS I HAVE ABOUT BEING MORE AUTHENTIC:

(1) I'm afraid that if I try to become authentic, it will turn into mundane realization, and I may go the way of a Godbrother who gave up guru and *sannyāsa* duties.

(2) If I become authentic, it may not be acceptable to ISKCON authorities. This fear I will attempt to subdivide under other numbers on this list.

(3) I'm afraid that authentic is something I don't really know. I'll go off on a blind alley.

(4) Or if I take authentic to be pure surrender to Kṛṣṇa, then I'm afraid I won't like it.

(5) If becoming an authentic devotee means I have to give up sweets with lunch, then how could I do that?

(6) If to be authentic means I shouldn't write anymore . . .

(7) Or if authentic means I have to write strict essays acceptable to the editors of *Back to Godhead* magazine and nothing else . . .

(In making this list I see I have two definitions of authentic. The absolute definition is to understand that I'm the eternal servant of Kṛṣṇa, so I should follow the six symptoms of surrender which begin with doing everything favorable for Kṛṣṇa consciousness and avoiding anything unfavorable to Kṛṣṇa consciousness. By this standard, I would have quite a different list. Thus my list has started off mixed because of the two definitions of authentic I am carrying in my mind. I need to find a synthesis. I need self-realization and self-fulfillment of my individual nature in the conditioned state before I can fully surrender. Or, to say it better, I *think* I need that kind of concession. I think if I can be satisfied and develop my psycho-physical nature, I'll be better able to give my love to Kṛṣṇa. If I am told too abruptly, "Your authentic nature is to do everything for Kṛṣṇa and nothing for yourself, Prabhu. We will now give you a detailed account of what you should be doing," that introduces another problem. That is, that different people inevitably have their own ideas of what it is for someone else to be authentic.

Well, who is the authentic Satsvarūpa dāsa? Someone might say, "Satsvarūpa used to be an authentic devotee of Prabhupāda and ISKCON, but now he's gone a little weird." I tend to think I've become authentic by searching on my own. This is what the psychologists refer to as the "acculturated self" and how it comes into conflict with the authentic self. Inauthentic means to live a lie. For example, a *brahmacārī* might be living a lie because in his heart he's not a *brahmacārī*. For him, it would be truth to admit something less than the highest standard of renunciation, something less than the fast lane for going back to Godhead. He'd have to go slower, but the true admittance would make him surer and stronger in the long run. That might be a humiliating position, but it's actually a more purifying one than pretending to be on a platform he's not.

This is all quite tricky and not easy to write down on paper—what is authentic and what is not, what my fears of authenticity are, etc. I'll proceed with the list, but I will add that I understand it's basically coming from a confused person who is not always sure which action is authentic—whether an act of indulgence toward the psycho-physical nature or an act which rejects an inner urge is the more honest approach to Kṛṣṇa.)

(8) I'm afraid that if I try to follow the path of the authentic self in terms of psycho-physical nature, I will miss out on the more single-minded path to Kṛṣṇa. Examples of this could

be thinking that it's useful for me to read nondevotee poetry. It *might* be useful to my writing, but it could also possibly cheat me from concentration on Kṛṣṇa. It will block me from the necessary practice that would make me the authentic Vrajavāsī that I want to be.

(9) One could also say that an authentic devotee of Lord Caitanya lives in Māyāpur or Vṛndāvana. I'm afraid that may be true, in which case I'm going to miss out. I am not even *trying* to live in Vṛndāvana or to renounce my Western ways. Rather, I'm dovetailing them in Kṛṣṇa's service. One might call it a gamble, but Prabhupāda authorized using Western ways as cultural weapons for preaching Kṛṣṇa consciousness. I'm afraid my being true to the authentic self in terms of my background, my knowledge of myself as growing up in New York, the literature I read and continue to read which is not devotional—I'm afraid that this authentic self will leave me at the end of life far short of being one who thinks of Vṛndāvana as his home in either this world or Goloka.

(10) On the other hand, if I try to live always in Vṛndāvana and develop my *bhajana* and the authentic meditation of a Vrajavāsī (i.e. meditating on Kṛṣṇa's *aṣṭa-kālīya-līlā* twenty-four hours a day), I could also become inauthentic in a different way. It would be false and imitative of me to turn myself into a so-called Hindu *sannyāsī* since I am not one. Neither could I make myself, by imitation, into one of the Six Gosvāmīs.

Regarding the fear of social condemnation or institutional reprimand, I'm afraid about that too. I'm afraid if I publish something criticizing the GBC, I'd be reprimanded. They could take away my freedom to lecture in the temples, to initiate disciples, to share my books with ISKCON devotees, and so on. This is not so much a conscious fear, but it may be lurking underneath, telling me, "Don't go *too* far. Don't make waves. You'll get into trouble."

I'm afraid if I followed my own nature I would gradually do less outward preaching. This might feel right for me, but it is different from what Prabhupāda writes in his purports. I'm afraid of not lining up with the image of a *sannyāsī* and devotee that Prabhupāda presented to us.

Since I'm not perfectly clear about my authentic self, I can't go ahead boldly and single-mindedly in this endeavor. Prabhupāda also discusses self-interest in Kṛṣṇa conscious terms. He says self-interest is good, but most people don't really know how to pursue their "super-self interest." They pursue a limited self-interest, starting with a kind of physical selfishness, then extending it to community and nation. *Na te viduḥ svārtha-gatiṁ hi viṣṇum.* They don't know that the real aim is to satisfy Viṣṇu. I'm aware of that, at least in a theoretical way. It seems that sometimes I have to make a concession and do things I may not feel to be authentic for me, but I know they're absolute. This is the nature of *vaidhi-bhakti*, which is regulative and not spontaneous. I have to do the things a devotee *should* do every day, and I have to do them even if they don't appear to correspond with my nature. The more I practice *vaidhi-bhakti*, the more my original nature will be uncovered. Prabhupāda said that when we uncover our pure intelligence, we won't know anything *but* surrender to Kṛṣṇa. We'll *want* to bow down to Rādhā and Kṛṣṇa, to get up early, to preach Kṛṣṇa consciousness. That's the hope we have in following the rules and regulations.

But it's a razor's edge. Prabhupāda also defines *niyamāgraha* as a too-rigid following of rules and regulations without knowing the ultimate goal. The ultimate goal is to love Kṛṣṇa. I can love Kṛṣṇa *now* by writing, and, strange as it may sound, I can do it by *doing things I love to do and offering them to Kṛṣṇa*.

I just said that sometimes I have to concede to my psychophysical nature, but it's not always a concession. Sometimes it's the bold, right, and most Kṛṣṇa conscious thing to do; it's surrender to be myself as I understand myself right now. Sometimes it may be more Kṛṣṇa conscious to give up that sense of self, to consider it an attachment to be sacrificed. Day by day, hour by hour we weigh the pros and cons and consider not only what is authentic but how much we're willing to *be* authentic. I know I can't claim that as soon as I find out what's authentic I'll immediately do it. I'm afraid, and maybe others are too, because it's hard. We think it's easier to remain imitators. Or if not easier, then safer. That's sad. Imagine going through an entire life with the blessings we have been given and choosing to remain mediocre. It's hard even to contemplate. To be governed by fear and repression, the consciousness absorbed in projecting a look-good persona rather than striving for the personal offering of self to Kṛṣṇa.

Devotees sometimes ask how much the psychologist's concept of an acculturated self is in conflict with the authentic self—how much this is true of the life of an ISKCON devotee. The psychologist would probably say that the religious institution is very much like other social institutions in that they apply pressure on the individual to conform. That pressure naturally causes the individual who wishes to be socialized to repress and/or deny what is authentic to himself. In ISKCON's more naive days we used to say with certainty that there was no conflict between the self ISKCON tried to bring out of an individual and the authentic self that *was* the individual. Anyone who saw a conflict was unsurrendered, in *māyā*. Now we admit that ISKCON does create certain social pressures that are just that, social, and not necessarily absolute for all individuals in all circumstances. An early absolute was that to be a good devotee you had to live in the temple. If someone decided otherwise in answer to some internal calling, he was obviously not *really* a devotee. Thank God that's changing, finally. Gradually ISKCON is providing more room for individual expression, for *individuals*, and devotees are also not waiting for the society to reform before they decide what's authentic for them.

Enough of this for now. "Whatever you desire to describe that is separate in vision from the Lord simply reacts, with different forms, names and results, to agitate the mind as the wind agitates a boat which has no resting place." *(Bhāg.* 1.5.14)

"Thus when all a man's activities are dedicated to the service of the Lord, those very activities which caused his perpetual bondage become the destroyer of the tree of work." *(Bhāg.* 1.5.34)

"Śrī Nārada said: The great sages, who had imparted scientific knowledge of transcendence to me, departed for other places, and I had to pass my life in this way." *(Bhāg.* 1.6.5)

LEAVING THE FALSE EGO BEHIND

I was moving with big-time writers like Allen Ginsberg and other persons of that generation. I was respected on a level with them and doing different crazy things like they were doing. Sometimes, though, I was opposed to them. I had certain powers. I realized that in order to keep up, I had to kill my ego. I had already killed my ego from when I was young, when I was Stephen, but now I had to continue killing my ego in order to remain with these people. There was a long scene where a truck caused me a problem. I shot my gun at it and it turned into an elephant, which I then drove away.

That's a fragment of the dream. The important thing to me now was the emotion I felt. It almost woke me up. I had already killed the false ego or a certain sense of self, but I realized I had to keep doing it.

Later in the dream we entered one person's house, and he looked up, awestruck, to see Allen Ginsberg and the other veterans. I was with them, but I was younger than they were and less of a veteran poet. I could see from that experience that I had given up my selfish desire to always be praised and given attention. It was gone and I was living in the moment.

Later: giving up the desire for praise is vital to advancement in Kṛṣṇa consciousness. It's not something you can do on your own; it's a grace that's bestowed by Kṛṣṇa. This is not abstract psychology; the ego is something we can actually perceive, namely, the false, material part of consciousness. We hope to kill it and to live in the moment of love for Kṛṣṇa.

9:10 A.M.

Can't go out now until around 8:30, it's so dark in the morning. Frost on window evaporates into water when I put on the gas heater in the shed. My head may have to diffuse pressure, but it may go down. Happy to see the rising sun and to walk in the cool outdoor air. Kṛṣṇa, Kṛṣṇa—chanting my sixteenth round at the desk in the shed. Now read.

LIST OF THINGS I WANT OR NEED

(1) A subtitle for this book.
(2) Hope.
(3) Faith.
(4) Charity.
(5) Lord Kṛṣṇa—at every moment. We all do. He holds the planets together.
(6) To know the *ślokas* I have already memorized and to quote them sometimes.
(7) To rest and to eat throughout the twenty-four hours at designated times.
(8) To publish books to please my spiritual master.
(9) To be rid of material attachments in the spirit of item two in *Śaraṇāgati:* "Avoid whatever is unfavorable to Kṛṣṇa consciousness."
(10) God's mercy.
(11) Ability, determination, and stamina to read Prabhupāda's books every day.
(12) Freedom from sex desire.
(13) To follow my *sannyāsa* vows until I die.
(14) The mercy of Kṛṣṇa's pure devotees.
(15) To keep that exclusive feeling of taking shelter at Prabhupāda's lotus feet.
(16) To hear his lectures daily.
(17) A sweet at the end of lunch.
(18) To keep writing letters to disciples and other friendly persons.

(19) Peace.

(20) Strength to endure pain.

(21) To honorably pass through old age up to the end.

(22) To think of Kṛṣṇa at the time of death favorably, desiring only to serve Him in the company of His pure devotees.

(23) To be free of faultfinding and other prominent *anarthas* which continue to linger in me.

(24) To chant Hare Kṛṣṇa with tears in my eyes, a throbbing heart, and a voice choked with love.

(25) To read scriptures in Vṛndāvana.

(26) To develop attachment for the dust of Vṛndāvana.

(27) Kṛṣṇa's mercy (already said that, I know).

(28) An easy way (even though that may not be right to desire).

(29) To be able to write like this.

(30) To write poems and poetic prose.

(31) To read *śāstra* and put it into my writing.

(32) To stay awake.

(33) Not to be afraid in times of danger, or at least to remember to chant God's names when I am afraid.

(34) To go on writing honestly through the end of this year and right into next year, enthusiastic to begin a new book as I go to India.

(35) To write deeply and spontaneously (hundreds of books, readable too).

(36) For people to take to Kṛṣṇa consciousness, and I want the Kṛṣṇa consciousness movement to be capable of sheltering them.

(37) To go back to Godhead.

(38) For the movement to grow and become pure.

You say, "I don't know what
to write, it's a beginner's way
each time I start from scratch."
You heard this writer's talk
and you pretend? Or is it that you
are now a disciple of Writing and
American writing teachers?

Dog barks. December 27 is gone.

Happy birthday
Dec 19,
1996
Moksade

my heroic father at a fire

I'm just saying I need help. I can't do it on my own.

Or are you your master's
spiritual son? Are you both
writer and disciple? Yes, that's
it. I write as my
offering. It's my service.
I keep digging,
paring away the layers.
I want to find something
and I do. I find worms
and brass rings and bones and
more dirt and borrowed
phrases, tulip bulbs, a picture
(in your mind) of a good-
looking woman. I keep
digging.

Sanskrit verses appear on a
lower level, with translations
and purports. That's me, too,
and down and more dirt, clean
earth dirt. Not dirty
factory rubble dirt,
clean dirt and juicy worms
and a mouse skeleton and
a prayer book,
piece of car tire, a memory, my own fingers digging,
a spade,
a pen and paper.

Down I go, digging, and if
someone asks what I am
looking for, I'll quip
that I'm digging for buried treasure
on the eastern side as the
astrologer said to do. I am
digging for love of God.

4:30 P.M.

Writing what comes, an old habit with me. Try to concentrate, but easy does it too. The pressure was rising in my head, so Madhu massaged my head, neck, and shoulders and for now I'm clear. Hoping to be clear for tomorrow's performances.

A flurry of mail came and I answered it. Mostly Vyāsa-pūjā homages. It's hard to deal with it with integrity and tenderness only because of the quantity, but I want to try. I read them and reply too quickly, though, so please forgive me for that. The best thing I can do for my disciples is to remain true to them by being true to Śrīla Prabhupāda.

5:48 P.M.

Birthday kid eats fudge sent by a lady disciple. Now I'm free and that's Kṛṣṇa's grace. He let me get through the tight squeeze.

Now if I can only do better, but how?

The head creates pressure, then I long for peace and quiet. But a preacher meets pressures. All right, I say to myself, then I'll stay quiet externally but write something valuable for others. What is that? I write my day.

I am a small-fry. A small-fry may also be permitted to enter the spiritual world if he or she is a pure devotee.

Kṛṣṇa, Kṛṣṇa.

I answered a small batch of mail, but when Baladeva comes on the 23rd, I think he'll have a bigger batch.

I'd like to write a passionate picture story in a sketchbook where I let go of my right-brain stuff, clustering.

BIRTHDAY:

You come out of your mother connected by the navel. Birthday candles. When you go to school, if the kids find out it's your birthday, they slap your behind hard. Seven years old, give me gifts. I'm eight years old. Give me, give me. Greedy kid. King for the day. He wants the *right* gift.

Birth? Not again! Suffering in the air-tight bag for nine months. No one is free no matter who his mother is. Don't come back.

Whew.

The real birthday is the *janma* of Kṛṣṇa or Bhaktisiddhānta Sarasvatī or Śrīla Prabhupāda. Birthdays of saints are *līlā*.

I'm fifty-seven this year, Bill Clinton is fifty, and next year I'll be fifty-eight. How many more? One of them will be my death-day.

December 1939, I came out with the navel, Mom, dead Dad. Birthday cake on my face.

Give me money. It's my birthday. Give me records, give me toys, give me plastic soldiers, cowboys and Indians on horses, give me records and toy guns.

December 20

12:30 A.M.

Hello, you're still breathing in this cool air. Write for effect like Emily Dickinson in "A Fly Buzzed When I Died"? Often can't figure out what she's saying. I want the meaning to be clear and easy for a reader to discern. So a simple fellow says to himself.

What you see in the mirror is the outer man. Where is the inner authentic self? He shivers to see it. Even the outer man is difficult—standing naked in line in a military situation with other men.

Will I have to return to the scenes of my dreams? Are dreams pushing the inner naked man into my consciousness? But, Dream Source, the messages you send are so puzzling.

In one scene last night I went onto a playing field where athletes were engaged in a game. I was caught way out in the outer field by two men from the sidelines. They were Brazilian athletes. They grabbed me and beat me around the eyes and forehead. Their blows were not staggering, but they hurt. I grabbed their hands and managed to drag them toward where people could see us. I considered the beating an injustice. I thought I could stop it if I brought it to people's attention. Was this symbolic for my headaches—the way they were beating me? Is the dream source some unconscious part of myself. (Some hint that the dream source is a person [or persons] of power beyond the self. Others say it's we ourselves who send ourselves dreams for our own benefit.)

I want to improve. I'm desperate, or like Thoreau said, living a life of "quiet desperation." I'm quietly desperate because I don't know by what method I'll make radical progress during the remainder of my life. I already have an expert guru, perfect scriptures, disciples, Godbrothers, a spiritual movement, a preaching field, and God in my heart. If *still* I don't cross the ocean of birth and death—I don't know what to say. Where else can I expect help to come from? As I grow older I'm less bold, less capable of making big changes in my way of thinking. Aging makes you complacent and in want of peace and quiet to heal your wounds and nurse your aching body. They say we should grow old gracefully. Does that mean seeking a niche in ISKCON? Is that what it means?

4 A.M.

I came out of the bathroom at 3:30 A.M. and Madhu said "Happy Birthday" with a little laugh. I responded by telling him that Śrīla Prabhupāda was speaking against Darwin and using such strong arguments. Whatever scientists claim as the origin of life, Prabhupāda replied, "Where did the ocean [or the explosion] come from?"

"It was an accident."

"There is no such thing as accident. Everything has a cause."

I read a news item that the Pope says the Church now accepts Darwin's theory. It is more than a theory, the Pope said, and recent findings lead us to accept it. They can no longer take the Bible as literal.

Sipping tea.

"Would you like a sweetener in it?"

"Yes, a little, thanks."

Then to poetry. I have no poetic heights to scale. I have only ten minutes to spare for this, then I must get back to chanting *hari-nāma* on my beads. Holding up so I'll be able to go out and sit in the chair my disciples have decorated for me.

It's the chair I use for chanting *japa*. They will cover it in saffron, but I told them not to use a lot of pins or stiff lumpy flowers because I have to sit on it. During the homages I may want to rest my head back for a little respite and check how I am doing.

Yes, pace yourself and get through this day.

Heaney wrote a poem about an imaginary land of conscience. He made it up. I don't make it up. The promised land is Kṛṣṇaloka. It exists and it's described in Vedic literature. As for the transformed material world and what it would be like, it would be filled with chanting and dancing, *varṇāśrama-dharma* would be intact, there would be many *brāhmaṇas* and real *kṣatriyas*, temples, farming, cow protection—it would be a bit of Vaikuṇṭha on earth. Kṛṣṇa would be adored and openly served, and everything would be in tune with the wishes of the *ācāryas*. The world would be safe—few thieves, and definitely no big rascals in charge. I can't imagine it actually taking place this Kali-yuga, but we have historical evidence of this in times past when Yudhiṣṭhira and others reigned.

"Are they right or are we right?"

"We are right," a disciple said, "the *Vedas*."

O Prabhupāda, you are my father. Jaya Gaurasundara dāsa's father died recently. He said he was not so attached to him, but he wishes his soul well. He's taking a few days off from work. Today they are having a party, a social-spiritual gathering for the disciples of Satsvarūpa Mahārāja, in the Baltimore area. It will include a feast and readings at Jaya Gaurasundara's house.

I am trying to get beyond pausing for the right word. I go barreling past that to whatever comes—the first frost, the nipple host, the crotchety . . . the, "Yes, I'm from New York"—the weird attachments. Pick up what others say. One disciple said that our material attachments lead us down many paths, some of which *seem* spiritual. Until we attain pure love of God, however, we may not find the right path. He promises to keep on practicing. He asks me to excuse him since he admits he cannot fully accept that I am not an ordinary man. What can I say? Shall I read his statement to others as exemplary or something to preach against? Did he hit the nail on the head? He put the blame on himself, says he has many doubts in the philosophy, but doesn't show them to others. Figures this is all because he is not a pure devotee. The fact remains he doubts his guru and thinks he may be an ordinary man. We say, "No, he is the representative of Kṛṣṇa." He is ordinary in one sense, in a *number* of senses with his ordinary body, ordinary life history before Kṛṣṇa consciousness, and you could even say his ordinary service to Śrīla Prabhupāda. He's got an ordinary (mad, uncontrolled) mind. But he's also extraordinary. He met Śrīla Prabhupāda in 1966 and is still following, he's not falling down, he's preaching in *paramparā*. Whatever he is, he has his spiritual master's mercy.

Out of time. Have to keep hale for today's performance. This was just to say hello on my birthday. Maybe someday in the future I may be able to write beautiful sonnets to Lord Kṛṣṇa or something exquisite. Or maybe I will always ramble on . . . In either case, I try to write every day to reach, squeaking for eloquence.

December 21

MIDNIGHT

Continuing the authentic search.

I gave out a lot yesterday in talks to disciples. Spoke of lifelong commitment to them and to maintaining a good personal example so that I can serve as guru. Heard their praises of me. Gave them my writing mind, writing life, as I read for almost two hours from my writings. Does that deplete me? It shouldn't. Still, I want to return now to my simple life and putting my thoughts down on paper. Yesterday I expressed my faith in and dedication to writing. One passage stated that whatever I hear in the world, I relate back to my metaphor for the writing life. I heard last night that ISKCON is threatened by an anti-cult inspired government investigation in several European countries. I worried about it as I fell asleep, but I still choose to write personally, to make this my contribution to helping an over-burdened ISKCON.

3:45 A.M.

"Follow the *mahājanas*!" Śrīla Prabhupāda says in a Vṛndāvana lecture. That doesn't mean you become a puppet. "Follow" means you use your brains, your life, and your imagination to visualize Kṛṣṇa from what you know. When Kṛṣṇa stood wearing a golden garment, holding a flower, the wives of the yajñic *brāhmaṇas* embraced Him in their minds. Can you picture it? Are you permitted to? You are not a dull stone.

Alas, then your attention slips and the train of thought moves past Kṛṣṇa into something else, falling into memories. Suddenly I am thinking of a letter I received from a devotee whose guru has given up his duties. She can't believe it because he told her their relationship was eternal. She wants to go on believing that. Why is she writing to me? I haven't read the letter closely enough yet to understand her mind.

Yesterday still lingers too—the room full of devotees reading homages. I tried to relax in the chair as soon as I felt the first sign of a headache. I learned that technique from biofeedback tapes. Maybe it helped, but the main relief came after the ceremony when I was allowed to go back to my room and use the shower for hot and cold therapy, then get into bed. Madhu took care of Prabhupāda so I could rest. Finally, I slept, and by Kṛṣṇa's grace the pain went down by lunch time.

Is it enough to say what happened? If more is permitted, what should I add? Should I embellish? They say every good storyteller departs from the truth.

Kṛṣṇa, Kṛṣṇa. At Krishna-Balaram Mandir, Śrīla Prabhupāda says that Prahlāda was a *mahā-bhāgavata* and that we could become one too, although it's unlikely we would. We should at least lift ourselves up from the *kaniṣṭha* stage, though, and become *madhyama-adhikārīs*. Prahlāda Mahārāja was a *mahā-bhāgavata* even when he was in the womb of his mother.

Hare Kṛṣṇa.

December 22

12:30 A.M.

Last night while lying in bed, I thought to quit the *Every Day, Just Write* title and series and start something new on January 1st. After all, it's a new year. Another trip to India. It deserves a fresh start.

It may be partly an illusion to think I can do something new at this stage. I don't claim that anything I write is completely different from anything I've ever written before, but I want to feel as free as possible. I want to write a unique combination of something for me and something for Kṛṣṇa conscious readers.

It's a paradox, so it's no wonder that I'm puzzled by it. I need to do whatever will help me throw off inner strait jackets.

8:33 A.M.

Bala's coming a day late, the 24th. Didn't feel like talking with M. at our usual time this morning. He was late. I had topics like (1) my writing—I can tell you about it, not now, but at the right time; (2) the writing I did in 1993 in Purī.

Went to sleep in dark—woke with first smudge of red on horizon over a calm, cold lake. Frost on the ground.

When is a journal not a journal but a free-writing practice? When am I on my own and following my master with no guilt? What would you like to read later in your own books? There is no narrator, my friend, but musings and moving of days. Now last days of the year slide away. I'll be traveling on January 1st. Changes liable to happen, as in Bala's delay. I could be delayed anywhere along the line—or worse. May the hand move off the line into loops and jots and struts of zigzag lightning and loop and jut and sketch—suddenly another man walking with a creature and no *tilaka*.

Where's the Kṛṣṇa conscious tag? Aren't we advised to "look for the Union label?" Well, where's the Kṛṣṇa conscious label? At least write out the holy name to keep away the Yamadūtas. Kṛṣṇa Caitanya Prabhu Nityānanda.

THINGS TO ACCOMPLISH NEXT YEAR:

(1) Travel to India—Jagannātha Purī and Vṛndāvana—and while there read and talk philosophy.

(2) Go on writing all year if that's what Kṛṣṇa wants.

(3) Accomplish more surrender—open myself to what Kṛṣṇa wants me to do.

(4) Accomplish steadiness in health. It's not up to me what happens, so how can I speak of an expected accomplishment? I can only say, "If Kṛṣṇa desires." Plan to go to the Caribbean, to speak there and to not lose hope.

(5) Remain celibate; follow strict *sannyāsa* vows.

(6) Remain true to disciples.

(7) Follow in ISKCON with good conscience.

(8) Be present, write, and urge them to go on publishing.
(9) Read better.

Talk to me so I don't go batty in solitude. Give me news, good news or light news or say something personal.

He said, "You can do the *nirjana-bhajana* stage now. Śrīla Prabhupāda has written it in his Fourth Canto. Your writings can go out to people." Yeah, yeah.

THINGS I NEVER MOURNED:

(1) My father's innocence, his ignorance.
(2) Death of love in that family. Did it ever exist?
(3) Your master's passing away—not enough.
(4) The passing away of ISKCON's innocence and my own enthusiasm in those days when I cared little about myself.
(5) The chance I missed to serve him as servant up until the end. I couldn't.
(6) The gone.
(7) The dead.

Hare Kṛṣṇa, I *mourn*. I do. Am I sorry I never loved a woman? A temple? Anyone? God—I mourn that thirty years have passed and I haven't attained *ruci* for *nāma* or for hearing *śāstra (satāṁ prasaṅgān mama vīrya-saṁvido)*.

BLESSINGS I FORGOT TO COUNT:

(1) I didn't forget to thank my Gurudeva for taking me as *śiṣya*. But say it at least three times a day.
(2) Blessing that I came to him and escaped death, escaped falldown, although I was a candidate for that.
(3) Thank you for getting me free of *karmī* family and devotee wife and now from management.
(4) I can write, am not broken up yet. Thank you for sending people to publish and edit and distribute what I write.
(5) I thank you for sparing my life.

(6) Kṛṣṇa, I thank You in advance for considering my service and when I go, for transferring me in the way that You think best to further my progress.

(7) Thanks that I'm not bitter.

(8) Thank You for peace and so far, thank You for reducing my suffering to a token of karmic sins.

THINGS THAT REALLY BOTHER ME:

(1) People who make loud noises.

(2) People who make me wait.

(3) Red tape holding up permission for us to go forward with our plans.

(4) Late meals.

(5) Mosquitoes.

(6) Blasphemers.

(7) Atheists and their propaganda.

(8) Oh, my own anger sometimes, but I'll keep trying to control it.

AFFIRMATIONS

Why do I want to continue this series under the title *Every Day, Just Write*? Because it feels right. It's comfortable. I like the idea of an "opus." But not something artificial. I like an opus to be authentic, something based on what I actually do each day rather than something I create or imagine that I do. I want nothing more or less than that. I like the lack of structure. That is, the freedom to write through intense periods of more structured work, then to naturally return to the less intense. I like it that there's no loss in doing so, and that I don't have to go through the big shift of quitting one work and starting another.

4 P.M.

Winter full moon bright rising over the island of Inis Rath. The sky is pale blue with a faint rosiness down toward the horizon. A jet trail passed in front of the moon's face, but now the moon has risen above it. Mr. Moon has an O mouth and deep cavernous eyes, reflecting my headache. Beam back to me, Mr. Moon, from far away. You are indeed mysterious and just a fragment of Kṛṣṇa's glories.

December 23

12:10 A.M.

I want to become deeply appreciative of what Śrīla Prabhupāda gave us—in the form in which he gave it. I may sometimes specialize by reading *Bhāgavatam* philosophy in Jīva Gosvāmī's *Ṣaṭ-sandarbha*, but I prefer much more to stay with Prabhupāda's books. By reading—daily reading.

The fact that Śrīla Prabhupāda writes basic philosophy implies that we should preach it to newcomers. It also implies that basic *Śrīmad-Bhāgavatam* philosophy is nourishing and necessary for us to hear again and again. It also implies that we will see things in deeper ways as we continue to study and think over what he has given.

As for my writing, I can simply trust in the process and where it is leading me. It's similar to Śrīla Prabhupāda's books in that it repeats the same thing and sticks to basics. But if I stay with it, it will reveal newer and deeper lights. It will also automatically lead to new and varied kinds of expressions and publishable works. This appears to be my particular form of discipline or craft: to write as much as possible. As I do, the process churns up varied shapes and products. I accept the theory that the diligent lab scientist will be the most likely candidate to hit on a brilliant discovery. The daily work I do, keenly and sometimes agonizingly, leads to discoveries of serendipity and synchronicity. That is, when you're in the right place at the right time, and when you are attuned to your craft by regular practice, the "universe" passes through you as you write. With this in mind, I'll look for what I can at Jagannātha Purī, and I won't fake it.

Yesterday I heard Sadāpūta explaining his current "three-pronged attack" on material science. He's trying to develop a presentation for showing Vedic astronomy in U.S. planetariums. People are interested in archeo-astronomy, the astronomical views of ancient cultures. There's also an interest in finding evidence for a pan-world culture to support unity in today's communally violent world. Sadāpūta Prabhu will also take the opportunity to present Vedic astronomy and *Śrīmad-Bhāgavatam* not as mythology but as an explanation of higher dimensional reality.

Hearing this prompted me to ask myself, "What is my three-pronged attack? Am I working on a way to win with my cultural weapons? Am I preparing a literature to conquer the American hearts and minds?" It appears I am not as keenly focused as Sadāpūta Prabhu as he scouts out the enemy and tries to penetrate ignorance and prejudice. I admire his meditation and his outreach.

By contrast I seem to write only for my own purification. An inner critic might say I'm just mewling around in my diary. That means that at best my writing is not a cultural weapon but a personal tool to help me cope with the day.

Continuing the authentic search.

Grrrr.

Man overboard!

KC

prasadam time

So speaks the inner critic. I say I want to make art. I'm not calculating what will work. I don't have the novelist's insidious cleverness to keep the reader within a world of imagination. My gamble (or tactic) is that the authentic will win out. I simply search for that. Gold will sell. My whole job is to write for truth.

Read in *Kṛṣṇa* book how some of the *gopīs* were conditioned souls enjoying with Kṛṣṇa while He was here performing His *līlā*. They associated with *nitya-siddha gopīs*. When Kṛṣṇa played His flute calling the *gopīs* for the *rāsa* dance, these not-completely-liberated *gopīs* were unable to escape from their houses. Yogamāyā arranged that they were prevented by their husbands or brothers. In the subsequent state of separation they meditated on Kṛṣṇa, became the greatest *yogīs*, and gave up their remaining material desires (their traces of material impiety or piety). "Their severely painful yearnings caused by their not being able to see Kṛṣṇa freed them from all sinful reactions, and their ecstasy of transcendental love for Kṛṣṇa in His absence ended all their reactions to material pious activities."

Śukadeva Gosvāmī then explains to Mahārāja Parīkṣit that any attraction to Kṛṣṇa, even out of fear or anger or lust, will grant freedom from material contamination and deliver liberation. Śrīla Prabhupāda then takes the opportunity to praise preachers who risk their lives to spread Kṛṣṇa consciousness. They are very, very dear to Kṛṣṇa. If Kṛṣṇa awards salvation even to His enemies, we can just imagine the good fortune of those who preach Kṛṣṇa consciousness.

On a morning walk in Māyāpur I heard Śrīla Prabhupāda talking with Hṛdayānanda Mahārāja, Bhavānanda Mahārāja, Tamal Krishna Mahārāja, and others who spoke, as well as those who didn't speak up to be identified and remembered on tape. One after another the devotees were telling stories of the effectiveness of Kṛṣṇa consciousness. Sudāmā Mahārāja told how the police came to the temple every day in answer to *maṅgala-ārati* noise complaints, but they told the devotees they actually liked them and asked for *prasādam*. Hari Śauri told how the City Council in Melbourne spent $10,000 in a case against them. The devotees decided not to contest it, but the judge threw it out of court. Hṛdayānanda Mahārāja told how the police, a judge, and the guests in Caracas were favorable to Prabhupāda in various ways. It was pleasing to hear the disciples telling these stories to their spiritual master. I liked them for this. Śrīla Prabhupāda heard it and was pleased, praising how Kṛṣṇa consciousness spreads and how although his men meet obstacles, they always go on. He said a preacher is very, very dear to Kṛṣṇa and that we should all preach. That is the definition of a *madhyama-adhikārī*. Prabhupāda also warned that we cannot imitate the perfect vision of the *paramahaṁsa* and we should never think we are already perfect. A tiny devotee should not think he is in complete control of his senses or that he does not need to chant his sixteen rounds. It was a good warning.

Starting to turn in the mind toward travel to India. Picking out which sketchbook to bring. Shall it be the 5 1/2" × 8" or the 6" × 9"? I consider the merits of each one. Hard to decide. But I can't take both. We are going as light as possible. They tried to buy me the usual portable, battery-run typewriter in America, but typewriters are harder to get these days. Now there are only word processors and computers. I belong to a former age. Go back even further then, to the pen and paper. Progress can't stop me.

Baladeva is due to arrive tomorrow, and then the next day is Christmas. There'll be entertainment at the temple. Time is running out for this volume. At least I've chosen the subtitle and have declared with hope that I will keep going with this banner into the new year. "O say can you see . . . that star-spangled banner yet wave." *Every Day, Just Write* is still in the air, lit up by the bombs and rockets of my doubts and the attacks of self-critics "O'er the land of the free and the home of the brave."

Kṛṣṇa, Kṛṣṇa, Kṛṣṇa. We now have tickets for the superficial carriage of these bodies to India. Of course, the soul will also fly. I am going to Nīlācala to find Kṛṣṇa consciousness in a place of Indian tourism, crummy hotels, the mixture of sense gratification and the town of prejudiced *paṇḍas* and so-called *brāhmaṇas*, real *brāhmaṇas* too who worship Lord Jagannātha. Nobody really seems to love anyone there—such party spirit —but they tolerate us and we tolerate them. That's the nature of this world.

Now I am alone with my master. He doesn't want to hear that I walk out to a shed and it is pleasant, just a little cold, and that my ankle sometimes aches. He already knows I get headaches almost every day. He knows what things I say that are untrue, and he knows I try to hide. Yes, I try to hide. But I can't hide from you, O master, so I always try to come out from hiding to tell you the truth.

It's just a few days before Christmas, Śrīla Prabhupāda. The *saṅkīrtana* results are rolling in over the computers, letting us know who is besting whom. All those newcomers and veterans distributing books, so many dollars liberated for Kṛṣṇa's service.

Here I am at your knee, sometimes dreaming of you and writing these pages. These are the things I say to those coming to Kṛṣṇa consciousness since your disappearance. They come to hear your teachings, and although they can get them directly from your books, some of them also want to see someone who has been following since he heard them from you and persisting despite America, the end of the century, old age, and all other bejabbers and sentiment.

8:43 A.M.

Too dark to read but soon I will. Kṛṣṇa speaking in fourth chapter when Arjuna asks Him how He could have spoken millions of years ago to the sun-god. Thank God we can receive this message today. This is *adbhuta*, most wonderful. Sañjaya says his hairs stand on end and he thrills at every moment when he recalls Kṛṣṇa's dialogue with Arjuna. Is this not better than any mundane thriller?

I asked Madhu to fix the tape that was chewed up in the machine yesterday. He didn't get back to me yet. I'll have to ask him for it.

Pink and white sky will lighten at any moment unless the clouds, already massive and blue-gray, mount a heavier campaign to darken this day. Manu's car is here. He's back, I think, from a weekend of book distribution in Dublin. O Hare Kṛṣṇa, O Hare Kṛṣṇa, I'm happy to begin that first round by candlelight. Joy you could say, that I am able to perform this most direct *yajña* to contact God. Surrender to Him by saying His names quickly as Śrīla Prabhupāda also says them on the *japa* tape.

Six pence two pence
a hen will do—let
the creatures run free
and don't eat them at your
Christmas feast. For
Christ was born not to
kill humankind or
its creatures but to save
us from sin.

3:30 P.M.

Walking out to the shed, a thought passed through my mind: what if I could have anything I wanted? I turned over a few options and settled for taste for the holy names. I desire pure devotion to Kṛṣṇa.

Then it occurred to me that I was *actually* being offered such a benediction right now. I stuck my walking cane into the mud, felt the cold air, and walked on toward my destination—the little orange shed by the water's edge.

Opening the cold *Bhagavad-gītā* I felt my heart and mind warmed. I turned to the purport of 4.11: "But Kṛṣṇa is fully realized only by His pure devotees. Consequently, Kṛṣṇa is the object of everyone's realization, and thus anyone and everyone is satisfied according to one's desire to have Him."

December 24

MIDNIGHT
THE TENTH CANTO

Tenth Canto is all Kṛṣṇa
Each chapter is also Him so
No way to avoid it.
To read it forever is fine.
However, you should also
Choose to read other cantos
As your master taught.
Now do it freely and pray
To render service to the best book
Over all considerations.

For three days in a row I had to close down my activities in the afternoon and take rest for the night by 5 or 6 P.M. due to headaches. It makes me want to work as best I can in the morning before it hits. Today Baladeva should arrive around lunch time with two weeks of mail and ready for me to work with him for two hours a day on a memory project. This signals the breakup of having my own time at Geaglum and the steady, quiet flow of writing and reading I have enjoyed here, the solitude. In a week we leave for England and India.

PRAYERS

Prayers are taught by Christian saints
Rūpa Gosvāmī prays in Vṛndāvana
and I would like to pray
yes, but need the desire to love or
else what is my cry, my prayer?
"Give me weather"? "Give me happiness"?

JAPA TIME

Japa time, sacred
inattentive mind I ask you
please attend to the holy names.

Time for chanting well spent
I'm a fool
bad habits but
even I can be saved.
O holy name
sprinkle
Your mercy upon me.

HEADACHES #1

Headaches come when they like
each one in its own time
to stop me from work.

Don't you know it's silly to write
and you shouldn't try to make a
cute poem fit into a concept?
"Headaches" is a subject but
each poem
should go its own way.

HEADACHES #2

How the headache develops:
each one new, right side, diffuse,
spoil my fun but
don't stop me from thinking of Kṛṣṇa.

Aches, aches—surrender you're
not lord now, headaches
your lot
each one
sent by the Supreme to
teach me
what I forget.

SEARCH FOR THE AUTHENTIC SELF

Authentic self I seek
under the moss, under law.
Teach me who I am through writing—it
haunts me to know so I can serve
the ends that justify the means.
No, no, Nanette, I don't
teach you what I don't know.
Is it authentic to
carp and cut and choose and pick?

See? It makes no sense to ask
each line is independent—
in authentic poem self,
forget the meaning and just flow.

TEMPLE

Temple is haven, hard work
each moment austere,
together
mostly for young devotees, they say.
Parents are not allowed mostly
instead it's the strain and the surety
every day you're in His house.

KEEPING VOWS

Vows I made it's a wonder
all these years I still follow
why I do it is my decision
surely it's His mercy on me.

A DREAM: VISITING MYSELF IN THE HOSPITAL BED

I went to the hospital and saw myself lying on a bed. I began to talk to myself. A doctor entered and I thought he would notice that I was identical with the man on the bed, but he didn't even look at me. He treated a boil on my arm. While I was sitting there, a few sailors came in. It turned out that I was a sailor and they were buddies of mine coming to see how I was. I sat and listened to the sailors talk.

I want to think more about that dream where I was talking to myself lying on a hospital bed. Obviously, I wanted to talk with myself about something. On re-entering the dream, I ask the self who is lying on the bed, "What do you really want? Do you want sex?"

"No," he says. "I don't want sex."

"Good. What do you want then? Do you want to be Kṛṣṇa conscious? Would you like me to get you out of the hospital?"

"I can't get out of the hospital because I have a problem."

"You mean the hospital is a symbol for being in the material world?"

"Yeah, you could say that."

I'd like to help him to get him out of the hospital, but he seems entangled, as if he's the property of the doctors. The coarse Navy fellows aren't helping much either.

No solution. This man wasn't very communicative; I had to do most of the talking.

SAṄKĪRTANA DEVOTEES

Saṅkīrtana devotees are the book
distributors
and other kinds of preachers
doesn't matter *how* they preach
as long as they sing for
Kṛṣṇa together and work
in harmony.

Lord Caitanya's devotees move in
ecstasy and rhythm
veering off into the blue I
mean the skies of Māyāpur.
Gone are material troubles
the *saṅkīrtana* devotees are free
and I bow down
to them, ask their forgiveness
for not loving as I should.

MEMORIES

Memories come, some of when
I was in *māyā*.
Does every memory have to be
authorized? But they
come and go, I
choose them or
they choose me.

Which memory will give
me pause and which
will I consecrate
by writing it down
preaching to it, letting it
reach out to me?
I am what I was and
remember when I cried—
those good days.

8:40 A.M.

I'm enjoying the rush of "alpha poems" while they last. An "alpha poem" is when you choose a phrase and then begin each line with a letter from that phrase in order. I know they're not great poetry, but they induce me to speak in a more Kṛṣṇa conscious way.

Black Kerry cows grouped by shed—four of them. Is Draupadī among them? Maybe not, because as I walked down here, none of them bellowed, although they watched me curiously. Now we're in separate worlds again.

Heavy, gray, blanket clouds, but way up toward the top of the sky I see light blue. Only gradually is it becoming light enough for me to read.

READING BOOKS

Reading books, singing brooks
each day less from my total.
I'd like to see you with your
nose in the scripture and
damn it, awake and alert.
And I want to be a fellow that
writes what he reads.

'Neath the oak the Swami stood
and spoke
no garland but all
praise to him now.
Beware the stinking body
and read his books.
O Māyā, don't stop me:
Kṛṣṇa's giving *darśana*
and I wanna go Home.

VṚNDĀVANA #1

Vraja, Ramaṇa finds His pleasure there.
Extraordinary donkeys, no ordinary monkeys
no plain folks,
and not a place to go if you want to make money.
I have no right to
stay there, and my master tells me to
"Keep moving"—
preach in ISKCON.

VṚNDĀVANA #2

Vṛndāvana, Vraja, Vṛndā,
Vṛndāvaneśvarī.
O Vṛndāvana
be kind and let me stay at least
nineteen days
writing like a child
in your lap,
holding twigs from the *tulasī*,
dust on my head,
writing day and night
of Your glories.

As I sit reading *Bhagavad-gītā*, one of the cows is giving herself a good rubdown by scraping her body against the side of the shed. Yes, it's Draupadī, who's now bellowing and looking in my window.

Reading, reading, a little at a time. We are spirits and Kṛṣṇa is the Supreme spirit. If you think you are apart from Kṛṣṇa, that's the illusion of the material identity. The bona fide spiritual master teaches us that we are part and parcel of the Supreme Person, Kṛṣṇa. Pink light through the white clouds, "indirect lighting." The blue heavy clouds pile in the sky. The fresh rain cloud is Kṛṣṇa's hue.

WRITING, WRITING

Writing is hard work and tends to
ride off the Kṛṣṇa conscious track.
Instead I advise you to enter
the truth of scripture.
I accept it on faith, with trust in Vyāsa
and the self-effulgent knowledge.
How is that? I can't completely know.
Go on writing and discover what you can.

Writing leads nowhere sometimes, but I'm indifferent to that now
and ride the swell waves as they come,
grateful.

Where is this uphill leading?
I don't always know.
To paradise? A peat bog?
A cottage for more writing? To
death?

In trance, in blear, in simple
humble prose we know
that nowhere—there's no such place in God's
kingdom.

2:20 P.M.

Christmas Eve afternoon. Nice lunch, no meat or alcohol or smokes or sex life. Listening to Śrīla Prabhupāda on morning walk tell how his father gave *gañjā* to "*sādhus*," but Śrīla Bhaktisiddhānta Sarasvatī Ṭhākura was very strict about "no intoxication."

Nice day so far for me—clear in head. Baladeva landed in Belfast with three or four big suitcases. KK's car is too small to carry them, so they're putting him on a bus. Sounds like Santa Claus is coming. Madhu and Aniruddha rehearsing Irish songs for tomorrow's show. Rehearse isn't the word—they're putting it together from scratch in one meeting.

So, mate, it is nice to have a soul mate. It is most fortunate to have taken the human form of life after wandering in so many lower species. *Uttiṣṭha*—get up! Don't sleep! Use this form of life for enlightenment in Kṛṣṇa consciousness. Don't come back to this material world.

Peace on earth to men of goodwill.

December 25

CHRISTMAS MORNING, 3:30 A.M.
CHRISTMAS STANZAS

1

Tea-lights they are called—little white
candles
each burning on the altar as I chant
and pray and mind-wander.
and count the quota.
Christmas Day in Geaglum.
We'll sing and dance and a play
will be put on by devotees before
Rādhā-Govinda.

2

When the body is dead
the soul lives on.
Vee go the ducks flying.
each keeps itself up in the air
and the master leads
the way.
Even when dead the soul
holds its head and goes
flying under order to
its destination on His will.
You choose and He
sends you. Dead ain't dead.

May you have a merry one
a holiday as you see on
recent morns the swans glide
smoothly and it's warm—no snow—
"Now peace be w' you"
and may everyone accept *bhakti-yoga*,
as blessed by Prahlāda.

2:45 P.M.

Waiting. Let my head pressure not build up. It's already up, but tolerable. Perhaps it will diffuse. One letter kept me awake last night. The devotee said that I don't remind him of Prabhupāda. My Godbrothers, he said, are preaching all over the world, "fighting hard in ISKCON for ISKCON." I admit it hurt me. I responded with my feelings and felt some release from them.

Waiting. There will be a play and some music. Now less than a week left in the year and in my peaceful Geaglum stay.

Who's afraid?

Listen . . .

December 26

12:35 A.M.

Last night after the show at the temple, Bala rowed us across to Geaglum. We could see by the light on in Manu's house—its beam was like a lighthouse beam across the water. We joked about capping the night with rum cake (I suggested an Aum cake instead) and I gave Baladeva and Madhu milk sweets and apple juice and had some myself. My head pressure had been bothersome but tolerable during the Nṛsiṁha skit and the concert that followed, but I'm all right now.

9:50 A.M.

Day after Christmas. Lay down your burden.
Not yet.
Then carry your Cross.

Free-write your way home to America. Pick up your travel pen from January 1st on. And when you're afraid, remember Lord Hari's names. Don't be afraid: no one can hurt you, not even with words. You are protected by your spiritual master, although you still have a long way to go.

DAY AFTER CHRISTMAS

Day after Christmas—are we in
a sorry state? No, we are with Kṛṣṇa
conscious society and on our own too.
Girls singing "Kṛṣṇa Carols"
last night—"no false joy" they
said.
I liked that. Yes, we are sober,
don't fake it, we have controlled senses and
for gravity's sake we don't hang
so loose
although cider and apples and sweets were
given out by me to men
from my hallway.
Each day left in calendar is to
pick up your old kit bag
remember Lord Hari
and go.

Christmas—the meaning
is holy—and we want holy
madhyama tasks. Mine is to
write and always respond. To
chant the holy name.

SPARE ME LORD

Spare me Lord, I pray but know
peace has got to be earned or
rather it's up to You, inexplicable
how You
are handling each one of us.

Rāma too, Your brother, smiles.
Each *bhakta* and *bhaktin* in Goloka
must know by Yogamāyā
that You are their loved one.
Each time I say it I make gains—
Lord, spare me
O Lord, I pray as aches visit
me. Let me realize
divine life is Your service and
this body is
not good
except for serving You.

4 P.M.

In the foreword to *Court of Memory*, James McConkey tells how one night he "underwent a change so radical that it transformed my apprehension both of the world and of valid modes for writing about people." He was sitting in his basement study feeling anxiety about the Cold War going on at that time between the Soviet Union and the United States. As a writer, he felt dissatisfied with a story he had just written because "what did *that* story have to do with my present feelings? What did it have to say about a society which might destroy itself with nuclear missiles very soon?" Out of this anxiety, McConkey suddenly felt the value of simple things perceived in the moment—the snow-covered ground outside his house where he saw a bird's nest in a tree, and right beside him in his study, the moist nose of his German shepherd. "The story I had written was unsatisfactory because it was 'made up,' a fiction, one devoid of the sacredness I saw everywhere about me. The only way open to me to communicate the strength of my feelings was through myself—through my intimate experiences, through memory, and personal observation."

McConkey begins to write autobiographically at this moment, but instead of writing about things immediately at hand, such as the bird's nest or his dog's nose, he turns to a memory of a "botched up nightstand I had built as a child for my mother." He says, "In re-reading that account, I realize that I was (as I still am) held by the old truths of literature, for my words turn into a statement of the momentary victory of the imagination not only over mortality but over those aspects of the real world I had wanted to celebrate. Whatever my wish I had not escaped fiction; I had simply made myself the central character of a story, finding in my own experiences and dreams a greater authenticity than I could in those of any character I might invent." That was the beginning of his writing several volumes of autobiography.

I like what he says about writing of real life and its familiar objects and perceptions as being more true to the sacredness of existence than what is possible in fiction. It's also interesting, however, that even when a writer decides to speak his own unvarnished truth, he still turns to an active imagination with an inevitable persona, a form or selection that might even be called fictional. I find I am doing that in an attempt to make an artistic form of presenting Kṛṣṇa consciousness. I write because of the personal satisfaction and the relief I get from it, and I write as a way to cope with life. I also write because I'm driven to do it. Fortunately, all these motives are dovetailed in presenting Kṛṣṇa consciousness.

December 27

11:20 A.M.

I've run out of time to write this volume and I would like to explain why. The main factor is that Baladeva is here for a week and we're working on a project. So far I've only been able to work once a day with Baladeva because of my headaches, but now I've decided that even if I'm up all day, I'll meet with him twice. Those are the same times I would be out in the shed, from 8:30–9:30 and from 3–4 in the afternoon.

A LETTER TO A FRIEND, WRITTEN IN THE MIND:

Dear Prabhu, you and I have been discussing the technical differences between conditional devotional service and pure devotional service. You understand it more analytically than I do. You describe an early stage of devotional service where you offer the fruits. That is not pure devotion. You discuss another stage where you're detached from the fruits and do your work dutifully, but it's not yet spontaneous. You describe a stage of pure devotion, which involves emphasis on *śravaṇaṁ kīrtanam*, but also doing only what Kṛṣṇa wants you to do—even beyond one's psycho-physical nature. What I want to express to you as a friend is a line of argument I'm compelled to take in answer to this request that you are making on Kṛṣṇa's behalf that I do only what Kṛṣṇa wants me to do if I want to attain pure devotion.

By way of replying I want to first tell you something I read years ago in Franz Kafka's diaries. He said something about the nature of Judaism. Although Kafka was not a religious man in the ordinary sense, in this one diary entry he spoke in praise of Judaism and said, "Now there's a real religion. It accepts the whole man." I don't know exactly what he was thinking, but it struck me. I thought in contrast of a stereotype that is given of renounced Christianity, which is that one surrenders in spirit and negatively renounces the flesh—perhaps Kafka was praising Judaism as one that accepts the human man in all his dimensions.

I like to think this is what I'm doing in my own Kṛṣṇa consciousness. Perhaps when I was younger and *appeared* to be more surrendered, I was partly pursuing that renounced version where one suppresses certain "impure" drives one has (and I don't mean sinful activities but personal natures) and does just what Kṛṣṇa wants, according to the spiritual master's order. It appears that one is on the higher platform of devotional service, but actually, the "whole man" has not been eliminated; neither has he been fully engaged in Kṛṣṇa's service.

I think now that I'm allowing myself to dovetail my creative nature in Kṛṣṇa's service I am more surrendered than when I was completely submerging those desires. I know there's a thin line between self-indulgence and offering something to Kṛṣṇa, but I try again and again to be honest about this, and the best I can come up with is that this is my surrendered offering to Kṛṣṇa. In other words, it's not a matter of theological discussion but existential reality. The theoretical discussion can go on as perfect talks from the *vyāsāsana*, or talks between you and I about what Kṛṣṇa is saying in the *Bhagavad-gītā*. If I say I now know what pure devotion is—to do only what Kṛṣṇa wants—then I have to ask, how do I follow it up? How do I know what Kṛṣṇa wants? How do I attain it?

I don't really know what Kṛṣṇa wants in my very specific, tiny life. I have to offer Him the best I can in terms of what I think He wants. Furthermore, even if I were to make a guess and say that Kṛṣṇa doesn't want me to be, say, a writer, I wouldn't know for sure that that's what He wants, and how could I give it up?

I don't want to define myself on a lower rung of devotional service, but neither can I artificially do something beyond my realization, so I try to surrender fully *(ātma-nivedanam)* in the sense of the impression I got from Kafka's line. I want to give the whole man and not just a renounced version of myself to Kṛṣṇa. I want to give Him what I love. I want to also let it serve energetically in a preaching way to show others how they can give their whole selves to Kṛṣṇa.

Here the words "whole selves" do not mean pure self; it means giving all aspects of our selves as we know them according to our conditional nature. Giving our money, giving our talents, and so on. Giving all the things we have. I expanded on this image while writing *Churning the Milk Ocean*. There I said that when I write I churn up things that are sometimes poison and sometimes nectar. We reject the poison and don't offer it to Kṛṣṇa, but we can't deny that it gets churned up in the process.

I am writing this to you personally. I wouldn't advocate it at an ISKCON forum for social living or as support for Western psychology—inviting devotees to do their own thing for Kṛṣṇa. I have to admit it's what I'm doing. I do restrict myself from expanding on inner desires I may have. But I'm going ahead as fully as possible to offer Kṛṣṇa my nature, to do the best I can to respond to the perfection that Kṛṣṇa desires—that we act only to please Him.

It may sound strange to say I don't know what Kṛṣṇa really wants, so I have to agonize over it on my own. What do you think? Do you think you know in vital aspects—and that other devotees in ISKCON know in vital aspects—exactly what Kṛṣṇa wants from them? Rather, isn't this part of our free will to struggle with this?

6 P.M., NIGHT NOTES

Night notes now it's running
into very last days but I get
a next life
go to Vṛndāvana, go to Nīlācala,
go to pilgrimage chant and wait.
Lord Hari will take away and
give you—
take away your dearmost
idea maybe and teach you
how to please Him.

"No, not that!
Oh, don't ask me to give up
being a retired writer."
To please the Lord you must
do whatever He wants
so learn it,
escape not,
"Śyāmasundara rules this
life"—let it be said of me.

A dog barks and December 27 is gone. The end rushes in on us. Fog almost all day—I could hear men shouting on the lake but saw nothing. Finally the sun cleared it all and the afternoon brightened.

I spoke with Baladeva and told a story-length memoir of my days as a wallflower at high school dances. Now I'm tired, and I'm finding it hard to write anything here at length. Telegraph messages only.

Alas, alack, am I going to ask for a sweater even when I don't need one? I already have a good warm scarf, a sweatshirt, and a coat. What more do I need?

No, I could use a warmer sweater.

All right, we won't let you freeze.

Well, I can live without it. I hate to take something I don't need because I'll have to pay for it later, right?

And what is this claim that you don't know what He wants of you?

I mean, as far as I can see He is pleased that I'm writing. He wants me to do this. But He wants much more too. I don't think He's *not* telling me, but what I'm hearing is "go on writing." But how can I say I'm absolutely sure that's what I'm hearing? I can't say there's a huge gap in my surrender because I refuse to act for Kṛṣṇa's pleasure even though I know what He wants of me. Rather I surrender this way, and if Kṛṣṇa wants, He will tell me otherwise.

December 28

12:45 A.M.

When I arose from bed this morning I made a few notes for the talk I have to give tomorrow morning at the disciples' meeting. I'm going to start out by saying that I'm going to Vṛndāvana. I'll read references from Prabhupāda's books. The first one will establish that Kṛṣṇa in Vṛndāvana is the object of our worship. Vṛndāvana in India is a replica of the spiritual world. It's important for us just to go there. Then I'll read a quote that says if you can't go to Vṛndāvana, you should think of Vṛndāvana in your mind. This refers to *rāgānuga-bhakti*, but it can also be applied on our level of devotional service. That means we can practice chanting and hearing in a Vṛndāvana-like mood, or to put it more simply, in an attentive and serious way. Then just to assure us that we don't need to travel to India, I'll read a quote by Prabhupāda where he says that we can think of Vṛndāvana wherever we are in the world.

But the real substance of my talk is to encourage devotees to establish a sacred space in their life for daily *sādhana*. One of the keys is regulation, then maintaining that regulation. And being creative so that we find it interesting, and we make gains by practicing it.

The ongoing drama about the management of this temple goes on. Several of the key devotees met yesterday and the temple president expressed why he finds it difficult to continue here. His main difficulty seems to be with only one devotee. He wrote me a letter last night telling from his point of view why this devotee is troublesome, but yesterday I received a letter from the "troublesome" devotee and his point of view seemed just as reasonable. I wrote a note to Madhu that it's time for us to leave. Otherwise, we'll be dragged into this controversy that seems headed for a "no win" result.

INSTRUCTION TO KILL A DEMON

I dreamt that a disciple had to fight a strong adversary who was coming to attack him in the temple. I encouraged him and helped him build an ax. When I gave him the ax, I said, "If you have to, you can kill the demon when you knock him unconscious."

He said, "I prefer not to. I'll just knock him out."

Then we waited. Finally the demon came and my disciple was confident he could defeat him.

On waking I thought about this particular disciple and the actual adversary he appears to be facing in his life in the temple. Of course, his "adversary" is a devotee, not a demon, and my role in discussing the problem with my disciple is not to encourage him to focus on his so-called adversary, but to see the adversary in his own heart. That's the demon I want to teach him to kill. I wonder if I can write a note to this disciple based on the insights of this dream. Maybe not, because I wonder what he could possibly apply. Reading and chanting helps overcome inner conflicts on the deepest level. At least I could say that.

11 P.M.

I wanted to write farewell pages at midnight but I'm prevented by a headache. It was unusually sharp behind the right eye all night and it continues. At least I can offer this dream fragment.

PRABHUPĀDA PRAISES HIS SANNYĀSĪ DISCIPLES: A DREAM

Prabhupāda was in a place but wasn't giving classes or *darśanas*. Finally he gave *darśana* to a group of mostly *sannyāsīs*. He said that *sannyāsa* was required, and he praised each devotee. He said Hṛdayānanda and another devotee from South America were learned. He called me Satsvarūpa dāsa Brahmacārī and people smiled. He said I was his personal servant. Then he said something else about me that I couldn't catch. Jayatīrtha turned and said, "He said you don't take even two minutes for Deity worship." He was praising me for following my schedule of *sādhana* so strictly. Prabhupāda went on to praise others.

December 29

5 A.M.

My headache persists, so we've canceled the disciples' meeting I was supposed to hold this morning. I muttered seven poor, silent rounds before 3 A.M., and then instead of going into the bathroom, I went back to bed. I knew the headache was getting worse, and there's nothing but rest that can help it go away.

9 A.M.

Farewell, Volume Two. You've certainly been a friend—and will continue to be one.

Farewell to shed visits twice a day, view of the swans, walks in the damp woods, mud puddles, wet leaves, Tilaka the collie trailing behind but independent.

The most significant thing about this volume of *Every Day, Just Right* is that I passed over two crossroads where I could have quit. Both times I decided to stay with it. Therefore, this is my "survivor" volume, my search for the authentic self.

Epilogue

DECEMBER 30, 1996

Baladeva Vidyābhūṣaṇa dāsa suggested that we skip Jagannātha Purī and go only to Vṛndāvana—or not go to India at all—when he observed me with all-day headaches, but we are going. We've planned it, we've calculated the risks, we want to go. Nine of us are meeting in Purī for two weeks. Then on to Vṛndāvana for eighteen days. It's an adventure and I want to appreciate it as such. We discussed some of the realities of Purī last night—arguments with rickshaw *wallas*, diseases lurking, sellers on the beach, the general attitude of "*brāhmaṇas*" and priests toward white-bodied devotees . . . But I also recall the sound of the ocean surf heard from the hotel room while I chant *japa* early in the morning, and the fact that despite Kali-yuga's covering, Purī is the *dhāma* where Lord Caitanya spent eighteen years of His life on earth. I hope to read *Caitanya-caritāmṛta* there to the devotees. And to write and draw. My conditioned self—I'll drag it there, not to indulge it, and not expecting to rise above physical and mental affliction, but to preach and to tell my story of struggling to be a devotee of my spiritual master.

END OF YEAR

End of year what does it matter?
No one cares. I mean it's just a
calendar notation and New Year's Eve
drunks and a chance for brave devotees to
chant in city streets at midnight.

Of years this was the Centennial,
ways to count and to be inspired to
preach, praise Prabhupāda—
year-end, year beginning and
we are fortunate to move to
India's *dhāmas* at start of 1997.

I asked my Lord and my spiritual master,
to please let me read their books,
every chance I get as I did
this morning
remembering that Kṛṣṇa is present in
every atom of the material worlds and
as He told the *gopīs*,
"You are always with Me, and there is
no cause for lamentation."

Now you're awake in Jagannātha Purī.

FLYING
RATH

RĀDHĀ-GOVINDA OF INIS RATH

Rādhā-Govinda, I did not visit You
as often as I planned.
On Christmas night I was in Your
temple but You were covered by a curtain
while the devotees performed their
skits and songs.

Rādhā-Govinda, You are beautiful,
a lame remark, I cannot say it
well. Please help me. I went to
see You. I hoped
devotees would keep You warm.
You are not different from Kṛṣṇa Himself and
Kṛṣṇa's dearmost devotee eternally.

Have mercy on the devotees of
Inis Rath, this island that is Your
setting. May they persevere,
remain dedicated to You.

As You desire, I too may return
to encourage them. We are all
Your puppets—although we
sometimes imagine we are self-willed.

God and His dearmost consort,
She blesses us, sometimes holds *tulasī* or
a garland for Him.
O black treasure, and fair-
hued Rādhā, sublime Lady
and the King of men and universes,
votives, votive praises
to You!
I bring Your picture as I travel,
never leave us day and night.

Appendix

BULLETIN BOARD

The following items gathered on my bulletin board during the two weeks that I wrote Volume Two of *Every Day, Just Write*:

Pretentious: Making claims, explicit or implicit, to some distinction, importance, dignity or excellence. Affectedly grand; ostentatious.

Avoid it, write (draw) without trying to show off, make claims of saintliness, art—just be.

Spend all now. Poems, etc. You can put them in this EJW diary and take them out later as you like—flashes—memory poems

raw dreams

don't worry regarding literary or neatness. Put it in rather than leave it out.

Inis Rath temple phone number
Śyāmānanda 21512

Write to find out where you are going. It's not for reading in a book.

Tell many fiction stories—even just a few lines.
Your prose is one poem after another in paragraphs.

Write more and trust that the process will lead you to good things. Present writing is harbinger for future projects, even if you don't know it.

More time on it helps. You'll know conclusively when a project arrives.

Make *Every Day, Just Write* all inclusive
dreams, poems,
drawings, f.w.,
write on Śrīla Prabhupāda's books
memories,
prayers
little life data, etc.

Free-write
don't forget to draw with colors.

I just reread *Castlegregory*. Good mood. Remember where it came from? Those many legal pads of writing *Forgetting the Audience*. In a similar way, I should write plenty here and then gather from it some excellent sentences and moods and Kṛṣṇa conscious teachings to share.

A Sojourn in Tapo-bhūmi

Every Day, Just Write

Volume 3

Jagannātha Purī, Vṛndāvana
December 30, 1996–February 9, 1997

Satsvarūpa dāsa Goswami

GN Press, Inc.

Contents

About the Title

The word *tapo-bhūmi* here refers to India as "the land of austerity." I experienced a particular kind of suffering during my visit to India in 1997 and I have recorded it here. I hope my experience was purifying. I know I committed offenses to the *dhāma* and the devotees. My reporting of them is also unredeemed. I can only ask forgiveness from the devotees for my transgressions and pray that I can stop such offenses in the future.

Foreword

DECEMBER 30, 1996

Aniruddha dāsa has left Inis Rath and I'm leaving tomorrow. My persona and I are feeling sad to leave this peaceful scene overlooking the lake. Yeah, so sad I could die. That's it, I'm sad I'll have to die and everyone else will too.

Well, brother, hitch up your *dhotī* and don't worry about it. We're starting out. Onward to London and the friendly faces there.

Aindra singing on tape as I write this. Conches blowing, echoing through the *mandira* Prabhupāda built. Yes, I will die, and I hope that's where—Vṛndāvana-dhāma—but I have thousands of miles—and pages—to go. And many days with my head filling up with pressure and stealing my time. But don't worry, I'll get my licks in.

Someone is down at the quay waiting for the rowboat.
Clear sky clouding over. Slow flowing days
and nights—pink clouds, blue
Kṛṣṇa's peaceful
harbor.
Facing the island across the lake I
see boats pushing off to cross
the strait and a two-week-long guest,
a spiritual seeker, finally leaving, his
pack on his back.
Water shimmering now as the blackness
moves in over
the Kerry cows in the grass.

December 31, 1996

12:05 A.M.

During the night I had one dream after another about *bābājīs* chanting. I experienced how it felt from the inside—they weren't eating but were sustaining themselves simply on chanting. In one dream I joined them, but I felt the challenge of convincing myself that I was pleasing Prabhupāda. I reasoned in the dream that although he may not have explicitly taught *bābājī* life (and even seemed to teach against it), it was something I had to follow with confidence, surrender, and trust that it was my unique calling. I thought if I accepted my life totally and sincerely, Prabhupāda would accept me.

As I awoke, it occurred to me that these dreams are what are called "compensatory" dreams. That is, dreams that fulfill something we are unable to have in waking life. My dreams contained good detail, such as how people tried to take advantage of the *bābājīs*, and how they were examined to see whether they were actually performing austerity. As I practiced this *bhajana*, one disciple found out about it and wanted to join me. This was a test for me because I knew devotees would complain that I was influencing others to give up their regular services.

It's interesting that I should have dreams like this the night before beginning the process of going to India. Today we will go by car to Dublin, then board a plane to England, and in a few days, go to Jagannātha Purī. I am not going on a solitary tour but on a preaching tour; I am not going to emphasize *bābājī* life but *goṣṭhyānandī* life. The dreams provide a contrast to my upcoming reality.

Dear Lord, I'm reading *Kṛṣṇa* book and desire to enter with faith and taste. I read the prayers made by the sages who saw Lord Kṛṣṇa at Kurukṣetra during the solar eclipse. This particular prayer reflects my own thoughts:

> Having concluded that Kṛṣṇa was the Supreme Personality of Godhead, the sages addressed Him thus: "Dear Lord, we, the leaders of human society, are supposed to possess the proper philosophy of life, yet we are bewildered by the spell of Your external energy. We are surprised to see Your behavior, which is just like that of an ordinary human being and which conceals Your real identity as the Supreme Personality of Godhead, and we therefore consider Your pastimes to be all-wonderful."
>
> —*Kṛṣṇa*, Chapter 84

Please grant me the vision to worship Your pastimes as all-wonderful, as the factual science of Godhead. They are not mythological. I am a tiny, bewildered creature. Unlike the sages in *Kṛṣṇa* book or the *bābājīs* in my dreams last night, I am unable to perform *vairāgya*. I live in comfort with amenities, and I seek to be insulated from stress to avoid the pain of headaches. Still, You are available to me in an easy-to-take form if I hear and chant. And You have provided me with the opportunity to preach and to help others understand the true mission of human life.

10:45 A.M.

Scheduled to leave the house in forty-five minutes in Manu's car bound for the Dublin airport. Everything is packed and I am now facing Śrīla Prabhupāda's empty *vyāsāsana* on the equally empty altar. Prabhupāda is in the "On Tour" luggage and ready to roll. I asked him to enter *samādhi* until we can worship his form again, which should be tonight at Guru-dakṣiṇā's house in London. Until then, let me recall him and chant or do *something* to maintain my connection.

1:45 P.M.

Approaching Dublin. Live for the moment and feel your cold *toes*. Manu said there's a debate Friday in London between ISKCON and the *ṛtvik* proponents. That's the day we fly to India, but now it's on my mind. My debate will be with my inner critics and I hope it will be short.

Before leaving Manu's house I read a few random pages in *Shack Notes*—lively, good writing. Talked about death, *Kṛṣṇa* book, poems.

Snow on the ground and flurries in the air. Hope it doesn't delay the flight. Was playing the nervous game of noticing cars ahead of us slowing, which means possible delay to the forward movement of *this* car. And the clock—its tedious marking of time.

Hare Kṛṣṇa, O Kṛṣṇa.

2:30 P.M.

Gate 27, Aer Lingus. Heavy snow falling and overcast. To get to the gate we had to pass through shops—a bewildering number of them. In some parts of the airport you're surrounded by open shops. You don't even have to enter them through a door. They're all around you and you can hardly find the trail that leads to the departure gates.

Sign describing Seamus Heaney as the winner of the Nobel Prize for poetry, then the names and pictures of other Irishmen who have won it. Yeats looking young and self-consciously handsome, Shaw looking old (he lived to be a hundred), Beckett, haggard and haunted, and Heaney himself.

No words for Manu other than an embrace and "I'll be back in April."

A woman just approached me and asked questions for a tourist questionnaire. I didn't mind answering them, but it wasn't preaching. I said "Kṛṣṇa" and "Hare Kṛṣṇa" a number of times, and she said I didn't look fifty-seven. She asked if I was happy in my religion. "Yes, I feel secure and fulfilled." She asked when I joined. "1966." "You must have been one of the first to join." She figured that the Hare Kṛṣṇa movement was thirty years old. Yes, I'm now old and feeble. Or better, fragile. I told her I wrote a hundred letters while I was in Ireland.

Onboard plane. Christmas music. "O Christmas Tree!" I have to focus. Take a risk that reading will bring on a headache and open the *Kṛṣṇa* book. Otherwise, I'll be stuck mildly coasting, spacing out, skipping along the surface of the *mahā-mantra* while the carols play in the background.

Sunbathers not far away.

Im gonna drink this milk on good conscious ness

Purī vacationers.

January 1, 1997

7:30 A.M.

After surviving the trip to England as well as the arrival chat in Guru-dakṣiṇā's living room, I went upstairs and promptly got a headache, the last one of the old year and the first of the new. The room was uncomfortably cold. I endured the night, but could not get up at midnight. With my earplugs in I heard revelers' fireworks and police sirens, but it was muffled and not so disturbing.

Well, here we are where we expected to be on this day. We have again managed to stumble into the new year with no radical change for the better, but steadily holding onto Prabhupāda's lotus feet.

FREE-WRITE '97

Another first for the year. Accuse me of loop-de-loop, loop dela. Bank holiday—can't get a typewriter. Anyway, they don't sell them anymore; only laptop computers available now.

Accuse me
of not taking care of a mother with Alzheimer's,
of Mickey Mantle
twelve zones
GBC man
not fighting hard for
ISKCON
in ISKCON
of past-life infamy
of avoiding the truth.
You mean?
Yes.

I mean, no bad words need enter my prose. I can avoid them easily. I can write like a devotee, even though I'm not one.

Harry James and Betty Grable jokes,
and Wa Wa "Sugar Blues"
my man laughs and I say, "Oh,
the truth."

Kṛṣṇa book, I read Vasudeva praising the Lord according to what he'd heard the sages say—that Kṛṣṇa and Balarāma are everything. Vasudeva repeated it out of love for his boys. They smiled and said, "We are your sons, but what you say about Us, that We are everything, We agree in toto. However," They said, "Everyone is everything. All is spirit. *Advaya-jñāna*."

Cone with whipped cream for dessert, and me, a persona greedy for sweaters, goods, hats, candy canes, praise, no bad news, stretch socks, easy journey to India and met and escorted by police from Bhub to Jag and put in a hotel there where you can do these f.w. each day for the remainder of your life.

Kṛṣṇa, Kṛṣṇa, the Truth. Don't go to Gambhīrā if rough-necked, ruffian, rip-off priests there will hound you for money and you can only peek anyway into the sacred room. Ready for a fight? We've got our Nārāyaṇa-kavaca, Rūpa-Raghunātha, and others to watch out for the *paṇḍas*.

3:55 P.M.

They just bought me a good, loud-playing portable tape recorder, and now I'm using a borrowed typewriter. Well, what do I have to say? That Kṛṣṇa is the Supreme Personality of Godhead and to serve Him is the perfection of life. The truth is in the *Vedas*. It's as simple as that. You work at it and say what you can to the people of the world. Don't stay away from hard preaching.

But sirs, I do get headaches, you see. Therefore, I can't attend your meetings, preach several lectures a day, or go into the streets. I have done that in the past, but now I have to slow down as I approach old age. Face it. I advise the younger ones who also feel ill that they needn't push themselves beyond their capacity. Do what you can.

Hell, I'm producing thick books. Śrīla Prabhupāda says everyone has to be active. If you want to go to the spiritual world, you must act. If you want to go to hell, you have to act. Even if you want to stay in this world, you have to act. Action brings realization.

Night of first day of year
ended,
I am here still,
still heart-beating
'tho everyone from long ago has
passed on,
gone from here but the souls
leave and then come back.
Hayagrīva dāsa gone and returned?
Or where is he? Is he *there*?
with the Swami?

In Goloka where
night and day are perpetual
and there is no fear
or death
or unhappiness.

Night notes on earth, cold this
first day of year, London 1997.

O time you are arbitrary
and we track you by calendars.
You are Kṛṣṇa and can't be changed.
Kṛṣṇa and Rādhā dance
beyond time—a night of *rāsa*
for a day of
Brahmā.
Night notes,
prayer,
Hare Kṛṣṇa
and then you go.

January 2

1:05 A.M.

Alarm didn't go off. I am well prepared with my topic and references. This little space to say hello and keep the hand moving.

It's January 2nd and I have a shopping list. I feel like I'm trying to arrange my life into paper bags or well-organized suitcases these days. Of course, I have my protected and sealed inner compartments, and I have enough money. Visa and face intact, back to India.

I am Prabhupāda's *śiṣya*. Do I fight hard in ISKCON for ISKCON? Do I remind people not of Prabhupāda but only of myself? So I've been accused.

I don't know the answer to that one. I only know that this traveler tries not to hurt others. He listens to Prabhupāda and hopes things will get better. But I don't know—going back to

Godhead requires rare qualifications. That's my big question: how can I make more progress? I mean, me, with all my limits? Can I even *wish* to go back to Godhead? Please help me, Lord. I'm so fragile and tenderfooted, afraid of austerities, wanting life to be painless. I know everything is there in the chanting and hearing. And in carrying the burden for the spiritual master. He said, "You have to do *something* for Śrīla Prabhupāda." It's a rocky path, but I have faith that it is made easier by hearing the transcendental message and the holy name.

A DREAM: I ASKED SRILA PRABHUPĀDA ABOUT THE CHANGES IN HIS MOVEMENT

I was walking with Prabhupāda and asked, "Prabhupāda, are you aware of the changes our movement is going through, that there is basic conflict in the approach or attitude toward Kṛṣṇa consciousness?" Prabhupāda said he had heard about this. "They were discussing it yesterday," he said.

I said, "I think there is something healthy about a movement going through such basic changes."

Then he went to his room to lie down. He indicated the floor. I was his servant, so I asked, "Should I take the mat from the bed?"

"No, go and get it from the other room." He said it with a little anger in his voice. I was afraid I had disturbed him with my earlier question, but I asked more.

"Some devotees feel that you aren't present in the movement anymore. I mean, they have been saying this since your disappearance. They also say that the managers are trying to take control."

Prabhupāda didn't say anything. I hoped he wasn't annoyed with me.

In the meantime, I was busy botching up my service—I was supposed to be taking the blankets off the bed. I couldn't seem to remember which way he wanted things done; I was too absorbed in asking troublesome questions.

While asking Prabhupāda my questions, he looked worried, but his general attitude seemed to be that we have to live in the present. Whether or not Prabhupāda knew the future after his disappearance, he knew that we have our free will to follow his movement or to choose something else. In 1974 there was no such thing as a split in Prabhupāda's movement; he said there was only sincerity and insincerity.

This dream may have come because I've been thinking about the controversies here in England—the *ṛtvik* debate and the other ones. It's so odd to be thinking of those things when today I have to speak my bit to a roomful of devotees who consider me their spiritual master. They may have faith in me, but I can never consider myself qualified. Rather, I simply endeavor to point them to Prabhupāda and Kṛṣṇa. Rūpa Gosvāmī says even a low-class man can light the wood in a *yajña* which will purify the heart. I try to act without pretense. Time would see through it eventually if I tried to bluff, and that would mean disaster.

12:30 P.M.

The disciples' meeting went well, although I felt the audience was a little stiff. There weren't that many—maybe a dozen—devotees. Or perhaps it was me who was stiff. I was too well-prepared, too structured or even formal. It was an officially important topic, a typical Satsvarūpa talk stressing *sādhana*. What else is there to talk about? I simply have to deliver the goods, and I feel I did that. If they would only listen carefully to what I said, they would benefit. They all know what I'm talking about. As I spoke about Vṛndāvana I thought of Paraśurāma dāsa (who was present) and who knows Vṛndāvana better than I do in terms of living in the *dhāma*, going on *parikrama*, and so on. Anyway, I did what I could.

4:45 P.M.

Second day of the year. Reading the opening pages to "Prayers by the Personified *Vedas.*" I love how the topic is passed from higher to higher authorities. Mahārāja Parīkṣit asks Śukadeva how the material mind and words can know the Absolute Truth, which is beyond matter. Śukadeva replies by saying that Nārada once asked this same question of Nārāyaṇa Ṛṣi at Badarikāśrama. At that time, Nārāyaṇa Ṛṣi replied by saying that the exact same question had been discussed by the four Kumāras on Janaloka and that Sananda-kumāra was chosen to answer the question. When Sananda began his reply, he referred the topic to an even earlier and higher discussion: when the personified *Vedas* prayed to Garbhodakaśāyī Viṣṇu.

I love it. It's better than a spiritual fiction. We climb the increasingly cold and snowy mountain to where the ascetics live and meditate. Up we travel on yogic air currents to Janaloka, where four eternal *brahmacārī* boys tell us how the *Vedas* personified approached the great form of Viṣṇu on the Causal Ocean at the time of creation. No fiction can match that, no dream, nothing. And no truth is more solid than that passed down in *paramparā*. If we are lucky, we receive it even here, sitting under a skylight in a London attic. Beams from outer space unfold as *Kṛṣṇa* book. As Śrutadeva prayed in the previous chapter, "You are always with each one of us in our hearts. It's up to us to realize it, by Your grace, but factually You never leave us."

Shopping items in London before we go off: sturdy rubber-covered Duracell flashlight, two Sony Dictaphones, a new portable tape recorder so I can hear Śrīla Prabhupāda's lectures as long as I live—all packed in my Delsey and Samsonite suitcases. Oh, and a new saffron sweatshirt to use carefully in His service. O master, I desire to serve you, although my service is not yet unalloyed.

January 3

12:55 A.M.

Beginning of a long day for me. Stayed in bed until 12:30, then got up and read "Syamantaka Jewel." Lord Kṛṣṇa in Dvārakā was addressed by the residents as Yadunandana, Nārāyaṇa, the child of Yaśodāmātā, and Dāmodara. They know Him to be the Supreme Personality of Godhead, and they are proud that they can see Him every day. They told Him the sun-god had come to visit Him. He smiled and said that this person is not the sun-god, he is Satrājit. Later in this chapter Lord Kṛṣṇa fights with Jāmbavān who, covered by attachment to his child and his anger, could not recognize his master. When Jāmbavān rendered service by fighting, however, Kṛṣṇa revealed Himself.

I'm feeling an auspicious wave lately of exclusive interest in Kṛṣṇa conscious topics. That gives me a non-hypocritical position for preaching. Yesterday when a devotee told me she liked to read *Time* magazine for its occasional topics relevant to Kṛṣṇa consciousness, I said to myself, "Why? It's not necessary." Fulfill your interests in Kṛṣṇa conscious reading and hearing.

This same devotee went to India at Kārttika. While there she saw a body being cremated on the bank of the Yamunā. She mentioned it in a letter to me. She was moved when the relatives were crying for the departed husband and friend, but the brown body went up in flames and the skull appeared in the white ashes. Nearby, a pack of dogs fought over the intestines of a recently cremated human.

5:50 A.M.

I have been keeping a separate notebook which I've labeled "What to write in India '97." On December 22nd I was saying that I should try directed free-writing because that would be compatible with a pilgrimage to India. I wrote this:

"One goes on pilgrimage to India with some kind of focus, usually how to be more Kṛṣṇa conscious. You beg and pray for insight in the *dhāma*. You can start by asking yourself what you want to achieve from the visit to Jagannātha Purī and Vṛndāvana. It may not be what you expect. *It's not something you already know*.

"But be open to and willing for Kṛṣṇa to reveal that purpose to you in His *dhāma*. '*Dhāma*' also means the place where Kṛṣṇa resides. At Kṛṣṇa's birth, the *dhāma* was in Vasudeva's heart (see *Kṛṣṇa*, Chapter 2). Do you dare ask Kṛṣṇa to appear and direct you? I think you should."

Since writing that I've decided to go on with the format of *Every Day, Just Write*, but the idea of a focus, of looking forward to Kṛṣṇa directing me in the *dhāma*, is good. Don't just go there thoughtlessly, but hope to improve your Kṛṣṇa consciousness. Writing should be for that.

11:25 A.M.

Very gray sky, sparse snowflakes floating. It looks like we're in for a heavy downfall. I'll try not to worry that our plane won't get off the ground today. Better to sit here and be Kṛṣṇa conscious.

Madhu and Bhakti-rasa were watching *Mahābhārata* TV episodes, so I went and joined them. Hindi voices and English subtitles. The special effects on the battlefield were well done —the arrows meeting in mid-air and splitting each other, the sword play, the elephants, club fights, blood, death . . . I don't so much like all the gore and sport. Madhu loves it.

HEATHROW, BRITISH AIRWAYS GATE, 2:50 P.M.

We met Jñānagamya in the airport. He's on the same plane as us, scheduled to depart at 4 P.M. to Delhi. A few moments later we met Ṛtadhvaja Mahārāja, who was ahead of us in line.

As we were standing in line, one of the Indian British Airways employees suddenly came up to me and ordered that I put my Prabhupāda *mūrti* luggage with the check-in baggage. I tried reasoning with her, but she wouldn't budge. I put Śrīla Prabhupāda in his wooden box into Madhu's knapsack, and I quickly emptied out reading and drawing materials from my shoulder bag so it would pass inspection. It was upsetting, but not so bad.

Now we're onboard. Said hello to Jñānagamya and had a more extended chat with Ṛtadhvaja Swami. We'll take off at 9:30 P.M. Delhi time, so I probably won't need the reading material. Can chant January 4 *japa* in flight and maybe get a little rest.

SHELTER

Shelter in Kṛṣṇa is what I want and
to remember Him.
How? By chanting you
end the day and start the next,

long day's journey
to India. Again I'm going
to end one life and start another.

We are really seriously past the gate; nobody goes through free. They catch you. They are playing English classical tunes on violins and showing film shots of merry royal England—all you can see in fifteen minutes.

Jñānagamya came down the aisle. I didn't look up at him, but Madhu did. I ought to be more friendly. I put my dictaphones into the luggage, but I don't know if I'll get them back. No lock on it.

January 4

So far so good. Another thing happened at immigration upon leaving England. The man looked through my passport and asked if I lived in Ireland. When I said yes, he had me fill out a form for the Irish government. This may cause trouble the next time I go to Ireland. More on that later.

7:40 A.M.

Arrived. Now a three-hour wait in the cramped domestic waiting area for Indian Airlines.

Things in this country work or they don't work. A big sign over the TV set: "Entertainment." It's not turned on, thank God. I go into the Gents toilet room. About six men standing around as janitors. "No tips. Suggestions please." Moth balls in sink. "Hare Rāma, Hare Kṛṣṇa."

Sitting on suitcase. Madhu pacing, chanting. Might as well relax if I can. Jñānagamya and Ṛtadhvaja Swami have gone their way. I ought to get into some spiritual focus. One piece of cabin luggage only. These things occupy the mind, at least while you travel. Fog on ground, drove in free bus from International terminal to domestic one. Along the way I saw a cheap housing development under construction, and ads: "Win a trip to Hollywood!" Daydreamed of the poor Hindu who won the trip to Hollywood and what he would see there. This kind of gently ironic "American in India" again. When several lackeys outside the airport doors called out, "Hare Rāma, Hare Kṛṣṇa!" I said, "Hare Kṛṣṇa" back and some men wanted to take us to Vṛndāvana.

INDIA

India land of tiger and odor special
a faceless Viṣṇu painting in air terminal.

Never forget India is the land of Kṛṣṇa
the immigration man is slow but
gentle.

Don't know those young Britishers,
boy and girl, venturing to India—
to find a true guru?

I am here again seeking time to
write my mission, my ministry.

Prabhupāda is rolling in the
trolley luggage. I think of him and
ease him over the bumps.

Can't help but indulge in sarcasm toward Indian inefficiency. They are consumer unfriendly. I'm the customer, a passenger on Indian Airlines, so I boil away with the others because of the way they treat us. Now our luggage is checked, but there's a big sign that says only a certain size cabin luggage will be allowed. We're trying to sneak through, so who is the nonsense, us or them? I may have to do what I did yesterday—take Śrīla Prabhupāda out of the trolley luggage and put him in Madhu's backpack. That will be harder to do here than with British Airlines. We'd have to go back to the main ticket desk and boldly cut the line to check our one bag—they won't do it for you. This is on my mind instead of Lord Caitanya and King Pratāparudra.

I've been finding it too taxing to read. Luckily I don't have a headache even though we didn't sleep much during our eight-hour overnight flight. I sit and finger my beads and watch all the stuff going on here. The poor employees. They're in illusion, but I'm entangled in it too as their passenger. We should live more simply. Why all this unnecessary air travel?

One kind of lowly employee here wears a sleeveless pullover with lettering on his chest: "Trolley Retriever." At least he's got a job. The bigger shots strut around giving orders to their lessers. As I write this, Madhu is talking with the old, uniformed policeman who was at the security check point. He's been sitting with him for awhile, preaching. That's the good side of India, but I'm in the mundane part, and it's chaotic, draining, and filled with delays. Estimated departure time now 11 A.M.

11:50 A.M.

Obviously the plane is not going to leave at noon. They haven't called it yet. For awhile I walked back and forth reading *Gītā* verses aloud. Guards looked at me oddly, but I didn't care. It felt good—sixth chapter on yoga. I thought of Rāmarāya dāsa's enthusiasm for book distribution. He's living compassion by giving people books.

Don't feel much of anything right now, so I pray to Kṛṣṇa to request connection with Him. Sixth chapter verses made me feel transcendental to the plane delay situation. Be detached, be situated in the self. It worked for a while. Now I'm back to grinding, waiting.

This is the bad luck flight, #877. Vārāṇasī left, Mumbai left, Patna left—all are leaving but us. Now it's noon. Paying a batch of India factor "dues" right away. How different from staying in my room at Geaglum. But to travel to the *dhāma* costs.

PRAY

Pray, fellow, don't be enamored by the
young woman in leather booties
sitting opposite you.
Really pray to God, Kṛṣṇa, as you sit
in noisy places—airport seats
are hard and your mind
always wanders. Someone left a
Times of India on a seat. You
ought to pray, say Hare Kṛṣṇa, Hare
Kṛṣṇa, I want to spend my time in India
serving and seeking Kṛṣṇa.
Each day is special, each hour
another chance to
really pray.

Flight delayed twice. We are invited to free coffee or tea. The radio volume has been increased. We're being bombarded by Indian pop rock. Many Japanese here, along with assorted Westerners . . .

Rāma-rāya joined us. He's coming straight from the book distribution marathon in Japan. Says he wants to always continue book distribution; no reason to stop. I talk with him, but it gets too intense hour after hour waiting for the plane. What will we do in Jagannātha Purī? Live for the moment? Hare Kṛṣṇa Hare Kṛṣṇa, Kṛṣṇa Kṛṣṇa Hare Hare/ Hare Rāma Hare Rāma, Rāma Rāma Hare Hare.

India is a good place to be alive.

Nīlācala ocean.

EEK!

We were finally allowed to board the plane at 12:30. It was difficult squeezing everything in, and I had to sit cross-legged in my seat with Prabhupāda beneath me. I began sketching nervously and then heard Madhu say, "Jayapatākā Mahārāja is getting on this flight." Sure enough, there he was. He sat a few rows ahead of us. I sent some of our *prasādam* up to him and a note excusing myself for not sitting with him, saying I'm not sociable because I get headaches. We talked a little. On arrival at Bhubaneshwar devotees met him with *kīrtana* and we caught a free garland in the process. Now at Hotel Prachi, Bhubaneshwar, ready to leave tomorrow for Purī. Prabhupāda was bathed by some of his servants and offered lunch.

January 5

HOTEL PRACHI, BHUBANESHWAR, 3:30 A.M.

Fortunately I was able to stay in bed, sleeping on and off from 6 P.M. to past 2 A.M. I was tired enough, and my earplugs helped block out the continual chatter of people in the courtyard and the hall. Indian factors galore. We're scheduled to leave at 5 A.M. for Jagannātha Purī. No place is fixed for our group yet, and we'll have to stay in one hotel for two days and then move to another. My writing here tells of that.

A DISCIPLE IS QUALIFIED: A DREAM

I was sitting with a Godbrother friend. He was showing me different things about his spiritual life. He also showed me a list of all the books that have been distributed under his jurisdiction. He was making the point that this list proved a devotee's qualification. I said, "Yes, I have heard devotees say that first you have to directly carry out the order of the spiritual master, then you can take care of your spiritual life."

I felt I gained a lot by this exchange with my Godbrother. I had used other words to praise devotees and he added, "Yes, but first he must be *qualified.*" That qualification comes by preaching, as he was demonstrating by the list of books he had arranged to have distributed. I felt grateful when he said this, and felt as if some important instruction had come through him. I think I even embraced him to show my gratitude.

I have to write what's actually happening rather than a pretension of a "pilgrim's journal." I hope a true pilgrim's journal will come out of this, but I can't wait and just put in rare gems of Gauḍīya Vaiṣṇava philosophy as if that's all that's passing through my mind. Neither is it a fact that so-called superficial events are all *māyā*. Rather, the things that are happening moment to moment are genuine struggles to remain on the spiritual platform.

One of the first challenges is to figure out who will cook for us. We're going to spend two weeks with a party of eleven in Purī. When I asked the devotees who were supposed to set everything up how it was going, they said, "Pretty good." It turns out, though, that we can't get into one hotel together until two days after we arrive. They arranged to have a "*brāhmaṇa*" cook. They were so satisfied with their arrangements—the *brāhmaṇa* in question cooks for the Hotel Birla, the only purely vegetarian hotel in Purī—that I didn't say anything at first. Then I read a purport in the *Caitanya-caritāmṛta* where Prabhupāda first says that it's all right to take food from non-devotees if we offer it to the Deity, then repeatedly says that an *avaiṣṇava* cannot cook food suitable for offerings. "Even if an *avaiṣṇava* cooks food without fault, he cannot offer it to Lord Viṣṇu and it cannot be accepted as *mahā-prasādam* . . . an *avaiṣṇava* may be a vegetarian and a very clean cook, but because he cannot offer the foodstuffs to Viṣṇu, the food he cooks cannot be accepted as *mahā-prasādam*. It is better that a Vaiṣṇava abandon such food as untouchable." (Cc. *Madhya* 9.53, purport) Prabhupāda said devotees shouldn't accept food cooked by *karmīs*.

When I mentioned this, the devotees who had organized the cooking brought up the various standards devotees use while in India. One of them said that he had heard that not only is everyone in the *dhāma* already a devotee, but everything is already offered. Prabhupāda didn't teach us that. We have been trained to live by a strict ISKCON temple standard. That's what I want to follow while we're in Purī.

But I realized I was talking big and yet asking the devotees to make the sacrifice to do our own cooking. Therefore, I suggested that perhaps we could get *prasādam* from a nearby Gaudiya Math temple. I was told that they too often hired cooks. Okay, then we'll cook for ourselves.

7:45 A.M., SAMUDRA HOTEL

Recording waking experience is similar in some ways to recording dreams. Unless you do it soon after it happens, you may lose the essence of the experience. Also, waking and dreaming life are both difficult to understand.

I'm back in India after a year. Poverty and inefficiency. Rāma-rāya dāsa straight from Japan speaks of its super-efficiency. Is it a national karma that one Oriental nation is rich and another so poor? Jesus said the poor we will have with us always; they live in all countries. Me and my friends—our present karma is high on the ladder because we're humans. Of course, by misbehavior we could become one of these street dogs. On the way to Purī I saw a skinny bitch with a bloated pregnant belly. I also saw a new, three-wheeled rick-shaw scooter with a sign, VANDE PURUSHOTTAM, and a billboard that read: "The heart and soul of the computer industry introduced to Sakshi Gopal."

Because our Purī visit was not well-planned, we are moving from one hotel to another. This morning we'll spend an hour at the Samudra, then the Vijaya, then in two days the Birla. It occurs to me that Americans become spontaneously cynical in India as a defense mechanism. Our sensibilities are shocked by the inefficiency and the poverty. Wisecracks are a way to make light of the experience. Yesterday while standing at the Indian Airlines counter delay after delay, we made jokes with the British fellows who had traveled with us all the way from London on British Airways. Our jokes were at the expense of Indian Airlines, but were not malicious. They were just a way to pass the time. We're not so pure (and neither are we naive) that we can just see spiritual *cintāmaṇi* dust everywhere we turn in India.

This dump, the Samudra, is a good place to read *Kṛṣṇa* book by the sunlight coming through the window.

VIJAYA HOTEL, 12:20 P.M.

Four stories up, facing the ocean. Surf sound at Purī. The beach area in front of us is now forested with small evergreens and fenced in. No dogs allowed. The fishing boats are out to sea and I see families playing on the beach. Awaiting our party, most of whom will arrive tomorrow.

Fruit for breakfast and lunch—fresh pomegranates, plump bananas. In this room, they've hung an Orissan-style painting of a large Mother Yaśodā—very curvy. She's making a face at Kṛṣṇa, who is cradled in her right arm, while a diminutive Balarāma is grasping at her left hand, begging for attention. Her attention in this painting is all on Kṛṣṇa. The artist has depicted her as gigantic compared to her boys. A Westerner who didn't know the pastime might think it's a painting depicting worship of the mother goddess and that the boys are insignificant.

The fishing boats have dropped their nets and now they appear to be waiting for the catch to fill them. I see one small canoe with two men standing in it and paddling violently. Are they trying to smash the poor fish to death? I see something protruding out of the water.

3 P.M., DREAM

I was holding a baby. I carried him to the floor and accidentally banged his head. I said, "I'm sorry." The baby said, "You were supposed to take care of me, but instead you banged my head." Then the baby's mother said, "Once when he banged your head, he performed a ceremony to ask forgiveness. He forgot this time, but that was the right thing to do. This is information from the second order."

I awoke thinking I had caused someone pain through neglect. Or perhaps, since they say the people in dreams are really parts of yourself, I have neglected some part of my self and caused myself pain. Anyway, I should do the forgiveness "ceremony," make a sincere gesture of regret and beg forgiveness from anyone I have hurt.

January 6

12:30 A.M.

A headache built up in the afternoon, and I had to get under the mosquito net and take rest at 5 P.M. At 6:30 P.M. I heard a knock on the door. They continued knocking, so I got out and went to the door without my dentures or eyeglasses. A hotel employee handed me something and said, "Goodnight . . . mosquitoes." I looked at my hand and saw the small blue object he had given me. Since the man had disappeared, I closed the door. Looking closely at it I realized it was a "Good Knight" mosquito killer. I put it aside and got back under the mosquito net.

DREAM: A SQUARE AUDIENCE CAN'T EVOKE MY CONFESSIONS

Disciples of another guru were pleased to hear me praise their guru. Later, Madhu said the audience was "square" and therefore didn't evoke my confessions. Then some women came forward and tried to help me confess.

This is a dream fragment, but there is a potentially powerful image in Madhu saying the audience is "square," meaning they didn't reciprocate with me, and thus I couldn't bring out my confessions. It had something to do with writing.

When I think of it now, awake, I think that on the superficial level I have to say that I don't write for an audience. It's not that I'm an entertainer who needs an audience's participation. Still, I do need a good audience to reciprocate with me. Otherwise, the "women" will come forward to evoke my confessions.

6:10 A.M.

Went back to bed for an hour hoping it would clear my right eye, but it didn't. Now I'm up and the dark night is gone. Look out at gray sky and sea. Hear the crows—those big black ones on the roofs below. If I get better, I'll write. This is a good place for it—new adventures. But basically I have to cope moment to moment.

12 NOON

Śrī Kṛṣṇa Caitanya. I want to write creatively and honestly and leave a record, a true record. Do it in words and pictures. I'd like it to be as Kṛṣṇa conscious as possible, but to the degree I fall short of pure Kṛṣṇa consciousness, I want to tell it, that record. When I learn to write honestly (I can also play with it) I'll be up for the times when I *do* feel genuine Kṛṣṇa conscious emotions and thoughts. It will come out on paper.

The faces. Orpheus (in Cocteau's film) told the artist, "Don't you know all you artists are capable of are self-portraits?"

Is that so?

I was talking with Madhu about a devotee I know who is facing a crossroads in his life. He sold his business and signed a contract that he wouldn't start a competitive business for the next five years. He likes to give donations to ISKCON, but he'd also like to get free of the material entanglement involved in making money.

Madhu said that people can't expect to do what they want in life. Life means you have to earn money even when you would rather not. He said the guy digging the ditch doesn't want to dig ditches, and the guy supervising him has got someone over him to make his life miserable. His point was that we simply have to accept the crunch if we have taken birth in the material world.

I replied that I had just heard Prabhupāda lecturing about the threefold miseries (*adhyātmika*, *adhibhautika*, *adhidaivika*). My headaches are *adhyātmika*, the dogs barking and the mosquitoes are *adhibautika*, and when it's either too hot or too cold, that's *adhidhaivika*.

A little later our conversation drifted to my reading. I've been reading *Kṛṣṇa* book—the Lord's Dvārakā pastimes. Now I'm turning to *Caitanya-caritāmṛta* because I'll be speaking to the devotees every day. I mentioned this to Madhu, and he said, "You have a wonderful life."

Something clicked when he said that, not in an emotional way, but intellectually. Although people have to work at things they don't want to do, I have an easy life. People give me money, a place to stay, and food. I have many places in the world where I can go and stay as a mendicant, places where I can write my books and lecture. I have a wonderful life, by Kṛṣṇa's grace.

At the same time, I'm still striving to have a better creative life. I want to be a better devotee. It isn't easy. I endeavor, I think it over, I use what energy I have left as I get older. It's a wonderful life, striving for Kṛṣṇa. I should be cheerful and emanate that to others.

5:50 P.M., NIGHT NOTES

We move out of this Vijaya Hotel at 5:30 A.M. tomorrow. Tonight I read *Vidagdha-mādhava*.

Kṛṣṇa's sweetest Vṛndāvana pastimes and
as we read I looked out at the waves.
The sky seemed different.
Hare Kṛṣṇa. May Prabhupāda be pleased.
India is a good place to be alive
despite the crows and loud voices despite
never being alone in your own heart—what
do you want?
Kṛṣṇa consciousness.

January 7

4 A.M.

Get ready for a short move. Then you can chant *gāyatrī* and eat breakfast after offering it with prayers to your Guru Mahārāja.

12:15 NOON

Moved to Birla Hotel, supposedly our home for the next two weeks (January 7–19). Looks good and feels good. Couch to sit on when I speak to devotees. I'll read from *Caitanya-caritāmṛta*, starting with the first mention of Jagannātha Purī in *Ādi-līlā* where the devotees from Nīlācala are listed.

Give me this, give me that—two pairs of sandals, one for indoors and one for outdoors, more earplugs than I need. Be careful not to ask for too much, such as a limousine or first-class air ticket. I'll be dying soon enough. Never dying—living on to write your little life without expecting people to read through your thousands of pages.

Craft and uncraft.

PURĪ BEACH

Purī beach sands, lifeguards wear
cone-shaped hats
they have come for fun
Godhead forgotten.

In the square a new statue of
Caitanya Mahāprabhu,
He appeared to have gray hair
but nice arms forward as if the
ocean is calling Him, He's running to
Caṭaka-parvaka.

This is good. We have finally moved, 8 A.M., in a taxi across Purī. On the beach road I saw a saffron-dressed man approaching us from a distance. People were around him, I said, "There's a *sannyāsī*" and saw it was a Godbrother.

4:30 P.M.

We had our first meeting. I read and spoke, straining my voice to rise above the sound of the surf and to keep their attention as they waned from jet lag. Are they interested in hearing the list of names of Lord Caitanya's devotees in Nīlācala? After the meeting, Rāma-rāya dāsa lent me his copy of Gaura-Govinda Swami's *The Embankment of Separation*. I read the account of how Lord Jagannātha appeared in that ecstatic shape and remembered when the story first surfaced in ISKCON in 1974. A devotee asked me to ask Śrīla Prabhupāda if it was authentic. He said, "Maybe." Then he said, "Our business is to worship Him."

SPEAKING

Speaking to devotees my brand
of humor and realization.
Prabhupāda taught me,
I assimilated, I don't know
exactly what I give but
I try
although this kid is still impure
Kṛṣṇa lets His mercy
come through.
Go on speaking, go on,
the Gambhīrā's not far away.
(Oh no?)

5:15 P.M.

I told the devotees, "You go first to Siddha-bakula and report back to me. If it's okay, I'll go out with you."

Oh jeez. You go out and have fun, then come back and tell me. I'll limp into a taxi and go out tomorrow. On the day I visit a *tīrtha*, will I also be able to lecture?

Lecture? Are you any smarter than the other devotees in this group? Just a little? A lot? How much? What's the difference between you and them? "Their disciples and granddisciples" form a *sampradāya*, branches of the great tree. Yes, we're part of a tree—guru and disciples and granddisciples and great-granddisciples. That's *sampradāya*.

I hear conch shells—and now see the man selling them, and peas, and pearls, on the beach.

Darker it grows
the soul tight and eternal
can't die. Eating
evening bananas is another
chance to hear your master
lecture on surrender, on
Kṛṣṇa, that the soul is

eternal, can't slay or
be slain.
Master, you've bound me
in a network of
lotus stems. You
in New York—
you brought me
to truth and gave grapes
as a reward
for my typing.

January 8

12:51 A.M.

Śrīla Prabhupāda is up with his dictaphone translating *Śrīmad-Bhāgavatam* or maybe the *Padma Purāṇa*, or some other work his disciples asked him to work on to satisfy their hankerings and curiosities. I'm up too, still wanting to be faithful. Please, world, let me go down as having remained faithful. And for being myself.

Read *Caitanya-caritāmṛta*. Who is Gaurāṅga? Only His devotees can know Him.

Gray sky worry rumbles. On veranda he's chanting the release from self in verse. Gray water and sky not like in the West. "Purī doesn't seem like a *dhāma*. I'm glad you explained it." They want to connect Lord Caitanya to this place. Soft-hearted *paṇḍa* at entrance to main *mandira* didn't beat him with sticks but said, "Jagannātha is everywhere." Tough, kid. You are white and saggy. Come back next lifetime as a Hindoo. Caw crow picks at tissue paper from our trash pail and nibbles something in it. I slap my sandaled foot on the stone floor to scare it away.

10:30 A.M.

Writing this on Indian, paper-like papyrus. *Veda* means "knowledge". It cannot be dated because it was given at creation by Brahmā, whose day is so long you can't calculate it. Śrīla Prabhupāda gave such answers to the doubting teacher, David Lawrence, who said the *Vedas* were not as old as the Old Testament or the Egyptian books.

Please nurture me, master, and keep me clean and strict. I don't want to say, "Use a stick on me if you think I need it," but I know you have the right. O master, I am entering your presence. I am also playing the role of a guru with his disciples. It's a happy role and it's not an illusion. This small group of people love me and are dedicated to helping me. I wish to reciprocate with them and give them the teachings of *Caitanya-caritāmṛta*.

O great grandfather, Bhaktivinoda Ṭhākura, I wish to read your books too, and my master gives permission, but mainly I want to return to his books with relish. That is my main happiness, although it requires discipline and the proper atmosphere. It requires my heart.

After lunch and after rest, I was sitting and some important thoughts came—about death, about wanting to advance, and about wanting to know the truth of myself. Then I lost track of them. They evaporated like dreams. I was almost sulking and couldn't write or read. I went back to bed to nap and asked for guidance or direction. I drifted off into a light sleep,

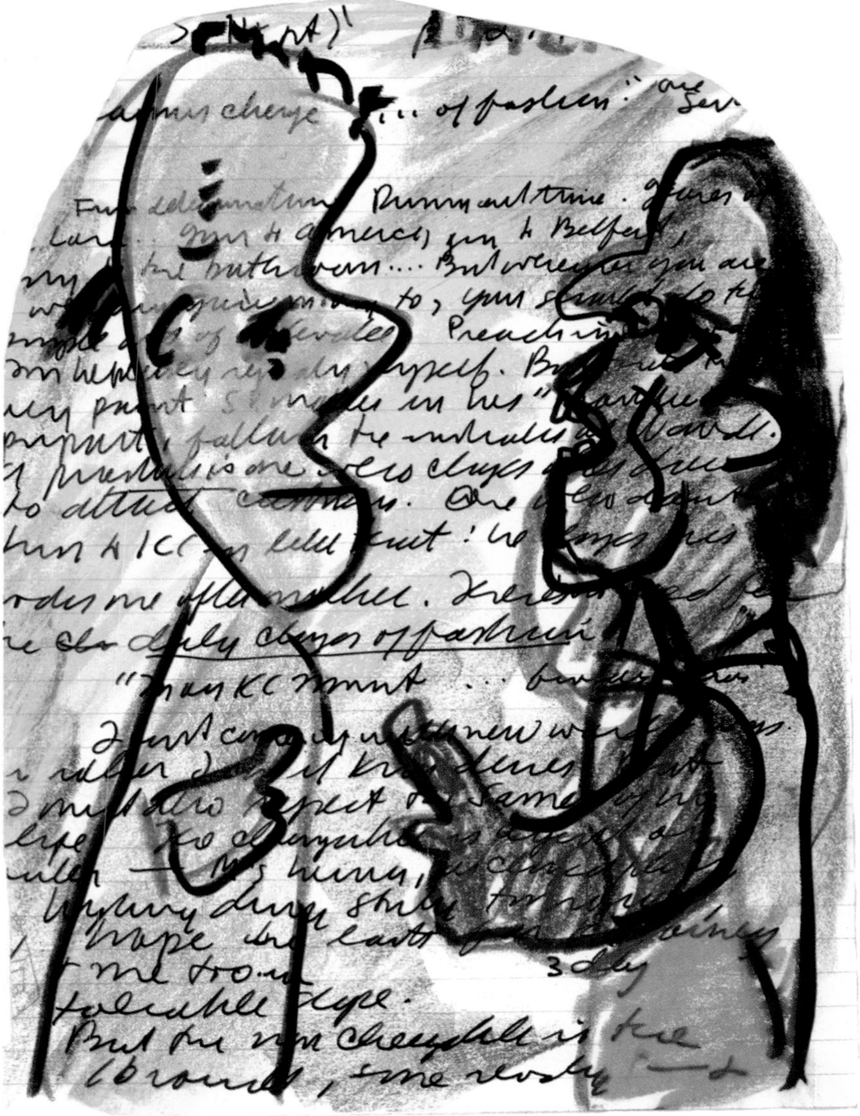

"It's better to always dwell on Kṛṣṇa."

Crow swaying in breeze on top branch of beach-growing evergreen.

If Jagannātha wants.

Nama Acarya
Haridas Thakur
HH
HK
HK
KK
"নামাচার্য"—শ্রীশ্রীহরিদাস ঠাকুর"
Hare Krsna
Hare Krsna
Krsna Krsna
Hare Hare
Hare Rama
Hare Rama
Rama Rama Hare Hare

but didn't dream, or rather, couldn't remember anything. All this on an overcast and uncomfortably cool day in Nīlācala.

5:15 P.M.

Read *Vidagdha-mādhava* with Rāma-rāya and Madhu. I couldn't pay attention during the second half. Read about forty minutes. Can't expect to be up for all of it—all the gems of Rūpa Gosvāmī's verses and the highest *rasa*. At least I was in good company.

Grayer as night falls. White breaker reminds me of flashing teeth. Some devotees on our party went out to *tīrthas*. I'm scheduled to go to Siddha-bakula tomorrow. Would like to have the taste, the *taste*.

Go ahead, tell us. You are not Lalitā talking to a swan or Madhumaṅgala joking with Kṛṣṇa or Paurṇamāsī arranging for a meeting between Rādhā and Kṛṣṇa. You are not even Kaṁsa planning to kill Kṛṣṇa. You are just you, picked up by His Divine Grace and transported to Jagannātha Purī, the latest of your stops. Remember reading that Rāmānuja was once thrown many miles by Lord Jagannātha? Have I been thrown here too?

NIGHT

Night, our group together
in Purī now go rest and
God will protect us
never, never forget
the Lord. I do I don't
I am a fool.
I am the *śiṣya*
never forget, never disobey
the rules, never go to
people who can't accept
those who love
Viṣṇu and Lord Caitanya
and Prabhupāda.

January 9

12:45 A.M.

A *yogī* cannot go without seeing the Lord within his heart at every moment. Bhaktivinoda Ṭhākura wrote hundreds of books. My head is fogged over. I dreamt last night, I lay awake. It seemed late when I heard men shouting, but it was only 8:30 P.M. I just wanted quiet so I could think in a peaceful, clear, spiritual way. Perhaps it's like straining to hear the Word, as the Christian monks say.

Ah yes.

Monks reading. Cassian observed them ruminating in the desert.

Raghunātha dāsa Gosvāmī, Rūpa Gosvāmī . . . we want to ingest information and *bhāva*. We can't do it all at once. Our attention span is the bottleneck. We have a passing desire to imbibe tons of Kṛṣṇa conscious messages of sweetness and surrender in order to transform ourselves, but we can't accommodate them all. Our heads are too small. Our minds balk. What can we do but rest in between? In the meantime, however, we should be careful not to divert ourselves to too many other subjects. Hare Kṛṣṇa.

Desires spew out like lava—Kṛṣṇa conscious desires too, and love, or at least an eruption of energy willing to be spent in a Kṛṣṇa conscious direction. Still the tiny conditioned self creates a bottleneck. Should I draw a diagram of it? The waves desire to pass through the person, but he's unable to see them.

O Kṛṣṇa, let it flow easily. Let it flow easily and constantly.

Madhu reminds me we have hectic, demanding days ahead. Traveling and lecturing in India, the Caribbean, and America. I'll have to perform. I have to adjust my attitude toward it. Try not to worry about performance. Or, learn to lecture in a way compatible to an inner life of śāstric reflection.

Our group in Nīlācala. We'll get along, share the cooking and cleaning duties, and gather to hear. We'll go to *tīrthas*, run errands, and I'll write. I'll also read Bhaktivinoda Ṭhākura, get aches, feel some fear, and then overcome it. (Two women devotees remained in Sarajevo during the war and kept the temple open. Fifteen refugees lived with them. The difference between the devotees and the nondevotees broke down). Overcome fear.

Flow, O life.

JAGANNĀTHA IS KIND

"Jagannātha is kind to crippled devotees,"
I prayed and wrote it to Swamijī.
All right, he replied, very nice.
God as *dāru-brahman*—
full spirit, not little. He
comes to us
nayana-patha-gāmī bhavatu me

nayana-patha-gāmī—Śrīla Prabhupāda told
Hayagrīva to chant at the installation
in San Francisco '67.

There's an early Bob Dylan song—
"Ten thousand dollars at the drop of a hat,
I'd give it all if I could get it back."
We loved those days, but these days
I am crotchety, faultfinding
aware of schisms! Who ever
thought it would turn out like this?
Or me, an old feeble guy—
but happy and more Kṛṣṇa conscious than I
was, free to write and read
free as a bird
in the cage of my own making.

DREAM: WINN BURGRAFF FORCES ME TO ADMIT I'M AFRAID OF THE DANGER OF LIFE

Winn Burgraff is an old friend from school. I saw him and said hello, but I kept myself aloof. He said, "You have to look closely at everything and you'll see around its edges."

"I don't see it."

He insisted that I should see it. He compared the act of looking to my religion. Because I couldn't see what he saw, I must have a different religion. Then he began to act threatening toward me, and even attacked me.

Finally, I broke down crying. I saw he wasn't vicious; he was just trying to tell me that this is how life is. I said, "Yes, I can understand that the only dangerous thing about life is the vicious characters we see in it. They are attacking and killing people at this very moment."

"Yes, it happened to me recently."

We drew closer as friends because he forced me by his threatening ways to break through my veneer and admit that I too was afraid, just as he had been. Nothing more was resolved.

I didn't talk about Kṛṣṇa or chant Hare Kṛṣṇa in this dream, but I still received a message. Life is dangerous, and I tend not to face that because my life appears to be safe. It makes it easy to take on a sophisticated front. But I should be more aware of my fears and use them as an impetus to turn to Kṛṣṇa. Real religion means to call out God's holy name. If I can't do it out of love, then I may be forced to do it out of the fear caused by witnessing the cruelty of one living being toward another.

Don't wait. Remember that man in London who ran after the devotees carrying Rādhā-Londonīśvara out of his house? "Wait, I'll bring Them to you in the right way."

No, they couldn't wait. In writing, words don't wait either. They are like *gopīs* running out in the night to the sound of Kṛṣṇa's flute. Their brothers and husbands call, "Stop!"

"No, we won't stop. We're going to Kṛṣṇa. No one can stop me. I'm going to the Lord of the horizon, the darkish one."

And they go.
And my words go
west and east in taxis
not stopping for
Thomas Wolfe
or cleverness or
bounce.
They want to be with Kṛṣṇa.

How brilliant the rhetoric, the archenemy, the faultfinding critic who scathes when I don't seem to make sense, when I just keep pressing the harrow down into the earth, hoping the
words will catch me
later.

THINGS TO DO IN PURĪ

(1) Scratch yourself.
(2) Hail your face.
(3) Say good-bye to Kay Adams.

(4) Say hello to Christ—can you face implications of his head with crown of thorns?

(5) Say hello to free-writing and Peter London.

(6) File your nails and a report.

(7) Think seriously about what to do with the remainder of your life—the boldest Kṛṣṇa consciousness.

(8) Think of a Godbrother's question about whether to do *bhajana* or constant preaching.

(9) Read Śrīla Prabhupāda's books.

(10) Check yourself with reference to Gaura-kiśora dāsa Bābājī.

(11) Order books.

(12) Write poetry.

(13) Fly your own plane.

(14) Recall frogs, Basho's.

(15) Get ready to die.

(16) Answer letters.

(17) Pray.

(18) Say "Kṛṣṇa, Kṛṣṇa, Kṛṣṇa."

(19) Draw pics of Lord Jagannātha, Baladeva, and Subhadrā.

(20) Draw pics of Rādhā-Kṛṣṇa.

(21) Draw a pic of Lyndon B. Johnson.

(22) Ha-ha your face in mirror.

(23) Resolve to read no more books except Prabhupāda's.

(24) Be pure, grave.

(25) Give up all else.

(26) Recall WCW's *Imaginations*.

(27) Drop names.

(28) Get bitten by tiny gnats.

(29) Wave incense.

(30) Try to look good.

(31) Try to look bad.

(32) Believe it and recall the name of Army aircraft carriers.

(33) Be crafty and dumb.

(34) Control your tongue.

(35) Behave.

(36) Be nice.
(37) Eat rice.
(38) Go to Siddha-bakula.
(39) Go to Ṭoṭā-gopīnātha.
(40) Go to Gambhīrā, but watch out for the tough guys.
(41) Laugh at your own jokes.
(42) Read your writings to favorable devotees.
(43) Plan how to print *Songs of a Hare Kṛṣṇa Man* even if nobody wants to read it.
(44) Be your own man.
(45) Behave.
(46) Count the waves.
(47) Pray to Kṛṣṇa, "Please save me."
(48) Say holy names.
(49) Chant rounds.
(50) Keep reading.
(51) Exchange with devotees who are dear to you.
(52) Let your heart beat.
(53) Eat more Jagannātha tongues.
(54) Think about going back to Godhead, Vraja.
(55) Plan to live in a log cabin in West Virginia and write a hundred million thousand six hundred and forty-two verses in '97.
(56) Find out how to hide out.
(57) Be on guard.
(58) Hare Kṛṣṇa Hare Kṛṣṇa, Kṛṣṇa Kṛṣṇa Hare Hare/ Hare Rāma Hare Rāma, Rāma Rāma Hare Hare: you can chant these holy names.

COMPROMISE

Can you believe it?
Old-timer in Levis, bare chest
man, you wander by waterfront
warehouses.

People you meet are ex-Hare Kṛṣṇas
or buried Hare Kṛṣṇas
real sadness in me for Viṣṇujana
old times of purity gone.

Man, I'm wandering and I too am lost
I talk to a guy who vaguely remembers
me and asks, "Do you expect us,
Sats, to be better? Is that
your trip?"

Hey, I'm half afraid he'll
beat me if I tell the truth,
or the cops will or the Navy
goons, someone
bound to get me
I keep wandering and
don't sing,
don't chant until I
wake up from this
nightmare
compromised.

10:10 A.M.

I gave the class. Maybe I carried on too much. I closed my eyes and ran through, like a computer scan, words to answer the questions. I grind axes about loyalty to Prabhupāda and yes or no about *gopī-bhāva*. I tire myself, *bore* myself, and bore them too to some degree. Is it possible to make it more interesting? Could they participate more? Maybe I should just shut up. Not read so many passages. Talk less. Sing off key.

SIDDHA-BAKULA GOING

Siddha-bakula going,
I and my friends
deliver us from commotion
of streets
deliver us from notions
of our inferior status
ha! We are white and black
and not *brāhmaṇas* or
Hindus of Purī.

Believe we will
go there, Prabhupāda our guide
and if I can find a corner
quiet enough, Kṛṣṇa will speak through
me and to me and
we will understand the holy names,
learn them again,
and chant, chant
chant.

Impressions while at Siddha-bakula
Back in room, feels like landing
awkwardly on the moon. I've been here before,
haven't I?
Rickshaw rides, heavy Indian voices demanding money and
Rūpa-Raghunātha soft and insistent
takes care of the business.
Dirt streets. The entrance? He points ahead toward more confusion and poverty and dirt to the sign, "Shri Siddha-bakul."

Bare feet on cold earth, silent man sitting at the altar of Siddha-bakula. Peaceful—you could say he's not preaching—but he's there.

Statue—is it Haridāsa? We bow down. A picture of Kṛṣṇa lying on a peacock feather playing the flute, a Sanskrit "*Aum*" beaming down on Him. There's the wall with English words, history of Siddha-bakula, the framed pictures high on the walls. I thought I remembered them as murals. The tree, petrified, hung with clay or stone slabs—prayers or wishes. Does it pain the tree to hold them all?

We circumambulate three times. It's like walking on the moon—a different atmosphere. Then into the next courtyard and the Deity room—Gaurāṅga with wig, Kṛṣṇa, etc., and a separate one of bearded Haridāsa wearing a crocheted hat and wrapped in a rough wool blanket. Jagannātha, Baladeva, and Subhadrā too, wrapped in Their winter blankets. Even the bas relief figure on an outer column has a blanket.

We bow. A Gauḍīya-looking *sādhu* in white cloth nods to us. Our group sits. I admit I feel alienated. My voice is slow and measured. Let it come out. I speak from my feelings, but soon move to discuss Haridāsa. Haridāsa Ṭhākura is similar to us in that he is born outside the Hindu culture. He kept himself humble. I give examples and speak some of the *līlās* of Siddha-bakula, hoping it will impress us enough to chant attentively, at least while we're here.

Preaching and *sādhana* come together in good *japa*. One who has enthusiasm, taste, and steadiness in chanting will progress beyond offensive chanting and will also become a potent preacher. Yes, it's true.

Then I ended, picked up leaves from the ground, got on the rickshaw, and left, elated.

6:30 P.M.

Good night. I'd go out onto the veranda, but what would I say if I met them in the dark—the members of our group? Eight-year-old Kālindī said the priest at Ṭoṭā-gopīnātha promised them if they come back at 7 A.M., he'll show them a golden line where Lord Caitanya entered the Deity.

Bala got me Jagannātha "stamps" for my collages at my request.

Solitude and good night. I pray for guidance. One attains the higher stages only by the mercy of guru and Kṛṣṇa. Śrīla Prabhupāda can confer on me all I need. All I deserve.

LEAVES

Leaves from Siddha-bakula, he said
it's easy to get them laminated but
they can't last forever—
will they help me chant?
V-shaped ducks flying—I miss them—
over Geaglum. How many lives
can I live at once?
Kṛṣṇa Kṛṣṇa Kṛṣṇa.

January 10

12:30 A.M.

Don't be selfish. That's what the *Bhagavad-gītā* teaches. A true *yogī* acts to please the Supreme. (See opening verses of sixth chapter and eighteenth chapter where renunciation is taught. One should not avoid duty; that is false renunciation.) These topics were wrongly taught or pushed in the painting *saṅkīrtana* sales days because we denied devotees, in some cases, their basic spiritual programs. We didn't show sufficient care that they were following the principles. The leaders mismanaged funds dearly gained. Now we have to return to the basic principles of faith in Kṛṣṇa and guru. We have to decide carefully what is best for our own self—with the help of the spiritual master.

DREAMS

Dreams lead nowhere
I want to go.
Really a maze, through
buildings, sex offers,
lost identity.
I'm a *sannyāsī*, not a
Senoi warrior,
my destination is Great Kills in
the dream
a distraction. When
I wake I ask,
"What *is* this Great Kills stuff? I want Kṛṣṇa!"
I go to Prabhupāda and
bow down, he
seems concerned and
he understands.
One of these days . . .

10:15 A.M.

I'm typing on the porch, but it's hard because the chair arms prevent movement. We talked of Lord Caitanya at Jagannātha Purī—the first time He entered the temple and fell unconscious. I said, "Yeah," and they said, "Yeah." I'm writing what comes now since I have done my duty.

Sunshine coming through clouds. Several times I said, "The people of India are innocent and religious," but what do I know? I mostly stay indoors and only know what I read in books or what someone else tells me. Secondhand reports. That's even how I wrote the *Līlāmṛta*. Others did the interviews and I examined the accounts. By the power of visualization and imagination, I could enter it and know what others thought of Śrīla Prabhupāda.

Yeah, I'm quite a guy. And yeah, it's quite an experience being a devotee of Lord Caitanya. Even living in Purī is quite a trip, although I'm quite an indoors man even here. I have chronics and as I write this, I hear two Indians laughing as they pass by on a burping-coughing motor scooter on the paved road just in front of the beach.

O holy place, this is better than Los Angeles, but the temple there is an okay place too because you can distribute books and see the Deities. Yes, as I was telling this guy, it sure is a happy picnic, and, it's a hard rain that's gonna fall. The worst is yet to come. *Karmī* pickles are going to fall. The Clinton administration is okay, they are trying real hard because they are liberal Democrats, and we don't want to put them down, but they are *doomed.* Come now, you have to call a spade a spade. The leaders are foolish.

Clap hands! Chase those gray and black Indian crows off the balcony. They keep cawing and I keep clawing at the page with my ink marks.

All glories to the Lord of the Universe and to the temple-like structure on the roof of the guest house here. All glories to Prabhupāda. Thank you, master, for allowing me to serve you and to speak of Kṛṣṇa. The devotees in our group are well experienced. I may not be teaching them anything new, but I go ahead anyway and speak what I have read.

3:45 P.M.

I'd like to write, I'd like to read, I'd like to talk about myself to those who will listen. But I'm afraid I'll worsen the head pain that has developed. I had to cancel the afternoon's activities. I . . . I am putting down another layer, like paint, whenever I write. Clean lines and sentences that create by-products, art-products to be left in the world even after I leave. Illusion? I wouldn't want to do anything that would slow my spiritual progress. I do it to please Kṛṣṇa, and I pray never to misuse my tiny free will.

Bored of the old presentations of Kṛṣṇa consciousness. We say all our preaching is for newcomers. I want to hear someone speak from the heart and soul, but not if he or she is obnoxious or sentimental. Often we say, "Go ahead, speak," and we get an earload of complaining, politics, or grief. Grief is okay, and complaining too, but we want universal grief, blues music that touches everyone's sadness or evokes the Kṛṣṇa conscious element in it, the yearning and appreciation we all want to feel despite the obstacles. I'm not saying that I'm the singer, just stating what I would like to hear.

So I give off by-products while I try to reach it. Then I will dwindle and die. At least I won't become a twig that snaps off the Caitanya tree in the wind. Bend and be flexible, headaches and all.

INDOORS MAN

Indoors I spend my time but
I'm free to go out
although I never hardly do.
Dat's me, he said, lookin'
in the mirror of
lonely pasts when he
was a kid on a sandlot baseball
field in Queens.
That's me indoors, happy
when the energy flows
well.

January 11

12:10 A.M., JĪVA GOSVĀMĪ'S APPEARANCE DAY

I wake up humming, "It would take, I know/ a Michelangelo . . . " and feel my head clearing after an all-night headache. Got one dream recorded, but refused to record the second one, now gone forever unless the unconscious wants to send it again. What messages?

Told M. last night that I doubt there's something wrong with me. He met a man yesterday who asked, "How is your Guru Mahārāja? Does he still get headaches?" They speak as if I'm supposed to get rid of something bad and become a better person. I live with my conditions and limits at this point.

Now is my chance to read Śrīla Prabhupāda's books. What about *Bhagavad-gītā*? You have clear consciousness, it's quiet,

I GOTTA WRITE
GIVE US This DAY OUR DAILY "BREAD"
Jan 17, 1997
Every Day

my service is not unalloyed
Hare Krsna Hare Krsna Krsna
Krsna Hare Hare
Rama Hare Rama
Rama Rama Hare
Hare Hare Krsna
Hare Krsna Krsna
Krsna Krsna Hare
Hare Hare

Śrī Viṣṇu, Śrī Viṣṇu, Śrī Viṣṇu.

The wealth of Tapo-bhumi—*sādhus* and *tulsī-pūjā*.

The sacred tree where Haridāsa Ṭhākura chanted.

and the predominate sound is the heavy surf washing and thudding for miles along the dark beach. The time is yours, and the free will to move in Kṛṣṇa's direction with faith.

I feel satisfaction whenever I engage in any act of devotion, such as offering food or praying to Śrīla Prabhupāda, chanting Hare Kṛṣṇa mantra or reading, but I also feel my lack of advancement. These two factors may always be with me, just as at the beach we will always hear the ocean's surf. "Hearing of the transcendental activities of Lord Kṛṣṇa is therefore expert treatment for the mad mind . . . " (Bg. 6.35, purport)

Bhaktivinoda Ṭhākura prays (in his last stanzas before his seclusion) that he may always live in his modest *bhajana-kuṭīr* at Navadvīpa and remember the pastimes of Rādhā-Kṛṣṇa. I'd also like to live somewhere and pursue my Kṛṣṇa consciousness in reading and writing. But I need to go out and preach too. Therefore, I've come to India with this select group. I'm here for them. I wish to give the reading and talk of *Caitanya-caritāmṛta* today and every day, and then travel on to speak in other places as is my duty. My writing and reading enhance this. I find topics to discuss and feel more prepared to try to help those who are entangled in worldly duties but who want to pursue Kṛṣṇa consciousness and find the peace and bliss therein, who want to actually achieve it.

10:15 A.M.

Very nice meeting today with devotees asking questions about the affectionate dealings of Lord Caitanya with His devotees. I told of Jagadānanda and Gadādhara Paṇḍita, how they were different, stories of Prabhupāda criticizing devotees, Sanātana Gosvāmī's intimate desires to be close to the Lord as Jagā was. All nice.

This afternoon we plan to walk to Ṭoṭā-gopīnātha temple. We will go to these places and hope to arouse sentiment in our hearts for Lord Caitanya's pastimes. I will ask the devotees to tell me of their experiences in the different places they visit.

The ocean is never exhausted. When I tell stories I think I will soon exhaust my stock, but it is never exhausted. It will go on and on and it will always find new connections, one to another. Today I connected Jāmbavān's fighting with Lord Kṛṣṇa with Lord Caitanya's defeating Sārvabhauma with argument. Both recognized, "This must be God." Let it come together. Strain your ear to hear the word of God.

Typing this while Kālindī plays in the backyard sand. She has no truck or shovel or friends, but spends an hour in her world building little mounds and playing with sticks. Who knows what she is thinking as she plays there.

Hands on typewriter. Girl playing in the sand, the wall beyond, the surf pounding, the big slide, barefoot walk through sand on this cool gray day, the constant crows.

Evergreens growing in sandy earth, and I haven't seen rodents since I've been in India, just mangy dogs and an elephant in a *Mahābhārata* video. Gaṇeśa rides a rat. In a dream I saw a rat in the water. The mosquitoes I see when I'm awake. They live in the corners, in cloth bags, in any dark place. They come to life at night, and as I turn the pages of the *Bhagavad-gītā* in the early morning hours, they bite. Kṛṣṇa says yoga is hard, but we can practice it with determination and devotion. I try to hear. Try to hear. Dear Lord, please clean me of wrong desires and make me Your devotee.

Now the sun is clear of clouds for the first time in a couple of days. I'm going inside to worship Śrīla Prabhupāda and hear him speak from 1973. May I be blessed, and tested, but successful.

4:15 P.M., ṬOṬĀ-GOPĪNĀTHA MANDIRA IMPRESSIONS

Pūjārī with swollen legs let us inside Deity rooms for *darśana;* group of Manipuri ladies arrived while we were there. After *darśana* at the three altars, we sat in the *kīrtana* hall, marble floor, walls painted green-blue. I read from Mahānidhi Swami's book and mine on Ṭoṭā-Gopīnātha Mandira. Then we chanted a round together. I was not so conscious of spiritual emotions, but wary of the possibility of a twinge in the head. Rūpa-Raghunātha gave me a walking stick. It was a leisurely outing and the air was warm. As we strolled, I stopped occasionally and spoke about Śrīla Prabhupāda's stay here in 1977. I also told of our past visits to Purī and how we were rejected. I seem to relish the stories of the insults we received. Walked near village where fisher families live. Two children, a girl with a basket of silver fish, boy with a crab and fish dangling from his hand, like toys. Walk and stop and point out buildings—Caitanya Sarasvati Math, etc.

5:45 P.M.

You can use writing to bring yourself closer to Kṛṣṇa consciousness, as you would in reading or *japa*. *Japa* . . . I felt a little wave to do it, then it passed, almost as if it was an illusion. When I actually begin a round, the mind goes off.

Good sections lined up in *Caitanya-caritāmṛta*. We are covering a lot of material. Devotees are commenting in the class and that allows me to springboard into other sections. My reading of the summer and fall has been useful for our discussions here. Always read *Caitanya-caritāmṛta*.

As we walked I turned and hoped that they would gather in close enough to hear me. I said, "You should go to many *tīrthas* and write me your impressions." How are you different from the guru act which you are seen as—pompous and too self-important? I'm more low-key. I come back to my room and draw a picture of two brown *sādhus* standing on either side of a *tulasī* pot. Then I hear Prabhupāda talking to a mathematician in Australia. The man said, "Mine is not a very transcendental occupation, is it?" Śrīla Prabhupāda said it doesn't matter. What matters is whether you do it for Kṛṣṇa. Come closer to Kṛṣṇa.

I do live as though I will always be here remembering experiences in India, times with Prabhupāda. It's not the case. I'm moving along to death—cold, scary, painful death, white as a sheet, stretched out and all that. "These are my final days," Śrīla Prabhupāda said to a few of us one day—so simply, so unafraid. He engaged in life right up until the end. For him, life was meant for preaching and encouraging us to carry on his mission. Deliver the fools and rascals and give them Kṛṣṇa consciousness. Maintain what I have set up, he said. Cooperate. Don't ruin it. Maybe we're not doing so well collectively.

January 12

12:45 A.M.

Reading scriptures. Getting a clearer idea of *bhakti* as the goal. Hearing from Kṛṣṇa about Himself, or from His pure devotees. Viśvanātha Cakravartī Ṭhākura tells us that in Vṛndāvana, Śrī Kṛṣṇa is worshiped without *aiśvarya-jñāna*. When Kṛṣṇa displays His divine potency, the eternal Vrajavāsīs don't waver in their affection for Him.

The ocean waves are always beating, but I only heard them when I awoke and took out my earplugs. Mosquitoes bit me a few times even under the mosquito net. Now I'm out in the room, but I've covered most of my flesh so they can't get through. I still hear their motors whine, and I brush them away.

Better to always dwell on Kṛṣṇa. He's always present in all things if we will just remember Him. Kṛṣṇa consciousness: to see Kṛṣṇa in all beings and all beings in Kṛṣṇa; to see Kṛṣṇa in all things and to see everything in Him. The desk, wood grain, varnish; the desk lamp, metal, and blue paint; the clock ticking each second and the minute hand moving each minute—these are Kṛṣṇa's energies in this world. Things don't work automatically or independently of Him. He is the Supreme controller. For the pure devotees, He is the object of their love. No one else but Kṛṣṇa and things and persons in relation to Kṛṣṇa. I work with this principle, but I am not absorbed in it in the highest way. I become disturbed by physical pain or concerned with material comfort and happiness. I don't chant His holy names in *samādhi*. I report (write) from this lesser platform in the name of honesty. I don't want to be a hypocrite.

Hear from *śāstra* and the mind-flow and sensual operation will naturally be closer to pure Kṛṣṇa consciousness.

6:25 A.M.

Soon cold breakfast, soon take off your long johns. How long it is before I can reach perfection. If we worship Rādhā and Kṛṣṇa as Deities with veneration in *vaidhī-bhakti*, the perfection we attain is Goloka in Vaikuṇṭha. I read this in *Rāga-vartma Candrikā*. "In Goloka the devotee becomes an eternal associate of Queen Satyabhāmā in Dvārakā, serving her and Kṛṣṇa in *svakīya-bhāva* with *mādhurya-jñāna* mixed with *aiśvarya-jñāna*. But in *rāga-bhakti* the devotee goes to the highest spiritual abode of Vraja where he resides as an eternal associate of Śrīmatī Rādhikā, serving Her in *parakīya-bhāva* and pure *mādhurya-jñāna*."

I don't understand this, and I don't understand how we're going to get to this stage. Recently I told a devotee that Prabhupāda's emphasis has to do with more immediate concerns: surrender to guru and Kṛṣṇa and freeing ourselves from *anarthas*. Then how will we realize the higher stages?

They say it will happen automatically. Well, does that mean you just sit around and wait for it to happen? No; you surrender to Kṛṣṇa and guru and by their mercy, everything will come about. Kṛṣṇa indicates something like that in the twelfth chapter of *Bhagavad-gītā*, verses 6 and 7, when He says that He is the swift deliver from the ocean of birth and death. Prabhupāda writes, "The devotee does not need to wait to become very experienced in order to transfer himself to the spiritual sky . . . The responsibility is taken by the Supreme Lord Himself." Prabhupāda is here referring to the fact that we don't need to practice *aṣṭāṅga-yoga*.

Nowadays, devotees are wondering whether it's enough to wait for Kṛṣṇa. They have heard a different emphasis from other gurus. They have been told that it's not enough to serve Prabhupāda's mission; we must also know Prabhupāda in his eternal form.

I prefer to think it *is* enough to wait for Kṛṣṇa simply because that's what Prabhupāda said. Therefore, we can only conclude that if we do what Prabhupāda says, we will reach the highest perfection. We have to have that confidence. Prabhupāda is not leading us to worship Satyabhāmā but Rādhā and Kṛṣṇa in Vraja. We may be so inexperienced that we don't understand how it will all come about. It's natural for children to have little understanding of the mechanics of life. Anyway, we will not be able to go to Vraja by academic or theoretical understanding. Actually, a premature understanding can hinder our progress and even delay us. It has been said that if we think ourselves female servants in our eternal form without becoming free from mundane bodily identification, we could be forced to take a female body next time around—in the material world.

2:30 P.M.

Rest doesn't always bring
the ease I want. I wake up
foggy. Tag on

Śrī Kṛṣṇa's name, keep
going
toward afternoon as
waves wash on Sunday.

More vacationers than usual today. Partly sunny. They jump into the waves. A big one rolls in and I watch to see whether it will wash them away or rub their faces on the ocean floor as happened to me in Varkala and once at a mountain seashore in Trinidad. I decided after that to stay like a seashell on the beach.

I call out Śrī Kṛṣṇa's names as if old age doesn't mean death.

Near the tall water tower is a sand elevation, "Caṭaka-parvata," and across the street from that is Ṭoṭā-gopīnātha. Yesterday, I said nothing about the Deities. There is Balarāma with His unpolished silver horn, Gaura-Gadādhara, who looked almost like dolls, and of course, Ṭoṭā-gopīnātha.

Clothes hanging out on balconies
of Hotel Raj some hundreds
of yards from here and
Frisbees have finally made it
to India.
Beep-beep Ambassadors,
waves break standard anywhere
but here you know it's
ocean at Poori.

A crow's conference in the sandy courtyard of Birla guest house. The unsteady whine-cough of the motor scooter rickshaw sailed down the beachside paved road. Our men went swimming. Bala made a do-it-yourself dessert where I could combine the ingredients myself—a thin custard, toasted crumbs, and an apple mash.

Oh wash
wash your heart.

MUSIC BOX

The words "music box"
drift into mind . . .
Jagannātha Swami calendar . . .
the nature of music.
I just write.
"In case of fire, break glass."

"Give me a little
peace," he said just when
he began hearing the *gopīs*
had anything but peace and
Kṛṣṇa told Arjuna, "If you don't
fight then I'd prefer you die."
"He was so dissatisfied
with Arjuna's decision,"
Prabhupāda said,
strong in lecturing in
England, '73.

Master, where are you? I
ask rhetorically, not expecting
an answer as
the wind rustles the page.

January 13

12:35 A.M.

Blessed be the meek, the poor, the peacemakers, and those who suffer on behalf of the son of God. These and other pure devotees with saintly qualities shall enter the kingdom of God.

Mosquitoes are more active this morning. Each day they seem worse. I am trying to remain nonviolent, but some will get killed as they come at my flesh. I have to defend myself or be eaten.

FREE-WRITE

"Music box." Śrīla Prabhupāda lecturing in Sweden: "I do not wish to take much of your time," but you should know the soul is different from the body. No matter how expert a swimmer one may be, he cannot be happy swimming in the vast ocean. He will be happy only when taken out of that foreign element. Go to the spiritual world and breathe and be happy there. What is the proof? The proof is that Kṛṣṇa says so.

You call that proof?!

Yes.

Foreign element. I chant Hare Kṛṣṇa and bat away roving mosquitoes. One lands in the warm lemon drink in Prabhupāda's cup.

Someone may say his *mūrti* is cumbersome to carry and we don't usually worship the guru in a statue. Why not worship a Govardhana-śilā instead? I could, but not at the expense of my worship of Prabhupāda *mūrti*. How could I give up massaging him every day?

Śrīla Prabhupāda talking to the Indian ambassador in Sweden, who said, "We have a problem in India in that we have many religions and can't favor one because we are secular."

Secular doesn't mean the government lets the people go to hell.

Difficult moments, but Prabhupāda is dedicated to Kṛṣṇa and spreading His glories. I follow him just for that reason.

Nārāyaṇa-kavaca said this get-together is giving the Gītā-nāgarī Press workers an identity together. It's a chance to work together at cleaning and cooking and being friends. He hopes we can do it again.

Yes, I said.

Little life, śāstric life. I'm reading Bhaktivinoda Ṭhākura's last twelve verses, which were written in Jagannātha Purī, and sharing them with the devotees.

MILK WORM

Milk worm I never
heard of but I like it
when
I, me, the servant
draws without caring how
it will
look
to an observer.

Kṛṣṇa, I love
to draw Your name and form
whenever I can but
if I don't You're there anyway
in all Your energies.
My truth is yours—
I'm part and parcel of
the one Supreme
color and
form pouring out
of hands like words,
"Kṛṣṇa" the best of all
to cry out at death
with knowledge and pleading
for devotional service life after life.

January 14

1 A.M.

Sharp headache all last night and this morning. Couldn't do anything else but tolerate it. Checking in now.

Sitting on the dark balcony, different thoughts going through my mind. As usual when I get a headache like this one, I question whether I can continue my traveling and preaching. I'll talk with Madhu about it later.

I am also recalling a conversation I had a few days ago with a couple of devotees here. We were discussing our mutual experience of fighting in the trenches of the *saṅkīrtana* war on behalf of our zone. We each concluded that we wouldn't do it again in this lifetime. One devotee spoke of a deep distrust of authority he now has. He felt he was a victim of the system.

Another devotee said that we couldn't condemn the *whole* system. We had to take personal responsibility for our parts in it.

That conversation lingers in my mind. Conversations are themselves acts of conscience and they are binding. Legally, if you discuss murdering someone, you can be convicted as a conspirator in the murder.

Do I really think that we should mistrust ISKCON authorities? My first response is to say that I wouldn't want to trust my *life* to them. I couldn't live subject to all the things that come up on the ISKCON calendar: "Okay, Prabhus, now it's World Relief Day and we have to go out and distribute food in such-and-such a way," or, "Okay, Prabhus, now it's the marathon. We have to surrender for the next month."

Some devotees tend to think that ISKCON is more suitable or geared for young idealists than older devotees. It's hard to imagine myself going back to live the way I lived years ago. At the same time, I have disciples who live in temples, and I don't think they're in a bad place or wrongly situated. I think of some of my old-timer disciples, and even some newcomers. They basically like where they are and accept the difficulties. Anyway, there are difficulties everywhere.

Recently I wrote a letter to a prominent author in the world in response to her book and note she sent me. The typist gave me the letter to sign and asked me whether I wanted it to be sent on ISKCON stationery or plain paper. I said offhand to use ISKCON stationery. Well, do I actually want to be known as a member of ISKCON? Am I proud of it? Am I willing to stand for all that goes on in the movement and represent it? As I walk in the world catching planes as a Hare Kṛṣṇa person, I think, "People won't really know *all* of what goes on in ISKCON, so it's okay if they see me as a member." Right?

9:40 A.M.

Oh yeah, man, we feel better finally, but don't know what to do with the little bit of energy and time left at our disposal. I think I'll have to revise my schedule so as not to go to the

Caribbean. It's too much for me right now. These days of pain are leaving me drained. I hate to disappoint devotees by not traveling to their country, but I don't know . . . I'm weak and can't do much without feeling pain.

In this condition, I'm asking You (Arjuna said) how I should act. Please instruct me. He was weak-hearted. Kṛṣṇa wanted him to fight. Should I also fight by going to the Caribbean?

M. says I should be realistic—not that I call off all lecturing and traveling after a bad day, but proceed according to what I can do. He says my criteria for action shouldn't be what will please (and not disappoint) the devotees. If that's the standard, there is no end to travel, lecture, and the dance.

Better I travel at a pace I can control, as I do in the van in Europe. If that fails, perhaps I can at last go home and stay in a cabin in America—at Gītā-nāgarī for a couple of weeks, then to Baltimore.

And then the bigger question: I want to show them the essence of love between guru and disciple, and I don't want to be guilty of hypocrisy. But how does my going there or not actually change their lives? How can I measure it? What's best to do? What's *possible* to do?

2:20 P.M.

Tired old pawpaw. Want to go to Kṛṣṇa. Someone says, "I'm very attached to Prabhupāda—more than I am to Kṛṣṇa. Is that bad?"

No, I say, he will lead you to Kṛṣṇa.

Kṛṣṇa dancing with flute. I saw Him in my mind's eye faintly, momentarily, above the hotel building's pre-dawn, while I was sitting on the balcony as a sharp headache was finally going down. Was thinking about what I'd read, and also how a Zen practitioner doesn't strive for enlightenment but realizes it's more a matter of tuning in than discovering. That seems similar to the *mahā-bhāgavata's* vision that everyone and everything is already perfect. Yes, but we want to add

Kṛṣṇa to that. Not that we click into enlightenment while looking at a hotel, sky, and ocean at Purī and feel, "This is it. It's perfect now and always was."

Kṛṣṇa
became superimposed
dancing, what we want,
but He's a long way off—
many lives.

MANY LIVES

Many lives both you and I
Arjuna, we've had, but
never can you remember them,
although I do.
Yes, Arjuna knew it too by
His grace.

Love to be there one day
but so far I struggle
for strength each day—
I want to be a devotee,
make a beeline to His lotus feet,
but ecstasies must be paid for and
samādhi is no joke.

DON'T MISS PRABHUPĀDA'S SPECIAL POTTERY CLASS: A DREAM

I'm talking to Rūpānuga and hear that Prabhupāda is going to teach a pottery class after school hours. I decide to go, but first have to pick up my coat from a store. Rūpānuga says to me, "You're not a clay-making man, are you? Even if you're not, though, I know you'll want to take advantage of Prabhupāda teaching pottery."

"Yeah, I was thinking of going home, but now that you mention what a special treat it is, I have decided to stay."

When I awoke I thought, "Pottery class?" More to the point is that I shouldn't miss the opportunity—any opportunity—to

I'll toot my horn in lines, poems, and pictures.

Bend, flexible, headaches and all.

Do you find your *japa's* better in the holy *dhāma*?

Fly your own plane.

be with Prabhupāda. We generally have to practice austerities to receive the guru's special mercy in the form of an extra class. Don't be dull, go to the trouble to get the nectar. Prabhupāda's teaching sculpture. Be awake for it.

4:30, OUTING IMPRESSIONS

Soft pleasant breezes. A young girl banging a can with a stick, her rag of a dress held together with a single button in back. Women carrying bricks on their heads. In the ISKCON *bhakti-kuṭīr* of Bhaktivinoda Ṭhākura, the bricks all have the word PREM stamped on them. The place is still under construction. We sat in their temple room and read of how the devotees gave Śrīla Prabhupāda an *abhiṣeka* at Jagannātha Purī at the ocean's edge. The temple president and others listened and gave me a mat to sit on. Then we climbed to the roof for a beautiful view of the Jagannātha Mandira dome (scaffolding around it) and on the other side, the ocean. On leaving, Nārāyaṇa-kavaca said, "There was an uproar when ISKCON tore down the original thatched hut to build their brick building." The president said there would be a museum to honor Bhaktivinoda Ṭhākura.

We walked as a group. "It's good to be among the living again," I thought after my hard day yesterday. Kids said Hare Kṛṣṇa to us. We also went to Purushottama Gaudiya Math. I remembered we had *kīrtana* there with Śrīla Prabhupāda in 1977. The Deities were closed today—no one in sight. We circumambulated. Madhu walked ahead of me so I wouldn't trip down the stairs. Then we went to Haridāsa Ṭhākura's *samādhi* Mandira. I could not enter an internal mood, just moved through the places, bowing down at altars, circumambulating, seeing paintings of Lord Nityānanda, Lord Caitanya, Advaitācārya, all done in bas relief to depict the passing away of Śrīla Haridāsa Ṭhākura.

Walking back. Do you hear the waves? I was thinking of asking the devotees, "Could you write me your impressions of the waves?" Could I ask the temple president, "Do you hear the surf at night?" Of course he does.

Crow on top branch of beach-growing evergreen. It sways in the breeze. It's good to be among the living.

January 15

12:30 A.M.

First thing I did on rising was to read *Caitanya-caritāmṛta*. As I began, however, other thoughts crept into my mind—notes I might write to Madhu or letters to others, editing and publishing topics, dreams. But I stayed with the book for twenty minutes and read about the cleansing of the Guṇḍicā temple. That section contains the long purport about cleansing the heart of *anarthas* before Kṛṣṇa will be pleased to sit there and reveal Himself. "Kṛṣṇa Himself will cleanse the heart because He is already seated there. Kṛṣṇa wants to continue living within the heart, and the Lord wants to give directions, but one has to keep his heart as clean as Lord Caitanya Mahāprabhu kept the Guṇḍicā temple." (Cc. *Madhya* 12.135, purport)

Some of the faults listed are those committed by outright materialists, but some are committed by neophyte devotees. Śrīla Prabhupāda says, "*Jīva-hiṁsā* (envy of other living entities) actually means to stop the preaching of Kṛṣṇa consciousness. . . . If one stops preaching and simply sits down in a solitary place, he is engaging in material activity."

With this in mind I think I ought to persist in trying to travel this year. I should go to the Caribbean and to America, then back to Europe. It may provoke headaches, but I get them regardless. We can only take as much caution as possible, be careful not to push beyond my limits, and hope the devotees will understand that I can only preach when I don't have a headache. My condition seems to be benign. That is, although I'm fragile, I don't have a life-threatening disease. When I stay in one place I can write. The more alone I can be at those times, allowing outer activities to calm themselves, the easier it is for me to turn within and to face *anarthas*, and to sometimes churn out a literary gem.

Later I had this dream, which seems related to my thinking about my health and whether or not to continue traveling:

DEATH DESPITE ALL SCIENTIFIC ATTEMPTS TO SAVE ONESELF: A DREAM

An old man dies. I watched him go. He had a great illness, but extremely sophisticated medicine and treatment. His son knew how to administer it all, and tried to revive him as he approached his end. His son's attempts went to the extreme—fiery potions, flashing lights—but it didn't work. Finally, people brought a pallet to take out the body.

On waking I remember the bas relief paintings of Haridāsa Ṭhākura's passing away. Death was depicted much simpler than in the dream. Haridāsa Ṭhākura's death was sublime. Lord Caitanya allowed him to give up his body in His presence, and then he was lowered into a simple grave.

Let's recall Prabhupāda's own practice, how at the end he didn't want to be put into a hospital and hooked up to tubes and machines. I realized that I have to try to be brave and simple and face not only death but my disease without resorting to contraptions and too much medication. Yes, it takes courage.

The surf sounds especially close, as if I'm near a dock. It almost sounds threatening, like it might overflow the beach.

6:15 A.M., FREE-WRITE

The surf is rolling.
Listen to the waves, listen to the waves
to the permanent waves,
to the joshing joshers, the avoidance of nonsense and sinful bad words. We have been made clean in mind, thoughts, and deeds by our spiritual master. In obedience to him I cut out bad words from my writing, although I leave in a little so you'll know I'm still human—as if that will help you.

Free-write like the hawk harassed by crows. We walked through the narrow dirt streets. Rāma-rāya said, "People are friendly here." Baladeva said this particular walk was through a neighborhood near the Gaudiya temples, so the kids were the offspring of devotees. I saw a group on the beach mocking us though. Did the others see it? Rancid piles of fish, two small dogs eating from their borders. The fishermen don't stop them, so why should I worry?

Don't worry about trying to reform others, Bhaktisiddhānta Sarasvatī Ṭhākura says. Providence will take care of reform. Here is a quote by him which someone says sums up what I am trying to do:

> The world stands in no need of any reformer. The world has a very competent person for guiding its minutest happenings. The person who finds that there is scope for reform of the world himself stands in need of reform. The world goes on its own perfect way. No person can deflect it but the breadth of

a hair from the course chalked out for it by Providence. When we perceive any change being actually affected in the course of events of this world by the agency of any particular individual, we also know very well that the agent possesses no real power at any stage. The agent finds himself driven forward by a force belonging to a different category from himself.

The course of the world does not require to be changed by the activity of any person. What is necessary is to change our outlook to this very world. This was done for the contemporary generation by the mercy of Śrī Caitanya. It could be known only to the recipients of His mercy . . .

The scriptures declare that it is only necessary to listen with an open mind to the name of Kṛṣṇa from the lips of a bona fide devotee. As soon as Kṛṣṇa enters the listening ear, He clears up the vision of the listener so that he no longer has any ambition of ever acting the part of a reformer of any other person, because he finds that nobody is left without the very highest guidance. It is therefore his own reform, by the grace of God, whose Supreme necessity and nature he is increasingly able to realize by the eternally continuing mercy of the Supreme Lord.

2:30 P.M.

I seem to be writing less each day. I'm tired—tired of meeting with disciples and giving a full class because it causes me physical pain. I don't have the spirit for it now. Neither do I feel comfortable acting as if I'm so much more advanced than they are. Still, there is no other scope for our relationship. I'm also feeling the tensions that exist between them. How many days left here? It was wonderful for awhile . . . probably still would be all right if I didn't feel so weak. Cāṇakya Paṇḍita says that if you don't have money, then everything is lost. Similarly, if you don't have physical strength, you can't do all the things that are demanded—editing, writing letters and books and poems, and on top of that, meeting daily with disciples for class and *parikrama*.

Yesterday when I felt relieved of the headache I was confident we would go to the Caribbean. This afternoon I'm feeling fed up with having to perform as a guru before disciples in one scene after another. Purī is only the beginning, and I'll have to do it again and again in many other places. I don't want to reach that point where I would actually despise the audience and myself for living out a role. I need to recognize my need for being alone and reforming myself, as Bhaktisiddhānta Sarasvatī Ṭhākura says. My children in the Caribbean . . . my children in America . . . my children who will gather to see me in Vṛndāvana. Me inside feeling that my time is being stolen. I hate myself for allowing it to happen.

I can argue that the *karmīs* have to go through this—they have to work every day whether they want to or not. Why not me? But that doesn't seem like a good argument. Why *shouldn't* I try for the best for myself? If I can be really satisfied, then I can give people the best thing. It's not a given that by showing up in their camp and saying "I love you" that I am giving the best part of myself to my disciples.

4:30 P.M., FREE-WRITE

So many different ideas of what to do. I could take a sixty-four-round *japa-vrata;* I could stay in India longer, alone; I could skip Vṛndāvana and go straight back to Geaglum to hear and chant and chant and chant; I can skip the Caribbean, go to America, and then return to Geaglum. Which one should I do?

Please see me as sincere. Do something.

Jibberty jibbish. Eight-year-old Kālindī looks up at me vacantly from her coloring work while I lecture on *japa*. Or did I touch a chord within her? She looks up at this old guy who is the Guru Mahārāja of everyone she knows. What's so special about him? Why does he raise his voice and why do they laugh? What's so funny? What's so serious? What's so interesting? She doesn't know, would prefer it her way.

Well, the truth is—

I have a stiff neck and head. Take rest early. I can't do a sixty-four-round *vrata* because of my headaches. It's too strenuous to chant for nine hours a day.

"I thought of practicing meditation to help my chanting."

"Yes," I say and glance at Nārāyaṇa-kavaca. "Remember how Mahākrama used to read books on *aṣṭāṅga-yoga* to improve his concentration on *japa*?" Someone else says, "The answer is earplugs."

"How do you get around the wall?"

"Associate with good chanters."

"Where do you find them?"

Pay attention to the *japa* genius within you, the *japa* reformer. If you give him room, he will awaken and reciprocate.

CHANGING MIND

Change mind twice a day—
are you
going to Vṛndāvana or the Caribbean?
Oh, go change your diapers,
your mind, your seat, your
college major, your girlfriend.
Each year you change your musical
tastes, but not your God
or guru.

5:45 P.M.

Madhu just came in with revised travel suggestions. Seems all of us are getting itchy feet at the same time, ready to leave our Purī conference. It was nice together, but now it seems the mood has passed. If we can catch a plane, we're going to leave the day after tomorrow for Bhubaneshwar.

January 16

12:12 A.M.

Yesterday was warmer, so more small mosquitoes are flying about, eager to bite me. Saw a dog yesterday suddenly flop on its back and roll in the sand in an effort to rub out some bug that was biting it. This world. Flea eat dog.

What's the value of unconscious over conscious writing?

See imprints on the page of handwriting from the previous page . . . ancient, uncoded marks . . . a few paper clips, the desk space limited as my books, papers, and Jagannātha stickers encroach upon it, leaving me a small area for the note pad.

Registering complaints,
aliases, alases,
laments, complaints,

bitch dog and male dog,
you saw the dogs and were impressed by their behavior. It's typical.

Words come out. I want something new or enduring.

I want to be left alone. Life is tough. We each have to contribute something. Be a little confident, determined, tolerant, accepting of your limits, doing what you can. I'm just so limited.

Put things out of your mind (like mosquitoes) that you can't handle right now—decisions, or world's horrors, or solutions or lack of solutions for ISKCON, the unsolaced, traumatic past—that stuff.

Also, why you don't have more taste, who can teach you, who can deliver you. My master did all he could. Now I have to carry my weight across the desert.

MERCY

Mercy of God will come to me
as He desires, as Gadādhara knows.
Each one has a chance.
When it comes
choose to act
receive the mercy by standing
in the right place.

ON THE BALCONY

I've been sitting out on the balcony since I began chanting *japa* at 12:20 A.M. I usually chant out here for a round or so, go inside, then come out again. When I first came out this morning I looked over to the hotel a few hundred yards from here. On their second floor there were two rooms that had red lights on the porch. One of the lights went out. I also noticed an electric line flashing on and off. It would flash on for a moment, then go off for several minutes, then come on again. I imagined myself as a forest fire watcher—when I saw this electric line I would report it to headquarters as something potentially dangerous. Now that flashing has become a constant burning light. I've seen that in other places in India—the electric line on the telephone pole suddenly blazes.

Out here I also have heard and seen a watchman in another hotel come out of a door and blow a sad whistle. Now it's raining pleasant dripping sounds. Rounds out here are "good" —wide awake and once or twice, I caught myself *listening* to the words Hare, Kṛṣṇa, and Rāma.

3:45 A.M.

I feel like apologizing to my Boots tape recorder for dropping it in the bathroom. I resolved previously never to do that. It was tucked under my clothes and I didn't notice it until it slid out and hit the stone floor. I'm grateful it's not broken. I need it to hear Prabhupāda. Turning it on I suddenly heard Prabhupāda come on loudly and it made me glad to be alive and awake. "Cats and dogs, cats and dogs," he said.

I'd like to do more things than it's possible for me to do today on this last day in Jagannātha Purī. Here's a partial list:

(1) I'd like to use up all the Jagannātha stickers and images I have in a flurry of drawings—many pages.

(2) I'd like to chant more than sixteen rounds—start it today and continue for a good amount of time. Face the desert and keep going. Be humbled.

(3) I'd like to go to the Gambhīrā in the afternoon even if you don't say something about Lord Caitanya's experience of the mood of Rādhā in separation.

(4) I'd like to be kind to others, starting with the devotees in our group. Extend yourself to them with intelligence.

(5) I'd like to write here my heart's ache outpouring.

(6) If a headache comes, I like to see it not as defeat but as purification, similar to extra chanting.

(7) I'd like to choose which book by Prabhupāda I'm going to read next and get started.

(8) I'd like to start thinking about Vṛndāvana. I did this this morning and considered staying in Vṛndāvana for months and not leaving—to increase my chanting and hearing.

11:35 A.M.

Gurujī. They met and discussed my writings. I wasn't there. They said good things, I heard. Now from my room I see fishermen and smell their catch. Two men bring a straw basket to a section of the beach where a cloth is spread out. They dump the fish there (reminds me of the "Jesus of Nazareth" film). A woman then spreads the pile out with her hands. A little way out in calm water, five men in a boat with four oars trail a net. The whole group works together, and I guess they share the profits, not exactly formally—they distribute no paychecks. They're no punch-in clock employees with full benefits. They share their profits simply and practically in the form of fish and the simple, smelly life.

Jagannāthaḥ svāmī nayana-patha-gāmī bhavatu me. It's settled: we're leaving tomorrow in a mini bus to Bhubaneshwar. Did what we could here. Devotees decided to work together to edit and print *Cc. Āśraya* while we're in India.

2:15 P.M.

No way to prepare for going to the Gambhīrā. Be grave if possible. What Lord Caitanya felt there no one can really understand. We dabble in it and hope to become purified by it. Let me at least look at *Caitanya-caritāmṛta* for references.

I decided to meet with the devotees before going to the Gambhīrā to read a few passages. I want to tell them what a sacred place it is. Since I'm acting as spiritual master, do it with deep subject matter and pass it on to them. Then when we go, we'll conduct ourselves in an internal way and know that the real meaning of the place is inexplicably deep.

"Śrī Caitanya Mahāprabhu's emotion of transcendental madness in separation from Kṛṣṇa is very deep and mysterious.

Even though one is very advanced and learned he cannot understand it." (Cc. *Antya* 14.5)

I will read the section where Prabhupāda said Lord Caitanya was in the mood of Śrīmatī Rādhārāṇī in separation from Kṛṣṇa, that He taught this method of separation from Kṛṣṇa for His devotees to follow.

I'll also read little scenes where we see Lord Caitanya in the Gambhīrā with Rāmānanda Rāya and Svarūpa Dāmodara. Svarūpa Dāmodara would sing a song that would increase the Lord's ecstasy, and Rāmānanda Rāya would also sing or recite verses from their favorite poets about Rādhā and Kṛṣṇa. The Lord would speak in madness, expanding on the meaning of the verses in Śrīmatī Rādharāṇī's mood. Rāmānanda Rāya would leave for the night, and the Lord would stay up chanting loudly in the Gambhīrā. Then during the night, He would suddenly be silent, and when Govinda would enter the room, he would find that the Lord had escaped, although all three doors were locked. It was on occasions like this that He went either to the Siṁha-dvāra gate or to some other place and manifested the extreme bodily transformations no one had ever seen before.

We have a right to hear these things because this is our movement and we are servants in this *sampradāya*. I'll tell them about the Lord injuring His face and the devotees suggesting that Śaṅkara Paṇḍita stay inside the Gambhīrā as the Lord's pillow. They wanted to prevent the Lord from injuring Himself. Finally, I'll give a glimpse of how the Lord, while composing verses or speaking and hearing others, spoke His "*Śikṣāṣṭakam*" to Svarūpa Dāmodara and Rāmānanda Rāya.

3:45 P.M.

Speaking to the devotees about the Gambhīrā, I was like a puffed-up college student who gets A's in his major and who likes to drop names and pat himself on the back. "I have read this section many times, and lately I have had the following realization . . . "

Yeah man, where's your drop of love for the holy name? Where's your single brick of *prema*?

You can't live forever.
Don't be afraid of others' opinions.
Just act your best for Śrīla Prabhupāda.

4:35 P.M., BACK FROM GAMBHĪRĀ

They were friendly. As you walk in, there's a Deity of Kṛṣṇa and the *gopīs* on the left—Kāśī Miśra's Deities. I moved toward Them, but Baladeva said, "No, first go into the Gambhīrā. The Kāśī Miśra Deity is where a troublesome *paṇḍa* stays." We went right into the Gambhīrā and the men there waved us in, "Come on, take a look." At first I thought, "Wow! I'm going right into the Gambhīrā itself!" Then I saw that there was an enclosure with pillars where one *bābājī* was sitting and singing. Nearby there was a small window through which you can see inside to the Gambhīrā.

Anyway, what would I *do* if I went in? I *belong* outside.

And I looked to my fill. I no longer cared what they were saying behind me or what we were supposed to pay or say. I knew the other men would take care of it. I just drank in the room with my eyes for a minute or so. I saw an electric lamp pressed down right on top of the place where the Lord's slippers were. I saw an excellent picture of Lord Caitanya with His hand on His heart. That was the main image in the Gambhīrā. There was also a *mūrti* in there—but of who?

I was conscious that the ten devotees in our party also wanted to look in the window, so I moved aside.

I was then invited to the open side doorway leading into the inner doorway of the Gambhīrā. Both doors were open. I took a step into the first room and was told to back out. The *pūjārī* in there gave me a *tulasī* leaf. Someone else gave me some sweet grains. I stood back while the devotees in our party squeezed up to the window and peered in. I looked at the bas relief over the window of the Gambhīrā—Lord Caitanya with His two dear friends on either side of Him. When the Gambhīrā window was clear, I went up and looked in for a second time. How much can you cram in?

Then we left. Took *darśana* of Kāśī Miśra's beautiful Deities. The priest invited us to step in closer. I said, "Kāśī Miśra" to show that I knew and to let the others know.

The devotees are going now to various places, shopping and temple visiting on our last night in Jagannātha Purī. Madhu and I came back in our puttering motor rickshaw. I regretted that we didn't go on to see Sārvabhauma Bhaṭṭācārya's house. Is that where the Gaura-Gopāl Swami *mūrti* is? But then some pressure started in my head, and I figured that I'd done enough, although it was so little.

January 17

12:15 A.M.

I'm carrying a notebook I'm calling, "In favor of staying with *Every Day, Just Write.*" I've been keeping it to encourage myself to maintain this format. It also contains some of the doubts. This morning as I complete a section of *Every Day, Just Write* and consider the next—which will be written in Vṛndavāna—a question arises:

Writing is my active service and preaching. Gītā-nāgarī Press is publishing the books and we will distribute them. People appreciate them. For example, Nārāyaṇa-kavaca wrote me that I am not futilely trying to tell people to become Indians, but I write from the Western mindset. He said I'm writing a literature as expert as any Western art, I'm delivering

Carrying the Lord of the universe.

He is in everything.

Prostrate in Vraja Mandir
Sands outside

morning
walk with
Prabhupada

Thank you Gurudev
Here.
GURU'S giving blessing of knowledge

Kṛṣṇa consciousness, I'm presenting myself as naked before the readers, and my books will have an impact on readers, especially of the future, etc.

I have a responsibility. I want to deliver the goods. Therefore, my question today is whether the 'effortless' true-to-self, true-to-day's-flow touch I've developed in *Every Day, Just Write* is in any way a relinquishing of the responsibility to work at making literature.

When I rise at midnight I give Śrīla Prabhupāda his dictaphone and I think, "You are writing the Bhaktivedanta purports. I am going to write too." Is *Every Day, Just Write* just for me? Or am I writing *my* equivalent of the Bhaktivedanta purports? I mean, is it worthy enough that others could read what I write? Will it help them in their Kṛṣṇa consciousness?

Well, the fact is, I don't know what else I can do except to be true to myself. For now, I've left *A Poor Man Reads the Bhāgavatam* behind. It was more on *paramparā* teachings than EJW is (whenever I write the initials, I keep thinking of "easy journey," as in *Easy Journey to Other Planets*. Easy Journey to where?), but after 1500 pages of *Poor Man*, I thought, "Enough. This is not my unique contribution." Nārāyaṇa-kavaca also said—as others do—that he especially likes the free-writing. I *do* have a responsibility to readers, and for now, EJW may be the best and only way I know how to fulfill it. But that doesn't mean I can't improve it, deepen it, make more effort to bring out the best in it. Natalie Goldberg quoted her guru as saying, "No one is asking us to open our hearts, but we must do it every day. Make a great effort for the truth." Yes, that's what I want to do. And I want to write it down, my secret report on the adventures of a *sādhaka* or whatever it is I am. I will probably never be completely certain of the value of what I'm doing—I tremble with uncertainty—because in a sense, Prabhupāda's mission is in my hands, as it is in the hands of each and every one of his followers.

A DREAM

I was chanting Hare Kṛṣṇa and playing with a kite. Just before this I saw a film depicting God in His holy name. Even large animals were bowing down before Him. Then this scene: as God's names are being chanted, the person chanting is flying a kite and feeling the pull of the wind. That pull, if you're daring enough to allow it, will lift you off the earth and into the sky, but you have to be willing to go. I was. Each kite had two strings, and a woman grabbed hold of the other string. I immediately thought, "She shouldn't be doing this!" She's an unreliable, unregulated person, and the kite immediately started to dip lower and finally come down by her interference. She said, "I should be allowed to fly kites too."

Some hours later, out of the twilight zone of the dream and faced with its contents, I have come to see it as an intriguing metaphor for chanting. The mantra can pull me into the sky if I'm daring enough to go with it, but I have to be careful of others who want the facility of the kite but who have a different purpose in flying it. I mean, mixed motives in chanting, impurities. I have to chant in pure consciousness. That woman was like my mind, or the world. I have to get beyond it, chant free of it, if I really want to be effective. Although that woman made a strong plea for democratic behavior, I realize that I can't give power over my kite to others. I have to fly my kite, and if others want to fly theirs and follow, that's better. I could go so far as to say also that if I get involved in too much *teaching* on the ground about *how* to chant, then where's the potency? Where's the high flight?

Oh, for the day when I will feel that pull in my hands as the kite begins to take me off the ground and I will go with it. When, oh when will that day be mine? Until then, I have to be determined to keep running along the ground, trying to get it going as we see the poor Indian kids do with their flimsy kites. Prabhupāda said he and his sister also used to fly kites when they were young. They would run together and pray, "Bhagavān, please let our kite fly."

3:45 A.M.

God is Kṛṣṇa, God is God. There is God. He's a person. Śrīla Prabhupāda tells 'em at Upsala University in Stockholm, 1973. It's preserved on tape.

"But it's inexplicable," the professor pleads and insists.

"God is a person," Śrīla Prabhupāda insists. God is a person and we are persons eternally.

They can't accept it and Śrīla Prabhupāda can't compromise. That's why he's so great. I hear him as I shave my face. I hear him faithfully, my master.

Took a group photo yesterday. I'll get a last chance to speak at 9 A.M. if my head is okay. I'll read them the letter I wrote to my Godbrother about how to surrender the whole self, all the limbs, the toes, the head, the lock, stock, and barrel active person in the Lord's mission.

We're all going to Vṛndavāna to Śrīla Prabhupāda's rooms and the Samādhi Mandir, to see Rādhā-Śyāmasundara, Kṛṣṇa-Balarāma, and the sands of Ramaṇa-reti.

Leaving this place in a few hours. I got under the mosquito net after breakfast with the intention to take a nap. The sun was already up and the room bright. Once inside the net with all the sides tucked in, however, I noticed a mosquito inside. It flashed through my mind that I could push the net open again at the bottom and let him out, but before I could act on that compassionate thought, my hasty hands moved over and slapped. My first slap missed him. I slapped again, this time pushing against the net while clapping. After that I didn't see him and presumed he was dead.

Then came the regret. With just a little trouble I could have pushed the net open and let him out. I wanted to blame Madhu, who I know kills mosquitoes once they get inside the net. He says he takes all care not to kill them when they're outside—doesn't use a Good Knight killer, etc.—but once they're *inside* the net, he says that's his territory. But why blame Madhu? I'm supposed to be his teacher and set a good example.

Then I thought how it's likely I'll receive a karmic reaction for this killing. Didn't Prabhupāda once say an astrologer told him that he had been a doctor in his past life and was sinless except that he had once killed an animal—was it a snake? We know about the *ṛṣi* who was almost speared through the anus because he once speared an ant when he was a child. With that selfish fear of my own skin, I lay back to take rest and pray to be forgiven, as I will, by constant engagement in Kṛṣṇa's service. Still, it's not right to kill. I have to make more of an effort to be nonviolent.

12:20 P.M.

Crows caw. "In your country I do not see so many crows, but in India there are many crows. They gather wherever garbage is thrown." What was his point? That we are like crows if we don't take to self-realization? Something like that. Newspaper readers and Indians in the West, new crows. Hogs, cats, and dogs Prabhupāda told them at Upsala University. I listen today, and it's not always easy to hear. It's a workout to hear him urge them to take to Kṛṣṇa consciousness. He recommends the Kṛṣṇa consciousness movement, his ISKCON which gets the LSD-addicted hippies free of intoxicants. He advises his audience to observe the boys and girls who dance in *brahma-bhūta*. "If you are not jubilant you cannot dance like this. It is not dog's dancing. And we have no anxiety over expenditures. We chant Hare Kṛṣṇa and Kṛṣṇa meets all our needs."

I particularly liked it when Prabhupāda spoke strongly in favor of nonviolence, of kindness to *all* creatures, not just humans. An Animal Liberation spokesperson couldn't have done better. He proved that the animal has a soul and shouldn't be slaughtered. Not even a plant should be killed, he said. He told the story of Nārada and the hunter. When converted, the ex-hunter wouldn't even step on an ant.

My head is clean-shaven. We are due to leave in two hours. It's over here.

In our last meeting I read a statement about full surrender to Kṛṣṇa. I was responding to a Godbrother's analysis of pure devotion in the *Bhagavad-gītā*. He said that when we serve Kṛṣṇa spontaneously according to our propensity, that's a less than ultimate stage. The final stage is when we do whatever Kṛṣṇa wants us to do, beyond our personal propensity.

While accepting this conclusion, I argued in favor of the existential reality whereby we have to surrender the "whole person" to the Lord. My propensity to write and read and avoid management may be considered "impure," but it is the way for me to purify myself. Furthermore, although we should do whatever Kṛṣṇa wants, it's not easy to understand what Kṛṣṇa actually wants, specifically, in our lives. We have to agonize over that, and then go ahead with our best intelligence, guided by guru, *śāstra*, and *sādhu*.

The devotees present made encouraging contributions to this discussion, and I'll note them here briefly.

Lalitāmṛta referred to a story about Śrīla Prabhupāda where a frustrated disciple had pleaded with him to make a solution, "Prabhupāda, you know Kṛṣṇa. What does He want us to do?" Prabhupāda replied, "Kṛṣṇa wants to know what *you* want to do."

Rāma-rāya referred to Prabhupāda's purport where he says freedom is the pivot in devotional service. We don't give up our initiative to serve Kṛṣṇa when we surrender.

I had mentioned that St. Francis of Assisi was praised for being able to give up not only many material things, but to conquer himself. Nārāyaṇa-kavaca said that sounded a bit impersonal. We have to *use* our self to surrender.

Although I read my defense of surrendering to Kṛṣṇa with one's own will and propensity, I went on to say that now we are going to Vṛndāvana and should pray to Kṛṣṇa there to tell us what He wants us to do. I said that maybe Kṛṣṇa doesn't want me to be a writer and to be away from ISKCON management, so I have to be open to that possibility. Kaiśorī remarked that it didn't sound right that I should think of renouncing the very means of my surrender. I agreed, just as I agreed to the other remarks which were all in favor of using the self and not thinking that it can be annihilated in the name of doing what Kṛṣṇa wants us to do.

Mādhurya-līlā quoted *The Nectar of Devotion* where it states that particular propensities are not just material but are spiritual tastes.

I'm grateful to the devotees for speaking in this way. I agree with this direction and I know that Kṛṣṇa is fully capable of stepping in and changing our service if He wants. I don't want to think that after thirty years of service I have no idea of how to please Kṛṣṇa. I want to go on doing what I'm doing, but ask Him to help me improve, deepen, become pure, and so on.

Go to Vṛndāvana in a humble mood and pray to Kṛṣṇa. He can do anything and it may not be what you think is going to happen.

2:30 P.M., OUTSIDE HOTEL

Good Deities, six inches tall or more of Lord Jagannātha, Subhadrā, and Baladeva on taxi dashboard, each dressed in cloth, Lord Jagannātha's *cakra* beside Him. An auspicious beginning. Flowers in pots throughout front yard of this Birla guest house. Luggage fills up the trunk. Nārāyaṇa-kavaca gently supervising the operation as the ladies get themselves into the other car. Kālindī plucks the strings of her violin. I breathe and wait.

It will be like this at the end, waiting, but I'll need tremendous reserves—more than today—because pain and fear are likely, are guaranteed, for any conditioned soul.

Good-bye to a nice time.

Nearing Bhubaneshwar. Temple on hill. Pleasant breeze around neck. We are traveling in two cars, a third one to come later. They say there is a guest house at ISKCON Bhubaneshwar. I will be on the alert for suggested etiquette to honor the unique position of His Holiness Gaura-Govinda Swami, who has passed on. I'm still living and he has left. Do I think that gives me an advantage?

Cab driver stopped at roadside Durgā temple to offer coins and receive blessings, the same as when we were here in 1993. I lay down with a pillow.

Shree Biswanatha Jewelers. Hawkins Cooking Pots. Tata Steel Cement.

Trees with red and white horizontal stripes as markers for night driving. Frequent speed bumps to protect the villages. Thatched cottages near lake.

OCM Suiting. Dhaula Santi Sup. Amber Saris. A&T Cement. It's all rather friendly, low-key materialism. Doesn't hit me as it would in America where slogans get under your skin and irritate your psyche.

Chanṭ on the old red beads. No love for Govinda, but I stay with His name. This cab has two Hare Kṛṣṇa mantra stickers on left and right upper sides of windshield. It's the ISKCON classic, "Chant Hare Kṛṣṇa Hare Kṛṣṇa, Kṛṣṇa Kṛṣṇa Hare Hare/ Hare Rāma Hare Rāma, Rāma Rāma Hare Hare and be happy."

Jagannātha Mastar . . . Bhand . . .

PL Tyre Works. Chariot Cement the Best. Emblem of Konark sun-god wheel.

In Purī the *paṇḍa* who sold us sweets every day (Jagannātha *prasādam*) informed us that there is a *bābājī* in Purī who speaks to Rādhārāṇī. If you go to him, he will tell you your eternal form, but only if you're ready for it.

It won't be long now—Bhubaneshwar temple.

January 18

1:30 A.M., ISKCON BHUBANESHWAR

Don't feel obliged to write an objective or even overly descriptive "pilgrim's progress" of what we saw at ISKCON Bhubaneshwar, but it is overwhelming how Gaura-Govinda Swami's followers have praised him since his disappearance. I respect and honor it. Who was he? Lord Caitanya said, when worshiping Advaita Ācārya, "You are who you are." Kṛṣṇa knows and I can't add to or subtract from any other person.

I've got an accessible *Śrīmad-Bhāgavatam* verse to speak on (3.2.20). Makes me want to revive my *Bhāgavatam* studies with this Third Canto. Arjuna's arrows liberated the enemy, and the enemy saw and appreciated *(nayanābhirāma)* Kṛṣṇa's beauty. This is the Lord's extraordinary morality. There are degrees of liberation; Goloka Vṛndāvana is the highest. Pure love is dormant in all souls and is awakened by chanting and hearing. The pure devotee is the agent of the Lord's mercy. I thank Lord Kṛṣṇa for allowing me to speak this today.

12:30 NOON, VIP LOUNGE, BHUBANESHWAR AIRPORT

You don't have to be a big politician to get sole possession of this VIP room, you just have to have rupees. The room contains two beds and a toilet, and it's away from the maddening crowd. Again, I don't have to tell you, dear reader, what happened at the temple, but I'll say this much. After my lecture, a questioner threw me a challenge. "As you probably know," he began (but I didn't know), "two hostile camps of Gurudeva's followers exist. Some don't accept ISKCON authority and have spilt and gone to His Holiness Nārāyaṇa Mahārāja, who, as you know, is a pure devotee. What do you think of that?"

I said I didn't know anything about it and that such a thing is best discussed in an *iṣṭa-goṣṭhī* and not in a *Bhāgavatam* class. Then I spoke in favor of maintaining the temple their spiritual master had worked so hard to build, and to keep it within ISKCON as Prabhupāda certainly would want.

Later, a devotee drove us to the airport in an Indian-made Mercedes. We were given tiffins full of nice *prasādam—iddlis, subjī*, a pasta preparation, and a clay vessel full of Kṣīra-corā-gopīnātha's condensed milk from Remuṇā.

Now to wait for the airplane to Delhi. Devotees in our party are flying together, but at Delhi they'll go on to Vṛndāvana. We'll stay overnight.

Spare your ink, your pages. This is India. Relax and as always, try to drop the pose.

January 19

3:30 A.M., NEW DELHI

Sharp headache behind right eye on plane yesterday. Lay down in back of car through the chaotic New Delhi traffic. Our driver said the bus drivers in Delhi cause most of the car accidents. Ninety-nine percent of the bus drivers come from the villages, don't have licenses, and don't know any traffic rules—or even how to drive.

We arrived at Tri-kāla-jñā Prabhu's flat, and although the room was cold and the street noisy, I lay down under the heavy quilt and the sharp ache gradually subsided. Now it's the morning of another day. I'm hoping I'll be able to lecture in the temple this morning and then move on to Vṛndāvana.

This morning at the apartment in Delhi I received a phone call from a GBC man. He wanted me to give judgment regarding a controversy. It is not a role I usually like to take. The controversy troubled me all morning, and it was on my mind as I tried to chant on the way to Vṛndāvana. This ruined my approach to Vṛndāvana. The day was also cold and rainy. We saw many car and truck wrecks along the road. Our taxi was a new one, not even a year old, but the windshield wipers didn't work. The driver had to keep reaching out his side window with a rag to rub off a small portion of the windshield so he could see. Somehow or other we made it without incident.

Outside the Guesthouse I took a couple of steps out of the taxi and prostrated myself in the sand. I felt the earth touch the different parts of my body, and I rubbed sand between my fingers. I thought, "This is it. This is the place where I'll want to be at the end. Life will be grit then, like this sand."

Now we've been here a few hours, but I don't feel like I'm in Vṛndāvana yet. I don't have anything to say to people, although Madhu wants me to meet with the devotees at 4 P.M. to say hello. I can't honestly say to them that I've come to Vṛndāvana to try to find what Kṛṣṇa wants me to do or that I want to enter the Vraja mood. Not yet. Our entry is a flurry of looking for things we'll need while we're here—a desk lamp, etc. I've been struggling to come out of the slough of a headache, and I'm looking for steadiness.

5 P.M.

Head cleared, then spoke for over an hour to disciples. Told them, "Be truthful." Ranged over subjects. Tried my best. Said, "Be happy in Vṛndāvana." Boasted a little. But head clear of pain.

Got desk lamp, scrounged memories, heard dogs bark, free-wrote in sacred land protected by amenities, prayed, "Kṛṣṇa, please make me truthful—but not too painfully."

"Does your *abhimāna* [mental conception] change?" Mahā-mantra dāsa asked.

Yes, it becomes (we hope) more genuine.

I'm here.

January 20

12:40 A.M.

I wake thinking I ought to read of Kṛṣṇa and the *gopīs* since I'm in Vṛndāvana. That's okay. But don't think other topics are not nourishing or inspiring. Reading of Kṛṣṇa as a baby in Vṛndāvana is also good and leads you to becoming eligible for appreciating the son of Mahārāja Nanda in the *rāsa* dance. How can I think I am eligible to hear of Kṛṣṇa's topmost pastimes? Rest assured, that when reading and hearing Śrīla Prabhupāda's lectures, you are preparing yourself for the highest Kṛṣṇa consciousness, and a stay in Vṛndāvana will impel this.

> If someone takes advantage of hearing the pastimes of the Lord, the material contamination of dust, accumulated in the

> heart due to long association with material nature, can be immediately cleansed. Lord Caitanya also instructed that simply by hearing the transcendental name of Lord Kṛṣṇa one can cleanse the heart of all material contamination. There are different processes for self-realization, but this process of devotional service—of which hearing is the most important function—when adopted by any conditioned soul, will automatically cleanse him of the material contamination and enable him to realize his real constitutional position. Conditional life is due to this contamination only, and as soon as it is cleared off, then naturally the dormant function of the living entity—rendering service to the Lord—awakens. . . . This Kṛṣṇa treatise is meant for that purpose, and the reader may take advantage of it to attain the ultimate goal of human life.
>
> —*Kṛṣṇa*, Chap. 7

Note the phrase, "The dormant function of rendering service to the Lord . . . awakens." As unconscious material desires are dormant in the self and come out in dreams and other expressions creating "wholeness" and "balance," even deeper than that is the unconscious (covered) spiritual nature of the self as pure soul. It's uncovered not simply by letting go in drawing or writing, etc., but by hearing from a higher source. That higher source, (*śāstra*, guru) appears to be something outside our self, but actually it touches off the inherent nature of the soul. The constitutional relationship between God and the soul is objective reality but covered. Self-improvement must come to this stage. Working alone with the self in the world is not enough. The ordinary psychologist can only bring you to a certain stage of improvement and awareness, say, from the modes of ignorance and passion up to goodness. Even then it's only God's mercy that keeps us alive. The real mercy descends from the spiritual world to clean us and awaken our spiritual nature—and grant us love of God (*hlādinī-śakti*). Don't think it is merely "religious," or blind faith in dogma.

January 21

MIDNIGHT

Yesterday was a bad pain day for me, although everything is good by Kṛṣṇa's will. I went to *maṅgala-ārati* in Prabhupāda's Samādhi bundled up in layers of clothes, including my shiny silver coat. It proved to be too much clothing. The air wasn't as frigid as I had expected it to be. I realize now that my worry about the temperature was partly due to last year's visit when Madhu and I were so depleted after returning from the Naturopath clinic.

Then I confidently led the singing. After a few moments I became nervous that I might forget the words, so I meditated on my own Prabhupāda *mūrti*, to whom I sing this song every day. Still, my knees shook at the surrender it required to sing the song without worrying about how I was about to forget the words. To those who heard me, I didn't miss a word and the singing was all right, but no one saw what was going on inside. Then Puruṣatraya Mahārāja, who lives in Vṛndāvana, welcomed me with a few formal words after the *ārati*.

Then we went into the temple room for the Deities' *ārati*. I was astonished and pleased at the new painting over Śrīla Prabhupāda's *vyāsāsana*. It depicts Rūpa Gosvāmī and Sanātana Gosvāmī sitting under a tree. One of them is composing Sanskrit verses with a pen, and the other is glancing at him with a sidelong glance. Rādhā and Kṛṣṇa and various *gopīs* appear in the tree. The artistry of this painting is nice, and it held my attention. It makes Prabhupāda look extra-appealing in that setting. We went through the usual stopping before the three altars. Although it was the first time I have seen the Deities here this year and my concentration wasn't so deep, I felt the sweetness of being in Vṛndāvana.

Yesterday was the day the devotee to whom I'm supposed to talk was to arrive in Vṛndāvana. I wanted to keep my day clear for him, but he never arrived. By 10 A.M. a headache started to build, and it became pain behind the right eye. It increased and I couldn't do any work. By 3:30 P.M. I went to bed and bolted the door. The headache didn't stop until 10 or 10:30 P.M.

Vṛndāvana is out there and also
in this room
as much as I can comprehend.

I'm in Vṛndāvana with body aches and Indian long underwear with no elastic at the ankles or waist, room enough for a big belly and only two straps to make it fit my size. I get annoyed with the constant Indian deficiencies—a bathroom with weak lights so you can't see if your *tilaka* is on straight, cars that overturn, "No Berm available." What the hell is this?

Another thing about the Indian mentality: they don't shoot straight; they're polite but not cooperative. They're also pious and know Kṛṣṇa and I don't.

The big, lovable Deity.

Your heart is beating in Purī.

Ocean at Puri

Jagannātha is kind to crippled devotees.

They are so poor . . .

You defend them wherever you go because they are the repository of Vedic wisdom.

Prabhupāda wouldn't let me criticize them. He said, "Mind your own business!"

I hope I never fall down.

I hope I attain attachment, love for Kṛṣṇa, but if I don't, I hope I can at least keep exposing the truth of myself.

I hope to keep strong in my commitment not to be manipulated by others. GBC committees, etc., have their work to do, and I'm glad they're protecting ISKCON, but I have a different mission. My role is not to judge relative issues. I'm not a politician. Going my way.

8:30 A.M.

To do in Vṛndāvana:

(1) Sit in this room.

(2) Pride myself on how I was strong not to be manipulated. I call it "aggressively neutral."

(3) Thank Madhu and all those who take care of me.

(4) Tell the cooks I want small pieces of ginger, soft *capātīs*, not so much cereal. Do I dare ask for papayas with the porridge?

(5) Think of how this is the land of Rādhā-rasa.

(6) Ask for a gossip report.

(7) Read *Vidagdha-mādhava*.

(8) Write an alpha poem on the word Mug.
(Mug would be okay for putting
pens in
unless you mean "face" mug—
God-awful wind and fog.)

(9) Write an alpha poem on Sorry.
Sorry I left you alone didn't
open up, didn't do a dirty-
good turn for a friend and

really break rules in
your favor. So when it's my
turn I'll
turn to Kṛṣṇa only and
say, "I did wrong, I admit, I admit.
Now do your worst."

(10) Think about the meaning of cover-up.

(11) Don't cooperate with hanky-panky.

(12) Turn mind away from pornography models that come back specifically from magazines of past.

(13) Fight for my life.

(14) Say, "My disease is not malignant" as if I'll live forever.

(15) Look out window of this room I never leave and see only fog.

(16) Don't attend *Śrīmad-Bhāgavatam* class two days in a row and hope I don't get caught, tarred, and feathered.

(17) I can get thrown out or get in trouble in ISKCON as I could in the Navy.

(18) What about Govardhana-śilā? Or a special little rock to sit beside Śrīla Prabhupāda *mūrti*. A piece of Vṛndāvana to take with me. I could do that with some Vraja sand *(cintāmaṇi)*.

(19) I could sail clear. No storms. He was polite, I was polite—both superficial.

(20) Hey man, what's the latest?

(21) Read it and weep. My eyes can see, but my mind refuses to read *Kṛṣṇa* book. Whaddya want? Higher *rasas*?

No, no . . .

(22) No mice, only a few monkeys I saw climbing on Samādhi Mandir dome.

(23) Get out and meet the people.

I will, I will.

11:30 A.M.

Vṛndāvana is cold this time of year. I'm afraid of the next eye twinge developing. Vṛndāvana is an adventure that I'm not up to. I can hardly venture out of this room to explore. I am . . . less than a grain of sand here, but somehow I'm caught in the tide of those who come from around the world.

Back to thinking of traveling in the van. So many ifs. If the European Economic Community allows my much-stamped and faded American passport through, and if the van holds up—if Europe holds up, and our travel money and the ISKCON temples' welcome and any excuses I need to get out on the road . . .

A friend and Godbrother asked me to side with him in a controversy. I declined. If I get into a jam of my own doing, I shouldn't ask a friend to take my side either. At least not if I have to make politics. Allow Kṛṣṇa to judge. Another lesson: I don't appear to be in favor of covering up a wrong, so if I do a wrong I ought to tell it.

Eyes on ISKCON and on me. How will I act? Will I join those who think it's best to cover up a scandal? They may be morally right, but others will criticize their actions. As a *sannyāsī* I wish to remain aloof.

VṚNDĀVANA IS

Vṛndāvana is known by the veterans who
refuse to leave summer or winter.
I don't know
neither do I want to suffer in
body to stay here.
Don't love the lanes, residents, not
touched by particles of the mercy of
attraction to Rādhārāṇī's abode.
Ask me. I'll say, "Whatever is
best for headaches."
Ask me, do you love
Rādhā's *sevā*?
I'll say only that I love to hear.

2:45 P.M.

Pray.
Pray: close your eyes
and right now, what you have just read
ask Kṛṣṇa to teach you
what it means.

Keep an inner dialogue with Kṛṣṇa in this place. May Acyuta protect your feet, head, etc. As you go out on the road, may He protect you from the front and behind. May the Lord guide you from within and without.

January 22

12:20 A.M.

Saw the art place of Bhaktisiddhānta Prabhu and the team of forty devotees, mostly Russians, who work with him. Splendid place. Area of several acres, walled in, a temple in Vṛndāvana near Madana-mohana temple. They work there at art day and night. He is the master of the new devotees coming to paint *kṛṣṇa-* and *caitanya-līlā*, and who work on sculptures, all for the museum at the New Delhi temple. What can I learn from it? Can I ever work like that with artists? I don't think so. I write alone. And give out my books. I don't train others to write diaries or free-write poems. I myself have to agonize whether it's right or wrong, so how can I tell others that *they* should do it? We would be inundated with bad poetry and other outpourings. Rather, I see myself as teaching not writing but honesty, self-searching. If some keep a diary, that's their business.

Meetings each day. The little knot of a twinge is always ready to go off behind the right eye. Cat and mouse game. The editor is taking out references to my illness in a book I wrote because people won't be interested in my condition. They want to hear the notes I kept while reading *Caitanya-caritāmṛta*, but what about the human element that I struggled? Aches and pains don't belong in a book.

I asked Bhaktisiddhānta Prabhu where he and his artists get their ideas. He said they paint out of their own heads and hearts; they don't use models, and I presume they don't study Western artists. He did mention Rodin in our conversation.

Large rat running across Rādhā-Kṛṣṇa's altar at Bhaktisiddhānta Prabhu's art compound.

Each day I try to fulfill a schedule, but it all depends on whether I get a headache. Too many references to headaches bores readers. I don't mind. What I'm writing is a medical record as much as a record of everything else. Why leave out the pain?

Bhaktisiddhānta Prabhu got brain malaria, which he said is like having twenty malarias at once. People die from it. Yet while the pain was great, he dragged himself from bed and continued drawing. These drawings are later used as models for sculptures. As soon as he drew one picture, he said the pain went away. He spoke of miraculous results. Artists who have never painted before do their first painting and it comes out beautifully. It's inconceivable. He said there is a group energy which brings out wonderful images in the paintings and sculptures that had never before appeared in his work. It happens automatically by working in Vṛndāvana on this project. He's positive.

Bhaktisiddhānta Prabhu has been an artist for forty-five years, and now he's writing a book on how to do it. He's writing several other books at the same time. I ask him, "Do you sleep and eat?"

He smiled, "Not much." In a flow of continual creativity. He has worked hard to reach this stage. He showed me two painted panels that formerly took him six months to complete. Now he can do a bunch of them in a week. He has learned how to increase, how to be more in touch with Kṛṣṇa, and so on.

I come back to my little scribblings. How can I presume to be an artist? This morning I drew three little doodles of tigers, like the tigers I saw in a dream last night. I was pleased with my doodles. I'm not trying to train myself to become a realistic artist. Rather, I am interested in primitive art, some way to make them come honestly from my hand.

What's the purpose of tapping your unconscious if you're a conditioned soul? Isn't that what the critics ask? They want to know why we should pretend to be spiritual masters if actually we're conditioned. You admit it in your books, don't you? We constantly have to refine and redefine our positions.

MAṄGALA-ĀRATI IMPRESSIONS:

Today I was properly suited up, no big Western coat, but a *cādar* over my sweatshirt, and I was carrying a *daṇḍa*. I met the old devotee who gives out the *tulasī* leaves and *caraṇāmṛta* in our temple, who has been here for years. We made obeisances to each other and then I embraced him. One of his legs is a little crooked, and he walks with a stiff gait. We didn't exchange any words, just that greeting. The stone floors are cold at this time of year. I'm still not looking with devotion at the *arcā-vigraha* at the main *maṅgala-ārati*, but the Prabhupāda *mūrti* in the Samādhi Mandir evokes a presence I cannot ignore. I like the way he looks so somber, almost gaunt, with his long face, warm *cādars*, knit cap, and bony wrinkled hands.

Standing in the ranks, everyone bundled in sweaters, *cādars*, jackets. I timed my participation carefully so that I could made a quick exit into the temple room. I wanted to be there before they blew the conches.

In Vṛndāvana the trees on Bhaktivedanta Mārg are flourishing. "*Jaya* Rādhe" painted on each of them. The new *tamāla* tree in the Krishna-Balaram courtyard is also growing nicely. *Gurukula* kids wear sleeveless maroon sweaters these days, yellow *dhotīs*—still distinctive. The kids are mostly brown-colored, although some are white from Europe and America.

I saw hogs and monkeys as I walked by. I am the servant of my master, ISKCON's founder-*ācārya*.

VṚNDĀ FREE-WRITE #1

Vṛndā's song I way lay
Rādhā songs I pronounce
not to speculate
damn the rockets I say
a free-write's got to
make sense.

VṚNDĀ FREE-WRITE #2

Vṛndā is Tulasī is favorite is
lore
Rādhā is yore and new always
but not allowed to speak of Her
unless you're pure.
She's Bhakti-mātā.
Follow Prabhupāda even when
you're dull, dogmatic, blind,
eyesore, unclean—
clean up this place, this heart!
Clean up crude oil from Yamunā
and all will be well—will you die entranced?
You'll die, period.

It will be a rainy sad day
sun will shine despite your
death and new baby monkeys will
frolic and pick lice and
pilgrims will go to temples as usual
while British Airways will run on time.
Into the sea,
into the Yamunā, ashes.
Don't bury me on the lone prairie
as if I was a *mahā-bhāg*.

7:15 A.M.

Śivarāma Swami is giving the *Śrīmad-Bhāgavatam* lecture this morning and I plan to attend. Hope I'll be warm enough. Perhaps I need to ignore my bodily pains, or at least tolerate them, and then the headache wouldn't come. Yesterday I met and spoke with a *bābā* who is eighty-five years old. He spoke in a lively way, although he had trouble raising himself out of the easy chair. He was certainly doing well for eighty-five. When he spoke he didn't complain of bodily pains, laughed a lot, spoke about Kṛṣṇa consciousness and other affairs with an alert mind. Here I am, a mere fifty-seven, and I can't take extended discussions. That *bābā* gave me and my friends apples, a garland, and a small yellow cloth.

O *bābājī*, O summit of
perfection of writing art,
O daily chores and all I try to do.

I asked M. to buy *Prema Pradīpa*, a novel by Bhaktivinoda Ṭhākura which I saw in the showcase of the temple bookstore. Two days went by and only when I asked for it again did Madhu bring it in. He told me he had just read it.

"How did you like it?"

"Very much!"

I find it hard to get into. M. breezed through it, the novel form and the primary-to-advanced topics of Kṛṣṇa consciousness catching his imagination.

Almost time to go to class.

After Śivarāma Swami finished giving the class, I hesitated and almost left without greeting him. Then I turned and we embraced and talked for about three minutes. We were heading out the door and he said, "So now you're going back upstairs?" I said, "Yes." He was gently letting me return to my reclusive situation. I felt a tinge of regret as I left. I suppose my regret is expressed by the part of me that would like to be more social. Or perhaps I don't like to be seen as such a weak person who always has to "go back upstairs," but I can't have everything. If I have chosen loneliness/ aloneness, that's not so bad, if only I can make something out of it.

Looking out the window I see a huge hornet's nest hanging just a few feet away on the bottom side of the extended flat roof. It's too cold for them right now. The majority of them are huddled around the swollen hive, but many of them are stuck onto the outside of the screen and railing, as if frozen there.

Madhu just came in and remarked that we have to be careful because we're in Vṛndāvana. This morning as we walked into the temple to attend the class, I forgot to take my sandals off until I had crossed the courtyard and was just about to enter the *kīrtana* hall. Then I noticed, took them off, and Madhu took them away. When Madhu was leaving the temple, a widow came up to him and asked, "Why did Mahārāja wear his shoes in the temple?"

Madhu replied that I didn't do it intentionally.

She muttered bitterly, "It's too much! It's just too much!"

Madhu later found out from other ladies that this widow keeps an eye out for any little thing that goes wrong. I was caught in error. I have to be careful. I can't claim I walked into the temple in transcendental ecstasy and that's why I forgot to remove my shoes.

Looking down from my fourth-floor window I see into the yard of the Māyāpur-Vṛndāvana Trust homes. They're really splendid. The whole area looks like a high-class neighborhood in poor Vṛndāvana. When I see the rows of buildings with their penthouses on top, it looks like a painting of the spiritual world. Just inside the wall there's a playground for children with a slide, sandbox, and swings. Two healthy-looking American girls about eight years old are playing in the sand. Some of the workers are sitting on the edge, two of them smoking. I could see the puffs of smoke and it seemed so incongruous. The girls must have thought so too because they retreated. You can't completely wall out the world even in a compound. On a distant roof within the compound I see a woman with a stylish coat pacing back and forth, chanting. On another roof I see a poor worker with a trowel spreading cement.

In his class Śivarāma Swami stated the Vedic maxim that one should speak the truth palatably. He said that sometimes the truth is painful, but we can speak it nicely. After the lecture Dadu Prabhu asked, "Can you give an example of how the truth is painful?" Śivarāma Mahārāja replied that if we are detached, the truth is always sweet, but if we have material attachment (false ego), when the source of attachment is taken, away that truth causes pain.

Are you sorry, literary man, that you are not an apex master loving and caring for artists and training them in the school of "Satsvarūpa art"? Are you garbled and gobbledegooked? "Are you able to chant *prema-nāma*?" A disciple just asked that question. He said that a devotee recommends they always play a tape of Prabhupāda chanting *japa* in the temple so that "we'll be assured we're hearing *prema-nāma*." My disciple wants to know if it's possible Prabhupāda could empower his disciples to chant *prema-nāma*. Well, Prabhupāda teaches, and if the devotees follow, of course it is possible. *Prema-nāma* comes from Kṛṣṇa. Of course, I haven't answered whether I have *prema-nāma*. I don't. I can state that frankly. In my chanting you'll only hear someone struggling to achieve it.

The truth may be too painful for a disciple to hear—that his spiritual master doesn't have *prema-nāma*, and he has to go to Prabhupāda for that. We could say that Śrīla Prabhupāda is not the only one who has it, although we don't like to say that. But I mean, aside from him, who has it? And who actually *knows* that Prabhupāda has it? It's heresy to consider that he doesn't. But I mean, how do you *know* that he has it?

One response is that he spread the holy name all over the world, so he must be empowered with *kṛṣṇa-śakti*. Is *kṛṣṇa-śakti* the same as *prema-nāma*? I don't know. I don't know the answers to all these questions. Leave me alone.

We have to *dig* for the truth, *dig* for it. I was saying that a crow came and did nonsense and then a monkey came and did the same. At this moment they are hammering in a nearby room in the Guesthouse. The guests are disturbed—no peace —just bang! Bang! Blocking out even the normal sounds of Vṛndāvana.

Yes, the truth is painful both to hear and to admit. I get tired of all the measuring of me and of falling short of expectations. "He walked into the temple with his shoes on! This indicates that he will fall down soon for this offense." Should I apologize to the widow who complained as if she is the caretaker of all etiquette in Vṛndāvana? But that would just give her a chance to vent her bitterness because she's got her gripes.

NOON

To avoid depression caused by shame or criticism I often turn to thinking of book production. In the shower (a good place to get ideas—one of the three Bs—the bed, the bus, and the bathroom)—I thought of a mosaic with all the pieces of memory. We could have a picture that is broken into mosaic like a jigsaw puzzle. The picture could depict a person who's half a devotee and half a nondevotee, as in my picture of a sailor with a *dhotī*. It would be something like the transmigration pictures in *Bhagavad-gītā* where someone is changing into a bear because he's sleeping too much. I always feel cheerful when I think of practical service.

I COULD DO A POEM

I could do a poem on rice paper or
whatever paper was available in India.
I could get off the self trip
the feel-sorry-for-yourself—
I'm-all-alone trip.
As he let me go, my brother said,
"Are you going back up to your room now?"
What should I say instead?
Say, "I want to go with you.
I want to walk beside you and be
very happy as I used to be
with friends in youth."

But it can't be.
I see from my window the eight-year-old
girls trying to be friends and play together
but they get bored with each other—
they try to invent games
to pass the time,
it doesn't work out,
they quarrel . . .

What I did last year may not
work this year. "Vṛndāvana is"—
I wrote and then each line came out.

When *prema-nāma* comes
when *prema-līlā* comes through
will I be eligible?

Walk a few blocks around corners in
Vṛndāvana, come to a one-room flat of a
sādhu and ask him what? Ask him
to show me the truth, to press his nose
like Guru Maharaj Ji used to do?
Show the gullible follower The Light?
Is this the Divine Light Society?
I could do a poem on rice paper, he said.
I could do a poem if I were a pure devotee
or imitate Ginsberg and say
I have seen the best devotees
of my generation bloop
back into the strobe lights of *māyā*.
I've seen all the strange things
that can be done—devotees
running off in the snow
with the temple's money in a satchel.
I have heard the *ṛtviks* storm
the castle. I hear
a revolution is about to take place
and they are waiting for a self-effulgent guru
(although he has already come as
this Mahārāja or that) and who knows what
in the holy *dhāmas* . . .

I have seen the best minds in ISKCON
blooped and furry, *sannyāsīs* returning
to householder life, those
who read *Bhagavad-gītā* seriously
yet fell down
and I have seen Carl Sandburg's poem—
"The women under the gas lamps

luring the farm boys"
seen innocent ladies luring *sannyāsīs*
and the other way around—
downfall and uprisings
endless meetings
resolving nothing
because nothing can be
resolved, finally.
We're doing our best.

"No one has a sense of humor anymore," he said.
Our skin is too thin.

2:10 P.M.

I'm grateful I can wake up in Vṛndāvana from a post-lunch nap. In dreams I was being attacked by a machine that ate my flesh. I attacked back. Also in the dream, my mother and I went upstairs and she attacked me with pencils. It's *nice* to wake up and to find myself here, ready to chant Hare Kṛṣṇa and to walk over to Baladeva's house. As I walk over the sands I think, "Vṛndāvana, Vṛndāvana."

5 P.M.

I showed Bhāgavata dāsa my idea for the cover of *Memories*, the man walking east, his front half a devotee with bead bag, his back half from the 1960s holding one of Coltrane's album. I told him that one devotee suggested the sky be light on the devotee side and dark on the pre-Kṛṣṇa conscious side, but I said I didn't want to over-exaggerate that effect. Bhāgavata dāsa said yes, in Russia some of his friends said, "You devotees say everything inside your movement is good and everything outside is bad. We find that hard to take." Bhāgavata added, "Coltrane is good."

Baladeva's house was nice. A sun-warmed breeze was blowing across the veranda as we sat facing the open field of the Oriental Institute. But the cricket match going on was not so good. Still, it was pleasing to be there, and it gave me a lazy, slowed-down feeling as if I could stay there forever, chant slowly, and write. It was such an open space after being in room 42 of the Guesthouse, which is closed in, cold, and noisy.

On the road, on the path
me with head and feet—
the same feet that wore shoes into the temple,
the same head that dreamed of ramparts
spilling over with spaghetti and
my own mother attacking me
with pencils that broke against me.
I defended myself
wearing Sir Lancelot's armor.
Yes, I defend myself against all attackers.

Me on the path, the sandy
path, grave, silent,
walking, listening to how
he's gonna turn the place into heaven—
a pond in the backyard
called Rādhā-kuṇḍa/ Śyāma-kuṇḍa—
how I can come there and write and
he's feeling the oncoming sadness because
he has to go back to
the States and these days are through.
I add, "We can meet again in America—
Baltimore, Gītā-nāgarī,"
although everything is changing, changing . . .

He's built a *japa-kuṭīr* with a little
shelf, authentic, you
sit up there on a thick grass mat
with no back rest. One swami said,

DOGS AT PURI

There's a *sannyāsī*.

He's a beggar and broke.

Waiting for a catch to fill their nets.

"Book me to use the *kuṭīr*
on Ekādaśīs. I'll do sixty-four rounds."
Boy, I thought, I can't do that much.
I've got no *prema-nāma*, no *ruci* for *nāma*,
only offensive chanting?
I'll never live it down.

Aching ankle, the distractions of cricketeers
with white knee pads and
Tommy Oakland and acorns on
Staten Island, autumn leaves, Edgar Allan
Poe, falling out of Tommy's
car and my new madras shirt ripped
the anger at his wildness.
I lived to tell the tale
in the Kṛṣṇa consciousness movement
where I live a retired life, hurling
accusations at myself: "Why are you
not thinking constantly of Rādhā and Kṛṣṇa in Vṛndāvana?"
I don't deserve to.

January 23

MIDNIGHT

You're trapped in a narrow passage, like in a ship's watertight passageway, only much tighter. Reminds me of Poe's tale of horror, "The Pit and the Pendulum." How evil and criminal of those sectists to trap us like this. We didn't know what we were getting into in our visits to the various religionists. I admire one of our devotees, a rower, who strongly demonstrates that he doesn't want to be mishandled. He revolts, but I suppose we are all trapped and put in separated compartments by the evil designs of some demons.

If it so happened and I became helpless, then all I could do is chant Hare Kṛṣṇa and save my soul. You think you'd like to be a reformer and reach other trapped brothers, but the more you think it out realistically, the less advisable that seems. Are you going to plead that we break down barriers and become liberated friends? Are you going to go to the GBC with this proposal? "I had a dream we were separated and trapped. We should come together in freedom and love and make ISKCON glorious and happy."

But is there nothing I can do? Yes, I can work to break loose of the fear I have. I think of my fear of breaking the rules and being criticized as happened yesterday when I thoughtlessly entered the temple with my shoes on. A bigger falldown could happen in an unconscious moment like that and my whole life could be ruined.

All right, then turn to Kṛṣṇa and pray. Pray as you read a book, Kṛṣṇa in Vṛndāvana. Pray for *śraddhā.* That seems most important. "The evil witches . . . and the evil spirits . . . are always ready to give trouble to the body, the life air and the senses, causing loss of memory, madness and bad dreams. Like the most experienced evil stars, they all create great disturbances, especially for children, but one can vanquish them simply by uttering Lord Viṣṇu's name, for when Lord Viṣṇu's name resounds, all of them become afraid and go away." (*Bhāg*. 10.6.27–29)

5:30 A.M.

I confessed to Madhu that I felt troubled when we read yesterday about Rādhā and Kṛṣṇa's conjugal pastimes. I prefaced my remarks to Madhu by saying that I hoped what I had to say wouldn't hurt his faith in me as his spiritual master. I said that my concept of spiritual master is someone who's sincere, dedicated to Prabhupāda, and who is also piercingly honest. He shouldn't have to make a show of being a perfect devotee on the highest level. Too often someone pretends and then later has to back down in embarrassment. Madhumaṅgala has a similar conviction about the nature of the spiritual master, so we proceeded to talk about my discomfort. Perhaps I shouldn't read that type of material—I still need to think about that—but I was relieved to have discussed it with a confidential friend. It also opens up the area of discussion that I lack *any* positive feelings of devotion for Rādhā and Kṛṣṇa.

Madhu told me that this morning at *maṅgala-ārati*, he stood before Rādhā-Śyāmasundara and prayed to Kṛṣṇa, "You are very beautiful and I know that You are a debauch." In other words, he wanted to see Kṛṣṇa not as Nārāyaṇa, but with an awareness of His sportive nature. Still, the question remains: how far do we investigate Rādhā, Kṛṣṇa, and the *gopīs*? We shouldn't think that if we hold back and maintain reverence for Rādhā and Kṛṣṇa, we will be disqualified from *mādhurya-rasa*. It's all rather complicated. We don't want to rush in where we don't belong, but neither do we want to remain dull and dead with no feelings at all.

7:35 A.M.

In a few minutes we'll go down for *Śrīmad-Bhāgavatam* class. Govinda Mahārāja is singing right now—I hear his amplified voice from my perch in room 42—but I think someone else is scheduled to speak. "Don't be critiquing everyone and everything, but examine your own motives," said Lakṣmī-Nṛsiṁha Prabhu in a class a few days ago. We all live together.

Just as I left the Prabhupāda Samādhi this morning at 4:25 A.M., a devotee stopped me and said he had something urgent to say. He spoke with a German accent. "Do you believe in violence?" he asked. He said that devotees were throwing him violently out of the temple. I said I didn't know anything about the issue, so it wasn't fair to ask me such a general question about violence. He said, "Do you think it's fair that they throw me out? I've been a devotee for eighteen years." I said I don't know anything about it, about this case. He had a *sādhu's* stubble and an old saffron *cādar*, like me. Then he said, "Will you speak up for me if they try to throw me out with violence?" Since I had twice told him I didn't know anything about it, I didn't answer but turned and walked away.

As I walked away I said to Madhu, "It's a madhouse." But of course, there are many sane devotees who live in the Kṛṣṇa consciousness movement.

SHORT LINES

Reach rich widows
serve hot hannas
believe tall *śāstras*
revile rascal misleaders
miss Rādhā and Kṛṣṇa
japa your rounds.
Refuse entry to misfits
"Don't listen to helpless."
"All glories to Camp Pendelton"
and the recovery of my senses.
Sweet almond oil to you.
May Kṛṣṇa give me a little
hint which way to go.

VṚNDĀ #3

Vṛndā's secrets are kept from
reprobates like me unredeemed
nerds and ne'er-do-wells. But
I may be better than
actually meets the eye.
Or worse.

11:15 A.M.

The *Śrīmad-Bhāgavatam* lecture was exhausting. The speaker demanded eye contact and even facial response. Tired out afterwards. Leaving the temple I met Lakṣmī-Nṛsiṁha Prabhu, who told me why he's leaving Towaco and what his next service will be. When he inquired about me, I told him my health was not good. He said, "But you're writing?" Yes. When we finished speaking at the bottom of the stairs, Bhakta

Rakesh was standing behind Lakṣmī-Nṛsiṁha. He stepped forward and made obeisances, but I kept going up the stairs and not until I was halfway up did I look down and smile at him. I can't keep up the reciprocation. I'm not complaining here, but writing it down. Went to my room, bolted the door, and answered half a dozen letters. Remember that dream about being in a tight maze? Remember you wanted to write some poems?

Vṛndāvana is out there in the
temples and Govardhana Hill and
Rādhā-kuṇḍa in winter in
poverty and Indian language and
esoteric to me, the secrets
of Rādhā and Kṛṣṇa—all these
are obstacles and reasons why
I'm not permitted.

VṚNDĀ #4

Vṛndā is the *tulasī* plant?
Realize who you are. See the twig
of *tulasī*.
Nevermind your foolishness
Don't ask me—I lost a shoe
outside the temple.
Ask my mother, ask Madhu
ask *śāstra*, "Who is Vṛndā?"

I sit here waiting for hot water, for the time to say *gāyatrī*, for lunch, for my 3 P.M. meeting, for whoever else I may meet, to be alone and feel the limits of my own association. I wait for a chance to read Śrīla Prabhupāda or Bhaktivinoda Ṭhākura, and then—and then—when all things are said and done, can I say I had a good time?

"Don't act as the enjoyer"—it sounds harsh. Kṛṣṇa should enjoy and you should serve His senses.

Serve

wave

no more Purī. But what was Purī? Thinned out milk. Loud music in America. Take what you can . . .

Momentarily I'm feeling like Arjuna's description of the riven cloud. I cannot be interested in introductory topics such as that this material world is a place of suffering, and I also tire when Prabhupāda speaks a lecture where the basic ingredients are items I've heard more times than I can count—the meaning of the word Bhagavān, the three phases of the Absolute Truth, the different stages in the yoga ladder, etc.

On the other hand, I see I'm not fit to hear about Rādhā and Kṛṣṇa's conjugal pastimes. Neither do I want to study Madhvācārya, Rāmānujācārya, or Christian theology, psychology, Beat poetry. "Like a riven cloud, with no position in any sphere."

5:45 P.M.

I'm tired of being around so many people. I can't accommodate all the different viewpoints. I can't think or feel for myself under what feels like a bombardment. It's good to hear their voices, but I want to be free from having to hear so many controversies. Relax, enter a pace where you can be on your own and be by yourself. Yah, yah, blah, blah.

I read each day. Not forced to lecture on it or spew forth wisdom I don't have.

I spoke honestly to that disciple, but he didn't want to hear what I had to say. He thinks I should move outside the institution since I have such broad vision. I have no desire. I stay in ISKCON despite the straitjacket dreams.

He said, "Oh, I have learned and grown personally by going outside the institution." Good for him. I will learn by staying inside.

A brother said, "Sometimes I think I feel a conflict between my love for Kṛṣṇa and my love for Śrīla Prabhupāda." He wants my opinion. I don't have one. I don't know anything. All I know is that I don't know a damned thing.

Write a poem. This beat.

VṚNDĀ #5

Vṛndā—the *sādhus*
were sitting around a slow smothering fire and
one invited my Madhu over. He
sat with them, but they spoke in Hindi and
he thanked them while ISKCON
sannyāsīs and gurus went by
and asked, "What
are you doing there?!"

He was sitting, waiting for me to come back from my meeting.

Meanwhile, I was with this disciple hearing his conviction in his *śikṣā-guru*. We talked around the point. He praised me for being a neutral *sādhu*. I said, "Yeah, yeah." He asked if it's okay to introduce my disciples to *rāgānuga-bhakti*. "Uh, I don't have a policy," and walked down the stairs. He had someone specific in mind. "Oh, he's a special person." I didn't tell him I was wondering whether I was fit to hear of the conjugal pastimes of Rādhā and Kṛṣṇa. After this meeting I thought I would stop. I just want to serve Prabhupāda and know Kṛṣṇa. I'm nobody special.

Did I see any hogs?

Yes, a pale one. He was gentle and aware of our presence, and he walked lightly somehow on his feet. If we attacked him, he would have squealed intelligently.

Did you see any monkeys? Low-class Indians? Anyone smoking a big cigar? Did you see your father in the streets of Vṛndāvana? Did you hear Allen Ginsberg's song over the rooftops of your brain? Did it stay with you? Will Bhūrijana Prabhu come to Vṛndāvana while I am here, and if so?

Listen, there are just too many people here that I know. If I talk with all of them, it will be exposed that I don't know anything, that I'm not the best anything, that I'm not anything at all.

Hey, are you trying to prove something?

Yes, I'm trying to prove I can be a rabbit free-writer. You don't understand, you who read this. You don't know. You misunderstand. I am a lover, a *śiṣya*.

January 24

12:35 A.M.

Read Tenth Canto. Hearing Kṛṣṇa's pastimes will relieve us from suffering. It solves any mental duality and diminishes any lingering doubts. Our natural affection for Prabhupāda comes into focus. I feel confident that hearing from him will bring me to Kṛṣṇa and does not need supplementation. The pastimes of other incarnations of the Lord are not as attractive to me as hearing about Kṛṣṇa. Mahārāja Parīkṣit praises Kṛṣṇa's childhood pastimes in Vṛndāvana. This time, reading as I rise at midnight will enable me to face the social demands of life in ISKCON.

5 A.M.

When I give my *Śrīmad-Bhāgavatam* lecture on Sunday *(karmīs* don't try to solve the problems of birth and death, etc., they don't know there's a spiritual world, *śāstra*, Śrīla Prabhupāda's preaching), they will see through me. They will see my shortcomings, my isolation, my loneliness, and my foolish, superior attitude. Hurt, wounded by what has gone down, he takes an inward, arrogant air.

Yeah, bundled up family members stood through two *maṅgala-āratis* on the cold marble floors. "How are you? Good to see you. Are you going out (from Vṛndāvana) to preach sometimes?" I asked.

Yes, he says, in summer I go to Malaysia and America and Afghan Karunya. I feel inspired to preach.

Oh, see you later.

You should come to Vṛndāvana every year.

How's your mom?

Bow down. Wealthy followers support him. Take your time, I know you get headaches and your disciples are here. Take your time.

"He takes such a strong stand, and you have to accommodate his reality."

Things gathered. What's their net worth?

At *maṅgala-ārati:* A junior devotee put a straw mat on the cold marble floor for me to stand on. I deferred, so he promptly stood on it himself. I glanced over and saw Dhanurdhara Mahārāja, who is barefoot, standing on one of those straw mats. As the *maṅgala-ārati kīrtana* progressed, I noticed the singer, who was playing *mṛdaṅga*, was just inches from me on my left. The drum was loud, so I moved and stood on the other side.

"Have you been away from here?"

"Yes, I attended a fund-raising ceremony in Bombay."

"How are things over at your house?"

"Oh, all right."
"Indian factors as usual?"
"Plenty of them."

"I'm an optimist. That's my problem." (That is, if I say something is good, you have to take it down a few notches.)
"Oh."
"Do you get more headaches when you come here?"
"No. I get the same amount of headaches here or there. But I try not to have too many meetings."

Ingratiating smile, the manager looks in my direction and bows his head. I do the same. Or was he looking at somebody in front of me? I didn't get a chance to go over and speak to Govinda Mahārāja. His body looks big in the layers of clothes. *Maṅgala-ārati* in the main temple. Stand at one altar, then move over. *Jaya* Kṛṣṇa-Balarāma, *Jaya* Kṛṣṇa-Balarāma, *Jaya* Kṛṣṇa-Balarāma.

How am I feeling toward those *arcā-vigrahas*? I can't say.

VṚNDĀ #6

Vṛndā, this jerk is your
maidservant? No, not yet.
Really, he said you've
really got to slow down. Tell
that rickshaw *walla*, "*Nyet, nyet. Bās.*"
No. Ouch! Pressure points hurt
loud pain is good for you—
"your organs are responding."
Vṛndā,
America, you grow there
too, O beloved of Kṛṣṇa.

A couple of ISKCON *sannyāsīs* have paid for the construction of a big building near Krishna-Balaram Mandir. They have their building and compound walled in. On the outer wall someone has written, "Is this the way Prabhupāda wanted his *sannyāsīs* to live?"

5 P.M.

All day long I've been opting to do something other than writing. I guess it's procrastination. Sometimes it seems like a duty. I've got a bunch of letters here, from both local devotees who are here in India and the usual letters forwarded from America. I answered letters instead of writing. Then I read and prepared my *Bhāgavatam* class instead of writing. Then I ate and slept instead of writing. Then I chanted an extra round or two. Then I went to a meeting to preach about surrender—all instead of writing.

I told myself, "You don't *always* have to write. Don't force yourself." And I said, "You're not *only* a writer. You could start spending more time reading instead."

So the pressure builds. I hope it will cause me to explode into irresistible writing full of realization.

SURRENDER

Surrender to what happens,
Lao Tze said, "Flow."
Unless Kṛṣṇa's in the center . . .

Rasa dāsa wrote me that his seventeen-year-
old son was killed by a train.
Rasa wrote me that *Litany* brought
him back.
End the day in surrender.
Never forget you're not a
special guru or Kafka
fan anymore, you're a
cela, a *śiṣya*,
a *dāsa*
Dee Dee Dee surrendered to Prabhupāda.
Each one. I met an American devotee at
the entrance gate, said, "Hello, hello"
smile fading out

like on a film
fade-out—
we're all vanishing . . .
Bring us to the master's feet
before it's too late
surrendered in love.

January 25

12:30 A.M.

I'm supposed to give the lecture tomorrow on *Bhāgavatam* 7.6.3. *Sukhaṁ aindriyakam:* happiness from the senses is available in any body, hog or human. Don't bother endeavoring for it; it comes automatically (just as the miseries come) by our karma. The special prerogative of human life is to stop the suffering of birth, death, disease, and old age by Kṛṣṇa consciousness. *Na te viduḥ-svārtha-gatiṁ hi viṣṇum.* Happiness comes without effort. Trust in Kṛṣṇa. You can't improve on happiness either for yourself or for others. What is my message from this verse? Work without fear and depend on Kṛṣṇa. Reform yourself and give your effort to that. There is no point trying to change others or fighting for happiness.

O Lord, don't let
them drop it, don't let
them drop that atom
bomb on me.
Stop it, bebop it,
O Lord . . .

He's complaining (the writing subperson?) that he's not writing much because of the mail and meetings at Krishna-Balaram Mandir.

Is he saying Kṛṣṇa-Balarāma have caused the lull? Is he actually complaining to Them?

Oh, They will drive you away. Don't complain. A little stress is good. Stress means you are making a contribution.

What are the stresses? One stress might be that your "big frog in a little pond" pride has been crushed. There are those who sing better than you, those who are more expert lecturers, those who are more humble. Someone wrote me, "I thought you were reclusive and aloof, so I didn't write to you, but then in one lecture I saw you were jolly."

Does she think a reclusive life means living a life of constant frustration? Isn't socializing just as frustrating?

Someone else wrote me, "What happened to the three hundred letters Śrīla Prabhupāda wrote to Nārāyaṇa Mahārāja which were once in your possession? Tell me truly."

Does he think I'm a sinister liar, that I destroyed the letters and now won't admit it? I wrote back that I never received any letters, and that if there had been three hundred letters in my possession, or even thirty, or even *three*, I would have long ago shared them with others.

And someone else wrote . . .

Śrīla Prabhupāda wrote that dreaming is simply mental life while you are asleep. Generally he seems to think it's material and therefore of no value, but a Kṛṣṇa conscious person may also dream spiritually, and that's precious. Sometimes

O master, I desire to serve you.

I will not abandon my worship of Śrīla Prabhupāda.

Your debts to
others will be
absolved if you
just worship
Govinda

GUYS
HANGIN'
around
but
they
are
Devotees

Kṛṣṇa gives messages through dreams. But it depends on your advanced state of Kṛṣṇa consciousness whether you can receive them. In my case, I don't claim that my dreams are valuable in themselves, or even that the messages I receive are from Kṛṣṇa, but they certainly are messages from my unconscious and they have more frankness and artistry than what I capture from the conscious state. I'm already writing as much as I can in the spirit of self-examination and purification. Sometimes I have writing blocks and don't know what to say, and I certainly can't see metaphors and symbols in my life in a way that I can put into prose or poetry. All that comes ready-made in a dream. How can I refuse to notice them? Therefore, in the spirit of *yukta-vairāgya* I sometimes record my dreams in writing and try to make sense out of them to improve my Kṛṣṇa consciousness.

Like this one:

A large troupe of actors and actresses are going to do *Hamlet*, but they don't have the determination to work together. Somehow they are thrust together on location, and gradually they decide they should work together. They make this decision partly because they see how much freedom they have to be with each other in various ways. For example, two members of the orchestra decide to get married. Others make different commitments to each other. Eventually, they decide to do the play.

The dream goes on to combine different images, and the actors and actresses are eventually cast in their roles. Some of them are outstanding, some minor. And there are elephants. The dream is not so much about the play, but about the actors and actresses arriving at commitment.

A dream from my own attempt to harmonize elements within myself and even outside of myself. I haven't become successful at that yet, but eventually I'll have to surrender and "put on the show."

If it actually takes so many subpersons to pull off this show, it is only by Kṛṣṇa's grace that they would all cooperate and become inspired. It reminds me of Bhaktisiddhānta Prabhu's art family where he has forty devotees pulling together and producing astounding artwork. I too would like to produce excellent works. Maybe the dream source is telling me that something more elevated and harmonized could be undertaken. But since I'm committed to free-writing, it will have to come spontaneously. Even Shakespeare wrote without blotting his page. It just came to him.

TRIBE DREAM

Tribe sends out dreamers—
"Don't come back until you get a good one."
Recent results? They sit around
campfire and discuss them. Look for peace—
Indians, Americans, rich and poor
share their dreams. Look for wisdom.
"But it's already in the *śāstras*."
Yes, but it must come through me.
Each one holds their post,
deploys, reports, seeks the good
of the whole.

Dreamer! We scorn them, we
practical people:
"Religious folks don't dream unless
they are pure devotees."
Each night, each sleep
another chance.
Ask your dream self, "Help me find
the deep inspirations."
May I commit myself to dreaming
even when awake—
See the dream of a Kṛṣṇa conscious
world and me working for it,
dream I'm serving my master,

I am with him,
accepted into his entourage,
dream my way
back to Godhead.

SUBLIME THEATER

Actors gather and
choose to work
beyond my control
past false ego . . .
The holy name Hare Kṛṣṇa Hare Rāma . . .
the birth of "theater"
despite the frivolity, the bid
for freedom they
come together and work
and commit themselves to art.

Oh, make it true
make it art for Kṛṣṇa
make it pleasing to Vaiṣṇavas
in verse, like Rūpa Gosvāmī
the best playwright
his actors and Vṛndāvana stage
to be read again and again!
Act it in love
to the best audience . . .
Each moment in Vṛndāvana precious:
given to me
a golden chance—

theater for Kṛṣṇa,
Rādhā-Kṛṣṇa *līlā*
in the universe of Goloka—
never mind the dirt and the hogs
and my own wretched surmises.
Banish it, bath it in His perfect words,
the dirty mind released.

5 A.M.

Śrīmatī Rādhārāṇī was wearing a heavy silk shawl this morning. Their warm clothing is not as warm as you'd like Them to have, or what a human being might require for comfort. That Kṛṣṇa and Balarāma are barefoot reminds me that They are spiritual; there is no question of Them being cold. The shawls are really an offering of service more than a practical necessity. Kṛṣṇa-Balarāma, Rādhā-Śyāma, and Gaura-Nitāi stand in transcendence. They're not marble statues, although I'm a statue before them, cold in heart and cold in body.

I've got my Post-its in the *Śrīmad-Bhāgavatam* for tomorrow's lecture. Material happiness and misery come automatically, so "don't bother about it." As soon as you try to find happiness, your miseries begin. The remedies that you seek to counteract suffering turn out to be worse than the suffering itself. (In 1967 I remember Prabhupāda saying that LSD was like that.) Later in his life, Prahlāda Mahārāja received similar good instructions from a *sannyāsī* who was found lying in the road like a python. That *avadhūta sannyāsī* said that from his observations, so-called sex pleasure brought only misery. Therefore, he was no longer taking part in such activities. He was just lying in the road and meeting his bodily necessities as Nature provided them and without any effort on his part at all. In another early lecture, Prabhupāda was pleased to remark that one of his disciples was depending on Kṛṣṇa for temple maintenance. Prabhupāda said that that doesn't mean we should be lazy and not do anything, but we should work fearlessly. Kṛṣṇa supplies His devotees' necessities. After this, I may give a reference to Bhaktisiddhānta Sarasvatī on this subject and whatever else Kṛṣṇa inspires me to speak.

As you see, I have solid references, so I will make a moderate trot through these topics one after another. Then I will have put another duty behind me.

11 A.M.

Just before going down to hear Dhanurdhara Mahārāja's class, I felt the budding of a twinge behind the right eye. I calculated that it might go down and that it was very important for me to attend the class. He'll be attending my class tomorrow.

As I sat in his class the headache gradually settled in, like a mole digging in the earth, and began to flower. Dhanurdhara Mahārāja's verse was about Prahlāda Mahārāja, but he soon shifted to praising Parīkṣit Mahārāja for tolerating the pain he was experiencing by not eating and drinking, and because he didn't lament even though he knew he would die within a few days. It was sincere praise, but I wondered what it had to do with us—that spiritual giant so far above us.

Now I've come back to my room. Tried sleeping off the pain, but it hasn't worked. Dhanurdhara Mahārāja once told me that when you're sick, the one pleasure you have is that you're the object of other's compassion. Mahārāja Parīkṣit renounced this in favor of feeling compassion for those who were consigned to hell. Instead of looking to his own suffering, he inquired how they could be saved.

As Dhanurdhara Mahārāja spoke, I doubted that a chronically ill person is always the object of compassion. Rather, he is often misunderstood.

The "story" of a headache may not be so interesting, but I track it as I track dreams, as I track the day. Literary soul. Record-maker. I just hope I'm well enough to give my class tomorrow. Big performance.

January 26

1 A.M.

I had to take rest for the night yesterday at 3:30 P.M., but all night long the sharp pain persisted behind the right eye. Sometimes I sat up in bed, but soon layed down again. I couldn't sleep. I heard the monkeys crying and grunting on the roof, or the noises they make when they jump and run up and down the boards in the light of the near-full moon.

I tried to think that this pain is Kṛṣṇa's will for me, but that didn't make it any easier. I kept worrying about not being able to give the *Bhāgavatam* class. Let it go. Wait out the pain. I'm no Mahārāja Parīkṣit with his quality of forbearance.

During the night I had a dream in which I had a headache. I walked into my father's room, but he was sleeping. Finally, he opened his eyes. He was handsome, like my father. "How are you?" I asked.

"All right."

"I'm having a really bad day. I have such a painful headache."

Then he noticed a few things wrong with me that were causing my headache—my neck beads were too tight and had something caught in them. He mentioned a few other things, then told me to rest and take it easy.

When I awoke I thought that my father had been loving and caring. He was a younger version of my father, and he resembled me. I took it that he was some part of myself, a male source coming to give me solace—not exactly the spiritual master, but a caretaker extension of the spiritual master. Śrīla Prabhupāda is my guide, and he has assistants who help him to guide me. It was a difficult night and it's a difficult life with a chronic illness, but I have help to get me through in a manly way.

Yesterday during the headache pain I was telling Madhu how difficult it is to be in ISKCON Vṛndāvana because of the social pressure, yet I would not want to come to Vṛndāvana and live outside the temple. I said that I might not come next year. He said he agreed, "but you're here now."

I'm here now and I'd better not complain while in the holy *dhāma* about being in the holy *dhāma*.

1 P.M.

I couldn't give the class today, but I'm scheduled to speak tomorrow. I'll use many of the same references I had for today's verse. I have a good opener: In the beginning of this chapter, Prahlāda Mahārāja says that human life is very rare and that one should use it to learn *bhāgavata-dharma.* He should start his education at five years old. Prahlāda then said that the Supreme Lord Kṛṣṇa is our dearmost friend. Therefore, we should search Him out. The children to whom he was preaching objected. They preferred to play now and search for Kṛṣṇa later in life. An adult might object in a similar way: "If I search out Kṛṣṇa, how will my material necessities be met?"

After this, I have a number of references, but my planned lecture seems to peter out with no relevant message for today's devotees. They're likely to ask me nitty-gritty questions about economic development and dependence on Kṛṣṇa. They'll want to know where the dividing line is between surrender and obligation.

I heard this morning that a woman devotee asked the lecturer, "Why does ISKCON mistreat its devotees when they grow older, or neglect them completely?" If I were asked such a question, I might reply, "Just because I'm giving the *Śrīmad-Bhāgavatam* lecture for half an hour today doesn't mean I have the answers to all of ISKCON's problems." But that probably wouldn't satisfy such a questioner.

2 P.M.

VṚNDĀ #7

Sitting on porch, I'm in Vṛndāvana.
Vṛndā, save me, my head gets—
you know.
Repeat Prabhupāda's messages and
never tire. Please bless me with that.
Don't let me stray from his feet.
Prabhupāda is "good enough"—
let my words help others.

VṚNDĀ #8

Vṛndāvana-dhāma, damn my
hard dull etcetera.
Rāma Rāma Ramaṇa
the words of the sense-
enjoyer can never know peace
nor soothe the hearing of
aspirant devotees.

Vṛndā. Baladeva's house. The cricket game continues. I'm facing away from it as I write, facing a man painting a railing on the building next door. Sitting on the veranda, four of us chanting *japa*. Peaceful, cool January afternoon at Sant Colony. Nārāyaṇa Mahārāja has gone to Australia, and his *śiṣya*, my one-time disciple, has gone to a book fair in Calcutta.

I've stacked up six books I've decided I'm not going to read in India. Find someone to carry them back to America. I probably won't read them there either. Then carry them to Ireland. Śrīla Prabhupāda says the scholar is like a donkey carrying books here and there and never reading them. Ah, me. Is Frankie Sinatra dead yet? If so, why didn't they tell me? And Sid Ceasar? And Imogene Coca? Did they get a divorce? Will I be able to let all this go?

I used to write of my sublime struggle here years ago in this house. It was 1992. Now I'm hardened to that particular struggle. I have stopped trying to learn all the technicalities of *bhakti* and am concentrating more on my need for honesty and heart. But I need *śāstra*, and in particular, Vraja-Kṛṣṇa.

Kṛṣṇa Kṛṣṇa, I filled up a glass vial with Vraja sand from just outside the Krishna-Balaram Mandir gate.

In Vṛndāvana I sprained a joint but never smoked one. In Vṛndāvana there are secrets revealed to sincere devotees. In the past, Śyāmānanda found a bracelet belonging to Śrīmatī Rādhārāṇī. That kind of miracle can't happen to me. Give me a red dot on the forehead. I belong to She who loves Śyāma. It would be nice to be marked as belonging to Śrīla Prabhupāda.

Listen, friend, there's no pen like this fat, black Sheaffer. I decided writing is as good as chanting or reading. Each has its place. Hare Kṛṣṇa Hare Kṛṣṇa, Kṛṣṇa Kṛṣṇa Hare Hare/ Hare Rāma Hare Rāma, Rāma Rāma Hare Hare.

January 27

12:15 A.M.
VṚNDĀ #9

Vṛndā, I'm rising
at midnight
"Never fear," the Lord says.
Don't you know I fear
and I'm seeking solace
in Your names—
O Kṛṣṇa, Lord of Vṛndā.

Just depend on Kṛṣṇa for protection. This was the standard of the residents of Vṛndāvana. When Tṛṇāvarta was killed falling from the sky, Kṛṣṇa was unharmed. Thus the

Vrajavāsīs concluded that the sinful demon died, but pious Kṛṣṇa was protected by God. *Āhāra-nidrā-bhaya-maithuna*—these four are always active in life, but a devotee transcends them. Even fear doesn't reach him because he fully depends on Kṛṣṇa for protection.

Why am I trying to figure things out by myself, to be truthful, nourished, gain a little wisdom, etc.? Just depend on Kṛṣṇa.

January 27, 1997

ISKCON Vṛndāvana

Dear Godbrother,

Please accept my humble obeisances. All glories to Śrīla Prabhupāda.

I wanted to place before you a problem I have been having for some years now regarding my visits to Vṛndāvana-dhāma. I don't think you will be able to solve this for me in a decisive way, because it's something like a personal problem and a situation I don't think can be entirely controlled, but I would be grateful to hear your realizations as a friend, and especially because you are so deeply acquainted with living in Vṛndāvana.

Whenever I come to Vṛndāvana, I find that it becomes an intense period of socializing, with pressure from Godbrothers and disciples. There really doesn't seem to be any off-season at ISKCON Vṛndāvana, because *whenever* I come it's the same. It's natural that at this temple more than any other temple in ISKCON, one is likely to meet devotees from anywhere in the world. Also, ISKCON controversies often seem to be focused here. This has been my experience in recent years, and although I tend to forget it when I'm away and again desire to return to Vṛndāvana, as soon as I arrive I have the same experience. Then the tension begins to build day after day, week after week, until the pressure becomes almost unbearable for me and I find myself looking forward to leaving. This pressure usually means more headaches than usual, and also anxiety because when I have pain, I can't perform the duties I am expected to perform. Neither do I find devotees overly sympathetic toward my chronic illness.

This year I decided not to give the VIHE seminar, but that doesn't seem to have alleviated the pressure.

One alternative I considered is coming to Vṛndāvana and living outside the ISKCON temple. I did that one year when I lived at Baladeva's house for four weeks to write. I didn't visit the temple at all during the period I was writing. The writing went well, and the fact is that I produced some of the best writing I have ever done about Vṛndāvana (it was included in the front of the book called *The Wild Garden*). After those four weeks, however, a great sense of obligation had built in me that now I should participate fully in temple life, and once I did, the usual pressures developed, devotees wanted to meet me, my refusing to meet displeased them, letters poured in, and there were so many demands and controversies.

Neither do I like to live outside ISKCON because I don't think it sets a good example. I mean, not just living a few blocks away from the temple, but the idea of living here and not going regularly to the programs. If sometime during the year I want to take a writing retreat, I would never think of doing it in Vṛndāvana for this very reason. I find some other more remote place in the world more suitable.

But I don't think this is a good attitude to take toward the most sacred place in the universe. I may be developing an offensive attitude toward Vṛndāvana as I come here, complain, and so on. This year I even said to Madhumaṅgala that next year we might not come. It almost seems like I'm starting to not like Vṛndāvana, and that's bad.

Also, I have a permanently crippled ankle. After walking about an hour on any one day, I can't walk the next day, or if I were to walk two days in a row, then I can only walk for a short period. This, my tendency for headaches, and my general temperament, prevent me from having much enthusiasm for going out. I can't even do the two- or three-hour *parikrama* around Vṛndāvana, although I know it's a blissful and purifying experience.

I like to *read* about the Vṛndāvana of the spiritual world in *Kṛṣṇa* book and other books, and I like it here also, despite my complaints. Even here in room 42 I can feel the blessings seeping through the walls. But mostly my stay in Vṛndāvana is rewarding because I feel I have fulfilled the obligations I have to meet disciples and Godbrothers. It's an austere *yajña*. I go away from Vṛndāvana thinking I have paid some dues, but not with the bliss of falling in love with the place, tasting its simple life, tasting its intense devotion to Kṛṣṇa even found in the ordinary residents—and what to speak of the deeper secrets of Vṛndāvana, of Rādhā-Kṛṣṇa *bhajana*.

I would be appreciative of your comments on this predicament. Thank you.

I hope this meets you in good health.

Your servant,

Satsvarūpa dāsa Goswami

7:30 A.M.

In just a few minutes I'll go down to give the *Bhāgavatam* class. I'm not afraid. The flurry of excitement for writing some kind of fiction of dream incidents has passed. If it wants to overpower me and come back with a novel-length dream, then fine, but I'm not up to it yet. Staying with *Every Day, Just Write*.

Of course, even within this *Every Day, Just Write*, I could tell small "stories" from my dreams, but I really have to want to do it. Seems odd to be thinking about such a thing here, a story set in Norway while I'm here in Vṛndāvana.

Well, what do I want? A sequel to *Choṭa* (as one devotee suggested)? Choṭa goes to India and meets a *mahā-bhāgavata*, who tells Choṭa to settle there. In response to this suggestion I wrote back, "But I have not met a *mahā-bhāgavata* who told me to do that." I have to experience these stories before I can write them. Yes, the whole thing should run through me.

That may be one of the reasons I can't plunge into telling dream stories. I don't even know what the dream story means, so how can I repeat it?

VṚNDĀ #10

Vṛndā, I'm so low-powered—
railroads don't know me
never make sense,
don't look behind
always wasting time.

VṚNDĀ #11

Vṛndā, there's the nicest *tulasī*
house in Wicklow
really you'd like it, kept
by Hare Kṛṣṇa dāsī—names
of *tulasīs* like "dear to Kṛṣṇa"
written on each pot.
Never missing care, the
plants thrive.
Dear Lord, please make
me a maidservant.
Always pray like
that? You don't?

IN VṚNDĀVANA

Oh, the parrots are singing or
is that the crows? Yes, it's caws.
How could I have mistaken it?
Low-powered listening, crawling
confession. Oh, I am not
a harmless loser . . .
I don't care. Get straight now.

This is Vṛndāvana where saints live—
go out and see them carrying
just the right staff for
walking down Bhaktivedanta Mārg.
Check them out.
Bhakti-rasa dāsa wandered
off the *parikrama* trail to what
looked like an ideal
little thatched roof mud-walled
village but the young boys gathered
and stoned him! He ran away
in his bright orange Western
winter coat and they
pursued and he felt purified.

In Vṛndāvana hot water's on the way, and I get at least two headaches a week. ISKCONites want to help relieve my pain—a girl from Ukraine said she can do it with acupressure, but I won't let her try. Bhāgavata dāsa from Russia says, "I'm different from those who cause pain trying to relieve a headache while it's on."

In Vṛndāvana I gave the lecture to over a hundred bundled up devotees in the temple room. We didn't speak about *rasa* or conjugal moods, only straight-from-Prabhupāda examples on the verse translated by Prabhupāda, our master. Was it okay? Passable.

I looked out and saw
one *sannyāsī* with scarf wrapped
over neck and mouth
and the other eccentric one,
eyes rolled up and
when I looked again he was asleep.
Someone asked me after the speech,
"Why did Bhaktisiddhānta Sarasvatī

chastise his disciples when they didn't
give the beggars some paisa?"
Because he saw they were hard-hearted.

In Vṛndāvana today it's cold and
dark-skied, yesterday it was sunny.
I like the sunny days
when the heart lightens and I think
I'm going to make it through.
But I can't chant with love
or remorse, or *anything*.
Lord, Lord, help me.

IN VṚNDĀVANA

Quiet, the bell is ringing for
noon. You just have to listen
as all Vṛndāvana chimes in
even in this room.
The heater hums except when
the electricity cuts off—
as it does at 6 A.M. when I eat breakfast
in the dark and light candles to see by.
Then the heater comes on
and I remember I was dreaming
awake in Vṛndāvana.

In Vṛndāvana while lecturing
I noticed Aindra Prabhu wrapped
in woolen robes
just like the ones Bhāgavata Purāṇa
dāsa is wearing—the uniform of the
twenty-four-hour *kīrtana*-ers.
My uniform is a knit cap from New York,
a sweatshirt from London,
a wrist watch from Hong Kong,

Tīrtha-going.

Vṛndāvana! Vṛndāvana!

Painting the holy form in the holy land.

Bundled up.

Glider slip-on shoes from Purī,
and Fixodent pasted-in teeth
from Brescia—
and all this paraphernalia
I'm carrying from state to state.

Vṛndāvana catechism: I believe in the holy ghost, the forgiveness of sins, in Akrūra-ghāṭ, and the old mother who wears saffron, and everyone's right to be disappointed in me. I believe in the sands of Ramaṇa-reti.

I believe I will get out there and see it.
I believe in Abhirāma's house and the reddish
flowers that grow there on that metal frame.
I believe Bhagatji lived there and
gave me an orange once.
I believe in Prabhupāda
who makes all this remembrance possible.

WALK

Walking your ankle says
okay, me too in Vṛndā-
ban.
Always look around for
sights to treasure—
laugh while you can
stumble your mantras
add to footprints in the sand,
Kṛṣṇa's calling you.

Impressions from a walk:

Madhumaṅgala, Śamīka Ṛṣi, and I walked down the *parikrama* trail in the direction of the Madana-mohana temple. Although the morning was cold, it was sunny and we soon found we were wearing too many clothes. I took off my scarf, sweatshirt, and hat. At one point we came upon two little boys no more than eight years old. They walked beside us for awhile. I asked one of them to chant Hare Kṛṣṇa. He didn't respond. Then Śamīka Ṛṣi asked him again in Hindi, "Hare Kṛṣṇa *bol*," and the boy responded. A little later a group of more than half a dozen older boys came toward us. They were boisterous, almost challenging, saying, "Hare Kṛṣṇa, *haribol*." We replied and they said a few other things—I don't know what—and had a laugh. We saw the old spots we've seen in previous years. Some things have changed, new walls built, etc. We bowed before the two trees—the Kṛṣṇa-Balarāma tree and the other tree at Ramaṇa-reti. We reached the ISKCON *gośālā* and saw many cows crowded onto their land. They were mooing and grunting. Walking on sand. I became tired and didn't want to walk further, but we at least got within sight of the Madana-mohana temple. I said that another day we could go by rickshaw to see Rādhā-Dāmodara.

So we returned, sometimes meeting *sādhus*. *Everyone* is colorful in Vṛndāvana. Even seeing a man and his wife is fascinating. I saw one man watering his large garden by holding a bucket in his left hand, reaching in with his right hand, and splashing water in the deft way Indians have. I saw the same thing yesterday from Baladeva's roof where a man was thinning a paint job by first spreading water out in that same hand-flicking way.

We walked under one tree which was full of loud crows. We saw many little chipmunks or Indian squirrels everywhere we went. And old trees with old vines wrapped around them. As we came up the road on our way home, a fifty-year-old Indian man wearing a *paṇḍita's* hat stopped us. Apparently, he was the leader of a group of about a dozen people. He spoke good English and had the verve of a professional interviewer. All he lacked was a microphone to hold in my face. He asked each of us which country we had come from and for our impressions of India. I said that my impression was that India is the land of truth and religion. Then he wanted to know my second impression, so I added that people in India have forgotten to practice their culture, but they seem to remember it at heart. He kept pushing for more impressions, and I didn't have anything else to say, so I introduced him to Śamīka Ṛṣi. Śamīka Ṛṣi is from Madhya Pradesh, and it turned out that this man was too. Finally, after interviewing us as much as he could, asking what holy places we had been to, how long we were going to stay in India, etc., he finally let us go. His name is Surendra Singh. A pleasant chap.

There were many more particular impressions that my senses took in which I hope to remember at another time—the shape of the cows and bulls, details of the chipmunks, the twist to the trees.

Toward the beginning of our walk in Ramaṇa-reti, a row of tractors drove by one after another. Each had the word "Svaraj" written on the side. Also, wherever that *sādhu* has written "Rādhā", someone has added "Kṛṣṇa." The signs now say, "*Jaya* Rādhā-Kṛṣṇa." I joked that the one who wrote Rādhā was like the parrot who praises Rādhā. Now the Kṛṣṇa parrot has come by and glorified his master.

From my bed on this fourth floor of the Guesthouse I have a good view of the end portion of the *prasādam* hall. It's outdoors and covered with a metal roof supported by brick columns. It's part of an old building that for many years wasn't part of ISKCON property but has since been acquired. I can just hear the men singing, "*Śarīra avidyā jāl . . .* "

In front of that area is a path where devotees walk when they cut across between the temple and the MVT buildings. It's interesting to see Western devotees mixing with the Vṛndāvana dust and with the brown-bodied Indian devotees. Sometimes you see a little kid from Sweden or America dressed in a combination of Western sports clothes and an Indian *dhotī*. And they mix right in with the stray dogs, *chaukīdārs*, crows, pigeons, parrots, and monkeys. The monkeys are never welcome down at the *prasādam* area. Sometimes I hear a yell as someone shouts to chase away a monkey that has comes too close. I'm sure the monkeys get their dinner later, after the devotees have gone.

On the *gurukula* roof I see yellow *dhotīs* hanging on the line to dry. In about twenty minutes Bhāgavata dāsa will be here to give me my evening's head and neck massage, then acupressure. I relax through the pain his hard pushing at the sore points causes. Without my asking for it, Śamīka Ṛṣi gave me an anesthetic aerosol called Lidocaine. You're supposed to stick it in your nostrils and spray, and it gets rid of headaches. I'm sure Madhu will be completely against it, and I ought to be also, but believe it or not, I'm thinking to try it in case it can do anything to help with those twenty-hour headaches.

January 28

12:20 A.M.

I'm reading about Kṛṣṇa showing Mother Yaśodā the universal form. A speculation occurred to me: how could Vyāsadeva write these pastimes? How did he know they happened? Lord Kṛṣṇa and Vyāsa collaborated to write the *Bhāgavatam*. Vyāsadeva is himself an incarnation of God, so it's not surprising that he knew the Lord's pastimes. After Nārada coached him, Vyāsadeva sat in meditation and saw the Lord with all His internal energies as well as the material energy.

Then I thought that the act of writing down the pastimes was almost as important as the pastimes themselves. Or, you could say one reason for Kṛṣṇa enacting the pastimes is that He wanted them to be recorded for the people of the future.

Otherwise, what is the meaning of our saying that Kṛṣṇa came to this earth to perform His pastimes in order to attract the living beings back to Kṛṣṇaloka? How would He attract them? He would perform His activities within the one hundred and twenty-five years He remained on earth, and then the billions of people who came after that would never hear about them—unless they were written down.

My next thought may seem a ridiculous application of this teaching to some, but I'll put it here anyway. It occurred to me that I'm living my life in order to write it down, and that's not such a bad thing. My life is not a "pastime," something glorious to be remembered forever, but it's still worth recording because I am following Prabhupāda's instructions. I drew two lessons from this: (1) I should live my life as ideally as possible so that I don't leave a disastrous, tawdry record; (2) I should take the recording of it as important.

I've got my material ready for today's disciples meeting. First I'll answer a written question that was handed me regarding how we can be confident as we practice Kṛṣṇa consciousness. Then I'll read a segment from *Cc. Āśraya* and discuss how to read Prabhupāda's books. Then I'll talk about *japa*, then ask Śamīka Ṛṣi to tell how he met Prabhupāda in 1973. He asked him how to control the mind while chanting. He can relate Prabhupāda's response. Then I'll read from *Nāmāmṛta* and comment that I have faith in the process of *japa*, even though I haven't yet achieved the desired result. Then we'll chant one round together.

After that, I'll read some segments from *Wild Garden* and talk about our relationship as guru and disciple, which includes their reading my books.

Some people say I'm not a guru. I should agree. But I have to dance. And it's not a monkey's dance. There's no turning back from this basic commitment. I simply have to purify it.

VṚNDĀVANA

Vṛndāvana, I'm on the surface,
scratching my skin.
I rest and read and write and work in
room 42.
Do I never go out? Walked to
within sight of Madana-mohana Mandir and turned
back with sore feet, head fogged.
Don't tell us.
I will.
Vṛndāvana is
my spiritual home. I aspire to die here.
That will be the end of
another ISKCON chapter when
Brahmānanda, Satsvarūpa, etc., finish up—
the class of '66 one by one goes
(we hope) to join with Swamijī.
And Vṛndāvana? Go to Kṛṣṇa
and His friends if you
have the *laulyam*, and *that* comes after
lives of sincere practice
with His full mercy.

5:30 A.M., ESCAPE ROUTES

Words worth black sonnets cutey-pie Everest crescents.

Doo be doo be doo be get away from your life sometimes. The way out is to avoid nerve endings and to write pleasantly here in this notepad without saving it for later.

Save it for Mother who dreams of Norway and two girls who tell him he can ride with them. Wink and wake up, you're free of pros and cons, potatoes, and nightly

accuse I don't
free runs down helicopters
Kṛṣṇa Kṛṣṇa Kṛṣṇa is
Soopreme and I'm tired of acting (like to just Be). Well, you can do it at least on this page.

Escape routes. Can this page take a little pen action, or is it too sorry for that? Seems to go okay. You can't always escape and don't want to, but I'd like to write it out.

Lie back and rest. You forgot to pray. I'm tired of reading my books, can't read Śrīla Prabhupāda's unless I'm *up* for it. And someone else's and passports and tired of Ready McFreddy. Tired of posing and passing Francs,
fake you gotta stay with it.

11:05 A.M.

Some good things are happening here in Vṛndāvana. I'm feeling a growing conviction about my exclusive dependence on Śrīla Prabhupāda. That came up strongly in 1993. It's still growing. It's fed by the challenge of ISKCON devotees taking shelter of Nārāyaṇa Mahārāja. My dependence on Śrīla Prabhupāda is also fed by my seeing a Godbrother leave his post—he gave up guru duties and *sannyāsa*—and by signs of others deviating. I can only depend on the strength I get from Prabhupāda. It's that strength that enabled me in 1966 to give up my nasty habits and to continue on the platform of decent obedience. I don't say it's only the chanting that has helped me; it's the chanting as Śrīla Prabhupāda gave it to me.

A Godbrother wrote me, "I feel our prime duty as the spiritual leaders of ISKCON is to bring *bhakti* more and more into our heart. Vṛndāvana has a special potency to facilitate that." He advised me to come to Vṛndāvana only for the purpose of deepening my attraction for the holy name, but he also acknowledged that as a senior man, I have to fulfill obligations wherever I am in ISKCON. He suggests I come here and not announce disciples' meetings. "You can meet them in America." He suggested I live outside ISKCON Vṛndāvana when I come here, and attend the temple two or three times at the beginning, then again at the end of my stay. Use Vṛndāvana for a retreat.

"I would strongly encourage you in this regard to take care of your own needs, but if it disturbs you that you are setting a bad example if you do—then that will also disturb you. I beg you not to be disturbed, and set the example of keeping Vṛndāvana sacred for yourself."

I like the principle of coming to Vṛndāvana to purify my heart and not thinking of it as a chore full of institutional obligations. I set myself up for suffering in that way, and the result is I may become offensive toward Vṛndāvana. On the other hand, I cannot conceive of using Vṛndāvana for a retreat without living or at least participating in the Krishna-Balaram temple. When we hear that someone has come to Vṛndāvana and doesn't come to Prabhupāda's temple, we think something is wrong with him.

I think I will no longer announce to my disciples in advance that I'm coming to Vṛndāvana. In that sense I will try to use Vṛndāvana for my own spiritual needs. I'll be discussing the details of this in coming weeks and months with Madhu, working out whether we'll actually come back next year and how. And when we do come, it can be for some specific function such as chanting sixty-four rounds a day, living near the temple, and participating a little, but especially making it known that I've come for a *japa-vrata*.

JAPA LOG, JANUARY 28
KRISHNA-BALARĀM MANDIR, VṚNDĀVANA

I propose to take notes during the day. At the end of the day I'll note the total rounds done and make a summary or final statement. This is an attempt to get my *japa* "going". It seems to have no feeling. My only purpose seems to be to count each round in the sixteen minimum quota. No prayer, no attention, hardly any hearing of the actual mantras, hardly any attempt to control the flickering mind.

This log is a small gesture to indicate that I'm seeking improvement. I might also write here other ideas I have for improvement, and anything to encourage me about the importance of *japa* in my life.

JAPA LOG, 9:45 A.M.

Seventeen rounds. I heard of a Godbrother who is in Vṛndāvana but who doesn't come to the ISKCON temple. I heard that he's chanting a high quota *japa-bhajana*. I thought of going to see him to talk about chanting on beads, but I decided not to. I'll talk with myself.

Want to increase the quantity?

I heard Bhakti-rasa dāsa chants *japa* on the roof. Maybe I could go up there and try it out. But in many ways, this room is an ideal *bhakti-kuṭīr*. The door is bolted, a sign on it in both Hindi and English says, "Do not disturb," and an arrow points all would-be intruders to Madhu's room. I am free to chant here. But I don't want to. Have no taste.

My health limits me from vigorous quotas.

A deadness prevents me from pushing on with extra rounds or from relishing the bare sixteen. For now I must proceed with firm faith in the principle that chanting will produce the sweet taste which I now find bitter.

JAPA LOG, 5:45 P.M.

Total of twenty rounds today. This writing makes me conscientious. Some devotees say, "I feel that my daily chanting starts only after I complete my sixteen rounds." A little extra quantity makes for hope—adventure in *japa*.

January 29

12:10 A.M.

My first impression on waking is that I gave too much at the disciples' meeting. Boasted of tangibly entering a sacred consciousness while reading Śrīla Prabhupāda's books. Asserted that firm faith in the chanting of Hare Kṛṣṇa will relieve *avidyā*. Boasted that my personal writing is a unique contribution to ISKCON—a search for the authentic. As a result I'm humbled, reduced.

To ashes?

No, to my real size. I even dreamt of being a tiny chanter. I'll tell it in my dream report. Right now, rather than give myself first preference, I'll try to read of Lord Kṛṣṇa, the Supreme Personality of Godhead, in Śrīla Prabhupāda's purports. I'm tiny—one ten-thousandth the upper portion of a hair in size—and I'm most fallen. I boasted that I depend utterly on Śrīla Prabhupāda. Let it be true. I presumed to be their teacher, and now I must set a good example.

While reading about Gargamuni approaching Nanda Mahārāja for Kṛṣṇa's name-giving ceremony this morning, I was struck by the importance of *believing*. This is why I depend on Prabhupāda and not someone else. The most important experience for me is to overcome doubts, and Prabhupāda is the one who can best do that for me.

I need to overcome doubts. Is what I'm reading real or just a relative Indian cultural expression? When Kṛṣṇa says *dehino 'smin yathā dehe*, "The soul takes another body at death," is this Hindu philosophy? Why doesn't it appear in other religions?

My answer to this doubt is that Kṛṣṇa is speaking the Absolute Truth regardless of whether it appears in other religions. How have I gained this conviction in Kṛṣṇa's words? I gained it from Śrīla Prabhupāda's presentation of *Bhagavad-gītā*. Therefore, I need to continue to overcome whatever doubts come up in my mind. Doubts arise from bad association. Prabhupāda is bringing me to Vedic culture and insisting that it's not foreign but the truth. This is my constant need when I read, when I'm taught by my guru, to enter the reality of what he is saying. Prabhupāda is convinced. No doubt other gurus are also convinced in what they say, but he is the one who convinced me. He is my spiritual master. I don't cling to him sentimentally, but because I know he can help me. If in any way I were to switch over to another, will he do a better job on this one particular thing I need—the conviction that the teachings are real? No, I don't think anyone can improve on that. Neither am I prepared to gamble.

I realize that people might say I'm not very adventurous. In fact, I'm not even very trusting. I should trust in the scriptures' description of the multiplicity of gurus and not think that it's such a fragile relationship that I'll lose hold of it by hearing from someone else. But Prabhupāda himself has not encouraged this kind of adventure. He warned us that his Godbrothers could not do help us; he even said they could do us great harm. I maintain this kind of "childhood" impression. I honor it. I want to please my guru and I don't get the impression from him that he would be happy to hear that I'm ranging wide in Vaiṣṇava readings and approaching other members in the Sarasvatī *gotra*. That's just the way it is. I admit that my position may not be the same as others have adopted, and it may not be the position that will be manifested by followers of Prabhupāda in succeeding generations. Right now, however, I am confident that it's right for me. And I don't feel it is harmful to those depending on my teachings. It's authentic. The idea of being more adventurous as a teacher seems extremely risky.

It occurred to me yesterday while asserting this faithfulness in Prabhupāda that I'm not the only one who's remaining faithful in ISKCON. Rather, the whole generation of ISKCON leaders, and the new devotees also, comprise a body of persons fiercely loyal to Prabhupāda. It has its excesses, I admit, but it's ISKCON's saving factor. ISKCON does have *guru-niṣṭhā*. We do express it sometimes in fanatical or superficial ways, and we sometimes misuse Prabhupāda's authority in our zeal—that's all unfortunate—but by maintaining single-minded faith in Prabhupāda, we remain fixed on the Gauḍīya Vaiṣṇava *siddhānta*. There's a jungle of possible misunderstandings in the name of being faithful to Prabhupāda, but that doesn't mean it's wrong to attempt it.

My Godbrother has done me a nice service by pointing out that I should use Vṛndāvana for its actual purpose—to increase *bhakti* in my heart. I propose that my future visits to Vṛndāvana will be more focused on this. Even now I should salvage the few remaining days I have here to be more Vṛndāvana conscious. That doesn't mean I have to try and imitate Rūpa Gosvāmī and live as a *bābājī* practicing severe austerities. It doesn't even mean I have to run out and visit many places.

Still, I should try to find out some essence, even if I mostly stay at the Krishna-Balaram Mandir. Today I'm planning to visit Prabhupāda's resident rooms. I hope to place renewed emphasis on my chanting.

We might have used the word "emphasis" too much to point out the importance of following Prabhupāda over any other teacher, yet the word "emphasis" has meaning. Here are the relevant meanings I found in my dictionary. First, it's a word that comes from that which shows, and to shine or polish. "The force of expression, thought, feeling, action. Special attention given to something so as to make it stand out; importance, stress, weight as in *to put less emphasis on athletics*." Out of the great kingdom of Vaiṣṇava thought a particular guru will give special prominence to certain aspects of the philosophy. Then it's a question of whether the follower accepts this as absolute or thinks, "My guru was on a particular trip, and I needn't emphasize the same things he did."

For example, in Śrīla Śrīdhara Mahārāja's book, *The Guru and His Grace*, a devotee asks if it's true that a preacher is better than a *bhajanānandī*. Śrīdhara Mahārāja replies that those who say so are expressing their own party spirit which favors preaching. His statement is an objective one about the relative merits of preaching over *bhajana*, and it is an intelligent analysis, but it's different than what Śrīla Prabhupāda says. Śrīla Prabhupāda is also aware that sincerity is all that counts in the attempt to please Kṛṣṇa, but he gave emphasis to preaching as the quickest way to catch Kṛṣṇa's attention. He said frankly that the *goṣṭhyānandī* is better than the *bhajanānandī*. If we, as Śrīla Prabhupāda's followers, accept Śrīla Śrīdhara Mahārāja's statement as having the same weight as Prabhupāda's statement, then we have to accept that Prabhupāda may be a party man who has overdone it. That's what I'm talking about. It reminds me of Prabhupāda telling Mukunda in 1967 that if one of his Godbrothers comes and changes one thing, everything will be upset.

5 A.M.

The electric current is weak this morning, but not weak enough to go out completely and switch on the generator. Everywhere around the *mandira* lights are dim—a brownout. The atmosphere at *maṅgala-ārati* was quiet, and taking *darśana* of Rādhā-Śyāmasundara in the low light was interesting. Then suddenly the power came on strong and the lights surged on to brighten the altar. Reminds me of my own energy level. Not enough umph to write a poem, even to just write a lot.

VṚNDĀVANA IS

Vṛndāvana is always reminding me
I will have to die.
I bow down in his *samādhi*,
"Prabhupāda," and suddenly remember
he's here, buried
here. What does it mean?
Why do we forget it in a
haze of vague Prabhupāda-isms?
Prabhupāda and the temple Deities, dark
maṅgala-āratis in the cold,
an electrical brownout.

In Vṛndāvana yesterday there was a
monkey fight—the devotees on
the ground were calling up to
the monkeys—excitement spread
between the species.
In the morning announcements he said,
"Beware of monkeys who steal eyeglasses
and cameras."

In Vṛndāvana Rādhā and Kṛṣṇa play and
pure devotees can partake but
don't imitate. Prabhupāda said
come here and then, surcharged,
go out and preach again.

Vṛndāvana is the place more
than any other where you can
contact Rādhā and Kṛṣṇa
and here I go sleepy
laying under heavy quilt and
dreaming—not of the perfection.
May Kṛṣṇa bless me with
a drop of *hari-nāma* nectar.

VṚNDĀ #12

Vṛndā, Tulasī, I saw you
one moment in the temple
in dim light your delicate
branches and leaves I didn't
have time or presence to
bow down . . .
release me from feeling
nowhere in Vṛndāvana.

I love you, Vṛndāvana.
When I
die, it's here I hope to come
to remember Śrīla Prabhupāda
and be born again in Vṛndāvana
in this world or *that*.

Chanting *japa* on the roof of the Guesthouse. Since it's five stories up, you get to peer down into everybody's backyard. It makes me feel like a voyeur. Sometimes they notice

Gaurāṅga in his heart.

Old crow.

Winter in Vṛndāvana.

Vraja
dhama

and look way up at me. On the roof of a building just outside Krishna-Balaram's walls, I saw a Western man. His head was mostly bald, but the remaining hairs were grown out long. He held a beadbag and wore a shawl. He also had a guitar up there with him.

In another direction I saw into the yard of a school where boys wore uniforms of dark blue shirts and gray pants. They were playing an orderly game of volleyball, but then one of the boys grabbed the ball and ran with it. Both teams broke ranks and ran after him as if the game had suddenly turned into a free-for-all.

When construction goes on in Vṛndāvana, it's often to repair temple domes. One nearby dome competes with Krishna-Balaram's. They're making their spire even higher. Some well-kept buildings seem to be empty; only a *chaukīdār* sleeping on one of the verandas or porches waits for the owners to come for their vacation.

Then there's the MVT buildings, a section of forests, monkeys on the domes of this temple, and me and my mind. I remember the time I went for a health retreat in Puerto Rico. The neurosurgeon recommended Migranol for headaches, and the iridologist recommended a vile-tasting cabbage drink. That was when I wrote a group of poems with peaceful, clear-cut images in the tradition of Kenneth Rexroth's translations of the old Chinese.

4:45 P.M.

A devotee named Anantaśaya came and filmed me talking about Prabhupāda for Russian television. He said that eighty percent of a person's effectiveness on TV is how he looks, fifteen percent is how he speaks, and only five percent is the actual substance of what he says. He requested that I smile as often as possible. Once the interview began, however, I couldn't crank out any smiles. He admitted that when one talks about a serious thing, he can't always be smiling. Ananta emphasized, however, that Russia is under the grips of an anti-cult movement pushed by the Russian Orthodox Church. The devotees want to break the image of the Hare Kṛṣṇas as fanatics.

He said the best part of my interview was when I talked about my "intense intellectual life" before becoming a devotee. He liked that I mentioned Allen Ginsberg, Franz Kafka, and Vincent Van Gogh. When we finished the interview, he discovered that his batteries had run dead for part of the interview, so we had to do it again. Again I talked about Kafka and Van Gogh, and this time laid it on even thicker. But I still couldn't smile.

As soon as Ananta left, I met with Śamīka Ṛṣi. We talked about how I could sometimes take a painkiller while on a long plane trip to alleviate a headache. I won't use them at other times.

Now I'm left with just a little bit of the day, but I'm disoriented—don't know how to use my time and still have fog in the head. I can't push myself.

VṚNDĀ #14

Vṛndā, Vṛndā, I can't direct this
one to you, I'm just a fellow who
met the Swami back then.
Really, Vṛndā, I could have
spent this day better, watered
Tulasī-devī and walked around her.
No, I didn't go to my Swami's
rooms and sit there and write.
Don't know if I'll take a pill
on that long plane journey . . .
And night is coming,
the parrots,
days running out
on another stay.

VṚNDĀ #15

Vṛndā, Vṛndā what do you think?
Will I be able to read and chant?
Realize you and Kṛṣṇa consciousness?
Earlier today was nice reading
of Rādhā's love.
Now the day is going down,
I didn't
achieve taste in *japa* but
I ask you, dear self, chant
another round.
Ask the Lord for
mercy to persist.

5:15 P.M. F.W.

Write what comes, fog head
look down into the dirt yard
where devotees walk through—
brahmacārī with cane
white-haired *gṛhastha*
mom and daughter

three men talking about what? Do they talk *rasika* talks or about how to make money? Are they more surrendered and *engaged* than I am? Look down through the screen. How agile the monkeys are! There goes my friend wearing a long white cloth wrapped around his waist, no white piece tucked up the back . . . There goes a stylish *mātājī*. Oh, a guy is checking *me* out from the *gurukula* roof.

They're putting up blue drapes to cover the sunlight and cold wind in the *prasādam* hall. Get your stainless steel *thālī* and sit down. Servers with buckets.

I'm not hungry, but I'll eat something with tea and hear Śrīla Prabhupāda in 1968 speaking about Aghāsura from *Kṛṣṇa* book.

Listen, we've got our free-wheelin',

we could go to Narottama dāsa Ṭhākura's tomb. We could sit somewhere and watch ants and pigeons. We could ride on a rickshaw.

Tee hee, tee hee, I giggles.

"Smile," he said, it's *very* important.

But I couldn't. I was telling him I read F. Kafka. I read B. Doffer and Bonhoeffer and G. Gestalt and Fried Sartre and Albee Camoo

and who else? Jack Gelber the Living Connection theater with Jackie McLean slicing angular alto sax.

Is this Vṛndāvana? Can you dream of Vṛndāvana?

"Don't come here except to take care of your soul, to chant and get *bhakti*," he said.

JAPA LOG, JANUARY 29, 5 A.M.

Fourteen "good" rounds. That means I chanted them vigorously with the motor running. Not attentive or prayerful.

The goal is not to increase mechanical rounds. Start with awareness that chanting is important, shouldn't be pushed aside, neglected. Here's a special chance to start a wave in Vṛndāvana and continue it after I leave. Hear the names, can you?

Chanted rounds fifteen and sixteen on the roof of the Guesthouse. Don't think I'll do it again. Nice sky and scenery, and interesting things for the mind to play with. My pleasant room 42 is more private, better for *japa*.

You would do well to stay there and chant extra, sit down when you want before Prabhupāda's altar . . . I wish I could—be content to stay in this room and chant Hare Kṛṣṇa Hare Kṛṣṇa, Kṛṣṇa Kṛṣṇa Hare Hare/ Hare Rāma Hare Rāma, Rāma Rāma Hare Hare.

JAPA LOG, 5:30 P.M.

Twenty rounds done. I can't report that it was a great day, but I did chant some extra rounds and *wanted to*. That's good. I can keep it up as long as I don't get head pain. When all is said and done, chanting is left. It's the first and last spiritual practice. It's what I do.

I actually heard the words of some mantras. If I keep on chanting, I'll start seeing clearer how bad my chanting is. Then I can chant in that space. Chanting supplies the answer.

Red beads are fine, thank you. Hope they last as long as I do.

January 30

12:45 A.M.

Lectio divina. I write what's in me. I say I am a devotee and carefully plan how to improve. I stopped him in the Samādhi Mandir and began talking, but to hear me he had to first remove his earplugs (was wearing them as an aid for concentration in *japa*).

When I concentrate too much I get a headache. Same if I push too much for an extended free-write (gone are days of full one-hour exercises, summer nights and days at Stroudsburg, *Shack Notes*).

Gone? Or can I return? Also, lost some faith that such a "slow" process—working through effluvia of mind—is the best way to go.

Be careful you don't write over-careful thoughts already in your psyche. Write to surprise yourself.

In Vṛndāvana a man was holy. In Vṛndāvana when you come here you may become automatically Kṛṣṇa conscious. To die here means to go to Kṛṣṇaloka. The monkeys will do that. Don't envy them. Don't hate anyone in the *dhāma*. Don't critique everyone. Don't be a faultfinder. (Fruit-finder.)

Oh, equations and geysers like "Old Faithful," American history books and road atlases, Jack's *On The Road*, and Salinger's Central Park merry-go-round, and—yeah they are so hip and hard-edged,

gowns, lice, hell, sex, they're so hard-edged.

I spoke to the Russian TV devotee. Now I think he shouldn't have chosen me since he says TV is eighty percent how you look and only five per cent what you say. Better to pick a young guy or a media-perfect girl. He said it is *very* important that you occasionally smile, but I didn't. Why waste my time and his?

This way leads to the exit. Yadu writes, "How can we tell people that Pūtanā witch was thirteen miles long and that Kṛṣṇa had millions of children and there were billions of people living in Dvārakā?" I will refer him to Sadāpūta Prabhu's higher dimensions, expansions of space, and to simple faith in *acintya*.

Strange dream, but now I'm awake. Fortunately I'm not like the little alienated cell member of that other world, the sensitive person wanting quiet and cleanliness but who somehow is being forced to live surrounded by low-class people and the loud noises of a tenement. Rather, I am a respected person in this Guesthouse. When I walk downstairs the guards stand in their long overcoats, hold their rifles at attention, and give me a little bow. I return it and say, "Hare Kṛṣṇa" or "*Jaya* Prabhupāda."

Yes, I'm living at least on the surface of Vṛndāvana. It's cold out and there's no central heating, but I have an electric heater in my room. I hear the poor but fortunate dogs barking outside. Do I believe that they'll go back to Godhead at the end of this life? Do I believe in the spiritual world? Do I understand who is Śrīmatī Rādhārāṇī? All *I* see is poverty, young kids who live here and don't seem so exalted, yet who have something special in their eyes. Kids who taunt you for being a Western "monkey." Kṛṣṇa, please help me to understand. I am going now to chant Your holy names. I beg to hear the syllables and to let the mercy work on me.

A disciple wrote requesting that I give him permission to worship a Govardhana-śilā. He has already given his heart to it and there's nothing I can do but agree to it. Last year another disciple made this request and I resisted, but this disciple's request sounds right for him. I know of his inner life and I think it would complement it. He is a book distributor and wishes to think of Rādhā-Kṛṣṇa's pastimes while he's out on the street; he wants the protection of Deity worship while he places himself so close to hell to distribute Prabhupāda's books.

As I read his letter I thought of my own occasional desire to worship Govardhana. I can't see how to do it because I don't want to increase the time I'm already giving to *pūjā*. I already bathe and dress Prabhupāda every day. Of course, I *could* do it, but this gives rise to another thought.

If I'm going to make any increase, I would rather it be in the direction of writing. It seems a long time since I've been able to write a one-hour timed sessions. I seem to be writing less and less. I don't want to arrange my life so that there will be less and less time for it. My *bhajana* is to rise at midnight and to write and read. I'm grateful to be able to do that. I go straight to Prabhupāda's books; that's certainly a kind of *pūjā*. Then I write, my worshipable practice, and then chant *japa*—the best worship. I worship the Prabhupāda deity at two different times in the day. I think I'm already complete. At least I have a complete schedule for purification. If I were to take up a Govardhana-śilā, I think the drive to do so would have to become more spontaneous for it to make sense for me.

I've been churning feelings about writing. Finally I let them out in three letters I addressed to my editor and to Madhu. In one letter I expressed my desire (almost a greed) to be able to again write high-powered one-hour writing sessions. I regretted that I don't have the health to do them, and also that I don't seem to have the conviction in their value. I also reasoned that maybe I'm just at a different stage where I'm flowing gently and more efficiently. I seem to be on the verge of praying here in Vṛndāvana for a new burst, a new dedication.

In the second letter I discussed how devotees, under the influence of *The Seven Habits of Highly Effective People*, are making "mission statements." They're careful about the words they choose to express their life's mission. One devotee told me that a mission statement is not for others; it's tailor-made for yourself and what you want to do with your own life. He's trying to decide whether his mission statement is to cultivate *bhakti* in his heart or to serve and please Śrīla Prabhupāda. I thought he should include both concepts, but he pointed out that it's subtle how you find your exact focus.

With this in mind I was thinking about my own focus in writing. I want to achieve several objectives: (1) To cope as a practicing devotee, and writing helps with that; (2) to preach, and publishing serves that purpose; (3) to make art. It's difficult to include all three objectives and yet have a most specific focus. I think the idea of a writing *process* fulfills it, and the idea of the "zigzag path of truth." And it may not be that each emphasis gets equal attention at every moment. Sometimes I'll be working toward one at the apparent expense of another.

In the third letter I recalled the metaphors used by Natalie Goldberg in *The Long Quiet Highway*. She spoke of the marathon-running monks who vow to complete a certain *vrata* (running quota) or else die trying. A writer has to be similarly determined. The other image is of a quiet, desolate highway in America, and of a driver driving down that road. This is similar to the often unrewarding, seemingly endless, even seemingly dull task of going on, writing all your life without expecting excitement or rewards.

3:20 P.M.

I'm in Śrīla Prabhupāda's room in Vṛndāvana. Best thing I can do here is write, read, chant, and pray to him. It's 1997. A disciple got the key and unlocked the door for us so we could go in alone, before other devotees began to arrive. Śrīla Prabhupāda is still resting, but they let me in anyway. The sign says, "Open to public at 4 P.M." Write until then? Oh, I can't write for so long without going crazy or getting a headache or becoming illegible.

Kṛṣṇa's *dhāma*. My heart is closed. I simply don't comprehend it. Just a tiny ray of light. I stand by the foot of his bed where I stood on November 14, 1977. Don't feel—because if I did, if I remembered everything I'd—what? Cry? Die? Or nothing. Stone now and stone then.

I feel I have passed through too much stress, although worse may be ahead in this life or the next. I seek peace, but even more than that, I seek devotion to my spiritual master. I seek it before I die. I am his disciple, his Satsvarūpa dāsa. The letter on his desk today is to Kṣīrodakaśāyī in Vṛndāvana 1971. This letter is entirely taken up with business for preaching—get the import number, I'm sending you devotees to keep up the work, do it nicely, etc. Prabhupāda had a mission to be accomplished, and he needed cool-brained, practical-minded people to help him.

It was hard then. Is it easier nowadays? Someone wants to concentrate on the study of *śāstra*, some *want* to bear the burden of pushing on the movement (corporate ISKCON they call it) forcefully.

Yeah, well I have another contribution. ISKCON strain. Failing trust. I must keep up my end.

I decided to go to my room as soon as I leave here. I'd prefer to look at the murals in the temple room, but I may bump into someone I know and waste time, become implicated. Hermit. Recluse. Dreamer. Writer. Looking out for rodents and possibly monkeys to enter your periphery vision, sneaking up to grab your eyeglasses. Drum rolls over the loudspeakers mixing with the dogs' growls.

Exhale. Don't die. Imagine, you too, you who write this with a bold pen—you too will die.

I can't get into literary convention or actual prayer talk like, "Dear Śrīla Prabhupāda, I'm here in your room. I feel your presence. Here is my prayer: I wish to always serve you." But he knows my intention to be his disciple. I need to know who I am so that I can serve him best.

Oh, the controversies. More to come, and me sitting here talking about death from a pleasant distance where it can't harm me, like being on the roof of the Guesthouse and looking down at the dogs and poor people in the dirt lane and thinking I'm above it all because I have a karmic cushion. There's more to come and when I die, I will leave it all behind. At least until next time. O Lord, O Vṛndāvana.

VṚNDĀVANA

Vṛndāvana, you are the summit
reserved for the best
not allowed am I—
Don't believe I'll
be born in Kṛṣṇaloka when
I die here?
Ah, ach!
Believe it, you fool. Don't
come back a monkey.
Austere I am not, but hope for
a special ticket to get to
head of line.
"Not allowed—loafers
and shnobs."
Her dirt, her secrets.

Prabhupāda's books in his room, in Hindi and other Indian languages—all Greek to me. Ah, the English ones. "*Duṣṭa mana*" written by his Guru Mahārāja. When was the last time I was deep and earnest and innocent in thinking of him? I wanted to write more and now it's coming. Thank you, thank you.

VṚNDĀ #16

Vṛndā is the plant—
Tulasī and a *gopī*—the one
who recreates Vṛndāvana in pleasant
kuñjas and bowers for Rādhā and
Kṛṣṇa.
Now you know? Oh, I don't,
it ain't that easy. I prefer
to eat marshes and mallows.
Wind in the Willows. I saw
that book on a shelf in the temple president's
home in Delhi—
intended for his kid.
Vṛndā—you are all things
but you exclude, kick out,
all that falls short
of pure devotion to
Rādhā-Śyāma.

O mind, why aren't you a Vaiṣṇava? Hear your master, hear and read. And write these seemingly endless letters.

Better save yourself. Śrīla Prabhupāda set a different example. He reached out to his disciples in his last days, and continued to write his *Bhāgavatam* purports. I should do what he says and develop *bhakti* for Rādhā-Govinda. *How*? By keeping the hand moving? GNP duties? Publishing books? Helping others.

Ten more minutes before they open the door to the public. Write until then and then chant one round here. My twenty-first. *Duṣṭa mana*! Do the needful to conquer the mind. At my age and as a *sannyāsī*, that means that my first duty is to read Prabhupāda's books. Prabhupāda himself told me that. So I will do it. Don't look to compromise that instruction. "Can I read other books?" You can, *but*. Can I write a lot? Yes, *but*. Can I live forever? No. Am I a devotee? Yes, *but*.

No ifs, ands, or buts.

But master . . .

"What impact did he make? What kind of a man was he? Tell us, sir, your impressions for the potential two hundred million people who want to see you smile on Russian TV"—damn those Orthodox priests who hate us!

Kṛṣṇa, please protect and improve the ISKCONites. Do as You will. You are always victorious, but that doesn't mean that ISKCON always wins the court cases or gains the famous multi-millionaire followers. Nor does it mean all temples will be saved from closing or all devotees will not desert. It simply means that You are always victorious. Your will is supreme, even if we cannot always understand what You intend.

JAPA LOG, 5:45 A.M.

Fourteen rounds so far. It's not going to be bliss and easy and feeling, "Wow, I'm on a wave of reform and new pleasure in chanting; I'm on an increase in quota like the one I did for three months and wrote about in *Japa Reform Notebook*."

It'll be something, however, if I can give that little extra push, that little extra effort to hear the names and to do a few extra rounds. Don't stop dead, cold-stone finished after sixteen. *Hari-nāma* awaits you.

> Reclining on the desk
> they invite me once again
> my red japa beads.

Take them up and finger and walk and sit. Push . . .

JAPA LOG, 5:10 P.M.

Twenty-two rounds done. I could do another. They are not "better," but I get more of a chance to chant with attention. The mind separates and notices the individual words as they occur: Hare, Kṛṣṇa, Hare, Kṛṣṇa, etc. That's a gain.

Don't say anything else in this log, as if all you do is live to chant.

CHANTING JAPA

Chanting makes chanting
and Hari takes all and gives more.
Always chant—sixteen,
twenty, twenty-five
and don't give up
'til you die.
Japa awards and
punishment.
Am saying what comes
just as in chanting rounds
please pay attention
and rescue your own
dharma.
Fishtail Purī
memories—
begin another round
on beads.

January 31

12:40 A.M.

Good morning. I just prepared for today's disciples' meeting. I hope I don't get a headache, but if I do, I'm prepared for the next meeting we can schedule. Do it like that, sane and easy and what you can actually do.

Śamīka Ṛṣi said some people take medicine all their lives, risking the side effects. They figure it's a better option than lying day after day in pain.

I dreamt all night and recorded a bunch.

10:15 A.M.

Sixteen rounds and whaddya get? Blah, chirp, chortle. Heart beats still. "My Foolish Heart." Little life in Vṛndāvana, *mixed*, like *jñāna-miśra-bhakti*, *māyā-miśra-bhakti*.

Vṛndāvana is. I am. Prabhupāda is. Kṛṣṇa is eternally. Rādhā is supreme.

The *rasa-śāstras*, *Bhagavad-gītā*, Kṛṣṇa is speaking.

Who gave class today?

Listen, prison is bad, but Dhīra-Kṛṣṇa dāsa meditates after chanting *japa* in the mornings in his cell. The rest of the day he tries to retain fragments of that prayer state.

Good. Look out the screened porch. See below. Hear Hindi.

Talk ISKCONese. Who's who. Who bowed down best? Who danced and strutted? Know yourself. Faultfinding is contagious. Keep it to yourself? Don't poison yourself. I spill a little of it and say, "I can't help it. Just don't take it seriously."

This morning between 5–6 A.M. I worked steadily at answering letters. A sense of accomplishment.

"Mahārāja, what is the meaning of Rādhā-kuṇḍa? How to think and behave toward the residents?"

Prabhu, Prabhu, my shoe.

She gave me a knit slipper. Carry it down to the Mandir in a book bag and put it on as you go inside. Step out of your shoes and on with the slippers, see?

But then can you walk from the Samādhi Mandir to the other Mandir in the same slippers? Not really. On and off. Oh, it's not worth all the trouble just to keep your feet warm. You can warm them when you return to your room by sticking them in front of the electric heater.

I've got friends at Krishna-Balaram Mandir, connections. I get Rādhā's garland, *mahā* sweets, a lady makes me Russian bread. I get a hoodwink, a broadside.

I didn't notice who was bowing at my feet. It was a brother, the keeper of this house, Gaṇapati Prabhu.

Hare Kṛṣṇa. Is someone knocking at my door? My ear strains. I here the smashing of rock on rock and the sound of parrots. Twenty-five days and nights in Vṛndāvana, the toe, the head, the plain man, the uncontrolled mind on surface of Vraja. Failure to enter, a failure . . . Here isn't soft enough. Hard, hard.

Walking the Vṛndāvana lanes.

Caught
IN

Let's see
living in Vrndavan
monkey steals his eye glasses
I get head-aches
Got a walking Staff
left hand japa

Inner music.

But I fall down at his feet, my Prabhupāda. That much.
Caw caw
awful how you
fail to tune into Vraja
Vṛndā poems calling
out from back seat of
old Studebaker and
Plymouth times and memories
crying out
Prabhodhānanda Sarasvatī,
I know the names too . . .

JAPA LOG, JANUARY 31

This log can't last. It doesn't matter. It's 10:30 A.M. and I did one extra above sixteen. Do another. Cool air. Someone at the door.

Chant, chant
can't, can't
red beads in hand—the essence of Vṛndāvana. Chant here and carry it west, extra is all I know to improve.

Zero, desert. Music of beads. New counters. Hear, man. The writing can help, but chanting is itself, is Hare Kṛṣṇa mantra.

JAPA LOG, 5:30 P.M.

Twenty-one rounds, the last one done in front of my disciples. Someone looked at me. Someone took a flash picture.

Kept on chanting. I spoke on the need for humility in a life dedicated to chanting. A devotee assigns himself to a lower position. How to do it practically?

Be humble when you chant and don't record brilliant ideas that come while you chant. Hare Kṛṣṇa Hare Kṛṣṇa, Kṛṣṇa Kṛṣṇa Hare Hare.

February 1, 1997

Good moment in disciples' meeting yesterday when a disciple asked a challenging question and I groped and found the right answer. I had just presented the four stages of *lectio divina* and demonstrated it with a purport in *Kṛṣṇa* book. He asked, "Is this from the Christians?" I answered with one word, "Yes." Then he asked, "Do any of our *ācāryas* teach this?" At first I couldn't think of any good examples, so I said that everything comes from the *Vedas*. Then I hit upon Lord Caitanya in the Gambhīrā. The Lord actually went through the four steps—(1) heard and comprehended a verse from *Śrīmad-Bhāgavatam*, usually Tenth Canto, about the *gopīs;* (2) took it personally in the mood of Śrīmatī Rādhārāṇī; (3) made prayers in His own words; and (4) attained "union with God." So there. It wasn't me speaking something *asampradāya*. Lord Caitanya did it.

M. and I have been saying that we may not come to India next year. While I'm here, however, I have been reading statements about how this is the best place to be. Perhaps I really could come again and have a more solitary stay. Or, I could recreate Vraja in the West if I read Prabhupāda's books or did a sixty-four-round *vrata*.

ROOM 42

Room 42 is where I stay because
of headaches I get here.
Open . . . I'm free of them for five days
in a row. I press a button and a bell
rings in room 41 and a lady's voice says,
"Open the door, please!"—
a source of endless jokes.

Madhu comes in and I say I don't
like this guy, I don't care for this trip.
The fourth floor where
monkeys come down from the roof.
Two monkeys, me and one at
top of stairs—in imagination I run
forward to him and he stands his ground
snarling and baring his teeth until he sees
the brick in my hand.
Land of Rādhā and Kṛṣṇa, next
year I won't come to 42
but I tell you
this is also a good place for
chanting
and reading *Śrīmad-Bhāgavatam*.

Reading Prabhupāda's books is like a medicine we constantly need to ingest, but it goes beyond that. It's a nourishing and tasty food. Why ever stop? It's a shame if we abandon such nourishing food or become disgusted with it and start to crave novelty for its own sake. Prabhupāda does say that "variety is the mother of enjoyment," but we can find it in his books.

One devotee wrote me on these points and said as follows: "Faith is a conscious choice. I do want to see Prabhupāda as absolute, but I can see that I won't attain that loyalty cheaply. I will have to make the first investment and then wait for reciprocation. This point makes me appreciate so much what you are saying. You say Prabhupāda saved you. He is the one who convinced you of Kṛṣṇa consciousness. It was Prabhupāda who quelled your doubts, not someone else. I honestly do appreciate your lack of adventurousness, as you call it, no matter how many gurus the *śāstras* say we may have. I want to learn to follow your mood with honesty and conviction."

There's more to it than the amazing but isolated historical act of Prabhupāda saving me in 1966. Even if that was *all* he did, I would owe him my life. It's such an extraordinary 180-degree change in my life. No, more than 180 degrees. It's beyond linear history. I was plucked out of a life that was mixed-bad or mixed-good and given something entirely different. I could never have found it on my own even if I had stumbled onto the *Bhagavad-gītā* or the *Upaniṣads*. (Emerson and Thoreau stumbled on the *Harivaṁśa* at Harvard University over a hundred years ago. That's quite an esoteric book, yet they didn't change and become devotees of Kṛṣṇa.)

Therefore, I love to remember 1966. It's not that Prabhupāda gave me initiation and has done little for me since, however. He has given me and so many others a life to continue in Kṛṣṇa consciousness. For the journey he has given us his books. When you surrender to guru it's comprehensive, total. If he says these are the books you should read, you can't jettison them later. It's an act of faith to constantly go back to them and work past the repetitiousness of what they contain.

Nowadays we face challenges we never had to face in the past. No one dared say that Prabhupāda didn't give us everything, that Prabhupāda only "cleaned the pot," that he only chopped down with a machete the rough weeds and jungle growth of Māyāvāda philosophy and only now are we ready for someone else to give us the nectar. The challenge has been made, and we have to meet it by finding everything in Prabhupāda's books. It's there in the *Caitanya-caritāmṛta* and in other places, but there are also the warnings. Don't take them cheaply. Therefore I pray and I work to find satisfaction in Prabhupāda's books alone.

5:55 A.M.

We went over to bow down before *tulasī*, but I saw women standing there so I bowed to *tulasī* from a distance.

Room 42. That's where I am in long johns, dental adhesive, and dream thoughts, sometimes feeling the body too hot, sometimes too cool.

He asks, "Please change my initiation name. Duḥkhī-Kṛṣṇa changed his name to Śyāmānanda."

"Keep your name. Rādhārāṇī changed Duḥkhī-Kṛṣṇa's name. Are you so extraordinary that your name should be changed?"

The guru in a righteous huff catches the errant disciple.

Get 'em! Go get 'em! O days in Vṛndāvana, please let something happen.

Bow in front of Śrīla Prabhupāda in his Samādhi and catch yourself thinking, "Rush through these *praṇāma-mantras* and get up so you can finish the fourteenth round before the conch blows." But I don't get up immediately, I stop and say the mantras slowly, and even when finished I stay there, "diving" in space downward, feeling blackness, and thinking, "You will die, you will die too," although it's a painless thought and therefore just a musing. But it's true, and you could do it every day—come here and say to Prabhupāda, "You're here and I'm coming to join you in this life and the next."

9 A.M.

Now they're chanting, "*Śarīra avidyā-jāl*" down in the outdoor *prasādam* hall. Sun filtering through the haze, gradually lifting the chill from the air. A large monkey sits on the wall of the temple and surveys the serve-out. He does not dare to come down. This is his last life in the material world.

Vṛndā, land of trees
forests of Vṛndāvana—
Rāmacandra is in Ayodhya
Nārāyaṇa in Vaikuṇṭha
does and bucks hear the flute
and here I am
dwelling in down
original mind covered.

The BBT asked me to write a pop book on Vedic culture. I said, "No, I only write books for those already won over to our side. I don't confront issues, I confront my own shortcomings."

A disciple wrote me about a dream he had after he broke the regulative principles. In the dream his guru (me) had transformed into a nondevotee. This disciple came upon him, and he had dirty blond hair, a goatee, and was playing basketball at an outdoor court. The devotee began to cry and confronted his one-time guru, "Why have you done this to me?"

The guru (me) still holding the basketball and looking through his sunglasses, fixed the devotee with his gaze and said, "Now you know what it's like to be shit upon."

The disciple said that the dream taught him that it was he who had done the wrong thing. I guess he means it forced his guru to fall down.

1:10 P.M.

I've got a headache rising behind the right eye. It started around 9:30 A.M., and we canceled our group reading. It's likely I'll cancel my 4 P.M. class on "Prabhupāda Appreciation" too. Naturopaths say that when you have pain you shouldn't eat, but I ate a moderate plate of spaghetti just now. It was tasty, but I couldn't enjoy it.

Along with the headaches, two ideas are growing about chalking something out that I could do for the whole year. In 1993 when I left Vṛndāvana, I gave myself the task of beginning and continuing worship of a Prabhupāda *mūrti*. I also resolved to read the whole *Bhāgavatam*. I dedicated 1994 to that reading and that was good for me.

Last year I began *A Poor Man Reads the Bhāgavatam* on January 11th and left Vṛndāvana with full sails and fair weather to cruise that ship. It lasted half a year, and I'm glad for it.

I want to make practical my desire to be faithful to Prabhupāda by reading his books. I want to prove to myself that the books are enlivening and enlightening, not that, "Swamijī had to clean the pot" and therefore he couldn't give us advanced teachings. My reading program has dwindled down to about fifteen minutes a day. I need some kind of reform, some kind of plan—but it can't be something forced. What?

It will become a discipline and I will have to work for it. Maybe again read the *Bhāgavatam*—from the beginning?

Another line of thinking is about my writing. I've noticed that I am writing less and less. I've had different thoughts about how to increase it, but there too it's not a matter of forcing myself. In both areas I'm wondering if there is some kind of foundational shift I can make. I'm hoping that Kṛṣṇa will give me some insight on this before I leave room 42.

Last year I was happy, almost euphoric, about starting PMRB. I therefore celebrated the fact that the inspiration came to me here in room 42 by gathering dust from under the bed and putting it in reticules, keeping one on my altar and giving a couple to my writing assistants. I won't be doing that this year, but maybe this could be the scene again of some directions for reading and writing.

Room 42: Dream lab, center of my universe, a cell in Prabhupāda's house.

Place where I lie down when I get headaches. Place where ideas come that I can follow for a year—inspiration to read *Bhāgavatam*, inspiration for a semi-fictive trip to the Caribbean, a Henry-type character (as in Berryman's *The Dream Songs*)—a place where it can all come together.

Room 42, located in Ramaṇa-reti, just off Bhaktivedanta Mārg. How noisy it is just outside the temple with all the shops and rickshaws . . .

Room 42 has an electric heater while I'm here because the temple president's wife is my disciple. How is it that a fellow like me can be a spiritual master? Some people would like to tear me down, but Prabhupāda protects me.

From room 42 I can look down to the *prasādam* hall with its blue drapes, and I can see people passing on the dirt path that connects the temple to the MVT houses. I can look out, but what can I see? Can't see the soul, can't see my Beloved. I can see young *mātājīs*, old *mātājīs*, young and old Indians, almost everyone wrapped in scarf or sweater in this weather.

JAPA LOG, 9 A.M.

Empty, but I did two rounds above sixteen so far. I *wanted* to chant them. I thought of other things while my voice said the mantras, and that makes me sad. I walked back and forth in my room carrying a bamboo walking stick until my ankle started to hurt.

If I come to Vṛndāvana next year with a plan to chant thirty-two or sixty-four rounds a day, would that help? O holy names . . .

February 2

12:50 A.M.

I took rest for the night at 4:30 P.M. The headache went down by 6:30 P.M. I was clear but then couldn't sleep. My mind went toward writing plans. I got up and began to write notes around 8 P.M.

I thought of a book I could write. It would have a basic fictive twist to it, just one change, then everything else could be writing from my actual life, starting with my trip to Trinidad. I would use the energy of the moment-to-moment realities of travel, temple visits, even free-writing in Kṛṣṇa consciousness, but it would be part of a "story." Just as Franz Kafka changed reality with the first sentence of his story "Metamorphosis"—he gave us the fantastic image of himself as a large bug lying in bed—but then wrote a realistic account of what would happen, so I'd like to do something similar. Probably not so wild.

I thought of different ways to make the fictive trip. I thought of telling a story that the BBT had ordered me to write a certain kind of book. I would be somewhat resistant to that assignment, but would carry it out of fear of censure and a desire to please them. I would work on it as I visited each Caribbean temple. My next thought was, "What assignment?"

I thought I could report on devotees' dreams, and I would do that by using my own dreams as the material. Or maybe I could be researching ISKCON's favorite self-help book, *The Seven Habits of Highly Effective People*. I could be working on my own "mission statement."

But it wasn't long after I wrote these notes that I decided against the proposal. It seems antithetical to my desire to continue and renew serious, lively reading in Prabhupāda's books. Whatever I do in my writing life should not create so much energy that I become deviated from my reading *sādhana*. I began to surrender to the idea that if I do find a way to improve my reading, I can just write what actually happens.

Yes, that's the kind of writer I am, as I wrote the other day in a letter to my editor, " . . . it's all right to have churning moods that maybe I can go in this direction, maybe I can go in that direction. It's all right to actually start a streak of something new, a poem series or whatever, but a commitment is a commitment, so I just have to accept it—that I'm a certain kind of writer who *wants* to write a lot every day, who doesn't want to work and re-work polished pieces. Therefore, drive your car and chant Hare Kṛṣṇa."

This is another victory for my continuance of *Every Day, Just Write*. I feel like I've weathered another challenge to it, similar to the one I weathered when I thought of writing a fable based on a dream. The challenges will continue, and perhaps one of these semi-fictive waves will carry me along with it. But overnight I returned to my little life and writing it out as it is. Somehow the fiction seemed to me like

Prabhupāda's example of reaching around your head to touch your nose. I'd be putting all this pressure on myself for a certain kind of writing, hype it up, and make it better for the devotees. Knock their socks off with a new fictive piece as good as *Photo Preaching* or better.

To some degree I sacrifice my identity as a "writer" for my desire to be a well-rounded devotee. Aside from that, I like what I'm writing. It doesn't drive the reader along in a suspenseful way, but if he or she quiets down to read, it's good. For example, my activities here in Vṛndāvana—I'm telling them as they actually are. As true as I can make them. I work to write more truly, more nakedly, and when I can take off on a good, deep free-write—which I can do whenever I am free in the day—that will allow me to combine different fictive touches, dreams, and so on.

I'm thinking of my disciple's request for a new name and how it can be applied to my seeking something new in Vṛndāvana. We hope when we come to Vṛndāvana that something special will happen to us. This disciple says the *pūjārī* in Prabhupāda's Mandir asked him, "What is your name?" When he said his name the *pūjārī* said, "That's not a good name. It should be changed to such-and-such." My disciple said that that's exactly what he was thinking also, so he wrote me asking for the change.

We hope some divine word will be whispered to us in Vṛndāvana, and we can come away with a new name, a new project, a new direction. Obviously, that can be hasty, and it might not last once we leave Vṛndāvana. Therefore, my expression of this in terms of wanting a new literary project is like asking for a new spiritual name. I already have a good project. Let me pray to continue to write every day, and let it come, let me come to it.

8:35 A.M.

Lots of notes and letters focusing on writing. Lots of letters to local devotees. What about actually writing and reading?

A Godbrother says, "Most of the *ācāryas* in our line have gone to other planets to preach. At the end of his life, Śrīla Prabhupāda also said he was going to another planet to preach and that his sincere followers would join him there."

The mood of this assertion is a challenge. It takes the edge off any salvation motive we may have in our service. I'd like to find out the source of these statements. Usually we hear that the *ācāryas* have rejoined Rādhā and Kṛṣṇa in eternal Vraja. Did Prabhupāda actually say this, and does it rule out any other possibility of Prabhupāda's location? We also have to ask, "What is preaching?" Different persons may answer in different ways.

Any good thing can be abused.

Hold on, mate. Get through this day until 4 P.M. when you can give your class on "Prabhupāda Appreciation"—which was canceled yesterday.

They say he's okay, a good writer. Get him to write a book we can use in the preaching mission: a list of ten ways to heal wounds, five reasons why book distribution is best, what ISKCON is doing to solve the *varṇāśrama-dharma* need, what to do with the *gurukula* mess. Hey Bol.

VṚNDĀ #18

Vṛndā, I need to know more
tales of your glories so
I can sing these irregulars,
not leave them so empty.
Don't abandon us, dear *tulasī.*
You grow even in the north,
asked to stay there by your devotees
who wanted
what Prabhupāda said.

VṚNDĀ #19

He was pleased when
tulasīs appeared first in Hawaii then
in a St. Louis, Missouri attic
with fluorescent bulb through snowy winters,
even Boston, even Sweden,
barometer of devotion—
now, the twigs are dry,
don't cut, take care, let her
bloom—
Devotee's plant
connected to Rādhā and Kṛṣṇa.

We are planning to go to Rādhā-Dāmodara, Śrīla Prabhupāda's room, and another day to Rādhā-Gokulānanda. "It's only the *puṣpa-samādhi*" (of Narottama dāsa Ṭhākura). That's all right—pray there, pray to write in American language with devotion, your own description of what happened as you tried.

Play tape and say, "See? He's great, he's fine. He said this because—

I chose it because it moved my sense of appreciation." Spontaneous, not prepared. All glories . . .

ROOM 42

Room 42 is where I do
open to Lord Kṛṣṇa
my heart I mean, and
Madhu when he knocks. I unbolt the door
to 42, a magic number.
Two is Rādhā and Kṛṣṇa—
mind and heart
beads and hand
books and brain.

JAPA LOG

I thought, "What's the use of keeping a *japa* log? I certainly won't keep it up after I leave Vṛndāvana."

Why? I think it's an artificial extra. I pretend to be more devoted to *japa* than I am. Besides, there's nothing to say. *Japa* is *japa*. It's inexplicable. It's either good or bad. What's the use of writing, "Today was better," "Today was worse"?

Okay, but I may just keep the log anyway. It's nice to write and thus think about *japa*. "Write your realizations," Prabhupāda said. I remember the editor of *Modern Haiku* used to publish his one- or two-sentence realizations and descriptions about haiku in each issue of his magazine. He numbered them. You could tell he loved haiku and liked writing about it. A haiku, like a Hare Kṛṣṇa mantra, may be inexplicable by nature, but a lover likes to talk of the one he loves. Even a struggler or offender like me wants to be focused on chanting.

February 3

Last week here. Class went all right yesterday. Played an excerpt where Prabhupāda pauses and cannot continue after saying that a pure devotee never asks Kṛṣṇa for anything; he simply *gives* to Kṛṣṇa, "Just like *gopīs*. They never asked Kṛṣṇa for anything . . . " Long pause. Then, "All right, chant." I stated an "appreciation" that Śrīla Prabhupāda himself was like that: he never asked Kṛṣṇa for boons, but gave everything to Kṛṣṇa by preaching—gave Him souls surrendered to Kṛṣṇa consciousness. We think that Kṛṣṇa sometimes indicated to Prabhupāda that He loved him very much, and Prabhupāda was overcome by Kṛṣṇa's love and could not speak. I didn't mention that when he said the word "*gopīs*," he might have merged into that *bhāva* and left the scene of lecturing to neophytes at the Los Angeles temple.

"We are *all* neophytes," he said in a New Vrindaban conversation as soon as a disciple said something about, "a neophyte devotee."

Jaya Prabhupāda. Thank you for allowing me to speak of you, and forgive me for making mistakes. I want to encourage the devotees to hear your tapes, even though I sometimes struggle to hear them myself. All glories to you.

Poor bodies get malaria and dozens of other diseases. I read of it in letters from disciples, how they went to the hospital and slept on ice packs. I too . . . have one of these bodies.

Keep a record. Nightly acupressure from Bhāgavata dāsa. He said I need to drink more water, rubbed on almond oil, Madhu watching and learning. Bhāgavata says, "At night I hurt the devotees with my fingers" (his description of acupressure).

O Vṛndāvana, I'll go to the *maṅgala-āratis* this morning, if Kṛṣṇa allows me, and if my body agrees. The impressions will come through my eyes—Śrīla Prabhupāda in his Samādhi Mandir, the Deities shining out from Their altars, the devotees who are truly attached to Them.

8:45 A.M.

We're going to travel to the Caribbean with only hand luggage. I asked Madhu to put my carry-on bag in my room, and I'll gradually decide what goes into it. Thus we have started our departure from Vṛndāvana.

One disciple wrote me that she regrets leaving Vṛndāvana and going back to her country. I wrote her that the only reason to leave Vṛndāvana is to preach, and preaching is often better outside Vṛndāvana. She wrote back and said that in her case, she wasn't going to preach. She had another whole life awaiting her. She's young and is at that point in her life where she's trying to see how to live it to her best capacity.

I answered, "You have to face the fact that you're not ready to surrender everything and live in Vṛndāvana either doing

Just depend on Kṛṣṇa for protection.

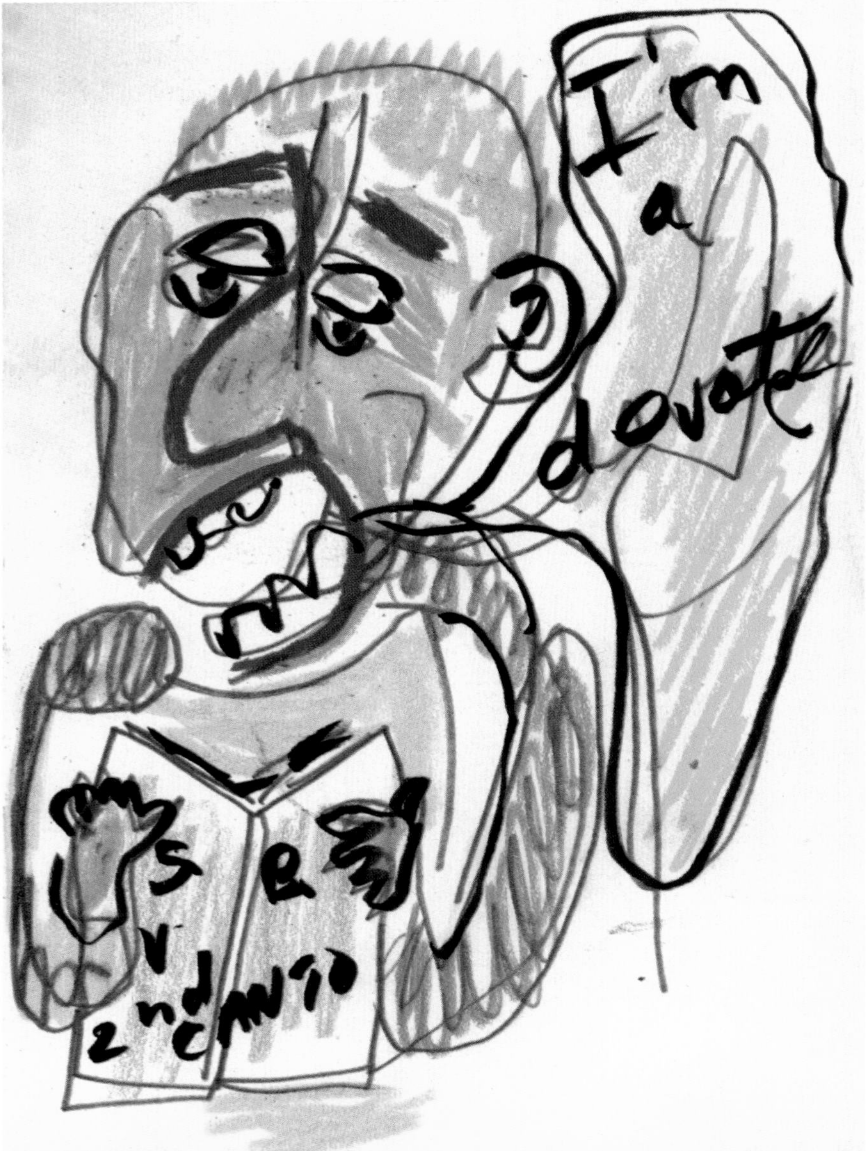
I'm a devotee
S B
V
2nd CANTO

Free-wheelin'.

full-time service at Krishna-Balaram Mandir or living under a bush chanting Hare Kṛṣṇa twenty-four hours a day. By staying in Vṛndāvana you're avoiding the fact that you have to go back and sort out your life. Besides that, even those of us who say that we're leaving Vṛndāvana to preach are leaving because we're not qualified to live here. That includes me."

And it does. I surely don't appreciate the dust of Vṛndāvana, the lanes for walking, the temples for *darśana*, the *parikramas*, monkeys, hogs, and people. I don't even appreciate the great devotees. But I'm also unhappy about leaving in this state. I wish to return to further my progress toward becoming attached to the lotus feet of Vṛndāvana.

Vṛndāvana can be saved for culturing *bhakti*. Don't come here and stay at the temple to teach seminars or invite disciples to be here with you. Stay outside and chant and hear and wander Vṛndāvana. Fulfill minimum obligations, and otherwise stay focused. When will I return?

3:20 P.M., ŚRĪLA PRABHUPĀDA'S ROOM

Devotees are quietly walking around the campus. Some are chanting on beads, some have stopped to talk to each other. I feel responsible to give them the best thing. That is, unadulterated Prabhupāda. Find him again in *Śrīmad-Bhāgavatam*. I'm thinking to start with the Second Canto.

He's ours. Each one finds him and keeps him. I can share him only partially. It's not the same as embracing him—his purports.

O Prabhupāda, I'm a phony, but you keep me on the right track.

He is who he is, Sats.

Don't point your feet at your spiritual master.

I'm not Norman Mailer. I don't have to read Allen Ginsberg to see how he divides his lines. Write on your own.

The audience will read you. Tell your life in Kṛṣṇa consciousness, and the life of devotees. Hare Kṛṣṇa.

Guys talking loudly in Hindi outside, something about work. It's pious, it's even "transcendental," but it's a distraction. I want pure *bhakti* and wish to find it by a discipline of chanting *japa* and reading Prabhupāda's books.

Recently I decided my writing should serve the interests of my pursuit for better *sādhana*. Also, *sādhana* should be done to please my spiritual master. Make it contribute to his movement. Stay in his movement, even though it's inconvenient sometimes.

Hare Kṛṣṇa, Hare Kṛṣṇa.

"Routinization of charisma" (Max Weber). *The Web and the Rock*, by Thomas Wolfe.

The pert girls, the sad boys who want a pert girl to love them. The guru in trouble with material desires. The dry, tired-out ISKCON sage.

Yapping, yapping Hindi workers. On and on they talk.

The monkeys of Vṛndāvana are not to be hated. Vṛndāvana is Vṛndāvana—worshipable. I have a great purport to read on this tomorrow.

I'm allowed to read *Śrīla Prabhupāda-līlāmṛta* to the devotees tomorrow since it's Ekādaśī. Don't ask me to chant sixty-four rounds or to do sixty fasts or sixteen pinpricks inflicted on purpose. *Tapasya* for me is to chant despite dryness, to worship, to go to Trinidad and Guyana and America with goodwill and gratitude.

They walk by, two devotees, talking quietly, and sometimes fingering their beads. They would like to help each other. How do they do it? Pray here in the *dhāma*.

The *gopīs* never asked Kṛṣṇa for anything, but we may ask Kṛṣṇa for help to serve. Be personal with Him, but don't bargain. Oh, I don't know.

If He wants me to stop writing . . .

If He wants to allow me to write better . . .

If He tells me what's best for me, will I be willing to follow?

Be sure, confident, patient, etc. Spill out intelligent instructions. Be confident. It will work. But when? It's already working. More will come.

I get agitated when I see my own disciples on campus and they seem to be waiting for something to happen. Or they may be talking about my books as if they are worthwhile. I become humbled, even unnerved. How can I assign myself to a lower position and yet be the guru whose books they edit and publish, print and sell?

Ask for protection from pride and falldown. If writing or dreamwork helps in that, then fine. If not, why are you doing it?

I am who I am. I remember '50s and '60s jazz as if it were good. I think of the old days before I was a devotee as if it's meaningful.

I'm thirsty. Wanton. Kṛṣṇa is out there. In my heart too. In books. In Name. Like butter in milk or fire in wood. Work and pray and He will manifest. They come after you begging, "Have you found Kṛṣṇa? If so, give Him to us." Greedy beggars.

The artist says, "All you're going to write is a diary?"

It will be an art diary, a smart one, a short-story essay personal poem diary.

You mean like Little Lulu kept?

Like Anne Frank's?

Thoreau's? Kafka's?

Yeah, and more. It's one book true for me.

Died on the road. Expired on the way to spiritual heaven. Had unfinished business and had to return. One of two dogs in Sweden?

No. I'll tell you, it's going to be all right.

Yellow straw mats with green elephants on them. Parrots outside, me in, inside this room where he sat and talked to so many. Preached and managed. Didn't want his disciples to be cheated or deviant or lazy. He reprimanded us: stay in ISKCON. Do your work. "Don't be like a monkey at

Rādhā-kuṇḍa." Don't be a monkey associating with the Rādhā-kuṇḍa *bābājīs*.

Yes, Prabhupāda, you sure did say those things. I'm still in your ISKCON and not well enough to even go out on a rickshaw to the Rādhā-Dāmodara temple. I figure your room here is as good as your room there. Better, in fact. I can write here freely and no one will kick me out. Guards will chase out the monkeys.

Kṛṣṇa-Balarāma statue on black mantle. Framed pictures of Rādhā-Gokulānanda from the old days, Rādhā-Dāmodara old days, 1977 when he was here. Nothing new to say.

After all the flood that has passed over, you mean you have nothing to say?

Peace and quiet
master is master
ISKCON is afloat despite . . .

I'm not adding to the trouble. I'm trying to "set a good example" as we say. Set it.

JAPA LOG, 1 P.M.

Sixteen rounds done. I'll try for extra. Just to say I've done more? Yes, because I see it as a virtue. To scale higher on the wall. Hare Kṛṣṇa. Maybe it will help me to overcome mechanical chanting.

Hear, please, your chanting. Early in the morning I did fourteen by 4:30 A.M. Hear and chant.

JAPA LOG, 5:35 P.M.

Four extra today. Caw, caw. I don't brag. Screech. Thud, Yap. Hindi. Crash. Hare Kṛṣṇa. You ate sweet bread? Tomorrow is Ekādaśī—I know, I don't expect you to do something Herculean. But at least four extra. Or, don't let me pressure you. You've got two lectures. Just make whatever chanting you do good quality. Start before 1:30 A.M.

February 4

12:30 A.M.

Thank you for assuring me that the diary form would accommodate the needs of art as well as the needs of my Kṛṣṇa conscious expression. What we are saying is write in a way that will not hinder my *sādhana* and that will also fulfill my desires to preach through literary art. Now if it *is* the diary form that does this, I should be glad for the discovery and go with it. I should push it to its limits for Kṛṣṇa conscious expression in the art of diary writing. Neither do I have to think of it as "diary" or "mere diary," but simply writing. Writing in a life of attempting to be a devotee.

Surrender here. You just read about Mother Yaśodā seeing the universal form. Praise it. Consider it. Pray for the vision of appreciation.

Surrender while reading and in writing it down. I have nothing extra to achieve. I am poor. Another day I may write a "great" poem, or rather it may pass through me. A powerful description may pass through my pen onto the page. I'll write in quiet and in excitement. I'll leave a trail of words. Some will be memorable and readers may wonder, "How was he able to evoke this, to flow like this? This piece is a breakthrough. He didn't used to be able to write so well." But often it will be the quiet walk to and from the shed in Geaglum. And who knows what is the best in the trail of words? I don't know; it's not up to me. I have to speak, write—and it must come from a life that is not diverted by literary aims (by greed for powerful writing pieces).

Approach Kṛṣṇa to surrender.

10:30 A.M.

I gave the Ekādaśī class in the temple room, reading and speaking from *Śrīla Prabhupāda-līlāmṛta*. The topic was Prabhupāda in Vṛndāvana. I was planning to read, but I decided to paraphrase. It came out all right. As soon as I began I felt a twinge behind the eye. It didn't develop immediately into a painful headache, but now I'm afraid that it may. Therefore, I haven't dared to write here, and neither am I able to chant extra rounds for Ekādaśī. Neither am I able to read to prepare for my 3 P.M. class. Gun-shy in Vṛndāvana.

NIGHT NOTES

Lying on my back while Bhāgavata dāsa does acupressure just before I take rest for the night. I hear the wonderful sounds of Vṛndāvana—the bell ringing at 6:30 P.M. for the evening *ārati*, the bell that I associate with Śrīla Prabhupāda and his last days here. At the same time a flock of peacocks starts calling out.

Not so "wonderful" are the screeching, chattering, and grunting monkeys nearby. But they're also part of it. Then during the night I'll hear the *chaukīdār* walking by loudly banging his stick, insensitive to the Guesthouse full of sleepers. He makes a gruff "ho-ho" sound to show the monkeys who's boss, and when I'm up here in the morning after *maṅgala-ārati*, I hear clearly the duet between a man and woman loud-speakered from a nearby *āśrama*. He sings, "Govinda-Rādhe, Rādhe" and she sings back, "Rādhe-Govinda, Rādhe-Govinda," back and forth in a musically interesting way. We may object that it's not a scientific mantra, but nevertheless it's nothing but Govinda, Rādhe, Rādhe and Govinda. All sounds in Vṛndāvana are different from sounds elsewhere.

As I said in the class this morning, Vṛndāvana was not just Prabhupāda's residence but it is the residence of all Gauḍīya Vaiṣṇavas. Although we may feel culturally foreign here, certainly we feel religiously at home. Nowhere else, even in India, do we find people of "our religion" with beadbags, the same *tilaka*, the chanting of Hare Kṛṣṇa, and with Rādhā and Kṛṣṇa as their worshipable Lords. So I'm appreciating Vṛndāvana even as I'm approaching the last days of this visit. Tonight Janmāṣṭamī dāsa, who's trying to live here as long as he can, said that the local devotees refer to a "transcendental boot" that kicks you out. They're always fearful it may happen. That boot is easily applied to a person like me who's just a tender visitor, but I hope there's something like a return permission and maybe some day in the future, a longer stay for me. Prabhupāda angrily denounced one of his own disciples who went to live outside of ISKCON at Rādhā-kuṇḍa with the *bābājīs* there, "Don't become a monkey!" Whatever I do I want it to please Prabhupāda, and I think that means contributing to his movement.

JAPA LOG, 3 P.M.

Chanted one extra round so far and will do another at the disciples' meeting. A Godbrother wrote me that he concentrates as he chants on Śrīla Prabhupāda's "just hear," and he regularly reviews as he chants, "Am I hearing? Am I hearing?"

Squeeze out an extra round. It's what counts. *Japa*. How serious am I? How good am I? I'm tired of trying to figure it out. Don't want to pose as a serious chanter, but neither do I want to fall into a negative cliché that I'm incorrigibly inattentive. I do care and there is hope for reform. Therefore, extra efforts are worthwhile.

How long will this log last? It's like a flickering flame that could blow out with a sudden gust.

February 5

MIDNIGHT

Is there something I should try to achieve in my remaining six days in Vṛndāvana? The program is chalked out. I should try to give several more classes and go on a few outings. My health limits me so that it will take my full effort to fulfill these obligations. I say this is not the real Vṛndāvana; even in my present neophyte stage I am capable of better worship and residence in Vṛndāvana. Therefore, we have been planning our return visit.

But this conclusion, "This is not the real Vṛndāvana where you wear yourself out with group obligations"—is it right? Seems so. Keep Vṛndāvana sacred in your life for personal development of that which is soft and sweet (as Vṛndāvana is described in *Caitanya-caritāmṛta*). Go to Vṛndāvana (as Lord

Caitanya did) without a crowd. Allow yourself to think that you have paid enough of the institutional dues to worship alone in Vṛndāvana, concentrating on chanting and reading instead of lecturing and meetings. Then you'll become a fit instrument to preach when you leave.

As for "doing something" during these last days, that may not be up to me. At least I can avoid making offenses and I can seek forgiveness for offenses I've made. Don't take entering Vṛndāvana for granted. Pray you'll be allowed to return. Pray to understand the essence of Vṛndāvana and how you will keep it alive even when you're not here.

A *sādhana-siddha-bhakta* cannot become Mother Yaśodā nor Śrīmatī Rādhārāṇī nor Nanda Mahārāja nor Śrīdāmā nor any of those eternally existing *pāriṣads*, but "by following the principles exhibited by Nanda Mahārāja and Yaśodā and their associates, the inhabitants of Vṛndāvana, ordinary living beings may attain such affection as exhibited by Nanda and Yaśodā." *(Bhāg.* 10.8.49, purport) This hints at *rāgānuga-bhakti*. Let us do what Śrīla Prabhupāda teaches, absorb what he writes, but don't think vital supplementation is needed from the teachings of a guru who is much more "*rasika*" than Śrīla Prabhupāda. Don't read into Śrīla Prabhupāda's teachings something concocted.

Will how to attain *prema-bhakti* be revealed "automatically"? How to show or develop the required greed *(laulyam)*? We say we accept the *bhakti* Śrīla Prabhupāda is teaching and recognize it as pure devotional service. It is our most crucial, immediate need. It will lead us on. I think Kṛṣṇa and Śrīla Prabhupāda are capable of revealing to me how I'll serve in Vṛndāvana when I'm liberated. I can't practice it now anyway. That would be artificial—to pretend I'm a *gopī-mañjarī* massaging Rādhā's feet or chasing Kṛṣṇa from Her *kuñja*.

Go for *bhakti;* pray to understand Prabhupāda's books. This morning I read and understood how we cannot become Yaśodā or Nanda (just as we can't become God—a Māyāvādī conception). I also appreciated reading that Mother Yaśodā surrendered to Kṛṣṇa as the Supreme when she couldn't understand the cause of the universal form appearing in His mouth. Then Yogamāyā covered Mother Yaśodā with maternal affection. She is beyond Bhagavān realization. I plan to speak on these topics in a class and say, "But we cannot imitate her."

How will a follower of Śrīla Prabhupāda receive specific *rāgānugā* practice, since Prabhupāda doesn't teach it? I have faith that we are all right as Prabhupādānugas, but I'd like more "scientific" information to answer this challenge: "You are merely practicing *vaidhi-sādhana-bhakti,* so you'll go to Vaikuṇṭha. You need to specifically hear and practice *rāgānugā-sādhana-bhakti,* hearing of the *gopīs'* service to Rādhā. You need to hear it from a *rasika-guru.* Unless you do so, you cannot reach the ultimate goal, certainly not in this lifetime."

But who is so great that he can achieve perfection in this lifetime? Our perfection is to attain pure love of Kṛṣṇa in His Vṛndāvana feature. Śrīla Prabhupāda *is* teaching this. Serve his mission in practical ways. Help his followers. Work for the spreading and strengthening of his movement. Your service will be rewarded.

In each of the disciples' meetings I've been citing references and speaking on the same items: (1) Living in Vṛndāvana; (2) reading *śāstras;* (3) *japa;* and (4) our spiritual master/disciple relationship. On the last topic I always read something from one of my books. My point is that the best way we can relate is by their reading my books. Only in my writings am I able to be most honest and intimate. Last night I read from the first chapter of *Radio Shows.* It ends with the words, "This has become the assumption of my writing life and the code I live by." In that session I describe my participation in a *harināma* party in Verona, Italy. My perceptions were those of the mechanical man, not very deep, but then I assert that it's worthwhile to write any experience in order to preserve the moment. "Rather than lose, lose, lose, *āyur harati vai puṁsām*

. . . An artist wants to hold onto what happens between sunrise and sunset, and if he can write it down, it will be saved."

I like this spirit. Here in Vṛndāvana I feel that I'm not preserving as much as I'd like. By following this code I have faith that life is not just trash or a series of trivial events. "Although I can't feel it when I walk on the street with the *harināma*, still, I know that even if I describe the mechanical level of existence, it will be meaningful. The essential Kṛṣṇa conscious impressions will be beautiful and worth saving." This is especially true in Vṛndāvana. At least I've accumulated a good number of pages in my weeks here. I look forward to traveling to Delhi, the long plane flights to the Caribbean, my stay in Trinidad, and going to Guyana. It's all worth saving, even though I'm in the mundane world, and my Kṛṣṇa conscious insights are not deep. I'll say it again: it's worth saving. As Prabhupāda said about his own writing, he gets up at midnight and writes because he must, he has to. He has taste.

MAṄGALA-ĀRATI

Maṅgala, auspicious
but all I can think and feel is who is
near me, pushing me, and can I fit my
skinny body between those two devotees?
God is here but I'm worried
how I look before others.
Prema escapes me.

ROOM 42

Room 42 contains me.
Open the door for *prasādam*
open your eyes after sleep
my heavens . . .
four days, two nights
six left . . .

42 is 24 backwards
and 14 is a number I used
when gambling with dimes
at the wheel of fortune
in Saint Clare's Church.
Did you win the Eucharist?
Naw. I won the prize for
sad
boobs.
Anyway, forget all that—
from room 42 I go out
surmising
that next year
I may return to Vṛndāvana
to stay somewhere else.
But this room is ever dear.

February 6

In a dream I go to see Rādhā-Vallabha dāsa about my health. He's a famous doctor from whose body light emanates and water trickles. I wonder if this is just a stunt he performs to gain followers or if it's true. My only fear is that he will prescribe a fruit-only diet. I also hear that this doctor very much respects someone who has the drive to get better.

When I awoke I realized that I'm feeling a little desperate about my health. The pain is intense and I have frequent bouts of it. Maybe I should adjust my diet again or try some new way to get better.

I do have a strong will to get better, but I don't have much hope. It seems that Kṛṣṇa is not allowing me to get better. If this is true, then I should go to the Caribbean despite the inevitable pain. If Kṛṣṇa wants me to have a headache, then it will be better to continue my duty as a preacher than to take a health retreat. "Die on the battlefield" is not necessarily a harsh philosophy. It just means you recognize that your health will be bad no matter where you are or what you do. You might as well preach.

It seems significant that the person I wanted to talk to about health was Rādhā-Vallabha. I think beyond Rādhā-Vallabha dāsa to the original Rādhā-Vallabha, Kṛṣṇa, who is dear to the *gopīs*. The dream source is asking why I don't take my case to Kṛṣṇa Himself. If my dream Rādhā-Vallabha dāsa is an instrument for the original Kṛṣṇa, he is reminding me of the importance of having a strong will to get better.

But I never got to talk to him; I only made an appointment. O Kṛṣṇa, O Śrīla Prabhupāda, what should I do about my health? Bhaktisiddhānta Prabhu, my Godbrother, told me that when he was very ill he dragged himself to the drawing table and went on with his work and the pain went away. I can't push myself like that. O Rādhā-Gopīvallabha, O Rādhā-Vallabha, You are my refuge. I'm not this body.

February 7

8:45 A.M.

Finding quotes to read this afternoon. I'm not living rightly in Vṛndāvana. No big offenses but . . . just choked up, dry. Always on the verge of another headache. Writing dwindled. Nothing to say. Most important is to use available energy to (1) prepare and give lectures; (2) answer letters; (3) chant *japa*—squeezing out extras.

Little waves do come and then I know I'm in Vṛndāvana. When I leave, my main regret will be that I didn't love this place and its residents. But I don't want phony trends or a "*bhāva*" of the imagination only. In that sense, this visit is real. I mainly want to come back with a proper attitude. I think only by going away from this straitjacketed life of temple obligations will I be able to read Prabhupāda's books more

Inner music 2.

Me 'n' you.

SURR-
ENDER

Encounter.

steadily. So the Vṛndāvana mood, loving Kṛṣṇa, may be better attained by leaving. Today an ISKCON guru will arrive, and his secretary has already invited me to lunch tomorrow. I don't want to go. Another leader is phoning me from abroad, probably to get me to cooperate with his side in a controversy, and I'm lying low from another big Godbrother—letters and requests pour in. People suffering. "My heart is full of pain," she said. What does she mean?

"The school needs a new headmaster. What do you think?" I don't think.

"Come see my newly installed *śilā*." No thanks. I'm not up to it and don't want to make a farce: "He looks cute. What's His name?"

"Come lecture to the children in our writing class. We like to invite ISKCON writers to come share their realizations about the craft." I don't know the craft. I wouldn't be a good influence on your junior craftsmen.

Arrogant sonofa . . .

"So and so is making huge amounts of money."

"What is my *varṇa*?"

Eating food cooked in butter is not good for you. Why don't you do yoga?

Vraja, Vraja . . . twenty-four-hour *kīrtana*. Look it up in his books.

You see what I mean?

ROOM 42

Room alone before 9 A.M., sounds
distant. Open your mouth, shut it, *saumya*.
Open-shut case. He's a nervous
wreck. A lazy piece. Too many pies
and creams
burning in gut.
Four, four. Two, two, his
room number. Give up the key when

you leave in
two days plus one and a half.
Then where do you go?
When do you return?

VṚNDĀ #21

Vṛndā I'm plumb out
realize I love Kṛṣṇa
somehow
and *tulasī*
oh, chant.

THE BELL AT KRISHNA-BALARAM MANDIR

Bell ringing 12:30, caw caw
elephant hand? No, little hand
of me
little life
little bell, moment gone
Swami, Prabhupāda is in
his rooms and I'm with him
dying—got a long (a little)
way to go. Not long now.
Hang on to the rail.

5:15 P.M.

Walking over to MVT buildings to give last disciples' meeting—met the bright warm sunshine. How nice! Small monkey on ledge of one-story building and me with strong pole in my hands. I read about leaving Vṛndāvana from *Wild Garden* 1992, on reading Śrīla Prabhupāda books from *Cc. Āśraya*, and on *japa* from *Begging For the Nectar of the Holy Name*. Didn't talk much in between. I didn't read sections I had lined up as examples of the intimacy of the relationship through my books. I said it's too intimate to read to a group. It's just between each one of you and me when you read my books. In this way I honored the precious relationship of reader and author. You can only go so far in an out loud reading with such a large, diverse group. Anyway, some of them know and I know.

February 8

A devotee praised me for pushing on with travels and lecturing even though I'm ill. She connected it to a line in Prabhupāda's purport, "One who lays down his life on the sacrificial altar, or in the proper battlefield, is at once cleansed of bodily reactions and promoted to a higher status of life." (Bg. 2.22, purport) She praised me for my determination, dedication, and sacrifice. "Still you are going and putting your body on the line for the cause of preaching and encouraging others in Kṛṣṇa consciousness." She doesn't know I have canceled my tour. From Vṛndāvana I'm going to a place where I can be free of obligations and can just repair my body.

I read this call to die on the battlefield just before bed last night. I thought I would probably think of it during the night, and worry whether it was cowardly of me to cancel my

Caribbean tour just because my health has broken down. I called Madhu and he asked me to rest peacefully. He said as far as he was concerned, my "proper battlefield" was first *sādhana*, then writing, and only thirdly traveling and speaking where people see me in the flesh (what's left of it). I accepted his assurance.

Realizations in Kṛṣṇa consciousness are ultimately meant to be shared among devotees and those eligible to come to Kṛṣṇa consciousness. *The Nectar of Instruction* states this in the *prīti-lakṣaṇam* verse, and Kṛṣṇa also says it in *Bhagavad-gītā*. But sometimes we need time to assimilate what we have read before we can express it deeply to others. Each person can read the book for themselves. "Hey, Prabhu, there's a great purport in *Bhāg*. 10.9.5 where Prabhupāda advises us, 'On the platform of love and affection, it is the duty of the devotee to do one thing first and other things later. The proper intuition by which to do this is given by Kṛṣṇa.' See? This means even when Śrīla Prabhupāda isn't directly available as he used to be, if we are sincere and pure in serving guru and Kṛṣṇa, the Lord will tell us what to do."

To this the Prabhu might reply, "You mean Kṛṣṇa is telling you how to write your books and telling you what to quote from *śāstra*?"

No, I don't make that claim, but Kṛṣṇa may be instructing me through my intelligence or through the material energy. Intuition.

Giving the Hindi class was fun. I restrained myself while speaking about Mother Yaśodā and the *gopīs* complaining to her about Kṛṣṇa's naughty activities, the accusations that Kṛṣṇa ate dirt. I didn't want to play it up too much or be too corny. Still, it's sweet to speak straight about the pastimes. Mother Yaśodā made an important philosophical point about surrender to Kṛṣṇa's will when we don't know the cause of some overwhelming situation. Śrīla Prabhupāda advised us to follow that path. Kṛṣṇa gave me the intelligence to speak in a balanced way.

It was fun speaking in Prabhupada's residence. He was present in his *mūrti* form, sitting at his desk. The audience was Hindi-speaking-only-devotees, almost all men. Their faces were brownish, wrapped in scarves, humble looking. There were also some Western devotees, mostly my disciples, blond-haired Trivikrama dāsa, Ekatvam from Puerto Rico in a big, green, winter jacket, and *mātājīs* from America, Australia, Finland, etc. I gave preference to the Hindi-speaking devotees during the question and answer session. I took a firmer control over their questions and spoke to them as a teacher. I played the role. When a devotee asked what to do if he can't fully surrender, I said, "Did you think you would be surrendered by now?" When a devotee said that his life is a failure and he wants to know why since Kṛṣṇa wants him to surrender, I replied, "Your life is not a failure, but you have to prove that your will to surrender is strong and that you won't accept *māyā*."

I've been complaining that I haven't been able to get the taste of Vṛndāvana-dhāma, but certainly this was a real Vṛndāvana event. ISKCON Vṛndāvana is also Vṛndāvana. And the heart of ISKCON Vṛndāvana is to be able to speak Prabhupāda's teachings from his *Bhāgavatam* purports to an audience like I had today.

NOON

Yesterday I told the devotees that they should examine themselves as to why they're leaving Vṛndāvana. Probably it's because they're not fit to live here. Maybe they're admitting that they don't want to live here, or they may hold some idealistic notion that they'd like to live in Vṛndāvana, but they know they're not fit.

To live in Vṛndāvana for an ISKCON devotee means finding some service at the Krishna-Balaram Mandir. That can be demanding. Maybe there's nothing here for us to do. Are we leaving because there's no service?

Or are we leaving because we want to preach? That's a good reason—the main reason—to leave. It's the reason Prabhupāda left Vṛndāvana-dhāma.

One devotee admitted that she's too shy to preach, so she can't claim she's leaving Vṛndāvana for that reason. She admits that she's leaving Vṛndāvana in order to pursue relative goals. She wants to go to school and figure out how to make money. She also wants to get married and thinks Vṛndāvana is not a good place for contemplating a marriage partner.

Later, I wrote this devotee a letter and said, "It's good to admit that you're leaving for those material reasons and it's not necessarily bad. You're leaving Vṛndāvana in order to make progress in your *varṇāśrama* evolution. It's natural to get married and you may have to develop career skills. Leave Vṛndāvana, then, with the idea to accomplish what you need to do and then eventually work on coming back."

Neither is it all or nothing—no Vṛndāvana or all Vṛndāvana. We can take Vṛndāvana with us in our hearts. We make resolutions here that we carry with us outside of Vṛndāvana. And we can come back to visit.

I spoke these things, but what about me? Why am *I* leaving? Remember that haiku I wrote about ten years ago? It was at the end of *The Dust of Vṛndāvana*. It went like this:

> Driven out of Vṛndāvana
> by a Sikh
> in a Mazda.

I'm leaving because I'm not fit to live here, because I don't *want* to stay here, because I have no service at the Krishna-Balaram Mandir. I'm not sure about making progress in my *varṇāśrama-dharma*. I'm a *sannyāsī*, and that's already the end of the *varṇāśrama* road. But I have to evolve in my devotion to Kṛṣṇa before I can come back to stay. Yes, I'm going to preach. That will help.

ROOM 42

Room 42 lease up,
I signed my name in Register
O. Stephen. O Satsfer
Oh, time is up "Time is
flying!" Madhu said.
I asked him, "*Which* time?"
Today you mean?
Or—he meant for our
stay in Vṛndāvana '97.

42, get it?
24 backwards
no more coming back
go to Vrajaloka with
Śrīla Prabhupāda.

PRABHUPĀDA

Phony Prabhupāda lover
real one I want to be
as reader and follower
Brahmānanda, Satsvarūpa '66
Hayagrīva, yeah, well now
Vṛndāvana means die and go—
Prabhupāda is waiting. I
always make sense but not
in this one.
Done poem done
always his *śiṣya*.

5:30 P.M.

I spoke with a *sannyāsī* Godbrother and asked him questions that were important to me.

I told him I'd heard that most of the *ācāryas* in our line have gone to another planet and are preaching there, and that at the end of his life Prabhupāda said he was going to preach on another planet too. He said his sincere followers would join him there.

Mahārāja said he didn't know of any references showing that our *ācāryas* are preaching on other planets. He said he knew of a story told about Śrīla Bhaktisiddhānta Sarasvatī Ṭhākura's last days. One night he looked at the moon and said, "Kṛṣṇa consciousness is diminishing on the moon." Some of his followers then surmised that when he left, he went to the moon to preach. But Mahārāja didn't think it would be correct to assume that our *ācāryas* have all gone to other planets to preach. We say of them *nitya-līlā praviṣṭha*—they have gone to join Kṛṣṇa's *nitya-līlā* in the spiritual world. I was satisfied by his replies.

I then asked him my questions about the challenge from Nārāyaṇa Mahārāja's followers. Nārāyaṇa Maharāja teaches that there are two paths of *sādhana-bhakti—vaidhi* and *rāgānuga*, and that *vaidhi* will lead us to Vaikuṇṭha while *rāgānuga*, which is difficult to obtain, will lead to Goloka Vṛndāvana. They also say that the only way to attain *rāgānuga-bhakti* is to associate with a *rāgānuga-bhakta*. This, of course, is our *siddhānta*. But they also say that ISKCON is following *vaidhi-bhakti* and that we will not attain Vraja. Therefore, we need to associate with a *rasika-guru* to receive more specific *rāgānuga* teachings.

Mahārāja replied by first reciting lines from a Bengali song composed by Śrīla Bhaktisiddhānta Sarasvatī Ṭhākura, which he sang on the day he and his disciples moved from their modest temple in Calcutta to their new temple. The general translation is this: "The path of *vaidhi-bhakti* has been abandoned and *rāgānuga-bhakti* has now taken over. The *sādhus* are engaged in apparent *viṣayi* [material activities]."

The purport of the song is that Bhaktisiddhānta Sarasvatī was engaging devotees, perhaps for the first time in

Vaiṣṇavism, in intense *yukta-vairāgya*—using cars and so many other apparently material things—to spread Lord Caitanya's movement. In this song he defined *yukta-vairāgya* as *rāgānuga*.

Mahārāja also quoted a song by Prabhodhānanda Sarasvatī stating that when one follows the path of Lord Caitanya, then Rādhā-Kṛṣṇa *bhāva* appears in the heart. Lord Caitanya, who is worshiped in *dāsya-rasa*, leads us to worshiping Rādhā-Kṛṣṇa in *mādhurya*. Ordinary *dāsya* performed in *vaidhi-bhakti* by which we see Kṛṣṇa always as master, will lead to Vaikuṇṭha, but *dāsya* rendered to Lord Caitanya brings us to Rādhā-Kṛṣṇa worship in *mādhurya*.

Those who concentrate only on hearing of Kṛṣṇa and Rādhā and Their intimate pastimes have to show us where they are strongly connected to Lord Caitanya. We know that we're connected to Lord Caitanya through the *saṅkīrtana* movement. It's by execution of *saṅkīrtana* that we become eligible to have Rādhā-Kṛṣṇa appear in our hearts.

Saṅkīrtana can be explained in various ways. Literally, it means the congregational singing of the holy names. It also means engaging everything in Kṛṣṇa's service. Prabhupāda was expert in doing this.

I told Mahārāja that his explanation was satisfying, but there's a further challenge. One could say that he is a learned devotee and has given references outside of Prabhupāda's books to support ISKCON as competent to lead us back to Godhead. One might say that these references are not in Prabhupāda's books specifically. Mahārāja admitted that he learned a lot from sources outside ISKCON years ago, but he said he began to feel that by hearing from those sources, he was minimizing his relationship with Prabhupāda. The point is, both Mahārāja and I agree that it would be all right for a devotee who is fixed in following Prabhupāda to sometimes explain Śrīla Prabhupāda's books by making references to other Gauḍīya Vaiṣṇava sources. If, however, this kind of commentary on Prabhupāda's teachings or on Gauḍīya Vaiṣṇavism in general is done separate from a connection with Prabhupāda, then it will not be good for

Prabhupāda's followers. They will risk losing their strong attachment to him and focus on his movement.

I then raised another challenge: could he give more support for his statement that *saṅkīrtana* activities could be considered *rāgānuga-bhakti*? He said that he could not deny that the highest aspect of *rāgānuga-bhakti* is to speak of Rādhā and Kṛṣṇa in Their loving pastimes, but the *ācāryas* warn us that since material sex is a reflection of spiritual sex, we should not talk about Rādhā and Kṛṣṇa's pastimes if we have that material sex still in our hearts. He gave the example of Lord Caitanya who certainly came to teach *rāgānuga-bhakti*, but who spoke about Rādhā and Kṛṣṇa only with a very few persons in the Gambhīrā. At the same time, He gave *prema-bhakti* through His *saṅkīrtana* movement.

I was also encouraged to think that if I am writing even experimentally in Kṛṣṇa's service, this is a kind of spontaneous devotional service.

Mahārāja added that those who follow the path Prabhupāda has given us are preaching around the world. The Rādhā-kuṇḍa *bābājīs* who jump ahead to talk of esoteric topics do not preach or do much of anything. He said Bhaktisiddhānta Sarasvatī's followers are strict about not openly discussing the highest pastimes of Rādhā and Kṛṣṇa.

He also said if you love what you're doing, that itself is spontaneous. I mentioned that in *The Nectar of Devotion* where Prabhupāda doesn't use many Sanskrit terms, he seems to define *rāgānuga-bhakti* as spontaneous service. Some people seem to think that *rāgānuga-bhakti* is *only* when you talk specifically of the liberated devotees in Vraja. Prabhupāda has said that the highest stage can only be practiced in the liberated state. Mahārāja affirmed that the spiritual master will reveal this in our hearts when we serve Lord Caitanya's *saṅkīrtana* movement. He quoted the song that we sing every day, *divya-jñān hṛde prokāśito*, "The spiritual master will reveal *prema-bhakti* in the heart."

I said sometimes I thought it was hype the way some ISKCON leaders say book distribution is *rāgānuga-bhakti*, but he was saying it in a way I could accept and appreciate. I said that for this to be true, *saṅkīrtana* would have to be done deeply. And, of course, it has to be done in a life where hearing and chanting are emphasized, not only that we concentrate on outer activities. He then confided in me about his own project and the boldness required to carry it out. It gave me confidence and inspiration in my own service.

At the meeting today, I heard a story about Prabhupāda. Once, an ordinary man came to Prabhupāda and demanded to know his *svarūpa*. Prabhupāda said, "Rascal *svarūpa*." Then he told the man that if he followed the principles of Kṛṣṇa consciousness nicely, the rules and regulations, then Prabhupāda himself would reveal the man's *svarūpa*.

I also heard another story that illustrated how one who actually has *bhakti* doesn't brag. He keeps himself humble and waits to be raised up. We shouldn't be presumptuous in our attempts to be Kṛṣṇa conscious.

February 9

MIDNIGHT

Nothing will work perfectly, but I write and live. This is the work of the Madman, Wink Pervis Bhakta. His hair in disarray. His . . .

You can split.

You can leave Vṛndāvana, but it's in your heart. I'm afraid of the Vṛndāvana underground and what may happen if I come back here, but I can find a space at the trough.

Serve in the *saṅkīrtana* movement wherever I am. Fashion an instrument, a cultural weapon.

But a morning walk, how is that serving?

The Vṛndāvana underground.

The *bhakti* rivers flow, she said, from many places, and she went off to collect it. I said, "I'll take what comes from Śrīla Prabhupāda. That way I'm sure I won't get poisonous water."

Commendable.

American cameras and gadgets tumble. They'll all be stolen. Better to procure a treasure moths and thieves can't destroy—*kṛṣṇa-bhakti*. But it's not found in the Vṛndāvana underground or Krishna-Balaram Mandir?

"I tried desperately to get in touch with you in November, but you're not on e-mail and no one in America knew where you were. They said only that you were traveling in Europe."

You sent it to the wrong address.

Blue-green algae. Tickets at twice the price.

Don't get fat. Don't go to the moon. You go where He takes you or sends you—like a boat going over the waterfall.

Write, Mistah, write. Get your second voice in order. Use any method you can. For Kṛṣṇa take a chance.

Saṅkīrtana has many meanings.

Today the 9th, then the 10th, on the 11th we leave. Therefore, if you are going to steal nectar, do it today.

Oh, this is Vṛndāvana, but I can't find it.

He came back shiny-eyed from Nanda-grāma. I came back shiny-eyed from a talk with a Godbrother.

Hit sturdy bamboo pole against the cement walk—there, I got it, the authentic *chaukīdār* sound.

I'm serious but petering out. I wanted to take Vṛndāvana home in a jar. It won't stay there. Jam it in your heart. No, I can't digest it. The gas in the intestines.

Please write an objective account for the BBT of whippersnappers you carried back from Vṛndāvana. My book will be called, "The Vṛndāvana Underground, Is There One? An Anthropologist's Delayed Apology."

Pigeons. Next life

stony heart

the pallet people—dread on feeling I've returned to America. Spend too much money to get there as if desperate, and hope your head won't split.

Too much. Too much—that's what the widow said of Satsva when he walked into the *mandira* in Glider shoes.

Too much, too little. Lord Kṛṣṇa is also the Judge and the Mercy. Too much.

In a dream there was so much fear. People were afraid to speak their truth or to be themselves. They did a lot of beating around the bush. Who can cut through? The fear is based on the reality that a young giant would kill them at any moment. Death could come and you would lose your nice things, your shelter, your friends, your good meals, your trip to Nanda-grāma or wherever you were planning to go and return from this afternoon. All your hopes for the future life could be similarly smashed because the body is fragile and can be killed. It's no wonder everyone was living a compromised life in the dream. Heroes get killed.

Nevertheless, you tried to express yourself. What do I mean? I mean by speaking obscure double-talk, I could get messages out. Or by accepting Kṛṣṇa's protection. Get your truth out and into the people's hearts somehow or other.

I have so many dreams. I can't expect any one dream is suddenly going to change my life. Such powerful dreams come but rarely. All these little ones, though, if I take them seriously and thoughtfully, can guide me. Now I'm awake in Vṛndāvana, but am I really?

Good-bye sir,
I've got it in the jar.

Tickets he didn't get yet, but we've got reservations. He could have bought them if he had had the money. "The full whack" we had to pay.

Determinists. Feminists. I'm tired of it. Palavar. Pancakes. He says it's all in the cooking; in the simple diet you'll find health. Ride smooth.

Another Russian doctor says, "Just smell this. Put some into your nostrils and around your ears. It should smell light, not heavy or sweet. What do you think?"

I think it smells sweet and heavy, but I don't know what it's *supposed* to smell like. I don't know what's right.

No Guru but one.

9:30 A.M.

This morning in the Prabhupāda Samādhi Mandir several more *sannyāsīs* and GBC men arrived. Madhu and I have the same thought: time to go. In fact, we've over-stayed. Two of the new arrivals mention to me that they will meet with me, but there's no time, given my limited capabilities.

We've decided to leave by 5 A.M. tomorrow and we have a place in Delhi to stay until final arrangements are made for the plane. It's an abrupt departure from Vṛndāvana, but I've already settled matters in my mind about my inability to enter Vṛndāvana. Staying here longer would not be good. I'll leave, but with hopes to return in a better frame of mind. We're purchasing round-trip tickets so that we can come back next year.

12:25 NOON

Chant or read. Don't think only writing will last (in print) and that chanting fades away. Kṛṣṇa hears. It's eternal credit when you chant. If only I could do it with more feeling. Maybe one day I'll stop writing and only chant. I *could* write, "The chanting of the holy names tastes like honey," as one Gauḍīya *bābājī* wrote in his diary in his last days. Or I may go on like this.

Kṛṣṇa escapes me. He doesn't call me because I don't sufficiently cry for Him.

List of things to do in last afternoon in Vṛndāvana:

(1) Make this list.

(2) Feel nonverbal.

(3) Feel nothing to say.

(4) Think over.

(5) Get a book like *Easy Journey to Other Planets* to read on the plane.

Tired old pawpaw.

Guru and disciple.

Be pure, be grave.

Keep on truckin'.

(6) Think in the vein of fictive lists *(A Fictive Diary*, Nemerov).

(7) Think, think, drink, drink.

(8) "Vṛndāvana! Vṛndāvana!"

(9) Say *jaya*.

(10) Answer letters.

(11) Avoid a headache.

(12) Maintain. Heart-beat.

(13) Live.

(14) Be confident your 4 P.M. class will be okay.

(15) Think of Trivikrama Swami.

(16) The lot.

(17) Be here as crows and parrots caw and screech your last day over.

(18) Sneak-away plan—keep it.

(19) Money bag pouch on wall—get it down.

(20) O ladies and gents, I tried to be a guru. Don't suck at my ear.

(21) I am the kitty in my dream—hurry, lick up the milk from the floor, get down and do it.

(22) Sorry R.R., I love you anyway.

(23) I'm going to stay fit.

(24) Phone, phone, write letters, notes—prove something.

(25) Make prayers to Rādhā and Kṛṣṇa—please give me strength to serve my guru.

(26) I can't go to his room, go to Rādhā-Dāmodara, Nanda-grāma, Yamunā. It's too late. I couldn't taste it if I went anyway, but it would have been good for me.

(27) Look out the window down into the edge of the *prasādam* hall—line of six devotees sitting on green mat facing a *brahmacārī* who's giving them a class. His hand gestures.

(28) Just outside the *prasādam* hall in the February afternoon sunlight, small *tulasī* in a pot on a table. Worship her.

(29) But Prabhu, this is a list of things to do. You're just talking about things that are. Yes, because to be is also as good

as to do. There's nothing to do but just carry out your duties as faithfully as you can.

(30) Vinay Aggarwal became Varuṇa dāsa, and his sister Madhu became Madhumatī.

(31) Looking for the bag to put my sleeping bag in.

(32) Waiting the last hour, chanting a round.

(33) Watch Prabhupāda's clothes dry.

Completed uncompleted on February 9, 1997
in room 42 of the Guesthouse at Krishna-Balaram
Mandir, Vṛndāvana

Appendix

DEAR GODBROTHER,

Please accept my humble obeisances. All glories to Śrīla Prabhupāda.

I want to write a letter to you which is a P.S. to my last letter and a further discussion with you about the nature of pure Kṛṣṇa consciousness or surrender to Kṛṣṇa.

You have been defining in an analytical way the further and further stages of pure devotion. Pure devotion is not simply offering the fruits of one's work or working in a dutiful way. It is serving spontaneously, in chanting and hearing, and doing what Kṛṣṇa actually wants us to do. This acting just to please Kṛṣṇa goes beyond wanting to serve according to one's personal nature.

What I want to express to you as a friend is a line of argument that I find compelled to take in answer to this request that you are making on behalf of Kṛṣṇa, that I just do what Kṛṣṇa wants me to do if I want to attain pure devotion.

First, however, I want to relate to you something I read many years ago, before I became a devotee, in the diaries of Franz Kafka. Kafka said something about the nature of Judaism. Although Kafka was not a religious man in the ordinary sense, in this one diary entry he spoke in praise of Judaism and said something like, "Now there's a real religion. It accepts the whole man." I don't know exactly of what he was speaking, but it struck me. I thought in contrast of the stereotype that is sometimes given of renounced Christianity, which is that one surrenders in spirit and negatively renounces the flesh. Perhaps Kafka was praising Judaism as a religion that accepts the human man in all his dimensions.

I like to think that this is what I am trying to do in my own Kṛṣṇa consciousness. Perhaps when I was younger and I *appeared* more surrendered, I was partly pursuing that renounced version where one suppresses certain "impure" drives one has (and I don't mean sinful activities, but personal natures) and does just what Kṛṣṇa wants according to the order of the spiritual master. Although it appears that one is on the higher platform of devotional service, that "whole man" has not been eliminated. Therefore, he has not been fully engaged in Kṛṣṇa's service.

I think that now that I am allowing myself to dovetail my creative nature in Kṛṣṇa's service, to be a writer for Kṛṣṇa, I am more surrendered than when I was completely submerging my desires to write in this way. I know there's a thin line between indulgence and offering something to Kṛṣṇa, but I try again and again to be honest about this. The best I can come up with so far is that this is my surrendered offering to Kṛṣṇa. In other words, it's not a matter of theological discussion but existential reality. A theoretical discussion can go on, on one hand, as perfect talks from the *vyāsāsana*, or talks between you and I about what Kṛṣṇa is actually saying in the *Bhagavad-gītā*, but if I ask myself, "All right, so now I know what pure devotion is, I have to do only what Kṛṣṇa wants," I have to ask further, "Then how do I follow it up? How do I know what Kṛṣṇa wants? And how do I attain it?"

First of all, I don't really know what He wants in my very specific, tiny life. I have to offer Him the best I can in terms of what I think He wants. Furthermore, even if I were to make a guess and say that Kṛṣṇa doesn't want me to be, say, a writer, first of all I wouldn't know for sure that that's what He wants, and second, how could I give it up?

I don't want to define myself on a lower rung of devotional service, but neither can I artificially do something beyond my realization. I try to fully surrender *(ātma-nivedanam)* in the sense of that impression I got from Kafka's line. I want to give the whole man and not just a renounced version of myself to Kṛṣṇa. I want to give Him what I love, and I want to also let it serve energetically in a preaching way to show others how they can give their whole selves to Kṛṣṇa.

Here the words "whole self" do not just mean pure self, but they mean giving all aspects of ourselves as we know them in the conditional nature—giving our money, giving our talents, and so on, giving all the things we have. I also expanded on this image while writing a book called *Churning The Milk Ocean.* There I said that when I write, I churn up things that are sometimes poison and sometimes nectar. We reject the poison and don't offer it to Kṛṣṇa, but still, in the process of living, it gets churned up.

I am writing this to you personally. I wouldn't advocate it at any kind of ISKCON forum for social living, or, in the name of Western psychology, inviting devotees to do their own thing for Kṛṣṇa. But I have to admit that it's what I'm doing. I do restrict myself from expanding on any inner desires I may have, say, for a woman's association or listening to nondevotee music or whatever. There is certainly a constant restraining of oneself from certain desires one has. But on the other hand, I'm going ahead as fully as possible to offer Kṛṣṇa my nature and to do the best I can to respond to the perfection that Kṛṣṇa desires—that we act only to please Him.

It may sound strange to say that I claim I don't know what Kṛṣṇa really wants, so I have to agonize on it on my own. But what do you think? Do you think you know in vital aspects, and that other devotees in ISKCON know in vital aspects, exactly what Kṛṣṇa wants? Rather, isn't this part of our free will to struggle with this?

I could say much more but I don't want to deluge you with letters that you may find a burden to answer. In fact, you don't have to answer, but just hear me. Thank you.

Glossary

A

Abhiṣekha—the bathing ceremony of the Deity.

Ācārya—a spiritual master who teaches by his personal behavior.

Adhyātmika (-kleśa)—miseries caused by one's own body and mind.

Adhibautika (-kleśa)—miseries caused by other living entities.

Adhidhaivika (-kleśa)—miseries caused by demigods (natural disasters, etc.).

Aiśvarya—majesty, opulence.

Anartha—unwanted things; material desire.

Anyābhilāṣitā-śūnyam—Srīla Rupa Gosvāmī's definition of pure devotional service as being free from any other desire.

Arcā-vigraha—Deity.

Arjuna—one of the five Pāṇḍavas. Kṛṣṇa spoke the *Bhagavad-gītā* to him on the Battlefield of Kurukṣetra.

Āśrama—a spiritual order: *brahmacārī* (celibate student), *gṛhastha* (householder), *vānaprastha* (retired), *sannyāsī* (renunciate); living quarters for those engaged in spiritual practices.

Avadhūta—a spirtually advanced person whose activities are not restricted by social convention.

B

Bābājī—one who devotes the major portion of his life to solitary devotional practices, especially chanting the Lord's names.

Badarikāśrama—a place of pilgrimage in the Himalayas.

Bhagavad-gītā—lit., "song of God." The discourse between Lord Kṛṣṇa and His devotee Arjuna, expounding devotional service as both the principal means and the ultimate end of spiritual perfection.

Bhāgavatam—*See: Śrīmad-Bhāgavatam.*

Bhajana—devotional activities.

Bhakta—a devotee of Kṛṣṇa.

Bhakti—devotional service to the Supreme Lord.

Bhaktisiddhānta Sarasvatī Ṭhākura—the spiritual master of His Divine Grace A. C. Bhaktivedanta Swami Prabhupāda; an *ācārya* in the Gauḍīya Vaiṣṇava-sampradāya.

Bhaktivinoda Ṭhākura—an *ācārya* in the Gaudīya Vaiṣṇava disciplic succession; the father of Bhaktisiddhānta Sarasvatī Ṭhākura.

Bhāva—the stage of transcendental ecstacy experienced after transcendental affection.

Brahmā—the first created living being and the secondary creator of the material universe.

Brahma-bhūta—the liberated or spiritual platform of consciousness.

Brahmacārī—a celibate student living under the care of a bona fide spiritual master.

Brahman—the impersonal aspect of the Absolute Truth; spirit.

Brāhmaṇa—those wise in the *Vedas* who can guide society; the first Vedic social order.

Bṛhat-mṛdaṅga—lit., "the great drum." A phrase coined by Śrīla Bhaktisiddhānta Sarasvatī Ṭhākura; refers to the power of publishing books as an instrument for preaching.

Buddhi-yoga—another term for *bhakti-yoga* (devotional service to Kṛṣṇa), indicating that it represents the highest use of intelligence (*buddhi*).

C

Cādar—a shawl.

Caitanya (Mahāprabhu)—lit. "Living force." An incarnation of Kṛṣṇa who appeared in the form of a devotee to teach love of God through the *saṅkīrtana* movement.

Caitanya-caritāmṛta—the biography and philosophy of Caitanya Mahāprabhu, written by Śrīla Kṛṣṇadāsa Kavirāja Gosvāmī.

Cāṇakya Paṇḍita—a legendary advisor to the Hindu king, Candragupta, renowned through history for his social and political wisdom.

Caraṇāmṛta—water that has washed the Deity.

Causal Ocean—the water upon which Mahā-Viṣṇu sleeps, and upon which float the innumerable material universes generated from His body.

Chaukīdār—a security guard.

Cintāmaṇi-dhāma—the spiritual world, where everything is made of touchstone *(cintāmaṇi)*.

D

Daṇḍa—a staff composed of three long sticks tied together, carried by Vaiṣṇava *sannyāsīs*.

Darśana—vision; audience.

Daru-brahman—the Absolute Truth manifest in a wooden form.

Dāsya-rasa—the spiritual relationship in which the devotee acts as the Lord's servant.

Dhāma—abode; the Lord's place of residence.

Dharma—the duties prescribed by one's nature and social position; ultimately, dharma means devotional service to the Supreme Lord.

Dhotī—Vedic men's dress.

Dvārakā—the city where Kṛṣṇa ruled in His later pastimes as a king.

E

Ekādaśī—a day on which Vaiṣṇavas fast from grains and beans and increase their remembrance of Kṛṣṇa. It falls on the eleventh day of both the waxing and waning moons.

G

Gambhīrā—a room in Jagannātha Purī where Śrī Caitanya Mahāprabhu would experience intense feelings of separation from Kṛṣṇa.

Gaṇeśa—the demigod in charge of material opulence and freedom from misfortune.

Garuḍa—Lord Viṣṇu's eternal carrier, a great devotee in a bird-like form.

Gaudiya Math—the preaching institution originally established by Śrīla Bhaktisiddhānta Sarasvatī Ṭhākura.

Gauḍīya Vaiṣṇava—a follower of Lord Caitanya.

Gaura-kiśora dāsa Bābājī—the spiritual master of Śrīla Bhaktisiddhānta Sarasvatī Ṭhākura.

Gaurāṅga—lit., "golden-limbed." A name of Śrī Caitanya Mahāprabhu.

Gāyatrī—a prayer chanted silently by *brāhmaṇas* at sunrise, noon, and sunset.

Goloka—Kṛṣṇaloka, the eternal abode of Lord Kṛṣṇa.

Gopa—a cowherd boy; one of Kṛṣṇa's eternal associates.

Gopī—a cowherd girl; one of Kṛṣṇa's most confidential servitors.

Goṣṭhyānandī—a devotee who desires to preach the glories of the holy name.

Gosvāmī—one who controls his mind and senses; title of one in the renounced order of life. May refer specifically to the Six Gosvāmīs of Vṛndāvana, who are direct followers of Lord Caitanya in disciplic succession, and who systematically presented His teachings.

Govardhana Hill—a hill in Vṛndāvana, the site of many of Kṛṣṇa's pastimes.

Gṛhastha—a married person living according to the Vedic social system.

H

Halavā—a sweet dish made from roasted grains, butter, sugar, and water or milk.

Hare—the vocative form of Harā, another name of Rādhārāṇī; refers specifically to the internal spiritual energy of the Lord.

Haridāsa Ṭhākura—a great devotee of Lord Caitanya Mahāprabhu; known as the *nāmācārya*, the master who taught the chanting of the holy names by his own example.

Harināma—public chanting of the Hare Kṛṣṇa *mahā-mantra.*

Hari-nāma—lit., "the name of the Lord."

I

ISKCON—acronym of the International Society for Krishna Consciousness.

J

Jagannātha—lit., "the Lord of the universe"; may refer specifically to the Deity of Lord Jagannātha in His temple at Purī.

Jāmbavān—a devotee of the Lord who fought with Kṛṣṇa for the Syamantaka jewel.

Janaloka—one of the higher planetary systems on which liberated sages reside.

Japa—individual chanting of the Hare Kṛṣṇa mantra while counting on beads.

Jāri—ornate embroidery with silver or gold thread.

Jaya—an acclamation meaning, "Victory!" or, "All glories!"

Jīva—the individual eternal soul or living entity; part and parcel of the Supreme Lord.

Jīva Gosvāmī—one of the Six Gosvāmīs of Vṛndāvana.

K

Kali-yuga—the present age, which is characterized by quarrel and hypocrisy.

Kāliya—a serpent-demon who was chastised by Kṛṣṇa in His Vṛndāvana pastimes.

Kāma-bīja—the seed of a particular *gāyatrī-mantra.*

Kaniṣṭha—neophyte.

Karatālas—hand cymbals used during *kīrtana.*

Karmī—one engaged in karma (fruitive activity); a materialist.

Kārttika—the Vedic month corresponding to October–November in which Lord Dāmodara is worshiped.

Kīrtana—chanting of the Lord's holy names.

Kṛpana—a miser.

Kṛṣṇa—the Supreme Personality of Godhead.

Kṛṣṇadāsa Kavirāja Gosvāmī—the author of *Śrī Caitanya-caritāmṛta.*

Kṛṣṇa-kathā—topics spoken by or about Kṛṣṇa.

Kṛṣṇa-prema—love of Kṛṣṇa.

Kṣatriya—administrative or warrior class. The second Vedic social order.

Kumāras—four great sages, devotees of the Lord, who exist eternally in the form of *brahmacārīs* of the *kumāra* (four- to five-year-old) age.

Kuñja—grove.

Kurukṣetra—a holy place where the war between the Pāṇḍavas and the Kurus took place and where Lord Kṛṣṇa spoke the *Bhagavad-gītā* to Arjuna.

L

Lakṣmī-Nārāyaṇa—expansions of Rādhārāṇī and Kṛṣṇa worshiped in the mood of awe and reverence, as in the Vaikuṇṭha planets.

Līlā—pastimes.

M

Madhuram—sweet.

Mādhurya-rasa—devotional service to Kṛṣṇa in the mood of sweetness and conjugal love.

Madhya-līlā—the pastimes Lord Caitanya performed during the middle part of His manifest presence, while He was traveling throughout India; the portion of *Śrī Caitanya-caritāmṛta* recounting those pastimes.

Madhyama-adhikārī—a devotee whose advancement in spiritual life is midway between the neophyte *(kaniṣṭha)* and advanced *(uttama)* levels.

Mahā-bhāgavata—a devotee in the highest stage of devotional life.

Mahābhārata—the history of ancient India, compiled by Śrīla Vyāsadeva and including the *Bhagavad-gītā.*

Mahājanas—refers to the twelve authorized agents of the Lord whose duty it is to preach the path of devotional service to the people in general.

Mahā-mantra—the great chant for deliverance: Hare Kṛṣṇa Hare Kṛṣṇa, Kṛṣṇa Kṛṣṇa Hare Hare/ Hare Rāma Hare Rāma, Rāma Rāma Hare Hare.

Mandira—temple.

Maṅgala-ārati—the first Deity worship of the day, performed an hour and a half before sunrise.

Mantra—sound vibration that can deliver the mind from illusion.

Mārga—path.

Mātājī—mother.

Māyā—the external, illusory energy of the Lord, comprising this material world; forgetfulness of one's relationship with Kṛṣṇa.

Māyāpur—a town in West Bengal, India, where Lord Caitanya appeared.

Mohinī—the Lord's incarnation as the most beautiful woman.

Mūḍha—fool, rascal.

Mūrti—a form, usually referring to a Deity.

N

Nāma—the holy name.

Nāmāmṛta—a compilation of Śrīla Prabhupāda's written instructions on the chanting of the Hare Kṛṣṇa *mahā-mantra.*

Nanda-grāma—the area in Vṛndāvana where Kṛṣṇa spent His childhood.

Nanda Mahārāja—Kṛṣṇa's father in Vṛndāvana.

Nārada Muni—a great devotee of Lord Kṛṣṇa who travels throughout the spiritual and material worlds singing the Lord's glories and preaching the path of devotional service.

Nārāyaṇa Ṛṣi—an incarnation of the Lord who advented as a sage.

The Nectar of Devotion—Śrīla Prabhupāda's summary study of Śrīla Rūpa Gosvāmī's *Bhakti-rasāmṛta-sindhu.*

New Vrindaban—a spiritual village established by Śrīla Prabhupāda near Wheeling, West Virginia.

Nīlācala—another name for Jagannātha Purī.

Nirjana-bhajana—solitary spiritual practices.

Nitya-līlā—the eternal pastimes of the Lord or His devotees in the spiritual world.

Nityānanda—the incarnation of Lord Balarāma who is a principal associate of Lord Caitanya.

Nitya-siddha—an eternally liberated soul.

Nṛsiṁha(deva)—the half-man, half-lion incarnation of Lord Kṛṣṇa who appeared to save Prahlāda Mahārāja from Hiraṇyakaśipu.

P

Paṇḍa—temple priest, usually of a caste *brāhmaṇa* family.

Pāṇḍavas—the five warrior-brothers, sons of King Pāṇḍu, and intimate friends of Lord Kṛṣṇa.

Paramparā—the disciplic succession of bona fide spiritual masters.

Parikrama—a walking pilgrimage.

Parīkṣit Mahārāja—the emperor of the world five thousand years ago who heard *Śrīmad-Bhāgavatam* from Śukadeva Gosvāmī and thus attained perfection.

Prabhupāda, A. C. Bhaktivedanta Swami—Founder-*ācārya* of ISKCON and foremost preacher of Kṛṣṇa consciousness in the Western world.

Prahlāda Mahārāja—a great devotee who was persecuted by his demoniac father, but who was protected and saved by Lord Nṛsiṁha.

Prasādam—lit. "mercy." Food which is spiritualized by being offered to Kṛṣṇa, and which helps purify the living entity; also referred to as *prasāda*.

Pratāparudra—the king of Orissa at the time of Lord Caitanya's manifest presence and a great devotee of the Lord.

Prema—love of Kṛṣṇa.

Purī—refers to Jagannātha Purī, a city in the province of Orissa, India, where the temple of Lord Jagannātha is located.

Pūrṇimā—the full moon day.

Pūrva-rāga—attachment before first meeting.

R

Rādhārāṇī (Rādhā)—the eternal consort and spiritual potency of Lord Kṛṣṇa.

Rāga—attachment; traditional Indian melodies.

Rāgānuga-bhakti—devotional service following the spontaneous loving service of the inhabitants of Vṛndāvana.

Rāma—as part of the Hare Kṛṣṇa *mahā-mantra*, refers to the highest eternal pleasure of Lord Kṛṣṇa; also refers to Lord Balarāma, the first plenary expansion of the Lord.

Rāmāyaṇa—the epic history of Lord Rāmacandra, written by Vālmīki Muni.

Rasa—the spiritual essence of a personal relationship with the Supreme Lord.

Rasābhasa—incompatible mixing of rasas.

Rāsa dance—refers to Kṛṣṇa's pastime of dancing with the *gopīs*.

Rasika—person or things absorbed in *rasa*.

Ṛtvik—lit. "Priest." Name given to a fallacious doctrine which holds that Śrīla Prabhupāda is the only initiating guru of ISKCON and that his followers may initiate new devotees only as officiating priests on his behalf.

Ruci—lit. "Taste." A stage in the practice of Kṛṣṇa consciousness in which one develops a natural attraction or "taste" for the activities of devotional service.

Rūpa Gosvāmī—one of the Six Gosvāmīs of Vṛndāvana.

S

Sādhaka—one who practices regulated devotional service.

Sādhana—regulated spiritual activites meant to increase one's attachment to Kṛṣṇa.

Sādhu—saintly person.

Sādhu-saṅga—the association of saintly persons.

Sakhī—girlfriend, refers to Śrīmatī Rādhārāṇī's intimate girlfriends, who assist Her in Her service to Kṛṣṇa.

Samādhi—trance or absorption in the service of the Lord.

Sampradāya—a chain of disciplic succession through which spiritual knowledge is transmitted.

Saṁsāra—cycle of repeated birth and death.

Saṅkīrtana—the congregational chanting of the holy name, fame, and pastimes of the Lord; preaching.

Sannyāsī—one in the renounced order of life.

Sārvabhauma Bhaṭṭācārya—a famous logician who surrendered to Lord Caitanya.

Śāstra—revealed scripture.

Ṣaṭ-sandarbha—treatises on the Vedic scriptures, written by Śrīla Jīva Gosvāmī.

Siddha-bakula—the tree in Purī under which Haridāsa Ṭhākura lived and chanted the holy name.

Śikhā—lit. "flag." A tuft of hair grown at the crown of the head of male Vaiṣṇavas.

Śiṣya—disciple or student.

Śiva—the personality in charge of the mode of ignorance.

Śloka—a stanza of Sanskrit verse.

Śraddhā—firm faith and confidence.

Śravaṇam—hearing about Kṛṣṇa.

Śreyas—activities which are ultimately beneficial and auspicious when performed over time.

Śrīla Prabhupāda-līlāmṛta—the biography of His Divine Grace A. C. Bhaktivedanta Swami Prabhupāda, written by Satsvarūpa dāsa Goswami.

Śrīmad-Bhāgavatam—the *Purāṇa*, written by Śrīla Vyāsadeva, which specifically points to the path of devotional love of God.

Śrutadeva—a poor *brāhmaṇa* whose simple service to Lord Kṛṣṇa was accepted by the Lord as equal to that of the king.
Subhadrā—Lord Kṛṣṇa's sister; Yogamāyā.
Śuddha-sattva—the transcendental state of pure goodness, uncontaminated by the modes of material nature.
Śūdra—a laborer; one of the four Vedic social orders.
Śukadeva Gosvāmī—the sage who originally spoke the *Śrīmad-Bhāgavatam* to King Parīkṣit just prior to the king's death.
Sūrya—the presiding demigod of the sun.
Svarūpa—one's original spiritual form.
Svarūpa Dāmodara Gosvāmī—Lord Caitanya's secretary and constant companion who helped the Lord experience the attitude of Rādhārāṇī.
Swami—one who controls his senses, a title of one in the renounced order of life.

T

Tapasya—austerity.
Tenth Canto—the part of the *Śrīmad-Bhāgavatam* describing the most confidential pastimes of Lord Kṛṣṇa.
Tilaka—auspicious clay markings that sanctify a devotee's body as a temple of the Lord.
Tīrtha—holy place of pilgrimage.
Ṭoṭā-gopīnātha temple—a temple in Jagannātha Purī near the tomb of Haridāsa Ṭhākura.
Tulasī—a great devotee in the form of a plant; her leaves are always offered to the lotus feet of the Lord.

U

Ujjvala—the mood of conjugal love with the Lord.
Upadeśa—instruction.
Upaniṣads—108 philosophical treatises that appear within the *Vedas*.

V

Vaidhi-bhakti—the process of following the regulative principles of devotional service under the guidance of a spiritual master, in accordance with revealed scriptures.
Vaikuṇṭha—the spiritual world.
Vairāgya—renunciation.
Vaiṣṇava—one who is a devotee of Viṣṇu or Kṛṣṇa.

Varṇāśrama—the Vedic social system of four social and four spiritual orders.

Vasudeva—the father of Lord Kṛṣṇa.

Vedas—the original revealed scriptures.

Vibhu—great.

Vipralambha—ecstasy in separation.

Viṣṇu—a fully empowered expansion of Kṛṣṇa.

Viśvanātha Cakravartī Ṭhākura—a great Vaiṣṇava *ācārya* and scholar.

Vrata—vow.

Vṛndāvana—Kṛṣṇa's personal abode, where He fully manifests His personal qualities.

Vyāsadeva—the original compiler of the *Vedas* and author of the *Vedānta-sūtra* and *Mahābhārata*, and the author of the *Śrīmad-Bhāgavatam.*

Vyāsa-pūjā—worship of the spiritual master, who represents Śrīla Vyāsadeva, on his appearance day.

Vyāsāsana—a special, elevated seat, reserved for the speaker of *Śrīmad-Bhāgavatam.*

W

Walla—a Hindi suffix signifying a vendor of goods or services.

Y

Yadu dynasty—the dynasty in which Lord Kṛṣṇa appeared.

Yajña—sacrifice.

Yamadūtas—the agents of Yamarāja, the superintendent of death and karmic justice.

Yamunā—a sacred river in India, which Lord Kṛṣṇa made famous by performing pastimes there.

Yaśodā—Kṛṣṇa's mother in Vṛndāvana.

Yogamāyā—the internal spiritual potency of the Lord.

Yukta-vairāgya—real renunciation by utilizing everything in the service of God.

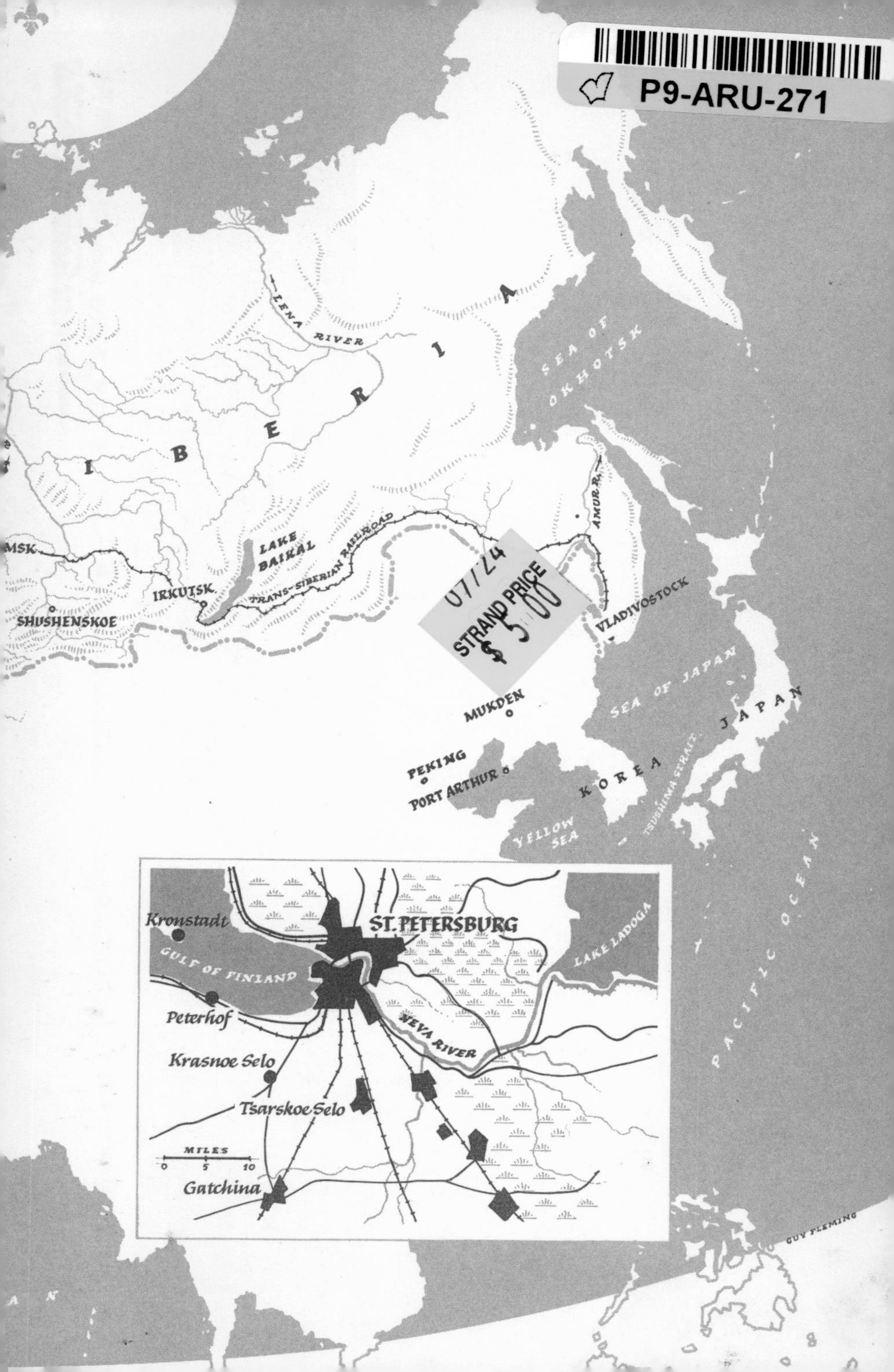
I B E R I A
LENA RIVER
SEA OF OKHOTSK
LAKE BAIKAL
TRANS-SIBERIAN RAILROAD
MSK
IRKUTSK
SHUSHENSKOE
AMUR R.
VLADIVOSTOCK
MUKDEN
PEKING
PORT ARTHUR
KOREA
YELLOW SEA
SEA OF JAPAN
TSUSHIMA STRAIT
JAPAN
PACIFIC OCEAN
ST. PETERSBURG
Kronstadt
GULF OF FINLAND
LAKE LADOGA
Peterhof
NEVA RIVER
Krasnoe Selo
Tsarskoe Selo
MILES
0 5 10
Gatchina
GUY FLEMING

Nicholas and Alexandra

Robert K. Massie

NICHOLAS AND ALEXANDRA

Atheneum

NEW YORK

Published simultaneously in Canada by McClelland and Stewart Ltd.
Manufactured in the United States of America

To Suzanne

"I have a firm, an absolute conviction that the fate of Russia—that my own fate and that of my family—is in the hands of God who has placed me where I am. Whatever may happen to me, I shall bow to His will with the consciousness of never having had any thought other than that of serving the country which He has entrusted to me."

NICHOLAS II

"After all, the nursery was the center of all Russia's troubles."

SIR BERNARD PARES

"The Empress refused to surrender to fate. She talked incessantly of the ignorance of the physicians. . . . She turned towards religion, and her prayers were tainted with a certain hysteria. The stage was ready for the appearance of a miracle worker. . . ."

GRAND DUKE ALEXANDER

"The illness of the Tsarevich cast its shadow over the whole of the concluding period of Tsar Nicholas II's reign and alone can explain it. Without appearing to be, it was one of the main causes of his fall, for it made possible the phenomenon of Rasputin and resulted in the fatal isolation of the sovereigns who lived in a world apart, wholly absorbed in a tragic anxiety which had to be concealed from all eyes."

PIERRE GILLIARD,
Tutor of Tsarevich Alexis

"Without Rasputin, there could have been no Lenin."

ALEXANDER KERENSKY

Introduction

THE WRITING of this book is the result, like most things in life, of a circumstance of Fate. Since the day, now over ten years ago, that my wife and I discovered that our son had hemophilia, I have tried to learn how other families dealt with the problems raised by this unique disease. In time, this led to curiosity about the response of the parents of the boy who was the most famous hemophiliac of all, the Tsarevich Alexis, the only son and heir of Nicholas II, last Tsar of all the Russias.

What I discovered was both fascinating and frustrating. There was general agreement that the child's hemophilia had been a significant factor in the lives of the parents, Tsar Nicholas and Empress Alexandra, and thereby in the fall of Imperial Russia. Thus, in the most comprehensive political study of the period, *The Fall of the Russian Monarchy*, Sir Bernard Pares declares categorically: "On August 12, 1904 . . . took place the event which more than anything else determined the whole later course of Russian history. On that day was at last born the heir to the throne, long expected and fervently prayed for." What Pares is saying, and what is scarcely disputed by anyone, is that in an effort to deal with the agonies hemophilia inflicted on her son, the distraught mother turned to Gregory Rasputin, the remarkable Siberian mystagogue. Thereafter, Rasputin's presence near the throne—his influence on the Empress and, through her, on the government of Russia—brought about or at least helped to speed the fall of the dynasty.

This was fascinating. But it was frustrating to discover that even those who attached the greatest significance to the effect of the disease on events did not explain, either in human or in medical terms, exactly what happened. This seemed a serious gap affecting larger areas than the one which first attracted my interest. If the illness of this boy and the aid given him by Rasputin had, in fact, brought down the ancient Romanov dynasty and led to the Russian Revolution with all its awesome consequences, why had there never been an attempt to decipher and interpret these episodes of grim suffering and dramatic healing? As for Rasputin, who has not heard something of this extraordinary man and his garish murder? But who knows precisely what he did to help the Tsarevich? In both historical and human terms, this seemed to me enormously important, for only by understanding the basis of this relationship does the rest of the story become coherent.

I have read the diaries, letters and memoirs left by the men and women who were intimately involved in this great drama. In the letters from Nicholas and Alexandra to each other and from the Tsar to his mother, scattered through the books by Imperial relatives, intimate friends of the Empress, ladies-in-waiting, court officials, government ministers and foreign ambassadors, there is a wealth of fragmented information. But it has never been collected and assembled. In this book, my purpose has been to weave together from all the threads, and interpret in the light of modern medicine and psychiatry and of the common experience which all families affected by hemophilia necessarily share, an account of one family whose struggle with the disease was to have momentous consequences for the entire world.

If at first my interest was primarily in tracing the role of hemophilia, I soon found it expanding to include the rich panorama of the reign of Nicholas II, his role as tsar, his place in history, and the glittering epoch over which he presided. In reading and conversation, I discovered that, despite the passage of fifty years, people still react strongly to Nicholas. A few, mostly Russian émigrés who see in him the symbol of an age now fading beyond recall, revere and even idolize him; by some members of the Russian Orthodox Church, he and all his martyred family are regarded as un-canonized saints.

On the opposite side, there still are those who for political or other reasons continue to insist that Nicholas was "Bloody Nicholas." Most commonly, he is described as shallow, weak, stupid—a one-dimensional figure presiding feebly over the last days of a corrupt and crumbling system. This, certainly, is the prevailing public image of the last Tsar.

Historians admit that Nicholas was a "good man"—the historical evidence of personal charm, gentleness, love of family, deep religious faith and strong Russian patriotism is too overwhelming to be denied —but they argue that personal factors are irrelevant; what matters is that Nicholas was a bad tsar. The virtues which we admire in private life and profess in our religion become secondary qualities in our rulers. The test of greatness in tsars or presidents is not in their private lives or even in their good intentions, but in their deeds.

By this standard, one has to agree: Nicholas was not a great tsar. Historically, the great leaders of the Russian people—Ivan the Terrible, Peter the Great, Lenin and Stalin—have been those who by sheer force and terror have thrust the backward nation forward. Until perhaps the present day, Russians have stood in awe of the ruthless man who wielded the whip and drove them forward. Peter, who broke his enemies on the rack and hanged them in Red Square, who had his son tortured to death, is Peter the Great. But Nicholas, whose hand was lighter than that of any tsar before him, is "Bloody Nicholas." In human terms, this is irony rich and dramatic, the more so because Nicholas knew what he was called.

In terms of accomplishment, it may be unfair to compare Nicholas II with his towering ancestors. No one can say how well they would have managed under the cascade of disasters which broke upon Nicholas. Perhaps a more equitable and revealing comparison might be made between Nicholas II and his contemporaries on the thrones of Europe: King Edward VII and King George V, Kaiser William II and Emperor Franz Joseph. Was there among this group one who could better have ridden the storm which Nicholas had to face? History itself provided part of the answer: the same catastrophic war which helped drive Nicholas off his throne also toppled the emperors of Germany and Austria-Hungary.

A comparison with the two kings of England, Edward VII and George V, Nicholas's uncle and first cousin, only deepens the irony. For if Nicholas had not been instructed from childhood that constitutions were anathema, he would have made an excellent constitutional monarch. He was at least as intelligent as any European monarch in his day or ours: his qualities and tastes were surprisingly similar to those of King George V, whom physically he so much resembled. In England, where a sovereign needed only to be a good man in order to be a good king, Nicholas II would have made an admirable monarch.

But Fate did not intend for the last Romanov Tsar so serene an existence or so comfortable a niche in history. He was Russian, not English, and he became, not a constitutional monarch, but Emperor-

Tsar-Autocrat over millions of people and a vast region of the earth. Once on the throne, he faced simultaneously two wholly extraordinary disasters: a son with hemophilia and the imminent disintegration of his great empire. From the moment his son was born, the two disasters were intertwined. Although he stood at the highest pinnacle of political power in a system which had clearly lived beyond its time, Imperial Russia was not necessarily marked for total destruction. There were chances to adapt the autocracy to the modern world. But then, as if to ensure the implacable ending, Fate introduced hemophilia and Rasputin. It was the blow from which Nicholas and Imperial Russia could not recover.

Essentially, the tragedy of Nicholas II was that he appeared in the wrong place in history. Equipped by education to rule in the nineteenth century, equipped by temperament to reign in England, he lived and reigned in Russia in the twentieth century. There, the world he understood was breaking up around him. Events were moving too swiftly, ideas were changing too radically. In the gigantic storm which swept over Russia, he and all he loved were carried away. To the end, he did his best, and for his wife and family that was a very great deal. For Russia, it was not enough.

The man who, sensing only imperfectly the dimensions of the storm which beats against him, still tries with courage to do his duty is a particularly recognizable twentieth-century figure. Perhaps for this reason we today are better equipped to understand the ordeal and the qualities of Nicholas II. In an earlier era when the world seemed ordered and disorder the result primarily of human weakness or folly, then wars or revolutions could be blamed on a single leader. Since then, two world wars, the Great Depression and twenty years of the Nuclear Age have taught us, among other things, tolerance. We have come to accept the fact that there are forces beyond the control of any single man, be he tsar or president. We have also adjusted our measure of human achievement. Facing together things which we only dimly see, uncertain which course to follow, we place a higher value on intentions and effort. We may lose—more often than not we will lose—but we must try: this is the essence of a rational twentieth-century morality.

Caught in a web he could not break, Nicholas paid for his mistakes —he died as a martyr with his wife and his five children. But Fate had not taken everything from them. The old values by which they had lived, the very faith for which they were derided, gave them the courage and dignity that over the years have redeemed everything else. These human qualities are eternal and will survive and transcend the rise and fall of every empire. It is for these qualities that Nicholas II was an exceptional man. For, in the end, he did succeed.

R.K.M.

Contents

Illustrations

FOLLOW PAGE 266

Cast of Characters

NICHOLAS II, TSAR OF RUSSIA, 1894–1917
Before 1894, the Tsarevich Nicholas

ALEXANDRA FEDOROVNA, EMPRESS OF RUSSIA
Born Princess Alix of Hesse-Darmstadt

ALEXIS, THE TSAREVICH
Fifth child and only son of Nicholas and Alexandra

OLGA
TATIANA
MARIE
ANASTASIA
Daughters of Nicholas and Alexandra

ALEXANDER III, TSAR OF RUSSIA, 1881–1894
Father of Nicholas II

MARIE FEDOROVNA, DOWAGER EMPRESS
Mother of Nicholas II. Born Princess Dagmar of Denmark

GRAND DUKE GEORGE
GRAND DUKE MICHAEL
Brothers of Nicholas II

GRAND DUCHESS XENIA
GRAND DUCHESS OLGA
Sisters of Nicholas II

GRAND DUKE VLADIMIR
GRAND DUKE ALEXIS
GRAND DUKE SERGE
GRAND DUKE PAUL
Brothers of Tsar Alexander III and uncles of Nicholas II

GRAND DUCHESS MARIE PAVLOVNA
Wife of Grand Duke Vladimir

GRAND DUKE CYRIL
GRAND DUKE BORIS
GRAND DUKE ANDREI
Sons of Vladimir and Marie Pavlovna and cousins of Nicholas II

GRAND DUCHESS ELIZABETH (*Ella*)
Sister of Empress Alexandra and wife of Grand Duke Serge

GRAND DUKE NICHOLAS NICOLAIEVICH
Commander-in-Chief of the Russian Army in World War I

GRAND DUKE ALEXANDER MIKHAILOVICH (*Sandro*)
Husband of Nicholas II's sister Xenia

PRINCE FELIX YUSSOUPOV
Murderer of Rasputin. Husband of Princess Irina, the daughter of Grand Duchess Xenia and Grand Duke Alexander Mikhailovich

GRAND DUKE DMITRY
Murderer of Rasputin. Son of Grand Duke Paul

EDWARD VII, KING OF ENGLAND, 1901–1910 (*Uncle Bertie*)
Brother-in-law of Dowager Empress Marie Fedorovna. Uncle of Empress Alexandra and Kaiser William II

GEORGE V, KING OF ENGLAND, 1910–1936 (*Georgie*)
Through his mother, first cousin of Nicholas II. Through his father, first cousin of Empress Alexandra

COUNT SERGIUS WITTE, 1905–1906
IVAN GOREMYKIN, 1906
PETER STOLYPIN, 1906–1911
VLADIMIR KOKOVTSOV, 1911–1914
IVAN GOREMYKIN, 1914–1916
BORIS STÜRMER, 1916
ALEXANDER TREPOV, 1916–1917
NICHOLAS GOLITSYN, 1917

Presidents of the Council of Ministers (Prime Ministers) after the 1905 Manifesto

WILLIAM II, KAISER OF GERMANY, 1888–1918 (*Willy*)
First cousin of Empress Alexandra. Distant cousin of Nicholas II

COUNT VLADIMIR FREDERICKS
Minister of the Imperial Court

COUNT PAUL BENCKENDORFF
Grand Marshal of the Imperial Court, Fredericks' subordinate

DR. EUGENE BOTKIN
Court physician. Botkin attended primarily the Empress Alexandra

DR. FEDOROV
A doctor who cared for the Tsarevich Alexis

DR. VLADIMIR DEREVENKO
A doctor permanently assigned to the Tsarevich Alexis

PIERRE GILLIARD
Swiss tutor of the Tsarevich Alexis

ANNA VYRUBOVA
The Empress Alexandra's closest friend and confidante

DEREVENKO
A sailor assigned to watch the Tsarevich Alexis night and day. No relation to Dr. Derevenko

MATHILDE KSCHESSINSKA
Ballerina. Mistress of Nicholas II before his marriage

GREGORY RASPUTIN
A Siberian peasant

ALEXANDER KERENSKY
Prime Minister of the Provisional Government, 1917

VLADIMIR ULYANOV (Lenin)
First leader of the Soviet State

PART ONE

NOTE

The titles EMPEROR *and* TSAR, *and* EMPRESS *and* TSARITSA, *are all correct and are used interchangeably in this book.* EMPEROR *was a higher rank, first taken by Peter the Great, but Nicholas II, a Slavophile, preferred the older, more Russian title,* TSAR.

Dates in Russian history can be confusing. Until 1918, Russia adhered to the old Julian calendar. In the nineteenth century, this calender was twelve days behind the Gregorian calender used almost everywhere else. In the twentieth century, the Russian calender fell thirteen days behind. In this book, all dates are given according to the newer, Gregorian calender, except those specifically indicated as Old Style (O.S.).

Every Russian has three names: his first or Christian name; the name of his father with VICH *added (meaning* SON OF*); and his family name. Thus, Nicholas was Nicholas Alexandrovich Romanov. For women, the second name is their father's with* EVNA *or* OVNA (DAUGHTER OF) *added. The Tsar's youngest daughter was Anastasia Nicolaevna.*

CHAPTER ONE

1894: *Imperial Russia*

FROM the Baltic city of St. Petersburg, built on a river marsh in a far northern corner of the empire, the Tsar ruled Russia. So immense were the Tsar's dominions that, as night began to fall along their western borders, day already was breaking on their Pacific coast. Between these distant frontiers lay a continent, one sixth of the land surface of the globe. Through the depth of Russia's winters, millions of tall pine trees stood silent under heavy snows. In the summer, clusters of white-trunked birch trees rustled their silvery leaves in the slanting rays of the afternoon sun. Rivers, wide and flat, flowed peacefully through the grassy plains of European Russia toward a limitless southern horizon. Eastward, in Siberia, even mightier rivers rolled north to the Arctic, sweeping through forests where no human had ever been, and across desolate marshes of frozen tundra.

Here and there, thinly scattered across the broad land, lived the one hundred and thirty million subjects of the Tsar: not only Slavs but Balts, Jews, Germans, Georgians, Armenians, Uzbeks and Tartars. Some were clustered in provincial cities and towns, dominated by onion-shaped church domes rising above the white-walled houses. Many more lived in straggling villages of unpainted log huts. Next to doorways, a few sunflowers might grow. Geese and pigs wandered freely through the muddy street. Both men and women worked all summer, planting and scything the high silken grain before the coming of the first September frost. For six interminable months of winter, the open country became a wasteland of freezing whiteness. Inside their huts, in an atmosphere thick with the aroma of steaming clothes and boiling tea, the peasants sat around their huge clay stoves and argued and pondered the dark mysteries of nature and God.

In the country, the Russian people lived their lives under a blanket of silence. Most died in the villages where they were born. Three fourths of them were peasants, freed from the land a generation before by the Tsar-Liberator Alexander II's emancipation of the serfs. But freedom did not produce food. When famine came and the black earth cracked for lack of rain, and the grain withered and crumbled to dust still on the stalks, then the peasants tore the thatch from their roofs to feed their livestock and sent their sons trudging into town to look for work. In famine, the hungry *moujiks* wrapped themselves in ragged cloaks and stood all day in silence along the snowy roads. Noble ladies, warm in furs, drove their *troikas* through the stricken countryside, delivering with handsome gestures of their slender arms a spray of silver coins. Soon, along came the tax collector to gather up the coins and ask for others.

When the *moujiks* grumbled, a squadron of Cossacks rode into town, with lances in their black-gloved hands and whips and sabers swinging from their saddles. Troublemakers were flogged, and bitterness flowed with blood. Landowner, police, local governor and functionaries were roundly cursed by Russia's peasants. But never the Tsar. The Tsar, far away in a place nearer heaven than earth, did no wrong. He was the *Batiushka-Tsar*, the Father of the Russian people, and he did not know what suffering they had to endure. "It is very high up to God! It is very far to the Tsar!" said the Russian proverb. If only we could get to the Tsar and tell him, our troubles would be at an end—so runs the plot of a hundred Russian fairy tales.

As the end of the century approached, the life of many of these scattered towns and villages was stirring. The railroad was coming. During these years, Russia built railroads faster than any other country in Europe. As in the American West, railroads bridged the vast spaces, linked farms to cities, industries to markets. Travelers could step aboard a train in Moscow and, after a day in a cozy compartment, sipping tea and watching the snowbound countryside float past, descend onto a station platform in St. Petersburg. In 1891 the Imperial government had begun the construction of Russia's greatest railway, the Trans-Siberian. Beginning in the eastern suburbs of Moscow, the ribbon of track would stretch more than four thousand miles to the Pacific Ocean.

Then, as now, Moscow was the hub of Russia, the center of railroads, waterways, trade and commerce. From a small twelfth-century village surrounded by a wooden stockade, Moscow had become the capital and Holy City of Russia. It was there that Ivan the Terrible announced, when he took the throne in 1547, that he would be crowned not as Grand Prince of Moscow, but as Tsar of all Russia.

Moscow was "The City of Forty Times Forty Churches." High above the green rooftops glistened the blue-and-gilded onion domes of hundreds of church towers. Below, the wide avenues were graced by the columned palaces of princes and the mansions of wealthy textile merchants. In the maze of back streets, rows of two-story wooden buildings and log cabins sheltered the city's clerks and factory workers. The streets themselves lay deep in the snows of winter, the spring mud or the thick dust of summer. Women and children who ventured out had to watch for the sudden dash of a carriage or a thundering band of Cossacks whooping like cowboys in a town of the American West.

In the heart of Moscow, its massive red walls jutting from the bank of the Moscow River, stood the somber medieval citadel of Russian power, the Kremlin. Not a single building but an entire walled city, it seemed to a romantic Frenchman no less than a mirror of Russia itself: "This curious conglomeration of palaces, towers, churches, monasteries, chapels, barracks, arsenals and bastions; this incoherent jumble of sacred and secular buildings; this complex of functions as fortress, sanctuary, seraglio, harem, necropolis, and orison; this blend of advanced civilization and archaic barbarism; this violent conflict of crudest materialism and most lofty spirituality; are they not the whole history of Russia, the whole epic of the Russian nation, the whole inward drama of the Russian soul?"

Moscow was the "Third Rome," the center of the Orthodox Faith. For millions of Russians, most of the drama and panoply of life on earth were found in the Orthodox Church. In the great cathedrals of Russia, peasant women with kerchiefs over their heads could mingle with princesses in furs and jewels. People of every class and age stood for hours holding candles, their minds and senses absorbed in the overwhelming display taking place around them. From every corner of the church, golden icons glittered in the glowing light. From the iconostasis, a high screen before the altar, from the miters and crosses of gold-robed bishops, blazed diamonds and emeralds and rubies. Priests with long beards trailing down their chests walked among the people, swinging smoking pots of incense. The service was not so much a chant as a linked succession of hymns, drawing unbelievable power from the surging notes of the deepest basses. Dazzled by sights and smells, washed clean by the soaring notes of the music, the congregation came forward at the end of the service to kiss the soft hand of the bishop and have him paint a cross in holy oil upon their foreheads. The Church offered the extremes of emotion, from gloom to ecstasy. It taught that suffering was good, that drabness and pain were inevitable. "As God wills," the Russian told himself and, with the aid of the Church, sought to find the humility and strength to bear his earthly burden.

For all its glory, Moscow in 1894 was no longer the capital of the Tsar's empire. Two hundred years before, Peter the Great had forcibly wrenched the nation from its ancient Slav heritage and thrust it into the culture of Western Europe. On the marshes of the Neva River, Peter built a new city, intended to become Russia's "Window on Europe." Millions of tons of red granite were dragged into the marshland, piles were driven, and two hundred thousand laborers died of fever and malnutrition, but before Peter himself died in 1725, he ruled his empire from this strange, artificial capital at the head of the Baltic Sea.

Peter's city was built on water. It spread across nineteen islands, chained by arching bridges, laced by winding canals. To the northeast lay the wide expanse of Lake Ladoga, to the west the Gulf of Finland; between them rolled the broad flood of the river Neva. "Cleaving the city down the center, the cold waters of the Neva move silently and swiftly like a slab of smooth grey metal . . . bringing with them the tang of the lonely wastes of forests and swamp from which they have emerged." The northern shore was dominated by the grim brown bastions of the Fortress of Peter and Paul, surmounted by a slim golden spire soaring four hundred feet into the air above the fortress cathedral. For three miles along the southern bank ran a solid granite quay lined by the Winter Palace, the Admiralty, the foreign embassies and the palaces of the nobility.

Called the Venice of the North, the Babylon of the Snows, St. Petersburg was European, not Russian. Its architecture, its styles, its morals and its thought were Western. The Italian flavor was distinct. Italian architects, Rastrelli, Rossi, Quarenghi, brought to Russia by Peter and his heirs, had molded huge baroque palaces in red and yellow, pale green or blue and white, placing them amid ornate gardens on broad and sweeping boulevards. Even the smaller buildings were painted, plastered and ornamented in the style and colors of the south. Massive public buildings were lightened by ornamented windows, balconies and columned doorways. St. Petersburg's enormous Cathedral of Our Lady of Kazan was a direct copy of St. Peter's Basilica in Rome.

Despite its Mediterranean style, St. Petersburg was a northern city where the Arctic latitudes played odd tricks with light and time. Winter nights began early in the afternoon and lasted until the middle of the following morning. Icy winds and whirling snowstorms swept across the flat plain surrounding the city to lash the walls and windows of the Renaissance palaces and freeze the Neva hard as steel. Over the baroque spires and the frozen canals danced the strange fires of the aurora borealis. Occasionally a brilliant day would break the gloomy monotony. The sky would turn a silvery blue and the crystal snowflakes on the trees, rooftops and gilded domes would sparkle with sunlight so bright that the eye could not bear the dazzling glare. Winter was a great leveler. Tsar, minister, priest and factory worker all layered themselves in clothing and, upon coming in from the street, headed straight to the bubbling *samovar* for a glass of hot tea.

Summer in St. Petersburg was as light as the winters were dark. For twenty-two hours the atmosphere of the city was suffused with light. By eleven in the evening the colors of the day had faded into a milky haze of silver and pearl, and the city, veiled in iridescence, slept in silence. Yet those who were up after midnight could look to the east and see, as a pink line against the horizon, the beginning of the next dawn. Summer could be hot in the capital. Windows opened to catch the river breezes also brought the salt air of the Gulf of Finland, the aromas of spice and tar, the sound of carriage wheels, the shouts of street vendors, the peal of bells from a nearby church.

St. Petersburg, in 1894, still was faithful to Tsar Peter's wish. It was the center of all that was advanced, all that was smart and much that was cynical in Russian life. Its great opera and ballet companies, its symphonies and chamber orchestras played the music of Glinka, Rimsky-Korsakov, Borodin, Mussorgsky and Tchaikovsky; its citizens read Pushkin, Gogol, Dostoyevsky, Turgenev and Tolstoy. But society spoke French, not Russian, and the best clothing and furniture were ordered from Paris. Russian noblemen vacationed in Biarritz and Italy and on the Riviera, rather than going back to the huge country estates which supplied the funds to finance their pleasures. Men went to the race track and the gambling clubs. Ladies slept until noon, received their hairdressers and went for a drive to the Islands.

Love affairs flourished, accompanied by the ceaseless rustle of delicious gossip.

Society went every night to the Imperial Ballet at the gorgeous blue-and-gold Maryinsky Theatre or to the Théatre Français, where "fashionable décolletage was compensated for by an abundance of jewels." After the theatre, ladies and their escorts bundled themselves into furs in little, bright red sleighs and sped noiselessly over the snows to the Restaurant Cuba for supper and dancing. "Nobody thought of leaving before 3 a.m. and the officers usually stayed until five . . . when the sky was colored with pearl, rose and silver tints."

The "season" in St. Petersburg began on New Year's Day and lasted until the beginning of Lent. Through these winter weeks, the aristocracy of the capital moved through a staggering round of concerts, banquets, balls, ballets, operas, private parties and midnight suppers. Everybody gave one and everybody went. There were receptions at which officers in brilliant uniforms with blazing decorations and old ladies in billowing white satin dresses milled about in high-ceilinged drawing rooms, plucking glasses of champagne from passing servants and filling their plates with cold sturgeon, chicken creams, stuffed eggs and three different kinds of caviar. There was the *Bal Blanc*, at which young, unmarried girls in virginal white danced quadrilles with young officers, carefully watched by vigilant chaperones sitting in stiff-backed gold chairs. For young married couples, there were the *Bals Roses*, a swirl of waltzes and gypsy music, of flashing jewels and blue, green and scarlet uniforms, that "made one feel one had wings on one's feet and one's head in the stars."

At the height of the season, ladies put on their diamonds in the morning, attended church, received at luncheon, took some air in the afternoon and then went home to dress for a ball. Traditionally, the finest balls of all were those given by Their Majesties at the Winter Palace. No palace in Europe was better suited for formal mass revelry. The Winter Palace possessed a row of gigantic galleries, each as wide and tall as a cathedral. Great columns of jasper, marble and malachite supported high gilded ceilings, hung with immense crystal and gold chandeliers. Outside, in the intense cold of a January night, the whole three blocks of the Winter Palace would be flooded with light. An endless procession of carriages drew up, depositing passengers who handed their furs or cloaks to attendants and then ascended the wide white marble staircases, covered with thick velvet carpets. Along the walls, baskets of orchids and palm trees in large pots framed huge mirrors in which dozens of people could examine and admire themselves. At intervals along the corridors troopers of the Chevaliers Gardes, in white uniforms with silver breastplates and silver eagle-crested helmets, and Cossack Life Guards in scarlet tunics stood rigidly at attention.

The three thousand guests included court officials in black, gold-laced uniforms, generals whose chests sagged with medals from the Turkish wars, and young Hussar officers in full dress with elkskin breeches so tight it had taken two soldiers to pull them on. At a great court ball, the passion of Russian women for jewels was displayed on every head, neck, ear, wrist, finger and waist.

An Imperial ball began precisely at 8:30 in the evening, when the Grand Master of Ceremonies appeared and tapped loudly three times on the floor with an ebony staff, embossed in gold with the double-headed eagle of the tsar. The sound brought an immediate hush. The great mahogany doors inlaid with gold swung open, the Grand Master of Ceremonies cried out, "Their Imperial Majesties," and hundreds of dresses rustled as ladies sank into a deep curtsy. This announcement in the winter of 1894 produced the appearance of a tall, powerful, bearded man, Tsar Alexander III. Beside him, in a silver brocade gown sewn with diamonds, her famous diamond tiara in her hair, was his dark-eyed Danish wife, Empress Marie. The orchestra broke into a polonaise, then as the evening progressed, a quadrille, a chaconne, a mazurka, a waltz. At midnight, in adjacent rooms, a supper was served. While demolishing plates of lobster salad, chicken patties, whipped cream and pastry tarts, the merrymakers could look through the double glass of the long windows to see the wind blowing gusts of fine powdered snow along the ice-bound river. Through clusters of tables, the Tsar, six feet four inches tall, ambled like a great Russian bear, stopping here and there to chat, until 1:30, when the Imperial couple withdrew and the guests reluctantly went home.

Tsar Alexander III had an enormous capacity for work and awesome physical strength. He could bend iron pokers or silver plates. Once at dinner the Austrian ambassador hinted at trouble in the Balkans and mentioned ominously that Austria might mobilize two or three army corps. Alexander III quietly picked up a silver fork, twisted it into a knot and tossed it onto the plate of the Austrian ambassador. "That," he said calmly, "is what I am going to do to your two or three army corps." Alexander's mode of relaxation was to rise before dawn, shoulder his gun and set off for a full day of hunting in the marshes or forests. Like a bear, he was gruff, blunt, narrow and suspicious. He had a strong mind, strong likes and dislikes and a purposeful will. After making a decision, he went to bed and slept soundly. He disliked Englishmen and Germans and had a passion for everything Russian. He hated pomp and felt that a true Russian should be simple in manners, table, speech and dress; he wore his own trousers and boots until they were threadbare. Queen Victoria once said frostily of this huge Tsar that he was "a sovereign whom she does not look upon as a gentleman."

Alexander III dominated his family as he did his empire. His wife achieved a role of her own by charming the gruff giant; his children, especially his three sons, scarcely had any independence at all. The Tsar's words were commands and, to one official of his court, when he spoke he "gave the impression of being on the point of striking you." When he gathered a small group to play chamber music together, the Tsar dominated the room, puffing away on his big bassoon.

Under Alexander III, the Russian system of autocracy appeared to work. The tsar personally was the government of Russia. His power was absolute, his responsibility only to God. From the tsar, power flowed downward and was exercised across the empire by an army of ministers, governors, clerks, tax collectors and policemen, all appointed in the name of the tsar. No parliament existed, and the people had no say in their government. Even members of the Imperial family, the grand dukes and grand duchesses, were subject to the tsar's will. Imperial grand dukes served as governors of provinces, or high-ranking officers in the army or navy, but they served only at the pleasure of the tsar. A snap of his finger and they stepped aside.

Alexander III was a dedicated autocrat, exercising to the limit the powers of his rank. He would have been a forceful tsar under any circumstances, but the fierceness of his belief in autocracy was inspired by his revulsion against those who had murdered his father, the Tsar-Liberator Alexander II. That his father's assassins were not liberals but revolutionary terrorists did not concern Alexander III; he lumped them all together.

Throughout the thirteen years of his reign, Alexander III devoted himself to crushing all opposition to autocracy. Hundreds of his political enemies made the long journey to exile in the lost towns of

Siberia. Heavy censorship shackled the press. Before long, the vigor of his policies actually began to create a psychological force in favor of autocracy, and the zeal of the assassins and revolutionaries began to wane.

Except in his reactionary political views, Alexander III was a forward-looking tsar. He made a military alliance with republican France and acquired the huge French loans he needed to build Russian railways. He began rebuilding the Russian army and resisted all temptations and provocations which might have dragged it into war. Although he disliked Germans, he encouraged German industrialists to bring their capital and develop the coal and iron mines of Russia.

The attempt to run this vast empire by himself required all of Alexander III's great energy. In order to work undisturbed, he chose to live in the palace at Gatchina, twenty-five miles southwest of St. Petersburg. The Empress Marie much preferred living in town, and every winter she brought him into the capital to preside over the season. Alexander III flatly refused, however, to live in the huge, ornate Winter Palace, which he thought cold and drafty, and the Imperial couple took up residence in the smaller Anitchkov Palace on the Nevsky Prospect.

It was Russia's good fortune that Alexander III was married to a woman whose talents exactly suited her position. Born Princess Dagmar of Denmark, she was a younger sister of Princess Alexandra, who married Edward, Prince of Wales, and became Queen of England. As a girl, Dagmar was engaged to Tsar Alexander III's older brother, Nicholas, then the heir to the Russian throne. When Nicholas died before their marriage, he bequeathed to Alexander not only his title of Tsarevich, but his dark-haired fiancée as well. Before her marriage, Princess Dagmar took the Russian name of Marie Fedorovna.

Russians loved this small, gay woman who became their Empress, and Marie gloried in the life of the Russian court. She delighted in parties and balls. "I danced and danced. I let myself be carried away," she wrote at the age of forty-four. Seated at dinner, she was an intelligent, witty conversationalist and, with her dark eyes flashing, her husky voice filled with warmth and humor, she dominated as much by charm as by rank. When something worth gossiping about occurred, Marie delightedly passed the tidbit along. "They danced the mazurka for half an hour," she once reported in a letter. "One poor lady lost her petticoat which remained at our feet until a general hid it behind a pot of flowers. The unfortunate one managed to hide herself in the crowd before anyone discovered who she was." Amused by human foibles, she was tolerant of human weaknesses. She regarded with droll pity the ordeal suffered by the Archduke Franz Ferdinand when he paid a ceremonial visit to St. Petersburg in 1891: "He is feted, he is stuffed with lunches and dinners everywhere so that he will end by having a monstrous indigestion. Last night at the theatre, he looked already rather pasty and left early with a migraine."

By the time she was thirty, Marie had met the requirements of royal motherhood by producing five children. Nicholas was born May 18, 1868, followed by George (1871), Xenia (1875), Michael (1878) and Olga (1882). Because of her husband's involvement in work, it was Marie who clucked over the children, supervised their studies, gave them advice and accepted their confidences. Frequently she acted as a maternal buffer between her growing brood and the strong, gruff man who was their father. Her oldest son, the shy Tsarevich Nicholas, was especially in need of his mother's support. Everything about Alexander inspired awe in his son. In October 1888, the Imperial train was derailed near Kharkov as the Tsar and his family were eating pudding in the dining car. The roof caved in, but, with his great strength, Alexander lifted it on his shoulders and held it long enough for his wife and children to crawl free, unhurt. The thought that one day he would have to succeed this Herculean father all but overwhelmed young Nicholas.

As the year 1894 began, Nicholas's fears appeared remote. Tsar Alexander III, only forty-nine years old, was still approaching the peak of his reign. The early years had been devoted to reestablishing the autocracy in effective form. Now, with the empire safe and the dynasty secure, he expected to use the great power he had gathered to put a distinctive stamp on Russia. Already there were those who, gazing confidently into the future, had begun to compare Alexander III to Peter the Great.

CHAPTER TWO

The Tsarevich Nicholas

IT WAS with special care that Fate had selected Nicholas to be Tsarevich and, later, Tsar. He was not a firstborn son. An older brother named Alexander, who had he lived would have been Tsar Alexander IV, had died in infancy. Nicholas's next brother, George, three years younger than the Tsarevich, was gay with quick intelligence. Throughout their childhood Nicholas admired George's sparkling humor, and whenever his brother cracked a joke, the Tsarevich carefully wrote it down on a slip of paper and filed it away in a box. Years later when Nicholas as Tsar was heard laughing alone in his study, he would be found rereading his collection of George's jokes. Unhappily, in adolescence George developed tuberculosis of both lungs and was sent to live, alone except for servants, in the high, sun-swept mountains of the Caucasus.

Although the palace at Gatchina had nine hundred rooms, Nicholas and his brothers and sisters were brought up in spartan simplicity. Every morning, Alexander III arose at seven, washed in cold water, dressed in peasant's clothes, made himself a pot of coffee and sat down at his desk. Later when Marie was up, she joined him for a breakfast of rye bread and boiled eggs. The children slept on simple army cots with hard pillows, took cold baths in the morning and ate porridge for breakfast. At lunch when they joined their parents, there was plenty of food, but as they were served last after all the guests and still had to leave the table when their father rose, they often went hungry. Ravenous, Nicholas once attacked the hollow gold cross filled with beeswax which he had been given at baptism; embedded in the wax was a tiny fragment of the True Cross. "Nicky was so hungry that he opened his cross and ate the contents—relic and all," recalled his sister Olga. "Later he felt ashamed of himself but admitted that it had tasted 'immorally good.'" The children ate more fully when they dined alone, although these meals without their parents' presence often turned into unmanageable free-for-alls, with brothers and sisters pelting one another across the table with pieces of bread.

Nicholas was educated by tutors. There were language tutors, history tutors, geography tutors and a whiskered dancing tutor who wore white gloves and insisted that a huge pot of fresh flowers always be placed on his accompanist's piano. Of all the tutors, however, the most important was Constantine Petrovich Pobedonostsev. A brilliant philosopher of reaction, Pobedonostsev has been called "The High Priest of Social Stagnation" and "the dominant and most baleful influence of the [last] reign." A wizened, balding man with coldly ascetic eyes staring out through steel-rimmed glasses, he first came to prominence when as a jurist at Moscow University he wrote a celebrated three-volume text on Russian law. He became a tutor to the children of Tsar Alexander II, and, as a young man, Alexander III was his faithful, believing pupil. When Alexander mounted the throne, Pobedonostsev already held the office of Procurator of the Holy Synod, or lay head of the Russian Orthodox Church. In addition, he assumed the tutorship of the new Tsarevich, Nicholas.

Pobedonostsev's brilliant mind was steeped in nationalism and bigotry. He took a misanthropic Hobbesian view of man in general. Slavs in particular he described as sluggish and lazy, requiring strong leadership, while Russia, he said, was "an icy desert and an abode of the 'Bad Man.'" Believing that national unity was essential to the survival of this sprawling, multi-racial empire, he insisted on the absolute authority of Russia's two great unifying institutions: the autocracy and the Orthodox Church. He insisted that opposition to them be ruthlessly crushed. He opposed all reforms, which he called "this whole bazaar of projects . . . this noise of cheap and shallow ecstasies." He regarded a constitution as "a fundamental evil," a free press as an "instrument of mass corruption" and universal suffrage as "a fatal error." But most of all Pobedonostsev hated parliaments.

"Among the falsest of political principles," he declared, "is the principle of the sovereignty of the people . . . which has unhappily infatuated certain foolish Russians. . . . Parliament is an institution serving for the satisfaction of the personal ambition, vanity, and self-interest of its members. The institution of Parliament is indeed one of the greatest illustrations of human delusion. . . . Providence has preserved our Russia, with its heterogeneous racial composition, from like misfortunes. It is terrible to think of our condition if destiny had sent us the fatal gift—an all-Russian Parliament. But that will never be."

For the same reason, and from his special position as—in effect—Minister of Religion, Pobedonostsev attacked all religious strains in Russia unwilling to be assimilated into Orthodoxy. Those who most strenuously resisted, he hated most. He was violently anti-Semitic and declared that the Jewish problem in Russia would be solved only when one third of Russia's Jews had emigrated, one third had been converted to Orthodoxy and one third had disappeared. It was the pupil of Pobedonostsev speaking in Alexander III when he wrote in the margin of a report depicting the plight of Russian Jewry in 1890, "We must not forget that it was the Jews who crucified our Lord and spilled his precious blood."

Pobedonostsev's virulent prejudice was not restricted to Jews. He also attacked the Catholic Poles and the Moslems scattered across the broad reaches of the empire. It was Pobedonostsev who wrote the document excommunicating Leo Tolstoy in 1901.*

The Russia described to Nicholas by Pobedonostsev had nothing to do with the restless giant stirring outside the palace windows. Instead, it was an ancient, stagnant, coercive land made up of the classical triumvirate of Tsar, Church and People. It was God, the tutor explained, who had chosen the Tsar. There was no place in God's design for representatives of the people to share in ruling the nation. Turning Pobedonostsev's argument around, a tsar who did not rule as an autocrat was failing his duty to God. Heard as a school lesson, the old man's teaching may have lacked a basis in reality, but it had the compelling purity of logic, and Nicholas eagerly accepted it.

For Nicholas, the most dramatic proof of Pobedonostsev's teachings against the dangers of liberalism was the brutal assassination of his grandfather, Alexander II, the most liberal of Russia's nineteenth-

* Tolstoy had left the Church, and the excommunication was only a formal acknowledgment of this fact. Still, Pobedonostsev may have taken a personal satisfaction in expelling the great novelist. Since 1877, when Tolstoy completed *Anna Karenina*, it had been rumored that the character of Alexis Karenin, the coldly pompous bureaucrat whom Anna cuckolds and then divorces, was modeled on an episode in the family life of Constantine Pobedonostsev.

century tsars. For his historic freeing of the serfs, Alexander II was known as the "Tsar-Liberator," yet his murder became the preeminent objective of Russian revolutionaries. The assassins went to extraordinary lengths. Once, near Moscow, they purchased a building near the railway track and tunneled a gallery from the building under the track, where they planted a huge mine. The Tsar was saved when his train left Moscow in a different direction. Six other attempts were made, and on March 13, 1881—ironically, only a few hours after the Tsar had approved the establishment of a national representative body to advise on legislation—the assassins succeeded. As his carriage rolled through the streets of St. Petersburg, a bomb, thrown from the sidewalk, sailed under it. The explosion shattered the vehicle and wounded his horses, his equerries and one of his Cossack escorts, but the Tsar himself was unhurt. Stepping from the splintered carriage, Alexander II spoke to the wounded men and even asked gently about the bomb thrower, who had been arrested. Just then a second assassin ran up, shouting, "It is too early to thank God," and threw a second bomb directly between the Tsar's feet. In the sheet of flame and metal Alexander II's legs were torn away, his stomach ripped open, his face mutilated. Still alive and conscious, he whispered, "To the palace, to die there." What remained of him was picked up and carried into the Winter Palace, leaving a trail of thick drops of black blood up the marble stairs. Unconscious, he was laid on a couch, his right leg torn off, his left leg shattered, one eye closed, the other open but vacant. One after another, the horrified members of the Imperial family crowded into the room. Nicholas, aged thirteen, wearing a blue sailor suit, came in deathly pale and watched from the end of the bed. His mother, who had been ice-skating, arrived still clutching her skates. At the window looking out stood his father, the Heir Apparent, his broad shoulders hunched and shaking, his fists clenching and unclenching. "The Emperor is dead," announced the surgeon, letting go of the blood-covered wrist. The new Tsar, Alexander III, nodded grimly and motioned to his wife. Together they walked out of the palace, now surrounded by guardsmen of the Preobrajensky Regiment with bayonets fixed. He stood for a moment, saluting, then jumped into his carriage and drove away "accompanied by a whole regiment of Don Cossacks, in attack formation, their red lances shining brightly in the last rays of a crimson March sunset." In his accession manifesto, Alexander III proclaimed that he would rule "with faith in the power and right of autocracy."

For the thirteen years of his father's reign, Nicholas saw Russia ruled according to the theories of Pobedonostsev.

Nicholas, at twenty-one, was a slender youth of five feet seven inches, with his father's square, open face and his mother's expressive eyes and magnetic personal charm. His own best qualities were gentleness, kindliness and friendliness. "Nicky smiled his usual tender, shy, slightly sad smile," wrote his young cousin and intimate companion Grand Duke Alexander Mikhailovich. Himself prepared to like everybody, Nicholas hoped that people liked him. As best he could tell through the thickets of flattery and etiquette surrounding his rank, they did.

In many respects, his education was excellent. He had an unusual memory and had done well in history. He spoke French and German, and his English was so good that he could have fooled an Oxford professor into mistaking him for an Englishman. He rode beautifully, danced gracefully and was an excellent shot. He had been taught to keep a diary and, in the style of innumerable princes and gentlemen of that era, he faithfully recorded, day after day, the state of the weather, the number of birds he shot and the names of those with whom he walked and dined. Nicholas's diary was identical to that of his cousin King George V; both were kept primarily as a catalogue of engagements, written in a terse, monotonous prose, and regarded as one of the daily disciplines of an ordered life. Curiously, Nicholas's diary, which lacks the expressive language of his private letters, has proved a rich mine for his detractors, while George's diary is often praised for its revelation of the honest character of this good King.

In May 1890, a few days before his twenty-second birthday, Nicholas wrote in his diary, "Today I finished definitely and forever my education." The young man then happily turned to the pleasant business of becoming a rake. His day usually began in mid-morning when he struggled out of bed exhausted from the previous night. "As always after a ball, I don't feel well. I have a weakness in the legs," he wrote in his diary. "I got up at 10:30. I am persuaded that I have some kind of sleeping sickness because there is no way to get me up."

Once on his feet, he went to a council meeting, or received the Swedish minister, or perhaps a Russian explorer just back from two years in Ethiopia. Occasionally he was lucky. "Today, there was not a meeting of the Imperial Council. I was not overwhelmed with sadness by the fact."

Most of the time, Nicholas was required to do absolutely nothing. The essential function of a tsarevich, once he had finished his schooling and reached manhood, was to wait as discreetly as possible until it came his turn to become tsar. In 1890 Alexander III still was only forty-five years old. Expecting that he would continue to occupy the throne for another twenty or thirty years, he dawdled about giving his son the experience to succeed him. Nicholas happily accepted the playboy role to which he had tacitly been assigned. He appeared at meetings of the Imperial Council, but his eyes were fixed on the clock. At the first reasonable opportunity, he bolted.

On winter afternoons, he collected his sister Xenia and went ice-skating. "Skating with Xenia and Aunt Ella. We amused ourselves and ran like fools. Put on skates and played ball with all my strength," he wrote. He fell on the ice, got sore knees, sore feet and had to hobble around in slippers, grumbling about the good luck of people still able to skate. At twilight, flushed by exercise and the freezing air, the skaters bundled themselves into a drawing room for glasses of steaming tea. Dinner might be anywhere: in a restaurant with a party of friends, or as a guest in a home where the host would provide an orchestra of balalaikas.

Every night during the winter season, Nicholas went out. In the month of January 1890, he attended twenty performances, sometimes two in a day, at the opera, theatre and ballet. It was during this month that Tchaikovsky's ballet *Sleeping Beauty* was first presented in St. Petersburg; Nicholas went to a dress rehearsal and two performances. He attended plays in German, French and English, including *The Merchant of Venice*. He was especially fond of *Eugene Onegin* and *Boris Godunov* and in February he even arranged to play a small part in a production of *Eugene Onegin*. He was a much-prized guest at exclusive late-evening soirees where the guests were entertained by the Imperial Navy Band, or a chorus of sixty singers, or a famous raconteur who told stories to amuse the guests. Two or three times a week, the Tsarevich attended a ball. "We danced to exhaustion . . . afterwards supper . . . to bed at 3:30 a.m." The arrival of Lent abruptly ended this round of festivities. The day after the ball and midnight supper which ended the winter season in 1892, he wrote in his diary, "All day I found myself in a state of gaiety which has little in common with the period of Lent."

During this quieter period, Nicholas stayed home, dined with his mother and played cards with his friends. A telephone was installed in his room at the palace so that he could listen to Tschaikovsky's opera *Queen of Spades* over an open line direct from the stage. He regularly accompanied his father on hunting parties, leaving the palace at dawn to spend a day in the forests and marshes outside the capital, shooting pheasants and hares.

Nicholas was never happier than when he was sitting on a white horse outside the Winter Palace, his arm frozen in salute as squadrons of Cossacks trotted past, their huge fur caps sitting down on their eyebrows, pennants fluttering from their lances. The army, its pageantry and history fascinated him all his life, and no title meant more to him than the rank of colonel awarded him by his father.

At nineteen, Nicholas was given command of a squadron of Horse Guards and went with them to Krasnoe Selo, the great military camp outside St. Petersburg used by regiments of the Imperial Guard for summer maneuvers. Installed in a private bungalow with a bedroom, study, dining room and a balcony overlooking a small garden, he lived the pleasant, mindless existence of any wealthy aristocratic young Russian officer. He participated fully in the life and chatter of the messrooms and his modesty made him popular among his fellow officers.

"I am happier than I can say to have joined the army and every day I become more and more used to camp life," he wrote to his mother, Empress Marie. "Each day we drill twice—there is either target practice in the morning and battalion drill in the evening or the other way round—battalion drill in the morning and target practice in the evening. . . . We have lunch at 12 o'clock and dine at 8, with siesta and tea in between. The dinners are very merry; they feed us well. After meals, the officers . . . play billiards, skittles, cards or dominoes."

The Empress worried that the eager subaltern would forget that he was also the Tsarevich. "Never forget that everyone's eyes are turned on you now, waiting to see what your first independent steps in life will be," she wrote. "Always be polite and courteous with everybody so that you get along with all your comrades without discrimination, although without too much familiarity or intimacy, and *never* listen to flatterers."

Nicholas wrote back dutifully, "I will always try to follow your advice, my dearest darling Mama. One has to be cautious with everybody at the start." But to his diary he confided more fully: "We got stewed," "tasted six sorts of Port and got a bit soused," "we wallowed in the grass and drank," "felt owlish," "the officers carried me out."

It was as a young officer in the spring of 1890 that Nicholas first met a seventeen-year-old dancer in the Imperial Ballet, Mathilde Kschessinska. A small, vivacious girl with a supple body, a full bosom, an arched neck, dark curls and merry eyes, Kschessinska had been rigorously schooled in ballet for ten years and in 1890 was the best dancer in her graduating class. By chance, that year the entire Imperial family attended the graduation performance and supper.

In her memoirs, Kschessinska recalled the arrival of Tsar Alexander III, towering over everyone else and calling in a loud voice, "Where is Kschessinska?" When the tiny girl was presented to him, he took her hand and said to her warmly, "Be the glory and adornment of our ballet." At supper, the Tsar first sat next to Mathilde; then he moved and his place was taken by the Tsarevich. When Kschessinska looked at Nicholas, she wrote, "in both our hearts an attraction had been born impelling us irresistibly towards each other." Nicholas's entry in his diary that night was more laconic: "We went to see the performance at the Theatre School. Saw a short play and a ballet. Delightful. Supper with the pupils."

From that moment, Kschessinska struggled to put herself in Nicholas's line of vision. Knowing that Nicholas and his sister Xenia often stood on a high stone balustrade of the Anitchkov Palace watching passers-by on the Nevsky Prospect, Kschessinska strolled past the building every day. In May, on Nicholas's birthday, she decorated her room with little white, blue and red Russian flags. That summer she was selected to join the troupe which danced in the wooden theatre for officers at Krasnoe Selo, where the Tsarevich was on duty with the Guards. He came every day to watch Kschessinska's performance. Once when Tsar Alexander III saw them talking, he said to her with a smile, "Ah, you must have been flirting."

As the Tsarevich and the dancer were never alone, the romance that summer did not go beyond flirting. "I thought that, without being in love with me, he did feel a certain affection for me, and I gave myself up to my dreams," she wrote. "I like Kschessinska very much," Nicholas admitted to his diary. A few days later he wrote, "Gossiped at her window with little Kschessinska." And just before leaving the camp, he added, "After lunch, went for the last time to the dear little theatre at Krasnoe Selo. Said goodbye to Kschessinska."

Nicholas did not see Mathilde again for almost a year. In Ocotober

1890, he set out with his brother George on a nine-month cruise which took them from the Mediterranean Sea through the Suez Canal to India and Japan. In George's case, his parents prayed that the weeks at sea in warm sunshine and salt air would clear his congested lungs. For Nicholas, they intended a royal grand tour, an education in diplomatic niceties and an interval which would help the Tsarevich forget the young women who had begun to complicate his life.

Kschessinska was not the only one. Nicholas found the dancer appealing; she was close at hand; she was pretty; and she was letting him know in every way possible how much she liked him. But his feelings for a tall, golden-haired German princess, Alix of Hesse, were more serious. Princess Alix was a younger sister of Grand Duchess Elizabeth, the twenty-five-year-old wife of Nicholas's uncle Grand Duke Serge. Elizabeth, called Ella, was a gay young woman whose skating parties and family theatricals had brought a youthful bounce into the Imperial family. Nicholas was a frequent visitor in the home of this young aunt; when Ella's sister Alix came to St. Petersburg, Nicholas's visits became even more frequent. Serious and shy, Alix burned with inner fires. When she set her blue-gray eyes on Nicholas, he was overwhelmed. Unfortunately, she lived far away in Hesse-Darmstadt and his parents saw little to recommend their matching a Russian tsarevich with a minor German princess.

Leaving St. Petersburg in a gloomy mood, Nicholas and George went to Athens, where they were joined by their cousin Prince George of Greece. There the three cousins, accompanied by several young Russian noblemen, including Prince Bariatinsky, Prince Obolensky and Prince Oukhtomsky, boarded a Russian battleship, the *Pamiat Azova*. By the time the battleship reached Egypt, the cruise had turned into a traveling house party and Nicholas's spirits had soared. On the Nile, they transferred to the Khedive's yacht and began a trip up the river. In the broiling heat, Nicholas stared at the riverbank, "always the same, from place to place, villages and clusters of palm trees." Stopping in towns along the river, the youthful Russians became increasingly interested in the local belly dancers. "Nothing worth talking about," Nicholas wrote after watching his first performance. But the following night: "This time it was much better. They undressed themselves." The travelers climbed two pyramids, dined like Arabs, using their fingers, and rode on camels. They got as far as the first cataracts of the

Nile at Aswan, where Nicholas watched Egyptian boys swimming in the foaming water.

In India, Bariatinsky and Oblensky each killed a tiger, but Nicholas, to his immense chagrin, shot nothing. The heat was intense and the Tsarevich grew irritable. From Delhi he complained to his mother, "How stifling it is to be surrounded again by the English and to see red uniforms everywhere." Hurriedly, Marie wrote back:

"I'd like to think you are very courteous to all the English who are taking such pains to give you the best possible reception, shoots, etc. I quite see that the balls and other official doings are not very amusing, especially in that heat, but you must understand that your position brings this with it. You have to set your personal comfort aside, be doubly polite and amiable, and above all, never show you are bored. You will do this, won't you, my dear Nicky? At balls you must consider it your duty to dance more and smoke less in the garden with officers just because it is more amusing. One simply cannot do this, my dear, but I know you understand all this so well and you know my only wish is that nothing can be said against you and for you to leave a good impression with everybody everywhere."

George suffered in the Indian heat. His cough persisted and he developed a constant fever. To his great disappointment, his father and mother ordered him to break off the tour. When the *Pamiat Azova* sailed from Bombay, George left on a destroyer in the opposite direction to return to his quiet life in the Caucasus.

Nicholas continued eastward, stopping in Colombo, Singapore, Batavia and in Bangkok, where he called on the King of Siam. He went on to Saigon and Hong Kong, and arrived in Japan just as the cherry trees were blooming in Tokyo parks. He visited Nagasaki and Kyoto and he was passing through the town of Otsu when his tour—and his life—nearly came to an abrupt end. Suddenly on a street a Japanese jumped at him swinging a sword. The blade, aimed at his head, glanced off his forehead, bringing a gush of blood but failing to bite deep. The assassin swung a second time, but Prince George of Greece forcefully parried the blow with his cane.

The assailant's motives have never been clear. Nicholas, although he bore a scar for the rest of his life and sometimes suffered headaches in that part of his skull, gave no explanation. Two stories, both largely rumor, have been offered. One attributes the assault to a fanatic outraged by the supposedly disrespectful behavior of Nicholas and his companions in a Japanese temple. The other describes it as the jealous lunge of a Samurai whose wife had received the Tsarevich's attention. The episode terminated the visit, and Alexander III telegraphed his son to return home immediately. Thereafter, Nicholas never liked Japan and customarily referred to most Japanese as "monkeys." A subsequent entry in his diary reads, "I received the Swedish minister and the Japanese monkey, the chargé d'affaires, who brought me a letter, a portrait and an ancient armor from Her Majesty [the Empress of Japan]."

On his way home, Nicholas stopped in Vladivostock long enough to lay the first stone of the eastern terminus of the Trans-Siberian Railway. He found Vladivostock a desolate frontier town of muddy, unpaved streets, open sewers, unpainted wooden houses and clusters of mud-plastered straw huts inhabited by Chinese and Koreans. On May 31, 1892, he attended an outdoor religious service swept by cold Siberian winds. He wielded a shovel to fill a wheelbarrow with dirt, trundled it along for several yards and emptied it down an embankment of the future railroad. Soon after, he grasped a trowel and cemented into place the first stone of the Vladivostock passenger station.

Upon his return to St. Petersburg, Nicholas again began to see Kschessinska. At first, they rendezvoused secretly in carriages on the bank of the Neva. Later, the Tsarevich began to call on Mathilde at her father's home. Usually, he brought with him three youthful cousins, Grand Dukes Serge, George and Alexander Mikhailovich. Kschessinska served the young men her father's champagne and listened while they sang songs from Russian Georgia. On Sundays, Mathilde went to the race track and sat just opposite the Imperial box, never failing to receive a bouquet of flowers, delivered for the Tsarevich by two fellow officers of the Guards.

As Nicholas's affection for Kschessinska grew stronger, he gave her a gold bracelet studded with diamonds and a large sapphire. The following summer, when Kschessinska returned to the military theatre at Krasnoe Selo, Nicholas came often to rehearsals, sitting in her dressing room, talking until the rehearsal began. After the performance, Nicholas came for Kschessinska, driving his own *troika.* Alone together they set off on starlit rides, galloping through the shadows on the great plain of Krasnoe Selo. Sometimes, after these blood-stirring rides, the Tsarevich stayed after supper until dawn.

At the end of that summer of 1892, Kschessinska decided that she needed a place of her own. "Though he did not openly mention it," she said, "I guessed that the Tsarevich shared this wish." Her father, shattered by her announcement, asked whether she understood that Nicholas could never marry her. Mathilde replied that she cared nothing about the future and wished only to seize whatever brief happiness Fate was offering her. Soon after, she rented a small two-story house in St. Petersburg, owned by the composer Rimsky-Korsakov.

When her house was ready, Nicholas celebrated the housewarming by giving her a vodka service of eight small gold glasses inlaid with jewels. Thereafter, she said, "we led a quiet, retiring life." Nicholas usually rode up on horseback in time for supper. They gave little parties, attended by the three young Grand Dukes, another dancer or two and a tenor of whom Nicholas was fond. After supper, in "an intimate and delightful atmosphere" the company played baccarat.

Nicholas, meanwhile, continued his functions at court. "I have been nominated a member of the Finance Committee," he wrote at one point. "A great honor, but not much pleasure. . . . I received six members of this institution; I admit that I never suspected its existence." He became president of a committee to aid those who were starving in a famine, and he worked hard at the job, raising money and donating substantial funds of his own. His relations with his father remained distant and deferential. "I would have liked to exercise with the Hussars today," he wrote, "but I forgot to ask Papa." Sergius Witte, the burly, efficient Finance Minister who built the Trans-Siberian Railway and later served Nicholas during the Japanese War and the 1905 Revolution, gave an account of a conversation he had with Alexander III. According to Witte, he began the conversation by suggesting to the Tsar that the Tsarevich be appointed president of the Trans-Siberian Railroad. Witte says Alexander III was astonished by his proposal.

"What? But you know the Tsarevich. Have you ever had a serious conversation with him?"

"No, Sire, I have never had the pleasure of having such a conversation with the Heir."

"He is still absolutely a child, he has only infantile judgments, how would he be able to be president of a committee?"

"Nevertheless, Sire, if you do not begin to initiate him to affairs of state, he will never understand them."

In 1893, Nicholas was sent to London to represent the family at the wedding of his first cousin George, Duke of York—later King

George V—to Princess Mary of Teck. The Tsarevich was lodged in Marlborough House with most of the royal personages of Europe living just down the hall. The Prince of Wales, always concerned with sartorial matters, immediately decided that the young visitor needed sprucing. "Uncle Bertie, of course, sent me at once a tailor, a bootmaker and a hatter," Nicholas reported to his mother. This was his first visit to London. "I never thought I would like it so much," he said, describing his visits to Westminster Abbey, St. Paul's and the Tower. Appropriately, he avoided that citadel of representative government, the Houses of Parliament.

Nicholas was immediately taken with Princess Mary. "May is delightful and much better looking than her photographs," he wrote. As for his cousin George, Nicholas and the bridegroom looked so much alike that even people who knew them well confused one with the other. George was shorter and slimmer than Nicholas, his face was thinner and his eyes somewhat more protuberant, but both parted their hair in the middle and wore similar Van Dyke beards. Standing side by side, they looked like brothers and almost like twins. Several times during the ceremonies, the resemblance caused embarrassment. At a garden party, Nicholas was taken for George and warmly congratulated, while George was asked whether he had come to London only to attend the wedding or whether he had other business to transact. The day before the wedding, George, mistaken for Nicholas, was begged by one gentleman of the court not to be late for the ceremony.

After the wedding, Nicholas visited Windsor Castle and had lunch with Queen Victoria. "She was very friendly, talked a lot, and gave me the Order of the Garter," he reported. He went to a ball at Buckingham Palace and, knowing his mother would be pleased, told her, "I danced a lot . . . but didn't see many beautiful ladies."

In St. Petersburg, meanwhile, little Kschessinska's career as a dancer was gathering momentum. Already, at nineteen, she was dancing such roles as the Sugar Plum Fairy in Tchaikovsky's *Nutcracker* and Princess Aurora in *Sleeping Beauty*. Tchaikovsky himself came to her rehearsals and accompanied the dancers on the piano. Once after Mathilde had danced Princess Aurora, the composer came to her dressing room especially to congratulate her. In later years Mathilde Kschessinska would rank with Anna Pavlova and Tamara Karsavina among the great ballerinas of pre-revolutionary Russia.

There were those, of course, who ascribed Mathilde's early success primarily to her connection with the Tsarevich. Not that society regarded the liaison on either side with moral disdain. For the Russian aristocracy, ballet was a supreme art and the mingling of great titles and pretty ankles was a common thing. Many a deep-bosomed young dancer in the back row of the Imperial Ballet left the Maryinsky Theatre pulling her cloak about her shoulders, gathered her skirts and stepped into the plush velvet interior of a waiting coach to be whirled away to a private supper in one of the city's elegant palaces.

Despite Mathilde's success on the stage, the flame between her and Nicholas began to flicker. Nicholas had never hidden from Kschessinska his interest in Princess Alix. Early in 1894, he told Mathilde that he hoped to make Alix his fiancée. Later that year, Nicholas and Mathilde parted, saying goodbye at a highway rendezvous, she seated in her carriage, he astride a horse. When he rode away, she wept. For months, she went through "the terrible boundless suffering . . . of losing my Niki." The great ballet master Marius Petipa consoled her by persuading her that suffering in love is necessary to art, especially to the great stage roles to which she aspired. "I was not alone in my grief and trouble. . . . The [younger] Grand Duke Serge . . . remained with me to console and protect me." Serge bought her a *dacha* with a garden by the sea. Later, at the height of her success, she met Grand Duke Andrei, another cousin of the Tsar. Although Andrei was seven years her junior, they traveled together on holidays to Biarritz and Venice. In 1902, Mathilde and Andrei had a son, and in 1921, in Cannes, they married.

CHAPTER THREE

Princess Alix

"MY DREAM is some day to marry Alix H. I have loved her a long while and still deeper and stronger since 1889 when she spent six weeks in St. Petersburg. For a long time, I resisted my feeling that my dearest dream will come true."

When Nicholas made this entry in his diary in 1892, he had not yet established his temporary little household with Kschessinska. He was discouraged about the prospects of his interest in Princess Alix. Russian society did not share Nicholas's rapture for this German girl with red-gold hair. Alix had made a bad impression during her visits to her sister Grand Duchess Elizabeth in the Russian capital. Badly dressed, clumsy, an awkward dancer, atrocious French accent, a schoolgirl blush, too shy, too nervous, too arrogant—these were some of the unkind things St. Petersburg said about Alix of Hesse.

Society sniped openly at Princess Alix, safe in the knowledge that Tsar Alexander III and Empress Marie, both vigorously anti-German, had no intention of permitting a match with the Tsarevich. Although Princess Alix was his godchild, it was generally known that Alexander III was angling for a bigger catch for his son, someone like Princess Hélène, the tall, dark-haired daughter of the Pretender to the throne of France, the Comte de Paris. Although a republic, France was Russia's ally, and Alexander III suspected that a link between the Romanov dynasty and the deposed House of Bourbon would strengthen the alliance in the hearts of the French people.

But the approach to Hélène did not please Nicholas. "Mama made a few allusions to Hélène, daughter of the Comte de Paris," he wrote in his diary. "I myself want to go in one direction and it is evident that Mama wants me to choose the other one."

Hélène also resisted. She was not at all willing to give up her Roman Catholicism for the Orthodox faith required of a future Russian empress. Frustrated, the Tsar next sent emissaries to Princess Margaret of Prussia. Nicholas flatly declared that he would rather become a monk than marry the plain and bony Margaret. Margaret spared him, however, by announcing that she, too, was unwilling to abandon Protestantism for Orthodoxy.

Through it all, Nicholas nurtured his hope that someday he would marry Alix. Before leaving for the Far East, he wrote in his diary, "Oh, Lord, how I want to go to Ilinskoe [Ella's country house, where Alix was visiting] . . . otherwise if I do not see her now, I shall have to wait a whole year and that will be hard." His parents continued to discourage his ardor. Alix, they said, would never change her religion in order to marry him. Nicholas asked permission only to see her and propose. If Alix were denied him, he stated, he would never marry.

As long as he was well, Alexander III ignored his son's demands. In the winter of 1894, however, the Tsar caught influenza and began having trouble with his kidneys. As his vitality began to ebb alarmingly, Alexander began to consider how Russia would manage without him. Nothing could be done immediately about the Tsarevich's lack of experience, but Alexander III decided that he could at least provide his heir with the stabilizing effect of marriage. As Princess Alix was the only girl whom Nicholas would even remotely consider, Alexander III and Marie reluctantly agreed that he should be allowed to propose.

For Nicholas, it was a great personal victory. For the first time in his life he had overcome every obstacle, pushed aside all objections, defeated his overpowering father and had his way.

Alix Victoria Helena Louise Beatrice, Princess of Hesse-Darmstadt, was born on June 6, 1872, in the medieval city of Darmstadt a few miles from the river Rhine. She was named Alix after her mother, Princess Alice of England, the third of Queen Victoria's nine children. "Alix" was the nearest euphonic rendering of "Alice" in German. "They murder my name here, Aliicé they pronounce it," her mother said.

Princess Alix was born "a sweet, merry little person, always laughing and a dimple in one cheek," her mother wrote to Queen

Victoria. When she was christened, with the future Tsar Alexander III and the future King Edward VII as godfathers, her mother already called her "Sunny." "Sunny in pink was immensely admired," Princess Alice reported to Windsor Castle.

If the emotional ties between England and the small grand duchy of Hesse-Darmstadt were strong, those between Hesse and Prussia, ruled by the House of Hohenzollern, were weak and embittered. Only two years before Alix's birth, Hesse had been forcibly incorporated into the newly created German Empire. As recently as 1866, Hesse had sided with Austria in an unsuccessful war against Prussia. Alix's father, Grand Duke Louis of Hesse, hated Prussia and the Hohenzollerns, and throughout her life Alix shared his bitterness.

Darmstadt itself was an old German city with narrow cobblestone streets and steeply roofed houses covered with ornamental fifteenth-century carvings. The palace of the Grand Duke stood in the middle of town, surrounded by a park filled with linden and chestnut trees. Inside, Victoria's daughter had filled its rooms with mementoes of England. The drawing rooms were hung with portraits of Queen Victoria, Prince Albert and all the living English cousins. Sketches of English scenes and English palaces lined the walls of the bedchambers. An English governess, Mrs. Orchard, ruled the nursery. Mrs. Orchard was not one for frills. The children's bedrooms were large and airy, but plainly furnished. Meals were simple; Alix grew up eating baked apples and rice puddings. Mrs. Orchard believed in strict daily schedules with fixed hours for every activity. Years later, when Alix had carried this training to Russia, the Russian Imperial family ate on the stroke of the hour and divided its mornings and afternoons into rigid little blocks of time while Mrs. Orchard watched and nodded approvingly. She, along with her well-drilled habits, had been brought to Russia.

Before she was six, Alix drove her own pony cart through the park, accompanied by a liveried footman who walked at the pony's head. In the summertime, her father, Grand Duke Louis, took his family to a hunting lodge called Wolfsgarten. There, Alix spent her mornings in a sun-filled courtyard, running up and down a flight of high stone steps and sitting by the courtyard fountain, dipping her hand in the water, trying to catch a goldfish. She liked to dress in her mother's cast-off dresses and prance down the hall engulfed in crinoline, imagining herself as a great lady or a character from a fairy story.

Christmas was celebrated with German lavishness and English trimmings. A giant tree stood in the palace ballroom, its green branches covered with apples and gilded nuts, while the room glowed with the light of small wax candles fixed to the boughs. Christmas dinner began with a traditional Christmas goose and ended with plum pudding and mince pies especially shipped from England.

Every year, the family visited Queen Victoria. The Hessian children loved these visits to Windsor Castle near London, to the granite castle of Balmoral in the Scottish Highlands and to Osborne, the tiled Renaissance palace by the sea. Many years afterward, in Russia, the Empress Alexandra was to dream of herself as a little girl again, fishing for crabs, bathing and building sand castles on an English beach.

In 1878, when Alix was six, diphtheria swept the palace in Hesse-Darmstadt. All but one of the Grand Duke's children were stricken. Victoria sent her own physician from England to help the German doctors, but, despite their efforts, Alix's four-year-old sister, May, died. Then, worn out from nursing her children, Alix's mother, Princess Alice, also fell ill. In less than a week she was dead.

The death of her mother at thirty-five, had a shattering effect on six-year-old Alix. She sat quiet and withdrawn in her playroom while her nurse stood in the corner, weeping. Even the toys she handled were new; the old, familiar toys had been burned as a precaution against the disease. Alix had been a merry, generous, warm little girl, obstinate but sensitive, with a hot temper. After this tragedy she began to seal herself off from other people. A hard shell of aloofness formed over her emotions, and her radiant smile appeared infrequently. Craving intimacy and affection, she held herself back. She grew to dislike unfamiliar places and to avoid unfamiliar people. Only in cozy family gatherings where she could count on warmth and understanding did Alix unwind. There, the shy, serious, cool Princess Alix became once again the merry, dimpled, loving "Sunny" of her early childhood.

After her daughter's death, Queen Victoria treated Grand Duke Louis as her own son and invited him often to England with his motherless children. Alix, now the youngest, was the aging Queen's special favorite and Victoria kept a close watch on her little grandchild. Tutors and governesses in Darmstadt were required to send special reports to Windsor and receive, in return, a steady flow of advice and instruction from the Queen. Under this tutelage, Alix's standards of taste and morality became thoroughly English and thoroughly Victorian. The future Empress of Russia developed steadily into that most recognizable and respectable of creatures, a proper young English gentlewoman.

Alix was an excellent student. By the time she was fifteen, she was thoroughly grounded in history, geography and English and German literature. She played the piano with a skill approaching brilliance, but she disliked playing in front of people. When Queen Victoria asked her to play for guests at Windsor, Alix obliged, but her reddened face betrayed her torment. Unlike Nicholas, who learned by rote, Alix loved to discuss abstract ideas. One of her tutors, an Englishwoman named Margaret Jackson—"Madgie" to Princess Alix—was interested in politics. Miss Jackson passed her fascination along to Alix, who grew up believing that politics was a subject not necessarily restricted to men. Alix's grandmother, after all, was a woman and still managed to be the dominant monarch in Europe.

Alix first traveled to St. Petersburg at the age of twelve for the marriage of her sister Ella to Grand Duke Serge, younger brother of Tsar Alexander III. She watched with interest as her sister was met at the station in St. Petersburg by a gilded coach drawn by white horses. During the wedding ceremony in the chapel of the Winter Palace, Alix stood to one side, wearing a white muslin dress, with roses in her hair. Between listening to the long, incomprehensible chant of the litany and smelling the sweet incense which filled the air, she stole side glances at the sixteen-year-old Tsarevich Nicholas. Nicholas responded and one day presented her with a small brooch. Overwhelmed, she accepted, but then shyly pressed it back into his hand during the excitement of a children's party. Nicholas was offended and gave the brooch to his sister Xenia, who, not knowing its history, accepted it cheerfully.

Nicholas and Alix met again five years later in 1889, when she visited Ella in St. Petersburg. This time, she was seventeen, he was twenty-one—ages when girls and young men fall in love. They saw each other at receptions, suppers and balls. He came for her in the afternoon and took her skating on frozen ponds and tobogganing down hills of ice. Before Alix departed, Nicholas persuaded his parents to give her a special tea dance, followed by a supper of *blinis* and fresh caviar, in the Alexander Palace at Tsarskoe Selo.

The following summer Alix returned to Russia, but not to St. Petersburg. She went instead to Ilinskoe, the Grand Duke Serge's country estate near Moscow. There Serge and Ella lived a simple country life with friends invited for prolonged visits. Summer was at its golden height, there were lazy rambles in the fields and searches through the woods for berries and mushrooms. It was Alix's first sight of the wide expanse of Russian meadowland, of the white birch groves and the peasants in their loose blouses and baggy knickers. She was impressed by the deep, respectful bows they gave to her, a visitor. When she visited a country fair with Ella, she happily bought wooden dolls and gingerbread to take back home to Darmstadt.

Alix and Nicholas did not meet on this trip, and that autumn he left on his long cruise to the Far East. Alix was increasingly sure, however, that she loved the Russian Tsarevich. From the beginning, Nicholas had been polite and gentle. She liked his wistful charm and his appealing blue eyes. She saw that Nicholas still was treated as a boy by his parents, but she also saw his quiet persistence in pursuit of her against their wishes. In his devotion, he was a person in whom she could confide.

For Alix, the insuperable obstacle to any thought of marrying this shy, affectionate youth was his religion. Confirmed into the Lutheran Church at sixteen, Alix had accepted its Protestant theology with all the fervor of her passionate nature. She took everything in life seriously, and religion was the most serious matter of all. To reject casually a faith she had just sworn to accept seemed to her a direct affront to God. Yet still she loved Nicholas. Princess Alix plunged herself into a turmoil of doubt and self-examination.

The fact that Nicholas would one day be one of the mightiest rulers in Europe influenced Alix not at all. She had no interest in titles or the size of empires. In 1889, she rejected the proposal of Prince Albert Victor, the oldest son of the Prince of Wales and, after him, the heir to the British throne. This gay, popular young man, known to the family as Prince Eddy, died in 1892 at the age of twenty-eight, a sad event which put his younger brother, George, in line for the throne. It is one of the fascinating "if's" of history that if Alix had accepted Prince Eddy's proposal and Eddy had lived, he and Alix, not King George V and Queen Mary, would have ruled England. In this case, today Alix's son might sit on the British throne.

In any case, Alix had no interest in Eddy, and even Queen Victoria, who favored the match, admired the strong-minded way in which her granddaughter rejected Eddy's suit. "I fear all hope of Alicky's marrying Eddy is at an end," the Queen wrote to a friend. "She has written to tell him how it pains her to pain him, but that she cannot marry him, much as she likes him as a Cousin, that she knows she would not be happy with him and that he would not be happy with her and that he must not think of her. . . . It is a real sorrow to us . . . but . . . she says—that if she is forced she will do it—but that she would be unhappy and he too. This shows great strength of character as all her family and all of us wish it, and she refuses the greatest position there is."

Alix played the part of a conscientious princess. She visited schools and hospitals and sponsored charities. She went to costume balls, sometimes dressed as a Renaissance princess in a gown of pale green velvet and silver with emeralds in her red-gold hair. With a friend, she sat in a palace window, singing songs and playing a banjo. She escorted Queen Victoria on a tour of the mining districts of Wales and insisted on being taken down the shafts and walking through the grimy labyrinthine tunnels. On a visit to Italy, she toured the palaces and galleries of Florence and settled herself into a gondola for a ride down the canals of Venice.

In the spring of 1894, Alix's older brother Ernest, who had succeeded his father as Grand Duke of Hesse-Darmstadt, was to be married. The wedding in Coburg had attracted Europe's most distinguished royalty. Queen Victoria, then seventy-five, was coming from England with her son Edward, Prince of Wales. Kaiser William II, Victoria's thirty-five-year-old grandson, was arriving from Berlin. And Nicholas, having wrung from his father permission to propose to Alix, was coming to represent Russia.

On a warm April night, Nicholas boarded a train in St. Petersburg accompanied by three of his four uncles, Grand Dukes Vladimir, Serge and Paul. When he arrived in Coburg a day and a half later, dressed in full uniform, Alix was waiting at the station. That night, they went to dinner and an operetta with the family. The following morning, unable to wait any longer, Nicholas went straight to Alix and proposed. In his diary and in a letter to his mother he described what happened.

"What a day!" he wrote in his diary. "After coffee about ten, I went with Aunt Ella to Alix. She looked particularly pretty, but extremely sad. They left us alone and then began between us the talk which I had long ago strongly wanted and at the same time very much feared. We talked till twelve, but with no result; she still objects to changing her religion. Poor girl, she cried a lot. She was calmer when we parted."

In his letter to Gatchina, Nicholas wrote: "I tried to explain that there was no other way for her than to give her consent and that she simply could not withhold it. She cried the whole time and only whispered now and then, 'No, I cannot.' Still I went on repeating and insisting . . . though this went on for two hours, it came to nothing."

But Nicholas was not alone in his suit. As the relatives gathered from all over Europe, there were so many people present that family dinners had to be divided into two sittings, one at seven, the second at nine. A few hours after Nicholas's first talk with Alix, Queen Victoria arrived, escorted by a squadron of British Dragoons. The Queen favored the Russian marriage and had a talk with the reluctant girl, taking the somewhat original tack that Orthodoxy was not really so very different from Lutheranism. The following day, the Kaiser appeared. Not at all unhappy at the prospect of marrying a German princess to the future Tsar of Russia, he too pressed Nicholas's suit with Alix. Above all, it was Ella who calmed Alix's fears and encouraged her ardor. Ella had not been required to change her religion to Orthodoxy when she married Serge, since her husband was not in line for the Russian throne. But she had accepted Orthodoxy voluntarily. She insisted to Alix that a change of faith was not really so enormous or unusual an experience.

Long before it took place, Grand Duke Ernest's wedding had been thoroughly overshadowed by the matter of Nicholas and Alix. During the wedding ceremony, Nicholas watched Alix closely. "At that moment," he wrote, "how much I would have liked to have been able to look into the depths of Alix's soul."

The very next day Alix capitulated. Nicholas wrote exultantly in his diary: "A marvelous, unforgettable day. Today is the day of my engagement to my darling, adorable Alix. After ten she came to Aunt Miechen * and after a talk with her, we came to an understanding. O God, what a mountain has rolled from my shoulders. . . . The whole day I have been walking in a dream, without fully realizing what was happening to me. William sat in the next room and waited with the uncles and aunts till our talk was over. I went straight with Alix to the Queen [Victoria]. . . . The whole family was simply enraptured. After lunch we went to Aunt Mary's Church and had a thanksgiving service. I cannot even believe that I am engaged."

To his mother, Nicholas wrote: "We were left alone and with her

* Grand Duchess Marie Pavlovna, the wife of Nicholas's eldest uncle, Grand Duke Vladimir.

first words she consented. . . . I cried like a child and she did too, but her expression had changed: her face was lit by a quiet content. . . . The whole world is changed for me: nature, mankind, everything, and all seem to be good and lovable. . . . She is quite changed. She is gay and amusing, talkative and tender."

Later, everyone present remembered the moment that this fateful match was made. "I remember I was sitting in my room," recalled Princess Marie Louise of England. "I was quietly getting ready for a luncheon party when Alix stormed into my room, threw her arms around my neck and said, 'I'm going to marry Nicky!' "

Nicholas awoke the next morning to the clatter of horses' hoofs on cobblestones and the hoarse shout of military commands. Under his window, Queen Victoria's Dragoons were executing a drill in his honor. "At ten o'clock," he wrote in his diary, "my superb Alix came to me and we went together to have coffee with the Queen." While they remained in Coburg, every day began with "coffee with Granny." Victoria was delighted with the young couple. An incurable romantic and an indefatigable royal matchmaker, she loved to surround herself with soft-eyed young people in love. Alix was her special pet, and now that the match was made, she wanted to revel in it.

The weather was cold and gray that day, Nicholas wrote, "but everything in my heart was bright." Uncle Bertie suggested that since so large a part of the family was present, there ought to be a photograph. The thirty members of the family trooped down to the garden, and the result was a remarkable panorama of royalty. The old Queen, tiny and indomitable, sat in the middle of the front row, holding her cane. The Kaiser was there, the only man seated, dressed in a uniform and his fierce mustache. Nicholas, small and mild in a bowler hat, stood next to Alix, who appeared pretty but unsmiling.

From everywhere came congratulatory telegrams. "We answered all day," Nicholas complained, "but the pile grew rather than diminished. It seems that everybody in Russia has sent flowers to my fiancée."

Whatever their opposition to the match, Tsar Alexander III and his wife responded gallantly, once it was made. Alix wrote the Empress calling her "Aunty-Mama," and Marie wrote back to Nicholas: "Your dear Alix already is quite like a daughter to me. . . . Do tell Alix that her . . . [letter] has touched me so deeply—only—I don't want her to call me 'Aunty-Mama'; 'Mother dear' that's what I am to her now. . . . Ask Alix which stones she likes most, sapphires or emeralds? I would like to know for the future." As a start, Marie sent Alix an emerald bracelet and a superb Easter egg encrusted with jewels.

Spring came suddenly to Darmstadt, and the park was filled with flowers, the air perfumed and warm. Nicholas couldn't believe what had happened. "She has changed so much these last days in her relationship with me, that I am brimming with pleasure. This morning she wrote two sentences in Russian without error." When the family went for drives in carriages, Nicholas and Alix followed behind in a pony cart, taking turns at the reins. They walked, gathered flowers and rested beside the fishponds. They dined together at every meal. "It isn't easy to talk with strangers present, one has to give up talking about so many things," Nicholas complained. In the evenings they went to concerts in the local theatre. At Nicholas's request, the choir of the Preobrajensky Regiment of the Imperial Guard arrived by train from Russia to sing for his fiancée and the other assembled guests.

Nicholas began spending the end of each day with Alix in her room. "We were together a long time, she was remarkably tender with me. . . . It is so strange to be able to come and go like this without the least restraint. . . . What a sorrow to part from her even for one night."

Finally, after ten days of bliss, the time came for Nicholas to say goodbye. He spent the last evening in Alix's room while warm spring rain fell on the trees outside her window. "What sadness to be obliged to part from her for a long time," he wrote. "How good we were together—a paradise."

The following day, as he traveled eastward to Russia, Nicholas's heart was suffused with love and sadness, and he wore a new ring on his finger. "For the first time in my life, I put a ring on my finger. It makes me feel funny," he said. At Gatchina, he found his family gathered to meet him, Tsar Alexander III still wearing the knickers in which he had just returned from shooting ducks. There were telegrams waiting from Alix and Queen Victoria to be answered. Then Nicholas took a long walk in the park with his mother and told her everything that had happened.

The month of May seemed interminable to the Tsarevich. He spent his days pacing among the lilacs in the park, then rushing off to write another letter to Alix. At last, in June, he boarded the Imperial yacht *Polar Star*, which carried him down the Baltic and across the North Sea to Alix in England. At the end of the four-day trip, nearing the English coast, he wrote, "Tomorrow I shall see my beloved again. . . . I'll go mad with joy." He landed at Gravesend and hurried by train to London's Waterloo Station "into the arms of my betrothed who looked lovely and more beautiful than ever."

Together, the pair went to a cottage at Walton-on-Thames belonging to Alix's eldest sister, Princess Victoria of Battenberg. For three memorable days, they relaxed on the banks of the gently flowing river. They walked on the bright green lawns and gathered fruit and flowers from nearby fields. Under an old chestnut tree in the cottage garden, they sat in the grass and Alix embroidered while Nicholas read to her. "We were out all day long in beautiful weather, boating up and down the river, picnicking on the shore. A veritable idyll," Nicholas wrote his mother. Years later, both Nicholas and Alix remembered every detail of those three shining days in the English countryside, and the mere mention of the name Walton was enough to bring tears of happiness to Alix's eyes.

When the three days were over, the young couple emerged from their private cocoon of happiness. "Granny" waited to greet them at Windsor Castle. Tsar Alexander III had sent his personal confessor, Father Yanishev, and the priest was anxious to begin Alix's religious instruction. At Windsor, Nicholas presented his formal engagement gifts: a pink pearl ring, a necklace of large pink pearls, a chain bracelet bearing a massive emerald, and a sapphire-and-diamond brooch. Grandest of all was a *sautoir* of pearls, a gift to his new daughter-in-law from the Tsar. Created by Fabergé, the famed Russian court jeweler, it was worth 250,000 gold roubles and was the largest single transaction Fabergé ever had with the Imperial family. Staring at this dazzling display of gems, Queen Victoria smilingly shook her head and said, "Now, Alix, do not get too proud."

The heat was stifling in England that summer. Nicholas began riding out from Windsor Castle in the morning while it still was cool. He liked to trot down Queen Anne's Way, a popular horse path bordered by magnificent trees, then come back home through open fields, "galloping like a fool." He was always back by ten to join Alix and the Queen for coffee. Lunch was at two, and afterward everybody rested and tried to ward off the heat. Before tea, Nicholas and Alix drove under the great oaks of Windsor Park and admired the blooming rhododendron. Nicholas admitted to his mother, "I can't complain. Granny has been very friendly and even allowed us to go for drives without a chaperone." In the evening, when the air had cooled, they dined with guests on a balcony or terrace and listened to music being played in the castle courtyard. Once when a violinist came up from London, Alix accompanied him on the piano.

Despite her lessons with Father Yanishev, Alix frequently popped into Nicholas's rooms. He apologized to his mother for not writing home more often. "Every moment," he pleaded, "I simply had to get up and embrace her." During one of these visits, apparently, Alix discovered that Nicholas was keeping a diary. She began to write in it herself. These entries, most of them in English, began with short notes—"Many loving kisses," "God bless you, my angel," "forever, forever"—and progressed to lines of verse and prayers:

"I dreamed that I was loved, I woke and found it true and thanked God on my knees for it. True love is the gift which God has given, daily, stronger, deeper, fuller, purer."

As the object of such overwhelming devotion, Nicholas felt that he had to speak about certain episodes in his past. He told her at this point about Kschessinska. Although she was only twenty-two, Alix rose to the occasion like a true granddaughter of Queen Victoria. She forgave him handsomely, even gushingly, but she also delivered a brief little lecture which cast Nicholas in the role of the male redeemed by the purity of love:

"What is past is past and will never return. We all are tempted in this world and when we are young we cannot always fight and hold our own against the temptation, but as long as we repent, God will forgive us. . . . Forgive my writing so much, but I want you to be quite sure of my love for you and that I love you even more since you told me that little story, your confidence in me touched me oh so deeply. . . . [May] I always show myself worthy of it. . . . God bless you, beloved Nicky. . . ."

Knowing Nicholas's love of military pageantry, the Queen arranged a succession of displays. At Windsor he watched a thousand cadets from the naval academy at Greenwich perform gymnastics to music. He reviewed six companies of the Coldstream Guards, and the officers invited him to dinner. Normally, Nicholas would have jumped at this invitation, "But . . . Granny loves me so and doesn't like me missing dinner, nor does Alix," he wrote, explaining to his mother why he refused. At Aldershot, the huge British military camp, they watched a torchlight retreat ceremony and listened to a massed choir of English, Scottish, Welsh and Irish voices. Next day, Nicholas, dressed in his uniform of the Imperial Hussars, took the salute of columns of British infantry, cavalry and horse artillery. He liked especially the pleated kilts and the skirling pipes of the Highland regiments.

While Nicholas was in England, a baby was born into the British royal family. "Yesterday, at 10 o'clock a son was born to Georgie and May to the general joy," he wrote. The baby, named Prince Edward, would become King Edward VIII, and later the Duke of Windsor. Nicholas and Alix were chosen as godparents of the little Prince. "Instead of plunging the infant into the water," noted the Tsarevich, "the archbishop sprinkled water on his head. . . . What a nice, healthy child." Afterward the baby's father dropped in on the engaged couple at Windsor. Even in his diary Nicholas showed a quaint touch of prudery as he described the visit: "Georgie came for lunch. Alix and he stayed in my room with me. I add these words 'with me' because otherwise it would sound a bit odd."

Before he left England, the Tsarevich and his fiancée went with the Queen to Osborne, the seaside royal residence on the Isle of Wight. From the palace lawns they could watch flotillas of sailboats scudding before the wind. Like a small boy, Nicholas took off his shoes and walked through the waves rolling up on the sand.

As the end of July approached, the six-week idyll came to an end. Alix had filled the diary with messages: "Love is caught, I have bound his wings. No longer will he roam or fly away. Within our two hearts forever, love sings." As the *Polar Star* slipped past Dover, north-bound for the Baltic, Nicholas read her prayer, "Sleep gently, and let the gentle waves rock you to sleep. Your Guardian Angel is keeping watch over you. A tender kiss."

Next day, Nicholas stood at the rail watching a fiery sunset off the coast of Jutland and gazing across the water as twenty ships of the Imperial German Navy dipped their flags in salute. Entering the Baltic through the Skaggerak, the *Polar Star* steamed slowly down the Danish coastline within sight of the ancient castle of Elsinore. But Nicholas's thoughts were far away.

"I am yours," Alix had written, "you are mine, of that be sure.

You are locked in my heart, the little key is lost and now you must stay there forever."

There was another entry, too—a strangely prophetic line from Marie Corelli: "For the past is past and will never return, the future we know not, and only the present can be called our own."

CHAPTER FOUR

Marriage

AT GATCHINA, Nicholas found his family in a state of alarm over his father's health. Troubled by headaches, insomnia and weakness in the legs, the Tsar had consulted doctors, who recommended that he rest, preferably in the warm climate of the Crimea. But Alexander III was not a man to disrupt his schedule simply because he was not feeling well. The family entrained in September, not for the Crimea, but for the Imperial hunting lodge at Spala in Poland.

There, the Tsar continued to feel ill, and a specialist, Professor Leyden, was summoned from Vienna. Leyden carefully looked over the bearlike frame and diagnosed nephritis. He insisted that his patient be moved to the Crimea immediately and forced to rest. This time, Alexander III agreed. Nicholas, meanwhile, found himself caught in a struggle between "my duty to remain here with my dear parents and follow them to the Crimea and the keen desire to hurry to Wolfsgarten to be near my dear Alix." Eventually, he suppressed his ardor and went with the family to the summer palace at Livadia in the Crimea.

There, amid warm breezes scented with grapes, the Tsar began to improve. He ate well, took sunbaths in the garden and even went down to walk on the beach. But this improvement was only temporary. After a few days, he again began to have trouble sleeping, his legs gave way and he took to his bed. His diet was rigidly restricted and, to his distress, he was forbidden ice cream. Sitting alone by his bedside, his sixteen-year-old daughter, Olga, suddenly heard her father whisper, "Baby, dear, I know there is some ice cream in the next room. Bring it here—but make sure nobody sees you." She smuggled him a plate and he enjoyed it immensely. A St. Petersburg priest, Father John of Kronstadt, whose followers believed him capable of miracles, was summoned. While the doctors worked, Father John prayed, but the Tsar grew steadily worse.

Sensing what was coming, Nicholas asked Alix to come to Livadia. She came immediately, traveling by train as an ordinary passenger. Normally the fiancée of a tsarevich would have been honored with a special train, but the Minister of the Imperial Court, whose job it was to make such arrangements, was so involved with the illness of the Tsar that he simply forgot. Approaching the Crimea, Alix wired ahead that she wanted the ceremony of her conversion to Orthodoxy to take place as soon as possible. Nicholas could not suppress his happiness. "My God, what a joy to meet her in my country and to have her near," he wrote. "Half my fears and sadness have disappeared."

He met her train in Simferopol and brought her to Livadia in an open carriage. During the four-hour drive, they were stopped repeatedly by Tartar villagers with welcoming bread and salt and armloads of grapes and flowers. When their carriage rolled up in front of the palace guard of honor, it was brimming with fruit and flowers. In his bedroom, seated in an armchair, Alexander III awaited the young couple. He was dressed in full-dress uniform. He had insisted, despite all objection, that this was the only way for the Tsar of Russia to greet a future Russian empress. Kneeling before the pale, enfeebled giant, Alix received his blessing, and she and Nicholas were formally betrothed.

For the ten days that followed, the life of the household revolved about the sickbed of the dying Tsar. Nicholas and Alix went quietly about the house, caught up in an unsettling swirl of happiness and despair. They walked through the vineyards and by the sea, although they never dared to go too far from the house. She sat at his side while he began reading over the reports submitted by his father's ministers. It was a difficult role. Plunged into the bosom of a grief-stricken family, she felt herself an outsider. Her one contact and confidant was Nicholas. Marie was too busy caring for her husband to worry about the niceties of welcoming her future daughter-in-law. It was natural, of course, in a household where the patient was husband, father and ruler of a great empire, that attention should be concentrated on him and his wife. Doctors, government ministers and court officials treated Marie not only with the normal deference due an empress, but with the extra consideration accorded a human being facing a great personal ordeal. Doctors hurried from the bedside to the Empress, scarcely noticing the shy young man and woman standing outside the door or waiting at the foot of the stairs. In time Alix became offended by this treatment. Her lover, whom she honored, was Heir to the Throne. If this huge Tsar whom she scarcely knew should die, her fiancée would be the Tsar. Yet he was treated like a nobody.

She put many of these feelings into a famous passage in his diary: "Sweet child, pray to God. He will comfort you. Don't feel too low. Your Sunny is praying for you and the beloved patient. . . . Be firm and make the doctors come to you every day and tell you how they find him . . . so that you are always the first to know. Don't let others be put first and you left out. You are Father's dear son and must be told all and asked about everything. Show your own mind and don't let others forget who you are. Forgive me, lovy."

For ten days after Alix's appearance at Livadia, the agony in the sickroom continued. Then, on the afternoon of November 1, 1894, Alexander III suddenly died. Marie fainted into Alix's arms. "God, God, what a day," wrote Nicholas. "The Lord has called to him our adored, our dear, our tenderly loved Papa. My head turns, it isn't possible to believe it. All day we rested upstairs near him. His respiration became difficult, suddenly it became necessary to give him oxygen. About 2:30 he received extreme unction; soon light trembling began and the end followed quickly. Father John remained with him an hour at the bedside, holding his head. It was the death of a saint, Lord assist us in these difficult days. Poor dear Mama."

No one better understood the significance of the death of the Tsar than the twenty-six-year-old youth who had inherited his throne. "I saw tears in his blue eyes," recalled Grand Duke Alexander, Nicholas's brother-in-law. "He took me by the arm and led me downstairs to his room. We embraced and cried together. He could not collect his thoughts. He knew that he was Emperor now, and the weight of this terrifying fact crushed him.

" 'Sandro, what am I going to do?' he exclaimed, pathetically. 'What is going to happen to me, to you, to Xenia, to Alix, to mother, to all of Russia? I am not prepared to be a Tsar. I never wanted to become one. I know nothing of the business of ruling. I have no idea of even how to talk to the ministers.' "

In the late afternoon, while the guns of the warships in Yalta harbor still thundered a last salute to the dead monarch, an altar was erected on the lawn in front of the palace. Courtiers, officials, servants and family formed a semicircle, and a priest in golden vestments solemnly administered the oath of allegiance to His Imperial Majesty, Tsar Nicholas II.

When morning came the following day, the palace was draped in black and a storm raged on the Black Sea. As the embalmers arrived to deal with the body, the priests effected the religious conversion of the Protestant German Princess who suddenly stood so close to the Russian throne. Before noon that very day, the new Tsar, his betrothed and his widowed mother went to the palace chapel for a special service.

"Even in our great grief, God gives us a sweet and luminous joy," wrote Nicholas. "At ten o'clock in the presence only of the family, my dear Alix has been consecrated to Orthodoxy." After the service, Alix, Marie and Nicholas took Holy Communion together and, said Nicholas, "Alix read beautifully and in a clear voice, the responses and the prayers." When they returned to the palace, the new Tsar Nicholas issued his first Imperial Decree. It proclaimed the new faith, new title and new name of the former Princess Alix of Hesse. Queen Victoria's Lutheran granddaughter had become "the truly believing Grand Duchess Alexandra Fedorovna."

The death of the powerful Tsar Alexander III at the age of forty-nine was a shock to all Russia. No arrangements had been made for a funeral, and the body of the dead Tsar was forced to wait for a week at Livadia while telegrams flew between the Crimea and St. Petersburg. The wedding, originally planned for the following spring, was moved forward at Nicholas's insistence. Staggering under the weight of his new office, he had no intention of allowing the one person who gave him confidence to leave his side.

"Mama, many others, and I think it would be better to celebrate the marriage here in peace, while Papa still is under this roof," he noted in his diary, "but all the uncles are against it, saying that I should marry in Petersburg after the funeral."

Nicholas's uncles, the four brothers of the dead Tsar, were independent, strong-minded men who carried great weight in the family. Their view, that the wedding of their young nephew was too important a national event to be performed privately at Livadia, prevailed. Meanwhile, the Orthodox ceremonies of death went on continuously. The family kissed the lips of the dead Tsar as he lay in his coffin, and went to the chapel twice a day to pray for his soul. "My dear Papa was transferred from the chapel to the large church," Nicholas wrote. "The coffin was carried by the Cossacks. . . . When we got back to the empty house, we absolutely broke down. God has afflicted us with heavy trials."

At the end of a week, the coffin, draped in purple and accompanied by the mourning family, left Livadia for Sevastopol, where a funeral train awaited. As the train rolled north from the Crimea across the Ukraine, clusters of peasants gathered along the track to watch the dead Tsar pass. In the cities of Kharkov, Kursk, Orel and Tula, the train halted and services were held in the presence of local nobility and officials. In Moscow, the coffin was transferred to a hearse and carried to the Kremlin for an overnight rest. Low clouds whipped across a gray November sky, and splinters of sleet bit into the faces of the Muscovites who lined the streets to watch the cortege. Ten times before reaching the Kremlin the procession stopped and separate litanies were sung from the steps of ten different churches.

In St. Petersburg, red-and-gold court carriages heavily draped in black waited at the station to pick up the family and move off through streets filled with the slush of an early thaw. For four excruciating hours the cortege advanced slowly across St. Petersburg to the Cathedral of the Fortress of Peter and Paul, where the Romanov tsars were buried. Throughout the city, the only sounds were the beat of muffled drums, the clatter of hoofs, the rumble of iron carriage wheels and the slow tolling of church bells. In the procession, the new Grand Duchess Alexandra Fedorovna rode alone, thickly veiled, behind the rest of the family. As she passed, the silent crowd strained to see their young Empress-to-be. Shaking their heads, old women crossed themselves and murmured darkly, "She has come to us behind a coffin."

The Kings of Greece, Denmark and Serbia arrived to join the royal mourners. Edward, Prince of Wales, and his son George, Duke of York, represented Queen Victoria; Prince Henry of Prussia represented his brother, the Kaiser. In all, sixty-one royal personages, each with an entourage, gathered that week in the marble palaces of St. Petersburg. In addition, the ministers of the Imperial government, the commanders of the Russian army and navy, the provincial governors and 460 delegates from across Russia came to pay their respects. "I have received so many delegations, I had to walk in the garden. My head is spinning," wrote Nicholas. At a banquet arranged in honor of the foreign guests, "I almost broke into sobs sitting down at the table because it was so difficult to see all this ceremony when my soul was so heavy."

For seventeen days, the body of Alexander III lay exposed in its coffin. Thousands of people shuffled past the open bier while a priest stood by chanting prayers and a hidden choir sang mournful hymns. Twice a day all the royal mourners rode through the dank and misty streets for services. During this period, the future King George V wrote to his wife, Mary:

"Every day, after lunch, we had another service at the church. After the service, we all went up to [the] coffin which was open and kissed the Holy Picture which he holds in his hand. It gave me a shock when I saw his dear face so close to mine when I stooped down. He looks so beautiful and peaceful, but of course he has changed very much. It is a fortnight today."

Amid the priests and their litanies, the rooms and streets decorated in black, the sad faces, the tears and the wringing hands, Alexandra suppressed her own small, pathetic happiness. "One's feelings one can imagine," she wrote to her sister. "One day in deepest mourning lamenting a beloved one, the next in smartest clothes being married. There cannot be a greater contrast, but it drew us more together, if possible." "Such was my entry into Russia," she added later. "Our marriage seemed to me a mere continuation of the masses for the dead with this difference, that now I wore a white dress instead of a black."

The wedding took place on November 26, one week after the funeral. The day selected was the birthday of Empress Marie, now the Dowager Empress, and for such an occasion protocol permitted a brief relaxation of mourning. Dressed in white, Alexandra and Marie drove together down the Nevsky Prospect to the Winter Palace. Before a famous gold mirror used by every Russian grand duchess on her wedding day, the bride was formally dressed by the ladies of the Imperial family. She wore a heavy, old-fashioned Russian court dress of silver brocade and a robe and train of cloth of gold lined with ermine. From a red velvet cushion, Marie herself lifted the sparkling diamond nuptial crown and settled it carefully onto Alexandra's head. Together the two women walked through the palace galleries to the chapel where Nicholas waited in the boots and uniform of a Hussar. Each holding a lighted candle, Nicholas and Alexandra faced the Metropolitan. A few minutes before one in the afternoon, they became man and wife.

Alexandra was radiant. "She looked too wonderfully lovely," said the Princess of Wales. George, the Duke of York, wrote to Mary in England, "I think Nicky is a very lucky man to have got such a lovely and charming wife and I must say I never saw two people more in love with each other or happier than they are. I told them both that I could not wish them more than that they should be as happy as you and I are together. Was that right?"

Because of the mourning, there was no reception after the wedding, and no honeymoon. The young couple returned immediately to the Anitchkov Palace. "When they drove from the Winter Palace after the wedding, they got a tremendous . . . ovation from the large crowds in the streets," George wrote to Queen Victoria. "The cheering was most hearty and reminded me of England. . . . Nicky has been kindness itself to me, he is the same dear boy he has always been and talks to me quite openly on every subject. . . . He does everything so quietly and naturally; everyone is struck by it and he is very popular already." At the Anitchkov Palace, Marie was waiting to welcome them with bread and salt. They stayed in that night, answered congratulatory telegrams, dined at eight and, according to Nicholas, "went to bed early because Alix had a headache."

The marriage that began that night remained unflawed for the rest of their lives. It was a Victorian marriage, outwardly serene and proper, but based on intensely passionate physical love. On her wedding night, before going to bed, Alexandra wrote in her husband's diary: "At last united, bound for life, and when this life is ended, we meet again in the other world and remain together for eternity. Yours, yours." The next morning, with fresh, new emotions surging through her, she wrote, "Never did I believe there could be such utter happiness in this world, such a feeling of unity between two mortal beings. I love you, those three words have my life in them."

They lived that first winter in six rooms of the Anitchkov Palace, where the Dowager Empress Marie remained mistress of the house. In his haste to be married, Nicholas had allowed no time for preparation of a place for himself and Alexandra to live, and they moved temporarily into the rooms which Nicholas and his brother George had shared as boys. Although he ruled a continent, the young Tsar conducted official business from a small sitting room while the new twenty-two-year-old Empress sat next door in the bedroom working on her Russian language. Between appointments, Nicholas joined her to chat and puff on a cigarette. At mealtime, because the apartment lacked a dining room, Nicholas and Alexandra went to dine with "Mother dear."

The young couple minded their cramped quarters less than the long hours apart. "Petitions and audiences without end," Nicholas grumbled, "saw Alix for an hour only," and "I am indescribably happy with Alix. It is sad that my work takes so many hours which I would prefer to spend exclusively with her." At night, Nicholas read to her in French, as she wanted to improve her use of the court language. They began by reading tales by Alphonse Daudet and a book about Napoleon's life on St. Helena.

Occasionally, on snowy nights, Nicholas bundled Alexandra into fur robes beside him in a sleigh. Then he set the horses to flying under the walls and domes of the city and across the frozen white landscape. Back in their apartment, they changed into dressing gowns and had a late supper before a roaring fire.

On the last day of 1894, Nicholas looked back at the enormous events of that fateful year. In his diary he wrote: "It is hard to think of the terrible changes of this year. But putting our hope in God, I look forward to the coming year without fear, because the worst thing that could have happened to me, the thing I have been fearing all my life [the death of his father and his own accession to the throne], has already passed. At the same time that He has sent me irreparable grief, God has sent me a happiness of which I never dared to dream, in giving me Alix."

Certain problems are universal. Nicholas, genuinely grieved for his abruptly widowed mother, tried to comfort her by his presence, dutifully dining with her and often staying to sit with her after dinner. During the early months of his reign, Nicholas turned to his mother for political advice. She gave it freely, never suspecting that Alexandra might be resenting her role. To Marie, Alexandra was still an awkward young German girl, only recently arrived in Russia, with no knowledge or background in affairs of state. As the period of mourning ended, Marie returned to public life, to the clothes, the jewelry, the brilliant lights she loved so much. She was constantly seen driving down the Nevsky Prospect in an open carriage or sleigh pulled by a pair of shiny blacks, with a huge, black-bearded Cossack on the runningboard behind her. In the protocol of the Russian court, a dowager empress took precedence over an empress. At public ceremonies, Marie, dressed all in white and blazing with diamonds, walked on the arm of her son while Alexandra followed behind on the arm of one of the grand dukes. So natural did the leading role seem to Marie that when she discovered that her daughter-in-law was bitter, Marie was surprised and hurt.

Alexandra, for her part, felt and behaved much like any young wife. She was shocked by the sudden blow which had struck Marie, and her first reaction toward her mother-in-law was sympathetic. Before long, however, the strains of living under the same roof and competing for the same man began to tell. At meals, Alexandra was doubly insulted. Not only was she completely ignored, but the older woman treated her beloved Nicky like a schoolboy. Despite elaborate politeness between "dear Alix" and "Mother dear," a veiled hostility began to appear.

One incident especially irritated Alexandra. Certain of the crown jewels traditionally passed from one Russian empress to the next, and, indeed, protocol required that Alexandra wear them on formal occasions. But Marie had a passion for jewelry and when Nicholas asked his mother to give up the gems, she bristled and refused. Humiliated, Alexandra then declared that she no longer cared about the jewelry and would not wear it in any case. Before a public scandal occurred, Marie submitted.

Like many a young bride, Alexandra sometimes had difficulty accepting the swift transition in her life. "I cannot yet realize that I am married," she wrote. "It seems like being on a visit." She alternated between despair and bliss. "I feel myself completely alone," she wrote to a friend in Germany. "I weep and I worry all day long because I feel that my husband is so young and so inexperienced. . . . I am alone most of the time. My husband is occupied all day and he spends his evenings with his mother." But at Christmas she wrote to one of her sisters, "How contented and happy I am with my beloved Nicky." In May she wrote in his diary, "Half a year now that we are married. How intensely happy you have made . . . [me] you cannot think."

The domestic tensions eased in the spring of 1895 when Nicholas and Alexandra moved to Peterhof for the summer and Marie left Russia on a long visit to her family home in Copenhagen. More important, Alexandra discovered that she was pregnant. Grand Duchess Elizabeth came to stay with her sister, and together the two young women painted, did needlework and went for carriage rides in the park. Both Nicholas and Alexandra marveled at the baby's growth. "It has become very big and kicks about and fights a great deal inside," the Tsar wrote to his mother. With the baby coming, Alexandra began planning and decorating her first real home in the Alexander Palace at Tsarskoe Selo, fifteen miles south of St. Petersburg. "Sad to leave Peterhof and . . . our little house on the shore where we spent our first summer so quietly together," Nicholas wrote to Marie. "But when we entered Alix's apartments [at Tsarskoe Selo] our mood changed instantly . . . to utter delight. . . . Sometimes, we simply sit in silence wherever we happen to be and admire the walls, the fireplaces, the furniture. . . . Twice we went up to the future nursery; here also the rooms are remarkably airy, light and cozy."

Both parents hoped that the new baby would be a son; a male heir would become the first tsarevich born directly to a reigning tsar since the eighteenth century. As the date approached, Marie returned, bubbling with excitement. "It is understood, isn't it, that you will let me know as soon as the first symptoms appear?" she wrote to Nicholas. "I shall fly to you, my dear children, and shall not be a nuisance except perhaps by acting as a policeman to keep everybody else away."

In mid-November 1895, when Alexandra began her labor, artillerymen in Kronstadt and St. Petersburg were posted beside their guns. A salute of 300 rounds would announce the birth of a male heir, 101 would mean that the child was a girl. Alexandra suffered intensely in labor, and birth was protracted. At last, however, the cannon began to fire, 99 . . . 100 . . . 101 . . . But the 102nd gun never fired. The first child born to Tsar Nicholas II and the Empress Alexandra Fedorovna was the Grand Duchess Olga Nicolaievna. At birth, she weighed nine pounds.

The joy of having their first baby instantly dispelled all worries about whether the child was a boy or a girl. When the father is twenty-seven and the mother only twenty-three, there seems infinite time to have more children. Alexandra nursed and bathed the baby herself and sang the infant to sleep with lullabies. While Olga slept, her mother sat by the crib, knitting a row of jackets, bonnets and socks. "You can imagine our intense happiness, now that we have such a precious little one to care for and look after," the Empress wrote to one of her sisters.

CHAPTER FIVE

The Coronation

IN THE spring, when the ice on the Neva, used all winter as a thoroughfare for sleighs and people, began to crack, the thoughts of all Russians turned to the coronation. The year was 1896, the twelve-month period of mourning was over and the new Tsar was to be crowned in Moscow in May.

Realizing that for the forty-nine-year-old Dowager Empress Marie the coronation would be partially a reminder of the sudden death of Alexander III, Nicholas attempted to console her. "I believe we should regard all these difficult ceremonies in Moscow as a great ordeal sent by God," he wrote his mother, "for at every step we shall have to repeat all we went through in the happy days thirteen years ago! One thought alone consoles me: That in the course of our life we shall not have to go through the rite again, that subsequent events will occur peacefully and smoothly."

The coronation of a Russian tsar was rigidly governed by history and tradition. The ceremony was held in Moscow; nothing so solemn, so meaningful to the nation, could be left to the artificial Western capital thrown up by Peter the Great. By tradition, the uncrowned tsar did not enter the city until the day before his coronation. Upon arriving in Moscow, Nicholas and Alexandra went into retreat, fasting and praying, in the Petrovsky Palace outside the city.

While the Tsar waited outside the city, the Muscovites painted and whitewashed buildings, hung strings of evergreen across the doorways and draped from the windows the white-blue-and-red Russian flag. Every hour thousands of people poured into the city. Bands of Cossacks galloped past creaking carts filled with peasant women whose heads were covered with brilliant kerchiefs of red, yellow, blue and orange. Trains disgorged tall Siberians in heavy coats with fur collars, Caucasians in long red coats, Turks in red fezzes and cavalry generals in bright red tunics with golden, fur-trimmed cloaks. The mood of the city was buoyant: besides excitement, pageantry and feasting, the coronation meant a three-day holiday, the granting of pardons to prisoners, the lifting of fines and taxes.

On the afternoon of May 25, the day of Nicholas's formal entry into Moscow, the sun sparkled on the city's domes and windows. Two ribbons of troops bordered the four-mile line of march, holding back the crowds. Every balcony and window above the street was jammed with people. On one of the viewing platforms built along the street sat Mathilde Kschessinska. "It was agonizing to watch the Tsar pass . . . the Tsar who was still 'Niki' to me, one I adored and who could not, could never, belong to me."

At two o'clock, the first squadrons of Imperial Guard cavalry rode into the streets, forming the van of the procession. Those watching from the windows could see the flash of the afternoon sun on their golden helmets and cuirasses. The Cossacks of the Guard came next, wearing long coats of red and purple, their curved sabers banging against their soft black boots. Behind the Cossacks rode Moscow's nobility in gold braid and crimson sashes with jeweled medals sparkling on their chests. Then, on foot, came the Court Orchestra, the Imperial Hunt and the court footmen in red knee breeches and white silk stockings.

The appearance of the officials of the court in gold-embroidered uniforms signaled the coming of the Tsar. Nicholas rode alone, on a white horse. Unlike the lavishly costumed ministers, generals and aides who wore rows of medals from shoulder to shoulder, he was dressed in a simple army tunic buttoned under his chin. His face was drawn and pale with excitement and he reined his horse with his left hand only. His right hand was raised to his visor in a fixed salute.

Behind Nicholas rode more clusters of horsemen, the Russian grand dukes and the foreign princes. Then came the sound of carriage wheels, mingled with the clatter of hoofs. First came the gilded carriage of Catherine the Great, drawn by eight white horses. On top was a replica of the Imperial Crown. Inside, beaming and bowing, sat the Dowager Empress Marie. Behind, in a second carriage, also made of gold and drawn by eight white horses, sat the uncrowned Empress, Alexandra Fedorovna. Dressed in a pure white gown sewn with jewels, she wore a diamond necklace around her neck which blazed in the brilliant sunlight. Leaning from left to right, bowing and smiling, the two Empresses followed the Tsar through the Nikolsky Gate into the Kremlin.

The following day, on coronation morning, the sky was a cloudless blue. In the city's streets, heralds wearing medieval dress proclaimed that on that day, May 26, 1896, a tsar would be crowned. Inside the Kremlin, servants laid a crimson velvet carpet down the steps of the famous Red Staircase which led to the Ouspensky Cathedral, where the ceremony would take place. Opposite the staircase, a wooden grandstand had been built to hold guests who could not squeeze inside the cathedral. From this vantage, hundreds of people watched as soldiers of the Imperial Guard in red-white-and-gold uniforms took up positions on the staircase, lining the crimson carpet.

In their apartment, Nicholas and Alexandra had been up since dawn. While Alexandra's hair was being done by her hairdresser, Nicholas sat nearby quietly talking and calming his wife. With her attendants, she practiced fastening and unfastening the clasps of her heavy coronation robe. Nicholas settled the crown on her head as he would do in the cathedral and the hairdresser stepped up with a diamond-studded hairpin to hold the crown in place. The pin went too far and the Empress cried with pain. The embarrassed hairdresser beat a retreat.

The formal procession down the Red Stairway was led by priests, trailing long beards and golden robes. Marie came next in a gown of embroidered white velvet, her long train carried by a dozen men. At last, Nicholas and Alexandra appeared at the top of the stairway. He wore the blue-green uniform of the Preobrajensky Guard with a red sash across his breast. At his side, Alexandra was in silver-white Russian court dress with a red ribbon running over her shoulder. Around her neck she wore a single strand of pink pearls. They walked slowly, followed by attendants who carried her train. On either side walked other attendants, carrying over their sovereigns' heads a canopy of cloth of gold with tall ostrich plumes waving from its top. At the bottom of the steps, the couple bowed to the crowd and stopped before the priests, who touched them on the forehead with holy water. Before an icon held by one of the priests, they said a prayer; then the churchmen in turn kissed the Imperial hands, and the pair walked into the cathedral.

Beneath the domes of its five golden cupolas, the interior of the

Ouspensky Cathedral glowed with light. Every inch of wall and ceiling was covered with luminous frescoes; before the altar stood the great iconostasis, a golden screen which was a mass of jewels. Light, filtering down from the cupolas and flickering from hundreds of candles, reflected off the surfaces of the jewels and the golden icons to bathe everyone present in iridescence. A choir, dressed in silver and light blue, filled the cathedral with the anthems of the Orthodox Church. Before the altar stood ranks of high clergy: metropolitans, archbishops, bishops and abbots. From their miters glittered more diamonds, sapphires, rubies and pearls, adding to the unearthly light.

At the front of the cathedral, two coronation chairs awaited the Tsar and his wife. Nicholas sat on the seventeenth-century Diamond Throne of Tsar Alexis, encrusted almost solidly with gems and pearls. Its name was derived from the 870 diamonds embedded in its surface; the armrest alone was set with 85 diamonds, 144 rubies and 129 pearls. Alexandra sat next to her husband on the famous Ivory Throne brought to Russia from Byzantium in 1472 by Ivan the Great's Byzantine bride, Sophia Paleologus.

The coronation ceremony lasted five hours. After a lengthy Mass came the formal robing of the Tsar and Tsaritsa. Then Alexandra knelt while the Metropolitan prayed for the Tsar. While everyone else remained standing, Nicholas alone dropped on his knees to pray for Russia and her people. After being anointed with Holy Oil, Nicholas swore his oath to rule the empire and preserve autocracy as Emperor and Autocrat of all the Russias.* Then, for the first time and only time in his life, the Tsar entered the sanctuary to receive the sacrament as a priest of the church. As Nicholas walked up the altar steps, the heavy chain of the Order of St. Andrew slipped from his shoulders and fell to the floor. It happened so quickly that no one noticed except those standing close to the Tsar. Later, lest it be taken as an omen, all these were sworn to secrecy.

* Nicholas's complete title was: Emperor and Autocrat of all the Russias, Tsar of Moscow, Kiev, Vladimir, Novgorod, Kazan, Astrakhan, of Poland, of Siberia, of Tauric Chersonese, of Georgia, Lord of Pskov, Grand Duke of Smolensk, of Lithuania, Volhynia, Podolia and Finland, Prince of Estonia, Livonia, Courland and Semigalia, Samogotia, Bialostock, Karelia, Tver, Yougouria, Perm, Viatka, Bulgaria, and other countries; Lord and Grand Duke of Lower Novgorod, of Tchernigov, Riazan, Polotsk, Rostov, Yaroslav, Belozero, Oudoria, Obdoria, Condia, Vitebsk, Mstislav and all the region of the North, Lord and Sovereign of the countries of Iveria, Cartalinia, Kabardinia and the provinces of Armenia, Sovereign of the Circassian Princes and the Mountain Princes, Lord of Turkestan, Heir of Norway, Duke of Schleswig Holstein, of Storman, of the Ditmars, and of Oldenbourg, etc.

By tradition, a tsar crowned himself, taking the crown from the hands of the Metropolitan and placing it on his own head. In planning his coronation, Nicholas had wished to use for this purpose the eight hundred-year-old Cap of Monomakh, a simple crown of gold filigree said to have been used by Vladimir Monomakh, twelfth-century ruler of Kievan Russia. Besides emphasizing his attachment to Russia's historic past, Monomakh's Cap had the distinct advantage of being light: it weighed only two pounds. But the iron etiquette of the ceremony made this impossible, and Nicholas lifted onto his head the huge nine-pound Imperial Crown of Russia made in 1762 for Catherine the Great. Shaped like a bishop's miter, it was crested with a cross of diamonds surmounting an enormous uncut ruby. Below, set in an arch supporting the cross and in the band surrounding the head, were forty-four diamonds, each an inch across, surrounded by solid masses of smaller diamonds. Thirty-eight perfect rosy pearls circled over the crown on either side of the central arch. Nicholas let the gem-encrusted crown rest on his head for a moment. Then, reaching up, he took it off and carefully placed it on Alexandra's head. Finally, he replaced it on his own head and Alexandra was given a smaller crown. Nicholas kissed her and, taking her hand, led her back to the two thrones. The ceremony ended with Empress Marie and every member of the Imperial family approaching to do homage to the crowned Tsar of all the Russias.

Despite the length of the ceremony, Alexandra later wrote to one of her sisters that she had never felt tired, so strong were her own emotions. To her, the ceremony seemed a kind of mystic marriage between herself and Russia. At the coronation, she left behind the girl who grew up in Darmstadt and England. In her heart she now truly thought of herself, not only as Empress, but as "*Matushka*," the Mother of the Russian people.

At the end of the service, the newly crowned monarchs walked from the church wearing brocaded mantles embroidered with the double-headed Imperial eagle. They climbed the Red Stairway, turned and bowed three times to the crowd. From thousands of throats roared a mighty cheer. From the muzzles of massed cannons, thunder rolled across the city. Above everything, making it impossible for a man to speak into the ear of his neighbor, clanged the thousands of bells of Moscow. From the towers and churches of the Kremlin the concentrated ringing of the bells obliterated all other sounds.

Among the seven thousand guests who dined at the coronation

banquet, among the grand dukes and royal princes, the emirs and ambassadors, was one room filled with plain Russian people in simple dress. They were there by hereditary right, for they were the descendants of people who, at one time or another, had saved the life of a Russian tsar. The most honored among them were the descendants of an old servant, Ivan Susanin, who had refused under torture to tell the Poles where young Michael Romanov, first of the Romanov tsars, was hiding. At hundreds of tables the guests sat down and found before them a roll of parchment tied with silken cords. Inside, in illuminated medieval lettering, was the menu. The meal consisted of borshch and pepper-pot soup, turnovers filled with meat, steamed fish, whole spring lamb, pheasants in cream sauce, salad, asparagus, sweet fruits in wine, and ice cream.

On a dais beneath a golden canopy, Nicholas and Alexandra dined alone, according to ancient tradition, watched from the galleries by the cream of the Russian nobility. The highest court officials personally passed them their golden plates. During the lengthy meal, foreign ambassadors were admitted one by one to drink the health of the Imperial couple. For the rest of the day, Nicholas and Alexandra greeted their other guests, moving through the great Kremlin halls, hung with blue silk and lined with gilt chairs. All day the Tsar wore the huge coronation crown, so big that it came down almost over his eyes. Resting directly on the scar made by the Japanese fanatic, its great weight soon gave him a headache. The Empress walked at his side, still in her silver-white dress, her train supported by a dozen pages.

At the coronation ball that night, the Kremlin shimmered with light and music. The gowns worn by Russian women were thought by foreign ladies to be shockingly far off the shoulder. There were tiaras, necklaces, bracelets, rings and earrings, some with stones as big as robins' eggs. Grand Duchess Xenia, Nicholas's sister, and Grand Duchess Elizabeth, his sister-in-law, were covered with emeralds. Other women were drowning in sapphires and rubies. Alexandra wore a thick girdle of diamonds around her waist. Nicholas himself was draped with an enormous collar, made of dozens of clusters of diamonds, reaching around his entire chest. Even in a day which had seen a thousand kingly fortunes, the jewels that appeared that night brought gasps of awe.

That night the entire city of Moscow glowed with the light of special illuminations. Within the Kremlin itself, the churches and public buildings were lit by thousands of electric light bulbs which all flashed on when Alexandra pressed a button hidden in a bouquet of roses. Outside, millions of candles flickered in the streets and homes. At ten o'clock, when Nicholas and Alexandra walked onto a Kremlin balcony overlooking the river to gaze at the city, their faces shone with reflected light. Even after they went to bed, the walls of their bedchamber in the Kremlin apartment still were covered with shadows from the illuminated city outside.

The day following the coronation belonged to the people of Moscow. Grand Duke Serge, who was Governor General of Moscow, had arranged the traditional huge open-air feast which the Tsar and the Empress would attend in a field outside the city. Cartloads of enameled cups, each stamped with the Imperial seal, were to be given away as souvenirs, and the authorities had ordered hundreds of barrels of free beer.

Khodynka Meadow, the field selected for this mass festivity, was a training ground for troops of the Moscow garrison and it was crisscrossed by a network of shallow trenches and ditches. It was the only place which could accommodate the hundreds of thousands of Muscovites expected to pour out of the city to see the new Tsar and Tsaritsa.

The night before, thousands of people walked to the meadow without bothering to go to bed. By dawn, five hundred thousand people waited, some already drunk. The wagons loaded with cups and beer began to arrive and draw up behind skimpy wooden railings. The crowd watched with interest and began moving forward, full of good nature. Suddenly a rumor passed that there were fewer wagons than had been expected and that there would be beer enough only for those who got there first. People began to run. The single squadron of Cossacks on hand to keep order was brushed aside. Men tripped and stumbled into the ditches. Women and children, knocked down in the mass of rushing, pushing bodies, felt feet on their backs and heads. Their noses and mouths were ground into the dirt. Over the mutilated, suffocating bodies, thousands of feet relentlessly trampled.

By the time police and more Cossacks arrived, the meadow resembled a battlefield. Hundreds were dead and thousands wounded. By afternoon, the city's hospitals were jammed with wounded and everybody knew what had happened. Nicholas and Alexandra were stunned.

The Tsar's first frantic impulse was to go immediately into a prayerful retreat. He declared that he could not possibly go to the ball being given that night by the French Ambassador, the Marquis de Montebello. Once again, the uncles, rallying around their brother Grand Duke Serge, intervened. To adorn the ball, the French government had sent priceless tapestries and treasures of silver plate from Paris and Versailles, along with one hundred thousand roses from the south of France. The uncles urged that Nicholas not magnify the disaster by failing to appear and thus giving offense to France's only European ally. Tragically, the young Tsar gave in and agreed.

"We expected that the party would be called off," said Sergius Witte, the Minister of Finance. "[Instead] it took place as if nothing had happened and the ball was opened by their Majesties dancing a quadrille." It was a painful evening. "The Empress appeared in great distress, her eyes reddened by tears," the British ambassador informed Queen Victoria. Alexander Izvolsky, later Russian Foreign Minister, declared that "far from being insensible, they [the Imperial couple] were deeply moved. The Emperor's first impulse was to order a suspension of the festivities and to retire to one of the monasteries. The Tsar's uncles urged him not to cancel anything to avoid greater scandal."

Expressing their grief, Nicholas and Alexandra spent a day going from one hospital to another. Nicholas ordered that the dead be buried in separate coffins at his own expense rather than dumped into the common grave customary for mass disasters. From the Tsar's private purse, the family of every victim received a thousand roubles. But no act of consideration could erase the terrible event. Masses of simple Russians took the disaster as an omen that the reign would be unhappy. Other Russians, more sophisticated or more vengeful, used the tragedy to underscore the heartlessness of the autocracy and the contemptible shallowness of the young Tsar and his "German woman."

After a coronation, the newly crowned monarch was expected to travel, making state visits and private courtesy calls on fellow sovereigns. In the summer of 1896, Nicholas and Alexandra went to Vienna to visit the aging Emperor of Austria-Hungary, Franz Joseph, called on the Kaiser at Breslau and spent ten quiet days in Copenhagen with Nicholas's grandparents, King Christian IX and Queen Louise of

Denmark. In September, taking with them ten-month-old Olga, they sailed to visit Queen Victoria.

The Queen was in Scotland at the great, turreted, granite castle of Balmoral deep in the Highlands of Aberdeen. In a driving rain, the Russian Imperial yacht *Standart* anchored in the roadstead at Leith, and Uncle Bertie, the Prince of Wales, came aboard to escort the Russian guests through the wild mountains. Thoroughly drenched from riding in open carriages, they arrived at the castle after dark. The Queen was waiting for them on the castle steps, surrounded by tall Highlanders holding flaming torches.

Overjoyed to see each other, grandmother and granddaughter spent hours playing with the baby. "She is marvelously kind and amiable to us, and so delighted to see our little daughter," Nicholas wrote to Marie. Nicholas was left in the hands of Bertie. "They seem to consider it necessary to take me out shooting all day long with the gentlemen," he complained. "The weather is awful, rain and wind every day and on top of it no luck at all—I haven't killed a stag yet. . . . I'm glad Georgie comes out to shoot too—we can at least talk."

From Scotland, the Russian party traveled to Portsmouth and then to France. Unlike the British visit, which had been a family holiday, the Tsar's visit to Paris was an event of the highest importance to both countries. Despite the great difference in their political systems, the needs of diplomacy had made military allies of Europe's greatest republic and its most absolute autocracy. Since 1870, when France lost the Franco-Prussian War and was stripped of its eastern provinces of Alsace and Lorraine, French statesmen and generals had dreamed of the day they would take revenge on Germany, aided by the countless soldiers of the Tsar. For his part, Tsar Alexander III had wanted a counterbalance to the immense military power of the German Empire which had grown up on his western frontier. Besides, France was willing to loan to Russia the enormous sums Alexander III needed to rebuild his army and to build his railways. In 1888 and 1889, the first of these loans was floated on the Paris Bourse at a low rate of interest. In 1891, the French fleet visited Kronstadt, and the Autocrat of all the Russias stood bareheaded while the bands played the "*Marseillaise*." Until that moment it had been a criminal offense to play this revolutionary song anywhere in the Tsar's dominions. In 1893, the Russian fleet visited Toulon, and in 1894, the year of Alexander III's death and his son's accession, Russia and France signed a treaty of alliance. In his *Memoirs*, Raymond Poincaré, President of France during World

War I, recorded, "Those of us who reached manhood in 1890 cannot recall without emotion the prodigious effect produced by the friendliness of the Emperor Alexander III."

Nicholas II was the first tsar to visit France since the *entente* had been formed, and the French government proposed to give him an overwhelming welcome. It being late September, Paris carpenters were ordered to wire artificial chestnut blooms to the famed chestnut trees to give the city its most pleasing appearance. Police were stationed every twenty yards along the line of parade to dampen the enthusiasm of revolutionaries or anarchists who might jump at the chance to assassinate an autocrat. The French fleet steamed to the middle of the English Channel with flags flying and bands playing to greet the Tsar as he crossed from England.

From the moment Nicholas's carriage appeared on the wide boulevards of Paris, the people of France raised a thunderous, unceasing ovation. Huge crowds frantically waved their handkerchiefs and shouted as Nicholas and Alexandra went by. Seeing Olga and her nurse in another carriage, the crowds shouted "*Vive le bébé,*" "*Vive la Grande Duchesse*" and even "*Vive la nounou.*" Nicholas was overcome. "I can only compare it with my entry into Moscow [for the coronation]." Together, the Imperial guests visited Notre Dame, the Ste. Chapelle, the Panthéon and the Louvre. At the Invalides, they looked down on the tomb of Russia's invader, Napoleon. With Alexandra in a blue satin gown standing at his side, Nicholas laid a foundation stone of the Pont Alexander III over the Seine. At Versailles for an evening, Alexandra was assigned the rooms of Marie Antoinette.

The French visit concluded with a huge military review on the river Marne. Nicholas, dressed in a Cossack uniform, sat on a sorrel horse and watched seventy thousand Chasseurs Alpins, African Zouaves, Spahi horsemen in flowing robes, and regiments of regular infantry in red pantaloons. Then, as a climax to the review, the Spahis whirled and charged *en masse,* engulfing the reviewing party in clouds of dust. Leaving the field to board his train, Nicholas rode down a road lined on both sides with battalions of French infantry. Spontaneously the French soldiers began to cheer "*Vive l'Empereur!*"

Exhilarated by their reception in France, Nicholas and Alexandra hated to begin the journey back to Russia by train across Germany. "We arrived at the frontier at eleven in the evening," Nicholas wrote to Marie. "There for the last time, we heard the strains of our national anthem. After this began German helmets and it was unpleasant to look out of the window. At every station in France one heard 'Hurrah' and saw kind and jolly faces, but here everything was black and dark and boring. Happily, it was time to go to bed; by daylight it would have been even more depressing."

Nicholas never forgot the outpouring of emotion displayed by the people and soldiers of France on his first visit as Tsar. In the future, this favorable impression in the mind and heart of the young Tsar was to serve France well.

CHAPTER SIX

The New Tsar

At home, Nicholas plunged into "the awful job I have feared all my life." He attacked the mountains of paper brought him every day and dutifully initialed them, wrote comments in their margins, signed orders, promotions and lists of honors. At first, feeling his way, he relied on Marie for guidance. "The various affairs you left me, petitions, etc. have all been attended to," he reported faithfully. Two weeks later she wrote back, "I am sorry to have still to forward you so many papers, but it is always like that in early summer just before the ministers go on leave."

But Nicholas did not always follow his mother's recommendations. When she asked as a favor the loan of one million roubles from the State Bank to a needy princess, Nicholas lectured her sternly: "I must talk to you, darling Mama, about some rather unpleasant things. . . . As regards . . . a loan of a million roubles from the Bank, I must tell you honestly that this is impossible. I should have liked to see how she would have dared even to hint at such a thing to Papa; and I can certainly hear the answer he would have given her. . . . It would be a fine state of affairs indeed at the Treasury if, in Witte's absence (he is at present on a holiday) I were to give a million to one, two millions to another, etc. . . . What forms one of the most brilliant pages in the history of dear Papa's reign is the sound condition of our finances—[this] would be destroyed in the course of a few years."

Far more difficult for Nicholas were the uncles, the four surviving brothers of Alexander III. Vladimir, the oldest, a hunter, gourmet and patron of the arts, was Commander of the Imperial Guard and President of the Academy of Fine Arts. Alexis, a man of infinite charm and enormous girth, was simultaneously Grand Admiral of the Russian Navy and an international *bon vivant*—"his was a case of fast women and slow ships." Serge, the husband of Grand Duchess Elizabeth, was the violently reactionary Governor General of Moscow, a man so narrow and despotic that he forbade his wife to read *Anna Karenina* for fear of arousing "unhealthy curiosity and violent emotions." Only Paul, a mere eight years older than his nephew, made no trouble for Nicholas.

"Nicholas II spent the first ten years of his reign sitting behind a massive desk in the palace and listening with near-awe to the well-rehearsed bellowing of his towering uncles," wrote Grand Duke Alexander, the Tsar's cousin. "He dreaded to be left alone with them. In the presence of witnesses his opinions were accepted as orders, but the instant the door of his study closed on the outsider—down on the table would go with a bang the weighty fist of Uncle Alexis . . . two hundred and fifty pounds . . . packed in the resplendent uniform of Grand Admiral of the Fleet. . . . Uncle Serge and Uncle Vladimir developed equally efficient methods of intimidation. . . . They all had their favorite generals and admirals . . . their ballerinas desirous of organizing a 'Russian season' in Paris; their wonderful preachers anxious to redeem the Emperor's soul . . . their clairvoyant peasants with a divine message."

It was not surprising that the uncles had a powerful influence; all were vigorous, relatively young men when their inexperienced twenty-six-year-old nephew suddenly became Tsar. Three of them had been present in Darmstadt to steer Nicholas through his proposal to Princess Alix; later it was they who decided that Nicholas should marry publicly in St. Petersburg, not privately at Livadia; at the coronation, the uncles insisted that Nicholas go on to the French ambassador's ball after the disaster at Khodynka Meadow. The uncles' influence continued over the first decade of the reign. It was not until Nicholas had gone through the fires of war with Japan and the 1905 Revolution and was himself thirty-six that their influence began to fade.

Along with becoming Tsar of Russia, Nicholas had suddenly become head of the House of Romanov and manager of the vast Imperial estate. His income, totaling 24 million gold roubles ($12 million) a year, came partly from an annual Treasury appropriation and partly from the profits of the millions of acres of crown lands—vineyards, farms and cotton plantations—purchased mainly by

Catherine the Great. In 1914 the value of these Romanov lands was estimated at $50 million. Another $80 million was frozen in the form of the immense treasures of jewelry bought in three centuries of rule. Along with the fabulous Russian Imperial Crown, these included the Orlov Diamond of 194.5 carats, which was set in the Imperial Scepter; the Moon of the Mountain diamond of 120 carats; and the Polar Star, a superb 40-carat ruby.

Despite this wealth, the Tsar's private purse was often empty. There were seven palaces to be kept up: the Winter Palace and the Anitchkov Palace in St. Petersburg; the Alexander and Catherine Palaces at Tsarskoe Selo; Peterhof; Gatchina; the Imperial apartments in the Kremlin; and Livadia Palace in the Crimea. In these palaces, fifteen thousand officials and servants required salaries, food, uniforms and appropriate presents on holidays. There were the Imperial trains and yachts. Three theatres in St. Petersburg and two in Moscow, the Imperial Academy of Arts and the Imperial Ballet with its 153 ballerinas and 73 male dancers, all were maintained from the Tsar's private purse. Even the little students at the Ballet School, wearing dark blue uniforms with silver lyres on their collars, and training in leaps and entrechats, were considered members of the personal household of the Tsar.

In addition, every member of the vast Imperial family received an allowance from the Tsar. Each of the grand dukes was given $100,000 a year and every grand duchess received a dowry of $500,000. Innumerable hospitals, orphanages and institutions for the blind depended on the Imperial charity. A flood of private petitions for financial aid poured in each year to the private chancery; many were worthy and had to be satisfied. Before the end of the year, the Tsar was usually penniless; sometimes he reached this embarrassing state by autumn.

In running his family and empire, Nicholas looked to his father and the Russian past. Nicholas preferred to be Russian down to the smallest details of personal life. At his desk, he wore a simple Russian peasant blouse, baggy breeches and soft leather boots. Once he toyed with the idea of converting formal court dress to the ancient long *caftans* of the days of Ivan the Great and Ivan the Terrible. He gave up the project only when he discovered that the cost of ornamenting these robes with jewels in the style of the ancient Muscovite *boyars* was more than any modern purse could bear. Although Nicholas's English, French and German were excellent, he preferred to speak Russian.

He spoke Russian to his children and wrote in Russian to his mother; only to the Empress Alexandra, whose Russian was awkward, did he speak and write in English. Although French was the popular language of the upper classes, he insisted that his ministers report to him in Russian and was displeased even by the insertion of a foreign phrase or expression. Even culturally, Nicholas was intensely nationalistic. He liked to read Pushkin, Gogol and the novels of Tolstoy. He was fond of Tchaikovsky and went to concerts, opera and ballet several times a week; his favorite ballet was *The Hunchback Horse*, based on a Russian fairy tale. Of all the tsars, Nicholas most admired Alexis the Mild, last of the purely Muscovite tsars and father of Peter the Great. In 1903, Nicholas's interest led to a lavish costume ball at which everyone present appeared in robes and gowns of the seventeenth century and danced old Russian dances which they had rehearsed for weeks. Once when an aide was talking enthusiastically about Peter the Great, Nicholas replied thoughtfully, "I recognize my ancestor's great merits, but . . . he is the ancestor who appeals to me least of all. He had too much admiration for European culture. . . . He stamped out Russian habits, the good customs, the usages, bequeathed by a nation."

In his work habits, Nicholas was solitary. Unlike most monarchs and chiefs of state—unlike even his own wife—he had no private secretary. He preferred to do things for himself. On his desk he kept a large calendar of his daily appointments, scrupulously entered in his own hand. When official papers arrived, he opened them, read them, signed them and put them in envelopes himself. He once explained that he placed things exactly because he liked to feel that he could enter his office in the dark and put his hand on any object he desired. With much the same sense of privacy, Nicholas disliked discussions of politics, especially in casual conversation. A new aide-de-camp, galloping at the side of the Tsar near Livadia on a morning ride, supposed that his duty was to amuse the Tsar with small talk. He chose politics as his subject. Nicholas replied reluctantly, and quickly switched the conversation to the weather, the mountain scenery, the horses and tennis. When the aide persisted, Nicholas put spurs to his horse and galloped ahead.

This sense of privacy, along with an unwillingness to provoke personal unpleasantness, created perennial difficulty between the Tsar and his ministers. Ministers were appointed and dismissed directly by the crown. In theory, they were the servants of the Tsar, and he was free to give these posts to whomever he liked, to listen to or ignore a minister's advice, and to hand down dismissals without explanation. In practice, the ministers were the heads of large government departments where continuity and coordination were administrative necessities. In addition, the ministers were also ambitious, proud and sensitive men. Nicholas never mastered the technique of forceful, efficient management of subordinates. He hated scenes and found it impossible to sternly criticize or dismiss a man to his face. If something was wrong, he preferred to give a minister a friendly reception, comment gently and shake hands warmly. Occasionally, after such an interview, the minister would return to his office, well pleased with himself, only to receive in the morning mail a letter regretfully asking for his resignation. Not unnaturally, these men complained that they had been deceived.

The major lines of Nicholas's character as Tsar were set in these early years of the reign. Coming to the throne unprepared, he was forced to develop his administration of the office as he went along. Because he was influenced at first by his mother, his uncles and his tutor (Pobedonostsev remained Procurator of the Holy Synod until 1905), his enemies declared that he had no will of his own. It would be more accurate to say that he was a man of narrow, special education; of strong and—unfortunately—unchanging conviction; of soft-spoken, kindly manner; and, underneath, of stubborn courage. Even Sergius Witte, whose abrupt dismissal from office later bred in him a venomous hatred of Nicholas, nevertheless wrote of the early years: "In those days, the young Emperor carried in himself the seeds of the best that the human mind and heart possess."

To the despair of Russian liberals who had hoped that the death of Alexander III would mean a modification of the autocracy, Nicholas quickly made it clear that he would closely abide by his father's principles. Even before the coronation, he struck this note. In sending to the new Tsar the traditional address of congratulation on his accession, the Zemstvo of Tver, a stronghold of liberalism, had voiced an appeal "that the voice of the people and the expression of its desires would be listened to" and that the law would stand "above the changing views of the individual instruments of supreme power." In this mild language Pobedonostsev discovered a dangerous challenge to the principle of autocracy, and with his help the young Tsar drafted a reply which he delivered in person to the Tver delegation. Admonishing them for their "senseless dreams of the participation of the Zemstvos' representatives in the affairs of internal administration," Nicholas added, "I shall maintain the principle of autocracy just as firmly and unflinchingly as it was preserved by my unforgettable dead father."

Nicholas's speech was a blunt dashing of liberal hopes and a renewed challenge to revolutionaries, who once again set to work to undermine the monarchy. Yet within the family he was widely congratulated. From Kaiser William II came a happy note: "I am delighted by your magnificent address. The principle of the monarchy must be maintained in all its strength."

In foreign affairs, Alexander III had left a legacy of thirteen peaceful years, but he had not considered it important to acquaint his heir with even the most basic information concerning Russia's international position. It was not until Nicholas's accession, therefore, that the young Tsar learned the terms of the Franco-Russian alliance." * Anxious to keep this peace and unwilling to trust it solely to a military alliance, Nicholas issued a dramatic appeal for disarmament and "universal peace" which led to the formation of the International Court of Justice. In August 1898, a Russian note lamenting the economic, financial and moral effects of the armaments race was delivered to all the governments of the world, proposing an international conference to study the problem. It has been suggested that the Tsar's proposal stemmed wholly from the fact that Austria was re-equipping her artillery with modern field guns which Russia was unable to match, but this was not entirely the case. Another reason was the publication that year of a six-volume work by Ivan Bliokh, an important Russian Jewish railroad financier, who depicted in a massive array of facts, statistics and projected casualty rates the grim horror of any future war. Bliokh had an audience with Nicholas and helped persuade the Tsar to issue the appeal.

The strange proposal from St. Petersburg astonished Europe. From some quarters Nicholas was hailed as a tsar who would be known in history as "Nicholas the Pacific." Sophisticated folk, on the other hand, dismissed it in the tones of the Prince of Wales, who described

* The strange phenomenon of powerful chiefs of state withholding vital government information from their immediate heirs has not been restricted to Russia or autocracies. Only when he suddenly became President on the death of Franklin D. Roosevelt did Harry Truman learn that the United States was in the final stage of an immense effort to build an atomic bomb.

it as "the greatest nonsense and rubbish I ever heard of." The Kaiser was instantly, frantically hostile. Imagine, he telegraphed the Tsar, "a Monarch . . . dissolving his regiments sacred with a hundred years of history and handing over his town to Anarchists and Democracy."

Despite apprehensions, in deference to the Tsar and Russia a conference was convened at The Hague in May 1899. Twenty European powers attended along with the United States, Mexico, Japan, China, Siam and Persia. The Russian proposals for freezing armament levels were defeated, but the convention did agree on rules of warfare and established a permanent court of arbitration. In 1905 Nicholas himself referred the Dogger Bank incident between Britain and Russia to the World Court, and in 1914, on the eve of the First World War, the Tsar pleaded with the Kaiser to help him send the dispute between Austria and Serbia to The Hague.

Europe's surprise that so unusual an idea as universal peace should come out of "semi-barbaric" Russia betrayed its lack of awareness of the richly creative culture which was flourishing there. The early years of Nicholas's reign were a period of such glittering intellectual and cultural achievement that they are known as the "Russian Renaissance" or the "Silver Age." The ferment of activity and new ideas included not only politics but philosophy and science, music and art.

In literature, Anton Chekov was writing the plays and short stories which would become world classics. In 1898, Constantine Stanislavsky first opened the doors of the famous Moscow Art Theatre, and its second play, Chekov's *The Sea Gull,* written in 1896, determined its success. Thereafter the appearance of *Uncle Vanya* (1899) and *The Cherry Orchard* (1904) confirmed the arrival of a new concept of naturalistic acting and a new era in the history of the theatre. In 1902, Stanislavsky directed *The Lower Depths,* a grimly realistic play by Maxim Gorky, hitherto known primarily for his massive novels. In Kiev, from 1900 to 1905, Sholom Aleichem, who had already lost a fortune trading on the grain and stock exchanges, was devoting himself entirely to writing in Yiddish the scores of short stories which have made him known as the "Jewish Mark Twain."

In philosophy, Vladimir Solov'ev, the preeminent religious philosopher and poet, had begun publishing his works in 1894. In 1904, the poems of Solov'ev's famous disciple Alexander Blok began to appear. At the Institute of Experimental Medicine in St. Petersburg, Ivan

Pavlov, one of a group of Russian scientists making significant advances in chemistry and medicine, was conducting the experiments in physiology which won him a Nobel Prize in 1904.

Russian painting was in transition. Ilya Repin, then a professor of historical painting at the St. Petersburg Academy of Fine Arts, was crowning a career of painting the great historical scenes of Russia's past. Victor Vasnetsov and Michael Nesterov had gone back even further and were attempting to re-create medieval religious art. Meanwhile, a rank of younger artists was responding excitedly to exhibitions in Russia of Cézanne, Gauguin and Picasso. Serov, influenced by the French Impressionists, painted evocative portraits of many contemporary Russians including, in 1900, the Tsar. In 1896, Vassily Kandinsky, a lawyer in Moscow, gave up his career and left Russia to begin painting in Munich. In 1907, Marc Chagall arrived in St. Petersburg to study with the famous contemporary painter Lev Bakst.

At the Imperial Ballet, Marius Petipa was in the midst of a half-century reign as choreographer which would last until he resigned in 1903. In richly magnificent succession, he staged sixty major ballets, among them Tchaikovsky's *Swan Lake*, *Nutcracker* and *Sleeping Beauty*. It was Petipa who thrust onto the stage the glittering parade of Russian dancers which included Mathilde Kschessinska, Tamara Karsavina, Anna Pavlova and Vaslav Nijinsky. Even today, the great ballet companies of the world are measured for excellence against the standards set by Petipa. In 1899, Serge Diaghilev founded the influential journal *The World of Art* and editorially began to criticize Petipa's conservative style. In 1909, Diaghilev, with a daring new choreographer, Michael Fokine, founded the Ballet Russe in Paris and took the world by storm.

In the superlative music conservatories of St. Petersburg and Moscow, an unbroken succession of famous teachers passed their art to talented pupils. Nicholas Rimsky-Korsakov was the conductor of the St. Petersburg Symphony. While writing his own magnificent *Golden Cockerel*, he was instructing a youthful Igor Stravinsky, whose brilliantly original ballet scores written for Diaghilev, *Firebird* (1910), *Petrushka* (1911) and *Rite of Spring* (1913), were to have gigantic influence on all twentieth-century music. Later, in 1914, another of Rimsky-Korsakov's pupils, Serge Prokoviev, was to graduate from the conservatory. Among the violinists and pianists trained in Imperial Russia were Serge Rachmaninov, Vladimir Horowitz, Efrem Zimbalist, Mischa Elman and Jascha Heifetz. Serge Koussevitsky conducted his own symphony orchestra in Moscow. In 1899, the matchless basso Fedor Chaliapin made his debut and thereafter dominated the opera stage.

Across Russia, people flocked to hear music and opera. Kiev, Odessa, Warsaw and Tiflis each had its own opera company with a season of eight to nine months. St. Petersburg alone had four opera houses. In 1901, Tsar Nicholas built one of these, the Narodny Dom or People's Palace. Believing that ordinary Russians should have an opportunity to savor the best in national music and drama, Nicholas had constructed a vast building which included theatres, concert halls and restaurants, with admission fees of only twenty kopecks. In time, the best orchestras and the leading actors and musicians appeared there. St. Petersburg society, enjoying the flavor of something new, trooped to follow.

During these years, the young Tsar's family grew rapidly. At two-year intervals, three more daughters were born. In 1897, when Alexandra was pregnant a second time and feeling ill, the Dowager Empress advised: "She ought to try eating raw ham in bed in the morning before breakfast. It really does help against nausea. I have tried it myself, and it is wholesome and nourishing, too. . . . It is your duty, my dear Nicky, to watch over her and to look after her in every possible way, to see she keeps her feet warm. . . ." That June, Grand Duchess Tatiana was born.

A year later, in October 1898, Alexandra was pregnant again. "I am now in a position to tell you, dear Mama, that with God's help we expect a new happy event in the family next May," wrote Nicholas. "Alix does not go driving any more, twice she fainted during Mass. . . ." A month later, in November: "The nausea is gone. She walks very little, and when it is warm sits on the balcony. . . . In the evening, when she is in bed, I read to her. We have finished *War and Peace*." Grand Duchess Marie was born in May 1899, and their fourth child, also a girl, arrived in June 1901. They named her Anastasia.

Along with births, there were illnesses and deaths. In the summer of 1899, Nicholas's brother Grand Duke George finally died at twenty-seven of tuberculosis, and in the fall of 1900, Nicholas himself came down with typhoid fever in the Crimea. Alexandra nursed him herself. "Nicky was really an angel," she wrote to her sister. "I rebelled at a nurse being taken and we managed perfectly ourselves.

Orchie [Mrs. Orchard] would wash his face and hands in the morning and bring my meals in always. I took them on the sofa. . . . When he was getting better, I read to him almost all day long." "Alix looked after me better than any nurse," Nicholas wrote to Marie once he was feeling better. "All through my illness I could not stand up. Now I can easily walk from the bed to the dresser."

Scarcely had Nicholas recovered when Queen Victoria died. Only the summer before, when the eighty-one-year-old Queen had invited the Empress to England, Alexandra had written to a friend: "How intensely I long to see her dear old face . . . never have we been separated so long, four whole years, and I have the feeling as tho' I should never see her any more. Were it not so far away, I should have gone off all alone for a few days to see her and left the children and my husband, as she has been as a mother to me, ever since Mama's death 22 years ago."

When the news of Victoria's death arrived in January 1901, Alexandra wanted to start immediately for Windsor, but, being pregnant with Anastasia, she was persuaded not to go. At the memorial service in the English church in St. Petersburg, the Empress wept in public. To her sister she wrote, "How I envy you being able to see beloved Grandmama being taken to her last rest. I cannot really believe she has gone, that we shall never see her any more. . . . Since one can remember, she was in our life, and a dearer, kinder being never was. . . . England without the Queen seems impossible."

The death of her grandmother did more than carry away the woman Alexandra loved best. It also removed an influence of stability and a source of encouragement. Ever since her marriage, the Empress and the Queen had written regularly, although Alexandra destroyed their letters in March 1917. The Queen had always worried about Alexandra's excessive shyness, fearing that the dramatic ascent in a single month from being a German princess to becoming Empress of Russia had left no time for developing ease in society.

This had, in fact, been a problem since Alexandra's first public appearance as Empress in the winter season of 1896. As she stood beside her husband at a ball, Alexandra's eyes were cold with fright and her tongue was stilled by nervousness. That night, Alexandra later admitted, she was terrified and would have liked to sink beneath the polished floors. But she stayed until midnight and then gratefully swept away.

The new Empress's first receptions for the ladies of St. Petersburg were blighted by the same shyness. As the reception line filed past, the invited ladies found themselves confronting a tall figure standing silent and cold before them. Alexandra rarely smiled and never spoke more than an automatic word of welcome. In an awkward way, her hand hung in the air, waiting to be kissed. Everything about her, the tight mouth, her occasional glance down the line to see how many more were coming, plainly indicated that the young Empress's only real desire was to get away as soon as possible.

It did not take many of these balls and receptions before nervousness and uncertainty turned on both sides to active dislike. Alexandra's childhood in the little court at Darmstadt, her training under the strict Victorian standards of Windsor, had not prepared her for the gay, loose society of St. Petersburg. She was shocked by the all-night parties, the flaunted love affairs, the malicious gossip. "The heads of the young ladies of St. Petersburg are filled with nothing but thoughts of young officers," she declared, accurately enough. Scandalized by the flourishing love affairs among the aristocracy, Alexandra took the palace invitation lists and began crossing off names. As one prominent name after another disappeared, the list was decimated.

Many people in St. Petersburg society quickly dismissed the young Empress as a prude and a bore. There is a story that at one of her first court balls she saw a young woman dancing whose décolletage she considered too low. One of her ladies-in-waiting was sent to tell the offender: "Madame, Her Majesty wants me to tell you that in Hesse-Darmstadt we don't wear our dresses that way."

"Really?" the young woman is said to have replied, at the same time pulling the front of her dress still lower. "Pray tell Her Majesty that in Russia we *do* wear our dresses this way."

Alexandra's new zeal over Orthodoxy embarrassed society. Themselves Orthodox from birth, they thought of the Empress with her aggressive collecting of rare icons, her wide reading of church history, her pilgrimages, her talks about abbots and holy hermits, as crankish. When she tried to organize a handiwork society in St. Petersburg whose members would knit three garments a year for the poor, most St. Petersburg ladies declared that they had no time for such rubbish.

Members of the Imperial family resented the way the Empress seemed to seal them off from the palace and the Tsar. Large and scattered though it was, the Russian Imperial family, like most Russian families, had always been closely knit. Uncles and aunts and cousins were accustomed to frequent visits and invitations to dine. Anxious to be alone with her young husband, Alexandra was slow to issue these invitations. The family became indignant. Imperial grand duchesses, themselves the sisters or daughters of a tsar, huffed that a mere German princess should attempt to come between them and their prerogatives.

Society enjoyed the friction between the two Empresses, Alexandra and Marie, siding openly with Marie and talking longingly of gayer days. But Marie lived mostly abroad, either in Copenhagen or visiting her sister, now Queen Alexandra of England, or staying in her villa on the French Riviera.

Perhaps, because of the shyness she carried from childhood, the Empress Alexandra could never successfully have acted the public role demanded of her. Yet, in addition to her own personality, every happenstance conspired against her. Marie had lived in Russia for seventeen years before she came to the throne; Alexandra barely one month. The new Empress spoke almost no Russian. Unable to grasp the intricate ranking of the court, she made errors and gave offense. Once she was Empress, there was no way for her to make friends; ladies could not simply drop in on her or casually invite her for tea. Her sister Grand Duchess Elizabeth, who might have acted as a bridge between the throne and society, had moved to Moscow. Alexandra's private plans to start giving lunches were interrupted by her recurring pregnancies and long confinements. Childbearing was not easy for her and, long before each birth was due, she canceled all appointments and went to bed. After the birth, she insisted on nursing each child and disliked being far from the nursery.

Between the Empress and the aristocracy it became an unhappy cycle of dislike and rebuff. In her own mind, Alexandra found the explanation for this by telling herself that they were not real Russians at all. Neither the jaded nobility, nor the workers who went on strike, nor the revolutionary students, nor the difficult ministers had anything to do with the real people of Russia. The real people were the peasants she had seen during her summer at Ilinskoe. These humble people, multiplied into millions, who walked through the birch groves on their way to the fields, who fell on their knees to pray for the Tsar, were the heart and soul of Holy Russia. To them, she was certain, she was more than just an Empress; she was *Matushka.*

CHAPTER SEVEN

Two Revolutionaries

ALEXANDRA's view of life in the provinces, although oversimplified, was generally accurate. Even at the turn of the century, the Russian countryside was studded with manor houses belonging to loyal country squires, and with villages inhabited by peasants whose fathers had been serfs and who themselves still clung to traditional patterns of life. Each sleepy provincial town was much like the next: at the top a crust of local nobility and gentry, then the bureaucrats and professional classes—judges, lawyers, doctors and teachers—and below them, priests and clerks, shopkeepers, artisans, workmen and servants. At times a current of unrest, a tricklet of liberalism, might run through one of these towns, but overwhelmingly the prevailing mood was conservative. Ironically, exactly such a town was Simbirsk on the Middle Volga, the childhood home of two men who in succession would play major roles in the overthrow of the Russia of Nicholas and Alexandra. One was Alexander Fedorovich Kerensky. The other, eleven years Kerensky's senior, was Vladimir Ilyich Ulyanov, called Lenin.

Simbirsk in the 1880's and 1890's was an isolated town perched on a hill above the Volga River. There was no railroad, and although paddlewheel steamers stopped at its quay during the summer, in winter the only highway was the ice of the frozen river. On the crest of the hill, looking out over the river and the meadowland stretching away to the eastern horizon, stood the town's cathedral, the governor's mansion, the high school, the library. "From the summit right down to the waterside," recalled Kerensky, "stretched luxuriant apple and cherry orchards. In the spring the whole mountain-side was white with blossom, fragrant, and at night breathless with the songs of the nightingales. From the summit . . . the view across the river over miles of meadowland was magnificent. With the melting of the snow, the river used to leave its banks and flood the low-lying fields . . . stretching like an endless sea over the fields which later in the heat of summer would be gay with the songs and games of peasants and townspeople come to mow the rich, fragrant grass."

In this pleasant place Vladimir Ulyanov was born in 1870, two years after the birth of Nicholas II. His father, Ilya Ulyanov, the son of a serf who had won his freedom, had graduated from Kazan University and begun his career as a teacher of mathematics. Ilya Ulyanov rose rapidly through the ranks of the state educational system and in 1863 he married Maria Blank, a Volga German whose father, a doctor, owned a large estate. Vladimir, named after the saint who became the first Christian ruler of Russia, was the third of Maria's six children.

In 1869, the year before Lenin's birth, Ilya Ulyanov became Inspector and, five years later, Director of Schools for the Province of Simbirsk. He worked zealously training teachers and opening new schools, and he was away from home for long periods, but in twelve years the number of primary schools in the province rose from 20 to 434. In recognition of this work, Ilya was promoted to the rank of Actual Councilor of State, a rank in the hereditary nobility equivalent to an army major general. When Tsar Alexander II was assassinated in 1881, Ilya Ulyanov "sadly buttoned on his official uniform and went off to the Simbirsk cathedral to mourn the death of the Tsar-Liberator."

Vladimir, called Volodya in the family, was a plump, red-haired boy with a large head, stocky body and short legs. In the summers, with his brothers and sisters, he swam in the Volga and hunted mushrooms in the birch woods; during the winters, he went ice-skating and sleighing. Unlike Alexander, his impulsive, idealistic older brother, Vladimir tended to be precise and sarcastic. When he played chess with his brothers and sisters, he established a strict rule: "Under no circumstances, take a move back. Once you have touched a piece, you have to move it." He was an excellent student in school, and when the other Ulyanov children brought their marks home and solemnly reported them to their parents, Volodya simply burst through the door and up the stairs, shouting, "Excellent in everything!"

Within a span of sixteen months in 1886 and 1887, the comfortable

Ulyanov household collapsed. In 1922, replying to a census questionnaire, Lenin wrote: "Nonbeliever [in God] since the age of 16"—this was his age when, in January 1886, his father died of a stroke before his eyes. In the spring of 1887, his older brother Alexander was arrested in St. Petersburg, along with four other university students, on the charge of trying to assassinate Tsar Alexander III. They had been apprehended with a crude, unworkable bomb concealed inside a hollowed medical dictionary. Alexander did not deny the charge. To his mother, who hurried to his side, he declared, "I tried to kill the Tsar. The attempt failed and that is all there is to it." In May 1887, Alexander Ulyanov was hanged. His mother walked beside him to the gallows, repeating over and over, "Have courage. Have courage."

The effect of his brother's death on Vladimir is a subject of dispute. "The execution of such a brother as Alexander Ulyanov was bound undoubtedly to have a crushing and destructive psychological result upon any normal mind," said Alexander Kerensky. But Lenin, of course, was very far from normal. In addition, there is evidence of friction between the two brothers, especially after their father's death. "Undoubtedly, a very gifted person but we don't get along," said Alexander of Vladimir during this period. Alexander particularly disliked Vladimir's impertinence, arrogance and mockery of their mother. Once when her two sons were playing chess, Maria reminded Vladimir of something she had asked him to do. Vladimir answered rudely and did not move. Maria insisted and Vladimir became ruder. At this point, Alexander said calmly, "You either go and do what Mama asks or I shall not play with you again."

Alexander was hanged in the spring of Vladimir's final year in the Simbirsk high school. Outwardly unperturbed, Vladimir took his final examinations and, wearing a tight-fitting blue uniform, graduated at the head of his class. When he did so, the school headmaster (at considerable risk, considering the scandal then hanging over the Ulyanovs) wrote a warm endorsement of Vladimir:

"Very gifted, always neat and assiduous, Ulyanov was first in all his subjects, and upon completing his studies received a gold medal as the most deserving pupil with regard to his ability, progress and behavior. Neither in the school, nor outside, has a single instance been observed when he has given cause for dissatisfaction by word or by deed to the school authorities. . . . Religion and discipline were the basis of this upbringing . . . , the fruits of which are apparent in Ulyanov's behavior. Looking more closely at Ulyanov's character and private life, I have had occasion to note a somewhat excessive tendency towards isolation and reserve, a tendency to avoid contact with acquaintances and even with the very best of his school fellows outside school hours."

The signature under this document was that of Fedor Kerensky, headmaster of the school, and friend and admirer of the deceased Ilya Ulyanov. Because of this friendship, the court temporarily entrusted Fedor Kerensky with the management of young Vladimir's affairs.

As the widow of a hereditary nobleman, Maria Ulyanov continued to draw her pension, but the scandal made it necessary for her to move from Simbirsk. Vladimir entered the University of Kazan and was quickly expelled for taking part in a mild student demonstration. Thereafter, hoping to save her second son from the course which had destroyed his brother, Maria bought a farm of 225 acres and installed Vladimir as farm manager. He did not like it. "My mother wanted me to engage in farming," he recalled. "I tried it but I saw that it would not work. My relations with the *moujiks* were not normal." The farm was sold and the family moved to Samara to live with Maria's parents. There, sitting beside his grandfather's fireplace, Vladimir read omnivorously: Pushkin, Turgenev, Dostoyevsky, Tolstoy. He began to study law at home and crammed four years of work into a single year; when he received permission to take his examinations, he was again first in his class. Despite his academic brilliance, he failed in his brief attempt at legal practice. He took a dozen cases in Samara on behalf of peasants and workmen accused of minor crimes; all were found guilty. For exercise, he swam every day. In the winter, he hung upside down and did gymnastics on a pair of cross-bars he made himself.

With the same intensity with which he had mastered law, he began to study Karl Marx. The totality of the Marxist dream and the compelling logic of Marx's style appealed to Vladimir far more than the impulsive emotionalism displayed by his brother Alexander Ulyanov. Alexander thought of assassinating a single man whose death would alter nothing. Marx—and after him, Lenin—wished to change everything. To his mother's despair, Vladimir turned every family meal into a heated discussion of *Das Kapital*. She despaired even more when he announced that, because Marx had declared that the core of the revolution would be the urban proletariat, he intended to follow his brother's footsteps to St. Petersburg.

In 1893, just one year before the youthful Tsar Nicholas mounted the throne, twenty-three-year-old Vladimir wearing his father's frock coat and top hat, arrived in St. Petersburg, where it was arranged that he would work in a law office. He joined a Marxist study group which met to debate in the evenings. At a traditional Russian Shrove Tuesday supper of *blinis*, Vladimir first met another dedicated Marxist, Nadezhda Krupskaya. A round-faced, snub-nosed schoolteacher with short hair, full lips and unusually large eyes, Krupskaya, as she was always called, was a year older than Vladimir. After the party, Vladimir walked her home along the banks of the Neva. Thereafter they attended meetings together. At one of these, someone suggested the establishment of literary committees to educate the masses. "Vladimir Ilyich laughed," recalled Krupskaya, "and somehow the laughter sounded so wicked and dry. . . . 'Well,' he said, 'anybody who likes to save the fatherland with a literacy committee, why, fine, we shall not interfere.' "

In 1895, Vladimir went abroad for the first time. He was eager to go to Geneva to meet George Plekhanov, the father of Russian Marxism and idol of all young Russian revolutionaries. Yet Plekhanov, after twenty years in exile, had begun to lose touch with the movement in Russia, and Vladimir, anxious to talk, found him cold and distant. He went on to Zurich, Berlin and Paris, where he admired the wide tree-lined boulevards. A few weeks later, he returned to Russia with a false-bottomed trunk stuffed with wads of illegal literature, and plunged into organizing strikes and printing anti-government leaflets and manifestoes. For the sake of expediency, he avoided personal attacks on the young Tsar, who had been on the throne for less than a year. "Of course, if you start right away talking against the Tsar and the existing social system, you only antagonize the workers," he explained. Arrested in December 1895, he spent a year in jail in St. Petersburg and then was exiled for three years to Siberia.

The life of a political exile in Siberia during the last years of tsarist rule was not always a frozen nightmare. It could be and often was a remarkably permissive arrangement. Punishment consisted only in the requirement that the exile live in a prescribed area. If the exile had money, he could live exactly as he did in European Russia, establishing a household, keeping servants, receiving mail, books and visitors.

Vladimir, released from prison in St. Petersburg, was given five days in St. Petersburg and four in Moscow to prepare for his exile. He traveled alone across the Urals, taking with him a thousand roubles and a trunk filled with a hundred books. His three years in the quiet backwater Siberian village of Shushenskoe near the Mongolian border were among the happiest of his life. The river Shush flowed nearby and was filled with fish, the woods teemed with bears, squirrels and sables. Vladimir rented rooms, went swimming twice a day, acquired a dog and a gun and went hunting for duck and snipe. He was the wealthiest man in the village and demonstrated to a local merchant how to keep his books. His mail was enormous, and through it he maintained contact with Marxists in every corner of Russia and Europe. Several hours each day he worked on his lengthy work, *The Development of Capitalism in Russia.*

He had been there a year when Krupskaya joined him. Herself arrested for organizing a strike, she had arranged to be sent to Shushenskoe by telling the police that she was Vladimir's fiancée. Vladimir was delighted to see her and to have the books she brought, but less happy to welcome her mother, whom she had brought along and whom he disliked. To his own mother he wrote that Nadezhda "has had a tragi-comic condition made to her; if she does not marry immediately, she has to return to Ufa." On July 10, 1898, to solve the problem, they married. As newlyweds, they settled down to translate *The Theory and Practice of Trade Unionism* by Sidney and Beatrice Webb; their Russian version ran to a thousand pages. In the winter, they ice-skated on the frozen river. Vladimir was expert; with his hands in his pockets, he glided quickly away. Krupskaya tried valiantly and stumbled behind. The mother-in-law went once and fell flat on her back. But all three loved the whiteness of the Siberian winter, the clear, glowing quality of the air, the peaceful silence of the snowy woods. "It was like living," said Krupskaya, "in an enchanted kingdom."

Because his term ended before hers, Vladimir left his wife and her mother in Siberia and returned to St. Petersburg. Soon after, he drew up a petition from "the hereditary noble, Vladimir Ilyich Ulyanov" asking the authorities to permit him to return to Siberia to see his wife before going abroad. The petition was granted, Vladimir said goodbye and began a lonely life as a Russian revolutionary in the cities of Europe. His work as an underground organizer and a forceful writer had already brought him a significant reputation; this was enhanced when he became an editor and regular contributor to *Iskra* (*The Spark*), a revolutionary magazine published abroad for smuggling into Russia. It was at this point that Vladimir began to use the pen name

"Lenin." He wrote a pamphlet titled *What Is to Be Done?* which attracted wide attention, and drafted a program for the Social Democratic Party, as the exiled Russian Marxists had begun to call themselves. He no longer feared to attack the Tsar personally; "Nicholas the Bloody" and "Nicholas the Hangman" were favorite expressions.

When Krupskaya's term of exile was ended, she joined her husband in Munich. In 1902 the offices of *Iskra* were moved to London, and Lenin and Krupskaya followed, arriving in a dense fog. For Krupskaya particularly, the transition from a peaceful Siberian village to an immense city with its noise and dirt and clanging traffic was painful. They rented an unfurnished two-room apartment at 30 Holford Square kept by a Mrs. Yeo, and Lenin, under the name "Jacob Richter," applied for entrance to the Reading Room of the British Museum. In the mornings he worked, and in the afternoons he and Krupskaya took trips around London on the top of a double-decker bus. There was trouble with Mrs. Yeo, who protested that Krupskaya did not hang curtains and wore no wedding ring. Finally a Russian friend warned the landlady that her lodgers were legally married and that if she persisted in chattering, she would be sued for defamation of character.

By his implacable certainty and singleness of purpose, his overwhelming energy and self-sacrifice, Lenin rapidly became a dominant figure within the party. Once recognized as a leader, he was fiercely intolerant and unwilling even to discuss his views with others unless circumstances forced him to do so. On the rock of Lenin's intransigence, the tiny party of exiles began to splinter.

It was to end this quarreling that the Social Democratic Party called a unity conference to be held in Brussels in July 1903. With forty-three delegates in attendance, the conference opened in an old flour warehouse draped with red cloth but infested with rats and fleas. The Belgian police, who had harassed the Russians by searching their rooms and opening their baggage, suddenly gave the exiles twenty-four hours to leave the country. In a body, they boarded a boat and crossed the English Channel to London, arguing all the way.

Continuing their sessions in a socialist church in London, the delegates soon realized that their momentous "unity" conference was leading to a dangerous split between Plekhanov and Lenin. Plekhanov's speeches were lyrical and moving; Lenin's were simpler, cruder, more logical and more forceful. The divisive issue was the organizational structure of the party. Lenin wanted the party restricted to a small, tightly disciplined, professional elite. Plekhanov and others wanted to embrace all who were willing to join. On a vote, Lenin was narrowly victorious; thereafter his followers took the name of Bolsheviks (Majorityites) and the losers became the Mensheviks (Minorityites). Half fearful, half admiring, Plekhanov looked at Lenin and said, "Of this dough, Robespierres are made."

If Lenin was Robespierre, Alexander Kerensky was Russia's Danton. Himself struck by the coincidence of their background and upbringing, Kerensky once wrote: "Let no one say that Lenin is an expression of some kind of allegedly Asiatic 'elemental Russian force.' I was born under the same sky, I breathed the same air, I heard the same peasant songs and played in the same college playground. I saw the same limitless horizons from the same high bank of the Volga and I know in my blood and bones . . . that it is only by losing all touch with our native land, only by stamping out all native feeling for it, only so could one do what Lenin did in deliberately and cruelly mutilating Russia."

Fedor Kerensky, Alexander's father, was a gentle, scholarly man, destined originally to become a priest, who instead became a teacher. Early in his career, he married one of his pupils, an officer's daughter whose grandfather had been a serf. As director of the high school in Simbirsk, Fedor Kerensky was a leading member of local society. "From my earliest glimpses of consciousness I remember an enormous, splendid flat provided by the government," wrote Fedor's son, Alexander. "A long row of reception rooms; governesses for the elder sisters, nurseries, children's parties in other 'society' households." At school, standing in chapel in a white suit and pink Eton bow, Alexander was an important boy, the headmaster's son. "I see myself in my early childhood as a very loyal little subject. I felt Russia deeply . . . the traditional Russia with its tsars and Orthodox Church, and the upper layer of provincial officialdom." In the same town of Simbirsk, the parish priest was Alexander's uncle. Alexander himself dreamed of becoming a "church bell-ringer, to stand on a high steeple, above everybody, near the clouds, and thence to call men to the service of God with the heavy peals of a huge bell."

In 1889, when Alexander was eight, Fedor Kerensky was promoted to become Director of Education for the Province of Turkestan, and the family moved to Tashkent. There, one night, Alexander overheard his parents discussing a pamphlet circulating illegally in which Leo Tolstoy protested the alliance of the backward Russian autocracy and the French republic which Tolstoy admired. But "my youthful adoration of the Tsar was in no way impaired through hearing Tolstoy," said Alexander; ". . . when Alexander III died, I read the official obituaries . . . and I wept long and copiously. I fervently attended every mass and requiem held for the Tsar and assiduously collected small contributions in my class for a wreath to the Emperor's memory."

In 1899, Kerensky arrived in St. Petersburg to study at the university. The city, bursting with creative excitement in every field of the arts and intellect, was packed with students from every social class and every province of the empire. "I doubt whether higher education before the war was so cheap and so generally accessible anywhere in the world as it was in Russia. . . . The lecture fees were practically negligible, while all laboratory experiments and other practical work . . . were completely free . . . one could have dinner for from five to ten kopecks . . . the poorest among us often lived in very bad conditions, ran about from house to house giving lessons and did not dine every day; still we all lived and studied."

At first Kerensky, the loyal son of a government bureaucrat, had little interest in politics. But politics was a part of student life in St. Petersburg, and he became caught up in the waves of student agitation, mass meetings and strikes. Student opinion was split between the two leading Russian revolutionary parties, the Marxists and the Narodniki or People's Party. Kerensky instinctively favored the latter. "Simbirsk, the memories of my childhood . . . the whole tradition of Russian literature drew me strongly towards . . . the Narodniki movement. . . . The Marxist teaching, borrowed in its entirety from abroad, deeply impressed youthful minds by its austere completeness and its orderly logic. But it tallied very badly with the social structure of Russia. In contrast . . . the Narodniki teaching was indistinct . . . inconsistent. . . . But it was the product of national Russian thought, rooted in the native soil, flowed entirely within the channel of the Russian humanitarian ideals."

Swept along by his youthful enthusiasm, Kerensky one day found himself making a speech at a student gathering; the following day, he was summoned before the rector and deans and temporarily sent home. He returned, planning an academic career, hoping to take up post-graduate study in criminal law. Before he had graduated, however, this "highly respectable pastime" began to pale for him—it "even, perhaps, repelled me a little. One does not want to attend to private interests when one dreams of serving the nation, of fighting for freedom. I decided to be a political lawyer."

For the next six years, Kerensky would travel to every corner of Russia, defending political prisoners against prosecution by the state. But before he left St. Petersburg, in 1905, an extraordinary episode occurred:

"It was Easter and I was returning late at night, or rather in the morning, about four o'clock from the traditional midnight celebration. I cannot attempt to describe the enchanting spell of St. Petersburg in the spring, in the early hours before dawn—particularly along the Neva or the embankments. . . . Happily aglow, I was walking home . . . and was about to cross the bridge by the Winter Palace. Suddenly, by the Admiralty, just opposite the Palace, I stopped involuntarily. On an overhanging corner balcony stood the young Emperor, quite alone, deep in thought. A keen presentiment [struck me]: we should meet sometime, somehow our paths would cross."

CHAPTER EIGHT

The Kaiser's Advice

IN the early years of the reign, along with his mother, the tutor Pobedonostsev and his uncles, Nicholas was also taken in hand by his cousin Kaiser William II of Germany. From the first months, William peered over the Tsar's shoulder, tapped him on the elbow, flattered him, lectured him and dominated him. William was nine years older than Nicholas and had become Kaiser in 1888, six years before Nicholas became Tsar. He thus had the advantage of experience as well as age, and he used it vigorously. For ten years, 1894–1904, the Kaiser manipulated Russian foreign policy by influencing the youthful, susceptible Tsar. Eventually, an older and wiser Nicholas shook off this meddlesome influence. But the harm was done. Urged on by William, Russia had suffered a military catastrophe in Asia.

In character, the two Emperors were totally unlike. Nicholas was gentle, shy and painfully aware of his own limitations; the Kaiser was a braggart, a bully and a strutting exhibitionist. Nicholas hated the idea of becoming a sovereign; William all but wrenched the crown from the head of his dying father, Frederick III. As Tsar, Nicholas tried to live quietly with his wife, avoiding fuss. William delighted in parading about in high black boots, white cloak, a silver breastplate and an evil-looking spiked helmet.

William II's thin face, bleak gray eyes and light-colored curly hair were partially masked behind his proudest possession, his mustache. This was a wide, brushy business with remarkable upturned points, the creation of a skillful barber who appeared at the palace every morning with a can of wax. In part, this elegant bush helped to compensate for another physical distinction, one which William tried desperately to hide. His left arm was miniaturized, a misfortune believed to have been caused by the excessive zeal with which an obstetrical surgeon used forceps at William's birth. William arrived in the world with his arm pulled almost from its socket; thereafter the arm grew much too slowly. As much as possible, he kept this damaged limb out of sight, tucking it into especially designed pockets in his clothes. At meals, the Kaiser could not cut his meat without the aid of a dinner companion.

In the military atmosphere of the Prussian court in which he grew up, William's bad arm had a pronounced effect on his character. A Prussian prince had to ride and shoot. William drove himself to do both expertly and went on to become a swimmer, rower, tennis player as well. His good right arm became extraordinarily powerful, and its grip was as strong as iron. William increased the sensation of pain in those he greeted by turning the rings on his right hand inward, so that the jewels would bite deep into the unlucky flesh.

When he was nineteen and a student in Bonn, William fell in love with Princess Elizabeth of Hesse, the Empress Alexandra's older sister. William often visited in Darmstadt with the Hessian family of his mother's sister. Even as a guest, he was selfish and rude. First he demanded to ride, then he wanted to shoot or row or play tennis. Often he would throw down his racket in the middle of a game or suddenly climb off his horse and demand that everybody go with him to do something else. When he was tired, he ordered his cousins to sit quietly around him and listen while he read aloud from the Bible. Alix was only six when these visits occurred, and she was ignored. But Ella was a blossoming fourteen, and William always wanted her to play with him, to sit near him, to listen closely. Ella thought he was dreadful. William left Bonn, burning with frustration, and four months later he became engaged to another German princess, Augusta of Schleswig-Holstein. After Ella married Grand Duke Serge of Russia, the Kaiser refused to see her. Later he admitted that he had spent most of his time in Bonn writing love poetry to his beautiful cousin.

William's restless temperament, his vanities and delusions, his rapid plunges from hysterical excitement to black despair kept his ministers in a state of constant apprehension. "The Kaiser," said Bismarck, "is like a balloon. If you don't keep fast hold of the string, you never know where he'll be off to." William scribbled furiously on the margins of official documents: "Nonsense!" "Lies!" "Rascals!"

"Stale fish!" "Typical oriental procrastinating lies!" "False as a Frenchman usually is!" "England's fault, not ours!" He treated his dignitaries with an odd familiarity, often giving venerable admirals and generals a friendly smack on the backside. Visitors, official and otherwise, were treated to dazzling displays of verbosity, but they could never be sure how much to believe. "The Kaiser," explained a dismayed official of the German Foreign Ministry, "has the unfortunate habit of talking all the more rapidly and incautiously the more a matter interests him. Hence it happens that he generally has committed himself . . . before the responsible advisors or the experts have been able to submit their opinions." To witness the Kaiser laughing was an awesome experience. "If the Kaiser laughs, which he is sure to do a good many times," wrote one observer, "he will laugh with absolute abandonment, throwing his head back, opening his mouth to the fullest possible extent, shaking his whole body, and often stamping with one foot to show his excessive enjoyment of any joke."

William was convinced of his own infallibility and signed his documents "The All Highest." He hated parliaments. Once, at a colonial exhibition, he was shown the hut of an African king, with the skulls of the king's enemies impaled on poles. "If only I could see the Reichstag stuck up like that," blurted the Kaiser.

William's bad manners were as offensive to his relatives as to everyone else. He publicly accused his own mother, formerly Princess Victoria of England, of being pro-English rather than pro-German. Writing to *her* mother, Queen Victoria of England, the Princess said of her twenty-eight-year-old son, "You ask how Willy was when he was here. He was as rude, as disagreeable and as impertinent to me as possible." Tsar Alexander III snubbed William, whom he considered "a badly brought up, untrustworthy boy." When he spoke to the Kaiser, Alexander III always turned his back and talked over his shoulder. Empress Marie loathed William. She saw in him the royal *nouveau riche* whose empire had been made in part by trampling over her beloved Denmark and wrenching away the Danish provinces of Schleswig-Holstein. Marie's feeling was that of her sister Alexandra, who was married to King Edward VII. "And so my Georgie boy has become a real, live, filthy, blue-coated Pickelhaube German soldier. I never thought I would live to see the day," Queen Alexandra wrote to her son, later King George V, when George became an honorary colonel in one of the Kaiser's regiments. When it came Russia's turn to make the Kaiser an admiral in the Russian navy, Nicholas tried to tell Marie gently. "I think, no matter how disagreeable it may be, we are obliged to let him wear our naval uniform; particularly since he made me last year a Captain in his own navy. . . . *C'est à vomir!*" After another visit from the Kaiser, he wrote, "Thank God the German visit is over. . . . She [William's wife] tried to be charming and looked very ugly in rich clothes chosen without taste. The hats she wore in the evening were particularly impossible." The Empress Alexandra could barely be civil to William. She turned away when he made his heavy jokes, and when the Kaiser picked up her daughters in his arms, she winced. A mutual loathing of William was perhaps the point of closest agreement between the young Empress and her mother-in-law.

Nicholas himself was both repelled and attracted by the Kaiser's flamboyance. From the first, William managed to restore the old custom of former monarchs who kept personal attachés in each other's private retinues. This, the Kaiser pointed out, would enable Nicholas "to quickly communicate with me . . . without the lumbering and indiscreet apparatus of Chancelleries, Embassies, etc."

The famous "Willy-Nicky" correspondence began. Writing in English and addressing himself to his "Dearest Nicky" and signing himself "Your affectionate Willy," the Kaiser drenched the Tsar with flattery and suggestions. Delighted by Nicholas's "senseless dreams" address to the Tver Zemstvo, he hammered on the importance of maintaining autocracy, "the task which has been set us by the Lord of Lords." He advised that "the great bulk of the Russian people still place their faith in their . . . Tsar and worship his hallowed person," and predicted that "the people will . . . cheer you and fall on their knees and pray for you." When they met in person, William tapped Nicholas on the shoulder and said, "My advice to you is more speeches and more parades."

Using this private channel, William bent himself to undo the anti-German alliance between Russia and France. Nicholas had been Tsar less than a year when the Kaiser wrote to him: "It is not the friendship of France and Russia that makes me uneasy, but the danger to our principle of monarchism from the lifting up of the Republicans on a pedestal. . . . The Republicans are revolutionaries *de nature*. The French Republic has arisen from the source of the great revolution and propagates its ideas. The blood of their Majesties is still on that country. Think—has it since then ever been happy or quiet again? Has it not staggered from bloodshed to bloodshed and from war to war, till it soused Europe and Russia in streams of Blood? Nicky, take my word, the curse of God has stricken that people forever. We Christian kings have one holy duty imposed on us by Heaven: to uphold the principle of the Divine Right of Kings."

Russia's alliance with France withstood these assaults, but on another theme the Kaiser's exhortations had a striking success. William hated Orientals, and often raved about "the Yellow Peril." In 1900, bidding farewell to a shipload of German marines bound for China to help disperse the Boxer revolutionaries, the Kaiser shouted blood-curdling instructions: "You must know, my men, that you are about to meet a crafty, well-armed, cruel foe! Meet him and beat him. Give no quarter. Take no prisoners. Kill him when he falls into your hands. Even as a thousand years ago, The Huns under King Attila made such a name for themselves as still resounds in terror through legend and fable, so may the name of German resound through Chinese history a thousand years from now. . . ."

In writing to the Tsar, William elevated his prejudice to a loftier pedestal. Russia, he declared, had a "Holy Mission" in Asia: "Clearly, it is the great task of the future for Russia to cultivate the Asian continent and to defend Europe from the inroads of the Great Yellow Race. In this you will always find me on your side, ready to help you as best I can. You have well understood the call of Providence . . . in the Defense of the Cross and the old Christian European culture against the inroads of the Mongols and Buddhism. . . . I would let nobody try to interfere with you and attack from behind in Europe during the time you were fulfilling the great mission which Heaven has shaped for you."

William pursued the theme into allegorical art. He sent the Tsar a portrait showing himself in shining armor, gripping a huge crucifix in his raised right arm. At his feet crouched the figure of Nicholas, clothed in a long Byzantine gown. On the Tsar's face, as he gazed up at the Kaiser, was a look of humble admiration. In the background, on a blue sea, cruised a fleet of German and Russian battleships. In 1902, after watching a fleet of real Russian battleships steam through naval maneuvers, William signaled from his yacht to the Tsar aboard the *Standart*, "The Admiral of the Atlantic salutes the Admiral of the Pacific."

William's hatred of Orientals was genuine, but there was more to his game than simple prejudice. For years, Bismarck had urgently promoted Russian expansion in Asia as a means of diminishing Russian influence in Europe. "Russia has nothing to do in the West," said the crafty German Chancellor. "There she can only catch Nihilism and other diseases. Her mission is in Asia; there she represents civilization." By turning Russia away from Europe, Germany decreased the danger of war in the Balkans between Russia and Austria, and Germany herself was left a free hand with Russia's ally, France. In addition, wherever Russia moved in Asia, she was certain to get into trouble: either with Britain in India or with Japan in the Pacific. William II enthusiastically revived Bismarck's design. "We must try to tie Russia down in East Asia," he confided to one of his ministers, "so that she pays less attention to Europe and the Near East."

The Kaiser was not the only man filling Nicholas's head with expansionist dreams; many Russians were equally anxious to go adventuring in Asia. The temptations were strong. Russia's only Pacific port, Vladivostock, was imprisoned in ice three months a year. Southward, the decrepit Chinese Empire stretched like a rotting carcass along the Pacific. In 1895, to Russia's chagrin, the vigorous, newly Westernized island empire of Japan occupied several Chinese territories which Russia coveted, among them the great warm-water port and fortress of Port Arthur. Six days after Japan had swallowed Port Arthur, Russia intervened, declaring that Japan's new arrangements "constituted a perpetual menace to the peace of the Far East." Japan, unwilling to risk a war, was forced to disgorge Port Arthur. Three years later, Russia extracted a ninety-nine-year lease on the port from the helpless Chinese.

The occupation of Port Arthur was heady stuff in St. Petersburg. "Glad news . . . ," wrote Nicholas. "At last we shall have an ice-free port." A new spur of the Trans-Siberian was constructed directly across Manchuria, and when the railroad was finished, the Russian workmen and Russian railway guards remained behind. In 1900, during the Boxer Rebellion, Russia "temporarily" occupied Manchuria. Only one further prize remained on the entire North Pacific coast, the peninsula of Korea. Although Japan clearly regarded Korea as essential to her security, a group of Russian adventurers resolved to steal it. Their plan was to establish a private company, the Yalu Timber Company, and begin moving Russian soldiers into Korea disguised as workmen. If they ran into trouble, the Russian government could always disclaim responsibility. If they succeeded, the empire would acquire a new province and they themselves would have vast economic concessions within it. Witte, the Finance Minister, vigorously opposed this risky policy. But Nicholas, impressed by the leader of the adventurers, a former cavalry officer named Bezobrazov, approved the plan, whereupon Witte in 1903 resigned from the government. Predictably, Kaiser William chimed in, "It is evident to every unbiased mind that Korea must and will be Russian."

The Russian advance into Korea made war with Japan inevitable. The Japanese would have preferred an agreement: Russia to keep Manchuria, leaving Japan a free hand in Korea. But the Mikado's ministers could not stand by and watch the Russians swarm along the whole coast of Asia, planting the Tsar's double-headed eagle in every port and promontory facing their islands. In 1901, the greatest of Japanese statesmen, Marquis Ito, came to St. Petersburg to negotiate. He was treated shamefully. Ignored, finding no one to talk to, he put his requests in writing; replies were delayed for days on trifling pretexts. Eventually, he left Russia in despair. Through 1903, the permanent Japanese Minister in St. Petersburg, Kurino, issued urgent warnings and begged in vain for an audience with the Tsar. On February 3, 1904, bowing grimly, Kurino also left Russia.

In Russia, it was taken for granted that if war came, Russia would win easily. It would not be necessary for the Russian army to fire even a single shot, gibed the drawing-room generals. The Russians would annihilate the Japanese "monkeys" simply by throwing their caps at them. Vyacheslav Plehve, the Minister of Interior, wrestling with a growing plague of rebellious outbursts, openly welcomed the idea of "a small victorious war" to distract the people. "Russia has been made by bayonets, not diplomacy," he declared.

Nicholas, lulled into belief in Russia's overwhelming superiority, assumed that the decision was his, that war would not come unless Russia began it. Foreign ambassadors and ministers, gathered for the annual gala diplomatic reception on New Year's Day, heard the Tsar talk grandly of Russia's military power and beg that there would not be a test of his patience and love of peace. Nevertheless, during the month of January 1904, Nicholas's indecision kept the Kaiser in a state of constant alarm. He wrote, urging that Russia accept no settlement with Japan, but go to war. He was appalled when Nicholas replied, "I am still in good hopes about a calm and peaceful understanding." William showed this letter to his Chancellor, von Bülow, and complained bitterly about the Tsar's unmanly attitude. "Nicholas is doing himself a lot of harm by his flabby way of going on," said the

Kaiser. Such behavior, he added, was "compromising all great sovereigns."

Japan made a Russian decision unnecessary. On the evening of February 6, 1904, Nicholas returned from the theatre to be handed a telegram from Admiral Alexeiev, Russian Viceroy and Commander-in-Chief in the Far East:

"About midnight, Japanese destroyers made a sudden attack on the squadron anchored in the outer harbor of Port Arthur. The battleships *Tsarevich*, *Retvizan* and the cruiser *Pallada* were torpedoed. The importance of the damage is being ascertained." Stunned, Nicholas copied the text of the telegram into his diary and added, "This without a declaration of war. May God come to our aid."

The next morning, huge, patriotic crowds filled the streets of St. Petersburg. Students carrying banners marched to the Winter Palace and stood before it singing hymns. Nicholas went to the window and saluted. Amid the rejoicing, he was depressed. He had flirted with war and tried to bluff his enemies, but the idea of bloodshed revolted him. The people now looked forward to a quick Russian victory; Nicholas knew better. As confidential reports of the damage at Port Arthur continued to arrive, Nicholas set down his "sharp grief for the fleet and for the opinion that people will have of Russia."

The disaster that followed was far greater than even Nicholas had feared. In scarcely a single generation, Japan had leaped from feudalism to modern industrial and military power. Military instructors from France and naval instructors from England had helped create an efficient army with skilled, imaginative commanders. In the two years since Ito returned, humiliated, from St. Petersburg, Japan's generals and admirals had perfected their plans for war against Russia. The moment further negotiations seemed futile, they struck.

From the beginning, the match was unequal. Although the Japanese army consisted of 600,000 men and the Russian army numbered almost three million, Japan threw 150,000 men into battle at once on the Asian mainland. There they faced only 80,000 regular Russian soldiers, along with 23,000 garrison troops and 30,000 railway guards. Japanese supply lines stretched back to the homeland over only a few hundred miles of water, and losses could be quickly replaced. The Russians had to haul guns, munitions, food and reinforcements four thousand miles over the single track of the Trans-Siberian Railroad. Even the railroad was not complete; around the mountainous southern end of Lake Baikal, a gap of a hundred miles yawned in the track.

In summer, the gap was bridged by lake ferries; in the winter, every soldier and shell had to be moved across the ice in horse-drawn sledges.

The Russian Far Eastern Fleet and the Imperial Japanese Navy were more equal in size; the Russians actually had more battleships and cruisers, the Japanese more destroyers and torpedo boats. But with their first surprise attack, the Japanese seized the initiative and gained command of the sea. Russian ships which survived the war's first blow were hemmed in by Japanese minefields and harassed at their moorings by further torpedo attacks. When Russia's most distinguished admiral, Makarov, sortied from the harbor of Port Arthur on April 13, his flagship, the battleship *Petropavlovsk*, hit a mine and sank with a loss of seven hundred men, Makarov included. "This morning came news of inexpressible sadness . . . ," Nicholas wrote of the disaster. "All day long I could think of nothing but this terrible blow. . . . May the will of God be done in all things, but we poor mortals must beg mercy of the Lord."

With the sea secured, Japanese expeditionary forces were free to land where they chose along the mainland coast. One army came ashore in Korea, overwhelmed five Siberian regiments, crossed the Yalu River and marched north into Manchuria. Another Japanese force landed at the head of the Yellow Sea and laid siege to Port Arthur with monster eleven-inch siege cannons. Through the summer and fall of 1904, the Japanese infantry stormed one fortified height around Port Arthur after another; by January 1905, when Port Arthur finally surrendered, it had cost Japan 57,780 men and Russia 28,200.

From St. Petersburg, Nicholas watched with dismay. His first instinct had been to go to the front and place himself at the head of his beleaguered troops. Once again, his uncles overruled his inclination. To his mother the Tsar wrote: "My conscience is often very troubled by my staying here instead of sharing the dangers and privations of the army. I asked Uncle Alexis yesterday what he thought about it: he thinks my presence with the army in this war is not necessary—still, to stay behind in times like these is very upsetting to me."

Instead, Nicholas toured military encampments, reviewing troops and passing out images of St. Seraphim to soldiers about to entrain for the Far East. The Empress canceled all social activities and turned the huge ballrooms of the Winter Palace into workrooms where hundreds of women of all classes sat at tables, making clothing and bandages. Every day Alexandra visited these rooms and often sat down herself to sew a dressing or a hospital shirt.

As the grim prospect of a Russian defeat seemed ever more likely, Nicholas, urged on by William, ordered the Russian Baltic Fleet to travel around the world to restore Russian naval supremacy in the Pacific. Admiral Rozhdestvensky, the fleet commander, viewed the project without much hope, but once the Tsar had commanded, he placed himself on his bridge and ordered his ships made ready for sea. In October 1904, Nicholas took the final salute from the deck of the *Standart*. As the fleet of gray battleships and cruisers slowly left its anchorage and steamed out into the Baltic, he wrote, "Bless its voyage, Lord. Permit that it arrive safe and sound at its destination, that it succeed in its terrible mission for the safety and happiness of Russia."

Unfortunately, long before he got anywhere near Japan, Admiral Rozhdestvensky almost involved Russia in a war with England. The Admiral had been much impressed by Japan's surprise torpedo attack on the fleet at Port Arthur. Assuming that such wily tactics would have a sequel, he suspected that Japanese ships flying false colors might slip through neutral European waters to deliver another frightful blow to the Russian navy. No man to be tricked, the Admiral ordered extra lookouts posted from the moment his ships left home port. Steaming at night through the North Sea in this trigger-happy state, Russian captains suddenly found themselves surrounded by a flotilla of small boats. Without asking questions, Russian guns sent shells crashing into the frail hulls of British fishing boats in the waters of Dogger Bank. After the first salvos, the Russians realized their mistake. Such was the Admiral's fear, however, that, rather than stopping to pick up survivors, he steamed off into the night.

Only one boat had been sunk and two men killed, but Britain was outraged. Nicholas, already irritated by Britain's diplomatic support of Japan, was in no mood to apologize. "The English are very angry and near the boiling point," he wrote to Marie. "They are even said to be getting their fleet ready for action. Yesterday I sent a telegram to Uncle Bertie, expressing my regret, but I did not apologize. . . . I do not think the English will have the cheek to go further than to indulge in threats."

The Russian Ambassador in London, Count Benckendorff, more accurately assessed the extent of Britain's anger and quickly recommended that both parties submit the matter to the International Court at The Hague. Nicholas reluctantly agreed, and eventually Russia paid £65,000 in damages.

Leaving this nasty crisis in his wake, Admiral Rozhdestvensky steamed into the Atlantic, bound for the Cape of Good Hope, the Indian Ocean and the Pacific. He stopped and lay at anchor for three months at the French island of Madagascar while Russian diplomatic agents scoured the world's shipyards seeking to buy extra battleships to reinforce the fleet. The Kaiser ordered German merchant vessels to fuel the Russian squadron. At secluded anchorages in Madagascar and Camranh Bay, Indochina, German seamen transferred hundreds of tons of coal into the bunkers of Admiral Rozhdestvensky's weatherbeaten ships.

At two o'clock in the afternoon on May 27, 1905, the Russian fleet, led by eight battleships steaming in columns, appeared in the Strait of Tsushima between Japan and Korea. Admiral Togo, the Japanese commander, ranged his ships seven thousand yards across the head of the Russian columns, bringing his guns to bear first on one Russian ship, then another. As this blizzard of Japanese shells ripped though them, Russian warships exploded, capsized or simply stopped and began to drift. Within forty-five minutes it was over. Togo flashed his torpedo boats to attack and finish the cripples. All eight Russian battleships were lost, along with seven of Rozhdestvensky's twelve cruisers and six of his nine destroyers.

Tsushima, the greatest sea battle since Trafalgar, had a powerful impact on naval thinking everywhere. It confronted Britain, whose whole existence depended on the Royal Navy, with the appalling prospect of losing a war in one afternoon in a general fleet engagement. The Kaiser, who cherished his High Seas Fleet, became equally frightened. As a result, during the four years of the First World War the huge British and German navies collided only once, at Jutland. In the United States, Tsushima convinced President Theodore Roosevelt that no nation could afford to divide its battle fleet as the Russians had done. Roosevelt immediately began pressing ahead with his plan to build a canal through Panama to link the two oceans that washed American shores.

The Tsar was traveling aboard the Imperial train when the news of the disaster reached him. He sent for the Minister of War, General Sakharov, who remained alone with him for a lengthy discussion. Returning to the lounge car where the staff was waiting to learn Nicholas's reaction, Sakharov declared, "His Majesty showed that he thoroughly recognized the problems ahead of us and he sketched a very sensible plan of action. His composure is admirable." In his diary that night, Nicholas wrote, "Definite confirmation of the terrible news concerning the almost complete destruction of our squadron."

Recognizing that Russia no longer had a chance of winning the war, Nicholas sent for Sergius Witte and dispatched him to America to make the best of a peace conference which Roosevelt had offered to mediate. Although the war was ending as he had predicted, Witte accepted the assignment grudgingly. "When a sewer has to be cleaned, they send for Witte," he grumbled. "But as soon as work of a cleaner and nicer kind appears, plenty of other candidates spring up."

Crossing the Atlantic on the German liner *Wilhelm der Grosse* accompanied by a swarm of European journalists, Witte struck a pose as the "representative of the greatest empire on earth, undismayed by the fact that that mighty empire had become temporarily involved in a slight difficulty." Arriving in Portsmouth, New Hampshire, the scene of the peace conference, to find Americans filled with admiration for the "plucky little Japs," Witte set out to reverse this image. "I may say that I succeeded in swerving American public opinion over to us," he noted afterward. "I gradually won the press over to my side. . . . In this regard, the Japanese plenipotentiary Komura committed a grave blunder. . . . He rather avoided the press. . . . I took advantage of my adversary's tactlessness to stir up the press against him and his cause. . . . My personal behavior may also partly account for the transformation of American public opinion. I took care to treat all the Americans with whom I came in contact with the utmost simplicity of manner. When traveling, whether on special trains, government motorcars or steamers, I thanked everyone, talked with the engineers and shook hands with them—in a word, I treated everybody, of whatever social position, as an equal. This behavior was a heavy strain on me as all acting is to the unaccustomed, but it surely was worth the trouble."

Maneuvered by Witte into the role of villains, the Japanese envoys had difficulty in pressing all of their demands. Finally Nicholas—knowing that Japan was financially unable to continue the war—told his Foreign Minister: "Send Witte my order to end the parley tomorrow in any event. I prefer to continue the war, rather than to wait for gracious concessions on the part of Japan." Komura, who had come as victor, accepted a compromise.

Lunching after the conference with President Theodore Roosevelt at Sagamore Hill in Oyster Bay, Long Island, Witte described the meal as "for a European, almost indigestible. There was no tablecloth and ice water instead of wine. . . . Americans have no culinary taste and . . . they can eat almost anything that comes their way." He was "struck by . . . [Roosevelt's] ignorance of international politics. . . . I heard the most naïve judgments." Nor did Roosevelt care much for Witte. "I cannot say that I liked him," said the President, "for I thought his bragging and bluster not only foolish, but shockingly vulgar when compared with the gentlemanly restraint of the Japanese. Moreover, he struck me as a very selfish man, totally without ideals."

Returning to Russia, Witte was pleased with himself. "I acquitted myself with complete success," he wrote, "so that in the end the Emperor Nicholas was morally compelled to reward me in an altogether exceptional manner by bestowing upon me the rank of count. This he did in spite of his and especially Her Majesty's personal dislike for me, and also in spite of all the base intrigues conducted against me by a host of bureaucrats and courtiers whose vileness was only equalled by their stupidity."

In fact, Witte had handled the negotiations brilliantly; "no diplomat by profession could have done it," said Alexander Izvolsky, who was soon to become Russia's Foreign Minister. Nicholas received the returning hero on his yacht in September 1905. "Witte came to see us," wrote the Tsar to his mother. "He was very charming and interesting. After a long talk, I told him of his new honor. I am creating him a Count. He went quite stiff with emotion and then tried three times to kiss my hand!"

Tsushima abruptly ended Russia's "Holy Mission" in Asia. Beaten and humiliated by the Japanese "monkeys," the Russian giant staggered back toward Europe. In Berlin, as he watched events unfold, the Kaiser was not displeased. With a sullen, defeated army, no navy and a disillusioned, embittered people, the Tsar was no longer a neighbor to fear. William assumed that he still possessed Nicholas's friendship. He soothed the Tsar, reminding him that even Frederick the Great and Napoleon had suffered defeats. He strutted in the loyalty he had shown to Russia by "guarding" Russia's frontier in Europe—presumably from his own ally, Austria. Now, stepping smoothly over the ruins of the Far Eastern adventure he had done so much to promote, the Kaiser reverted to his original purpose: breaking the Russian alliance with France by seducing Nicholas into a new alliance of autocrats between Russia and Germany.

This last spectacular attempt by the Kaiser to manipulate the Tsar was the episode at Björkö on the coast of Finland in July 1905. It had its immediate origins in the international furor arising from the incident at Dogger Bank. The British press, loudly advocating that the Royal Navy prevent German steamers from coaling the Russian warships, had driven the Kaiser to frenzy. Nicholas replied to a letter from William by saying, "I agree fully with your complaints about England's behavior . . . it is certainly high time to put a stop to this. The only way, as you say, would be that Germany, Russia and France should at once unite to abolish Anglo-Japanese arrogance and insolence. Would you like to lay down and frame the outlines of such a treaty? As soon as it is accepted by us, France is bound to join as an ally."

William was overjoyed and feverishly began to draw up the treaty. The following summer, the Kaiser privately telegraphed the Tsar, inviting him to come as a "simple tourist" to a rendezvous at sea. Nicholas agreed and left Peterhof one afternoon without taking any of his ministers. The two Imperial yachts, *Hohenzollern* and *Standart*, anchored that night in the remote Finnish fjord and the two Emperors had dinner together. The next morning William reached into his pocket and "by chance" found the draft of a treaty of alliance between Russia and Germany. Among its provisions was an agreement that France was to be told only after Russia and Germany had signed and then invited to join if she wished. Nicholas read it and, according to William, said, "That is quite excellent. I agree."

"Should you like to sign it," said the Kaiser casually, "it would be a very nice souvenir of our interview."

Nicholas signed and William was jubilant. With tears of joy, he told Nicholas that he was sure that all of their mutual ancestors were looking down on them from heaven in ecstatic approval.

Upon returning to their respective capitals, both Emperors received unpleasant shocks. Von Bülow, the German Chancellor, criticized the treaty as useless to Germany and threatened to resign. The deflated Kaiser wrote his Chancellor a hysterical letter: "The morning after the arrival of your letter of resignation would no longer find your Emperor alive. Think of my poor wife and children." In St. Petersburg, Lamsdorf, the Russian Foreign Minister, was aghast; he could not believe his eyes and ears. The French alliance, he pointed out to Nicholas, was the cornerstone of Russian foreign policy; it could not be lightly thrown aside. France, said Lamsdorf, would never join an alliance with Germany, and Russia could not join such an alliance without first consulting France.

Eventually William was informed that, as written, the treaty could not be honored. The Kaiser responded with an impassioned plea to the Tsar to reconsider: "Your Ally notoriously left you in the lurch during the whole war, whereas Germany helped you in every way. . . . We joined hands and signed before God who heard our vows. What is signed is signed! God is our testator!" But the Björkö treaty was never invoked, and the private Willy-Nicky correspondence soon dwindled away. Thereafter, the Kaiser's influence over the Tsar also faded rapidly. But Nicholas's eyes were opened late. By 1905, he had lost a war and his country was rushing full tilt into revolution.

CHAPTER NINE

1905

THE "small victorious war" so ardently desired by Plehve, the Minister of Interior, was over, but Plehve did not live to see it. Vyacheslav Plehve was a professional policeman: his most spectacular piece of work had been the rounding up of everyone involved in the plot which killed Alexander II. Appointed Minister of Interior in 1902 after his predecessor had been killed by a terrorist, Plehve was described by a colleague as "a splendid man for little things, a stupid man for affairs of state." As Minister, he permitted no political assemblies of any kind. Students were not allowed to walk together on the streets of Moscow or St. Petersburg. It was impossible to give a party for more than a few people without first getting written permission from the police.

Russia's five million Jews were a special object of Plehve's hatred.* In a bitter cycle of repression and retaliation, Russian Jews were

* Anti-Semitism, an endemic disease in Russia, stemmed from the oldest traditions of the Orthodox Church. "To the devoutly . . . Orthodox Russians," explains a Jewish historian, " . . . the Jew was an infidel, the poisoner of the true faith, the killer of Christ." Every tsar supported this faith. Peter the Great, refusing to admit Jewish merchants to Russia, declared, "It is my endeavor to eradicate evil, not to multiply it." Catherine the Great endorsed Peter's decision, saying, "From the enemies of Christ, I desire neither gain nor profit." It was Catherine who, upon absorbing heavily Jewish regions of eastern Poland into her empire, established the Jewish Pale of Settlement, an area in Poland and the Ukraine to which all Russian Jews supposedly were restricted. The restrictions were porous, but the life of a Jew in nineteenth-century Russia remained subject to harassment and persecution. That this antagonism was religious rather than racial was repeatedly illustrated by cases of Jews who gave up their faith, accepted Orthodoxy and moved freely into the general structure of Russian society.

driven in numbers into the ranks of revolutionary terrorism. Under Plehve, local police were encouraged to turn a blind eye toward anti-Semites. On Easter Day, Plehve's policy led to the most celebrated pogrom of Nicholas's reign: a mob running wild in the town of Kishenev in Bessarabia murdered forty-five Jews and destroyed six hundred houses; the police did not trouble to intervene until the end of the second day. The pogrom was condemned by the government, the governor of the province was dismissed and the rioters tried and punished, but Plehve remained in power. Witte bluntly told the Interior Minister that his policies were making his own assassination inevitable. In July 1904, Plehve was blown to pieces by an assassin's bomb.

Plehve's death did not destroy his most inventive project, a workers' movement created and secretly guided by the police. The movement was led by a youthful St. Petersburg priest, Father George Gapon, who hoped by his efforts to immunize the workers against revolutionary viruses and strengthen their monarchist feelings. Economic grievances were to be channeled away from the government in the general direction of the employers. The employers, understandably touchy, were persuaded in turn that it was better to have an organization watched and controlled by the police than to leave the workers to the dangerous blandishments of clandestine socialist propagandists.

Gapon was not an ordinary hack police agent. His interest in the people was genuine, and in the working-class districts of St. Petersburg where he had worked and preached for several years, he was a popular figure. He sincerely believed that the purpose of his Assembly of Russian Workingmen was to strive "in a noble manner under the leadership of educated, genuinely Russian people and clergymen toward a philosophy of life and the status of the working man in a sound Christian spirit." By some, Gapon's police connections were suspected, but the mass of workers, happy enough to have any machinery which enabled them to meet and protest, looked to him for leadership.

Early in January 1905, the humiliating news of Port Arthur's surrender sent a wave of protest against mismanagement of the war sweeping across the country. In St. Petersburg, a minor strike at the huge Putilov steel works suddenly spread until thousands of disillusioned, restless workers were out on strike.* Swept along by this surge of feeling, Gapon had a choice: he could lead or be left behind. Rejecting his role as agent of the police, he chose to lead. For a week he went from meeting hall to meeting hall, giving dozens of speeches, whipping up impassioned support and, day by day, enlarging his list of demands. Before the end of the week, carried away by his sense of mission, he was rallying the workers with an extravagant theatrical vision: He personally would lead a mass march to the Winter Palace, where he would hand to Nicholas a petition on behalf of the Russian people. Gapon visualized the scene taking place on a balcony above the vast sea of Russian faces, where the *Batiushka-Tsar*, acting out the Russian fairy tale, would deliver his people from their evil oppressors, named in the petition as the "despotic and irresponsible government" and the "capitalistic exploiters, crooks and robbers of the Russian people." Along with deliverance, the petition also demanded, specifically, a constituent assembly, universal suffrage, universal education, separation of church and state, amnesty for all political prisoners, an income tax, a minimum wage and an eight-hour day.

Gapon did not communicate the extent of his intentions to any responsible government official; had he done so, they probably would not have listened. Prince Sviatopolk-Mirsky, the newly appointed liberal Minister of Interior, was concerned for most of the week about the Tsar's ceremonial visit to St. Petersburg on Thursday, January 19, for the traditional religious service of the Blessing of the Waters. In balance, that day was a success: Nicholas was received with cheers as he drove past dense crowds in the streets. While he stood on the Neva bank, a cannon employed in the ceremonial salute fired a live charge which landed near the Tsar and wounded a policeman, but investigation proved that the shot was an accident, not part of a plot.

Only on Saturday, January 21, when Gapon informed the government that the march would take place the following day and asked

* The era was one of bitter labor strife in all industrial nations. In the United States, for example, during the Pullman strike of 1894, Judge William Howard Taft, a future President, wrote to his wife, "It will be necessary for the military to kill some of the mob before the trouble can be stayed. They have killed only six as yet. This is hardly enough to make an impression." In the end, 30 were killed, 60 wounded and 700 arrested. Six years later, Theodore Roosevelt, campaigning for Vice President, said privately, "The sentiment now animating a large proportion of our people can only be suppressed . . . by taking ten or a dozen of their leaders out, standing them against the wall and shooting them dead. I believe it will come to that. These leaders are planning a social revolution and the subversion of the American Republic."

that the Tsar be present to receive his petition, did Mirsky suddenly become alarmed. The ministers met hurriedly to consider the problem. There was never any thought that the Tsar, who was at Tsarskoe Selo and had been told of neither the march nor the petition, would actually be asked to meet Gapon. The suggestion that some other member of the Imperial family receive the petition was rejected. Finally, informed by the Prefect of Police that he lacked the men to pluck Gapon from among his followers and place him under arrest, Mirsky and his colleagues could think of nothing to do except bring additional troops into the city and hope that matters would not get out of hand.

On Saturday night, Nicholas learned for the first time from Mirsky what the morrow might bring. "Troops have been brought from the outskirts to reinforce the garrison," he wrote in his diary. "Up to now the workers have been calm. Their number is estimated at 120,000. At the head of their union is a kind of socialist priest named Gapon. Mirsky came this evening to present his report on the measures taken."

Sunday morning, January 22, 1905, with an icy wind driving flurries of snow, Father Gapon began his march. In the workers' quarters, processions formed to converge on the center of the city. Locking arms, they streamed peacefully through the streets in rivers of cheerful, expectant humanity. Some carried crosses, icons and religious banners, others carried national flags and portraits of the Tsar. As they walked, they sang religious hymns and the Imperial anthem, "God Save the Tsar." At two p.m. all of the converging processions were scheduled to arrive at the Winter Palace.

There was no single confrontation with the troops. Throughout the city, at bridges and on strategic boulevards, the marchers found their way blocked by lines of infantry, backed by Cossacks and Hussars. Uncertain what this meant, still not expecting violence, anxious not to be late to see the Tsar, the processions moved forward. In a moment of horror, the soldiers opened fire. Bullets smacked into the bodies of men, women and children. Crimson blotches stained the hard-packed snow. The official number of victims was ninety-two dead and several hundred wounded; the actual number was probably several times higher. Gapon vanished and the other leaders of the march were seized. Expelled from the capital, they circulated through the empire, exaggerating the casualties into thousands.

The day, which became known as "Bloody Sunday," was a turning point in Russian history. It shattered the ancient, legendary belief that tsar and the people were one. As bullets riddled their icons, their banners and their portraits of Nicholas, the people shrieked, "The Tsar will not help us!" It would not be long before they added the grim corollary, "And so we have no Tsar." Abroad, the clumsy action seemed premeditated cruelty, and Ramsay MacDonald, a future Labor Prime Minister of Britain, attacked the Tsar as a "blood-stained creature" and a "common murderer."

Father Gapon, from his place of hiding, issued a public letter, bitterly denouncing "Nicholas Romanov, formerly Tsar and at present soul-murderer of the Russian empire. The innocent blood of workers, their wives and children lies forever between you and the Russian people. . . . May all the blood which must be spilled fall upon you, you Hangman!" Gapon became a full-fledged revolutionary: "I call upon all the socialist parties of Russia to come to an immediate agreement among themselves and begin an armed uprising against Tsarism." But Gapon's reputation was cloudy, and the leaders of the Social Revolutionary Party were convinced that he still had ties with the police. They sentenced him to death and his body was found hanging in an abandoned cottage in Finland in April 1906.

At Tsarskoe Selo, Nicholas was stunned when he heard what had happened. "A painful day," he wrote that night. "Serious disorders took place in Petersburg when the workers tried to come to the Winter Palace. The troops have been forced to fire in several parts of the city and there are many killed and wounded. Lord, how painful and sad this is!" The ministers met in great alarm and Witte immediately suggested that the Tsar publicly dissociate himself from the massacre by declaring that the troops had fired without orders. Nicholas refused to cast this unfair aspersion upon the army and instead decided to receive a delegation of thirty-four hand-picked workers at Tsarskoe Selo. The workers arrived at the palace and were given tea while Nicholas lectured them, as father to sons, on the need to support the army in the field and to reject the wicked advice of treacherous revolutionaries. The workers returned to St. Petersburg, where they were ignored, laughed at or beaten up.

The Empress was in a state of despair. Five days after "Bloody Sunday," she wrote to her sister Princess Victoria of Battenberg:

"You understand the crisis we are going through! It is a time full of trials indeed. My poor Nicky's cross is a heavy one to bear, all the more as he has nobody on whom he can thoroughly rely and who can be a real help to him. He has had so many bitter disappointments, but through it all he remains brave and full of faith in God's mercy. He tries so hard, works with such perseverance, but the lack of what I call 'real' men is great. . . . The bad are always close at hand, the others through false humility keep in the background. We shall try to see more people, but it is difficult. On my knees I pray to God to give me wisdom to help him in his heavy task. . . .

"Don't believe all the horrors the foreign papers say. They make one's hair stand on end—foul exaggeration. Yes, the troops, alas, were obliged to fire. Repeatedly the crowd was told to retreat and that Nicky was not in town (as we are living here this winter) and that one would be forced to shoot, but they would not heed and so blood was shed. On the whole, 92 killed and between 200–300 wounded. It is a ghastly thing, but had one not done it the crowd would have grown colossal and 1,000 would have been crushed. All over the country, of course, it is spreading. The Petition had only two questions concerning the workmen and all the rest was atrocious: separation of the Church from the Government, etc. etc. Had a small deputation brought, calmly, a real petition for the workmen's good, all would have been otherwise. Many of the workmen were in despair, when they heard later what the petition contained and begged to work again under the protection of the troops.

"Petersburg is a rotten town, not one atom Russian. The Russian people are deeply and truly devoted to their Sovereign and the revolutionaries use his name for provoking them against landlords, etc. but I don't know how. How I wish I were clever and could be of real use. I love my new country. It's so young, powerful and has so much good in it, only utterly unbalanced and childlike. Poor Nicky, he has a bitter, hard life to lead. Had his father seen more men, drawn them around him, we should have had lots to fill the necessary posts; now only old men or quite young ones, nobody to turn to. The uncles no good, Mischa [Grand Duke Michael, the Tsar's younger brother] a darling child still. . . ."

But "Bloody Sunday" was only the beginning of a year of terror. Three weeks later, in February, Grand Duke Serge, the Tsar's uncle and Ella's husband, was assassinated in Moscow. The Grand Duke, who took a harsh pride in knowing how bitterly he was hated by revolutionaries, had just said goodbye to his wife in their Kremlin apartment and was driving through one of the gates when a bomb exploded on top of him. Hearing the shuddering blast, Ella cried, "It's

Serge," and rushed to him. What she found was not her husband, but a hundred unrecognizable pieces of flesh, bleeding into the snow. Courageously the Grand Duchess went to her husband's dying coachman and eased his last moments by telling him that the Grand Duke had survived the explosion. Later she visited the assassin, a Social Revolutionary named Kaliayev, in prison and offered to plead for his life if he would beg the Tsar for pardon. Kaliayev refused, saying that his death would aid his cause, the overthrow of the autocracy.

The murder of her husband changed Ella's life. The gay, irrepressible girl who had guided her small, motherless sister Alix; who had fended off the attentions of William II; who had skated and danced with the Tsarevich Nicholas—this woman disappeared. All of the gentle, saintly qualities suggested by her quiet acceptance of her husband's character now came strongly forward. A few years later, the Grand Duchess built an abbey, the Convent of Mary and Martha, in Moscow and herself became the abbess. In a last gesture of worldly flair, she had the robes of her order designed by the fashionable religious painter Michael Nesterov. He designed a long, hooded robe of fine, pearl-gray wool and a white veil, which she wore for the rest of her life.

As the months rolled by, violence spread to every corner of Russia. "It makes me sick to read the news," said Nicholas, "strikes in schools and factories, murdered policemen, Cossacks, riots. But the ministers instead of acting with quick decision, only assemble in council like a lot of frightened hens and cackle about providing united ministerial action." The slaughter of Rozhdestvensky's fleet in Tsushima raised a storm of mutiny in the ships remaining in the Baltic and Black Sea fleets. Sailors of the battleship *Potemkin*, angered when they were served portions of bad meat, threw their officers overboard, raised the red flag and steamed their ship along the Black Sea coast, bombarding towns, until the need for fuel forced them to intern at the Rumanian port of Constanza.

By mid-October 1905, all Russia was paralyzed by a general strike. From Warsaw to the Urals, trains stopped running, factories closed down, ships lay idle alongside piers. In St. Petersburg, food was no longer delivered, schools and hospitals closed, newspapers disappeared, even the electric lights flickered out. By day, crowds marched through the streets cheering orators, and red flags flew from the rooftops. At night, the streets were empty and dark. In the countryside, peasants raided estates, crippled and stole cattle, and the flames of burning manor houses glowed through the night.

Overnight, a new workers' organization bloomed. Consisting of elected delegates, one for each thousand workers, it called itself a soviet, or council. Like the strike itself, it came from nowhere, but grew rapidly in numbers and power. Within four days, a leader emerged in Leon Trotsky, a fiery orator and a member of the Menshevik branch of the Marxist Social Democratic Party. When the Soviet threatened to wreck every factory which did not close down, companies of soldiers were brought into the city. Sentries paced in front of all the public buildings, and squadrons of Cossacks clattered up and down the boulevards. The revolution was at hand; it needed only a spark.

In one of his most famous letters, written to his mother at the height of the crisis, Nicholas described what happened next:

"So the ominous quiet days began. Complete order in the streets, but at the same time everybody knew that something was going to happen. The troops were waiting for the signal but the other side would not begin. One had the same feeling as before a thunder storm in summer. Everybody was on edge and extremely nervous. . . . Through all those horrible days I constantly met with Witte. We very often met in the early morning to part only in the evening when night fell. There were only two ways open: to find an energetic soldier to crush the rebellion by sheer force. There would be time to breathe then but as likely as not, one would have to use force again in a few months, and that would mean rivers of blood and in the end we should be where we started.

"The other way out would be to give to the people their civil rights, freedom of speech and press, also to have all laws confirmed by a state Duma—that of course would be a constitution. Witte defends this energetically. He says that, while it is not without risk, it is the only way out at the present moment. Almost everybody I had an opportunity of consulting is of the same opinion. Witte put it to me quite clearly that he would accept the Presidency of the Council of Ministers only on condition that his program was agreed to and his action not interfered with. He . . . drew up the Manifesto. We discussed it for two days and in the end, invoking God's help, I signed it. . . . My only consolation is that such is the will of God and this grave decision will lead my dear Russia out of the intolerable chaos she has been in for nearly a year."

Sergius Witte, who gave Russia its first constitution and its first parliament, believed in neither constitutions nor parliaments. "I have a constitution in my head, but as to my heart—" Witte spat on the floor. Witte was a huge, burly man with massive shoulders, great height and a head the size of a pumpkin. Inside this head Witte carried the ablest administrative brain in Russia. It had guided him from humble beginnings in the Georgian city of Tiflis, where he was born in 1849, to the role of leading minister of two tsars.

Witte's mother was Russian, but on his father's side his ancestry was Dutch. His father, a native of Russia's Baltic provinces, was a cultured man who lost his fortune in a Georgian mining scheme, leaving Witte to battle upward on wits and ego alone. In both respects, Witte was handsomely equipped. "At the University [of Odessa]," he wrote, "I worked day and night and achieved great proficiency in all my studies. I was so thoroughly familiar with the subjects that I passed all my examinations with flying colors without making any special preparations for them. My final academic thesis was entitled, 'On Infinitesimal Quantities.' The work was rather original in conception and distinguished by a philosophical breadth of view."

Hoping to become a professor of pure mathematics, Witte was compelled instead to go to work for the Southwestern District Railroad. During Russia's 1877 war with Turkey, he served as a traffic supervisor in charge of transporting troops and supplies. "I acquitted myself with success of my difficult task," he declared. "I owed my success to energetic and well thought-out action." In February 1892, he was promoted to Minister of Communications (including railroads). "It will not be an exaggeration," he noted, "to say that the vast enterprise of constructing the great Siberian railway was carried out by my efforts, supported, of course, first by Emperor Alexander III and then by Emperor Nicholas II." In August 1892, Witte was transferred to the key post of Minister of Finance. "As Minister of Finance, I was also in charge of our commerce and industry. As such, I increased our industry threefold. This again is held against me. Fools!" Even in his private life, Witte took care to ensure that he was not outsmarted. He married twice; both wives had previously been divorced from other men. Of his first wife he said, "With my assistance she obtained her divorce and followed me to St. Petersburg. Out of consideration for my wife I adopted the girl who was her only child, with the understanding, however, that should our marriage prove childless, she would not succeed me as heiress."

Along with the throne, Nicholas inherited Witte from his father. Both the new Tsar and the veteran Minister hoped for the best. "I knew him [Nicholas] to be inexperienced in the extreme but rather intelligent and . . . he had always impressed me as a kindly and well-bred youth," Witte wrote. "As a matter of fact, I had rarely come across a better-mannered young man than Nicholas II." The Empress Witte liked less, although he was forced to admit that "Alexandra does not lack physical charms." As Minister of Finance, he struggled successfully to put Russia on the gold standard. He brought in armies of foreign traders and industrialists, tempting them with tax exemptions, subsidies and government orders. His state monopoly on vodka brought millions into the treasury every year. Nicholas disliked Witte's cynicism and arrogance, but admitted his genius. When Witte brought the Portsmouth peace negotiations to what under the circumstances amounted to a brilliant conclusion for Russia, the Tsar recognized his indebtedness by making Witte a count.

Experienced, shrewd and freshly crowned as a peacemaker, Witte was the obvious choice to deal with the spreading revolutionary upheavals. Even the Dowager Empress Marie advised her son, "I am sure that the only man who can help you now is Witte. . . . He certainly is a man of genius." At the Tsar's request, Witte drew up a memorandum in which he analyzed the situation and concluded that only two alternatives existed: a military dictatorship or a constitution. Witte himself urged that granting a constitution would be a cheaper, easier way of ending the turmoil. This recommendation gained further weight when it was vehemently endorsed by Grand Duke Nicholas Nicolaievich, the Tsar's six-foot-six-inch cousin, then in command of the St. Petersburg Military District. So violently did the Grand Duke object to the idea that he become military dictator, that he brandished the revolver in his holster and shouted, "If the Emperor does not accept the Witte program, if he wants to force me to become Dictator, I shall kill myself in his presence with this revolver. We must support Witte at all cost. It is necessary for the good of Russia."

The Imperial Manifesto of October 30, 1905, transformed Russia from an absolute autocracy into a semi-constitutional monarchy. It promised "freedom of conscience, speech, assembly and association" to the Russian people. It granted an elected parliament, the Duma, and pledged that "no law may go into force without the consent of the State Duma." It did not go as far as the constitutional monarchy in England; the Tsar retained his prerogative over defense and foreign affairs and the sole power to appoint and dismiss ministers. But the Manifesto did propel Russia with great rapidity over difficult political terrain which it had taken Western Europe several centuries to travel.

Witte now had maneuvered himself into an awkward corner. Having forced a reluctant sovereign to grant a constitution, Witte was expected to make it work. He was installed as President of the Council of Ministers, where he quickly obtained the resignation of Constantine Pobedonostsev. After twenty-six years as Procurator of the Holy Synod, Pobedonostsev left, but not before he had scathingly referred to his successor, Prince Alexis Obolensky, as a man in whose head "three cocks were crowing at the same time."

To Witte's despair, rather than getting better, the situation grew steadily worse. The Right hated him for degrading the autocracy, the Liberals did not trust him, the Left feared that the revolution which it was anticipating would slip from its grasp. "Nothing has changed, the struggle goes on," declared Paul Miliukov, a leading Russian historian and Liberal. Leon Trotsky, writing in the newly formed *Isvestia*, was more vivid: "The proletariat knows what it does not want. It wants neither the police thug Trepov [commander of the police throughout the empire] nor the liberal financial shark Witte: neither the wolf's snout, nor the fox's tail. It rejects the police whip wrapped in the parchment of the constitution."

In parts of Russia, the Manifesto, by stripping the local police of many of their powers, led directly to violence. In the Baltic states, the peasants rose against their German landlords and proclaimed a rash of little village republics. In the Ukraine and White Russia, bands of Ultra-Rightists, calling themselves Black Hundreds, turned against the familiar scapegoats, the Jews. In Kiev and Odessa, pogroms erupted, often with the open support of the Church. In the Trans-Caucasus, similar attacks, under the guise of patriotism and religion, were made on Armenians. In Poland and Finland, the Manifesto was taken as a sign of weakness; there was a sense that the empire was crumbling, and mass demonstrations clamored for autonomy and independence. At Kronstadt on the Baltic and Sevastopol on the Black Sea, there were naval mutinies. In December, the Moscow Soviet led two thousand workers and students to the barricades. For ten days they held off government forces, proclaiming a new "Provisional Government." The revolt was crushed only by bringing from St. Petersburg the Semenovsky Regiment of the Guard, which cleared the streets with artillery and bayonets. During these weeks, Lenin slipped back into Russia to lead the Bolsheviks; the police soon found his trail and he was forced to flit secretly from place to place, diminishing his effectiveness. Still, he was gleeful. "Go ahead and shoot," he cried. "Summon the Austrian and German regiments against the Russian peasants and workers. We are for a broadening of the struggle, we are for an international revolution."

Nicholas, meanwhile, waited impatiently for his experiment in constitutionalism to produce results. As Witte stumbled, the Tsar became bitter. His letters to his mother mark the progression of his disillusionments:

November 9: "It is strange that such a clever man [Witte] should be wrong in his forecast of an easy pacification."

November 23: "Everybody is afraid of taking courageous action. I keep trying to force them—even Witte himself—to behave more energetically. With us nobody is accustomed to shouldering responsibility, all expect to be given orders which, however, they disobey as often as not."

December 14: "He [Witte] is now prepared to arrest all the principal leaders of the outbreak. I have been trying for some time past to get him to do it, but he always hoped to be able to manage without drastic measures."

January 25, 1906: "As for Witte, since the happenings in Moscow he has radically changed his views; now he wants to hang and shoot everybody. I have never seen such a chameleon of a man. That, naturally, is the reason why no one believes in him any more."

Feeling his status slipping, Witte tried to recapture the Tsar's good will by cynically chopping away most of the strength from the Manifesto he had only recently written. Without waiting for the Duma to be elected, Witte arbitrarily drafted a series of Fundamental Laws based on the declaration: "To the Emperor of all the Russias belongs the supreme autocratic power." To make the government financially independent of Duma appropriations, Witte used his own great personal reputation abroad to obtain from France a massive loan of over two billion francs.

Despite these efforts, Sergius Witte took no part in the affairs of the Russian parliament which he had helped to create. On the eve of its first meeting, Nicholas asked for his resignation. Witte pretended to be pleased by the move. "You see before you the happiest of mortals," he said to a colleague. "The Tsar could not have shown me greater mercy than by dismissing me from this prison where I have been languishing. I am going abroad at once to take a cure. I do not want to hear about anything and shall merely imagine what is happening over here. All Russia is one vast madhouse." This was nonsense, of course; for the rest of his life, Witte itched to return to office. His hopes were illusory. "As long as I live, I will never trust that man again with the smallest thing," said Nicholas. "I had quite enough of last year's experiment. It is still like a nightmare to me." Eventually, Witte returned to Russia, and Nicholas made him a grant of two hundred thousand roubles from the Treasury. But in the nine years which were to pass before Witte died, he would see the Tsar only twice again, each time for a brief interview of twenty minutes.

In all these months of war with Japan and the 1905 Revolution, Nicholas and Alexandra had had only one brief moment of unshadowed joy. On August 12, 1904, Nicholas wrote in his diary: "A great never-to-be-forgotten day when the mercy of God has visited us so clearly. Alix gave birth to a son at one o'clock. The child has been called Alexis."

The long-awaited boy arrived suddenly. At noon on a hot summer day, the Tsar and his wife sat down to lunch at Peterhof. The Empress had just managed to finish her soup when she was forced to excuse herself and hurry to her room. Less than an hour later, the boy, weighing eight pounds, was born. As the saluting cannon at Peterhof began to boom, other guns sounded at Kronstadt. Twenty miles away, in the heart of St. Petersburg, the batteries of the Fortress of Peter and Paul began to thunder—this time the salute was three hundred guns. Across Russia, cannons roared, churchbells clanged and flags waved. Alexis, named after Tsar Alexis, Nicholas's favorite, was the first male heir born to a reigning Russian tsar since the seventeenth century. It seemed an omen of hope.

His Imperial Highness Alexis Nicolaievich, Sovereign Heir Tsarevich, Grand Duke of Russia, was a fat, fair baby with yellow curls and clear blue eyes. As soon as they were permitted, Olga, nine, Tatiana, seven, Marie, five, and Anastasia, three, tiptoed into the nursery to peek into the crib and inspect their infant brother.

The christening of this august little Prince was performed in the Peterhof chapel. Alexis lay on a pillow of cloth of gold in the arms of Princess Marie Golitsyn, a lady-in-waiting who, traditionally, carried

Imperial babies to the baptismal font. Because of her advanced age, the Princess came to the ceremony especially equipped. For greater support, the baby's pillow was attached to a broad gold band slung around her shoulders. To keep them from slipping, her shoes were fitted with rubber soles.

The Tsarevich was christened in the presence of most of his large family, including his great-grandfather King Christian IX of Denmark, then in his eighty-seventh year. Only the Tsar and the Empress were absent; custom forbade parents to attend the baptism of their child. The service was performed by Father Yanishev, the elderly priest who had served for years as confessor to the Imperial family. He pronounced the name Alexis, which had been carried by the second Romanov Tsar, Alexis the Peaceful, in the seventeenth century. Then he dipped the new Alexis bodily into the font, and the Tsarevich screeched his fury. As soon as the service was over, the Tsar hurried into the church. He had been waiting anxiously outside, hoping that the aged Princess and the elderly priest would not drop his son into the font. That afternoon, the Imperial couple received a stream of visitors. The Empress, lying on a couch, was seen to smile frequently at the Tsar, who stood nearby.

Six weeks later, in a very different mood, Nicholas wrote again in his diary: "Alix and I have been very much worried. A hemorrhage began this morning without the slightest cause from the navel of our small Alexis. It lasted with but a few interruptions until evening. We had to call . . . the surgeon Fedorov who at seven o'clock applied a bandage. The child was remarkably quiet and even merry but it was a dreadful thing to have to live through such anxiety."

The next day: "This morning there again was some blood on the bandage but the bleeding stopped at noon. The child spent a quiet day and his healthy appearance somewhat quieted our anxiety."

On the third day, the bleeding stopped. But the fear born those days in the Tsar and his wife continued to grow. The months passed and Alexis stood up in his crib and began to crawl and to try to walk. When he stumbled and fell, little bumps and bruises appeared on his arms and legs. Within a few hours, they grew to dark blue swellings. Beneath the skin, his blood was failing to clot. The terrifying suspicion of his parents was confirmed. Alexis had hemophilia.

This grim knowledge, unknown outside the family, lay in Nicholas's heart even as he learned of Bloody Sunday and Tsushima, and when he signed the Manifesto. It would remain with him for the rest of his life. It was during this period that those who saw Nicholas regularly, without knowing about Alexis, began to notice a deepening fatalism in the Tsar. Nicholas had always been struck by the fact that he was born on the day in the Russian calendar set aside for Job. With the passage of time, this fatalism came to dominate his outlook. "I have a secret conviction," he once told one of his ministers, "that I am destined for a terrible trial, that I shall not receive my reward on this earth."

It is one of the supreme ironies of history that the blessed birth of an only son should have proved the mortal blow. Even as the saluting cannons boomed and the flags waved, Fate had prepared a terrible story. Along with the lost battles and sunken ships, the bombs, the revolutionaries and their plots, the strikes and revolts, Imperial Russia was toppled by a tiny defect in the body of a little boy. Hidden from public view, veiled in rumor, working from within, this unseen tragedy would change the history of Russia and the world.

PART TWO

CHAPTER TEN

The Tsar's Village

THE secret of Alexis's disease was hidden and carefully guarded within the inner world of Tsarskoe Selo, "the Tsar's village." "Tsarskoe Selo was a world apart, an enchanted fairyland to which only a small number of people had the right of entry," wrote Gleb Botkin, the son of Nicholas II's court physician. "It became a legendary place. To the loyal monarchists, it was a sort of terrestrial paradise, the abode of the earthly gods. To the revolutionaries, it was a sinister place where blood-thirsty tyrants were hatching their terrible plots against the innocent population."

Tsarskoe Selo was a magnificent symbol, a supreme gesture, of the Russian autocracy. At the edge of the great St. Petersburg plain, fifteen miles south of the capital, a succession of Russian tsars and empresses had created an isolated, miniature world, as artificial and fantastic as a precisely ordered mechanical toy. Around the high iron fence of the Imperial Park, bearded Cossack horsemen in scarlet tunics, black fur caps, boots and shining sabers rode night and day, on ceaseless patrol. Inside the park, monuments, obelisks and triumphal arches studded eight hundred acres of velvet green lawn. An artificial lake, big enough for small sailboats, could be emptied and filled like a bathtub. At one end of the lake stood a pink Turkish bath; not far off, a dazzling red-and-gold Chinese pagoda crowned an artificial hillock. Winding paths led through groves of ancient trees, their massive branches latticed for safety with cables and iron bars. A pony track curved through gardens planted with exotic flowers. Scattered in clumps throughout the park were lilacs planted by a dozen empresses. Over the years, the shrubs had grown into lush and fragrant jungles. When the spring rain fell, the sweet smell of wet lilacs drenched the air.

Tsarskoe Selo sprang up when Catherine I, the lusty wife of Peter the Great, wanted a country retreat from the granite city her husband was building on the Neva marshes. Peter's daughter, Elizabeth, displayed her parents' instinct for grand construction. At a cost of ten million roubles, she built the Winter Palace in St. Petersburg and then turned her attention to Tsarskoe Selo. Disliking the joggling carriages which bore her in and out of the city, she began constructing a canal so that she could make the journey entirely by water. Elizabeth died before the canal was finished, but the completed sections provided excellent bathing for the inhabitants of Tsarskoe Selo.

The two palaces standing five hundred yards apart in the Imperial Park during the reign of Nicholas II had been built by Empress Elizabeth and by Catherine the Great. In 1752, Elizabeth ordered the famous architect Rastrelli to build a palace at Tsarskoe Selo which would outshine Versailles. Rastrelli erected the big blue-and-white palace now called the Catherine Palace, an ornate structure with more than two hundred rooms. It pleased Elizabeth so much that she made Rastrelli a Russian count. Mingling taste with exquisite diplomacy, the French ambassador at Elizabeth's court told the Empress that her beautiful palace lacked only one thing—a cover of glass to protect so breathtaking a masterpiece. In 1729, Catherine the Great commissioned another Italian, Quarenghi, to build a second, smaller palace at Tsarskoe Selo for her beloved grandson, the boy who was to become Alexander I. Quarenghi's building, the Alexander Palace, was as simple as the Catherine Palace was ornate. It was here, to the Alexander Palace, that Nicholas II brought his bride to live in the spring of 1895. It remained their home for twenty-two years.

In describing palaces, simplicity becomes a relative term. The Alexander Palace had over one hundred rooms. From the tall windows of the Catherine Palace, the Tsar and his wife gazed down on terraces, pavilions, statues, gardens and ornate carriages drawn by magnificent horses. Inside the palace were long, polished halls and tall, shaded rooms furnished in marble, mahogany, gold, crystal, velvet and silk. Beneath huge chandeliers, rich Oriental rugs were spread on gleaming parquet floors. In winter, sapphire-and-silver brocade curtains helped to shut out the murky chills of Russian twilight. Large multicolored porcelain stoves warmed the cold rooms, mingling the smell of burning wood with the fragrant scent provided by smoking pots of incense carried by footmen from room to room. In every season, Empress Alexandra filled the palace with flowers. When autumn frosts ended the growing in the gardens and greenhouses at Tsarskoe Selo, flowers were brought by train from the Crimea. Every room had its swirl of odors; the sweetness of lilies in tall Chinese vases, the delicate fragrance of violets and lilies of the valley bunched in silver bowls, the perfume of hyacinths in rare lacquered pots.

To guard this paradise, to tend its lawns and pick its flowers, to groom its horses, polish its motorcars, clean its floors, make its beds, polish its crystal, serve its banquets and bathe and dress its Imperial children took thousands of human hands. Besides the Cossacks, a permanent garrison of five thousand infantrymen carefully chosen from all the regiments of the Imperial Guard provided guard detachments at the palace gates and foot patrols in the Imperial Park. Thirty sentries were always stationed inside the palace, in vestibules, corridors, staircases, kitchens and even in the cellars. The guardsmen were supplemented by plainclothes police who inspected the servants, tradesmen and workmen and kept notebook records of all who came and went. In bad weather, the Tsar could look from any window and see a tall soldier in a long greatcoat, cap and boots pacing his round. Not far away, there was usually a forlorn policeman with galoshes and umbrella.

Inside, an army of servants in gorgeous livery moved through the polished halls and silken chambers. Equerries in red capes bordered with Imperial eagles, and hats waving long red, yellow and black ostrich plumes, stepped noiselessly on the soft soles of their patent-leather shoes. "Resplendent in snow white garters, the footmen ran before us up the carpeted staircases," wrote one visitor to the Imperial palace. "We passed through drawing rooms, ante-rooms, banqueting rooms, passing from carpets to glittering parquet, then back to carpets. . . . At every door stood lackeys petrified in pairs in most varied costumes, according to the room to which they were attached; now the traditional black frock coats, now Polish surcoats, with red shoes and white stockings and gaiters. At one of the doors [stood] two handsome lackeys with . . . crimson scarves on their heads, caught up with tinsel clasps."

Nothing had changed, neither the trappings nor the rhythm of palace life, since the days of Catherine the Great. Court protocol, handed down from a forgotten era, remained as obstinately rigid as a block of granite. In the palace, courtiers backed away from the presence of the sovereigns. No one ever contradicted a member of the Imperial family. It was improper to speak to a member of the family without being spoken to, and when walking with the sovereigns, friends did not greet each other or even notice each other's existence unless an Imperial personage did so first.

Frequently, court protocol almost seemed to conduct itself, taking its own course, making its own decisions, running on its own vast internal energies of tradition, exclusive of all human management. One day Dr. Botkin, the court physician, was surprised to receive the award of the Grand Cordon of the Order of St. Anna. According to protocol, he asked for a formal audience with the Tsar to thank him for the decoration. As he saw Botkin daily in his capacity as physician, Nicholas was surprised by the request. "Has anything happened that you want to see me officially?" he asked. "No, Sire," said Botkin, "I came only to thank Your Majesty for this." He pointed to the star pinned on his chest. "Congratulations," said Nicholas, smiling. "I had no idea I had given it to you."

Everything at Tsarskoe Selo centered on the Tsar. Outside the palace gates, Tsarskoe Selo was an elegant provincial town dominated by the life and gossip of the court. The mansions of the aristocracy, lining the wide tree-shaded boulevard which led from the railway station to the gates of the Imperial Park, pulsed with the rhythm that emanated from the Imperial household. A week of excited conversation could follow a nod, a smile or a word sent by the sovereign in an unusual direction. Severe crises arose over matters of promotion, decorations and clashing appointments for tea. Invitations to the palace were hoarded like diamonds. No greater delight offered itself than to have the telephone ring and hear one of the deep male voices of the palace telephone operators announce, "You are called from the apartments of Her Imperial Majesty" or, if the caller was one of Her Majesty's daughters, "You are called from the apartments of Their Imperial Highnesses."

The master of court life, the impresario of all court ceremonies, the bestower of all stars and ribbons, the arbitrator of all court disputes, was a Finnish nobleman advanced in years, Count Vladimir Fredericks. In 1897, at the age of sixty, Fredericks became chief minister of the Imperial court; he held the post until 1917, when it ceased to exist. Nicholas and Alexandra were devoted to "the Old Man," as they referred to Fredericks. He, in turn, treated them as his own children and in private addressed them as "*mes enfants*."

Fredericks, according to Paléologue, the French Ambassador, was "the very personification of court life. Of all the subjects of the Tsar, none has received more honors and titles. He is Minister of the Imperial court and household, aide-de-camp to the Tsar, cavalry general, member of the Council of Empire. . . . He has passed the whole of his long life in palaces and ceremonies, in carriages and processions, under gold lace and decorations. . . . He knows all the secrets of the Imperial family. In the Tsar's name he dispenses all the favors and gifts, all the reproofs and punishments. The grand dukes and grand duchesses overwhelm him with attention for he it is who controls their households, hushes up their scandals and pays their debts. For all the difficulties of his task he is not known to have an enemy, such is the charm of his manner and his tact. He is also one of the handsomest men of his generation, one of the finest horsemen, and his successes with women were past counting. He has kept his lithe figure, his fine drooping mustache, and his charming manners . . . he is the ideal type for his office, the supreme arbitrator of the rites and precedences, conventions and traditions, manners and etiquette."

As old age crept over him, Fredericks became ill and his energies sagged. He dozed off in the middle of conferences. He became forgetful. During the war, Prince Bariatinsky arrived at the palace to present the Tsar with the military order of the Cross of St. George. "Fredericks went to announce the Prince to His Majesty," wrote Botkin, "but on his way from one room to the other, forgot what he was supposed to do, and wandered off, leaving the Emperor to wait for the Prince in one room and the Prince to wait for the Emperor in an adjoining room, both bewildered and angry at the delay." Another time, Fredericks approached the Tsar and said, "I say, did His Majesty invite you for dinner tonight?" When Nicholas looked at him in utter bewilderment, Fredericks said, "Oh, I thought you were somebody else."

After Fredericks, Nicholas's favorite among the inhabitants of his court was Prince Vladimir Orlov, Chief of the Tsar's Private Secretariat. A highly cultivated, sarcastic man and a descendant of one of the lovers of Catherine the Great, the Prince was known as "Fat Orlov" because he was so obese that, when sitting, he was unable to see his own knees. Orlov had been a cavalry officer, but in middle age he no longer was able to mount a horse. At parades when the Tsar and the Imperial suite rode by on horseback, Orlov was seen in the middle of the cavalcade, marching along on foot.

Naturally, these courtiers were fervent monarchists, "*plus royaliste que le roi*." The Russia that men like Orlov preferred to see was a land of meek, sentimental, devoutly religious *moujiks*, overwhelmingly loyal to the Tsar. Russia's enemies, they believed, were those who degraded the autocracy—the politicians and parliamentarians as well as the revolutionaries. This view, sounded in Nicholas's ear whenever he would listen, survived defeats in war, revolutionary upheavals, the rise and fall of ministers and Imperial Dumas. Year after year slipped away, wrote Botkin, and "the enchanted little fairyland of Tsarskoe Selo slumbered peacefully on the brink of an abyss, lulled by the sweet songs of bewhiskered sirens who gently hummed 'God Save the Tsar,' attended church with great regularity . . . and from time to time asked discreetly when they were going to receive their next grand cordon or advance in rank or raise in salary."

A graceful two-story building in simple classical style, the Alexander Palace at Tsarskoe Selo was made up of a center and two wings. In the central building were clustered the state apartments and formal chambers. The ministers of court and ladies- and gentlemen-in-waiting had apartments in one of the two wings. In the other wing, Nicholas and Alexandra established a world and led a carefully scheduled and domestic existence.

The Empress Alexandra's first command as a bride was that the rooms of this wing be redecorated. Curtains, rugs, upholstering and pillows were done in bright English chintzes and in mauve, her favorite color. On the second floor, the rooms selected as nurseries were cleared of heavy furniture, and simple beds and dressers of lemonwood were installed, with covers of cheerful English cretonne. Under her direction, the general appearance of the private wing became that of a comfortable English country house.

Mounting guard over the frontier between this private world and the rest of the palace was a gaudily fantastic quartet of bodyguards. Four gigantic Negroes dressed in scarlet trousers, gold-embroidered jackets, curved shoes and white turbans stood guard outside the study where the Tsar was at work, or the boudoir where the Empress was resting. "They were not soldiers," wrote Alexandra's friend Anna Vyrubova, "and had no function except to open and close doors and to signal by a sudden noiseless entrance into a room that one of Their

Majesties was about to appear." Although all of these men were referred to at court as Ethiopians, one was an American Negro named Jim Hercules. Originally a servant of Alexander III, Hercules was an employee, bound to the family only by loyalty. He took his vacations in America and brought back jars of guava jelly as presents for the children.

Behind the heavy doors guarded by this flamboyant quartet, the Imperial family lived a punctual existence. In the winter, Tsarskoe Selo lay under a heavy blanket of snow and the sun did not come until nine o'clock. Nicholas rose at seven, dressed by lamplight, had breakfast with his daughters and disappeared into his study to work. Alexandra rarely left her room before noon. Her mornings were spent propped up on pillows in bed or on a chaise-longue, reading and writing long emotional letters to her friends. Unlike Nicholas, who wrote painstakingly and sometimes took hours to compose a letter, Alexandra wrote voluminously, dashing off lengthy sentences across page after page, punctuating only with dots and dashes and exclamation points. At her feet, while she wrote, lay a small shaggy Scotch terrier named Eira. Most people considered Eira disagreeable; he liked to dart from under tables and nip at heels. Alexandra doted on him and carried him from room to room—even to the dinner table.

Unlike many a royal couple, Nicholas and Alexandra shared the same bed. The bedroom was a large chamber with tall windows opening onto the park. A large double bed made of light-colored wood stood between two windows. Chairs and couches covered in flowered tapestry were scattered about on a thick carpet of mauve pile. To the right of the bed, a door led to a small chapel used by the Empress for her private prayers. Dimly lit by hanging lamps, the room contained only an icon on one wall and a table holding a Bible. Another door led from the bedroom to Alexandra's private bathroom, where a collection of old-fashioned fixtures were set in a dark recess. Primly Victorian, Alexandra insisted that both bath and toilet be covered during the day by cloths.

The most famous room in the palace—for a time the most famous room in Russia—was the Empress's mauve boudoir. Everything in it was mauve: curtains, carpet, pillows; even the furniture was mauve-and-white Hepplewhite. Masses of fresh white and purple lilacs, vases of roses and orchids and bowls of violets perfumed the air. Tables and shelves were cluttered with books, papers and porcelain and enamel knicknacks.* In this room, Alexandra surrounded herself with mementoes of her family and her religion. The walls were covered with icons. Over her chaise-longue hung a picture of the Virgin Mary. A portrait of her mother, Princess Alice, looked down from another wall. On a table in a place of honor stood a large photograph of Queen Victoria. The only portrait in the room other than religious and family pictures was a portrait of Marie Antoinette.

In this cluttered, cozy room, surrounded by her treasured objects, Alexandra felt secure. Here, in the morning, she talked to her daughters, helping them choose their dresses and plan their schedules. It was to this room that Nicholas hurried to sit with his wife, sip tea, read the papers and discuss their children and their empire. They talked to each other in English, although Nicholas and all the children spoke Russian to each other. To Alexandra, Nicholas was always "Nicky." To him, she was "Alix" or "Sunshine" or "Sunny." Sometimes through the rooms of this private wing, a clear, musical whistle like the warbling song of a bird would sound. This was Nicholas's way of summoning his wife. Early in her marriage, Alexandra, hearing the call, would blush red and drop whatever she was doing to hurry to him. Later, as his children grew up, Nicholas used it to call them, and the birdlike whistle became a familiar and regular sound in the Alexander Palace.

Next to the mauve boudoir was the Empress's dressing room, an array of closets for her gowns, shelves for her hats and trays for her jewels. Alexandra had six wardrobe maids, but her modesty severely limited their duties. No one ever saw the Empress Alexandra undressed or in her bath. She bathed herself, and when she was ready to have her hair arranged, she appeared in a Japanese kimono. Often it was Grand Duchess Tatiana who came to comb her mother's hair and pile the long red-gold strands on top of her head. After the Empress was almost dressed, her maids were summoned to fasten buttons and clasp on jewelry. "Only rubies today," the Empress would say, or "Pearls and sapphires with this gown." She preferred pearls to all other jewels, and several ropes of pearls usually cascaded from her neck to her waist.

* Along with religious crosses, icons and images of every description, Alexandra was fascinated by the symbol of the swastika. Its origins buried deep in the past, the swastika has been for thousands of years the symbol of the sun, of continuing re-creation and of infinity. Swastikas have been found on relics unearthed at the site of Troy, woven into Inca textiles and scrawled in the catacombs of Rome. Only to the generation that grew up after Alexandra's death has the meaning of the swastika been perverted and the symbol transformed into a despised emblem of violence, intolerance and terror.

For daytime, Alexandra wore loose, flowing clothes trimmed at the throat and waist with lace. She considered the famous "hobble skirts" of the Edwardian era a nuisance. "Do you really like this skirt?" she asked Lili Dehn, whose husband was an officer on the Imperial yacht. "Well, Madame, *c'est la mode*," replied the lady. "It's no use whatever as a skirt," said the Empress. "Now, Lili, prove to me that it is comfortable—run, Lili, run, and let me see how fast you can cover ground in it."

The Empress's gowns were designed by St. Petersburg's reigning fashion dictator of the day, a Mme. Brissac, who made a fortune as a *couturière* and lived in a mansion in the capital. Her clients, including the Empress, all complained about her prices. To the Empress, Mme. Brissac confided, "I beg Your Majesty not to mention it to anyone, but I always cut my prices for Your Majesty." Subsequently, Alexandra discovered that Mme. Brissac had met similar complaints from her sister-in-law Grand Duchess Olga Alexandrovna with the whispered plea, "I beg Your Imperial Highness not to mention these things at Tsarskoe Selo, but I always cut my prices for you."

In the evening, Alexandra wore white or cream silk gowns embroidered in silver and blue and worn with diamonds in her hair and pearls at her throat. She disliked filmy lingerie; her undergarments and her sleeping gowns were made of fine, embroidered linen. Her shoes were low-heeled and pointed, usually bronze or white suede. Outdoors she carried a parasol against the sun, even when wearing a wide-brimmed hat.

Lili Dehn, recalling her presentation to the Empress in the garden at Tsarskoe Selo in 1907, gives a vivid first impression of the Empress Alexandra: "Advancing through the masses of greenery came a tall and slender figure. . . . The Empress was dressed entirely in white with a thin white veil draped around her hat. Her complexion was delicately fair . . . her hair was reddish gold, her eyes . . . were dark blue and her figure was supple as a willow wand. I remember that her pearls were magnificent and that diamond earrings flashed colored fires whenever she moved her head. . . . I noticed that she spoke Russian with a strong English accent."

For the children of the Imperial family, winter was a time of interminable lessons. Beginning at nine in the morning, tutors drilled them in arithmetic, geography, history, Russian, French and English.

Before beginning their classwork, they submitted themselves every morning to the examination of Dr. Eugene Botkin, the court physician, who came daily to look at throats and rashes. Botkin was not solely responsible for the children; a specialist, Dr. Ostrogorsky, came from St. Petersburg to render his services. Later, young Dr. Vladimir Derevenko was especially assigned to care for the Tsarevich's hemophilia. But Botkin always remained the children's favorite. A tall, stout man who wore blue suits with a gold watch chain across his stomach, he exuded a strong perfume imported from Paris. When they were free, the young Grand Duchesses liked to track him from room to room, following his trail by sniffing his scent.

At eleven every morning, the Tsar and his children stopped work and went outdoors for an hour. Sometimes Nicholas took his gun and shot crows in the park. He had a kennel of eleven magnificent English collies and he enjoyed walking with the dogs frisking and racing about him. In winter, he joined the children and their tutors in building "ice mountains," big mounds of snow covered with water which froze and made a handsome run for sleds and small toboggans.

Dinner at midday was the ceremonial meal at Tsarskoe Selo. Although the Empress was usually absent, Nicholas dined with his daughters and members of his suite. The meal began, according to the Russian custom, with a priest rising from the table to face an icon and intone his blessing. At the Imperial table this role was filled by Father Vassiliev, the confessor to the Imperial family. Of peasant origin, Vassiliev had never graduated from the Theological Academy, but what he lacked in schooling he made up in fervor. As he shouted his prayers in a cracked voice, Alexandra was convinced that he represented the simple, essential Orthodoxy of the Russian people. As a confessor, Vassiliev was comforting. No matter what sin was confessed to him, he smiled beatifically and said, "Don't worry. Don't worry. The Devil does none of these things. He neither smokes nor drinks nor engages in revelry, and yet he is The Devil." At the Imperial table, among the gold-braided uniforms of the court officials, Vassiliev cut a starkly dramatic figure. Wearing a long, black robe with wide sleeves, a black beard that stretched to his waist, a five-inch silver cross that dangled from his neck, he gave the impression that a great black raven had settled down at the table of the Tsar.

Another presence, not always visible, graced the Imperial table. It was that of Cubat, the palace chef. At Tsarskoe Selo, Cubat labored under a heavy burden. Neither Nicholas nor Alexandra cared for the rich, complicated dishes which the great French chefs had brought from their homeland to spread across the princely tables of Russia. Nicholas especially enjoyed slices of suckling pig with horseradish, taken with a glass of port. Fresh caviar had once given him severe indigestion and he rarely ate this supreme Russian delicacy. Most of all, he relished the simple cooking of the Russian peasant—cabbage soup or *borshch* or *kasha* (buckwheat) with boiled fish and fruit. Alexandra cared nothing for food and merely pecked at anything set before her. Nevertheless, Cubat, one of the greatest French chefs of his day, struggled on, happily anticipating the time when the Tsar's guests would include a renowned gourmet. Sometimes when an especially elegant dish was being served, Cubat would stand hopefully in the doorway, immaculate in his white chef's apron and hat, waiting to receive the compliments of master and guests.

In the afternoon, while her children continued their lessons, Alexandra often went for a drive. The order "Prepare Her Majesty's carriage for two o'clock" stimulated a burst of activity at the stables. The carriage, an open, polished black rig of English design, was rolled out; the horses were harnessed into place and two footmen, in tall hats and blue coats, mounted the steps in the rear. Not until all else was ready did the coachman appear. He was a tall, heavy man amplified to greater size by an immense padded coat which he wore covered with medals. Two grooms placed themselves behind him and, at his grunt of command, boosted him into place. Taking the reins, he crossed himself, gave the reins a flick and, with a mounted Cossack officer trotting behind, the carriage moved under an arch toward the palace to wait for the Empress.

Not only the stables but also the vast and cumbersome apparatus of police surveillance was alerted when Alexandra asked for her carriage. Squads of detectives were hastily dispatched, and when the Empress drove out the gate an hour later, every tree and bush along her route concealed a crouching policeman. If she stopped to speak to someone along the way, no sooner had she driven on than an agent of the police stepped forward, notebook in hand, to ask, "What is your name and what reason had you for conversation with Her Imperial Majesty?"

Nicholas rarely accompanied his wife on these excursions by carriage. He preferred instead to ride out on horseback accompanied by Count Fredericks or by a friend, the Commander of Her Majesty's Uhlans, General Alexander Orlov. Usually they went through the countryside in the direction of Krasnoe Selo, passing through villages along the way. Often, during these outings, the Tsar stopped to talk informally to peasants, asking them about themselves, their village problems and the success of the harvest. Sometimes, knowing that the Tsar frequently rode that way, peasants from other districts waited by the road to hand him petitions or make special requests. In almost every case, Nicholas saw to it that these requests were granted.*

At four, the family gathered for tea. Teas at Tsarskoe Selo were always the same. Year after year, the same small, white-draped tables were set with the same glasses in silver holders, the same plates of hot bread, the same English biscuits. Cakes and sweetmeats never appeared. To her friend Anna Vyrubova, Alexandra complained that "other people had much more interesting teas." Although she was Empress of Russia, wrote Vyrubova, she "seemed unable to change a single detail of the routine of the Russian court. The same plates of hot bread and butter had been on the same tea tables . . . [since the days of] Catherine the Great."

* There is a story told by General Spiridovich which has all the quality of a fairy tale except that Spiridovich, a sternly practical and conscientious policeman, filled his book with nothing but precise and exhaustive descriptions of fact. The story is this:

Late one night in the room of the Peterhof palace set aside for the receiving of petitions, General Orlov heard a strange sound coming from the anteroom. He found a girl hiding there, sobbing. Throwing herself on the floor before him, she explained that her fiancé had been condemned to death and that he would be executed the next morning. He was a student, she said, who had tuberculosis and who had gotten mixed up in revolutionary activities. Just before his arrest, he had tried to extricate himself from the movement, but had forcibly been prevented from doing so. He would die anyway in a short time from his disease. Clutching Orlov about the knees, her eyes brimming with tears, she begged him to ask the Tsar for a pardon.

Moved by her plea, Orlov decided to act despite the lateness of the hour. He ordered a troika and dashed to the Alexandra Villa, where the Tsar was staying. Bursting through the door, he was stopped by a valet who told him that the Tsar already had retired. Nevertheless, Orlov insisted. A few minutes later, Nicholas appeared in his pajamas and asked quietly, "What is happening?" Orlov told him the story.

"I thank you very much for acting the way you did," said Nicholas. "One must never hesitate when one has the chance to save the life of a man. Thank God that neither your conscience nor mine will have anything to reproach themselves for." Quickly, he wrote a telegram to the Minister of Justice: "Defer the execution of S. Await orders." He handed the paper to a court messenger and added, "Run!"

Orlov returned to the girl and told her what had happened. She fainted and Orlov had to revive her. When she could speak, her first words were, "Whatever happens to us, we are ready to give our lives for the Emperor." Later, when Orlov saw Nicholas and told him her words, the Tsar smiled and said, "You see, you have made two people, her and me, very happy."

As with everything else at Tsarskoe Selo, there was a rigid routine for tea. "Every day at the same moment," Anna Vyrubova recalled, "the door opened, the Emperor came in, sat down at the tea table, buttered a piece of bread and began to sip his tea. He drank two glasses every day, never more, never less, and as he drank, he glanced over his telegrams and newspapers. The children found teatime exciting. They dressed for it in fresh white frocks and colored sashes, and spent most of the hour playing on the floor with toys. As they grew older, needlework and embroidery were substituted. The Empress did not like to see her daughters sitting with idle hands."

After tea, Nicholas returned to his study. Between five and eight p.m. he received a stream of callers. Those having business with him were brought by train from St. Petersburg, arriving at Tsarskoe Selo just as dusk was falling. They were escorted through the palace to a waiting room where they could sit and leaf through books and magazines until the Tsar was ready to see them.

"Although my audience was a private one," wrote the French Ambassador, Paléologue, "I had put on my full dress uniform, as is fitting for a meeting with the Tsar, Autocrat of all the Russias. The Director of Ceremonies, Evreinov, went with me. He also was a symphony of gold braid. . . . My escort consisted only of Evreinov, a household officer in undress uniform and a footman in his picturesque (Tsaritsa Elizabeth) dress with the hat adorned with long red, black and yellow plumes. I was taken through the audience rooms, then the Empress's private drawing room, down a long corridor leading to the private apartments of the sovereigns in which I passed a servant in very plain livery who was carrying a tea tray. Further on was the foot of a little private staircase leading to the rooms of the Imperial children. A ladies' maid flitted away from the landing above. The last room at the end of the corridor was occupied by . . . [the Tsar's] personal aide-de-camp. I waited there barely a minute. The gaily and weirdly bedecked Ethiopian who mounted guard outside His Majesty's study opened the door almost at once.

"The Emperor received me with that gracious and somewhat shy kindness which is all his own. The room in which he received me is small and has only one window. The furniture is plain and comfortable. There are plain leather chairs, a sofa covered with a Persian rug, a bureau and shelves arranged with meticulous care, a table spread with maps and a low book case with photographs, busts and family souvenirs."

Nicholas received most visitors informally. Standing in front of his desk, he gestured them into an armchair, asked if they would like to smoke and lighted a cigarette. He was a careful listener, and although he often grasped the conclusion before his visitor had reached it, he never interrupted.

Precisely at eight, all official interviews ended so that the Tsar could go to supper. Nicholas always terminated an audience by rising and walking to a window. There was no mistaking this signal, and newcomers were sternly briefed to withdraw, no matter how pleasant or regretful His Majesty might seem. "I'm afraid I've wearied you," said Nicholas, politely breaking off his conversation.

Family suppers were informal, although the Empress invariably appeared at the table in an evening gown and jewels. Afterward, Alexandra went to the nursery to hear the Tsarevich say his prayers. In the evening after supper, Nicholas often sat in the family drawing room reading aloud while his wife and daughters sewed or embroidered. His choice, said Anna Vyrubova, who spent many of these cozy evenings with the Imperial family, might be Tolstoy, Turgenev or his own favorite, Gogol. On the other hand, to please the ladies, it might be a fashionable English novel. Nicholas read equally well in Russian, English and French and he could manage in German and Danish. His voice, said Anna, was "pleasant and [he had] remarkably clear enunciation." Books were supplied by his private librarian, whose job it was to provide the Tsar each month with twenty of the best books from all countries. This collection was laid out on a table and Nicholas arranged them in order of preference; thereafter the Tsar's valets saw to it that no one disarranged them until the end of the month.

Sometimes, instead of reading, the family spent evenings pasting snapshots taken by the court photographers or by themselves into green leather albums stamped in gold with the Imperial monograph. Nicholas enjoyed supervising the placement and pasting of the photographs and insisted that the work be done with painstaking neatness. "He could not endure the sight of the least drop of glue on the table," wrote Vyrubova.

The end of these pleasant, monotonous days arrived at eleven with the serving of evening tea. Before retiring, Nicholas wrote in his diary and soaked himself in his large, white-tiled bathtub. Once in bed, he usually went right to sleep. The exceptions were those occasions when his wife kept him awake, still reading and crunching English biscuits on the other side of the bed.

CHAPTER ELEVEN

"*OTMA*" *and Alexis*

DIRECTLY over the mauve boudoir of the Empress were the nurseries. In the morning, Alexandra could lie back on her couch and through the ceiling hear the footsteps of her children and the sound of their pianos. A private elevator and a private stairway led directly to the rooms above.

In these large, well-aired chambers, the four Grand Duchesses were brought up simply, in a manner befitting granddaughters of the spartan Alexander III. They slept on hard camp beds without pillows and took cold baths every morning. Their nurses, both Russian and English, were strict, although not without their own weaknesses. A Russian nurse assigned to little Olga was fond of tippling. Later she was found in bed with a Cossack and dismissed on the spot. Marie's English nurse, a Miss Eager, was fascinated by politics and talked incessantly about the Dreyfus case. "Once she even forgot that Marie was in her bath and started discussing the case with a friend," wrote the Tsar's younger sister, Grand Duchess Olga Alexandrovna. "Marie, naked and dripping, scrambled out of the bath and started running up and down the palace corridor. Fortunately, I arrived just at that moment, picked her up and carried her back to Miss Eager, who was still talking about Dreyfus."

The passage of time and the shortness of their lives have blurred the qualities of the four daughters of the last Tsar. Only Anastasia, the youngest, stands out distinctly, not for what she was as a child, but because of the extraordinary, often fascinating claims made on her behalf in the years after the massacre at Ekaterinburg. Yet the four girls were quite different, and as they became young women, the differences between them became more distinct.

Olga, the eldest, was most like her father. Shy and subdued, she had long chestnut-blond hair and blue eyes set in a wide Russian face. She impressed people by her kindness, her innocence and the depth of her private feelings. Olga had a good mind and was quick to grasp ideas. Talking to someone she knew well, she spoke rapidly and with frankness and wit. She read widely, both fiction and poetry, often borrowing books from her mother's tables before the Empress had read them. "You must wait, Mama, until I find out whether this book is a proper one for you to read," she parried when Alexandra spotted her reading a missing book.

Reading *Les Misérables* in French under the guidance of her Swiss tutor, Pierre Gilliard, Olga almost brought the tutor to calamity. Gilliard had instructed his pupil to underline all the French words she did not recognize. Arriving at the word spoken at Waterloo when the commander of Napoleon's Guard was asked to surrender, Olga dutifully underlined "*Merde!*" That night at dinner, not having seen Gilliard, she asked her father what it meant. The following day, walking in the park, Nicholas said to the tutor, "You are teaching my daughter a curious vocabulary, Monsieur." Gilliard was overcome with confusion and embarrassment. "Don't worry," said Nicholas, breaking into a smile, "I quite understand what happened."

If Olga was closest to her father, Tatiana, eighteen months younger than Olga, was closest to Alexandra. In public and private, she surrounded her mother with unwearying attentions. The tallest, slenderest and most elegant of the sisters, Tatiana had rich auburn hair and deep gray eyes. She was organized, energetic and purposeful and held strong opinions. "You felt that she was the daughter of an Emperor," declared an officer of the Imperial Guard.

In public, Grand Duchess Tatiana regularly outshone her older sister. Her piano technique was better than Olga's although she practiced less and cared less. With her good looks and self-assurance, she was far more anxious than Olga to go out into society. Among the five children, it was Tatiana who made the decisions; her younger sisters and brother called her "the Governess." If a favor was needed, all the children agreed that "Tatiana must ask Papa to grant it." Surprisingly, Olga did not mind being managed by Tatiana; the two, in fact, were devoted to each other.

Marie, the third daughter, was the prettiest of the four. She had red cheeks, thick, light brown hair and dark blue eyes so large that they were known in the family as "Marie's saucers." As a small child, she was chubby and glowing with health. In adolescence, she was merry and flirtatious. Marie liked to paint, but she was too lazy and gay to apply herself seriously. What Marie—whom everyone called "Mashka"—liked most was to talk about marriage and children. More than one observer has noted that, had she not been the daughter of the Tsar, this strong, warmhearted girl would have made some man an excellent wife.

Anastasia, the youngest daughter, destined to become the most famous of the children of Nicholas II, was a short, dumpy, blue-eyed child renowned in her family chiefly as a wag. When the saluting cannon on the Imperial yacht fired at sunset, Anastasia liked to retreat into a corner, stick her fingers into her ears, widen her eyes and loll her tongue in mock terror. Witty and vivacious, Anastasia also had a streak of stubbornness, mischief and impertinence. The same gift of ear and tongue that made her quickest to pick up a perfect accent in foreign languages also equipped her admirably as a mimic. Comically, sometimes cuttingly, the little girl aped precisely the speech and mannerisms of those about her.

Anastasia, the *enfant terrible*, was also a tomboy. She climbed trees to dizzying heights, refusing to come down until specifically commanded by her father. She rarely cried. Her aunt and godmother, Grand Duchess Olga Alexandrovna, remembered a time when Anastasia was teasing so ruthlessly that she slapped the child. The little girl's face went crimson, but instead of crying, she ran out of the room without uttering a sound. Sometimes Anastasia's practical jokes got out of hand. Once in a snowball fight, she rolled a rock into a snowball and threw it at Tatiana. The missile hit Tatiana in the face and knocked her, stunned, to the ground. Truly frightened at last, Anastasia broke down and cried.

As daughters of the Tsar, cloistered at Tsarskoe Selo without a normal range of friends and acquaintances, the four young Grand Duchesses were even closer to each other than most sisters. Olga, the eldest, was only six years older than Anastasia, the youngest. In adolescence, the four proclaimed their unity by choosing for themselves a single autograph, OTMA, derived from the first letter of each of their names. As OTMA, they jointly gave gifts and signed letters. They shared dresses and jewels. On one occasion, Baroness Buxhoeveden, one of the Empress's ladies-in-waiting, was dressing for a ball when the sisters decided that her jewels were inappropriate. Tatiana rushed off and reappeared with some ruby brooches of her own. When the Baroness refused them, Tatiana was surprised. "We sisters always borrow from each other when we think the jewels of one will suit the dress of the other," she said.

Rank meant little to the girls. They worked alongside their maids in making their own beds and straightening their rooms. Often, they visited the maids in their quarters and played with their children. When they gave instructions, it was never as a command. Instead, the Grand Duchesses said, "If it isn't too difficult for you, my mother asks you to come." Within the household, they were addressed in simple Russian fashion, using their names and patronyms: Olga Nicolaievna, Tatiana Nicolaievna. When they were addressed in public by their full ceremonial titles, the girls were embarrassed. Once at a meeting of a committee of which Tatiana was honorary president, Baroness Buxhoeveden began by saying, "May it please Your Imperial Highness . . ." Tatiana stared in astonishment and, when the Baroness sat down, kicked her violently under the table. "Are you crazy to speak to me like that?" she whispered.

Cut off from other children, knowing little about the outside world, they took the keenest interest in the people and affairs of the household. They knew the names of the Cossacks of the Tsar's escort and of the sailors on the Imperial yacht. Talking freely to these men, they learned the names of their wives and children. They listened to letters, looked at photographs and made small gifts. As children they each had an allowance of only nine dollars a month to spend on notepaper and perfume. When they gave a present, it meant sacrificing something they wanted for themselves.

In their youthful aunt Grand Duchess Olga Alexandrovna, the girls had an intimate friend and benefactress. Every Saturday she came from St. Petersburg to spend the day with her nieces at Tsarskoe Selo. Convinced that the girls needed to get away from the palace, she persuaded the Empress to let her take them into town. Accordingly, every Sunday morning, the aunt and her four excited nieces boarded a train for the capital. Their first stop was a formal luncheon with their grandmother, the Dowager Empress, at the Anitchkov Palace. From there they went on to tea, games and dancing at Olga Alexandrovna's house. Other young people were always present. "The girls enjoyed every minute of it," wrote the Grand Duchess over fifty years later. "Especially my dear god-daughter [Anastasia]. Why

I can still hear her laughter rippling all over the room. Dancing, music, games—why she threw herself wholeheartedly into them all." The day ended when one of the Empress's ladies-in-waiting arrived to take the girls back to Tsarskoe Selo.

In the palace, the two oldest girls shared a bedroom and were known generally as "The Big Pair." Marie and Anastasia shared another bedroom and were called "The Little Pair." When they were children, the Empress dressed them by pairs, the two oldest and the two youngest wearing matching dresses. As they grew up, the sisters gradually made changes in the spare surroundings arranged for them by their parents. The camp beds remained, but icons, paintings and photographs went up along the walls. Frilly dressing tables and couches with green and white embroidered cushions were installed. A large room, divided by a curtain, was used by all four as a combination bath and dressing room. Half the room was filled with wardrobes; behind the curtain stood a large bath of solid silver. In their teens, the girls stopped taking cold baths in the morning and began taking warm baths at night with perfumed bath water. All four girls used Coty perfumes. Olga preferred "*Rose Thé*," Tatiana favored "*Jasmin de Corse*," Anastasia stayed faithfully with "*Violette*" and Marie, who tried many scents, always came back to "*Lilas*."

As Olga and Tatiana grew older, they played a more serious role at public functions. Although in private they still referred to their parents as "Mama" and "Papa," in public they referred to "the Empress" and "the Emperor." Each of the girls was colonel-in-chief of an elite regiment. Wearing its uniform with a broad skirt and boots, they attended military reviews sitting side-saddle on their horses, riding behind the Tsar. Escorted by their father, they began attending theatres and concerts. Carefully chaperoned, they were allowed to play tennis, ride and dance with eligible young officers. At twenty, Olga obtained the use of part of her large fortune and began to respond to appeals for charity. Seeing a child on crutches when she was out for a drive, Olga inquired and found that the parents were too poor to afford treatment. Quietly, Olga began putting aside a monthly allowance to pay the bills.

Nicholas and Alexandra intended that both their older daughters should make their official debuts in 1914 when Olga was nineteen and Tatiana seventeen. But the war intervened and the plans were canceled. The girls remained secluded with the family at Tsarskoe Selo. By 1917, the four daughters of Nicholas II had blossomed into young women whose talents and personalities were, as fate decreed, never to be unfolded and revealed.

"Alexis was the center of this united family, the focus of all its hopes and affections," wrote Pierre Gilliard. "His sisters worshipped him. He was his parents' pride and joy. When he was well, the palace was transformed. Everyone and everything in it seemed bathed in sunshine."

The Tsarevich was a handsome little boy with blue eyes and golden curls which later turned to auburn and became quite straight. From the beginning, he was a happy, high-spirited infant, and his parents never missed an opportunity to show him off. When the baby was only a few months old, the Tsar met A. A. Mosolov, director of the Court Chancellery, just outside the nursery. "I don't think that you have yet seen my dear little Tsarevich," said Nicholas. "Come along and I will show him to you."

"We went in," said Mosolov. "The baby was being given his daily bath. He was lustily kicking out in the water. . . . The Tsar took the child out of his bath towels and put his little feet in the hollow of his hand, supporting him with the other arm. There he was, naked, chubby, rosy—a wonderful boy!"

"Don't you think he's a beauty?" said the Tsar, beaming.

Next day Nicholas said proudly to the Empress, "Yesterday I had the Tsarevich on parade before Mosolov."

In the spring following his birth, the Empress took Alexis for rides in her carriage and was delighted to see the people along the road bowing and smiling before the tiny Heir. When he was still less than a year old, his father took him to a review of the Preobrajensky Regiment. The soldiers gave the baby a mighty "Hurrah!" and Alexis responded with delighted laughter.

From the beginning, the disease of hemophilia hung over this sunny child like a dark cloud. The first ominous evidence had appeared at six weeks, when the boy bled from his navel. As he began to crawl and toddle, the evidence grew stronger: his tumbles caused large, dark blue swellings on his legs and arms. When he was three and a half, a blow on the face brought a swelling which completely closed both eyes. From London, Empress Marie wrote in alarm: "[I heard] that poor little Alexei fell on his forehead and his face was so swollen that it was dreadful to look at him and his eyes were closed. Poor boy, it is terrible, I can imagine how frightened you were. But what did he stumble against? I hope that it is all over now and that his charming little face has not suffered from it." Three weeks later, Nicholas was able to write back: "Thank God the bumps and bruises have left no trace. He is as well and cheerful as his sisters. I constantly work with them in the garden."

Medically, hemophilia meant that the Tsarevich's blood did not clot normally. Any bump or bruise rupturing a tiny blood vessel beneath the skin could begin the slow seepage of blood into surrounding muscle and tissue. Instead of clotting quickly as it would in a normal person, the blood continued to flow unchecked for hours, making a swelling or hematoma as big as a grapefruit. Eventually, when the skin was hard and tight, filled with blood like a balloon, pressure slowed the hemorrhage and a clot finally formed. Then, gradually, a process of re-absorption took place, with the skin turning from a shiny purple to a mottled yellowish-green.

A simple scratch on the Tsarevich's finger was not dangerous. Minor external cuts and scratches anywhere on the surface of the body were treated by pressure and tight bandaging which pinched off the blood and allowed the flesh to heal over. Exceptions, of course, were hemorrhages from the inside of the mouth or nose—areas which could not be bandaged. Once, although no pain was involved, the Tsarevich almost died from a nosebleed.

The worst pain and the permanent crippling effects of Alexis's hemophilia came from bleeding into the joints. Blood entering the confined space of an ankle, knee or elbow joint caused pressure on the nerves and brought nightmarish pain. Sometimes the cause of the injury was apparent, sometimes not. In either case, Alexis awakened in the morning to call, "Mama, I can't walk today," or "Mama, I can't bend my elbow." At first, as the limb flexed, leaving the largest possible area in the joint socket for the incoming fluids, the pain was small. Then, as this space filled up, it began to hurt. Morphine was available, but because of its destructive habit-forming quality, the Tsarevich was never given the drug. His only release from pain was fainting.

Once inside the joint, the blood had a corrosive effect, destroying bone, cartilage and tissue. As the bone formation changed, the limbs locked in a rigid, bent position. The best therapy for this condition was constant exercise and massage, but it was undertaken at the risk of once again beginning the hemorrhage. As a result, Alexis's normal treatment included a grim catalogue of heavy iron orthopedic devices which, along with constant hot mud baths, were designed to straighten his limbs. Needless to say, each such episode meant weeks in bed.*

The combination of exalted rank and hemophilia saw to it that Alexis grew up under a degree of care rarely lavished on any child. While he was very young, nurses surrounded him every minute. When he was five, his doctors suggested that he be given a pair of male companions and bodyguards. Two sailors from the Imperial Navy, named Derevenko and Nagorny, were selected and assigned to protect the Tsarevich from harm. When Alexis was ill, they acted as nurses. "Derevenko was so patient and resourceful, that he often did wonders in alleviating the pain," wrote Anna Vyrubova, an intimate friend of the Empress. "I can still hear the plaintive voice of Alexis begging the big sailor, 'Lift my arm,' 'Put up my leg,' 'Warm my hands,' and I can see the patient, calm-eyed man working for hours to give comfort to the little pain-wracked limbs."

Hemophilia is a fickle disease, and for weeks, sometimes months, Alexis seemed as well as any child. By nature he was as noisy, lively and mischievous as Anastasia. As a toddler, he liked to scoot down the hall and break into his sisters' classroom, interrupting their lessons, only to be carried off, arms waving. As a child of three or four, he often made appearances at the table, making the round from place to place to shake hands and chatter with each guest. Once he plunged beneath the table, pulled off the slipper of one of the maids-of-honor and carried it proudly as a trophy to his father. Nicholas sternly ordered him to put it back, and the Tsarevich disappeared again under the table. Suddenly the lady screamed. Before replacing the slipper on her foot, Alexis had inserted into its toe an enormous ripe strawberry. Thereafter, for several weeks he was not allowed at the dinner table.

"He thoroughly enjoyed life—when it let him—and he was a happy, romping boy," wrote Gilliard. "He was very simple in his tastes and he entertained no false satisfaction because he was the Heir; there was nothing he thought less about." Like any small boy's, his pockets were

* Today, at the first sign of severe bleeding, hemophiliacs are given transfusions of frozen fresh blood plasma or plasma concentrates. New non-habit-forming drugs are used to lessen pain. Where necessary, joints are protected by intricate plastic and light metal braces. Most of these developments in the treatment of hemophilia are quite recent. The use of plasma, for example, was a medical outgrowth of the Second World War, while the design of new lightweight braces is the result of new syntheses of metals and plastics. Hemophilia today is a severe but more manageable disease, and most hemophiliacs can survive the difficult years of childhood to live relatively normal adult lives.

filled with string, nails and pebbles. Within the family, he obeyed his older sisters and wore their outgrown nightgowns. Nevertheless, outside the family, Alexis understood that he was more important than his sisters. In public, it was he who sat or stood beside his father. He was the one greeted by shouts of "The Heir!" and the one whom people crowded around and often tried to touch. When a deputation of peasants brought him a gift, they dropped to their knees. Gilliard asked him why he received them thus, and Alexis replied, "I don't know. Derevenko says it must be so." Told that a group of officers of his regiment had arrived to call on him, he interrupted a romp with his sisters. "Now girls, run away," the six-year-old boy said, "I am busy. Someone has just called to see me on business."

Sometimes, impressed by the deference shown him, Alexis was rude. At six, he walked into the waiting room of his father's study and found the Foreign Minister, Alexander Izvolsky, waiting to see the Tsar. Izvolsky remained seated. Alexis marched up to the Minister and said in a loud voice, "When the Heir to the Russian Throne enters a room, people must get up." More often, he was gracious. To one of his mother's ladies-in-waiting who had done him a favor, the Tsarevich extended his hand in an exact imitation of his father and said with a smile, "It is really nice of you, you know." As he grew older, he became sensitive to the subtleties of rank and etiquette. At nine, he sent a collection of his favorite jingles to Gleb Botkin, the doctor's son, who drew well. Along with the jingles he sent a note, "To illustrate and write the jingles under the drawings. Alexis." Then, before handing the note to Dr. Botkin to take to Gleb, Alexis abruptly crossed out his signature. "If I send that paper to Gleb with my signature on it, then it would be an order which Gleb would have to obey," the Tsarevich explained. "But I mean it only as a request and he doesn't have to do it if he doesn't want to."

As Alexis grew older, his parents carefully explained to him the need to avoid bumps and blows. Yet, being an active child, Alexis was attracted to the very things that involved the greatest danger. "Can't I have my own bicycle?" he would beg his mother. "Alexei, you know you can't." "May I please play tennis?" "Dear, you know you mustn't." Then, with a gush of tears, Alexis would cry, "Why can other boys have everything and I nothing?" There were times when Alexis simply ignored all restraints and did as he pleased. This risk-taking behavior, common enough among hemophiliac boys to be medically labeled the "Daredevil reaction," was compounded of many things: rebellion against constant overprotection, a subconscious need to prove invulnerability to harm and, most important, the simple desire to be and play like a normal child.

Once, at seven, he appeared in the middle of a review of the palace guard, riding a secretly borrowed bicycle across the parade ground. The astonished Tsar promptly halted the review and ordered every man to pursue, surround and capture the wobbling vehicle and its delighted novice rider. At a children's party at which movies had been shown, Alexis suddenly led the children on top of the tables and began leaping wildly from table to table. When Derevenko and others tried to calm him, he shouted gaily, "All grown-ups have to go," and tried to push them out the door.

By deluging him with expensive gifts, his parents hoped to make him forget the games he was forbidden to play. His room was filled with elaborate toys: There were "great railways with dolls in the carriages as passengers, with barriers, stations, buildings and signal boxes, flashing engines and marvelous signalling apparatus, whole battalions of tin soldiers, models of towns with church towers and domes, floating models of ships, perfectly equipped factories with doll workers and mines in exact imitation of the real thing, with miners ascending and descending. All the toys were mechanically operated and the little Prince had only to press a button to set the workers in motion, to drive the warships up and down the tank, to set the church-bells ringing and the soldiers marching."

Like his father, Alexis was enthralled by military pageantry. From birth, he had borne the title of Hetman of all the Cossacks and, along with his toy soldiers, toy forts and toy guns, he had his own Cossack uniform with fur cap, boots and dagger. In the summer, he wore a miniature uniform of a sailor of the Russian navy. As a child, he said that he wanted most to be like one of the ancient tsars, riding his white horse, leading his troops into battle. As he began spending more and more time in bed, he realized that he would never be that kind of tsar.

Alexis had an ear for music. Unlike his sisters, who played the piano, he preferred the balalaika and learned to play it well. He liked nature and kept a number of pets. His favorite was a silky spaniel named Joy, whose long ears dragged on the ground. From a circus the Tsar acquired an aged performing donkey with a repertory of tricks. When Alexis visited the stable, Vanka, the donkey, expected to find sugar in his master's pocket; if it was there, he turned it out with his nose. In the winter, Vanka was harnessed to a sled and pulled Alexis about the park.

Once Alexis was presented with the rarest pet of all, a tame sable. Caught by an old hunter in the depths of Siberia, it had been tamed by the old man and his wife, who decided to bring it as a present to the Tsar. The couple arrived, having spent every kopeck on the long journey. After the palace authorities had checked by telegram with their home village to make sure that the two were not revolutionaries, the Empress was informed. An hour later a message came back, instructing the old man and woman to come with the sable "as quickly as possible. The children are wild with impatience." Later the old hunter himself described to a palace official what had happened:

"Father Tsar came in. We threw ourselves at his feet. The sable looked at him as if it understood that it was the Tsar himself. We went into the children's room. The Tsar told me to let the sable go and the children began to play with it. Then the Tsar told us to sit down on chairs. He began to ask me questions. What made me think of coming to see him . . . What things are like in Siberia, How we go hunting . . . [The sable, meanwhile, was racing around the room, pursued by the children, leaving a trail of ruin.] Father Tsar asked what had to be done for the sable. When I explained, he told me to send it to the Hunters village at Gatchina. But I said,

" 'Father Tsar, that won't do. All the hunters will be wanting to sell the skin of my sable. They will kill it and say the animal had an accident. . . . '

"The Tsar said:

" 'I would have chosen a hunter I could trust. But perhaps after all you are right. Take it back with you to Siberia. Look after it as long as it lives. That is an order you have received from me. . . . But mind, don't forget to look well after the sable; it's my sable now. God be with you!' "

The old man was given a watch crested with the Imperial eagle and the old woman a brooch. They were paid generously for the sable and also given money to travel home. But the children were inconsolable. "There was no help for it," they said. "Papa had made up his mind."

Pets were only a substitute for what Alexis really wanted: boys his own age as playmates. Because of his hemophilia, the Empress did not want him to play often with the small Romanov cousins who appeared infrequently at the palace with their parents. She considered most of them rough and rude, and she was afraid that they would knock Alexis down while playing their games. His most constant companions were the two young sons of Derevenko the sailor, who played with Alexis while their father watched. If the play got rough, Derevenko growled and the three children obeyed immediately. Later, carefully selected young cadets from the military academy were instructed as to the danger involved and then brought to the palace to play with the Tsarevich.

More often, Alexis played with his sisters or by himself. "Luckily," wrote Gilliard, "his sisters liked playing with him. They brought into his life an element of youthful merriment that otherwise would have been sorely missed." Sometimes, by himself, he simply lay on his back staring up at the blue sky. When he was ten, his sister Olga asked him what he was doing so quietly. "I like to think and wonder," said Alexis. "What about?" Olga persisted. "Oh, so many things," he said. "I enjoy the sun and the beauty of summer as long as I can. Who knows whether one of these days I shall not be prevented from doing it?"

More than anyone else outside the family, Pierre Gilliard understood the nature of hemophilia and what it meant to the Tsarevich and his family. His understanding developed gradually. He came to Russia from Switzerland in 1904 at the age of twenty-five. In 1906, he began tutoring Alexis's sisters in French. For six years, he came to the palace almost every day to tutor the girls without ever really knowing the Tsarevich. He saw the boy as a baby in his mother's arms; later he caught glimpses of him running down a corridor or out in the snow riding his sled, but nothing more. Of Alexis's disease the tutor was almost completely ignorant.

"At times, his visits [to his sisters' classroom] would suddenly cease and he would be seen no more for a long time," Gilliard wrote. "Every time he disappeared, the palace was smitten with the greatest depression. My pupils' [the girls] mood was melancholy which they tried in vain to conceal. When I asked them the cause, they replied evasively, 'Alexis Nicolaievich is not well.' I knew that he was prey to a disease . . . the nature of which no one told me."

In 1912, at the request of the Empress, Gilliard began tutoring Alexis in French. He found himself confronted with an eight-and-a-half-year-old boy "rather tall for his age . . . a long, finely chiseled face, delicate features, auburn hair with a coppery glint, and large grey-blue eyes like his mother. . . . He had a quick wit and a keen, penetrating mind. He surprised me with questions beyond his years which bore witness to a delicate and intuitive spirit. Those not forced to teach him habits of discipline as I was, could quickly fall under the spell of his charm. Under the capricious little creature I had first known, I discovered a child of a naturally affectionate disposition, sensitive to suffering in others just because he suffered so much himself."

Gilliard's first problem was establishing discipline. Because of her love and fear for him, the Empress could not be firm with her son. Alexis obeyed only the Tsar, who was not always present. His illness interrupted his lessons for weeks at a time, sapping his energy and his interest, so that even when he was well he tended to laziness. "At this time, he was the kind of child who can hardly bear correction," Gilliard wrote. "He had never been under any regular discipline. In his eyes, I was the person appointed to extract work from him. . . . I had the definite impression of his mute hostility. . . . As time passed, my authority took hold, the more the boy opened his heart to me, the better I realized the treasures of his nature and I began to feel that with so many precious gifts, it was unjust to give up hope."

Gilliard also worried about the isolation which surrounded Alexis. Princes inevitably live outside the normal routine of normal boys and, in Alexis's case, this isolation was greatly intensified by his hemophilic condition. Gilliard was determined to do something about it. His account of what happened—of the decision by Nicholas and Alexandra to accept his advice and of the anguish they and Alexis suffered when a bleeding episode ensued—is the most intimate and moving eyewitness account available of how life was really lived in the inner world of Tsarskoe Selo:

"At first I was astonished and disappointed at the lack of support given me by the Tsaritsa," wrote Gilliard. . . . "Dr. Derevenko [coincidentally, the Tsarevich's doctor had the same name as his sailor attendant, although the two were unrelated] told me that in view of the constant danger of the boy's relapse and as a result of the religious fatalism developed by the Tsaritsa, she tended to leave the decision to circumstance and kept postponing her intervention which would inflict useless suffering on her son if he were not to survive. . . ."

Gilliard disagreed with Dr. Derevenko. "I considered that the perpetual presence of the sailor Derevenko and his assistant Nagorny were harmful to the child. The external power which intervened whenever danger threatened seemed to me to hinder the development of will-power and the faculty of observation. What the child gained possibly in safety, he lost in real discipline. I thought it would be better to give him more freedom and accustom him to resist the impulses of his own motion.

"Besides, accidents continued to happen. It was impossible to guard against everything and the closer the supervision, the more irritating and humiliating it seemed to the boy and the greater the risk that it would develop his skill at evasion and make him cunning and deceitful. It was the best way to turn an already physically delicate child into a characterless individual without self-control and backbone even in the moral sense.

"I spoke . . . to Dr. Derevenko, but he was so obsessed by fears of a fatal attack and so conscious of the terrible responsibility that devolved on him as a doctor that I could not bring him around to share my view. It was for the parents and the parents alone to take a decision which might have serious consequences for their child. To my great astonishment, they entirely agreed with me and said they were ready to accept all risks of an experiment on which I did not enter myself without terrible anxiety. No doubt they realized how much harm the existing system was doing to all the best in their son and if they loved him to distraction . . . their love itself gave them the strength to run the risk of an accident . . . rather than see him grow up a man without strength of character. . . . Alexis Nicolaievich was delighted at this decision. In his relations with his playmates, he was always suffering from the incessant supervision to which he was subject. He promised me to repay the confidence reposed in him.

"Everything went well at first and I was beginning to be easy in my mind when the accident I had so much feared happened without warning. The Tsarevich was in the classroom standing on a chair, when he slipped and in falling hit his right knee against the corner of some piece of furniture. The next day he could not walk. On the day after, the subcutaneous hemorrhage had progressed and the swelling which formed below the knee rapidly spread down the leg. The skin, which was greatly distended, had hardened under the force of the blood and . . . caused pain which worsened every hour.

"I was thunderstruck. Yet neither the Tsar nor the Tsaritsa blamed me in the slightest. So far from it, they seemed intent on preventing me from despairing. . . . The Tsaritsa was at her son's bedside from the first onset of the attack. She watched over him, surrounding him with her tender love and care and trying a thousand attentions to alleviate his sufferings. The Tsar came the moment he was free. He tried to comfort and amuse the boy, but the pain was stronger than his mother's caresses or his father's stories and moans and tears began once more. Every now and then, the door opened and one of the Grand Duchesses came in on tiptoe and kissed her little brother, bringing a gust of sweetness and health into the room. For a moment, the boy would open his great eyes, around which the malady had already painted black circles, and then almost immediately, close them again.

"One morning I found the mother at her son's bedside. He had had a very bad night. Dr. Derevenko was anxious as the hemorrhage had not stopped and his temperature was rising. The inflammation had spread and the pain was worse than the day before. The Tsarevich lay in bed groaning piteously. His head rested on his mother's arm and his small, deadly white face was unrecognizable. At times the groans ceased and he murmured the one word, 'Mummy.' His mother kissed him on the hair, forehead, and eyes as if the touch of her lips would relieve him of his pain and restore some of the life which was leaving him. Think of the torture of that mother, an impotent witness of her son's martyrdom in those hours of anguish—a mother who knew that she herself was the cause of those sufferings, that she had transmitted the terrible disease against which human science was powerless. Now I understood the secret tragedy of her life. How easy it was to reconstruct the stages of that long Calvary."

CHAPTER TWELVE

A Mother's Agony

HEMOPHILIA is as old as man. It has come down through the centuries, misted in legend, shrouded with the dark dread of a hereditary curse. In the Egypt of the Pharaohs, a woman was forbidden to bear further children if her firstborn son bled to death from a minor wound. The ancient Talmud barred circumcision in a family if two successive male children had suffered fatal hemorrhages.

Because over the last one hundred years it has appeared in the ruling houses of Britain, Russia and Spain, it has been called "the royal disease." It has also been called "the disease of the Hapsburgs"; this is inaccurate, for no prince of the Austrian dynasty has ever suffered from hemophilia. It remains one of the most mysterious and malicious of all the genetic, chronic diseases. Even today, both the cause and the cure are unknown.

In medical terms, hemophilia is an inherited blood-clotting deficiency, transmitted by women according to the sex-linked recessive Mendelian pattern. Thus, while women carry the defective genes, they almost never suffer from the disease. With rare exceptions, it strikes only males. Yet it does not necessarily strike all the males in a family. Genetically as well as clinically, hemophilia is capricious. Members of a family in which hemophilia has appeared never know, on the birth of a new son, whether or not the child will have hemophilia. If the child is a girl, the family cannot know with certainty whether she is a hemophilic carrier until she grows and has children of her own. The secret is locked inside the structure of the chromosomes.*

If modern science has made little progress in finding the cause of or a cure for hemophilia, it has achieved an extensive charting of the scope of the disease. Hemophilia follows no geographical or racial pattern; it appears on all continents, in all races at a statistical ratio of one hemophiliac among every 5,000 males. In the United States, there are 200,000 hemophiliacs. Theoretically, the disease should appear only in families which have a previous history of hemophilia. But today, in the United States, forty percent of all cases appearing have no traceable family history. One explanation for this is that the defective gene can remain hidden for as many as seven or eight generations. A more probable explanation is that the genes are spontaneously changing or mutating. What causes these spontaneous mutations, no one knows. Some researchers believe they are the result of new and rapidly changing environmental factors such as drugs or radiation. In any case, their number apparently is increasing.

The most famous case of spontaneous mutation occurred in the family of Queen Victoria. The tiny indomitable woman who ruled England for sixty-four years and who was "Granny" to most of Europe's royalty was, unknowingly at her marriage, a hemophilic carrier. The youngest of her four sons, Prince Leopold, Duke of Albany, had hemophilia. Two of her five daughters, Princess Alice

* At the heart of the problem of hemophilia are the genes which issue the biochemical instructions that tell the body how to grow and nourish itself. Gathered in curiously shaped agglomerations of matter called chromosomes, they are probably the most intricate bundles of information known. They determine the nature of every one of the trillions of highly specialized cells that make up a human being. Scientists know that the defective gene which causes hemophilia appears on one of the female sex chromosomes, known as X chromosomes, but they have never precisely pinpointed the location of the faulty gene or determined the nature of the flaw. Chemically, most doctors believe that hemophilia is caused by the absence of some ingredient, probably a protein factor, which causes normal blood to coagulate. But one eminent hematologist, the late Dr. Leandro Tocantins of Philadelphia, believed that hemophilia is caused by the presence of an extra ingredient, an inhibitor, which blocks the normal clotting process. Nobody really knows.

There is a remote prospect that current research into the structure of chromosomes will help hemophiliacs. If it should become possible to locate the genes responsible—and then to correct or substitute for the faulty gene—hemophilia could be cured. But medical researchers hold out little hope for the immediate future. So far, science has been unable to change genetic characteristics in any form of life except bacteria.

and Princess Beatrice, were hemophilic carriers. When the daughters of Alice and Beatrice—Queen Victoria's granddaughters—married into the royal houses of Russia and Spain, their sons, the heirs to those two thrones, were born with hemophilia.

The Queen, on learning that her own son had hemophilia, was astonished. Bewildered, she protested that "this disease is not in our family," and indeed it had not appeared until that point. A spontaneous mutation had occurred, either in the genetic material of Victoria herself or on the X chromosome passed to her at conception by her father, the Duke of Kent. Nevertheless, soon after Leopold's birth in 1853, the evidence of the disease in the form of bumps and bruises was unmistakable. At the age of ten, he was assigned to tend, during a family wedding, his equally stubborn, four-year-old nephew William, the future Kaiser. When William fidgeted and Leopold reprimanded, the small German boy bit his uncle on the leg. Leopold was unharmed, but Queen Victoria was angry. Leopold grew up a tall, intelligent, affectionate and stubborn prince. Throughout his boyhood and adolescence, his wilfulness often led to hemorrhaging, and he was left with a chronically lame knee. In 1868, the *British Medical Journal* reported one of his bleeding episodes: "His Royal Highness . . . who has previously been in full health and activity, has been suffering during the last week from severe accidental hemorrhage. The Prince was reduced to a state of extreme and dangerous exhaustion by the loss of blood." In 1875, when Leopold was twenty-two, the same journal recorded: "The peculiar ability of the Prince to suffer severe hemorrhage, from which he has always been a sufferer . . . is essentially a case for vigilant medical attendance and most careful nursing. . . . He is in the hands of those who have watched him from the cradle and who are armed by the special experience of his constitution, as well as the most ample command of professional resources."

The Queen reacted in a manner typical of hemophilic parents. She was unusually attached to this son, worried about him, overprotected him, and as a result of her constant admonitions to be careful, she often fought with him. When he was fifteen, she gave him the Order of the Garter at a younger age than his brothers "because he was far more advanced in mind and because I wish to give him this encouragement and pleasure as he has so many privations and disappointments." When Leopold was twenty-six, his mother wrote to the Prime Minister, Benjamin Disraeli, that Leopold could not represent her at the opening of an Australian exposition as Disraeli had asked. Using the royal third person, the Queen wrote: "She cannot bring herself to consent to send her very delicate son who has been *four or five times at death's door* [italics the Queen's] and who is *never* hardly a *few* months without being laid up, to a great *distance*, to a climate to which he is a stranger and to expose him to dangers which he may not be able to avert. Even if he did not suffer, the terrible anxiety which the Queen would undergo would unfit her for her duties at home and might undermine her health."

Constantly frustrated by his mother's attempts to shelter him, Leopold looked for something to do. His older brother Bertie, the Prince of Wales, suggested giving him command of the Balmoral Volunteers, a military company stationed near the royal castle in Scotland. The Queen, fearing for Leopold's knee, declined, and Leopold thereafter refused to go to Balmoral. When the Queen tried to keep her son sequestered on an upper floor of Buckingham Palace, Leopold slipped away for two weeks to Paris. At twenty-nine, to his mother's surprise, he found a German princess, Helen of Waldeck, who was unafraid of the disease and willing to marry him. They lived happily for two years and she bore him a daughter. Helen was pregnant a second time when, in Cannes, Leopold fell, suffered a minor blow on the head and died, at thirty-one, of a brain hemorrhage. His mother sorrowed for herself and the family, but, she wrote in her journal, "for dear Leopold himself, we could not repine . . . there was such a restless longing for what he could not have . . . that seemed to increase rather than lessen."

Prince Leopold, the first of the royal hemophiliacs, was the Empress Alexandra's uncle. His affliction meant that all of his five sisters were potential carriers, but only Alice and Beatrice actually transmitted the mutant gene into their offspring. Of Alice's eight children, two of the girls—Alix and Irene—were carriers. One son, Alix's brother Frederick, called "Frittie," was a hemophiliac. At two, he bled for three days from a cut on the ear. At three, Frittie and his older brother Ernest burst romping into their mother's room one morning while she was still in bed. The windows which reached to the floor were open. Frittie tumbled out and fell twenty feet to the stone terrace below. No bones were broken and at first he seemed only shaken and bruised. But bleeding in the brain had begun, and by nightfall Frittie was dead.

The Empress Alexandra was a year-old baby when Frittie died, and she was twelve at the death of Leopold. Neither tragedy struck her personally. Her first meaningful contact with hemophilia occurred when it appeared in her two nephews, the sons of her older sister Irene and Prince Henry of Prussia. One of these boys, a younger Prince Henry, died, apparently of bleeding, at the age of four in 1904, just before the birth of Alexis. His short life was lived behind palace walls and his disease was concealed, probably to hide the fact that hemophilia had appeared in the German Imperial family. The older brother, Prince Waldemar, survived to the age of fifty-six and died in 1945.

Under normal circumstances, the appearance of hemophilia in her uncle, her brother and her nephews should have indicated to Alexandra the possibility that she was carrying the hemophilic gene. The genetic pattern had long been known: it was discovered in 1803 by Dr. John Conrad Otto of Philadelphia and confirmed in 1820 by Dr. Christian Nasse of Bonn. In 1865, the Austrian monk and botanist Gregor Johann Mendel formulated his law of genetics, based on twenty-five years of cross-breeding garden peas. In 1876, a French doctor named Grandidier declared that "all members of bleeder families should be advised against marriage." And by 1905, a year after Alexis was born, Dr. M. Litten, a New Yorker, had had sufficient experience with the disease to write that hemophilic boys should be supervised while playing with other children and that they should not be subjected to corporal punishment. "Bleeders with means," he added, "should take up some learned profession; if they are students, dueling is forbidden."

Why, then, did it come as such an overwhelming shock to Alexandra that her son had hemophilia?

One reason suggested by the late British geneticist J. B. S. Haldane is that although the genetic pattern was known to doctors, this knowledge never penetrated the closed circles of royal courts: "It is predictable," wrote Haldane, "that Nicholas knew that his fiancée had hemophiliac brothers although nothing is said in his diaries or letters, but by virtue of his education, he attached no importance to this knowledge. It is possible that they or their counselors consulted doctors. We do not know and doubtless will never know if . . . the court doctor counseled against marriage. If a distinguished doctor outside court circles had desired to warn Nicholas of the dangerous character of his approaching marriage, I do not believe he would have been able to do it, either directly or in the columns of the press. Kings are carefully protected against disagreeable realities. . . . The hemophilia of the Tsarevich was a symptom of the divorce between royalty and reality."

There is, as Haldane says, no evidence that either Nicholas or Alexandra ever interpreted the laws of genetics to determine their own chance of having a hemophilic son. Almost certainly, both considered the mystery of the disease, of who would and would not be afflicted, to be a matter in the hands of God. This also seems to have been the attitude of Queen Victoria, who apparently did not understand the hereditary pattern of the disease she had spread so widely. When one of her grandchildren died in childhood, she wrote simply, "Our poor family seems persecuted by this awful disease, the worst I know."

If Alexandra was surrounded by hemophilic relatives before she married, so were most of the princesses of Europe. So numerous were Queen Victoria's royal progeny—nine children and thirty-four grandchildren—that the defective gene had been spread far and wide. In marrying and having children, hemophilia was considered one of the hazards royal parents faced, along with diphtheria, pneumonia, smallpox and scarlet fever. Royal princes, even those who were heirs to a throne, did not shy away from a prospective mate because there was hemophilia in her family. Prince Albert Victor of England, who, had he lived, would have been king in place of his younger brother, George V, sought Princess Alix's hand before Nicholas won it. Had they married, hemophilia would have come down through the line of the British royal family. Kaiser William II was surrounded on all sides by hemophilia. He and his six sons escaped, but his uncle and two of his nephews were victims. William himself was in love with Ella, Empress Alexandra's older sister. Had Ella married William instead of Grand Duke Serge (they were childless), the Kaiser also might have had a hemophilic heir.

In that era, every family, including royal families, had a long string of children and expected to lose one or two in the process of growing up. The death of a child was never a casual experience, but it rarely brought the life of a family to more than a temporary halt. Nevertheless, in Alexandra's case the mere threat of death of her youngest child involved her totally, and through her, the fate of an ancient dynasty and the history of a great nation. Why was this so?

It is important to understand what the birth of Alexis meant to Alexandra. Her greatest desire after her marriage had been to give the Russian autocracy a male heir. Over the next ten years, she had four daughters, each healthy, charming and loved, but still not an Heir to the Throne. The Russian crown no longer passed down through the female as well as the male line, as it had to the daughters of Peter the Great and to Catherine the Great. Catherine's son, Tsar Paul, hated his mother and changed the law of succession so that only males could inherit the throne. Thus, if Alexandra could not produce a son, the succession would pass first to Nicholas's younger brother Michael and after that, into the family of his uncle Grand Duke Vladimir. Each time Alexandra became pregnant, she prayed fervently for a boy. Each time, it seemed, her prayers were ignored. When Anastasia, their fourth daughter, was born, Nicholas had to leave the palace and walk in the park to overcome his disappointment before facing his wife. The birth of the Tsarevich, therefore, meant far more to his mother than the arrival of just another child. This baby was the crowning of her marriage, the fruit of her hours of prayer, God's blessing on her, on her husband and on the people of Russia.

All who saw the Empress with her infant son in those first months were struck with her happiness. At thirty-two, Alexandra was tall, still slender, with gray-blue eyes and long red-gold hair. The child in her arms appeared to be glowing with health. "I saw the Tsarevich in the Empress's arms," wrote Anna Vyrubova. "How beautiful he was, how healthy, how normal, with his golden hair, his blue eyes, and his expression of intelligence so rare for so young a child." Pierre Gilliard first saw the Tsarevich when his future pupil was eighteen months old. "I could see she [Alexandra] was transfused by the delirious joy of a mother who had at last seen her dearest wish fulfilled. She was proud and happy in the beauty of her child. The Tsarevich certainly was one of the handsomest babies one could imagine, with lovely fair curls, great grey-blue eyes under the fringe of long curling lashes and the fresh pink color of a healthy child. When he smiled, there were two little dimples in his chubby cheeks."

Because she had waited so long and prayed so hard for her son, the revelation that Alexis suffered from hemophilia struck Alexandra with savage force. From that moment, she lived in the particular sunless world reserved for the mothers of hemophiliacs. For any woman, there is no more exquisite torture than watching helplessly as a beloved child suffers in extreme pain. Alexis, like every other child, looked to his mother for protection. When he hemorrhaged into a joint and the pounding pain obliterated everything else from his consciousness, he still was able to cry, "Mama, help me, help me!" For Alexandra sitting beside him, unable to help, each cry seemed a sword thrust into the bottom of her heart.

Almost worse for the Empress than the actual episodes of bleeding was the terrible Damoclean uncertainty of hemophilia. Other chronic diseases may handicap a child and dismay the mother, but in time both learn to adjust their lives to the medical facts. In hemophilia, however, there is no *status quo*. One minute Alexis could be playing happily and normally. The next, he might stumble, fall and begin a bleeding episode that would take him to the brink of death. It could strike at any time in any part of the body: the head, nose, mouth, kidneys, joints, or muscles.

Like Queen Victoria's, Alexandra's natural reaction was to overprotect her child. The royal family of Spain put its hemophilic sons in padded suits and padded the trees in the park when they went out to play. Alexandra's solution was to assign the two sailors to hover so closely over Alexis that they could reach out and catch him before he fell. Yet, as Gilliard pointed out to the Empress, this kind of protection can stifle the spirit, producing a dependent, warped and crippled mind. Alexandra responded gallantly, withdrawing the two guardians to permit her son to make his own mistakes, take his own steps and—if necessary—fall and bruise. But it was she who accepted the risk and who bore the additional burden of guilt when an accident followed.

To maintain the balance which provides adequate protection as well as attempting a degree of normalcy is a cruel strain for a mother. Except when the child is asleep, there are no hours of relaxation. The toll on the Empress was like battle fatigue; after too long a period of sustained alertness, her emotions were drained. This often happens to soldiers in war, and when it does, they are withdrawn from the front to rest. But for the mother of a hemophiliac there is no withdrawal. The battle goes on forever and the battlefield is everywhere.

Hemophilia means great loneliness for a woman. At first, when a hemophilic boy is born, the characteristic maternal reaction is a vigorous resolve to fight: somehow, somewhere, there must be a specialist who can declare that a mistake has been made, or that a cure is just around the corner. One by one, all the specialists are consulted. One by one, they sadly shake their heads. The particular emotional security that doctors normally provide when confronting illness is gone. The mother realizes that she is alone.

Having discovered this and accepted it, she begins to prefer it that way. The normal world, going about its everyday life, seems coldly unfeeling. Since the normal world cannot help and does not understand, she prefers to cut herself off from it. Her family becomes her refuge. Here, where sadness need not be hidden, there are no questions and no pretensions. This inner world becomes the mother's reality. So it was for the Empress Alexandra in the little world of Tsarskoe Selo. Alexandra, trying to control the waves of anxiety and frustration that kept rolling over her, sought answers by throwing herself into the Church. The Russian Orthodox Church is an emotional church with a strong belief in the healing power of faith and prayer. As soon as the Empress realized that no doctor could aid her son, she determined to wrest from God the miracle which science denied. "God is just," she declared, and plunged into renewed attempts to win His mercy by the fervent passion of her prayers.

Hour after hour, she prayed, either in the small room off her bedroom or in the palace chapel, a darkened chamber lined with silken tapestries. For greater privacy, she established a small chapel in the crypt of the Fedorovski Sobor, a church in the Imperial Park used by the household and soldiers of the Guard. Here, alone on the stone floors, by the light of oil lamps, she begged for the health of her son.

In periods when Alexis was well, she dared to hope. "God has heard me," she cried. Even as the years passed and one hemorrhage followed another, Alexandra refused to believe that God had deserted her. Instead, she decided that she herself must be unworthy of receiving a miracle. Knowing that the disease had been transmitted through her body, she began to dwell on her own guilt. Obviously, she told herself, if she had been the instrument of her son's torture, she could not also become the instrument of his salvation. God had rejected her prayers; therefore she must find someone who was closer to God to intercede on her behalf. When Gregory Rasputin, the Siberian peasant who was reported to have miraculous powers of faith healing, arrived in St. Petersburg, Alexandra believed that God had at last given her an answer.

For most young mothers of hemophilic sons, encircled by corrosive fear and ignorance, hope is thin and help is uncertain. The greatest support which any woman can have in this lonely torment is the love and understanding of her husband. In this respect, Nicholas's contribution was remarkable. No man ever was gentler or more compassionate to his wife, or spent more time with his afflicted son. However this last Russian tsar may be judged as a monarch, his behavior as a husband and father was something which shone nobly apart.

The other support which the mother of a hemophiliac can hope for is the understanding of her friends. Here, Alexandra was at a special disadvantage. She had never made friends easily. The friends of her childhood had been left behind in Germany; when she came to Russia at twenty-two, it was to move onto the lofty isolation of the throne. Even before Alexis was born, Alexandra disliked the gay balls and empty life of society and the court. After his birth, she was wholly involved in her private struggle, and the normal life of a woman of her station seemed even emptier and more superficial. What she longed to find was, not the stylized attentions and conversations of most ladies of the court, but the simple, profound friendship of the heart which leaps all barriers and reaches from one soul into another, sharing the most intimate fears, dreams and hopes.

Once in a letter to Princess Marie Bariatinsky, one of the few close friends of her first years in Russia, the Empress described what she sought in her friends: "I must have a person to myself; if I want to be my *real* self. I am not made to shine before an assembly—I have not got the easy nor the witty talk one needs for that. I like the *internal being*, and that attracts me with great force. As you know, I am of the preacher type. I want to help others in life, to help them to fight their battles and bear their crosses."

The compulsion to fight other people's battles and help bear their crosses stemmed in part from Alexandra's own frustration. Nothing is more discouraging and debilitating than to be permanently confronted with a situation which never changes and which cannot be changed, no matter how hard one tries. Frequently, mothers of hemophiliacs experience an overwhelming urge to throw themselves into helping others who *can* be helped. Many of the problems of this world, unlike hemophilia, hold out some promise of hope. By helping others, Alexandra was actually trying to keep a grip on her own faith and sanity.

One of those whom the Empress helped in this way was Princess Sonia Orbeliani. A Georgian girl who arrived at court in 1898 at the age of twenty-three, Sonia Orbeliani was small, blonde and high-spirited, an excellent sportswoman and a fine musician. The Empress was always fond of Sonia's cleverness and cheerfulness, but it was not until the girl fell ill while accompanying the Imperial party on a visit to Darmstadt that Alexandra's feelings were fully aroused. As soon as Sonia became sick, Alexandra dropped everything to care for her, despite the criticism of her German relations and of members of the Imperial suite. The illness was a wasting spinal disease which all knew was hopeless. But for nine years, until Sonia died, Alexandra made her life worth living.

"The Empress had great moral influence over her," wrote Baroness Buxhoeveden, a lady-in-waiting who witnessed the long ordeal. "It was she who led the doomed woman who knew what was awaiting her, to the attainment of that wonderful Christian submission with which she not only patiently bore her malady but managed to keep a cheerful spirit and keen interest in life. For nine long years, whatever her own health was, the Empress never paid her daily visit to her children without going to Sonia's rooms, which adjoined those of the Grand Duchesses. When Sonia had an acute attack of illness . . . the Empress went to her not only several times a day but often at night when she was very ill: indeed no mother could have been more loving. Special carriages and special appliances were made for Sonia so that she could share the general life as if she were well. . . . She followed the Empress everywhere."

Sonia Orbeliani died in 1915 in the hospital at Tsarskoe Selo where the Empress Alexandra was tending wounded soldiers from the battlefront. Rather than change into black mourning clothes, Alexandra came directly to the memorial service in her nurse's uniform. "I feel somehow nearer to her like this, more human, less Empress," she said. Late that evening, before the coffin was closed, Alexandra sat beside the body of her friend, staring at the peaceful face, stroking the golden hair. "Leave me here," she said to those who wanted to take her away to rest. "I would like to be a little more with Sonia."

Sonia Orbeliani came close to being what Alexandra so fervently desired at the Russian court: a friend of the heart. But even Sonia never fully tapped the immense reservoir of emotion inside the Empress. Outside her own family, the only person to whom Alexandra ever fully opened her whole soul was a heavy, round-faced young woman named Anna Vyrubova.

Anna Vyrubova, born Anna Taneyeva, was twelve years younger than the Empress Alexandra. Her family was distinguished; her father, Alexander Taneyev, was both Director of the Imperial Chancellery and a noted composer. Through his house moved government ministers, artists, musicians and ladies of society. Anna herself attended an exclusive dancing class where an occasional partner was young Prince Felix Yussoupov, the son of the wealthiest family of the Russian nobility.

In 1901, at seventeen, Anna Taneyeva fell ill, and the Empress paid her a short visit in the hospital. It was one of many such calls that Alexandra made, but the romantic girl was overwhelmed by the gesture. Anna conceived a passionate admiration for the twenty-nine-year-old Empress. After her recovery, Anna was invited to the palace, where Alexandra discovered that she could sing and play the piano, and the two began to play and sing duets.

An unhappy romance further strengthened the bond. Although Anna Taneyeva was too heavy and soft to be considered beautiful, she had clear blue eyes, a pretty mouth and a trusting, innocent charm. "I remember Vyrubova when she came to visit my mother," said Botkin's daughter Tatiana. "She was pink-cheeked, full, and all dressed in fluffy fur. It seemed to me that she was too sweet talking to us and petting us and we didn't like her very much." In 1907, Anna was being courted by Lieutenant Boris Vyrubov, a survivor of the Battle of Tsushima. Anna was reluctant to marry Vyrubov, but Alexandra overrode her objections and urged her to go ahead. Anna agreed, and the marriage was performed with the Tsar and his wife as witnesses. Within a few months, the marriage collapsed. Vyrubov, whose ship had been sunk from under him, had shattered nerves and never managed to consummate his marriage.

The Empress blamed herself for Anna's misfortune. For a while, she devoted most of her time to her romantic and lonely young friend. Anna was invited that summer to join the Imperial family for its annual two-week cruise aboard the Imperial yacht through the Finnish fjords. Sitting on deck during the day or under lamplight in the yacht's salon at night, Anna poured her heart out. Alexandra responded by talking of her own childhood, her dreams before her marriage, her loneliness in Russia, her hopes and fears for her son. From those days on board the yacht there sprang one of those intimate, confiding relationships such as exist only between women. The tie between them grew so strong that they could sit for hours in silence, secure in unexpressed affection. On each side, anxieties were calmed, wounds healed and faith encouraged. When the cruise ended, Alexandra cried out, "I thank God for at last having sent me a true friend." Nicholas, who liked Anna, told her good-naturedly, "Now you have subscribed to come with us regularly."

From that summer, Anna Vyrubova centered her life on the Empress Alexandra. If for some reason Alexandra could not see her for a day or so, Anna pouted. At these times, the Empress teased her, calling her "our big baby" and "our little daughter." To bring her closer, Anna was moved into a small house inside the Imperial Park, just two hundred yards from the Alexander Palace. It was a summer house with no foundations, and in the winter an icy chill rose up through the floors. Often after dinner Nicholas and Alexandra came to visit.

"When their Majesties came to tea with me in the evening," Anna wrote, "the Empress generally brought fruit and sweetmeats with her and the Emperor sometimes brought a bottle of cherry brandy. We used to sit around the table with our legs drawn up so as to avoid contact with the cold floor. Their Majesties regarded my primitive way of life from the humorous side. Sitting before the blazing hearth, we drank our tea and ate little toasted cracknels, handed around by my servant. . . . I remember the Emperor once laughingly saying to me that, after such an evening, nothing but a hot bath could make him warm again."

When not playing hostess in her cottage, Anna was at the palace. She came after dinner, joining in the family's puzzles, games and reading aloud. In conversation, she rarely proposed a political subject or urged an original opinion, preferring instead to endorse whatever the Tsar and the Empress had just said. If husband and wife disagreed, her role was to come down ever so gently on the side of the Empress.

Unlike most famous royal favorites, Anna Vyrubova asked nothing for herself except attention and affection. She was without ambition. She never appeared at court ceremonies and never asked for favors, titles or money for herself or her own relatives. Occasionally, Alexandra made her accept a dress or a few hundred roubles; usually Anna gave the money away. During the war, she spent most of her small inheritance on equipment for one of the military hospitals at Tsarskoe Selo.

In a court where the sharp edges of petty intrigue and ambition showed all too plainly, Anna Vyrubova outraged many people. Some scorned her unattractiveness and her naïveté, others felt simply that an empress of Russia deserved a more glittering companion. Grand duchesses of the Imperial blood who were never invited to the Imperial palace were irked to think that the dumpy Vyrubova was sitting night after night in the intimate circle of the Imperial family. Maurice Paléologue, the French Ambassador during the war, was shocked by Anna's inelegant appearance. "No royal favorite ever looked more unpretentious," he wrote. "She was rather stout, of coarse and ample build, with thick, shining hair, a fat neck, a pretty, innocent face with rosy, shining cheeks, large strikingly clear bright eyes and full, fleshy lips. She was always very simply dressed and with her worthless adornments had a provincial appearance."

For the same reasons that others scorned Anna Vyrubova, the Empress prized her. Where others thought only of themselves, Anna's apparent selflessness set her apart and made her seem all the more rare and valuable. On no account would Alexandra listen to criticism of her young protégée. When Anna sensed dislike in a person and reported it to the Empress, Alexandra bristled toward the antagonist and increased her attentions to Anna. Almost belligerently, the Empress refused to make Anna an official lady-in-waiting and allow her to become enmeshed in the duties and intrigues which went with that rank. "I will never give Anna an official position," she said. "She is my friend, I wish to retain her as such. Surely an Empress is allowed the right of a woman to choose her friends."

Later, during the war, when the Empress assumed an important part in the government of Russia, Alexandra's friendship for Anna took on political significance. Because she was known as the Empress's most intimate confidante, every gesture Anna made, every word she uttered, was watched and commented on. Correctly or incorrectly, Anna's opinions, activities, tastes and mistakes were associated in the public mind with Alexandra Fedorovna. This association was especially significant in connection with Anna's unqualified devotion to the extraordinary Siberian miracle-worker Gregory Rasputin, whose influence on the Imperial couple and therefore on Russia was to grow to towering proportions. Anna met Rasputin when he first arrived in St. Petersburg; he prophesied the collapse of her marriage, and she became convinced that he was a man divinely blessed. Certain that Rasputin could help ease the burdens carried by her mistress, Anna became his most passionate advocate. When Alexandra and Rasputin communicated, Anna was often the physical link. She carried messages in person and telephoned Rasputin daily. She transmitted his opinions faithfully and urged them upon the Empress. But Anna herself was not a source of ideas or political action. Everyone who dealt with her personally—ministers, ambassadors, even Rasputin's secretary—described her in the same terms: "a vehicle," "an ideal gramophone disc," "she understood nothing."

Nevertheless, in the tumultuous days culminating in the fall of the dynasty, the unpretentious Anna was accused of holding major political influence over the Tsar and his wife. Rumor inflated her into a monster of depravity who was said to reign over sinister orgies at the palace. She was accused of conniving with Rasputin to hypnotize or drug the Tsar; she was described as sharing the beds of both Nicholas and Rasputin, with a preference for the latter and a lewd dominion over both. Ironically, both the aristocracy and the revolutionaries told the same stories with the same relish and the same small grunts of rage. After the fall of the monarchy, with the rumors swirling viciously around her head, Anna Vyrubova was dragged off to prison by the Provisional Minister of Justice, Alexander Kerensky. Later, put on trial for her "political activities," Anna pathetically defended herself in the only way she knew: she asked for a medical examination to prove her sexual innocence. The examination was performed in May 1917 and, to the astonishment of all Russia, Anna Vyrubova, the notorious confidante of the Empress Alexandra, was medically certified to be a virgin.

As one precarious year followed another, emotional stress took a terrible toll on Alexandra's physical health. As a girl, she suffered from sciatica, a severe pain in the back and legs. Her pregnancies, four in the first six years of marriage, were difficult. The battle against her son's hemophilia left her physically and emotionally drained. At times of crisis, she spared herself nothing, sitting up day and night beside Alexis's bed. But once the danger had passed, she collapsed, lying for weeks in bed or on a couch, moving about only in a wheelchair. In 1908, when the Tsarevich was four, she began to develop a whole series of symptoms which she referred to as the result of "an enlarged heart." She had shortness of breath, and exertion became an effort. She was "indeed a sick woman," wrote Grand Duchess Olga Alexandrovna, the Tsar's sister. "Her breath often came in quick, obviously painful gasps. I often saw her lips turn blue. Constant worry over Alexis had completely undermined her health." Dr. Botkin, who came every day at nine in the morning and five in the afternoon to listen to her heart, mentioned years later to an officer in Siberia that the Empress has "inherited a family weakness of the blood vessels" which often led to "progressive hysteria." In modern medical terminology, the Empress Alexandra undoubtedly was suffering from psychosomatic anxiety symptoms brought on by worry over the health of her son.

Alexandra's own letters occasionally mentioned her poor health. In 1911, she wrote to her former tutor, Miss Jackson: "I have been ill nearly all the time. . . . The children are growing up quite fast. . . . I send them to reviews with their father and once they went to a big military luncheon . . . as I could not go—they must get accustomed to replace me as I rarely can appear anywhere, and when I do, am afterwards long laid up—overtired muscles of the heart."

To her sister Princess Victoria of Battenberg she wrote: "Don't think my ill health depresses me personally. I don't care except to see my dear ones suffer on my account and that I cannot fulfill my duties. But once God sends such a cross it must be borne. . . . I have had so much, that, willingly I give up any pleasure—they mean so little to me, and my family life is such an ideal one, that it is a recompense for anything I cannot take part in. Baby [Alexis] is growing a little companion to his father. They row together daily. All 5 lunch with me even when I am laid up."

Alexandra's inability to participate in public life worried her husband. "She keeps to her bed most of the day, does not receive anyone, does not come out to lunches and remains on the balcony day after day," he wrote to his mother. "Botkin has persuaded her to go to Nauheim [a German health spa] for a cure in the early autumn. It is very important for her to get better, for her own sake, and the children's and mine. I am completely run down mentally by worrying over her health."

Marie was sympathetic. "It is too sad and painful to see her [Alexandra] always ailing and incapable of taking part in anything. You have enough worries in life as it is without having the ordeal added of seeing the person you love most in the world suffer. . . . The best thing would be for you to travel . . . that would do her a lot of good."

Taking Botkin's and his mother's advice, Nicholas escorted his wife to the German spa of Nauheim so that the Empress could take the cure. Nicholas enjoyed himself on these trips. Dressed in a dark suit and bowler hat, he strolled, unrecognized, through the streets of the little German town. Alexandra, meanwhile, bathed in the warm waters, drank bottled water and went shopping in Nauheim with an attendant pushing her wheelchair. At the end of several weeks, she went back to Russia, rested but not cured. For the mother of a hemophiliac, as for the son, no cure has ever been found.

Russians are a compassionate people, warm in their love of children and deeply perceptive in their understanding of suffering. Why did they not open their hearts to this anguished mother and her stricken child?

The answer, incredibly, is that Russia did not know. Most people in Moscow or Kiev or St. Petersburg did not know that the Tsarevich had hemophilia, and the few who had some inkling had only hazy ideas as to the nature of the disease. As late as 1916, George T. Marye, the American Ambassador, reported, "We hear all sorts of stories about what was the matter with him [Alexis] but the best authenticated seems to be that he has some trouble of the circulation, the blood circulates too close or too freely near the surface . . . [of] the skin." Even within the Imperial household, people such as Pierre Gilliard who saw the family regularly did not know for many years precisely what was wrong with Alexis. When he missed a public function, it was announced that he had a cold or had suffered a sprained ankle. No one believed these explanations and the boy became the subject of incredible rumors. Alexis, it was said, was mentally retarded, an epileptic, the victim of anarchists' bombs. Whatever it was, the mystery made it worse, for there was never a focus for sympathy and understanding. Just as at Khodynka Meadow after their coronation, Nicholas and Alexandra attempted to continue in the midst of disaster by pretending that nothing unusual had happened. The trouble was that everyone knew that behind the façade of normalcy something terrible was happening.

Alexis's secret was deliberately withheld at the wish of the Tsar and the Empress. There was a basis for this in court etiquette: traditionally, the health of members of the Imperial family was never mentioned. In Alexis's case, this secrecy was vastly extended. Doctors and intimate servants were begged not to reveal the staggering misfortune.* Alexis, his parents reasoned, was the Heir to the Throne of the world's largest and most absolute autocracy. What would be the fate of the boy, the dynasty and the nation if the Russian people knew that their future Tsar was an invalid living under the constant shadow of death? Not knowing the answer and fearing to discover it, Nicholas and Alexandra surrounded the subject with silence.

* Dr. Botkin kept the secret well and never discussed the illness with his own family. In 1921, his daughter Tatiana wrote a book about the Imperial family without mentioning the nature of the Tsarevich's illness or the word "hemophilia." This suggests either that she still did not know or that, true to her father's code, she still felt bound by secrecy.

A revelation of Alexis's condition would inevitably have put new pressures on the Tsar and the monarchy. But the erection of a wall of secrecy was worse. It left the family vulnerable to every vicious rumor. It undermined the nation's respect for the Empress and, through her, for the Tsar and the throne. Because the condition of the Tsarevich was never revealed, Russians never understood the power which Rasputin held over the Empress. Nor were they able to form a true picture of Alexandra herself. Unaware of her ordeal, they wrongly ascribed her remoteness to distaste for Russia and its people. The years of worry left a look of sadness settled permanently on her face; when she spoke to people, she often appeared preoccupied and deep in gloom. As she devoted herself to hours of prayer, the life of the court became stricter and her own public appearances were reduced. When she did emerge, she was silent, seemingly cold, haughty and indifferent. Never a popular consort, Alexandra Fedorovna became steadily less popular. During the war, with national passions aroused, all the complaints Russians had about the Empress—her German birth, her coldness, her devotion to Rasputin—blended into a single, sweeping torrent of hatred.

The fall of Imperial Russia was a titanic drama in which the individual destinies of thousands of men all played their part. Yet in making allowance for the impersonal flow of historic forces, in counting the contributions made by ministers, peasants and revolutionaries, it still remains essential to understand the character and motivation of the central figures. To the Empress Alexandra Fedorovna this understanding has never been given. From the time her son was born, the central concern of her life was her fight against hemophilia.

CHAPTER THIRTEEN

The Royal Progress

EACH year as spring crept north across Russia, the Imperial family fled the frosts and snows of Tsarskoe Selo for the flowering gardens of the Crimea. As the moment of departure approached, the Tsar's spirits always lifted. "I am only sorry for you who have to remain in this bog," he said cheerfully to the cluster of grand dukes and government ministers who came to see him off in March 1912.

There was a regular cyclical pattern to these annual migrations. March brought the spring exodus to the Crimea; in May, the family moved to the villa on the Baltic coast at Peterhof; in June, they cruised the Finnish fjords on the Imperial yacht; August found them at a hunting lodge deep in the Polish forest; in September, they came back to the Crimea; in November, they returned to Tsarskoe Selo for the winter.

The Imperial train which bore the Tsar and his family on these trips across Russia was a traveling miniature palace. It consisted of a string of luxurious royal-blue salon cars with the double-eagled crest emblazoned in gold on their sides, pulled by a gleaming black locomotive. The private car of Nicholas and Alexandra contained a bedroom the size of three normal compartments, a sitting room for the Empress upholstered in mauve and gray, and a private study for the Tsar furnished with a desk and green leather chairs. The white-tiled bathroom off the Imperial bedroom boasted a tub with such ingeniously designed overhangs that water could not slosh out even when the train was rounding a curve.

Elsewhere in the train, there was an entire car of rooms for the four Grand Duchesses and the Tsarevich, with all the furniture painted white. A mahogany-paneled lounge car with deep rugs and damask-covered chairs and sofas served as a gathering place for the ladies-in-waiting, aides-de-camp and other members of the Imperial suite, each of whom had a private compartment. One car was devoted entirely to dining. It included a kitchen equipped with three stoves, an icebox and a wine cabinet; a dining room with a table for twenty; and a small anteroom, where before every meal *zakouski* were served. Even while traveling, the Imperial suite observed the Russian custom of standing and helping themselves from a table spread with caviar, cold salmon, sardines, reindeer tongue, sausages, pickled mushrooms, radishes, smoked herring, sliced cucumber and other dishes. At dinner, Nicholas always sat at the middle of a long table with his daughters beside him, while Count Fredericks and other court functionaries sat opposite. With rare exceptions, the Empress ate alone on the train or had her meals with Alexis.

Despite the excitement of leaving St. Petersburg, a trip on the Imperial train was not an unmitigated pleasure. There was always the nagging thought that, at any moment, the train might be blown up by revolutionaries. To make this less likely, two identical Imperial trains made every trip, traveling a few miles apart; potential assassins could never know on which the Tsar and his family were riding. Worse for the travelers were the normal discomforts and boredom of long train trips. Although it could go faster, the train customarily rattled along at fifteen to twenty miles an hour. Accordingly, the trip from St. Petersburg to the Crimea meant two nights and a day of bumping and jostling across the interminable vastness of the Russian landscape. In the summer, the sun beat down on the metal roofs, turning the salon cars into carpeted ovens. It was a regular practice to halt the train for half an hour wherever a grove of trees or a river offered an opportunity for the passengers to get out, stretch their legs and cool themselves in the shade or by the water.

Once when the train was stopped in open country at the top of a high embankment, the children took large silver trays from the pantry and used them to toboggan down the sandy slope. After dinner, in the presence of the Tsar and Empress, General Strukov, an aide-de-camp, shouted to the children that he would beat them on foot to the bottom. Wearing his dinner uniform with the ribbon of Alexander Nevsky over his shoulder and his diamond-studded sword of honor in hand, the General threw himself down the bank. He slid for twenty feet, became mired up to his knees and gallantly waved as the children glided past, giggling with pleasure, on their silver saucers.

If the Imperial train was a means of travel, the Imperial yachts were a mode of relaxation. For two weeks every June, the Tsar gave himself completely to a slow, seaborne meandering along the rocky coast of Finland. By day, the yacht steamed among the islands, finding an anchorage at night in a cove deserted except for the lonely hut of an isolated fisherman. The following morning, when the passengers awoke, they found themselves surrounded by sparkling blue water, beaches of yellow sand, red granite islands and dark forests of green pines.

Nicholas's favorite yacht was a 4,500-ton, black-hulled beauty named the *Standart*, especially built for him in a Danish shipyard. Moored in a Baltic cove or tied up beneath the Crimean cliffs in Yalta harbor, the *Standart* was a marvel of nautical elegance. As big as a small cruiser, fueled by coal and propelled by steam, the *Standart* nevertheless was designed with the graceful majesty of a great sailing ship. An immense bowsprit encrusted with gold leaf jutted forward from her clipper bow. Three tall varnished masts towered above her twin white funnels. The gleaming decks were covered with white canvas awnings and lined with wicker tables and chairs. Below were drawing rooms, lounges and dining rooms paneled in mahogany, with polished floors, crystal chandeliers and velvet drapes; only the private staterooms of the family were done in chintz. Along with a chapel and spacious rooms for the Imperial suite, there were quarters for the ship's officers, engineers, stokers, deckhands, stewards, valets, maids and a whole platoon of Marine Guards. In addition, somewhere in the yacht's lower decks, space had been found to house the members of the *Standart's* brass band and balalaika orchestra.

Life aboard the *Standart* was easy and informal. The family mingled freely with the crew and knew many of the sailors by their first names. Often a group of ship's officers was invited to dine at the Imperial table. During the day, the girls wandered the decks unescorted, wearing white blouses and polka-dotted skirts. Conversations and bantering shipboard flirtations sprang up between young officers and the blossoming Grand Duchesses. Even in the winter, when the yacht was laid up for refurbishing, the special bonds of shipboard life held firm. "During the performances of the opera, especially *Aïda*, . . . sailors from the Imperial yacht *Standart* would often be called upon to play parts of warriors," wrote the Tsar's sister Grand Duchess Olga. "It was a riot to see those tall husky men standing awkwardly on the stage, wearing helmets and sandals and showing their bare, hairy legs. Despite the frantic signals of the producer, they would stare up at us [in the Imperial box] with broad grins."

When the children were young, each was assigned a sailor whose duty it was to prevent his small charge from toddling overboard. As the children grew older and went ashore to swim, the sailor-nannies went along. At the end of each year's cruise, the Tsar rewarded these husky seafaring nursemaids by giving each man a gold watch.

Even aboard the *Standart*, Nicholas was not free of the burdens of office. Although he barred government ministers and police security agents from the decks of the yacht, courier boats from St. Petersburg churned up daily to the foot of the *Standart's* ladder, bringing reports and documents. As a further reminder of the presence of its august passenger, the yacht was never without an escort of navy torpedo boats anchored nearby or cruising slowly along the horizon.

At sea, Nicholas worked two days a week. The other five he relaxed. In the morning, he rowed ashore to take long walks through the wild Finnish forests. When the *Standart* moored near the country estate of a Russian or Finnish nobleman, the owner might awake to find the Tsar at his door asking politely if he might use a court for tennis. Sometimes Nicholas dismissed the gentlemen who accompanied him on these hikes and walked alone with his children, searching the woods for mushrooms or wandering down a beach looking for bright-colored rocks.

Because her sciatica made it difficult for her to move, Alexandra rarely left the yacht. She spent the days peacefully sitting on deck, knitting, doing needlework, writing letters, watching the gulls and the sea. Alone in the lounge, she played Bach, Beethoven and Tchaikovsky at the piano. As they grew older, the girls took turns staying aboard the ship, keeping their mother company. In 1907, when Anna Vyrubova began making these cruises, the two women spent their days sitting in the sun, knitting and talking.

At teatime, the Tsar and the children returned with stories, wildflowers, mosses, cups of berries and pieces of quartz. Tea was served on deck while the ship's band thumped out marches or the balalaika orchestra strummed Russian folk melodies. Occasionally, the girls acted out skits. Anna Vyrubova recalled the day that the older Imperial yacht, *Polar Star,* carrying the Dowager Empress, anchored nearby and the girls' grandmother came on board the *Standart* for tea and a play. Afterward, Vyrubova saw Marie "sitting on Alexis's bed talking to him gaily and helping him peel an apple just like any other grandmother."

The part of the day Alexandra liked best was sunset. As the last slanting rays touched trees, rocks, water and boats with golden light, she sat on deck watching the lowering of the flag and listening to the deep, echoing male voices of the crew singing the Orthodox service of Evening Prayer. Later in the evening, while Nicholas played billiards and smoked with his staff, the Empress read and sewed by lamplight. Everyone went to bed early. By eleven p.m. the waves had rocked them to sleep, and stewards bringing evening tea into the drawing room invariably found the place deserted.

In 1907, the cruise on the *Standart* ended in near-calamity. The yacht was moving out to sea through a narrow channel while, on deck, the passengers were having afternoon tea. Suddenly, with a shuddering crash, the ship hit a rock. Teacups flew, chairs overturned, the band went sprawling. As water poured into the hull, the ship listed and began to settle. Sirens wailed and lifeboats were lowered. For a moment, the three-year-old Tsarevich was missing, and both parents were distraught until he was located. Then Alexandra herded her children and maids into boats and, with Anna Vyrubova, bustled back to her own stateroom. Stripping sheets from the bed, she tossed jewels, icons and mementoes into a bundle. When she left the yacht, the last woman to depart, she carried this priceless bundle securely in her lap.

Nicholas, meanwhile, stood at the rail supervising the lowering and casting off of the lifeboats. As he did so, he bent over the side every few seconds and looked at the waterline, then consulted a pocket watch he held in his hand. The Tsar explained that he intended to stay aboard to the last, and that he was calculating how many inches a minute the boat was sinking; he estimated that twenty minutes remained. Nevertheless, due to its watertight compartments, the *Standart* did not sink, and it was later pulled off the rock and repaired. That night the family slept in crowded quarters aboard the navy cruiser *Asia.* "The Emperor, rather disheveled, brought basins of water to the Empress and me to wash our faces and hands," said Anna. "The next morning, the *Polar Star* appeared and we transferred to its more spacious quarters."

In August 1909, the *Standart* steamed slowly past the Isle of Wight, carrying the Russian Imperial family on its last visit to England. The Tsar arrived just before Regatta Week, and before the races began, King Edward VII honored Nicholas with a formal review of the Royal Navy. In three lines, the world's mightiest armada of battleships and dreadnoughts lay at anchor. As the British royal yacht, *Victoria and Albert*, steamed slowly under the rail of each of these mountains of gray steel, pennants dipped, saluting cannon boomed, bands played "God Save the Tsar" and "God Save the King," and hundreds of British seamen burst into rippling cheers. On the deck of the yacht, the portly King and his Russian guest, wearing the white uniform of a British admiral, stood at salute.

After the naval review, the sailing races which climaxed the summer social season began. A great fleet of hundreds of yachts lay in the roadstead, their varnished masts gleaming in the sunlight like a forest of golden spars. "Ashore and afloat," wrote a British observer, "there were dinner parties and balls. Steam launches, with gleaming brass funnels, and slender cutters and gigs, pulled by their crews at the long white oars, plied between the yachts and the Squadron steps. By day, the sails of the racing yachts spread across the blue waters of the Solent like the wings of giant butterflies, by night the riding lights and lanterns gleamed and shone like glow-worms against the onyx water and fireworks burst and spent themselves in the night sky."

This visit was the only time that Prince Edward, the present Duke of Windsor, met his Russian cousins. Prince Edward, then fifteen, and his younger brother Prince Albert, who became King George VI, were cadets at the Naval College of Osborne, near Cowes on the Isle of Wight. Both British Princes were scheduled to show the Russian party through their school, but, at the last minute, Albert developed a cold which rapidly worsened into whooping cough. Dr. Botkin feared that if Albert passed the disease along to Alexis, the fits of coughing might trigger bleeding. Accordingly, Albert was quarantined.

"[This] was the one and only time I ever saw Tsar Nicholas," wrote the Duke of Windsor, looking back on the event. "Because of assassination plots . . . the Imperial government would not risk their Little Father's life in a great metropolis. Therefore the meeting was set for Cowes on the Isle of Wight, which could be sealed off almost completely. Uncle Nicky came for the regatta with his Empress and their numerous children aboard the *Standart*. I do remember being astonished at the elaborate police guard thrown around his every movement when I showed him through Osborne College."

The Empress Alexandra was overjoyed to be back in the land where she had spent the happiest days of her childhood. Pleased with the warm hospitality offered by King Edward, she wrote that "dear Uncle" has "been most kind and attentive." Less than a year later, "dear Uncle" was dead. His son, King George V, was on the throne and the young Prince Edward became the Prince of Wales.

Every emperor, king and president in Europe trod at one time or another upon the polished decks of the *Standart*. The Kaiser, whose own 4,000-ton white-and-gold *Hohenzollern* was slightly smaller than the *Standart*, openly proclaimed his envy of the Russian yacht. "He said he would have been happy to get it as a present," Nicholas wrote to Marie after William had come aboard for the first time. In reply, Marie sputtered indignantly, "His joke . . . was in very doubtful taste. I hope he will not have the cheek to order himself a similar one here [in Denmark]. This really would be the limit, though just like him, with the tact that distinguishes him."

The Tsar and the Kaiser saw each other for the last time in June 1912, when the two Imperial yachts *Standart* and *Hohenzollern* anchored side by side at the Russian Baltic port of Reval. "Emperor William's visit was a success," Nicholas reported to Marie. "He remained three days and . . . he was very gay and affable and would have his joke with Anastasia. . . . He gave very fine presents to the children and quite a lot of toys to Alexei. . . . On his last day he invited all the officers to a morning reception on board his yacht. It lasted about an hour and a half and afterwards he . . . said that our officers had got through sixty bottles of his champagne."

To every other place in Russia, Nicholas and Alexandra preferred the Crimea. To the traveler coming down from the north by train, wearied by hour after hour of the flatness and emptiness of the Ukrainian steppe, the scenery of the Russian Crimea is lushly dramatic. On this southern peninsula washed by the Black Sea, rugged mountain peaks rise from the blue and emerald waters. On the upper slopes of this Haila range, there are forests of tall pines. In the valleys and along the sea cliffs, there are groves of cypresses, orchards, vineyards, villages and pastures. The flowers and grapes of the Crimea have always been famous. In Nicholas's day, no winter ball in St. Petersburg was complete without a carload of fresh flowers rushed north by train from the Crimea. No grand-ducal or princely table anywhere in Russia was set without bottles of red and white wine from the host's Crimean estate. The Crimean climate was mild the year around, but in the spring the sudden massive flowering of fruit trees, shrubs, vines and wildflowers transformed the wild valleys of the peninsula into a vast perfumed garden. Lilacs, wisteria, violets and white acacias bloomed. Apple, peach and cherry trees burst into pink and white blossoms. Wild strawberries covered every slope. Grapes of every taste and color could be plucked wild along the road. Most spectacular of all were the roses. Huge, thick vines curled over buildings and walls, dropping petals across paths, courtyards, lawns and fields. With its swirl of colors and delicate odors, with its bright sun and warm sea breezes, with the aura of health and freedom that it bestowed, it is not surprising that of all the Imperial estates scattered across Russia, Nicholas and Alexandra preferred to be at the Livadia Palace in the Crimea.

Before 1917, the Crimea was deliberately maintained as an unspoiled wilderness. Along the coast between Yalta and Sevastopol, the handsome villas of the Imperial family and the aristocracy nestled between the cliffs and the sea. Half the peninsula lay behind the high posts surmounted by golden eagles which marked the lands of the Imperial family. To preserve the natural seclusion and beauty of these valleys, Alexander III and Nicholas II had forbidden the building of railways, except for the track coming down from the north through Simferopol to Sevastopol. From this port, one traveled overland by carriage or by boat along the sea cliffs to reach Yalta, the little harbor on the edge of the Imperial estate. The voyage took four hours, the carriage ride all day.

The people of the Crimea were Tartars of the Moslem faith, the residue of the thunderous Tartar invasions of Russia in the thirteenth century. Until they were conquered by Prince Gregory Potemkin for Catherine the Great in the eighteenth century, the Tartars were ruled by their own khans. Under the tsars, they lived in picturesque whitewashed villages scattered along the slopes and marked from afar by the delicately laced minarets of their Moslem mosques rising gracefully into the blue sky. Tartar men, sinewy and dark-complexioned, wore round black hats, short embroidered coats and tight white trousers. "To see a cavalcade of Tartars sweep by was to imagine a race of Centaurs come back to earth," wrote the admiring Anna

Vyrubova. Tartar women were handsome creatures who dyed their hair bright red and wore floating veils to hide their faces. At the summit of all fervent Tartar loyalties stood the tsar, successor to the khan. When the Imperial carriage passed through Tartar villages, it had first to be halted so that the ranking Tartar chief could exercise his duty and privilege of riding through his village before his Imperial master.

The Imperial palace at Livadia was the special pride of the Empress Alexandra. Built in 1911 to replace an older wooden structure, it was made of white limestone and perched on the edge of a cliff overlooking the sea. Its columned balconies and courtyards were in an Italianate style admired by the Empress from her fond recollection of the palaces and cloisters she had seen in Florence before her marriage. The gardens, laid out in large, triangular flower beds, were studded with ancient Greek marbles excavated from Crimean ruins. On the ground floor, a white state dining room was also used—with tables and chairs removed—for dances. From the dining room, glass doors opened directly into the rose garden; at night, the sweet smell filled every corner of the palace. Upstairs, from her rooms furnished in pink chintz with mauve flowers, Alexandra had magnificent vistas. From her boudoir she could see the mountains, still glistening with snow in May; from her bedroom, she could see the sweeping sea horizon. Nearby was Nicholas's study; down the corridor were rooms for the children and a private family dining room. On the day in April 1911 when the new palace was opened, it was blessed in the Orthodox fashion by priests going from room to room, swinging smoldering censers of incense and sprinkling holy water. When they finished, Alexandra hustled in to unpack and arrange her favorite pictures and icons on the walls and tables.

For Alexandra and Alexis, the warm days at Livadia meant recovery from illness and renewal of strength. The Empress and her son spent their mornings together, she lying in a chair on her balcony, he playing nearby with his toys. In the afternoon, she went into the garden or drove her pony cart along the paths around the palace, while Alexis went swimming with his father in the warm sea. Once in 1906, Nicholas was swimming in the surf with his four daughters when a large wave swept over them. The Tsar and the three older girls rose to the crest of the wave, but Anastasia, then five, disappeared. "Little Alexis [aged two] and I saw it happen from the beach," wrote the Tsar's sister Olga Alexandrovna. "The child, of course, didn't realize the danger, and kept clapping his hands at the tidal wave. Then Nicky dived again, grabbed Anastasia by her long hair, and swam back with her to the beach. I had gone cold with terror."

Despite this accident, Nicholas enjoyed the water so much and considered it so healthy for his children that he had a large indoor bath constructed and filled with warm salt water so that their daily swimming would not be affected by wind or rain or a drop in the temperature of the sea. When Alexis appeared healthy, Nicholas was overjoyed. In 1909, in the middle of writing to Empress Marie, the Tsar interrupted himself to report cheerfully, "Just now, Alexei has come in after his bath and insists that I write to you that he kisses 'Granny' very tenderly. He is very sunburned, so are his sisters and I."

At Livadia, Nicholas and Alexandra could live more informally than anywhere else. The Empress drove into Yalta to shop, something she never did in St. Petersburg or Tsarskoe Selo. Once, entering a store from a rainy street, she lowered her umbrella, allowing a stream of water to form a puddle on the floor. Annoyed, the salesman indicated a rack near the door, saying sharply, "Madame, this is for umbrellas." The Empress meekly obeyed. Only when Anna Vyrubova, who was with the Empress, addressed her in conversation as "Alexandra Fedorovna" did the astonished salesman begin to realize who his customer was.

Nicholas spent most of his days at Livadia outdoors. Every morning, he played tennis. He made horseback excursions with his daughters to neighboring villas, to the farm which supplied their table, to a mountain waterfall. As in Finland, the children and their father collected berries and mushrooms in the woods. Sometimes in the fall, Nicholas built a small fire of twigs and dry leaves and cooked mushrooms in wine, stirring the bubbling tidbit in a tin cup. In 1909, when the Russian Ministry of War was redesigning the clothing and equipment of the Russian infantryman, Nicholas decided to test it himself for lightness and comfort and ordered an entire kit in his size brought to Livadia. He put on shirt, breeches and boots, shouldered the rifle, cartridges, knapsack and bedding roll and, leaving the palace, marched alone for nine hours, covering twenty-five miles. He was stopped at one point by a security policeman who did not recognize him and roughly ordered him to leave the vicinity. Returning at dusk, Nicholas pronounced the uniform satisfactory. When the Kaiser heard about this exploit, he was vexed that the idea had not occurred to him and asked his military attaché for a full report. Later, the commander of the regiment whose uniform the Tsar had worn asked Nicholas to fill out a common soldier's identity booklet as a memento. In the booklet, Nicholas filled in the form: *Last name:* "Romanov"; *Home:* "Tsarskoe Selo"; *Service Completed:* "When I am in my grave."

If possible, the Imperial family always spent Easter at Livadia. The celebration of Easter was an exhausting but exhilarating experience for the Empress. During the days of the great religious festival, she spent freely of the strength she had been carefully hoarding. In Imperial Russia, Easter was the climax of the Orthodox Church year. More profoundly holy and more joyous than Christmas, it brought an intense outpouring of emotion. Across Russia on Easter night, huge, reverent crowds packed into cathedrals and stood, holding lighted candles, to hear the great choral litany. Beginning just before midnight, they waited for the moment when the priest, the bishop, the Metropolitan, or all of them in procession, went in search of the Savior. Followed by the entire congregation, making a river of candles, they circled the outside of the church. Then, returning to the door, they reenacted the discovery of Christ's tomb when the stone before it was rolled away. Looking inside, seeing that the church was empty, the priest turned his face to the crowd. His features lighted with joy, he shouted, "*Khristos Voskres!*": "Christ is risen!" The congregation, the candles lighting their own glowing faces, responded with a mighty shout, "*Voistinu Voskrese!*": "Indeed he is risen!" Everywhere in Russia—in Red Square before St. Basil's Cathedral, at the doors of the Cathedral of Our Lady of Kazan in St. Petersburg, in tiny churches in lost villages—this was the moment when the Russian people, peasants and princes alike, laughed and wept in unison.

At the conclusion of the religious service, the Russian Easter festival began. It was an unbelievable surge of eating, visiting and exchanging gifts. Most Russians hurried from the church to begin, in the middle of the night, the sumptuous feasting which broke the long Lenten fast. Because butter, cheese and eggs had been denied, the climax of these meals was *paskha,* a rich, creamy dessert, and *kulich,* the round Easter cake, crowned with white icing and the symbol XB, "Christ is risen." It was a tradition that any stranger who entered the house was welcome, and the table was set with food night and day. In the Crimea, the Imperial palace became a vast banqueting hall. Presiding over this gaiety, Nicholas and Alexandra greeted the entire household with the traditional three kisses of blessing, welcome and joy. Schoolchildren came the following morning from Yalta to stand in line and receive little cakes of *kulich* from the Empress and her daughters. To members of the court and the Imperial Guard, the sovereigns gave their famous Easter eggs. Some were simple: exquisitely painted eggshells from which the yolks had been drawn through tiny pinholes. Others were the fabulous gem-encrusted miracles made by the immortal master jeweler Fabergé.

Peter Carl Fabergé was a Russian of French descent. At the peak of his success, around the turn of the century, his workshops in St. Petersburg employed five hundred jewelers, smiths and apprentices. He had branch offices in Moscow, London and Paris, and he did an enormous business in silver and gold, especially in large dinner services. His lasting fame, however, rests on the extraordinary quality of his jewelry. It was Fabergé's genius to ignore the usual flamboyant emphasis on precious stones and to subordinate gems to the over-all pattern of the work. In designing a cigarette box, for example, Fabergé's craftsmen used translucent blue, red or rose enamel as the primary material, lining the edges with a row of tiny diamonds. The result was a masterpiece of restraint, elegance and beauty.

Fabergé was officially the court jeweler to the Tsar of Russia, but his clients were international. King Edward VII was a regular customer, always demanding, "We must have no duplicates," to which Fabergé could always reply with serene assurance, "Your Majesty will be content." In a single day in 1898, the House of Fabergé played host to the King and Queen of Norway, the Kings of Denmark and Greece, and Queen Alexandra of England, Edward VII's consort. In Russia, no princely wedding, no grand-ducal birthday, no regimental or society jubilee was complete without a shower of Fabergé brooches, necklaces, pendants, cigarette cases, cufflinks, writing sets and clocks. To satisfy his eager patrons, Fabergé produced a breathtaking array of imaginative jewelry. In an endless, gorgeous stream, his craftsmen turned out jeweled flowers, a menagerie of tiny animals, and figures of Russian peasants, gypsy singers and Cossack horsemen. His miniatures included tiny parasols, garden watering cans ornamented in diamonds, an equestrian statue of Peter the Great done in gold and less than an inch high, a gold Louis XVI cabinet only five inches tall, and three-inch sedan chairs made of gold and enamel with interiors of mother-of-pearl.

The supreme expressions of Fabergé's art were the fifty-six fabled Imperial Easter eggs which he created for two Russian tsars, Alexander III and Nicholas II. Alexander began the custom in 1884 when he presented a Fabergé egg to his wife, Marie. After his father's death, Nicholas continued the custom, ordering two eggs each year, one for his wife and one for his mother. The choice of materials and the design were left entirely to Fabergé, who surrounded their construction in his workshops with enormous secrecy. From the first of these commissions, Fabergé hit upon the idea of using the egg only as a shell which would open, revealing a "surprise." Inside, there might be a basket of wildflowers made with milky chalcedony petals and gold leaves. Or the top of the egg might fly open every hour on the hour to elevate a jeweled and enameled cockerel which crowed and flapped its wings.

Fabergé's problem was that every year's masterpiece made his task that much more difficult in the year that followed. He never really excelled the Great Siberian Railway Easter Egg which he made in 1900. Because Nicholas as Tsarevich had been chairman of the railway committee, Fabergé created an egg of blue, green and yellow enamel on which delicate inlays of silver traced the map of Siberia and the route of the Trans-Siberian. The top could be lifted from the egg by touching the golden double-headed eagle which surmounted it, revealing the "surprise" within. It was a scale model, one foot long, five eighths of an inch wide, of the five cars and a locomotive of the Siberian express. "Driving wheels, double trucks under carriages, and other moving parts were precision made to work so that, given a few turns with the gold key . . . the gold and platinum locomotive, with a ruby gleaming from its headlight, could actually pull the train," wrote an observer. "Coupled to the baggage car are a carriage with half the seats reserved for ladies, another car for children, . . . still another car for smokers . . . [and a] church car with a Russian cross and gold bells on the roof."

Fabergé himself survived the Revolution, but his art did not. With his workshops broken up and his master craftsmen scattered, Fabergé escaped Russia in 1918 disguised as a diplomat and lived his last two years in Switzerland. An artist and purveyor to emperors, he had created works of art that survive as symbols of a vanished age, an age of opulence but also of craftsmanship, integrity and beauty.

Along with the palaces and villas of the Russian aristocracy, the seaside hills of the Crimea were dotted with hospitals and sanatoria for tuberculosis. Alexandra often visited these institutions; when she could not go herself, she sent her daughters. "They should realize the sadness that lies beneath all this beauty," she said to a lady-in-waiting. The Empress herself founded two hospitals in the Crimea, and every year she sold her own needlework and embroidery at a charity bazaar in Yalta to raise money for these institutions. The bazaar was held near the Yalta pier, with the *Standart*, tied alongside, used as a lounge and stockroom. Sometimes Alexis appeared at his mother's table. When this happened, a crowd gathered and men and women begged that the boy be lifted up high so they could see him. Smiling, Alexandra placed the small Tsarevich on the tabletop, where he sat cross-legged and, at her whisper, made a courtly bow.

Nicholas and Alexandra preferred to live quietly at Livadia, but the inhabitants of the neighboring estates followed a lively existence of picnics, sailing parties and summer balls. As they grew up, Olga and Tatiana were invited to these parties, and occasionally, well chaperoned, they were allowed to attend. Even the Tsar's household life was more active than at Tsarskoe Selo. The palace was usually filled with visitors—ministers down from St. Petersburg to report to the Tsar, local residents or guests from neighboring palaces, officers of the *Standart* or one of the army regiments stationed in the Crimea—and unlike the procedure at Tsarskoe Selo, visitors were always invited to lunch. The children's favorite guest was the Emir of Bokhara, the ruler of an autonomous state within the Russian Empire, near the border of Afghanistan. The Emir was a tall, dark man whose beard flowed down over a robe topped with a Russian general's epaulets encrusted with diamonds. Although he had been educated in St. Petersburg and spoke perfect Russian, the Emir followed the custom of Bokhara, and when he spoke officially to the Tsar, he used an interpreter. When the Emir arrived, escorted by two of his ministers wearing long beards dyed bright red, he gave extraordinary gifts. The Tsar's sister remembered receiving from the Emir "an enormous gold necklace from which, like tongues of flame, hung tassels of rubies."

At Livadia in 1911, to celebrate the sixteenth birthday of her oldest daughter, Grand Duchess Olga, the Empress gave a full-dress ball. Before the dance, Olga's parents gave her a diamond ring and a necklace of thirty-two diamonds and pearls. These were Olga's first jewels, intended to symbolize her coming into young womanhood. Olga was dressed in pink in her first ballgown. With her thick blond hair coiled for the first time in womanly style atop her head, she arrived at the dance, flushed and fair.

The ball was held in the state dining room of the new white Livadia Palace. The glass doors were thrown open and the fragrance of the roses in the garden filled the room. The lights in the chandeliers blazed in clusters, catching the gowns and jewels of the women and the bright decorations on the white uniforms of the men. Afterward, a cotillion supper was served and the dancers strolled in the garden and along the marble balconies at the top of the cliffs. As they stood watching from the palace of the Tsar, a huge autumn moon came up and cast its silver light across the shining waters of the Black Sea.

CHAPTER FOURTEEN

"The Little One Will Not Die"

On August 19, 1912 (O.S.), Empress Alexandra wrote a letter from Peterhof to her old tutor, Miss Jackson, who was retired and living in England:

Darling Madgie:

Loving thanks for yr last letter—forgive me for being such a shockingly bad correspondent. I had Victoria's visit for a week wh. was delightful, and Ella came also for 3 days, and I shall see her again in Moscow. Ernie and family we had in the Crimea, Waldemar came for 3 days on the *Standart* in Finland and Irene will come at the end of September to us in Poland, Spala. . . . Next week we leave for Borodino and Moscow, terribly tiring festivities, don't know how I shall get through them. After Moscow in spring, I was for a long time quite done up—now I am, on the whole, better. . . . Here we had colossal heat and scarcely ever a drop of rain.

If you know of any interesting historical books for girls, could you tell me, as I read to them and they have begun reading English for themselves. They read a great deal of French and the 2 youngest acted out of the *Bourg. Gentilhomme* and really so well. . . . Four languages is a lot, but they need them absolutely, and this summer we had Germans and Swedes, and I made all 4 lunch and dine, as it is good practice for them.

I have begun painting flowers, as alas, have had to leave singing and playing as too tiring.

Must end. Goodbye and God bless and keep you.

A tender kiss from Your fondly
Loving old P.Q. No. III
Alix

Despite the stream of visitors, the summer of 1912 was peaceful for the Imperial family. The girls were getting older: Olga was seventeen, Tatiana fifteen, Marie thirteen and Anastasia eleven. Alexis, who was eight, was a source of pride and relief. He was cheerful, mischievous and lively; he had been so well that year that Alexandra had begun to hope her prayers had been answered and he might be getting permanently better.

At Spala, six weeks after this letter was written, this hope disintegrated. That autumn, in the depths of the Polish forest, Nicholas and Alexandra were plunged into a crisis that seared them both forever.

The Borodino ceremonies mentioned in Alexandra's letter were a centenary celebration of the great battle before Moscow in 1812 when Kutuzov's army finally gave battle to Napoleon. For the centenary, Russian army engineers had reconstructed the battlefield, rebuilding the famous redoubts marking the positions of French and Russian batteries, and identifying the spots where infantry and cavalry charged. Nicholas, mounted on a white horse, rode slowly across the battlefield, which was lined with detachments of soldiers from the regiments that had fought at Borodino. As a climax to the ceremony, an ancient Sergeant Voitinuik, said to be 122 years old and a survivor of the famous battle, was led forward and presented to the Tsar. Nicholas, deeply moved, warmly grasped the hand of the tottering veteran and congratulated him. "A common feeling of deep reverence for our forebears seized us there," he wrote to Marie.

The ceremonies concluded in Moscow, which one hundred years before had burned before Napoleon's eyes. Nicholas moved through cathedral services, receptions, parades and processions. He visited museums, attended balls and reviewed seventy-five thousand soldiers and seventy-two thousand schoolchildren. As she had predicted, Alexandra exhausted herself trying to keep up. With relief, she and her family boarded the Imperial train in mid-September for the westward journey to the Polish hunting lodges of Bialowieza and Spala. They stopped only once along the way; in Smolensk they took tea with the local nobility. That afternoon, reported the Tsar to his mother, "Alexis got hold of a glass of champagne and drank it unnoticed after which he became rather gay and began entertaining the ladies to our great surprise. When we returned to the train, he kept telling us about his conversations at the party and also that he heard his tummy rumbling."

The hunting lodge at Bialowieza in eastern Poland was surrounded by thirty thousand acres of deep forest filled with big game. Along with elk and stag, it was the only place in Europe where the auroch, or European bison, were still to be found. At Bialowieza, the Imperial family began a pleasant holiday routine. "The weather is warm, but we have constant rain," the Tsar wrote to his mother. "In the mornings my daughters and I go for rides on these perfect woodland paths." Alexis, not permitted to ride, went rowing on a nearby lake. On one of these excursions, while jumping into a boat, he fell. An oarlock ground itself into the upper part of his left thigh. Dr. Botkin examined the spot and found a small swelling just below the groin. The bruise hurt Alexis, and for several days Botkin made him stay in bed. A week later, the pain and swelling had dwindled and Botkin believed that the incident was closed.

After two weeks at Bialowieza, the family moved on to Spala, the ancient hunting seat of the kings of Poland. Lost at the end of a sandy road, the wooden villa resembled a small country inn. Inside, it was cramped and dark; electric lights were left burning all day so that people could find their way through the tiny rooms and narrow hallways. Outside, the forest was magnificent. A clear, fast-flowing stream cut through the middle of a wide green lawn. From the edge of the lawn, small paths branched off into the forest. One was called the Road of Mushrooms because it ended at a bench surrounded by a fairy ring of mushrooms.

Nicholas threw himself eagerly into hunting. Every day, he rode off with the Polish noblemen who came to visit. At night, after dinner, the slain stags were laid out on the grass in front of the villa. While huntsmen stood beside the beasts holding flaming torches, the Tsar and his guests came out and examined their kill.

It was while Alexis was convalescing from his original fall in the boat that Alexandra first asked Pierre Gilliard to begin tutoring her son in French. This was Gilliard's first intimate contact with the Tsarevich. He still did not know the nature of the boy's disease. The lessons were soon interrupted. "[Alexis] had looked . . . ill from the outset," Gilliard recalled. "Soon he had to take to his bed. . . . [I was] struck by his lack of color and the fact that he was carried as if he could not walk."

Alexandra, like any mother, worried about her son being cooped up in the gloomy house without sunlight and fresh air. Deciding to take him for a drive, she had him placed in her carriage between herself and Anna Vyrubova. Bouncing and jostling, the carriage set off down the sandy roads. Not long after starting, Alexis winced and began to complain of pain in his lower leg and abdomen. Frightened, the Empress ordered the driver to return to the villa immediately. There were several miles to travel. Every time the carriage jolted, Alexis, pale and contorted, cried out. Alexandra, now in terror, urged the driver first to hurry, then to go slowly. Anna Vyrubova remembered the ride as "an experience in horror. Every movement of the carriage, every rough place in the road, caused the child the most exquisite torture and by the time we reached home, the boy was almost unconscious with pain."

Botkin, examining the boy, found a severe hemorrhage in the thigh and groin. That night, a stream of telegrams flew off from Spala. One by one, the doctors began to arrive from St. Petersburg: Ostrogorsky, the pediatrician, and Rauchfuss, the surgeon, joined Fedorov and Dr. Derevenko. Their presence at Spala added worried faces and urgent whispers, but none of them could aid the suffering child. The bleeding could not be stopped and no pain-killers were given. Blood flowed steadily from the torn blood vessels inside the leg, seeping slowly through the other tissues and forming an enormous hematoma, or swelling, through the leg, groin and lower abdomen. The leg drew up against the chest to give the blood a larger socket to fill. But there came a point when there was no place else for the blood to go. Yet still it flowed. It was the beginning of a nightmare.

"The days between the 6th and the 10th were the worst," Nicholas wrote his mother. "The poor darling suffered intensely, the pains came in spasms and recurred every quarter of an hour. His high temperature made him delirious night and day; and he would sit up in bed and every movement brought the pain on again. He hardly slept at all, had not even the strength to cry, and kept repeating, 'Oh Lord, have mercy upon me.'"

Day and night, screams pierced the walls and filled the corridors. Many in the household stuffed their ears with cotton in order to continue their work. Yet for eleven days, the most critical part of the crisis, Alexandra scarcely left her son's side. Hour after hour, she sat by the bed where the groaning, half-conscious child lay huddled on his side. His face was bloodless, his body contorted, his eyes, with hollow black circles under them, were rolled back in his head. The Empress never undressed or went to bed. When she had to sleep, she lay back on a sofa next to his bed and dozed. After a while, his groans and shrieks dwindled to a constant wail that tore her heart. Through the pain, he called to his mother, "Mama, help me. Won't you help me?" Alexandra sat holding his hand, smoothing his forehead, tears running down her cheeks as she prayed mutely to God to deliver her little boy from torture. During these eleven days, her golden hair became tinged with gray.

Even so, she stood it better than the Tsar. "I was hardly able to stay in the room, but of course had to take turns with Alix for she was exhausted by spending whole nights by his bed," he wrote to his mother. "She bore the ordeal better than I did." Anna Vyrubova says that once when Nicholas came into the room and saw his son in agony, his courage gave away and he rushed out of the house, weeping.

Both parents were certain that the boy was dying. Alexis himself thought so and hoped so. "When I am dead, it will not hurt any more, will it, Mama?" he asked. In another moment of relative calm, he said quietly, "When I am dead, build me a little monument of stones in the woods."

Nevertheless—incredibly, it seemed to Gilliard—outside the sickroom, the surface household routines went on unchanged. Polish noblemen continued to arrive to hunt with the Tsar, and Nicholas rode off with them into the forest. In the evenings, the Empress would briefly leave the bedside and appear, pale but composed, to act as hostess for her husband. Desperately, they played this charade, trying to conceal from the world not only the extent of the Tsarevich's illness, but their own anguish.

Gilliard, watching from his newly intimate vantage point, could scarcely believe what he saw. One night after dinner, his pupils Marie and Anastasia were to present two scenes from Molière's *Bourgeois Gentilhomme* before their parents, the suite and some guests. As prompter, Gilliard stood in the wings of the makeshift stage behind a screen. From there, he could see the company as well as whisper to the girls.

"I could see the Tsaritsa in the front row, smiling and talking gaily to her neighbors," the tutor wrote. "When the play was over, I went out by the service door and found myself in the corridor opposite Alexis Nicolaievich's room from which a moaning sound came distinctly to my ears. Suddenly I noticed the Tsaritsa running up holding her long, awkward train in her two hands. I shrank back against the wall and she passed me without observing my presence. There was a distracted and terror-stricken look on her face. I returned to the dining room. There all were happy. Footmen in livery were handing around refreshments and everyone was laughing and exchanging jokes. . . .

"A few minutes later the Tsaritsa came back. She had resumed the mask. She smiled pleasantly at the guests who crowded around her. But I noticed that the Tsar, even while engaged in conversation, had taken up a position from which he could watch the door, and I caught the despairing glance which the Tsaritsa threw him as she came in. The scene . . . suddenly brought home to me the tragedy of a double life."

Despite all precautions, the shroud of secrecy surrounding the illness began to tear. St. Petersburg buzzed with talk, none of it accurate. There were blind guesses as to what had happened; a lengthy article in the *London Daily Mail* declared that the boy had been attacked by an anarchist and gravely wounded by a bomb. At last, after Dr. Fedorov warned Nicholas that the hemorrhage in the stomach, still unchecked, could be fatal at any hour, Count Fredericks received permission to begin publishing medical bulletins. Still, there was no mention of the cause.

Official announcements of the grave illness of the Heir to the Throne plunged Russia into national prayer. Special services were held in great cathedrals and in small churches in lonely villages. Before the blessed icon in the Cathedral of Our Lady of Kazan in St. Petersburg, Russians stood and prayed night and day. There was no church at Spala, but a large green tent was erected for that purpose in the garden. "All the servants, the Cossacks, the soldiers and all the rest were wonderfully sympathetic," Nicholas wrote to his mother. "At the beginning of Alexei's illness, they begged the priest, Vassiliev, to hold a *Te Deum* in the open. They begged him to repeat it every day until he recovered. Polish peasants came in crowds and wept while he read the sermon to them."

More than once, it seemed the end had come. At lunch one day, the Tsar was handed a note scribbled by the Empress from her place beside Alexis's bed. Alexis was suffering so terribly, she said, that she knew he was about to die. Pale but collected, Nicholas made a sign to Fedorov, who hastily left the table and went to the sickroom. But Alexis continued to breathe and the agony continued. The following night, when the suite was sitting helplessly in the Empress's boudoir, Princess Irene of Prussia, Alexandra's sister, came to the doorway. With a white face, she begged the suite to retire, saying the boy's condition was desperate. The last sacrament was administered, and the bulletin sent to St. Petersburg that night was worded so that the one to follow could announce that His Imperial Highness the Tsarevich was dead.

It was on this night, at the end of hope, that Alexandra called on Rasputin. She asked Anna Vyrubova to telegraph him in Pokrovskoe, his home in Siberia, begging him to pray for the life of her son. Rasputin immediately cabled back: "God has seen your tears and heard your prayers. Do not grieve. The Little One will not die. Do not allow the doctors to bother him too much."

The next morning, Alexandra came down to the drawing room, thin and pale, but she was smiling. "The doctors notice no improvement yet," she said, "but I am not a bit anxious myself now. During the night, I received a telegram from Father Gregory and he has reassured me completely." A day later, the hemorrhage stopped. The boy was spent, utterly wasted, but alive.

The part played by Rasputin's telegram in Alexis's recovery at Spala remains one of the most mysterious episodes of the whole Rasputin legend. None of the doctors present ever discussed it in writing. Anna Vyrubova, the link between Rasputin and the Empress, writes of the telegram and the boy's recovery without comment or evaluation. Pierre Gilliard, at that time a minor member of the household to whom many doors still remained closed, does not even mention Rasputin's telegram. Strangely, even Nicholas, in writing to his mother, fails to mention the dramatic telegram from Siberia. His account, written after the ordeal had ended, was this:

"On Oct. 10 [O.S.] we decided to give him Holy Communion and his condition began to improve at once. The temperature fell and the pain almost disappeared and he fell quickly into a sound sleep for the first time. The family suite received Holy Communion and the priest took the Holy Sacrament to Alexis. It snowed all day yesterday, but it thawed last night. It was cold standing in Church but all that is nothing when the heart and soul rejoice."

The Tsar's silence in this letter on the matter of Rasputin's telegram does not mean that he was unaware of it, or of the significance attached to it by his wife. Rather, it indicated his own uncertainty as to what had happened and his unwillingness to commit himself to belief in Rasputin, especially in a letter to his mother. Marie considered Rasputin a fraud, and a letter from Nicholas announcing that Rasputin had saved Alexis by sending a telegram from Siberia would have dismayed the Dowager Empress. Knowing this, Nicholas tactfully left Rasputin out of his account.

The remaining evidence is skimpy. Mosolov was at Spala. He suggests that Fedorov, the surgeon, may have had something to do with the recovery. Mosolov's story is that at the height of the crisis Fedorov came to him and said, "I do not agree with my colleagues. It is most urgently necessary to apply far more drastic measures, but they involve a risk. Ought I to say so to the Empress? Or would it be better to prescribe without letting her know?" Later, after the bleeding had stopped, Mosolov asked Fedorov, "Did you apply the remedy you spoke of?" Fedorov threw up his hands and said, "If I had done so, I should not have admitted it. You can see for yourself what is going on here." The implication that Fedorov did nothing is strengthened by the fact that later that year Fedorov met Grand Duchess Olga Alexandrovna and told her that "the recovery was wholly inexplicable from a medical point of view."

Despite what Fedorov said, there is a possible medical explanation of this episode. After a greatly prolonged period of time, hemophilic bleeding may stop of its own accord. As long ago as 1905, Dr. M. Litten wrote: "It is impossible to predict in any individual case when the hemorrhage will be arrested; the great loss of blood itself seems to exercise a beneficent effect in the direction of constricting the hemorrhage. Anemia of the brain produces fainting accompanied by a reduction in blood pressure, and the hemorrhage eases soon after. Occasionally, on the other hand, it persists for so long a time that the patient bleeds to death."

Today, long before a hemophiliac is allowed to reach this state, hemorrhage is arrested with transfusions of plasma. If plasma were not available, however, hemotologists agree that hemophiliacs often would find themselves in the state described.

Because the crisis at Spala is so obscure and yet so enormously important to what happened later, every possible explanation should be examined. In this context, it is reasonable to speculate that the arrival of Rasputin's telegram did, of itself, have a beneficial effect on the desperate medical situation.

To begin with, one passage in Rasputin's telegram—"Do not allow the doctors to bother him too much"—was excellent medical advice. With four doctors hovering anxiously around the bed, taking his temperature, probing his leg and groin, Alexis probably was denied the total absence of trauma he desperately needed. A clot, gradually formed, still fragile, could easily have been dislodged in the course of one of the doctors' frequent examinations. When at last they left Alexis alone, either because they had given up or because of Rasputin's advice to the Empress, the effect could only have been good.

There is another possibility, more shadowy, but important to consider. That emotion plays a role in bleeding has long been suspected. Recently, the hypothesis has been greatly strengthened. In 1957, Dr. Paul J. Poinsard, of Jefferson Hospital in Philadelphia, described to an international symposium on hemophilia his belief "that the hemophiliac patient bleeds more profusely under a condition of emotional stress." Turning the thesis around, Dr. Poinsard continued, "Emotional tranquillity with a feeling state of well-being appears to be conducive to less severe and less frequent bleeding than in the subject who is emotionally distressed."

At the moment Rasputin's telegram arrived at Spala, Alexandra, the only person with whom the semi-conscious Alexis had strong emotional communication, was in a state of frantic, if exhausted, hysteria. Alexis must have felt her fear and despair. Perhaps, in the manner Dr. Poinsard suggested, his condition was affected by these emotions. If it was, then the sudden overwhelming change in his mother's emotional state produced by Rasputin's telegram may also have affected Alexis. Alone, the new aura of calm and confidence probably could not have stopped the hemorrhage. But together with the natural reduction of the loss of blood caused by lowered blood pressure and the slow formation of clots, it may have helped. It could even, as Alexandra believed, have been the factor which turned back the tide of death.

Whatever the cause, everyone—doctors, court officials, grand duchesses, people who believed in Rasputin and those who hated him—recognized that a remarkably eerie coincidence had occurred. Only to one person was the mystery not a mystery. In her own mind, Alexandra understood clearly what had happened. To her, it seemed quite natural: after the best doctors in Russia had failed, after her own hours of prayer had gone unanswered, her plea to Rasputin had brought the intervention of God and a miracle had taken place. From that time, Alexandra was unshakably convinced that her son's life lay in Rasputin's hands. From this belief, enormous consequences were to flow.

Once the crisis had passed, most of the Imperial household quickly returned to their normal pursuits. Nicholas received his ministers to discuss the war which Bulgaria and Serbia were waging against Turkey. He hunted, played tennis, walked in the woods and went rowing on the river. He took Anna Vyrubova out in a boat which hit a rock in a rapid current and almost capsized.

But for the two most intimately involved in the ordeal, recovery was slow. For weeks, Alexandra and Alexis sat together in his room. He was propped against pillows in his bed, while she sat in a chair beside him, reading aloud or knitting. "I must warn you that according to the doctors, Alexei's recovery will be very slow," Nicholas wrote to Marie. "He still has a pain in his left knee and cannot bend it. It has to be propped up on a pillow. But that does not worry the doctors for the chief thing is that the process of internal absorption continues and for this, complete immobility is necessary. His complexion is quite good now, but at one time he looked like wax, his hands, his feet, his face, everything. He has grown terribly thin but the doctors are now stuffing him for all they are worth."

A month later, Alexis had recovered sufficiently to be moved back to Tsarskoe Selo. At the Empress's command, the road from the house to the station had been smoothed and graded so that there should not be the slightest jolt. On the homeward journey, the Imperial train crawled at fifteen miles an hour.

Almost a year was to pass before Alexis could walk again. For months, his left leg, drawn up against his chest, refused to straighten. The doctors applied a metal triangle with sliding sides which could be moved to varying points as the leg permitted. Bit by bit, the triangle was widened and the leg extended. But even a year later, at Livadia, Alexis still was undergoing a series of hot mudbaths as a treatment for the limp he had acquired at Spala. Through all this time, official photographs of the Heir were posed either seated or on steps so that the bent leg would appear to be normal.

After Spala, Alexis became a more serious child, more reflective and more considerate of other people. For an eight-year-old boy, it was a matter to ponder that his father was autocrat over millions of men and the master of the largest empire on earth, and yet had no power to spare him the pain he had felt in his leg. For Alexandra, Spala was a supreme religious experience. She had been, for what seemed an eternity, in Hell. The power that vanquished Hell and saved her son had been a sign from Heaven. Beneath that sign stood Gregory Rasputin.

CHAPTER FIFTEEN

Rasputin

THERE was much about Gregory Rasputin that was repulsive. When he first appeared in 1905 in several of St. Petersburg's most elegant drawing rooms, the heralded Siberian "miracle worker" was in his early thirties, broad-shouldered, muscular, of average height. He dressed roughly in loose peasant blouses and baggy trousers tucked into the top of heavy, crudely made leather boots. He was filthy. He rose and slept and rose again without ever bothering to wash himself or change his clothes. His hands were grimy, his nails black, his beard tangled and encrusted with debris. His hair was long and greasy. Parted loosely in the middle, it hung in thin strands to his shoulders. Not surprisingly, he gave off a powerful, acrid odor.

To his devotees, none of these details mattered. Women who found him disgusting discovered later that disgust was a new and thrilling sensation; that the rough and strong-smelling peasant was an alluring change from a surfeit of perfumed and pomaded cavalry officers and society gentlemen. Others, less sensual, reasoned that his coarse appearance was a sure sign of his spirituality. Were he not a Holy Man, they said to themselves, such a ragged *moujik* would not be here among us. Satisfied with this conclusion, they went out, adding their voices to the growing chorus which chanted that Rasputin was indeed a Man of God.

Rasputin's eyes were his most remarkable feature. Friends and enemies alike described their strange power. Anna Vyrubova, who worshipped Rasputin, spoke of him as having a "pale face, long hair, un-cared for beard and the most extraordinary eyes, large, light, brilliant." The monk Iliodor, who hated Rasputin, described his "steely grey eyes, deep set under their bushy eyebrows, which almost sank into pinpoints." Paléologue, who had to consider Rasputin as a political phenomenon, found himself focusing on the eyes: "Rasputin was dark, with long stiff hair, a thick black beard, a high forehead, a broad prominent nose, and sensuous mouth. The full expression of his personality, however, seemed concentrated in his eyes. They were pale blue, of exceptional brilliance, depth and attraction. His gaze was at once piercing and caressing, naïve and cunning, far-off and intent. When he was in earnest conversation, his pupils seemed to radiate magnetism. He carried with him a strong animal smell, like the smell of a goat."

It was difficult to resist the power of Rasputin's steady gaze. Men and women who met him out of curiosity found themselves fascinated, lured and compelled by the glimmering eyes and the urgent, mysterious will behind them. Prince Yussoupov, who murdered Rasputin, went to him first, coolly announcing that he was sick, to learn more about Rasputin's methods of "healing."

"The '*starets*' made me lie down on the sofa," Yussoupov wrote later. "Then, staring intently at me, he gently ran his hand over my chest, neck and head, after which he knelt down, laid both hands on my forehead and murmured a prayer. His face was so close to mine that I could see only his eyes. He remained in this position for some time, then rising brusquely, he made mesmeric passes over my body.

"Rasputin had tremendous hypnotic power. I felt as if some active energy were pouring heat, like a warm current into my whole being. I fell into a torpor, and my body grew numb; I tried to speak but my tongue no longer obeyed me and I gradually slipped into a drowsy state, as though a powerful narcotic had been administered to me. All I could see was Rasputin's glittering eyes; two phosphorescent beams of light melting into a great luminous ring which at times drew nearer and then moved farther away. I heard the voice of the *starets* but could not understand what he said.

"I remained in this state without being able to cry out or to move. My mind alone was free, and I fully realized that I was gradually falling into the power of this evil man. Then I felt stir in me the will to fight his hypnosis. Little by little the desire to resist grew stronger and stronger, forming a protective armour around me. I had the feeling that a merciless struggle was being fought out between Rasputin and me. I knew that I was preventing him from getting complete mastery over me, but still I could not move: I had to wait until he ordered me to get up." Rasputin closed the interview with "Well, my dear, that'll be enough for the first time."

A story told by Fülöp-Miller, Rasputin's biographer, indicates the strange duality of Rasputin's nature:

"A young girl who had heard of the strange new saint came from her province to the capital and visited him in search of . . . spiritual instruction. His gentle monastic gaze and the plainly parted light brown hair . . . all at first inspired her with confidence. But when he came closer to her, she felt immediately that another quite different man, mysterious, crafty, and corrupting, looked out from behind the eyes that radiated goodness and gentleness.

"He sat down opposite her, edged quite near and his light blue eyes changed color and became deep and dark. A keen glance reached her from the corner of his eyes, bored into her, and held her fascinated. A leaden heaviness overpowered her limbs as his great wrinkled face, distorted with desire, came closer to hers. She felt his hot breath on her cheeks, and saw how his eyes, burning from the depths of their sockets, furtively roved over her helpless body, until he dropped his lids with a sensuous expression. His voice had fallen to a passionate whisper and he murmured strange, voluptuous words in her ear.

"Just as she was on the point of abandoning herself to her seducer, a memory stirred in her dimly . . . she recalled that she had come to ask him about God . . . she gradually awoke . . . the heaviness disappeared . . . she began to struggle. . . . He was at once aware of the increasing inner resistance, his half-shut eyes opened again, he stood up, bent over her . . . and pressed a passionless, gentle, fatherly kiss on her forehead. His face distorted with desire became smooth again and was once more the kindly face of the wandering teacher. He spoke to his visitor in a benevolent, patronizing tone, his right hand raised to his forehead in blessing. He stood before her in the attitude in which Christ is depicted on old Russian icons; his glance was again gentle and friendly, almost humble, and only in the depth of those little eyes still lurked, almost invisible, the other man, the sensual beast."

Rasputin focused his eyes not only on feverish women, but on ministers of the Imperial government. At the request of the Empress, he called on and was received by two successive Prime Ministers of Russia, Peter Stolypin and Vladimir Kokovtsov.

Stolypin, a man of great strength and will, later described the visit of Rasputin to his friend Michael Rodzianko, President of the Duma: "He [Rasputin] ran his pale eyes over me, mumbled mysterious and inarticulate words from the Scriptures, made strange movements with his hands, and I began to feel an indescribable loathing for this vermin sitting opposite me. Still, I did realize that the man possessed great hypnotic power, which was beginning to produce a fairly strong moral impression on me, though certainly one of repulsion. I pulled myself together. . . ."

To a remarkable degree, the same scene was repeated with Stolypin's successor, Kokovtsov: "When Rasputin came into my study and sat down in an arm chair, I was struck by the repulsive expression of his eyes," Kokovtsov wrote. "Deep seated and close set, they glued on me and for a long time, Rasputin would not turn them away as though trying to exercise some hypnotic influence. When tea was served, Rasputin seized a handful of biscuits, threw them into his tea and again fixed his lynx eyes on me. I was getting tired of his attempts at hypnotism and told him in as many words that it was useless to stare at me so hard because his eyes had not the slightest effect on me."

Both Stolypin and Kokovtsov departed from their interviews convinced that they, at least, had triumphed over the Siberian *moujik*. In fact, both had simply made more certain their own political fates. The interviews had been arranged by Alexandra so that Rasputin could evaluate the two ministers. Leaving each of them, he reported to her that neither man seemed attentive to him or to the will of God. Upon these reports, unknown to them, the palace reputations of both of these Prime Ministers, the best men that Russia had, began to decline.

Rasputin's eyes were the foundation of his power, but when they failed him, he was quick to use his wheedling tongue.

The rise of Gregory Rasputin would have been impossible in any country other than Russia. Even in Russia, pungent, shaggy, semiliterate peasants did not normally take tea with prime ministers. Yet neither Kokovtsov nor Rasputin considered the scene quite as bizarre as it seems today; it was not, as someone put it, "as if Og had entered the White House."

Rasputin appeared in St. Petersburg as a *starets*—a Man of God who lived in poverty, asceticism and solitude, offering himself as a guide to other souls in moments of suffering and turmoil. Sometimes, as in his case, the *starets* might also be a *strannik*—a pilgrim who carried his poverty and his offerings of guidance in wanderings from place to place. These were types that all Russians could recognize. Through Russian history, armies of impoverished pilgrims had walked across the steppes from village to village and monastery to monastery, living on whatever the peasants or monks might choose to give them. Many ascetics walked barefoot in the winter or wrapped their legs with heavy chains. Some preached, others claimed powers of healing. If the Orthodox Church caught them preaching heresy, they went to prison, but their poverty and self-sacrifice often made them seem holier than the local priests.

All Russians listened to these holy men. To illiterate peasants who had never walked beyond the nearest river, they talked of mighty cities, foreign lands, mysterious healings and miracles of God. Even educated Russians treated them with respect. Dostoyevsky wrote in *The Brothers Karamasov*, "The *starets* is he who takes your soul and will and makes them his. When you select your *starets*, you surrender your will. You give it to him in utter submission, in full renunciation." Before his death, Count Leo Tolstoy visited the revered *starets* of Optina Poustin for counsel. Traditionally, the rags, the chains, the clear renunciation of the world gave these men freedoms that others lacked. They could rebuke the mighty, sometimes even the tsars themselves.

Rasputin was a fraudulent *starets*. Most were saintly old men who had left all temptation and worldly goods behind. Rasputin was young, he was married and had three children, and his powerful friends later bought him the grandest house in his village. His mind was impure and his moral behavior was gross. But he had in lavish abundance some of the dramatic trappings of holiness. Along with his burning eyes, he had a fluent tongue. His head was filled with Scriptures, and his deep, powerful voice made him a compelling preacher. Besides, he had wandered the length and breadth of Russia and twice made pilgrimages to the Holy Land. He presented himself as a humble penitent, a man who had sinned greatly, been forgiven and commanded to do God's work. It was a touching symbol of his humility, people said, that he kept the nickname "Rasputin" which he had earned as a young man in his native village. "Rasputin" in Russian means "dissolute."

Rasputin was born Gregory Efimovich, the son of Efim, a farmer who once had been a coachman in the Imperial Mail. The year was 1872; thus he was thirty-three when he first met the Imperial family, and forty-four when he died. His birthplace was Pokrovskoe, a village on the Tura River in western Siberia, 250 miles east of the Ural

Mountains. It was a hard, wind-swept land where the temperature in winter dropped to forty below zero and to survive took great strength and hard physical work. Climate and isolation had their effect on the mind, and more mystics, more holy men and more outlandish sects came out of Siberia than any other part of Russia.

There is a story that, as a boy, Gregory uttered his first startling bit of prophecy. He lay in bed with fever while a group of villagers gathered in his father's house to discuss the theft of a horse. From his bed, the story goes, Gregory arose, flushed and excited, and pointed his finger at a peasant in the room, declaring that he was the thief. Outraged, the peasant denied it, and Gregory was beaten. That night, however, a pair of distrustful villagers followed the accused man and saw him take the horse from his shed into the forest. Gregory acquired a modest local reputation as a seer, a heady thing for a boy of twelve.

As a young man, the seer became a rake. He drank and fought and made free with the village girls. He became a wagoner, carrying goods and passengers to other villages, an occupation that extended the range of his conquests. A good talker, sure of himself, he tried every girl he met. His method was direct: he grabbed and started undoing buttons. Naturally, he was frequently kicked and scratched and bitten, but the sheer volume of his efforts brought him notable success. He learned that even in the shyest and primmest of girls, the emptiness and loneliness of life in a Siberian village had bred a flickering appetite for romance and adventure. Gregory's talent was for stimulating those appetites and overcoming all hesitations by direct, good-natured aggression.

On one of his trips, Gregory—now dubbed Rasputin by his snickering neighbors—carried a traveler to the monastery of Verkhoturye, a place used both as a retreat for monks and as a seat of ecclesiastical imprisonment for heretical sectarians. Rasputin was fascinated by both groups of inhabitants and remained at the monastery for four months.

Most of those confined at Verkhoturye were members of the Khlysty, a sect which believed in reaching God through the raptures of sexual encounter. Their secret nocturnal orgies took place on Saturday nights in curtained houses or clearings deep in the forest. Both men and women arrived dressed in clean white linen gowns and began singing hymns by candlelight. As the candles burned lower, the singers began to dance, slowly and reverently at first, then more wildly. In a fever of excitement, they stripped their bodies and submitted to the whip brandished by the local leader of the sect. At the peak of their frenzy, men and women fell on each other, regardless of age or family relationship, and climaxed their devotions with indiscriminate intercourse.

In later years, Rasputin's enemies often charged him with membership in the Khlysty. Had they been able to prove it, even the Empress might have been shocked, but solid evidence was never available. The most that could be proved—and Rasputin freely admitted this—was that, like the Khlysty, Rasputin believed that to sin was the first step toward holiness.

Soon after returning to Pokrovskoe, Rasputin, then barely twenty, married a blonde peasant girl four years older than he. Through all his life, even at the height of his notoriety, his wife, Praskovie, remained at home in Pokrovskoe. She knew about his womanizing and never complained. "He has enough for all," she said with a curious pride. She bore him four children—two sons and two daughters. The eldest son died in infancy and the other was mentally deficient; the two girls, Maria and Varvara, later came to live with their father and be educated in St. Petersburg.

To support his family, Rasputin took up farming. One day while plowing, he thought he saw a vision and declared that he had been directed to make a pilgrimage. His father scoffed—"Gregory has turned pilgrim out of laziness," said Efim—but Gregory set out and walked two thousand miles to the monastery at Mount Athos in Greece. At the end of two years, when Gregory returned, he carried an aura of mystery and holiness. He began to pray at length, to bless other peasants, to kneel at their beds in supplication when they were sick. He gave up his drinking and curbed his public lunges at women. It began to be said that Gregory Rasputin, the profligate, was a man who was close to God. The village priest, alarmed at this sudden blossoming of a vigorous young Holy Man within his sphere, suggested heresy and threatened an investigation. Unwilling to argue and bored by life in Pokrovskoe, Rasputin left the village and began once again to wander.

Rasputin's first appearance in St. Petersburg occurred in 1903 and lasted for five months. Even in the capital, remote and sophisticated, his reputation had preceded him. He was said to be a strange Siberian *moujik* who, having sinned and repented, had been blessed with extraordinary powers. As such, he was received by the city's most famous churchman, Father John of Kronstadt. John was a saintly figure noted for the power of his prayers, and his church at Kronstadt was an object of pilgrimages from across Russia. He had been the private confessor to Tsar Alexander III and had sat with the family by Alexander's bed at Livadia while the Tsar was dying. To be received and blessed by this most revered priest in Russia was an impressive step in Rasputin's progress.

In 1905, Rasputin was back in St. Petersburg. This time, he was taken to meet the aged Archimandrite Theophan, Inspector of the St. Petersburg Theological Academy and former confessor to the Empress Alexandra. Like Father John, Theophan was struck by the apparent fervor of Rasputin's faith and arranged for him to meet another ranking churchman, Bishop Hermogen of Saratov. With all of these priests and bishops, Rasputin's approach was the same. He refused to bow and treated them with jolly, spontaneous good humor, as if they were friends and equals. Put off balance by his egalitarianism and simple sincerity, they were also impressed by his obvious gifts as a preacher. He was a phenomenon, it seemed to them, which had been given to the Church and which the Church, then trying to strengthen its roots among the peasants, could put to valuable use. They welcomed him as a genuine *starets*.

In addition to the blessing of the Holy Fathers of the Church, Rasputin began his life in the capital with the endorsement of two ladies of the highest society, the Montenegrin sister princesses, Grand Duchess Militsa and Grand Duchess Anastasia. The daughters of King Nicholas I of Montenegro, each had married a cousin of Tsar Nicholas II, and both were prominent practitioners of the pseudo-Oriental brand of mysticism then in vogue in many of the capital's most elegant drawing rooms. This upper layer of society, bored with the old church routines of traditional Orthodoxy, looked for meaning and sensation in the occult. Amid an atmosphere of decadence, of cards and gold lying on green baize tables, of couples flushed with champagne dancing all night, of galloping *troikas*, of fortunes staked at the race track, the mediums and clairvoyants flourished. Grand dukes and princes gathered around tables, the curtains drawn behind their backs, to hold seances and try feverishly to communicate with the other world. There were table-rappings in darkened rooms where strange voices were said to speak and the tables themselves were declared to have risen and floated in the air. Numerous great mansions had their domestic ghosts. Footsteps sounded, doors creaked and a certain tune was always played on the piano by invisible hands whenever a member of the family was dying. Rasputin, who had so impressed the saintly men of the Church, was received with equal excitement by this coterie of the occult.

It was Grand Duchess Militsa who first brought Rasputin to Tsarskoe Selo. The fateful date, November 1, 1905 (O.S.), is fixed by an entry in Nicholas's diary: "We have got to know a man of God, Gregory, from Tobolsk Province." A year later, Nicholas wrote: "Gregory arrived at 6:45. He saw the children and talked to us until 7:45." Still later: "Militsa and Stana [Grand Duchess Anastasia] dined with us. They talked about Gregory the whole evening."

Rasputin was not, in fact, the first "Holy Man" brought to the palace by the Grand Duchess Militsa. In 1900, when Alexandra was desperately anxious to give her husband a male heir, Militsa advised her of the existence of a French mystic and "soul doctor" named Philippe Vachot. Vachot had begun as a butcher's assistant in Lyon, but he had found life easier as a faith healer; many believed he could also determine the sex of unborn children. This did not impress the French authorities, who three times had prosecuted him for practicing medicine without a license. In 1901, Nicholas and Alexandra paid an official visit to France, and Militsa arranged for them to meet Vachot. He proved to be a childlike little man with a high forehead and penetrating eyes. When the Imperial couple returned to Russia, Vachot went along as part of their baggage.

Unfortunately for Vachot, the Empress's next child, like the preceding three, proved to be a girl, Anastasia. In 1903, Vachot declared that the Empress was pregnant and would have a son. She was not even pregnant and Vachot's stock plummeted. Despairing, Alexandra was persuaded to give up Vachot and he was sent home, lavishly remunerated, to die in obscurity. But before he left, he told the Empress, "You will someday have another friend like me who will speak to you of God."

At first, Rasputin's reception at the palace caused little comment. His credentials on all sides were impeccable. He had the blessing of the most saintly men of the church; Father John and the Archimandrite Theophan had both advised the Empress to have a talk with the devout peasant, and he was introduced from the highest social circle of the capital.

None of these people, however, expected the degree of intimacy with which Rasputin came to be accepted at the palace. Usually, he came in the hour before dinner when Alexis was playing on the floor in his blue bathrobe before going to bed. When Rasputin arrived, he sat down with the boy beside him and told stories of travels and adventures and old Russian tales. There was the story of the hump-backed horse, of the legless rider and the eyeless rider, of Alyonushka and Ivanushka, of the unfaithful Tsaritsa who was turned into a white duck, of the evil witch Baba Yaga, of the Tsarevich Vasily and the beautiful Princess Elena. Often, the girls, the Empress and the Tsar himself found themselves listening.

It was on such an evening in the autumn of 1907 that Grand Duchess Olga, the Tsar's youngest sister, first met Rasputin. Nicholas said to her, "Will you come and meet a Russian peasant?" and Olga followed him to the nurseries. There, the four girls and their small brother, all wearing white nightgowns, were waiting to go to bed. In the middle of the room stood Rasputin.

"All the children seemed to like him," said Olga. "They were completely at ease with him. I still remember little Alexis [then three], deciding he was a rabbit, jumped up and down the room. And then, quite suddenly, Rasputin caught the child's hand and led him to his bedroom, and we three followed. There was something like a hush as though we had found ourselves in Church. In Alexis's bedroom no lamps were lit; the only light came from the candles burning in front of some beautiful icons. The child stood very still by the side of the giant, whose head was bowed. I knew he was praying. It was all most impressive. I also knew that my little nephew had joined him in prayer. I really cannot describe it—but I was then conscious of the man's sincerity. . . . I realized that both Nicky and Alicky were hoping that I would come to like Rasputin. . . ."

Rasputin's manner with Nicholas and Alexandra exactly suited his role. He was respectful but never fawning; he felt free to laugh loudly and to criticize freely, although he larded his language heavily with biblical quotes and old Russian proverbs. He referred to the sovereigns not as "Your Majesty" or "Your Imperial Majesty," but as *Batiushka* and *Matushka*, the "Father" and "Mother" of the Russian peasants. In these ways he deepened the contrasts between himself, the Man of God and representative of the Russian people, and the polished figures of court and society whom Alexandra despised.

Both Nicholas and Alexandra spoke freely to Rasputin. To the Tsar, Rasputin was exactly what he had described to his sister, "a Russian peasant." Once, speaking to one of the officers of his guard, Nicholas elaborated: "He [Rasputin] is just a good, religious, simple-minded

Russian. When in trouble or assailed by doubts, I like to have a talk with him, and invariably feel at peace with myself afterward." To Alexandra, Rasputin became much more important. Gradually, Alexandra became convinced that the *starets* was a personal emissary from God to her, to her husband and to Russia. He had all the trappings: he was a peasant, devoted to the Tsar and the Orthodox faith; he represented the historic triumvirate: Tsar-Church-People; in addition, as an irrefutable proof of his divine mission, Rasputin was able to help her son.

This was the key. "It was the boy's illness that brought Rasputin to the palace," writes Sir Bernard Pares. "What was the nature of Rasputin's influence in the family circle?" Pares goes on to ask. "The foundation of it all was that he could undoubtedly bring relief to the boy, and of this there was no question whatsoever." The eyewitnesses agree. "Call it what you will," declared Alexandra Tegleva, Alexis's last nurse, "he [Rasputin] could promise her [the Empress] her boy's life while he lived." Mosolov, the court official, writes of Rasputin's "incontestable success in healing." Gilliard states that "Rasputin's presence in the palace was intimately connected with the prince's illness. She [Alexandra] believed that she had no choice. Rasputin was the intermediary between her and God. Her own prayers went unanswered but his seemed to be." Kerensky, intruding on the family circle after Rasputin was dead, nevertheless declares that "it was a fact that more than once before the eyes of the Tsar and the Tsaritsa, Rasputin's appearance by the bedside of the apparently dying Alexis caused a critical change."

What was it, exactly, that Rasputin did? The common belief, never verified, is that Rasputin used his extraordinary eyes to hypnotize the Tsarevich and then, with the boy in a hypnotic state, suggested that the bleeding would stop. Medically, it could not have been that simple. No doctor established in this field accepts the possibility that hypnosis alone could suddenly stop a severe hemorrhage. Nevertheless, there is a strong body of responsible opinion which believes that hypnosis, properly used, can play a part in controlling hemophilic bleeding.

"Rasputin took the empire by stopping the bleeding of the Tsarevich," wrote J. B. S. Haldane, the British geneticist. "It was perhaps an imposture, but it is also possible that by hypnotism or a similar method, he was able to produce a contraction of the small arteries. These last were placed under the regulation of the [autonomic] nervous system and although they are not normally controlled by the will, their contraction can be provoked in the body of a hypnotized subject."*

If it is medically possible that Rasputin could have controlled Alexis's bleeding by using hypnosis, it is far from historically certain that he did. Stephen Beletsky, Director of the Police Department, which monitored all Rasputin's activities, declared that in 1913 Rasputin was taking lessons in hypnotism from a teacher in St. Petersburg; Beletsky put an end to the lessons by expelling the teacher from the capital. Rasputin's successes with Alexis, however, began well before 1913. If he had been using hypnosis all the while, why did he need lessons?

The probable answer to this mystery derives from recent explorations into the shadowy links between the working of mind and body and between emotions and health. In hematology, for example, it has been proved that bleeding in hemophiliacs can be aggravated or even spontaneously induced by emotional stress. Anger, anxiety, resentment and embarrassment cause an increase in blood flow through the smallest blood vessels, the capillaries. In addition, there is evidence that overwrought emotions can adversely affect the strength and integrity of the capillary walls. As these tend to become more fragile and break down under stress while at the same time they are attempting to handle an increased flow of blood, the likelihood of abnormal bleeding becomes greater.

There is an opposite side to this proposition: It is strongly suspected that a decrease in emotional stress has a beneficial effect on bleeding. As calm and a sense of well-being return to a patient, his capillary

* Recently, over a three-year period, 1961–1964, at Jefferson Hospital in Philadelphia, Dr. Oscar Lucas used hypnosis to extract 150 teeth from hemophilic patients without transfusing a single pint of blood or plasma. Normally, for hemophiliacs, tooth extraction means a major operation requiring the transfusion of dozens of units of plasma before, during and for days after an operation. Lucas uses hypnosis in his work primarily to dissipate the fears that hemophiliacs naturally suffer when faced with the prospect of surgery and the accompanying major bleeding. "An emotionally tranquil patient has less bleeding difficulty than one emotionally distressed," Lucas has explained. "Bleeding engenders fear and fear of bleeding is considerably greater in the hemophiliac than in non-bleeders. The anxiety which results may be averted through hypnosis." Generally, Lucas suppressed anxiety by asking patients to recall pleasurable experiences. One patient enjoyed himself hugely during surgery by returning himself to a baseball park for the climactic inning of a crucial game. Whether Rasputin actually hypnotized the Tsarevich or not, the distraction a contemporary American receives from watching an exciting baseball game cannot be far different from that a small Russian boy would find in hearing the dramatic stories and legends told by a mysterious wanderer. Interestingly, Oscar Lucas was inspired to begin his own work in hypnosis after reading about Rasputin.

blood flow will decline and the strength of his vascular walls increase. In this context, the question of whether Rasputin hypnotized the Tsarevich becomes a matter of degree. If, technically, it was not hypnosis that he practiced, it was nevertheless a powerful suggestion —Prince Yussoupov's account gives an indication of its strength. When Rasputin used this power on Alexis, weaving his tales, filling a darkened room with his commanding voice, he did in effect cast a spell over a boy overwhelmed by pain. Then, as Rasputin assured him in tones which left no room for doubt, Alexis believed that the torment was receding, that soon he would be walking again, that perhaps they would go together to see the wonders of Siberia. The calm and sense of well-being produced by this powerful flow of reassuring language produced a dramatic emotional change in the Tsarevich. And, as if by a miracle, the emotional change affected Alexis's body. The bleeding slowed, the exhausted child dropped off to sleep and eventually the bleeding stopped altogether. No one else could have done it, neither the anguished parents nor the terrified doctors. Only a man supreme in his own self-confidence could transmit this self-confidence to a child.

Like every other explanation, this one is only a guess. It is supported, however, by current medical knowledge. It is also suggested by a wisp of testimony from Maria Rasputin, the *starets's* daughter: "The power, the nervous force that emanated from my father's eyes, from his exceptionally long and beautiful hands, from his whole being impregnated with willpower, from his mind concentrated on one desire . . . [were] transmitted to the child—a particularly nervous and impressionable subject—and . . . in some way . . . galvanized him. At first through the stream of emotion and later through the power of confidence, the child's nervous system reacted, the envelope of the blood vessels contracted, the hemorrhage ceased."

The truth about Rasputin's effect on the Tsarevich will never be precisely known. Few medical records of these episodes were kept and none survived the Revolution. Not even persons intimate with most of the family secrets were privy to these dramatic episodes. Grand Duchess Olga Alexandrovna, the Tsarevich's aunt, declares, "There is no doubt about that [Rasputin's healing powers]. I saw those miraculous effects with my own eyes and that more than once. I also know that the most prominent doctors of the day had to admit it. Professor Fedorov, who stood at the very peak of his profession and whose patient Alexis was, told me so on more than one occasion, but all the doctors disliked Rasputin intensely."

It turns out, however, that if Olga saw the "miraculous effects," she never saw the cause. She did not ever see with her own eyes what happened at Alexis's bedside. The sole experience she cites is this:

"The poor child lay in pain, dark patches under his eyes and his little body all distorted, and the leg terribly swollen. The doctors were just useless . . . more frightened than any of us . . . whispering among themselves. . . . It was getting late and I was persuaded to go to my rooms. Alicky then sent a message to Rasputin in St. Petersburg. He reached the palace about midnight or even later. By that time, I had reached my apartments and early in the morning Alicky called me to go to Alexis's room. I just could not believe my eyes. The little boy was not just alive—but well. He was sitting up in bed, the fever gone, the eyes clear and bright, not a sign of any swelling in the leg— Later I learned from Alicky that Rasputin had not even touched the child but merely stood at the foot of the bed and prayed."

Olga may have been misled, both about the severity of the hemorrhage and about the speed of recovery. But not necessarily. It is one of the mysteries of the disease that the recuperative powers of its victims, especially when they are children, are extraordinary. A child who has been totally disabled and in great pain can be quickly restored. Even a night's sleep can bring color into the cheeks and life into the eyes. Swellings recede more slowly and afflicted joints may be weeks or months returning to normal. But to observers like Olga Alexandrovna, the difference between a night and the following morning could well have seemed miraculous.

There were those who, in regard to Rasputin, expressed skepticism that his presence had any effect at all. Pierre Gilliard mentions the theory that Rasputin was a clever cheat who had an accomplice in the palace; the one most suspected, of course, was Anna Vyrubova. When Alexis fell sick, this theory runs, Rasputin waited until the crisis reached its peak. Then, signaled by his ally, he appeared at the precise moment the crisis was passing and took credit for the recovery. This theory, as Gilliard himself admits, is shaky. For one thing, it presupposes a medical knowledge on Anna Vyrubova's part which her subsequent book does not reveal. It would have been risky; had Rasputin been summoned too soon or too late, his game would have been exposed. Most damaging of all to this theory is the fact that it assumes that Anna Vyrubova owed a greater allegiance to Rasputin than she did to the Empress. Overwhelmingly, the evidence denies this last assumption.

Whatever it was that Rasputin did or did not do, there was only one judge of his effectiveness who mattered. This was the Empress Alexandra. She believed that Rasputin was able to stop Alexis's hemorrhages and she believed that he did it through the power of prayer. Whenever Alexis began to recover from an illness, she attributed it exclusively to the prayers of the Man of God.

CHAPTER SIXTEEN

The Holy Devil

SUCCESS at Tsarskoe Selo ensured Rasputin's success in society. As his social position improved, his wardrobe became more elegant. The rough linen shirts were exchanged for silk blouses of pale blue, brilliant red, violet and light yellow, some of them made and embroidered with flowers by the Empress herself. Black velvet trousers and soft kid leather boots replaced the mud-spattered garb of the peasant. The plain leather thong belted around his waist gave way to silken cords of sky blue or raspberry with big, soft, dangling tassels. On a chain around his neck, Rasputin wore a handsome gold cross. It too was a gift from Alexandra.

In his new trappings, Rasputin strode confidently into crowded parlors and became the immediate center of attention. His rich clothes were in striking contrast to his rude, open, peasant's face with its unkempt hair, matted beard, broad, pockmarked nose and wrinkled, weather-beaten skin. Advancing on the guests, Rasputin seized the hands of every new acquaintance between his own wide, horny palms and stared fiercely into the other's eyes. Holding them with his gaze, Rasputin began his familiar banter, studded with impertinent questions. Asked what she liked least about Rasputin, Grand Duchess Olga Alexandrovna cited his "curiosity, unbridled and embarrassing." Olga had a strong taste of this in her first meeting with Rasputin at Tsarskoe Selo.

"In Alicky's boudoir," Olga wrote, "having talked to her and Nicky for a few minutes, Rasputin waited for the servants to get the table for evening tea and then began plying me with most impertinent questions. Was I happy? Did I love my husband? Why didn't I have any children? He had no right to ask such questions, nor did I answer them. I am afraid Nicky and Alicky looked rather uncomfortable. I do remember I was relieved at leaving the palace that evening and saying 'Thank God he hasn't followed me to the station' as I boarded my private coach in the train for St. Petersburg."

Rasputin was always ready, even in public gatherings, to offer intimate personal advice. The Empress's friend Lili Dehn first met Rasputin at a moment when she was wondering whether to go on a trip with her husband or stay behind with her infant son. "Our eyes met," she wrote. ". . . His eyes held mine, those shining, steel-like eyes which seemed to read one's inmost thoughts. He came forward and took my hand. . . . 'Thou art worried. . . . Well, nothing in life is worth worrying over—*tout passe*—you understand. That's the best outlook.' He became serious. 'It is necessary to have Faith. God alone is thy help. Thou art torn between thy husband and thy child. Which is weaker? Thou thinks't that thy child is the more helpless. This is not so. A child can do nothing in his weakness. A man can do much.' "

Beneath his new finery, Rasputin remained the *moujik*. He gloried in the fact that a peasant was accepted in the silken drawing rooms of the aristocracy and he strutted his origins before his titled admirers. Amid a stream of guests coming in from the street and divesting themselves of furs and velvet capes, Rasputin handed the footman his plain, long, black *caftan*, the age-old coat of the Russian peasant. In polite conversation, Rasputin used coarse barnyard expressions. It was not a matter of the words slipping out accidentally; Rasputin used them often and with gusto, and he enjoyed the little gasps they invariably produced. He liked to describe in detail the sexual life of horses which he had observed as a child in Pokrovskoe, then turn to a beautiful woman in a décolleté dress and say, "Come, my lovely mare." He found that society was as fascinated by his stories and tales of Siberia as the Imperial family. Frequently, seated in an elegant parlor, he would shake his head reprovingly and say, "Yes, yes, my dears, you are all much too pampered. Follow me in the summer to Pokrovskoe, to the great freedom of Siberia. We will catch fish and work in the fields and then you will really learn to understand God." His table manners left people aghast. There is no more vivid image of Rasputin than that left by Simanovich, his aide and partner, who described Rasputin "plunging his dirty hands into his favorite fish soup." Yet, this raw confirmation of Rasputin's nature seemed to attract rather than repel. For a jaded, mannered, restless society, Rasputin was an exotic diversion.

At first, Rasputin walked carefully in this new world of the wealthy. He soon discovered, however, that to many of the women who thronged around him, his sensual side was as interesting as his spiritual nature. Rasputin responded quickly. His lusts flared up, his gestures became excited, his eyes and voice turned suggestive, lewd and insinuating. His first conquests were easy and those that followed even easier; talk of his amorous adventures only increased his mysterious reputation. Noble ladies, wives of officers on duty far away, actresses and women of lower classes sought the rough, humiliating caresses of the *moujik*. Making love to the unwashed peasant with his dirty beard and filthy hands was a new and thrilling sensation. "He had too many offers," said Simanovich.

Rasputin made it easier for the ladies by preaching his personal doctrine of redemption: salvation is impossible unless one has been redeemed from sin, and true redemption cannot be achieved unless sin has been committed. In himself, Rasputin offered all three: sin, redemption and salvation. "Women," says Fülöp-Miller, "found in Gregory Efimovich the fulfillment of two desires which had hitherto seemed irreconcilable, religious salvation and the satisfaction of carnal appetites. . . . As in the eyes of his disciples, Rasputin was a reincarnation of the Lord, intercourse with him, in particular, could not possibly be a sin; and these women found for the first time in their lives a pure happiness, untroubled by the gnawings of conscience."

For some, bestowal of this supreme honor by Father Gregory was a matter for boasting, not only by the ladies but also by their husbands. "Would you be ready to accede to him?" an outsider once incredulously asked one of Rasputin's disciples. "Of course. I have already belonged to him, and I am proud and happy to have done so," the lady supposedly replied. "But you are married! What does your husband say to it?" "He considers it a very great honor. If Rasputin desires a woman, we all think it a blessing and distinction, our husbands as well as ourselves."

Every day, numbers of admiring women came to Rasputin's apartment to sit in his dining room, sip wine or tea, gossip and listen to the Father's wisdom. Those who could not come telephoned tearful apologies. One frequent visitor, an opera singer, often rang up Rasputin simply to sing to him his favorite songs over the telephone. Taking the telephone, Rasputin danced around the room, holding the earpiece to his ear. At the table, Rasputin stroked the arms and hair of the women sitting next to him. Sometimes he put down his glass of Madeira and took a young girl on his lap. When he felt inspired, he rose before everyone and openly led his choice to the bedroom, a sanctum which his adoring disciples referred to as "The Holy of Holies." Inside, if necessary, he whispered reassurance into the ear of his partner: "You think that I am polluting you, but I am not. I am purifying you."

Giddy at his success, not knowing where to stop, Rasputin even made advances to Grand Duchess Olga. One evening after dinner, Olga had gone with her brother and Alexandra to Anna Vyrubova's cottage. "Rasputin was there," she wrote, "and seemed very pleased to meet me again, and when the hostess with Nicky and Alicky left the drawing room for a few moments, Rasputin got up, put his arm about my shoulders, and began stroking my arm. I moved away at once, saying nothing. I just got up and joined the others. . . ."

Not many days afterward, Anna Vyrubova arrived, flushed and disheveled, at Olga's palace in town. She begged the Grand Duchess to receive Rasputin again, pleading, "Oh please, he wants to see you so much." "I refused very curtly. . . . To the best of my knowledge Nicky put up with the man solely on account of the help he gave to Alexis and that, as I happen to know very well, was genuine enough."

Although the moments were wholly innocent, Rasputin's visits to the palace nurseries touched the Tsar's young daughters with rumors of scandal. On the pretext of saying prayers with the Tsarevich and his sisters, Rasputin sometimes hung about their upstairs bedrooms after the girls had changed into their long white nightgowns. The girls' governess, Mlle. Tiutcheva, was horrified to see a peasant staring at her charges and demanded that he be barred. As a result, Alexandra became angy not at Rasputin, but at Tiutcheva, who dared to question the saintliness of the "Man of God." Nicholas, seeing the impropriety of Rasputin's presence, intervened in the quarrel and instructed Rasputin to avoid his daughters' rooms. Later, Tiutcheva was dismissed, and blamed her downfall on Rasputin's hold over the Empress. Tiutcheva returned to Moscow, where her family had important connections and were especially close to Alexandra's sister Grand Duchess Elizabeth. Busily spreading her story across Moscow, Tiutcheva at the same time implored the Grand Duchess to speak bluntly to her younger sister the Empress. Ella was more than willing; having herself entered into religious retreat, she regarded Rasputin as a blasphemous and lascivious impostor. At every opportunity she spoke, sometimes gently, sometimes bitterly, to Alexandra about the *starets*. Her efforts had no effect except to open a breach between the two sisters which, as time went on, became so wide that neither could touch the other.

By 1911, St. Petersburg was in an uproar over Rasputin. Not all the husbands were *complaisant*, nor did all the ladies of St. Petersburg enjoy having their buttons undone. The Montenegrin princesses, Grand Duchess Militsa and Grand Duchess Anastasia, closed their doors to their former protégé. Anastasia's soldier-husband, Grand Duke Nicholas, swore "never to see the devil again." The two Montenegrins even went to Tsarskoe Selo to report to the Empress their "sad discovery" about Gregory, but Alexandra received them coolly.

It was the Church which initiated the first formal investigation of Rasputin's activities and carried the first official complaints to the Tsar. Bishop Theophan, the saintly Inspector of the Theological Academy, who had been impressed by Rasputin's faith and had recommended him to the Empress, was the first to entertain doubts. When women who had given in to Rasputin began coming to him with their confessions, Theophan went to the Empress. Once he had been Alexandra's confessor; now he advised her that something was fearfully wrong about the "Holy Man" he had recommended to her. Alexandra sent for the *starets* and questioned him. Rasputin affected surprise, innocence and humility. The result was that Theophan, a distinguished theologian, was transferred from the Theological Academy to become Bishop of the Crimea. "I have shut his trap," gloated Rasputin in private.

Next, the Metropolitan Anthony called on the Tsar to discuss Rasputin. Nicholas replied that the private affairs of the Imperial family were no concern of the Church. "No, Sire," the Metropolitan replied, "this is not merely a family affair, but the affair of all Russia. The Tsarevich is not only your son, but our future sovereign and belongs to all Russia." Nicholas nodded and quietly ended the interview. But soon afterward, Anthony fell ill and died.

The single most damaging attack on Rasputin came from a flamboyant young zealot of a monk named Iliodor. Iliodor was even younger than Rasputin, but he had built a reputation as a fiery orator and crowds flocked to hear him whenever he spoke. Simply by telling the multitude that he wanted to build a great monastery ("Let one man bring a plank, let another bring a rusty nail"), he attracted thousands of volunteers who erected a vast spiritual retreat near Tsaritsyn [later Stalingrad, now Volgograd] on the banks of the Volga.

Austere in his behavior, Iliodor was fanatical in his beliefs. He preached strict adherence to the Orthodox faith and the absolute autocracy of the tsar. Yet alongside his extreme monarchism, he advocated a vague peasant communism. The tsar should rule, he said, but beneath the autocrat all other men should be brothers with equal rights and no distinctions of rank or class. As a result, Iliodor was as unpopular with government officials, local governors, aristocrats and the hierarchy of the Church as he was popular with the masses.

In Rasputin, Iliodor saw an ally. When Rasputin was first brought to him by Theophan, Iliodor welcomed the primitive religious fervor manifested by the *starets*. In 1909, Iliodor discovered Rasputin's other face. He invited Rasputin to come with him to his spiritual retreat near Tsaritsyn. There, to Iliodor's surprise, Rasputin responded to the respect and humility of the women they met by grabbing the prettiest and smacking their lips with kisses. From Tsaritsyn, the monk and the *starets* set out for Pokrovskoe, Rasputin's home. On the train, Iliodor was even more dismayed when Rasputin, bragging about his past, boasted openly of his sexual exploits and jibed at Iliodor's innocence. He gave a swaggering account of his relations with the Imperial family. The Tsar, said Rasputin, knelt before him and told him, "Gregory, you are Christ." He boasted that he had kissed the Empress in her daughters' rooms.

Once they had reached Pokrovskoe, Rasputin supported his boasts by showing Iliodor a collection of letters he had received from Alexandra and her children. He even gave several of these letters to Iliodor—or so Iliodor said—saying, "Take your choice. Only leave the Tsarevich's letter. It's the only one I have." Three years later, portions of these letters from the Empress to Rasputin began appearing in public. They became the basic incriminating documents for the lurid charge that the Empress was Rasputin's lover. Of them, the most damning was this:

> My beloved, unforgettable teacher, redeemer and mentor! How tiresome it is without you! My soul is quiet and I relax only when you, my teacher, are sitting beside me. I kiss your hands and lean my head on your blessed shoulder. Oh how light, how

light do I feel then. I only wish one thing: to fall asleep, to fall asleep, forever on your shoulders and in your arms. What happiness to feel your presence near me. Where are you? Where have you gone? Oh, I am so sad and my heart is longing. . . . Will you soon be again close to me? Come quickly, I am waiting for you and I am tormenting myself for you. I am asking for your holy blessing and I am kissing your blessed hands. I love you forever.

Yours,
M. [Mama]

Assuming for a moment that Alexandra wrote this letter to Rasputin, did it, as their enemies charged, prove that they were lovers? No responsible participant in the events of these years and no serious historian who subsequently has chronicled these events has accepted this charge. Sir Bernard Pares says of this letter, "Alexandra, it appears, had inadvisedly used some expressions which a cynical reader might interpret into an admission of personal attraction." Pares was putting it too carefully. The fact is that Alexandra wrote to all of her intimate friends in this florid, emotional style. Almost all of these sentences could have been addressed to Anna Vyrubova or any one of a number of friends. It is equally possible that the letters were faked. Only Iliodor saw them, and his credentials as an objective source were thoroughly undermined by subsequent events.

Despite Iliodor's surprise and disgust at what he saw and read in 1909, he and Rasputin remained friendly for another two years. He continued to urge Rasputin to change his ways. At the same time, Iliodor stoutly defended Rasputin when others attacked him. Then, in 1911, Rasputin attempted to seduce—and when that failed, to rape—a nun.

Hearing about it, Iliodor was sickened and enraged. Along with Bishop Hermogen of Saratov, he invited Rasputin into his room and confronted him with the story. "Is it true?" thundered Hermogen. Rasputin looked around and then mumbled, "It's true, it's true, it's all true." Hermogen, a powerful man, was beside himself. He hit Rasputin in the head with his fist and then beat him with a heavy wooden cross. "You are smashing our sacred vessels," bellowed the outraged Bishop. Subdued, Rasputin was dragged into a little chapel, where Hermogen and Iliodor made him swear on an icon that he would leave women alone and that he would stay away from the

Imperial family. Rasputin swore enthusiastically. The following day, Rasputin appeared before Iliodor, begging, "Save me! Save me!" Iliodor softened and took Rasputin with him to Hermogen. But the Bishop turned his back on the humbled *starets*, rejecting his pleas with the haughty words, "Never and nowhere."

Rasputin recovered quickly from his beating and from his brush with abstinence. Within a few days, he was back at the palace, giving his version of the episode. Soon afterward, by Imperial order, Hermogen was sent to seclusion in a monastery. Iliodor was ordered into seclusion also, but he refused to submit. Instead, he wandered from place to place, bitterly and ever more hysterically denouncing Rasputin. The peasant "Holy Man" to whom he had extended his friendship, whom he had meant to use as a tool in purifying the Church and in steering the Russian people back to their historic values—this same unwashed, lewd, immoral peasant—had shattered his own bright dreams. The great career as an orator and prophet had tumbled into the dust. And the knave who had destroyed him walked freely in and out of the palace, had the ear of the Empress and could move bishops and prophets around like pieces on a chessboard. It was at this point, when Iliodor was in this mood, that the letters from Alexandra allegedly taken from Rasputin's desk first appeared.

Iliodor surrendered himself and was imprisoned for several months in a monastery to await a trial. From his cell, Iliodor scribbled feverish letters to the Holy Synod: "You have bowed down to the Devil. My whole being is for holy vengeance against you. You have sold the glory of God, forgotten the friendship of Christ. . . . Oh, cheats, serpents, murderers of Christ . . . I will tear off your cloaks. . . . Traitors and renegades . . . You are all careerists; you despise the poor; you ride in carriages, proud and arrogant . . . you are not servants of the people, you put present-day prophets to the stake. . . . Godless anti-Christs, I will not be in spiritual communion with you. . . . You are animals fed with the people's blood."

The addressees retaliated by unfrocking Iliodor. Raging, he screamed, "I will not allow myself ever to be pardoned," and renounced Orthodoxy. Uncertain what to do with himself, he considered becoming a shepherd and "borrowed sufficient money to buy a flock of fifty sheep." But this idea seemed tame, and, instead, he decided to start a revolution. "It was my intention to start a revolution on October 6, 1913. I planned the assassination on that day of sixty lieutenant governors and forty bishops throughout Russia. . . . I chose a hundred men to execute this plan." But the plan was uncovered by the police and Iliodor went into hiding. As a fugitive, he gave his blessing to the formation of an organization of women and girls, most of them wronged by Rasputin, which had as its sole purpose Father Gregory's castration. One of the women, a pretty twenty-six-year-old former prostitute named Khina Gusseva whom Rasputin had used and then spurned, wished to go further and kill the *starets*. Iliodor pondered the thought, agreed, opened her blouse and hung a knife on a chain around her neck, instructing her, "With this knife, kill Grishka."

Eventually, Iliodor slipped across the frontier into Finland disguised as a woman and began writing a book about himself and Rasputin. When his book was finished, Iliodor first offered it to the Empress for sixty thousand roubles. This piece of blackmail was rejected and the vengeful former monk then took his manuscript to an American publisher. Later, even he admitted that into the book he had put "a bit extra."

Although he wielded great influence, Rasputin was not a frequent visitor at the Alexander Palace. He lived in St. Petersburg, and when he came to Tsarskoe Selo, it was usually to the little house of Anna Vyrubova. Avoiding the palace was not Rasputin's idea. Rather, it represented a decision by the Imperial couple to observe a certain circumspection in their interviews with the controversial *starets*. The palace police saw everything. It was impossible even to creep up a back staircase without the event being noted and recorded; the following day, the news was all over St. Petersburg. In the later years, so rarely did Rasputin come that Gilliard never met him inside the palace. Baroness Buxhoeveden, who lived just down the hall from the young Grand Duchesses, never met him at all.

Nevertheless, despite the fact that she saw Rasputin infrequently and then under circumstances ideal for him, Alexandra refused to consider that there might be another side to her Man of God. "Saints are always calumniated," she told Dr. Botkin. "He is hated because we love him." The family despised the police who surrounded them day and night; they took it for granted that the police reports of Rasputin's activities were fabrications. The Empress flatly refused to accept any hint of Rasputin's debauchery. "They accuse Rasputin of kissing women, etc.," she later wrote to the Tsar. "Read the apostles;

they kissed everybody as a form of greeting." Alexandra's opinion was confirmed by the faithful Anna Vyrubova. "I went often to Rasputin's lodging," said Anna, "bringing messages from the Empress, usually referring to the health of Alexis." But Anna saw nothing of which she did not devotedly approve. "Rasputin had no harem," she insisted. "In fact, I cannot remotely imagine a woman of education and refinement being attracted to him in a personal way. I never knew of one being so attracted."

Neither by temperament nor by experience was Anna Vyrubova equipped to judge the matter of physical attraction. Nevertheless, her innocent reports of Rasputin's behavior were not the result of blindness or stupidity. When Anna was present—and her visits were always announced in advance—Rasputin's behavior was rigidly correct. The ladies of his circle, knowing Anna's importance to their hero, followed suit.

After the Revolution, Basil Shulgin, an intensely monarchist member of the Duma and one of the two men who, trying to preserve the monarchy, obtained the abdication of Nicholas II, analyzed Rasputin's role: "Rasputin was a Janus. . . . To the Imperial family he had turned his face as a humble *starets* and, looking at it, the Empress cannot but be convinced that the spirit of God rests upon this man. And to the country he has turned the beastly, drunken unclean face of a bald satyr from Tobolsk. Here we have the key to it all. The country is indignant that such a man should be received under the Tsar's roof. And under the roof there is bewilderment and a sense of bitter hurt. Why should they all be enraged? That a saintly man came to pray over the unhappy Heir, a desperately sick child whose least imprudent movement may end in death? So the Tsar and the Empress are hurt and indignant. Why should there be such a storm? The man has done nothing but good. Thus a messenger of death has placed himself between the throne and the nation. . . . And because of the man's fateful duality, understood by neither [Tsar nor people], neither side can understand the other. So the Tsar and his people, however apart, are leading each other to the edge of the abyss."

Pierre Gilliard was more succinct. "The fatal influence of that man [Rasputin] was the principal cause of death of those who thought to find in him their salvation."

CHAPTER SEVENTEEN

"*We Want a Great Russia*"

If any man outside of the Imperial Family could have saved Imperial Russia, it was the burly, bearded country squire who served as prime minister from 1906 to 1911, Peter Arkadyevich Stolypin. A man of the country with roots in the rural nobility, Stolypin had little in common with either the great figures of the princely aristocracy or the dry, professional civil servants who scrambled diligently up the ladders of promotion to the seats of power in the St. Petersburg bureaucracy. Stolypin brought to the Imperial government a clean, strong breath of youth and fresh country air. Direct, outspoken, brimming with impassioned patriotism and overwhelming in his physical energy, Stolypin grappled with the fundamental causes of Russia's troubles. A passionate monarchist, he hated the revolutionaries and ruthlessly crushed the last outbursts of the 1905 Revolution. But Stolypin was also a realist who sensed that the monarchy would survive only if the government and the structure of society itself could adapt to the times. Accordingly, he reconstructed the system of peasant land ownership and began the transformation of an absolute autocracy into a form of government more responsive to the popular will.

No Russian statesman of the day was more admired. In the Duma, Stolypin's big, bearlike figure attracted every eye. Dressed in a frock coat with a watch chain across his chest, he spoke with such eloquence and such evident sincerity that even his adversaries respected him. "We are not frightened," he boomed at his enemies on the Left in the Second Duma. "You want great upheavals, but we want a great Russia." His ministerial colleagues were unanimous in their praise. "His capacity for work and his moral power of endurance were prodigious," wrote Alexander Izvolsky, the Foreign Minister. Vladimir Kokovtsov, the Finance Minister, declared that Stolypin's "nobility, courage and devotion to the State were indisputable." Sir George Buchanan, the British Ambassador, called him "an ideal man to transact business with . . . his promises were always kept." Most important of all, Stolypin pleased the Tsar. In October 1906, after Stolypin had been in office for only three months, Nicholas wrote to his mother, "I cannot tell you how much I have come to like and respect this man."

Peter Stolypin was born in 1863 while his mother rested at the Rhineland spa of Baden-Baden. He was educated in St. Petersburg, where his father had a position at court and his mother was in society. Stolypin himself preferred the country, and most of his career was spent away from the capital. In 1905, at the height of the first revolution, he was governor of Saratov province, charged with suppressing local peasant uprisings that were among the most violent in Russia. Stolypin accomplished his task with a minimum loss of life. Often, rather than ordering government troops to bombard an insurgent village, Stolypin himself would walk into the village alone to talk to the rebel leader and persuade him to have his men lay down their arms.

Because of his success in Saratov province, Stolypin was brought to St. Petersburg in 1906 to become Minister of Interior. He arrived as Witte was departing and took office under Witte's successor, an elderly bureaucratic relic named Ivan Logginovich Goremykin. Goremykin conducted his office on the simple, undeviating principle that ministers were servants of the tsar, appointed to execute, not initiate, policy. Sir Arthur Nicolson, who preceded Buchanan as British Ambassador, called on Goremykin at this time, expecting to find a harried, overworked statesman. Instead, he found himself confronting "an elderly man with a sleepy face and Piccadilly whiskers" reclining on a sofa surrounded by French novels. Goremykin foundered after only three months in office, and before departing, he recommended to the Tsar that Stolypin be appointed in his place.

On the evening of July 7, 1906, Stolypin was summoned to Nicholas's study at Tsarskoe Selo and asked to become Prime Minister. Kokovtsov wrote later: "Stolypin told us that he had attempted to point out his lack of experience and his unfamiliarity with the crosscurrents of St. Petersburg society, but the Tsar had not let him finish: 'No, Peter Arkadyevich, here is the icon before which I often pray. Let us make the sign of the Cross over ourselves and let us ask the Lord to help us both in this difficult, perhaps historic, moment.' Then the Tsar made the sign of the cross over Stolypin, embraced him and kissed him, and asked him on what day it would be best to dissolve the Duma."

Once in power, Stolypin became a whirlwind of energy. He meant to attack root problems such as the peasants' long-suppressed thirst for land of their own, but nothing could be done about these matters until the terrorist attacks on local officials and police had been suppressed. To restore law and order, Stolypin established special field courts-martial. Within three days of their arrest, assassins swung from the gallows. Before the end of the summer, six hundred men had been strung up and Russians had named the hangman's noose "Stolypin's necktie." Yet, the number of men hanged by the government was smaller than the sixteen hundred governors, generals, soldiers and village policemen killed by terrorists' bombs and bullets.

Inevitably, Stolypin himself became the assassins' target. On a Saturday afternoon, scarcely a month after taking office, he was writing at his desk in his country villa outside St. Petersburg when a bomb exploded. A wall of the house collapsed and thirty-two people, including visitors and servants, were killed. Stolypin's young son, playing on an upstairs balcony, was hurt, and his daughter, Natalia, was badly maimed. But Stolypin himself was merely splattered with ink. "A day and a half after the explosion, the Ministers' Council resumed its work as if nothing unusual had happened," Kokovtsov wrote. "Stolypin's calm and self-control won the admiration of everyone."

The government's repression, to which the bomb plot was a reaction, was only a harsh preliminary to reform. While terrorists still dangled at the end of government ropes, the new Prime Minister attacked the basic problem of land. In 1906, three quarters of the people of Russia coaxed a living from the soil. Since 1861, when Alexander II freed the serfs, most of Russia's peasants lived in village communes, made communal plans for the land and worked it in partnership. The system was ridiculously inefficient; within each commune, a single peasant might farm as many as fifty small strips, each containing a few thin rows of corn or wheat. Often, the peasant spent more time walking between his scattered furrows than he did plowing the earth or scything the grain. Stolypin overturned this communal system and introduced the concept of private property. By government decree, he declared that any peasant who wished to do so could withdraw from the commune and claim from it a share of ground to farm for himself. Further, the new plot was to be a single piece, not in scattered strips, and the peasant was expected to pass it along to his sons.

Nicholas strongly approved Stolypin's program and, in order to make more land available, proposed that four million acres of the crown lands be sold to the government, which in turn would sell them on easy terms to the peasants. Although the Tsar needed the consent of the Imperial family to take this step, and both Grand Duke Vladimir and the Dowager Empress opposed him, eventually he had his way. The land was sold and Nicholas waited hopefully for members of the nobility to follow his example. But none did so.

The impact of Stolypin's law was political as well as economic. At a stroke, it created a new class of millions of small peasant landowners whose future was tied to an atmosphere of stability which could be provided only by the Imperial government. As it happened, the most vociferous peasant troublemakers were often the first to claim land, and thus became supporters of law and order. By 1914, nine million Russian peasant families owned their own farms.

At bottom, political success or failure in Russia depended on the crop. For five fruitful years, nature smiled on Peter Stolypin. From 1906 to 1911, Russia was blessed with warm summers, mild winters and steady, gentle rain. Acre for acre, the crops were the best in Russia's history. As food became plentiful, government tax revenues rose; the budget was balanced and even showed a surplus. With the help of large French loans, the railroad network expanded rapidly. Coal and iron mines broke records for production. American firms such as International Harvester and Singer Sewing Machine Company established offices in Russia. In the Duma, the government introduced and passed bills raising the salaries of primary-school teachers and establishing the principle of free primary-school education. Censorship of the press was lifted, and the government became more liberal in the sphere of religious tolerance. "It is all wrong," said Stolypin, explaining these changes to Sir Bernard Pares, "that every proposal of reform should come from the opposition."

Ironically, the fiercest opposition to Stolypin's programs came from the extreme Right and the extreme Left. Reactionaries disliked all reforms which transformed the old, traditional ways. Revolutionaries hated to see any amelioration of a system which bred discontent. For Lenin and his dwindling band of exiles, the Stolypin era was a time of fading hope. Sadly convinced that a "revolutionary situation" no longer existed in Russia, Lenin wandered from library to library through Zurich, Geneva, Berne, Paris, Munich, Vienna and Cracow. Gloomily, he watched the success of Stolypin's land reforms. "If this should continue," he wrote, "it might force us to renounce any agricultural program at all." For some dedicated Marxists, it seemed that the dream was entirely dead; in 1909, Karl Marx's despairing daughter and son-in-law Laura and Paul Lafargue committed suicide. Lenin took the news with grim approval. "If one cannot work for the Party any longer," he said, "one must be able to look truth in the face and die the way the Lafargues did."

The appearance in May 1906 of the First Imperial Duma was so new, so alien to everything that had gone before in Russia, that neither the Tsar nor the members of the fledgling representative body knew quite how to behave. Everything had to be begun at the beginning and be constructed overnight: constitution, parliament and political parties. Before October 1905, there were no political parties in Russia other than the Social Democrats and Socialist Revolutionaries, both revolutionary parties which had worked underground. Under the circumstances, it was remarkable that two responsible liberal parties sprang up quickly: the Constitutional Democrats or Cadets, led by the historian Paul Miliukov, and the Octobrists, who took their name from their adherence to the 1905 October Manifesto and were led by Alexander Guchkov.

Nevertheless, the gap in understanding between monarch and parliament remained too wide. The Duma was received by the Tsar in the throne room of the Winter Palace. It was not a promising occasion. Masses of police and soldiers waited outside in the palace square. The newly elected deputies, some in evening clothes, others in peasant blouses, stood on one side of the room, staring at the huge crimson-and-gold throne, at the court officials in gold braid, and at the Empress and her ladies in formal court dress. On the other side stood the court and the ministers, among them Count Fredericks. "The deputies," he said. "They give one the impression of a gang of criminals who are only waiting for the signal to throw themselves upon the ministers and cut their throats. What wicked faces! I will never again set foot among those people." Fredericks was not the only one who felt uncomfortable. The Dowager Empress Marie noticed the "incomprehensible hatred" on the deputies' faces. Kokovtsov found himself staring at one of the deputies particularly, "a man of tall stature, dressed in a worker's blouse and high oiled boots, who examined the throne and those about it with a derisive and insolent air." Stolypin, standing near Kokovtsov, whispered to him, "We both seem engrossed in the same spectacle. I even have the feeling that this man might throw a bomb."

The feelings of the Duma were quickly manifested. Scarcely had the 524 members taken their seats in a hall of the Tauride Palace when they formulated a sweepingly aggressive "Address to the Throne." To Nicholas's horror, it demanded universal suffrage, radical land reform, the release of all political prisoners and the dismissal of ministers appointed by the Tsar in favor of ministers acceptable to the Duma. At Nicholas's command, old Goremykin tottered down to the Duma and, with trembling hands and in a scarcely audible voice, rejected everything the Duma had asked. When Goremykin sat down, there was a moment of complete silence. Then one member leaped to the rostrum and cried, "Let the executive power bow before the legislative." He was greeted by deafening applause. Other speakers followed, each more stinging in his attack on the government. When those ministers who were present rose and attempted to speak, they were shouted down with cries of "Retire! Retire!"

Appalled by these scenes, Nicholas was eager to dissolve the Duma, but he recognized that Goremykin was not the man to ride out the turmoil which would follow dissolution. It was at this point, in July 1906, that Goremykin resigned and Stolypin was appointed. Two days later, Stolypin locked the doors of the Tauride Palace and posted the Imperial decree dissolving the Duma. That afternoon, a number of members took trains across the nearby border into Finland. Meeting in a forest, they declared, "The sessions of the Duma are hereby resumed," and called on the nation to refuse to pay taxes and to send no recruits to the army until the Duma was restored. But this appeal, the famous Vyborg Manifesto, had no effect. Numbed by revolution, Russians were not willing to fight again to preserve their parliament.

Nicholas, disgusted by this experience, would have been happy to end the experiment in representative government. It was Stolypin who insisted that the Tsar's signature on the October Manifesto constituted a solemn promise to the nation which must not be broken. Grudgingly, Nicholas abandoned his plans for eliminating the Duma altogether and gave permission for the election of a Second Duma.

As the Second Duma met for the first time, in February 1907, the ceiling of the hall caved in over their heads. It was an appropriate beginning for a Duma session which, in every way, was worse than the first. The Leftist parties, including the Social Democrats and the Social Revolutionaries, which had boycotted the First Duma, had won two hundred seats in the Second, more than a third of the membership. Determined to defy the government in every way, they turned the Duma into a madhouse of shouts, insults and brawls. At the other extreme, the reactionaries were determined to discredit and abolish the Duma once and for all. Police plots were arranged to incriminate the Leftist members, accusations were hurled, debates became violent and meaningless. At one point, Stolypin stood up amid a torrent of abuse and thundered, "All your attacks are intended to cause a paralysis of will and thought in the government and the executive; all these attacks can be expressed in two words which you address to authority: 'Hands up!' Gentlemen, to these words the government, confident in its right, answers calmly with two other words: 'Not afraid!' "

Again, Nicholas waited impatiently to rid himself of the Duma. In two letters to Marie, he let his bitterness flow:

"A grotesque deputation is coming from England [to see liberal members of the Duma]. Uncle Bertie informed us that they were very sorry but were unable to take action to stop their coming. Their famous 'liberty,' of course. How angry they would be if a deputation went from us to the Irish to wish them success in their struggle against their government."

A little later he wrote: "All would be well if everything said in the Duma remained within its walls. Every word spoken, however, comes out in the next day's papers which are avidly read by everyone. In many places the populace is getting restive again. They begin to talk about land once more and are waiting to see what the Duma is going to say on the question. I am getting telegrams from everywhere, petitioning me to order a dissolution, but it is too early for that. One has to let them do something manifestly stupid or mean and then—slap! And they are gone!"

Three months later, the moment came. A deputy named Zurabov rose in the Duma and, in insulting and occasionally profane language, accused the army of training its soldiers exclusively for repressing civilians. Zurabov directly appealed to the troops to revolt and join the people in overthrowing the government. This insult to the Russian army was more than enough for Nicholas. He issued a manifesto accusing the Duma of plotting against the sovereign, troops were brought into St. Petersburg and the Duma was dissolved. Thirty Social Democratic members were exiled to Siberia and most other Leftist members were placed under police surveillance.

Stolypin followed this dissolution by publishing a new electoral law which abandoned all pretense of universal suffrage and concentrated elective power largely in the hands of the country gentry. As a result, the Third Duma, elected in the autumn of 1907, was a thoroughly conservative body; its membership even included forty-five Orthodox priests. With this carefully tailored representative body, Stolypin generally got along well. He did not share the innate dislike for any legislature expressed by Nicholas and by most of his fellow ministers. In debate in the Duma, Stolypin's great voice allowed him to argue his policies effectively. Nevertheless, when the Duma remained hostile, Stolypin had no qualms about invoking Article 87 of the Fundamental Laws, which empowered the Tsar to issue "urgent and extraordinary" emergency decrees "during the recess of the State Duma." Stolypin's most famous legislative act, the change in peasant land tenure, was promulgated under Article 87.

Despite its prevailing conservatism, the Third Duma remained an independent body. This time, however, the members proceeded cautiously. Instead of hurling themselves at the government, opposing parties within the Duma worked to develop the role of the body as a whole. In the classic manner of the British Parliament, the Duma reached for power by grasping for the national purse strings. The Duma had the right to question ministers behind closed doors as to their proposed expenditures. These sessions, endorsed by Stolypin, were educational for both sides, and, in time, mutual antagonism was replaced by mutual respect. Even in the sensitive area of military expenditures, where the October Manifesto clearly had reserved decisions to the throne, a Duma commission began to operate. Composed of aggressive patriots no less anxious than Nicholas to restore the fallen honor of Russian arms, the Duma commission frequently recommended expenditures even larger than those proposed.

Sir Bernard Pares, who was on the closest personal terms with many members of the Duma, looked back on the period with nostalgia: "May an Englishman, bred in the tradition of Gladstone, to whom the Duma was almost a home with many friends of all parties, recall that vanished past? At the bottom was a feeling of reassurance, and founded on it one saw a growing courage and initiative and a growing mutual understanding and goodwill. The Duma had the freshness of a school, with something of surprise at the simplicity with which differences that had seemed formidable could be removed. One could feel the pleasure with which the members were finding their way into common work for the good of the whole country. . . . Some seventy persons at least, forming the nucleus of the most important commissions, were learning in detail to understand both each other and the Government. One could see political competence growing day by day. And to a constant observer it was becoming more and more an open secret that the distinctions of party meant little, and that in the social warmth of their public work for Russia, all these men were becoming friends."

With the passage of time, Nicholas also began to have confidence in the Duma. "This Duma cannot be reproached with an attempt to seize power and there is no need at all to quarrel with it," he said to Stolypin in 1909. In 1912, a Fourth Duma was elected with almost the same membership as the Third. "The Duma started too fast," Nicholas explained to Pares in 1912. "Now it is slower, but better. And more lasting."

Despite Stolypin's successes, there were influences constantly working to poison the relationship between the Tsar and his Prime Minister. Reactionaries, including such powerful men at court as Prince Vladimir Orlov, never tired of telling the Tsar that the very existence of the Duma was a blot on the autocracy. Stolypin, they whispered, was a traitor and a secret revolutionary who was conniving with the Duma to steal the prerogatives assigned the Tsar by God. Witte also engaged in constant intrigue against Stolypin. Although Stolypin had had nothing to do with Witte's fall or with Nicholas's contempt for Witte, the former Premier blamed the incumbent. Witte himself had written the 1905 Manifesto creating the Duma, but now, overflowing with spite, he allied himself with the reactionaries and worked a gradual corrosion on Stolypin's power.

Unfortunately, without intending it, Stolypin also had angered the Empress. Early in 1911, alarmed that a man such as Rasputin should have influence at the palace, Stolypin ordered an investigation and presented a report to the Tsar. Nicholas read it, but did nothing. Stolypin, on his own authority, then commanded Rasputin to leave St. Petersburg. Alexandra protested vehemently, but Nicholas refused to overrule his Prime Minister. Rasputin departed on a long pilgrimage to Jerusalem, during which he scrawled lengthy, flowery and mystical letters to the Empress.

Stolypin's banishing of Rasputin was still another example of the tragic isolation and lack of understanding which surrounded the Imperial family. Stolypin was not a heartless man. Had he once been present when the Tsarevich lay in pain and observed the relief which Rasputin brought to mother and child, he would not have ordered this forcible separation. Yet, in political terms, the abrupt purging of this dangerous influence from the palace must have seemed the essence of wisdom. To Alexandra, however, it seemed that Stolypin had deliberately severed the bond on which her son depended for life, and for this she hated the Prime Minister.

Stolypin, meanwhile, was beginning to weary in office. Attempting to overturn the traditions of centuries in five years was more than even so robust a figure as Stolypin could manage. His health waned in repeated attacks of grippe and he became constantly irritable. For a man who preferred clear, decisive action, working with a sovereign who believed in fatalism and mysticism was frustrating. As an example, Nicholas once returned to Stolypin a document unsigned with the note: "Despite most convincing arguments in favor of adopting a positive decision in this matter, an inner voice keeps on insisting more and more that I do not accept responsibility for it. So far my conscience has not deceived me. Therefore, I intend in this case to follow its dictates. I know that you, too, believe that 'a Tsar's heart is in God's hands.' Let it be so. For all laws established by me I bear a great responsibility before God, and I am ready to answer for my decision at any time."

In March 1911, Stolypin lost his temper when the State Council rejected a bill which Stolypin had ushered through the Duma. Stolypin concluded erroneously that the Council had acted as it did because Nicholas had been maneuvering behind his back. In a fit of anger, stating that he obviously no longer commanded the Imperial confidence, he asked to be relieved of his office. The move was unprecedented. Two years before, when Stolypin had casually mentioned resigning, Nicholas had written: "This is not a question of confidence or lack of it; it is my will. Remember that we live in Russia, not abroad . . . and therefore I shall not consider the possibility of any resignation."

In the interim, Nicholas had not softened these views, and when Stolypin insisted, a heated argument took place. It was the Tsar who backed away. "I cannot accept your resignation," he said to Stolypin, "and I hope that you will not insist upon it, for you must perceive that in accepting your resignation I not only should lose you but also should create a precedent. What would become of a government responsible to me if ministers came and went, today, because of a conflict with the Council, tomorrow, because of a conflict with the Duma? Think of some other way out and let me hear it."

At this moment of impasse, the Dowager Empress sent for Kokovtsov to get his impressions. She took Stolypin's part. "Unfortunately, my son is too kind," she said. "I can well understand that Stolypin is almost in despair and is losing confidence in his ability to conduct the affairs of state." Then Marie began a frank discussion of Nicholas's problems: "I am perfectly sure that the Tsar cannot part with Stolypin. . . . If Stolypin were to insist, I have not the slightest doubt that in the end the Tsar would give in. He has not given his answer because he is trying to find some other way out of the situation. He seeks advice from no one. He has too much pride and, with the Empress, goes through such crises without letting anyone see that he is agitated. . . . As time goes by, the Tsar will become more and more rooted in his displeasure with Stolypin. I feel sure that Stolypin will win for the present but for a short time only; he will soon be removed which would be a great pity both for the Tsar and for Russia. . . . My poor son has so little luck with people."

Marie's prophecy was accurate. Nicholas arranged for Stolypin to stay by permitting him to suspend sittings of the Duma for three days to enact his law by decree in the interim. But a coolness sprang up between the two men. Stolypin, knowing how much encouragement the episode had given his enemies, lived in expectation of dismissal. He complained to his friends that he was being ignored at court, that petty slights such as forgetting to assign him a carriage or a place on an Imperial boat were being administered.

In September 1911, Stolypin and Kokovtsov accompanied Nicholas to Kiev to unveil a statue of Alexander III. As the procession wound through the streets, the Tsar was surrounded by guards and police, but the carriage in which the two ministers were riding was completely unprotected. "You see, we are superfluous," Stolypin said to Kokovtsov.

By a startling but purely coincidental meshing of fates, Rasputin was in Kiev that day, standing in the crowd, observing the procession. As Stolypin's carriage clattered past, Rasputin became agitated and began to mumble. Suddenly, he called out in a dramatic voice, "Death is after him! Death is driving behind him!" For the rest of the night, Rasputin continued muttering about Stolypin's death.

The following day, before the eyes of the Tsar, Peter Stolypin was assassinated. The Imperial party was attending a performance of Rimsky-Korsakov's opera *Tsar Sultan* at the Kiev Opera House. Nicholas was sitting with his two eldest daughters in a box overlooking the stage, while Stolypin and other officials were seated in the first row of the orchestra. During the second intermission, Stolypin rose and stood with his back to the stage. As he did so, a young man in evening clothes walked down the aisle from the rear of the house. The Prime Minister looked at him questioningly. In response, the man drew a Browning revolver and fired two shots which struck Stolypin in the chest.

From his box, Nicholas saw what happened next. He described the lurid scene in a letter to the Dowager Empress:

"Olga and Tatiana were with me at the time. During the second interval, we had just left the box as it was so hot, when we heard two sounds as if something was dropped. I thought an opera glass might have fallen on somebody's head and ran back into the box to look. To the right I saw a group of officers and other people. They seemed to be dragging someone along. Women were shrieking and directly in front of me in the stalls Stolypin was standing. He slowly turned his face towards me and with his left hand made the sign of the Cross in the air. Only then did I notice that he was very pale and that his right hand and uniform were bloodstained. He slowly sank into his chair and began to unbutton his tunic. Fredericks . . . helped him. Olga and Tatiana . . . saw what happened.

"While Stolypin was being helped out of the theatre, there was a great noise in the corridor near our box; people were trying to lynch the assassin. I am sorry to say the police rescued him from the crowd and took him to an isolated room for his first examination. . . . Two of his front teeth were knocked out. The theatre filled up again, the national anthem was sung and I left with the girls at 11. You can imagine with what emotions. . . . Tatiana was very upset and she cried a lot. . . . Poor Stolypin had a bad night."

The plot against Stolypin was intricate and sordid. The assassin, Mordka Bogrov, was a revolutionary and, at the same time, a police informer. Allowed to continue his underground work while making regular reports to the police, Bogrov apparently gave his primary allegiance to the revolution. The commonly accepted and most likely version of the plot is that Bogrov used his police connections to achieve a revolutionary goal. Before the Tsar and Stolypin arrived in Kiev, Bogrov had given the police detailed information about a plot against Stolypin's life. The police followed the trail and discovered, too late, that it was false. Meanwhile, Bogrov, using a police ticket to gain admittance, was striding into the opera, where his mission, supposedly, was to guard Stolypin by spotting and pointing out potential "assassins" who might have slipped through the police net. Inside, Bogrov drew a revolver from under his cape and fired.

This was the official version and the one accepted by all of the Imperial family. "I cannot say how distressed and indignant I am about the murder of Stolypin," wrote Empress Marie. "It is horrible and scandalous and one can say nothing good of the police whose choice fell upon such a swine as that revolutionary to act as informer and as guard to Stolypin. It exceeds all bounds and shows the stupidity of the people at the top." Nevertheless, a question remains which this account does not answer: Why, if Nicholas was also present, did the assassin shoot the Prime Minister and not the Tsar? Although Bogrov was hanged and four officials of the police were suspended for negligence, the suspicion has always remained that Stolypin's murder was the work of powerful reactionaries who had connections with the police.

Nicholas's shock over the murder of his Prime Minister was genuine. Stolypin lived for five days after the shooting, and the Tsar, although urged by palace security officials to leave Kiev immediately for the safety of Livadia, remained in the vicinity. "I returned to Kiev in the evening of September 3rd, called at the nursing home where Stolypin was lying, and met his wife who would not let me see him," he wrote to Marie. Nicholas continued his program, making a short trip down the Dnieper. "On September 6th at 9 A.M. I returned to Kiev. Here on the pier I heard from Kokovtsov that Stolypin had died. I went at once to the nursing home, and a memorial service was afterwards held in my presence. The poor widow stood as though turned to stone and was unable to weep."

It was Kokovtsov who, on the night of the assassination, took the reins of government and averted a second disaster. Because Bogrov was a Jew, the Orthodox population of Kiev was noisily preparing for a retaliatory pogrom. Frantic with fear, the city's Jewish population spent the night packing their belongings. The first light of the following day found the square before the railway station jammed with carts and people trying to squeeze themselves onto departing trains. Even as they waited, the terrified people heard the clatter of hoofs. An endless stream of Cossacks, their long lances dark against the dawn sky, rode past. On his own, Kokovtsov had ordered three full regiments of Cossacks into the city to prevent violence. Asked on what authority he had issued the command, Kokovtsov replied, "As head of the government." Later, a local official came up to the Finance Minister to complain, "Well, Your Excellency, by calling in the troops you have missed a fine chance to answer Bogrov's shot with a nice Jewish pogrom." Kokovtsov was indignant, but, he added, "his sally suggested to me that the measures I had taken at Kiev were not sufficient . . . therefore I sent an open telegram to all governors of the region demanding that they use every possible means—force if necessary—to prevent possible pogroms. When I submitted this telegram to the Tsar, he expressed his approval of it and of the measure I had taken in Kiev."

Nicholas also quickly confirmed Kokovtsov's official position, naming him as Stolypin's successor. One month later, the new Prime Minister visited the Tsar at Livadia to discuss future policy. "I . . . was accorded a most hearty welcome. The members of the court . . . vied with each other in their graciousness to me," Kokovtsov wrote. ". . . The next day, after lunch, the Empress who found it painful to stand for any length of time, sat down in an armchair and called me to her side. . . . A part of this conversation impressed itself upon my memory because it . . . showed me the peculiar, mystic nature of this woman who was called to play such an extraordinary part in the history of Russia. . . .

"The Empress said . . . 'I notice that you keep on making comparisons between yourself and Stolypin. You seem to do too much honor to his memory and ascribe too much importance to his activities and his personality. Believe me, one must not feel sorry for those who are no more. I am sure that everybody does only one's duty and fulfills one's destiny, and when one dies that means that his role is ended and that he was bound to go since his destiny was fulfilled. Life continually assumes new forms, and you must not try to follow blindly the work of your predecessor. Remain yourself; do not look for support in political parties; they are of so little consequence in Russia. Find support in the confidence of the Tsar—the Lord will help you. I am sure that Stolypin died to make room for you, and this is all for the good of Russia.' "

In 1911, when Stolypin ordered an investigation of Rasputin's activities, the outcry against the *starets* was still a matter for private conversation. By 1912, when Kokovtsov inherited Stolypin's office, the scandal had burst into the public arena. In the Duma, broad hints at "dark forces" near the throne began to creep into the speeches of Leftist deputies. Soon the "Rasputin question" dominated the political scene.

"Strange as it may seem," wrote Kokovtsov, "the question of Rasputin became the central question of the immediate future; nor did it disappear during my entire term of office as Chairman of the Ministers' Council." Censorship had been abolished by the Manifesto, and the press began to speak openly of Rasputin as a sinister adventurer who controlled appointments in the Church and had the ear of the Empress. Newspapers began to print accusations and confessions from Rasputin's victims and the cries of anguished mothers. Alexander Guchkov, leader of the Octobrists, obtained copies of Iliodor's letters allegedly written by the Empress to Rasputin; he had them copied and circulated through the city. "Although they were absolutely impeccable, they gave rise to the most revolting comments," said Kokovtsov. ". . . We [Kokovtsov and Makarov, the Minister of Interior] both believed that the letters were apocryphal and were being circulated for the purpose of undermining the prestige of the sovereign but we could do nothing. . . . The public, of course, greedy for any sensation, was according them a very warm reception."

As the attack on Rasputin intensified, the Moscow newspaper *Golos Moskvy* denounced "that cunning conspirator against our Holy Church, that fornicator of human souls and bodies—Gregory Rasputin" as well as "the unheard-of tolerance exhibited toward the said Gregory Rasputin by the highest dignitaries of the Church." Nicholas issued an order banning any mention of Rasputin in the press on pain of fine. But Rasputin made much too good copy for editors to worry about fines; they published and cheerfully paid. The unprintable stories, passed from mouth to mouth, were infinitely worse. The Empress and Anna Vyrubova, it was said, shared the peasant's bed. He ordered the Tsar to pull off his boots and wash his feet and then pushed Nicholas out of the room while he lay with Alexandra. He had raped all the young Grand Duchesses and turned the nurseries into a harem, where the girls, mad with love, fought for his attentions. "Grishka," the diminutive of Gregory, appeared in obscene drawings chalked on walls and buildings; he was the subject of a hundred smutty rhymes.

Nicholas was bitterly offended at the dragging of his wife's name and honor through the mud. "I am simply stifling in this atmosphere of gossip and malice," he told Kokovtsov. "This disgusting affair must be ended." Neither Nicholas nor Alexandra understood the meaning of freedom of the press; they did not understand why the ministers could not prevent the appearance in print of what they both knew was inaccurate and libelous. On the other hand, for the ministers, the Duma and even the Dowager Empress, the solution lay not in repressing the newspapers, but in ridding the throne of Rasputin. Once again, Marie invited Kokovtsov to call on her, and for an hour and a half they discussed Rasputin. "She wept bitterly and promised to speak to the Tsar," Kokovtsov wrote. "But she had little hope of success." "My poor daughter-in-law does not perceive that she is ruining both the dynasty and herself," said Marie. "She sincerely believes in the holiness of an adventurer and we are powerless to ward off the misfortune which is sure to come."

Inevitably, the demand rose for an open debate in the Duma on the role of Rasputin. The Duma President, Michael Rodzianko, a massive figure weighing 280 pounds, was a former cavalry officer of aristocratic family whose political views were not much different from those of a Tory country squire in England. To him, the idea of a public debate in the Duma on Rasputin's relations with the Imperial family seemed highly offensive. Seeking advice, he too visited Empress Marie and heard the same depressing views that Marie had addressed to Kokovtsov. "The Emperor . . . is so pure of heart," she concluded, "that he does not believe in evil."

Nevertheless, Rodzianko persisted and he was granted an audience with the Tsar. So important did he consider his mission that before going to the palace, he went to pray in the cathedral before the holy icon of Our Lady of Kazan. At the palace, Rodzianko bravely told the Tsar that he meant to "speak of the *starets,* Rasputin, and the inadmissible fact of his presence at Your Majesty's Court." Then, before going any further, he said, "I beseech you, Sire, as Your Majesty's loyal subject, will it be your pleasure to hear me to the end? If not, say but one word and I will remain silent." Nicholas looked away, bowed his head and murmured, "Speak." Rodzianko spoke at length, reminding Nicholas of those such as Theophan and Iliodor who had condemned Rasputin and suffered for it. He mentioned the major charges against Rasputin. "Have you read Stolypin's report?" asked Nicholas. "No," said Rodzianko, "I've heard it spoken of, but never read it." "I rejected it," said the Tsar. "It is a pity," said the Duma President, "for all this would not have happened."

Moved by Rodzianko's honest fervor, Nicholas gave way and authorized a new investigation of Rasputin's character and activities to be conducted by Rodzianko himself. Rodzianko immediately demanded and received the evidence which had been collected by the Holy Synod and passed along to Stolypin to form the basis of his earlier report. The following day, an official of the Holy Synod appeared and ordered Rodzianko to hand the papers back. "He explained," Rodzianko wrote, "that the demand came from a very exalted person. 'Who is it, Sabler [Minister of Religion]?' 'No, someone much more highly placed.' . . . 'Who is it?' I repeated. 'The Empress, Alexandra Fedorovna.' 'If that is the case,' I said, 'will you kindly inform Her Majesty that she is as much a subject of her august consort as I myself, and that it is the duty of us both to obey his commands. I am, therefore, not in a position to comply with her wishes.' "

Rodzianko kept the papers and wrote his report, but when he asked for another audience to present it, the request was denied. He sent it to the Tsar, nevertheless, and Sazonov, the Foreign Minister, was present when Nicholas read it at Livadia. Afterward, Sazonov spoke to Grand Duke Ernest of Hesse, the Empress's brother, who also was present. Sadly, the Grand Duke shook his head and commented, "The Emperor is a saint and an angel, but he does not know how to deal with her."

Two years after his appointment as Prime Minister, Kokovtsov toppled from power. Once again, it was Rasputin who poisoned this political career. Upon appointing Kokovtsov Minister of Finance, Nicholas had told him, "Remember, Vladimir Nicolaievich, that the doors of this study are always open to you at any time you need to come." When Kokovtsov sent the Tsar his proposed budget speech to the Duma in 1907, Nicholas returned it with a personal note reading, "God grant that the new Duma may study calmly this splendid explanation and appreciate the improvement we have made in so short a time after all the trials sent to us." The Empress also was initially well disposed toward Kokovtsov. During their first interview after he became Finance Minister, she said, "I wished to see you to tell you that both the Tsar and I beg you always to be quite frank with us and to tell us the truth, not hesitating lest it be unpleasant for us. Believe me, even if it be so at first, we shall be grateful to you for it later."

But Alexandra's warmth and her desire to hear the truth faded quickly once the newspapers began their attack on Rasputin. Kokovtsov himself understood clearly what had happened and even sympathized with Alexandra:

"At first, I enjoyed Her Majesty's favor," he wrote. "In fact, I was appointed Chairman of the Ministers' Council with her knowledge and consent. Hence, when the Duma and press began a violent campaign against Rasputin . . . she expected me to put a stop to it. Yet it was not my opposition to the Tsar's proposal to take measures against the press that won me Her Majesty's displeasure; it was my report to His Majesty about Rasputin after the *starets* had visited me. From that time on, although the Tsar continued to show me his favor for another two years, my dismissal was assured. This changed attitude of Her Majesty is not hard to understand. . . . In her mind, Rasputin was closely associated with the health of her son, and the welfare of the Monarchy. To attack him was to attack the protector of what she held most dear. Moreover, like any righteous person, she was offended to think that the sanctity of her home had been questioned in the press and in the Duma. She thought that I, as head of the government, was responsible for permitting these attacks, and could not understand why I could not stop them by giving orders in the name of the Tsar. She considered me, therefore, not a servant of the Tsar, but a tool of the enemies of the state and, as such, deserving dismissal."

Despite his wife's animosity, Nicholas retained his affection for Kokovtsov. Nevertheless, on February 12, 1914, the Prime Minister received a letter from the Tsar:

> VLADIMIR NICOLAIEVICH:
>
> It is not a feeling of displeasure but a long-standing and deep realization of a state need that now forces me to tell you that we have to part.
>
> I am doing this in writing, for it is easier to select the right words when putting them on paper than during an unsettling conversation.
>
> The happenings of the past eight years have persuaded me definitely that the idea of combining in one person the duties of Chairman of the Ministers' Council and those of Minister of Finance or of the Interior is both awkward and wrong in a country such as Russia.
>
> Moreover, the swift tempo of our domestic life and the striking

development of the economic forces of our country both demand the undertaking of most definite and serious measures, a task which should be best entrusted to a man fresh for the work.

During the last two years, unfortunately, I have not always approved of the policy of the Ministry of Finance, and I perceive that this can go no farther.

I appreciate highly your devotion to me and the great service you have performed in achieving remarkable improvements in Russia's state credit; I am grateful to you for this from the bottom of my heart. Believe me, I am sorry to part with you who have been my assistant for ten years. Believe also, that I shall not forget to take suitable care of you and your family. I expect you with your last report on Friday, at 11:00 a.m. as always, and ever as a friend.

With sincere regards,
NICHOLAS

Kokovtsov found little solace in Nicholas's description of his successor as "a man fresh for the work," especially when he discovered that this successor was to be Goremykin. Certainly Goremykin made no such estimate of his talents. "I am like an old fur coat," he said. "For many months I have been packed away in camphor. I am being taken out now merely for the occasion; when it is passed I shall be packed away again till I am wanted the next time."

After his dismissal, Kokovtsov was asked to call on the Dowager Empress. "I know you are an honorable man and I know that you bear no ill will toward my son. You must also understand my fears for the future. My daughter-in-law does not like me; she thinks that I am jealous of her power. She does not perceive that my one aspiration is to see my son happy. Yet I see that we are nearing some catastrophe and the Tsar listens to no one but flatterers, not perceiving or even suspecting what goes on all around him. Why do you not decide to tell the Tsar frankly all you think and know, now that you are at liberty to do so, warning him, if it is not already too late?"

Almost as distressed as Marie, Kokovtsov replied that he "could do nothing. I told her that no one would listen to me or believe me. The young Empress thought me her enemy." This animosity, Kokovtsov explained, had been present ever since February 1912.

It was in the middle of February 1912 that Kokovtsov and Rasputin had met and disliked each other over tea.

When he first came to St. Petersburg, Gregory Rasputin had no plan for making himself the power behind the Russian throne. Like many successful opportunists, he lived from day to day, cleverly making the most of what was offered to him. In his case, the path led to the upper reaches of Russian society, and from there, because of Alexis's illness, to the throne. Even then he remained indifferent to politics until his own behavior became a political issue. Then, with government ministers, members of the Duma, the church hierarchy and the press all attacking him, Rasputin counterattacked in the only way open to him: by going to the Empress. Rasputin became a political influence in Russia in self-defense.

Alexandra was a faithful patron. When government ministers or bishops of the church leveled accusations at the *starets*, she retaliated by urging their dismissal. When the Duma debated "the Rasputin question" and the press cried out against his excesses, the Empress demanded dissolution of the one and suppression of the other. She defended Rasputin so strongly that it became difficult for people to associate in their minds the Empress and the *moujik*. If she had determined to hate all his enemies, it was not surprising that his enemies decided to hate her.

Stephen Beletsky, Director of the Police Department, later reckoned that Rasputin's power was firmly established by 1913. Simanovich, who worked with Rasputin in St. Petersburg, estimated that it took Rasputin five years, 1906–1911, to gain power and that he then exercised it for another five, 1911–1916. In both estimates, the turning point falls in the neighborhood of 1912, the year that the Tsarevich Alexis almost died at Spala.

CHAPTER EIGHTEEN

The Romanov Dynasty

In 1913, the gilded world of the European aristocracy seemed at its zenith. In fact, fashionable society, like the rest of mankind, stood one step from the abyss. Within five years, three European empires would be defeated, three emperors would die or flee into exile and the ancient dynasties of Hapsburg, Hohenzollern and Romanov would crumble. Twenty million men, aristocrats and commoners alike, would perish.

Even by 1913, there were omens of danger. The aristocracy of Europe continued to move through a world of elegant spas, magnificent yachts, top hats, tailcoats, long skirts and parasols, but the old monarchs who had given character to this world were vanishing. In Vienna, the aged Emperor Franz Joseph was eighty-seven; already he had sat on the throne for sixty-four years. In England, not only Queen Victoria but also her son King Edward VII were in their graves. King Edward's death left his nephew the Kaiser the dominant monarch in Europe. William reveled in his new preeminence and scorned the pair of gentle cousins who occupied the thrones of England and Russia. William, meanwhile, changed uniforms five times a day and let it be known that when he commanded troops at army maneuvers, the side he was leading was expected to win.

Beneath the polished sphere of kings and society, there was a wider world where millions of ordinary people lived and worked. Here, the portents were even more ominous. Nations ruled by kings and emperors had grown into industrial behemoths. The new machines had given the monarchs vastly greater power to make war; by 1913, it was scientifically assured that a dynastic quarrel would lead to the death not of thousands, but of millions of men. In the upheaval of such murderous wars lay promise of revolution. "A war with Austria would be a splendid little thing for the revolution," Lenin wrote to Maxim Gorky in 1913. "But the chances are small that Franz Joseph and Nikolasha will give us such a treat." Even without war, the stresses produced by industrialization promised future storms of frustration and unrest. Governments shuddered under the impact of strikes and assassinations. The red banners of Syndicalism and Socialism floated beside the golden standards of militant nationalism. These were the days when, in Churchill's words, "the vials of wrath were full."

Nowhere was there greater contrast between the effortless lives of the aristocracy and the dark existence of the masses than in Russia. Between the nobility and the peasants lay a vast gulf of ignorance. Between the nobility and the intellectuals there was massive contempt and flourishing hatred. Each considered that if Russia was to survive, the other must be eliminated.

It was in this atmosphere of gloom and suspicion that Russia began a national celebration of the ancient institution of autocracy. The occasion was the tercentenary of the Romanov dynasty, which had come to power in 1613. The hope of the Tsar and his advisors was that by raising again the giant figures of Russia's past they might submerge class hostility and unite the nation around the throne.

To an astonishing degree, the tercentenary succeeded. Huge crowds—workers and students among them—flooded the city boulevards to cheer Imperial processions. In the villages, peasants flocked to catch a glimpse of the Tsar as he passed by. No one then dreamed that this was the sunset of autocracy, that after three hundred years of Romanov rule no tsar would ever pass that way again.

In February 1913, Nicholas and Alexandra prepared for the tercentenary celebrations by moving with their children from Tsarskoe Selo to the Winter Palace. None of them was fond of the palace. It was too large, too gloomy, too drafty, and the tiny enclosed garden was much too small for the children to play. Besides, Alexandra had a special reason for disliking the Winter Palace: it reminded her of the weeks she had spent in St Petersburg as a bride, going to the theatre, speeding along in a *troika*, having cozy suppers before a blazing fire. "I was so happy then, so well and strong," she told Anna Vyrubova. "Now I am a wreck."

The official tercentenary celebration began with a great choral *Te Deum* in the Cathedral of Our Lady of Kazan. On the morning of the service, the Nevsky Prospect, down which the Imperial carriages would pass, was jammed with excited crowds. Despite lines of soldiers holding the people back, the crowd, cheering wildly, burst the cordons and mobbed the carriage containing the Tsar and the Empress.

Under its great golden dome, the cathedral was packed to capacity. Although most of those present were standing, seats in front had been saved for members of the Imperial family, foreign ambassadors, government ministers and members of the Duma. Shortly before the Tsar arrived, a dramatic squabble had occurred over the Duma seats. Michael Rodzianko, the President of the Duma, had with great difficulty secured these seats for his members. As he entered the church, a guard whispered to him that a peasant had sat down in one of them and refused to move.

"Sure enough," wrote Rodzianko, "it was Rasputin. He was dressed in a magnificent Russian tunic of crimson silk, patent leather top boots, black cloth trousers and a peasant's overcoat. Over his dress he wore a pectoral cross on a finely wrought chain." Rodzianko firmly ordered the *starets* out of the seat. Then, according to Rodzianko, Rasputin tried to mesmerize him on the spot. "He stared me in the eyes. . . . I felt myself confronted by an unknown power of tremendous force. I suddenly became possessed of an almost animal fury, the blood rushed to my heart and I realized I was working myself into a state of absolute frenzy. I, too, stared straight into Rasputin's eyes, and, speaking literally, felt my own staring out of my head. . . . 'You are a notorious swindler,' I said." Rasputin fell on his knees, and Rodzianko, who was bigger and stronger, began to kick him in the ribs. Finally the Duma President lifted Rasputin by the scruff of his neck and threw him bodily out of the seat. Murmuring, "Lord, forgive him his sin," Rasputin slunk away.

The days after the service were crowded with ceremonies. From all parts of the empire, delegations in national dress arrived to be presented to the Tsar. In honor of the sovereign, his wife and all the Romanov grand dukes and grand duchesses, the nobility of St. Petersburg jointly gave a ball attended by thousands of guests. Together, the Imperial couple attended a state performance of Glinka's *A Life for the Tsar* at the opera. "The orchestra was a mass of officers in uniform and the boxes were filled with ladies in jewels," wrote Anna

Vyrubova. "When Their Majesties appeared, the whole house rose and gave them tumultuous applause."

The strain of these activities, coming only four months after Spala, was intense. At receptions in the Winter Palace, the Empress stood for hours in the middle of the enormous crowds jamming the state rooms. She looked magnificent in dark blue velvet with a diamond tiara and diamond necklace; for one ball she wore white with pearls and emeralds. Several times, as a reminder of Russia's past, she wore a long Oriental gown of silk brocade and the tall cone-shaped *kokoshnik* worn by Russian empresses before the court was Westernized by Peter the Great. Her daughters appeared in shimmering white gowns wearing the Order of St. Catherine, a scarlet ribbon blazing with diamonds. But Alexandra's strength was fragile. At one ball, wrote Baroness Buxhoeveden, "she felt so ill that she could scarcely keep her feet . . . she was able to attract the attention of the Emperor who was talking at the other end of the room. When he came up it was only just in time to lead her away and prevent her from fainting in public."

One night at the Maryinsky Theatre, she appeared pale and silent in a white velvet dress with the pale blue ribbon of the Order of St. Andrew across her breast. From an adjacent box, Meriel Buchanan watched her closely: "Her lovely, tragic face was expressionless . . . her eyes enigmatic in their dark gravity, seeming fixed on some secret inner thought that was certainly far removed from the crowded theatre. . . . Presently it seemed that this emotion or distress mastered her completely, and with a few whispered words to the Emperor she rose and withdrew. . . . A little wave of resentment rippled over the theatre."

For Easter that year, Nicholas gave Alexandra a Fabergé egg which bore miniature portraits of all the reigning Romanov tsars and empresses framed in Russian double eagles. Inside, the surprise was a globe of blued steel with two maps of the Russian Empire inset in gold, one of the year 1613, the other of 1913. In May, the Imperial family set off on a dynastic pilgrimage to trace the route taken by Michael Romanov, the first of the Romanov tsars, from his birthplace to the throne. On the Upper Volga, where the great river curves north and west of Moscow, they boarded a steamer to sail to the ancient Romanov seat of Kostroma, where in March 1613 sixteen-year-old Michael was notified of his election to the throne. Along the way, peasants lined the banks to watch the little flotilla pass; some even plunged into the water to get a closer look. On this trip, Grand Duchess

Olga Alexandrovna remembered, "Wherever we went we met with manifestations of loyalty bordering on wildness. When our steamer went down the Volga we saw crowds of peasants wading waist-high in the water to catch a glimpse of Nicky. In some of the towns I would see artisans and workmen falling down to kiss his shadow as we passed. Cheers were deafening."

The climax of the tercentenary came in Moscow. On a brilliant blue day in June, Nicholas rode into the city alone, sixty feet in advance of his Cossack escort. In Red Square, he dismounted and walked, behind a line of chanting priests, across the square and through a gate into the Kremlin. Alexandra and Alexis, following in an open car, also were supposed to walk the last few hundred yards. But Alexis was ill. "The Tsarevich was carried along in the arms of a Cossack of the bodyguard," wrote Kokovtsov. "As the procession paused . . . I clearly heard exclamations of sorrow at the sight of this poor helpless child, the heir to the throne of the Romanovs."

Looking back on the tercentenary once it was over, the principals drew different conclusions. In Alexandra, it confirmed once more her belief in the bond between the Tsar and his people. "Now you can see for yourself what cowards those State Ministers are," she told a lady-in-waiting. "They are constantly frightening the Emperor with threats of revolution and here—you see it yourself—we need merely to show ourselves and at once their hearts are ours." In Nicholas, it aroused a desire to travel further within Russia's borders; he talked of sailing again along the Volga, of visiting the Caucasus, of going perhaps even to Siberia. Grand Duchess Olga Alexandrovna, writing in retrospect, knowing what was to come, declared, "Nobody seeing those enthusiastic crowds, could have imagined that in less than four years, Nicky's very name would be splattered with mud and hatred."

Even Kokovtsov, who felt that the ministers and Duma had been ignored, admitted that the celebrations appeared successful. "The Tsar's journey was to be in the nature of a family celebration," he wrote. "The concepts of state and government were to be pushed into the background and the personality of the Tsar was to dominate the scene. The current attitude seemed to suggest that the government was a barrier between the people and their Tsar, whom they regarded with blind devotion as anointed by God. . . . The Tsar's closest friends at the court became persuaded that the Sovereign could do anything by relying on the unbounded love and utter loyalty of the people. The ministers of the government, on the other hand, [and] . . . the

Duma . . . both were of the opinion that the Sovereign should recognize that conditions had changed since the day the Romanovs became Tsars of Russia and lords of the Russian domains."

The Romanov dynasty was the fruit of a marriage in 1547. The bride was Anastasia, daughter of the Romanovs, a popular family of the Moscow nobility. The groom was the seventeen-year-old Muscovite prince Ivan IV, who had just proclaimed himself Tsar of Russia. Ivan's technique of choosing a wife was in the grand manner: he ordered two thousand girls lined up for his inspection; from this assembly he chose Anastasia. Nevertheless, Ivan was deeply in love with his young wife. When she died ten years later, Ivan suspected that she had been poisoned. His grief turned to rage and perhaps to madness. His reign thereafter was such a crescendo of cruelties that he became known as Ivan the Terrible. He carried an iron staff with which he impaled courtiers who irritated him. When the city of Novgorod rebelled, Ivan surrounded the city and for five weeks sat on a throne in the open air while before his eyes sixty thousand people were tortured to death.

Torn between good and evil, Ivan talked incessantly of leaving the throne. He did leave Moscow midway in his reign for a monastery, where he alternated between spectacular debauchery, bloody executions and abject remorse. Returning to the throne, he soon fell into a rage and stabbed his eldest and favorite son. When the young man died, Ivan tried to atone by reading the Bible and interminable prayers. He sobbed that his life had been ruined by the death of his beloved Anastasia Romanovna. Writing to his enemy Prince Kurbsky, he said, "And why did you separate me from my wife? If only you had not taken from me my young wife . . . none of this would have happened." Toward the end, he was haunted by his victims. His hair fell out and he howled every night. When he died, supposedly in the middle of a game of chess with his courtier Boris Godunov, his last act was to call for a cowl and become a monk.

Ivan was succeeded by his feeble second son, Fedor, who was succeeded in turn by the regent, Boris Godunov. Boris ruled as Tsar for five years. His death opened the door to a horde of claimants and pretenders—in Russian history, this period is known as the Time of Troubles. At one point, the throne was claimed by a son of the King of Poland. A Polish army occupied Moscow, entrenched itself in the Kremlin and burned the rest of the city. Besieged by the Russians, the Poles held out in the Kremlin for eighteen months, fending off starvation by eating their own dead. In November 1612, the Kremlin surrendered. Russia, which had had no tsar for three years, convened a national assembly, the Zemsky Sobor, to elect a new tsar.

The choice fell on another boy, 16-year-old Michael Romanov. By blood, Michael's claim was weak; he was no more than the grandnephew of Ivan the Terrible. But he remained the only candidate on whom all the quarreling factions could agree. On a cold, windy day, March 13, 1613, a delegation of nobles, clergy, gentry, traders, artisans and peasants, representing "all the classes and all the towns of Russia," arrived at Kostroma on the Upper Volga to inform Michael Romanov that he had been elected Tsar. Michael's mother, who was present, demurred, pointing out that all previous tsars had found their subjects disloyal. The delegates admitted that this was true, but, they added, "now we have been punished and we have come to an agreement in all the towns." Michael tearfully accepted and on July 11, 1613, in the Kremlin, the first Romanov tsar was crowned.

The greatest of the Romanovs was Michael's grandson, Peter the Great. Peter became tsar in 1689 and reigned for thirty-six years. From boyhood, Peter was interested in Europe. As an adolescent in Moscow, he shunned the Kremlin and played outside the city with three older companions, a Scot, a German and a Swiss. In 1697, Peter became the first tsar to leave Russia, when, traveling under an alias, he toured Western Europe for a year and a half. His incognito was difficult to maintain: Peter was almost seven feet tall, he traveled with a retinue of 250 people including dwarfs and jesters, his language was Russian, his manners barbarous. Fascinated by the art of surgery being practiced at the Anatomical Theatre in Leyden, Peter noticed squeamish looks on the faces of his courtiers; instantly, he ordered them to descend into the arena and sever the muscles of the cadavers with their teeth.

When he returned to Russia, Peter wrenched his empire violently from East to West. He personally shaved the waist-long beards and sheared the *caftans* of his *boyars* (nobles). To modernize their sleeping habits, he declared, "Ladies and gentlemen of the court caught sleeping with their boots on will be instantly decapitated." Wielding a new pair of dental pliers which he had acquired in Europe, he collected teeth from the jaws of unwary and terrified subjects. When he considered that St. Petersburg, his European capital, was sufficiently finished to be inhabitable, he gave his *boyars* twenty-four hours to pack their belongings in Moscow and leave for the north.

There was no side of Russian life that Peter did not touch. Along with the new capital, he built the Russian army and navy and the Academy of Science. He simplified the Russian alphabet and edited the first Russian newspaper. He flooded Russia with new books, new ideas, new words and new titles, mostly German. He wreaked such havoc on the old Russian culture and religion that the Orthodox Church considered him the Antichrist. For all his modern ideas, Peter retained the impulses of an ancient, absolute autocrat. Suspecting that his son and heir, the Tsarevich Alexis, was intriguing against him, Peter had the youth tortured and beaten to death.

The other towering figure of the Romanov dynasty was not a Romanov or even a Russian. Catherine the Great was born an obscure German princess, Sophie of Anhalt-Zerbst. At fourteen, she married Peter the Great's grandson, Peter III. For eighteen years they lived together, first more as brother and sister, then as antagonists when Peter insulted her in public and lived openly with his mistress. In 1762, a conspiracy was organized on her behalf and Peter was forced to abdicate. Soon afterward, at a dinner party, he died in a scuffle. Prince Alexis Orlov, one of the conspirators entrusted with his custody, declared, "We cannot ourselves remember what we did." Because it has never been established that Peter III fathered Catherine's son Paul, there is a strong chance that the original Romanov line ended in this scuffle.

Catherine's reign brought classical style to the Russian autocracy. Diderot, Locke, Blackstone, Voltaire and Montesquieu were her favorite authors. She wrote frequently to Voltaire and Frederick the Great; she built the Hermitage to serve as a guest house if Voltaire should ever come to Russia, but he never did. Catherine herself wrote a history of Russia, painted and sculpted. She never remarried. She lived alone, rising at five to light her own fire and begin fifteen hours of work. Over the years, she took dozens of lovers. A few, such as Prince Gregory Orlov and Prince Gregory Potemkin, helped her rule Russia. Of Potemkin, she wrote that their letters might almost be man to man, except that "one of the two friends was a very attractive woman."

Catherine died in 1796, the year that Napoleon Bonaparte was winning his first military triumphs in Italy. Eighteen years later, Napoleon invaded Russia and entered Moscow only to see his army destroyed by winds and snows. Two years after that, in 1814, Catherine's grandson, Tsar Alexander I, rode into Paris at the head of a Russian army. After Alexander I came his brother, Nicholas I. Nicholas II, descendant and heir to Michael Romanov, Peter the Great and Catherine the Great, was the great-grandson of Nicholas I.

Maurice Paléologue once did some idle arithmetic and calculated that, by blood, Tsar Nicholas II was only 1/128th Russian, while his son, the Tsarevich Alexis, was only 1/256th Russian. The habit Russian tsars had of marrying German and Danish wives was responsible for these startling fractions; they suggest better than anything else the extent to which the original Romanov blood had been diluted by the beginning of the twentieth century.

As head of the family, Nicholas II presided over an immense clan of Romanov cousins, uncles, aunts, nieces and nephews. Although keenly jealous of name and rank, they were often casual about duties and obligations. By education, language and taste, they were part of the cosmopolitan aristocracy of Europe. They spoke French better than they spoke Russian, they traveled in private railway coaches from hotels at Biarritz to villas on the Riviera, they were more often seen as guests in English country houses or palaces in Rome than on their family estates beside the Volga or the Dnieper or the Don. Wealthy, sophisticated, charming and bored, most of the Romanovs considered "Nicky," with his naïve fatalism, and "Alicky," with her passionate religious fervor, to be pathetically quaint and obsolete.

Unfortunately, in the public mind, all the Romanovs were lumped together. If Nicholas's inadequacies as tsar weakened the logic of autocracy, the family's indifference to its reputation helped to corrode the prestige of the dynasty. Nicholas's sister Grand Duchess Olga Alexandrovna recognized the family's failure. Shortly before her death in 1960 she observed sorrowfully:

"It is certainly the last generation that helped to bring about the disintegration of the Empire. . . . All those critical years, the Romanovs, who should have been the staunchest supporters of the throne, did not live up to their standards or to the traditions of the family. . . . Too many of us Romanovs had . . . gone to live in a world of self-interest where little mattered except the unending gratification of personal desire and ambition. Nothing proved it better than the appalling marital mess in which the last generation of my family involved themselves. That chain of domestic scandals could not but shock the nation . . . but did any of them care for the impression they created? Never."

The problem was divorce. By law, members of the Imperial family were forbidden to marry without the sovereign's consent. They were also forbidden to marry commoners or persons who had been divorced. The Orthodox Church permits divorce in cases where adultery has been committed; indeed, in the eyes of the Church, the act of adultery itself dissolves a Christian marriage. But what is permitted is certainly not encouraged. In the Imperial family, whose private life was supposed to set an example, divorce was considered a stain and a disgrace.

Yet, scarcely was Nicholas II on the throne before the strict code began to crumble. First, his cousin Grand Duke Michael Mikhailovich casually married a commoner and went to live in England. Next, the Montenegrin princess Grand Duchess Anastasia divorced her husband, the Duke of Leuchtenberg, to marry Grand Duke Nicholas, the tall soldier who commanded the Russian armies in World War I. Soon afterward, the Tsar's youngest uncle, Grand Duke Paul, having been left a widower, married a commoner and a divorcée.

"I had a rather stern talk with Uncle Paul which ended by my warning him of all the consequences his proposed marriage would have for him," Nicholas wrote to Marie on this occasion. "It had no effect. . . . How painful and distressing it all is and how ashamed one feels for the family before the world. What guarantee is there now that Cyril won't start at the same sort of thing tomorrow, and Boris and Serge the day after? And in the end, I fear, a whole colony of members of the Russian Imperial family will be established in Paris with their semi-legitimate and illegitimate wives. God alone knows what times we are living in when undisguised selfishness stifles all feelings of conscience, duty, or even ordinary decency."

Three years later, Grand Duke Cyril, Nicholas's first cousin, fulfilled the Tsar's gloomy prophecy by marrying a divorcée. To make matters more delicate, Cyril's new wife was Princess Victoria Melita, whose former husband was Empress Alexandra's brother Grand Duke Ernest of Hesse. It had been at the wedding of "Vicky" and "Ernie" that Nicholas had proposed to Alexandra. Nicholas reacted to Cyril's move by dismissing him from the Imperial Navy and banishing him from Russia. This action, in turn, infuriated Cyril's father, Grand Duke Vladimir, who threatened to resign all *his* official posts. In the end, Nicholas retreated. "I wonder whether it was wise to punish a man publicly to such an extent, especially when the family was against it," he wrote to Marie. "After much thought which in the end gave me a headache, I decided to take advantage of the name day of your grandson and I telegraphed to Uncle Vladimir that I would return to Cyril the title which he had lost."

Of all the blows delivered against the dynasty by the Romanov family itself, none was more damaging or more personally painful to the Tsar than the one which came from his brother Michael. Like many another youngest son and younger brother of a reigning monarch, Michael was ignored in public and indulged in private. Even as a child, he had been the only one able to tease his redoubtable father, Alexander III. A family story told of the morning that father and son were strolling in a garden when the Tsar, suddenly angry at Michael's behavior, snatched a watering hose and drenched his son. Michael accepted the dousing, changed his dripping clothes and joined his father at breakfast. Later in the morning, Alexander got up from his desk and, as was his habit, leaned meditatively out of the window of his study. A torrent of water descended on his head and shoulders. Michael, waiting at a window above with a bucket, had had his revenge.

Grand Duke Michael, ten years younger than Nicholas, grew up a handsome, affectionate nonentity. Although from the death of his brother George in 1898 until the birth of his nephew Alexis in 1904 Michael was Heir to the Throne, no one seriously considered the possibility of "darling Misha" becoming tsar. It was unthinkable. Even in public, surrounded by government ministers, his sister Olga Alexandrovna blithely addressed Michael by her own pet name for him, "Floppy."

Michael himself enjoyed automobiles and pretty girls. He had a garage filled with shiny motorcars which he loved to drive. Unfortunately, the Grand Duke had the troublesome habit of falling asleep at the wheel. Once, with Olga beside him, speeding to Gatchina to dine with their mother, "Floppy" nodded off and the car rolled over. Both brother and sister were thrown clear, unhurt.

Among his relatives, Michael was closest to Olga, the other baby of the family. Consequently, he was often around Olga's attractive young female friends and maids-of-honor. In 1901, at the age of twenty-three, Michael decided that he was in love with the prettiest of these girls, Alexandra Kossikovsky, whom Olga called "Dina." Romantically, he followed his sister and her suite to Italy, and in Sorrento he and Dina began planning an elopement. Before the scheme had advanced beyond the planning stage, Empress Marie heard about it. Summoning Michael, she overwhelmed him with anger and scorn. Dina was summarily dismissed.

Five years later, in 1906, Michael, now twenty-eight, again fell in love. This time, he wrote to his brother asking permission to marry a woman who was not only a commoner but who had twice been divorced. In dismay, Nicholas wrote to Marie: "Three days ago, Misha wrote asking my permission to marry. . . . I will never give my consent. . . . It is infinitely easier to give one's consent than to refuse it. God forbid that this sad affair should cause misunderstanding in our family."

This time, Michael did not give up. The lady involved was born Nathalie Cheremetevskaya, the daughter of a Moscow lawyer. At sixteen, she had married a merchant named Mamontov, then divorced him three years later to marry a Captain Wulfert of the Blue Cuirassier Guards. The colonel of her new husband's regiment was none other than His Imperial Highness Grand Duke Michael. Within a few months Nathalie managed to become Michael's mistress. From that moment on, she dominated his life.

Nathalie Cheremetevskaya was a beautiful woman of great allure. Paléologue encountered her once in a St. Petersburg shop during the war and hurried home to describe her to his diary with Gallic exuberance: "I saw a slender young woman of about 30. She was a delight to watch. Her whole style revealed great personal charm and refined taste. Her chinchilla coat, opened at the neck, gave a glimpse of a dress of silver grey taffeta with trimmings of lace. A light fur cap blended with her glistening fair hair. Her pure and aristocratic face is charmingly modeled and she has light velvety eyes. Around her neck a string of superb pearls sparkled in the light. There was a dignified, sinuous soft gracefulness about her every movement."

At first, Michael respected the Tsar's denial of permission to marry. Nevertheless, he and Nathalie left Russia to live together abroad. In 1910, Nathalie bore the Grand Duke a son whose name became George. In July 1912, the lovers took up residence in the Bavarian resort village of Berchtesgaden. One morning in October of that year, they secretly crossed the border into Austria and in a small Orthodox church in Vienna they were married. Only after their return to Berchtesgaden as man and wife did they notify the Tsar.

Their telegram was delivered to Nicholas at Spala. Coming immediately after the crisis with Alexis, it staggered the Tsar. "He broke his word, his word of honor," Nicholas said, agitatedly rubbing his brow as he showed the telegram to Anna Vyrubova. "How in the midst of the boy's illness and all our trouble, could they have done such a thing?" At first, Nicholas wanted to keep the marriage a secret. "A terrible blow . . . It must be kept absolutely secret," he wrote to Mama. The impossibility of this soon became obvious. Nevertheless, Nicholas deprived his brother of the right of regency on Alexis's behalf, and put Michael in a state of tutelage as if he were a minor or a mental incompetent. Grand Duke Michael, second in line for the Russian throne, was then forbidden to return to Russia.

Later, the reason for Michael's seemingly impetuous decision to marry became clearer. From the medical bulletins and news reports that were filtering across Europe, Michael suddenly became aware of the fact that his nephew might die at any moment. If Alexis died, Michael knew that he would be compelled to return to Russia under circumstances which would make it impossible for him to marry a woman of Nathalie's standing. Before this could happen, he—or she—decided to act. "What revolts me more than anything else," said Alexandra, "is [Michael's] reference to poor Alexis's illness which, he says, has hurried things up."

Despite his anger, Nicholas could not ignore his brother's *fait accompli*. Nathalie was now his brother's wife. Reluctantly, he granted her the title of Countess Brassova and consented that her infant son, his nephew, should be styled Count Brassov. When the war began, Nicholas permitted the couple to return to Russia and Michael went to the front in command of a Caucasian division. But neither Nicholas nor Alexandra ever received or uttered a word to the bold and beautiful Nathalie Cheremetevskaya.

To those who remember it, the winter season in St. Petersburg following the tercentenary seemed especially brilliant. The tall windows in the great palaces along the Neva blazed with light. The streets and shops were filled with bustling crowds. Fabergé, with its heavy granite pillars and air of Byzantine opulence, was thronged with customers. In elegant hair-dressing salons, ladies sat on blue-and-gold chairs, congratulating themselves on getting an appointment and exchanging the latest gossip. The most delicious story that year concerned Vaslav Nijinsky's expulsion from the Imperial Ballet. The banishment followed a performance of *Giselle* in which the magnificent dancer had worn an unusually brief and revealing costume. When he appeared on stage, there was a commotion in the Imperial box. The Dowager Empress was seen to rise, fix the stage with a devastating glare and then sweep out of the theatre. The dancer's expulsion followed immediately.

The mood of the capital was one of hope. Russia was prosperous, memories of the war with Japan had faded, the tercentenary had provided a surge of enthusiasm for the ancient monarchy. There were rumors that court balls would be held again, now that the Tsar's daughters were growing up. Grand Duchess Olga, golden-haired and blue-eyed, had already made her first appearances at St. Petersburg balls. Grand Duchess Tatiana, slender, with dark hair and amber eyes, was ready to be presented. The court balls did not take place that winter, but the social event of the season was a ball which the Dowager Empress gave for her granddaughters at the Anitchkov Palace. The Empress came, but left at midnight, and it was the Tsar who remained until 4:30 a.m. to escort his daughters home. On the train back to Tsarskoe Selo, he sipped a cup of tea and listened while the girls discussed the party and planned how late they would sleep the next morning.

Beyond the circle of sparkling light, the enthusiasm of the tercentenary quickly dissipated. Unrest among the workers and peasants continued to grow. In April 1912, an incident had taken place in the remote Lena goldfields of Siberia. The miners had gone on strike and were walking in protest toward the office of the Anglo-Russian Lena Gold Mining Company when a drunken police officer ordered his men to open fire. Two hundred people were killed, and Russia seethed with anger. In the Duma and the press, the massacre was called "a second Bloody Sunday." The government ordered a Commission of Inquiry, and the Duma, unwilling to rely on the report of a government commission, decided to conduct its own investigation. The head of the Duma commission was Alexander Kerensky.

Since leaving the university in St. Petersburg in 1905, Kerensky had become a familiar figure as he defended political prisoners in courtrooms all across Russia. Although his arguments and his successes frequently were embarrassing to the government, "I was not subject to the slightest pressure," he said. "No one could oust us from the courts, no one could lift a finger against us." The same sense of legal fair play prevailed at the Lena goldfields investigation: "The government commission sat in one house and we sat in another. Both commissions were summoning and cross-examining witnesses . . . both were recording the testimony of the employees, both were writing official reports. . . . The gold fields administration greatly resented our intrusion but neither the . . . [government investigators] nor the local officials interfered in any way; on the contrary . . . the Governor actually helped." Kerensky's report bitterly damned the police, and not long afterward the Minister of Interior resigned.

From the goldfields, Kerensky went straight to the Volga region to run for election to the Fourth Duma. He ran as a critic of the government, was elected, and for the two years before the war he traveled across Russia making speeches, holding meetings and doing "strenuous political organizing and revolutionary work . . . The whole of Russia," he wrote, "was now covered with a network of labor and liberal organizations—the co-operatives, trade unions, labor clubs." It was no longer even necessary for agitators to be secretive about their work. "In those days a man as openly and bitterly hostile to the government as myself toured from town to town quite freely making speeches at public meetings. At these meetings, I criticized the government sharply. . . . [Never] did it enter the heads of the Tsarist Cheka to infringe on my parliamentary inviolability."

Kerensky's work, and that of others like him, had an effect. In 1913, the year of the tercentenary, seven hundred thousand Russian workers were on strike. By January 1914, the number had grown to one million. In the Baku region, fighting broke out between the oil workers and the police, and, as it had always been in Russia, the Cossacks came at a gallop. By July 1914, the number of strikers had swollen to one and a half million. In St. Petersburg, mobs of strikers were smashing windows and erecting barricades in the streets. That month, Count Pourtalès, the German Ambassador, repeatedly assured the Kaiser that in these chaotic circumstances Russia could not possibly fight.

The end of the Old World was very near. After three hundred years of Romanov rule, the final storm was about to break over Imperial Russia.

CHAPTER NINETEEN

The Long Summer of 1914

By the spring of 1914, the nine-year-old Tsarevich had made a good recovery from the attack at Spala eighteen months before. His leg had straightened and, to his parents' delight, he walked with only a trace of a limp. In celebration of Alexis's return to health, the Tsar decided one clear May morning to abandon his papers and take his son on an outing. The excursion from Livadia into the mountains was to be entirely male. Alexis was overjoyed.

Two touring cars set out after breakfast. Alexis and his father were in the first, along with Gilliard and an officer from the *Standart*; the sailor Derevenko and a single Cossack guard followed in the second. Trailing long plumes of dust, the cars climbed the slopes of the mountains behind the Imperial palace, passing through cool forests of towering pines. Their destination was a great rust-colored cliff called Red Rock, which offered a majestic view of the valleys, the white palaces and the turquoise sea below. After lunch, descending the northern slope, the little cavalcade came on patches of still unmelted winter snow. Alexis begged that the cars be stopped, and Nicholas agreed. "He [Alexis] ran around us, skipping about, rolling in the snow, and picking himself up only to fall again a few seconds later," wrote Gilliard. "The Tsar watched his son's frolics with obvious pleasure." Although he intervened from time to time to caution his son to be careful, Nicholas was convinced for the first time that the ordeal at Spala was finally over.

"The day drew to a close," Gilliard continued, "and we were quite sorry to have to start back. The Tsar was in high spirits during the drive. We had an impression that this holiday devoted to his son had been a tremendous pleasure to him. For a few hours, he had escaped his imperial duties."

Despite her shyness and the close family circle that surrounded her, talk of marriage began to focus that year on eighteen-year-old Grand Duchess Olga. A match with Edward, the Prince of Wales, was mentioned. Nothing came of it, and the Prince remained unmarried until 1936, when he gave up his throne to marry Wallis Warfield Simpson. More serious discussion centered on Crown Prince Carol of Rumania. Sazonov, the Russian Foreign Minister, was an advocate of this match; he saw in it a possibility of detaching Rumania from her alliance with Germany and Austria-Hungary. Nicholas and Alexandra were receptive to Carol's suit, but Olga herself was implacably opposed.

On June 13, the Russian Imperial family paid a brief, formal visit to the Rumanian Black Sea port of Constanza. Carol and his family waited on the pier as the *Standart* brought the Russian visitors from Yalta. The single day was crowded with ceremonies: a cathedral service, a naval review and luncheon in the morning, followed by a military review, a formal tea, a state dinner, a torchlight parade and fireworks in the evening. All day long, the Rumanians stared at Olga, aware that in the Russian girl they might be observing their future queen.

In that sense, the visit was a waste of time. Even before the *Standart* arrived in Constanza, Olga found Gilliard on deck. "Tell me the truth, Monsieur," she said, "do you know why we are going to Rumania?" Tactfully, the tutor replied that he understood it was a matter of diplomacy. Tossing her head, Olga declared that Gilliard obviously knew the real reason. "I don't want it to happen," she said fiercely. "Papa has promised not to make me, and I don't want to leave Russia. I am a Russian and I mean to remain a Russian."

Olga's parents respected her feelings. Alexandra, sitting one day on the terrace at Livadia, explained their viewpoint to Sazonov. "I think with terror that the time draws near when I shall have to part with my daughters," she said. "I could desire nothing better than that they should remain in Russia after their marriage. But I have four daughters and it is, of course, impossible. You know how difficult marriages are in reigning families. I know it by experience, although I was never in the position my daughters occupy, being [only] the daughter of the Grand Duke of Hesse, and running little risk of being obliged to make a political match. Still, I was once threatened with the danger of marrying without love or even affection, and I vividly remember the torments I endured when . . . (the Empress named a member of one of the German reigning houses) arrived at Darmstadt and I was informed that he intended to marry me. I did not know him at all and I shall never forget what I suffered when I met him for the first time. My grandmother, Queen Victoria, took pity on me, and I was left in peace. God disposed otherwise of my fate, and granted me undreamed-of happiness. All the more then do I feel it my duty to leave my daughters free to marry according to their inclination. The Emperor will have to decide whether he considers this or that marriage suitable for his daughters, but parental authority must not extend beyond that."

Carol did not give up hope of marrying a Romanov grand duchess. Two years later, he suggested to Nicholas that he marry Marie, then sixteen. Nicholas laughingly declared that Marie was only a schoolgirl. In 1947, having abdicated the throne of Rumania, Carol made the third of his three marriages. His wife was the woman who had been his mistress for twenty-two years, Magda Lupescu.

In Europe, the early summer of 1914 was marked by glorious weather. Millions of men and women went off on holidays, forgetting their fears of war in the warmth of the sun. Kings and emperors continued to visit each other, dine at state dinners, review armies and fleets and bounce each other's children on their knees. Beneath the surface, however, differences were detectable. The important visits took place between allies: King George V visited Paris; the Kaiser visited the Austrian Archduke Franz Ferdinand; Raymond Poincaré, President of France, visited the Tsar in St. Petersburg. In their entourages, the chiefs of state brought generals and diplomats who sat down quietly with their opposite numbers to compare plans and confirm understandings. Military reviews took on special significance. Troops on parade were carefully watched for signs of *élan*, vigor and readiness for war.

An event of special symbolic importance took place at the end of June when the dashing British Admiral Sir David Beatty led the First Battle Cruiser Squadron of the Royal Navy up the Baltic on a visit to Russia. England, alarmed by the rapid building of the Kaiser's powerful High Seas Fleet, was reluctantly abandoning a century of "splendid isolation." A closer tie with Tsarist Russia, hitherto despised in press and parliament as the land of the Cossack and the knout, was part of Britain's new diplomacy. On June 20, a blazing, cloudless day, Beatty's four huge gray ships, *Lion*, *Queen Mary*, *Princess Royal* and *New Zealand*, steamed slowly past the *Standart* and anchored at Kronstadt. The Imperial family went aboard Beatty's flagship, *Lion*, for lunch. "Never have I seen happier faces than those of the young grand duchesses escorted over *Lion* by a little band of middies especially told off for their amusement," reported the British Ambassador, Sir George Buchanan. "When I think of them as I saw them that day," he added, "the tragic story of their deaths seems like some hideous nightmare."

The following day, while thousands of Russians stared at the English ships swinging silently on the Baltic tide, Beatty and his officers visited Tsarskoe Selo. Beatty himself, the youngest British admiral since Nelson, made a tremendous impression. His youthful, clean-shaven face caused many Russians, accustomed to seeing admirals with beards to their waists, to mistake Beatty for his own flag lieutenant. But Beatty's manner was unmistakably one of command. His square jaw and the jaunty angle at which he wore his cap suggested the sea dog. He spoke in a voice which would have carried over the howl of a gale. It was as if the solid reality of Britain's enormous seapower, a thing few Russians understood, had suddenly been revealed in Beatty's person.

After Beatty's departure, the Imperial family boarded the *Standart* for their annual two-week cruise along the coast of Finland. They were at sea four days later, June 28, when the terrible day arrived which is known in European history simply as "Sarajevo."

A hot Balkan sun shone down that morning on the white, flat-roofed houses of the Bosnian capital of Sarajevo. The streets were crowded with people who had come from miles away to see the middle-aged Hapsburg prince who one day would be their emperor. Tall and fleshy, the Archduke Franz Ferdinand was not ragingly popular anywhere within the sprawling Austro-Hungarian Empire, which had been ruled for sixty-six years by his aged uncle, Emperor Franz Joseph. Yet Franz Ferdinand was sufficiently enlightened politically to see—as his uncle and the government in Vienna did not—that unless something was done about the Slav nationalism burning inside the empire, the empire itself would disintegrate.

Austria-Hungary in 1914 was a hodge-podge of races, provinces and nationalities scattered across central Europe and the upper Balkans. Three fifths of these forty million people were Slavs—Poles,

Czechs, Slovaks, Serbs, Bosnians and Montenegrins—yet the empire was ruled by its two non-Slavic races, the Austrians and the Magyars of Hungary. Not surprisingly, most of the Slavic peoples within the empire restlessly longed for the day they would be free.

On these turbulent Slav provinces within the empire, the small independent Slav kingdom of Serbia acted as a magnet. Inside Serbia, passionate Slav nationalists plotted to break up the crumbling Austro-Hungarian Empire and weld the dissident Slav provinces into a single Greater South Slav Kingdom. Serbia lacked the military strength to wrest the provinces away by force, but Belgrade, the Serb capital, became a fountainhead of inflammatory Slav nationalist propaganda. Belgrade also became the headquarters of a secret terrorist organization called the Black Hand, designed to strike at Austria-Hungary by sabotage and murder.

In Vienna, the Imperial capital, the disruptive influence of Serbia was greatly feared. Field Marshal von Conrad-Hötzendorf, Chief of the Austrian General Staff, described Serbia as "a dangerous little viper." For years, Conrad-Hötzendorf had impatiently awaited orders to crush the Serb menace. But in 1914 the Emperor Franz Joseph was eighty-four. He had come to the throne in 1848; the years of his reign had been marked by tragedy. His brother Maximilian had become Emperor of Mexico and had been shot by a firing squad on a Mexican hillside. His only son, Crown Prince Rudolf, had died with his mistress in a love-pact suicide at Mayerling. His wife, Empress Elizabeth, had been struck down by an assassin's knife. His nephew and heir, Franz Ferdinand, had defied his will and married a commoner, Countess Sophie Chotek. Before settling the succession on Franz Ferdinand, the old Emperor forced the Archduke to renounce the throne for any children he should have by Sophie. On public occasions, Sophie, wife of the heir, was forced to walk behind the least important ladies of the royal blood and to sit at a distant end of the Imperial table. She found the humiliations unbearable; the Archduke made violent scenes with his family, but the Emperor refused to give way. His last hope was to die in peace with his Imperial dignity and his empire intact.

Busy soothing his wife, absent from the court, Franz Ferdinand knew nevertheless that the Emperor would not live forever. Politically, he understood that the policy of drift could not continue. His proposal was to appease the Slavs within the empire by bringing them into active participation within the government: he foresaw an eventual broadening of Austro-Hungarian "dualism" into a "trialism" which would include in the government Austrians, Magyars and Slavs. His solution was opposed by all concerned: by Austrian and Magyar ministers who did not wish to share their power, and by Slav nationalists who feared that the plan's success would destroy their own dreams of a South Slav kingdom. Yet Franz Ferdinand persisted. As a preliminary step, he decided that while he was watching Austrian army maneuvers in the Bosnian mountains, he would also pay a ceremonial visit to the provincial capital of Sarajevo. To expand this gesture of friendship, the Archduke brought his wife, the mother of his three disinherited children. In addition, he asked that the troops which normally lined the streets during an Imperial visit be dispensed with. Except for 150 local policemen, the crowds were to have free access to the Heir to the Throne.

Franz Ferdinand was dressed that day in the green uniform of an Austrian field marshal, with feathers waving from his military cap. As his six-car motorcade entered the town, he was in the open back seat of the second car with Sophie beside him. On the streets, he saw smiling faces and waving arms. Flags and bright-colored rugs hung as decorations, and from the windows of shops and houses his own portrait stared back at him. Franz Ferdinand was enormously pleased.

As the procession neared the city hall, the Archduke's chauffeur glimpsed an object hurled from the crowd. He pressed the accelerator, the car jumped forward and a bomb which would have landed in Sophie's lap bounced off the rear of the car and exploded under the wheels of the car behind. Two officers were wounded. The young Serb who had thrown the bomb ran across a bridge, but was apprehended by the police.

Franz Ferdinand, meanwhile, arrived at Sarajevo's city hall. He was pale, shaken and furious. "One comes here for a visit," he shouted, "and is welcomed by bombs!" There was a quick, urgent conference. One of the Archduke's suite asked if a military guard could be arranged. The provincial governor replied acidly, "Do you think Sarajevo is filled with assassins?" It was decided to go back through the city by a different route. On the way, however, the driver of the first car, forgetting the alteration, turned into one of the prearranged streets. The Archduke's chauffeur, following behind, was momentarily misled. He too started to turn. An official shouted, "Not that way, you fool!" The chauffeur braked, pausing to shift gears not five feet from the watching crowd. At that moment, a slim nineteen-year-old boy stepped forward, aimed a pistol into the car and fired twice. Sophie sank forward onto her husband's breast. Franz Ferdinand remained sitting upright, and for a minute no one noticed that he had been hit. Then the governor, sitting in front, heard him murmur, "Sophie! Sophie! Don't die! Stay alive for our children!" His body sagged and blood from a wound in his neck spurted across his green uniform. Sophie, the wife who could never become an empress, died first from a bullet in the abdomen. Fifteen minutes later, in a room next to the ballroom where waiters were preparing chilled champagne for his reception, the Archduke died. His last muttered words were "It is nothing."

The assassin, Gabriel Princip, was a native Bosnian of Serb extraction. On trial, the boy declared that he had acted to "kill an enemy of the South Slavs" and to "avenge the Serbian people." The Archduke, Princip explained to the court, was "an energetic man who as ruler would have carried through ideas and reforms which stood in our way." Years later, after Princip had died of tuberculosis in an Austrian prison, the truth came out: the plot had been laid in Belgrade, capital of Serbia, by the Serbian terrorist society known as the Black Hand. Its leader was none other than the chief of Serbian Army Intelligence.

The Austrian government reacted violently to Princip's act. The Heir to the Throne had been killed in a Slav province by a Serb. The time and the pretext had arrived to crush "the Serbian viper." Field Marshal von Conrad-Hötzendorf immediately declared that the assassination was "Serbia's declaration of war on Austria-Hungary." Count Berchtold, the Chancellor, who hitherto had opposed preventive war against Serbia, changed his mind and demanded that "the Monarchy with unflinching hand . . . tear asunder the threads which its foes are endeavoring to weave into a net above its head." The most candid appraisal of the situation came in a personal letter from the Emperor Franz Joseph to the Kaiser:

"The bloody deed was not the work of a single individual but a well organized plot whose threads extend to Belgrade. Although it may be impossible to establish the complicity of the Serbian government, no one can doubt that its policy of uniting all Southern Slavs under the Serbian flag encourages such crimes and that the continuation of this situation is a chronic peril for my house and my territories. Serbia," the Emperor concluded, "must be eliminated as a political factor in the Balkans."

Despite the excitement in Vienna, most Europeans refused to consider the Archduke's assassination a final act of doom. War, revolution, conspiracy and assassinations were the normal ingredients of Balkan politics. "Nothing to cause anxiety," said the Paris newspaper *Figaro*. "Terrible shock for the dear old Emperor," Britain's King George V wrote in his diary. The Kaiser received the news three hours later aboard his sailing yacht, *Meteor*, as he was setting out from Kiel to take part in a race. A motor launch sped toward the yacht and William leaned over the stern to hear the shouted news. "The cowardly detestable crime . . . has shaken me to the depths of my soul," he wired his Chancellor, Bethmann-Hollweg. But William did not think that the assassination meant war. What appalled him was the occurrence of that most monstrous of crimes, a regicide.

Three days before the events at Sarajevo, the Russian Imperial family sailed from Peterhof on their annual summer cruise along the Baltic coast. As they were boarding the *Standart*, Alexis, jumping for the ladder leading up to the deck of the yacht, caught his foot on a rung and twisted his ankle. Toward evening that day, he began to feel serious pain.

The following morning, the *Standart* was anchored in the heart of one of the Finnish fjords. Gilliard, making his way to Alexis's cabin, found both Dr. Botkin and the Empress with his pupil, who was suffering intensely. The hemorrhage into the ankle was continuing, the joint swollen and rigid. Alexis was weeping; every few minutes, as the throbbing pain mounted, he screamed. Alexandra's face was white. Gilliard went back to collect his books and then settled down to read to him as a distraction. Despite the illness, the cruise continued.

It was aboard the *Standart* that Nicholas and Alexandra learned what had happened at Sarajevo. Because neither he nor his ministers expected the assassination to lead to war, the Tsar did not return to his capital. On the day following the Archduke's death, other news, even more sensational for every Russian, arrived on the *Standart*. It passed quickly through the ship in excited whispers: an attempt had been made on Rasputin's life. None dared speak openly, but almost every person aboard hoped that the *starets* was finished. Alexandra, struggling with Alexis's illness, became frantic with worry. She prayed continually and telegraphed daily to Pokrovskoe.

What had happened was this: Rasputin, returning to his village on June 27, had been followed there without his knowledge by Khina Gusseva, Iliodor's agent. Gusseva caught the *starets* alone in a village street. She accosted him and, when he turned, drove Iliodor's knife deep into his stomach. "I have killed the Antichrist," she screamed hysterically and then attempted unsuccessfully to stab herself.

Rasputin was gravely hurt; the slash in his stomach had exposed his entrails. He was taken to a hospital in Tyumen, where a specialist sent by his friends in St. Petersburg performed an operation. For two weeks, his life was uncertain. Then, with the enormous physical strength which marked his life, he began to recover. He remained in bed for the rest of the summer and, accordingly, exercised no influence on the momentous events which were to come. Gusseva was placed on trial, declared insane and put into an asylum.

It was sheer coincidence that placed the two assassination attempts, the one at Sarajevo and the one at Pokrovskoe, so close together in time. Yet the coincidence alone is enough to provoke a tantalizing bit of speculation: Suppose the outcome of these two violent episodes had been reversed. Suppose the Hapsburg Prince, a well-meaning man, the heir and the hope of a crumbling dynasty, had lived, while the surging life and mischievous influence of the Siberian peasant had ended forever. How different the course of that long summer—and perhaps of our twentieth century—might have been.

On July 19, the *Standart* returned its passengers to Peterhof. Alexis, still suffering from a swollen ankle, was carried ashore. Nicholas and Alexandra plunged immediately into preparations for the state visit of the President of France, Raymond Poincaré, who was due in St. Petersburg the following day.

Raymond Poincaré was ten years old in 1870 when Prussian armies seized his native province of Lorraine, exiling him for most of his life from the place of his birth. Poincaré became a lawyer and then, successively, Foreign Minister, Premier and President of France. A short, dark-haired, robust man, he impressed all who met him. Sazonov, the Russian Foreign Minister, reported to the Tsar: "In him [Poincaré], Russia possesses a reliable and true friend endowed with a statesmanlike understanding that is exceptional and with an indomitable will." The German ambassador in Paris had much the same impression. "M. Poincaré differs from many of his countrymen by a deliberate avoidance of that smooth and fulsome tone characteristic of the Frenchman," he wrote. "His manner is measured, his words unadorned and carefully weighed. He makes the impression of a man with a lawyer's mind who expresses his conditions with stubborn emphasis and pursues his aims with a powerful will." Nicholas, who had met Poincaré once before, said simply, "I like him very much. He is a calm and clever man of small build."

Only a few weeks before Poincaré's arrival in Russia, he had been preceded to St. Petersburg by the new French Ambassador, Maurice Paléologue. A veteran career diplomat, Paléologue was also a brilliant writer whose talents later brought him membership in the French Academy. From the moment of his arrival in Russia, Paléologue began keeping a diary of people, events, conversations and impressions, providing an extraordinarily vivid account of Imperial Russia in the Great War.

Paléologue's diary began on July 20, 1914, the day that Poincaré arrived in Russia. The President was steaming up the Baltic aboard the battleship *France*; that morning the Tsar invited Paléologue to lunch with him aboard his yacht before the arrival of the *France*. "Nicholas II [was] in the uniform of an admiral," wrote Paléologue. "Luncheon was served immediately. We had at least an hour and three quarters before us until the arrival of the *France*. But the Tsar likes to linger over his meals. There are always long intervals between the courses in which he chats and smokes cigarettes. . . ." Paléologue mentioned the possibility of war. "The Tsar reflected a moment. 'I can't believe the Emperor [William II] wants war. . . . If you knew him as I do! If you knew how much theatricality there is in his posing!' Coffee had just arrived when the French squadron was signalled. The Tsar made me go up on the bridge with him. It was a magnificent spectacle. In a quivering silvery light, the *France* slowly surged forward over the turquoise and emerald waves, leaving a long white furrow behind her. Then she stopped majestically. The mighty warship which had brought the head of the French state is well worthy of her name. She was indeed France coming to Russia. I felt my heart beating. For a few minutes there was a prodigious din in the harbor; the guns and the shore batteries firing, the crews cheering, the *Marseillaise* answering the Russian national anthem, the cheers of thousands of spectators who had come from St. Petersburg on pleasure boats."

That night, at Peterhof, the Tsar welcomed his guest at a formal banquet. "I shall long remember the dazzling display of jewels on the women's shoulders," wrote Paléologue. "It was simply a fantastic shower of diamonds, pearls, rubies, sapphires, emeralds, topaz, beryls —a blaze of fire and flame. In this fiery milieu, Poincaré's black coat was a drab touch. But the wide, sky-blue ribbon of St. Andrew across his breast increased his importance in the eyes of the Russians. . . . During the dinner I kept an eye on the Tsaritsa Alexandra Fedorovna opposite whom I was sitting. She was a beautiful sight with her low brocade gown and a diamond tiara on her head. Her forty-two years have left her face and figure still pleasant to look at."

Two days later, Paléologue attended the review of sixty thousand troops at the army encampment at Krasnoe Selo. "A blazing sun lit up the vast plain," he wrote. "The elite of St. Petersburg society were crowded into some stands. The light toilettes of the women, their white hats and parasols made the stands look like azalea beds. Before long the Imperial party arrived. In a court horse *calèche* was the Tsaritsa with the President of the Republic on her right and her two elder daughters opposite her. The Tsar was galloping by the side of the carriage, followed by a brilliant escort of the grand dukes and aides de camp. . . . The troops, without arms, were drawn up in serried ranks as far as the eye could reach. . . .

"The sun was dropping towards the horizon in a sky of purple and gold," Paléologue continued. "On a sign from the Tsar an artillery salvo signalled evening prayer. The bands played a hymn. Everyone uncovered. A non-commissioned officer recited the *Pater* in a loud voice. All those men, thousands upon thousands, prayed for the Tsar and Holy Russia. The silence and composure of that multitude in that plain, the magic poetry of the hour . . . gave the ceremony a touching majesty."

The following night, the last of Poincaré's visit, the President entertained the Tsar and the Empress at dinner aboard the *France*. "It had indeed a kind of terrifying grandeur with the four gigantic 304 cm. guns raising their huge muzzles above the heads of the guests," wrote Paléologue. "The sky was soon clear again; a light breeze kissed the waves; the moon rose above the horizon. . . . I found myself alone with the Tsaritsa, who asked me to take a chair on her left. The poor lady seemed worn out. . . . Suddenly she put her hands to her ears. Then with a pained and pleading glance she timidly pointed to the ship's band quite near to us which had just started on a furious allegro with a full battery of brass and big drums.

"'Couldn't you?' . . . she murmured.

"I signalled sharply to the conductor. . . . The young Grand Duchess Olga had been observing us for some minutes with an anxious eye. She suddenly rose, glided towards her mother with graceful ease and whispered two or three words in her ear. Then addressing me, she continued, 'The Empress is rather tired, but she asks you to stay, Monsieur l'Ambassadeur, and to go on talking to her.' "

As the *France* prepared to leave, Nicholas invited Paléologue to remain aboard the Imperial yacht. "It was a splendid night," Paléologue wrote. "The Milky Way stretched, a pure band of silver, into unending space. Not a breath of wind. The *France* and her escorting division sped rapidly away to the west, leaving behind long ribbons of foam which glistened in the moonlight like silvery streams. . . . Admiral Nilov came to the Tsar for orders. The latter said to me, 'It's a wonderful night. Suppose we go for a sail.' " The Tsar told the Ambassador of the conversation he had just had with Poincaré. "He said, 'Notwithstanding appearances the Emperor William is too cautious to launch his country on some wild adventure and the Emperor Franz Joseph's only wish is to die in peace.' "

At 12:45 a.m., July 25, Paléologue said goodnight to the Tsar, and at half past two he reached his bed in St. Petersburg. At seven the next morning, he was awakened and informed that the previous evening, while he had been out for a sail, Austria had presented Serbia with an ultimatum.

The wording and the timing of the Austrian ultimatum had been carefully planned in Vienna. With the Emperor Franz Joseph's approval, the Austro-Hungarian Empire had decided to make war on Serbia. Conrad-Hötzendorf, the Chief-of-Staff, wanted to mobilize and attack Serbia immediately. But Count Berchtold, the Chancellor, took a subtler line. He persuaded his colleagues to send the Serbs an ultimatum so outrageous that Serbia would be forced to reject it.

The ultimatum declared the the Archduke Franz Ferdinand's murder had been plotted in Belgrade, that Serb officials had supplied the assassin's bomb and pistol, and that Serb frontier guards had arranged their secret entry into Bosnia. As satisfaction, Austria demanded that Austrian officers be allowed to enter Serbia to conduct their own investigation. In addition, the ultimatum demanded suppression of all Serb nationalist propaganda directed at the empire, dissolution of Serb nationalist societies and dismissal of all Serbian officers who were "anti-Austrian." Serbia was given forty-eight hours to answer.

The ultimatum was drafted and approved by Franz Joseph on July 19. Then it was deliberately withheld for four days during the visit of

President Poincaré to St. Petersburg so that the President and the Tsar would not be able to coordinate the response of France and Russia. Only at midnight on July 23, after Poincaré was at sea, headed down the Gulf of Finland, was the ultimatum delivered.

Every diplomat in Europe, reading the document, understood its implications. In Vienna, a government official, Count Hoyos, said flatly, "The Austrian demands are such that no state possessing the smallest amount of national pride or dignity could accept them." In London, the British Foreign Secretary, Sir Edward Grey, told the Austrian Ambassador that he had never before seen one state address to another so formidable a document. In St. Petersburg, the Russian Foreign Minister, Sazonov, said simply, "*C'est la guerre Européenne.*"

Upon receiving the ultimatum, Serbia immediately appealed to Russia, traditional protector of the Slavs. From Tsarskoe Selo, Nicholas telegraphed to the Serbian Crown Prince: "As long as there remains the faintest hope of avoiding bloodshed, all my efforts will tend in that direction. If we fail to attain this object, in spite of our sincere desire for peace, Your Royal Highness may rest assured that Russia will in no case remain indifferent to the fate of Serbia." A military council was convened at Krasnoe Selo on July 24, and on July 25 the Tsar summoned his ministers to Tsarskoe Selo.

To the men seated in Nicholas's study that summer day, the Austrian ultimatum to Serbia appeared aimed directly at Russia. Russia's classic role as protector of the Slavs and Nicholas II's personal guarantees of Serbian independence were part of the permanent fabric of European diplomacy; a threat to Serbia, therefore, could be interpreted only as a challenge to Russian power and influence in the Balkans. In the discussions that took place near St. Petersburg those hectic two days, both Sazonov and Grand Duke Nicholas, Inspector General of the Army, declared that Russia could not stand by and permit Serbia's humiliation without herself losing her rank as a great power.

The roots of this Russian dilemma in July 1914 went back seven years to another European diplomatic crisis, provoked in 1907 by Austria's sudden annexation of Bosnia. On that occasion, when Russia had been humiliated before the world, the fault lay primarily in the ornate secret diplomacy and personal character of the Russian Foreign Minister of the day, Alexander Izvolsky.

Izvolsky came to power at the end of the disastrous war with

Japan and promptly proceeded to liquidate what remained of Russia's Far Eastern adventure. From the moment he took office with Stolypin in 1906, Izvolsky concentrated on a historical Russian objective: the opening of the Dardenelles. Izvolsky himself was simply for grabbing both the Strait and the city of Constantinople from the decrepit Turkish Empire, but Stolypin absolutely prohibited any such provocative aggressive act, at least until Russian strength had grown. Then, said Stolypin, "Russia could speak as in the past."

Izvolsky did not give up his dream. Alert, able and ambitious, Alexander Izvolsky was the archetype of the Old World professional diplomat. A plumpish, dandified man, he wore a pearl pin in his white waistcoat, affected white spats, carried a lorgnette and always trailed a faint touch of violet *eau de cologne*. In his world of secret diplomatic intrigue, achievement of one objective might mean betrayal of another; Izvolsky took such arrangements easily in stride.

It was entirely in character, therefore, when Alexander Izvolsky secretly met his Austrian counterpart, Foreign Minister Freiherr von Aehrenthal, in 1907 and reached a private agreement from which both countries would benefit. In return for Austrian support of a Russian demand that Turkey open the Dardenelles to free passage by Russian warships, Izvolsky agreed to turn his back when Austria-Hungary annexed the Balkan provinces of Bosnia and Herzegovina. Both halves of this bargain were in violation of general European treaties signed by all the great powers. Recognizing this, the two statesmen agreed—or so Izvolsky afterward claimed—that the two moves should be made simultaneously, in order to present Europe with a *fait accompli*. No date was set for the moves. In Izvolsky's case, the bargain involved not only defiance of treaties but, infinitely worse, the betrayal of a small Slavic people. His willingness to go ahead indicated the importance he attached to opening the Strait.

Unfortunately for Izvolsky, before he was ready to betray the Bosnians, he himself was betrayed by Aehrenthal. Three weeks after the secret meeting, long before Izvolsky was ready to press Russia's demand on Turkey, the Emperor Franz Joseph suddenly proclaimed the annexation of Bosnia to Austria-Hungary. Caught red-handed, without a thing to show for his betrayal, Izvolsky hurried to London and Paris, attempting to get support for a belated Russian move on the Strait. He failed. Nicholas, informed of the bargain after it had been secretly struck, was furious. "Brazen impudence gets away with anything," he wrote to Marie. "The main culprit is Aehrenthal. He is simply a scoundrel. He made Izvolsky his dupe." Serbia mobilized and called on Russia for aid. Russian troops began to assemble on the Austrian frontier.

At this point, Germany intervened to save her Austrian ally. The intervention was performed in the bluntest possible manner; the Kaiser himself later described it as appearing in "shining armor" beside his ally. The German government asked Izvolsky whether he was prepared to back down. "We expect a precise answer, yes or no. Any vague, complicated or ambiguous reply will be regarded as a refusal." Izvolsky had no choice; Russia was unready for war. "If we are not attacked," Nicholas wrote Marie, "of course we are not going to fight." Later, he explained the situation to her more fully. "Germany," he wrote, "told us we could help solve the difficulty by agreeing to the annexation, while if we refused the consequences might be very serious and hard to foretell. Once the matter had been put as definitely and unequivocally as that, there was nothing for it but to swallow one's pride, give in, and agree. . . . But," added the Tsar, "German action towards us has simply been brutal and we won't forget it."

Russia's humiliation in the Bosnia crisis was spectacular. Sir Arthur Nicolson, then the British Ambassador to St. Petersburg, wrote, "In the recent history of Russia . . . there has never previously been a moment when the country has undergone such humiliation and, though Russia has had her troubles and trials both external and internal and has suffered defeats in the field, she has never, for apparently no valid reason, had to submit to the dictation of a foreign power."

It was in the depths of this humiliation that Russian statesmen, generals and the Tsar himself had formed their resolve never to withdraw again from a similar challenge. From 1909 onward, the commander of Kiev military district in the Ukraine had standing orders to be ready within forty-eight hours to repel an invasion from the West. Izvolsky left his post in St. Petersburg to become Russian Ambassador to France, where vengefully he worked night and day to strengthen the alliance. In 1914, when war came, Alexander Izvolsky boasted happily in Paris, "This is my war! My war!"

Nicholas recognized that the Austrian ultimatum to Serbia was the feared second challenge to Russia. For years, he had faced the fact that Russia could not back down again. But against this resolution he had balanced a hope that the challenge would not come until Russia was ready.

In 1911, Nicholas stressed this point in an interview with his new Ambassador to Bulgaria, Nekliudov. "The Tsar," Nekliudov later recalled, "after an intentional pause, stepping back and fixing me with a penetrating stare, said, 'Listen to me, Nekliudov, do not for one instant lose sight of the fact that we cannot go to war. I do not wish for war; as a rule I shall do all in my power to preserve for my people the benefits of peace. But at this moment of all moments everything that might lead to war must be avoided. It would be out of the question for us to face a war for five or six years—in fact until 1917—although if the most vital interests and the honor of Russia were at stake we might, if it were absolutely necessary, accept a challenge in 1915; but not a moment sooner in any circumstances or under any pretext whatsoever.' "

With Russia's unpreparedness in mind, the Tsar hoped desperately that this new crisis could be negotiated. He instructed Sazonov to play for time. Sazonov's first move, accordingly, was a plea that the limit on the Austrian ultimatum be extended beyond forty-eight hours. Vienna, determined to let nothing prevent its destruction of Serbia, refused. Next, Sazonov attempted to persuade Austria's ally Germany to mediate the Balkan quarrel. The German government refused, declaring that the matter was an issue solely between Austria and Serbia and that all other states, including Russia, should stand aside. Sazonov then asked Sir Edward Grey to mediate. Grey agreed, and proposed a conference of ambassadors in London. Sazanov hurriedly accepted Grey's proposal, but the German government refused. Finally, in reply to Serbia's appeals for aid, Sazonov advised the Serbian Premier, Pashich, to accept all the Austrian demands which did not actually compromise Serbian independence.

The Serbs, no less anxious to avoid a military showdown than their Russian patron, agreed, and replied to the Austrian ultimatum in extravagantly conciliatory terms. So humble was their reply, in fact, that it took Vienna entirely by surprise. Count Berchtold was aghast and didn't know what to do with the document. Accordingly, for two days, July 26 and July 27, he hid it. When the German Ambassador in Vienna asked to see it, he was told that he would have to wait because of the pile-up of paperwork in the Austrian Foreign Ministry.

By July 28, however, Berchtold and his colleagues had reached a decision. Austria, rejecting the Serb reply, issued a declaration of war. At 5 a.m. the following morning, July 29, Austro-Hungarian artillery began hurling shells across the Danube into Belgrade, the Serbian capital. The bombardment continued all day, in disregard of the white flags fluttering from Belgrade rooftops. In St. Petersburg, Tsar Nicholas gave the order to mobilize all Russian military districts along the Austrian frontier.

How fast and how far the war was to spread now depended on the reaction of Germany. Despite the urgent demands of the Russian General Staff for general mobilization, Nicholas had permitted only partial mobilization against Austria. The long frontier with Germany running through Poland and East Prussia still slumbered in peace. The Tsar believed, as he had said to Paléologue, that the Kaiser did not want war.

Predictably, the Kaiser's views had changed several times during the crisis. He first assumed that the cringing Slavs could be bullied into backing down before the shining Teutons. In October 1913, William had spoken of just such a situation to Count Berchtold, the Austrian Chancellor: "If His Majesty the Emperor Franz Joseph makes a demand, the Serbian government must obey," said William. "If not, Belgrade must be bombarded and occupied until his wish is fulfilled. And rest assured that I am behind you and ready to draw the sword wherever your action requires."

As he spoke, William rested his hand on the hilt of his ceremonial sword. Berchtold was suitably impressed. After Franz Ferdinand's assassination, the Kaiser's militancy appeared to increase. "Now or never," he scribbled on the margin of a telegram from Vienna. "It is time to settle accounts with the Serbs and the sooner the better." "We could reckon on Germany's full support," cabled Count Szogyeny, the Austrian Ambassador in Berlin, after a talk with the Kaiser. "His Majesty [the Kaiser] said . . . Austria must judge what is to be done to clear up her relations with Serbia. Whatever Austria's decision may turn out to be, Austria can count with certainty upon it that Germany will stand by her friend and ally." Having given his pledge, William cheerfully left for Kiel to board the *Hohenzollern* for a cruise through the Norwegian fjords.

Wreathed in his own bluster, the Kaiser miscalculated the reaction of each of Germany's three major antagonists. According to Sazonov's estimate: "The authorities in Berlin were not convinced that Russi

Nicholas II, painted by Serov

The Tsarevich Alexis

mpress Alexandra

Nicholas's family: (LEFT TO RIGHT) *Michael, Empress Marie, Nicholas, Xenia, Georg*
Seated: *Tsar Alexander III holding Olga*

Mathilde Kschessinska

The Grand Tour: Nicholas, a Maharajah, Prince George of Greece

Alix at seventeen before her first ball.

Mrs. Orchard, Alix (seated), *Grand Duchess Elizabeth*

Nicholas II and the Prince of Wales, later King George V, at Cowes, 1909

Alexandra and her daughters arriving aboard the Imperial yacht Standart

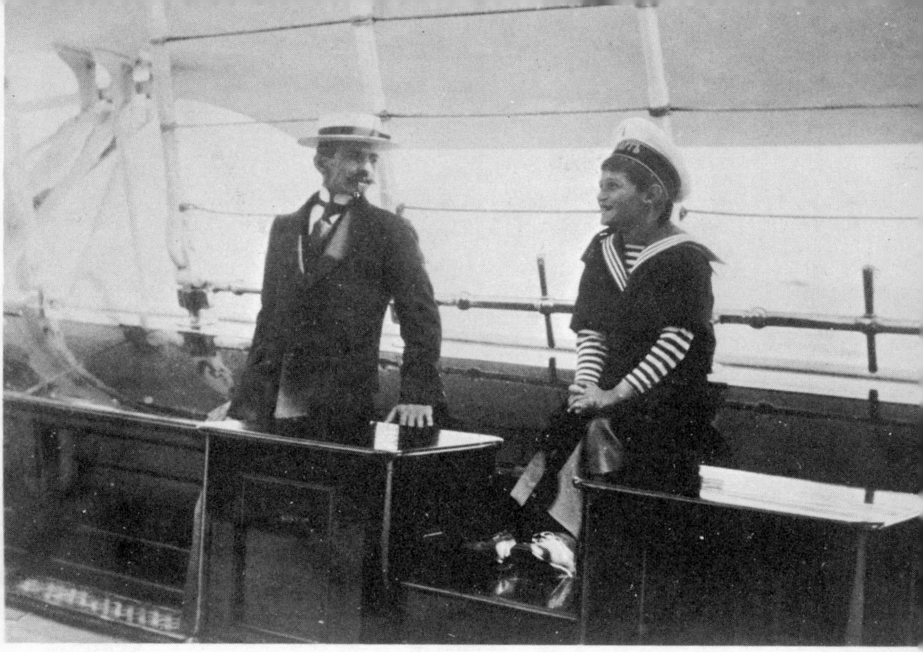

Pierre Gilliard and Alexis

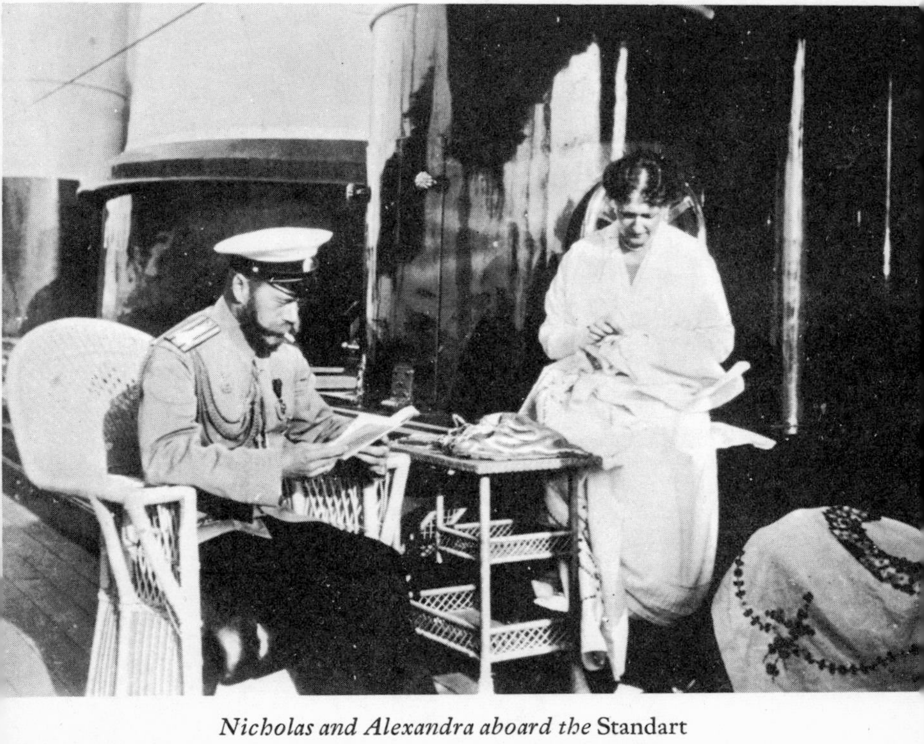

Nicholas and Alexandra aboard the Standart

The Empress

The Tsar

Facing: ABOVE, *Picnicking on the coast of Finland: Alexandra, Anna Vyrubova, and Olga, the Empress's eldest daughter;* BELOW, *Derevenko and Alexis*

Nicholas with his officers

Nicholas with Alexis, just before setting out on an all-day march to test the Russian private soldier's uniform and equipment

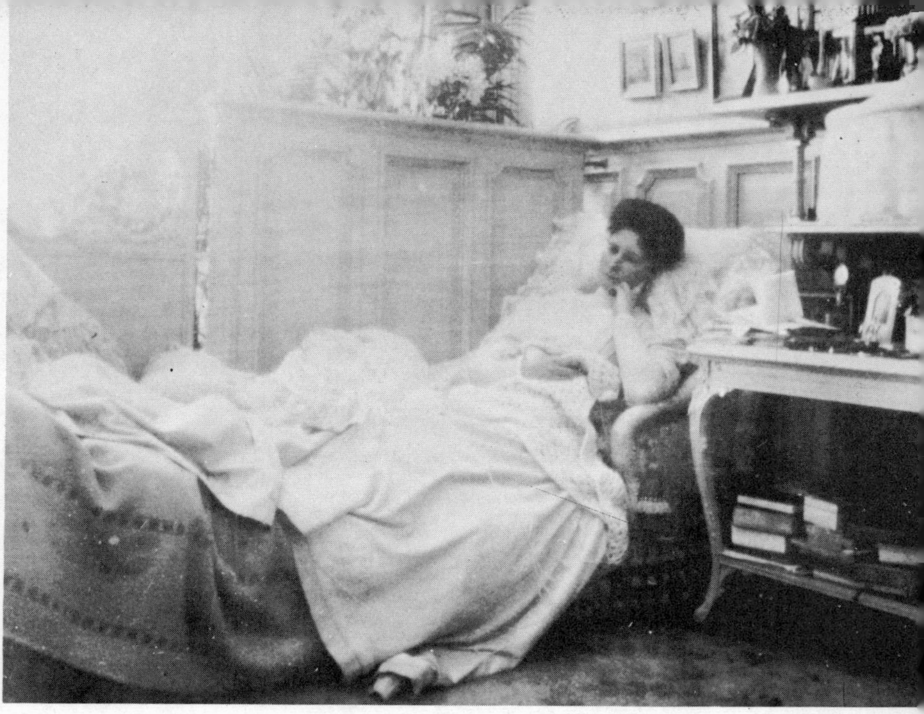

Alexandra in her mauve boudoir

With Alexis

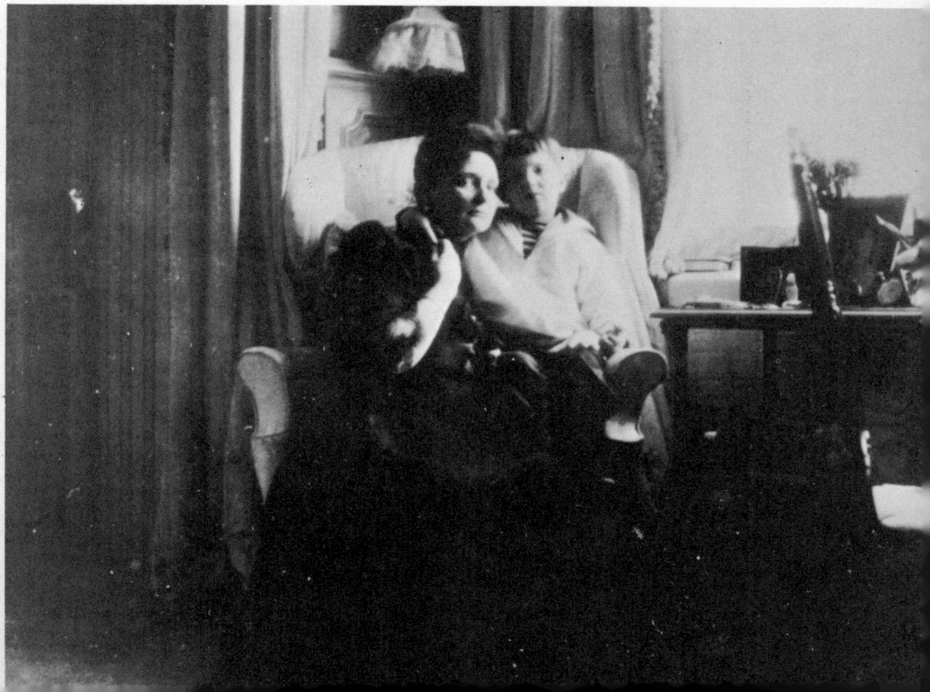

Nagorny pulling Alexis (third from left) and his friends

Derevenko and Alexis (third from right)

Livadia: Pierre Gilliard with Olga and Tatiana

At Spala: Alexandra

After Spala: Alexis.
The Tsarevich's left leg is bent and a metal brace is attached to his shoe

Facing: *Gregory Rasputin*

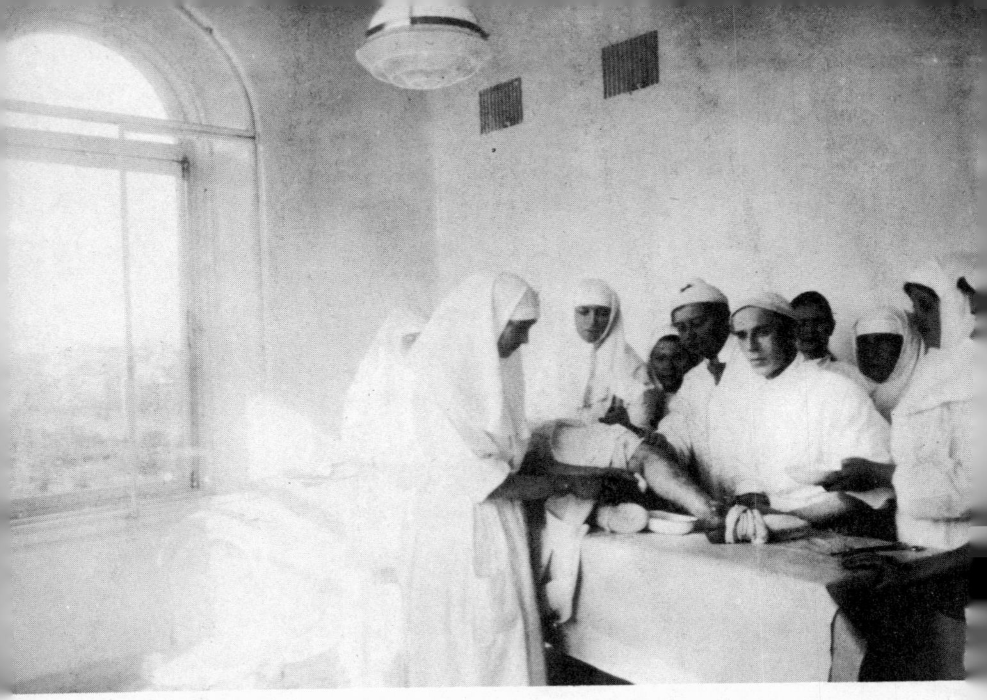

In a hospital: (from left) *Olga* (partly hidden), *Tatiana* (foreground), *Alexandra*

Nicholas and Alexis inspecting a Cossack regiment during the war

The Tsar with Grand Duke Nicholas

Facing: *Anastasia* *Marie, Tatiana, and Olga* (seated)

Nicholas, Alexis, and Tatiana, 1916

The Empress

Imprisoned at Tsarskoe Selo, 1917

would care to risk a war in order to preserve her position in the Balkans. . . . In any case, they scarcely believed her capable of carrying on a war. Nor did they entertain a very high opinion of France as a military power. As for the possibility of England siding with their enemies, no one in Germany ever thought of it; the warnings of the German Ambassador in London, Prince Lichnowsky, were derided, and he was indulgently referred to as 'good old Lichnowsky' at the Berlin Foreign Office."

The wisdom of presenting Austria-Hungary with exactly this kind of *carte blanche* to determine the fate of Germany had often been questioned in Berlin. As late as May 1914, the German Ambassador to Vienna wrote to Berlin wondering "whether it really pays to bind ourselves so tightly to this phantasm of a state which is cracking in every direction." The dominant view in Berlin, however, was expressed in a résumé from the German Foreign Ministry to the German Embassy in London summarizing the factors determining German policy:

"Austria is now going to come to a reckoning with Serbia. . . . We have not at the present time forced Austria to her decision. But neither should we attempt to stay her hand. If we should do that, Austria would have the right to reproach us with having deprived her of her last chance of political rehabilitation. And then the process of her wasting away and of her internal decay would be still further accelerated. Her standing in the Balkans would be gone forever. . . . The maintenance of Austria, and in fact of the most powerful Austria possible is a necessity for us. . . . That she cannot be maintained forever I willingly admit. But in the meanwhile we may be able to arrange other combinations."

The Kaiser's endorsement of this position was significantly reinforced by the reports he was getting from his elderly Ambassador in St. Petersburg, Count Pourtalès. Pourtalès, the dean of the St. Petersburg diplomatic corps, had spent seven years in his post. He was enormously fond of Russia. But he knew that, in July 1914, a million and a half Russian workers were out on strike; he had seen with his own eyes the barricades erected in the streets of the capital. Citing these factors, he repeatedly assured his sovereign that Russia could not go to war. On July 28, Pourtalès lunched at the British Embassy with his British colleague, Sir George Buchanan. Over cigars, Pourtalès expressed his views on Russia's weakness, declaring that he was regularly forwarding these views to Berlin. Appalled, Buchanan grasped his guest by the shoulders and said, "Count Pourtalès, Russia means it." Nevertheless, as late as July 31, the Kaiser was speaking confidently of the "mood of a sick Tom-cat" which, his Ambassador had assured him, infected the Russian court and army.

To the end, William expected to bluff his way. On July 28, back from his cruise, he saw the abject Serb reply to Austria's ultimatum. His expectations seemed brilliantly confirmed. "A capitulation of the most humiliating character," he exulted. "Now that Serbia has given in, all grounds for war have disappeared." When, that same night, Austria declared war on Serbia, William was astonished and frustrated. Nevertheless, the war was still only an affair in the Balkans. Unless Russia moved, Germany need not become involved. With this in mind, William personally telegraphed the Tsar:

> It is with the gravest concern that I hear of the impression which the action of Austria against Serbia is creating in your country. The unscrupulous agitation that has been going on in Serbia for years has resulted in the outrageous crime to which Archduke Franz Ferdinand fell victim. You will doubtless agree with me that we both, you and I, have a common interest, as well as all Sovereigns, to insist that all the persons morally responsible for this dastardly murder should receive their deserved punishment. In this, politics play no part at all.
>
> On the other hand, I fully understand how difficult it is for you and your government to face the drift of public opinion. Therefore, with regard to the hearty and tender friendship which binds us both from long ago with firm ties, I am exerting my utmost influence to induce the Austrians to deal straightly to arrive at a satisfactory understanding with you. I confidently hope you will help me in my efforts to smooth over difficulties that may still arise. Your very sincere and devoted friend and cousin.
>
> Willy

The Kaiser's telegram crossed a message to him from the Tsar:

> Am glad you are back. In this most serious moment I appeal to you to help me. An ignoble war has been declared on a weak country. The indignation in Russia, shared fully by me, is enormous. I foresee that very soon I shall be overwhelmed by pressure brought upon me, and forced to take extreme measures which will lead to war. To try and avoid such a calamity as a European war, I

beg you in the name of our old friendship to do what you can to stop your allies from going too far.

Nicky

The "pressure" on Nicholas to which he referred in his telegram came from the Russian General Staff, which was insisting on full mobilization. Sazonov, once he had heard that the Austrians were firing on Belgrade, had abandoned his protests and endorsed the generals' request.

On the 29th, William replied to the Tsar's telegram:

It would be quite possible for Russia to remain a spectator of the Austro-Serbian conflict, without involving Europe in the most horrible war she ever witnessed. I think a direct understanding between your government and Vienna possible and desirable and as I already telegraphed you, my government is continuing its exertions to promote it. Of course, military measures on the part of Russia which would be looked upon by Austria as threatening, would precipitate a calamity we both wish to avoid, and jeopardize my position as mediator which I readily accepted on your appeal to my friendship and help.

Willy

Nicholas replied, suggesting that the dispute be sent to the Hague.

I thank you for your conciliatory and friendly telegram, whereas the communications of your Ambassador to my Minister today have been in a very different tone. Please clear up this difference. The Austro-Serbian problem must be submitted to the Hague Conference. I trust to your wisdom and friendship.

Nicholas

On the morning of the 30th, Nicholas wired the Kaiser an explanation of Russia's partial mobilization:

The military measures which have now come into force were decided five days ago for reasons of defense on account of Austria's preparations. I hope with all my heart that these measures won't interfere with your part as mediator which I greatly value. We need your strong pressure on Austria to come to an understanding with us.

Nicky

The Tsar's telegram announcing that Russia had mobilized against

Austria put the Kaiser into a rage. "And these measures are for defense against Austria which is no way attacking him!!! I cannot agree to any more mediation since the Tsar who requested it has at the same time secretly mobilized behind my back." After reading Nicholas's plea; "We need your strong pressure on Austria . . . ," William scribbled: "No, there is no thought of anything of that sort!!!"

On the afternoon of July 30, Sazonov telephoned Tsarskoe Selo to ask for an immediate interview. Nicholas came to the telephone and, suspecting the purpose, reluctantly asked his Foreign Minister to come to the palace at three p.m. When the two men met, Sazonov sadly told his sovereign, "I don't think Your Majesty can postpone the order for general mobilization." He added that, in his opinion, general war was unavoidable. Nicholas, pale and speaking in a choked voice, replied, "Think of the responsibility you are advising me to take. Remember, it would mean sending hundreds of thousands of Russian people to their deaths." Sazonov pointed out that everything had been done to avoid war. Germany and Austria, he declared, were "determined to increase their power by enslaving our natural allies in the Balkans, destroying our influence there, and reducing Russia to a pitiful dependence on the arbitrary will of the Central Powers." "The Tsar," Sazonov wrote later, "remained silent and his face showed the traces of a terrible inner struggle. At last, speaking with difficulty, he said, 'You are right. There is nothing left for us to do but get ready for an attack upon us. Give . . . my order for [general] mobilization.' "

Before news of Russia's general mobilization reached Berlin, two more telegrams passed between Potsdam and Tsarskoe Selo. First, Nicholas cabled to the Kaiser:

> It is technically impossible for me to suspend my military preparations. But as long as conversations with Austria are not broken off, my troops will refrain from taking the offensive anyway, I give you my word of honor on that.
>
> Nicky

William replied:

> I have gone to the utmost limits of the possible in my efforts to save peace. It is not I who will bear the responsibility for the terrible disaster which now threatens the civilized world. You and you alone can still avert it. My friendship for you and your empire which my grandfather bequeathed to me on his deathbed is still

sacred to me and I have been loyal to Russia when she was in trouble, notably during your last war. Even now, you can still save the peace of Europe by stopping your military measures.

Willy

News of the general mobilization of the huge Russian army caused consternation in Berlin. At midnight on July 31, Count Pourtalès appeared in Sazonov's office with a German ultimatum to Russia to halt her mobilization within twelve hours. At noon the following day, August 1, Russia had not replied, and the Kaiser ordered general mobilization.

Nicholas hurriedly telegraphed to William:

> I understand that you are compelled to mobilize but I should like to have the same guarantee from you that I gave you myself —that these measures do not mean war and that we shall continue to negotiate to save the general peace so dear to our hearts. With God's help our long and tried friendship should be able to prevent bloodshed. I confidently await your reply.
>
> Nicky

Before this message arrived in Berlin, however, coded instructions had been sent by the German government to Count Pourtalès in St. Petersburg. He was instructed to declare war on Russia at five p.m. The Count was tardy and it was not until 7:10 p.m. that he appeared ashen-faced before Sazonov. Three times Pourtalès asked if Sazonov could not assure him that Russia would cancel its mobilization; three times Sazonov refused. "In that case, sir," said Pourtalès, "my government charges me to hand you this note. His Majesty the Emperor, my august sovereign, in the name of the empire accepts the challenge and considers himself in a state of war with Russia." Pourtalès was overcome with emotion. He leaned against a window and wept openly. "Who could have thought I should be leaving St. Petersburg under such circumstances," he said. Sazonov rose from his desk, embraced the elderly Count and helped him from the room.

At Peterhof, the Tsar and his family had just come from evening prayer. Before going to dinner, Nicholas went to his study to read the latest dispatches. The Empress and her daughters went straight to the dinner table to await the Tsar. Nicholas was in his study when Count

Fredericks brought him the message from Sazonov that Germany had declared war. Shaken but calm, the Tsar instructed his ministers to come to the palace at nine p.m.

Meanwhile, Alexandra and the girls waited with growing uneasiness. The Empress had just asked Tatiana to go and bring her father to the table when Nicholas appeared in the doorway. In a tense voice he told them what had happened. Alexandra began to weep. The girls, badly frightened, followed their mother's example. Nicholas did what he could to calm them and then withdrew, without dinner. At nine p.m., Sazonov, Goremykin and other ministers arrived at the palace along with the French and British Ambassadors, Paléologue and Buchanan.

Four months later, in another conversation with Paléologue, Nicholas revealed how the day had ended for him. Late that night, after war had been declared, he had received another telegram from the Kaiser. It read:

> An immediate, clear and unmistakable reply of your government [to the German ultimatum] is the sole way to avoid endless misery. Until I receive this reply, I am unable to my great grief to enter upon the subject of your telegram. I must ask most earnestly that you, without delay, order your troops under no circumstances to commit the slightest violation of our frontiers.

Almost certainly this message had been intended for delivery before the declaration of war and had been caught in the crowded bureaucratic pipeline. Yet it was composed during the same hours that his country was declaring war, an indication of the Kaiser's state of mind. To Nicholas, this last message he ever received from the German Emperor seemed a final revelation of William's character.

"He was never sincere; not a moment," Nicholas told Paléologue, speaking of the Kaiser. "In the end he was hopelessly entangled in the net of his own perfidy and lies. . . . It was half past one in the morning of August 2. . . . I went to the Empress's room, as she was already in bed, to have a cup of tea with her before retiring myself. I stayed with her until two in the morning. Then I wanted to have a bath as I was very tired. I was just getting in when my servant knocked at the door saying he had 'a very important telegram . . . from His Majesty the Emperor William.' I read the telegram, read it again, and then repeated it aloud, but I couldn't understand a word. What on earth does William mean, I thought, pretending that it still depends on me whether war is averted or not? He implores me not to let my troops cross the frontier! Have I suddenly gone mad? Didn't the Minister of the Court, my trusted Fredericks, at least six hours ago bring me the declaration of war the German ambassador had just handed to Sazonov? I returned to the Empress's room and read her William's telegram. . . . She said immediately: 'You're not going to answer it, are you?' 'Certainly not!'

"There is no doubt that the object of this strange and farcical telegram was to shake my resolution, disconcert me and inspire me to some absurd and dishonorable step. It produced the opposite effect. As I left the Empress's room I felt that all was over forever between me and William. I slept extremely well. When I woke at my usual hour, I felt as if a weight had fallen from my mind. My responsibility to God and my people was still enormous, but at least I knew what I had to do."

PART THREE

CHAPTER TWENTY

For the Defense of Holy Russia

THE next afternoon, August 2, 1914, the Tsar issued a formal proclamation of hostilities at the Winter Palace. It was a blazing-hot midsummer day. The palace square, one of the largest in Europe, was packed with thousands of sweltering, excited people carrying banners, flags and icons and waiting impatiently for the moment when they could pour out their emotion in the presence of the sovereign himself. On the Neva side, where the Tsar would arrive by boat from Peterhof, crowds of people swarmed along the bridges and quays, singing and cheering. The river itself was teeming with yachts, steamers, sailboats, fishing smacks and rowboats, all streaming flags and crowded with spectators.

When Nicholas and Alexandra stepped onto the quay at the Palace Bridge, wave on wave of cheers rolled over them: "*Batiushka, Batiushka*, lead us to victory!" Nicholas wore the plain uniform of an infantry regiment. Alexandra, in a pure white dress, had turned up the brim of her picture hat so that the crowds could see her face. The four young Grand Duchesses walked behind, but the Tsarevich, still unable to walk because of his injury on the *Standart*, remained at Peterhof, weeping in disappointment.

Inside the palace, the Tsar and the Empress slowly made their way through the crush of people lining the grand staircases and wide corridors. As Nicholas passed, bowing and nodding, men and women dropped to their knees and frantically tried to kiss his hand. The service was held in the great white marble Salle de Nicholas, where five thousand people had jammed themselves beneath the glittering chandeliers. An altar had been erected in the center of the hall, and on it stood the miraculous icon, the Vladimir Mother of God. The icon, brought to Moscow in 1395, was said to have turned back Tamerlane. Before the icon in 1812 the grizzled General Kutuzov had prayed as he was leaving to take command of Tsar Alexander I's armies in the war against Napoleon. Now, at the beginning of a new war, Nicholas II invoked the icon's blessing. Raising his right hand, he pronounced in a low voice the oath taken by Alexander I in 1812: "I solemnly swear that I will never make peace so long as a single enemy remains on Russian soil."

After taking the oath, Nicholas and Alexandra went to meet the expectant masses waiting outside. When the two small figures appeared alone on a red-draped balcony high above them, the great crowd knelt. Nicholas raised his hand and tried to speak; the front rows hushed, but at the rear the excitement and commotion were too great and his words were drowned. Overwhelmed, Nicholas bowed his head. Seeing him, the crowd spontaneously began to sing the Imperial anthem whose chords make up the final crescendo of Tchaikovsky's "1812 Overture":

God save the Tsar,
Mighty and powerful,
Let him reign for our glory,
For the confusion of our enemies,
The Orthodox Tsar,
God save the Tsar.

Hand in hand, the man in the khaki uniform and the woman in the white dress stood on the balcony and wept with the crowd. "To those thousands on their knees," declared Paléologue, "at that moment the Tsar was really the Autocrat, the military, political and religious director of his people, the absolute master of their bodies and souls."

It was the same throughout the empire: wild excitement, crowds filling the streets, laughing, weeping, singing, cheering, kissing. Overnight, a wave of patriotism swept over Russia. In Moscow, Kiev, Odessa, Kharkov, Kazan, Tula, Rostov, Tiflis, Tomsk and Irkutsk, workmen exchanged their red flags of revolution for the icons of Holy Russia and portraits of the Tsar. Students rushed from the universities to enlist. Army officers, caught in the street, were happily tossed in the air.

In St. Petersburg, every day brought new demonstrations in favor of the Tsar and Russia's allies. From his window in the French Embassy, Paléologue looked down on huge processions carrying flags and icons, shouting "*Vive la France!*" On August 5, as the German armies crossed the frontiers of neutral Belgium, a telegram from London to Sir George Buchanan, the British Ambassador, announced that England had entered the war. The same day, the Union Jack was hoisted into line with the Tricolor and the Russian Imperial banner. With a fine Gallic sense of detail, Paléologue noted that "the flags of the three nations blend eloquently. Composed of the same colors, blue, white and red, they are a picturesque and striking expression of the coalition."

At the German Embassy, an immense granite building surmounted on the roof by two huge bronze horses, the violent mob predicted by Count Pourtalès made a sudden vengeful appearance. Their rage was directed not at their own government, as Pourtalès had promised, but at his. Invading the building, they smashed windows, ripped tapestries and pictures and hurled into the street not only the Embassy furniture, china and glassware, but the Count's own priceless collection of Renaissance marbles and brasses. Ropes were coiled around the equestrian statues on the roof, hundreds of hands pulled and tugged, and with a crash the Kaiser's prancing horses toppled into the street.

In those early days, patriotism was closely tied to a deep-rooted fear of the Germans. "For Faith, Tsar and Country!" and "For the defense of Holy Russia!" were the calls that stirred the barracks, factories and villages. "The war with Japan," wrote Kerensky, was "dynastic and colonial," but "in 1914 the people immediately recognized the conflict with Germany as its own war . . . a war which meant that the destinies of Russia were at stake." Rodzianko, walking in the streets of Petersburg, mingled with workers who a few days earlier had been chopping down telegraph poles, overturning streetcars and building barricades. "Now all Russia is involved," they told him. "We want to rally to our Tsar to make certain of victory over the Germans." Nobility and peasants burned with the same emotions. "This is not a political war," said Grand Duchess Marie Pavlovna, widow of the Tsar's uncle Vladimir. "It is a duel to the death between Slavism and Germanism. One of the two must succumb." An old peasant from Novgorod told Kokovtsov, the former Prime Minister, "If we are unlucky enough not to destroy the Germans, they'll come here. They'll reign over the whole of Russia and then they'll harness you and me—yes, you as well as me—to their plows."

The Duma sat only one day, August 8, passing the government's military budget without a dissenting vote. "War was declared and all at once, not a trace was left of the revolutionary movement," declared Kerensky. "Even the Bolshevik members of the Duma were forced to admit—though somewhat sullenly—that it was the duty of the proletariat to cooperate in the defense."

That Germany would be defeated, few Russians doubted; Britain's entry made the outcome certain. There was controversy as to how long the war would go on. "Six months," said the pessimists, who argued that the Germans might fight. "The Germans don't know how to fight," replied the optimists. "They only know how to make sausages. All the Russians will have to do to annihilate the whole German army is simply to throw their caps at them."

Ancient tradition prescribed that Russian tsars begin their wars by going to Moscow to ask the blessing of God in the historic seat of tsarist rule, the Kremlin. If anything, when Nicholas and his family arrived in Moscow on August 17, the city was more wildly enthusiastic than St. Petersburg. A million people lined the streets, jammed balconies, windows and rooftops or clung from the branches of trees as the Imperial procession wound through the streets to the Kremlin's Iberian Gate. That night, inside the Kremlin, a private worry reappeared. "Alexis Nicolaievich is complaining a good deal of his leg tonight," Pierre Gilliard wrote in his diary. "Will he be able to walk tomorrow or will he have to be carried? The Tsar and Tsaritsa are in despair. The boy was not able to be present at the ceremony in the Winter Palace. It is always the same when he is supposed to appear in public . . . some complication will prevent it. Fate seems to pursue him."

On the following day, Gilliard continued: "When Alexis Nicolaievich found he could not walk this morning, he was in a terrible state. Their Majesties have decided he shall be present at the ceremony all the same. He will be carried by one of the Tsar's Cossacks. But it is a dreadful disappointment to the parents who do not wish the idea to gain ground among the people that the Heir to the Throne is an invalid."

At eleven, the Tsar, the Empress, their four daughters, the Tsarevich, in the arms of a huge Cossack, and Grand Duchess Elizabeth, wearing the gray robe of her religious order, appeared in the St.

George Hall of the Kremlin. In the center of the hall, Nicholas proclaimed to the nobility and people of Moscow: "From this place, the very heart of Russia, I send my soul's greeting to my valiant troops and my noble allies. God is with us!" Moving into the Ouspensky Sobor—the Cathedral of the Assumption—where eighteen years earlier they had been crowned, the Tsar and the Empress prayed before the lofty, jeweled iconostasis. In the flickering glow of hundreds of candles, through pungent clouds of sweet incense, they walked around the church to kneel and pray before the tombs of Russia's patriarchs. The triumphant setting and the glorious display of pomp and piety seemed an eloquent dramatization of the basic principle of the Russian autocracy: "As it is God Himself who has given us our supreme power, it is before His altar that we are responsible for the destinies of Russia."

The following morning, while Moscow still seethed with excitement, Gilliard and his young pupil slipped quietly out of the Kremlin for a drive into the hills outside the city. Returning through narrow streets clogged with workmen and peasants, their unescorted automobile was slowed and halted by the mass. Surging on all sides of the auto, the crowd suddenly recognized its young passenger. "The Heir! The Heir!" they shouted, struggling for a better view. As those nearest the car were crushed against its sides, the bolder of them thrust their arms inside and touched Alexis. "I've touched him! I've touched the Heir!" shouted a woman in triumph. Frightened and pale, the Tsarevich huddled back in the seat while Gilliard frantically tried to get the car moving. Eventually the auto was rescued by two large Moscow policemen who happened on the scene and moved the crowd back with much puffing and shouting.

When the Imperial family returned to Tsarskoe Selo on August 22, Nicholas was exhilarated. The two largest cities of his empire had given spontaneous, overwhelming demonstrations of affection and patriotism. Determined to be worthy, Nicholas issued a decree intended to expunge every blemish from the holy crusade on which Russia was embarking. Throughout the empire, the sale of vodka was banned for the duration of the war. The gesture, coming at a moment when military expenditures were soaring, was more noble than wise, for the sale of vodka was a state monopoly from which the Imperial government drew a substantial proportion of its revenue. Nor did the ban stop drinking in Russia; the rich drew from their well-stocked cellars, the poor made alcohol at home. In a second burst of enthusiastic patriotism, after returning from Moscow, Nicholas suddenly changed the name of his own capital. On August 31, 1914, the German St. Petersburg was changed to the Slav Petrograd.

In the opening days of the war, the same heady emotions surged through Paris, London and Berlin. But after the trumpets had sounded, the hymns had been sung and the men had marched away, then war began its stern testing of the nations. In the terrible years ahead, Britain, France and Germany each called up deep reserves of national purpose and strength. But in Russia, behind the massive façade of an enormous empire, the apparatus of government, the structure of society and economy were too primitive, too inflexible, and too brittle to withstand the enormous strains of a great four-year war.

Two shrewd and cunning Russians sensed this danger immediately. From the beginning, although their voices were drowned in the gush of war excitement, Rasputin and Witte opposed the war. Still close to the villages, Rasputin sensed what war would cost in peasant blood. Once before, in 1908, he had argued against fighting Austria over the annexation of Bosnia: "The Balkans are not worth fighting for," he had said. In 1914, still lying in bed in Siberia recovering from his stab wounds, he telegraphed, "Let Papa not plan war, for with the war will come the end of Russia and yourselves and you will lose to the last man." Anna Vyrubova, who delivered the telegram to the Tsar, reported that he angrily tore it to pieces before her eyes. Rasputin was undeterred. Taking a large piece of paper, writing in almost illegible letters, he scrawled this ominous prophecy:

> Dear friend, I will say again a menacing cloud is over Russia lots of sorrow and grief it is dark and there is no lightening to be seen. A sea of tears immeasurable and as to blood? What can I say? There are no words the horror of it is indescribable. I know they keep wanting war from you evidently not knowing that this is destruction. Heavy is God's punishment when he takes away reason that is the beginning of the end. Thou art the Tsar Father of the People don't allow the madmen to triumph and destroy themselves and the People. Well, they will conquer Germany and what about Russia? If one thinks then verily there has not been a greater sufferer since the beginning of time she is all drowned in blood. Terrible is the destruction and without end the grief.
>
> Gregory

Witte, abroad when the war broke out, hurried home to urge that

Russia withdraw immediately. He spoke bluntly to Paléologue: "This war is madness. . . . Why should Russia fight? Our prestige in the Balkans, our pious duty to help our blood brothers? . . . That is a romantic, old-fashioned chimera. No one here, no thinking man at least, cares a fig for these turbulent and vain Balkan folk who have nothing Slav about them and are only Turks christened by the wrong name. We ought to have let the Serbs suffer the chastisement they deserved. So much for the origin of the war. Now let's talk about the profits and rewards it will bring us. What can we hope to get? An increase of territory. Great Heavens! Isn't His Majesty's empire big enough already? Haven't we in Siberia, Turkestan, the Caucasus, Russia itself, enormous areas which have not yet been opened up? Then what are the conquests they dangle before our eyes? East Prussia? Hasn't the Emperor too many Germans among his subjects already? Galicia? It's full of Jews! . . . Constantinople, the Cross on Santa Sophia, the Bosporous, the Dardanelles. It's too mad a notion to be worth a moment's consideration. And even if we assume a complete victory, the Hohenzollerns and Hapsburgs reduced to begging for peace and submitting to our terms—it means not only the end of German domination, but the proclamation of republics throughout central Europe. That means the simultaneous end of Tsarism. I prefer to remain silent as to what we may expect on the hypothesis of our defeat. . . . My practical conclusion is that we must liquidate this stupid adventure as soon as possible."

Paléologue, whose job it was to do everything possible to keep Russia in the war fighting on France's side, watched Witte go and mused on the old stateman's character: "an enigmatic, unnerving individual, a great intellect, despotic, disdainful, conscious of his powers, a prey to ambition, jealousy, and pride." Witte's views, he reflected, were "evil" and "dangerous" to France as well as to Russia.

Nowhere was Nicholas's optimism more keenly shared than among the officers of the Russian army. Those unlucky enough to be stationed with regiments far from the frontier were frantic with worry lest it all be over before they had a chance to see action. Guards officers, fortunate enough to be leaving immediately for the front, asked whether they should pack their dress uniforms for the ceremonial parade down the Unter den Linden. They were advised to go ahead and let their braid and plumes follow by the next courier.

Day after day, the capital trembled to the cadence of marching men. From dawn until nightfall, infantry regiments marched down the Nevsky Prospect, bound for the Warsaw Station and the front. Outside the city, other regiments of infantry, cavalry squadrons and batteries of horse artillery clogged the roads leading toward the Baltic provinces and East Prussia. In motion with only casual organization, the soldiers walked rather than marched, followed in no particular order by long columns of baggage carts, ammunition wagons, ambulances, field kitchens and remount horses. So dense were the moving columns that in places they left the roads and spread out across the dry summer fields, swarming in a jumbled confusion of dust, shouts, horses' hoofs and rumbling wheels, recalling the Tartar hordes of the thirteenth century.

Paléologue, driving back to the capital from an audience with the Tsar, encountered one of these regiments marching along a road. The general, recognizing the Ambassador, saluted and boomed out, "We'll destroy those filthy Prussians! No more Prussia! No more Germany! William to St. Helena!" As each company paraded past Paléologue's car, the general rose in his stirrups and bellowed, "The French Ambassador! Hurrah!" The soldiers cheered frantically, "Hurrah! Hurrah!" Finally, the general galloped away, shouting over his shoulder, "William to St. Helena! William to St. Helena!"

Sometimes, women with children followed for the first few miles: "One . . . was very young . . . and she was pressing a baby to her breast. She was striding out as well as she could to keep pace with the man at the rear of the file, a fine fellow, tanned and muscular. They did not exchange a word, but gazed fixedly at each other with loving, haggard eyes. Three times in succession, I saw the young mother offer the baby to the soldier for a kiss."

The same scenes were repeated in railway stations in every town and village in Russia. In Moscow, British Consul R. H. Bruce Lockhart remembered: "the troops grey with dust and closely packed in cattle trucks; the vast crowd on the platform to wish them Godspeed; grave, bearded fathers, wives and mothers, smiling bravely through their tears . . . ; fat priests to bless the happy warriors. The crowd sways forward for a last handshake and last embrace. There is a shrill whistle from the engine. Then, with many false starts, the overloaded train, as though reluctant to depart, crawls slowly out of the station and disappears in the grey twilight of the Moscow night. Silent and bareheaded, the crowd remains motionless until the last faint echo of the song of the men, who are never to return, has faded into nothing."

Somehow, it was the men rather than the officers who sensed what was coming. Beneath the gaudy talk of parades in Berlin and cries of "William to St. Helena!" many a Russian soldier marched to war suffused with a melancholy resignation that he would never see his family or his village again. At the front, General Alfred Knox, a British military attaché, found a tall young recruit from Kiev downhearted because he had left his wife and five children. Knox tried to cheer him, telling him he would come back, but the soldier only shook his head and said, "They say it is a wide road that leads to war and only a narrow path that leads home again."

In sheer numbers of soldiers, the Russian army was a colossus. The pre-war regular strength of the army was 1,400,000; mobilization immediately added 3,100,000 reserves. Behind this initial mass stood millions more. During three years of war, 15,500,000 men marched away to fight for the Tsar and Holy Russia. In the British press, this mass of bodies ready to bleed was reassuringly described as "the Russian steamroller."

In every respect except numbers of men, Russia was unprepared for war. The railroads were hopelessly inadequate; for every yard of Russian track per square mile, Germany had ten. French and German reserves moving to the front traveled 150 to 200 miles; in Russia, the average journey was 800 miles. A general commanding a Siberian corps told Knox that he had been on a train for twenty-three days bringing men to the front. Once the operations began, the supremacy of German railroads allowed the German command to move whole armies rapidly from one front to another. On the Russian side, said Knox, "the Supreme Command ordered, but the railroads decided."

Russian industry was small and primitive. For every factory in Russia, there were 150 in Great Britain. Russian generals, expecting a short war, had accumulated limited reserves of weapons and ammunition. Russian guns, having fired all their ammunition, quickly fell silent, while enemy shells, arriving steadily from German factories, burst continually overhead. At one point, Russian artillerymen were threatened with court-martial if they fired more than three rounds per day.

Russia's immense and isolated geography made it impossible for the Western Allies to help. Germany easily blockaded the Baltic, and

Turkey, entering the war against the Allies in November 1914, barred the Dardanelles and the Black Sea. Communication remained only through Archangel, frozen solid in the winter, and Vladivostock on the Pacific. Russian exports dropped 98 percent and imports 95 percent. An average of 1,250 ships called at Russian ports *annually* during the war, while arrivals in British ports amounted to 2,200 *weekly*. Once the British and French attempt to break the blockade by storming the Dardanelles at Gallipoli had failed, Russia became a "barred house which could be entered only through the chimney."

Not all the flaws lay in technology and geography. At its summit, the Russian army was commanded by two men who hated each other: General Vladimir Sukhomlinov, the Minister of War, and Grand Duke Nicholas Nicolaievich, the Tsar's distant cousin, who commanded the armies in the field. Sukhomlinov was a small chubby man with a fat feline face of whom Paléologue observed, "with his sly look, his eyes always gleaming watchfully under the heavy folds of his eyelids, I know few men who inspire more distrust at first sight." Although totally bald and advancing on seventy, Sukhomlinov retained a strong taste for expensive pleasures including a voluptuous wife thirty-two years his junior. Mme. Sukhomlinov enjoyed giving enormous parties, clothing herself in Paris and vacationing on the Riviera; her husband was left to pay the bills as best he could. Allowed a handsome traveling allowance based on mileage, he conducted frequent inspection trips to Vladivostock, eight thousand round-trip miles from his office. Once there, local officers found that the War Minister disliked leaving his train.

Sukhomlinov's reputation was not so much bad as a mournful joke. "The true picture of a drawing room soldier, scented, pomaded, with gold chain bracelets on his white wrists," recalled a lady who met him in society. "In spite of his mature age, Sukhomlinov was . . . eager for pleasure like a youth," wrote Sazonov, his ministerial colleague. "He enjoyed life and disliked work. . . . It was very difficult to make him work, but to get him to tell the truth was well-nigh impossible." Nevertheless, along with supporting his wife, it was Sukhomlinov's responsibility to organize and equip the Russian army. A former cavalry officer who had won the Cross of St. George in the 1878 war against the Turks, he believed in the charge—the cavalry with sabers, the infantry with bayonets. Modern weapons, such as machine guns and rapid-firing artillery, he thought unworthy of brave men. As a result, the Russian army entered the war with half as much field artillery as the Germans—seven field-gun batteries per division as opposed to fourteen—and 60 batteries of heavy artillery compared to 381. "Sukhomlinov," explained General Nicholas Golovine, who served under him, "believed that knowledge acquired by him in the 'seventies of the last century and largely of no further practical importance, was permanent truth. His ignorance went hand in hand with an extraordinary light-mindedness. These two personal characteristics enabled him to treat the most complicated military questions with astonishing levity. His attitude of easy assurance made the impression on those not familiar with the complicated technique of modern military art that Sukhomlinov handled such problems well and took the right decisions quickly."

Most significantly, Sukhomlinov made this impression on the Tsar. Like many rogues, he could be enormously charming, and he carefully did everything in his power to please Nicholas. His reports, unlike those of other ministers, were brief and free from gloomy predictions. Knowing that the Tsar took pride in the army, he gave constant assurance that morale and equipment were in splendid condition. When he reported in person, he larded his talk with selections from his vast fund of funny stories. At court, he was known as "*General Fly-Off*" because of his alertness and speed in anticipating the Tsar's wishes. Nicholas enjoyed him greatly, and, watching the superbly polished regiments of the Imperial Guard march past on parade, could not believe that the Russian army was unready for war.

Sukhomlinov was a courtier who used high military rank to support a lavish way of life. His arch-rival, the Commander-in-Chief in the field, Grand Duke Nicholas Nicolaievich, was a prince of the Imperial blood, a grandson of Tsar Nicholas I. Although born to great wealth and impeccable position, Nicholas Nicolaievich devoted his life to service in the army. In appearance, the fifty-seven-year-old Grand Duke was awesome. Standing six feet six inches tall, with a thin body, blazing blue eyes in a narrow face, his beard trimmed to a neat point, a dagger or sword hanging from his belt, he was the ancient warrior chieftain. "He was the most admired man in the army, not only an old-fashioned soldier, but deeply Slav," wrote Paléologue. "His whole being exuded a fierce energy. His incisive measured speech, flashing eyes and quick, nervous movements, hard, steel-trap mouth and gigantic stature personify imperious and impetuous audacity."

In the army, the Grand Duke inspired feelings of awe. By "the peasant soldiers of the Russian army," declared Knox, " . . . he was regarded as a sort of legendary champion of Holy Russia. . . . They felt that, though he was a strict disciplinarian and very exacting . . . he would ask from the private soldier no greater effort than he . . . imposed upon himself."

Naturally enough, the Commander-in-Chief and the Minister of War despised each other. The Grand Duke took his responsibilities as seriously as Sukhomlinov took his lightly. In 1908, when the Duma had criticized the appearance of members of the Imperial family in high military ranks, Nicholas Nicolaievich resigned from active command. Sukhomlinov, appointed War Minister in 1909, had seen a clear field for his own advancement to the more glamorous role of Commander-in-Chief once war was declared. To his chagrin, in 1914 the Tsar, having been dissuaded from assuming personal command of the armies in the field, appointed his cousin to the post. Thereafter, both in word and in deed, the jealous War Minister did what he could to undercut the Grand Duke. At one point, with messages streaming in begging for more shells, Sukhomlinov refused to raise the order for more ammunition. When the Chief of Artillery came to him weeping to say that Russia would have to make peace because of the shortage of shells, Sukhomlinov told him curtly to "go to the devil and shut up."

Both in Berlin and in Paris, strategy was tailored to the size and clumsiness of the Russian colossus. Aware that the state of Russia's railroads would not permit a rapid concentration of the Tsar's millions of soldiers, the German General Staff planned that the weeks before the cumbersome giant could move should be used to destroy France. "We hope in six weeks after the beginning of operations to have finished with France, or at least so far as to enable us to direct our principal forces against the East," General von Moltke, Chief of the German General Staff, told his nervous Austrian counterpart in May 1914. The Kaiser characteristically expressed the German plan more crudely: "Lunch in Paris, dinner in St. Petersburg."

Knowing that the blow was coming, French generals and diplomats had struggled single-mindedly for twenty years to ensure that the Russians would move quickly in the East once war began. To speed up Russian mobilization, France had poured money into her ally; the loans were given strictly on condition that they be used to build railroads leading to the German frontier. Even with this new track, the number of men in position by M–15—fifteen days after mobilization—

would be only a fraction of Russia's strength. Nevertheless, France insisted that the Russians attack on M–15 with whatever they had ready; the French counted on seven hundred thousand men. To wait longer meant catastrophe for France.

In its first weeks, the war ran brilliantly according to the German timetable. Through the hot weeks of August, the cream of the German army, one million men in gray uniforms, moved like a human scythe across Belgium and northern France. On September 2, less than a month after crossing the frontier, the Kaiser's weary advance guard stood thirty miles north of Paris. With a single lunge, they would be on the Champs-Elysées.

From the day war began, the primary mission of the French Ambassador in St. Petersburg was to urge the Russians to hurry. With a stream of anguished telegrams from Paris flowing into his Embassy, Paléologue bustled from one office to the next, begging, imploring and demanding haste. On August 5, he told the Tsar, "The French army will have to face the formidable onslaught of twenty-five German corps. I, therefore, implore Your Majesty to order your troops to take the offensive immediately. If they do not, there is danger that the French army may be crushed." Nicholas responded emotionally. Reaching out and clasping Paléologue in his arms, he said, "*Monsieur l'Ambassadeur*, let me embrace in you my dear and glorious France. . . . The moment mobilization is complete I shall order an advance. My troops are most enthusiastic. The attack will be pressed with the greatest vigor. No doubt you know that the Grand Duke Nicholas is extraordinarily forceful."

On the same day, the Ambassador called on the Grand Duke: "The generalissimo received me in his enormous study where maps were spread out on all the tables. He came towards me with his quick firm strides. 'God and Joan of Arc are with us,' he exclaimed. 'We shall win. . . .' " "How soon will you order the offensive, Monseigneur?" asked Paléologue. "Perhaps I shan't even wait until the concentration of all my corps is complete. As soon as I feel myself strong enough, I shall attack. It will probably be the 14th of August." Escorting Paléologue to the door, he vigorously shook the Ambassador's hand, crying, "And now, into God's hands."

The Grand Duke was as good as his word. The front he commanded was 550 miles long, beginning in the north on the Baltic where the

Russian Baltic provinces bordered East Prussia. From there, the front curved south and west around the enormous bulge that made up Russian Poland. Then, along the bottom of the Polish bulge, it ran eastward to the frontier of the Ukraine. On the southern sector of this long line, in the Austrian province of Galicia, an Austro-Hungarian army of one million men was massing. West of Warsaw, on the direct line to Berlin, the Russians could not advance because of the danger on their lengthy Galician and East Prussian flanks. The Russian attack, therefore, was delivered in the north, against East Prussia.

Two Russian armies were selected to make the attack. The First Army, consisting of 200,000 men under General Rennenkampf, was to move southwest parallel to the Baltic coast, while the Second Army, 170,000 men under General Samsonov, would advance northward from Poland. Rennenkampf's army was to start first, drawing on itself the bulk of the German forces in East Prussia. Two days later, once the Germans were fully engaged, Samsonov was to strike north for the Baltic, putting himself across the rear of the Germans fighting Rennenkampf. Each of the Russian armies individually was larger than the German force. If the Grand Duke's strategy worked, the Germans would be ground up between the two armies, and the Russians would begin crossing the Vistula River below Danzig. Ahead of them, the road to Berlin—only 150 miles away—would lie open.

Because of the need for haste, the Russian offensive was assembled piecemeal. Grand Duke Nicholas did not leave the capital for field headquarters until midnight of August 13. Allowing his train to be shunted onto sidings so that troop trains could pass, he took fifty-seven hours for the journey and arrived on the morning of the 16th. General Samsonov, commander of the Second Army, was an asthmatic and had been on leave with his wife in the Caucasus. He arrived at his headquarters on the 16th to find his troops already on the march toward the frontier. General Rennenkampf, a swashbuckling cavalry officer, sent his Cossacks raiding across the border as early as the 12th. A German machine gun, captured on one of these forays, appeared as a trophy two days later on the lawn at Peterhof, where it was examined with interest by the Tsar and the Tsarevich. On August 17, Rennenkampf's entire army advanced, driving the German frontier troops before them. In these first skirmishes, Rennenkampf's tactics recalled the Napoleonic Wars one hundred years before. Under fire from German cannon, the General sent his cavalry to charge the guns. As a result, in the war's first engagements many young Guards officers, the flower of Russia's aristocratic youth, were shot from their saddles.

Although the German General Staff had anticipated a Russian advance into East Prussia, the news that Cossack horsemen were riding over the rich farms and estates of Junker aristocrats sent a thrill of horror through Berlin. Temporarily ignoring the Russian Second Army moving up from the south, the Germans engaged Rennenkampf's force on August 20. The Russian artillery, firing 440 shells per day, was effective, and the result was a partial German defeat. In desperation, the German General Staff hastily dispatched a new pair of generals to take command. On August 22, Paul Hindenburg and Erich Ludendorff, the formidable military duo which was to lead Germany through four years of war, were both aboard the same train bound for East Prussia.

While Rennenkampf rested—too long—from his victory, Samsonov's army was struggling north through the wild, uninhabited country north of the Polish border. The route lay through a maze of pine and birch forests intersected by streams and marshes, with few inhabitants, poor roads and no railroads. There were few farms on this sandy soil, and the army ate only what it could pull behind it in carts. On the eve of battle, some of the men had been without their full ration of bread for five days.

Despite their hardships, Samsonov's men struggled forward. Many of the men, coming from small Russian villages, were pleased at the sight of the East Prussian towns. Soldiers of the 23rd Corps, reaching the town of Allenstein, cheered enthusiastically, believing themselves to be entering Berlin. Samsonov himself was less sanguine. At the end of a long chain which began in Paris, passed through Paléologue, the Grand Duke and the Northwest Front commander, Samsonov received constant signals to hurry. "Advancing according to timetable, without halting, covering marches of more than 12 miles a day over sand. I cannot go more quickly," he telegraphed back. As it was, his men were hungry, his horses without oats, his supply columns disorganized, his artillery mired.

On August 24, a day after their arrival in East Prussia, Hindenburg and Ludendorff decided on a sweeping gamble. Leaving only two brigades of cavalry to face Rennenkampf, whose army still was motionless five days after its victory, they loaded every other German soldier onto trains and trundled them south to meet Samsonov. By August 25, the transfer was complete. Rennenkampf still had not resumed his advance, and Samsonov was now confronted by an army equal in size and vastly superior in artillery. Informing General Jilinsky, commander of the Russian Northern Front, of his predicament, Samsonov was rudely told, "To see the enemy where he does not exist is cowardice. I will not allow General Samsonov to play the coward. I insist that he continue the offensive."

In four days of battle, Samsonov's exhausted troops did what they could. Nevertheless, faced with hurricane barrages of German artillery, enveloped on three sides by German infantry, the Second Army disintegrated. Samsonov was fatalistic. "The enemy has luck one day, we will have luck another," he said and rode off alone into the forest to shoot himself.

The Germans named their victory the Battle of Tannenberg in revenge for a famous Slav defeat of the Teutonic Knights near the same site in 1410. At Tannenberg, the Russians lost 110,000 men, including 90,000 prisoners. Blame fell on General Jilinsky, who was replaced, and on Rennenkampf, who was discharged from the army. Grand Duke Nicholas, whose southern armies were winning a great victory against the Austrians in Galicia, met the defeat at Tannenberg with equanimity. "We are happy to have made such sacrifices for our allies," he declared when the French military attaché at his headquarters offered condolences. In St. Petersburg, Sazonov told Paléologue, "Samsonov's army has been destroyed. That's all I know," and then added quietly, "We owed this sacrifice to France, as she has showed herself a perfect ally." Paléologue, thanking the Foreign Minister for the generosity of his thought, hurried on to discuss the only thing that truly concerned him: the massive threat to Paris which was mounting by the hour.

For all the reckless gallantry and foolish ineptitude of the premature Russian offensive, it nevertheless achieved its primary objective: the diversion of German forces from the West. The limited penetration of East Prussia had had a magnified effect. Refugees, many of them high-born, had descended in fury and despair on Berlin, the Kaiser was outraged, and von Moltke himself admitted that "all the success on the Western front will be unavailing if the Russians arrive in Berlin." On August 25, before the decisive blow against Samsonov, von Moltke violated his supposedly inviolable war plan of ignoring the Russians until France was finished. On urgent orders, two army corps and a cavalry division were stripped from the German right wing in France and rushed to the East. They arrived too late for Tannenberg; they could not be returned before the Marne. "This was perhaps our salvation," wrote General Dupont, one of Joffre's aides. "Such a mistake made by the Chief of the German General Staff in 1914 must have made the other Moltke, his uncle, turn in his grave."

As France's generals had foreseen, one key to the salvation of France lay in immediately setting the Russian colossus in motion. Whether the colossus met victory or defeat mattered little as long as the Germans were distracted from their overwhelming lunge at Paris. In that sense the Russian soldiers who died in the forests of East Prussia contributed as much to the Allied cause as the Frenchmen who died on the Marne.

CHAPTER TWENTY-ONE

Stavka

At the outbreak of war, Nicholas's first impulse had been to take command of the army himself, assuming the ancient role of warrior-tsar at the head of his troops. He was urgently dissuaded by his ministers, who pleaded that he not risk his prestige as sovereign, especially—as Sazonov put it—"as it is to be expected that we may be forced to retreat during the first weeks." The supreme command went to Grand Duke Nicholas, who departed with his staff from Petrograd on August 13 to establish field headquarters at Baranovichi, a Polish railway junction midway between the German and Austrian fronts. The camp, called *Stavka* after an old Russian word meaning the military camp of a chief, was set off the main Moscow-Warsaw track in a forest of birch and pine. Here, surrounded by three concentric rings of sentries, the Grand Duke and his officers lived and worked in a dozen army trains drawn up fanwise beneath the trees. In time, as the encampment became semi-permanent, roofs were built over the cars to shield them from heat and snow, and wooden sidewalks were laid so that officers could walk from train to train without slipping on mud or ice.

From his private railway car spread with bearskins and Oriental rugs, the Grand Duke dominated the life of the camp. On the wall of his sleeping compartment, crowded between the windows, were more than two hundred icons. Over the doors of all the rooms frequented by the Grand Duke, small pieces of white paper were affixed to remind the six-foot-six-inch Nicholas Nicolaievich to duck so as not to bump his head.

General Sir John Hanbury-Williams, British military attaché in

Petrograd, arrived at *Stavka* on Grand Duke Nicholas's train and remained there until the Tsar's abdication. His diary of these two and a half years gives a vivid portrait of Imperial Russian Headquarters during the First World War: "We all attended the little wooden church in the camp. All the headquarters troops were drawn up at the entrance to the church, Guards and Cossacks of the Guard . . . all in khaki with long, grey overcoats reaching to their feet—still as rocks—looking almost like a line of statues against the pine forests. Here we waited till suddenly a fanfare of trumpets rang out and in the distance, coming along a road from the train, there marched, stern-faced and head erect, that great and to the army he loved so well, almost mystical figure, Grand Duke Nicholas. . . . He reached the line and swung around facing his men . . . looking them absolutely straight in the eye, and called out to all ranks the customary 'Good day.' With the rattle of presenting arms came the answering shout from every man in reply . . . and so we all slowly filed into church."

It was to this vigorous, masculine atmosphere that the Tsar came often as an enthusiastic visitor. When the Imperial train, its long line of blue salon cars emblazoned with golden crests, glided slowly under the sunlit foliage onto a siding alongside the Grand Duke's, the Tsar stepped happily into the routine of army life. He loved the disciplined sense of purpose at *Stavka*, the clear-cut giving and taking of orders, the professional talk at the officers' mess, the rough, hardy, outdoor life. It called back memories of his days as a junior officer when his heaviest responsibility was getting out of bed in time to stand morning parade. It was a release from government and ministers and a change from Tsarskoe Selo, where, no matter how devoted he was to wife and children, the world was small, closed and predominantly feminine.

Nicholas was careful during his visits to Headquarters not to intrude on the authority of the Grand Duke. Sitting beside the Commander-in-Chief at morning staff conferences, the Tsar played the part of the interested, honored guest. Together, the two men listened to reports of the previous day's operations at the front; together, they bent over the huge maps of Poland, East Prussia and Galicia, studying the red and blue lines which marked the positions of the opposing armies. But when the moment came to issue commands, the Tsar was silent and the Grand Duke spoke.

It was when the Tsar was in this relaxed, happy mood at Headquarters that General Hanbury-Williams first met him. "At 2:30 I was summoned to meet the Emperor," he wrote. "On arrival, I found two huge Cossacks at the door of His Imperial Majesty's train. . . . The Emperor received me alone. He was dressed in perfectly plain khaki uniform, the coat being more of a blouse than ours, with blue breeches and long black riding boots, and was standing at a high writing desk. As I saluted, he came forward at once and shook me warmly by the hand. I was at once struck by his extraordinary likeness to our own King, and the way he smiled, his face lighting up, as if it were a real pleasure to him to receive one. His first question was one of inquiry after our King and Queen and the Royal family. . . . I had always pictured him to myself as a somewhat sad and anxious-looking monarch, with cares of state and other things hanging heavily over him. Instead of that I found a bright, keen, happy face, plenty of humor and a fresh-air man."

Meals at Headquarters were hearty and masculine: plentiful *zakouski*, roast beef, Yorkshire pudding, vodka and wines. The vodka, wrote Hanbury-Williams, "went down my throat like a torchlight procession." At the table, surrounded by men he considered his fellow officers, Nicholas spoke freely without the inhibitions imposed at court. Once he offered an analysis of the difference between Russia and the United States:

"At dinner tonight, H.I.M. [His Imperial Majesty] talked about empires and republics. His own ideas as a young man were that he had a great responsibility and he felt that the people over whom he ruled were so numerous and so varying in blood and temperament, different altogether from our Western Europeans, that an Emperor was a vital necessity to them. His first visit to the Caucasus had made a vital impression on him and confirmed him in his views.

"The United States of America, he said, was an entirely different matter, and the two cases could not be compared. In this country [Russia], many as were the problems and the difficulties, their sense of imagination, their intense religious feeling and their habits and customs generally made a crown necessary, and he believed this must be so for a very long time, that a certain amount of decentralizing of authority was, of course, necessary but that the great and decisive power must rest with the Crown. The powers of the Duma must go slowly, because of the difficulties of pushing on education at any reasonably fast rate among all these masses of his subjects."

As for the personal role of the Autocrat, Nicholas admitted that, while he could give any order he liked, he could not ensure that it was carried out. Often, when he found that something he had asked had not been properly done, he said wistfully to Hanbury-Williams, "You see what it is to be an autocrat."

At Headquarters, the Tsar took long afternoon walks along country roads thoroughly scouted in advance by Cossack patrols. In warm weather, he rowed on the Dnieper, often removing his blouse so that the sun could tan him. Occasionally, for variety, he challenged other officers to a race. Nicholas liked to win, but he would row only against men who had a chance of beating him.

In November 1914, the Tsar left Headquarters for a long journey to the southern Causasus, where his troops were fighting the Turks. "We are passing through picturesque country," he wrote to Alexandra, " . . . with beautiful high mountains on one side and the steppes on the other. At each station, the platforms are crowded with people . . . thousands of them. . . . We are running along by the Caspian Sea. It rests the eyes to look on the blue distance, it reminded me of the Black Sea . . . not far off are the mountains, beautifully lit by the sun." In Kuban province, passing Cossack villages, he admired the people and their rich orchards. "They are beginning to be wealthy, and above all they have an inconceivably high number of small infants. All future subjects. This all fills me with joy and faith in God's mercy. I look forward in peace and confidence to what lies in store for Russia."

On trips, when outdoor exercise was impossible, Nicholas solved the problem by rigging an apparatus inside the train. "My hanging trapeze has proved very practical and useful," he wrote. "I swung on it many times and climbed it before meals. It really is an excellent thing for the train, it stirs up the blood and the whole organism." From this description arises a piquant image of the Imperial train rolling through dusty villages, past platforms crowded with curious and worshipful peasants, while inside, hidden from view, the Little Father hangs by his heels, swinging back and forth on his trapeze.

In the autumn of 1915, the Tsar brought his son, the eleven-year-old Tsarevich, to live with him at Army Headquarters. It was a startling move, not simply because of the boy's age but also because of his hemophilia. Yet, Nicholas did not make his decision impetuously. His reasons, laboriously weighed for months in advance, were both sentimental and shrewd.

The Russian army, battered and retreating after a summer of terrible losses, badly needed a lift in morale. Nicholas himself made constant appearances, and his presence, embodying the cause of Holy Russia, raised tremendous enthusiasm among the men who saw him. It was his hope that the appearance of the Heir at his side, symbolizing the future, would further bolster their drooping spirits. It was a reasonable hope, and, in fact, wherever Alexis appeared he became a center of great excitement.

Perhaps more important, the Tsar was thinking of the distant future and the day his son would sit on the throne. Alexis's education, up to that point, had been anything but normal. As a prince, he lived in a restricted world; because of his illness, it was primarily a world of adoring women. By taking his son from the muffled, silken-pillowed atmosphere of the palace and bringing him into the bracing air of beards, leather and uniforms at *Stavka*, Nicholas proposed to broaden the education of the future tsar.

It was enormously difficult for the Empress to let Alexis go. During his entire lifetime, he had not been out of her sight for more than a few hours; whenever he was gone, she imagined dangers which others would never dream of. On his trips to Headquarters, the Tsarevich was surrounded with protection by his personal retinue: Fedorov and Derevenko the doctors, Gilliard the tutor, Derevenko and Nagorny the sailor bodyguards. Yet real risks were involved and the Empress was acutely aware of them. In traveling on the Imperial train, there was danger of stumbling and falling in the corridors as the carriages lurched. Bouncing in automobiles over dirt roads, traveling in a zone where German airplanes might appear, walking long distances and standing for hours as thousands of men marched by—no doctor would permit this activity for any other hemophiliac. While he was away, Alexandra's letters to the Tsar were filled with concern for him: "See that Tiny [Alexis] doesn't tire himself on the stairs. He cannot take walks. . . . Tiny loves digging and working and he is so strong and forgets that he must be careful. . . . Take care of Baby's arm, don't let him run about on the train so as not to knock his arms. . . . Before you decide, speak with Mr. Gilliard, he is such a sensible man and knows all so well about Baby." Every night at nine p.m., the Empress went to Alexis's room as if he were there saying his prayers. There, on her knees, she prayed to God that her son would come home safely.

Once when Gilliard had returned alone to Tsarskoe Selo, leaving Alexis at Headquarters, the Empress explained to him why she had let her son go at all. "After the meal, we went out on the terrace," wrote the tutor. "It was a beautiful evening, warm and still. Her Majesty was stretched on a sofa and two of her daughters were knitting woollen clothing for the soldiers. The other two Grand Duchesses were sewing. Alexis Nicolaievich was naturally the principal topic of conversation. They never tired of asking me what he did and said . . . with a candor which utterly amazed me [the Empress then] said that all his life the Tsar had suffered from his natural timidity and from the fact that, as he had been kept too much in the background, he had found himself badly prepared for the duties of a ruler on the sudden death of Alexander III. The Tsar had vowed to avoid the same mistakes in the education of his own son." Suppressing her own terrible fears, the Empress agreed with her husband.

Alexis himself was longing to escape from the Alexander Palace. For months, his greatest excitement had been a series of afternoon automobile drives taken within a radius of twenty miles of Tsarskoe Selo. "We used to start out immediately after lunch," wrote Gilliard, who arranged the excursions. "[We] often stopped at villages to watch the peasants at work. Alexis Nicolaievich liked questioning them, and they always answered him with the frank, kindly simplicity of the Russian *moujik*, not having the slightest idea whom they were speaking to. The railway lines of the suburbs of St. Petersburg had a great attraction for the boy. He took the liveliest interest in the activities of the little stations we passed and the work of repair on track and bridges. . . . The palace police grew alarmed at these excursions which took us beyond the guarded zone. . . . Whenever we left the park, we were certain to see a car appear and follow in our tracks. It was one of Alexis Nicolaievich's greatest delights to try and throw it off the scent."

For a lively, intelligent eleven-year-old boy, the chance to visit Army Headquarters was a promise of high adventure. On an October morning in 1915, the Tsarevich, dressed in the uniform of an army private, delightedly kissed his mother goodbye and boarded his father's train. Even before reaching Headquarters, Alexis saw his first review of front-line troops. As the Tsar walked down the ranks, Gilliard wrote, "Alexis Nicolaievich was at his father's heels, listening intently to the stories of these men who had often stared death in the face. His features, which were always expressive, became quite strained in an effort not to lose a single word of what the men were saying. His presence at the Tsar's side greatly interested the soldiers . . . they were heard whispering their ideas about his age, size and looks. But the point that made the greatest impression on them was the fact that the Tsarevich was wearing the uniform of a private soldier."

A series of German victories in the summer of 1915 had forced relocation of *Stavka* from Baranovichi to Mogilev, a Russian town on the upper Dnieper River. Here, the trains had been abandoned and Headquarters established in the house of the provincial governor, a mansion on the crest of a hill overlooking a bend in the river. As the building was crowded, Nicholas reserved only two rooms for himself—a bedroom and an office. For Alexis, a second cot was placed in the Tsar's bedroom.

"It is very cosy sleeping side by side," Nicholas wrote to Alexandra. "I say prayers with him every night. . . . He says his prayers too fast and it is difficult to stop him. . . . I read all [your] letters aloud to him. He listens lying in bed and kisses your signature. . . . He sleeps well and likes the window left open. . . . Noise in the street does not disturb him. . . . Yesterday evening when Alexei was already in bed, a thunderstorm broke out; the lightning struck somewhere near the town, it rained hard after which the air became delightful and much fresher. We slept well with the window open. . . . Thank God he looks so well and has become sunburnt. . . . He wakes up early in the morning between 7 and 8, sits up in bed and begins to talk quietly to me. I answer drowsily, he settles down and lies quietly until I am called."

There was a tender charm in this intimate companionship between father and son, briefly shared in the middle of a great war; for them, the room at Mogilev became a tiny haven of peace and affection set in the eye of the hurricane. "He brings much light into my life here," Nicholas wrote. Later, he said, "His company gives light and life to all of us."

Every morning at Headquarters, the Tsarevich did lessons with Gilliard on the veranda. Afterward, he played in the garden with a toy rifle. "He always carries his little gun with him and walks backwards and forwards on the path marching and singing loudly," wrote Nicholas. "I went into the little garden where Alexei was marching about singing loudly and Derevenko was walking on another path, whistling. . . . His left hand hurts him a little because yesterday he worked in the sand on the river bank but he pays no attention and is very cheerful. After lunch, he rests for about a half an hour and Mr. Gilliard reads to him while I write. At the table, he sits on my left hand. . . . Alexei loves to tease. It is extraordinary how he has lost his shyness. He always follows me when I greet my gentlemen."

In the afternoons, "we go out in the car . . . either into a wood or on the bank of the river, where we light a fire and I walk about nearby." On hot days in summer, they swam in the Dnieper: "He splashes about near the bank. I bathe not far away." Once "we found a lovely place with soft sand where he played happily. The sand was as soft and white as on the seashore. Baby [Alexis] ran about shouting. Fedorov allowed him to go barefoot. Naturally, he was delighted." Sometimes, playmates appeared. "Did he [Alexis] describe to you how the peasant boys played all sorts of games with him?"

In Mogilev, meals were served in the dining room of the governor's house or, in warm weather, in a large green tent set up in the garden. Along with the regular Headquarters staff, there were always "colonels and generals who are returning from the front. . . . [I] invite them to lunch and dinner. Mogilev is like an enormous hotel where crowds of people pass through." Alexis plunged happily into this bustling atmosphere. "He sits on my left hand and behaves well but sometimes becomes inordinately gay and noisy, especially when I am talking with the others in the drawing room. In any case, it is pleasant for them and makes them smile."

The Tsarevich's favorites at Headquarters were "the foreigners—the military attachés of Britain, France, Italy, Serbia, Belgium and Japan. Before long, they had, in effect, adopted the high-spirited boy as their mascot. "I had expected to find a very delicate and not very lively boy," wrote Hanbury-Williams, who became one of the Tsarevich's favorites. "But in the periods of what may be called his good health, he had all the spirits and the mischief of any ordinary boy of that age. . . . He wore a khaki uniform and long Russian boots and was very proud of himself as a soldier, had excellent manners and spoke various languages well and clearly.

"As time went on and his first shyness wore off, he treated us as old friends and . . . had always some bit of fun with us. With me it was to make sure that each button on my coat was properly fastened, a habit which naturally made me take great care to have one or two unbuttoned, in which case he used at once to stop and tell me I was 'untidy again,' give a sigh at my lack of attention to these details and stop and carefully button me all up again."

Once Alexis had made sure of his new friends, quite incredible things began to happen, especially at lunch: "While the rest of the party were eating *zakouska*, every conceivable game went on, a 'rag' in fact, ending most likely in a game of football with anything that came handy. The Belgian general of whom he was very fond, and used always to call 'Papa de Ricquel,' being a man of no mean girth, gave great opportunities for attack. The devoted tutor was almost in despair and it generally ended with the intervention of the Emperor, by which time the small boy was carefully hidden behind a curtain. He then used to reappear with a twinkle in his eye and solemnly march to take his place at the table. There he would begin again by a bread pellet attack . . . which risked all the Imperial china and glasses. If, however, he had a stranger sitting next to him he had all the courtesy and charm of his father, talking freely and asking sensible questions. The moment, however, that we adjourned to the anteroom the games used to begin again, and went on fast and furious till either the Emperor or his tutor carried him off."

After lunch, the games often continued in the garden: "He dragged some of us off after lunch in the tent to a round fountain in the garden which had porpoise heads all round it, with two holes in each to represent the eyes. The game is to plug up these holes with one's fingers, then turn on the fountain full split and suddenly let go. The result was that I nearly drowned the Emperor and his son and they returned the compliment, and we all had to go back and change, laughing till we nearly cried." Nicholas, expecting that the Empress might disapprove of such rough games, wrote an explanatory note: "I am writing . . . having come in from the garden with wet sleeves and boots as Alexei has sprayed us at the fountain. It is his favorite game . . . peals of laughter ring out. I keep an eye in order to see that things do not go too far."

Late in October, to show his son that war was not all games and toy forts and lead soldiers, the Tsar took Alexis on a month-long trip the length of the battlefront. In Galicia, returning after dark from a mass review, Nicholas and Alexis made a surprise visit to a front-line dressing station. The rooms were lit only by torches. Moving from one bandaged body to the next, Nicholas spoke to the suffering men, many of whom could scarcely believe that the Tsar himself was walking among them. Close behind came Alexis, deeply moved by the groaning and suffering all around him. Later, standing before a field of men on parade, Nicholas asked those who had served since the beginning of the war to raise their hands. "But very few hands were lifted above those thousands of heads," wrote Gilliard. "There were whole companies in which not a man moved. . . . [This] made a very great impression on Alexis Nicolaievich."

Wherever they went, Alexis was insatiably curious. At Reval, on the Baltic coast, they visited four British submarines which had been sinking German ships in the Baltic. The hulls and conning towers were sheathed in sparkling ice as Nicholas thanked the officers and men and awarded the St. George Cross to the four Royal Navy captains. For Alexis, the submarines had an extraordinary fascination. "Alexei . . . crept into every possible hole," wrote Nicholas. "I even overheard him talking freely to a lieutenant asking him questions." That night, to the Tsarevich's delight, the Tsar brought the four submarine captains back to the train for dinner.

In the south, the Tsar and his son inspected four regiments of Caucasian cavalry. Alexis was thrilled, and even the stolid Gilliard was impressed: "Among other units were the Kuban and Terek Cossacks, perched high in the saddle and wearing the huge fur caps which make them look so fierce. As we started to return, the whole mass of cavalry suddenly moved forward, took stations on both sides of the road, broke into a gallop, tearing up the hills, sweeping down the banks of ravines, clearing all obstacles, and thus escorted us to the station in a terrific charge in which men and animals crashed together on the ground while the *melée* rose the raucous yells of the Caucasian mountaineers. It was a spectacle at once magnificent and terrible."

Besides visiting troops, father and son toured cities, factories, shipyards and hospitals. In Odessa, wrote Nicholas, "the streets were crowded with young soldiers and . . . people. . . . Our Treasure [Alexis] sat with a serious face, saluting all the time. Through the tumult of the crowd and the shouts of 'Hurrah!' I managed to hear women's voices calling out, 'The Heir!, The Angel!, The pretty boy!' . . . He heard them too and smiled at them." Once when the train stopped outside a town, "Alexei's cat ran away and hid under a big pile of board. We put on our great coats and went to look for her. Nagorny found her at once with a flashlight, but it took a long time to make the wretch come out. She would not listen to Alexei. At last, he caught her by one of her hind legs and dragged her through the narrow chink." Returning to Headquarters after a month on the train, Nicholas reported happily to Alexandra, "Alexei has borne the strain . . . astonishingly well, only occasionally he suffered from a little bleeding at the nose."

The Empress, as if unable to stay away from the exclusive male retreat of her husband and son, made occasional visits to Headquarters. Bringing her daughters and sometimes Anna Vyrubova, she lived aboard her train. During the mornings, while the Tsar was at work, she sat by the river or visited the families of peasants and railway workers. At noon, staff motorcars arrived to bring the ladies to the governor's house for lunch. In the afternoon, while the family went driving together, the cars went back to the train for the maids, gowns and jewels needed to costume the women for dinner. In a house crowded with men, the ladies changed as best they could in niches and closets.

At dinner, Hanbury-Williams found her "much easier to get on with than I expected. . . . She told me how terribly shy she felt on coming into the room where we all were assembled . . . the chiefs of the Allied military missions . . . and a galaxy of Russian officers. . . . The moment one began to laugh over things, she brightened up and talk became easy and unaffected. . . . It seems extraordinary how little it takes to cheer her up. . . . She is so proud of Russia and so anxious that the Allies should win the war. . . . War to her seems almost more terrible, if such a thing is possible, than to other people. But she spoke of it to me as the 'passing out of darkness into the light of victory. Victory we must have.' "

As long as Alexis was alone with his father, the Tsar carried the day-to-day burden of caring for his son's health. His letters to Alexandra were filled with detailed descriptions: "When we arrived by train in the evening, Baby played the fool," he wrote late in November 1915. "[He] pretended to fall off his chair and hurt his left arm (under the armpit). It did not hurt afterwards but swelled up instead. And so the first night here, he slept very restlessly, kept on sitting up in bed, groaning, calling for you and talking to me. Every few minutes he fell off to sleep again. This went on till 4 o'clock. Yesterday he spent in bed. I explained to everyone that he had simply slept badly. . . . Thank God, it is all over today except for paleness and a slight bleeding at the nose. For the rest, he is exactly as he usually is and we walked together in the little garden."

The following summer, in July 1916, Nicholas wrote: "This morning while we were still in bed, Alexei showed me that his elbow would not bend; then he took his temperature and calmly announced that he had better stay in bed all day." In November 1916: "The Little One is suffering from a strained vein in the upper part of his right leg. . . . During the night, he kept waking and groaned in his sleep. Fedorov has ordered him to lie quietly in bed." On the following day: "Baby's leg hurts from time to time and he cannot get off to sleep the first part of the night. When I come to bed, he tries not to groan."

Although the situation was unprecedented in the history of war and monarchy—an emperor, the commander-in-chief of the world's largest army, spending his nights caring for a groaning child—Nicholas carefully avoided any specific discussion of his son's illness. "He rarely refers to the Tsarevich's health but tonight I could see that he was anxious about him," wrote Hanbury-Williams. "I suppose he recognizes that the boy's health can never be satisfactory and no doubt wonders what will happen if he lives to succeed to the throne. Anyhow, he is doing all he possibly can to train him on what, if he ever succeeds, will be a very heavy task. He wishes very much that he may be able to travel about and see something of the world, and gain experiences from other countries which will be of use to him in Russia, with all the complications, as he put it to me, of this enormous Empire."

For the most part, all went well, the disease remained under control, and Nicholas enjoyed the deceptive sense of calm and stability which often comes to the parents of hemophiliacs. But the disease, capricious and malevolent, awaits precisely these moments to strike. In December 1915, the Tsarevich suffered a severe nosebleed. The attack was the worst since Spala, the kind which haunted the dreams of the Empress. Unlike other external bleeding which can be checked by pressure and bandaging, nosebleeds pose an extreme danger to hemophiliacs. Difficult to treat, unsusceptible to pressure, once started they are almost impossible to check.

Nicholas and Alexis were on the train headed for Galicia to inspect a number of regiments of the Imperial Guard. "On the morning of our departure," recalled Gilliard, "Alexis Nicolaievich, who had caught cold the previous day and was suffering from a heavy catarrh in the head, began to bleed heavily at the nose as a result of sneezing violently. I summoned Professor Fedorov but he could not entirely stop the bleeding. . . . During the night, the boy got worse. His temperature had gone up and he was getting weaker. At three o'clock in the morning Professor Fedorov, alarmed at his responsibilities, decided to have the Tsar roused and ask him to return to Mogilev where he could attend to the Tsarevich under more favorable conditions.

"The next morning we were on our way back to GHQ, but the boy's state was so alarming that it was decided to take him back to Tsarskoe Selo. . . . The patient's strength was failing rapidly. We had to have the train stopped several times to be able to change the [nose] plugs. Alexis Nicolaievich was supported in bed by his sailor Nagorny (he could not be allowed to lie full length), and twice in the night he swooned away and I thought the end had come."

During the crisis, Anna Vyrubova was with the Empress: "I was with the Empress when the telegram came announcing the return of the Emperor and the boy to Tsarskoe Selo, and I can never forget the anguish of mind with which the poor mother awaited the arrival of her sick, perhaps dying child. Nor can I ever forget the waxen, grave-like pallor of the little pointed face as the boy with infinite care was borne into the palace and laid on his little white bed. Above the blood-soaked bandages his large blue eyes gazed at us with pathos unspeakable, and it seemed to all around the bed that the last hour of the unhappy child was at hand. The physicians kept up their ministrations, exhausting every means known to science to stop the incessant bleeding. In despair, the Empress sent for Rasputin. He came into the room, made the sign of the cross over the bed and, looking intently at the almost moribund child, said quietly to the kneeling parents: 'Don't be alarmed. Nothing will happen.' Then he walked out of the room and out of the palace. That was all. The child fell asleep and the next day was so well that the Emperor left for the *Stavka*. Dr. Derevenko and Professor Fedorov told me afterwards that they did not even attempt to explain the cure."

Gilliard's account gives more credit to the doctors' efforts, but does not challenge Vyrubova's assertion that the Empress was convinced that only Rasputin had saved her son: "At last we reached Tsarskoe Selo. It was eleven o'clock. The Empress, who had been torn with anguish and anxiety, was on the platform with the Grand Duchesses. With infinite care the invalid was taken to the palace. The doctors ultimately succeeded in cauterizing the scar which had formed at the spot where a little blood vessel had burst. Once more the Empress attributed the improvement in her son's condition to the prayers of Rasputin, and she remained convinced that the boy had been saved thanks to his intervention."

Nicholas, sadly leaving his son surrounded again by women and pillows, returned to his life at the front. From Galicia, where he reviewed the Guards, he wrote, "They did not march past owing to the deep, thick mud—they would have lost their boots under my very eyes. . . . It was already getting dark. . . . A Te Deum [was held] in the center of a huge square in complete darkness. Having sat down in the car, I shouted 'Good bye' to the troops and from the invisible field rose a terrible roar. . . . On that day, I inspected 84,000 soldiers, Guards alone, and fed 105 commanding officers [on the train]. . . . Tell the Little One I miss him terribly."

At Mogilev, a stillness settled over the governor's house. Conversations at meals became formal and professional. "Tell him," Nicholas wrote to Alexandra, "that they [the foreigners] always finish their *zakouski* in the little room and remember him. I also think of him very often, especially in the garden and in the evenings and I miss my cup of chocolate [with him]."

The Tsarevich remained at Tsarskoe Selo the rest of the winter, regaining his strength. The Empress reported his progress in every letter: "Thank God, your heart can be quiet about Alexei . . . Baby has got up and will lunch in my room. He looks sweet, thin, with big eyes. . . . Sunbeam is at last going out and I hope he will regain his pink cheeks again. . . . He received a charming telegram from all the foreigners at Headquarters in remembrance of the little room in which they used to sit and chat during *zakouski*."

By February, he was well enough to go out into the park to play in the snow. One day, the Tsar—home for a few days—and his sisters were with him. "He [Alexis] slipped behind his youngest sister, who had not seen him coming, and threw a huge snowball at her," wrote Gilliard. "His father . . . called the boy to him and talked to him severely: 'You ought to be ashamed of yourself, Alexis! You're behaving like a German to attack anyone from behind when they can't defend themselves. It's horrid and cowardly. Leave that sort of behavior to the Germans!' "

In May 1916, six months after Alexis was stricken, the Empress reluctantly allowed him to return to Headquarters. He was promoted from private to corporal. "He is very proud of his stripes and more mischievous than ever," reported Hanbury-Williams. "At lunch the Tsarevich pushed all the cups, bread, toast, menus, etc. which he could get hold of across to me and then called the attention of his father to count all the pieces I had."

On December 20, 1916, the Tsarevich paid his last visit to Army

Headquarters. A few days later, he was to leave for Tsarskoe Selo for the winter; before spring, revolution would sweep his father off the throne. On that night, General Hanbury-Williams received word from England that his eldest son, an officer with the British army in France, had died as a result of wounds. As the General sat alone with his grief in his tiny, barren room, the door quietly opened. It was Alexis, saying, "Papa told me to come to sit with you as he thought you might feel lonely tonight."

CHAPTER TWENTY-TWO

"Poor Fellows, They Are Ready to Give Their Lives for a Smile"

VICTORY on the Marne and disaster at Tannenberg tended to dim the result of a third great battle fought in the opening weeks of war. Even as Rennenkampf's Cossacks rode through East Prussian barnyards, the main mass of the Austro-Hungarian army, one million strong, launched itself north from Galicia intending to amputate Poland from Russia. Within less than three weeks, the Russians had stopped and smashed these invaders. Four Austro-Hungarian armies were routed, two hundred thousand prisoners and Lemberg, the capital of the province, were taken, and Russian cavalry crossed the Carpathians to ride out onto the great Danube plain toward Budapest and Vienna. In terror, hinting that it might be forced to a separate peace, the Austrian government appealed to Berlin for help.

The German General Staff ordered Hindenburg to rush reinforcements. On September 14, 1914, two German army corps headed south from East Prussia; four days later, Hindenburg raised the rescue force by two additional army corps and a cavalry division. Even this help might not have been enough if the Russian offensive had not suddenly halted of its own accord. The source of this command—inexplicable and keenly frustrating to front-line generals who sensed a chance to knock Austria-Hungary out of the war—was Paris. On September 14, Paléologue received a telegram from his government. "It instructs me to impress on the Russian government that it is essential for the Russian armies to press home their direct offensive against Germany," he wrote. "[We are] afraid that our Allies may have had their heads turned by their relatively easy successes in Galicia and may neglect the German front in order to concentrate on forcing their way to

Vienna." On the Tsar's command, to accommodate the wishes of his ally, the triumphant Russians began receding from the Carpathians. Two of the four Russian armies in Galicia were shifted north to begin a fruitless attack on German Silesia. Again, Russia had made a gallant and expensive gesture toward her hard-pressed ally. But it represented a gross violation of sound military strategy as nicely expressed by the old Russian proverb: "If you chase two hares, you won't catch either." Russia's chance to crush Austria-Hungary at the outset was lost.

In the early battles of 1914, the Russians learned that the Austrians were a far weaker foe than the Germans. Fighting Austrians soon came to be considered almost unworthy by Russian officers. Knox discovered this feeling among twenty young subalterns just posted from artillery school: "The poor boys were keen as mustard and told me that their one fear was lest they might be employed till the end of the war against the Austrians and never have a dash at the Prussians."

The Russians also discovered on every battlefield that dash and bravery were not enough. The Russian cavalry, carrying long lances and swinging sabers, rode exuberantly to meet the Prussian Uhlans and Austrian Hussars. The Russian infantry, wielding vicious four-edged bayonets, willingly attacked whatever positions their officers indicated. But where those positions were defended by superior artillery and plentiful machine guns, the charging Russian ranks were scythed like rows of wheat. By the end of 1914, after only five months of war, one million Russians—one quarter of the army—had been killed, wounded or taken prisoner.

Among the officers, the ratio of loss was far higher. Unlike German and Austrian officers, who took sensible precautions, Russian officers considered it cowardly to take cover. Attacking in the face of murderous enemy fire, the officers made their men crawl forward on the ground while they themselves stood erect and walked into the enemy bullets. The famous Preobrajensky Guard Regiment lost 48 of its 70 officers; the 18th Division had only 40 of its original 370 officers. "These people play at war," said Knox sadly.

To make good these losses, three thousand military cadets were commissioned early and sent to the front. Fifteen thousand university students, originally deferred from military service, were ordered to take four months of military training and become lieutenants. Orders were given to curb the flamboyant, wasteful bravery of young officers. "Remember what I am going to say to you," said the Tsar on October 1, 1914, addressing a company of cadets promoted to lieutenant. "I have not the slightest doubt of your courage and bravery, but I need your lives, because useless losses in the officer corps may lead to serious consequences. I am sure that every one of you will give his life willingly when it becomes necessary, but do it only in cases of exceptional emergency. In other words, I am asking you to care for yourselves."

Despite their sacrifices, the Russians began the war as a gentlemanly undertaking. Captured enemy officers were not questioned; it was considered improper to ask a brother officer to inform on his compatriots. In time, the relentlessness of the German combative spirit was to alter these generous feelings. One German officer, being carried wounded from the battlefield, drew his revolver and shot his stretcher bearers. Later, the Tsar was to write, "We take no prisoners where the enemy uses explosive bullets."

Much of the power and resilience of the Russian army lay in its religious faith. Knox was enormously impressed by the simple, unquestioning belief, permeating all ranks, that prayer would lead to victory. In an underground hut near the front, he once listened to a Russian general discussing tactics with a group of Russian officers. "Then," wrote Knox, "in the simplest possible way, without any hypocritical flourish . . . he added, 'You must always remember, too, the value of prayer—with prayer you can do anything.' So sudden a transition from professional technicalities to simple primary truths seemed incongruous, and gave me almost a shock, but was taken quite naturally by the officers crowding around, with serious, bearded faces, in the little dugout. This religious belief is a power in the Russian army."

Knox watched a regiment of veterans drawn up on parade. Near the front, "The General . . . thanked them in the name of the Emperor and the country for their gallant service. . . . It was touching to see how the men were moved by his simple words of praise. . . . The latter leaned over and chucked men here and there under the chin as he rode along. 'Poor fellows,' he said as we drove away, 'they are ready to give their lives for a smile.' "

The difference that faith could make was demonstrated on every battlefront. At Easter in 1916, a German attack was launched near the

Baltic. At five a.m., German artillery began pounding the Russian trenches cut into the marshy ground. At the same time, the Germans released gas into the Russian lines. The Russians, lacking both gas masks and steel helmets, endured. After each hour of bombardment, the German artillery paused to learn the effect on the Russian trenches. Always, there was a resumption of rifle fire from the Russians, followed by a new German bombardment. After five hours of this devastation, Russian battalions of 500 men were reduced to 90 or 100. Yet when the German infantry finally advanced, it was met by a Russian bayonet charge. In all that day, the Russians gave up only a mile and half of front. That night, from within the Russian lines the Germans heard the sound of hundreds of men singing the Easter hymn, "Christ is risen from the dead, conquering death by death."

Despite the huge losses of the previous autumn, the coming of spring 1915 found the Russian army again ready for battle. Its strength, down to 2,000,000 men in December 1914, had swollen to 4,200,000 as new drafts of recruits arrived at the front. In March, the Russians attacked, hurling themselves again on the Austrians in Galicia. They had immediate, brilliant success. Przemysl, the strongest fortress in the Austro-Hungarian Empire, fell on March 19 with 120,000 prisoners and 900 guns. "Nikolasha [Grand Duke Nicholas] came running into my carriage out of breath and with tears in his eyes and told me," wrote Nicholas. A *Te Deum* in the church "was packed with officers and my splendid Cossacks. What beaming faces!" In his joy, the Tsar presented the Grand Duke with an ornamental golden sword of victory, its hilt and scabbard studded with diamonds. Early in April, the Tsar himself entered the conquered province, driving along hot roads covered with white dust. In Przemysl, he admired the fortress—"colossal works, terribly fortified, not an inch of ground remained undefended." In Lemberg, he spent the night in the house of the Austrian governor-general, occupying a bed hitherto reserved exclusively for the Emperor Franz Joseph.

Once again, waves of Russian infantry and horsemen rolled exultantly up to the Carpathians. The peaks, craggy and thickly forested, were desperately defended by crack Hungarian regiments. Because of their pitiful lack of heavy artillery and ammunition, the Russians were unable to bombard the heights before their attacks. Instead, each hill, each ridge, each crest had to be stormed by bayonet. Advancing with what Ludendorff described as "supreme contempt for death," the Russian infantry swept upward, leaving the hillsides soaked with blood. By mid-April, the Carpathian passes were in Russian hands and General Brusilov's Eighth Army was descending onto the Danubian plain. Again Vienna trembled; again there was talk of a separate peace. On April 26, 1915, convinced that the Hapsburg empire was collapsing, Italy declared war on Austria-Hungary.

It was at this moment that Hindenburg and Ludendorff let fall on Russia the monster blow which for months they had been preparing. Having failed to destroy France in 1914, the German General Staff had selected 1915 as the year to drive Russia out of the war. Through March and April, while the Russians devastated the Austrians in Galicia and the Carpathians, the German generals calmly and efficiently massed men and artillery in southern Poland. On May 2, 1,500 German guns opened fire on a single sector of the Russian line. Within a four-hour period, 700,000 shells fell into the Russian trenches.

"From a neighboring height one could see an uninterrupted line of enemy fire for five miles to each side," wrote Sir Bernard Pares, who witnessed the bombardment. "The Russian artillery was practically silent. The elementary Russian trenches were completely wiped out and so, to all intents and purposes, was human life in that area. The Russian division stationed at this point was reduced from a normal 16,000 to 500."

In this maelstrom, the Russian line disintegrated. Reinforcements were brought by train directly to the battlefield and detrained under fire. The Third Caucasian Corps, rushed into the breach, was quickly reduced from 40,000 men to 6,000; even this remnant, attacking at night with bayonets, took 7,000 prisoners. The Russian Third Army, which took the brunt of the German blow, had—said its commander—"lost all its blood." On June 2, the fortress of Przemysl was lost. Lemberg fell on June 22. "Poor Nikolasha," wrote the Tsar, "while telling me this, wept in my private room and even asked whether I thought of replacing him by a more capable man. . . . He kept thanking me for staying here, because my presence here supported him personally."

In the retreat, men lost their rifles or flung them away. The shortage quickly became desperate; one officer suggested arming some battalions with long-handled axes. "In recent battles, a third of the men had no rifles," reported General Belaiev from *Stavka.* "These poor devils had to wait patiently until their comrades fell before their eyes and they could pick up weapons. The army is drowning in its own blood." Unarmed men, waiting in support trenches until casualties on the firing line made weapons available, were "churned into gruel" by exploding shells and bursting shrapnel. The men understood what was happening. "You know, sir, we have no weapons except the soldier's breast," an infantry private said to Pares. "This is not war, sir, this is slaughter."

Nothing could stem the German columns advancing through the deep summer dust of Poland. Ahead of them came the long, slow-moving lines of refugees, trudging eastward. So intense was their suffering that a Russian general who had always been friendly suddenly turned on Knox and demanded to know what the British were doing in the war. "We are playing the game," said the Russian, distracted with anguish. "We are giving everything. Do you think it is easy for us to look at those long columns of refugees flying before the German advance? We know that all those children crowded on those carts will die before the winter is out." Knox, overcome by the tragedy, bowed his head and did not speak.

On August 5, 1915, Warsaw fell. For Grand Duke Nicholas, Russian strategy had become a question not of saving Warsaw or even Poland, but of preserving the army. Like Kutuzov in 1812, he retreated, giving up villages, towns, even provinces, intent only on keeping the army intact. Through it all, the Russian soldiers never lost their fighting spirit. On the day Warsaw fell, Knox visited officers of the Preobrajensky Guard. He found them still joking. "We will retire to the Urals," they explained, "and when we get there the enemy's pursuing army will have dwindled to a single German and a single Austrian. The Austrian will, according to custom, give himself up as a prisoner, and we will kill the German."

The ordeal of the Russian army in the spring and summer of 1915 seared all who survived. Half of the army was destroyed: 1,400,000 men were killed or wounded, 976,000 became prisoners. "The spring of 1915 I shall remember all my life," wrote General Deniken. "The retreat from Galicia was one vast tragedy for the Russian army. . . . The German heavy artillery swept away whole lines of trenches, and their defenders with them. We hardly replied—there was nothing with which we could reply. Our regiments, although completely exhausted, were beating off one attack after another by bayonet. . . . Blood flowed unendingly, the ranks became thinner and thinner. The number of graves constantly multiplied. . . . " *

It was impossible to hide from the country what was happening at the front. The gaudy optimism which had placed the Russian Guards on the Unter den Linden in less than six months was replaced by pessimism and gloom. There were no great balls that winter in the gray, snow-covered cities of Russia; the young men who had danced so gaily two winters before lay dead in the forests of East Prussia or on the slopes of the Carpathians. On the Nevsky Prospect, there were no flags, no bands playing the national anthem, no cheering crowds, only silent groups standing in the cold reading the casualty lists posted in shopwindows. In hospital wards across the land lay the wounded soldiers, patient, gentle, grateful as children. "*Nitchevo*—it is nothing, little sister," they responded to sympathy. Only rarely did the nurses hear a low-voiced "I suffer, little sister."

The thrilling sense of national unity which had so profoundly moved the Tsar in the Winter Palace and the Kremlin had evaporated, and in its place surged all the old suspicions, quarrels and hatreds. Worst was the hatred of everything German. In Petrograd, Bach, Brahms and Beethoven were banned from orchestra programs. The windows of German bakeries were broken, and exclusive German schools were threatened with arson. At Christmas in 1914, the Holy Synod had foolishly banned Christmas trees as being a German custom. "I am going to make a row," wrote the Empress to the Tsar when she heard about it. "Why take away the pleasure from the wounded and children because it originally comes from Germany? The narrow mindedness is too colossal."

Anti-German feeling was strongest in Moscow. French-speaking people riding Moscow streetcars found themselves hissed as "*Nemtsy*" [Germans] by Russians who understood no foreign tongue. Bitter stories were told about the German-born Empress. The most popular of these tales concerned a general, walking along a corridor of the Winter Palace, who came upon the Tsarevich, weeping. Patting the boy on the head, the general asked, "What is wrong, my little man?" Half smiling, half crying, the Tsarevich replied, "When the Russians

* Not surprisingly, those Russian soldiers who survived this maelstrom came to regard artillery as the God of War. Thirty years later, in April 1945, when Marshal Zhukov began the Red Army's final assault on Berlin, his attack was preceded by a barrage from 20,000 guns.

are beaten, Papa cries. When the Germans are beaten, Mama cries. When am I to cry?"

With the defeat of the supposedly invincible Russian army, the people of Moscow rushed into the streets to take vengeance. For three days beginning June 10, 1915, shops, factories and private houses belonging to people with German names were sacked and burned. "The country house of Knop, the great Russo-German millionaire who more than any man helped to build up the Russian cotton industry . . . was burned to the ground," wrote the British Consul, R. H. Bruce Lockhart. "The police could or would do nothing. . . . I stood and watched while hooligans sacked the leading piano store of Moscow. Bechsteins, Blüthners, grand pianos, baby grands, and uprights, were hurled one by one from the various stories to the ground."

In Red Square, a mob shouted open insults to the Imperial family, demanding that the Empress be shut up in a convent, the Tsar deposed, Rasputin hanged and Grand Duke Nicholas crowned as Nicholas III. From Red Square, the crowd surged to the Convent of Mary and Martha, where the Empress's sister Grand Duchess Elizabeth met them at the gate. There were wild, accusing shouts that she was giving sanctuary to a German spy and that she was hiding her brother Grand Duke Ernest of Hesse. The Grand Duchess, standing alone in white-and-gray robes, calmly invited the leaders to search the house to see for themselves that her brother was not there. As she answered, a stone landed at her feet. "Away with the German woman!" shouted the crowd, just as a company of soldiers arrived to drive them off.

Within the government, military defeat and the nation's anger brought swift political repercussions. General Sukhomlinov, at last at a loss to explain away the desperate lack of guns and munitions with another amusing story, was swept away on June 20. On June 27, the Tsar, calling on "all faithful sons of the Fatherland without distinction of class or opinion, to work together with one heart and mind to supply the needs of the army," announced that the Duma would be summoned "in order to hear the voice of the land of Russia." A new Special Defense Council, including both ministers of the government and leaders of the Duma, was formed. These were hopeful signs, but they were appearing late. General Polivanov, Sukhomlinov's successor as Minister of War, a vigorous, brusque, efficient man, spoke frankly to his fellow ministers at a meeting of the ministerial council on July 16. "I consider it my duty to declare to the Council of Ministers that the country is in danger," he declared. "Where our retreat will end, only God knows."

With his soldiers retreating, the Tsar's intense feelings about being with the army were revived. On July 16, walking restlessly in the park at Tsarskoe Selo with the Tsarevich and Gilliard, he said to the tutor, "You have no idea how depressing it is to be away from the front. It seems as if everything here saps energy and enfeebles resolution. . . . Out at the front men fight and die for their country. At the front there is only one thought—the determination to conquer."

Nicholas's strong feelings about the army were constantly stimulated from another, less noble source: the personal animosity of the Empress against Grand Duke Nicholas. Alexandra had never liked the fiery, impetuous soldier who towered over her less colorful husband. She had never forgotten that it was his melodramatic threat to blow out his brains in the presence of the Tsar and Witte which had forced the signing of the 1905 Manifesto, creating the Duma. At the front, she knew that "Nikolasha's" heroic size gave him the aura of the warrior grand duke, the real strong man of the Imperial family. There were rumors that among his intimates the Grand Duke did nothing to correct the stories that he would one day be crowned as Nicholas III. Worst, she knew that Nicholas Nicolaievich had sworn implacable hatred against Rasputin. Once Rasputin, hoping to regain favor with the man who had been his most prominent patron and had first introduced him at the Imperial palace, telegraphed the Grand Duke offering to come to Headquarters to bless an icon. "Yes, do come," replied Grand Duke Nicholas. "I'll hang you."

Against this powerful, dangerous enemy Rasputin fought back skillfully. He quickly discovered the arguments to which the Empress was most susceptible, and whenever he was in her presence, he used them with poisonous effect against the Commander-in-Chief: The Grand Duke is deliberately currying favor in the army and overshadowing the Tsar so that one day he can claim the throne. The Grand Duke cannot possibly succeed on the battlefield because God will not bless him. How can God bless a man who has turned his back on me, the Man of God? In all probability, if the Grand Duke is allowed to keep his power, he will kill me, and then what will happen to the Tsarevich, the Tsar and Russia?

As long as the Russian army continued to advance, Grand Duke

Nicholas's command remained secure. But once his soldiers began to retreat, his position became increasingly vulnerable. Through the summer, Alexandra's letters to the Tsar maintained a steady drumfire of criticism against the Grand Duke, echoing and re-echoing Rasputin's arguments:

June 11 (O.S.): "Please my angel, make N. [Nikolasha, the Grand Duke] see with your eyes. . . . I hope my letter did not displease but I am haunted by our Friend's [Rasputin's] wish and know it will be fatal for us and the country if not fulfilled. He means what he says when He speaks so seriously."

June 12: "Would to God N. were another man and not turned against a Man of God's."

June 16: "I have absolutely no faith in N.—know him to be far from clever and having gone against a Man of God, his work can't be blessed or his advice good. . . . Russia will not be blessed if her sovereign lets a Man of God sent to help him be persecuted, I am sure. . . . You know N.'s hatred for Gregory is intense."

June 17: "N's fault and Witte's that the Duma exists, and it has caused you more worry than joy. Oh, I do not like N. having anything to do with these big sittings which concern interior questions, he understands our country so little and imposes upon the ministers with his loud voice and gesticulations. I can go wild sometimes at his false position. . . . Nobody knows who is the Emperor now. . . . It is as though N. settles all, makes the choices and changes. It makes me utterly wretched."

June 25: "I loathe your being at Headquarters . . . listening to N.'s advice which is not good and cannot be—he has no right to act as he does, mixing in your concerns. All are shocked that the ministers go with reports to him, as though he were now the sovereign. Ah, my Nicky, things are not as they ought to be and therefore N. keeps you near to have a hold over you with his ideas and bad counsels."

The Tsar did not share his wife's strong views of Grand Duke Nicholas. He respected the Grand Duke and had full—and thoroughly justified—confidence in his loyalty. Paléologue, visiting *Stavka*, once attempted to discuss the Tsar's views with the Commander-in-Chief. Drawing himself up, the Grand Duke replied coldly, "I never discuss an opinion of His Majesty's except when he does me the honor of asking my advice." To suppress talk in some ranks of the army that Russia could not go on fighting, the Grand Duke issued an Order of the Day: "All faithful subjects know that in Russia, everyone from the

Commander-in-Chief to the private soldier, obeys and obeys only the sacred and august will of the Anointed of God, our deeply revered Emperor, who alone has the power to begin and end a war."

Wherever possible the Tsar tried to buffer relations between the Empress and Grand Duke Nicholas. In April 1915, when Nicholas was to visit Lemberg and Przemysl, Alexandra wanted the Grand Duke to remain behind so that her husband alone could receive the cheers of the troops. Calmly, Nicholas dissuaded her: "Darling mine, I do not agree with you that N. ought to remain here during my visit to Galicia. On the contrary, precisely because I am going in wartime to a conquered province, the commander-in-chief ought to be accompanying me. It is he who accompanies me, not I who am in his suite."

Nevertheless, as the retreat continued, the Tsar's determination to take personal command of the army intensified. With the army and the nation in danger, he was convinced that it was his duty to unify civil and military authority and take on his own person the full weight of responsibility for Russia's destiny. In the Council of Ministers, where bitter attacks had been made on Grand Duke Nicholas's handling of military operations, Prime Minister Goremykin warned his colleagues, "I consider it my duty to repeat to the members of the Council my emphatic advice to be extremely careful in what they are going to say to the Emperor about . . . those questions that relate to General Headquarters and the Grand Duke. Irritation against the Grand Duke at Tsarskoe Selo has become of a character which threatens serious consequences. I fear that your representations may serve as a pretext to bring about grave complications."

On August 5, Warsaw fell. "The Emperor, white and trembling, brought this news to the Empress as we sat at tea on her balcony in the warm autumn air," wrote Anna Vyrubova. "The Emperor was fairly overcome with grief and humiliation. 'It cannot go on like this,' he exclaimed bitterly."

Three weeks later, Nicholas and Alexandra made an unannounced, private visit by automobile to Petrograd. They drove first to the cathedral in the Fortress of Peter and Paul, where they knelt before the tombs of the tsars. From there they went to the Cathedral of Our Lady of Kazan, where they remained for several hours kneeling at the miraculous icon of the Virgin, praying for guidance. That night, the Council of Ministers was summoned to the Alexander Palace. Nicholas dined that evening with his wife and Anna Vyrubova. Before leaving for the meeting, he asked them to pray that his resolution remain strong. Silently, Anna pressed into his hand a tiny icon which she always wore around her neck. Carrying the icon, Nicholas walked out of the room and the two women settled down to wait. As the minutes stretched into hours, Alexandra grew impatient. Throwing a cloak around her shoulders and motioning Anna to follow, she slipped out onto a balcony which led past the windows of the council chamber. Through the lace curtains inside, they could see the Tsar, sitting very straight in his chair, surrounded by his ministers. One of the ministers was on his feet, arguing passionately.

Without exception, the ministers were aghast at the Tsar's proposal. They pointed to the disorganization of governmental machinery that would come if the head of state were to spend all his time at Headquarters, more than five hundred miles from the seat of government. They declared that the unity of administration which Nicholas sought would merely become a concentration of all blame for military defeats and political turmoil on the head of the sovereign. In the last resort, they begged him not to go to the front at a moment when the army was defeated. Nicholas listened, his brows and hands covered with perspiration, until every minister had spoken. Then he thanked them and announced quietly, "Gentlemen, in two days I leave for *Stavka.*"

His public letter to the Grand Duke, explaining his decision, was characteristic of the Tsar. Eloquent and felicitous, it managed to spare the Grand Duke's pride while gracefully easing him out of his post:

> To Your Imperial Highness:
>
> At the beginning of the war there were reasons of a political nature which prevented me from following my personal inclinations and immediately putting myself at the head of the army. Hence the fact that I conferred upon you the supreme command of all the military and naval forces.
>
> Before the eyes of all Russia, Your Imperial Highness has during the war displayed an invincible courage, which has given me and all Russians the greatest confidence in you, and roused the ardent hopes with which your name was everywhere associated in the inevitable vicissitudes of military fortune. Now that the enemy has penetrated far into the empire, my duty to the country which God has committed to my keeping ordains that I shall assume supreme command of the fighting forces, share the bur-

dens and toils of war with my army and help it to protect Russian soil against the onslaught of the foe.

The ways of Providence are inscrutable; but my duty and my own desires strengthen me in a determination which has been inspired by concern for the common weal.

The hostile invasion which is making more progress every day on the western front, demands above all an extreme concentration of all civil and military authority, unity of command during the war, and intensification of the activities of the whole administrative services. But all these duties distract our attention from the southern front, and in these circumstances, I feel the necessity for your advice and help on that front. I therefore appoint you my lieutenant in the Caucasus and Commander-in-Chief of the brave army operating in that region.

To Your Imperial Highness I wish to express my profound gratitude and that of the country for all your work in the war.

Nicholas

The letter was personally delivered to Grand Duke Nicholas at Headquarters by the War Minister, Polivanov. "God be praised," said Nicholas Nicolaievich simply. "The Emperor releases me from a task which was wearing me out." When the Tsar himself arrived at *Stavka*, he wrote: "N. came in with a kind, brave smile and asked simply when I would order him to go. The following day at lunch and dinner he was very talkative and in a very good mood."

The fall of the Grand Duke was a source of grim satisfaction to the Germans. "The Grand Duke," Ludendorff wrote later, "was really a great soldier and strategist." In the Russian army, officers and men were sad to see him go, but the summer of disaster had dimmed his hero's luster. Within the mauve boudoir at Tsarskoe Selo, the change was hailed as a supreme personal triumph. When Nicholas left for *Stavka*, he carried with him a letter of ecstasy from Alexandra:

My very own beloved one, I cannot find words to express all I want to—my heart is too full. I only long to hold you tight in my arms and whisper words of intense love, courage, strength and endless blessings. . . . You have fought this great fight for your country and throne—alone and with bravery and decision. Never have they seen such firmness in you before. . . . I know what it costs you . . . forgive me, I beseech you, my Angel, for having left you no peace and worried you so much, but I too well know your marvelously gentle character and you had to shake it off this time, had to win your fight alone against all. It will be a glorious page in your reign and Russian history, the story of these weeks and days. . . . God anointed you at your coronation, he placed you where you stand and you have done your duty, be sure, quite sure of that and He forsaketh not his anointed. Our Friend's prayers arise day and night for you to Heaven and God will hear them. . . . It is the beginning of the great glory of your reign, He said so and I absolutely believe it. . . . Sleep well, my Sunshine, Russia's Savior. Remember last night how tenderly we clung together. I shall yearn for your caresses. . . . I kiss you without end and bless you. Holy Angels guard your slumber. I am near and with you forever and ever and none shall separate us.

Your very own wife,
Sunny

In France and England, the Tsar's decision was greeted with a sigh of relief. Russian defeats had aroused fear in both countries that the Tsar's government might be forced to withdraw from the war. By taking personal command, Nicholas was regarded as pledging himself and his empire once again to the alliance.

In the Russian army, it was clearly understood that the Tsar's role would be that of a figurehead, and that the actual military decisions would be made by whichever professional soldier became his chief of staff. Nicholas's choice for this post was reassuring. Michael Vasilevich Alexeiev was an energetic soldier of humble beginnings who had risen to the top by sheer ability and hard work. A former professor at the military staff college, he had served in the southwest against the Austrians and had commanded the Northern Front. Now, as Chief of Staff, he was in fact, if not in name, Commander-in-Chief of the Russian armies.

In appearance, Alexeiev compared poorly with the Grand Duke. He was short, with a simple, wide Russian face which, unlike most Russian generals, he chose to expose without a beard. He had trouble with an eye muscle, and Nicholas once described him to Alexandra as "Alexeiev, my cross-eyed friend." At Headquarters, he was solitary, avoiding contact with the Imperial suite. His weakness was a failure to delegate authority; he tried to do everything himself, including checking map references on the huge war maps spread out on Headquarters tables. Nevertheless, Nicholas was delighted with him. "I have such good help from Alexeiev," he telegraphed immediately after taking command. And a few days later: "I cannot tell you how pleased I am with Alexeiev. Conscientious, clever, modest and what a worker!"

In September 1915, soon after the change of command at Russian Headquarters, the German offensive began to lose impetus. Russian troops, fighting now on the soil of Russia itself, gave ground slowly, contesting every river, hill and marsh. By November, as winter closed down most of the front, Alexeiev had managed to stabilize a line which ran, on the average, two hundred miles east of the front in May. Firmly in German hands lay all of Russian Poland and the lower Baltic territories. Indeed, the battle line at the end of 1915 became almost precisely the western frontier of Soviet Russia until 1939 and the outbreak of the Second World War.

There were no further great German offensives in the East during the war. Assuming that the losses of 1915 had broken the back of the Russian army, the German General Staff transferred its main effort back to the Western Front. Beginning in February 1916, all of the great mass of German artillery and a million infantrymen were hurled at the pivotal French fortress of Verdun. To the utter astonishment and intense dismay of the Kaiser's generals, no sooner were they committed in the West than the Russians attacked again in the East. From May until October, the Russians pressed forward; by July, eighteen German divisions had been transferred from West to East and the assault on Verdun had been abandoned. But the cost to the Russian army of the 1916 campaign again was a terrible one: 1,200,000 men.

After the war, Hindenburg paid tribute to the bravery and sacrifices of his Russian enemies: "In the Great War ledger the page on which the Russian losses were written has been torn out. No one knows the figures. Five or eight millions? We too have no idea. All we know is that sometimes in our battles with the Russians we had to remove the mounds of enemy corpses from before our trenches in order to get a clear field of fire against fresh assaulting waves." Ten years after Hindenburg wrote, a careful analysis of Russian casualties was made by Nicholas Golovine, a former general of the Imperial army. Weighing all the evidence, he estimated that 1,300,000 men were killed in action; 4,200,000 were wounded, of whom 350,000 later died of wounds; and 2,400,000 were taken prisoner. The total is 7,900,000—over half of the 15,500,000 men who were mobilized.

Thus, the military collapse of 1915 played a major part in all that was to happen afterward. For it was the tragic and bloody defeat of the army which weakened the grip of Grand Duke Nicholas and persuaded the Tsar to take personal command of his troops. By going to the army, hundreds of miles from the seat of government, the Tsar gave up all but a vague, supervisory control over affairs of state. In an autocracy, this arrangement was impossible; a substitute autocrat had to be found. Uncertainly at first, then with growing self-confidence, this role was filled by the Empress Alexandra. At her shoulder, his "prayers arising day and night," stood her Friend, Rasputin. Together they would finally bring down the Russian Empire.

CHAPTER TWENTY-THREE

The Fateful Deception

THE Empress had thrown herself heart and soul into the war. Burning with patriotism, filled with energy and enthusiasm, she forgot her own illness to plunge into hospital work. Alexandra was happiest when immersed in other people's problems, and the war gave endless scope to this side of her nature. "To some it may seem unnecessary my doing this," she said, "but . . . help is much needed and every hand is useful." Nursing became her passion. The huge Catherine Palace at Tsarskoe Selo was converted into a military hospital, and before the end of 1914 eighty-five hospitals were operated under her patronage in the Petrograd area alone. This activity, although on a grand scale, was not unique; many Russian ladies at this time established themselves as patrons of hospitals and hospital trains. But only a few followed the Empress's example by enrolling in nursing courses and coming daily in person to tend the wounded.

Life inside the Alexander Palace was transformed. The Empress, who had stayed in bed nursing her ills until noon, now was up for Mass at seven. Promptly at nine, dressed in the gray uniform of a nursing sister, she arrived at the hospital along with her two eldest daughters, Olga and Tatiana, and Anna Vyrubova for her nursing course. The hospital atmosphere was brutal and pathetic. Every day, Red Cross trains brought long lines of wounded and dying men back from the front. Most had had only first aid in the trenches and front-line dressing stations. They arrived dirty, bloodstained, feverish and groaning. Under the direction of trained nurses, the students washed and bandaged the ripped flesh and mangled bodies. "I have seen the Empress of Russia in the operating room," wrote Anna Vyrubova, ' . . . holding ether cones, handling sterilized instruments, assisting in the most difficult operations, taking from the hands of busy surgeons amputated legs and arms, removing bloody and even vermin-ridden field dressings, enduring all the sights and smells and agonies of the most dreadful of all places, a military hospital in the midst of war." Nevertheless, wrote Anna, "I never saw her happier than on the day, at the end of her two months training, she marched at the head of the procession of nurses to receive the Red Cross . . . diploma of a certified war nurse."

After a morning in the operating room, Alexandra ate a hurried lunch and spent the afternoon visiting other hospitals. Moving through the aisles between hospital beds, the tall figure of the Empress in her nurse's uniform stirred the wounded men. They reached out bandaged hands to touch her; they wept as she knelt beside their beds to pray. Officers and peasant boys alike, facing amputations, cried from their beds, "Tsaritsa, stand near me. Hold my hand that I may have courage."

To Alexandra, this was Russia, bleeding and dying. She was the Russian Empress, the *matushka* of all the brave men and boys who had given themselves for Russia. "Very bad wounds," she wrote to Nicholas on October 21, 1914 (O.S.). "For the first time, I shaved one of the soldiers' legs near and around the wound. . . . " Later, the same day, in a second letter: "Three operations, 3 fingers were taken off as blood poisoning had set in and they were quite rotten. . . . My nose is full of hideous smells from those blood poisoning wounds." And again: "I went in to see the wound of our standard bearer—awful, bones quite smashed, he suffered hideously during bandaging, but did not say a word, only got pale and perspiration ran down his face and body. . . ." On November 19 (O.S.): "An officer of the 2nd Rifles, poor boy, whose legs are getting quite dark and one fears an amputation may be necessary. I was with the boy yesterday during his dressing, awful to see, and he clung to me and kept quiet, poor child." On November 20 (O.S.): "This morning we were present (I help as always giving the instruments and Olga threaded the needles) at our first big amputation. Whole arm was cut off."

Alexandra spared herself nothing, not even terrible, shattering wounds in the groin: "I had wretched fellows with awful wounds—scarcely a man any more, so shot to pieces, perhaps it must be cut off as so black, but hope to save it—terrible to look at. I washed and cleaned and painted with iodine and smeared with vasoline and tied them up and bandaged all up. . . . I did three such—and one had a little tube in it. One's heart bleeds for them—I won't describe any more details as it's so sad, but being a wife and mother I feel for them quite particularly—a young nurse (girl) I sent out of the room."

To Nicholas, at Army Headquarters, death was remote, a question of arithmetic, as regiments, brigades and divisions shriveled away and then were restored by new recruits. To Alexandra, death was familiar and immediate. "During an operation a soldier died . . . hemorrhage," she wrote on November 25, 1914 (O.S.). "All behaved well, none lost their heads [Olga and Tatiana] were brave—They and Ania [Vyrubova] had never seen a death. But he died in a minute. . . . How near death always is."

In November, she formed a special attachment to a young boy, mentioning him repeatedly in her letters: "A young boy kept begging for me . . . the little boy begged me to come earlier today . . . I find the young boy gradually getting worse . . . in the evenings he is off his head and so weak . . . He will pass away gradually. I only hope not whilst we are away."

Early in March, he died. She wrote: "My poor wounded friend has gone. God has taken him quietly and peacefully to himself. I was as usual with him in the morning and more than an hour in the afternoon. He talked a lot—in a whisper always—all about his service in the Caucasus—awfully interesting and so bright with his big shiny eyes. . . . Olga and I went to see him. He lay there so peacefully covered under my flowers I daily brought him, with his lovely peaceful smile—the forehead yet quite warm. I came home with my tears. The elder sister [nurse] cannot either realize it—he was quite calm, cheery, said felt a wee bit not comfy and when the sister 10 minutes after she had gone away, came in, found him with staring eyes, quite blue, breathed twice—and all was over—peaceful to the end. Never did he complain, never asked for anything, sweetness itself—all loved him and that shining smile. You, lovy mine, can understand what that is, when daily one has been there, thinking only of giving him pleasure—and suddenly—finished. . . . Forgive my writing so much about him, but going there and all that, had been a help with you away and I felt God let me bring him a little sunshine in his loneliness. Such is life! Another brave soul left this world to be added to the shining stars above. It must not make you sad what I wrote, only I could not bear it any longer."

The Empress's letters to the Tsar were never meant for any eyes but his. In all, 630 letters were found in a black leather suitcase in Ekaterinburg after her death; of these, 230 were written over the period from their first acquaintance to the outbreak of war in 1914. The other 400 were written during the war years 1914–1916. They were written with no inkling that anyone else would ever read them, far less that they would one day be published and become key historical documents used to explain events, personalities and decisions on the eve of the Russian Revolution. Today, they offer this and even more: an intimate window into a soul, a unique portrait of a woman which none of her contemporaries in Russia could possibly have seen.

Alexandra wrote voluminously. She would begin early in the morning, add paragraphs during the day, go on for pages late at night and perhaps add even more the next day. In a bold, rounded hand, she wrote to the Tsar in English in the same telegraphic style she used for her friends: breathless prose with irregular spelling, many abbreviations, frequent omissions of words that seemed obvious, and punctuation largely with dots and dashes. Both the length and the style of her letters are unfortunate. Often by skipping and jumping, she gives an impression of light-mindedness on subjects about which she actually cared deeply. Similarly, the intense fervor of other passages is strong evidence of the great passions of which Alexandra was capable, but not—as some have charged—sufficient proof that the Empress was mad. The sheer length of her letters has made their interpretation difficult for historians and biographers. It is arduous to read them all and impossible to quote more than a minuscule fraction. Yet, in her case to an extraordinary extent, excerpting has been misleading. A thought whose germination has been proceeding for sentences—perhaps paragraphs—suddenly arrives full strength in a stark and damning phrase. These phrases, plucked from the mass of verbiage, make a loquacious woman seem hopelessly hysterical.

A remarkable feature of these letters was the freshness of Alexandra's love. After two decades of marriage, she still wrote like a young girl. The Empress, so shy and even icy about expressing emotion in public, released all her romantic passion in her letters. Beneath the Victorian surface of reserve, she revealed the extravagant, flowery emotions of the Victorian poets.

The letters, usually arriving with petals of lilies or violets pressed between their pages, begin "Good morning, my darling . . . My beloved one . . . My sweetest treasure . . . My Own Beloved Angel." They end: "Sleep well, my treasure . . . I yearn to hold you in my arms and rest my head upon your shoulder . . . I yearn for your kisses, for your arms and shy Childy [Nicholas] gives them me [only] in the dark and wify lives by them." She was in anguish whenever he left for the front: "Oh, my love! It was hard bidding you goodbye and seeing that lonely, pale face with big sad eyes at the . . . [train] window—my heart cried out, take me with you . . . I gave my goodnight kiss to your cushion and longed to have you near me—in thoughts I see you lying in your compartment, bend over you, bless you, and gently kiss your sweet face all over—oh my Darling, how intensely dear you are to me—could I but help you in carrying your heavy burdens, there are so many that weigh on you." Their burdens were much on her mind: "I . . . try to forget everything, gazing into your lovely eyes. . . . So much sorrow and pain, worries and trials—one gets so tired and one must keep up and be strong and face everything. . . . We show nothing of what we feel when together. Each keeps up for the other's sake and suffers in silence. We have lived through so much together in these 20 years—and without words have understood each other." Although her language had the fresh, gushing quality of young love, Alexandra did not deceive herself about the passing of time: "32 years ago my child's heart already went out to you in deep love. . . . I know I ought not to say this, and for an old married woman it may seem ridiculous, but I cannot help it. With the years, love increases and the time without your sweet presence is hard to bear. Oh, could but our children be equally blessed in their married lives."

Nicholas read her letters in bed at night, the last thing before going to sleep. His replies, if more restrained, were no less intimate and tender. "My beloved Sunny," he wrote, "when I read your letters my eyes are moist . . . it seems that you are lying on your sofa and that I am listening to you, sitting in my armchair by the lamp. . . . I don't know how I could have endured it all if God had not decreed to give you to me as a wife and friend. I speak in earnest. At times it is difficult to speak of such things and it is easier for me to put it down on paper, owing to stupid shyness. . . . Goodbye, my beloved sweet Sunny. . . . I kiss you and the children tenderly. Ever your old hubby, Nicky."

Sitting on her balcony, the Empress described the changing seasons at Tsarskoe Selo: "the sun behind the trees, a soft haze over all, the swans swimming on the pond, steam rising off the grass," and later, "the leaves are turning very yellow and red," and then, "the pink sky behind the kitchen and the trees thickly covered in snow look quite fairy like." From Mogilev, in early spring, Nicholas wrote "the Dnieper broke up yesterday. The whole river was covered with blocks of ice, they moved swiftly but noiselessly and only occasionally could be heard the sharp sound of the clashing of two large ice blocks. It was a magnificent spectacle." A few weeks later: "the birches are growing green, the chestnuts are shimmering and soon will burst into bud. Everything smells good. I noticed two small dogs chasing each other while I stood washing at my window."

Knowing how much he missed his children, Alexandra filled her letters with homey details of their activities: "Baby has his lessons and goes out in the donkey sled twice a day. We take tea in his room and he likes it. . . . Baby madly enjoys your bath and made us all come and look on his pranks in the water. All the daughters beg too for the same treat some evening. May they?" When the Tsar's permission arrived: "The girls are wild that they may bathe in your bath." And later: "Baby ate lots of blinis. . . . Baby improves playing on the balalaika. Tatiana too. I want them to learn to play together. . . . Marie stands at the door and, alas! picks her nose. . . . On the train, the girls are sprawling on the floor with the sun shining full upon them to get brown. From whom have they got that craze? . . . "

Despite the distraction of hospital work, the Empress continued to suffer from shortness of breath and used a wheelchair when not in public. Her feet were swollen and her teeth ached. During the spring of 1916, the dentist came daily; sometimes she saw him three separate times in a day. Alexis was bothered with recurring bleeding into his elbows and knees. When he was unable to walk, the Empress spent hours lying on a sofa in his room and took her dinner beside his bed. As evening approached and his pain became stronger—"he dreads the night," she wrote—his sisters Olga and Tatiana came to distract him.

"Baby was awfully gay and cheery all day . . . in the night he woke up from pain in his left arm and from 2 on scarcely got a moment's sleep," she wrote on April 6, 1916. "The girls sat with him a good while. It seems he worked with a dirk and must have done too much—he is so strong that it's difficult for him always to remember and think that he must not do strong movements. But as the pain came with such force in the night and the arm won't bend I think it will pass quicker—generally three nights pain. . . . I cried like a baby in church. Cannot bear when the sweet child suffers."

That night, she wrote again: "This afternoon I spent in Baby's room whilst Mr. G. [Gilliard] read to him. . . . He suffered almost the whole time, then would doze for a few minutes, and then again strong pains. . . . Reading is the best thing, as for a time it distracts the thoughts. . . . Seeing him suffer makes me utterly wretched. Mr. G. is so gentle and kind with him, knows exactly how to be with him."

For those who knew her, there never was any question of the Empress's Russian patriotism. War between Germany and Russia was personally excruciating—her brother Grand Duke Ernest of Hesse was in the German army—but her allegiance was fervently Russian. "Twenty years have I spent in Russia," she explained to a lady-in-waiting. "It is the country of my husband and my son. I have lived the life of a happy wife and mother in Russia. All my heart is bound to this country." Nevertheless, she grieved at the change that had come over Germany. "What has happened to the Germany of my childhood?" she asked Pierre Gilliard. "I have such happy, poetic memories of my early years at Darmstadt. But on my later visits, Germany seemed to me a changed country, a country I did not know and had never known. . . . I had no community of thought or feeling with anyone." She blamed the change on Prussia and the Kaiser. "Prussia has meant Germany's ruin," she declared. "I have no news of my brother. I shiver to think that the Emperor William may avenge himself against me by sending him to the Russian front. He is quite capable of such monstrous behavior."

Because of her awkward personal position, Alexandra was especially sensitive to the national reputation of the soldiers on both sides. When the German army savagely burned the Belgian library town of Louvain, she cried, "I blush to have been a German." On September 25, 1914 (O.S.), she wrote to the Tsar, "I long that our troops should behave exemplarily in every sense and not rob and pillage—leave that horror to the Prussian troops. . . . I want our Russian troops to be remembered hereafter with awe and respect—and admiration. . . . Now I am bothering you with things that do not concern me, but only out of love for your soldiers and their reputation."

Her deep sorrow was war itself and the suffering it brought. Like so many others, she yearned that the suffering would have meaning: "I do wonder what will be after this great war is over. Will there be a reawakening and new birth in all—shall once more ideals exist, will people become more pure and poetic, or will they continue to be dry materialists? So many things one longs to know. But such terrible misery as the whole world has suffered must clean hearts and minds and purify the stagnant brains and sleeping souls. Oh, only to guide all wisely into the right and fruitful channel."

Sharing the Tsar's patriotism, convinced that she and her husband were the center of a great national movement which was sweeping Russia, the Empress worked in the hospitals and awaited victory which would surely come. It was not until the spring of 1915, when the prospect of early victory had faded, that Alexandra's letters first showed a serious interest in her husband's work.

Her concern began, curiously enough, with the matter of the Tsar's personal bearing. Wholly imbued with the principle of autocracy, convinced that it was the only form of government for Russia, Alexandra worried that her gentle husband, whom she loved for his kindness and charm, was not sufficiently regal. "Forgive me, precious one," she began to write in April 1915, "but you know you are too kind and gentle—sometimes a good loud voice can do wonders and a severe look—do, my love, be more decided and sure of yourself. You know perfectly well what is right. They [the ministers] must remember who you are. You think me a meddlesome bore, but a woman feels and sees things sometimes clearer than my too humble sweetheart. Humility is God's greatest gift but a sovereign needs to show his will more often."

At the same time, she was advising, "Be more autocratic, my very own sweetheart . . . Be the master and lord, you are the autocrat," Alexandra also began to warn against those she thought were encroaching on the Imperial prerogatives. Grand Duke Nicholas was one target of her criticism; she continued her chiding until he fell. Simultaneously, the Empress bitterly inveighed against the Duma. "Deary, I heard that that horrid Rodzianko and others . . . beg the Duma to be called at once together," she wrote in July 1915. "Oh, please don't it's not their business, they want to discuss things not concerning them and bring more discontent—they must be kept away." Over and over in her letters, she sounds the theme: "We're not a constitutional country and dare not be, our people are not educated for it. . . . Never forget that you are and must remain autocratic Emperor. We are not ready for constitutional government." It was not only her husband's prerogative she was protecting, but also the rights of her son, the future tsar: "For Baby's sake we must be firm as otherwise his inheritance will be awful, as with his character he won't bow down to others but be his own master, as one must in Russia whilst people are still so uneducated."

Seen from Alexandra's viewpoint, the next step was entirely logical. In waging this great fight to save Russia and the autocracy, she needed a powerful ally. Rasputin, she was convinced, was a Man of God; his credentials had been proved in the hours when his prayers had seemed miraculously to check the Tsarevich's hemorrhages. Now, in a time of war, he also appeared the living embodiment of the soul of the Russian people: coarse, simple, uneducated, but close to God and devoted to the Tsar. From these premises, it was no great step for her to conclude that God intended Rasputin to guide Russia through the ordeal of war. If she could trust him with the dearest thing she possessed—the life of her son—why should she not also trust him with choosing ministers, commanding the army or directing the life of the entire nation?

For a while in the first autumn of war, Rasputin's influence at Tsarskoe Selo had dwindled. Nicholas could not forgive him his opposition to what the Tsar considered a patriotic war; the Empress was busy from morning until night with hospitals, fulfilling herself in nursing. Once when Rasputin telephoned Anna Vyrubova and asked to see the Empress, Anna replied that the Empress was busy and that he had better wait a few days. Rasputin put down the phone with loud annoyance.

Early in the winter of 1915, however, Rasputin's influence over the Empress was sweepingly restored by another of those remarkable episodes which studded his life. Late on the afternoon of January 15, 1915, a train carrying Anna Vyrubova from Tsarskoe Selo into Petrograd was wrecked. When Anna was found and extricated from the wreckage, she was in critical condition. Her legs had been crushed by the coils of a steam radiator; a steel girder had fallen across her face and pinned her head; her skull and her spine were badly injured. At the hospital where she was taken, a surgeon declared, "Do not disturb her. She is dying." Nicholas and Alexandra came to her bedside and waited helplessly for the end. Rasputin, quite out of touch, did not hear about the accident until the following day. When he did, he jumped up from his table and drove straight to the hospital in a car sent to him by Countess Witte. When he entered the room, Anna was in a delirium, murmuring, "Father Gregory, pray for me," while the

Tsar and the Empress stood by. Rasputin strode to Anna's side, took her hand and called out "Annushka! Annushka! Annushka!"

The third time he called, Anna slowly opened her eyes.

Rasputin ordered her, "Now wake up and rise."

She made an effort to get up.

"Speak to me," he commanded.

She spoke in a feeble voice.

"She will recover, but she will remain a cripple," said Rasputin, turning to the others. Then he staggered from the room and collapsed in a wave of dizziness and perspiration.

Exactly as Rasputin had predicted, Anna recovered but thereafter moved only on crutches or in a wheelchair. Her devotion to Rasputin became unquestioning. Convinced that he was sent by Heaven to save the Imperial family, she dedicated herself to assisting Rasputin in his mission. Acting as intermediary, she did everything in her power to smooth over differences between her mistress and the *starets.*

In Alexandra, the episode overwhelmingly revived her conviction that Rasputin was a true saint capable of accomplishing miracles. Utterly convinced herself, she did her utmost to transfer her conviction to Nicholas. "No, harken unto Our Friend," she wrote in June 1915. "Believe him. He has your interest and Russia's at heart. It is not for nothing God sent him to us, only we must pay more attention to what He says. His words are not lightly spoken and the importance of having not only his prayers but his advice is great. . . . I am haunted by Our Friend's wish and know it will be fatal for us and for the country if not fulfilled. He means what he says when he speaks so seriously." In September 1916: "I fully trust in our Friend's wisdom, endowed by God to counsel what is right for you and our country. He sees far ahead and therefore his judgement can be relied upon."

One block from the Fontanka Canal, at 64 Gorokhovaya Street in Petrograd, stood the building where Rasputin lived during these crucial years, 1914–1916. A five-story brick apartment house, entered through a small paved courtyard, with a concierge's room at the foot of the wide stairs, it was architecturally similar to thousands of buildings erected in that era in Paris, London, Berlin or New York. Socially there was nothing distinguished about the house of the Imperial favorite. Rasputin's neighbors were working people: a clerk, a seamstress, a masseuse. The staircase was thick with pungent smells leather, sheepskin coats, thick clouds of cabbage soup and the rancid odor of hot sheep's cheese.

Rasputin's apartment on the third floor of this building was surprisingly small and sedate. It consisted of five rooms. "The bedroom . . . was small and very simply furnished," wrote Prince Felix Yussoupov, who often visited Rasputin. "In a corner close to the wall was a narrow bed with a red fox bedspread, a present from Anna Vyrubova. Near the bed was a big chest of painted wood; in the opposite corner were lamps which burned before a small icon. Portraits of the Tsar and Tsarina hung on the walls along with crude engravings representing biblical scenes." [In the dining room] "water was boiling in the samovar; on the tables were a number of plates filled with biscuits, cakes and nuts; glass bowls contained jam and fruit and other delicacies; in the center stood a great basket of flowers. The furniture was of massive oak, the chairs had very high backs, a bulky dresser full of crockery took up most of one wall. There were a few badly-painted pictures. A bronze chandelier with glass shades lighted the table. The flat had an air of middle-class solidity."

Here, on days when he had not been drinking late, Rasputin rose early and went to Mass. By the time he returned for a breakfast of bread and tea, the first of his petitioners already was climbing the stairs. Rasputin's influence at court brought him people from all walks of life: bankers, bishops, officers, society women, actresses, adventurers and speculators, peasant girls, old women who had traveled miles simply to get his blessing. The callers came in such numbers that many had to wait in line on the staircase. Outside, the curb was lined with the automobiles of important people visiting Rasputin.

If Rasputin liked a visitor and decided to help, he took his pen and scrawled a few clumsy lines: "My dear and valued friend. Do this for me. Gregory." These scraps of paper, carrying the aura of great connections, were often all that was needed to obtain a position, win a promotion, delay a transfer or confirm a contract. Some of these notes, attached to petitions, went straight to the Empress, who forwarded them to the Tsar. Because Mosolov was head of the Court Secretariat, Rasputin's notes often arrived on his desk. "All were drawn up the same way," he wrote, "a little cross at the top of the page, then one or two lines giving a recommendation from the *starets*. They opened all doors in Petrograd." In one case, Mosolov was unable to help. "A lady in a low cut dress, suitable for a ball . . . handed me an envelope: inside was Rasputin's calligraphy with his erratic spelling: 'My dear chap, Fix it up for her. She is all right. Gregory.' The lady explained that she wanted to become a prima donna in the Imperial Opera. I did my utmost to explain to her clearly and patiently that the post did not depend in any way on me."

Usually, because he wrote poorly and slowly, Rasputin did not bother to name the service to be performed, leaving it to the petitioner to supply these details. Often, he did not even name the addressee, assuming that the petitioner would place it in the most appropriate hands. Eventually, to save time, Rasputin made up a supply of these notes in advance. As his petitioners arrived, he simply handed them out.

In return for his services, Rasputin accepted whatever his visitors might offer. Financiers and wealthy women put bundles of money on the table and Rasputin stuffed them into his drawers without bothering to count. If his next petitioner was a person in need, he might pull out the whole bundle and give it away. He had little need of money himself; his flat was simple, most of his wines and foods were brought as gifts. His only real interest in acquiring money was to accumulate a dowry for his daughter Maria, who was in school in Petrograd and lived in a room in his apartment.

For pretty women, there were other methods of payment. Many an attractive visitor, thinking she could win his help with words and smiles, rushed suddenly out of his apartment, weeping or trembling with rage. Helped down the stairs, she went off to the police station to complain that Rasputin had tried to rape her. There, her name and the circumstances of her plight were duly noted, but Father Gregory was never punished.

Along with his droves of petitioners, another cluster of people attended faithfully on Rasputin. Day after day, in front of the house, in the concierge's lodge and on the stairs leading to Rasputin's door, lounged a squad of detectives. They had a double function: to guard the *starets's* life and to take careful notes of everyone he saw and everything that happened to him. Bored, shifting their feet on the stairs to let the petitioners pass, they scribbled down minute details: "Anastasia Shapovalenkova, the wife of a doctor, has given Rasputin a carpet. . . . An unknown clergyman brought fish for Rasputin. . . Councilor von Kok brought Rasputin a case of wine." When a visitor left Rasputin's apartment, the plainclothesmen swarmed around, hoping to learn what had happened inside. If the visitor was garrulous, little dramas were scrawled deadpan into the notebooks:

November 2: "An unknown woman visited Rasputin in order to try to prevent her husband, a lieutenant at present in hospital, from being transferred from St. Petersburg. . . . [She said] 'A servant opened the door to me and showed me to a room where Rasputin, whom I had never seen before, appeared immediately. He told me at once to take off my clothes. I complied with his wish, and went with him into an adjoining room. He hardly listened to my request; but kept on touching my face and breasts and asking me to kiss him. Then he wrote a note but did not give it to me, saying that he was displeased with me and bidding me to come back next day."

December 3: "Madame Likart visited Rasputin . . . to ask him to intervene on her husband's behalf. Rasputin proposed that she should kiss him; she refused, however, and departed. Then the mistress of Senator Mamontov arrived. Rasputin asked her to return at 1 a.m."

January 29: "The wife of Colonel Tatarinov visited Rasputin and . . . the *starets* embraced and kissed a young girl in her presence; she found the incident so painful that she had decided never to visit Rasputin again."

The staircase watch was maintained at night as well as by day, and the police kept track of Rasputin's evening companions: "Maria Gill, the wife of a Captain in the 145th Regiment, slept at Rasputin's. . . . About 1 a.m. Rasputin brought an unknown woman back to the house; she spent the night with him. . . . Rasputin brought a prostitute back to the flat and locked her in his room. The servants, however, afterwards let her out. . . . Vararova, the actress, slept at Rasputin's."

Sometimes when Rasputin had been aroused but left unsatisfied by his female visitors, he wandered up and down the stairs, pounding on doors:

May 9: "Rasputin sent the concierge's wife for the masseuse but she refused to come. He then went himself to Katia, the seamstress who lives in the house, and asked her to 'keep him company.' The seamstress refused. . . . Rasputin said 'Come next week and I will give you fifty roubles.' "

June 2: "Rasputin sent the porter's wife to fetch the masseuse, Utilia, but she was not at home. . . . He went to the seamstress Katia in Flat 31. He was apparently refused admittance, for he came down the stairs again, and asked the porter's wife to kiss him. She, however, disengaged herself from his embrace, and rang his flat bell, whereupon the servant appeared and put Rasputin to bed."

In time, Rasputin became friendly with the detectives. As his door opened and his powerful figure and weather-beaten face appeared, the detectives would bow, lift their hats and wish him good morning. Often, they were able to be of service to him. One night, two gentlemen with drawn revolvers dashed up the stairs, declaring that their wives were spending the night with Rasputin and that they had come to avenge the dishonor. While one group of agents staved off the angry husbands, others raced up the stairs to give warning. In haste, Rasputin managed to bundle the ladies down the back stairs before their husbands burst in the front door.

Late at night, Rasputin thundered down the stairs, jumped into his car and drove off to carouse until dawn. The police, stuffing their pencils and notebooks into their pockets, scurried to follow:

December 14: "On the night of 13th to 14th December, Rasputin, accompanied by the 28 year old wife of . . . Yazininski, left . . . about 2 a.m. in a car for the restaurant Villa Rode. . . . He was refused admittance on account of the lateness of the hour; but he began to hammer on the doors and wrenched the bell off. He gave five roubles to the police officer on guard, not to annoy him. Then he went off with his companion to the Mazalksi gypsy choir at Number 49 and remained there until 10 a.m. The pair, in a very tipsy state, then proceeded to Madame Yazininskaia's flat, from which Rasputin did not return home until midday. In the evening, he drove to Tsarskoe Selo."

April 15: "Rasputin . . . called on the honorary burgess Pestrikov. . . . As Pestrikov was not at home, he took part in a drinking party which Pestrikov's son was giving to some students. A musician struck up and there was singing and Rasputin danced with a maidservant."

His revels ended, Rasputin staggered home, still accompanied by the exhausted but dogged detectives:

October 14: "Rasputin came home dead drunk at 1 a.m. and insulted the concierge's wife."

November 6: "Rasputin . . . came back drunk . . . as he went up to his flat he inquired if there were any visitors for him. On hearing that there were two ladies, he asked 'Are they pretty. Very pretty? That's good. I need pretty ones.' "

January 14: "Rasputin came home at 7 a.m. He was dead drunk. . . . He smashed a pane of glass in the house door; apparently he had had one fall already, for his nose was swollen."

Day after day, these reports piled up in huge bundles on the desks of the police. From there, they were passed to some whose duty it was to read them, and to many who, although unauthorized, paid handsomely to savor their lusty flavor. Ministers, court officials, grand dukes, countesses, foreign ambassadors, great industrialists, merchants and stockbrokers all pored over them. The talk of Petrograd, they titillated or outraged every important citizen. Marye, the American Ambassador, wrote breathlessly in his diary: "Rasputin's apartments are the scene of the wildest orgies. They beggar all description and from the current accounts of them which pass freely from mouth to mouth, the storied infamies of the Emperor Tiberius on the Isle of Capri are made to seem moderate and tame." The notes convinced all who read them that the man they described was coarse, unscrupulous, a satyr. Only one person, offered the chance, refused to read them. The Empress was convinced that the senior officials of the police hated Rasputin and would do what they could to blacken his name. For her, the famous "staircase notes" were only fiction.

The sheer, blind obstinacy of Alexandra's refusal to see the truth was never more dramatically displayed than in the notorious incident of the Yar in April 1915. Rasputin had arrived in Moscow, supposedly to pray at the tombs of the patriarchs in the Ouspensky Sobor inside the Kremlin. At night, however, he decided to visit the popular Yar restaurant, where he soon became roaring drunk. Bruce Lockhart happened to be present. "I was at Yar, the most luxurious night haunt of Moscow, with some English visitors," he wrote. "As we watched the music hall performance in the main hall, there was a violent fracas in one of the private rooms. Wild shrieks of women, a man's curses, broken glass, and the banging of doors. Headwaiters rushed upstairs. The manager sent for policemen. . . . But the row and the roaring continued. . . . The cause of the disturbance was Rasputin—drunk and lecherous, and neither police nor management dared evict him." Eventually, a telephone call reached the Assistant Minister of Interior, who gave permission to arrest him, and Rasputin was led away "snarling and vowing vengeance." According to witnesses, Rasputin had exposed himself, shouting boastfully that he often behaved this way in the company of the Tsar and that he could do what he liked with "the Old Girl."

A report including every detail of Rasputin's behavior was drawn up and personally submitted to the Tsar by General Dzhunkovsky, an aide-de-camp who was commander of all the police in the empire.

It was assumed by those who knew its contents that this time Rasputin was finally finished. Nicholas summoned Rasputin and angrily asked for an explanation. Rasputin's excuse was ingenious and contained at least a kernel of truth. He explained that he was a simple peasant who had been lured to an evil spot and tempted to drink more than he should. He denied the grosser parts of the report and swore that he had never made any statement about the Imperial family. Nevertheless, without showing the report to Alexandra, the Tsar ordered Rasputin to leave Petrograd for a while and return to Pokrovskoe.

Later, the Empress read the report and exploded with wrath. "My enemy Dzhunkovsky has shown that vile, filthy paper to Dmitry [Grand Duke Dmitry, later one of Rasputin's assassins]. If we let our Friend be persecuted, we and our country will suffer for it." Dzhunkovsky's days were numbered. From that moment, the Empress's letters were filled with a stream of pleadings to "get rid of Dzhunkovsky," and in September 1915 he was dismissed.*

Whatever else he might be doing, Rasputin always took exquisite care to preserve the image of piety he had created at Tsarskoe Selo. It was the keystone of everything, his career and his life, and he protected it with cunning and zeal. Sometimes, an unexpected telephone call from Tsarskoe Selo would break in and upset his evening plans. He growled, but even when thoroughly drunk, managed to sober himself immediately and rush off to consult with "Mama," as he called the Empress, on matters of state.

Alexandra's disbelief in the evil half of Rasputin's nature was considerably more complicated than a simple, prudishly Victorian blindness to that side of life. She was certainly moralistic, but she was not ignorant or squeamish about sex and vice. She had heard most of the stories about Rasputin's villainous behavior and she had consciously rejected them as false and slanderous. For this fateful misjudgment on her part, Rasputin himself was shamefully—and yet, as an actor, brilliantly—responsible.

* A novel explanation of Rasputin's two violently contrasting images—the holy man and the debauchee—is offered by Maria Rasputin in her book, *Rasputin, My Father*. According to this faithful daughter, her saintly father's good name was blackened by the monstrous device, concocted by the Tsar's enemies, of hiring an actor who resembled the *starets* and instructing him to debauch himself in the most obscene manner in the most public places. It is a dutiful effort, but it breaks under the weight of contrary evidence.

Gregory Rasputin was one of the most extraordinary and enigmatic men to appear on earth. He was an overwhelming personality and a superbly convincing actor. He had prodigious physical strength and caroused night and day at a pace that would kill a normal man. His physical presence projected enormous magnetism: prime ministers, princes, bishops and grand dukes as well as society women and peasant girls had felt his powerful attraction and, when the relationship soured, had been as powerfully repelled.

Now, all of the terrible power of this remarkable personality was concentrated on a single objective: convincing the Empress that he was as she saw him, the pure, devoted Man of God, sprung from the soil of peasant Russia. Because of his painstaking care, Alexandra never saw him as anything else. His superb performance was strongly enhanced by the miracles she had seen take place at the bedsides of Alexis and Anna. Whenever he felt himself threatened, Rasputin skillfully played on the Empress's fears and her religious nature. "Remember that I need neither the Emperor or yourself," he would say. "If you abandon me to my enemies, it will not worry me. I am quite able to cope with them. But neither the Emperor nor you can do without me. If I am not there to protect you, you will lose your son and your crown within six months." Even had she begun to doubt the *starets*'s purity, Alexandra—having been through Spala and the nosebleed on the train—was not willing to take risks. Rasputin must be what he said he was and he must stay with her or her world would collapse.

Shrewdly, Rasputin secured his position and enhanced his hold by meeting the Empress's more prosaic need for constant reassurance and encouragement. His conversation and telegrams were an artful blend of religion and prophecy, often sounding like the gloriously meaningless forecasts which fall from penny machines at county fairs: "Be crowned with earthly happiness, the heavenly wreaths will follow. . . . Do not fear our present embarrassments, the protection of the Holy Mother is over you—go to the hospitals though the enemies are menacing—have faith. . . . Don't fear, it will not be worse than it was, faith and the banner will favor us." Blurred though these messages were, the Empress, weary and harassed, found them comforting.

Politically, Rasputin's advice was usually confined to carefully endorsing policies which the Empress already believed in, making certain that the idea was rephrased in his own language so that it would seem freshly inspired. Where his ideas were in fact original and specific, they accurately and realistically represented peasant Russia. Throughout the war, he warned of the bloodletting. "It is getting empty in the villages," he told the Tsar. Yet, when challenged by Paléologue that he had been urging the Tsar to end the war, Rasputin retorted, "Those who told you that are just idiots. I am always telling the Tsar that he must fight until complete victory is won. But I am also telling him that the war has brought unbearable suffering to the Russian people. I know of villages where there is no one left but the blind and the wounded, the widows and the orphans."

As the war continued, Rasputin, like Lenin, saw that along with peace the other predominant concern of the Russian people was bread. He recognized that the shortage of food was mainly a problem of distribution, and never ceased to warn the Empress that the most critical of Russia's problems was the railways. At one point in October 1915, he urged Alexandra to insist that the Tsar cancel all passenger trains for three days so that supplies of food and fuel might flow into the cities.

When it came to the choice of ministers to rule the country, the area in which he exercised his most destructive influence, Rasputin had no design at all. He nominated men for the highest positions in the Russian government simply because they liked him, or said they liked him, or at the very least did not oppose him. Rasputin had no burning ambition to rule Russia. He simply wished to be left untroubled in his free-wheeling, dissolute life. When powerful ministers, despising his influence over the Empress, opposed him, he wanted them out of the way. By placing his own men in every office of major importance, he could ensure, not that he would rule, but that he would be left alone.

In time, every appointment in the highest echelon of the government ministries and in the leadership of the church passed through his hands. Some of Rasputin's choices would have been comical except that the joke was too grim. Rasputin once found a court chamberlain named A. N. Khvostov dining at the nightclub Villa Rode. When the gypsy chorus began to sing, Rasputin was not satisfied; he thought the basses much too weak. Spotting Khvostov, who was large and stout, he clapped him on the back and said, "Brother, go and help them sing. You are fat and can make a lot of noise." Khvostov, tipsy and cheerful, leaped onto the stage and boomed out a thundering bass. Delighted, Rasputin clapped and shouted his approval. Not long afterward, Khvostov unexpectedly became Minister of Interior. His appointment provoked Vladimir Purishkevich, a member of the Duma, to declare in disgust that new ministers now were asked to pass examinations, not in government, but in gypsy music.

Similarly, Rasputin's ardent endorsement of the Empress's belief in autocracy was at least in part self-defensive. Only under a system in which his patron and patroness were all-powerful would he survive. He resisted the demands of those in the Duma and elsewhere who urged responsible government, because the first act of such a government would have been to eliminate him. Furthermore, Rasputin honestly did not believe in responsible government. He did not believe that the Duma members or Rodzianko, their President, represented the real Russia. Certainly they did not represent the peasant Russia from which he had sprung. He believed in the monarchy not simply as an opportunist, but because it was the only form of government known in the villages. Traditionally, the peasants looked to the Tsar. Aristocrats, courtiers, landowners—precisely the men who sat in the Duma—were the classes which, historically, had barred the peasants' access to the Tsar. Seen in this light, it became the Duma members, not Rasputin, who were the unscrupulous opportunists trying to steal the Tsar's powers. To give the Duma more power than it had, to further dilute the role of autocracy, would bring to an end the old, traditional Russia of Tsar, Church and People. Rasputin understood this and resisted it. "Responsible government," wrote the Empress to the Tsar, "as our Friend says, would be the ruin of everything."

How did Nicholas regard these ardent, persistent letters exhorting him to choose this or that minister and, above all, to believe more in "our Friend"? There were times when he reacted by quietly ignoring her advice, wrapping himself in a mantle of silence, avoiding direct answers and calmly going his own way. The very vociferousness of Alexandra's letters is evidence that she was often dissatisfied with his response; had she truly been ruling the empire and Nicholas merely a pawn executing her commands, these insistent, repetitive exhortations would not have been necessary.

But if Nicholas did not always gratify his wife's entreaties, he rarely confronted her with an overt refusal. This was especially true in any matter involving Rasputin. Toward the *starets*, the Tsar's own attitude was one of tolerant respect tinged with an amiable skepticism. At times, he confessed himself soothed by Rasputin's semi-religious chatter. Leaving for the front in March 1915, he wrote to Alexandra, "I am going with such a calm in my soul that I am myself surprised. Whether it is because I had a talk with our Friend or because of the newspaper telling of the death of Witte [who had died of a stroke at sixty-seven] I don't know." On other occasions, Nicholas was annoyed at Rasputin's intrusion into political matters and begged his wife "do not drag our Friend into this."

Nevertheless, when the Empress threw herself at him verbally, pleading that he follow the advice of "the Man of God," Nicholas often bowed. He knew very well how much she counted on the presence and prayers of Rasputin; he had seen with his own eyes what had happened at the bedsides of Alexis and Anna. To comfort her, encourage her and appease her fears, he endorsed her suggestions and recommendations. This relationship was greatly accentuated once Nicholas had left for Headquarters. Then, having left the management of internal affairs in the Empress's hands, Nicholas regularly deferred to her suggestions in the appointment of ministers. And it was her choice of ministers, proposed by Rasputin, beseechingly pressed on and unwisely endorsed by the absentee Tsar, which lost the Tsar his throne.

CHAPTER TWENTY-FOUR

The Government Disintegrates

In the early autumn of 1915, Alexandra Fedorovna had been Empress of Russia for twenty-one years. During this time, she had shown little interest in politics and no personal ambition. Except in defense of Rasputin, she rarely even mentioned government affairs to the Tsar. She scarcely knew her husband's ministers and, during the first decade of her marriage, held them completely in awe. In 1905, Count Fredericks persuaded her with difficulty to speak to the Tsar on a political matter. When he came back and asked her a second time, Alexandra burst into tears. After her son was born and Rasputin appeared, she intervened when he seemed threatened. Then her power could become formidable: Kokovtsov's dismissal as Premier was primarily her work. But she remained shy and silent in the presence of the ministers and she still had no experience in government affairs.

All this changed when Nicholas took command of the army. Then the gap he left behind in the civil administration was filled by his wife. It was not a formal regency; rather, it was an almost domestic division of family duties. As such, it was wholly within the tradition of the Russian autocracy. "When the Emperor went to war, of course his wife governed instead of him," said Grand Duke Alexander, explaining what he considered a natural sequence of events.

That Nicholas regarded her role in this light is clear from his letters. "Think, my wify, will you not come to the assistance of your hubby now that he is absent," he wrote cheerfully after leaving for Headquarters. "What a pity that you have not been fulfilling this duty long ago or at least during the war." On September 23, 1916 (O.S.), he said, "Yes, truly, you ought to be my eyes and ears there in the capital while I have to stay here. It rests with you to keep peace and harmony among the Ministers—thereby you do a great service to me and to our country. . . . I am so happy to think that you have found at last a worthy occupation. Now I shall naturally be calm and at least not worry over internal affairs." And the next day: "You will really help me a great deal by speaking to the ministers and watching them." When she felt unsure and apologized for her presumption, he reassured her: "There is nothing to forgive you for, on the contrary, I must be deeply grateful to you for so far advancing this serious matter by your help."

Once the Tsar had asked for her help, Alexandra threw herself into the task. To "keeping peace and harmony among the ministers" and managing internal affairs, she brought the same intense devotion and narrow stubbornness she had shown in fighting for the life of her son. Lacking experience, she made numerous, outsized mistakes. She groped blindly for people and facts, unable to verify what she was told, often depending on the impressions of a single short interview. As she went along, her self-confidence improved, and it was a personal triumph when in September 1916 she delightedly wrote to the Tsar, "I am no longer the slightest bit shy or afraid of ministers and speak like a waterfall in Russian."

Rasputin was not only her advisor, he was also her yardstick for measuring other men. "Good" men esteemed Rasputin's advice and respected him. "Bad" men hated him and made up disgusting stories about him. The work of "good" men would be blessed, and therefore they should be appointed to high office. "Bad" men were sure to fail, and those already in office should be driven out. Alexandra did not particularly care whether a prospective minister had special aptness or expertise for his new role. What mattered was that he be acceptable to the Man of God. It was far more important that he like Rasputin than that he understand anything about munitions or diplomacy or the distribution of food.

Every new candidate for the Council of Ministers was scrutinized and measured in this manner: "He likes our Friend. . . . He venerates our Friend. . . . He calls our Friend Father Gregory. . . . Is he not our Friend's enemy?" Unlike the Duma, whose very existence she considered a stain on the autocracy, the Empress accepted the Council of Ministers as a legitimate institution. Ministers, appointed by the Tsar and responsible only to him, were necessary to govern the country. What Alexandra could not abide were ministers who opposed the autocratic will. Any sign that a minister disagreed with the Tsar made her suspicious; the thought that ministers and Duma might be working together drove her frantic.

For her, the ideal minister was personified by the aged Prime Minister, Ivan Goremykin. Having stepped down as Prime Minister in 1906 to make way for Stolypin, Goremykin had been restored to power before the outbreak of war. Now seventy-six and in failing health, Goremykin had no illusions about his role. As far back as 1896, Pobedonostsev had written to Nicholas that Goremykin needed a rest, otherwise "he would not last throughout the winter." Goremykin had repeatedly asked—and been denied—permission to resign. "The Emperor can't see that the candles have already been lit around my coffin and that the only thing required to complete the ceremony is myself," he said mournfully.

Nevertheless, Goremykin's stubborn, old-fashioned views of autocracy and the role of the minister were much too rare and valuable for him to be let go. "I am a man of the old school and an Imperial Command is for me a law," he declared. "To me, His Majesty is the anointed one, the rightful sovereign. He personifies the whole of Russia. He is forty-seven and it is not just since yesterday that he has been reigning and deciding the fate of the Russian people. When the decision of such a man is made and his course of action is determined, his faithful subjects must accept it whatever may be the consequences. And then let God's will be fulfilled. These views I have held all my life and with them I shall die." Not surprisingly, the Empress was delighted with Goremykin, whom she always affectionately called the "Old Man." "He sees and understands all so clearly and it is a pleasure speaking to him," she declared.

Just how unique Goremykin and his views of autocracy were became glaringly apparent in the severe ministerial crisis which followed the Tsar's decision to take command of the army. Of all the ministers, Goremykin alone supported his master's decision. In vain, he urged them, "I call upon you, gentlemen, in the face of events of extraordinary importance to bow to the will of His Majesty, to lend him your full support in the moment of trial, and to devote all your powers to the service of the Sovereign." When they refused, he said wearily, "I beg you to inform the Emperor that I am not fitted for my position and that it is necessary to appoint a man of more modern views in my place. I shall be grateful to you for the service."

Instead, the majority of the ministerial council decided that, as the Tsar refused to heed its advice, there was nothing to do but resign. "It is our duty," declared Sazonov, the Foreign Minister, ". . . to tell the Tsar frankly that under existing conditions we cannot govern the country, that we cannot serve conscientiously and that we are doing harm to the country. . . . The Cabinet cannot perform its functions while it does not enjoy the confidence of the Sovereign." A collective letter of resignation, signed by eight of the thirteen ministers, was addressed to the Tsar. It had no effect whatsoever. Nicholas summoned the ministers to Headquarters and told them that until he saw fit to replace them, they were not permitted to resign.

A few days later, in a letter to Alexandra, he ruminated on the gap between himself and his ministers. "The behavior of some of the Ministers continues to amaze me. After all I told them at that famous evening sitting, I thought they understood . . . precisely what I thought. What matter—so much the worse for them. They were afraid to close the Duma—it was done. I came away here and replaced N. [Grand Duke Nicholas] in spite of their advice; the people accepted this move as a natural thing and understood it as we did. The proof—numbers of telegrams which I receive from all sides with the most touching expressions. All this shows me clearly one thing: that the Ministers always living in town, know terribly little of what is happening in the country as a whole. Here I can judge correctly the real mood among the various classes of people. . . . Petrograd and Moscow constitute the only exceptions on the map of the fatherland."

The Empress was less interested in finding excuses for ministerial behavior than she was in driving each man who had signed the letter out of office. Thus, the next sixteen months saw a sad parade of dismissals, reshuffles and intrigues. In that time, Russia had four different prime ministers, five ministers of interior, four ministers of agriculture and three ministers of war. "After the middle of 1915," wrote Florinsky, "the fairly honorable and efficient group who formed the top of the bureaucratic pyramid degenerated into a rapidly changing succession of the appointees of Rasputin. It was an amazing, extravagant, and pitiful spectacle, and one without parallel in the history of civilized nations."

Two of the signers, Prince Shcherbatov, the Minister of Interior, and Samarin, the Procurator of the Holy Synod (Minister of Religion), went quickly, dismissed without explanation early in October. Krivoshein, the Minister of Agriculture, left in November, and Kharitonov, the State Controller, departed in January. The next to go, in February 1916, was the faithful Goremykin. "The ministers do not wish to work well with old Goremykin . . . therefore, on my return some changes must take place," had written Nicholas. At first, the Empress was reluctant. "If in any way you feel he hinders, is an obstacle for you, then you better let him go," she wrote, "but if you keep him he will do all you order and try to do his best. . . . To my mind, much better clear out ministers who strike and not change the President who with decent, energetic, well-intentioned . . . [colleagues] can serve still perfectly well. He only lives and serves you and your country and knows his days are counted and fears not death of age, or by knife or shot." Rasputin also hated the idea of losing Goremykin: "He cannot bear the idea of the Old Man being sent away, has been worrying and thinking over that question without end. Says he is so very wise and when others make a row . . . he sits merely with his head down—it is because he understands that today the crowd howls, tomorrow rejoices, that one need not be crushed by the changing waves."

Nevertheless, in Goremykin's enfeebled hands, the government had almost ceased to function. His fellow ministers avoided or ignored him. When he appeared in the Duma, the elderly man was greeted by a prolonged hiss which made it impossible for him to speak. The Tsar, the Empress and Goremykin himself understood that the situation could not continue. "I keep wracking my brains over the question of a successor for the Old Man," wrote Nicholas. Alexandra sadly agreed, and for a while they thought of appointing Alexander Khvostov, the conservative Minister of Justice. An uncle of the singing Minister of Interior, this older Khvostov was one of the ministers who had refused to sign the infamous letter. First, however, Khvostov was to have a visit from Rasputin.

"Our Friend told me to wait about the Old Man until he had seen Uncle Khvostov on Thursday, what impression he will have of him," Alexandra wrote to the Tsar. "He [Rasputin] is miserable about the dear Old Man, says he is such a righteous man, but he dreads the Duma hissing him and then you will be in an awful position." The following day, the Empress wrote, "Tomorrow Gregory sees old Khvostov and then I see him in the evening. He wants to tell his impression if a worthy successor to Goremykin." But Khvostov did not survive the interview; Alexandra wrote indignantly that Rasputin was received "like a petitioner in the ministry."

The next candidate brought forward, Boris Stürmer, was more successful. Equipped with Goremykin's arch-conservative instincts while lacking completely the old man's courage and honesty, Stürmer, then sixty-seven, was an obscure and dismal product of the professional Russian bureaucracy. His family origins were German; his great-uncle, Baron Stürmer, had been Austria's representative on the guard which sat on St. Helena keeping watch on Napoleon. Stürmer himself, first as Master of Ceremonies at court, then as the reactionary governor of Yaroslav province, had attracted a universally bad reputation. "A man who had left a bad memory wherever he occupied an administrative post," declared Sazonov. "An utter nonentity," groaned Rodzianko. "A false and double-faced man," said Khvostov.

When Stürmer first appeared, Paléologue, who had scarcely heard of him, busied himself for three days gathering information. Then he penned this discouraging portrait: "He . . . is worse than a mediocrity—third rate intellect, mean spirit, low character, doubtful honesty, no experience and no idea of State business. The most that can be said for him is that he has a rather pretty talent for cunning and flattery. . . . His appointment becomes intelligible on the supposition that he has been selected solely as a tool; in other words, actually on account of his insignificance and servility. . . . [He] has been . . . warmly recommended to the Emperor by Rasputin."

In fact, Stürmer was first recommended to the Tsar by Rasputin's friend and protégé Pitirim, who, with Rasputin's aid, had been named Metropolitan of the Orthodox Church in Petrograd. "I begat Pitirim and Pitirim begat Stürmer" was the way Rasputin sardonically put it. Nevertheless, Stürmer's name was the one that filled the Empress's letters. "Lovy, I don't know but I should still think of Stürmer. . . . Stürmer would do for a time. He very much values Gregory which is a great thing. . . . Our Friend said about Stürmer to take him for a time at least, as he is such a decided loyal man."

To the astonishment of Russia and even of the faithful Goremykin, who had no inkling that his wish for retirement was about to be granted, the unknown Stürmer was suddenly named Prime Minister in February 1916. The Duma regarded the appointment as a crushing humiliation, an insult to all of their work and aspirations. There was no doubt that when the new Prime Minister appeared before them, their outrage would exceed anything they had directed at Goremykin. At this point, Rasputin offered an ingenious suggestion. The *starets* had no love for the Duma, but he understood its usefulness. "Dogs collected to keep other dogs quiet," he called the members. Under the circumstances, he advised Nicholas to make a placating gesture. "Of course if you could have turned up for a few words, quite unexpected at the Duma . . . that might change everything," Alexandra explained the scheme to her husband. Nicholas agreed, and on February 22, 1916, the Tsar appeared in person before the Imperial Duma. The gesture was an overwhelming success. A *Te Deum* was sung, Nicholas greeted the members as "representatives of the Russian people" and presented the Order of St. Anne to Rodzianko. Although Stürmer was present at the side of the Tsar, his appointment was temporarily forgotten—as Rasputin had cunningly foreseen—amid a storm of cheers.

With Stürmer installed at the top, the Empress, urged on by Rasputin, continued to weed among the ministerial ranks. Her next major target was Polivanov, the Minister of War. The Empress had never liked him. "Forgive me," she had written the Tsar when Polivanov was appointed, "but I don't like the choice of Minister of War Polivanov. Is he not our Friend's enemy?" In the short time since he replaced the indolent Sukhomlinov, the brusque, efficient Polivanov had worked wonders in training and equipping the army. It was primarily due to his efforts that the beaten Russian army of 1915 was able to recover and launch the great offensive of 1916. Nevertheless, Polivanov was marked, not only by his rough refusal to have anything to do with Rasputin, but also by his eagerness to work closely with the Duma in obtaining maximum support for his army program. In the end, Polivanov's doom was sealed when he discovered that Rasputin had been supplied by Stürmer with four high-powered War Office cars too fast to be followed by the police when he set off for one of his steamy nocturnal haunts. Polivanov sternly objected, and soon Alexandra was writing to Nicholas, "Get rid of Polivanov . . . any honest man better than him. . . . Remember about Polivanov. . . . Lovy, don't dawdle, make up your mind, it's far too serious." On March 25, Polivanov fell. "Oh, the relief! Now I shall sleep well," she said when she heard the news. Others were appalled. Polivanov was "undoubtedly the ablest military organizer in Russia and his dismissal was a disaster," wrote Knox. General Shuvaiev, Polivanov's successor, Knox described as "a nice old man, quite straight and honest. He had no knowledge of his work, but his devotion to the Emperor was such that if the door were to open and His Majesty were to come into the room and ask him to throw himself out of the window, he would do so at once."

The next to go was Sazonov, the Foreign Minister. A brother-in-law of Stolypin, Sazonov was a cultivated man of liberal background and a close friend of both Buchanan and Paléologue. He had been Foreign Minister since 1910 and was completely trusted both by the Tsar and by the Allied governments. Nevertheless, since his signing of the ministerial letter, Alexandra had wanted him removed. She suspected, rightly, that along with his friendship with England and France, he also wanted a responsible government in Russia; both, she believed, would undermine the autocratic Russia she hoped to pass along to her son. Through the winter, she kept up a barrage at "long-nosed Sazonov . . . Sazonov is such a pancake." Then, in March 1916, she wrote to Nicholas, "Wish you could think of a good successor to Sazonov—need not be a diplomat. So as . . . to see we are not later sat upon by England and that when questions of ultimate peace come we should be firm. Old Goremykin and Stürmer always disapproved of him as he is such a coward towards Europe and a parliamentarist—and that would be Russia's ruin."

Sazonov's downfall came in July 1916, and was actually precipitated by the question of autonomy for Poland. At the outbreak of war, Russia had promised a virtually independent, united Polish kingdom, linked to Russia only in the person of the Tsar. The Poles were enthusiastic, and on first entering Galicia, Russian troops were welcomed as liberators. Military defeat and the loss of most Polish territory in 1915 had delayed action on the pledge, at the same time encouraging those Russian conservatives who resisted its enactment, fearing that autonomy for one part of the empire would stimulate other provinces to seek the same thing. Alexandra, spurred by Rasputin, argued that "Baby's future rights" were challenged. Nevertheless, Sazonov, backed by Britain and France, continued to insist.

On July 12, Sazonov saw Nicholas at Headquarters. "The Emperor has entirely adopted my views. . . . I won all along the line," he reported jubilantly to Buchanan and Paléologue. In enormous good humor, the Foreign Minister left for a Finnish holiday during which he planned to draft an Imperial proclamation on Poland. Meanwhile, both Stürmer and the Empress hurried to Headquarters, and while he was still in Finland, Sazonov was abruptly dismissed. Appalled, Buchanan and Paléologue pleaded that the dismissal be set aside. Failing, Buchanan then boldly asked the Tsar's permission to have King George V grant the fallen minister a British court decoration in recognition of his services to the alliance. Nicholas agreed and was genuinely pleased that Sazonov, whom he liked and had dealt with shabbily, was receiving the honor.

Sazanov's replacement at the Foreign Ministry was none other than Stürmer, who took on the office in addition to the Premiership. The appointment was a further hideous shock to Buchanan and Paléologue, who would now be dealing daily on an intimate professional level with Russia's new Foreign Minister. Each Ambassador reacted in character: Buchanan stiffly wrote London that "I can never hope to have confidential relations with a man on whose word no reliance can be placed." Paléologue, after an interview, confided to his diary, "His [Stürmer's] look, sharp and honeyed, furtive and blinking, is the very expression of hypocrisy . . . he emits an intolerable odor of falseness. In his bonhomie and his affected politeness one feels that he is low, intriguing, and treacherous."*

The key ministry in troubled times was not Foreign Affairs or even the presidency of the ministerial council. It was the Ministry of Interior, which was responsible for the preservation of law and order. Under this office came the police, the secret police, informers and counterespionage—all the devices which, as a regime grows more unpopular, become all the more necessary to its preservation. In October 1916, the Tsar suddenly appointed to this critical post the Vice-President of the Duma, Alexander Protopopov. The choice was a disaster, yet, ironically, Nicholas made it at least in part as a gesture to Rodzianko and the Duma.

Alexander Protopopov was sixty-four, a small, sleek man with white hair, a mustache and bright black eyes. In his native Simbirsk, the Volga town which also gave Russia Kerensky and Lenin, Protopopov's social position was far higher than that of either of his famous fellow townsmen. His father was a nobleman and landowner who also owned

* Buchanan and Paléologue, as representatives of Russia's allies, were naturally the preeminent members of the Petrograd diplomatic corps, but American representation was unusually and unnecessarily weak due to President Wilson's appointment of nonprofessionals to the post. From 1914 to 1916, the U.S. Ambassador was George T. Marye, a San Franciscan who had little contact or interest in Russia and got most of his information from the newspapers he received from Paris. At his farewell audience with the Tsar, Marye mentioned that he hoped that after the war American businessmen would flock to invest in Russia. "Russia needed American energy, American money and the Americans who engaged in business in Russia would find the field immensely profitable. No one, of course, is in business for his health—the Emperor smiled slightly as I indulged in this somewhat homely expression," reported Marye. Marye's successor was David R. Francis, a wealthy businessman and former Governor of Missouri who arrived in Russia with a portable cuspidor with a foot-operated lid.

a large textile factory; the son went to cadet cavalry school, studied law and became a director of his father's factory. An important local personage, he was elected to the Duma, where, although he showed little political distinction, his smooth and ingratiating air made him thoroughly popular. "He was handsome, elegant, captivating in a drawing room, moderately liberal and always pleasant. . . . There was a slightly cunning air about him but this seemed very innocent and goodnatured," wrote Kerensky, who also sat in the Fourth Duma.

Protopopov's charm and his membership in the large, moderately liberal Octobrist Party saw him repeatedly elected to the Duma vice-presidency. Rodzianko, as President, respected his deputy's abilities. In June 1916 he suggested to Nicholas that Protopopov would make a good minister. "For the post [of Minister of Trade] he proposed his *tovarish* Protopopov," Nicholas wrote to Alexandra, adding, "I have an idea that our Friend mentioned him [Protopopov] on some occasion." But no changes were made at that time, and Protopopov remained as the second man in the Duma. In this capacity, he led a delegation of Duma members on good-will visits to England and France in July 1916; on the way home, he stopped at Stockholm and had a mysterious talk with a Swedish financier known to be close to the German Embassy. Upon arriving in Russia, he traveled to Headquarters to make an official call on the Tsar. "Yesterday I met a man I like very much, Protopopov, Vice President of the State Duma," Nicholas wrote. "He traveled abroad with members of the Duma and told me much of interest."

All of the ingredients necessary for Protopopov's elevation to the Ministry now were present: he had charmed the Tsar with his manner, he had been recommended as a solid worker by Rodzianko and, most important of all, he had the sweeping endorsement of Rasputin and therefore of the Empress. Protopopov's acquaintance with Rasputin stretched back over several years. The prospective Minister was not in good health. He suffered from a disease variously described as progressive paralysis of the spine or advanced syphilis, depending on the informant's feelings about Protopopov. When doctors were unable to help, Protopopov went to Badmayev, a quackish Siberian herb doctor then fashionable in Petrograd. Badmayev knew Rasputin, and Protopopov, who was fascinated by mysticism and the occult, was introduced into an outer ring of the *starets's* circle. Now, struck by the news that Nicholas was pleased by his amiable protégé, Rasputin seized the initiative and began proposing that Protopopov be named Minister of Interior.

"Gregory earnestly begs you to name Protopopov," Alexandra wrote in September. "He likes our Friend for at least 4 years and that says much for a man." Two days later, she repeated: "Please take Protopopov as Minister of Interior. As he is one of the Duma, it will make a great effect and shut their mouths." Nicholas balked and chided his wife for accepting every one of Rasputin's whims: "This Protopopov is a good man. . . . Rodzianko has for a long time suggested him for the post of Minister of Trade. [But] I must consider this question as it has taken me completely by surprise. Our Friend's opinions of people are sometimes very strange as you know yourself—therefore this must be thought out very carefully." Nevertheless, a few days later the Tsar gave in and telegraphed, "It shall be done." In a letter, he added, "God grant that Protopopov may turn out to be the man of whom we are now in need." Overjoyed, the Empress wrote back, "God bless your new choice of Protopopov. Our Friend says you have done a very wise act in naming him."

The appointment caused a sensation. In the Duma, Protopopov's acceptance of office under Stürmer was regarded as a scandalous betrayal. When an old friend in the Duma bluntly told the new Minister that his appointment was a scandal and that he ought to resign immediately, Protopopov, bubbling with excitement over his promotion, replied candidly, "How can you ask me to resign? All my life it was my dream to be a vice-governor and here I am a minister."

Rodzianko was angriest of all. Shaking with rage, he confronted the turncoat and lambasted him for his treachery. When, in servile tones, Protopopov explained, "I hope I shall succeed in bringing about some changes," Rodzianko replied scornfully, "You haven't sufficient strength for the fight and will never dare to speak outright to the Emperor." Soon afterward, Protopopov returned to Rodzianko, hinting that, with his help, the Duma President might be appointed Premier and Foreign Minister in place of Stürmer. Rodzianko, fully aware that neither Nicholas nor Alexandra would dream of such an appointment, stated his terms: "I alone shall have the power to choose the Ministers . . . the Empress must remain . . . at Livadia until the end of the war." Hastily, Protopopov suggested that Rodzianko speak to the Empress herself.

Once he was in office, Protopopov's behavior became wholly eccentric. Although a minister, he kept his seat in the Duma and appeared at meetings wearing the uniform of a general of gendarmes, to which, as head of the police, he was entitled. Beside his desk he kept an icon which he addressed as a person. "He helps me do everything; everything I do is by His advice," Protopopov explained to Kerensky, indicating the icon. Even more astonishing was the sudden transformation of Protopopov the Duma liberal into Protopopov the arch-reactionary. He was determined to become the savior of tsarism and Orthodox Russia. Not only was he not afraid of revolution; he hoped to provoke it in order to crush it by force. At meetings, Rodzianko wrote, "he rolled his eyes repeatedly, in a kind of unnatural ecstasy. 'I feel that I shall save Russia. I feel that I alone can save her.' "

In addition to controlling the police, Protopopov also assumed responsibility for the most critical problem facing Russia, the organization of food supplies. The idea was Rasputin's. Not without logic, he proposed that authority should be transferred from the Ministry of Agriculture, which was floundering, to the Ministry of Interior, which had the police to enforce its orders. Seizing the idea, the Empress issued the transfer command herself. It was the only episode in which Alexandra did not bother first to get the Tsar's approval. "Forgive me for what I have done—but I had to—our Friend said it was absolutely necessary," she wrote. "Stürmer sends you by this messenger a new paper to sign giving the whole food supply at once to the Minister of Interior. . . . I had to take this step upon myself as Gregory says Protopopov will have all in his hands . . . and by that will save Russia. . . . Forgive me, but I had to take this responsibility for your sweet sake." Nicholas acquiesced, and thereby, as Russia moved into the critical winter of 1916–1917, both the police and the food supply remained in the trembling, ineffectual hands of Alexander Protopopov.

Although her informal mandate from Nicholas was only to oversee internal affairs, Alexandra also began to trespass on the area of military operations. "Sweet Angel," she wrote in November 1915, "long to ask you heaps about your plans concerning Rumania. Our Friend is so anxious to know." That same month: "Our Friend was afraid that, if we had not a big army to pass through Rumania, we might be caught in a trap from behind."

With supreme self-confidence, Rasputin soon passed from asking questions about the army to transmitting instructions as to the timing and location of Russian attacks. His inspiration, he told the Empress, had come to him in dreams while he slept: "Now before I forget, I must give you a message from our Friend prompted by what he saw in the night," she wrote in November 1915. "He begs you to order that one should advance near Riga, says it is necessary, otherwise the Germans will settle down so firmly through all the winter that it will cost endless bloodshed and trouble to make them move . . . he says this is just now the most essential thing and begs you seriously to order ours to advance, he says we can and we must, and I was to write to you at once."

In June 1916: "Our Friend sends his blessing to the whole orthodox army. He begs we should not yet strongly advance in the north because he says if our successes continue being good in the south, they will themselves retreat in the north, or advance and then their losses will be very great—if we begin there, our losses will be very heavy. He says this is . . . [his] advice."

At Headquarters, General Alexeiev was less than charmed to hear of this new interest in the army. "I told Alexeiev how interested you were in military affairs and of those details you asked for in your last letter," Nicholas wrote on June 7, 1916 (O.S.). "He [Alexeiev] smiled and listened silently." Alexeiev's silence concealed his worry over the possible leakage of his plans. After the abdication, he explained, "When the Empress's papers were examined, she was found to be in possession of a map indicating in detail the disposition of the troops along the entire front. Only two copies were prepared of this map, one for the Emperor and one for myself. I was very painfully impressed. God knows who may have made use of this map."

Although the Tsar thought it quite natural to admit his wife to military secrets, he did not want them passed to Rasputin. Repeatedly, after giving her a number of military details, he would write, "I beg you, my love, do not communicate these details to anyone. I have written them only for you. . . . I beg you, keep it to yourself, not a single soul must know of it." Almost as frequently, Alexandra ignored her husband's request and told Rasputin. "He won't mention it to a soul," she assured Nicholas, "but I had to ask his blessing for your decision."

Rasputin's intervention in military affairs appeared most conspicuously during the great Russian offensive of 1916. Following Polivanov's miracles in supply and manpower, wrought during the winter of 1915–

1916, the Russian army erupted in June 1916 with a heavy attack on the Austrians in Galicia. The Austrian line sagged and broke. Brusilov, the Russian commander, inflicted a million casualties, took 400,000 prisoners, pulled 18 German divisions away from Verdun and prevented the Austrians from exploiting their great victory over the Italians at Caporetto. In August, Rumania, sensing an Allied victory, entered the war against Germany and Austria.

Yet, all this was done at heavy cost to Russia. Through the summer, as Brusilov ground forward, Russian losses reached 1,200,000. As the army moved forward, leaving behind a carpet of dead, it seemed to the Empress and to Rasputin that Russia was choking in her own blood. As early as July 25 (O.S.), she wrote: "Our Friend . . . finds better one should not advance too obstinately as the losses will be too great." On August 8 (O.S.): "Our Friend hopes we won't climb over the Carpathians and try to take them, as he repeats the losses will be too great again." On September 21 (O.S.), Nicholas wrote: "I told Alexeiev to order Brusilov to stop our hopeless attacks." Alexandra replied happily, "Our Friend says about the new orders you gave to Brusilov: 'Very satisfied with Father's [the Tsar's] orders, all will be well.' "

Meanwhile, at *Stavka*, Alexeiev had discussed the operation with the Tsar, and even as the Empress was congratulating herself, Nicholas was writing: "Alexeiev has asked permission to continue the attack . . . and I have permitted it." Surprised, Alexandra responded: "Our Friend is much put out that Brusilov has not listened to your order to stop the advance—says you were inspired from above to give that order . . . and God would bless it. Now he says again useless losses." On the 24th (O.S.), Nicholas wrote, "I have only just received your telegram in which you inform me that our Friend is very disturbed about my plan not being carried out." Carefully, he explained that an additional army had been massed which "doubles our forces . . . and gives hope for the possibility of success. That is why . . . I gave my consent." He added that the decision, "from a military point of view is quite correct," and implored, "these details are for you only—I beg you, my dear. Tell him [Rasputin] only 'Papa has ordered that sensible measures be taken.' "

But the Empress was now in full cry. On the 25th (O.S.), she wrote: "Oh give your order again to Brusilov—stop this useless slaughter. . . . Why repeat the madness of the Germans at Verdun. Your plan, so wise [was] approved by our Friend. . . . Stick to it. . . . Our generals don't count the lives any—hardened to losses—and that is sin." On September 27 (O.S.), two days later, Nicholas finally gave in: "My dear, Brusilov has, on the receipt of my instructions, immediately given order to stop." As a result, Brusilov's great offensive ground to a halt. After the war, General Vladimir Gurko, who participated in the operation, wrote, "The weariness of the troops had its effect . . . but there can be no question that the stoppage of the advance was premature and founded on orders from Headquarters." The hard-bitten Brusilov responded impatiently, "An offensive without casualties may be staged only during maneuvers; no action at the present time is taken at random and the enemy suffer as heavy losses as we do . . . but to defeat the enemy or to beat him off, we must suffer losses and they may be considerable."

By October 1916, with Stürmer and Protopopov occupying the key ministries of the Russian government, the Empress had apparently achieved what she had set out a year before to do. The ministers who signed the collective letter were gone; those in power fawned on Rasputin. "Stürmer and Protopopov both completely believe in our Friend's wonderful, God-sent wisdom," she wrote happily.

In fact, the entire arrangement—and with it, all Russia—was beginning to disintegrate. A new governmental scandal loomed up when Manuilov, Stürmer's private secretary, was arrested for blackmailing a bank. Two episodes put the army's loyalty in question. In Marseilles, a Russian brigade on its way from Archangel to fight in Greece suddenly mutinied and killed its colonel. French troops intervened and twenty Russian soldiers were executed. Far more serious, two infantry regiments in Petrograd, called out in October to disperse a crowd of striking workers, turned instead and fired on the police. Only when four regiments of Cossacks charged and drove the infantry back to their barracks at lance point was the mutiny subdued. This time, 150 soldiers went to the firing squad.

Worst of all was the growing economic breakdown. Nicholas, more perceptive than the Empress, had seen this coming for months. "Stürmer . . . is an excellent, honest man," he wrote in June, "only, it seems to me, he cannot make up his mind to do what is necessary. The gravest and most urgent question just now is the question of fuels and metals—iron and copper for munitions—because with the shortage of metals, the factories cannot produce a sufficient quantity of cartridges and shells. It is the same with the railways. . . . These affairs are a regular curse. . . . But it is imperative to act energetically." In August, he confessed that the load was becoming unbearable. "At times when I turn over in my mind the names of one person and another for appointments, and think how things will go, it seems that my head will burst. The greatest problem now is the question of supplies. . . ." In September, as Alexandra was urging the appointment of Protopopov: "And whom am I to begin with? All these changes make my head go round. In my opinion, they are too frequent. In any case, they are not good for the internal situation of the country, as each new man brings with him alterations in the administration." In November: "The eternal question of supplies troubles me most of all . . . prices are soaring and the people are beginning to starve. It is obvious where this situation may lead the country. Old Stürmer cannot overcome these difficulties. . . . It is the most damnable problem I have ever come across."

Early in November, Nicholas, with Alexis, went to Kiev to inspect hospitals and to visit his mother, who was living away from Petrograd. On this visit, everyone noticed the change that had come over the Tsar. "I was shocked to see . . . Nicky so pale, thin and tired," wrote his sister Grand Duchess Olga Alexandrovna, who was with her mother in Kiev. "My mother was worried about his excessive quiet." Gilliard saw the same thing: "He had never seemed to me so worried before. He was usually very self-controlled, but on this occasion he showed himself nervous and irritable, and once or twice he spoke roughly to Alexis Nicolaievich."

Under the pressure of his dual role as Tsar and Commander-in-Chief, Nicholas's health and morale were beginning to suffer. Old friends such as Prince Vladimir Orlov had gone, driven away by their disapproval of Rasputin. Even old Count Fredericks managed to remain near the Tsar only by talking about the weather and other inconsequentia. In Kiev, Nicholas had thought to relax from the problems of war and government. Instead, in their first conversation Marie demanded that he dismiss Stürmer and push Rasputin away from the throne.

Although bowed by the cares of his office, Nicholas in Kiev made a graceful Imperial gesture. In the ward of the hospital where his sister worked, "we had a young, wounded deserter, court-martialed and condemned to death," she wrote. "Two soldiers were guarding him. All of us felt very troubled about him—he looked such a decent boy.

The doctor spoke of him to Nicky who at once made for that corner of the ward. I followed him, and I could see the young man was petrified with fear. Nicky put his hand on the boy's shoulder and asked very quietly why he had deserted. The young man stammered that, having run out of ammunition, he had got frightened, turned and ran. We all waited, our breath held, and Nicky told him that he was free. The next moment the lad scrambled out of bed, fell on the floor, his arms around Nicky's knees, and sobbed like a child. I believe all of us were in tears. . . . I have cherished the memory all down the years. I never saw Nicky again."

While the Tsar was in Kiev, the Duma met and the storm began to break. Party lines no longer mattered: from extreme Right to revolutionary Left, every party opposed the government. Miliukov, the leader of the liberals, made a direct attack on Stürmer and Rasputin, and indirectly attacked the Empress. Stürmer he accused outright of being a German agent. One by one, as he ticked off his charges of inefficiency and corruption against the government, he asked after each accusation, "Is this stupidity or is it treason?" Miliukov was followed by Basil Maklakov, a Right-wing liberal, who declared, "The old regime and the interests of Russia have now parted company." Quoting from Pushkin, he shouted, "Woe to that country where only the slave and the liar are close to the throne."

By the time Nicholas had returned from Kiev to Headquarters, the outrage in the Duma could no longer be ignored. With his mother's pleas ringing in his ears, the Tsar decided to dismiss Stürmer. The Empress was not entirely opposed, but she suggested a holiday rather than dismissal: "Protopopov . . . [and] our Friend both find for the quiet of the Duma, Stürmer ought to say he is ill and go for a rest for 3 weeks. It's true . . . he is really quite unwell and broken by those vile assaults—and being the red flag for that madhouse, it's better he should disappear a bit."

Nicholas quickly agreed, and on November 8 (O.S.), he wrote, "All these days I have been thinking of old Stürmer. He, as you say rightly, acts as a red flag, not only to the Duma, but to the whole country, alas. I hear this from all sides; nobody believes in him and everyone is angry because we stand up for him. It is much worse than with Goremykin last year. I reproach him for his excessive prudence and his incapacity for taking on himself the responsibility of making them all work as they should. He is coming here tomorrow. I will give him leave for the present. . . . As to the future, we shall see; we will talk it over when you come here."

Rasputin's suggestion was that Stürmer give up one of his offices, the Ministry of Foreign Affairs, to appease the Duma, but not both: "Our Friend says Stürmer can remain still some time as President of Council of Ministers," Alexandra reminded. But Nicholas, this time, had made up his mind. "I am receiving Stürmer in an hour," he wrote on November 9 (O.S.), "and shall insist on his taking leave. Alas, I am afraid he will have to go altogether [i.e., give up the presidency of the Council of Ministers as well as the Ministry of Foreign Affairs]—nobody has confidence in him. I remember even Buchanan telling me at our last meeting the English consuls in their reports predict serious disturbances if he remains. And every day I hear more and more about it."

The Empress was surprised at the Tsar's decision. "It gave me a painful shock you also take away from him the Council of Ministers. I had a big lump in my throat—such a devoted, honest, sure man. . . . I regret because he likes our Friend and was so right in that way. Trepov [the new Premier], I personally do not like and can never have the same feeling for him as to old Goremykin and Stürmer—they were of the good old sort . . . those two loved me and came for every question that worried them, so as not to disturb you—this one [Trepov] I, alas, doubt caring for me and if he does not trust me and our Friend, things will be difficult. I too told Stürmer to tell him how to behave about Gregory and to safeguard him always."

But Alexander Trepov, the new Prime Minister, already had decided how he would behave about Gregory. A former Minister of Communications, builder of the newly completed Murmansk railroad, Trepov was at once a conservative monarchist and a stern enemy of Rasputin. He was determined to purge the government of Rasputin's influence. As a first important step, he meant to evict Protopopov, Rasputin's instrument. On accepting appointment to the premiership, he had won the Tsar's promise that Protopopov would be dismissed. "I am sorry for Protopopov," Nicholas wrote Alexandra, explaining his decision. "He is a good, honest man, but he jumps from one idea to another, and cannot make up his mind on anything. I noticed that from the beginning. They say that a few years ago he was not quite normal after a certain illness. . . . It is risky to leave the Ministry of Interior in such hands in these times." Then, anticipating her reaction, he added significantly, "Only I beg, do not drag Our

Friend into this. The responsibility is with me, and therefore I wish to be free in my choice."

On hearing that both Stürmer and Protopopov were to be eliminated, Alexandra became desperate: "Forgive me, dear, believe me—I entreat you don't go and change Protopopov now, he will be alright, give him the chance to get the food supply into his hands and, I assure you, all will go [well]. . . . Oh, Lovy, you can trust me. I may not be clever enough—but I have a strong feeling and that helps more than the brain often. Don't change anybody until we meet, I entreat you, let's speak it over quietly together. . . ."

The next day, Alexandra's letter rose in pitch: "Lovy, my angel . . . don't change Protopopov. I had a long talk with him yesterday—the man is as sane as anyone . . . he is quiet and calm and utterly devoted which one can, alas, say of but few and he will succeed—already things are going better. . . . Change nobody now, otherwise the Duma will think it's their doing and that they have succeeded in clearing everybody out. . . . Darling, remember that it does not lie in the man Protopopov or x.y.z. but it's the question of monarchy and your prestige now, which must not be shattered in the time of the Duma. Don't think they will stop at him, but will make all others leave who are devoted to you one by one—and then ourselves. Remember . . . the Tsar rules and not the Duma. Forgive my again writing but I am fighting for your reign and Baby's future."

Two days later, the Empress arrived at Headquarters on a visit already planned. Together, in the privacy of their room, they wrestled out the problem of Protopopov; the Empress won—and Protopopov remained in office. Nevertheless, the trial of strength was not easy for either of them. In Nicholas's letter bidding farewell to the Empress at the end of her visit, there is evidence of the tension. It is, in fact, the only evidence in the whole of their correspondence of a serious personal quarrel. "Yes," wrote the Tsar, "those days spent together were difficult, but only thanks to you have I spent them more or less calmly. You were so strong and steadfast—I admire you more than I can say. Forgive me if I was moody or unrestrained—sometime's one's temper must come out! . . . now I firmly believe that the most painful is behind us and that it will not be hard as it was before. And henceforth I intend to become sharp and bitter. . . . Sleep sweetly and calmly."

Alexandra, sending her husband back to the front, could not help being pleased with her great triumph. Over the following days, a torrent of exhortation poured from her pen: "I am fully convinced that great and beautiful times are coming for your reign and Russia . . . we must give a strong country to Baby, and dare not be weak for his sake, else he will have a yet harder reign, setting our faults right and drawing the reins in tightly which you let loose. You have to suffer for faults in the reigns of your predecessors and God knows what hardships are yours. Let our legacy be a lighter one for Alexei. He has a strong will and mind of his own, don't let things slip through your fingers and make him build all over again. Be firm . . . one wants to feel your hand—how long, years, people have told me the same 'Russia loves to feel the whip'—it's their nature—tender love and then the iron hand to punish and guide. How I wish I could pour my will into your veins. . . . Be Peter the Great, Ivan the Terrible, Emperor Paul—crush them all under you—now don't you laugh, naughty one."

Nicholas took these exhortations calmly. With a touch of acid, he replied: "My dear, Tender thanks for the severe scolding. I read it with a smile, because you speak to me as though I was a child. . . . Your 'poor little weak-willed' hubby, Nicky." The immediate loser, however, was Trepov. Having failed to eliminate Protopopov, he tried to resign himself. Nicholas, freshly spurred by his wife's letters, refused, telling him sternly, "Alexander Fedorovich, I order you to carry out your duties with the colleagues I have thought fit to give you." Trepov, desperate, tried another way. He sent his brother-in-law, Mosolov, to call on Rasputin and offer him a handsome bribe. Rasputin was to get a house in Petrograd, all living expenses and a paid bodyguard, plus the equivalent of $95,000, if he would arrange Protopopov's dismissal and then himself quit any further interference in government. As a sop, Trepov offered Rasputin a continued free hand with the clergy. Rasputin, already wielding immense power and having little use for wealth, simply laughed.

By the autumn of 1916, Petrograd society mingled a deep loathing of Rasputin with a blithe indifference to the war. At the Astoria and the Europa, the two best hotels in Petrograd, the crowds drinking champagne in bars and salons included many officers who should have been at the front; now there was no disgrace in taking extended leave and shirking the trenches. Late in September, the season began when society appeared at the Maryinsky Theatre to watch Karsavina dance in *Sylvia* and *The Water Lily*. Paléologue, taking his seat in the sumptuous blue-and-gold hall, was struck by the unreality of the scene: "From the stalls to the back row of the highest circle, I could see nothing but a sea of cheery, smiling faces . . . sinister visions of war . . . vanished as if by magic the moment the orchestra struck up." Through the autumn, the splendid evenings continued. At the Narodny Dom, the matchless basso Fedor Chaliapin sang his great roles, *Boris Godunov* and *Don Quixote*. At the Maryinsky, a series of gorgeous ballets, *Nuits Egyptiennes*, *Islamey* and *Eros*, wrapped the audience in fairy tales and enchantment. Mathilde Kschessinska, the prima ballerina assoluta of the Imperial Ballet, danced her famous role in *Pharaoh's Daughter*. In the treetops high above the ballerina's head, a twelve-year-old student playing the part of a monkey jumped from branch to branch while Kschessinska tried to shoot him down with a bow and arrow. After the performance on December 6, the student, George Balanchine, was taken to the Imperial box to be presented to the Tsar and the Empress. Nicholas gave the boy a gentle smile, patted him on the shoulder and handed him a silver box filled with chocolates.*

To most of Russia, however, the Empress was an object of contempt and hatred. The German-spy mania was now flowering to its fullest, ugliest growth. Most Russians firmly believed in the existence of a secret pro-German cabal which was systematically betraying them from the top. The Tsar was not included in its supposed membership; whenever the subject of reconciliation with Germany came up, Nicholas always said bluntly that those who said he would make peace separately from his allies or while German soldiers stood on Russian land were traitors. But the unpopular Empress, along with Stürmer, a reactionary with a German name, and Protopopov, who had met a German agent in Stockholm, were widely and loudly accused. After the abdication, the entire Alexander Palace at Tsarskoe Selo was searched for the clandestine wireless stations through which these plotters were supposed to have been in secret communication with the enemy.

Rasputin, everyone assumed, was a paid German spy. In all the years since 1916, however, no evidence of any kind has ever been offered from either the German or the Russian side that this was so. On balance, it seems unlikely. For the same reason that Rasputin rejected Trepov's bribe, he would have refused money. No foreigner could

* Fifty years later, struggling to convey his strong impression of the Empress, Balanchine said, "Beautiful, beautiful—like Grace Kelly."

offer him more power than he already possessed; besides, he disliked foreigners, especially the English and Germans. What is more likely is that Rasputin was used and drained of the information he acquired by others who were German agents. In this sense, Kerensky argues, "it would have been inexplicable if the German General Staff had not made use of him [Rasputin]." It was not difficult to infiltrate Rasputin's circle. He hated the war and did not avoid people who spoke against it. His entourage already was filled with so wide a variety of people, many of them shady and disreputable, that a few additional faces would scarcely have been noticed. Rasputin was loud and boastful; all an agent would have had to do was sit and listen carefully.

There is some evidence that this is exactly what happened. Every Wednesday night, Rasputin was invited to dinner by Manus, a Petrograd banker. A number of charming and attractive ladies always were on hand. Everybody drank a great deal and Rasputin talked indiscriminately. Manus, Rasputin's host for these evenings, was openly in favor of reconciliation with Germany. Paléologue, whose own local intelligence service was efficient, believed that Manus was the leading German agent in Russia.

On far flimsier evidence, the Empress was accused of treason. When Alexandra sent prayerbooks to wounded German officers in Russian hospitals, it was taken as evidence of collusion. Knox, at the front, met a Russian artillery general who shrugged his shoulders and said, "What can we do? We have Germans everywhere. The Empress is a German." Even at Headquarters, Admiral Nilov, the Tsar's devoted flag captain, cursed the Empress in violent language. "I cannot believe she is a traitoress," he cried, "but it is evident she is in sympathy with them."

Alexandra's support of Rasputin seemed to confirm the worst. Most people took it for granted that the connection was sexual. In society drawing rooms, municipal council meetings, trade-union conferences and in the trenches, the Empress was openly described as Rasputin's mistress. Alexeiev even mentioned the prevalence of this gossip to the Tsar, warning him that censorship of the soldiers' letters revealed that they were writing continuously of his wife and Rasputin. As these rumors flew and feeling against Alexandra rose higher, many of the outward signs of respect in her presence were discarded. In the summer and fall of 1916, in hospital wards she was treated by some surgeons and wounded officers with careless disrespect and sometimes with open rudeness. Behind her back, she was referred to everywhere simply as *Nemka* (the German woman), just as the hated Marie Antoinette had been known to the people of France as *L'Autrichienne* (the Austrian woman). The Tsar's brother-in-law Grand Duke Alexander, trying at this time to locate the source of some of these "incomprehensible libels" on the Empress, talked to a member of the Duma. Bitingly, the member asked, "If the young Tsarina is such a great Russian patriot, why does she tolerate the presence of that drunken beast who is openly seen around the capital in the company of German spies and sympathizers?" Try as he could, the Grand Duke could not supply an answer.

By the end of 1916, some form of change at the top was regarded as inevitable in Russia. Many still hoped that the change could be made without violence, that the monarchy could be modified to make the government responsive to the nation. Others felt that if the dynasty was to be preserved, it had to be brutally purged. One group of officers revealed to Kerensky their plan to "bomb the Tsar's motorcar from an aeroplane at a particular point on its route." A famous fighter pilot, Captain Kostenko, plotted to nose-dive his plane into the Imperial car. There were rumors that General Alexeiev was plotting with Guchkov to force the Tsar to send the Empress to the Crimea. Alexeiev, however, came down with a high fever, and it was he who went to the Crimea to rest and recover in the sun.

The growing peril was obvious to other members of the Imperial family. In November, after his return from Kiev, the Tsar received a visit from his cousin Grand Duke Nicholas Mikhailovich, a well-known historian who was President of the Imperial Historical Society. The Grand Duke, a wealthy man-about-town and a habitué of Petrograd clubs, was an outspoken liberal; already he had written the Tsar a number of letters stressing the importance of broadening the government's support in the Duma. At Headquarters, he had a long talk with Nicholas and then handed the Tsar a letter. The Tsar, believing that he already had fully understood his cousin's views, forwarded the letter to the Empress without reading it. To her horror, Alexandra found in the letter a direct and scathing accusation against herself: "You trust her, that is quite natural," the Grand Duke had written to the Tsar. "Still what she tells you is not the truth; she is only repeating what has been cleverly suggested to her. If you are not able to remove this influence from her, at least protect yourself." Indignantly, the Empress wrote to her husband, "I read Nicholas's [letter] and am utterly disgusted . . . it becomes next to high treason."

Despite this setback, the family persisted. At a meeting of all the members in and near Petrograd, Grand Duke Paul, the Tsar's only surviving uncle, was chosen to go to the Tsar and ask that he grant a constitution. On December 16, Paul had tea with Nicholas and Alexandra and made his request. Nicholas refused, saying that he had sworn at his coronation to deliver his autocratic power intact to his son. While he was speaking, the Empress looked at Paul and silently shook her head. Then the Grand Duke talked openly of the damaging influence of Rasputin. This time, Nicholas remained silent, calmly smoking his cigarette, while the Empress earnestly defended Rasputin, declaring that in his own time every prophet was damned.

The most poignant of all the warning visits was that of Grand Duchess Elizabeth. Dressed in the gray-and-white robes of her religious order, Ella came from Moscow especially to speak to her younger sister about Rasputin. At the mention of his name, the Empress's face grew cold. She was sorry, she said, to find her sister accepting the "lies" told about Father Gregory; if that was all she had to discuss, her visit might as well end immediately. Desperate, the Grand Duchess persisted, whereupon the Empress cut off the conversation, rose and ordered a carriage to take her sister to the station.

"Perhaps it would have been better if I had not come," said Ella sadly as she prepared to leave.

"Yes," said Alexandra. On this cold note, the sisters parted. It was their last meeting.

On one matter, grand dukes, generals and members of the Duma all agreed: Rasputin had to be removed. The question was how. On December 2, a stinging public denunciation was delivered by Vladimir Purishkevich in the Duma. Then in his fifties, a man of sparkling intelligence and wit, the writer of brilliantly satiric political verse, Purishkevich was an orator of such renown that when he rose to speak the entire Duma, including his enemies, beamed in anticipation of what they were about to hear. Politically, Purishkevich was on the extreme Right, the most ardent monarchist in the Duma. He believed in absolute autocracy and rigid orthodoxy, in the Tsar Autocrat as the emissary of God. A fervent patriot, Purishkevich had thrown himself into war work, going to the front to organize a system of relief for the wounded and personally administrating a Red Cross train which traveled back and forth from Petrograd to the front. Invited to dine with the Tsar at Headquarters, Purishkevich had left a highly favorable impression: "wonderful energy and a remarkable organizer," wrote Nicholas.

Devoted to the monarchy, Purishkevich stood before the Duma and for two hours thundered his denunciation of the "dark forces" which were destroying the dynasty. "It requires only the recommendation of Rasputin to raise the most abject citizen to high office," he cried. Then in a ringing finale which brought his audience to a tumultuous standing ovation, he roared a challenge at the ministers who sat before him. "If you are truly loyal, if the glory of Russia, her mighty future which is closely bound up with the brightness of the name of the Tsar mean anything to you, then on your feet, you Ministers. Be off to Headquarters and throw yourselves at the feet of the Tsar. Have the courage to tell him that the multitude is threatening in its wrath. Revolution threatens and an obscure *moujik* shall govern Russia no longer."

Amid the storm of cheers which rolled through the Tauride Palace when Purishkevich had finished, a slender young man sitting in the visitors' box remained utterly silent. Staring at him, another visitor noticed that Prince Felix Yussoupov had turned pale and was trembling.

CHAPTER TWENTY-FIVE

The Prince and the Peasant

At twenty-nine, Prince Felix Yussoupov was the sole heir to the largest fortune in Russia. There were four Yussoupov palaces in Petrograd, three in Moscow and thirty-seven Yussoupov estates scattered across Russia. The family's coal and iron mines, oil fields, mills and factories churned out wealth which exceeded even the wealth of the tsars. "One of our estates," wrote Yussoupov, "stretched for one hundred and twenty-five miles along the Caspian Sea; crude petroleum was so abundant that the ground seemed soaked with it and the peasants used it to grease their cart wheels." Once, on a whim, Prince Yussoupov's father had given his mother the highest mountain in the Crimea as a birthday present. In all, the size of the Yussoupov fortune was estimated fifty years ago at $350 million to $500 million. What the same possessions would be worth today, no one can guess.

The wealth of the Yussoupovs had been accumulated by centuries of standing at the elbows of Russia's tsars and empresses. Prince Dmitry Yussoupov, descended from a Tartar khan named Yusuf, had whispered in the ear of Peter the Great. Prince Boris Yussoupov was a favorite of Empress Elizabeth. Prince Nicholas, the greatest Yussoupov of all, was a friend of Catherine the Great, an advisor to Catherine's son, Tsar Paul, and a counselor to her two grandsons, Tsar Alexander I and Tsar Nicholas I. Prince Nicholas Yussoupov's estate at Archangelskoe near Moscow was a city in itself, boasting huge parks and gardens with heated greenhouses, a zoo, private glass and porcelain factories, a private theatre and the Prince's own companies of actors, musicians and ballet dancers. Seated in the audience, Prince Nicholas could, with a wave of his cane, produce an extraordinary effect: all the dancers would suddenly appear on stage, stark naked. A gallery on this Archangelskoe estate contained portraits of the Prince's three hundred mistresses. When the old grandee died at eighty-one, he had just concluded a liaison with a girl of eighteen.

At his birth in 1887, Felix Yussoupov stepped into a fairyland of art and treasure left behind by these lusty progenitors. The drawing rooms and galleries of the Moika Palace, where he was born, were lined with a finer collection of paintings than those hanging in most of the museums of Europe. There was furniture which had belonged to Marie Antoinette and a chandelier which had lighted the boudoir of Mme. de Pompadour. Jewel-encrusted cigarette boxes by Fabergé were scattered idly about on tables. Dinner parties brought two thousand guests to sit before golden plates and be served by costumed Arab and Tartar footmen. One Yussoupov mansion in Moscow had been built in 1551 as a hunting lodge for Ivan the Terrible; it was still connected by tunnel with the Kremlin several miles away. Beneath its vaulted halls, filled with medieval tapestries and furniture, there were sealed underground chambers which, when opened in Felix's boyhood, revealed rows of skeletons still hanging in chains from the walls.

Cradled in wealth, Felix nevertheless was a spindly, lonely child whose birth caused his mother great disappointment. Princess Zenaide Yussoupov, one of the most famous beauties of her day, had borne three previous sons of whom only one had survived. She had prayed that her next child would be a girl. To console herself when Felix was born, she kept him in long hair and dresses until he was five. Surprisingly, this pleased him and he used to cry out to strangers in the street, "Look, isn't Baby pretty?" "My mother's caprice," Prince Yussoupov wrote later, "was to have a lasting influence on my character."

In adolescence, Felix Yussoupov was slender, with soft eyes and long lashes; he was often described as "the most beautiful young man in Europe." Encouraged by his older brother, he took to dressing up in his mother's gowns, donning her jewels and wigs and strolling in this costume on public boulevards. At The Bear, a fashionable St. Petersburg restaurant, he attracted enthusiastic attention from Guards officers, who sent notes inviting him to supper. Delighted, Felix accepted and disappeared into intimate private dining rooms. In Paris, continuing these masquerades, he once noticed a fat, whiskered gentleman staring persistently at him from the opposite side of the

Théatre des Capucines. A note arrived which Felix hastily returned; his beaming admirer was King Edward VII of England.

Yussoupov's first sexual experience occurred at the age of twelve in the company of a young man from Argentina and his girl friend. At fifteen, roaming Italy with his tutor, Felix first visited a Neapolitan bordello. Thereafter, he wrote, "I flung myself passionately into a life of pleasure, thinking only of satisfying my desires. . . . I loved beauty, luxury, comfort, the color and scent of flowers." He also tried opium and a liaison with "a charming young girl" in Paris. Bored, he enrolled as a student at Oxford, maintaining at the university a chef, a chauffeur, a valet, a housekeeper and a groom to look after his three horses. From Oxford, he moved on to a flat in London, where he installed black carpets, orange silk curtains, modern furniture, a grand piano, a dog, a pet macaw and a French couple to cook and serve. He moved in a gay circle which included ballerina Anna Pavlova, Prince Serge Obolensky and ex-King Manuel of Portugal. Day or night, when friends visited Felix Yussoupov, he took out his guitar and sang gypsy songs.

Felix, the younger Yussoupov brother, became the family heir when Nicholas, his older brother, was killed in a duel by an outraged husband. In 1914, Felix returned to Russia to marry. His bride, Princess Irina, was the niece of the Tsar and the most eligible girl in the empire. At their wedding, Felix wore the uniform of the Russian nobility: a black frock coat with lapels and collar embroidered in gold, and white broadcloth trousers. Irina wore Marie Antoinette's lace veil. The Tsar gave her in marriage and presented as his gift a bag of twenty-nine diamonds, ranging in size from three to seven carats apiece.

During the war, Yussoupov was not called for military service. Remaining in Petrograd, he achieved a glittering reputation as a bohemian. "Prince Felix Yussoupov is twenty-nine," Paléologue observed, "and gifted with quick wits and aesthetic tastes; but his dilettantism is rather too prone to perverse imaginings and literary representations of vice and death . . . his favorite author is Oscar Wilde . . . his instincts, countenance and manner make him much closer akin to . . . Dorian Grey than to Brutus."

Yussoupov first met Rasputin before his marriage. He saw him often, and they caroused together at dubious night spots. As treatment for an illness, Yussoupov submitted himself to Rasputin's caressing eyes and hands. During this time, he often heard Rasputin speak of his Imperial patrons: "The Empress is a very wise ruler. She is a second Catherine but as for him, well, he is no Tsar Emperor, he is just a child of God." According to Yussoupov, Rasputin suggested that Nicholas should abdicate in favor of Alexis, with the Empress installed as Regent. One year before he finally acted, Yussoupov concluded that Rasputin's presence was destroying the monarchy and that the *starets* had to be killed.

Purishkevich spoke in the Duma on December 2. The following morning Yussoupov called on Purishkevich in a fever of excitement. He said that he planned to kill Rasputin, but that he needed assistance. Enthusiastically, Purishkevich agreed to help. Three other conspirators were brought into the plot: an officer named Sukhotin, an army doctor named Lazovert and Yussoupov's youthful friend Grand Duke Dmitry Pavlovich. At twenty-six, Dmitry was the son of Nicholas II's last surviving uncle, Grand Duke Paul. Because of the difference in age, Dmitry referred to the Tsar—actually his first cousin—as "Uncle Nicky." Elegant and charming, Dmitry was a special favorite of the Empress, who often found herself laughing at his jokes and stories. Nevertheless, she worried about his character. "Dmitry is doing no work and drinking constantly," she complained to Nicholas during the war. ". . . order Dmitry back to his regiment; town and women are poison for him."

As December progressed, the five conspirators met regularly, weaving the threads of entrapment, death and disposal of the corpse. The date was determined by Grand Duke Dmitry's heavy social calender; December 31 was the first evening he had free. To cancel one of his previous engagements, the conspirators decided, might arouse suspicion. The place selected for the murder was the cellar of Yussoupov's Moika Palace. It was remote and quiet and Princess Irina was away in the Crimea for her health. Yussoupov himself was to bring Rasputin there in a car driven by Dr. Lazovert disguised as a chauffeur. Once in the cellar, Yussoupov would feed Rasputin poison, while the others, waiting upstairs, would take charge of removing the body.

As the heavy December snows swirled through the streets of Petrograd, Rasputin sensed that his life was in danger. After the impassioned denunciations hurled at him in the Duma, he understood that a crisis was coming. The ebullient Purishkevich, unable to abide by his pledge of secrecy, soon was bubbling with hints to other Duma members that something was about to happen to Rasputin. Catching wisps of these rumors, Rasputin became moody and cautious. He avoided as much as possible going out in daylight. He was preoccupied with the idea of death. Once after a lonely walk along the Neva he came home and declared that he had seen the river filled with the blood of grand dukes. In his last meeting with the Tsar, he refused to give Nicholas his customary blessing, saying instead, "This time it is for you to bless me, not I you."

According to Simanovich, Rasputin's secretary and confidant, it was during these last weeks of December 1916 that Rasputin produced the mystically prophetic letter which has become part of the legend of this extraordinary man. Headed "The Spirit of Gregory Efimovich Rasputin-Novykh of the village of Pokrovskoe," its message of warning is directed mainly at Nicholas:

> I write and leave behind me this letter at St. Petersburg. I feel that I shall leave life before January 1. I wish to make known to the Russian people, to Papa, to the Russian Mother and to the Children, to the land of Russia, what they must understand. If I am killed by common assassins, and especially by my brothers the Russian peasants, you, Tsar of Russia, have nothing to fear, remain on your throne and govern, and you, Russian Tsar, will have nothing to fear for your children, they will reign for hundreds of years in Russia. But if I am murdered by *boyars*, nobles, and if they shed my blood, their hands will remain soiled with my blood, for twenty-five years they will not wash their hands from my blood. They will leave Russia. Brothers will kill brothers, and they will kill each other and hate each other, and for twenty-five years there will be no nobles in the country. Tsar of the land of Russia, if you hear the sound of the bell which will tell you that Gregory has been killed, you must know this: if it was your relations who have wrought my death then no one of your family, that is to say, none of your children or relations will remain alive for more than two years. They will be killed by the Russian people. . . . I shall be killed. I am no longer among the living. Pray, pray, be strong, think of your blessed family.
>
> Gregory

Because the plot hinged on Yussoupov being able to bring Rasputin to the cellar of the Moika Palace, the young Prince intensified his approaches to Rasputin. "My intimacy with Rasputin—so indispensable to our plan—increased each day," he wrote. When near the end of the month Yussoupov invited him "to spend an evening with me soon," Rasputin readily accepted.

But there was more to Rasputin's acceptance than friendship for a charming dilettante and a taste for midnight tea. Yussoupov deliberately encouraged Rasputin's belief that Princess Irina, widely known for her beauty but a stranger to Rasputin, would be present. "He [Rasputin] had long wished to meet my wife," wrote Yussoupov. "Believing her to be in St. Petersburg, and knowing that my parents were in the Crimea, he accepted my invitation. The truth was that Irina was also in the Crimea, but I thought Rasputin would be more likely to accept my invitation if he thought he had a chance of meeting her."

The bait was attractive and Rasputin swallowed it. Both Simanovich and Anna Vyrubova, hearing of the forthcoming supper, tried to dissuade Rasputin from going. Anna Vyrubova visited him in his flat that afternoon, bringing him an icon as a gift from the Empress. "I heard Rasputin say that he expected to pay a late evening visit to the Yussoupov palace to meet Princess Irina, wife of Prince Felix Yussoupov," wrote Anna. "I knew that Felix often visited Rasputin, but it struck me as odd that he should go to their house at such an unseemly hour. . . . I mentioned this proposed midnight visit that night in the Empress's boudoir, and the Empress said in some surprise, 'But there must be some mistake, Irina is in the Crimea.' . . . Once again she repeated thoughtfully, 'There must be some mistake.' "

By evening, the cellar room had been prepared. Yussoupov described the scene: "A low vaulted ceiling . . . walls of gray stone, the flooring of granite . . . carved wooden chairs of oak . . . small tables covered with ancient embroideries . . . a cabinet of inlaid ebony which was a mass of little mirrors, tiny bronze columns and secret drawers. On it stood a crucifix of rock crystal and silver, a beautiful specimen of sixteenth century Italian workmanship. . . . A large Persian carpet covered the floor and, in a corner, in front of the ebony cabinet, lay a white bear skin rug. . . . In the middle of the room stood the table at which Rasputin was to drink his last cup of tea.

"On the table the samovar smoked, surrounded by plates filled with the cakes and dainties that Rasputin liked so much. An array of bottles and glasses sat on a sideboard. . . . On the granite hearth a log fire crackled and scattered sparks on the hearthstones. . . . I took from the ebony cabinet a box containing the poison and laid it on the table. Doctor Lazovert put on rubber gloves and ground the cyanide of potassium crystals to powder. Then, lifting the top of each cake, he sprinkled the inside with a dose of poison which, according to him, was sufficient to kill several men instantly," When he finished, Lazovert convulsively tossed the contaminated gloves into the fire. It was a mistake; within a few moments the fireplace was smoking heavily and the air became temporarily unbreathable.

Rasputin also prepared himself carefully for the rendezvous. When Yussoupov went alone at midnight to Rasputin's flat, he found the *starets* smelling of cheap soap and dressed in his best embroidered silk blouse, black velvet trousers and shiny new boots. Yussoupov promised, as he took his victim away and led him down into the cellar, that Princess Irina was upstairs at a party but would be down shortly. From overhead came the sounds of "Yankee Doodle" played on a phonograph by the other conspirators, simulating the Princess's "party."

Alone in the cellar with his victim, Yussoupov nervously offered Rasputin the poisoned cakes. Rasputin refused. Then, changing his mind, he gobbled two. Yussoupov watched, expecting to see him crumple in agony, but nothing happened. Then, Rasputin asked for the Madeira, which had also been poisoned. He swallowed two glasses, still with no effect. Seeing this, wrote Yussoupov, "my head swam." Rasputin took some tea to clear his head and, while sipping it, asked Yussoupov to sing for him with his guitar. Through one song after another, the terrified murderer sang on while the happy "corpse" sat nodding and grinning with pleasure. Huddled at the top of the stairs, scarcely daring to breathe, Purishkevich, Dmitry and the others could hear only the quavering sound of Yussoupov's singing and the indistinguishable murmur of the two voices.

After this game had gone on for two and a half hours, Yussoupov could stand it no longer. In desperation, he rushed upstairs to ask what he should do. Lazovert had no answer: his nerves had failed and he had already fainted once. Grand Duke Dmitry suggested giving up and going home. It was Purishkevich, the oldest and steadiest of the group, who kept his head and declared that Rasputin could not be allowed to leave half dead. Steeling himself, Yussoupov volunteered to return to the cellar and complete the murder. Holding Dmitry's Browning revolver behind his back, he went back down the stairs and found Rasputin seated, breathing heavily and calling for more wine. Reviving, Rasputin suggested a visit to the gypsies. "With God in thought, but mankind in the flesh," he said with a heavy wink.

Yussoupov then led Rasputin to the mirrored cabinet and showed him the ornate crucifix. Rasputin stared at the crucifix and declared that he liked the cabinet better. "Gregory Efimovich," said Yussoupov, "you'd far better look at the crucifix and say a prayer." Rasputin glared at the Prince, then turned briefly to look again at the cross. As he did so, Yussoupov fired. The bullet plunged into the broad back. With a scream, Rasputin fell backward onto the white bearskin.

Hearing the shot, Yussoupov's friends rushed into the cellar. They found Yussoupov, revolver in hand, calmly staring down at the dying man with a look of inexpressible disgust in his eyes. Although there was not a trace of blood, Dr. Lazovert, clutching Rasputin's pulse, quickly pronounced him dead. The diagnosis was premature. A moment later, when Yussoupov, having surrendered the revolver, was temporarily alone with the "corpse," Rasputin's face twitched and his left eye fluttered open. A few seconds later, his right eye also rolled open. "I then saw both eyes—the green eyes of a viper—staring at me with an expression of diabolical hatred," Yussoupov wrote. Suddenly, while Yussoupov stood rooted to the floor, Rasputin, foaming at the mouth, leaped to his feet, grabbed his murderer by the throat and tore an epaulet off his shoulder. In terror, Yussoupov broke away and fled up the stairs. Behind him, clambering on all fours, roaring with fury, came Rasputin.

Purishkevich, upstairs, heard "a savage, inhuman cry." It was Yussoupov: "Purishkevich, fire, fire! He's alive! He's getting away!" Purishkevich ran to the stairs and almost collided with the frantic Prince, whose eyes were "bulging out of their sockets. Without seeing me . . . he hurled himself towards the door . . . [and into] his parents' apartment."

Recovering, Purishkevich dashed outside into the courtyard. "What I saw would have been a dream if it hadn't been a terrible reality. Rasputin, who half an hour before lay dying in the cellar, was running quickly across the snow-covered courtyard towards the iron gate which led to the street. . . . I couldn't believe my eyes. But a harsh cry which broke the silence of the night persuaded me. 'Felix! Felix! I will tell everything to the Empress!' It was him, all right, Rasputin. In a few seconds, he would reach the iron gate. . . . I fired. The night echoed with the shot. I missed. I fired again. Again I missed. I raged at myself. Rasputin neared the gate. I bit with all my force the end of my left hand to force myself to concentrate and I fired a third time. The bullet hit him in the shoulders. He stopped. I fired a fourth time and hit him probably in the head. I ran up and kicked him as hard as I could with my boot in the temple. He fell into the snow, tried to rise, but he could only grind his teeth."

With Rasputin prostrate once again, Yussoupov reappeared and struck hysterically at the bleeding man with a rubber club. When at last the body lay still in the crimson snow, it was rolled up in a blue curtain, bound with a rope and taken to a hole in the frozen Neva, where Purishkevich and Lazovert pushed it through a hole in the ice. Three days later, when the body was found, the lungs were filled with water. Gregory Rasputin, his bloodstream filled with poison, his body punctured by bullets, had died by drowning.

"Next morning," wrote Anna Vyrubova, "soon after breakfast, I was called on the telephone by one of the daughters of Rasputin. . . . In some anxiety, the young girl told me that her father had gone out the night before in Yussoupov's motor car and had not returned. When I reached the palace, I gave the message to the Empress who listened with a grave face but little comment. A few minutes later, there came a telephone call from Protopopov in Petrograd. The police . . . had reported to him that a patrolman standing near the entrance of the Yussoupov palace had been startled by the report of a pistol. Ringing the doorbell, he was met by . . . Purishkevich who appeared to be in advance stages of intoxication. [He said] they had just killed Rasputin."

In the excitement of the moment, Purishkevich had again completely forgotten the need for secrecy. After the sharp report of his four pistol shots had split the dry winter air and roused a policeman, Purishkevich had thrown his arms around the man and shouted exultantly, "I have killed Grishka Rasputin, the enemy of Russia and the Tsar." Twenty-four hours later, the story, embroidered with a thousand colorful details, was all over Petrograd.

The Empress, remaining calm, ordered Protopopov to make a complete investigation. A squad of detectives, entering the Yussoupov palace, found the stains of a trail of blood running up the stairs and across the courtyard. Yussoupov explained this as the result of a wild party the night before at which one of his guests had shot a dog—the body of the dog was lying in the court for the police to see. Nevertheless, Protopopov advised Alexandra that Rasputin's disappearance was almost certainly linked to the commotion at Yussoupov's house;

Purishkevich's boast and the blood found by the police suggested that the *starets* had probably been murdered. Technically, only the Tsar could order the arrest of a grand duke, but Alexandra ordered that both Dmitry and Felix be confined to their houses. Late that day, when Felix telephoned asking permission to see the Empress, she refused, telling him to put his message into a letter. When the letter arrived, it contained a denial of any part in the rumored assassination. Grand Duke Paul, shocked at rumors of his son's complicity, confronted Dmitry with a holy icon and a photograph of Dmitry's mother. On these two sacred objects, he asked his son to swear that he had not killed Rasputin. "I swear it," said Dmitry solemnly.

On the afternoon after the murder, the Empress's friend Lili Dehn found Alexandra lying on a couch in her mauve boudoir, surrounded by flowers and the fragrant odor of burning wood. Anna Vyrubova and the four young Grand Duchesses sat nearby. Although Anna's eyes were red from weeping, Alexandra's blue eyes were clear. Only her extreme pallor and the frantic disjointedness of the letter she was writing to the Tsar betrayed her anxiety.

> My own beloved sweetheart,
>
> We are sitting together—you can imagine our feelings—thoughts—Our Friend has disappeared.
>
> Yesterday A. [Anna] saw him, and he said Felix asked him to come in the night, a motor would fetch him, to see Irina. A motor fetched him (military one) with two civilians and he went away.
>
> This night big scandal at Yussoupov's house—big meeting, Dmitry, Purishkevich, etc. all drunk; police heard shots, Purishkevich ran out screaming to the police that Our Friend was killed.
>
> . . . Our Friend was in good spirits but nervous these days. Felix pretends he [Rasputin] never came to the house. . . . I shall still trust in God's mercy that one has only driven Him off somewhere. Protopopov is doing all he can. . . .
>
> I cannot and won't believe that He has been killed. God have mercy. Such utter anguish (am calm and can't believe it) . . . Come quickly. . . .
>
> Felix came often to him lately.
>
> Kisses,
>
> Sunny

The following day, when Rasputin still had not appeared, Alexandra telegraphed: "No trace yet. . . . The police are continuing the search.

I fear that these two wretched boys have committed a frightful crime, but have not yet lost all hope. Start today, I need you terribly."

On the third day, January 1, 1917, Rasputin's body was found. In their haste, the murderers had left one of his boots on the ice near the hole. Divers probing beneath the ice in that vicinity brought up the corpse. Incredibly, before he died, Rasputin had struggled with sufficient strength to free one of his hands from the ropes around him. The freed arm was raised above the shoulder; the effect was that Rasputin's last gesture on earth had been a sign of benediction.

In Petrograd, where everyone knew the details and juicy stories of the Rasputin scandal, confirmation that the Beast was slain set off an orgy of wild rejoicing. People kissed each other in the streets and hailed Yussoupov, Purishkevich and Grand Duke Dmitry as heroes. At the Cathedral of Our Lady of Kazan, there was a crush to light a sea of candles around the icons of St. Dmitry. Far off in the provinces, however, where the peasants knew only that a *moujik*, a man like themselves, had become powerful at the court of the Tsar, the murder was regarded differently. "To the *moujiks*, Rasputin has become a martyr," an old prince just returned from his estate on the Volga reported to Paléologue. "He was a man of the people; he let the Tsar hear the voice of the people; he defended the people against the court folk, the *pridvorny*. So the *pridvorny* killed him. That's what's being said."

History, with all its sweep and diversity, produces few characters as original and extravagant as Gregory Rasputin. The source and extent of his extraordinary powers will never be fully known; the shadow of this uncertainty perpetually will refresh the legend. The duality of his countenance—the one face peaceful, soothing, offering the blessings of God; the other cynical, crafty, reddened by lust—is the core of his mysterious appeal. In his single, remarkable life, he represents not only the two sides of Russia's history, half compassionate and long-suffering, half savage and pagan, but the constant struggle in every soul between good and evil.

As for the evil in Gregory Rasputin, it should be carefully weighed. He has been called a monster, yet, unlike most monsters in history, he took not a single life. He schemed against his enemies and toppled men from high places, yet, once they had fallen, he sought no vengeance. In his relations with women he was undoubtedly villainous, but most of these episodes occurred with the consent of the women involved. Unquestionably, he used his "holy" aura to seductive advantage and, failing all else, forced himself upon unwilling victims. But even here the screams of outrage were greatly amplified by rumor.

Rasputin's greatest crime was his delusion of the Empress Alexandra. Deliberately, he encouraged her to believe that there was only one side of him: Father Gregory, Our Friend, the Man of God who gave relief to her son and calmed her fears. The other Rasputin—drunken, leering, arrogant—did not exist for the Empress except in the malicious reports of their common enemies. An obvious rogue to everyone else, he carefully hid this side from her. Yet no one could believe that the Empress did not know; therefore, her acceptance of him was taken as acceptance of his worst behavior. On her part, this can be called foolishness, blindness, ignorance. But on his part, the deliberate exploitation of weakness and devotion was nothing less than monstrous evil.

Predictably, the impact of Rasputin's death fell less severely on Nicholas than on Alexandra. Told of Rasputin's disappearance while he sat in a staff meeting at Headquarters, the Tsar left the room immediately and telegraphed "Am horrified, shaken." Nevertheless, he did not leave for Petrograd until January 1, when Rasputin's death was confirmed. Once again, in death as in life, Nicholas was less concerned about Rasputin than about the effect that the murder would have on his wife. In the months preceding the assassination, Rasputin's advice had become less welcome. Often Nicholas was irritated by what he regarded as clumsy intrusions by Rasputin into political and military matters. The Tsar, wrote Gilliard, "had tolerated him [Rasputin] because he dared not weaken the Empress's faith in him—a faith that kept her alive. He did not like to send him away, for if Alexis Nicolaievich died, in the eyes of the mother, he would have been the murderer of his own son."

For Nicholas himself, the quickest pang of Rasputin's death lay in the fact that the murder had been committed by members of the Imperial family. "I am filled with shame that the hands of my kinsmen are stained with the blood of a simple peasant," he exclaimed. "A murder is always a murder," he replied stiffly in refusing an appeal from his relatives on behalf of Dmitry. Almost fifty years later, the

Tsar's sister Grand Duchess Olga Alexandrovna still showed the same shame and scorn for her family's behavior: "There was nothing heroic about Rasputin's murder," she said. "It was . . . premeditated most vilely. Just think of the two names most closely associated with it even to this day—a Grand Duke, one of the grandsons of the Tsar-Liberator, and then a scion of one of our great houses whose wife was a Grand Duke's daughter. That proved how low we had fallen."

Soon after Nicholas's return to Petrograd, enough evidence had been amassed to incriminate the three leading conspirators. Grand Duke Dmitry was ordered to leave Petrograd immediately for duty with the Russian troops operating in Persia; the sentence undoubtedly saved his life, as it put him out of reach of the revolution which was soon to follow. Yussoupov was banished to one of his estates in the center of Russia; a year later, he left his homeland with Princess Irina, taking with him, from all his vast fortune, only a million dollars in jewels and two Rembrandts. Purishkevich was allowed to go free. His part in the murder had placed his prestige at a peak. To strike down a member of the Duma who had also become a hero was no longer possible even for the Autocrat of all the Russias.

In secrecy, Rasputin's body was taken to the chapel of a veterans' home halfway between Petrograd and Tsarskoe Selo, where an autopsy was performed and the body was washed and dressed and laid in a coffin. Two days later, on January 3, Rasputin was buried in a corner of the Imperial Park where Anna Vyrubova was building a church. Lili Dehn was present: "It was a glorious morning," she wrote. "The sky was a deep blue, the sun was shining and the hard snow sparkled like masses of diamonds. My carriage stopped on the road . . . and I was directed to walk across a frozen field towards the unfinished church. Planks had been placed on the snow to serve as a footpath, and when I arrived at the church I noticed that a police motor van was drawn up near the open grave. After waiting several moments, I heard the sound of sleigh bells and Anna Vyrubova came slowly across the field. Almost immediately afterwards, a closed automobile stopped and the Imperial family joined us. They were dressed in mourning and the Empress carried some white flowers; she was very pale but quite composed although I saw her tears fall when the oak coffin was taken out of the police van . . . the burial service was read by the chaplain and after the Emperor and Empress had thrown earth on the coffin, the Empress distributed her flowers between the Grand Duchesses and ourselves and we scattered them on the coffin."

Inside the coffin, before the lid was sealed, the Empress had two objects placed on Rasputin's breast. One was an icon, signed by herself, her husband, her son and her daughters. The other was a letter: "My dear martyr, give me thy blessing that it may follow me always on the sad and dreary path I have yet to follow here below. And remember us from on high in your holy prayers. Alexandra."

CHAPTER TWENTY-SIX

Last Winter at Tsarskoe Selo

DURING the dreary weeks of winter that followed Rasputin's murder, the Tsar of all the Russias suffered something close to a nervous collapse. Utterly weary, craving only tranquillity and rest, he remained secluded at Tsarskoe Selo. There, in the bosom of his family, surrounded by a narrow circle of familiar figures, he lived quietly, avoiding decisions that affected ministers, munitions, his millions of soldiers and tens of millions of subjects. Rodzianko, who saw him twice during this period, recalled the audience in which Nicholas got up and went to the window. "How lovely it was in the woods today," he said, looking out. "It is so quiet there. One forgets all these intrigues and paltry human restlessness. My soul felt so peaceful. One is nearer to Nature there, nearer to God."

Nicholas remained all day in his private quarters. He converted his billiard room into a map room, and there, behind a door guarded by his motionless Ethiopian, he stood for hours over huge maps of the battlefields spread out on the billiard tables. When he left the room, he carefully locked the door and carried the key in his own pocket. At night, he sat with his wife and Anna Vyrubova in the Empress's mauve boudoir, reading aloud. His public utterances were vague. He issued a manifesto to the army which, although written for him by General Gurko, was molded of Nicholas's own continuing patriotic dream: "The time for peace has not yet come. . . . Russia has not yet performed the tasks this war has set her. . . . The possession of Constantinople and the Straits . . . the restoration of a free Poland. . . . We remain unshaken in our confidence in victory. God will bless our arms. He will cover them with everlasting glory and give us a peace worthy of your glorious deeds. Oh, my glorious troops, a peace such that generations to come will bless your sacred memory!" Paléologue, reading the manifesto and wondering at Nicholas's meaning, decided that it "can only be . . . a kind of political will, a final announcement of the glorious vision which he had imagined for Russia and which he now sees dissolving into thin air."

Visitors were shocked by the Tsar's appearance; there were wild rumors that Alexandra was giving him drugs. On the Russian New Year, the diplomatic corps arrived at Tsarskoe Selo for its annual reception. Nicholas appeared, surrounded by his generals and aides, to exchange handshakes, smiles and congratulations. "As usual," wrote Paléologue, "Nicholas II was kind and natural and he even affected a certain care-free air; but his pale, thin face betrayed the nature of his secret thoughts." A private audience left the French Ambassador filled with gloom. "The Emperor's words, his silences and reticences, his grave, drawn features and furtive, distant thoughts and the thoroughly vague and enigmatical quality of his personality, confirm in me . . . the notion that Nicholas II feels himself overwhelmed and dominated by events, that he has lost all faith in his mission . . . that he has . . . abdicated inwardly and is now resigned to disaster."

Nicholas made a similar impression on Vladimir Kokovtsov, the former Prime Minister. Kokovtsov had always had a high regard for Nicholas's quick, intuitive grasp of most subjects and his exceptional memory. Entering the Tsar's study on February 1, Kokovtsov was deeply alarmed by the change in his sovereign: "During the year that I had not seen him, he became almost unrecognizable. His face had become very thin and hollow and covered with small wrinkles. His eyes . . . had become quite faded and wandered aimlessly from object to object. . . . The whites were of a decidedly yellow tinge, and the dark retinas had become colorless, grey and lifeless. . . . The face of the Tsar bore an expression of helplessness. A forced, mirthless smile was fixed upon his lips and he answered, repeating several times: 'I am perfectly well and sound, but I spend too much time without exercise and I am used to much activity. I repeat to you, Vladimir Nicolaievich, I am perfectly all right. You have not seen me for a long time, and possibly I did not have a good night. Presently I shall go for a walk and shall look better."

Throughout the interview, Kokovtsov continued, "the Tsar listened to me with the same sickly smile, glancing nervously about him." Asked a "question which seemed to me perfectly simple . . . the Tsar became reduced to a perfectly incomprehensible state of helplessness. The strange, almost vacant smile remained fixed on his face; he looked at me as if to seek support and to ask me to remind him of a matter that had absolutely slipped his memory. . . . For a long time, he looked at me in silence as if trying to collect his thoughts or to recall what had escaped his memory."

Kokovtsov left the room in tears. Outside, he found Dr. Botkin and Count Paul Benckendorff, the Grand Marshal of the court. "Do you not see the state of the Tsar?" he asked. "He is on the verge of some mental disturbance if not already in its power." Botkin and Benckendorff both said that Nicholas was not ill, merely tired. Nevertheless, Kokovtsov returned to Petrograd with the strong impression "that the Tsar was seriously ill and that his illness was of a nervous character."

Alexandra was bowed by Rasputin's murder, but, drawing on the same reserves of inner fortitude which were to sustain her during the pitiless months ahead, she did not break. Rasputin had often told her, "If I die or you desert me, you will lose your son and your crown within six months." The Empress had never doubted him. Rasputin's death removed the savior of her son and her link with God. Without his prayers and counsel, any disaster was possible. The fact that the blow had come from within the Imperial family did not surprise her. She knew their feelings and understood that she had been the real target of the assassins.

After the murder, she sat quietly for a number of days, with tear-stained face, staring in front of her. Then, she rallied, and the face she showed even to those in the palace was calm and resolute. If God had taken her Friend, she was still on earth. While life remained, she would persevere in her faith, in her devotion to husband and family, in her resolve, sealed now by Gregory's martyrdom, to maintain the autocracy given to Russia by God. Touched by the same sense of earthly doom that afflicted the Tsar, she steeled herself for the shocks to come. From that point, through the months left to her to live, Alexandra never wavered.

It was the Empress who took matters in hand. Since the day of the assassination, Anna Vyrubova's mail had been filled with anonymous threatening letters. By the Empress's command, Anna was moved for greater safety from her small house to an apartment in the Alexander

Palace. Although the Tsar was in the palace, the Empress continued to exert a predominant influence on political affairs. The main telephone in the palace was not on his desk but in her boudoir on a table beneath the portrait of Marie Antoinette. Protopopov's reports at the palace were given to either Nicholas or Alexandra, whoever was available, sometimes to both of them together. In addition, with her husband's knowledge, the Empress took to eavesdropping on the Tsar's official conversations. Kokovtsov sensed something of this kind in his interview. "I thought that the door leading from the [Tsar's] study to his dressing room was half open, which had never occurred before, and that someone was standing just inside," he wrote. "It may have been just an illusion but this impression stayed with me throughout my brief audience." It was not an illusion, but it was a temporary device. Soon afterward, for greater convenience, the Empress had a wooden staircase cut through the walls to a small balcony overlooking the Tsar's formal audience chamber. There, concealed by curtains, the Empress could lie on a couch and listen in comfort.

In the conduct of Russia's government, Rasputin's death changed nothing. Ministers came and went. Trepov, who had replaced Stürmer as Prime Minister in November, was allowed to resign in January to be replaced by Prince Nicholas Golitsyn, an elderly man whom the Empress had known as deputy chairman of one of her charitable committees. Golitsyn was horrified by his appointment and unsuccessfully begged the Tsar to choose another. "If someone else had used the language I used to describe myself, I should have been obliged to challenge him to a duel," he said.

It made little difference. Protopopov was the only minister in whom the Empress had genuine confidence. The rest of the Cabinet scarcely mattered, and Protopopov rarely bothered even to attend its meetings. Rodzianko refused even to speak to him. At a New Year's Day reception, the Duma President tried to avoid his former deputy. "I noticed he was following me. . . . I moved to another part of the hall and stood with my back [to him]. Notwithstanding . . . Protopopov held out his hand. I replied, 'Nowhere and never.' Protopopov . . . took me in a friendly manner by the elbow, saying, 'My dear fellow, surely we can come to an understanding.' I felt disgusted by him. 'Leave me alone. You are repellent to me,' I said."

Dependent, like Rasputin, solely on the favor of the Empress, the Interior Minister hastened to clothe himself in Rasputin's spiritual trappings. As the *starets* had done, he telephoned every morning at ten, to either the Empress or Anna Vyrubova. He reported that Rasputin's spirit sometimes came to him at night; that he could feel the familiar presence and hear the familiar voice as it gave him advice. A story making the rounds in Petrograd depicted Protopopov in the middle of an audience with Alexandra suddenly falling on his knees and moaning, "Oh, Majesty, I see Christ behind you."

Although the Empress was resolute, she had no joy in her work. Every Thursday evening, a concert of chamber music was given in a palace drawing room by a Rumanian orchestra. The Empress's chair always was placed near the fire burning in the grate, and she sat absorbed by the music, staring into the glowing flames. On one of these nights, only two weeks before the Revolution, her friend Lili Dehn slid into a chair behind her. "The Empress seemed unusually sad," she wrote. "I whispered anxiously, 'Oh, Madame, why are you so sad tonight?' The Empress turned and looked at me. . . . 'Why am I sad, Lili? . . . I can't say, really, but . . . I think my heart is broken.' "

A British visitor calling on the Empress during these same weeks was struck by her air of sadness and resignation. General Sir Henry Wilson, visiting Russia with an Allied mission, had known Alexandra as a girl in Darmstadt. Now, "taken down a long passage to the Empress's own boudoir—a room full of pictures and bric-a-brac . . . ," he reminded her of "our tennis parties in the old days, 36 years ago, at Darmstadt. . . . She was so delighted with the reminiscences, and remembered some of the names I had forgotten. After this it was easy. She said her lot was harder than most people's because she had relations and friends in England, Russia and Germany. She told me of her experiences and her eyes filled with tears. She has a beautiful face, but very, very sad. She is tall and graceful, divides her hair simply on one side, and it is done up at the back. The hair is powdered with grey. When I said I was going to leave her, as she must be tired of seeing strangers and making conversation, she nearly laughed and kept me on for a little while."

Wilson was moved by this talk. "What a tragedy there is in that life," he wrote. Nevertheless, when he left Russia a week later, he added, "It seems as certain as anything can be that the Emperor and Empress are riding for a fall. Everyone—officers, merchants, ladies—talks openly of the absolute necessity of doing away with them."

The killing of Rasputin was a monarchist act. It was intended by the Grand Duke, the Prince and the Right-wing deputy to cleanse the throne and restore the prestige of the dynasty. It was also intended, by removing what they conceived to be the power behind the Empress, to eliminate the Empress herself as a force in the government of Russia. The Tsar, they thought, would then be free to choose ministers and follow policies which would save the monarchy and Russia. This was the hope of many members of the Imperial family, most of whom disliked the murder, but were glad the murdered man was dead.

The Tsar's punishment of Grand Duke Dmitry and Prince Felix Yussoupov, mild though it was, disappointed these hopes. The family addressed a collective letter to Nicholas which combined a plea for pardon for Dmitry with a request for a responsible ministry. Nicholas, still outraged that members of his family had been involved in the assassination, was further offended by the letter. "I allow no one to give me advice," he replied indignantly. "A murder is always a murder. In any case, I know that the consciences of several who signed that letter are not clear." A few days later, hearing that one of the signers, the liberal Grand Duke Nicholas Mikhailovich, was going around his Petrograd clubs openly berating the government, the Tsar ordered him to leave the capital and remain in residence on one of his country estates.

The murder, far from closing the breach within the Romanov family, had widened it further. The Dowager Empress was greatly alarmed. "One should . . . forgive," Marie wrote from Kiev. "I am sure you are aware yourself how deeply you have offended all the family by your brusque reply, throwing at their heads a dreadful and entirely unjustified accusation. I hope that you will alleviate the fate of poor Dmitry by not leaving him in Persia. . . . Poor Uncle Paul [Dmitry's father] wrote me in despair that he had not even been given a chance to say goodbye. . . . It is not like you to behave this way. . . . It upsets me very much."

From his home in Kiev, the Tsar's cousin and brother-in-law Grand Duke Alexander Mikhailovich hurried to Tsarskoe Selo to plead that the Empress withdraw from politics and the Tsar grant a government acceptable to the Duma. This was the "Sandro" of Nicholas's youth, the gay companion of his suppers with Kschessinska, the husband of his sister Xenia and the father-in-law of Prince Felix Yussoupov. He found the Empress lying in bed, dressed in a white negligee embroidered with lace. Although the Tsar was present, sitting and quietly smoking on the other side of their large double bed, the Grand Duke spoke plainly: "Your interference with affairs of state is causing harm . . . to Nicky's prestige. I have been your faithful friend, Alix, for twenty-four years . . . as a friend, I point out to you that all the classes of the population are opposed to your policies. You have a beautiful family of children, why can you not . . . please, Alix, leave the cares of state to your husband?"

When the Empress replied that it was impossible for an autocrat to share his powers with a parliament, the Grand Duke said, "You are very much mistaken, Alix. Your husband ceased to be an autocrat on October 17, 1905."

The interview ended badly, with Grand Duke Alexander shouting in a wild rage: "Remember, Alix, I remained silent for thirty months. For thirty months I never said . . . a word to you about the disgraceful goings on in our government, better to say in *your* government. I realize that you are willing to perish and that your husband feels the same way, but what about us? . . . You have no right to drag your relatives with you down a precipice." At this point, Nicholas quietly interrupted and led his cousin from the room. Later, from Kiev, Grand Duke Alexander wrote, "One cannot govern a country without listening to the voice of the people. . . . Strange as it may appear, it is the Government which is preparing the Revolution . . . the Government is doing all it can to increase the number of malcontents and it is succeeding admirably. We are watching an unprecedented spectacle, revolution coming from above and not from below."

One branch of the Imperial family, the "Vladimirs," were not content to write letters, but talked openly of a palace revolution which would replace their cousin by force. Grand Duchess Marie Pavlovna and Grand Dukes Cyril, Boris and Andrei—the widow and sons of the Tsar's eldest uncle, Grand Duke Vladimir—carried resentments which stretched deep into the past. Vladimir himself, a forceful, ambitious man, always jealous of his older brother, Tsar Alexander III, had accepted with difficulty the accession to the throne of his mild-mannered nephew. A vociferous Anglophobe, he was infuriated when Nicholas chose as his consort a princess who, although born in Darmstadt, was a granddaughter of Queen Victoria. Vladimir's widow, Marie Pavlovna, also was German, a Mecklenberger, and the third lady of the Russian Empire, ranking directly after the two Empresses. Socially, Marie Pavlovna was everything that Alexandra was not. Energetic, poised, intelligent, well read, devoted to gossip and intrigue, openly ambitious for her three sons, she turned her grand palace on the Neva into a glittering court which far outshone Tsarskoe Selo. In the lively conversations which dominated her dinner parties and soirees, amusement and scorn directed at the ruling couple were frequent themes. Never did the Grand Duchess forget that after the Tsarevich, who was ill, and the Tsar's brother, who had married a commoner, the next in line for the throne was her eldest son, Cyril.

In addition, each of the Vladimir sons had separate personal reasons for prickly relations with the Tsar and the Empress. Cyril was married to the divorced wife of Alexandra's brother Grand Duke Ernest of Hesse. Andrei kept as his mistress the ballerina, Mathilde Kschessinska, who had been in love with Nicholas II before his marriage. Boris, the middle Vladimir son, had proposed to his cousin Olga, the Tsar's eldest daughter. The Empress, in writing to her husband, expressed some of the flavor of her rebuff to Boris: "What an awful set his wife would be dragged into . . . intrigues without end, fast manners and conversations . . . a half-worn, blasé . . . man of 38 to a pure fresh girl 18 years his junior and live in a house in which many a woman has 'shared' his life!! An inexperienced girl would suffer terribly to have her husband 4–5th hand—or more!" As the proposal had been transmitted not only in the name of Boris, but in that of his mother as well, Marie Pavlovna bore great bitterness toward Alexandra.

Rodzianko got a taste of this bitterness, and the conspiracy growing out of it, when in January 1917 he was urgently invited to lunch at the Vladimir Palace. After lunch, he wrote, the Grand Duchess "began to talk of the general state of affairs, of the Government's incompetence, of Protopopov and of the Empress. She mentioned the latter's name, becoming more and more excited, dwelling on her nefarious influence and interference in everything, and said she was driving the country to destruction; that she was the cause of the danger which threatened the Emperor and the rest of the Imperial family; that such conditions could no longer be tolerated; that things must be changed, something done, removed, destroyed. . . . "

Wishing to understand her meaning more precisely, Rodzianko asked, "What do you mean by 'removed'?"

"The Duma must do something. She must be annihilated."

"Who?"

"The Empress."

"Your Highness," said Rodzianko, "allow me to treat this conversation as if it had never taken place, because if you address me as the

President of the Duma, my oath of allegiance compels me to wait at once on His Imperial Majesty and report to him that the Grand Duchess Marie Pavlovna has declared to me that the Empress must be annihilated."

For weeks, the grand-ducal plot was the talk of Petrograd. Everyone knew the details: four regiments of the Guard were to make a night march on Tsarskoe Selo and seize the Imperial family. The Empress was to be shut up in a convent—the classic Russian method of disposing of unwanted empresses—and the Tsar was to be forced to abdicate in favor of his son, with the Grand Duke Nicholas as Regent. No one, not even the secret police who had collected all the details, took the Grand Dukes seriously. "Yesterday evening," Paléologue wrote on January 9, "Prince Gabriel Constantinovich gave a supper for his mistress, formerly an actress. The guests included the Grand Duke Boris . . . a few officers and a squad of elegant courtesans. During the evening the only topic was the conspiracy—the regiments of the Guard which can be relied on, the most favorable moment for the outbreak, etc. And all this with the servants moving about, harlots looking on and listening, gypsies singing and the whole company bathed in the aroma of Moët and Chandon *brut impérial* which flowed in streams."

The Imperial government was crumbling and among those who watched the process with dismay were some who were not Russian. The war and the alliance had conferred on the Ambassadors of France and Britain, Maurice Paléologue and Sir George Buchanan, positions of vast importance. Through the two Embassies in Petrograd and across the desks of the two Ambassadors flowed major questions of supply, munitions and military operations, as well as matters of diplomacy. As it became increasingly apparent that Russia's domestic political crisis was affecting her capacity as a military ally, Buchanan and Paléologue found themselves in a delicate situation. Accredited personally to the Tsar, they had no right to speak on matters affecting Russian internal policy. Nevertheless, by the winter of 1917 both Ambassadors found themselves begged on all sides to use their access to the Tsar to plead for a government acceptable to the Duma. Personally convinced that nothing else could save Russia as an ally, they both agreed. Paléologue's attempt, put off by Nicholas's vagueness and gentle courtesy, failed completely. On January 12, Buchanan, in turn, was received at Tsarskoe Selo.

Sir George Buchanan was an old-school diplomat, distinguished by discretion, silvery hair and a monocle. Seven years' service in Russia had left him weary and frail, but with a host of friends and admirers, including the Tsar himself. His only handicap in fulfilling his post was his inability to speak Russian. This made no difference in Petrograd, where everyone who mattered also spoke French or English. In 1916, however, Buchanan visited Moscow, where he was made an honorary citizen of the city and given a priceless icon and a massive silver loving cup. "In the heart of Russia," wrote R. H. Bruce Lockhart, the British Consul General, who was assisting in Buchanan's visit, "he had to say at least a word or two in Russian. We had carefully rehearsed the ambassador to hold it up and say to the distinguished audience, '*Spasibo*' which is the short form of Russian for 'thank you.' Instead, Sir George, in a firm voice, held up the cup and said, '*Za pivo*' which means 'for beer.' "

At Tsarskoe Selo, Buchanan was surprised to be received by the Tsar in the formal audience chamber rather than in Nicholas's study, where they usually talked. Nevertheless, he asked whether he could speak frankly, and Nicholas assented. Buchanan came straight to the point, telling the Tsar that Russia needed a government in which the nation could have confidence. "Your Majesty, if I may be permitted to say so, has but one safe course open to you—namely, to break down the barrier that separates you from your people and to regain their confidence."

Drawing himself up and giving Buchanan a hard look, Nicholas asked, "Do you mean that I am to regain the confidence of my people or that they are to regain *my* confidence?"

"Both, Sire," Buchanan replied, "for without such mutual confidence Russia will never win this war."

The Ambassador criticized Protopopov, "who, if Your Majesty will forgive my saying so, is bringing Russia to the verge of ruin."

"I chose M. Protopopov," Nicholas interjected, "from the ranks of the Duma in order to be agreeable to them—and this is my reward."

Buchanan warned that revolutionary language was being spoken not only in Petrograd but all over Russia, and that "in the event of revolution only a small portion of the army can be counted on to defend the dynasty." Then he concluded with a surge of personal feeling:

"An ambassador, I am well aware, has no right to hold the language which I have held to Your Majesty, and I had to take my courage in both hands before speaking as I have done. . . . [But] if I were to see a friend walking through a wood on a dark night along a path which I knew ended in a precipice, would it not be my duty, Sire, to warn him of his danger? And is it not equally my duty to warn Your Majesty of the abyss that lies ahead of you?"

The Tsar was moved by Buchanan's appeal and, pressing the Ambassador's hand as he left, said, "I thank you, Sir George." The Empress, however, was outraged by Buchanan's presumption. "The Grand Duke Serge remarked that had I been a Russian subject, I should have been sent to Siberia," Buchanan wrote later.

Although Rodzianko had disdained Marie Pavlovna's suggestion that the Empress be "annihilated," he agreed with the Grand Duchess that the Empress must be stripped of political powers. Earlier in the fall, when Protopopov had come to him and mentioned that the Tsar might appoint the Duma President as Premier, Rodzianko had stated as one of his terms that "the Empress must renounce all interference in affairs of state and remain at Livadia until the end of the war." Now, in the middle of winter, he received a visit from the Tsar's younger brother Grand Duke Michael. Michael, the handsome, good-natured "Misha," was living with his wife, Countess Brassova, at Gatchina, outside the capital. Although after the Tsarevich he was next in line for the throne, he had absolutely no influence on his brother. Worried and realizing his own helplessness, he asked how the desperate situation might be saved. Again Rodzianko declared that "Alexandra Fedorovna is fiercely and universally hated, and all circles are clamoring for her removal. While she remains in power, we shall continue on the road to ruin." The Grand Duke agreed with him and begged Rodzianko to go again to tell the Tsar. On January 20, Nicholas received him.

"Your Majesty," said Rodzianko, "I consider the state of the country to have become more critical and menacing than ever. The spirit of all the people is such that the gravest upheavals may be expected. . . . All Russia is unanimous in claiming a change of government and the appointment of a responsible premier invested with the confidence of the nation. . . . Sire, there is not a single honest or reliable man left in your entourage; all the best have either been eliminated or have resigned. . . . It is an open secret that the Empress issues orders without your knowledge, that Ministers report to her on matters of state.

. . . Indignation against and hatred of the Empress are growing throughout the country. She is looked upon as Germany's champion. Even the common people are speaking of it. . . . "

Nicholas interrupted: "Give me the facts. There are no facts to confirm your statements."

"There are no facts," Rodzianko admitted, "but the whole trend of policy directed by Her Majesty gives ground for such ideas. To save your family, Your Majesty ought to find some way of preventing the Empress from exercising any influence on politics. . . . Your Majesty, do not compel the people to choose between you and the good of the country."

Nicholas pressed his head between his hands. "Is it possible," he asked, "that for twenty-two years I tried to act for the best and that for twenty-two years it was all a mistake?"

The question was astonishing. It was completely beyond the bounds of propriety for Rodzianko to answer, yet, realizing that it had been asked honestly, man to man, he summoned his courage and said, "Yes, Your Majesty, for twenty-two years you followed a wrong course."

A month later, on February 23, Rodzianko saw Nicholas for the last time. This time the Tsar's attitude was "positively harsh" and Rodzianko, in turn, was blunt. Announcing that revolution was imminent, he declared, "I consider it my duty, Sire, to express to you my profound foreboding and conviction that this will be my last report to you."

Nicholas said nothing and Rodzianko was curtly excused.

Rodzianko's was the last of the great warnings to the Tsar. Nicholas rejected them all. He had pledged to preserve the autocracy and hand it on intact to his son. In his mind, urbane grand dukes, foreign ambassadors and members of the Duma did not represent the peasant masses of the real Russia. Most of all, he felt that to give way during the war would be taken as a sign of personal weakness which would only accelerate revolution. Perhaps when the war was ended, he would modify the autocracy and reorganize the government. "I will do everything afterwards," he said. "But I cannot act now. I cannot do more than one thing at a time."

The attacks on the Empress and the suggestions that she be sent away only angered him. "The Empress is a foreigner," he declared fervently. "She has no one to protect her but myself. I shall never abandon her under any circumstances. In any case, all the charges made against her are false. Wicked lies are being told about her. But I shall know how to make her respected."

Early in March, after two months of rest with his family, Nicholas's spirits began to improve. He was optimistic that the army, equipped with new arms from Britain and France, could finish the war by the end of the year. Complaining of the "poisoned air" of Petrograd, he was anxious to return to *Stavka* to plan the spring offensive.

Protopopov, meanwhile, sensing the approach of a crisis, tried to mask his fears by recommending forcible countermeasures. Four cavalry regiments of the Guard were ordered from the front to Petrograd, and the city police began training in the use of machine guns. The cavalry never arrived. At *Stavka,* General Gurko was disgusted at the prospect of fighting the people and countermanded the order. On March 7, the day before the Tsar left for Headquarters, Protopopov arrived at the palace. He saw the Empress first; she told him that the Tsar insisted on spending a month at the front and that she could not change his mind. Nicholas entered the room and, taking Protopopov aside, said that he had decided to return in three weeks. Protopopov in agitation said, "The time is such, Sire, that you are wanted both here and there. . . . I very much fear the consequences." Nicholas, struck by his minister's alarm, promised if possible to return within a week.

There was one moment, according to Rodzianko, when Nicholas wavered in his determination to refuse a responsible ministry. On the eve of his departure, the Tsar summoned several of his ministers, including Prince Golitsyn, the Prime Minister, and announced that he intended to go to the Duma the next day and personally announce the appointment of a responsible government. That same evening, Golitsyn was summoned again to the palace and told that the Tsar was leaving for Headquarters.

"How is that, Your Majesty?" asked Golitsyn, amazed. "What about a responsible ministry? You intended to go to the Duma tomorrow."

"I have changed my mind," said Nicholas. "I am leaving for the *Stavka* tonight."

This conversation took place on Wednesday, March 7. Five days later, on Monday, March 12, the Imperial government in Petrograd collapsed.

CHAPTER TWENTY-SEVEN

Revolution: March 1917

IN the grip of an intense thirty-five-degree-below-zero cold, the people of Petrograd shivered and were hungry. Outside the bakeries, long lines of women stood for hours waiting for their daily ration of bread while the snow fell gently on their coats and shawls. Workers, whose factories had closed for lack of coal, milled in the streets, worried, grumbling and waiting for something to happen. In their stuffy, smoke-filled barracks, soldiers of the garrison gathered around stoves and listened from supper until dawn to the speeches and exhortations of revolutionary agitators. This was Petrograd in the first week of March 1917, ripening for revolution.

On February 27, the Duma reconvened and Kerensky shouted defiance not only at the government but at the Tsar. "The ministers are but fleeting shadows," he cried. "To prevent a catastrophe, the Tsar himself must be removed, by terrorist methods if there is no other way. If you will not listen to the voice of warning, you will find yourselves face to face with facts, not warnings. Look up at the distant flashes that are lighting the skies of Russia." Incitement to assassination of the Tsar was treason, and Protopopov began proceedings to deprive Kerensky of his parliamentary immunity so that he could be prosecuted. Rodzianko told Kerensky privately, however, "Be sure we shall never give you up to them."

In the mood which lay over the capital, even Kerensky's inflammatory speech did not seem abnormal. On the very day of the speech, Buchanan, whose political antennae were acutely sensitive, concluded that the city was quiet enough for him to slip away on a much-needed ten-day holiday in Finland.

The underlying problem was the shortage of food and fuel. The war had taken fifteen million men off the farms, while at the same time the army was consuming huge quantities of food. The railroads which brought supplies into the capital were collapsing. Barely adequate in peacetime, the Russian railroads had now the added load of supplying six million men at the front with food and ammunition, as well as moving the men themselves according to the dictates of Army Headquarters. In addition, hundreds of coal trains had necessarily been added to the overtaxed system. Before the war, the entire St. Petersburg industrial region, with its giant metallurgical industries, had used cheap Cardiff coal imported up the Baltic. The blockade required that coal be brought by train from the Donets basin in the Ukraine. Creaking under this enormous military and industrial load, the railroads' actual capacity had drastically decreased. Russia began the war with 20,071 locomotives; by early 1917, only 9,021 were in service. Similar deterioration had reduced the number of cars from 539,549 to 174,346.

The cities, naturally, suffered more than the countryside, and Petrograd, farthest from the regions producing food and coal, suffered most. Scarcities sent prices soaring: an egg cost four times what it had in 1914, butter and soap cost five times as much. Rasputin, closer to the people than either the Tsar or his ministers, had seen the danger long before. In October 1915, Alexandra had written to her husband: "Our Friend . . . spoke scarcely about anything else for two hours. It is this: that you must give an order that wagons with flour, butter and sugar should be obliged to pass. He saw the whole thing in the night like a vision, all the towns, railway lines, etc. . . . He wishes me to speak to you about all this very earnestly, severely even. . . . He would propose three days no other trains should go except those with flour, butter and sugar—it's even more necessary than meat or ammunition."

In February 1917, winter weather dealt Russia's railroads a final blow. In a month of extreme cold and heavy snowfall, 1,200 locomotive boilers froze and burst, deep drifts blocked long sections of track and 57,000 railway cars stood motionless. In Petrograd, supplies of flour, coal and wood dwindled and disappeared.

Ironically, there were not, in the winter of 1917, any serious revolutionary plans among either workers or revolutionaries. Lenin, living in Zurich in the house of a shoemaker, felt marooned, depressed and defeated. Nothing he tried seemed to succeed. The pamphlets he wrote drew little response, while the hair oil which he bought in quantity and rubbed assiduously into his skull failed to stimulate even the slightest growth of hair.* In January 1917, addressing a group of Swiss workers, he gloomily declared that while "popular risings must flare up in Europe within a few years . . . we older men may not live to see the decisive battles of the approaching revolution." Kerensky, the Duma's most vociferous advocate of revolution, said later, "No party of the Left and no revolutionary organization had made any plan for a revolution." None was needed. Revolutionary plots and political programs became insignificant in the face of the growing hunger and bitterness of the people. "They [the revolutionaries] were not ready," wrote Basil Shulgin, a monarchist deputy, "but all the rest was ready."

On Thursday, March 8, as Nicholas's train was carrying him away from the capital back to Headquarters, the silent, long-suffering breadlines suddenly erupted. Unwilling to wait any longer, people broke into the bakeries and helped themselves. Columns of protesting workers from the industrial Vyborg section marched across the Neva bridges toward the center of the city. A procession, composed mainly of women chanting "Give us bread," filled the Nevsky Prospect. The demonstration was peaceful; nevertheless, at dusk a squadron of Cossacks trotted down the Nevsky Prospect, the clatter of their hoofs sounding the government's warning. Despite the disorders, no one was seriously alarmed. At the French Embassy that night, the guests threw themselves into a passionate argument as to which of the reigning ballerinas of the Imperial Ballet—Anna Pavlova, Tamara Karsavina or Mathilde Kschessinska—was supreme in her art.

On Friday morning, March 9, the crowds poured into the streets in greater numbers. More bakeries were sacked and again the Cossack patrols appeared, although without their whips, the traditional instrument of mob control in Russia. The crowd, noting this absence, treated the Cossacks cheerfully and parted readily to let them pass. The

* Krupskaya's mother died while Lenin was in Switzerland. There is a story that one night Krupskaya rose exhausted from her vigil beside her dying mother and asked Lenin, who was writing at a table, to awaken her if her mother needed her. Lenin agreed and Krupskaya collapsed into bed. The next morning she awoke to find her mother dead and Lenin still at work. Distraught, she confronted Lenin, who replied, "You told me to wake you if your mother needed you. She died. She didn't need you."

Cossacks, in turn, bantered with the crowd and assured them, "Don't worry. We won't shoot."

On Saturday, most of the workers of Petrograd went on strike. Trains, trolley cars and cabs stopped running, and no newspapers appeared. Huge crowds surged through the streets, carrying, for the first time, red banners and shouting, "Down with the German woman! Down with Protopopov! Down with the war!" A sense of alarm began to speed through the city. That night the violinist Georges Enesco gave a recital in the concert hall of the Maryinsky Theatre. The theatre was practically empty; not more than fifty people sat in the audience, and there were wide gaps in the orchestra. Enesco came up to a corner of the huge stage and played an intimate, private concert for the few people sitting close together in the front of the deserted hall.

The Cabinet, trying desperately to solve the problem of food supply, met all day and through the night. By telegram, they begged Nicholas to return. With the exception of Protopopov, the entire Cabinet also offered to resign, urging the Tsar to appoint a new ministry acceptable to the Duma. Nicholas refused. Five hundred miles away, misinformed by Protopopov as to the seriousness of the situation, believing the crisis to be only another of the turbulent strikes which had plagued his entire reign, he replied to Prince Golitsyn, the Prime Minister, that Cabinet resignations were out of the question. To General Khabalov, Military Governor of Petrograd, he telegraphed brusquely: "I order that the disorders in the capital, intolerable during these difficult times of war with Germany and Austria, be ended tomorrow. Nicholas."

The Tsar's order clearly meant that, where necessary, troops were to be used to clear the streets. The sequence, arranged by Protopopov, entailed meeting disorders first with the police, then with Cossacks wielding whips and, as a last resort, with soldiers using rifles and machine guns. Ultimately, of course, the plan and the security of the capital depended on the quality of the troops available.

As it happened, the quality of the troops in Petrograd could not have been worse. The regular soldiers of the pre-war army—the proud infantry and the cavalry of the Imperial Guard, the veteran Cossacks and regiments of the line—had long since perished in the icy wastes of Poland and Galicia. The best men who remained were still in the trenches facing the Germans. The Petrograd garrison in the winter of 1917 consisted of 170,000 men, most of them raw recruits crowded into training barracks. The Cossacks of the garrison were young country boys, fresh from the villages, wholly inexperienced in street fighting. Many of the infantry recruits were older men, in their thirties and forties, drawn in part from the working-class suburbs of Petrograd itself. Poor fighting material, not wanted by the generals at the front, they were left in the capital, where it was hoped that their proximity to home would keep them from stirring up trouble. There were too few officers; those on hand had been invalided back from the front or were boys from military schools incapable of maintaining discipline in a crisis. Lacking both officers and rifles, many units of the garrison never bothered to train.

Despite the caliber of his garrison, General Khabalov prepared to obey the Tsar's command. Early risers, venturing into the city's streets on Sunday morning, found huge posters bearing Khabalov's orders: All assemblies and public meetings were forbidden and would be dispersed by force. All strikers who were not back at their jobs the following morning would be drafted and sent to the front.

The posters were ignored completely. Huge crowds swarmed from the Vyborg quarter across the Neva bridges into the city. In response, lines of soldiers began issuing silently from their barracks. At 4:30 p.m. there was shooting on the Nevsky Prospect opposite the Anitchkov Palace. Fifty people were killed or wounded; throughout the city that day, two hundred people died. Many of the soldiers were bitter, and only reluctantly obeyed orders. Before the Nicholas Station, a company of the Volinsky Regiment refused to fire into a crowd, and emptied its rifles into the air. A company of the Pavlovsky Life Guards refused to fire at all and, when its commander insisted, turned and shot the officer instead. The situation was quickly restored when a loyal company of the crack Preobrajensky Guard moved in to disarm the mutineers and send them back to their barracks.

That night, Rodzianko, who had been meeting with the helpless ministers, sent an anguished telegram to the Tsar: "The position is serious," he said. "There is anarchy in the capital. The government is paralyzed. Transportation of food and fuel is completely disorganized. . . . There is disorderly firing in the streets. A person trusted by the country must be charged immediately to form a ministry." Rodzianko ended with a heartfelt plea: "May the blame not fall on the wearer of the crown." Nicholas, scornful of what he considered hysterics, turned to Alexeiev and declared, "That fat Rodzianko has sent me some nonsense which I shall not even bother to answer."

Instead of concessions, Nicholas decided to send reinforcements. He ordered General Ivanov, an elderly commander from the Galician front, to collect four of the best regiments from the front line, march on the capital and subdue it by force, if necessary. He telegraphed Prince Golitsyn to instruct Rodzianko that the Duma session was to be suspended. And he decided to return to Petrograd himself within a few days. "Am leaving day after tomorrow [the 13th]," he telegraphed Alexandra. "Have finished here with all important questions. Sleep well. God bless you." In Petrograd that night, although two hundred people lay dead, most of the city was quiet. Buchanan, returning at last from his Finnish holiday, noted that "the part of the city through which we passed on our short drive to the Embassy was perfectly quiet and, except for a few patrols of soldiers on the quays and the absence of trams and cabs, there was nothing unusual." Paléologue, returning home at eleven p.m., passed the Radziwill mansion, blazing with the lights of a gala party. Outside, among a long line of elegant cars and carriages, Paléologue happened to spot the car of Grand Duke Boris.

Monday, March 12, was the turning point in Petrograd. On Monday morning, the Tsar's government still clung to a last shred of power. By Monday night, power had passed to the Duma.

The key to this swift, overwhelming change was the massive defection of the Petrograd soldiery. Many of the workers had had enough of going to the Nevsky Prospect to be killed. Indeed, on Sunday night, Iurenev, the leader of the Bolshevik Party in Petrograd, had gloomily concluded that the uprising had failed. "The Reaction is gaining strength," he said to a group of extreme Left party leaders meeting in Kerensky's study. "The unrest in the barracks is subsiding. Indeed, it is clear that the working class and the soldiery must go different ways. We must not rely on day dreams . . . for a revolution, but on systematic propaganda at the works and the factories in store for better days."

Iurenev was wrong: the unrest in the barracks was not subsiding. On Sunday afternoon, the Volinsky Regiment, which had displayed reluctance to fire on the crowd, had retreated to its barracks in confusion and anger. All night the soldiers argued. Then, at six in the morning, a Volinsky sergeant named Kirpichnikov killed a captain who had struck him the previous day. The other officers fled from the barracks and, soon after, the Volinsky marched out, band playing, to join the revolution. The mutiny spread quickly to other famous regiments, the Semonovsky, the Ismailovsky, the Litovsky, the Oranienbaum Machine Gun Regiment and, finally, to the legendary Preobrajensky Guard, the oldest and finest regiment in the army, created by Peter the Great himself. In all of these cases, the units that went over were recruit battalions of inferior quality; nevertheless, they carried the colors and wore the uniforms of the proudest regiments of the Russian army.

In most parts of the city, the morning of March 12 broke with deadly stillness. From a window of the British Embassy, Meriel Buchanan, the Ambassador's daughter, stared out at "the same wide streets, the same great palaces, the same gold spires and domes rising out of the pearl-colored morning mists, and yet . . . everywhere emptiness, no lines of toiling carts, no crowded scarlet trams, no little sledges. . . . [Only] the waste of deserted streets and ice-bound river . . . [and] on the opposite shore the low grim walls of the Fortress and the Imperial flag of Russia that for the last time fluttered against the winter sky."

A few minutes later, from a window in his own Embassy, Paléologue witnessed the dramatic scene when the army confronted the mob: "At half past eight this morning just as I finished dressing, I heard a strange and prolonged din which seemed to come from the Alexander Bridge. I looked out; there was no one on the bridge which usually presents a busy scene. But almost immediately, a disorderly mob carrying red flags appeared at the end . . . on the right bank of the Neva and a regiment came towards them from the opposite side. It looked as if there would be a violent collision, but on the contrary, the two bodies coalesced. The army was fraternizing with the revolution."

Two hours later, General Knox heard "that the depot troops of the garrison had mutinied and were coming down the street. We went to the window. . . . Craning our necks, we first saw two soldiers—a sort of advance guard—who strode along the middle of the street, pointing their rifles at loiterers to clear the road. . . . Then came a great disorderly mass of soldiery, stretching right across the wide street and both pavements. They were led by a diminutive but immensely dignified student. All were armed and many had red flags fastened to their bayonets. . . . What struck me most was the uncanny silence of it all. We were like spectators in a gigantic cinema."

A few minutes later, Paléologue, trying to find out what was happening, went out into the street: "Frightened inhabitants were scattering through the streets. . . . At one corner of the Liteiny, soldiers were helping civilians to erect a barricade. Flames mounted from the Law Courts. The gates of the Arsenal burst open with a crash. Suddenly, the crack of machine-gun fire split the air; it was the regulars who had just taken up position near the Nevsky Prospect. . . . The Law Courts had become nothing but an enormous furnace; the Arsenal on the Liteiny, the Ministry of the Interior, the Military Government Building . . . the headquarters of the Okhrana and a score of police stations were in flames, the prisons were open and all the prisoners had been liberated." By noon, the Fortress of Peter and Paul had fallen with its heavy artillery, and 25,000 soldiers had joined the revolution. By nightfall, the number had swollen to 66,000.

During Monday morning, the Imperial Cabinet held its last meeting. Protopopov, who was present, was urged to resign. He rose and walked out of the room, melodramatically mumbling, "Now there is nothing left to do but shoot myself." The Tsar's younger brother Grand Duke Michael arrived and, after listening to the ministers, decided to appeal to Nicholas himself. Leaving the meeting, he telephoned directly to Headquarters and urged the immediate appointment of a government which could command the nation's confidence. General Alexeiev, at the other end of the line, asked the Grand Duke to wait while he spoke to the Tsar. Forty minutes later, Alexeiev called back: "The Emperor wishes to express his thanks," he said. "He is leaving for Tsarskoe Selo and will decide there." Hearing this, the Cabinet simply gave up. It adjourned itself—forever, as it turned out—and the ministers walked out of the building. By nightfall, most of them had arrived at the Tauride Palace to have themselves arrested and placed under the protection of the Duma.

At the Duma, events were moving with breathtaking speed. The Imperial order suspending the Duma had reached Rodzianko the previous night. At eight the next morning, he summoned the leaders of all the political parties to a meeting in his office. There it was decided that, in view of the collapse of law and order, the Imperial order should be ignored and the Duma kept in session. At half past one, the first large crowds of workers and soldiers, carrying red banners and singing the "*Marseillaise*," arrived at the Duma to offer their support and to ask for instructions. Swarming through the unguarded doors, they surged through the corridors and chambers and engulfed the parliament. It was a motley, exuberant mob. There were soldiers, tall and hot in their rough wool uniforms; students shouting exultantly; and here and there a few gray-bearded old men, just released from prison, their knees trembling, their eyes shining.

"I must know what I can tell them," Kerensky cried to Rodzianko, as the mob jostled and crowded the uncertain deputies. "Can I say that the Imperial Duma is with them, that it takes the responsibility on itself, that it stands at the head of the government?"

Rodzianko had little choice but to agree. Still personally loyal to the Tsar, he protested to Shulgin, a monarchist deputy, "I don't want to revolt." Shulgin, a realist as well as a monarchist, overrode him, saying, "Take the power . . . if you don't, others will." Reluctantly, Rodzianko mounted a platform which creaked under his bulk, and assured the crowd that the Duma would refuse to be dissolved and would accept the responsibilities of government. At three in the afternoon, the Duma met and appointed a temporary executive committee for the purpose of restoring order and gaining control over the mutinous troops. The committee included the leaders of all the parties of the Duma except the extreme Right.

Nor was the collapse of the Imperial government and the rise of the Duma all that happened on that remarkable day. On the same day, there arose a second, rival assembly, the Soviet of Soldiers' and Workers' Deputies, consisting of one delegate from each company of revolutionary soldiers and one delegate for each thousand workers. Incredibly, by nightfall, the Soviet was sitting under the same roof as the Duma.

It was Kerensky who created this astonishing situation. As he explained it later: "The entire garrison had mutinied and . . . the troops were marching towards the Duma. . . . Naturally a question arose . . . as to how and by whom the soldiers and workmen were to be led; for until then their movement was completely unorganized, uncoordinated and anarchical. 'A Soviet?' The memory of 1905 prompted this cry. . . . The need of some kind of center for the mass movement was realized by everyone. The Duma itself needed some representatives of the rebel populace; without them, it would have been impossible to reestablish order in the capital. For this reason the Soviet was formed quickly and not by any means as a matter of class war: simply about three or four o'clock in the afternoon, the organizers applied to me for suitable premises; I mentioned the matter to Rodzianko and the thing was arranged."

The Tauride Palace, an eighteenth-century building presented by

Catherine the Great to her favorite Prince Potemkin, possessed two large wings; one was the chamber of the Duma, the other, formerly the budget committee room of the Duma, was given to the Soviet. Thereafter, wrote Kerensky, "two different Russias settled side by side: the Russia of the ruling classes who had lost (though they did not realize it yet) . . . and the Russia of Labor, marching towards power, without suspecting it."

Although Rodzianko assumed the chairmanship of the temporary Duma committee, from the first it was Kerensky who became the central figure. Only thirty-six years old, he became the bridge between the Soviet and the Duma committee. He was elected Vice-Chairman of the Soviet; within three days, he was also Minister of Justice in the new Provisional Government. "His words and his gestures were sharp and clear-cut and his eyes shone," wrote Shulgin. "He seemed to grow every minute." A stream of important prisoners—Prince Golitsyn, Stürmer, the Metropolitan Pitirim, all the ministers of the Cabinet—were brought in or presented themselves for arrest. It was Kerensky who saved their lives. "Ivan Gregorovich," he said, striding up to one prisoner and speaking in a ringing tone, "you are arrested. Your life is not in danger. The Imperial Duma does not shed blood."

With justification, Kerensky later took credit for averting a massacre. "During the first days of the Revolution, the Duma was full of the most hated officials of the monarchy . . . ," he wrote. "Day and night the revolutionary tempest raged around the arrested men. The huge halls and endless corridors of the Duma were flooded with armed soldiers, workmen and students. The waves of hatred . . . beat against the walls. If I moved a finger, if I had simply closed my eyes and washed my hands of it, the entire Duma, all St. Petersburg, the whole of Russia might have been drenched in torrents of human blood as [it was] under Lenin in October."

Toward midnight, Protopopov came to ask for protection. After leaving the final meeting of the Council, he had spent the night hiding in a tailor shop. He arrived now in a makeshift disguise: an overlong overcoat and a hat down over his eyes. Sighting Kerensky in one of the corridors, he crept alongside and whispered, "It is I, Protopopov." Shulgin, at that moment, was in the adjoining room. "Suddenly," he wrote, "there was coming something especially exciting; and at once the reason was whispered to me. 'Protopopov is arrested,' and at that moment I saw in the mirror the door burst open violently and Kerensky broke in. He was pale and his eyes shone, his arm was raised; with this stretched out arm, he seemed to cut through the crowd; everyone recognized him and stood back on either side. And then in the mirror I saw that behind Kerensky there were soldiers with rifles and, between the bayonets, a miserable little figure with a hopelessly harassed and sunken face—it was with difficulty that I recognized Protopopov. 'Don't dare touch that man!' shouted Kerensky—pushing his way on, pallid, with impossible eyes, one arm raised, cutting through the crowd, the other tragically dropped, pointing at 'that man.' . . . It looked as if he were leading him to execution, to something dreadful. And the crowd fell apart. Kerensky dashed past like the flaming torch of revolutionary justice and behind him they dragged that miserable little figure in the rumpled greatcoat surrounded by bayonets."

By Tuesday morning, March 13, except for a last outpost of tsarism in the Winter Palace, which General Khabalov held with 1,500 loyal troops, the city was in the hands of the revolution. In the afternoon, the revolutionaries in the Fortress of Peter and Paul across the river gave Khabalov's men twenty minutes to abandon the palace or face bombardment; having lost all hope, the dejected loyalists marched out and simply melted away.

In the anarchy that followed, wild celebrations were mingled with violent outbursts of mob fury. In Kronstadt, the naval base outside the city, the sailors brutally slaughtered their officers, killing one and burying a second, still living, side by side with the corpse. In Petrograd, armored cars, with clusters of rebel soldiers perched on their tops, roared up and down the streets, flying red flags. Firemen, arriving to put out the fires blazing in public buildings, were driven away by soldiers and workmen who wanted to see the buildings burn. Kschessinska's mansion was sacked by the mob from top to bottom, the grand piano smashed, the carpets stained with ink, the bathtubs filled with cigarette butts.*

On Wednesday, March 14, even those who had wavered flocked to join the victors. That morning saw the mass obeisance to the Duma of the Imperial Guard. From his Embassy window, Paléologue watched three regiments pass on their way to the Tauride Palace: "They marched in perfect order," he wrote, "with their band at the

* One elegant Petrograd mansion was saved by the quick wits of its owner, the artful Countess Kleinmichel. Before the mob arrived, she barred her doors, shuttered her windows and placed in front of her house a sign which read: "No trespassing. This house is the property of the Petrograd Soviet. Countess Kleinmichel has been taken to the Fortress of St. Peter and Paul." Inside, Countess Kleinmichel then packed her bags and planned her escape.

head. A few officers came first, wearing a large red cockade in their caps, a knot of red ribbon on their shoulders and red stripes on their sleeves. The old regimental standard, covered with icons, was surrounded by red flags." Behind came the Guard, including units from the garrison at Tsarskoe Selo. "At the head were the Cossacks of the Escort, those magnificent horsemen who are the flower . . . and privileged elite of the Imperial Guard. Then came His Majesty's Regiment, the sacred legion which is recruited from all the units of the Guard and whose special function it is to secure the personal safety of their sovereigns."

Even more spectacular was the march of the Marine Guard, the *Garde Equipage*, most of whom had served aboard the *Standart* and personally knew the Imperial family. At the head of the marines strode their commanding officer, Grand Duke Cyril. Leading his men to the Tauride Palace, Cyril became the first of the Romanovs publicly to break his oath of allegiance to the Tsar, who still sat on the throne. In the presence of Rodzianko, Cyril pledged allegiance to the Duma. Then, returning to his palace on Glinka Street, he hoisted a red flag over his roof. Writing to his Uncle Paul, Cyril coolly explained, "These last few days, I have been alone in carrying out my duties to Nicky and the country and in saving the situation by my recognition of the Provisional Government." A week later, Cyril gave an interview to a Petrograd newspaper: "I have asked myself several times if the ex-Empress were an accomplice of William [the Kaiser]," he said, "but each time forced myself to recoil from the horror of such a thought."

Cyril's behavior drew a terse, prophetic comment from Paléologue: "Who can tell whether this treacherous insinuation will not before long provide the foundation for a terrible charge against the unfortunate Empress. The Grand Duke Cyril should . . . be reminded that the most infamous calumnies which Marie Antoinette had to meet when she faced the Revolutionary Tribunal, first took wing at the elegant suppers of the Comte d'Artois [the jealous younger brother of Louis XVI]."

Petrograd had fallen. Everywhere in the city, the revolution was triumphant. At the Tauride Palace, two rival assemblies, both convinced that tsarism was ended, were embarking on a struggle for survival and power. Yet, Russia was immense and Petrograd only a tiny, artificial mound, scarcely Russian, in a corner of the Tsar's empire. The two million people of Petrograd were only a fraction of the scores of millions of subjects; even in Petrograd, the revolutionary workers and soldiers were less than a quarter of the city's population. A week had gone by since Nicholas had left for Headquarters and the first disorders had broken out. In that week, he had lost his capital, but still he kept his throne. How much longer could he keep it?

The Allied ambassadors, desperately concerned that the fall of tsarism would mean Russia's withdrawal from the war, clung to the hope that the Tsar would not topple. Buchanan still talked in terms of Nicholas "granting a constitution and empowering Rodzianko to select the members of a new government." Paléologue thought that the Tsar had a chance if he pardoned the rebels, appointed the Duma committee as his ministers and "appeared in person . . . and solemnly announced on the steps of Our Lady of Kazan that a new era is beginning for Russia. But if he waits a day it will be too late." It was Knox who sensed more accurately the ominous future. Standing at a corner of the Liteiny Prospect, watching the burning of the district court across the street, he heard a soldier say, "We have only one wish: to beat the Germans. We will begin with the Germans here and with a family that you know called Romanov."

CHAPTER TWENTY-EIGHT

Abdication

NICHOLAS, leaving home for Headquarters on the night of March 7, was subdued and downhearted. Twice, from the train, he sent melancholy telegrams tinged with the loneliness that overwhelmed him on leaving his family after two months at Tsarskoe Selo. In Mogilev, he missed the buoyant presence of the Tsarevich. "Here in the house it is so still," he wrote to Alexandra. "No noise, no excited shouts. I imagine him sleeping—all his little things, photographs and knicknacks, in exemplary order in his bedroom."

Nicholas's last letters as Tsar, written as it were from the brink of the abyss, have often been cited as evidence of his incorrigible stupidity. The most famous remark of all, invariably quoted in even the briefest estimate of Nicholas's character, is the line: "I shall take up dominoes again in my spare time." Taken by itself, the remark is devastating. Any tsar with so little wit as to sit playing dominoes while his capital revolts deserves nothing: neither his throne nor understanding.

Yet, there is more to it than that. It was the Tsar's first night back at Army Headquarters and he was writing to his wife of familiar things. Immediately before this much-quoted line, he is talking about his son. He says that he will greatly miss the games they had played every evening; in lieu of them, he will take up dominoes again to relax in his spare moments. Even more significantly, the letter was written not against a backdrop of revolution, but at a moment when Nicholas believed that the capital was quiet. The date on the letter is March 8, the day on which the first bread riots occurred in the city. The first reports of these disorders arrived at Headquarters on the morning of the 9th; Nicholas did not learn until the 11th that anyone in Petrograd considered them serious.

Despite the weeks of rest with his family, Nicholas returned to Mogilev still mentally fatigued and physically exhausted. A vivid warning signal on the state of his health flashed on Sunday morning, March 11. As he stood in church, Nicholas suffered "an excruciating pain in the chest" which lasted for fifteen minutes. "I could hardly stand the service out," he wrote, "and my forehead was covered with drops of perspiration. I cannot understand what it could have been because I had no palpitation of the heart. . . . If this occurs again, I shall tell Fedorov [the doctor]." The symptoms are those of a coronary occlusion.

If the revolution in the streets of Petrograd came as a shock to everyone in the city, it is not entirely surprising that the Tsar, at Headquarters five hundred miles away, was neither more alert nor more prescient. Indeed, Nicholas had less information than those who continued blithely to attend dinners, parties and concerts in the capital. He depended on reports passed to him through a chain of officials which included Protopopov in Petrograd and General Voeikov at Headquarters. Both Protopopov and Voeikov served him badly, deliberately underplaying the seriousness of the situation as it developed. Protopopov was defending his own position; disorders which he could not control were a damning reflection on his abilities as Minister of Interior. Voeikov, at the other end of the line, was a conservative, unimaginative man who simply could not face the prospect of walking into the presence of the Tsar and announcing a revolution.

From Thursday, March 8, until Sunday, the 11th, Nicholas heard nothing which caused him serious alarm. He was told that the capital was afflicted with "street disorders." "Street disorders" were not a matter to worry Nicholas: he had faced them innumerable times in the twenty-three years of his reign. There were officials to deal with them: Khabalov, the Military Governor, and above him Protopopov, the Minister of Interior. The Tsar of all the Russias, the Commander-in-Chief of the Russian Army, need not bother himself with an affair which was a matter for the city police.

On the night of the 11th, after the troops had been called out and had fired into the crowd and two hundred people lay dead, Nicholas was told that the "street disorders" were becoming nasty. Reacting quickly, he sent an order to Khabalov commanding that the disorders, "intolerable in these difficult times of war with Germany and Austria," be ended immediately. That same night, he wrote to Alexandra, "I hope Khabalov will be able to stop these street disorders. Protopopov must give him clear and definite instructions."

On Monday, the 12th, the news was much worse. "After yesterday's news from town, I saw many frightened faces here," Nicholas wrote. "Fortunately, Alexeiev is calm, but he thinks it is necessary to appoint a very energetic man, so as to compel the ministers to work out the solution of the problems—supplies, railways, coal, etc." Late that night, a jolting telegram arrived from the Empress—"Concessions inevitable. Street fighting continues. Many units gone over to the enemy. Alix." At midnight he ordered his train, and at five a.m. he was under way for Tsarskoe Selo. Nevertheless, even at this point Nicholas did not proceed straight to the capital. Knowing that the most direct route was heavily used by troop supply trains, he chose a longer route to avoid dislocations. He still could not believe that his presence was so urgently required that supplies for the army and hungry civilians should be shunted aside.

As the Imperial train traveled north on Tuesday, the 13th, rumbling through village stations where local dignitaries still stood saluting on the platform to honor the passage of the Tsar, the grim news continued to come. Telegrams from the capital announced the fall of the Winter Palace and the formation of an executive committee of the Duma under Rodzianko. At two a.m. on the morning of the 14th, the train was at Malaya Vishera, just a hundred miles south of the capital, when it was slowed to a halt. An officer boarded the train and informed Voeikov that revolutionary soldiers with machine guns and artillery were just up the track. Nicholas was awakened, and in the middle of the night, alternative possibilities were discussed. If they could not go north to Petrograd and Tsarskoe Selo, they might go east to Moscow, south to Mogilev or west to Pskov, headquarters of the Northern Group of Armies, commanded by General Ruzsky. The discussion leaned in the last direction. Nicholas concurred and declared, "Well, then, to Pskov."

It was eight o'clock in the evening when the Imperial train glided slowly into the station at Pskov. The platform, usually lined with a guard of honor, was deserted except for General Ruzsky and his deputy, General Danilov. Ruzsky, entering the Tsar's car, brought more bad news: the entire garrison of Petrograd and Tsarskoe Selo had gone over, including the Guard, the Cossack Escort and the *Garde Equipage* with Grand Duke Cyril marching in front. Ivanov's expedition, sent ahead to restore order, had reached Tsarskoe Selo earlier in the day, where the trains had stopped and been surrounded by revolutionary soldiers calling on Ivanov's men to join them. Ivanov himself had received a telegram from Alexeiev advising that order had been restored in the capital, and that if there was no further bloodshed, the monarchy might be saved. Alexeiev had suggested that he withdraw; Ivanov had done so, and his little force had quickly melted away.

The report that his personal guard had defected was a heavy blow to Nicholas. Along with the revelation of personal betrayal, it clearly indicated the end of hope for support from within the city, while the loss of Ivanov's men displayed the futility of sending more troops from the front. Nicholas's freedom of action was narrowing rapidly, and as he sat listening to Ruzsky, he made a decision. He asked Ruzsky to telephone to Rodzianko and offer what he had so long refused: a ministry acceptable to the Duma, with a prime minister, presumably Rodzianko, who would have full power over internal affairs. Ruzsky left the railway car and hurried to the telegraph.

Rodzianko, answering Ruzsky's message, was surrounded by people pushing, shouting, asking advice and yelling instructions. Above the din, the harassed Rodzianko wired melodramatically to Ruzsky: "His Majesty and yourself apparently are unable to realize what is happening in the capital. A terrible revolution has broken out. Hatred of the Empress has reached a fever pitch. To prevent bloodshed, I have been forced to arrest all the ministers. . . . Don't send any more troops. I am hanging by a thread myself. Power is slipping from my hands. The measures you propose are too late. The time for them is gone. There is no return."

Rodzianko spoke truly in describing his own position. A compromise reached that morning between the Duma committee and the Soviet had produced the nucleus of a Provisional Government. Miliukov, leader of the Cadet Party in the Duma, was Foreign Minister; Kerensky, representing the Soviet, became Minister of Justice; Guchkov, leader of the Octobrists, was War Minister. The Prime Minister, however, was not Rodzianko, to whom the Soviet would not agree, but Prince George Lvov, the liberal and popular chairman of the Zemstvo Red Cross. Rodzianko continued to take part in the government's discussions, but his influence, like that of the Duma itself, faded rapidly.

Rodzianko was entirely accurate when he said that it was too late for concessions. Already the Duma committee and the Soviet had agreed that Nicholas must abdicate in favor of his son, with the Tsar's brother Grand Duke Michael as Regent. Even those on the committee who wished to preserve the throne—Guchkov, Miliukov and Basil Shulgin, a Right-wing deputy who participated in all the discussions—had concluded that if the Imperial system and the Romanov dynasty were to be saved, Nicholas would have to be sacrificed. "It is of vital importance that Nicholas II should not be overthrown by violence," declared Guchkov. "The only thing which can secure the permanent establishment of a new order, without too great a shock, is his voluntary abdication."

On this matter, the leaders of the new government in Petrograd already had been in touch with the leaders of the army. On the 14th, as the Tsar's train was approaching Pskov, Rodzianko had talked to Alexeiev at Headquarters. Alexeiev himself found abdication the only solution and agreed to collect the opinions of the generals commanding the different fronts. By the morning of the 15th, these replies had come back to Alexeiev and were forwarded to Ruzsky in Pskov. They were grimly unanimous: Nicholas must abdicate. Admiral Nepenin of the Baltic Fleet had stated: "It is only with the greatest difficulty that I keep the troops and fleet under my command in check." Grand Duke Nicholas, in the Caucasus, telegraphed that he begged "on my knees" for his cousin's abdication.

In Pskov, after breakfast on the morning of March 15, Ruzsky brought the generals' telegrams to the Imperial train and laid them before the Tsar. Nicholas was overwhelmed. His face became white, he turned away from Ruzsky and walked to the window. Absentmindedly, he lifted the shade and peeped out. Inside, the car was absolutely still. No one spoke, and most of those present could scarcely breathe.

If the anguish felt by Nicholas at this last, climactic moment of his reign is impossible to know, the logic of his reasoning is relatively clear. If he rejected the advice of the political leaders in Petrograd and of his generals, what could he do next? He knew from the defection of the Guard and from Ivanov's experience that it would not be easy to find loyal regiments to march on the city; without the support of his generals, it probably would be impossible. If he could find the men and fighting broke out, there was a risk to his family, still at Tsarskoe Selo, now firmly in the hands of the Provisional Government. On top of this, Nicholas had no real stomach for a bloody, pitched battle in the streets of his capital. Years of rule, years of war, years of personal strain and anguish had left him few inner resources with which to face the prospect of plunging his country into civil war.

Ultimately, the factor which swung the Tsar's decision was the advice of his generals. For Nicholas, each one of these telegrams was more significant than a dozen messages from Rodzianko. These were his fellow soldiers, his comrades, his brothers-in-arms. Nicholas loved the army, and he truly loved his country. He cared far more about winning the war than he did for his crown. To start a civil war, with Russians killing Russians while the hated Germans looked on, would be a negation of all that he deeply believed. If it was the advice of his generals that the highest act of patriotism he could perform would be to abdicate, then it became impossible for Nicholas to refuse.

All at once, with a sudden movement, the Tsar spun around from the window and announced in a clear, firm voice, "I have decided that I shall give up the throne in favor of my son, Alexis." Nicholas made the sign of the cross, and the others in the car crossed themselves. "I thank you gentlemen for your distinguished and faithful service," he continued. "I hope it will continue under my son."

A form of abdication, prepared at Alexeiev's direction and forwarded from Headquarters, was produced. Nicholas signed it, and the document was dated 3 p.m., March 15. The throne had passed from father to son, as prescribed by law. His Imperial Majesty Tsar Alexis II, aged twelve, was the Autocrat of all the Russias.

At this point, with the signing completed, a confusion in procedure arose. The night before, in Petrograd, the monarchists on the governing committee had decided that Guchkov and Shulgin should be present to witness the signing and to bring the document back to Petrograd. A train for them was provided at dawn, and throughout that day the two delegates were traveling toward Pskov. As they were not expected before evening, Ruzsky was instructed simply to hold on to the document which Nicholas already had signed.

This interval—almost six hours—gave Nicholas time to reflect on the consequences of the act he had just performed. For himself, the shedding of power came as a relief. He assumed that he would be allowed to retire with his family to Livadia, that Alexis would remain with them at least until he had finished his education, and that the actual responsibility of government would pass to his brother Michael as Regent. It was a conversation with Fedorov, the doctor, which caused Nicholas to change his mind. Sending for Fedorov, Nicholas first asked for a frank estimate of Alexis's prospects with hemophilia.

Fedorov, fully aware of the political significance of the question, replied carefully, "Science teaches us, Sire, that it is an incurable disease. Yet those who are afflicted with it sometimes reach an advanced old age. Still, Alexis Nicolaievich is at the mercy of an accident." The young Tsar would never be able to ride, the doctor explained, and he would be forced to avoid all activity which might tire him and strain his joints. Then Fedorov went beyond a purely medical opinion. He pointed out that Nicholas, once off the throne, would almost certainly be exiled with the Empress from Russia. If that happened, the new government would never allow its sovereign to be educated abroad by the deposed parents. Even if the entire family was allowed to remain in Russia, Alexis's upbringing was certain to be transferred to other hands.

Fedorov's words confronted Nicholas with a heart-breaking dilemma. As Tsar, he knew that his son was the rightful heir to the Russian throne; as a father, he could not bring himself to abandon his beloved child to strangers ignorant of all the ramifications of his disease. For the second time that fateful day, Nicholas was forced to a dramatic decision, a decision which would affect not only the fate of himself and his family, but the history of Russia.

At nine in the evening, Guchkov and Shulgin arrived in Pskov and were led across the tracks to the brightly lit Imperial train. Nicholas, wearing a simple gray tunic, greeted them with a handshake and invited them to sit. With his own back to the green silken wall of the drawing-room car, he listened as Guchkov began to explain why the abdication was necessary. Before Guchkov had finished, Nicholas interrupted. "This long speech is unnecessary," he said calmly, almost apologetically. "I have decided to renounce my throne. Until three o'clock today, I thought I would abdicate in favor of my son, Alexis. But now I have changed my decision in favor of my brother Michael. I trust you will understand the feelings of a father." As Nicholas spoke this last sentence, his voice dropped into a low, hushed tone.

When the Tsar had spoken, Guchkov handed him a new text prepared in Petrograd. Nicholas took it and left the room. Some time afterward, he reappeared with a document which he had written himself, editing in several points from Guchkov's text. This final version was splendidly and yet pathetically illuminated by the patriotism of its author:

In this great struggle with a foreign enemy, who for nearly three years had tried to enslave our country, the Lord God has been pleased to send down on Russia a new, heavy trial. The internal popular disturbances which have begun, threaten to have a disastrous effect on the future conduct of this persistent war. The destiny of Russia, the honor of our heroic army, the good of the people, the whole future of our dear country demand that whatever it cost, the war should be brought to a victorious end.

The cruel enemy is gathering his last forces, and already the hour is near when our gallant army, together with our glorious allies, will be able finally to crush the enemy.

In these decisive days in the life of Russia, we have thought it a duty of conscience to facilitate for our people a close union and consolidation of all national forces for the speedy attainment of victory; and, in agreement with the Imperial Duma, we have thought it good to abdicate from the throne of the Russian State, and to lay down the supreme power.

Not wishing to part with our dear son, we hand over our inheritance to our brother, the Grand Duke Michael Alexandrovich, and give him our blessing to mount the throne of the Russian State. We bequeath it to our brother to direct the forces of the State in full and inviolable union with the representatives of the people in the legislative institutions, on those principles which will by them be established.

In the name of our dearly loved country, we call on all faithful sons of the Fatherland to fulfill their sacred duty to him by obedience to the Tsar at a heavy moment of national trials, to help him, together with the representatives of the people, to bring the Russian State on to the road of victory, prosperity, and glory.

May the Lord God help Russia!

Nicholas

The historic scene was almost concluded. Before it broke up, Nicholas's signature was obtained on two final appointments nominated by the Provisional Government. The first was Prince Lvov as premier, the other was Grand Duke Nicholas, who once again was appointed commander-in-chief of the armies. When this was done, Nicholas rose. At this point, Shulgin, whose heart was bursting with affection and pity for the man who had just been humbled, moved with Nicholas into a corner of the car. "The Emperor looked at me," wrote Shulgin, "and perhaps he read in my eyes the feelings which were distressing me, because in his own there was something like an invitation to speak and my words came of themselves: 'Oh, Your Majesty, if you had done all this earlier, even as late as the last summoning of the Duma, perhaps all that . . . ' and I could not finish. The Tsar looked at me in a curiously . . . [unaffected] way: 'Do you think it might have been avoided?' "

The meeting was over. A coat of varnish was placed over Nicholas's signature on the abdication, and Guchkov and Shulgin left immediately for Petrograd. At 1 a.m. on March 16, after thirty hours in Pskov, the Imperial train left the silent railway platform, bound for Mogilev, where Nicholas would say goodbye to his armies. Through the long day when, with a stroke of his pen, he had removed two Romanovs from the throne of Russia, he had remained calm and almost kindly to those around him. That night in his diary, normally a repository of only the most cryptic and phlegmatic observations on the day's events, Nicholas finally uttered a heartfelt cry: "For the sake of Russia, and to keep the armies in the field, I decided to take this step. . . . Left Pskov at one in the morning. All around me I see treason, cowardice and deceit."

The Tsar had fallen. It was an event of gigantic significance, and yet, neither in Russia nor abroad was this significance more than dimly understood. On the Sunday following the abdication, Paléologue visited three Petrograd churches: "The same scene met me everywhere; a grave and silent congregation exchanging grave and melancholy glances. Some of the *moujiks* looked bewildered and horrified and several had tears in their eyes. Yet even among those who seemed the most moved I could not find one who did not sport a red cockade or armband. They had all been working for the Revolution; all of them were for it, body and soul. But that did not prevent them from shedding tears for their Father, the Tsar. Buchanan had the same impression: "It was not so much the Emperor as the regime of which the nation as a whole was weary. As a soldier remarked . . . 'Oh yes, we must have a Republic, but we must have a good Tsar at the head.' " Far away in a peasant village on the steppe of southern Russia, the peasants clustered around the notice of abdication. "Well, so he's gone, just think of that," said one, "and he's been our Tsar for God knows how many years, and when he leaves us everything will be the same as ever. I suppose he will go to manage his estates somewhere; he always liked farming." "Poor man," said an old woman, "he never did anyone any harm. Why did they put him away?"

"Shut thy mouth, old fool," she was told. "They aren't going to kill him. He's run away, that's all."

"Oh, but he was our Tsar, and now we have *no one!*"

If anything, the governments of England, France and the United States had even less understanding of the event than the Russian peasants. In England, where the Tsar was seen as the tyrant wielding the knout, most Liberals and Laborites were exuberant. In the House of Commons, Andrew Bonar Law, leader of the House, quoted Wordsworth: "Bliss was it in that dawn to be alive, But to be young was very heaven." From Paris, the French Socialist Minister of Munitions, Albert Thomas, telegraphed Kerensky his "congratulations and fraternal greetings."

In the United States, the news was greeted even more extravagantly. On March 22, only one week after the abdication, the United States became the first foreign government to recognize the Provisional Government. For America, on the verge of entering the war because of the German policy of unrestricted U-boat sinkings, the fall of tsarism removed the taint of fighting beside an autocratic Russia. On April 2, 1917, President Woodrow Wilson asked Congress to declare war and make the world "safe for democracy." In the same speech, he spoke glowingly of "the wonderful and heartening things that have been happening within the last few weeks in Russia. . . . The autocracy . . . has been shaken off and the great, generous Russian people have been added in all their naïve majesty and might to the forces that are fighting for freedom in the world, for justice and for peace. Here is a fit partner for a League of Honor."

This almost universal ardor and optimism was not shared by the brilliantly erratic Englishman whose mercurial career had been temporarily blighted by the failure of his special brainchild, the attack on Gallipoli. Even a decade later, when the wartime role of Nicholas II and Imperial Russia still was ignored or derided, Winston Churchill, alone in his viewpoint, gave this estimate:

"It is the shallow fashion of these times to dismiss the Tsarist regime as a purblind, corrupt, incompetent tyranny. But a survey of its thirty months' war with Germany and Austria should correct these loose impressions and expose the dominant facts. We may measure the strength of the Russian Empire by the battering it had endured, by the disasters it had survived, by the inexhaustible forces it had developed, and by the recovery it had made. In the governments of states, when great events are afoot, the leader of the nation, whoever he be, is held accountable for failure and vindicated by success. No matter who wrought the toil, who planned the struggle, to the supreme responsible authority belongs the blame or credit.

"Why should this stern test be denied to Nicholas II? He had made many mistakes, what ruler has not? He was neither a great captain nor a great prince. He was only a true, simple man of average ability, of merciful disposition, upheld in all his daily life by his faith in God. But the brunt of supreme decisions centered upon him. At the summit where all problems are reduced to Yea or Nay, where events transcend the faculties of man and where all is inscrutable, he had to give the answers. His was the function of the compass needle. War or no war? Advance or retreat? Right or left? Democratise or hold firm? Quit or persevere? These were the battlefields of Nicholas II. Why should he reap no honor from them? The devoted onset of the Russian armies which saved Paris in 1914; the mastered agony of the munitionless retreat; the slowly regathered forces; the victories of Brusilov; the Russian entry upon the campaign of 1917, unconquered, stronger than ever; has he no share in these? In spite of errors vast and terrible, the regime he personified, over which he presided, to which his personal character gave the vital spark, had at this moment won the war for Russia.

"He is about to be struck down. A dark hand, gloved at first in folly, now intervenes. Exit Tsar. Deliver him and all he loved to wounds and death. Belittle his efforts, asperse his conduct, insult his memory; but pause then to tell us who else was found capable. Who or what could guide the Russian state? Men gifted and daring; men ambitious and fierce, spirits audacious and commanding—of these there were no lack. But none could answer the few plain questions on which the life and fame of Russia turned."

Inevitably, members of the Imperial family greeted news of the Tsar's abdication with dismay. Some, thinking only of the awkwardness of their own situation, leaped to attack. "Nicky must have lost his mind," wrote Grand Duke Alexander. "Since when does a sovereign abdicate because of a shortage of bread and partial disorders in his capital? . . . He had an army of fifteen million men at his disposal. The whole thing . . . seemed ludicrous."

Far more widely criticized was Nicholas's decision to sign away the rights of his son. Shulgin and Guchkov, both strong monarchists, were surprised by the change from Alexis to Michael. They knew it would make trouble, but in the emotion of the moment on the train, they bowed to a "father's feelings." Among the legalistic, bureaucratic classes whose main concern was to obey whatever government was properly legal, and among the devout monarchists, faithful to tradition, who might have rallied to the legitimate heir, the change created consternation. "The immediate accession of the Tsarevich was the only means of stopping the Revolution," declared Nicholas Basily, an official at Headquarters, who had drafted the first abdication document and been shocked to see the switch from son to brother. "In the first place, the young Alexis Nicolaievich would have had the law on his side. He would also have benefited by the sympathetic feeling of the nation and army towards him."

Even those who had served Nicholas long and faithfully failed to completely understand that the Tsar was also the father of a delicate twelve-year-old boy. Sazonov, who had been Nicholas's Minister of Foreign Affairs for some years, spoke of the matter to Paléologue. "I needn't tell you of my love for the Emperor and with what devotion I have served him," he said with tears in his eyes. "But as long as I live, I shall never forgive him for abdicating for his son. He had no shadow of right to do so. Is there a body of law in the world which allows the rights of a minor to be abandoned? And what's to be said when those rights are the most sacred and august on earth? Fancy destroying a three-hundred-year-old dynasty, and the stupendous work of Peter the Great, Catherine II and Alexander I. What a tragedy! What a disaster!"

With Nicholas and Alexis both removed, Michael now was Tsar. There was an old Russian legend that when Tsar Michael II sat on the throne, Russia would win her eternal goal, Constantinople. There had been no tsar named Michael since the founder of the Romanov dynasty; Nicholas's younger brother, therefore, would be Michael II. There were other propitious omens. Britain and France, which always before had blocked Russia's advance to the south, now were her allies, and had promised Constantinople as a prize of victory. If Michael took the throne and the Allies won the war, the ancient legend might at last be fulfilled.

As it happened, the reign of the new Tsar Michael was ludicrously brief. The news burst upon him at Gatchina in a telegram from his older brother: "To His Majesty the Emperor Michael: Recent events have forced me to decide irrevocably to take this extreme step. Forgive me if it grieves you and also for no warning—there was no time. Shall always remain a faithful and devoted brother. Now returning to Headquarters where hope to come back shortly to Tsarskoe Selo. Fervently pray God to help you and our country. Nicky."

Michael, now thirty-nine, was wholly unprepared for this abrupt transformation. Before the birth of the Tsarevich, he had for six years been Heir to the Throne. During Alexis's periods of illness, he had faced the possibility of becoming Heir again. But he had never dreamed that both his brother and his nephew would be removed simultaneously and that, with the arrival of a telegram, he would suddenly find himself Tsar. Michael was no coward; he had won the St. George Cross commanding troops in the Carpathians. Nor was he politically insensitive: watching the disintegration of the government earlier that winter, he had come to Rodzianko to see what he could do to help. But he was not a bold, decisive man with extraordinary energies and will power, and it was a man of this character who was required. Nevertheless, taking leave of his wife, now beside herself with excitement at the prospect of becoming the consort of an emperor, Michael traveled from Gatchina into Petrograd to make his historic decision.

In Petrograd, the anti-monarchical tide was running strong. Even as Guchkov and Shulgin were in Pskov obtaining Nicholas's abdication, the Soviet had decided that replacing one tsar with another was not enough. "No more Romanovs! We want a Republic!" became their cry. Guchkov and Shulgin, returning to Petrograd with the document of abdication, were invited to address the railway workers at the station. Shulgin, believing it would please them to hear of Nicholas's abdication, fervently shouted, "Long live the Emperor Michael!" To his horror, the workers were outraged. Closing the doors, they attempted to seize both Guchkov and Shulgin, who barely managed to slip away to a waiting automobile. From the station, the two delegates drove straight to a private house where the new government was meeting. Rodzianko was present, and in an armchair at the head of the table, waiting to hear the advice of the men who would become his ministers if he accepted the throne, sat Michael.

The debate that followed was waged with passionate intensity. Miliukov, Guchkov and Shulgin pleaded that Michael had no right to evade the throne. They argued that the monarchy was the single unifying force in Russia, without which Russia would be destroyed. With equal force and conviction on the other side, Rodzianko and Kerensky threatened that if a new tsar took the throne against the people's will, a new torrent of revolution would be released. The first victim, they predicted, would be Michael himself. "He asked me point-blank whether I could vouch for his life if he accepted the crown," Rodzianko wrote later, "and I was compelled to answer in the negative because there was no armed force I could rely on."

Kerensky was even more vehement than Rodzianko. Knowing the fury that the proclamation of a new tsar would rouse in the Soviet, he declared, "In any case, I cannot answer for the life of Your Highness." Michael asked for a few minutes to think the matter over and left the room with Rodzianko and Prince Lvov. Five minutes later, he returned and announced, "I have decided to abdicate." He added that he would accept the throne later only if invited to do so by a constituent assembly.

Kerensky was overjoyed. "Monseigneur, you are the noblest of men," he shouted. The second deed of abdication was typed out on the desk of a children's schoolroom in the house next door, and Michael signed it.

Three hundred and four years after a shy sixteen-year-old boy had reluctantly accepted the throne at the plea of the Russian nation, his descendant, also named Michael, had given it back. The Romanov dynasty was swept away.

Although it was the defection of his trusted generals which ultimately swung his decision to abdication, Nicholas could not abandon the throne without saying goodbye to the army. In Pskov, immediately after signing the abdication, Nicholas applied for permission to return to Headquarters. The Provisional Government agreed without hesitation. Nicholas was not hostile but submissive; at Headquarters, Alexeiev was with them; at all the battlefronts, the commanding generals had united to urge the abdication. The likelihood that Nicholas would suddenly change his mind, revoke his abdication, rally his troops and march on the capital simply did not exist.

As the train approached Mogilev, Alexeiev sent Basily to meet the Tsar. "He was absolutely calm, but it shocked me to see him with a haggard look and hollow eyes," Basily wrote of his former sovereign. ". . . I took the liberty of saying that we at the *Stavka* were greatly distressed because he had not transferred his crown to the Tsarevich. He answered quietly: 'I cannot be separated from my son.' A few minutes later dinner was served. It was a melancholy meal. All of us felt our hearts bursting; we couldn't eat or drink. Yet the Emperor retained wonderful self-control and asked me several questions about the men who form the Provisional Government; but he was wearing a rather low collar and I could see that he was continually choking down his emotion."

In Mogilev, Alexeiev met the train at the station and drove with the Tsar in an open car back to the governor's house. Sitting down at his desk, Nicholas drafted as an Order of the Day his farewell to the army:

"My dearly beloved troops," he wrote, "I address you for the last time. Since my abdication, for myself and my son, from the throne of Russia, the power has passed to the Provisional Government, which has arisen on the initiative of the Imperial Duma. . . . Submit yourselves to the Provisional Government, obey your commanders. . . . May the Lord God bless you and may the Holy Martyr and Conqueror St. George lead you to victory." Sadly, the message never reached the troops. Forwarded for approval to Petrograd, it was suppressed by the same Provisional Government which Nicholas was so loyally recommending. The Soviet, sitting under the same roof of the Tauride Palace, had let it be known that it did not favor the issuance of Orders of the Day by deposed monarchs.

During these last five days in Mogilev, Nicholas exhibited the same steady restraint and self-control which he had been taught since boyhood. At a ceremonial farewell arranged by Alexeiev, the main hall of the house was packed with officers of the Headquarters staff. Nicholas, appearing at the front of the crowded room, quietly thanked the officers for their loyalty, begged them to forget all feuds and lead the army and Russia to victory. His modesty made a vivid impression; when he had finished, the room burst into loud cheers and most of those present wept openly. But none spoke up to urge him to change his mind, and Nicholas quietly bowed and left.

Alone in his room, he said goodbye to the foreign military observers. General Hanbury-Williams found Nicholas in a khaki uniform, looking tired and pale, with large black lines under his eyes. He smiled and got up from his desk to join his guest on the sofa. "He said that he had meant to carry out . . . [reforms]," wrote Hanbury-Williams, "but that matters had advanced so quickly and it was too late. The proposal that the Tsarevich should take his place with a regent he could not accept as he could not bear the separation from his only son, and he knew that the Empress would feel the same. He . . . hoped that he would not have to leave Russia. He did not see that there would be any objection to his going to the Crimea . . . and if not, he would sooner go to England than anywhere. . . . He . . . added that the right thing to do was to support the present Government, as that was the best way to keep Russia in the alliance to conclude the war. . . . He feared the revolution would ruin the armies. . . . As I said 'Good-bye' . . . he turned to me and added: 'Remember, nothing matters but beating Germany.' "

The change in his status was tactfully concealed by the continuing personal courtesy with which he was treated. It appeared, nevertheless, in the little matters of procedure and ceremony which are the visible trappings of power. On the morning following his last meeting with the staff, the same officers assembled to take the oath of allegiance to the Provisional Government. While Nicholas sat alone in his room, his suite, the staff and the troops of his escort lined up outside the house and pronounced the new oath in an audible chorus. In the prayers that followed, for the first time in hundreds of years the names of the Tsar and the Imperial family were omitted. The town of Mogilev greeted the abdication with noisy celebrations. At night, the town was illuminated and excited crowds stayed up shouting in the streets. From the windows of the local city hall, just opposite Nicholas's window, two large red flags were draped. One by one, as the days moved along, the officers of the suite began removing the Tsar's initials from their epaulets and cutting away the golden shoulder knots which marked them as aides-de-camp. Nicholas reacted gracefully to this melancholy sight: on March 21, Alexeiev telegraphed Brusilov: "The deposed Emperor understands and has given permission to remove initials and shoulder knots immediately."

On the second day of Nicholas's stay at Headquarters, his mother, the Dowager Empress, arrived from her home in Kiev. "The news of Nicky's abdication came like a thunderbolt," wrote the Tsar's sister Grand Duchess Olga Alexandrovna, who was with her mother in Kiev. "We were stunned. My mother was in a terrible state. She kept telling me it was the greatest humiliation of her life. . . . She blamed poor Alicky for . . . everything." In Mogilev, the Dowager Empress's train was brought to the Imperial platform and a few minutes later Nicholas drove up in his automobile. He said good morning to the two Cossacks standing at the entrance to Marie's car and went inside. For two hours, mother and son were alone. Then Grand Duke Alexander, who had accompanied Marie, entered the car. He found the Dowager Empress collapsed in a chair, sobbing aloud, while Nicholas stood smoking quietly and staring at his feet.

For three days, Marie remained in Mogilev, living aboard her train. She and Nicholas spent most of their time together, going for long drives in the afternoon and dining together every evening. It was the son who comforted the mother. Marie, always gay, witty, brilliant, decisive and totally in control of her emotions, had lost the regal bearing which was her emblem; for once she was frightened, ashamed and miserable. It was Nicholas, the son she had always lectured on behavior, who carefully steered his mother back toward courage and self-control.

While at Mogilev, Nicholas had only the scantiest communication with his family at Tsarskoe Selo. Anxious to return to them as soon as possible, he applied for permission to the Provisional Government, which again had no objections. In Petrograd, however, the position of the Imperial family had deteriorated. Rumors circulated through the city that Nicholas had returned to Headquarters to lead the army against the revolution or to "let the Germans in." Newspapers were filled with garish accounts of the sexual relationship of Rasputin and the Empress, along with stories detailing the Empress's "treason." On March 20, therefore, primarily to assure their own safety, the Provisional Government resolved "to deprive the deposed emperor and his consort of their liberty." The Empress was to be arrested at Tsarskoe Selo on March 21. That same day, Nicholas was to be arrested at Mogilev and then, escorted by four commissioners sent by the Government, brought back to his family at Tsarskoe Selo.

On March 21, the Tsar, knowing that he was to become a prisoner, had lunch alone with his mother. At three p.m., the express from Petrograd arrived, bearing the government envoys. At a quarter to four, the delegation, accompanied by Alexeiev, arrived to claim the Tsar. Nicholas stood up and tenderly kissed his mother goodbye. Neither could guess the future; both hoped that they would soon be reunited either in the Crimea or in England. Nevertheless, Marie cried unrestrainedly. Nicholas left her car, walked across the platform and entered the drawing-room car of his own train, which stood on the adjacent track. Whistles blew, there was a lurch and the Tsar's train started to move. Nicholas, standing at the window, smiled and waved his hand; Marie, still in tears, made the sign of the cross. A few minutes later, when his train was only a blur of smoke on the northern horizon, her car rolled out of the station headed southwest for Kiev. Neither could know it at the time, but the proud Empress and her quiet eldest son were never to meet again.

On the platform a few minutes before, as the Tsar's train was leaving, Alexeiev and other officers of the Headquarters staff had stood at attention as the train bearing their former sovereign departed. As the car carrying the Tsar moved past him, Alexeiev saluted. A second later, as the last car of the same train, bearing the representatives of the Duma, rolled by, Alexeiev took off his cap and made a deep bow.

CHAPTER TWENTY-NINE

The Empress Alone

At ten A.M. on Monday, March 12, a telephone rang in the Petrograd house of the Empress's friend Lili Dehn. Lili, still in bed, got up to answer. It was the Empress. "I want you to come to Tsarskoe Selo by the ten-forty-five train," said Alexandra. "It's a lovely morning. We'll go for a run in the car. You can see the girls and Anna and return to Petrograd at four p.m. . . . I'll be at the station."

With only forty-five minutes to catch her train, Lili dressed rapidly, snatching her gloves, rings and a bracelet, and rushed to the station. She managed to scramble aboard the train just as it was leaving the platform.

It was a superb winter morning. The sky was a rich blue and the sun sparkled on the deep drifts of white snow. True to her word, the Empress was waiting at the Tsarskoe Selo station. "How is it in Petrograd?" she asked anxiously. "I hear things are serious." Lili replied that the general strike had made things inconvenient, but that she herself had seen nothing alarming. Still troubled, the Empress stopped the car on the way to the palace to question a captain of the marine *Garde Equipage*. The captain smiled. "There is no danger, Your Majesty," he said.

Over the weekend, Alexandra had paid less attention than usual to events in Petrograd. From Protopopov and others, she had heard that there had been disturbances and that in places the police had had difficulty in calming and dispersing the crowds. Soothingly, Protopopov had assured her that matters were under control. In any case, the Empress had little time to worry about street disorders. At the palace, she faced an urgent family crisis.

Three of her children had come down with the measles. A week before, a group of young military cadets had come to the palace to play with the Tsarevich. One of these boys arrived with a flushed face and spent the afternoon coughing. The following day, the Empress learned that he had measles. Then, on Thursday, March 8, just after the Tsar's train had departed for Mogilev, both Olga and Alexis had developed a rash and high fever.

The disease spread quickly. Olga and Alexis were followed to bed by Tatiana and Anna Vyrubova. The Empress, in her white Red Cross uniform, nursed the invalids herself. "She spent all the succeeding days between her children's rooms and mine," wrote Anna Vyrubova. "Half-conscious, I felt gratefully her capable hands arranging my pillows, smoothing my burning forehead, and holding to my lips medicines and cooling drinks." Despite her efforts, the patients grew worse. On the night of March 12, Olga had a temperature of 103 degrees, Tatiana 102 and both Anna and Alexis 104.

It was during Lili Dehn's visit that the Empress learned that the Petrograd soldiery had joined the mob. Lili was upstairs, sitting in a darkened room with the ill Grand Duchesses; Alexandra had gone to talk to two officers of the palace guard. When the Empress returned, she beckoned Lili into another room: "Lili," she said, breathlessly, "it is *very* bad. . . . The Litovsky Regiment has mutinied, murdered the officers and left barracks; the Volinsky Regiment has followed suit. I can't understand it. I'll never believe in the possibility of revolution. . . . I'm sure that the trouble is confined to Petrograd alone."

Nevertheless, as the day wore on, the news got worse. The Empress tried to telephone the Tsar and was unable to get through. "But I have wired him, asking him to return immediately. He'll be here on Wednesday morning [the 14th]," she said. Alexander Taneyev, Anna Vyrubova's father, arrived puffing and footsore, his face crimson with excitement and anger. "Petrograd is in the hands of the mob," he declared. "They are stopping all cars. They commandeered mine, and I've had to walk every step of the way."

That night, rather than attempt to return to the capital under these conditions, Lili decided to remain at the palace. So that she could stay in the private family wing where there were no extra bedrooms, a couch was arranged for her in the red drawing room. There, while the Empress talked with Count Benckendorff, the elderly Grand

Marshal of the Court and senior court official at the palace, Lili and Anastasia sat on the red carpet and assembled jigsaw puzzles. When the Empress returned from her conference with Benckendorff, she sent her daughter to bed and said to Lili, "I don't want the girls to know anything until it is impossible to keep the truth from them, but people are drinking to excess, and there is indiscriminate shooting in the streets. Oh, Lili, what a blessing that we have here the most devoted troops. There is the *Garde Equipage*; they are all our personal friends."

That night, a message arrived from Rodzianko, now the chairman of the Temporary Committee of the Duma, warning that the Empress and her children were in danger and should leave Tsarskoe Selo as soon as possible. On his own initiative, Benckendorff withheld this message from the Empress and instead communicated it to Mogilev, asking the Tsar for instructions. Nicholas telegraphed that a train should be made ready for his family, but that his wife should not be told until the following morning. Meanwhile, he himself was leaving Mogilev and would arrive in Tsarskoe Selo early on the morning of the 14th.

On Tuesday, March 13, a fresh blizzard swept down from a gray sky, and an icy wind howled dismally outside the palace windows. The Empress was up early, taking *café au lait* in the sickroom with Olga and Tatiana. From Petrograd, the news was grim: the mob had swept all before it, and General Khabalov with his 1,500 men holding the Winter Palace constituted the only tsarist island in the entire city. Benckendorff informed the Empress of his previous night's conversations: Rodzianko's warning and appeal, and the Tsar's command that a train be prepared for her. The train itself was already only a hope; on telephoning the Petrograd yards, the palace staff had learned that it was doubtful that workers would roll out a train for any member of the Imperial family.

As it happened, this obstructionism became irrelevant. Alexandra refused to go. To Rodzianko and the Duma committee, as Benckendorff transmitted her message, she declared that she would never leave by herself and, "owing to the state of her children's health, especially that of the Heir Apparent, departure with them was completely out of the question." Rodzianko, more alarmed than ever at the rising pitch of revolutionary fever all around him, argued with Benckendorff, saying "when a house is burning the invalids are the first to be taken out," but Alexandra's mind was made up. At 11:30 that morning,

Benckendorff was informed by railway officials that within two hours all railway lines would be cut, and that if there was any idea of leaving Tsarskoe Selo they should do so at once. Knowing the Empress's mind, the Count did not even bother to give her this message. At four in the afternoon, Dr. Derevenko returned to the palace from visiting hospitals in Tsarskoe Selo village. He brought with him the news that the entire network of railways around Petrograd was in the hands of the revolutionaries. "We could not leave," wrote Gilliard, "and it was highly improbable that the Tsar would be able to reach us."

Even before that day was over, it seemed that Alexandra's decision would lead to calamity. From Petrograd, on a sudden inspiration, a crowd of mutinous soldiers set off by truck for Tsarskoe Selo. Their plan, shouted gleefully from truck to truck, was to seize "the German woman" and her son and bring them back to the capital. Arriving in the village of Tsarskoe Selo, they became distracted and began smashing into wine shops, looting and drinking. At the Alexander Palace, where the sounds of shooting and cheering were plainly heard, the size of the crowd was magnified by rumor. "Lili," the Empress said, "they say that a hostile crowd of three hundred thousand is marching on the palace. We shall not be, must not be afraid. Everything is in the hands of God. Tomorrow the Emperor is sure to come. I know that when he does, all will be well."

The Alexander Palace was not completely defenseless. That morning, before the arrival of the mutineers, Count Benckendorff had ordered a battalion of the *Garde Equipage*, two battalions of the picked Composite Regiment of the Imperial Guard, two squadrons of Cossacks of the Emperor's Escort, a company of the Railway Regiment and a battery of field artillery—in all, about 1,500 men—to take up defensive positions around the palace. By nightfall, their soup kitchens and warming fires were established in the palace courtyard. The Empress was reassured, and her younger daughters, seeing the familiar faces of the marines, declared happily, "It's just like being on the yacht again."

The night was spent awaiting an attack. At nine p.m. a telephone call advised that the rebels were on their way. A moment later, a sentry was shot less than five hundred yards from the palace. Through the trees of the park, the sound of firing grew steadily closer. From a palace window, the Empress looked down on General Ressine, commander of the defense forces, standing in the courtyard before his men. On impulse, she decided to go out to speak to the soldiers. Throwing a black fur cloak over her white nurse's uniform, accompanied by seventeen-year-old Grand Duchess Marie and Count Benckendorff, she walked out into the frigid night.

"The scene was unforgettable," wrote Baroness Buxhoeveden, who watched from above. "It was dark, except for a faint light thrown up from the snow and reflected on the polished barrels of the rifles. The troops were lined up in battle order . . . the first line kneeling in the snow, the others standing behind, their rifles in readiness for a sudden attack. The figures of the Empress and her daughter passed from line to line, the white palace looming a ghostly mass in the background." Walking from man to man, she told them that she trusted them completely, and that the life of the Heir was in their hands. Count Benckendorff, a rigid old soldier, thought that some of the men answered in surly fashion, but the Empress, according to Lili Dehn, returned to the palace "apparently possessed by some inward exaltation. She was radiant; her trust in the 'people' was complete. . . . 'They are all our friends,' she kept on repeating. 'They are so devoted to us.' " She asked that the men, many of whom were stiff with cold, be brought into the palace to warm themselves and be given cups of scalding tea.

During the night, Alexandra lay down, but did not undress. From time to time, she arose: first to bring extra blankets to Countess Benckendorff and Baroness Buxhoeveden, who were camping on sofas in the drawing room; later, appearing in her stockinged feet, she offered them fruit and biscuits from the table beside her bed.

Outside, the night was filled with confusion and occasional skirmishing. Mutinous soldiers had pressed as close as the Chinese Pagoda near the great Catherine Palace. There, hearing rumors that the Alexander Palace was defended by immense forces and that the roof was studded with many machine guns, they lost their nerve and withdrew.

Although the palace was not assaulted, the sound of shooting carried clearly into the children's rooms. The sick children, still feverish, were told that the shots came from manuevers; Lili and Anastasia, sleeping together in the same room, went to the window. In the courtyard, a big field gun was emplaced, with sentries and gunners stamping their feet around it to keep warm. "How astonished Papa will be," said Anastasia, staring at the huge gun.

The following morning—Wednesday, March 14—the Empress was up at five a.m., expecting the Tsar to arrive at six. She was told that he had been delayed. "Perhaps the blizzard detains him," she said and lay back on her couch to wait. Anastasia was instantly alarmed. "Lili, the train is *never* late. Oh, if only Papa would come quickly." At eight, Alexandra learned that Nicholas's train had been stopped at Malaya Vishera. She rose and sent a telegram. There was no reply. Other telegrams followed in an anxious stream. Over the next several days, all were returned marked in blue pencil: "Address of person mentioned unknown."

During the day, the loyalty of the troops guarding the Alexander Palace began to deteriorate. Standing at the window, the Empress noticed that many of the soldiers in the courtyard had bound white handkerchiefs to their wrists. The handkerchiefs were symbols of a truce worked out between the palace guards and the revolutionary troops in the village: if the Alexander Palace was not attacked, the loyal troops would not intervene against the mutineers in the village. The truce had been arranged by a member of the Duma. Learning this, the Empress said bitterly, "Well, so everything is in the hands of the Duma."

On the following morning, Thursday, March 15, the Empress had a far heavier blow. Very early that morning, deathly pale, she came up to Lili and said in an anguished whisper, "Lili, the troops have deserted!"

"Why, Madame? In the name of God, why?"

"Their commander—the Grand Duke Cyril—has sent for them." Then, unable to contain herself, the Empress said brokenly, "My sailors—my own sailors—I can't believe it."

In Pskov, on the 15th, the Tsar on his train was amending and signing the instrument of abdication. At Tsarskoe Selo, unaware even of her husband's whereabouts, Alexandra was coping with new difficulties. Alexis was better, but Anastasia and Marie were beginning to display unmistakable signs of oncoming measles. Both electricity and water had been cut off. Water was supplied only by breaking the ice on the pond. The Empress's small elevator, running between her rooms and the nurseries upstairs, stopped running. To reach her children, she had to climb slowly up the stairs, supported under the arms and gasping for breath. The lights were out. To visit Anna Vyrubova, whose room was in another wing of the palace, Alexandra was wheeled through the vast, darkened halls, now empty of all servants. Yet, knowing that others were watching for any sign of panic, she said to Lili, "I must not give way. I keep on saying, 'I must not'—it helps me."

Friday, March 16, another blizzard roared in, rattling the windows and piling the snowdrifts deeper in the park. Through the storm, more unsettling reports and rumors began to seep into the palace. At 3:30 a.m., a member of the Duma committee had telephoned Dr. Botkin, asking for news of the Tsarevich's health. During the afternoon, household servants making their way back from Petrograd on foot said that leaflets announcing the Tsar's abdication were being distributed in the capital. The Empress refused to believe them. At five p.m., the printed sheets announcing Nicholas's abdication, the renunciation of the throne by Grand Duke Michael and the establishment of a Provisional Government reached the palace. Officers of the Guard and members of the suite read them with tears in their eyes. At seven, Grand Duke Paul, the Tsar's uncle, arrived and went straight to the Empress. Grand Duchess Marie and Lili Dehn, waiting in the next room, heard agitated voices.

Then, wrote Lili, "the door opened and the Empress appeared. Her face was distorted with agony, her eyes were full of tears. She tottered rather than walked, and I rushed forward and supported her until she reached the writing table between the windows. She leaned heavily against it and taking my hands in hers, she said brokenly: '*Abdiqué!*' I could not believe my ears. I waited for her next words. They were hardly audible. 'The poor dear . . . all alone down there . . . what he has gone through, oh my God, what he has gone through . . . And I was not there to console him. . . .' "

That night, wrote Gilliard, "I saw her in Alexis Nicolaievich's room. . . . Her face was terrible to see, but with a strength of will which was almost superhuman, she had forced herself to come to the children's rooms as usual so that the young invalids . . . should suspect nothing."

The same evening, Count Benckendorff, Baroness Buxhoeveden and others went to see the Empress to assure her of their personal loyalty. "She was deadly pale," wrote Baroness Buxhoeveden. ". . . When the Empress kissed me, I could only cling to her and murmur some broken words of affection. Count Benckendorff held her hand, tears running down his usually immobile face. . . . 'It's for the best,' she said. 'It is the will of God. God gives this to save Russia. That is the only thing that matters.' Before we shut the door, we could see her sinking into her chair by the table, sobbing bitterly, covering her face with her hands."

Painful as it was, the Tsar's abdication improved the immediate situation at Tsarskoe Selo. The virtual state of siege surrounding the palace ended as officers and men of the palace guard, absolved by the abdication from their oath to the Tsar, swore allegiance to the Provisional Government. Communication between the deposed sovereigns, no longer a danger to the revolution, was restored. On March 17, upon his arrival at Headquarters, Nicholas was allowed to telephone his wife. Word of the call was brought by an aged servant, trembling with excitement. Oblivious of etiquette, he stammered: "The Emperor is on the phone!" Alexandra stared at him as if he had taken leave of his senses; then, realizing what he was saying, jumped up like a girl of sixteen and rushed to the telephone. Knowing that other people were listening in at both ends of the line, Nicholas said only "You know?" Alexandra answered nothing more than "Yes," before they went on to discuss the health of their children.

After ten o'clock at night on March 18, Count Benckendorff was startled to hear that Guchkov, now Minister of War in the Provisional Government, and General Kornilov, a regular soldier who had come from the front to take command of the Petrograd garrison, were on their way to Tsarskoe Selo to see the Empress. Guchkov was an avowed enemy—a former President of the Duma, an early antagonist of Rasputin, just back from overseeing the Tsar's abdication at Pskov. His coming, plus the lateness of the hour, seemed to indicate imminent arrest. Benckendorff informed Alexandra, who sent for Grand Duke Paul. The Grand Duke got out of bed and hurried from his house in Tsarskoe Selo. At eleven, Guchkov and Kornilov arrived, accompanied by twenty members of the new revolutionary council of the village of Tsarskoe Selo. While the Empress and the Grand Duke received the two envoys, these men, mostly workers and soldiers, wandered through the palace, abusing the servants and addressing the suite as "bloodsuckers."

As it happened, Guchkov and Kornilov had come only to investigate the state of affairs at the palace and to offer the protection of the Provisional Government to the Empress and her children. Guchkov respectfully asked whether the Empress had what she needed, especially medicines. Alexandra, relieved and grateful, replied that their own supplies were adequate, but she asked Guchkov to look into the supplies for the numerous hospitals around Tsarskoe Selo. In addition, she asked, for the children's sake, that order be maintained around the palace. Guchkov promised to arrange both of these matters. The first interview between the Empress and her captors had gone well. Returning home after the interview, Grand Duke Paul told his wife that he had never seen Alexandra more "beautiful, tranquil and dignified."

Nevertheless, the future still seemed precarious. During the days which preceded the Tsar's return, the Empress began burning her diaries, bound either in white satin or leather, and much of her private correspondence. All of her letters from Queen Victoria and her own letters to the Queen, which had been returned from Windsor after her grandmother's death, were destroyed. "A fierce fire was burning in the huge grate in the red drawing room," wrote Lili Dehn. ". . . She reread some of them. . . . I heard stifled sobs and . . . sighs. . . . Still weeping, [she] laid her letters one by one on the heart of the fire. The writing glowed for an instant . . . then it faded and the paper became a little heap of white ash." There were some letters which Alexandra did not burn. With rumors flying that one or both of them would be placed on trial, she carefully saved all of her letters to Nicholas and his to her to use as evidence of their patriotism.

Morale among the defending garrison began to erode. Following the dictate of Order Number One of the Petrograd Soviet, the troops began electing their officers. The Cossacks all reelected their former commanders, but General Ressine, commanding the Guard, was voted out. Discipline slackened, the men began to slouch on duty and argue when given a command. Those who remained loyal were frustrated and helpless because of the abdication. One devoted squadron of the Chevalier Guards, stationed at Novgorod, a hundred miles south of Tsarskoe Selo, had set out through the snow to defend tsar and dynasty. They rode for two days through bitter cold, reaching the palace gates, bedraggled and exhausted, to find that they had come too late. There no longer was a tsar or a dynasty for them to defend.

On the morning of March 21, General Kornilov returned to the palace. His mission this time was to place Alexandra Fedorovna under arrest. The Empress, dressed in her white nurse's uniform, received him in the green drawing room. Apprised of his mission, she stood icily silent and did not hold out her hand to receive him. Kornilov carefully explained that the arrest was purely precautionary, designed to safeguard her and her children from the excesses of the Soviet and the revolutionary soldiery. Her husband, he said, had been arrested at

Mogilev and would be returned to Tsarskoe Selo the following day. As soon as the children's health permitted, he declared, the Provisional Government intended to send the entire family to Murmansk, where a British cruiser would be waiting to take them to England. Kornilov's reassuring words overcame Alexandra's reserve. Half an hour later, an aide returned to find the Empress and the General sitting together at a small table. She was weeping and there were tears in his eyes. When she rose to say goodbye, she held out both her hands.

Moving to the Tsar's audience chamber, Kornilov addressed the assembled officers of the guard and the palace suite. He announced that, as the Tsar and his wife both were under arrest, the officers' duties at the palace had come to an end and that their men would be relieved by other troops. He told the suite that those who wished to leave were free to go; having gone, however, no one could return. Those who stayed would be placed under house arrest with Her Majesty. At that point, a majority rose and left the hall. Kornilov, disgusted, muttered under his breath: "Lackeys!" Kornilov informed Benckendorff that except for two entrances, the kitchen and the main entrance, the palace would be sealed. Captain Kotzebue, who had accompanied Kornilov, was assigned as palace commander, and the General warned that all in the palace must submit absolutely to the Captain's orders.

At two in the afternoon, the men of the Composite Regiment were relieved of their posts. "The soldiers of the new guard were horrible to look at," said Benckendorff. "Untidy, noisy, quarreling with everybody. The officers, who were afraid of them, had the greatest difficulty in preventing them from roaming about the palace and entering every room. . . . There were many quarrels between them and the household staff whom they reproached for wearing livery and for the attention they paid to the Imperial family."

As soon as Kornilov left her, the Empress sent for Gilliard. "The Tsar is coming back tomorrow," she said. "Alexis must be told everything. Will you do it? I am going to tell the girls myself." Both Tatiana and Anastasia then were suffering from painful ear abscesses as a result of secondary infections. Tatiana temporarily was quite deaf and could not hear what her mother was saying. Not until her sisters wrote the details down on paper did she understand what had happened.

Meanwhile, Gilliard went to the Tsarevich:

"[I] told him that the Tsar would be returning from Mogilev next morning and would never go back again.

" 'Why?'

" 'Your father does not want to be Commander-in-Chief any more.'

"He was greatly moved at this, as he was very fond of going to G.H.Q. After a moment or two, I added:

" 'You know your father does not want to be Tsar any more, Alexis Nicolaievich.'

"He looked at me in astonishment, trying to read in my face what had happened.

" 'What! Why?'

" 'He is very tired and has had a lot of trouble lately.'

" 'Oh yes! Mother told me they had stopped his train when he wanted to come here. But won't Papa be Tsar again afterwards?'

"I then told him that the Tsar had abdicated in favor of the Grand Duke Michael, who had also renounced the throne.

" 'But who's going to be Tsar, then?'

" 'I don't know. Perhaps nobody now . . . '

"Not a word about himself. Not a single allusion to his rights as the Heir. He was very red and agitated. . . . Then he said:

" 'But if there isn't a Tsar, who's going to govern Russia?'

"I explained that a Provisional Government had been formed. . . . "

At four that afternoon, the palace doors were locked. That night, the first of their imprisonment, a bright moon came up. From the park came the sounds of rifle shots; this time, it was the soldiers of the new guard killing the tame deer. Inside, the private wing of the palace was silent; from elsewhere in the building came sounds of laughter, broken by occasional snatches of song and drunken shouts.

Lili Dehn offered to sleep outside the Empress's door: "I went quietly downstairs to the mauve boudoir," she wrote. "The Empress was waiting for me and as she stood there, I thought how girlish she looked. Her long hair fell in a heavy plait, down her back, and she wore a loose silk dressing gown over her night clothes. She was very pale, very ethereal, but unutterably pathetic. As I stumbled into the boudoir with my . . . sheets and blankets, she smiled. . . . As she watched me trying to arrange my bed on the couch, she came forward, still smiling. 'Oh Lili, you Russian ladies don't know how to be useful. When I was a girl, my grandmother, Queen Victoria, showed me how to make a bed. I'll teach you. . . .'

"Sleep for me was impossible. I lay on the mauve couch—her couch—unable to realize that this strange happening was a part of ordinary life. Surely I was dreaming; surely I would suddenly awake in my own bed at Petrograd, and find that the Revolution and its attendant horrors were only a nightmare! But the sound of coughing in the Empress's bedroom told me that, alas! it was no dream. . . . The mauve boudoir was flooded with moonlight. . . . All was silent save for the footsteps of the Red sentry as he passed and repassed up and down the corridor."

The morning of March 22, the day scheduled for the Tsar's return, was cold and gray. Alexandra, both excited and worried that her hopes might be disappointed, went to wait with her children. Alexis, like his mother, in a state of nervous agitation, kept looking at his watch and counting aloud the minutes until his father arrived.

Nicholas's train arrived on schedule and pulled into the private siding at Tsarskoe Selo station. On the platform, the representatives of the Duma turned their prisoner over to the newly appointed palace commander. As the Tsar was taken away, the members of his suite peeked out the windows of the train and, seeing that the coast was clear, quickly scuttled across the platform in all directions. Only Prince Vassily Dolgoruky, Count Benckendorff's son-in-law, chose to accompany his former sovereign to whatever awaited him at the Alexander Palace.

At the palace gate, about a hundred yards from the entrance hall, Nicholas faced another humiliation. The gates were locked when his car drove up. The sentry asked who was inside and telephoned an officer, who came out on the palace steps and again asked in a shout "Who is there?" The sentry bawled back, "Nicholas Romanov." "Let him pass," cried the officer. "After this offensive comedy," wrote Benckendorff, "the motor arrived at the steps and the Emperor and Dolgoruky descended." They entered the antechamber, which was filled with people, most of them soldiers crowding to catch a glimpse of the Tsar. Some were smoking, others had not bothered to remove their caps. By habit, as he walked through the crowd, Nicholas touched the brim of his cap, returning salutes which had never been given. He shook hands with Benckendorff and left for the private apartments without saying a word.

Upstairs, just as the Empress heard the sound of the arriving automobile, the door flew open and a servant, in a tone which ignored the events of recent days, boomed out: "His Majesty the Emperor!"

With a cry, Alexandra sprang to her feet and ran to meet her husband. Alone, in the children's room, they fell into each other's arms. With tears in her eyes, Alexandra assured him that the husband and father was infinitely more precious to her than the tsar whose throne she had shared. Nicholas finally broke. Laying his head on his wife's breast, he sobbed like a child.

PART FOUR

CHAPTER THIRTY

Citizen Romanov

IN the afternoon, the Tsar reappeared, walking alone through the hushed rooms of the palace. In the red drawing room, he met Lili Dehn. Taking her hands in his, he said simply, "Thank you, Lili, for all you have done for us." She was shocked to see how much he had changed. "The Emperor was deathly pale," she observed. "His face was covered with innumerable wrinkles, his hair was quite grey at the temples, and blue shadows encircled his eyes. He looked like an old man." Nicholas smiled sadly at Lili's expression. "I think I'll go for a walk," he said. "Walking always does me good."

Before going out, Nicholas spoke to Count Benckendorff, who explained the arrangements made with General Kornilov. At first, Kornilov had wished to keep the Imperial family locked inside the palace, but Benckendorff, knowing the Tsar's intense need for outdoor exercise, had arranged for a small section of the park to be used. Nevertheless, it was required that every excursion be arranged in advance so that sentries could be posted. On this first afternoon, none of these arrangements had been made, and Nicholas was forced to wait for twenty minutes before an officer appeared with a key. When at last he did go outside, the Empress, Lili and Anna Vyrubova were watching from an upstairs window.

They saw Nicholas marching briskly across the park when a soldier stepped up and blocked his path. Surprised, the Tsar made a nervous gesture with his hand and started in a different direction. Another sentinel appeared and ordered him back. A moment later, Nicholas was surrounded by six soldiers armed with rifles. Anna was horrified: "With their fists and with the butts of their guns they pushed the

Emperor this way and that as though he were some wretched vagrant they were baiting on a country road. 'You can't go there, *Gospodin Polkovnik* (Mr. Colonel).' 'We don't permit you to walk in that direction, *Gospodin Polkovnik.*' 'Stand back when you are commanded, *Gospodin Polkovnik.*' The Emperor, apparently unmoved, looked from one of these coarse brutes to another and with great dignity turned and walked back to the palace." In the window above, Alexandra said nothing, but reached out and tightly clutched Lili's hand. "I do not think that until this moment we had realized the crushing grip of the Revolution," said Lili. "But it was brought home to us most forcibly when we saw the passage of the Lord of all the Russias, the Emperor whose domains extended over millions of miles, now restricted to a few yards in his own park."

Still, the long, tumultuous day was not over. At dusk, three armored cars packed with revolutionary soldiers from Petrograd burst through the palace gates. Leaping from the steel turrets, the soldiers demanded that Nicholas be given to them. The Soviet had unanimously resolved that the former Tsar be removed to a cell in the Fortress of Peter and Paul; this detachment had come to seize him. The palace guard, surly and disorganized, made no move to resist, but their officers hurriedly mustered to defend the entryway. Rebuffed, the invaders backed away and agreed not to take the Tsar if they were allowed to see him. Benckendorff reluctantly agreed to arrange an "inspection." "I found the Emperor with his sick children," recalled the Count, "informed him of what had happened, and begged him to come down and walk slowly along the long corridor. . . . He did this a quarter of an hour later. In the meantime, the Commandant, all the officers of the Guard . . . and myself, stationed ourselves at the end of the corridor so as to be between the Emperor and . . . [the invading band]. . . . The corridor was lit up brightly, the Emperor walked slowly from one door to the other, and . . . [the leader of the intruders] declared himself satisfied. He could, he said, reassure those who sent him."

Even when the armored cars had rumbled off into the night, Fate was to add a lurid epilogue to this extraordinary day. Sometime after midnight, another band of soldiers broke into the tiny chapel in the Imperial Park which had become Rasputin's tomb and exhumed the coffin. They took it to a clearing in the forest, pried off the lid and, using sticks to avoid touching the putrefying corpse, lifted what remained of Rasputin onto a pile of pine logs. The body and logs were drenched with gasoline and set on fire. For more than six hours, the body burned while an icy wind howled through the clearing and clouds of pungent smoke rose from the pyre. Along with the soldiers, a group of peasants gathered, silent and afraid, to watch through the night as the final scene of this baleful drama was played. It had happened as Rasputin once predicted: he would be killed and his body not left in peace, but burned, with his ashes scattered to the winds.

The small group which had ignored the offer to leave and remained with the family in the palace seemed, in Anna Vyrubova's words, "like the survivors of a shipwreck." It included, besides Anna herself and Lili Dehn, Count Benckendorff and his wife; Prince Dolgoruky; two ladies-in-waiting, Baroness Buxhoeveden and Countess Hendrikov; the tutors Pierre Gilliard and Mlle. Schneider; and Doctors Botkin and Derevenko. The two doctors were coping as best they could with Marie, who had developed pneumonia on top of measles. Dr. Ostrogorsky, the Petrograd children's specialist who for many years had made regular visits, had declined to return, informing the Empress that he "found the roads too dirty" to make further calls at the palace.

Inside the palace, the little band of captives was entirely isolated. All letters passing in and out were left unsealed so that the commander of the guard could read them. All telephone lines were cut except one connected to a single telephone in the guardroom. It could be used only if both an officer and a private soldier were present and the conversation was entirely in Russian. Every parcel entering the palace was minutely examined: tubes of toothpaste were ripped open, jars of yogurt stirred by dirty fingers, and pieces of chocolate bitten apart. When Dr. Botkin visited the ill Grand Duchesses, he was accompanied by soldiers who wanted to come right into the sickroom and hear everything that was said. With difficulty, Botkin persuaded the soldiers to wait at the open doorway while he examined his patients.

The attitude and appearance of the guards grated on Nicholas's precise military sensibilities. Their hair was shaggy and uncombed, they went unshaven, their blouses were unbuttoned and their boots were filthy. To others, such as Baroness Buxhoeveden, this crumbling discipline offered moments of comic relief. "One day," she remembered, "the Grand Duchess Tatiana and I saw from the window that one of the guards on duty in front of the palace, struck evidently with the injustice of having to stand at his post, had brought a gilt armchair from the hall and had comfortably ensconced himself therein, leaning back, enjoying the view, with his rifle across his knee. I remarked that the man only wanted cushions to complete the picture. There was evidently telepathy in my eye, for when we looked out again, he had actually got some sofa cushions out of one of the rooms, and with a footstool under his feet, was reading the papers, his discarded rifle lying on the ground." In time, even Nicholas saw the humor in this behavior: "When I got up," he told Alexandra one morning, "I put on my dressing gown and looked through the window. . . . The sentinel who was usually stationed there was now sitting on the steps—his rifle had slipped out of his hand—he was dozing! I called my valet, and showed him the unusual sight, and I couldn't help laughing—it was really absurd. At the sound of my laughter the soldier awoke . . . he scowled at us and we withdrew."

Off duty, the soldiers wandered freely through the palace. Baroness Buxhoeveden awoke one night to find a soldier in her bedroom, busily pocketing a number of small gold and silver trinkets from her table. Alexis attracted the most attention. Groups of soldiers kept tramping into the nursery, asking, "Where is Alexis?" Gilliard once came on ten of them standing uncertainly in a passage outside the boy's room.

"We want to see the Heir," they said.

"He is in bed and can't be seen," replied the tutor.

"And the others?"

"They are also unwell."

"And where is the Tsar?"

"I don't know; but come, don't hang about here," said the determined Swiss, at last losing patience. "There must be no noise because of the invalids." Nodding, the men tiptoed away, whispering to each other.

Gilliard became even closer to the Tsarevich at this time because Alexis had just been abruptly and cruelly deserted by another of the key figures in his small, intimate world. Derevenko, the sailor-attendant who for ten years had lived at the boy's side, catching him before he fell, devotedly massaging his injured legs when he could not walk, now saw his chance to escape this life which apparently he had hated. He did not leave without an act of petty but heartless vengeance. The scene was witnessed by Anna Vyrubova: "I passed the open door of Alexis's room and . . . I saw lying sprawled in a chair . . . the sailor Derevenko. . . . Insolently, he bawled at the boy whom he had formerly loved and cherished, to bring him this or that, to perform any menial service. . . . Dazed and apparently only half conscious of what he was being forced to do, the child moved about trying to obey." Derevenko immediately left the palace. Nagorny, the Tsarevich's other sailor-attendant, was outraged by the betrayal and remained.

In the long imprisonment that followed, Alexis found happy distraction in a movie projector and a number of films given him before the revolution by the Pathé film company. Using the equipment, he gave a number of "performances," inviting everyone to come to his room, where with grave delight he played the role of host. Count Benckendorff, a guest at these soirees, found himself thinking, "He is very intelligent, has a great deal of character and an excellent heart. If his disease could be mastered, and should God grant him life, he should one day play a part in the restoration of our poor country. He is the representative of the legitimate principle; his character has been formed by the misfortunes of his parents and of his childhood. May God protect him and save him and all his family from the claws of the fanatics in which they are at present."

Once all the children were well enough, the parents decided to resume their lessons, dividing their subjects among the people available. Nicholas himself became an instructor in history and geography, Baroness Buxhoeveden gave lessons in English and piano, Mlle. Schneider taught arithmetic, Countess Hendrikov taught art, and the Empress, religion. Gilliard, besides teaching French, became informal headmaster. After Nicholas had given his first lesson, the Tsar greeted Gilliard, "Good morning, dear colleague."

The tranquillity of Nicholas's behavior during his imprisonment, beginning with the five months he and his family were held at Tsarskoe Selo, has attracted both contemptuous scorn and glowing praise. In general, the scorn has come from those who, distant in place or time, have wondered how a man could fall from the pinnacle of earthly power without lapsing into bitter, impotent fury. Yet those who were closest to Nicholas during these months and saw him as a man; who had been with him during the years of supreme power and knew what a burden, however conscientiously carried, that power had been—these witnesses regarded his calm as evidence of courage and nobility of spirit. It was not a secret inside the palace that the Tsar's immense shield of reserve and self-control had broken when he returned to the palace; everyone knew that Nicholas had wept, and for a moment, for everyone, the anchor was gone. Then, he recovered and his bearing became once again the anchor which held everything and everyone else. "The Tsar accepted all these restraints with extraordinary serenity and moral grandeur," said Pierre Gilliard. "No word of reproach ever passed his lips. The fact was that his whole being was dominated by one passion, which was more powerful even than the bonds between himself and his family—his love of country. We felt that he was ready to forgive everything to those who were inflicting such humiliations upon him so long as they were capable of saving Russia."

Through the Russian newspapers and French and English magazines he was allowed to have, Nicholas followed military and political events with keen interest. At his request, the priest in church prayed for the success of the Russian and Allied armies, and when the priest offered a prayer for the Provisional Government, Nicholas fervently crossed himself. Above all, he was anxious that the army be kept disciplined and strong and that the country remain faithful to its allies. Having seen with his own eyes the collapse of discipline at the palace, he worried about the decay taking place at the front. Hearing that General Ruzsky had resigned, Nicholas said indignantly, "He [Ruzsky] asked that an offensive be undertaken. The Soldiers' Committee refused. What humilation! We are going to let our allies be crushed and then it will be our turn." The following day, he mellowed and consoled himself. "What gives me a little hope," he said, "is our love of exaggeration. I can't believe that our army at the front is as bad as they say."

Purely in a physical sense, the abdication and imprisonment at Tsarskoe Selo were a blessing for the fearfully weary man whom Nicholas had become. For the first time in twenty-three years, there were no reports to read, no ministers to see, no supreme decisions to make. Nicholas was free to spend his days reading and smoking cigarettes, playing with his children, shoveling snow and walking in the garden. He read the Bible from the beginning. At night, sitting with his wife and daughters, he read aloud to them from the Russian classics. Gently, by example, he tried to make easier for Alexandra the painful transition from empress to prisoner. After the long midnight service on Easter Eve, Nicholas quietly asked the two officers of the guard on duty to join his family for the traditional Easter meal in the library. There, he embraced them, not as prisoner and jailor, but as Russian and Russian, Christian and Christian.

Alexandra, unlike Nicholas, faced the overthrow of the monarchy and the beginning of captivity with deep bitterness. Proud and silent, thinner than ever before, her hair now predominantly gray, she remained most of the day on the sofa in the girls' room. In the evening, she traveled by wheelchair to visit Anna, with Nicholas himself usually pushing the chair. Everything spoke to her of humiliation. Used to filling her rooms with violets, lilies of the valley and hyacinths from the park greenhouses or brought fresh from the Crimea, she was now forbidden these as "luxuries unnecessary for prisoners." Occasionally when a maid or footman brought her a single branch of lilac, the Empress wept in gratitude.

For weeks, Alexandra remained convinced that, despite what had happened in Petrograd, the real Russia—the millions of peasants and the army—remained faithful. Only gradually, with a kind of bitter humor, did she begin to accept reality. Nicholas showed her the way. "He would sometimes laugh at the idea of being what he called 'an Ex,'" said Lili Dehn. Alexandra picked up the expression. "Don't call me an Empress any more—I'm only an Ex," she would say. One day at lunch when an especially unpalatable ham appeared on the table, Nicholas made everyone laugh by shrugging and saying, "Well, this may have once been a ham, but now it's nothing but an ex-ham."

In Petrograd during the weeks after the abdication, feelings mounted against all Romanovs. On March 24, Grand Duke Nicholas, reappointed by the Provisional Government to his old post of Commander-in-Chief of the Armies, arrived to take up his duties at Mogilev only to find a letter from Prince Lvov awaiting him. In the letter, the new Premier asked the Grand Duke to resign, explaining apologetically that "the national feeling is decidedly and insistently against the employment of any members of the House of Romanov in any official position." Rigidly loyal, the Grand Duke immediately acquiesced, handing the command to Alexeiev with the grandiloquent declaration, "I am happy once more to be able to prove my love for my country which so far Russia has not doubted." Then the old soldier retired from the army and retreated to his estate in the Crimea.

Still, the focus of popular hatred was always the Tsar and his family at Tsarskoe Selo. From the moment of abdication, rumors spread through Petrograd that "Citizen Romanov" and his wife, "Alexandra the German," were working secretly to betray the country to the Germans and with their help restore the autocracy. The press, freed of censorship and restraint, rushed into print with lurid tales of Rasputin and the Empress which hitherto had been passed only by word of mouth. The "private lives" of the Tsar's four daughters were written by their "lovers." A Rabelaisian palace dinner menu, described as "typical," was published so that the hungry people of Petrograd could read how "Nikolasha" and his family were gorging themselves: "Caviar, lobster soup, mushroom patties, macaroni, pudding, roast goose, chicken pie, veal cutlets, orange jelly, pork chops, rice pudding, herrings with cucumber, omelet, rissoles in cream, fresh pineapple, sturgeon." Cartoons depicted Nicholas clapping his hands with joy while he watched the hanging of a political prisoner, and Alexandra bathing in a tub filled with blood and saying, "If Nicky killed a few more of these revolutionaries, I could have such a bath more often."

It was at this point, with public opinion thoroughly aroused and the Soviet demanding that Nicholas be thrown into the Fortress, that the Provisional Government placed responsibility for the safety of the Imperial family entirely on Kerensky's shoulders. On April 3, the new warden decided to take a personal look at his prisoners.

He arrived early in the afternoon in one of the Tsar's automobiles driven by a chauffeur from the Imperial Garage. Alighting at the kitchen door, he assembled the soldiers of the guard and the palace servants in a passageway and delivered an impassioned revolutionary speech. The servants, he announced, were now the servants of the people, who paid their salaries, and who expected them to keep a close eye and report everything suspicious that happened in the palace. Next, in the Tsar's waiting room, Kerensky met Benckendorff. "He was dressed in a blue shirt buttoned to the neck, with no cuffs or collar, big boots, and he affected the air of a workman in his Sunday clothes," recalled the Count. ". . . He introduced himself and said, 'I have come here to see how you live, to inspect your Palace and to talk to Nicholas Alexandrovich.' " According to Kerensky, "the old dignitary [Benckendorff] with a monocle in his eye replied that he would put the matter before His Majesty." In the meantime, Benckendorff, knowing that Nicholas and Alexandra were still at lunch with the children, distracted Kerensky by proposing a tour of the palace. Kerensky agreed. "His manner was abrupt and nervous," Benckendorff recalled. "He did not walk but ran through the rooms, talking very loudly. . . . He had the Emperor's private rooms opened; and all the doors, drawers and cupboards searched, and told those who accompanied him to look in every corner and under the furniture." Without saying a word to them, Kerensky went through the rooms of the ladies-in-waiting, who stood and watched him. Eventually, he came to the door of Anna Vyrubova.

Nearly recovered from measles, Anna had been up having lunch with Lili Dehn when the noise and confusion in the palace signaled Kerensky's arrival. In terror, she grabbed a pile of her private papers and threw them into her fire, then jumped into bed and pulled the covers up to her head. As the commotion outside grew louder, Anna, "with an icy hand" upon her heart, whispered to Lili, "They are coming." A moment later, Kerensky entered, noting the fireplace filled with the glowing ash of burning paper. "The room seemed to fill up with men," Anna wrote, "and walking arrogantly before them I beheld a small, clean-shaven, theatrical person whose essentially weak face was disguised in a Napoleonic frown. Standing over me . . . right hand thrust into the bosom of his jacket, the man boomed out, 'I am the Minister of Justice. You are to dress and go at once to Petrograd.' I answered not a word but lay still on my pillows. . . . This seemed to disconcert him somewhat for he turned . . . and said nervously 'Ask the doctors if she is fit to go.'" Botkin and Derevenko were questioned and both declared that, from a medical viewpoint, it would not harm her to leave. Later, Anna bitterly attributed the doctors' decision to "craven fear."

Leaving Anna, Kerensky passed Gilliard's room. Assuming that the Swiss—being a citizen of a republic—was a friend, Kerensky nodded pleasantly and said, "Everything is going well."

By then, Nicholas and Alexandra were ready. Kerensky was conducted to the children's schoolroom, where Benckendorff left him standing before a closed door while he stepped in to announce the new Minister. Then, swinging wide open the double door, the Count announced grandly, "His Majesty bids you welcome." "Kerensky," Benckendorff recalled, "was in a state of feverish agitation; he could not stand still, touched all the objects which were on the table and seemed like a madman. He spoke incoherently."

Kerensky admitted his extreme nervousness: "To be frank I was anything but calm before this first meeting with Nicholas II. Too many hard, terrible things had been connected in the past with his name. . . . All the way along the endless chain of official apartments I was struggling for control over my emotions. . . . [Entering the room] my feelings underwent a lightning change. . . . The Imperial family . . . were standing . . . near the window, around a small table, in a huddled, perplexed little group. From this cluster of frightened humanity, there stepped out somewhat hesitantly, a man of medium height in military kit, who walked forward to meet me with a slight peculiar smile. It was the Emperor . . . he stopped in confusion. He did not know what to do, he did not know how I would act, what attitude I would adopt. Should he walk forward to meet me as a host, or ought he to wait for me to speak first? Should he hold out his hand?

"In a flash, instinctively, I knew the exact position: the family's confusion, its fear at finding itself alone with a revolutionary whose objects in bursting in upon it were unknown. . . . With an answering smile, I hurriedly walked over to the Emperor, shook hands and sharply said, 'Kerensky'—as I always do, by way of introduction. . . . Nicholas II gave my hand a firm grasp, immediately recovering from his confusion, and smiling once again, led me to his family.

"His daughters and the Heir Apparent were obviously burning with curiosity and their eyes were simply glued to me. But Alexandra Fedorovna stood tense and erect—proud, domineering, irreconcilable; she held out her hand to me slowly and unwillingly. . . . When the hand-shaking was over, I inquired after their health [and] told them that their relatives abroad were taking a keen interest in their welfare. . . . [I] told them not to be frightened . . . but to have complete confidence in the Provisional Government. After that the Emperor and I went into the next room where I again assured him that they were safe. . . . He had fully recovered his impressive calm. He asked me about the military situation and wished us success in our difficult new task."

In recalling the events of this day, Kerensky makes no mention of the arrest of Anna Vyrubova and Lili Dehn. Before leaving, both women briefly said goodbye to the Empress. "The last thing I remember," wrote Anna, "was the white hand of the Empress pointing upward and her voice, 'There we are always together.' " Alexandra's last words to Lili were similar: "With a tremendous effort of will, she [Alexandra] forced herself to smile; then, in a voice whose every accent bespoke intense love and deep religious conviction, she said: 'Lili, by suffering, we are purified for Heaven. This goodbye matters little. We shall meet in another world.' " Leaving her pet spaniel Jimmy behind, Anna stumbled on her crutches to the waiting car and climbed in beside Lili. "The car shot forward, and I left the palace at Tsarskoe Selo forever," Anna later wrote. "Both Lili and I pressed our faces to the glass in a last effort to see those beloved we were leaving behind, and through the mist and rain we could just discern a group of white-clad figures crowded close to the nursery windows to see us go. In a moment of time the picture was blotted out and we saw only the wet landscape, the storm-bent trees, the rapidly creeping twilight." In Petrograd, Lili was released the following day, but Anna was sent to spend five chilling months in the Fortress of Peter and Paul.

Six days later, on April 9, Kerensky returned to the palace to begin an investigation of the Empress's "treasonable, pro-German" activities. While the interrogation was under way, he ordered the Empress separated from her husband and children. At once, he ran into a storm of protest from both doctors and ladies-in-waiting, who declared that it was inhuman to separate a mother from her sick children. Kerensky relented and named Nicholas as the parent who would have to live apart. The couple were permitted to meet at prayers and meals, providing an officer was always present and only Russian was spoken.

Although the separation lasted for eighteen days, the investigation was casual and Kerensky learned nothing. His questioning of Alexandra was confined to a single session lasting one hour. As Benckendorff later described it, Kerensky began politely and mildly by asking about "the part the Empress had played in politics, [and] her influence on the Emperor in the choice of ministers whom she often had received in the absence of the Emperor. Her Majesty answered that the Emperor and herself were the most united of couples, whose whole joy and pleasure was in their family life, and that they had no secrets from each other; that they discussed everything, and that it was not astonishing that in the last years which had been so troubled, they had often discussed politics. . . . It was true that they had discussed the different appointments of ministers, but this could not be otherwise in a marriage such as theirs." Benckendorff learned afterward that Alexandra had been impressed by Kerensky's politeness and that Kerensky had been "struck by the clarity, the energy and the frankness of her words." When the Minister came out, he said to the Tsar, who was waiting outside, "Your wife does not lie." Quietly, Nicholas observed that this was scarcely news to him.

Questioning Nicholas, Kerensky learned even less. He asked why the Tsar had changed ministers so frequently, why he had appointed Stürmer and Protopopov and dismissed Sazonov, but Nicholas avoided answering directly and Kerensky quickly let the conversation drop. There was no further discussion of "treason" and Kerensky himself declared to his colleagues in the Provisional Government that the Empress Alexandra had been loyal to Russia.

As time passed and Kerensky continued to visit the palace, the relationship between the socialist minister and the deposed sovereign and his wife markedly improved. "Kerensky's attitude toward the Tsar is no longer what it was at the beginning. . . . [He] has requested the papers to put an end to their campaign against the Tsar and more especially the Empress," Gilliard wrote in his diary on April 25. Kerensky admitted that, during these weeks, he was affected by Nicholas's "unassuming manner and complete absence of pose. Perhaps it was this natural, quite artless simplicity that gave the Emperor that peculiar fascination, that charm which was further increased by his wonderful eyes, deep and sorrowful. . . . It cannot be said that my talks with the Tsar were due to a special desire on his part; he was obliged to see me . . . yet the former Emperor never once lost his equilibrium, never failed to act as a courteous man of the world." On Nicholas's part, Benckendorff noted that "the confidence which the Emperor felt in Kerensky increased still more . . . and the Empress shared this confidence." Nicholas himself declared of Kerensky, "He is not a bad sort. He's a good fellow. One can talk to him." Later, Nicholas was to add, "He [Kerensky] is a man who loves Russia, and I wish I could have known him earlier because he could have been useful to me."

Spring melted the snow, and in the afternoons the family began to go out together into the park. At first, they had to wait in the semicircular entry hall for an officer to come with the key, then file out, the Empress being pushed in her wheelchair, through a gauntlet of gaping, loitering soldiers, many of whom gibed and snickered as they passed. Sometimes, the men did more than mock: when Nicholas got his bicycle and started to pedal along a path, a soldier thrust his bayonet between the spokes. The Tsar fell and the soldiers guffawed.

Yet Nicholas was unfailingly friendly even to those who insulted him. He always said "Good morning" and held out his hand. "Not for anything in the world," declared one soldier, turning his back on the outstretched hand. "But, my dear fellow, why? What have you got against me?" asked Nicholas, genuinely astonished.

The news that the former Tsar and his family were walking under guard in the park attracted crowds who lined the iron fence to watch, whistle and jeer. At one point, an officer of the guard went up to Nicholas and asked him to move to avoid provoking the crowd any further. Nicholas, surprised, replied that he was not afraid and said that "the good people were not annoying him in any way."

The line of guards with fixed bayonets, the restriction of movement to a corner of the park and, especially, the humilation of his father were hard for Alexis to understand and to bear. He had seen his father treated only with respect and reverence, and he blushed with shame whenever an incident occurred. Alexandra, too, flushed deeply when her husband was insulted, but she learned to keep silent. When the weather was fine, she sat near the pond on a rug spread beneath a tree. Usually, she was surrounded by a ring of curious soldiers. Once when Baroness Buxhoeveden, who had been sitting next to the Empress, got up, one of the men dropped with a belligerent grunt onto the rug beside Alexandra. "The Empress edged a little bit away," wrote the Baroness, "making a sign to me to be silent, for she was afraid that the whole family would be taken home and the children robbed of an hour's fresh air. The man seemed to her not to have a bad face, and she was soon engaged in conversation with him. At first he cross-questioned her, accusing her of 'despising' the people, of showing by not travelling about that she did not want to know Russia. Alexandra Fedorovna quietly explained to him that, as in her young days she had had five children and nursed them all herself, she had not had time to go about the country and that, afterwards, her health had prevented her. He seemed to be struck by this reasoning and, little by little, he grew more friendly. He asked the Empress about her life, about her children, her attitude towards Germany, etc. She answered in simple words that she had been a German in her youth, but that that was long past. Her husband and her children were Russians and she was a Russian, too, now, with all her heart. When I came back with the officer . . . to whom I had risked appealing, fearing that the soldier might annoy the Empress, I found them peacefully discussing questions of religion. The soldier got up on our approach, and took the Empress's hand, saying, 'Do you know, Alexandra Fedorovna, I had quite a different idea of you. I was mistaken about you."

In May, a new officer assumed command of the Tsarskoe Selo garrison. Colonel Eugene Kobylinsky was a thirty-nine-year-old veteran of the Petrograd Life Guards who had twice been wounded at the front and then reassigned to one of the hospitals at Tsarskoe Selo. Kobylinsky was not a revolutionary, simply an officer doing the duty assigned him by General Kornilov. Although in name he was their jailer, in fact Kobylinsky was deeply loyal to the Imperial family and, during the twelve months that he was with them, did much to buffer them from shocks. Nicholas well understood Kobylinsky's situation, and from Siberia he wrote to his mother that Kobylinsky was "my last friend."

There were limits, however, to what any officer could do with the obstreperous soldiery, and unpleasant incidents continued to happen. In June, Alexis was playing outside with the toy rifle which he had played with in the garden at *Stavka.* Suddenly, the soldiers spotted the gun and began to shout to each other, "They are armed." Alexis, hearing the hubbub, went to this mother, who was sitting on the grass. A minute later, the soldiers arrived and demanded "the weapon." Gilliard tried to intervene and explain that the gun was a toy, but the soldiers insisted and walked off with the gun. Alexis, in tears, looked from the Empress to the tutor; both were helpless. The gun was turned over to Colonel Kobylinsky, who was furious that his men had bothered the child. Carefully, he took the gun apart and, carrying it under his coat, returned it piece by piece to the Tsarevich. Thereafter, Alexis played with his rifle only behind the door of his room.

Despite harassment and humiliation, the family continued to go out every day, happy for the chance to spend time in the fresh air. In the middle of May, they began digging up part of the park lawn to plant a vegetable garden. Together, they carried the grassy sod away, turned the soil, planted the seeds and brought water in tubs from the kitchen. Many of the servants helped; so did some of the soldiers, who discovered more pleasure in working beside the Tsar than in mocking him. In June, once the seeds were in, Nicholas turned to sawing up the dead trees in the park for firewood. Soon, piles of wood, neatly stacked, began to appear all over the park.

At night, tired from this exercise, the family sat quietly together before going to bed. One stifling evening in July, he was reading to the Empress and his daughters when an officer and two soldiers burst into the room shouting excitedly that a sentry in the park had seen someone signaling from the open window by flashing red and green lights. The men searched the room and found nothing. Despite the heat, the officer ordered the heavy curtains to be pulled shut—and at this moment the mystery was unraveled. Anastasia had been sitting in a window ledge doing needlework as she listened to her father. As she moved, bending to pick things up from a table, she had covered and uncovered two lamps, one with a red and the other with a green shade.

Harmless in themselves, these incidents revealed the underlying tension which prevailed at Tsarskoe Selo. Day and night, the sentries paced their rounds, believing that at any moment a rescue attempt might be made, for which, if successful, they would be held responsible. The prisoners waited inside the palace, living from day to day, uncertain as to who and where were friends, wondering whether the following morning would find them released or flung into a Soviet dungeon.

From the beginning, they most expected to be sent abroad. This was what every representative of the Provisional Government—Guchkov, Kornilov and Kerensky—had promised; that they would be powerless to keep this promise, no one could know. "Our captivity at Tsarskoe Selo did not seem likely to last long," said Gilliard, "and there was talk about our imminent transfer to England. Yet the days passed and our departure was always being postponed. . . . We were only a few hours by railway from the Finnish frontier, and the necessity of passing through Petrograd was the only serious obstacle. It would thus appear that if the authorities had acted resolutely and secretly it would not have been difficult to get the Imperial family to one of the Finnish ports and thus to some foreign country. But they were afraid of responsibilities, and no one dared compromise himself."

CHAPTER THIRTY-ONE

"His Majesty's Government Does Not Insist"

GILLIARD could not have known it, but, from the earliest days of the revolution, an overriding preoccupation of the Provisional Government had been to get the Tsar and his family to safety. "The former Emperor and the Imperial family were no longer political enemies but simply human beings who had come under our protection. We regarded any display of revengefulness as unworthy of Free Russia," said Kerensky. In keeping with this spirit, the new government had immediately abolished capital punishment in Russia. As Minister of Justice, Kerensky initiated this law, partly because he knew it would help forestall demands for the Tsar's execution. Stubbornly, Nicholas objected to the law. "It's a mistake. The abolition of the death penalty will ruin the discipline of the army," said the Tsar. "If he [Kerensky] is abolishing it to save me from danger, tell him that I am ready to give my life for the good of my country." Nevertheless, Kerensky held to his view. On March 20, he appeared in Moscow before the Moscow Soviet of Workers' Deputies and listened to an angry cacophony of cries for the Tsar's execution. Boldly, Kerensky replied, "I will not be the Marat of the Russian Revolution. I will take the Tsar to Murmansk myself. The Russian Revolution does not take vengeance."

Murmansk was the gateway to England and it was to England that all of Kerensky's fellow ministers hoped that the Tsar could be sent. As early as March 19, while Nicholas was still with his mother at *Stavka,* Paul Miliukov, the new Foreign Minister, was saying anxiously, "He should lose no time in getting away." On the 21st, when Buchanan and Paléologue confronted Miliukov with the news of the

Tsar's arrest at Mogilev, Miliukov eagerly explained that Nicholas had simply been "deprived of his liberty" in order to ensure his safety. Buchanan officially reminded Miliukov that Nicholas was a relative of King George V of England, who was expressing a strong interest in his cousin's welfare. Seizing upon the relationship, Miliukov agreed that the Tsar must be saved and begged Buchanan to wire London immediately asking for asylum for the Imperial family. Imploring Buchanan to hurry, he explained, "It's the last chance of securing these poor unfortunates' freedom and perhaps of saving their lives."

Buchanan was equally concerned, and the following day his urgent telegram was placed before the British War Cabinet. At the head of the table at 10 Downing Street sat the Liberal Prime Minister, David Lloyd George. The fiery Welshman had little sympathy for the Russian autocracy. In a famous speech made in August 1915, he had thundered grim approval of Russia's terrible defeats: "The Eastern sky is dark and lowering. The stars have been clouded over. I regard that stormy horizon with anxiety but with no dread. Today I can see the colour of a new hope beginning to empurple the sky. The enemy in their victorious march know not what they are doing. Let them beware, for they are unshackling Russia. With their monster artillery they are shattering the rusty bars that fettered the strength of the people of Russia."

When Imperial Russia fell, Lloyd George exuberantly telegraphed the Provisional Government: "It is with sentiments of the profoundest satisfaction that the people of Great Britain . . . have learned that their great ally Russia now stands with the nations which base their institutions upon responsible government. . . . We believe that the Revolution is the greatest service which they [the Russian people] have yet made to the cause for which the Allied peoples have been fighting since August 1914. It reveals the fundamental truth that this war is at bottom a struggle for popular Government as well as for liberty."

In his own heart, Lloyd George was highly reluctant to permit the deposed Tsar and his family to come to England. Nevertheless, he and his ministers agreed that, as the request for asylum had come not from the Tsar but from Britain's new ally, the Provisional Government, it could not be refused. Buchanan was signaled that Britain would receive Nicholas but that the Russian government would be expected to pay his bills.

On March 23, Buchanan carried this message to Miliukov. Pleased but increasingly anxious—the unauthorized descent on Tsarskoe Selo by armored cars filled with soldiers had occurred the day before—Miliukov assured the Ambassador that Russia would make a generous financial allowance for the Imperial family. He begged, however, that Buchanan not reveal that the Provisional Government had taken the initiative in making the arrangement. If the Soviet knew, he explained, the project was doomed.

But the Soviet, rigidly hostile to the idea of the Tsar leaving Russia, already knew. Kerensky had told them, in Moscow, that he would personally escort the Imperial family to a British ship. On March 22—the same day that Nicholas returned to his family, that Rasputin's corpse was disinterred, that the British Cabinet decided to offer asylum—the chairman of the Petrograd Soviet was shouting hoarsely, "The Republic must be safeguarded against the Romanovs returning to the historical arena. That means that the dangerous persons must be directly in the hands of the Petrograd Soviet." Telegrams were wired to all towns along the railways leading from Tsarskoe Selo with instructions to the workers to block the passage of the Tsar's train. At the same time, the Soviet resolved that the Tsar should be taken from Tsarskoe Selo, properly arrested and clapped into the bastion of the Fortress of Peter and Paul until the time of his trial and execution. The fact that this last resolution was never carried out was attributed by one scornful Bolshevik writer to the domination of the Soviet at that point by irresolute Mensheviks and Social Revolutionaries.

For the moment, the question of the Tsar's fate became a stand-off between the Soviet and the Provisional Government. The Soviet lacked the strength to penetrate the Alexander Palace and simply drag the family off to the Fortress. The government, on the other hand, was not sufficiently master of the country, and especially of the railways, to embark on an enterprise such as moving Nicholas to Murmansk. This journey, from Tsarskoe Selo, south of the capital, through the heart of Petrograd, meant running the very real risk that the train would be stopped, the Imperial family pulled off and carted away to the Fortress or worse.

Unwilling to take this risk, Kerensky, Miliukov and their colleagues decided to postpone the trip until the psychological atmosphere improved. In the meantime, they appeased the Soviet. On the 24th, the day after the British offer of asylum arrived, the Provisional Government pledged to the Soviet that the deposed sovereigns would remain in Russia. On the 25th, Miliukov informed Buchanan that he could not even deliver to the Tsar a personal telegram from King George which declared harmlessly, "Events of last week have deeply distressed me. My thoughts are constantly with you and I shall always remain your true and devoted friend, as you know I always have been in the past." When Buchanan argued that the telegram had no political significance, Miliukov replied that he understood this, but that others would misinterpret it as part of a plot to escape. The only indication Nicholas and Alexandra ever had of this telegram was Kerensky's comment during his first visit to Tsarskoe Selo that the King and Queen of England were asking for news of their Russian relatives.

Days passed and the impasse remained. On April 2, Buchanan wrote to the Foreign Office, "Nothing has yet been decided about the Emperor's journey to England." On April 9, Buchanan talked to Kerensky, who declared that the Tsar's departure would be delayed for several more weeks while his papers were examined and he and his wife were questioned. In England, meanwhile, the news that asylum had been offered had been received coldly by the Labor Party and many Liberals. As opposition to the invitation began to mount, the British government began backing away. On April 10, a semi-official Foreign Office statement coolly announced that "His Majesty's Government does not insist on its former offer of hospitality to the Imperial family."

On April 15, even Buchanan began to withdraw his support for asylum, explaining to London that the Tsar's presence in England might easily be used by the extreme Left in Russia "as an excuse for rousing public opinion against us." He suggested that perhaps Nicholas might be received in France. Hearing this, Lord Francis Bertie, the British Ambassador in Paris, wrote a scathing personal letter to the Foreign Secretary, brimming with vicious misinformation about the Empress Alexandra. "I do not think that the ex-Emperor and his family would be welcome in France," wrote Bertie. "The Empress is not only a Boche by birth but in sentiment. She did all she could to bring about an understanding with Germany. She is regarded as a criminal or a criminal lunatic and the ex-Emperor as a criminal from his weakness and submission to her promptings. Yours ever, Bertie."

From April until June, the plan remained suspended. Kerensky admitted later that, during this period, the suspension had nothing to do with the views of English Liberals and Laborites but was determined by the internal political situation in Russia. By early summer, however, conditions in Russia had changed and the moment seemed ripe for a discreet transfer of the Imperial family to Murmansk. Once again, the Russian government approached England on the matter of asylum.

"[We] inquired of Sir George Buchanan as to when a cruiser could be sent to take on board the deposed ruler and his family," said Kerensky. "Simultaneously, a promise was obtained from the German Government through the medium of the Danish minister, Skavenius, that German submarines would not attack the particular warship which carried the Royal exiles. Sir George Buchanan and ourselves were impatiently awaiting a reply from London. I do not remember exactly whether it was late in June or early in July when the British ambassador called, greatly distressed. . . . With tears in his eyes, scarcely able to control his emotions, Sir George informed . . . [us] of the British Government's final refusal to give refuge to the former Emperor of Russia. I cannot quote the exact text of the letter. . . . But I can say definitely that this refusal was due exclusively to considerations of internal British politics." Apparently, Bertie's letter from Paris had done its poisonous work, for Kerensky remembers the letter explaining that "the Prime Minister was unable to offer hospitality to people whose pro-German sympathies were well-known."

Subsequently, confusion, accusations and a sense of guilt appeared to permeate the recollections of all those involved in this inglorious episode. Both Sir George Buchanan and Lloyd George flatly contradicted Kerensky, insisting that Britain's offer of asylum was never withdrawn and that the failure of the project was solely due to the fact that the Provisional Government—in Buchanan's words—"were not masters in their house." Meriel Buchanan, the Ambassador's daughter, later overrode her father's account, explaining that he had offered it in order to protect Lloyd George, who was responsible for the refusal. She recalled that a telegram refusing to let the Tsar come to England did arrive in Petrograd on April 10; she remembered the words her father used and the anguished expression on his face as he described the telegram. Lloyd George did not respond formally to her charge, but she noted that the former Prime Minister "is reported to have said in an interview that he does not remember refusing the late Emperor admission to England, but that, if the matter had been considered, he probably would have given such advice." In his memoirs, Lloyd George left no doubt of his lack of sympathy for Imperial

Russia or its Tsar. The Russian Empire, he said, was "an unseaworthy Ark. The timbers were rotten and most of the crew not much better. The captain was suited for a pleasure yacht in still waters, and his sailing master had been chosen by his wife, reclining in the cabin below." Nicholas he dismissed as "only a crown without a head . . . the end was tragedy . . . but for that tragedy this country cannot be in any way held responsible."

King George's attitude on the matter vacillated. At first, he wanted to help his relatives, but by March 30, his private secretary was writing to the Foreign Secretary, "His Majesty cannot help doubting not only on account of the dangers of the voyage, but on general grounds of expediency, whether it is advisable that the Imperial family should take up their residence in this country." By April 10, the King was concerned about the widespread indignation felt in England against the Tsar. He realized that if Nicholas came to England he would be obliged to receive his cousin, an act which would bring considerable unpopularity down on him. Accordingly, he suggested to Lloyd George that, because of the outburst of public opinion, the Russian government should perhaps be informed that Britain was obliged to withdraw its offer.

Later, of course, when the murder of the Imperial family had outraged the King, memories tended to blur. "The Russian Revolution of 1917 with the murder of the Tsar Nicholas II and his family had shaken my father's confidence in the innate decency of mankind," recalled the Duke of Windsor. "There was a very real bond between him and his first cousin, Nicky. . . . Both wore beards of a distinctive character and as young men, they had looked much alike. . . . It has long been my impression that, just before the Bolsheviks seized the Tsar, my father had personally planned to rescue him with a British cruiser, but in some way the plan was blocked. In any case, it hurt my father that Britain had not raised a hand to save his cousin Nicky. 'Those politicians,' he used to say. 'If it had been one of their kind, they would have acted fast enough. But merely because the poor man was an emperor—' "

In Switzerland, Lenin's first reaction to the revolution in Russia was skepticism. Only seven weeks had passed since his statement on January 22, 1917, that "we older men may not live to see the decisive battles of the approaching revolution." Even the news of the Tsar's abdication and the establishment of a Provisional Government left him with reservations. In his view, the replacement of an autocracy by a bourgeois republic was not a genuine proletarian revolution; it was simply the substitution of one capitalist system for another. The fact that Miliukov and the Provisional Government intended to continue the war confirmed in his mind that they were no more than tools of Britain and France, which were capitalist, imperialist powers. On March 25, Lenin telegraphed instructions to the Bolsheviks in Petrograd, "Our tactics: absolute distrust, no support of the new government, Kerensky especially suspect, no rapprochement with the other parties."

Lenin became desperate to reach Russia himself. "From the moment the news of the revolution came, Ilyich did not sleep and at night all sorts of incredible plans were made," Krupskaya recalled. "We could travel by airplane. But such things could be thought of only in the semi-delirium of the night." He considered donning a wig and traveling via France, England and the North Sea, but there was the chance of arrest or of being torpedoed by a U-boat. Suddenly, through the German minister in Berne, it was arranged that he should travel through Germany itself to Sweden, Finland and then to Russia. The German motive in this bizarre arrangement was sheer military necessity. Germany had gained little from the fall of tsarism, as the Provisional Government meant to continue the war. Germany needed a regime which would make peace. This Lenin promised to do. Even if he failed, the Germans knew that his presence inside Russia would create turmoil. Accordingly, on April 9, Lenin, Krupskaya and seventeen other Bolshevik exiles left Zurich to cross Germany in a "sealed" train. "The German leaders," said Winston Churchill, "turned upon Russia the most grisly of all weapons. They transported Lenin in a sealed truck like a plague bacillus from Switzerland into Russia."

On the night of April 16, after ten years away from Russia, Lenin arrived in Petrograd at the Finland Station. He stepped from his train into a vast crowd and a sea of red banners. In an armored car, he drove to Mathilde Kschessinska's mansion, which had been commandeered as Bolshevik headquarters. From the dancer's balcony, he addressed a cheering crowd, shouting to them that the war was "shameful imperialist slaughter."

Although Lenin had been welcomed with the blaring triumph due a returning prophet, neither the Petrograd Soviet as a whole nor the Bolshevik minority within the Soviet were by any means ready to accept all of his dogma. In the early days of the revolution, the Social Revolutionaries and Mensheviks who dominated the Soviet believed that some degree of cooperation should be shown the Provisional Government, if only to prevent the restoration of the monarchy. Besides, Marxist theory called for a transitional period between the overthrow of absolutism and the dictatorship of the proletariat. The Soviet might argue whether Nicholas belonged in his palace or in a cell, but its over-all policy was to support the policies of the Provisional Government "insofar as they correspond to the interests of the proletariat and of the broad masses of the people." Even some Bolsheviks supported this program.

Lenin would have none of this. Speaking to the All-Russian Conference of Soviets on the morning after his return, he issued his famous April Theses, demanding overthrow of the Provisional Government, the abolition of the police, the army and the bureaucracy. Most important, he demanded an end to the war and urged the troops at the front to begin fraternizing with the enemy. Amazement and consternation greeted Lenin's words; he was interrupted in the middle of his speech by shouts, laughter and cries of "That is raving! That is the raving of a lunatic!" Even Molotov, who had remained one of the Bolshevik leaders in Petrograd, and Stalin, who returned on March 26 from three years' exile in Siberia, were caught off guard. *Pravda*, the Bolshevik newspaper which they had been editing, had been agreeing that a protracted period of bourgeois government was necessary before proceeding to the final stage of the socialist revolution. Lenin's enemies hastened to gibe. He had been away too long, they said, living comfortably in exile; he had taken no part in the overthrow of tsarism; he had been transported back to Russia under the protection of the most autocratic and imperialistic regime remaining in Europe. As word got around that the Soviet had disowned him, the Provisional Government was vastly relieved. "Lenin was a hopeless failure with the Soviet yesterday," said Miliukov gleefully on April 18. "He was compelled to leave the room amidst a storm of booing. He will never survive it."

Yet Lenin scarcely noticed his defeat. A brilliant dialectician, prepared to argue all night, he gained ascendancy over his Bolshevik colleagues by sheer force of intellect and physical stamina. On May 17, Trotsky, who had been living on East 162nd Street in New York City and writing for *Novy Mir*, an émigré Russian newspaper, while studying the American economy in the New York Public Library, returned to Petrograd. Nominally a Menshevik, within weeks of his return he and Lenin were working together. Of the two, Lenin was leader.

Through the spring and summer, Lenin hammered away at the Provisional Government. The Marxian subtleties of the April Theses were laid aside; for the masses, the Bolsheviks coined an irresistible slogan combining the two deepest desires of the Russian people: "Peace, Land, All Power to the Soviet." In May, when Miliukov once again proclaimed that Russia would honor its obligations and continue to fight, a massive public outcry forced him from office. Guchkov also resigned and, early in July, Prince Lvov decided that he could no longer continue as Prime Minister. Kerensky became simultaneously Prime Minister and Minister of War.

In constantly urging that Russia continue to fight, Russia's allies played directly into Lenin's hands. Terrified that Russia's withdrawal from the war would release dozens of enemy divisions for use in the west, Britain, France and the newly belligerent United States exerted heavy pressure on the shaky Provisional Government. Beginning in June, the U.S. government extended loans of $325 million to the Provisional Government. But Elihu Root, who led President Wilson's mission to Russia, made clear that the terms were: "No war, no loan."

Pressed by the Allies, the Provisional Government began to prepare another offensive. Kerensky made a personal tour of the front to exhort the soldiers. In early July, Russian artillery opened a heavy bombardment along forty miles of the Galician front. For the first time, supplies and munitions were plentiful, and the thirty-one Russian divisions attacking the Austrians quickly broke through. For two weeks, they advanced while Kerensky exulted and Nicholas, at Tsarskoe Selo, radiated happiness and ordered *Te Deums* to celebrate the victories. Then, on July 14, the news darkened. German reserves arrived and checked the advance. On the Russian side, Soldiers' Committees debated the wisdom of further attacks and whole divisions refused to move. When the enemy counterattacked, there was no resistance. The Russian retreat became a rout.

In Petrograd, news of the debacle provided the spark for an atmosphere already electrically charged. On July 16, half a million people marched through the streets carrying huge scarlet banners proclaiming "Down with the War!" "Down with the Provisional Government!" Lenin and the Bolsheviks were not prepared for the rising, and the Provisional Government crushed it, mainly by circulating among the loyal regiments a document purporting to prove that Lenin was a German agent and that the uprising was intended to betray Russia from the rear while the Germans advanced at the front. The disclosure was temporarily effective. The Bolshevik strongholds—Kschessinka's house, the offices of *Pravda*, the Fortress of Peter and Paul—were stormed and occupied. Trotsky gave himself up to the police, and Lenin, after spending the night hidden in a haystack, escaped over the border into Finland disguised as a fireman on a locomotive. The first Bolshevik uprising, later known as "the July uprising," was over. Admitting that it had been halfhearted, Lenin was to describe it later as "something considerably more than a demonstration but less than a revolution."

Despite his narrow victory, the rising made plain to Kerensky the danger of any further delay in moving the Imperial family away from Petrograd. Even before the rising, the new Prime Minister had come to warn Nicholas, "The Bolsheviks are after me and then will be after you." He suggested that the family would be safer in some distant part of Russia, far from the seething revolutionary passions of the capital. Nicholas asked if they might go to Livadia. Kerensky replied that Livadia might be possible, but he explained that he was also investigating a number of other spots. He suggested that the family begin packing in secret to avoid arousing the suspicions of the palace guard.

The thought that they might soon be leaving for Livadia was a tonic to the family's spirits. In their excitement, they talked openly about it until Benckendorff begged them to keep silent. Yet, as Kerensky weighed the advantages and disadvantages of the Crimea, it became increasingly obvious that it could not be managed. It was remote, the Tartar population was favorable and many of the Tsar's relatives, including the Dowager Empress, were already there, but it was a thousand miles away across the breadth of Russia. To reach Livadia, a train would have to pass through densely populated industrial towns and rural provinces where a revolutionary peasantry was already terrorizing landlords and expropriating land. Under these conditions, Kerensky felt no greater certainty that he could safely deliver his prisoners to Livadia than that he could place them aboard a British cruiser in Murmansk. The same considerations ruled out the country estate of Grand Duke Michael near Orel in central Russia, which Kerensky himself was inclined to favor.

Eventually, by elimination, he settled on Tobolsk, a commercial river town in western Siberia. The choice had nothing to do with a vengeful poetic justice. Rather, it was a matter of security on the railways. The Northern Route across the Urals to Siberia passed through wide expanses of virgin forest, with towns and villages thinly scattered along the track. Once in Tobolsk, the Imperial family would be relatively safe. "I chose Tobolsk," Kerensky later explained, "because it was an out-and-out backwater . . . had a very small garrison, no industrial proletariat, and a population which was prosperous and contented, not to say old-fashioned. In addition . . . the climate was excellent and the town could boast a very passable Governor's residence where the Imperial family could live with some measure of comfort."

On August 11, Kerensky returned to the palace and, without telling Nicholas where he was being taken, warned that they would leave within a few days and should take plenty of warm clothes. Nicholas immediately understood that their destination was not to be Livadia. When Kerensky, embarrassed, began to explain vociferously why the family's safety required this decision, Nicholas interrupted him with a penetrating look. "I have no fear. We trust you," he said quietly. "If you say we must move, it must be. We trust you," he repeated.

Preparations went ahead rapidly. The Tsar and the Empress chose the people they wanted to accompany them: Countess Hendrikov and Prince Dolgoruky as lady- and gentleman-in-waiting; Dr. Botkin; and Pierre Gilliard and Mlle. Schneider, the tutors. Baroness Buxhoeveden was to remain behind for an operation and would join the family in Tobolsk. To his immense regret, Count Benckendorff had to remain behind because of his wife's severe bronchitis. Asked whom he wished to replace the Count, Nicholas named General Tatishchev, an aide-de-camp. Without hesitation, Tatishchev packed a small suitcase and reported to the palace.

August 12 was the Tsarevich's thirteenth birthday, and at the Empress's request a holy icon was brought for the celebration from the Church of Our Lady of Znamenie. The icon arrived in a procession of clergy from the village which was admitted to the palace, proceeded to the chapel and there asked prayers for the safe journey of the Imperial family. "The ceremony was poignant . . . all were in tears," wrote Benckendorff. "The soldiers themselves seemed touched and approached the holy icon to kiss it. [Afterward, the family] followed the procession as far as the balcony, and saw it disappear through the park. It was as if the past were taking leave, never to come back."

The following day, August 13, 1917, was the last which Nicholas and Alexandra were to spend at Tsarskoe Selo. Through the day, the children rushed excitedly about, saying goodbye to the servants, their belongings and their favorite island in the pond. Nicholas carefully instructed Benckendorff to see that the vegetables they had raised and the piles of sawed wood were fairly distributed among the servants who helped with the work.

Within the government, Kerensky's plan had been kept a successful secret. Only four men including the Premier knew about the transfer to Tobolsk. The subject was never discussed at Cabinet meetings; Kerensky managed all the details by himself. On the night of departure, Kerensky left a Cabinet meeting at eleven p.m. to supervise the final arrangements. His first task was to speak to the troops selected to act as guards when the family reached Tobolsk. For this assignment, three companies—six officers and 330 men—had been culled from the 1st, 2nd and 4th Regiments of Sharpshooter Guards on duty at Tsarskoe Selo. Most of the men selected were noncommissioned officers who had been at the front. Many had been decorated for bravery. On Kerensky's orders, they had been issued new uniforms and new rifles and told that they would receive special pay. Despite these blandishments, some of the men were reluctant to go. Through the barracks ran a current of restlessness, grumbling and uncertainty.

With Colonel Kobylinsky, who was to command the detachment, Kerensky made for the barracks, gathered the new guard around him and addressed them persuasively: "You have guarded the Imperial family here; now you must guard it at Tobolsk where it is being transferred by order of the Provisional Government. Remember: no hitting a man when he is down. Behave like gentlemen, not like cads. Remember that he is a former Emperor and that neither he nor his family must suffer any hardships." Kerensky's oratory worked. The men, partially shamed, prepared to leave. The Prime Minister then wrote a document for Kobylinsky which said simply: "Colonel Kobylinsky's orders are to be obeyed as if they were my own. Alexander Kerensky."

By evening, the family had finished packing and was ready to leave except for trunks and chests scattered through the palace. Fifty soldiers, ordered to pick up the baggage and assemble it in the semicircular hall, flatly refused to work for nothing. Benckendorff, disgusted, eventually agreed to pay them three roubles each.

In the middle of these preparations, as the semicircular hall was filling with trunks and suitcases, Grand Duke Michael arrived to say goodbye to his older brother. Kerensky, who had arranged the meeting, entered the Tsar's study with the Grand Duke and watched the brothers embrace. Not wishing to leave them completely alone, he retreated to a table and began thumbing through the Tsar's scrapbook. He overheard the awkward conversation: "The brothers . . . were most deeply moved. For a long time they were silent . . . then they plunged into that fragmentary, irrelevant small-talk which is so characteristic of short meetings. How is Alix? How is Mother? Where are you living now? and so on. They stood opposite each other, shuffling their feet in curious embarrassment, sometimes getting hold of one another's arm or coat button."

The Tsarevich, nervous and excited, had spotted Michael upon his arrival. "Is that Uncle Misha who has just come?" he asked Kobylinsky. Told that it was, but that he could not go in, Alexis hid behind the door and peeked through a crack. "I want to see him when he goes out," he said. Ten minutes later, Michael walked out of the room in tears. He quickly kissed Alexis goodbye and left the palace.

The night was confused and sleepless. Alexis, holding his excited spaniel Joy on a leash, kept running from the semicircular hall into the family rooms to see what was happening. The Empress, sitting up all night in her traveling clothes, was unable to hide her anxieties. "It was then," wrote Kerensky, "that I first saw Alexandra Fedorovna worried and weeping like any ordinary woman." The soldiers, milling about carrying trunks into the hall and out to the railroad station, kept their caps on and cursed and grumbled at the work they were doing. Their officers sat at a table drinking tea with Countess Benckendorff and the other ladies. When the Tsar approached and asked for a glass, the officers stood up and loudly declared that they would not sit at the same table with Nicholas Romanov. Later, when the soldiers were not looking, most of the officers apologized, explaining that they feared being brought before the soldiers' tribunal and accused of being counterrevolutionaries.

The hours passed, but the train, ordered for one a.m., did not appear. The railwaymen, suspicious and hostile, had refused to shunt the cars together, then refused to couple them. Kerensky himself went repeatedly to telephone the yards. Kobylinsky, exhausted and still unwell, collapsed into a chair and fell asleep. At one point, Benckendorff got Kerensky's attention and asked him before witnesses how long the Imperial family would stay in Tobolsk. Kerensky confidently assured the Count that, once the Constituent Assembly had met in November, Nicholas could freely return to Tsarskoe Selo or go anywhere he wished. Undoubtedly, Kerensky was sincere. But in November he himself was a fugitive from the Bolsheviks.

Between five and six a.m., the waiting group at last heard the blare of automobile horns in the courtyard. Kerensky informed Nicholas that the train was ready and the baggage loaded. The family entered the automobiles, and the little procession was surrounded by a mounted escort of Cossacks. As they left the palace grounds, the early-morning sun cast its first rays on the sleeping village. The train, wearing Japanese flags and bearing placards proclaiming "Japanese Red Cross Mission," was standing on a siding outside the station. The family walked beside the track to the first car, where, for lack of steps, the men lifted Alexandra, her daughters and the other women onto the car platform. As soon as all were aboard, the train began moving eastward, toward Siberia.

CHAPTER THIRTY-TWO

Siberia

If the train which Kerensky provided for the Tsar's journey to Siberia was not of Imperial quality, it was nevertheless a luxurious vehicle for the transfer of prisoners. It consisted of comfortable *wagon-lits* of the International Sleeping Car Company, a restaurant car stocked with wines from the Imperial cellar, and baggage compartments filled with favorite rugs, pictures and knickknacks from the palace. In their portable jewel chests, the Empress and her daughters brought personal gems worth at least a million roubles ($500,000). In addition to the ladies and gentlemen of their suite, the Imperial family was accompanied to Siberia by two valets, six chambermaids, ten footmen, three cooks, four assistant cooks, a butler, a wine steward, a nurse, a clerk, a barber and two pet spaniels. Colonel Kobylinsky also rode aboard the Tsar's train, while most of his 330 soldiers followed on a second train.

The train routine deferred entirely to the established habits of the Imperial family: breakfast at eight, morning coffee at ten, lunch at one, tea at five and dinner at eight. Between six and seven every evening, the train came to a stop in open country so that Nicholas and the children could walk the dogs for half an hour along the track. Alexandra did not attempt these excursions. She sat fanning herself in the heat by an open window and was delighted one afternoon when a soldier reached up and handed her a cornflower.

For four days, the train rolled eastward, clicking monotonously over the rails through the heat and dust of European Russia. The passengers saw no one. At every village, the station was surrounded by troops, the blinds in the coaches were drawn and no one was permitted to show himself at the window. Only once was the train forced to halt by curious local officials. At Perm, on the edge of the Urals, a tall, white-bearded man entered Kobylinsky's compartment, introduced himself as head of the railroad workmen in that district and said that the comrades wanted to know who was on the train. Kobylinsky produced his paper bearing Kerensky's signature, and the workers immediately stood aside.

On the evening of the third day, as the train was crossing the Urals, the air grew noticeably cooler. East of this low range of forested hills lay the beginnings of the Siberian steppe. From the windows of the puffing, rattling train, the Empress and her children saw for the first time the meadowland stretching to the horizon. In late afternoon, the immense dome of sky overhead turned bright crimson and gold as the last rays of sunset glowed on the white trunks of the birches and the green stems of marsh grasses.

Near midnight on August 17, the train crawled slowly into Tyumen on the Tura River. At a dock across from the station, the river steamer *Rus* was waiting. Tobolsk lay two hundred miles to the northeast, a two-day journey on the Tura and Tobol rivers. Nicholas spent the voyage pacing the steamer's upper deck and staring at the villages scattered along the bare river shores. One of these villages was Pokrovskoe, Rasputin's home. As Pokrovskoe glided past, the family gathered on deck to look. They saw a prosperous village with flowers in the windowboxes and cows and pigs in the barnyards. Rasputin's house was unmistakable: two stories tall, it loomed above the simple peasant huts. The passengers were fascinated to see this remote but famous hamlet. Long before, Rasputin had predicted to the Empress that one day she would visit his village. He had not foretold the circumstances, and the family accepted this glimpse as a fulfillment of the prophecy.

Before sunset on the afternoon of the second day, the boat rounded a bend in the river and the passengers saw the silhouette of the old Tobolsk fortress and the onion bulbs of the city's churches. At dusk, the steamer docked at the wharf of the West Siberian Steamship and Trading Company, and Kobylinsky went ashore to inspect the governor's house, where the prisoners would live. He found the house dilapidated and bare of furnishings. The following morning, postponing the family's occupancy, he hired painters and paperers and bought furniture and a piano from stores and private families in Tobolsk. Electricians were summoned to improve the wiring, and plumbers came to install bathtubs. During the eight days it took to refurbish the house, the family lived aboard the *Rus*. To break the monotony, the steamer made afternoon excursions along the river, stopping so that Nicholas and the children could walk along the bank. Finally, on August 26, the house was ready, and at eight in the morning the Tsar, the Tsarevich and three of the Grand Duchesses walked from the dock to the house along a road lined with soldiers. Alexandra and Tatiana followed in a carriage.

Tobolsk, where the Tsar and his family were to live for the next eight months, lay at the juncture of the Tobol and the mighty Irtysh River. Once it had been an important trading center for fish and furs, a link with the Arctic, which lay farther north. But the builders of the Trans-Siberian Railroad had by-passed Tobolsk, going two hundred miles to the south, through Tyumen. In 1917, Tobolsk was, as Kerensky described it, "a backwater." Its twenty thousand people still lived mostly from trade with the north. In the summer, all transport moved by river steamer; in the winter, when the rivers were frozen, people traveled in sledges along the river ice or paths cut through the snow along the banks. The town itself was a sprawl of whitewashed churches, wooden commercial buildings and log houses scattered along streets thick with dust in the summer. In spring and fall, the dust turned to thick, syrupy mud, and the wooden planks laid down as sidewalks often sank out of sight.

The governor's house, a big, white, two-story structure fringed on each side with second-floor balconies, was the largest residence in town. Still, it was not large enough for the Imperial entourage. The family itself filled up the mansion's second floor, with the four Grand Duchesses sharing a corner room and Nagorny sleeping in a room next to Alexis. Gilliard lived downstairs off the big central drawing room in what had been the governor's study. The remainder of the household lived across the street in a house commandeered from a merchant named Kornilov.

At first, Kobylinsky posted no guards inside the governor's house and allowed the family considerable freedom of movement. On their first morning in Tobolsk, they all walked across the street to see how the suite was settling into the Kornilov house. The soldiers immediately objected to this degree of freedom for prisoners, and Kobylinsky reluctantly authorized the building of a high wooden fence around the house, enclosing a section of a small side street which ran beside the house. Inside this muddy, treeless compound, the family took all its exercise. The suite, on the other hand, was permitted to come and go freely, and when Sidney Gibbs, the Tsarevich's English tutor, arrived from Petrograd, he had no difficulty entering the house and joining the family. Several of the Empress's maids took apartments in town, and Dr. Botkin was even allowed to establish a small medical practice in Tobolsk.

Evening prayer services were held in a corner of the downstairs drawing room which was decorated with icons and lamps. A local priest came in to conduct these prayers, but because there was no consecrated altar he was unable to offer Mass. On September 21, Kobylinsky arranged for the family to begin attending a private early Mass at a nearby church. On these occasions, two lines of soldiers formed in the public garden which lay between the house and the church. As the Imperial family walked between the two lines, people standing behind the soldiers crossed themselves and some dropped to their knees.

As Kerensky had suspected, the people of Tobolsk remained strongly attached to both the symbol and the person of the Tsar. Walking past the governor's house, they removed their caps and crossed themselves. When the Empress appeared to sit in her window, they bowed to her. The soldiers repeatedly had to intervene and break up clusters of people who gathered in the muddy street whenever the Grand Duchesses came out on a balcony. Merchants openly sent gifts of food, nuns from the local convent brought sugar and cakes, and peasant farmers arrived regularly with butter and eggs.

Removed from the inflammatory atmosphere of Petrograd, Colonel Kobylinsky managed to restore some discipline in his men. The soldiers, watching the once august and unapproachable personages walking a few feet away, were surprised to find them a simple, united family. Although the men of the 2nd Regiment remained hostile, the soldiers of the 1st and 4th Regiments warmed, especially to the children. The Grand Duchesses talked often to these men, asking them about their villages and families. Marie quickly learned the names of all the wives and children. To many of the men, Alexis remained "the Heir," an object of special respect and affection. When one favorite section of the 4th Regiment was on duty, Alexis and his father sometimes slipped quietly into the guardhouse to play games with these men.

Kobylinsky remained in sole authority until late in September, when two civilian commissars arrived to take charge of the captives, although Kobylinsky was ordered to keep his command of the military guard. The two commissars, Vasily Pankratov and his deputy, Alexander Nikolsky, both were Social Revolutionaries who had spent years in exile in Siberia. Although they were friends, Pankratov and Nikolsky were opposite in character. Pankratov, a small, earnest man with bushy hair and thick glasses, presented himself formally upon arrival to the Tsar.

"Not wishing to infringe the rules of politeness," he wrote, "I requested the valet of the former Tsar to report my arrival and to state that I wished to see his master. . . .

" 'Good morning,' said Nicholas Alexandrovich, stretching out his hand. 'Did you have a good journey?'

" 'Thank you, yes,' I replied, grasping his hand.

" 'How is Alexander Fedorovich Kerensky?' asked the former Tsar. . . ."

Pankratov asked whether Nicholas was in need of anything.

" 'Could you allow me to saw wood? . . . I like that kind of work.'

" 'Perhaps you would like to have a carpenter's shop? It is more interesting work.'

" 'No, just see that they bring some logs into the yard and give me a saw,' replied Nicholas Alexandrovich.

" 'Tomorrow it shall be done.'

" 'May I correspond with my relatives?'

" 'Certainly. Have you enough books?'

" 'Plenty, but why do we not receive our foreign journals; is this forbidden?'

" 'Probably it is the fault of the post. I shall make enquiries.' "

Pankratov pitied the Tsar and was genuinely fond of the children. Alexis's illness disturbed him, and he sometimes sat, just as Rasputin had done, and spun long stories of his years in Siberia. Once, entering the guardhouse, he was astonished to discover Nicholas and his children sitting and talking to the guards. The Tsar graciously asked Pankratov to sit and join them at the table, but Pankratov, disconcerted by this scene, excused himself and fled.

Nikolsky, tall, with a broad face and thick, uncombed hair, felt differently about the captive family. Rough and unmannered, he bitterly blamed the Tsar personally for his imprisonment and tried in petty ways to even the score. He burst into rooms without knocking and spoke to the prisoners without removing his cap. He liked to offer his hand in apparent innocence and then, seizing the hand proffered in return, squeeze with his bony fingers until his victim winced with pain. As soon as he arrived, Nikolsky announced that the entire Imperial party would have to be photographed for identification. Kobylinsky objected, saying the sentries already knew everyone by sight. Nikolsky flew into a rage, shouting, "We were once ordered by the police to have our pictures taken, full face and profile, and so now their pictures shall be taken." As the pictures were being taken, Alexis peeped to watch, which brought another bellow from the angry Nikolsky. The Tsarevich, who had never been yelled at before, retreated in astonishment. Later, a case of wine for the family arrived from Petrograd. Its appearance in Tobolsk fired a passionate debate among the soldiers on the issue of pampering prisoners. The soldier who accompanied the case from Petrograd declared that it had been packed not only with Kerensky's permission but in Kerensky's presence. Dr. Derevenko pleaded that if the alcohol was not to be given to the Imperial family, he be allowed to take it for use in the city hospital. The arguments were useless; Nikolsky sternly saw his duty. Without being opened, the bottles were dropped into the river.

As old, doctinaire Social Revolutionaries, both Pankratov and Nikolsky believed it their duty to assist the political education of the soldiers. Unfortunately, said Kobylinsky, who watched these proceedings with apprehension, "the result of these lectures was that the soldiers were converted [not to Social Revolutionary principles] but to Bolshevism." There were more complaints about pay and food.

Nevertheless, the family was not markedly affected. They had endured worse treatment at Tsarskoe Selo, and they remained unafraid and hopeful for the future. All of the survivors remarked that, despite the narrow confinement, the peaceful autumn months in Tobolsk were not wholly unpleasant.

In October, the long Siberian winter descended from the Arctic upon Tobolsk. At noon, the sun still shone brightly, but by midafternoon the light had faded, and in the gathering darkness, crisp, heavy frosts formed on the ground. As the days grew shorter, Nicholas's greatest privation was lack of news. Despite Pankratov's assurances, the mail did not arrive regularly, and he depended for information on the blend of rumor and fact which drifted into Tobolsk and appeared in the local newspapers. It was through this medium that he morosely followed the rapid crumbling of Kerensky and the Provisional Government.

Ironically, Kerensky himself had assisted in making this tragedy inevitable. Despite the government's narrow triumph over the July Uprising, General Kornilov, now Commander-in-Chief of the Army, concluded that the government was too weak to resist the growing power of the Bolsheviks. Accordingly, at the end of August, Kornilov ordered a cavalry corps to occupy Petrograd and disperse the Soviet. He proposed to replace the Provisional Government with a military dictatorship, keeping Kerensky in the Cabinet but assuming the dominant role himself. Kerensky, as strongly socialist as he was anti-Bolshevik, resisted Kornilov's Rightist coup by what seemed to him the only means available: he appealed to the Soviet for help. The Bolsheviks responded enthusiastically and began forming the workers into Red Guard battalions. Meanwhile, as part of the arrangement, Kerensky released Trotsky and the other Bolshevik leaders.

As it happened, Kornilov's threat evaporated quickly; his cavalrymen immediately began to fraternize with the militia sent to oppose them. Kerensky then asked the Red Guards to return the weapons they had been issued, and they refused. In September, the Bolsheviks gained a majority within the Petrograd Soviet. From Finland, Lenin urged an immediate lunge for supreme power: "History will not forgive us if we do not take power now . . . to delay is a crime." On October 23, Lenin, in disguise, slipped back into Petrograd to attend a meeting of the Bolshevik Central Committee, which voted 10 to 2 that "insurrection is inevitable and the time fully ripe."

On November 6, the Bolsheviks struck. That day, the cruiser *Aurora*, flying the red flag, anchored in the Neva opposite the Winter Palace. Armed Bolshevik squads occupied the railway stations, bridges, banks, telephone exchanges, post office and other public buildings. There was no bloodshed. The next morning, November 7, Kerensky left the Winter Palace in an open Pierce-Arrow touring car accompanied by another car flying the American flag. Passing unmolested through streets filled with Bolshevik soldiers, he drove south to try to raise help from the army. The remaining ministers of the Provisional Government remained in the Malachite Hall of the Winter Palace, protected by a women's battalion and a troop of cadets. Sitting around a green baize table, filling the ashtrays with cigarette butts, the ministers covered their scratch pads with abstract doodles and drafts of pathetic last-minute proclamations: "The Provisional Government appeals to all classes to support the Provisional Government—" At nine p.m., the *Aurora* fired a single blank shell, and at ten, the women's battalion surrendered. At eleven, another thirty or forty shells whistled across the river from the batteries in the Fortress of Peter and Paul. Only two shells hit the palace, slightly damaging the plaster. Nevertheless, at 2:10 a.m. on November 8, the ministers gave up.

This skirmish was the Bolshevik November Revolution, later magnified in Communist mythology into an epic of struggle and heroism. In fact, life in the capital was largely undisturbed. Restaurants, stores and cinemas on the Nevsky Prospect remained open. Streetcars moved as usual through most of the city, and the ballet performed at the Maryinsky Theatre. On the afternoon of the 7th, Sir George Buchanan walked in the vicinity of the Winter Palace and found "the aspect of the quay was more or less normal." Nevertheless, this flick of Lenin's finger was all that was necessary to finish Kerensky. Unsuccessful in raising help, Kerensky never returned to Petrograd. In May, after months in hiding, he appeared secretly in Moscow, where Bruce Lockhart issued him a false visa identifying him as a Siberian soldier being repatriated home. Three days later, Kerensky left Murmansk to begin fifty years of restless exile. Trotsky later, in exile himself, scornfully wrote Kerensky's political epitaph: "Kerensky was not a revolutionist; he merely hung around the revolution. . . . He had no theoretical preparation, no political schooling, no ability to think, no political will. The place of these qualities was occupied by a nimble susceptibility, an inflammable temperament, and that kind of eloquence which operates neither upon mind or will but upon the nerves." Nevertheless, when Kerensky left, he carried with him the vanishing dream of a humane, liberal, democratic Russia.

From distant Tobolsk, Nicholas followed these events with keen interest. He blamed Kerensky for the collapse of the army in the July offensive and for not accepting Kornilov's help in routing the Bolsheviks. At first, he could not believe that Lenin and Trotsky were as formidable as they seemed; to him, they appeared as outright German agents sent to Russia to corrupt the army and overthrow the government. When these two men whom he regarded as unsavory blackguards and traitors became the rulers of Russia, he was gravely shocked. "I then for the first time heard the Tsar regret his abdication," said Gilliard. "It now gave him pain to see that his renunciation had been in vain and that by his departure in the interests of his country, he had in reality done her an ill turn. This idea was to haunt him more and more."

At first, the Bolshevik Revolution had little practical effect on far-off Tobolsk. Officials appointed by the Provisional Government—including Pankratov, Nikolsky and Kobylinsky—remained in office; the banks and lawcourts remained open doing business as before. Inside the governor's house, the Imperial family had settled into a routine which, although restricted, was almost cozy.

"Lessons begin at nine," the Empress wrote in December to Anna Vyrubova. "Up at noon for religious lessons with Tatiana, Marie, Anastasia, and Alexei. I have a German lesson three times a week with Tatiana and once with Marie. . . . Also I sew, embroider and paint, with spectacles on because my eyes have become too weak to do without them. I read 'good books' a great deal, love the Bible, and from time to time read novels. I am so sad because they are allowed no walks except before the house and behind a high fence. But at least they have fresh air, and we are grateful for anything. He [Nicholas] is simply marvelous. Such meekness while all the time suffering intensely for the country. . . . The others are all good and brave and uncomplaining, and Alexei is an angel. He and I dine a deux and generally lunch so.

". . . One by one all earthly things slip away, houses and possessions ruined, friends vanished. One lives from day to day. But God is in all, and nature never changes. I can see all around me churches. . . and hills, the lovely world. Volkov [her attendant] wheels me in my chair to church across the street . . . some of the people bow and bless us but others don't dare. . . . I feel old, oh, so old, but I am still the mother of this country, and I suffer its pains as my own child's pains and I love it in spite of all its sins and horrors. No one can tear a child from its mother's heart and neither can you tear away one's country, although Russia's black ingratitude to the Emperor breaks my heart. Not that it is the whole country though. God have mercy and save Russia."

A few days later, she wrote again to Anna: "It is bright sunshine and everything glitters with hoarfrost. There are such moonlight nights, it must be ideal on the hills. But my poor unfortunates can only pace up and down the narrow yard. . . . I am knitting stockings for the small one [Alexis]. He asks for a pair as all his are in holes. . . . I make everything now. Father's [the Tsar's] trousers are torn and darned, the girls' under-linen in rags. . . . I have grown quite grey.

Anastasia, to her despair is now very fat, as Marie was, round and fat to the waist, with short legs. I do hope she will grow. Olga and Tatiana are both thin."

In December, the full force of the Siberian winter hit Tobolsk. The thermometer dropped to 68 degress below zero Fahrenheit, the rivers were frozen solid, and no walls or windows could keep out the icy chill. The girls' corner bedroom became, in Gilliard's words, "a real ice house." A fire burned all day in the drawing-room grate, but the temperature inside the house remained 44 degrees. Sitting near the fire, the Empress shivered and suffered from chilblains, with her fingers so stiff she could hardly move her knitting needles.

For Alexis, the winter weather and the family coziness were an exhilarating treat. "Today there are 29 degrees of frost, a strong wind and sunshine," he wrote cheerfully to Anna. "We walked and I went on skees in the yard. Yesterday, I acted with Tatiana and . . . [Gilliard] a French piece. We are now preparing another piece. We have a few good soldiers with whom I play games in their rooms. . . . It is time to go to lunch. . . . Alexis."

Through the winter, the Tsarevich was lively and in excellent health. Despite the cold, he went out every morning, dressed in boots, overcoat and cap, with his father. Usually his sisters, in gray capes and red and blue angora caps, came too. While the Tsar walked back and forth with his fast military step from one side of the yard to the other with his daughters hurrying to keep up, Alexis wandered through the sheds attached to the house, collecting old nails and pieces of string. "You never know when they might be useful," he explained. After lunch, he lay on a sofa while Gilliard read to him. Afterward, he went out again to join his father and sisters in the yard. When he returned, he had his history lesson from his father. At four, tea was served, and afterward, Anastasia wrote to Anna, "We often sit in the windows looking at the people passing and this gives us distraction."

For the four Grand Duchesses, all active and healthy young women —that winter Olga was twenty-two, Tatiana twenty, Marie eighteen and Anastasia sixteen—life in the governor's house was acutely boring. To provide them with entertainment, Gilliard and Gibbs began directing them in scenes from plays. Soon, everybody was eager to participate. Both Nicholas and Alexandra carefully wrote out formal programs, and the Tsar acted the title role of Smirnov in Chekov's *The Bear.* Alexis gleefully joined in, accepting any part, overjoyed to put on a beard and speak in a hoarse basso. Only Dr. Botkin categorically refused to take part on stage, pleading that spectators also were essential. Taking Botkin's reluctance as a challenge, Alexis purposefully set himself to overcome it. After dinner one night, he approached the doctor and said in a serious tone, "I want to talk to you about something, Eugene Sergeievich." Taking Botkin's arm, the boy walked him back and forth through the room, arguing that the part in question was that of an old country doctor and that only Botkin could supply the necessary realism. Botkin broke down and agreed.

After dinner, the little group all huddled near the fire, drinking tea, coffee and hot chocolate, trying to keep warm. Nicholas read aloud while the others played quiet games and the grand duchesses did needlework. "In this atmosphere of family peace," said Gilliard, "we passed the long winter evenings, lost in the immensity of distant Siberia."

At Christmas, the group became especially intimate. "The children were filled with delight. We now felt part of one large family," recalled Gilliard. The Empress and her daughters presented to the suite and servants the gifts on which they had been working for many weeks: knitted waistcoats and painted ribbons for use as bookmarks. On Christmas morning, the family crossed the public garden for early Mass. At the end of the service, the priest offered the prayer for the health and long life of the Imperial family which had been dropped from the Orthodox service after the abdication. Hearing it, the soldiers became angry and thereafter refused the family permission to go to church. This was a great hardship, especially for Alexandra. At the same time, soldiers of the guard were posted inside the house, ostensibly to make certain that the same prayer was not uttered again. Their presence led to closer surveillance and stricter supervision.

One night after the inside watch had been established, the guard on duty reported, "at about 11 p.m. . . . I heard an extraordinary noise upstairs where the Romanovs lived. It was some family holiday with them, and dinner had lasted until far into the evening. Finally the noise grew louder, and soon a cheerful company, consisting of the Romanov family and their suite in evening dress came down the staircase. Nicholas headed the procession in Cossack uniform with a colonel's epaulets and a Circassian dagger at his belt. The whole company went into the room of Gibbs, the tutor, where they made merry until 2 a.m." In the morning, the guard reported the incident and the soldiers grumbled, "They have weapons. They must be searched." Kobylinsky went to Nicholas and obtained the dagger.

The same minor episode led to the affair of the epaulets. As the meaning of the Bolshevik Revolution penetrated through to Tobolsk, the soldiers of the 2nd Regiment became increasingly hostile. They elected a Soldiers' Committee which encroached increasingly on Kobylinsky's authority. Soon after Nicholas was seen wearing epaulets, the Soldiers' Committee voted 100–85 to forbid all officers, including the Tsar, to wear epaulets. At first, Nicholas refused to comply. He had been awarded his colonel's epaulets by his father and he had never taken a higher rank, even as Commander-in-Chief of the Russian Army. Kobylinsky did what he could to override the order, telling the soldiers that Nicholas could not be humiliated in that manner, that even if he no longer was Tsar he remained the cousin of the King of England and the Emperor of Germany. The soldiers brushed Kobylinsky rudely aside, threatening violence. "After dinner," Gilliard wrote, "General Tatishchev and Prince Dolgoruky came to beg the Tsar to remove his epaulets in order to avoid a hostile demonstration by the soldiers. At first it seemed as though the Tsar would refuse but after exchanging a look and a few words with the Empress, he recovered his self control and yielded for the sake of his family. He continued nevertheless to wear epaulets in his room and when he went out, concealed them from the soldiers under a Caucasian cloak."

To the faithful Kobylinsky, the affair of the epaulets seemed a final blow. "I felt I could bear it no more," he said. "I knew that I had absolutely lost all control of the men and I fully realized my impotence. I . . . begged the Emperor to receive me . . . and I said to him, 'Your Majesty, all authority is fast slipping out of my hands. . . . I cannot be useful to you any more, so I wish to resign. . . . My nerves are strained. I am exhausted.' The Emperor put his arm on my shoulder, his eyes filled with tears. He replied: 'I implore you to remain. Eugene Stepanovich, remain for my sake, for the sake of my wife and for the sake of my children. You must stand by us.' . . . Then he embraced me. . . . I resolved to remain."

Kobylinsky's decision was fortunate, for on February 8, the Soldiers' Committee decided that Pankratov and Nikolsky must reign. Simultaneously, the Bolshevik government issued an order demobilizing all older soldiers of the Imperial Army. "All the old soldiers (the most friendly) are to leave us," Gilliard wrote in his diary on February 13. "The Tsar seems very depressed at this prospect; the change may have disastrous results for us." Two days later, he added: "A certain number of soldiers have already left. They came secretly to take leave of the Tsar and his family."

Their effort to say goodbye to the men of the 4th Regiment of Sharpshooters cost the family heavily. In January, amid the heavy snows, Nicholas and his family had begun to pile up a "snow mountain" in the courtyard. For ten days they worked, shoveling snow and carrying water from the kitchen to pour on the snow and freeze it into a small toboggan run. Everybody helped—Dolgoruky, Gilliard, the servants and even members of the guard. Often they had to run from the kitchen to pour the water before it froze solid in the bucket. When it was finished, the children were delighted. A number of wild games were developed by Alexis, Anastasia and Marie, involving pell-mell racing down the slide and tumbling and wrestling in the snow, all accompanied by shrieks of laughter. Then, early in March, Nicholas and Alexandra used the hill to stand on in order to see over the stockade and watch the departure of the 4th Regiment. The Soldiers' Committee immediately declared that the Tsar and the Empress, exposed in this manner, might be shot from the street, an event for which they would be held responsible. The committee ordered that the hill be demolished. The following day, Gilliard wrote in his diary, "The soldiers with a hang-dog look, began to destroy the snow mountain with picks. The children are disconsolate."

The new guards sent from the regimental depots at Tsarskoe Selo were younger men, strongly affected by the currents of revolutionary excitement. Many enjoyed offering little insults to the captives. On a pair of swings used by the Grand Duchesses, they carved obscene words into the wooden seats. Alexis spotted them first, but before he could study them Nicholas arrived and removed the seats. Thereafter, the soldiers amused themselves by drawing lewd pictures and inscriptions on the fence where the girls could not avoid seeing them.

Through the winter, Kobylinsky's increasing difficulty with the soldiers had stemmed as much from problems of pay as those of politics. He had arrived in Tobolsk entrusted by the Provisional Government with a large sum of money out of which to pay the expenses of the Tsar's table and household. The soldiers were to be paid from separate funds to be forwarded later. When the Provisional Government was replaced by the Bolsheviks, the sums promised by Kerensky stopped coming and Kobylinsky had to pay the soldiers from his original sum. When it was gone, he and General Tatishchev twice visited the local District Commissioner and each time borrowed fifteen thousand roubles. Meanwhile, in Petrograd, Count Benckendorff visited government offices pleading for money to maintain the Tsar and his family. As news of the Tsar's circumstances spread, offers of money began to flow in. One foreign ambassador anonymously offered enough to keep the Tsar's household for six months. A prominent Russian quietly offered even more. Eventually, Benckendorff collected two hundred thousand roubles, which was sent to Tobolsk. Unhappily, it fell into other hands and never reached the Imperial family.

In Tobolsk, meanwhile, the captives were living on credit which soon began to wear thin. Just as the cook announced that he was no longer welcome or trusted in the local stores, a strongly monarchist Tobolsk merchant advanced another twenty thousand roubles. Finally, the matter was settled by a telegram which announced that, as of March 1, "Nicholas Romanov and his family must be put on soldier's rations and that each member of the family will receive 600 roubles per month drawn from the interest of their personal estate." As the family consisted of seven, that meant 4,200 roubles a month to support the entire household. Nicholas, facing the novel task of drawing up a family budget, asked for help. "The Tsar said jokingly that since everyone is appointing committees, he is going to appoint one to look after the welfare of his own community," said Gilliard. "It is to consist of General Tatishchev, Prince Dolgoruky, and myself. We held a 'sitting' this afternoon and came to the conclusion that the personnel must be reduced. This is a wrench; we shall have to dismiss ten servants, several of whom have their families with them in Tobolsk. When we informed Their Majesties we could see the grief it caused them. They must part with servants whose very devotion will reduce them to beggary."

The new self-imposed regime was harsh. As of the following morning, butter and coffee were excluded as luxuries. Soon, the townspeople, hearing of the situation, began to send packages of eggs, sweetmeats and delicacies which the Empress referred to as little "gifts from Heaven." Musing over the nature of the Russian people, she wrote, "The strange thing about the Russian character is that it can so suddenly change to evil, cruelty and unreason and as suddenly change back again."

At times, it seemed to the exiles in Tobolsk that they were living on a separate planet—remote, forgotten, beyond all help. "To-day is Carnival Sunday," wrote Gilliard on March 17. "Everyone is merry.

The sledges pass to and fro under our windows; sound of bells, mouth-organs, and singing. . . . The children wistfully watch the fun. . . . Their Majesties still cherish hope that among their loyal friends some may be found to attempt their release. Never was the situation more favourable for escape, for there is as yet no representative of the Bolshevik Government at Tobolsk. With the complicity of Colonel Kobylinsky, already on our side, it would be easy to trick the insolent but careless vigilance of our guards. All that is required is the organized and resolute efforts of a few bold spirits outside."

CHAPTER THIRTY-THREE

Good Russian Men

THE idea of escape grew slowly inside the governor's house. At first, it had scarcely seemed necessary. Had not Kerensky promised the safety of the Imperial family? Had he not assured them that Tobolsk was intended only as a winter refuge? "From there," Kerensky wrote later, "we thought it would be possible in the spring of 1918 to send them abroad after all, via Japan. Fate decided otherwise."

Despite Kerensky's promises, even before the Bolshevik Revolution there were Russians who were secretly planning to liberate the Imperial family. Both in Moscow and in Petrograd, strong monarchist organizations with substantial funds were anxious to attempt a rescue. The problem was not money but planning, coordination and, above all, clarity of purpose. Nicholas himself raised one serious obstacle whenever the question of escape was mentioned: he insisted that the family not be separated from one another. This increased the logistical problem: an escape involving a number of women and a handicapped boy could not be improvised. It would require horses, food and loyal soldiery. If it was to take place in summer, it would need carriages and boats; if it was planned for winter, there would have to be sledges and possibly a train.

Soon after the Imperial family arrived in Tobolsk, a number of monarchist organizations began sending agents to Siberia. Former officers using assumed names stepped off the train in Tyumen and strode onto the river steamers bound for Tobolsk. Mysterious visitors with fine-combed beards and precise Petrograd accents mingled with the well-to-do merchants and shopkeepers of Tobolsk. They made veiled remarks and vague promises about the Imperial family, then quietly disappeared, accomplishing nothing. It was easy at first to establish contact with the Imperial family. Servants and members of the suite passed freely in and out of the governor's house, carrying letters, messages and gifts. Only when the couriers attempted deception did the guards object. The clumsiest of these cases, involved Mlle. Margaret Khitrivo, a friend and maid-of-honor of young Grand Duchess Olga. In Petrograd, this girl decided on her own to share the family's imprisonment. She traveled openly to Tobolsk, carrying a thick wad of letters to the family concealed in a pillow. Upon arrival, she was searched and the letters came tumbling out. They were harmless, but the guards were angered, and thereafter access to the governor's house became more limited.

The major obstacle to rescue was always lack of leadership. There were too many groups, each jealous of the others. The Dowager Empress Marie, assuming that she should take precedence in arranging the rescue of her son, sent an officer to Bishop Hermogen of Tobolsk, proudly demanding his aid. "My lord," wrote the Tsar's mother, "you bear the name of St. Hermogen who fought for Russia. It is an omen. The hour has come for you to serve the motherland." An equal claim was made by members of the Petrograd group which had clustered around Rasputin and Anna Vyrubova. Feeling the Empress to be their special patroness, they demanded leadership of the effort to save her. Count Benckendorff and a group of former government officials were active in raising money and interest. Acting independently, each of these groups dissipated its energy in milling about, squabbling over money and arguing who was to have the honor of conducting so glorious an enterprise as the rescue of the Imperial family.

Eventually, a leader seemed to appear in the person of Boris Soloviev. Establishing himself in Tyumen, Soloviev gathered into his hands all the threads of the various rescue enterprises. So clear was his authority that monarchists arriving in Tyumen to assist the Imperial family automatically reported to Soloviev for instructions. His mandate, it appeared, came from the Empress herself. In fact, this was true; Alexandra trusted Soloviev implicitly for what seemed to her an overwhelming, unchallengeable reason: he was the son-in-law of Gregory Rasputin.

Boris Soloviev, the adventurous son of the Treasurer of the Holy Synod, had studied in Berlin and then become private secretary to a German tourist who was traveling to India. Once there, Soloviev left his employer and entered a school of mysticism founded by a Russian woman, Mme. Blavatskaya. For a year, Soloviev trained himself in hypnotism.

During the war, as an officer of a machine-gun regiment, Soloviev managed to avoid serving at the front. In Petrograd, where he was stationed, his background in mysticism provided splendid credentials for entering the occult gatherings which still amused society. In 1915, he became friendly with Rasputin and Anna Vyrubova. At the time, he showed little enthusiasm for their august Imperial patrons. On the second day of the March Revolution, Soloviev led his entire unit to the Tauride Palace to pledge his allegiance to the Duma.

Neither Rasputin's death, the fall of the Tsar nor Anna's imprisonment disturbed the faith of those who believed in Rasputin's mystical powers. During the spring and summer of 1917, groups of fervent admirers continued through spiritualistic prayer meetings and seances to attempt to converse with the departed *starets*. Soloviev continued to attend these meetings. Maria Rasputin, Gregory's daughter, was also present and a romance was hastily induced. "I went to Anya's house last night," she wrote in her diary. "Daddy spoke to us again. . . . Why do they all say the same thing: 'Love Boris—you must love Boris. . . . I don't like him at all.' "

In August, immediately after the Imperial family was transferred to Tobolsk, Soloviev now acting as agent for this group in Petrograd, went to Siberia to explore the situation. He returned to Petrograd and on October 5, 1917, married Maria Rasputin in the Duma chapel. With Maria, he returned to Siberia and lived for several weeks in her father's house in Pokrovskoe.

Upon arriving in the region, Soloviev quickly established contact with the Empress through one of her maids, Romanova, who had an apartment in Tobolsk. Through her, he passed on notes and a part of the money with which he had been entrusted. More important, Soloviev used Romanova to raise the captives' hopes by promising that "Gregory's family and his friends are active."

It was impossible, given Soloviev's family connection, for Alexandra to doubt his word. Confident that plans were proceeding for their liberation, she even passed along to him her choice for the name of the rescue organization which he was building. It was to be "The Brotherhood of St. John of Tobolsk" in honor of the town's famous saint. Frequently, when her family became gloomy, she cheered them with the reminder that "three hundred faithful officers" of the Brotherhood were disguised in the vicinity, only waiting for Soloviev's signal.

Before long, however, Soloviev's behavior began showing odd twists. He left Pokrovskoe and settled not in Tobolsk, where the prisoners were, but in Tyumen, where he could keep watch on the railroad and monitor all contact between Tobolsk and the outside world. In time, his careful scrutiny of every north-bound traveler became unnecessary; those who were involved in anything to do with the Imperial family came straight to him, handed over the money they had brought and asked for instructions. Soloviev operated with ruthless efficiency. He insisted that all agents and funds be channeled through him. When other conservative monarchist groups attempted to operate outside his control, he announced that any additional attempts to contact the Imperial family would jeopardize the efforts which were already going forward. Occasionally, when necessary, Soloviev went so far as to declare that the Empress herself believed that the work of groups other than his was endangering their chance of escape.

In time, of course, the other groups began to ask for evidence of Soloviev's rescue plans. He replied that he had converted eight regiments of Red soldiers in the area to monarchism. To prove it, he took skeptics to watch the cavalry of the Tyumen garrison at drill. There, just as Soloviev had promised, the officer at the head of the squadron made a prearranged hand signal, indicating his adherence to the plot. When skeptics proved unusually stubborn, Soloviev sent them to Tobolsk to stand in the street near the governor's house. As arranged through Romanova, a member of the Imperial family would step onto the balcony and make a carefully prescribed gesture.

Despite these persuasive indications, there remained four stubbornly suspicious officers who still did not trust Soloviev. Why, they asked, was he passing his messages through a parlormaid when Dr. Botkin—more intelligent, more devoted and more trusted by the Imperial family—was available? Why, because a single officer responded at drill to Soloviev's presence, did it follow that eight regiments stood ready to fight for the Tsar? Why did Soloviev continually assure Petrograd and Moscow that no more men should be sent but that they should show their support by advancing more money? The officers put these questions to Soloviev in January after the Bolsheviks had seized control of Tyumen. Immediately, three of the four officers were handed over to the Bolsheviks and shot; the fourth escaped.

Needless to say, no rescue attempts occurred under Soloviev's command. A few months later, when the Imperial family was moved from Tobolsk, Soloviev was conveniently arrested by the Bolsheviks, held for a few days and then released, thus providing him with a suitable alibi for doing nothing to prevent the transfer. During the civil war, he wandered with his wife through Siberia in the rear of the White armies, eventually reaching Vladivostock. From there, he made his way to Berlin, where he was hailed by unknowing Russians as the man who had tried to save the Imperial family; some of these grateful folk made him the manager of a restaurant.

Subsequently, a number of isolated facts relating to Soloviev came to light. The cavalry officer who supplied hand signals at his squadron's drill admitted that, of all his men, he alone had had anything to do with Soloviev. A Petrograd banker declared that he had raised 175,000 roubles and given them to Anna Vyrubova for transmission to the Imperial family. Of this sum, Soloviev had delivered only 35,000 roubles. As soon as the Imperial family left Tobolsk, Soloviev hurried there to talk to the maid Romanova; later, Romanova was to marry a Bolshevik commissar. In Vladivostock, Soloviev was arrested by the Whites and found to be in possession of documents indicating that he might be a German agent. However, his reputation as the gallant—if unsuccessful—"savior" of the Imperial family was strong, and he was released.

Soloviev's motives during his adventure in Tyumen have remained cloudy. He may have been only greedy. Having established an enormously profitable enterprise—in effect, a tollgate at Tyumen for everyone concerned with helping the Imperial family—he may have wished to extract what he could before he was forced to flee. But many believe that his intrigue was far more sinister. Kerensky later wrote, "In the Tobolsk region . . . the royalists were captained by the traitor Soloviev . . . who was sent there . . . to save and protect the family, but who was actually betraying to the Bolsheviks the royalist officers who came to Tobolsk."

It is possible that Soloviev was working for both the Bolsheviks and the Germans. It may be that his eager acceptance by Rasputin's devotees, his introduction and marriage to Maria and his mission to Siberia were all arranged by the same shadowy people who lurked around Rasputin before his death. Unquestionably, this marriage was the surest way to gain the Empress's confidence and persuade her not to seek other avenues of escape. With the Empress convinced that a strong, secret "Brotherhood" operating in the name of Rasputin stood ready to help, she naturally assisted Soloviev in discouraging other monarchists from making conflicting plans. In the end, whatever Soloviev's motives, the effect was the same. When the moment came for the laboriously constructed, lavishly financed escape machinery to swing into action, it did not do so because it did not exist.

In March, spring brought hope with the first warming rays of the sun. Sitting on her balcony in the sunshine, Alexandra closed her eyes and dreamed of English gardens. As Easter approached, she began to hope that some miraculous resurrection might happen for Russia. "God will not leave it like this," she wrote to Anna. "He will send wisdom and save Russia I am sure. . . . The nation is strong and young and soft as wax. Just now it is in bad hands and darkness and anarchy reign. But the King of Glory will come and will save, strengthen, and give wisdom to the people who are now deceived." Alexandra considered it a sign of this coming transformation that the soldiers changed their rules and allowed her to go frequently to church.

Just at this point, an enemy older than the Bolsheviks rose up to shatter her hopes. Alexis had been well all winter and was filled with energy and high spirits. The destruction of the snow mountain had deprived him of an activity which had absorbed much of his vitality; in its place, he was devising new and reckless games which no one seemed able to inhibit. One of these—riding down the inside stairs on a boat with runners which he had used on the snow mountain—led to calamity. He fell and began to bleed into the groin. The hemorrhage was the worst since Spala five years before. The pain increased rapidly and became excruciating. When it became intolerable, Alexis gasped between his screams, "Mama, I would like to die. I am not afraid of death, but I am so afraid of what they will do to us here." Alexandra, alone, without Rasputin to come or telegraph or pray, could do nothing. "He is frightfully thin and yellow, reminding me of Spala," she wrote to Anna. "I sit all day beside him holding his aching legs and I have grown about as thin as he."

A few days later, in her last letter to Anna Vyrubova, the Empress described Alexis's progress and mentioned a source of new alarm. "Yesterday for the first time, he smiled and talked with us, even played cards, and slept two hours during the day. He is frightfully thin with enormous eyes, just as Spala. He likes to be read to, eats little. . . .

I am with him the whole day, Tatiana or Mr. Gilliard relieving me at intervals. Mr. Gilliard reads to him tirelessly, or warms his legs with the Fohn apparatus. . . . A great number of new troops have come from everywhere. A new commissar has arrived from Moscow, a man named Yakovlev and today we shall have to make his acquaintance. . . . They are always hinting to us that we shall have to travel either very far away or to the center of Siberia. . . . Just now eleven men have passed on horseback, good faces, mere boys. . . . They are the guard of the new commissar. Sometimes we see men with the most awful faces. . . . The atmosphere around us is . . . electrified. We feel that a storm is approaching, but we know that God is merciful . . . our souls are at peace. Whatever happens will be through God's will."

Alexandra sensed accurately that the political storm was upon them; what she could not know was that her son would never walk again.

The collapse of Kerensky's government had been even more swift and bloodless than the overthrow of the autocracy. In scarcely more than the passage of a single night, Lenin stood at the helm of the new Soviet state. Nevertheless, his control over the huge territory of Russia was precarious. To consolidate their grip, the Bolsheviks had to have peace—at any price. The price set by the Germans was a terrible one: loss of most of the territory won by Russia since the days of Peter the Great, including Poland, Finland, the Baltic States, the Ukraine, the Crimea and most of the Caucasus. Within these four hundred thousand square miles lived sixty million people, more than one third of the population of the empire. Yet Lenin had no choice. "Peace" was the cry which had brought him to power. Russian soldiers, prodded by the Bolsheviks' own propaganda, were deserting by the millions. A German army was advancing on Petrograd, and the capital was moved to Moscow, but Russian soldiers could not be recalled to arms, least of all by the party which had promised them peace. Therefore, to save the revolution until, as he confidently expected, it spread to Germany itself, Lenin made peace. On March 3, 1918, in the town of Brest-Litovsk, now headquarters of the German Eastern Front, a Bolshevik delegation signed the German treaty. So humiliating were the terms and the German treatment of the Russian delegation that, after observing the ceremony, one Russian general went out and shot himself.

When news of the treaty reached Tobolsk, Nicholas was overwhelmed with grief and shame. It was, as Lenin was well aware, a total rejection of Russian patriotism. Nicholas called it "a disgrace" and "suicide for Russia." "To think that they called Her Majesty a traitor." he said bitterly. The Tsar was appalled that the Kaiser, Europe's most strident spokesman of the monarchical principle, had been willing to deal with the Bolsheviks. "I should never have thought the Emperor William and the German Government could stoop to shake hands with these miserable traitors," he cried. "But they [the Germans] will get no good from it; it won't save them from ruin." Hearing a rumor that the Germans were demanding that the Tsar and his family be handed over to them unharmed, Nicholas called it "either a maneuver to discredit me or an insult." Defiantly, Alexandra added, "They [the Germans] must never dare to attempt any conversations with Father [Nicholas] or Mother [herself]. . . . After what they have done to the Tsar, I would rather die in Russia than be saved by the Germans."

Inevitably, once the fighting had ended, both Germans and Russians had more time to think of the Tsar and his family. Nicholas remained a symbol, a human pawn with potential value. To the Kaiser, who was indeed ashamed of his embrace of the Bolsheviks, a pliable Nicholas willing to endorse the Treaty of Brest-Litovsk would have had great value. The Bolsheviks, sensing this German interest, immediately understood that in whatever bargaining and maneuvering lay ahead, the Tsar must be kept beyond the Kaiser's reach. As the soldiers in Tobolsk and their commander, Kobylinsky, were all still holdovers, from the Kerensky regime, the Bolshevik leaders resolved to place the Imperial family under more reliable guard.

There was another factor which was to influence the fate of the Imperial family. Of all the regional Soviets which had sprung up in Russia, none was more fiercely Bolshevik than that which sat in the Ural Mountain city of Ekaterinburg. For years, the Ural miners and workers, toiling underground or before open blast-furnaces, had maintained a tradition of discontent and rebellion which had earned the area the name of the Red Urals. In 1917, well before the Bolsheviks seized power in Petrograd, the Ekaterinburg Soviet had nationalized the local mines and factories. For a reason quite different from the central government's, this group of militant Bolsheviks was anxious to lay hands on the Tsar. Once in Ekaterinburg, the Tsar and his family would become not pawns in a game of international politics, but victims in a grim drama of retribution. In March, the Ural Regional

Soviet asked permission from Moscow to bring the Imperial family to Ekaterinburg.

Before Moscow could reply, a Bolshevik detachment from the city of Omsk suddenly arrived in Tobolsk. Omsk was the administrative capital of the province of Western Siberia and a rival of Ekaterinburg for supremacy in the regions east of the Urals. Technically, Tobolsk lay within the sway of Omsk, and this band of soldiers had come not to take away the Tsar, but to dissolve the local government and impose Bolshevism on the town. Pathetically, the Imperial family persisted in hoping that the Omsk soldiers were rescuers. The Empress, looking down from her window as they dashed by in *troikas* festooned with tinkling bells, happily waved and called her daughters to come and look out at "the good Russian men." Nicholas also was hopeful. "His Majesty tells me he has reason to believe that there are among these men many officers who have enlisted in the ranks," said Gilliard, who did not share this optimism. "He also asserts, without telling me definitely the source of his information, that there are three hundred officers at Tyumen."

On April 13, a detachment from Ekaterinburg under a commissar named Zaslavsky finally arrived in Tobolsk. Moscow still had not replied to the request to remove the Tsar from Tobolsk, and without this permission, neither Kobylinsky's men nor the soldiers from Omsk would allow the family to be taken. Zaslavsky then suggested that they at least be moved to the local prison, where they could be strongly guarded. Kobylinsky refused and Zaslavsky's men thereupon launched a campaign of propaganda, urging Kobylinsky's soldiers to ignore the orders of their commandant. It was at this low point that Moscow directly intervened in the form of Commissar Vasily Vaslevich Yakovlev.

From the beginning, an air of mystery attended Yakovlev. The prisoners were aware that someone important was coming from Moscow; there were rumors that it might be Trotsky himself. Instead, on April 22, Yakovlev arrived at the head of 150 horsemen, bringing with him a private telegraph operator through whom he communicated directly with the Kremlin. On his first evening in Tobolsk, he had tea with the Tsar and the Empress, but said nothing about his mission. They noted that he was around thirty-two or thirty-three, tall and muscular with jet-black hair and that, although he was dressed like an ordinary sailor, there was unmistakable evidence of a more cultured background. His language was refined, he addressed Nicholas as "Your Majesty" and greeted Gilliard by saying "*Bonjour, Monsieur.*" His hands were clean and his fingers long and thin. Despite these observations, the prisoners were not necessarily reassured. "Everyone is restless and distraught," Gilliard wrote in his diary that night. "The commissar's arrival is felt to be an evil portent, vague but real."

On the second morning, April 24, Yakovlev summoned Kobylinsky and showed him documents signed by Jacob Sverdlov, an intimate of Lenin who occupied the key administrative post of President of the Central Executive Committee of the All-Russian Congress of Soviets. "The first document was addressed to me," wrote Kobylinsky, "and ordered me to comply without delay with all requests of the Special Commissar Tovarich Yakovlev who had been assigned a mission of great importance. My refusal to execute these orders would result in my being instantly killed. The second document was addressed to the soldiers of our detachment. . . . It also carried a threat of the same penalty—i.e. courtmartial by a revolutionary tribunal and instant death."

Kobylinsky did not argue and, at Yakovlev's request, took him to see Nicholas and Alexis. The Tsarevich was lying in bed, his leg still badly flexed from the recent hemorrhage. The commissar was disturbed by this sight. Later in the day, he returned with an army doctor, who examined Alexis and assured Yakovlev that the boy was seriously ill.

Observing these movements, Gilliard became thoroughly alarmed. "We feel we are forgotten by everyone, abandoned to our own resources and at the mercy of this man. Is it possible that no one will raise a finger to save the Imperial family? Where are those who have remained loyal to the Tsar? Why do they delay?"

On the morning of the 25th, Yakovlev finally revealed his mission to Kobylinsky. He explained that originally he had been assigned by the Central Executive Committee to take the entire Imperial family from Tobolsk. On arriving, his discovery that the Tsarevich was seriously ill had forced a reconsideration. By telegraph, he had been communicating steadily with Moscow. Now, he concluded, "I have received an order to leave the family in Tobolsk and only to take the Emperor away." He asked to see the Tsar as soon as possible.

"After lunch, at two o'clock," said Kobylinsky, "Yakovlev and I entered the hall. The Emperor and Empress stood in the middle of the hall, and Yakovlev stopped a little distance away from them and bowed. Then he said, 'I must tell you that I am the Special Representative of the Moscow Central Executive Committee and my mission is to take all your family away from Tobolsk, but, as your son is ill, I have received a second order which says that you alone must leave.' The Emperor replied: 'I refuse to go.' Upon hearing this Yakovlev said: 'I beg you not to refuse. I am compelled to execute the order. In case of your refusal I must take you by force or I must resign my position. In the latter case the Committee would probably send a far less scrupulous man to replace me. Be calm, I am responsible with my life for your safety. If you do not want to go alone, you can take with you any people you wish. Be ready, we are leaving tomorrow [morning] at four o'clock."

Yakovlev bowed again, first to the Tsar, then to the Empress, and left. As soon as he was gone, Nicholas summoned Kobylinsky and asked where he thought Yakovlev intended to take him. Kobylinsky did not know, but Yakovlev had mentioned that the journey would take four or five days; therefore, he assumed the destination was Moscow. Nicholas nodded and, turning to Alexandra, said bitterly, "They want to force me to sign the Treaty of Brest-Litovsk. But I would rather cut off my right hand than sign such a treaty." The Empress agreed and, harking back to the abdication, declared emotionally, "I shall also go. If I am not there, they will force him to do something in exactly the same way they did before."

The news spread quickly through the house. Tatiana, weeping, knocked at Gilliard's door and asked him to come to her mother. The tutor found the Empress greatly upset. She told him that the Tsar was being taken that night and explained her own painful dilemma:

"The commissar says that no harm will come to the Tsar and that if anyone wishes to accompany him there will be no objection. I can't let the Tsar go alone. They want to separate him from his family as they did before. . . . They're going to try to force his hand by making him anxious about his family. The Tsar is necessary to them; they feel that he alone represents Russia. Together, we shall be in a better position to resist them and I ought to be at his side in the time of trial. But the boy is still so ill. Suppose some complication sets in. Oh, God, what ghastly torture. For the first time in my life, I don't know what to do. I've always felt inspired whenever I had to take a decision and now I can't think. But God won't allow the Tsar's departure; it can't, it must not be."

Tatiana, watching her mother, urged her to make a decision. "But,

Mother," she said, "if Father has to go, whatever we say, something must be decided." Gilliard suggested that if she went with the Tsar, he and the others would take excellent care of Alexis. He pointed out that the Tsarevich was over the worst of the crisis.

"Her Majesty," he wrote, "was obviously tortured by indecision; she paced up and down the room and went on talking rather to herself than to us. At last she came up to me and said: 'Yes that will be best; I'll go with the Tsar. I shall trust Alexis to you.' A moment later the Tsar came in. The Empress walked towards him saying, 'It's all settled. I'll go with you and Marie will come too.' The Tsar replied: 'Very well, if you wish it.' " The decision that Marie should accompany the parents had been made by the girls themselves. Hurriedly meeting, they decided that Olga was not well enough, that Tatiana would be needed in Tobolsk to supervise the household and manage Alexis, and that Anastasia was too young to be helpful to their mother, and so Marie was chosen.

Somehow, during this hectic day, General Tatishchev managed to send a telegram to Count Benckendorff's group in Moscow, pleading for advice: "Doctors demand immediate departure to health resort. Much perturbed by this demand and consider journey undesirable. Please send advice. Extremely difficult position."

The monarchists in Moscow knew nothing of Yakovlev's mission and could only reply: "Unfortunately we have no data which could shed light on reason for this demand. Hesitate to give definite opinion since state of health and circumstances of patient unknown. Advise postpone journey if possible, agreeing only if doctors insist."

Later, a single, last message was received from Tobolsk: "Had to submit to doctors decision."

During these hours, Yakovlev also was nervous. He had discovered that Zaslavsky, the commissar from Ekaterinburg, had left Tobolsk suddenly that morning. Yakovlev was so worried that he scarcely noticed when Kobylinsky arrived to discuss the departure and the luggage. "It makes no difference to me," he said distractedly. "All I know is we must leave tomorrow at all costs. There is no time to waste."

Meanwhile, Alexis, who was still unable to walk, was lying upstairs awaiting the visit his mother had promised to make after lunch. When she did not appear, he began to call, "Mama, Mama!" His shouts rang through the house even as the Tsar and the Empress were talking to Yakovlev. When Alexandra still did not come, Alexis became frightened. Between four and five, she quietly came into his bedroom, her eyes reddened, and explained to him that she and his father were leaving that night.

The entire family spent the rest of the afternoon and evening beside Alexis's bed. The Empress, with her hope for earthly rescue fading, prayed for help from heaven. As they would have to cross frozen rivers, she prayed for the thaw and the melting of the ice. "I know, I am convinced that the river will overflow tonight, and then our departure must be postponed," she said. "This will give us time to get out of this terrible position. If a miracle is necessary, I am sure a miracle will take place."

At 10:30 p.m., the suite went in to join them for evening tea. They found Alexandra sitting on a sofa surrounded by her daughters, their faces swollen from crying. Nicholas and Alexandra both were calm. "This splendid serenity of theirs, this wonderful faith, proved infectious," said Gilliard. At 11:30 p.m., they came downstairs to say goodbye to the servants in the main hall. Nicholas embraced every man, Alexandra every woman.

From the Kornilov house across the street, those watching from their windows saw the governor's house and its sheds blazing with lights throughout the night. Near dawn, the clatter of horses and the creak of carriages signaled Yakovlev's arrival in the courtyard. The vehicles, which had to carry the Tsar and the Empress across two hundred miles of mud and melting snow to Tyumen, were crude, uncomfortable peasant *tarantasses*, more cart than carriage, lacking both springs and seats. Passengers could only sit or lie on the floor. As cushioning, the servants swept up straw from the pigsty and spread it on the floor of the carts. In the only one which had a roof, a mattress was placed for Alexandra to lie on.

When the family came downstairs, the Empress, seeing Gilliard, begged him to go back up and stay with Alexis. He went up to the boy's room and found him lying in bed, his face to the wall, weeping uncontrollably. Outside, Yakovlev was infinitely courteous, repeatedly touching the brim of his hat in salute to the Tsar and Empress. Escorting Alexandra to her cart, he insisted that she put on a warmer coat and wrapped her in Botkin's large fur overcoat while sending for a new wrap for the doctor. Nicholas started to climb into the same cart with his wife, but Yakovlev intervened and insisted that the Tsar ride with him in a separate, open carriage. Marie sat beside her mother, and Prince Dolgoruky, Dr. Botkin, a valet, a maid and a footman were distributed among the other carriages.

When all was ready, the drivers flicked their whips and the carts lurched into motion. The cavalry escort spurred their horses, the procession passed out the gates and down the street. Gilliard, sitting beside Alexis on the Tsarevich's bed, heard Olga, Tatiana and Anastasia climb slowly up the stairs and pass, sobbing, to their room. The months in Tobolsk were ended. There was no "Brotherhood," no "good Russian men," no rescue. Only a boy and his sisters, frightened and utterly alone.

The journey to Tyumen was difficult and exhausting. The cavalcade crossed the river Irtysh on the melting ice with wheels sloshing axle-deep in water. Farther south, reaching the Tobol River, they found the ice beginning to crack. For safety's sake, the entire party dismounted and crossed the river on foot. They changed horses frequently. The last of these remount stations was Pokrovskoe, and the change was carried out directly beneath the windows of Rasputin's house. There sat the Tsar and the Empress, prisoners in a caravan of peasant carts, while in the windows above them the family of the man who had done so much to destroy them stood looking down, waving white handkerchiefs. Before the procession moved on, Rasputin's widow, Praskovie, looked directly at Alexandra and carefully made the sign of the cross.

Fourteen miles north of Tyumen, the little cavalcade was met by another squadron of Red cavalry, who surrounded the carts and escorted them into town. As the horsemen rode alongside, the Empress leaned to look at them, scrutinizing their faces, full of hope that they might be the "good Russian men" who would have been alerted by the news that the Tsar was being moved. Totally oblivious of this pathetic hope, the soldiers escorted the carts into town to the station where a special train was waiting. Yakovlev transferred his prisoners into a first-class coach and then, taking his telegraph operator, installed himself at the station telegraph office. His first message went back to Tobolsk: "Proceeding safely. God bless you. How is the Little One." It was signed Yakovlev, but those in Tobolsk knew who had written it. Then the commissar began sending a signal to Moscow.

When Yakovlev left the telegraph office some time later, he had made a startling decision. His orders had been to bring the former

Tsar and Empress to Moscow. Either during his conversation with the Kremlin or perhaps from what he had learned in Tyumen, he realized that if he took the direct route to Moscow, his train would be stopped in Ekaterinburg and his prisoners removed by the Ural Regional Soviet. Accordingly, to avoid Ekaterinburg, he decided to go eastward rather than westward from Tyumen. Traveling east, they would reach Omsk, where they could join the southern section of the Trans-Siberian track and then double back through Chelyabinsk, Ufa and Samara to Moscow. Returning to the coach, he confided this plan to the captives. At five a.m., with all lights extinguished, the train left Tyumen, headed east for Omsk. Yakovlev did not mention it, but he knew that beyond Omsk lay thousands of miles of clear track to the Pacific.

As soon as the train left Tyumen, Ekaterinburg was informed that Yakovlev was traveling in the wrong direction. A special meeting of the Ural Soviet Presidium was hastily summoned and Yakovlev was proclaimed "a traitor to the revolution" and an outlaw. Desperate telegrams addressed "to all, to all, to all" were sent to every Soviet and party headquarters in the region. At the same time, the Ural Soviet directly contacted the West Siberian Soviet in Omsk, asking that it block Yakovlev. The Omsk Soviet, having received no contrary instructions from Moscow, agreed to do so, and when Yakovlev's train reached the town of Kulomzino, sixty miles from Omsk, it was surrounded by troops. Yakovlev was told of the telegram declaring him a traitor. Unhitching the engine and one coach of his train, he left the Tsar and Empress behind and proceeded alone into Omsk to argue with the Omsk Soviet. When he failed to convince them, he insisted on contacting Moscow. He talked by telegraph directly to Sverdlov, explaining why he had changed his route. Sverdlov replied that, under the circumstances, there was nothing for Yakovlev to do but give in, take his prisoners to Ekaterinburg and hand them over to the Ural Soviet. Sadly, Yakovlev returned to his engine, rejoined the stranded train and told Nicholas and Alexandra, "I have orders to take you to Ekaterinburg." "I would have gone anywhere but to the Urals," said Nicholas. "Judging from the local papers, people there are bitterly hostile to me."

What should be made of this strange tangle of cross-purposes, murky intrigue and reversed directions? Later, when Yakovlev defected from the Bolsheviks to the Whites, the Bolsheviks charged that Yakovlev's enterprise had been all along a monarchist escape plot. Failing to break through Omsk to the Pacific—this theory goes—he turned back, but still considered stopping the train and taking the captives with him to hide in the hills. There is no serious evidence of this, and although Yakovlev was sympathetic to the plight of his prisoners, it is much more likely that he was exactly what he said he was: Moscow's agent, trying to carry out Moscow's order to bring Nicholas to the capital. When the most direct way was blocked and it looked as if he might lose his prisoners, he tried another way, via Omsk. But he became caught up in a struggle between the far-off Central Committee and the Ural Soviet, and, with the acquiescence of Sverdlov, he finally gave in to superior force.

But if Yakovlev's motives and objectives seem reasonably clear, those of other parties involved in this intrigue are more blurred and sinister. In addition to the two possible characterizations of Yakovlev already suggested—the monarchist cavalier attempting to save the Imperial couple, and the agent of Moscow bowing to Ekaterinburg's superior force—there is another role which Yakovlev may have been playing: that of dupe in an evil conspiracy involving the Ural Soviet in Ekaterinburg, the Bolshevik rulers in Moscow, and the German government of Kaiser William.

After the Treaty of Brest-Litovsk and Russia's withdrawal from the war, it became clear that the Western Allies had completely lost interest in the fate of the Russian Imperial family. The Tsar, who had summoned fifteen million Russians into the trenches, who had sacrificed an army to help save Paris, who had refused even when his country was being broken by war to make a separate peace, now was forgotten, scorned, despised. If the Tsar and his family were to be saved by the intervention of a foreign power, that power could only be Germany. In Russia, the Germans now spoke as conquerors. German troops had moved into the Ukraine to collect the food desperately needed by the Kaiser's hungry people. The Germans had not occupied Petrograd or Moscow because it was easier to leave the administration of these chaotic areas to the enfeebled Bolsheviks. But, if necessary, German regiments could march on the two cities and scatter Lenin and his lieutenants like dry leaves.

For this reason, a number of Russian conservatives, including Benckendorff and Alexander Trepov, the former Prime Minister, turned for help to Count William Mirbach, the newly appointed

German Ambassador. Mirbach's answer was always the same: "Be calm. I know all about the situation in Tobolsk, and when the time comes, the German Empire will act." Unsatisfied, Trepov and Count Benckendorff wrote Mirbach a letter, pointing out that Germany alone was in a position to save the Imperial family and warning that if the Tsar and his wife and children died, Kaiser William would be personally responsible.

Quite apart from the question of guilt, the Germans again were anxiously studying their eastern horizon. By injecting the Bolshevik bacillus into Russia, they had destroyed an enemy army. But they had also created a new menace which, they were beginning to sense, might become even more dangerous. Lenin's openly pronounced goal was world revolution; even now, his creed was exerting a pull on the war-weary soldiers and workers of Germany. With this in mind, the German government had a growing interest in restoring in Russia a monarchy which would crush the Bolsheviks and at the same time be friendly to Germany. Nicholas and Alexandra were known to be bitterly hostile to Germany. But the German government presumed that if it was the Kaiser who saved them and restored them to the throne, the Russian sovereigns would be grateful and submissive to the German will.

To achieve this goal, Mirbach began playing a delicate game. He insisted that Nicholas be brought to Moscow, where he would be within reach of German power. The request had to be made in such a way that the Bolsheviks would not take fright and guess the ultimate purpose, and yet also in a way which made clear that the request was backed by a threat of German military intervention. Sverdlov, apparently agreeing to Mirbach's demand, deputized Yakovlev to bring Nicholas to Moscow.

Sverdlov, of course, easily saw the German game and the need for thwarting it. He could not simply refuse; German power was too great. What he could do was to arrange secretly with Ekaterinburg, which was eight hundred miles east of Moscow and beyond the German reach, that they should intercept the Tsar and hold him in apparent defiance of the central government. This way, he could appear before Mirbach and say that he deplored the seizure but unfortunately was powerless to prevent it. The central government would appear all the more innocent as the fiercely Bolshevik sentiments of the Ural Soviet were widely known.

Thus, Sverdlov was betraying both the Germans and his own agent

Yakovlev, who was not in on Sverdlov's scheme. With his right hand, Sverdlov was directing Yakovlev, urging him to skirt Ekaterinburg and bring the Tsar to Moscow; with his left hand, he was closing the net tighter around Yakovlev to ensure that Nicholas would go to Ekaterinburg. Finally, to complete this circle of deception, it is possible that Yakovlev, beginning the game as Sverdlov's dupe, began to guess what was afoot and actually did attempt to escape with the Tsar to freedom.

In the end, once his train had been stopped, Yakovlev had no choice but to obey Sverdlov. Followed by another train filled with Bolshevik soldiers, he proceeded into Ekaterinburg. There, the train was surrounded by troops, and officials of the Regional Soviet immediately took charge of the captives. Yakovlev wired again to Sverdlov, who confirmed his order to give up the prisoners and return directly to Moscow. That night, at a meeting of the Regional Soviet, Yakovlev's arrest was demanded. He argued that he had been attempting only to follow orders and bring his charges to Moscow as directed. As this could not be disproved and Yakovlev was still plainly a deputy of Sverdlov, he was allowed to go. Six months later, he deserted to the White Army of Admiral Kolchak.

Mirbach, realizing that he had been outwitted, was furious. Sverdlov was deeply apologetic, wringing his hands and telling the German Ambassador, "What can we do? We have no proper administrative machinery as yet, and must let the local Soviets have their way in many matters. Give Ekaterinburg time to calm down." But Mirbach, knowing that this game was lost, decided to try another tack. Later, in May, one of the Kaiser's aides-de-camp appeared in the Crimea, where a scattering of Russian grand dukes had gathered. With him, this officer carried an offer from the Kaiser to proclaim Tsar of all the Russias any member of the Imperial family who would agree to countersign the Treaty of Brest-Litovsk. When every Romanov present refused, the German emissary even asked for a meeting with Felix Yussoupov. The meeting never took place and Rasputin's murderer was spared the temptation of visualizing on his own head the Russian Imperial Crown.

Mirbach wasted no more time on Nicholas. When the Russian monarchists came back to him in June, imploring him to save the Tsar from his captors in Ekaterinburg, Mirbach washed his hands, declaring, "The fate of the Russian Emperor is in the hands of his people. Had we been defeated, we would have been treated no better. It is the old, old story—woe to the vanquished!"

Woe indeed! Early in July, Mirbach was assassinated in his Embassy in Moscow. His murderers were two Russian Social-Revolutionaries who were convinced that Lenin and the Bolsheviks had betrayed the revolution to the Germans: "The dictatorship of the proletariat," they cried, "has become the dictatorship of Mirbach!" Four months later, in November 1918, Germany itself was vanquished.

CHAPTER THIRTY-FOUR

Ekaterinburg

THE city of Ekaterinburg lies on a cluster of low hills on the eastern slope of the Urals. Atop the highest of these hills, near the center of town, a successful merchant named N. N. Ipatiev had built himself a handsome, two-story house. Constructed into a slight incline on the side of the hill, the lower story was at street level on one side of the house and became a semi-basement on the other. At the end of April, as Nicholas and Alexandra were being taken from Tobolsk, Ipatiev was suddenly given twenty-four hours to vacate his house. After he left, a group of workmen arrived and hurriedly erected a high wooden fence shutting off the house and garden from the street. Five rooms on the upper floor were sealed as a prison, with the glass on the windows painted white so that those inside could not see out. The lower floor was hastily converted into guardrooms and offices. When it was ready, the house was given the ominous official designation "The House of Special Purpose."

As Yakovlev's train bearing the captives arrived in the city's main railway station, the mood of Ekaterinburg was all too evident. An angry mob surged around the coaches, shouting, "Show us the Romanovs!" So threatening did the crowd become that even the officials of the local Soviet agreed to let Yakovlev move the train back to an outer station before handing over his prisoners. Nicholas stepped out, wearing an officer's greatcoat with the epaulets removed, and carried his own luggage to a waiting car. Then, with Alexandra and Marie beside him, followed by only one other car, he was driven quickly through back streets to the Ipatiev house. There at the door stood Isiah Goloshchekin, a member of the Presidium of the Ural

Soviet and personal friend of Sverdlov. Goloshchekin greeted the Tsar ironically: "Citizen Romanov, you may enter."

At once, the captives were ordered to open their hand luggage. Nicholas was willing, but the Empress objected. Seeing his wife upset, Nicholas paced up and down the room, saying bitterly, "So far we have had polite treatment and men who were gentlemen, but now . . ." The guards cut him short. Roughly, they told him to remember that he was no longer at Tsarskoe Selo, and that if he continued to act provocatively, they would isolate him from his family. A second offense, they warned, would result in hard labor. Frightened for him, Alexandra quickly submitted. Upstairs in their new room, she took a pencil and drew on a window a swastika as a symbol of faith. Beneath, she added the date of their first day in Ekaterinburg, "17/30 Apr. 1918."

In Tobolsk, meanwhile, the remaining four children waited anxiously to hear what had happened to their parents. On May 3, a telegram to Kobylinsky announced that the Tsar and Empress had been detained at Ekaterinburg. Soon after, a letter from Ekaterinburg, written by the maid Demidova but dictated by the Empress, said noncommittally that all were well and advised the Grand Duchesses to "dispose of the medicines as had been agreed." In the code worked out by the family before separating, "medicines" meant "jewels." All of the gems brought from Tsarskoe Selo had been left in Tobolsk, as Nicholas and Alexandra, leaving on hours' notice, had had no time to hide them on their own persons. Now, having been thoroughly and roughly searched, Alexandra was advising her daughters to take the steps agreed on. Accordingly, for several days the girls and trusted servants sewed jewels into their clothing. Diamonds were sewed inside cloth buttons, rubies were hidden inside bodices and corsets. Tatiana, rather than Olga, supervised this work. She was regarded by prisoners and guards alike as head of the family remaining in Tobolsk.

The Bolsheviks had no intention of leaving the family separated. On May 11, Colonel Kobylinsky, who had held his command for twelve difficult months, was relieved, and on May 17, the soldiers of the Tsarskoe Selo regiments acting as guard on the governor's house were replaced by Red Guards from Ekaterinburg. Kobylinsky's place was taken by a bullying young commissar named Rodionov, whose orders were to bring the remainder of the party to Ekaterinburg as soon as the Tsarevich could travel. When Rodionov arrived, he went immediately to see Alexis. Finding the boy in bed, Rodionov stepped out of the room, waited a minute and then reentered, thinking to catch him up, using his malady as a pretext for not moving. Determined not to let anyone deceive him, Rodionov instituted daily roll-call of all the prisoners. He refused to allow the young Grand Duchesses to lock their doors at night, explaining that he had to be able to enter at any time to make certain that they were there. One morning, Anastasia came to the window and seeing Dr. Botkin's son Gleb in the street below, began to wave. Rodionov dashed into the street and pushed Gleb away, shouting, "Nobody is permitted to look at the windows! Comrades," he cried to the sentries, "shoot everybody who so much as looks in this direction." Anastasia continued to smile as Gleb bowed to her and walked away.

By May 19, Alexis was well enough to travel, and at noon the following day, Nagorny carried him aboard the steamer *Rus*, which had brought them to Tobolsk the previous summer. On the river voyage, Rodionov again refused to permit the girls to lock their doors at night. He insisted, nevertheless, on padlocking Alexis and Nagorny into their room. Both Gilliard and Nagorny protested, "The child is ill and the doctor ought to have access to him at any time." Nagorny was enraged and bellowed at Rodionov, but the commissar merely stared with slitted eyes at the loyal sailor.

At the Tyumen railway station, Gilliard was separated from Alexis and placed in a fourth-class carriage at the rear of the train. They traveled all day and reached Ekaterinburg in the middle of the night. The following morning, looking out his window through a steady drizzle of rain, the tutor had a last glimpse of the Imperial children:

"Several carriages were drawn up alongside our train and I saw four men go towards the children's carriage. A few minutes passed and then Nagorny the sailor . . . passed my window carrying the sick boy in his arms; behind him came the Grand Duchesses, loaded with valises and small personal belongings. I tried to get out but was roughly pushed back into the carriage by the sentry. I came back to the window. Tatiana Nicolaievna came last, carrying her little dog and struggling to drag a heavy brown valise. It was raining and I saw her feet sink into the mud at every step. Nagorny tried to come to her assistance; he was roughly pushed back by one of the commissars. . . . A few minutes later the carriages drove off with the children. . . . How little I suspected that I was never to see them again."

Once the children and Nagorny had disappeared, the guards divided up the rest of the party. General Tatishchev, Countess Hendrikov and Mlle. Schneider were sent to prison to join Prince Dolgoruky, who had been there since arriving with the Tsar. Kharitonov the cook, Trup the footman, and Leonid Sednev the fourteen-year-old kitchen boy were sent to join the Imperial family and Dr. Botkin in the Ipatiev house. When these people had gone, Rodionov entered the coach and announced, to their amazement that everyone else—Dr. Derevenko, Baroness Buxhoeveden, Sidney Gibbs and Gilliard himself—were free. For ten days, they remained in Ekaterinburg, living in the fourth-class railway carriage, until ordered by the Bolsheviks to leave the city. On July 20, in Tyumen, Gilliard and the others were rescued by the advancing White Army.

At the Ipatiev house, the children's arrival brought a burst of happiness. Marie slept that night on the floor so that Alexis could have her bed. Thereafter, twelve people were crowded into five rooms. Nicholas, Alexandra and Alexis shared a room, the girls had another, and the rest were divided between the male and female retainers.

In Ekaterinburg, Nicholas and his family were truly prisoners. Their guards were divided into two quite separate groups. Outside the fence and at intervals along the street, the guard consisted of ordinary Red soldiers. Inside, the guards were Bolshevik shock troops made up of former workers from the Zlokazovsky and Syseretsky factories in Ekaterinburg. All were old, hard-core revolutionaries, seasoned by years of privation and bitterness. Night and day, three of these men, armed with revolvers, kept watch outside the five rooms occupied by the Imperial family.

The leader of the inner guard was a tall, thin-faced man who habitually referred to the Tsar as "Nicholas the Blood-Drinker." Alexander Avadeyev had been a commissar at the Zlokazovsky works, where in the autumn of 1917 he personally had arrested the owner and had become head of the factory Soviet. Avadeyev hated the Tsar and dinned into the heads of his subordinates that Nicholas had forced Russia into war in order to spill the blood of larger numbers of workers. Avadeyev drank heavily and encouraged his men to join him. Together, they pilfered the Imperial family's baggage, which was stored in a downstairs room. Following Avadeyev's example, the guards went beltless and unbuttoned. They were deliberately rude. If a member of the family asked, for example, that a window be opened on a sweltering day, the guards either ignored the request or transmitted it to Avadeyev, whose customary response was, "Let them go to hell." Then, pleased with themselves, they would go downstairs and brag that they had just refused this or that to "Nikolasha" and "the German woman." The family had no privacy. The guards entered the rooms whenever they liked, swearing, telling dirty jokes or singing lewd ditties. When the girls went to the lavatory, the soldiers followed with loud guffaws to "guard" them. Inside the lavatory, they had scrawled obscene pictures depicting the Empress with Rasputin. Before one of the Grand Duchesses entered, the guard would tell her to be sure to notice.

Except for a walk in the garden every afternoon, family activity was limited to what could be done within the walls of their rooms. Nicholas and Alexandra read, the girls knitted and embroidered, and Alexis played in bed with a model of a ship. The Empress and her daughters often sang hymns to drown out the noise of the soldiers singing revolutionary songs around a piano on the floor below. Birthdays passed and were scarcely noticed: on May 19, Nicholas was fifty, and on May 25, Alexandra became forty-six.

Every morning, the family arose at eight and assembled for morning prayers. Breakfast was black bread and tea. The main meal arrived at two p.m., when soup and cutlets, sent from the local Soviet soup kitchen, were rewarmed and served by Kharitonov, the cook. They dined on a bare table lacking linen and silverware, and while they ate, Avadeyev and his men often came to watch. Sometimes, Avadeyev would reach past the Tsar, brushing Nicholas's face with his elbow, to fetch himself a piece of meat from the pot. "You've had enough, you idle rich," he would say. "There is enough for you, so I will take some myself."

Nagorny, whose arguments with Rodionov had already marked him, soon ran into more difficulty. The guards insisted that Alexis was to keep only one pair of boots. Nagorny insisted on two pairs, explaining that if one became wet, the Tsarevich needed a second as he was unable to walk without shoes. Soon afterward, one of the guards noticed a thin gold chain hanging from Alexis's bed on which the boy had strung his collection of Holy Images. The man began to take the chain for himself, and Nagorny, outraged, stopped him. It was his last service to Alexis. He was immediately arrested. As he stepped out of the house surrounded by Red Guards, Gilliard, Dr. Derevenko and Gibbs happened to be walking past in the street. "Nagorny was going to the . . . carriage," wrote Gilliard. "He was just setting foot on the step with his hand on the side of the carriage when, raising his head, he saw us all there standing motionless a few yards from him. For a few seconds he looked fixedly at us, then without a single gesture that might have betrayed us, he took his seat. The carriages were driven off . . . in the direction of the prison." Nagorny was put in the same cell with Prince George Lvov, the first Prime Minister of the Provisional Government, who had been sent to Ekaterinburg. Their time as cellmates was brief; four days later, Nagorny was taken out and shot.

With Nagorny gone, it became Nicholas's task to carry Alexis into the garden. There, the Tsar placed his son in a chair and Alexis sat quietly while the others walked back and forth under the eyes of the guards. In time, the sight of Nicholas and his family began to change the impressions of even these seasoned revolutionaries. "I have still an impression of them that will always remain in my soul," said Anatoly Yakimov, a member of the guard who was captured by the Whites. "The Tsar was no longer young, his beard was getting grey. . . . [He wore] a soldier's shirt with an officer's belt fastened by a buckle around his waist. The buckle was yellow . . . the shirt was khaki color, the same color as his trousers and his old worn-out boots. His eyes were kind and he had altogether a kind expression. I got the impression that he was a kind, simple, frank and talkative person. Sometimes I felt that he was going to speak to me. He looked as if he would like to talk to us.

"The Tsaritsa was not a bit like him. She was severe looking and she had the appearance and manners of a haughty, grave woman. Sometimes we used to discuss them amongst ourselves and we decided that she was different and looked exactly like a Tsaritsa. She seemed older than the Tsar. Grey hair was plainly visible on her temples and her face was not the face of a young woman. . . .

"All my evil thoughts about the Tsar disappeared after I had stayed a certain time amongst the guards. After I had seen them several times I began to feel entirely different towards them; I began to pity them. I pitied them as human beings. I am telling you the entire truth. You may or may not believe me, but I kept on saying to myself, 'Let them escape . . . do something to let them escape.' "

In the few days before Pierre Gilliard was forced to leave Ekaterinburg, he, along with Gibbs and Baroness Buxhoeveden, paid frequent calls on Thomas H. Preston, the British Consul in Ekaterinburg, urging him to do something to help the Imperial family. Preston was pessimistic.

"We spent long hours discussing ways and means of saving the royal family," said Preston later. "With 10,000 Red soldiers in the town and with Red spies at every corner and in every house, to have attempted anything in the nature of an escape would have been madness and fraught with the greatest danger to the royal family themselves. . . . There was never any organized attempt at Ekaterinburg to do so."

Preston's statement has been disputed by P. M. Bykov, Chairman of the Ekaterinburg Soviet, who saw a monarchist behind every tree. "From the first days of the Romanovs' transfer to Ekaterinburg," he wrote, "there began to flock in monarchists in great numbers, beginning with half-crazy ladies, countesses and baronesses of every calibre and ending with nuns, clergy, and representatives of foreign powers." According to Bykov, contact between these persons and the Imperial family was maintained through Dr. Derevenko, who was still allowed to enter the Ipatiev house to treat Alexis. In addition, Bykov said, notes were intercepted inside loaves of bread and bottles of milk, containing messages such as: "The hour of liberation is approaching and the days of the usurpers are numbered," "The Slav armies are coming nearer and nearer Ekaterinburg. . . . The time has come for action," "Your friends sleep no longer."

Preston knew nothing of attempts to rescue the Tsar, and Bykov found plots seething on every corner. Almost certainly, the truth was that there were people anxious to rescue the Imperial family who were never able to put their intentions into a workable plan. Two letters of reasonable authenticity supporting this view are quoted by General M. K. Dieterichs, Chief-of-Staff of Admiral Kolchak's White Army, who assisted in the subsequent exhaustive White inquiry into the Tsar's imprisonment and murder. The first letter was a message from an anonymous White officer to the Tsar:

"With God's help and your prudence we hope to achieve our object without running any risk. It is necessary to unfasten one of your windows, so that you can open it; please let me know exactly which. If the little Tsarevich cannot walk, matters will be very complicated, but we have weighed this up too, and I do not consider it an insurmountable obstacle. Let us know definitely whether you need two men to carry him and whether any of you could undertake this work. Could not the little one be put to sleep for an hour or two with some drug? Let the doctor decide, only you must know the time exactly beforehand. We will supply all that is necessary. Be sure that we shall undertake nothing unless we are absolutely certain of success beforehand. We give you our solemn pledge of this before God, history and our own conscience." The letter was signed: "Officer."

The second letter quoted by Dieterichs is Nicholas's reply:

"The second window from the corner, looking out onto the square, has been kept open for two days already, even at night. The seventh and eight windows near the main entrance . . . are likewise kept open. The room is occupied by the commandant and his assistants who constitute the inner guard at the present time. They number thirteen, armed with rifles, revolvers and grenades. No room but ours has keys. The commandant and their assistants can enter our quarters whenever they please. The orderly officer makes the round of the house twice an hour at night and we hear his arms clattering under our windows. One machine gun stands on the balcony and one above it, for an emergency. Opposite our windows on the other side of the street is the [outside] guard in a little house. It consists of fifty men. . . . In any case, inform us when there is a chance and let us know whether we can take our people [servants]. . . . From every post there is a bell to the commandant and a signal to the guard room and other places. If our people stay behind, can we be certain that nothing will happen to them?"

Along with the letters, Nicholas's diary clearly indicates that something was up. On June 27, he wrote: "We spent an anxious night, and kept up our spirits, fully dressed. All this was because a few days ago we received two letters, one after the other, in which we were told to get ready to be rescued by some devoted people, but days passed and nothing happened and the waiting and the uncertainty were very painful."

On July 4, uncertainty was replaced by fear. On that day, Avadeyev, whose drunkenness and thieving had become well known, was suddenly replaced along with his factory-worker guards. Their places were taken by a quietly efficient squad of ten "Letts" of the Bolshevik Cheka, or Secret Police, sent from Cheka headquarters in Ekaterinburg's Hotel America. In fact, the new men were not Letts, as uneducated Russians tended to call any foreigners who spoke in strange Germanic tongues. At least five of them were Magyars, taken as prisoners of war from the Austro-Hungarian army and hired by the Cheka for use in jobs at which they suspected native Russians might balk. Their leader, Jacob Yurovsky, was a Russian who had been a watchmaker in Tomsk and had become a photographic dealer in Ekaterinburg. When the Bolsheviks seized power, he became an active, efficient member of the secret police. Although Yurovsky's behavior was entirely correct, he was so chillingly cold that Nicholas immediately found him sinister. "This specimen we like least of all," he wrote in his diary. His apprehension was thoroughly justified. From the moment of Yurovsky's appearance, the fate of the Imperial family was sealed. The Cheka squad were not guards, but executioners.

Of everything that was to follow, Sverdlov and Moscow had full knowledge. Avadeyev had been replaced not only because of his pilfering, but because members of the Regional Soviet and the Central Executive Committee had sensed the change in the feelings of his men for the prisoners and realized that he was losing control. On July 4, the reassuring news of his replacement was telegraphed to Sverdlov: "Anxiety unnecessary. Useless to worry. . . . Avadeyev replaced by Yurovsky. Inside guard changed, replaced by others." The planning of the prisoners' fate now moved swiftly forward.

The Ural Soviet had never been in any doubt as to what to do with Nicholas. Soon after his arrival in Ekaterinburg, the Soviet decided unanimously in favor of execution. Unwilling to take this responsibility upon themselves, they sent Goloshchekin to Moscow to learn the attitude of the central government. Goloshchekin was not a local Ekaterinburg man. Born in the Baltic provinces, he was a professional revolutionary who had escaped abroad and attached himself to Lenin. He knew Sverdlov well and while in Moscow stayed with him. Goloshchekin learned on his visit that the leaders had not yet decided what to do with the Tsar; they were still toying with Trotsky's idea of holding a public trial at the end of July with Trotsky himself as prosecutor.

Before this could be arranged, however, there was a sudden dip in Bolshevik fortunes which, ironically, was to have a disastrous effect on the prisoners' fate. Civil war and foreign intervention had begun to challenge Boshevism's feeble grip on Russia. Already American marines and British soldiers had landed at Murmansk. In the Ukraine, Generals Alexeiev, Kornilov and Deniken had organized a White Volunteer Army in cooperation with the fiercely independent Don Cossacks. In Siberia, an independent Czech Legion of forty-five thousand men was advancing westward. They had taken Omsk and were moving rapidly toward Tyumen and Ekaterinburg. The Czechs were former prisoners of war taken from the Austro-Hungarian army, reorganized and equipped by Kerensky to fight on the Russian front for the freedom of their homeland. When the Bolsheviks arrived and made peace, Trotsky had agreed that the stranded Czechs be permitted to leave Russia by way of Siberia, Vladivostock and the Pacific to sail around the world to France and there resume the fight. The Czechs were already in Siberia headed eastward in a string of trains on the Trans-Siberian Railroad when the German General Staff vigorously objected to their passage and demanded that the Bolsheviks block and disarm them. The Bolsheviks tried, but the Czechs fought back. Already a formidable force in that chaotic arena, the Czechs were strengthened by anti-Bolshevik Russian officers and soldiers. It was the rapidly mounting threat of this advancing army which forced the Bolsheviks to abandon their thoughts of a show trial of the former Tsar and make other plans for Nicholas and his family.

On July 12, Goloshchekin returned from Moscow and appeared before the Ural Soviet to declare that the party leaders were willing to leave the fate of the Romanovs in their hands. The commander of the Red military forces was asked how long Ekaterinburg could hold out against the Whites. He reported that the Czechs already had outflanked the city from the south, and that Ekaterinburg might fall within three days. Upon hearing this, the Ural Soviet decided to shoot the entire family as soon as possible and to destroy all evidence of the act.

Yurovsky was given this order on the 13th, and at once preparations for the massacre began. For the next three days, Yurovsky and Goloshchekin made trips into the woods around the city, looking for a place to hide the remains. Fourteen miles from Ekaterinburg, near the village of Koptyaki, they discovered a suitable site: an abandoned mine shaft close to four lonely pine trees known to the peasants as the "Four Brothers." At the same time, Voikov, another member of the Ural Soviet, began buying drums containing 150 gallons of gasoline and 400 pounds of sulfuric acid.

The prisoners quickly sensed the change in mood. Yurovsky was not the drunken bully that Avadeyev had been. He did not rant about "Bloody Nicholas" and appeared to have no strong feelings about his captives. He was a professional; they were simply his next assignment. Two women who came to the house to scrub the floors saw Yurovsky sitting and asking the Tsarevich about his health. Earlier that same day, Yurovsky had been at the "Four Brothers" supervising preparations.

The great change in the family's attitude these last days was noted by an Ekaterinburg priest who had been permitted once before to enter the House of Special Purpose to read the service. On his first visit, at the end of May, he noticed that although the Empress seemed tired and ill, Nicholas and his daughters were in good spirits. Alexis, although unable to walk, had been carried to the service on a cot. He seemed happy, and when Father Storozhov approached with the crucifix, the boy looked up at him with bright, merry eyes. On July 14, when the priest returned, the change was marked. The family appeared extremely anxious and depressed. When the deacon sang the prayer "At Rest with the Saints," the family knelt and one of the girls sobbed openly. This time, when the crucifix was brought to Alexis, the priest found him pale and thin, lying in a white nightshirt with a blanket covering him up to the waist. His eyes, looking up, were still clear, but sad and distracted.

On July 16, the day of the murder, Yurovsky ordered the kitchen boy sent away from the house. At four in the afternoon, the Tsar and his four daughters went for their usual walk in the garden. At seven p.m., Yurovsky summoned all the Cheka men into his room and ordered them to collect all the revolvers from the outside guards. With twelve heavy military revolvers lying before him on the table, he said, "Tonight, we will shoot the whole family, everybody. Notify the guards outside not to be alarmed if they hear shots."

The decision was carefully hidden from the family. That night, at 10:30, they went innocently to bed. At midnight, Yurovsky awakened them, telling them to dress quickly and come downstairs. He explained that the Czechs and the White Army were approaching Ekaterinburg and that the Regional Soviet had decided that they must be moved. Still unsuspecting, the family dressed and Nicholas and Alexis put on their military caps. Nicholas came down the stairs first, carrying Alexis. The sleepy boy had his arms tightly around his father's neck. The others followed, with Anastasia clutching the spaniel Jimmy. On the ground floor, Yurovsky led them to a small semi-basement room, sixteen by eighteen feet, with a heavy iron grill over the window. Here, he asked them to wait until the automobiles arrived.

Nicholas asked for chairs so that his wife and son could sit while they waited. Yurovsky ordered three chairs brought and Alexandra took one. Nicholas took another, using his arm and shoulder to support Alexis, who lay back across the third chair. Behind their mother stood the four girls and Dr. Botkin, the valet Trupp, the cook Kharitonov and Demidova, the Empress's parlormaid. Demidova carried two pillows, one of which she placed in the chair behind the Empress's back. The other pillow she clutched tightly. Inside, sewed deep into the feathers, was a box containing a collection of the Imperial jewels.

When all were assembled, Yurovsky reentered the room, followed by his entire Cheka squad carrying revolvers. He stepped forward and declared quickly, "Your relations have tried to save you. They have failed and we must now shoot you."

Nicholas, his arm still around Alexis, began to rise from his chair to protect his wife and son. He had just time to say "What . . . ?" before Yurovsky pointed his revolver directly at the Tsar's head and fired. Nicholas died instantly. At this signal, the entire squad of executioners began to shoot. Alexandra had time only to raise her hand and make the sign of the cross before she too was killed by a single bullet. Olga, Tatiana and Marie, standing behind their mother, were hit and died quickly. Botkin, Kharitonov and Trupp also fell in the hail of bullets. Demidova, the maid, survived the first volley, and rather than reload, the executioners took rifles from the next room and pursued her, stabbing with bayonets. Screaming, running back and forth along the wall like a trapped animal, she tried to fend them off with the cushion. At last she fell, pierced by bayonets more than thirty times. Jimmy the spaniel was killed when his head was crushed by a rifle butt.

The room, filled with the smoke and stench of gunpowder, became suddenly quiet. Blood was running in streams from the bodies on the floor. Then there was a movement and a low groan. Alexis, lying on the floor still in the arms of the Tsar, feebly moved his hand to clutch his father's coat. Savagely, one of the executioners kicked the Tsarevich in the head with his heavy boot. Yurovsky stepped up and fired two shots into the boy's ear. Just at that moment, Anastasia, who had only fainted, regained consciousness and screamed. With bayonets and rifle butts, the entire band turned on her. In a moment, she too lay still. It was ended.

Epilogue

THE bodies were wrapped in sheets and placed in a truck outside the cellar. Before dawn, the vehicle with its sickening cargo reached the "Four Brothers" and the process of dismembering and destroying the bodies began. Each body was carefully cut into pieces with axes and saws, then placed in a bonfire kept burning fiercely with frequent soakings of gasoline. As the ax blades cut into the clothing, many of the jewels sewed inside were crushed, and the fragments spilled out into the high grass or were ground into the mud. As expected, many of the larger bones resisted fire and had to be dissolved with sulfuric acid. The process was neither easy nor quick; for three days, Yurovsky's ghouls labored at their macabre work. Finally, the ashes and residue were thrown into the pool of water at the bottom of the mine shaft. So satisfied were the murderers that they had obliterated all traces that Voikov, the member of the Ural Soviet who purchased the gasoline and acid, proudly declared, "The world will never know what we did with them." Later Voikov became Soviet Ambassador to Poland.

Eight days after the murder, Ekaterinburg fell to the advancing Whites, and a group of officers rushed to the Ipatiev house. In the courtyard, half famished, they found the Tsarevich's spaniel Joy, wandering about as if in search of his master. The house itself was empty, but its appearance was sinister. The basement room had been thoroughly mopped and scrubbed, but the walls and floors bore the scratches and scars of bullets and bayonets. From the wall against which the family had been standing, large pieces of plaster had fallen away. It was obvious that some kind of massacre had taken place in the room. But it was impossible to tell how many victims there had been.

An immediate search for the family led nowhere. Not until the following January (1919) did a thorough investigation begin when Admiral Kolchak, "Supreme Ruler" of the White government in Siberia, selected Nicholas Sokolov, a trained legal investigator, to undertake the task. Sokolov, assisted by both of the Tsarevich's tutors, Gilliard and Gibbs, located the mine and uncovered a wealth of tragic evidence. For Gilliard, especially, the work was excruciating. "But the children—the children?" he cried when Sokolov first told him of the preliminary findings. "The children have suffered the same fate as their parents," replied Sokolov sadly. "There is not a shadow of doubt in my mind on that point."

Before the investigation was concluded, hundreds of articles and fragments had been collected, identified and catalogued. Even the heart-broken Gilliard was convinced. Among the objects collected were these: the Tsar's belt buckle; the Tsarevich's belt buckle; an emerald cross given to the Empress Alexandra by the Dowager Empress Marie; a pearl earring from a pair always worn by Alexandra; the Ulm Cross, a jubilee badge adorned with sapphires and diamonds, presented by Her Majesty's Own Uhlan Guards; and fragments of a sapphire ring which had become so tight on Nicholas's finger that he could not take it off.

In addition, the investigators found a metal pocket case in which Nicholas always carried his wife's portrait; three small icons worn by the Grand Duchess (on each icon, the face of the saint had been destroyed by heavy blows); the Empress's spectacle case; six sets of women's corsets (the Empress, her four daughters and Demidova made exactly six); fragments of the military caps worn by Nicholas and Alexis; shoe buckles belonging to the Grand Duchesses; and Dr. Botkin's eyeglasses and false teeth.

There were also a number of charred bones, partly destroyed by acid but still bearing the mark of ax and saw; revolver bullets, many of which had been reduced by heat to molten blobs; and a severed human finger belonging to a middle-aged woman. It was slender and manicured like the Empress's.

The investigators collected an assortment of nails, tinfoil, copper coins and a small lock which puzzled them until they were shown to Gilliard. He immediately identified them as part of the pocketful of odds and ends always carried by the Tsarevich. Finally, mangled but unburned, the little corpse of the spaniel Jimmy was found at the bottom of the pit. For some reason, the murderers had taken great care to destroy the bodies of the owners, but had ignored the still recognizable body of their pet.

Later, to confirm this evidence, the Whites added the depositions of captured members of the guard at the House of Special Purpose, who described the execution. Later still, Sokolov's findings were fully confirmed from the Bolshevik side by P. M. Bykov, Chairman of the Ekaterinburg Soviet.

Within a few hours of the murder, a report was telegraphed to Moscow. On July 18, the Presidium of the Central Executive Council approved the action. That night, as the Commissar of Health was reading a draft of a new public-health law to the Council of People's Commissars, Sverdlov came into the hall and whispered to Lenin, who interrupted the speaker.

"Comrade Sverdlov wants to make a statement," said Lenin.

"I have to say," declared Sverdlov, "that we have had a communication that at Ekaterinburg, by a decision of the Regional Soviet, Nicholas has been shot. The Presidium has resolved to approve."

A hush fell over the room.

Then Lenin spoke up calmly: "Let us now go on to read the draft [of the health law] clause by clause."

Although only Nicholas's name was publicly mentioned, Lenin and Sverdlov knew that the entire family was dead. In their haste to evacuate Ekaterinburg, the Bolsheviks left behind the tapes of several telegrams exchanged with the Kremlin after the murder. "Tell Sverdlov," said one, "that the whole family met the same fate as its head. Officially, the family will perish during the evacuation." Another message asked how Moscow wished the news to be broken. Apparently the Bolshevik leaders decided that one murder was enough to announce at that time, and on July 20, the official proclamation mentioned only Nicholas. It came in the form of an announcement by the Ural Soviet with an endorsement by the Central Executive Committee:

DECISION

of the Presidium of the Divisional Council of Deputies of Workmen, Peasants, and Red Guards of the Urals:

In view of the fact that Czechoslovakian bands are threatening the Red Capital of the Urals, Ekaterinburg; that the crowned executioner may escape from the tribunal of the people (a White Guard Plot to carry off the whole Imperial family has just been discovered) the Presidium of the Divisional Committee in pursuance of the will of the people, has decided that the ex-Tsar Nicholas Romanov, guilty before the people of innumerable bloody crimes, shall be shot.

The decision of the Presidium of the Divisional Council was carried into execution on the Night of July 16th–17th.

Romanov's family has been transferred from Ekaterinburg to a place of greater safety.

Moscow's endorsement was worded:

DECISION

of the Presidium of the Central Executive Committee of all the Russias of July 18th:

The Central Executive Committee of the Councils of Deputies of Workmen, Peasants, Red Guards and Cossacks, in the person of their president, approve the action of the Presidium of the Council of the Urals.

The President of the Central Executive Committee
Sverdlov

A year later, unable to maintain their fiction, the Bolsheviks admitted that the entire family was dead. They still did not admit their own responsibility for the murders. Instead, they arrested and brought to trial twenty-eight people, all Social Revolutionaries, who, it was charged, had murdered the Tsar in order to discredit the Bolsheviks. Five of the defendants were executed. The hypocrisy of this second crime was later admitted by the Bolsheviks themselves in Bykov's book.

The link between the party leaders in Moscow who authorized the murder and the Ural Soviet which determined the time and method of execution was later described by Trotsky. He explained that he had proposed a public trial to be broadcast by radio throughout the country, but before anything could come of it, he had to leave for the front.

"My next visit to Moscow took place after the fall of Ekaterinburg.

Talking to Sverdlov, I asked in passing: 'Oh, yes, and where is the Tsar?'

" 'It's all over,' he answered. 'He has been shot.'

" 'And where is the family?'

" 'And the family along with him.'

" 'All of them?' I asked, apparently with a touch of surprise.

" 'All of them,' replied Sverdlov. 'What about it?' He was waiting to see my reaction, I made no reply.

" 'And who made the decision?' I asked.

" 'We decided it here. Ilyich believed that we shouldn't leave the Whites a live banner to rally around, especially under the present difficult circumstances.'

"I did not ask any further questions and considered the matter closed. Actually, the decision was not only expedient but necessary. The severity of this summary justice showed the world that we would continue to fight on mercilessly, stopping at nothing. The execution of the Tsar's family was needed not only in order to frighten, horrify, and dishearten the enemy, but also in order to shake up our own ranks to show that there was no turning back, that ahead lay either complete victory or complete ruin. . . . This Lenin sensed well."

The ruthlessness of Lenin's logic had an effect on many in the world who remained uncertain as to the nature of Bolshevism. Woodrow Wilson, still struggling to keep his idealism about the course of events in Russia, heard the news of the murder while at dinner in the home of his Secretary of the Interior, Franklin K. Lane. Rising from the table, the President declared that "a great menace to the world has taken shape." He added that he was sure everyone present would share his view that "it was not the time for gaiety." The dinner party broke up immediately.

The same ruthless logic dictated the murder of every member of the Romanov family on whom the Bolsheviks could lay their hands. Grand Duke Michael, the Tsar's younger brother, was shot in Perm six days before Nicholas's death in Ekaterinburg. On July 17, the day after the murder of the Tsar, an Imperial party including the Empress's sister Grand Duchess Elizabeth, Grand Duke Serge Mikhailovich, three sons of Grand Duke Constantine and a son of Grand Duke Paul were brutally murdered. Grand Duchess Elizabeth had refused all offers of security and escape. In March 1917, the Provisional Government had asked her to leave her abbey and take refuge in the Kremlin, but she refused. In 1918, the Kaiser tried several times, first through the Swedish Embassy and then through Mirbach, to bring the woman he once had loved to shelter in Germany. Again, Ella refused. Moved by the Bolsheviks to the town of Alapayevsk in the Urals, she and the other victims were taken in peasant carts to the mouth of another abandoned mine shaft. They were thrown down the shaft still living, with heavy timbers and hand grenades thrown after them to complete the work. Not all of the victims were killed immediately, for a peasant who crept up to the pit after the murderers had left heard hymns being sung at the bottom of the shaft. In addition, when the bodies were removed by the Whites, the injured head of one of the boys was found to have been carefully bound with the Grand Duchess's handkerchief. In January 1919, four more grand dukes, including Paul, the Tsar's uncle, and Nicholas Mikhailovich, the liberal historian, were executed in the Fortress of Peter and Paul. On the basis of Nicholas Mikhailovich's historical reputation and his liberalism, Lenin's friend, the writer Maxim Gorky, pleaded that the life of this Grand Duke be spared. Lenin refused, declaring, "The Revolution does not need historians."

Ironically, within a very few years, the Revolution also did not need either Lenin or Trotsky. Lenin died in 1924 after a series of strokes already had removed him from power. Trotsky, exiled once again in 1927, later wrote that Lenin had been poisoned by Stalin, an accusation about which Lenin's biographers still argue. There is no question that Trotsky's own assassination by a pickax in the brain in Mexico City in 1940 was ordered by Stalin. It was Stalin who inherited the revolution and for thirty years ruled Russia more cruelly than any tsar since Ivan the Terrible. In January 1945, near the peak of his power, Stalin received his allies, President Franklin D. Roosevelt and Prime Minister Winston Churchill, at Yalta in the Crimea. The American party was housed in the Livadia Palace. Because the President was ill, the other two leaders came to him and the Yalta conference was held around a circular table in the state dining room where, thirty-four years earlier, Nicholas and Alexandra's daughter Olga had appeared, flushed and fair, at her first ball to dance and celebrate her sixteenth birthday.

Jacob Sverdlov died within six months of the Ekaterinburg murder. The Bolshevik leaders gave pneumonia as his cause of death, although there were persistent rumors that he had been assassinated by a Moscow workman. In belated acknowledgment that it was

Sverdlov who arranged the murder of the Imperial family, the town of Ekaterinburg was renamed Sverdlovsk. For years, the House of Special Purpose was kept as a Bolshevik museum and visitors were led down into the cellar where the family was shot. In 1959, a group of American correspondents accompanying Vice President Nixon's tour of Russia quietly visited the house. They found the museum had been closed, but the house, now a repository for the archives of the local Communist Party, was freshly painted in cream and white and brown. The basement room, they were told, was now occupied by dusty bins filled with old documents. In the decades since 1918, Sverdlovsk has grown from a small city to a huge, grimy coal and steel metropolis. It was over Sverdlovsk in May 1960 that the U-2 piloted by Francis Gary Powers was shot down.

The list of members of the Imperial family who escaped the Bolsheviks by leaving Russia was headed by the Tsar's mother, the Dowager Empress Marie Fedorovna. In April 1919, as the Red Army approached the Crimea, the seventy-two-year-old Empress left on board a British battleship, H.M.S. *Marlborough.* Marie rejected what she called the "rumors" of the Ekaterinburg murders and left Russia reluctantly only at the insistent urging of her sister Queen Alexandra of England and Alexandra's son, King George V. Returning to her native Denmark, the Empress lived in a wing of the royal palace of her nephew King Christian X. The King and his aunt disliked each other and argued over money. Marie had brought many of her jewels from Russia, and the King suggested that she sell or pawn them to pay her expenses. The Empress adamantly refused and kept the jewels in a box under her bed. In retaliation, King Christian subjected her to numerous petty humiliations. One night in 1920, as she sat with Grand Duchess Olga, one of the King's footmen entered the room. "His Majesty has sent me over to ask you to switch off all these lights," he said. "His Majesty said to mention to you that the electricity bill he had to pay recently was excessive." The Dowager Empress paled and stared at the footman with stony eyes. Then, while the man still stood before her, she rang for her own servant and ordered him to light the palace from cellar to attic. In the end, the Empress's finances and dignity were saved by King George V, who forwarded a pension of £10,000 ($48,000) a year to his "dear Aunt Minnie." Marie never accepted the fact that Nicholas and his family were dead, although, contrary to general belief, she never met and interviewed any of the women who claimed to be her granddaughter

Anastasia. In October 1928, the gay Danish Princess who had captivated Russia as the consort of the giant Tsar Alexander III died in Copenhagen at the age of eighty-one.

Marie's daughters, Grand Duchess Xenia and Grand Duchess Olga, also left Russia on board British warships. Xenia came to London, where her servants, upon first seeing King George V, fell on their knees and kissed the hem of his coat, believing him to be the Tsar miraculously resurrected. She lived her last twenty-five years in a "grace and favor" mansion provided by the British royal family and named—perhaps appropriately—Wilderness House. In 1960, Xenia died at eighty-five. Olga, Nicholas II's younger sister, lived quietly in Denmark until 1948, when she moved to a small farm outside Toronto, Canada. There, she lived in such peaceful obscurity that her rural neighbors were much surprised in 1959 when she was invited to lunch aboard the royal yacht *Britannia* with Queen Elizabeth and Prince Philip. In 1960, Olga became too ill to live alone and went to live with a Russian couple in an apartment over a barbershop in a poor section of East Toronto. There, in November 1960, seven months after her sister Xenia, she died at seventy-eight.

Among the Russian grand dukes who got away was the Tsar's first cousin Cyril. Ironically, although by leading the *Garde Equipage* to the Duma he was the first Romanov to break his allegiance to Nicholas II, Cyril was still the eldest son of the senior surviving branch of the family, and thereby he became Nicholas's heir. In 1924, Cyril proclaimed himself "Tsar of all the Russias" and established his "court" in a village in Brittany. In 1930, he visited Paris for a "military review" of two thousand former officers of the Imperial Army in a forest outside the city. At Cyril's appearance, the officers shouted Cossack battle cries and yelled, "The day of glory is near!" Unfortunately for Cyril's cause, the Dowager Empress never recognized his title. He died at sixty-two in 1938 in the American Hospital in Paris. Today, Cyril's forty-nine-year-old son Vladimir, who lives in Madrid, is considered head of the House of Romanov.

Grand Duke Nicholas remained in the Crimea until 1919, when he left with the Dowager Empress aboard H.M.S. *Marlborough*. To many Russian émigrés, he seemed a more suitable pretender than Cyril, but the proud Grand Duke would have little to do with these maneuvers. When he died at Antibes in southern France in 1929, his funeral was attended with the elaborate military ceremony due a former commander-in-chief of one of the Allied armies.

For a while, another claimant to the nonexistent throne was Grand Duke Dmitry, whose life was saved by his banishment to Persia following Rasputin's murder. In 1926, Dmitry married an American heiress in Biarritz, and for a while in the 1930's he was a champagne salesman in Palm Beach, Florida. Unlike the other prominent murderers, Yussoupov and Purishkevich, he did not write a book and refused even to talk about his role in the assassination. Dmitry died of tuberculosis in 1941 at the age of fifty in Davos, Switzerland.

The Bolshevik toll of those who served the Tsar in one role or another was high. Countess Hendrikov and Mlle. Schneider, who shared the long captivity at Tsarskoe Selo and in Tobolsk, were executed in Siberia in September 1918. Prince Dolgoruky and General Tatishchev disappeared at the same time, but two bodies answering to their description were found. Baroness Buxhoeveden and Sidney Gibbs crossed Siberia and reached safety in England.

Of the Tsarist ministers, the aged Goremykin was caught by a Petrograd mob in 1918 and strangled on the spot. Stürmer and Protopopov were shot by the Bolsheviks. Kokovtsov and Sazonov escaped and went to live in France. Rodzianko, the Duma President, left Russia through the Crimea and died in 1924 in Belgrade, harassed to the end by Russian monarchists who blamed him for the overthrow of the monarchy. Purishkevich fought with the Whites in southern Russia and died there of typhus. Among the ministers of the Provisional Government, Prince Lvov, Miliukov and Guchkov all went to France, where they were active in anti-Bolshevik organizations.

Only two of Imperial Russia's leading World War generals left their homeland. These were the two arch-rivals Grand Duke Nicholas and Sukhomlinov. Alexeiev and Kornilov both died leading White armies, while Polivanov and Brusilov sided with the Bolsheviks. Brusilov, at least, saw this new allegiance as Russian patriotism. With the Allies landing troops in the Crimea, at Murmansk and at Vladivostock, with the Poles at the gates of Kiev and Smolensk, Brusilov declared, "The Poles are besieging Russian fortresses with the help of nations whom we rescued from certain defeat at the beginning of the war. With every drop of my blood, I wish success to the Red Army, so help me God." Sukhomlinov had no such patriotic feelings. In a sailboat, he escaped across the Gulf of Finland with his voluptuous wife and went to live in Berlin. Before he died in 1926, he wrote his memoirs, thoughtfully dedicating them to the Kaiser. William was so flattered that he proposed in turn to dedicate *his* memoirs to Sukhomlinov, but his publishers successfully suppressed this odd gesture. The youthful Mme. Sukhomlinov was not present to assist in her elderly husband's literary effort. Having seen him safely to Finland, she divorced him and returned to Russia to marry a young Georgian officer. They died together in the Bolshevik terror.

Buchanan and Paléologue both were transferred from Russia after the revolution to other diplomatic assignments, but for each, the years in the beautiful capital on the Neva remained the crown of his career. Buchanan became Ambassador in Rome, where his last years were troubled by those who alleged that in the spring and summer of 1917 he had not done enough to help Nicholas and his family escape. Paléologue returned to Paris to become a senior official of the French Ministry of Foreign Affairs and was elected to the Académie Française. He died in August 1944, just as his beloved Paris was liberated from the Germans.

The two dedicated officials of the Imperial court, Count Fredericks and Count Benckendorff, died only a few years after their Imperial master. Benckendorff painstakingly traced all rumors concerning the murder of the Imperial family and the disappearance of his stepson, Prince Dolgoruky. Only when he sincerely believed that all were dead did he attempt to leave Russia. He was held up by visa difficulties on the Estonian frontier and died in a dilapidated border-town hospital in 1921. Count Fredericks lived for a while in Petrograd, which was shortly to become Leningrad. Defiantly, he wore his fading gold court uniform in walks along the Nevsky Prospect. For the last year of his life, he was allowed to return to his native Finland, where he died in 1922 at the age of eighty-four.

Anna Vyrubova, after being taken by Kerensky from Tsarskoe Selo, was imprisoned for five months in the Fortress of Peter and Paul, released, then re-imprisoned several times, once in the stoker's quarters of the former Imperial yacht *Polar Star*, whose polished decks she had walked with the Empress. For a while, she lived in obscurity in Petrograd and even became friendly with the revolutionary writer Maxim Gorky, who urged her to write her memoirs. Finally, pursued again, she escaped to Finland in 1920. She lived there quietly for forty-four years until her death in 1964 at the age of eighty.

Pierre Gilliard remained in Siberia for three years, assisting in the work of Sokolov's investigation. With his wife, Alexandra Tegleva, who had been Grand Duchess Anastasia's nurse, he returned to Switzerland by way of Japan and the United States and there, in his early forties resumed the education interrupted almost twenty years before when he went to Russia. He became a noted Professor of the French language at the University of Lausanne and was awarded the French Legion of Honor. To the end, through his writing and speaking, Gilliard defended the memory of the family he had served. He died in 1962 at eighty-three.

Iliodor, the fiery monk-priest who had been Rasputin's arch-foe, went back to Russia after the revolution with a quixotic plan to revamp the Orthodox Church to suit the Bolsheviks and make himself the new "Russian Pope." The Bolsheviks were uninterested, and in 1921, Iliodor came to New York City and became a Baptist. He lived in obscurity, working for a while as a janitor in the Metropolitan Life Insurance Building on Madison Square. In 1952, at the age of seventy-one, he died of heart trouble in Bellevue Hospital.

Maria Rasputin, the *starets's* eldest daughter, left Russia with her husband, Boris Soloviev, and became a lion-tamer. In the 1930's, she toured Europe and the United States, billed as "the daughter of the famous mad monk whose feats in Russia astonished the world." She now lives near the Hollywood Freeway in Los Angeles.

Now, in the winter of 1967, only a handful of the major characters in this immense historical drama remain alive. Mathilde Kschessinska, whose house was Lenin's headquarters in Petrograd, left Russia in 1920 and married Grand Duke Andrei at Cannes in 1921. For thirty years, she conducted a ballet studio in Paris, instructing, among many others, Margot Fonteyn. In 1936, at the age of sixty-three, she danced in a jubilee performance at Covent Garden. Today, the young ballerina who rode through the snowy nights in a *troika* beside Nicholas II still lives in Paris. She is ninety-four.

Prince Felix Yussoupov and his wife, Princess Irina, have lived mostly in Paris, where Yussoupov's generosity to other Russian émigrés has become legend. Two famous court cases have brought the Yussoupov name back into prominence. The first occurred in 1934, when Princess Irina sued Metro-Goldwyn-Mayer for libel in London over a movie titled *Rasputin the Mad Monk*. The Yussoupovs won this case and MGM paid them $375,000. In 1965, Prince Yussoupov came to New York City to sue the Columbia Broadcasting System for invasion of privacy over a television play depicting the murder of Rasputin. This time, the Yussoupovs lost. Today, at seventy-nine, Prince Yussoupov lives in the Paris district of Auteuil in a small house converted from a barn.

Alexander Kerensky has lived in London, Paris, Palo Alto, California, and New York City. In the near half-century since leaving Russia, he has written a series of books, most of them an impassioned retelling of the story of the brief, hectic seven months in which he stood at the center of Russian history. Today, still vigorous at eighty-five, he lives in New York City and Palo Alto.

It is impossible to trace exactly the course of one of the overwhelming influences in this drama: the defective gene which Queen Victoria passed to her descendants. Until recently, when plasma and powerful plasma concentrates become available, hemophilia, like other recessive hereditary diseases, tended to die out of afflicted families by the process of attrition. In Queen Victoria's enormous clan, this pattern has been followed. Among the fourth generation—the Queen's great-grandchildren—there were six hemophiliacs. Alexis was one of these. Two of the others were Crown Prince Alfonso and Prince Gonzalo, the sons of Alfonso XIII, the last king of Spain. Both brothers were killed as young men in automobile accidents, Gonzalo in Austria in 1934 and Alfonso in Miami in 1938. In both cases, except for uncontrolled hemorrhaging, their injuries would have been minor. The fifth generation of Victoria's family, which includes both Queen Elizabeth II and her husband, Prince Philip, has been free of hemophilia, as has the sixth. It is possible that the mutant gene may still exist in the carrier state among Queen Victoria's female descendants and could suddenly appear in a future boy. But with the passing of successive generations, that possibility, already distant, will become exceedingly remote.

There is a durable legend that an immense pile of Romanov gold lies somewhere in a sealed bank vault awaiting the arrival of any member of the Tsar's immediate family who can positively identify himself or herself. The facts do little to support the legend. Nothing was left of the Imperial family's wealth inside Russia. Even before the Bolshevik Revolution, all the Romanov estates and properties were taken by the Provisional Government. When Nicholas abdicated, his personal capital in Russia amounted to a million roubles, or $500,000; the Empress's capital was one and a half million roubles, or $750,000. Portions of these sums were withdrawn by Count Benckendorff and used to pay the expenses of the Imperial family at Tobolsk; the rest was seized by the Bolsheviks. The jewelry belonging to the crown became the property of the state. Part of it was broken up and sold by the Soviet government; the residue makes up a dazzling permanent display in the Kremlin. Most of the personal jewelry taken by the Empress and her daughters to Tobolsk was discovered during the destruction of their bodies. The broken fragments later found by Sokolov were preserved as relics and later buried in the Russian cemetery outside Paris. Empress Marie's personal jewelry, once estimated at a value over $2 million, was sold after her death for a fraction of that sum. A number of pieces found their way into the collection of Queen Mary. Today, Queen Elizabeth II often wears the Empress Marie's spectacular diamond necklace and diamond tiara.

Before the First World War, the Russian Imperial family had deposits abroad, and it is here that many glowing expectations have been focused. There were funds in a bank in Berlin, but after the war, with the collapse of the mark in runaway inflation, the sum became insignificant. Today, there might be $1,500, but the bank is in East Berlin. The remaining hopes center on the Bank of England, but these too appear groundless. During the war, Nicholas and Alexandra devoted their private fortunes to the war effort. Deposits in England were withdrawn and brought back to Russia to help pay for the network of hospitals and hospital trains under the Empress's patronage. The money was transferred through the British Embassy in Petrograd; on August 26, 1915 (O.S.), Alexandra wrote to Nicholas: "I see [Sir George] Buchanan tomorrow as he brings me again over 100,000 p. [pounds] from England." By the end of the war, there was nothing left.

In 1960, the late Sir Edward Peacock, Director of the Bank of England from 1920 to 1924 and again from 1929 to 1946, discussed the question with a Canadian writer, Ian Vorres, who was collaborating with Grand Duchess Olga on her memoirs. Peacock had been personally instructed by King George V to look after his cousin Olga's financial affairs. From this vantage, he wrote:

"I am pretty sure there never was any money of the Imperial family of Russia in the Bank of England nor any other bank in England. Of course, it is difficult to say 'never' but I am positive at least there never was any money after World War I and during my long years as director of the bank."

Nevertheless, despite all evidence to the contrary, the alluring idea that a lost fortune exists has continued to stimulate extraordinary activity. As in every case of the death of royal persons in mysterious circumstances, rumors persisted that some or all members of the Imperial family were still alive. In 1920, the Tsar himself was said to have been seen in the streets of London, his hair snow white. Another story placed him in Rome, secretly hidden in the Vatican by the Pope. The entire Imperial family was said to be aboard a ship, cruising eternally through the waters of the White Sea, never touching any land.

Over the years, dozens of claimants have stepped forward, proclaiming themselves this or that member of the Imperial family. The Tsarevich Alexis reappeared for the first time in Siberia soon after the murder. Gilliard saw him and found a young man who looked vaguely like Alexis but understood only Russian. Eventually, the boy admitted that he was an impostor. The pathetic story of Mrs. Anna Anderson's lifelong attempt to prove herself the Grand Duchess Anastasia has become world famous. Nevertheless, she has been challenged by numerous other Anastasias living in far corners of the globe. It was the fate of Grand Duchess Olga, who had been closer to her niece Anastasia than any other Romanov survivor, to meet many of these women. Occasionally, she met them willingly, as in Berlin in 1925 when she interviewed Mrs. Anderson and, after four days at her bedside, sadly pronounced her false. More often, the pretenders pursued Olga relentlessly and flung themselves upon her, loudly crying, "Dear Aunt Olga!" Olga endured these intrusions, recognizing them as the inevitable consequence of public fascination with an exciting tale of miraculous escape from death. "My telling the truth does not help in the least," she once said, "because the public simply wants to believe the mystery."

Infinitely more remarkable and more fatefully enigmatic than the riddle of Anastasia is the awesome, overwhelming drama of the Russian Revolution itself. The rise of Communism, brought by Lenin to Russia, its rooting there and the spreading of its doctrines and power around the globe are the pivotal historical events of our time. Ironically, the two great Communist nations, Russia and China, are the only world powers with which the United States has never warred. The current struggle dividing the world is not over trade or territory, but over ideology. This is the legacy of Lenin.

And also the legacy of Rasputin and hemophilia. Kerensky once said, "If there had been no Rasputin, there would have been no Lenin." If this is true, it is also true that if there had been no hemophilia, there would have been no Rasputin. This is not to say that everything that happened in Russia and the world has stemmed entirely from the personal tragedy of a single boy. It is not to overlook the backwardness and restlessness of Russian society, the clamor for reform, the strain and battering of a world war, the gentle, retiring nature of the last Tsar. All of these had a powerful bruising impact on events. Even before the birth of the Tsarevich, autocracy was in retreat.

Here, precisely, is the point. Had it not been for the agony of Alexis's hemophilia, had it not been for the desperation which made his mother turn to Rasputin, first to save her son, then to save the pure autocracy, might not Nicholas II have continued retreating into the role of constitutional monarch so happily filled by his cousin King George V? It might have happened, and, in fact, it was in this direction that Russian history was headed. In 1905, the Russian people had had a partial revolution. Absolute power was struck from the hands of the Tsar with the creation of the Duma. In the era of Stolypin and the Third Duma, cooperation between the throne and parliament reached a level of high promise for the future. During the war, the nation asked not for revolution but for reform—for a share of responsibility in fighting and winning the victory. But Alexandra, goaded by Rasputin, passionately objected to any sharing of the Imperial power. By giving way to his wife, by fighting to save the autocracy and denying every plea for responsible government, Nicholas made revolution and the eventual triumph of Lenin inevitable.

Why Lenin triumphed, why Nicholas failed, why Alexandra placed the fate of her son, her husband and his empire in the hands of a wandering holy man, why Alexis suffered from hemophilia—these are the true riddles of this historical tale. All of them have answers except, perhaps, the last.

Family Trees

Acknowledgments

Notes

Bibliography

Index

Nicholas II's Family Tree (*partial*)

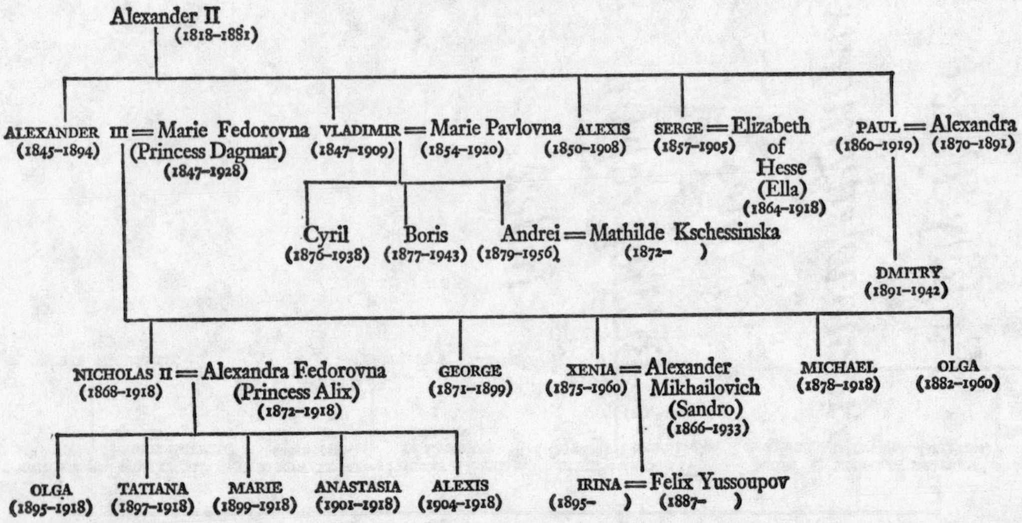

Empress Alexandra's Family Tree (partial)

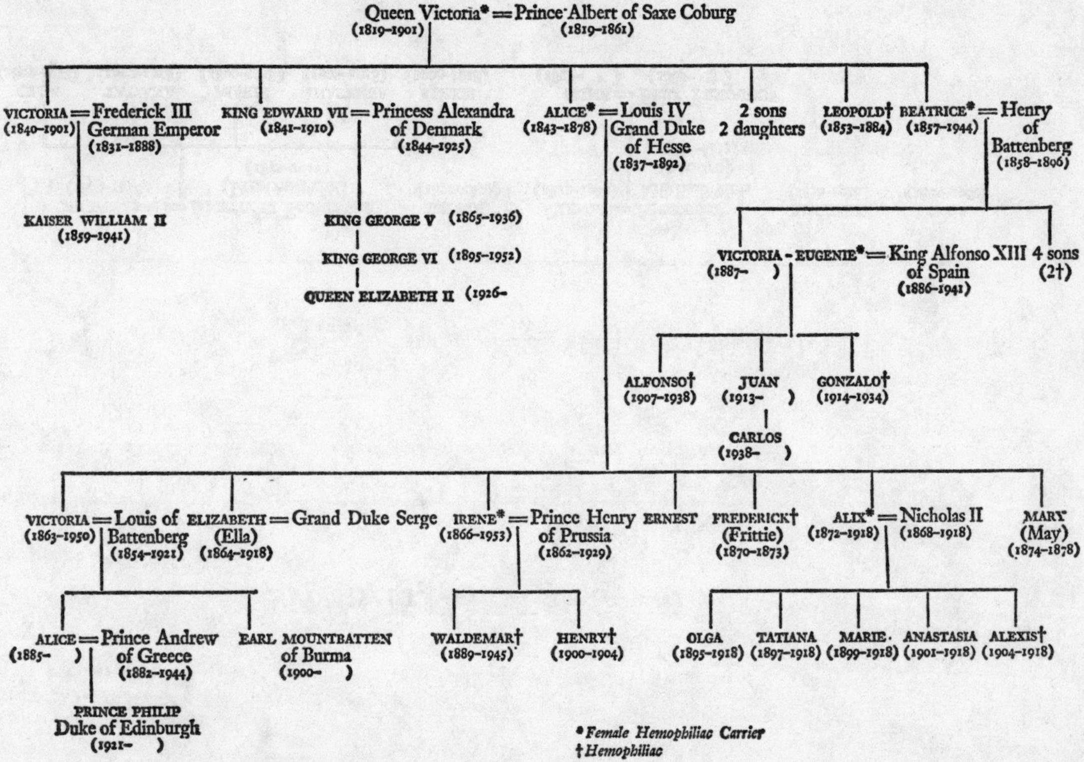

* *Female Hemophiliac Carrier*
† *Hemophiliac*

Acknowledgments

In writing this book I worked in and drew material from the New York Public Library, the Butler Library of Columbia University, and the Beinecke Rare Book Library of Yale University. I am grateful to the staffs of these institutions for their courtesy and efficiency. I especially appreciate the assistance of Miss Margery Wynne for making available the unique collection of Romanov albums and papers at the Beinecke Library. Without the help of Mr. Richard Orlando, who painstakingly traced numerous volumes, my research would have been thinner and more difficult.

I am greatly indebted to Mr. Dimitry Lehovich and to Professor Robert Williams of Williams College, each of whom read the entire manuscript and offered numerous helpful suggestions. Neither is responsible for any errors of fact or judgment which may appear in the book. On specific points, I drew on the knowledge of Father James Griffiths of the Orthodox Church, Mrs. Svetlana Umrichin, and Mrs. Evgenia Lehovich. These three also gave their constant encouragement to the project as a whole.

My understanding of the medical problems of hemophilia has been guided by a succession of interviews and conversations with Dr. Kenneth Brinkhous, Dr. Martin Rosenthal, the late Dr. Leandro Tocantins, Dr. Oscar Lucas, Dr. David Agle and Dr. Ake Mattson. For specific questions relating to this book, and for their devoted support over the years, I am profoundly grateful to Dr. Leroy Engel and Dr. Herbert Newman.

Among those who by word and deed gave me steady encouragement during the many long months of writing were Suzanne and

Maurice Rohrbach, the late N. Hardin Massie, Simon Michael Bessie, Alfred Knopf, Jr., Robert Lantz, and Janet Dowling, who, along with Terry Conover, typed the manuscript. My children have sustained me with their unfailing optimism and with dozens of cheerful drawings.

The contribution made by my wife, Suzanne, is immeasurable. Along with her own career in journalism, she produced a constant flow of research for this book. At nights and on weekends, she read and edited every line. Her ideas and suggestions, carefully recorded by me on hundreds of hours of tape, provided a constant environment of creative stimulus. Without this help, the book would never have been written. Now that it is finished, it is hers as much as mine.

ROBERT K. MASSIE

Notes

Four primary sources are cited in abbreviated form throughout these Notes. Nicholas II's *Journal Intime* is cited as "N's Diary." *The Letters of the Tsar to the Tsaritsa 1914–1917* is cited as "N to AF," and *Letters of the Tsaritsa to the Tsar 1914–1916* is cited as "AF to N." *The Secret Letters of the Last Tsar: The Confidential Correspondence Between Nicholas II and His Mother, Dowager Empress Marie Feodorovna* is cited as "N to MF" for letters from Nicholas to his mother, and as "MF to N" for letters from the Empress to her son.

CHAPTER 1 1894: IMPERIAL RUSSIA

5 "This curious conglomeration": Paléologue, I, 93.
6 "Cleaving the city down the center": Kennan, 3.
7 River breezes and salt air: Paléologue, I, 348.
8 "Fashionable décolletage": Dehn, 44. "Nobody thought of leaving": *ibid.*, 44.
8 Receptions and balls: Meriel Buchanan, 13; Vorres, 99.
8–9 Imperial balls: Mosolov, 192–202; Vorres, 100–1; Alexander, 55–6, 161–2.
9–10 "That is what I'm going to do to your . . . army corps": Alexander, 67.
10 Alexander III: Mosolov, 4. "A sovereign whom she does not look upon": Bainbridge, 13.
10 "On the point of striking you": Kaun, 130.
10 The bassoon: Pares, 30
11 Dagmar engaged to Alexander's brother: Vorres, 21.
11 Empress Marie: Alexander, 73; Mosolov, 65; Vorres, 53, 57.

11 "They danced the mazurka for half an hour": MF to N, 44.
12 "He is feted, he is stuffed": MF to N, 45. The Imperial train derailed: Alexander, 168; Vorres, 29.

CHAPTER 2 THE TSAREVICH NICHOLAS

13 An older brother, Alexander: Alexander, 165; Vorres, 21.
13 Nicholas admired George's humor: Vorres, 34. George's tuberculosis: Alexander, 120.
13 Gatchina, 900 rooms: Vorres, 24. Alexander III up at seven: *ibid.*, 26. Simple army cots: *ibid.*, 23.
13–14 "Nicky was so hungry": *ibid.*, 36. Pelting each other with bread: Mosolov, 5.
14 Dancing tutor: Vorres, 35.
14 "The High Priest of Social Stagnation": Mazour, 36. "The dominant and most baleful influence": Charques, 51. Coldly ascetic: Vorres, 38.
14 "Abode of the 'Bad Man' ": Alexander, 188.
14–15 "Among the falsest of political principles": Pobedonostsev, 32. "Parliament is an institution": *ibid.*, 34–5. "Providence has preserved our Russia": *ibid.*, 49.
15 Pobedonostsev's philosophy: Pares, *History*, 426–7. The Jewish problem: Harcave, 21. "We must not forget": Florinsky, 1119.
15 Pobedonostsev excommunicated Tolstoy: Introduction to Pobedonostsev, ix.
15 *Anna Karenina:* Paléologue, I, 314.
16 "It is too early to thank God": Pares, *History*, 403. "To the palace, to die there": *ibid.*, 403.
16 The death scene: Alexander, 59–61.
16 "Their red lances shining brightly": *ibid.*, 61.
16 "With faith in the power and right of autocracy": Pares, *History*, 407.
17 A slender youth, five feet seven inches: Alexander, 173. "His usual tender, shy, slightly sad smile": *ibid.*, 77.
17 Languages: Alexander, 165.
17 N's Diary: Pares, 15. The cryptic, emotionless style of Nicholas's diary often is cited as evidence of a shallow character. "It is the diary of a nobody," writes Charques, "of a man of transparently immature and of patently insignificant interests . . . triviality piled on triviality."

Nevertheless, this kind of diary is not universally condemned. In certain circumstances, these terse, monotonous Edwardian diaries have been found admirable and praiseworthy: "On May 3, 1880 . . . [he] began to keep a diary," begins one account of a royal diarist, "and from then onward he continued it without intermission until three days before his death. For fifty-six years, in his clear handwriting, he recorded daily the moment at which he got up, the times of his meals, and the hour when he went to bed. He acquired the nautical habit of registering the direction of the wind, the condition of the barometer and the state of the weather throughout the day. He would take careful notes of the places which he visited, the people whom he met, or the number of birds and other animals which he shot. Seldom did he indulge in any comment upon personal or public affairs; his diary is little more than a detailed catalogue of his engagements. He was not one of those to whom the physical act of writing comes easily and with pleasure; his pen would travel slowly across the page. Yet only when he was seriously ill would he allow his mother, his sisters or, later, his wife, to make the entries for him. His diaries swelled to twenty-four bound and locked volumes, each opening with a small golden key. They became for him part of the discipline of life."

This description, with only minor alterations, could have been written of Nicholas II. In fact, it was written by Harold Nicolson in his biography of Nicholas's cousin, King George V, pp. 15–16.

17 "Today I finished . . . my education: Radziwill, 37.

17 "As always after a ball": N's Diary, 13. "I got up at 10:30": *ibid.*, 16. "I was not overwhelmed with sadness": *ibid.*, 21.

18 "Ran like fools": *ibid.*, 14. His life in St. Petersburg: *ibid.*, 12–31.

18–19 "All day I found myself in a state of gaiety": *ibid.*, 25. A direct telephone line: *ibid.*, 43. Reviewing Cossacks: *ibid.*, 23.

19 Bungalow at Krasnoe Selo: Alexander, 166.

19 "I am happier than I can say": N to MF, 35.

19 "Never forget that everyone's eyes": MF to N, 33. "I will always try": N to MF, 36.

19–20 "We got stewed," etc.: Kaun, 133.

20 "Where is Kschessinska?": Kschessinska, 28. "Be the glory and adornment of our ballet": *ibid.*, 28. "In both our hearts, an attraction": *ibid.*, 29. "Supper with the pupils": *ibid.*, 29.

20 "Ah, you must have been flirting": *ibid.*, 33. "I thought that, without being in love with me": *ibid.*, 33. "Gossiped at her window": *ibid.*, 34.

21 "Villages and clusters of palm trees": N's Diary, 33. "Nothing worth talking about": *ibid.*, 33. "This time it was much better": *ibid.*, 34.

22 "Red uniforms everywhere": *ibid.*, 36. "I'd like to think": MF to N, 42.

22 The assassination attempt: N's Diary, 37–8; MF to N, 51; Alexander, 167; Kschessinska, 35. "I received the Swedish minister": N's Diary, 45.

23 Vladivostock: Tupper, 83, 85.

23 Kschessinska again: Kschessinska, 37–42.

23–4 "Though he did not openly mention it": *ibid.*, 42. "We led a quiet, retiring life": *ibid.*, 44.

24 "I have been nominated a member": N's Diary, 46. Exercise with the Hussars: *ibid.*, 14. "What, but you know the Tsarevich?": Quoted in an introductory passage in N's Diary, 45.

25 "Uncle Bertie, of course": N to MF, 59. "May is delightful": *ibid.*, 59. Nicholas mistaken for George: Buxhoeveden, 37; Hanbury-Williams, 89.

25 "She was very friendly": N to MF, 60. Kschessinska's career: Kschessinska, 47.

26 The end of the affair: *ibid.*, 50–1. "The terrible, boundless suffering": *ibid.*, 52.

26 "I was not alone in my grief and trouble": *ibid.*, 53. Grand Duke Andrei: *ibid.*, 78. A son: *ibid.*, 89. Married in Cannes: *ibid.*, 209.

CHAPTER 3 PRINCESS ALIX

27 "My dream is some day to marry Alix H.": Pares, 33.

27 "Mama made a few allusions": Radziwill, 38.

28 Princess Helene and Princess Margaret: N to MF, 61.

28 "Oh, Lord, how I want to go to Ilinskoe": Pares, 33.

28 Nicholas insists on Alix: Buxhoeveden, 33.

28 Alexander III's health: Mosolov, 44.

28–9 "They murder my name here": Buxhoeveden, 4. "A sweet, merry little person": *ibid.*, 4. "Sunny in pink": *ibid.*, 4.

29 Prussia and Hesse-Darmstadt: *ibid.*, 3; Botkin, 24.

29 Darmstadt: Buxhoeveden, 1; Almedingen, 7.

29–30 English mementoes: Buxhoeveden, 2. Mrs. Orchard: *ibid.*, 5. Pony cart: *ibid.*, 6. Goldfish: Almedingen, 14. Crinoline: Buxhoeveden, 6. Christmas: *ibid.*, 7. Visits to England: *ibid.*, 7, 9. Diphtheria: *ibid.*, 9–10.

30 Alix withdraws: *ibid.*, 12. Queen Victoria's interest: *ibid.*, 12.

31 A student: *ibid.*, 13–15. Ella's marriage: *ibid.*, 18–19. Nicholas presents a brooch: Vyrubova, 19.

31 Alix's visit to Russia, 1889: Buxhoeveden, 23–4. Ilinskoe: *ibid.*, 26–7.

32 Alix's feeling about Nicholas: *ibid.*, 21, 34. Prince Eddy: Pope-Hennessy, 183; Longford, 512.

33 Banjo: Buxhoeveden, 22. Italy: *ibid.*, 31.

33 Nicholas's arrival in Coburg: N's Diary, 48. "What a day": *ibid.*, 49. "I tried to explain": N to MF, 63.

34 Two sittings at dinner: N's Diary, 50. Queen Victoria's Dragoons: *ibid.*, 49. The Kaiser helps: N to MF, 64. "The depths of Alix's soul": N's Diary, 51.

34 "A marvelous, unforgettable day": *ibid.*, 52. "We were left alone": N to MF, 64. "'I'm going to marry Nicky'": Almedingen, 23.

35 Military drill: N's Diary, 52. "My superb Alix came to me": *ibid.*, 52. "Everything in my heart was bright": *ibid.*, 52. "We answered all day": *ibid.*, 53.
36 "Your dear Alix": MF to N, 65, 66.
36 "She has changed so much": N's Diary, 54.
36 "We were together a long time": *ibid.*, 59. "It is so strange": *ibid.*, 57. "What a sorrow": *ibid.*, 54. "What sadness": *ibid.*, 60. "A ring on my finger": *ibid.*, 57. Gatchina: *ibid.*, 62–3.
37 "Into the arms of my betrothed": N to MF, 71. Walton-on-Thames: *ibid.*, 71.
37 Engagement gifts: Buxhoeveden, 38. Fabergé's *sautoir* of pearls: Bainbridge, 56. "Alix, do not get too proud": Buxhoeveden, 38; Dehn, 59.
37–8 "Galloping like a fool": N's Diary, 63. "I can't complain": N to MF, 71.
38 "I simply had to get up": N to MF, 73.
38 "I dreamed that I was loved": N's Diary, 76–7. "What is past is past": *ibid.*, 78.
38 "Granny loves me so": N to MF, 74. Aldershot: N's Diary, 71.
39 "A son was born to Georgie and May": N's Diary, quoted by Catherine Radziwill, *The Intimate Life of the Last Tsarina* (New York, L. MacVeagh, Dial Press, 1928), 26.
39 "Instead of plunging the infant": N's Diary, 75. "What a nice, healthy child": N to MF, 73. "Georgie came for lunch": N's Diary, 76.
39 "Love is caught": *ibid.*, 81. "Sleep gently": *ibid.*, 83.
39–40 German fleet: *ibid.*, 83. "I am yours": *ibid.*, 86. "For the past is past": *ibid.*, 85.

CHAPTER 4 MARRIAGE

41 Nephritis: Witte, 46; Mosolov, 44; Vorres, 63.
41 "My duty to remain here": N's Diary, 90.
41–2 "There is some ice cream in the next room": Vorres, 64.
42 "My God, what a joy to meet her": N's Diary, 101. Welcome in the Crimea: *ibid.*, 101. The Tsar in dress uniform: Vyrubova, 20.
43 "Sweet child, pray to God": N's Diary, 103. "Be firm and make the doctors come to you": *ibid.*, 104.
43 "The Lord has called to him . . . Papa": *ibid.*, 107.
43 "I saw tears in his blue eyes": Alexander, 168–9.
44 The embalmers: N's Diary, 111. At that time the Orthodox Church did not normally permit embalming of the dead. Exceptions were made, however, in the cases of sovereigns who were to lie in state for many days.

44 "Even in our great grief": *ibid.*, 110. "Alix read beautifully": *ibid.*, 110. "The truly believing Grand Duchess Alexandra Fedorovna": Buxhoeveden, 41.
44–5 "Mama, many others and I": N's Diary, 110. The uncles' view: Buxhoeveden, 41. "My dear Papa was transferred": N's Diary, 112.
45 Across the Ukraine: *ibid.*, 114. Moscow: *ibid.*, 114; Almedingen, 37. St. Petersburg: N's Diary, 115; Almedingen, 37–8. "Behind a coffin": Gilliard, 48.
46 "I have received so many delegations": N's Diary, 120. "I almost broke into sobs": *ibid.*, 122.
46 "Every day, after lunch . . . another service": Pope-Hennessy, 301–2. "One's feelings": Buxhoeveden, 44. "Such was my entry into Russia": Fülöp-Miller, 80.
46 The wedding: N's Diary, 125; Buxhoeveden, 43; Vyrubova, 21.
47 "Nicky is a very lucky man": Pope-Hennessy, 300. "When they drove from the Winter Palace": Nicolson, 57. "Alix had a headache": N's Diary, 125.
47 "At last, united": Buxhoeveden, 50. "Never did I believe": N's Diary, 125; Buxhoeveden, 50.
47 Six rooms: Vorres, 71; Buxhoeveden, 45–6.
48 "I am indescribably happy with Alix": N's Diary, 125. Reading at night: *ibid.*, 131. Sleigh rides: Buxhoeveden, 47.
48 "It is hard to think": N's Diary, 126.
48 The mother-in-law: Vorres, 72, 93; Buxhoeveden, 49; Vyrubova, 87.
49 The jewels: Almedingen, 43.
49 "I cannot yet realize that I am married": Buxhoeveden, 44. "I feel myself completely alone": Vyrubova, 21–2.
49 "How contented and happy I am": Buxhoeveden, 51.
50 "It has become very big and kicks about": N to MF, 96. "Sad to leave Peterhof": *ibid.*, 93–4.
50 "It is understood, isn't it": MF to N, 100.
50 Birth of Olga: N's Diary, 132; Buxhoeveden, 56.
51 "You can imagine our intense happiness": Buxhoeveden, 56.

CHAPTER 5 THE CORONATION

52 River ice beginning to crack: N to MF, 101.
52 "I believe we should regard": *ibid.*, 107.
52 Petrovsky Palace: Vorres, 74.
52–3 Whitewash, evergreens, flags: Bovey, 10, 32. Cossacks, peasant women, Caucasians, Turks: *ibid.*, 14–15, 22.
53 Nicholas enters Moscow: Bovey, 13; Kschessinska, 58. "It was agonizing": Kschessinska, 58.
53 The procession: Bovey, 15–17; Kschessinska, 58.
54 The Red Staircase: Bovey, 21.

54 The hairdresser: Naryishkin-Kurakin, 148.
54 Down the Red Staircase: Bovey, 23–4.
55 Diamond Throne and Ivory Throne: Duncan, 165, 160.
55 Coronation ceremony: Buxhoeveden, 64–5. Chain of St. Andrew: Izvolsky, 262.
55 Nicholas's title: *Almanach de Gotha,* 79–80.
56 Nicholas preferred Monomakh's Cap: Buxhoeveden, 64. The Imperial Crown of Russia: Alexander, 157.
56 Homage from the family: Vorres, 76.
56 Leaving the cathedral: Bovey, 25.
57 Susanin's descendants: Buxhoeveden, 66. Scroll and menu: Bovey, 26. Nicholas and Alexandra dined alone: Vorres, 76.
57 Crown over his eyes: Bovey, 27.
57 Coronation ball: *ibid.,* 28, 30, 40.
57–8 Illuminations: *ibid.,* 33: Vorres, 77; Kschessinska, 59; Buxhoeveden, 66.
58 Khodynka Meadow: Alexander, 171–2; Bovey, 35, 36. Buxhoeveden, 67–9.
59 French tapestries and roses: Vorres, 79. "Far from being insensible": Izvolsky, 259.
60 Balmoral in the rain: N to MF, 109–10.
60 "She is marvelously kind": *ibid.,* 110.
60–1 Poincaré, "Those of us who reached manhood": quoted by Mansergh, 35.
61 Artificial chestnuts: Buxhoeveden, 74. Police every twenty yards: N to MF, 112.
61 The visit to France: N to MF, 112–17; Buxhoeveden, 74–6.
62 "German helmets . . . dark and boring": N to MF, 117.

CHAPTER 6 THE NEW TSAR

63 "The various affairs you left me": N to MF, 82. "Just before the ministers go on leave": *ibid.,* 83.
63 "I must talk to you, darling Mama": *ibid.,* 88–9.
63–4 The uncles: Alexander, 137–40. "Fast women and slow ships": *ibid.,* 139. *Anna Karenina*: Paléologue, I, 152.
64 "Bellowing of his towering uncles": Alexander, 173.
64–5 Imperial estates and income: *ibid.,* 156–63; Vorres, 94–6.
65–6 Nicholas preferred to be Russian: Mosolov, 19–21. Peter the Great: *ibid.,* 16. Tsar Alexis his favorite: Izvolsky, 269. The 1903 Court Ball: Alexander, 210–11; Buxhoeveden, 98–9; Izvolsky, 264.
66 Kept his own calendar: Vyrubova, 55.
66 Nicholas ignores his aide-de-camp at Livadia: Mosolov, 14.

66–7 Nicholas and his ministers: Pares, 52, 59; Mosolov, 8–10.

67 A man of narrow conviction: Harcave, 50.

67 "The young Emperor . . . seeds of the best": Witte, 96.

68 The Tver Zemstvo: Pares, 57; Florinsky, 1147.

68 "I am delighted": Kaun, 134.

68 Nicholas's unawareness of Franco-Russian alliance: Florinsky, 1141.

68–9 The Disarmament Conference of 1898: Florinsky, 1260–1. Witte's view: Witte, 96–7. Bliokh's book: Billington, 758.

69 "Nonsense and rubbish": Tuchman, *Proud Tower*, 239. "Dissolving his regiments": *ibid.*, 241. Establishment of the Hague Court: Florinsky, 1261.

69–71 "The Silver Age": Billington, 446; Florinsky, 1241–51; Mazour, 236–94. Sholom Aleichem: The *Universal Jewish Encyclopedia*, 516–18.

71 *Narodny Dom*: Paléologue, II, 206–7.

71 "Eating raw ham": MF to N, 128.

71 "A new happy event": N to MF, 130. "We have finished *War and Peace*," *ibid.*, 132.

71 Death of Grand Duke George: Buxhoeveden, 84.

71 "Nicky was really an angel": *ibid.*, 87.

72 "Alix looked after me": N to MF, 140.

72 "I long to see her dear old face": Buxhoeveden, 90.

72 "I cannot really believe she is gone": *ibid.*, 90. Alexandra destroyed Victoria's letters: *ibid.*, 91.

72 Alexandra terrified at a ball: *ibid.*, 58

73 Silent and cold: *ibid.*, 58–9.

73 "The heads of the young ladies": Vyrubova, 4; Botkin, 26.

73 The décolleté dress: Botkin, 26.

73 Ladies refuse to knit: Vyrubova, 5. The family antagonized: Buxhoeveden, 60.

74 Alexandra and Marie compared: Alexander, 169. No way to make friends: Buxhoeveden, 59.

74 To the real Russians, she was *Matushka*: Pares, 55.

CHAPTER 7 TWO REVOLUTIONARIES

75 Simbirsk: Kerensky, *Crucifixion*, 3; Fischer, 5; Payne, 47; Wolfe, I, 38.

75 "From the summit": Kerensky, *Crucifixion*, 3.

76 Ilya Ulyanov: Wolfe, I, 45; Fischer, 6–8; Payne, 62. "Sadly buttoned on his official's uniform": Fischer, 8.

76 Chess: Fischer, 8. "Excellent in everything": *ibid.*, 7; Payne, 53. Ilya's death: Fischer, 9; Payne, 62; Wolfe, I, 52.

77 Bomb inside a medical dictionary: Wolfe, I, 69; Payne, 68.

77 "I tried to kill the Tsar": Payne, 70. "Have courage. Have courage": Fischer, 11.

77 "The execution of such a brother": Kerensky, *Crucifixion*, 6.

77 "Undoubtedly a very gifted person": Fischer, 12. "Go and do what Mama asks": *ibid.*, 12.

77 Vladimir's graduation: Wolfe, I, 60. Blue uniform: Kerensky, *Crucifixion*, 60.

77 "Very gifted, always neat": *ibid.*, 10.

78 Vladimir expelled from Kazan University: Fischer, 18. The farm: Payne, 83. "My relations with the *moujiks*": Wolfe, I, 95.

78 Reading law: Payne, 82; Wolfe, I, 96. Failure as a lawyer: Payne, 89; Wolfe, I, 96. Reading Marx: Wolfe, I, 108–9; Fischer, 20.

79 To St. Petersburg: Wolfe, I, 111; Payne, 93. "Vladimir Ilyich laughed": Fischer, 22. Vladimir abroad: Payne, 105–7.

79 False-bottomed trunk: Payne, 108. "Of course, if you start right away talking against the Tsar": Fischer, 31.

79 Political exiles: Payne 111–13. To Shushenskoe: Fischer, 31–2; Payne, 111; Wolfe, I, 159–62.

80 Life in Shushenskoe: Fischer, 32–3; Payne, 127–8. "A tragicomic condition": Fischer, 33.

80 "It was like living in an enchanted kingdom": Payne, 128.

80 "The hereditary noble, Vladimir Ilyich Ulyanov": Fischer, 34.

81 "Lenin": Wolfe, I, 183.

81 "Nicholas the Bloody": Fischer, 37.

81 London: Payne, 155–67; Fischer, 22, 38.

81 Lenin's growing dominance: Fischer, 42–3; Payne, 170.

81 The Brussels conference: Fischer, 39. "Rats and fleas": Wolfe, I, 286.

81 Crossed the channel: *ibid.*, 296.

82 The split, Bolsheviks and Mensheviks: Payne, 174; Fischer, 40–1; Wolfe, I, 301–2.

82 "Of this dough, Robespierres are made": Wolfe, I, 302.

82 "Lenin . . . Asiatic 'elemental force' ": Kerensky, *Crucifixion*, 13.

82 Fedor Kerensky: *ibid.*, 58–9.

82 "From my earliest glimpses": *ibid.*, 59. "I see myself in early childhood": *ibid.*, 58.

82–3 "A church bell-ringer": *ibid.*, 61. "My youthful adoration of the Tsar": *ibid.*, 65. "I doubt whether higher education": *ibid.*, 84.

83 Narodniks and Marxists: *ibid.*, 112. "This highly respectable pastime": *ibid.*, 116.

84 "It was Easter": *ibid.*, 162.

CHAPTER 8 THE KAISER'S ADVICE

85 The Kaiser's encouragement of Russia's advance in the Far East: Izvolsky, 24, 48; Pares, 67.

85–6 William's appearance: Balfour, 139. His mustache: *ibid.*, 138. His left arm: *ibid.*, 74; Cowles, 9. His powerful grip: Balfour, 139.
86 In love with Princess Elizabeth: Cowles, 47–8.
86 "The Kaiser is like a balloon": Balfour, 126.
86–7 "Nonsense!" "Lies!": *ibid.*, 159. A friendly smack on the backside: Mosolov, 203. "Talking all the more rapidly": Balfour, 145. "If the Kaiser laughs": *ibid.*, 138.
87 "The All Highest": Cowles, 77. African skulls: Balfour, 159.
87 "You ask how Willy was": *ibid.*, 111. "Picklehaube German soldier": Cowles, 124.
88 "We are obliged to let him": N to MF, 120. "Thank God the German visit is over": *ibid.*, 121.
88 Alexandra's dislike of William: Mosolov, 203.
88 "Without the lumbering and indiscreet apparatus": Pares, 166. "The task set us by the Lord of Lords": *ibid.*, 166.
88 "The people will fall on their knees": *ibid.*, 167. "More speeches and more parades": Botkin, 103.
88 "It is not the friendship of France and Russia": Mansergh, 63–4.
89 "You must know, my men": *ibid.*, 55. "Clearly, it is the great task of the future": *ibid.*, 52; Pares, 167; Balfour, 189.
89 "The Admiral of the Atlantic": Mosolov, 203.
90 "Russia has nothing to do in the West": Pares, *History*, 423.
90 "We must try to tie Russia down in East Asia": Balfour, 189. "Glad news": N to MF, 130.
91 "It is evident to every unbiased mind": Pares, 168.
91 "A small victorious war": Witte, 250. New Year's Day, 1904: Harcave, 37.
91 "I am still in good hopes": Mansergh, 103. "Nicholas is doing himself a lot of harm": *ibid.*, 104.
92 Admiral Alexeiev's telegram: N to MF, 171–2. N's Diary, 157.
92 "Sharp grief for the fleet": *ibid.*, 159.
92 The opposing armies and navies: Pares, *History*, 440.
93 "News of inexpressible sadness": N's Diary, 162.
93 "My conscience is often very troubled": N to MF, 173.
93 Alexandra at the Winter Palace: Vyrubova, 9.
94 Rozhdestvensky's pessimism: Kokovtsov, 46.
94 "Bless its voyage, Lord": N's Diary, 179.
94 Dogger Bank: Novikoff-Priboy, 26–32.
94 "The English are very angry": N to MF, 174.
95 Buying extra battleships: Kokovtsov, 46–9.
95 Tsushima: Novikoff-Priboy, *passim.* Mahan, 82–4, 263–82; Florinsky, 1276; Pares, *History*, 445; Charques, 117.
95 Nicholas learns of Tsushima: Mosolov, 14–15.
96 "When a sewer has to be cleaned": Kokovtsov, 53.
96 "Representative of the greatest empire on earth": Witte, 138–9.

96 "I may say that I succeeded": *ibid.*, 140.
96 "Send Witte my order": *ibid.*, 158.
97 "Ice water instead of wine": *ibid.*, 144. "No culinary taste": *ibid.*, 151. "The most naïve judgments": *ibid.*, 162. "I cannot say that I liked him": quoted by Florinsky, 1261 n.
97 "The Emperor Nicholas was morally compelled": Witte, 161.
97 "No diplomat by profession could have done it": Izvolsky, 24. "I am creating him a count": N to MF, 175.
97 The Kaiser's attitude: Kokovtsov, 391.
98 "I agree fully": *Willy-Nicky*, 74–5.
98 Björkö: Cowles, 215; Balfour, 258.
98 "No longer find your emperor alive": Cowles, 219.
99 "Your ally notoriously left you": *Willy-Nicky*, 130–2.

CHAPTER 9 1905

100 Plehve: Pares, *History*, 408, 425.
100–1 Kishenev pogrom: Harcave, 35. "To the devoutly Orthodox Russians": Sacher, 80–1.
101 "Police socialism": Harcave, 39.
101 Father Gapon: Harcave, 66; Mazour, 352–3.
101–2 The Putilov strike: Harcave, 70–2. Gapon's vision: *ibid.*, 81, 88.
102 William Howard Taft: Tuchman, *Proud Tower*, 409. Theodore Roosevelt: *ibid.*, 424.
102 "Capitalistic exploiters, crooks": Mazour, 354–5.
102 The Blessing of the Waters: Harcave, 77–8.
103 The day before: *ibid.*, 83–5.
103 "Troops have been brought": N's Diary, 207.
103 The march: Harcave, 88–9.
103 Casualty figures for Bloody Sunday: Pares, 79.
104 "And so we have no Tsar": Mazour, 355. "Bloodstained creature" and "common murderer": Virginia Cowles, *The Gay Monarch* (New York, Harper, 1956), 346.
104 "Nicholas Romanov . . . soul murderer": Mazour, 356. Gapon's death: Harcave, 95; Mazour, 357; Florinsky, 1172.
104 "A painful day": N's Diary, 207.
104 Witte's suggestion: Harcave, 121. The workers at the palace: Kokovtsov, 39–40.
104 Alexandra's letter: Buxhoeveden, 108–10.
105 Grand Duke Serge: Vyrubova, 13; Paléologue, I, 156–60. The Convent of Mary and Martha: Paléologue, I, 161.
106 "It makes me sick to read the news": N to MF, 183.
106 The *Potemkin*: Harcave, 156. The October general strike: *ibid.*, 179, 183; Charques, 124.

106 The Soviet: Pares, 85; Harcave, 188; Mazour, 358.
107 "So the ominous quiet days began": N to MF, 184–5.
108 "I have a constitution in my head": von Laue, 25.
108 "At the University, I worked day and night": Witte, 13.
108 "I acquitted myself with success": *ibid.*, 19.
108 "It will not be an exaggeration": *ibid.*, 52.
108 "Fools!": *ibid.*, 76.
108 "She obtained her divorce": *ibid.*, 35.
109 "A kindly, well-bred youth": *ibid.*, 179.
109 "Alexandra does not lack physical charms": *ibid.*, 198
109 "The only man who can help you now is Witte": MF to N, 180.
109 "I shall kill myself": Witte, 247; Mosolov, 90; Vyrubova 26; Pares, 86.
109 The text of the October Manifesto: Harcave, 196.
110 "Three cocks were crowing at the same time": *ibid.*, 211.
110 "The proletariat knows": Florinsky, 1178–9.
110 Black Hundreds: Harcave, 204.
110–11 Lenin in Russia: Fischer, 51. "Go ahead and shoot": *ibid.*, 54.
111 Nicholas's letters on Witte: N to MF, 188, 192, 195, 211.
111 "To the Emperor of all the Russias": Harcave, 249.
111 "You see before you the happiest of mortals": Kokovtsov, 124.
112 "As long as I live": N to MF, 120.
112 200,000 roubles: Kokovtsov, 332.
112 "A great never-to-be-forgotten day": N's Diary, 174.
112 Alexis's birth: Vyrubova, 10. Russia celebrates: Buxhoeveden, 103.
112 His Imperial Highness: Almedingen, 80.
112 The christening: N's Diary, quoted by Catherine Radziwill, *The Taint of the Romanovs* (London, Cassell, 1931), 179–80; Buxhoeveden, 104.
113 "Alix and I have been very much worried": N's Diary, quoted by Radziwill, *op. cit.*, 181.
113 "There again was some blood": *ibid.*, 181.
114 "I have a secret conviction": Paléologue, I, 98.

CHAPTER 10 THE TSAR'S VILLAGE

117 "Tsarskoe Selo was a world apart": Botkin, 18.
117 The park at Tsarskoe Selo: *ibid.*, 15–17; Alexander, 158, 163; Meriel Buchanan, 66. The Cossacks: Paléologue, I, 244.
118 Building of the palaces: Botkin, 16. A masterpiece under glass: *ibid.*, 17.
118–19 Inside the palace: Almedingen, 187–8. The Imperial Guard: Paléologue, I, 243–5.

119 Palace police: Vyrubova, 158; Botkin, 62.
119 "Resplendent in snow-white garters": Bykov, 34.
119 Court protocol: Botkin, 32.
120 "Has anything happened?": *ibid.*, 58.
120 "You are called": *ibid.*, 83.
120–1 Count Fredericks: Mosolov, 101, 111, 127; Vyrubova, 93. "The very personification of court life": Paléologue, I, 20–1.
121 "Fredericks went to announce the Prince": Botkin, 41. "Oh, I thought you were somebody else": *ibid.*, 41.
121 Orlov: Mosolov, 122, 163; *ibid.*, 43–4.
122 "The enchanted little fairyland": Botkin, 61.
122 "They were not soldiers": Vyrubova, 9. Jim Hercules: Vorres, 26.
123 Alexandra's routine: Vyrubova, 56, 84. Shared the same bed: Vorres, 128. The bedroom: Dehn, 66. Chapel and bathroom: *ibid.*, 67.
123 The mauve boudoir: Vyrubova, 54, 70; Dehn, 70; Buxhoeveden, 51–2.
124 Talked in English: Vyrubova, 73.
124 "Sunny": *ibid.*, 59. The bird call: *ibid.*, 3–4.
125 Alexandra's gowns: *ibid.*, 55. Her bath: Dehn, 66. Her hair: Vyrubova, 74. "Only rubies today": *ibid.*, 74.
125 "Do you really like this skirt?": Dehn, 68.
125 Brissac: Vorres, 93. Lingerie and shoes: Dehn, 68.
125 "Advancing through the masses of greenery": *ibid.*, 39.
126 Dr. Botkin: Botkin, 29–30. English collies: Vyrubova, 16.
126 Father Vassiliev: Botkin, 80–1.
126 The Imperial table: Mosolov, 225–9; Almedingen, 120–1. Cubat: Vyrubova, 76.
127–8 "Prepare Her Majesty's carriage": *ibid.*, 159. The coachman: Botkina, 8. Policemen: Vyrubova, 159. Petitions for the Tsar: Spiridovitch, I, 72. Orlov and the young girl: *ibid.*, I, 73.
128 Tea: Vyrubova, 57–8.
129 "Although my audience was a private one": Paléologue, I, 190.
130 "I'm afraid I've wearied you": *ibid.*, 197.
130 Evenings: Vyrubova, 58–9.
130 "Remarkably clear enunciation": *ibid.*, 61. The Tsar's books: Mosolov, 31. "He could not endure the sight": Vyrubova, 56.
130 English biscuits: Vorres, 128.

CHAPTER 11 OTMA AND ALEXIS

131 Footsteps overhead: Vyrubova, 54. The girls' rooms and nurses: *ibid.*, 77; Vorres, 107.
131 "Once she even forgot that Marie was in her bath": Vorres, 107.

132–3 Descriptions of the four girls: Gilliard, 73–7; Buxhoeveden, 153–60; Dehn, 75–80; Vorres, 108–12; Kobylinsky, 220–1; Gibbs, in Wilton, 254–5.
132 "You must wait, Mama": Botkin, 65.
132 "Merde": Gilliard, 74.
132 "You felt that she was the daughter of an Emperor": Kobylinsky, 220.
133 OTMA: Gilliard, 73.
134 "We sisters always borrow from each other": Buxhoeveden, 159.
134 "My mother asks you to come": Botkina, 11.
134 "May it please Your Imperial Highness": Buxhoeveden, 158.
134 "The girls enjoyed every minute of it": Vorres, 112.
135 "The Big Pair" and "The Little Pair": Vyrubova, 77; Gilliard, 75.
135 Frilly dressing tables, perfumes, etc.: Dehn, 78.
135 The crippled child: Buxhoeveden, 159.
136 "Alexis was the center": Gilliard, 72.
136 "My dear little Tsarevich": Mosolov, 29–30.
136 First signs of hemophilia: Vyrubova, 81.
136 "Poor little Alexei fell on his forehead: MF to N, 231.
137 Orthopedic devices: Pares, 132.
138 Derevenko and Nagorny: Gilliard, 38.
138 "Lift my arm. Put up my leg": Vyrubova, 81.
138 The strawberry episode: Mosolov, 53.
138 "He thoroughly enjoyed life": Gilliard, 40.
139 "Derevenko says it must be so": *ibid.*, 85.
139 "Now girls, run away": Dehn, 82.
139 "When the Heir to the Russian throne": Catherine Radziwill, *The Taint of the Romanovs* (London, Cassell, 1931), 197. "It's really nice of you": Buxhoeveden, 151. "To illustrate and write the jingles": Botkin, 76.
139 "Can't I have my own bicycle?" Vyrubova, 81.
139 "Daredevil Reaction": Agle, 79.
140 Bicycle on the parade ground: Told to the author by the late Mr. Oleg Rodomar, who witnessed the scene.
140 "All grownups have to go": Botkina, 13.
140 "Great railways with dolls": Fülöp-Miller, 82.
140 Joy: Vyrubova, 84. Vanka: Gilliard, 71.
141 The sable: Mosolov, 55–9.
141 Playmates: Vyrubova, 83–4.
142 "Luckily, his sisters liked playing with him": Gilliard, 71.
142 "I like to think and wonder": Radziwill, *op. cit.*, 199.
142 "At times his visits would suddenly cease": Gilliard, 26.
142 "Rather tall for his age": *ibid.*, 40. "The kind of child who can hardly bear correction": *ibid.*, 39.
143–5 Gilliard's account: *ibid.*, 38–43.

CHAPTER 12 A MOTHER'S AGONY

147–8 Prince Leopold: *ibid.*, 257–8, 398. Bitten on the knee: Balfour, 75.
148 "Not in our family": Longford, 235.
148 "His Royal Highness": McKusick, 89. "The peculiar ability of the Prince to suffer severe hemorrhage": *ibid.*, 90.
148 Victoria's reaction: Longford, 398. The Order of the Garter: *ibid.*, 367.
149 "She cannot bring herself to consent": McKusick, 90.
149 Balmoral Volunteers: Longford, 398. Slipped away to Paris: *ibid.*, 422. Married: *ibid.*, 447.
149 Leopold's death: McKusick, 90. "For dear Leopold himself": Longford, 461.
149 Frittie: McKusick, 91.
150 Drs. Otto and Nasse: *ibid.*, 88.
150 "It is predictable": Haldane, *Sang Royal*, 39.
151 "Our poor family seems persecuted": McKusick, 88.
152 "I saw the Tsarevich": Vyrubova, 16.
152 "I could see she was transfused": Gilliard, 205.
153 Doctors shake their heads: *ibid.*, 251.
154 "God is just": Pares, 133. The private chapel: Kokovtsov, 449; Pares, 132; Fülöp-Miller, 112, 122.
154 "God has heard me": Gilliard, 52. Guilt feeling: Kokovtsov, 451; Gilliard, 53.
155 "I must have a person to myself": Buxhoeveden, 166.
155 Urge to help others: Gilliard, 127.
156 "The Empress had great moral influence": Buxhoeveden, 169.
156 "I feel somehow nearer her like this": *ibid.*, 214.
156 Anna and Alexandra: Vyrubova, 28; Dehn, 48. "I remember Vyrubova": Botkina, 8.
157 Lieutenant Vyrubov: Vyrubova, 30; Pares, 128.
157 "I thank God": Vyrubova, 23. "Now you have subscribed": Pares, 128.
158 "When Their Majesties came to tea with me": Vyrubova, 35.
158 Anna at the palace: Paléologue, I, 229.
158 "No royal favorite": Fülöp-Miller, 95; Paléologue, I, 229.
159 "I will never give Anna an official position": Dehn, 49.
159 "A vehicle," "A gramophone disc": Pares, 129.
160 A virgin: Vyrubova, 395; Kerensky, *Crucifixion*, 170.
160 The Empress's health: AF to N, 272, 284, 289, 295, 296, 298, 299, 301, 302, 305, 308, 360; Vyrubova, 10–11; Buxhoeveden, 197.
160 "Indeed a sick woman": Vorres, 130.
160 "A family weakness of the blood vessels": Kobylinsky, 219.

161 "I have been ill nearly all the time": Buxhoeveden, 128. "Don't think my ill health depresses me": *ibid.*, 126.
161 "She keeps to her bed": N to MF, 248. "Botkin has persuaded her": *ibid.*, 254. "It is too sad and painful": MF to N, 237–8.
162 "Some trouble of the circulation": Marye, 394.

CHAPTER 13 THE ROYAL PROGRESS

164 "This bog": Kokovtsov, 304.
164 The Imperial train: Mosolov, 241–5; Vyrubova, 97.
165 *Zakouski:* Vyrubova, 97; Bruce Lockhart, 57; Mosolov, 224.
165 Heat and discomfort: N to MF, 247. Silver toboggans: Mosolov, 55.
166 The Finnish fjords: Gilliard, 97.
166 The *Standart:* Mosolov, 246.
166 Informality aboard the yacht: Botkin, 10; Almedingen, 120.
166–7 "During performances of the opera": Vorres, 92. Sailor-nannies: Vyrubova, 29.
167 Nicholas ashore: *ibid.*, 18, 28–9. Alexandra aboard: *ibid.*, 18, 29.
168 "Just like any other grandmother": *ibid.*, 88. Evening prayer: *ibid.*, 29. Rocked to sleep: *ibid.*, 18.
168 Shipwrecked: Mosolov, 247; Vyrubova, 33; Buxhoeveden, 114.
168 "The Emperor rather disheveled": Vyrubova, 33.
169 "Ashore and afloat, there were dinner parties and balls": Heckstall-Smith, 77.
169 Prince Albert's whooping cough: Wheeler-Bennett, 42.
169 "The one and only time I ever saw Tsar Nicholas": Windsor, 69.
170 "Dear uncle . . . most kind": Buxhoeveden, 122.
170 "He said he would be happy": N to MF, 122. "His joke . . . was in very doubtful taste": MF to N, 125.
170 "Emperor William's visit was a success": N to MF, 269.
170 The flowering of the Crimea: Vyrubova, 36.
171 "To see a cavalcade of Tartars": *ibid.*, 38.
172 Livadia Palace: *ibid.*, 41–3; Botkina, 13.
172 The Empress at Livadia: Vyrubova, 39.
172 "Little Alexis and I saw it happen": Vorres, 110.
173 "Just now, Alexei has come in": N to MF, 250.
173 "Madame, this is for umbrellas": Botkina, 9.
173 The Tsar at Livadia: Vyrubova, 39.
173 Nicholas's march in private's uniform: Mosolov, 22; Botkina, 9–10.
174–5 Easter at Livadia: Vyrubova, 47.
175–6 Fabergé: This account of the master jeweler and his art draws heavily on Bainbridge and Dennis. In addition, I have seen Fabergé collections at the Metropolitan Museum in New York, at Mrs. Merriweather Post's home in Washington, D.C., in the Kremlin in Moscow and in the Hermitage in Leningrad.

176 The Great Siberian Railway Easter Egg: Tupper, 269–70.
177 "They should realize the sadness": Buxhoeveden, 180.
177 Alexis at the charity bazaars: Vyrubova, 26.
177 Yalta parties: Vorres, 56; Vyrubova, 44.
177 The Emir of Bokhara: Vorres, 92; Vyrubova, 39.
177 Olga's necklace: Vyrubova, 43.
177 Olga's birthday ball: *ibid.*, 44–5.

CHAPTER 14 "THE LITTLE ONE WILL NOT DIE"

179 "Darling Madgie": Buxhoeveden, 129.
180 Borodino Centenary: Botkin, 89. "A common feeling of deep reverence": N to MF, 270.
180 Moscow ceremonies: N to MF, 273; Bruce Lockhart, 74. "Alexis got hold of a glass of champagne": N to MF, 274.
181 Bialowieza: Mosolov, 251. "The weather is warm": N to MF, 274. Alexis fell jumping into a boat: *ibid.*, 275.
181 The house at Spala: Vyrubova, 91. The Road of Mushrooms: *ibid.*, 92. Flaming torches: *ibid.*, 91.
181 "Alexis had looked to me ill": Gilliard, 28.
182 "An experience in horror": Vyrubova, 92.
182 Botkin's examination: N to MF, 276. "The days between the 6th and the 10th were the worst": *ibid.*, 276. Screams pierced the walls: Gilliard, 29.
183 "Mama, help me!": Buxhoeveden, 132.
183 "I was hardly able to stay in the room": N to MF, 276. Nicholas weeping: Vyrubova, 93.
183 "It will not hurt any more, will it?": Buxhoeveden, 132. "Build me a little monument": Vyrubova, 93.
183 The household routine unchanged: Gilliard, 29, 31.
183 "I could see the Tsaritsa in the front row": *ibid.*, 29.
184 Medical bulletins: *ibid.*, 30. Prayers: *ibid.*, 31.
184 "All the servants, the Cossacks": N to MF, 277.
184 The end had come: Vyrubova, 93.
185 "The Little One will not die": *ibid.*, 94.
185 "The doctors notice no improvement yet": Paléologue, I, 148.
185 "We decided to give him Holy Communion": N to MF, 276–8.
186 "I do not agree with my colleagues": Mosolov, 151–2. "The recovery was wholly inexplicable": Vorres, 143.
186 "It is impossible to predict": M. Litten, *Hemorrhagic Diseases* (New York, W. B. Saunders and Co., 1905).
187 Poinsard: Brinkhous, 249–53.

188 Resumption of normal life: Vyrubova, 95–6.
188 "Alexis's recovery will be very slow": N to MF, 277–8. The journey home: Mosolov, 152; Vyrubova, 97.
188 Alexis's leg: Gilliard, 32; Vyrubova, 93. Hot mudbaths: Gilliard, 37.

CHAPTER 15 RASPUTIN

190 Rasputin's appearance: Fülöp-Miller, 3–4; Iliodor, 92; Pares, 135.
190–1 Rasputin's eyes: Vyrubova, 153; Iliodor, 209; Paléologue, I, 292.
191 "The starets made me lie down on the sofa": Yussoupov, 208.
192 "Well, my dear": Yussoupov, *Rasputin*, 103.
192 Rasputin and the country girl: Fülöp-Miller, 6–7.
192 "He ran his pale eyes over me": Rodzianko, 24.
193 "When Rasputin came into my study": Kerensky, *Murder*, 46.
194 "When you select your starets": qtd. by Gilliard, 54.
194 "Rasputin" means "dissolute": Paléologue, I, 138; Pares, 134.
195 The horsethief: Fülöp-Miller, 14–15. The rake: *ibid.*, 16.
195 Verkhoturye: *ibid.*, 17–18; Pares, 134.
195–6 The *Khlysty:* Paléologue, I, 139; Fülöp-Miller, 19, 30–2; Wilson, 38. Praskovie Rasputin: Rasputin, 45; Fülöp-Miller, 45. "He has enough for all": Pares, 145.
196 "Gregory has turned pilgrim": Wilson, 33.
196 John of Kronstadt, Theophan, Hermogen: Fülöp-Miller, 54–7.
198 "We have got to know a man of God, Gregory": Pares, 137; Fülöp-Miller, 145; Almedingen, 117.
198 Philippe Vachot: Paléologue, I, 203–10; Pares, 131.
198 Impeccable credentials: Gilliard, 62.
199 Bedtime stories: Vyrubova, 161; Fülöp-Miller, 141.
199 "Will you come and meet a Russian peasant?": Vorres, 138.
199 Rasputin's behavior at the palace: *ibid.*, 140.
199–200 "A good, religious, simple-minded Russian": Rodzianko, 11; Pares, 139; Paléologue, II, 93.
200 "It was the boy's illness: Pares, 138. "Call it what you will": *ibid.*, 138. "Rasputin's presence in the palace": Gilliard, 84.
200 "Rasputin took the empire": Haldane, 39.
201 General Beletsky: Pares, 138.
201 Dr. Lucas: Lucas, *passim.*
201–2 Relationship between emotions and bleeding: Drs. Agle, Mattsson and Gross, Poinsard (in Brinkhous) and Lucas all describe this relationship.
202 "The power, the nervous force . . . from my father's eyes": Rasputin, 39.

202 "There is no doubt": Vorres, 142.
203 "The poor child lay in pain": *ibid.*, 142.

CHAPTER 16 THE HOLY DEVIL

205 Rasputin's costume: Vorres, 141.
205 "Curiosity, unbridled and embarrassing": *ibid.*, 139.
205 "In Alicky's boudoir": *ibid.*, 139.
206 "Our eyes met": Dehn, 100.
206 "Come, my lovely mare": Fülöp-Miller, 271. "Yes, yes, my dears": *ibid.*, 271.
206 "Dirty hands into his favorite fish soup": Pares, 140.
207 "He had too many offers": Pares, 142.
207 "Women found in Gregory Efimovich": Fülöp-Miller, 207.
207 "Would you be ready?": *ibid.*, 206–7.
208 "You think that I am polluting you": *ibid.*, 215.
208 "Rasputin was there": Vorres, 139.
208 "Oh please, he wants to see you so much": *ibid.*, 140.
208 The Tiutcheva episode: Fülöp-Miller, 146; Gilliard, 62–3; Mosolov, 163–4.
209 Breach between the sisters: Paléologue, I, 161.
209 St. Petersburg in an uproar: Rodzianko, 31.
209 "I have shut his trap": Iliodor, 202.
209 "This is not a family affair": Rodzianko, 27–8.
210 "Let one man bring a plank": Iliodor, 67; Fülöp-Miller, 60.
210 Rasputin in Tsaritsyn: Iliodor, 108. "Gregory, you are Christ": *ibid.*, 111.
210 "Take your choice": *ibid.*, 116.
210–11 "My beloved, unforgettable teacher": Moorehead, 72.
211 Were they lovers?: Pares, 145; Kokovtsov, 299.
211 "You are smashing our sacred vessels": Pares, 146; Iliodor, 233–4.
212 "Never and nowhere": Pares, 146; Iliodor, 238. Rasputin's revenge: Kokovtsov, 293.
212 Iliodor produces the letters: Iliodor, 255.
212 "You have bowed down to the Devil": Pares, 150.
212 "It was my intention to start a revolution": Iliodor, 269.
213 60,000 roubles: Vyrubova, 172, 399.
213 Rasputin avoided the palace: *ibid.*, 160.
213 "Saints are always calumniated": Botkin, 123. "He is hated because we love him": Vyrubova, 162.
214 "I went often to Rasputin's lodgings": *ibid.*, 165. "Rasputin had no harem": *ibid.*, 166.
214 "Rasputin was a Janus": quoted by Almedingen, 127.

CHAPTER 17 "WE WANT A GREAT RUSSIA"

215 "We are not frightened. . . . We want a Great Russia": Kokovtsov, 184; Pares, 112.

215–16 "His capacity for work": Izvolsky, 98. "His nobility, courage and devotion": Kokovtsov, 165. "An ideal man to transact business with": Buchanan, I, 160.

216 "I cannot tell you": Pares, 111.

216 Stolypin in Saratov: Pares, 94.

216 "An elderly man . . . with Picadilly whiskers": Virginia Cowles, *The Gay Monarch* (New York, Harper, 1956), 340.

216 "Stolypin told us": Kokovtsov, 153.

217 "Stolypin's necktie": Charques, 161; Kerensky, *Crucifixion*, 121.

217 The attempt on Stolypin's life: Kokovtsov, 163–4; Florinsky, 1195.

218 Nicholas's proposal to sell crown lands: Harcave, 251–2.

219 "If this should continue": Wolfe, II, 31. "One must be able to look truth in the face": Fischer, 54.

219–20 The opening of the First Duma: Kokovtsov, 129–31. "Let the executive power bow": *ibid.*, 140. "Retire! Retire!": *ibid.*, 143, 145.

220 "The sessions of the Duma are hereby resumed": *ibid.*, 155.

221 The ceiling caved in: *ibid.*, 170.

221 A madhouse: *ibid.*, 171. Police plots: *ibid.*, 182–3. "Hands up! . . . Not afraid!": *ibid.*, 172.

221 "A grotesque deputation is coming from England": N to MF, 219.

221 "All would be well": N to MF, 228. Zurabov: Kokovtsov, 179–80.

222 The Third Duma: *ibid.*, 197–8, 209; Florinsky, 1200; Pares, 109.

222 "May an Englishman": Pares, 117.

223 "This Duma cannot be reproached": Kokovtsov, 222. "The Duma started too fast": Pares, 118.

223 Stolypin and Witte: Pares, 110.

223 Stolypin and Rasputin: Rodzianko, 24. Stolypin's failing health: Kokovtsov, 249.

224 "A Tsar's heart is in God's hands": *ibid.*, 167.

224 Stolypin resigns: *ibid.*, 263; Pares, 123. "This is not a question of confidence": Kokovtsov, 223.

225 "I cannot accept your resignation": *ibid.*, 264.

225 "Unfortunately, my son is too kind": *ibid.*, 266.

225 Stolypin expects dismissal: *ibid.*, 268. Petty slights: *ibid.*, 271.

225 "We are superfluous": Pares, 124. "Death is after him!": *ibid.*, 143.

226 Stolypin's assassination: Kokovtsov, 272; Vorres, 126.

226 "Olga and Tatiana were with me at the time": N to MF, 264–5.

226 Bogrov: Buchanan, I, 156–7; Florinsky, 1204.

227 "I cannot say how distressed": MF to N, 262.

227 The Tsar urged to leave Kiev immediately: MF to N, 262. "I returned to Kiev in the evening": N to MF, 265–6. "I went at once to the nursing home": *ibid.*, 266. The Tsar attended the service: Kokovtsov, 276.
227 Kokovtsov averts a pogrom: *ibid.*, 273–4.
228 "I was accorded a most hearty welcome": *ibid.*, 281. "I notice you keep on making comparisons": *ibid.*, 283.
229 "Strange as it may seem": *ibid.*, 291. "Although they were absolutely impeccable": *ibid.*, 290. "We believed that the letters were apocryphal": *ibid.*, 293.
229 "That cunning conspirator": Rodzianko, 33–4. Censorship fails: *ibid.*, 8, 31. Unprintable stories: Almedingen, 124.
230 "I am simply stifling": Pares, 152. "This disgusting affair": Kokovtsov, 294, 303–4. The Imperial couple fails to understand: Mosolov, 176–7.
230 "She wept bitterly": Kokovtsov, 295–6. "The Emperor is so pure of heart": Rodzianko, 38.
230 Rodzianko's interview: *ibid.*, 40–1. "Have you read Stolypin's report?": *ibid.*, 46.
231 "Who is it, Sabler?": *ibid.*, 53. Livadia: *ibid.*, 59. "The Emperor is a saint": Pares, 149.
231 "Remember, Vladimir Nicolaievich": Kokovtsov, 78.
231 "God grant that the new Duma": *ibid.*, 192. "Tell us the truth": *ibid.*, 12.
232 "At first I enjoyed Her Majesty's favor": *ibid.*, 454.
232 Nicholas's letter to Kokovtsov: *ibid.*, 418.
233 "I am like an old fur coat": *ibid.*, 439.
233 "I know you are an honorable man": *ibid.*, 470.
234 General Beletsky: Pares, 151.

CHAPTER 18 THE ROMANOV DYNASTY

236 "A war with Austria would be a splendid little thing": Wolfe, II, 306.
236 "I was so happy then": Vyrubova, 98.
237 "Sure enough, it was Rasputin": Rodzianko, 76–7.
237 "The orchestra was a mass of uniforms": Vyrubova, 99.
238 Alexandra's gowns and jewels: *ibid.*, 99; Almedingen, 130.
238 "She felt so ill": Buxhoeveden, 175. The Maryinsky appearance: Meriel Buchanan, 35–7.
238 Fabergé egg: Bainbridge, 72.
238 Peasants waded into the water: Vyrubova, 100. "Wherever we went": Vorres, 130.
239 Moscow: Vyrubova, 101. "The Tsarevich was carried": Kokovtsov, 361–2.

239 "Nobody seeing those enthusiastic crowds": Vorres, 130.
239 "The Tsar's journey": Kokovtsov, 360.
240 "And why did you separate me from my wife?": Fennell, 193.
241 "Ladies and gentlemen . . . sleeping with their boots on": Vorres, 47.
243 Idle arithmetic: Paléologue, I, 325.
243 "It is certainly the last generation": Vorres, 114–15.
244 Divorce within the Imperial family: N to MF, 165; Vorres, 116.
244 "I had a rather stern talk": N to MF, 164–5.
245 Michael and Alexander III: Witte, 40–1. "Floppy": Vorres, 83.
245 Automobile accident: *ibid.*, 93.
245 "Dina": *ibid.*, 80, 89.
246 "Three weeks ago Misha wrote": N to MF, 213.
246 Michael's mistress: Paléologue, II, 172.
246 "I saw a slender young woman": *ibid.*, 171.
246 Michael's marriage: Vorres, 118.
246–7 "He broke his word": Vyrubova, 96.
247 "A terrible blow": N to MF, 253.
247 "What revolts me more than anything else": *ibid.*, 284.
247 Winter, 1913–1914: Meriel Buchanan, 71; Almedingen, 132. Nijinsky: Almedingen, 132.
248 Olga and Tatiana: Meriel Buchanan, 71. The train to Tsarskoe Selo: Buxhoeveden, 181.
248 Lena Goldfields: Kerensky, *Crucifixion*, 135–6.
248 "No one could oust us from the courts": *ibid.*, 135. "The government commission sat in one house": *ibid.*, 137.
249 "Strenuous political organizing": *ibid.*, 181. "In those days": *ibid.*, 193.
249 "The Tsarist Cheka": *ibid.*, 194.

CHAPTER 19 THE LONG SUMMER OF 1914

250 Red Rock: Gilliard, 92.
251 Visit to Rumania: Buxhoeveden, 181–3.
251 "Tell me the truth, Monsieur": Gilliard, 94.
251 "I think with terror": Sazonov, 110.
252 Marie only a schoolgirl: Vyrubova, 89.
253 "Never have I seen happier faces": Buchanan, I, 188.
253 Beatty: Bruce Lockhart, 88–90.
253–4 Austria-Hungary: Mansergh, 116–20.
256 "The Archduke was an energetic man": *ibid.*, 216.
256 The Black Hand: Balfour, 344.
256 "Serbia's declaration of war": Mansergh, 219. Crush "the Serbian viper": *ibid.*, 132. "The Monarchy with unflinching hand": *ibid.*,

219. "The bloody deed": *ibid.*, 219. "Serbia must be eliminated": Pares, 182.

257 Alexis hurt aboard the *Standart:* Gilliard, 97.

257 Whispers that Rasputin was stabbed: *ibid.*, 97.

258 "I have killed the anti-Christ": Rasputin, 21; Paléologue, I, 78–9.

258 "In him Russia possesses a reliable and true friend": Mansergh, 170.

258 "M. Poincaré differs from many of his countrymen": *ibid.*, 170. "I like him very much": Sazonov, 270.

259 "Nicholas II in the uniform of an admiral": Paléologue, I, 12–13.

259 "I shall long remember the dazzling display of jewels": *ibid.*, 14.

260 "A blazing sun lit up the vast plain": *ibid.*, 21–2.

260 "It had indeed a kind of terrifying grandeur": *ibid.*, 24–5. "It was a splendid night": *ibid.*, 27–8.

261 The Austrian ultimatum: Mansergh, 345.

262 "The Austrian demands are such": Pares, 181.

262 "*C'est la guerre Européenne*": Mansergh, 225; Florinsky, 1315.

262 "As long as there remains the faintest hope": Sazonov, 178.

263 Izvolsky and the Strait: Kokovtsov, 215; Sazonov, 32. "Russia could speak as in the past": Mansergh, 124. Izvolsky a dandy: *ibid.*, 122.

263 The Bosnian annexation: *ibid.*, 122–37.

263 "Brazen impudence": N to MF, 234.

264 "We expect a precise answer": Mansergh, 133. "Of course we are not going to fight": N to MF, 236. "German action . . . has simply been brutal": *ibid.*, 239–40.

264 "In the recent history of Russia": Mansergh, 134. The Kiev military district: Pares, *History*, 471.

264 "This is my war! My war!": Alexander, 259; Florinsky, 1299; Mansergh, 136.

265 "Listen to me, Nekliudov": Mansergh, 196.

265 Sazonov plays for time: Sazonov, 153, 177.

266 "If His Majesty, the Emperor Franz Joseph": Mansergh, 205. "Now or never": Sazonov, 160; Pares, 182. The Austrian Ambassador's message: Sazonov, 156.

267 "Good old Lichnowsky": *ibid.*, 165.

267 "This phantasm of a state": Mansergh, 204.

267 "Austria is now going to come to a reckoning with Serbia": *ibid.*, 221.

268 "Count Pourtalès, Russia means it": Pares, 184.

268 "Now that Serbia has given in": Mansergh, 226.

268–71 Willy-Nicky telegrams: Buchanan, I, 200–4. The telegram referring to The Hague was not included by Buchanan and is taken from Paléologue, I, 270.

270 The Kaiser's rage: Cowles, 356.

270 "I don't think Your Majesty can postpone": Sazonov, 201.

270 "Think of the responsibility": Paléologue, I, 45.

270 "The Tsar remained silent": Sazonov, 204–5.
271 Sazonov and Pourtalès: *ibid.*, 212–13. "In that case, my government charges me": Paléologue, I, 48.
271–2 Alexandra and her daughters at Peterhof: Gilliard, 105–6.
272 "He was never sincere, not for a moment": Paléologue, I, 196–7.

CHAPTER 20 FOR THE DEFENSE OF HOLY RUSSIA

277 The ceremony at the Winter Palace: Vyrubova, 106; Pares, 187; Almedingen, 133–4.
277 The Tsarevich, weeping: Gilliard, 106.
277 Salle de Nicholas: Paléologue, I, 50; Buchanan, I, 212; Vyrubova, 107.
278 "I solemnly swear": Paléologue, I, 51.
278 The crowd knelt: Rodzianko, 109. "God Save the Tsar": Gilliard, 112. "The absolute master of their bodies and souls": Paléologue, I, 52.
278 Moscow, Kiev, Odessa, etc.: *ibid.*, 74; Botkin, 105.
279 "Vive la France": Paléologue, I, 57. "The flags of the three nations": *ibid.*, 59.
279 Sack of the German Embassy: *ibid.*, 58.
279 "For the defense of Holy Russia": Golovine, 205.
279 "The war with Japan": Kerensky, *Crucifixion*, 235.
279 "Now all Russia is involved": Rodzianko, 109.
279 "This is not a political war": Paléologue, I, 71. "If we are unlucky": *ibid.*, 135.
280 "Not a trace was left": Kerensky, *Crucifixion*, 195.
280 "Six months": Botkin, 111. "Sausages": *ibid.*, 68.
280 Moscow: Gilliard, 113; Buchanan, 214–15.
280 "Alexis is complaining of his leg": Gilliard, 113. "When Alexis found he could not walk": *ibid.*, 113.
281 "From this place": Paléologue, I, 90.
281 "As it is God himself": *ibid.*, 95.
281 "The Heir! The Heir!": Gilliard, 115.
282 St. Petersburg becomes Petrograd: Paléologue, I, 108. Nicholas's patriotism: Gilliard, 121.
282 "Let Papa not plan war": Pares, 188. Nicholas tore up the telegram: Vyrubova, 104, 173.
282 "Dear Friend, I will say again": The original of this letter is in the Beinecke Rare Book Library at Yale, where I saw it. A version of the same letter is published by Maria Rasputin, *My Father*, page 77. She describes it as "the last letter my father wrote to Nicholas II before the declaration of war."
283 "This war is madness": Paléologue, I, 122–3.

283 Dress uniforms for the ceremonial parade: Botkin, 112.
284 Russian army on the march: Paléologue, I, 63, 77.
284 "William to St. Helena!": *ibid.*, 65–6.
284 "One . . . was very young": *ibid.*, 64.
284 "The troops grey with dust": Bruce Lockhart, 95.
285 "A wide road that leads to war": Knox, 50.
285 Numbers of soldiers: Golovine, 45, 50. "Russian steamroller": *ibid.*, 53. Railroads compared to France and Germany: *ibid.*, 34.
285 Twenty-three days on the train: Knox, 17. "The railroads decided": *ibid.*, 449. Factories in Russia and Britain, *ibid.*, xxxiii. Court-martial for firing more than three rounds per day: *ibid.*, 255.
286 Russian imports and exports: Golovine, 37. Russian and British seaport traffic: Knox, xxxiii.
286 "A barred house": Golovine, 37.
286 "His sly look": Paléologue, I, 83. 8,000-mile round trips: Knox, 220.
286 "A drawing room soldier": Meriel Buchanan, 107.
286 "Eager for pleasure like a youth": Sazonov, 286.
286–7 German and Russian artillery: Golovine, 32. "Sukhomlinov believed": *ibid.*, 12. Funny stories: Knox, 220.
287 "General Fly-Off": Pares, 194.
287 Grand Duke Nicholas: Paléologue, I, 62; Knox, 43.
288 Sukhomlinov and the Grand Duke hated each other: Paléologue, I, 57.
288 "Go to the devil": Knox, 220.
288 "We hope in six weeks": Mansergh, 214.
288 "Lunch in Paris": Pares, 195.
289 France wants 700,000 men on M-15: Golovine, 35; Mansergh, 37.
289 Paléologue urges the Russians to hurry: Golovine, 212–13.
289 Paléologue's interview with Nicholas: Paléologue, I, 60–1.
289 Paléologue's interview with Grand Duke Nicholas: *ibid.*, 61–3.
290 Russian strategy in East Prussia: Knox, 56; Tuchman, 65–6.
290 Grand Duke Nicholas leaves St. Petersburg: Knox, 43. Samsonov: *ibid.*, 60. Rennenkampf, *ibid.*, 204–5. The German machine gun: Gilliard, 111.
290 Russian cavalry charges the guns: Pares, 198.
291 Russian invasion of East Prussia: Tuchman, 293, 274. The terrain: *ibid.*, 66.
291 Russians believe Allenstein is Berlin: Knox, 84. "Advancing according to timetable": Tuchman, 287.
292 "To see the enemy where he does not exist": Tuchman, 295.
292 Tannenberg. German artillery the decisive factor: Golovine, 133.
292 "The enemy has luck one day": Knox, 74. Russian losses: Paléologue, I, 107.
292 "We are happy to have made such sacrifices": Knox, 90. "We owed this sacrifice to France": Paléologue, I, 106.

292 "If the Russians arrive in Berlin": Tuchman, 293.
293 "This was perhaps our salvation": Golovine, 214.

CHAPTER 21 STAVKA

294 Nicholas's desire to take command of the army: Florinsky, *End*, 61.
294 "We may be forced to retreat": Paléologue, I, 56.
294 *Stavka: ibid.*, 302–5; Knox, 46, 233; Hanbury-Williams, 13.
295 "We all attended the little wooden church": Hanbury-Williams, 246.
295 The Tsar's train at *Stavka:* Paléologue, I, 302.
295 Red and blue lines on the maps: N to AF, 3.
295 "I was summoned to meet the Emperor": Hanbury-Williams, 14.
296 Yorkshire pudding: *ibid.*, 15. "A torchlight procession": *ibid.*, 18.
296 Nicholas's comparison of Russia and the U.S.: *ibid.*, 75.
297 "You see what it is to be an autocrat": *ibid.*, 58.
297 The Tsar walking, rowing: *ibid.*, 40, 56.
297 "We are passing through picturesque country": N to AF, 16.
297 "My hanging trapeze": *ibid.*, 13.
298 Alexis to *Stavka:* Gilliard, 148.
298 "See that Tiny": AF to N, 182. "Tiny loves digging": *ibid.*, 192.
298 "Take care of Baby's arm": *ibid.*, 225. The Empress went to his empty room: Vyrubova, 127.
298 Gilliard and the Empress: Gilliard, 167–8.
299 "We used to start out immediately after lunch": *ibid.*, 125.
299 "At his father's heels": *ibid.*, 149.
300 The Governor's house: N to AF, 73; Gilliard, 150; Vyrubova, 143.
300 "It is very cosy": N to AF, 95. "I read all letters aloud": *ibid.*, 197.
300 "A thunderstorm broke out": *ibid.*, 186.
300 "He wakes up early": *ibid.*, 96. "He always carries his little gun": *ibid.*, 97.
301 "We go out in the car": *ibid.*, 96. "Soft sand": *ibid.*, 184.
301 "Peasant boys": *ibid.*, 211. "An enormous hotel": *ibid.*, 227. "He sits on my left hand": *ibid.*, 96.
301 Alexis at *Stavka:* Hanbury-Williams, 237–9.
302 "He dragged some of us off after lunch": *ibid.*, 109.
302 "Wet sleeves and boots": N to AF, 225.
302 Front-line dressing station: Gilliard, 152. "Very few hands were lifted": *ibid.*, 154. Four British submarines: *ibid.*, 153.
303 "Alexei crept into every possible hole": N to AF, 102.
303 The cavalry charge: Gilliard, 154–5.
303 "The Heir! The Angel! The pretty boy!": N to AF, 108. "Alexei's cat ran away": *ibid.*, 284. "Alexei has borne the strain": *ibid.*, 110.
304 The Empress visits *Stavka:* Vyrubova, 142–3.
304 "Much easier to get on with": Hanbury-Williams, 93. "She is so proud of Russia": *ibid.*, 117.

304 "Baby played the fool": N to AF, 104. "His elbow would not bend": *ibid.*, 236.
304 "The Little One is suffering": *ibid.*, 291. "Baby's leg hurts": *ibid.*, 292.
305 "He rarely refers to the Tsarevich's health": Hanbury-Williams, 57.
305–6 The nosebleed: Gilliard, 155–6; Vyrubova, 169–70.
307 "Owing to the deep, thick mud": N to AF, 119. "Tell him that they always finish their *zakouska*": *ibid.*, 124.
307 "Thank God, your heart can be quiet": AF to N, 235. "Baby has got up": *ibid.*, 240. "Sunbeam is at last going out": *ibid.*, 243. "He received a charming telegram": *ibid.*, 248.
307 The snowball: Gilliard, 165 *n.*
307 "He is very proud of his stripes": Hanbury-Williams, 104.
308 "Papa told me to come to sit with you": *ibid.*, 138.

CHAPTER 22 "POOR FELLOWS, THEY ARE READY TO DIE FOR A SMILE"

309 Austrian defeat in Galicia: Golovine, 214; Pares, 204–5.
309 "It instructs me to impress": Paléologue, I, 129.
310 "If you chase two hares": Knox, 144.
310 "The poor boys were keen as mustard": *ibid.*, 102.
310 Russian cavalry and infantry tactics: *ibid.*, 103, 109.
310 One million casualties: Golovine, 217.
310 The officers walked erect: Pares, 211. Losses in the Preobrajensky Guard: Knox, 189. In the 18th Division: *ibid.*, 194. "These people play at war": *ibid.*, 249.
310 3,000 cadets: *ibid.*, 177. 15,000 students: Paléologue, I, 171.
311 "Remember what I am going to say": Golovine, 66.
311 Officers asked no questions: Knox, 115. German officer shot his stretcher bearers: *ibid.*, 65.
311 "The value of prayer": Knox, 262. "Poor fellows": *ibid.*, 262.
311 The German attack at Easter: Pares, 358.
312 New recruits: Golovine, 107. Przemysl fell: Pares, 227. "Nicolasha came running": N to AF, 38.
312 "Colossal works": *ibid.*, 48.
312 The Russians storm the Carpathians: Pares, 228–9.
313 The German General Staff decided to destroy Russia in 1915: Golovine, 145. 1,500 guns, 700,000 shells: Knox, 282.
313 "From a neighboring height": Pares, 230.
313 "Lost all its blood": *ibid.*, 231. "Poor Nicolasha": N to AF, 55.
313–14 Arm the infantry with axes: Golovine, 127. "These poor devils had to wait": Paléologue, II, 34. "Churned into gruel": Knox, 270, 319.

314 "You know, sir, we have no weapons": Pares, 232.
314 "We are playing the game": Golovine, 240.
314 Preserve the army: *ibid.*, 224. "We will retire to the Urals": Knox, 309. Half the army was destroyed: Golovine, 98.
314 "The spring of 1915": *ibid.*, 145.
315 20,000 guns: Cornelius Ryan, *The Last Battle* (New York, Simon and Shuster, 1966), 352.
315 Silent crowds: Meriel Buchanan, 108. "Nitchevo, little sister": *ibid.*, 121.
315 Anti-Germanism: Almedingen, 137. "I am going to make a row": AF to N, 37.
315 *Nemtsy:* Paléologue, I, 238. The story about the Tsarevich: Bruce Lockhart, 102–3.
316 Pianos thrown into the street: *ibid.*, 110.
316 Grand Duchess Elizabeth: Paléologue, II, 13; Almedingen, 143.
316 "All faithful sons of the fatherland": Paléologue, II, 23.
316 Polivanov: Knox, 415.
317 "Where our retreat will end": Golovine, 231.
317 The Tsar's patriotism: Florinsky, *End*, 60–1. "You have no idea": Gilliard, 137.
317 Alexandra distrusted the Grand Duke: Mosolov, 87. "Nicholas III": Pares, 250. "Yes, do come. I'll hang you": Knox, 334; Buchanan, I, 238.
317 Rasputin's arguments: Paléologue, I, 286, 341.
318 "Please my angel": AF to N, 87. "Would to God": *ibid.*, 89. "I have absolutely no faith in N": *ibid.*, 97. "N's fault and Witte's": *ibid.*, 100. "I loathe your being at Headquarters": *ibid.*, 110.
318 "I never discuss an opinion": Paléologue, I, 305. "All faithful subjects know": *ibid.*, 261.
319 "Darling mine, I do not agree": N to AF, 43.
319 "I consider it my duty": Golovine, 231–2.
319 "The Emperor, white and trembling": Vyrubova, 123.
319 Private visit to Petrograd: Paléologue, II, 68.
319 Anna and the Empress: Vyrubova, 124.
320 The ministers aghast: Pares, 139; Gilliard, 265.
320 "Gentlemen, . . . I leave for *Stavka*": Vyrubova, 125.
320 The Tsar's letter: Paléologue, II, 70–1.
321 "God be praised": *ibid.*, 62–3. "N. came in with a kind, brave smile": N to AF, 70.
321 "The Grand Duke was really a great soldier": Pares, 201.
321 Alexandra's letter to Nicholas: AF to N, 113–16.
322 Relief in England and France: Gilliard, 138–9. Nicholas a figurehead: Golovine, 235; Pares, 275.
322–3 Alexeiev: Knox, 49; Hanbury-Williams, 261. "My cross-eyed friend": N to AF, 55. "I have such good help": *ibid.*, 74.
323 The front stabilized: Golovine, 237.

323 Germans transferred: Florinsky, 1333. 1.2 million men: Golovine, 98.

322–4 Hindenburg: Pares, 367. Total casualties were 7.9 million: Golovine, 93.

324 Importance of the military collapse of 1915: Mosolov, 23–4; Florinsky, *End*, 75.

CHAPTER 23 THE FATEFUL DECEPTION

325 "To some it may seem unnecessary": Buxhoeveden, 192.

325 Hospitals: Vyrubova, 108–9.

325 "I have seen the Empress of Russia": *ibid.*, 109–10.

326 "Tsaritsa, stand near me": *ibid.*, 110.

326 "Very bad wounds": AF to N, 11. "Three operations": *ibid.*, 12. "My nose is full of hideous smells": *ibid.*, 26. "I went in to see the wound of our standard bearer": *ibid.*, 41. "An officer of the 2nd Rifles": *ibid.*, 24. "Whole arm was cut off": *ibid.*, 25. "I had wretched fellows": *ibid.*, 26.

327 "During an operation a soldier died": *ibid.*, 31. "A young boy kept begging for me": *ibid.*, 32. "The young boy gradually getting worse": *ibid.*, 33.

327 "My poor wounded friend is gone": *ibid.*, 53.

328 630 letters in a black suitcase: AF to N, Pares's Introduction, vi; Pares, 248.

329 "I yearn for your kisses": AF to N, 248. "It was hard bidding you goodbye": *ibid.*, 3. "I gave my goodnight kiss": *ibid.*, 14. "I try to forget everything": *ibid.*, 246.

329 "So much sorrow and pain": *ibid.*, 256. "We show nothing of what we feel": *ibid.*, 21. "32 years ago my child's heart": *ibid.*, 249. "Our children be equally blessed": *ibid.*, 267.

329 "My eyes are moist": N to AF, 169. "I do not know how I could have endured it all": *ibid.*, 122.

329 "The sun behind the trees": AF to N, 108. "The pink sky": *ibid.*, 237. "The Dnieper broke up yesterday": N to AF, 160.

330 "Baby madly enjoys your bath": AF to N, 51. "The girls are wild": *ibid.*, 58. "Baby eats lots of blini": *ibid.*, 272. "Baby . . . on the balalaika": *ibid.*, 310. "Marie, alas": *ibid.*, 43. "To get brown": *ibid.*, 334.

330 "He dreads the night": *ibid.*, 41. "Baby was awfully cheery and gay": *ibid.*, 318. "This afternoon I spent in Baby's room": *ibid.*, 318.

331 "Twenty years have I spent in Russia": Buxhoeveden, 186.

331 "What has happened to the Germany of my childhood?": Gilliard, 110. "I have no news of my brother": *ibid.*, 109.

331 "I blush to have been a German": Paléologue, I, 239.

331 "I long that our troops": AF to N, 9. "I do wonder what will be": *ibid.*, 288.
332 "Forgive me, precious one": *ibid.*, 62. "Be more autocratic": *ibid.*, 57.
332 "That horrid Rodzianko": *ibid.*, 110. "We're not a constitutional country": *ibid.*, 145. "For Baby's sake, we must be firm": *ibid.*, 305.
333 Rasputin: Gilliard, 141.
333 Rasputin's call to Anna: Paléologue, I, 137.
333 Anna's accident: Vyrubova, 118–19; Pares, 223; Paléologue, I, 257.
334 "No, harken unto Our Friend": AF to N, 86.
334 "I am haunted by Our Friend's wish": *ibid.*, 87. "I fully trust in Our Friend's wisdom": *ibid.*, 390.
335 "The bedroom was small": Yussoupov, 203.
335 "All were drawn up the same way": Mosolov, 153. "A lady in a low-cut dress": *ibid.*, 153. A supply prepared in advance: Fülöp-Miller, 236.
336 Payment for Rasputin's services: Mosolov, 148.
336 "Anastasia Shapovalenkova": Fülöp-Miller, 183. "An unknown woman": *ibid.*, 184. "Madame Likart": *ibid.*, 185. "The wife of Colonel Tatarinov": *ibid.*, 185. These episodes also appear in the *Red Archives* (Krasnyi Arkhiv), 25, 42, 44, 50.
337 "Maria Gill": Fülöp-Miller, 188. Katia: *ibid.*, 189. *Utilia: ibid.*, 190; *Red Archives*, 47, 29, 30.
338 The detectives: Fülöp-Miller, 190. Two angry husbands: *ibid.*, 294; Pares, 298. The Villa Rode: Fülöp-Miller, 196–7; *Red Archives*, 45.
338 Drunkenness: Fülöp-Miller, 199; *Red Archives*, 28, 41, 43, 48.
339 Titillated Petrograd: Fülöp-Miller, 200. "The Emperor Tiberius": Marye, 446.
339–40 The Yar: Paléologue, I, 331. "I was at Yar": Bruce Lockhart, 125–6. Exposed himself; the "Old Girl": Paléologue, I, 331. Nicholas summons Rasputin: Pares, 225. "My enemy Dzhunkovsky": AF to N, 105.
341 "Remember that I need neither the Emperor or yourself": Paléologue, I, 147.
341 Rasputin's telegrams: AF to N: 35, 144, 149.
342 "It is getting empty in the villages": Pares, 253.
342 Rasputin and Paléologue: Paléologue, I, 292–3.
342 Cancel all passenger trains: AF to N, 195.
342 "Brother, go and help them sing": Fülöp-Miller, 269. Khvostov's appointment due to Rasputin: Kerensky, *Crucifixion*, 221.
343 "Responsible government . . . would be the ruin": AF to N, 290.
343 Nicholas's reaction to her letters: Pares, 252.
344 Witte's death: N to AF, 29. "Do not drag Our Friend into this": *ibid.*, 298.
344 Nicholas unwilling to deprive Alexandra of Rasputin: Gilliard, 177.

CHAPTER 24 THE GOVERNMENT DISINTEGRATES

345 Fredericks in 1905: Buxhoeveden, 232.
345 "When the Emperor went to war": Pares, 280.
345–6 "Think, my wify": N to AF, 71–2. "Yes, truly, you ought to be my eyes and ears": *ibid.*, 269. "You will truly help me": *ibid.*, 270. "There is nothing to forgive you for": *ibid.*, 289.
346 "Speak like a waterfall in Russian": AF to N, 409.
347 Goremykin: Pares, 194. "He would not last through the winter": Florinsky, *End*, 77.
347 "The candles have already been lit around my coffin": Paléologue, II, 14.
347 "To me, His Majesty is the annointed one": Florinsky, *End*, 77.
347 "He sees and understands all so clearly": AF to N, 103.
347 "I call upon you, gentlemen": Florinsky, *End*, 79. "I beg you to inform the Emperor": *ibid.*, 83. "It is our duty to tell the Tsar": *ibid.*, 82.
348 "The behavior of some of the ministers": N to AF, 85.
348 The "Ministerial Leapfrog": Rodzianko, 239; Florinsky, *End*, 86–7.
348 "After the middle of 1915": *ibid.*, 67.
349 "The ministers do not wish to work well": N to AF, 91. "If in any way": AF to N, 145. "He cannot bear the idea": *ibid.*, 219.
349 "I keep wracking my brains": N to AF, 131. "Our Friend told me to wait": AF to N, 214. "Tomorrow, Gregory sees old Khvostov": *ibid.*, 216.
350 Stürmer: Florinsky, *End*, 88; Paléologue, II, 166: Pares, 317.
350 "A bad memory": Sazonov, 306. "An utter nonentity": Rodzianko, 178. "False and double-faced": Pares, 317. "Worse than a mediocrity": Paléologue, II, 166.
350 "I begat Pitirim": Pares, 315. "Lovy, I don't know": AF to N, 256.
350–1 "Dogs collected": Pares, 304. "For a few words": AF to N, 219.
351 Nicholas at the Duma: Rodzianko, 175–6; Paléologue, II, 187: Pares, 308.
351 "Is he not Our Friend's enemy?" AF to N, 91.
351 Polivanov: Pares, 299. Four automobiles: Rodzianko, 183. "Get rid of Polivanov": AF to N, 260. "Any honest man": *ibid.*, 297. "Lovy, don't dawdle": *ibid.*, 297. "Oh the relief!": *ibid.*, 297. "The ablest military organizer": Knox, 412.
351 "A nice old man": *ibid.*, 415.
352 "Long-nosed Sazonov": AF to N, 210. "Such a pancake": *ibid.*, 156.
352 "Wish you could think of a good successor": *ibid.*, 305.

352 Sazonov and Poland: Pares, 341; Paléologue, I, 81, 84.

352 "I won all along the line": Paléologue, II, 297. Dismissed: Sazonov, 313–14; Buchanan, II, 15–18. Nicholas pleased with British decoration of Sazonov: Hanbury-Williams, 119.

353 "I can never hope to have confidential relations": Buchanan, II, 18. Paléologue's view: Pares, 344; Paléologue, II, 224, 257.

353 Marye's interview with Nicholas: Marye, 475.

353 Protopopov: Pares, 379; Vyrubova, 188; Kerensky, *Crucifixion*, 214. "I chose Protopopov": Rodzianko, 260. "He was handsome, elegant, captivating": Kerensky, *Crucifixion*, 214.

354 "He proposed his *tovarich* Protopopov": N to AF, 219. Protopopov's mission to England, France and Sweden: Paléologue, III, 46. "Yesterday, I met a man I like very much": N to AF, 223.

354 Protopopov's health: Paléologue, II, 46; Kerensky, *Crucifixion*, 214.

354 Badmayev: Paléologue, III, 51–2.

355 "Gregory earnestly begs": AF to N, 394. "Please take Protopopov": *ibid.*, 295. "This Protopopov is a good man": N to AF, 256. "God grant": *ibid.*, 269. "God bless your new choice": AF to N, 398. "I hope I shall succeed": Rodzianko, 213. "I alone shall have the power": *ibid.*, 214.

355 Protopopov's eccentric behavior: *ibid.*, 218; Paléologue, III, 51, 88.

356 The icon: Kerensky, *Crucifixion*, 218.

356 "I feel that I shall save Russia": Rodzianko, 219.

356 Food supply: *ibid.*, 217; Pares, 383. "Forgive me for what I have done": AF to N, 428.

356 "Sweet angel . . . Rumania": *ibid.*, 211. "Our Friend was afraid": *ibid.*, 210. "Advance near Riga": *ibid.*, 221. "Our Friend sends his blessing": *ibid.*, 346.

357 "I told Alexeiev": N to AF, 202. "I was very painfully impressed": *ibid.*, editor's note, 203. "I beg you, my love": *ibid.*, 78. "Only for you": *ibid.*, 154. "Not a single soul must know": *ibid.*, 203. "He won't mention it to a soul": AF to N, 411.

358 Brusilov's offensive: Golovine, 98, 241.

358 "Our Friend finds better": AF to N, 377. "Hope we won't climb over the Carpathians": *ibid.*, 382. "Very satisfied with Father's orders": *ibid.*, 411.

358 "Alexeiev has asked permission": N to AF, 268. "Our Friend was much put out": AF to N, 412. "I have only just received your telegram": N to AF, 270.

358–9 "Stop this useless slaughter": AF to N, 413. "My dear, Brusilov . . .": N to AF, 272. Gurko: N to AF, 273 *n.* "An offensive without casualties": Golovine, 95.

359 "Stürmer and Protopopov both completely believe": AF to N, 428.

359 Manuilov: Rodzianko, 211; Paléologue, III, 17. The October Mutiny: Paléologue, III, 74, 83.

359 "Stürmer is an excellent, honest man": N to AF, 206. "It seems that my head will burst": *ibid.*, 248. "These changes make my head go round": *ibid.*, 257. "The eternal question of supplies": *ibid.*, 266.

360 "Nicky so pale": Vorres, 150. "He had never seemed to me so worried": Gilliard, 178.

360 "A young, wounded deserter": Vorres, 150–1.

361 Miliukov's attack: Paléologue, III, 92. "Woe to that country": Pares, 392.

361 "Protopopov and Our Friend both find": AF to N, 436.

361–2 "All these days I have been thinking": N to AF, 295. "Our Friend says Stürmer can remain": AF to N, 437. "I am receiving Stürmer in an hour": N to AF, 296. "It gave me a painful shock": AF to N, 438.

362–3 Trepov: Pares, 395; Paléologue, III, 107. "I am sorry for Protopopov": N to AF, 297. "Only I beg, do not drag Our Friend into this": *ibid.*, 298.

363 "Don't go and change Protopopov now": AF to N, 439. "The man is as sane as anyone": *ibid.*, 441. "The man Protopopov or x.y.z.": AF to N, 442.

363–4 "Those days spent together were difficult": N to AF, 299. "Great and beautiful times": AF to N, 453–5.

364 "Tender thanks for the severe scolding": N to AF, 307.

364 "Alexander Fedorovich, I order you": Paléologue, III, 108.

364 The bribe: Mosolov, 170–3; Moorehead, 107; Pares, 395.

364–5 Petrograd society: Pares, 301. Officers drinking champagne: Bruce Lockhart, 157.

365 "From the stalls to the back row": Paléologue, III, 26. The Narodny Dom: *ibid.*, 80.

Balanchine in the treetops: Taper, 47.

365 "Beautiful, beautiful—like Grace Kelly": George Balanchine to Suzanne Massie, January 12, 1965.

365 German spy mania: Florinsky, *End*, 69. The Tsar not included: Buchanan, I, 245. Clandestine wireless station: Buxhoeveden, 225.

365–7 No evidence that Rasputin was a spy: Pares, 335. "It would have been inexplicable": Kerensky, *Crucifixion*, 220.

366 Dinner with Manus: Paléologue, III, 63, 115.

366–7 "The Empress is a German": Knox, 515. "I cannot believe she is a traitoress": Kerensky, *Murder*, 55. Soldiers' letters: Knox, 515. Disrespect in hospitals: Vyrubova, 136. "Nemka": Paléologue, III, 121; Florinsky, *End*, 70. "If the young Tsarina": Alexander, 271.

367 "Bomb the Tsar's motorcar": Kerensky, *Crucifixion*, 244. Captain Kostenko: Kerensky, *Russia*, 147.

367–8 Nicholas Mikhailovich: Pares, 390. Grand Duke Paul: *ibid.*, 419.

368 Grand Duchess Elizabeth: Pares, 420; Gilliard, 181–2; Paléologue, III, 159.

368 Purishkevich: Pares, 376.

369 "Wonderful energy": N to AF, 196. Purishkevich's speech: Pares, 396–7; Paléologue, III, 111.

369 Yussoupov turned pale and trembled: Paléologue, III, 153.

CHAPTER 25 THE PRINCE AND THE PEASANT

370 Yussoupov wealth exceeded that of the tsars: Vorres, 98.

370 "One of our estates": Yussoupov, 65. A mountain as a birthday present: *ibid.*, 101.

370 Yussoupov genealogy: *ibid.*, 13–28. Archangelskoe and Prince Nicholas's amusements: *ibid.*, 21–5.

371 The Moika Palace: *ibid.*, 67–71. Moscow palace, *ibid.*, 78–79.

371 "Look, isn't baby pretty": *ibid.*, 29. The bear: *ibid.*, 75. King Edward VII: *ibid.*, 90.

372 "I flung myself passionately into a life of pleasure": *ibid.*, 87. "A charming young girl": *ibid.*, 115.

372 "Prince Felix Yussoupov is twenty-nine": Paléologue, III, 132. "The Empress is a very wise ruler": Yussoupov, 211–12.

373 "Town and women are poison for him": AF to N, 294.

374 "This time it is for you to bless me": Vyrubova, 174.

374 "The spirit of Gregory Efimovich": quoted by Pares, 399.

374 "My intimacy with Rasputin": Yussoupov, 202. "Spend the evening with me soon": *ibid.*, 218.

375 "He had long wished to meet my wife": *ibid.*, 218.

375 "I heard Rasputin say that he expected to pay a late evening visit": Vyrubova, 178.

375 "A low vaulted ceiling": Yussoupov, 219–20.

376 "My head swam": *ibid.*, 226.

376–7 "With God in thought": *ibid.*, 227. "You'd far better look at the crucifix": *ibid.*, 228. "I then saw both eyes": *ibid.*, 229.

377 "A savage, inhuman cry": Purishkevich, 105. "What I saw would have been a dream": *ibid.*, 106–7.

378 Rasputin died by drowning: Vyrubova, 182. "Next morning": *ibid.*, 179.

378 "I have killed Grishka Rasputin": Purishkevich, 108. The dog alibi: Vyrubova, 181. Felix telephoned the Empress: *ibid.*, 180.

379 "I swear it": Paléologue, III, 171. Alexandra lying on a couch: Dehn, 118. "My own beloved sweetheart": AF to N, 461.

379 "No trace yet": Fülöp-Miller, 365. The Beast was slain: Paléologue, III, 135.

380 "To the moujiks, Rasputin has become a martyr": *ibid.*, 189.

381 "Am horrified, shaken": N to AF, 312. "A faith that kept her alive": Gilliard, 177. "Before all Russia, I am filled with shame": Vyrubova, 183. "A murder is always a murder": Paléologue, III, 164.

382 "There was nothing heroic about Rasputin's murder": Vorres, 145.
382 "It was a glorious morning": Dehn, 123. The signatures on the icon: Kerensky, *Murder*, 106.
383 "My dear martyr": Paléologue, III, 136.

CHAPTER 26 LAST WINTER AT TSARSKOE SELO

384 Nicholas at Tsarskoe Selo: Pares, 413. "How lovely it was in the woods": Rodzianko, 254. Maps on the billiard table: Vyrubova, 196.
384–5 "The time for peace has not yet come": Paléologue, III, 125–6. "A kind of political will": *ibid.*, 152.
385 "As usual, Nicholas II was kind and natural": *ibid.*, 166. "The Emperor's words": *ibid.*, 151–2.
385 "During the year that I had not seen him": Kokovtsov, 478–9.
386 "Do you not see?" *ibid.*, 480. "The Tsar was seriously ill": *ibid.*, 480.
386 "If I die or you desert me": Paléologue, III, 191.
386 Alexandra's reaction to the murder: Pares, 412; Gilliard, 183.
386–7 Anna moved to the palace: Vyrubova, 185. The telephone, portrait of Marie Antoinette: Pares, 414. "I thought that the door": Kokovtsov, 478.
387 The concealed balcony: Pares, 414. "If someone else had used the language": Kaun, 134.
387 Protopopov the only minister who mattered: Pares, 416. "I noticed he was following me": Rodzianko, 251.
387–8 Telephoned every morning at ten: Pares, 416. "Oh, Majesty, I see Christ behind you": Paléologue, III, 119.
388 "Oh, Madame, why are you so sad?": Dehn, 137.
388 "Taken down a long passage": quoted by Frankland, 88. "It seems as certain as anything": *ibid.*, 87.
389 "I allow no one to give me advice": Paléologue, III, 167.
389 "One should forgive": MF to N, 302.
390 "Your interference . . . is causing harm": Alexander, 283.
390 "Remember, Alix": *ibid.*, 283. "One cannot govern": *ibid.*, 184.
390 The Vladimirs: Vorres, 58; Paléologue, III, 160–1; Buchanan, I, 175–6.
391 "What an awful set": AF to N, 280.
391 Rodzianko's conversation with Marie Pavlovna: Rodzianko, 246.
392 The grand-ducal plot: Paléologue, III, 140-1. "Prince Gabriel Constantinovich": *ibid.*, 157.
392 Paléologue's interview with Nicholas: *ibid.*, 149-52.
393 Sir George Buchanan: Bruce Lockhart, 115, 119.
393 "*Za Pivo*": *ibid.*, 150.

393 Buchanan's interview with Nicholas: Buchanan, II, 43-9.
394 "The Empress must renounce all interference": Rodzianko, 214.
394 "Alexandra Fedorovna is fiercely and universally hated": *ibid.*, 249.
394–5 Rodzianko's interview with Nicholas: *ibid.*, 252. "I consider it my duty, Sire": *ibid.*, 261.
395 "I will do everything afterwards": Vyrubova, 146. "The Empress is a foreigner": Paléologue, III, 172.
396 Protopopov's countermeasures: Pares, 437. "The time is such, Sire": *ibid.*, 437.
396 "What about a responsible ministry?" Rodzianko, 263.

CHAPTER 27 REVOLUTION, MARCH 1917

397 The women, the workers, the soldiers: Paléologue, III, 213, 264.
397 "The ministers are but fleeting shadows": Kerensky, *Crucifixion*, 261.
397 "Be sure, we shall never give you up": *ibid.*, 262.
398 The overburdened railroads: *ibid.*, 204. Cars and locomotives: Florinsky, *End*, 42.
398 Food prices: Paléologue, III, 44.
398 "Our Friend . . . spoke scarcely about anything else": AF to N, 195.
398 Boilers burst: Paléologue, III, 213.
399 "We older men may not live": Payne, 252. Hair oil: *ibid.*, 251. Lenin's mother-in-law: *ibid.*, 250.
399 The events of March 8: Paléologue, III, 213; Pares, 440; Moorehead, 141. Pavlova, Karsavina and Kschessinska: Paléologue, III, 214.
399–400 The events of March 9: *ibid.*, 214; Pares, 440-1; Knox, 558. Enesco: Paléologue, III, 215-16.
400 "I order that the disorders in the capital": Pares, 442.
400 Condition of the Petrograd garrison: Knox, 551; Paléologue, III, 81.
401 The events of March 11: Pares, 442; Moorehead, 143; Knox, 558; Paléologue, III, 216.
401 Rodzianko's telegram, "May the blame not fall," and "That fat
401 Rodzianko has sent me some nonsense": Pares, 443.
402 Ivanov's expedition: *ibid.*, 457.
402 "The part of the city through which we passed": Buchanan, II, 58.
402 The Radziwill party: Paléologue, III, 214, 217.
402 The workers were tired of being killed: *ibid.*, 217.
402 "The Reaction is gaining strength": Kerensky, *Crucifixion*, 266–7; Pares, 443.
402 Sergeant Kirpichnikov: Pares, 445; Moorehead, 146.
403 "The same wide streets": Meriel Buchanan, 164.
403 "At half past eight": Paléologue, III, 221.
403 "The depot troops . . . had mutinied": Knox, 553.
403 "Frightened inhabitants were scattering": Paléologue, III, 222–3.

404 Soldiers join the revolution: Moorehead presents a timetable of defections, 149.
404 "Now there is nothing left . . . but shoot myself": Pares, 451.
404 "The Emperor wishes to express thanks": Kerensky, *Murder*, 78.
404 The mob arrives at the Duma: Knox, 556; Pares, 453.
405 "I must know what I can tell them": Pares, 449.
405 "I don't want to revolt" and "If you don't, others will": *ibid.*, 451.
405 The appearance of the Soviet: *ibid.*, 460. "The entire garrison had mutinied": Kerensky, *Crucifixion*, 274.
406 "Two different Russias settled side by side": *ibid.*, 275.
406 "He seemed to grow every minute": Pares, 450.
406 "Waves of hatred . . . beat against the walls": Kerensky, *Crucifixion*, 219.
406 "It is I, Protopopov": Pares, 454.
407 Fall of the Winter Palace: *ibid.*, 453.
407 Butchery at Kronstadt: Botkin, 139; Paléologue, III, 282. Wild celebrations: Paléologue, III, 225. Kschessinska's mansion: *ibid.*, 229; Kschessinska, 169.
407 "They marched in perfect order": Paléologue, III, 232.
407 Countess Kleinmichel: Vorres, 99.
408 Grand Duke Cyril: Pares, 460; Kerensky, *Murder*, 89. The Red Flag on his roof: Paléologue, III, 259. "I have been alone in carrying out my duties": Kerensky, *Murder*, 89. "I have asked myself several times" Paléologue, III, 265. "Who can tell?" *ibid.*, 265.
409 "On the steps of Our Lady of Kazan": *ibid.*, 226.
409 "We will begin with the Germans here": Knox, 558.

CHAPTER 28 ABDICATION

410 "Here in the house it is so still": N to AF, 313.
410 "I shall take up dominoes again": *ibid.*, 313.
411 "An excruciating pain in the chest": *ibid.*, 316.
411 Voeikov: Buchanan, II, 61.
412 "I hope Khabalov will be able to stop these street disorders": N to AF, 316.
412 "After yesterday's news from town": *ibid.*, 317.
412 "Concessions inevitable": Kerensky, *Murder*, 79.
412 Nicholas chose a longer route: Pares, 458–9.
412 Stopped at Malaya Vishera: Kerensky, *Murder*, 86-7.
412 "Well, then, to Pskov": Pares, 459.
412 Met by Ruzsky: Kerensky, *Murder*, 87.
413 Failure of Ivanov's expedition: Pares, 458.
413 Ruzsky's exchange with Rodzianko: Kerensky, *Murder*, 90–2.
413 Formation of a Provisional Government: Paléologue, III, 236.

414 Nicholas must abdicate: *ibid.*, 234. "It is of vital importance": *ibid.*, 233.
414 The generals unanimous: Pares, 465.
414 "On my knees": Mosolov, 27.
414 Peeped out the window: Kerensky, *Murder*, 93.
414–15 Unwilling to start a civil war: Pares, 465.
415 "In favor of my son, Alexis": Kerensky, *Murder*, 93.
415 Shulgin and Guchkov to Pskov: Pares, 466.
415–16 Nicholas's conversation with Fedorov: Benckendorff, 46–7; Mosolov, 124. "Science teaches us, Sire": Gilliard, 195.
416 "This long speech is unnecessary": Bykov, 25–6; Pares, 467.
417 The abdication document: The text quoted is from Pares, 467. Slightly different translations from the Russian can be found in Gilliard, 196, and Paléologue, III, 237.
417 "The Emperor looked at me": quoted by Pares, 468.
418 "Treason, cowardice and deceit": Kerensky, *Murder*, 94–5.
418 "The same scene met me everywhere": Paléologue, III, 247.
418 "It was not so much the Emperor": Buchanan, II, 86.
418 "Well, so he's gone": Gorer and Rickman, 71.
419 "Bliss was it in that dawn": quoted by J. C. Squire in his Introduction to Buxhoeveden, xvii.
419 Congratulations and fraternal greetings": Paléologue, III, 254.
419 Wilson's speech: quoted by Kennan, 18.
419 "It is the shallow fashion of these purblind times": Churchill, *World Crisis* (Scribner), 695–7.
420 "Nicky must have lost his mind,": Alexander, 287–8.
421 "The immediate accession of the Tsarevich": Paléologue, III, 251.
421 "I needn't tell you of my love for the Emperor": *ibid.*, 265–6.
421 Michael and Constantinople: Pares, 470.
422 "To His Majesty, the Emperor Michael": Kerensky, *Murder*, 95.
422 "No more Romanovs": Paléologue, III, 238.
422 "Long live the Emperor Michael": Kerensky, *Murder*, 94.
423 The meeting on Michael's future: Pares, 470. "He asked me point-blank": Kerensky, *Murder*, 94. "I cannot answer for the life of Your Highness": Bykov, 29. "Monseigneur, you are the noblest of men": Paléologue, III, 241. Children's schoolroom: Pares, 470.
423 Nicholas not considered a threat: Kerensky, *Crucifixion*, 269.
424 "He was absolutely calm": Paléologue, III, 251.
424 Nicholas's address to the army: Pares, 472–3. Other translations in Gilliard, 203–4; Paléologue, III, 259.
424 Nicholas says goodbye to his staff: Alexander, 290; Kerensky, *Murder*, 102.
424 Hanbury-Williams's last interview: Hanbury-Williams, 168.
425 The new oath of allegiance: Alexander, 290–1; Kerensky, *Murder*,

102. The town was illuminated: Alexander, 291. Two red flags: Hanbury-Williams, 171.
425 "The deposed Emperor understands": Kerensky, *Murder*, 99.
425 "The news of Nicky's abdication came like a thunderbolt": Vorres, 151–2.
426 Nicholas greets Marie: Alexander, 288; Kerensky, *Murder*, 101.
426 "Let the Germans in": Kerensky, *Crucifixion*, 269.
426 Nicholas's farewell to Marie: Alexander, 292; Kerensky, *Murder*, 103–4.
427 Alexeiev's bow to the Duma representatives: Bulygin, 188.

CHAPTER 29 THE EMPRESS ALONE

428 "I want you to come to Tsarskoe Selo": Dehn, 147.
428 "How is it in Petrograd?": *ibid.*, 148. "There is no danger, Your Majesty": *ibid.*, 148.
429 The cadet with measles: Vyrubova, 204–5. "She spent all the succeeding days": *ibid.*, 205. The children's temperatures: Buxhoeveden, 251.
429 "Lili, it is very bad": Dehn, 148. "I have wired him": *ibid.*, 150.
429 "Petrograd is in the hands of the mob": *ibid.*, 149.
430 "I don't want the girls to know anything": *ibid.*, 152.
430 Benckendorff's messages from Rodzianko and from the Tsar: Benckendorff, 2–3.
430 The morning of March 13: Benckendorff, 3. "Owing to the state of her children's health": *ibid.*, 5. "When a house is burning": Gilliard, 211. The railway lines would be cut: Benckendorff, 5.
431 "We could not leave": Gilliard, 211.
431 "Lili, they say that a hostile mob": Dehn, 155. The troops defending the palace: Benckendorff, 6–7.
431 "It's just like being on the yacht": Dehn, 153. The rebels were on their way: Gilliard, 212.
432 "The scene was unforgettable": Buxhoeveden, 255. Benckendorff displeased: Benckendorff, 8. "Some inward exaltation": Dehn, 156.
432 Extra blankets: Benckendorff, 9.
432 "How astonished Papa will be": Dehn, 158.
433 "Perhaps the blizzard detains him": *ibid.*, 158. "Address of person mentioned unknown": Vyrubova, 209; Bykov, 32.
433–4 White handkerchiefs: Benckendorff, 14–15. "In the hands of the Duma": Dehn, 160. "Why, Madame? In the name of God, why?": *ibid.*, 162.
433 Electricity and water: *ibid.*, 67, 160; Buxhoeveden, 256. "I must not give way": Dehn, 163.
434 The leaflets: Benckendorff, 16–17.

434 *"Abdiqué!"*: Dehn, 165. "I saw her in Alexis's room": Gilliard, 213. "She was deadly pale": Buxhoeveden, 261–2.
435 State of siege lifted: Benckendorff, 18.
435 "The Emperor is on the phone": Dehn, 174. "You know?": Buxhoeveden, 264.
435 Guchkov's visit: Benckendorff, 20–2. "Bloodsuckers!" Buxhoeveden, 266.
436 Queen Victoria's letters: *ibid.*, 91. "A fierce fire": Dehn, 176.
436 Troops electing officers: Benckendorff, 25. Chevalier Guards: Buxhoeveden, 267–8.
436 Kornilov arrests Alexandra: Benckendorff, 30–5. Sitting together at a table: Bulygin, 190.
437 Kornilov addresses the suite: Benckendorff, 31. "Lackeys!": Bulygin, 191.
437 "The soldiers of the new guard:" Benckendorff, 38.
437 Gilliard's explanation to Alexis: Gilliard, 214–15.
438 Killing the deer: Benckendorff, 39.
438 "I went quietly downstairs": Dehn, 185–7.
439 Nicholas's arrival at the station: Kobylinsky, 170. "This offensive comedy": Benckendorff, 43. "Nicholas Romanov": Buxhoeveden, 271.
439 "His Majesty, the Emperor": Dehn, 188.
440 Nicholas wept: Vyrubova, 212.

CHAPTER 30 CITIZEN ROMANOV

443 "The Emperor was deathly pale": Dehn, 189.
443 Arrangements for outdoor exercise: Benckendorff, 33, 48.
444 "You can't go there, *Gospodin Polkovnik*": Vyrubova, 213.
444 "The crushing grip of the Revolution": Dehn, 190.
444 Three armored cars at Tsarskoe Selo: Kerensky, *Murder*, 110.
444 "I found the Emperor with his sick children": Benckendorff, 50.
444 Burning of Rasputin's body: Paléologue, III, 266; Kerensky, *Murder*, 105; Kobylinsky, 172.
445 "Like the survivors of a shipwreck": Vyrubova, 218.
445 "The roads too dirty": Botkin, 142.
445 Letters, telephone calls, toothpaste tubes and chocolate bars: Benckendorff, 34; Buxhoeveden 285–6.
445 Soldiers at the sickroom door: Benckendorff, 52.
446 "The man only wanted cushions": Buxhoeveden, 284.
446 "He was dozing": Dehn, 192.
446 Stealing gold trinkets: Buxhoeveden, 285.
446 "Where is Alexei?": Vyrubova, 211. "Don't hang about here": Gilliard 222.
447 "Derevenko . . . bawled at the boy": Vyrubova, 222.

447 The film performances: Benckendorff, 95–6.
447 Lessons resumed: *ibid.*, 78–9.
447 "Good morning, dear colleague": Gilliard, 228.
448 "The Tsar accepted all these restraints": *ibid.*, 216.
448 Nicholas followed military and political events: Kobylinsky, 179. "The Soldiers' Committee refused. What humiliation!": Gilliard, 229. "Our love of exaggeration": *ibid.*, 229.
448 Easter service: *ibid.*, 221, 225; Benckendorff, 68; Buxhoeveden, 296–7; Paléologue, III, 319.
449 "Luxuries unnecessary for prisoners": Buxhoeveden, 286.
449 "I'm only an Ex": Dehn, 199. Alexandra believes the country still loyal: Buxhoeveden, 275.
449 Prince Lvov's letter and Grand Duke Nicholas's reply: Hanbury-Williams, 179, 182.
450 "Citizen Romanov" and "Alexandra the German"; Paléologue, III, 257.
450 The menu: Almedingen, 209. "If Nicky killed a few more": *ibid.*, 209–10.
450 Kerensky's speech to the servants: Benckendorff, 54; "He was dressed in a blue shirt": *ibid.*, 55. "His manner was abrupt and nervous": *ibid.*, 55–6.
451 Kerensky and Vyrubova: Vyrubova, 223–4.
451 "Everything is going well": Benckendorff, 59.
451 "A state of feverish agitation": *ibid.*, 59.
451–2 Kerensky's first meeting with the Imperial family: Kerensky, *Murder*, 122–3.
452 "The white hand of the Empress": Vyrubova, 225.
452 "By suffering we are purified": Dehn, 215.
453 "A group of white-clad figures," Anna Vyrubova and Lili Dehn leave Tsarskoe Selo for the last time: Vyrubova, 226; Dehn, 215.
453 Inhuman to separate a mother from her sick children: Benckendorff, 66.
453–4 Kerensky's interview with Alexandra: *ibid.*, 75–6. "Your wife does not lie": *ibid.*, 76.
454 Kerensky's interview with Nicholas: *ibid.*, 77.
454 "Kerensky's attitude toward the Tsar is no longer what it was": Gilliard, 227. "The confidence which the Emperor felt in Kerensky increased": Benckendorff, 77. "He is a man who loves Russia": Pares in the Introduction to Kerensky, *Murder*, 15.
454–5 Bayonet in the bicycle spokes: Buxhoeveden, 299. "Not for anything in the world": Kobylinsky, 177. "What have you got against me?": Benckendorff, 71.
455 The crowds whistle and jeer: Kerensky, *Murder*, 114; Bulygin, 192.
455 Alexandra talks to the soldier: Buxhoeveden, 300, Benckendorff, 80.

456 Colonel Kobylinsky: Kobylinsky, 167–8; Benckendorff, 91; Bulygin, 189–90. "My last friend": Bulygin, 190.
456 The toy-gun episode: Benckendorff, 83; Gilliard, 230–1; Kobylinsky, 177.
456 The kitchen garden and cutting firewood: Benckendorff, 79–80; Gilliard, 229–31.
457 Red and green lights: Benckendorff, 87; Gilliard, 232; Kerensky, *Murder*, 114–15.
457 "Our Captivity at Tsarskoe Selo": Gilliard, 217–18.

CHAPTER 31 "HIS MAJESTY'S GOVERNMENT DOES NOT INSIST"

458 "Simply human beings": Kerensky, *Murder*, 112.
458 "It's a mistake": Buchanan, II, 73.
458 "I will not be the Marat of the Russian Revolution": Kerensky, *Crucifixion*, 161.
458 "He should lose no time in getting away": Paléologue, III, 253.
459 "It's the last chance": *ibid.*, III, 258.
459 Lloyd George's speech: quoted by Pares, 260; by Paléologue, II, 43.
459 Lloyd George's telegram: Lloyd George, 507. The decision to invite the Russian Imperial family: Nicolson, 300.
459 Buchanan's conversations with Miliukov: Buchanan, II, 104–6.
460 "The Republic must be safeguarded": Bykov, 33. One scornful Bolshevik writer, *ibid.*, 35.
460 Provisional Government pledges to the Soviet that the sovereigns will remain in Russia: Paléologue, III, 268. Miliukov cannot deliver
461 King George V's telegram: Buchanan II, 103; Paléologue, III, 278. Text of the telegram: Nicolson, 299.
461 The King and Queen . . . were asking for news of their Russian relatives: Gilliard, 222.
461 "Nothing has yet been decided": Lloyd George, 512.
461 "His Majesty's Government does not insist": Kerensky, *Murder*, 117.
461 "An excuse for rousing public opinion against us": Buchanan's message quoted by Lloyd George, 512.
461 Bertie's letter: quoted by Lloyd George, 514.
461 The plan suspended until early summer: Kerensky, *Murder*, 116–17.
462 "The British Government's final refusal": *ibid.*, 118.
462 "Not masters in their own house": Buchanan, II, 106. Meriel Buchanan's account of the episode: Meriel Buchanan, 195–7. Lloyd George "probably would have given such advice": quoted by Meriel Buchanan, viii a.
463 "An unseaworthy Ark": Lloyd George, 480. "A crown without a

head": *ibid.*, 483. "This country cannot be . . . held responsible": *ibid.*, 516.

463 "His Majesty cannot help doubting": Nicolson, 301. The King suggests that Britain withdraw its offer: *ibid.*, 301.

463 The Duke of Windsor's recollection: Windsor, 131.

463 "We older ones . . .": Payne, 252.

464 "Our tactics": Fischer, 108. "Ilyich did not sleep": *ibid.*, 108.

464 "A plague bacillus": Churchill, *World Crisis: The Aftermath*, 71.

464 Lenin's return: Trotsky, I, 295–8; Moorehead, 184–7.

465 Lenin's initial failure: Trotsky, I, 309–11; Florinsky, 1401–3; Fischer, 128. "Why, that is raving": Trotsky, I, 310. "Lenin was a hopeless failure": Paléologue, III, 302.

465–6 Trotsky in America: Kennan, 31–2. The Root Mission, *ibid.*, 19–23.

466 The Kerensky offensive: Florinsky, 1409–10. Nicholas's happiness: Benckendorff, 94. The "July Uprising": Florinsky, 1431. "More than a demonstration but less than a revolution": *ibid.*, 1432.

467 "The Bolsheviks are after me": Pares in Introduction to Kerensky, *Murder;* Benckendorff, 98.

467 Kerensky's search for a haven: Kerensky, *Murder*, 119. "I chose Tobolsk": *ibid.*, 120.

468 "I have no fear": *ibid.*, 121.

468 The suite: Benckendorff, 99.

468 "The ceremony was poignant": *ibid.*, 103.

469 The family's departure a secret: Kerensky, *Murder*, 128.

469 "No hitting a man when he is down": Kobylinsky, 183; Bykov, 40; Kerensky, *Murder*, 128.

469 "Colonel Kobylinsky's orders": Bulygin, 194. The soldiers refuse to work: Benckendorff, 105–6.

470 Grand Duke Michael: Benckendorff, 107. "How is Alix? How is Mother?": Kerensky, *Murder*, 129.

470 "Is that Uncle Misha?": Kobylinsky, 184.

470 "Weeping like any ordinary woman": Kerensky, *Murder*, 130.

470 The soldiers cursed and grumbled: Benckendorff, 108. The officers would not sit with Nicholas Romanov: *ibid.*, 110.

471 Nicholas could freely return: *ibid.*, 107.

471 Departure from Tsarskoe Selo: *ibid.*, 111–12; Gilliard, 234–5.

CHAPTER 32 SIBERIA

472 The train to Siberia. Stocked with wines: Benckendorff, 121. Gems worth a million roubles: Wilton, 74. Suite and servants: Bykov, 40, and Kobylinsky, who lists them by name, 187–8.

472 Train routine: Kerensky, *Murder*, 131. Walks by the track: Benckendorff, 121.

472 Heat, shades drawn: N's Diary, quoted by Kerensky, *Murder*, 134.

473 Stopped at Perm: Kobylinsky, 185.
473 The boat trip: Kerensky, *Murder*, 135. Pokrovskoe and Rasputin's house: Gilliard, 239–40; Yussoupov, *Rasputin*, 28–9.
473 Arrival in Tobolsk: Kerensky, *Murder*, 132–3; Gilliard, 240; Benckendorff, 121; Botkina, 37.
474 Tobolsk and the governor's house: Botkin, 156; Botkina, 39; Gilliard, 240.
474 Kornilov house: Benckendorff, 122; Bulygin, 194.
474 Enclosed yard: Gilliard, 240. Suite has free access: Gibbs, in Wilton, 244.
475 Attitude toward the Imperial family. Townspeople: Gilliard, 242. Soldiers: Bykov, 60.
476 Pankratov and Nikolsky: Kobylinsky, 190–1; Bulygin, 196; Botkina, 42.
476 "Not wishing to infringe the rules of politeness": Pankratov, *With the Tsar in Tobolsk,* quoted by Bykov, 43–4.
476 Pankratov's tales: Wilton, 61.
477 "We were once ordered by the police": Kobylinsky, 191.
477 Case of wine: Bykov, 45; Botkina, 43.
477 Political education of the soldiers: Bulygin, 196. "The result of these lectures": Kobylinsky, 192.
478 The Kornilov affair: Florinsky, 1436–42.
478 "History will not forgive us": Florinsky, 1445.
478–9 The October/November Revolution. There are innumerable accounts of the Bolshevik *coup d'état.* Most draw heavily on John Reed's vivid eyewitness account, *Ten Days That Shook the World.* I also consulted Trotsky, III, 200–75; Florinsky, 1447–50; and Kennan, 4–6, 71–3. "The Provisional Government appeals": Reed, 103;
479 "Kerensky . . . merely hung around the revolution": Trotsky, I, 183.
479 "The Tsar regret his abdication": Gilliard, 243.
480 "Lessons began at nine": Vyrubova, 311.
480 "One by one all earthly things": *ibid.*, 313.
480 "It is bright sunshine": *ibid.*, 314–16.
481 "A real ice house": Gilliard, 253.
481 "Today there are 29 degrees of frost": Vyrubova, 325.
481 "You never know when they might be useful": Gibbs, in Wilton, 256.
481 "We often sit in the windows": Vyrubova, 309.
481 The plays: Botkina, 49. "I want to talk to you": *ibid.*, 50.
482 "In this atmosphere of family peace": Gilliard, 243.
482 Christmas. "The children were filled with delight": Gilliard, 246. Ribbons and waistcoats: Vyrubova, 302. The church service: Kobylinsky, 194–5; Bykov, 48, 53.
482 "I heard an extraordinary noise": Bykov, 54. "They have weapons": Kobylinsky, 196.

483 The epaulets. 100 votes to 85: Gilliard, 251. "After dinner": *ibid.*, 252. "I felt I could bear it no more": Kobylinsky, 197–8.

483 "All the old soldiers . . . are to leave us": Gilliard, 253.

484 The snow mountain: Gilliard, 252–5. The Soldiers' Committee disapproves: Kobylinsky, 196. "The soldiers with a hang-dog look": Gilliard, 255.

484 Obscene words: Kobylinsky, 198; Gilliard, in Wilton, 229.

484–5 Money. Kobylinsky arrived entrusted with a large sum: Benckendorff, 127. The sums stopped coming: Kobylinsky, 197. An anonymous offer of enough for six months: Benckendorff 129. An advance of 20,000 roubles: Kobylinsky, 197. "Nicholas Romanov . . . must be put on soldier's rations": *ibid.*, 199; Bykov, 57. "Since everyone is appointing committees": Gilliard, 255. Eggs, sweetmeats and delicacies: Bykov, 44–5.

485 "The strange thing about the Russian character": Vyrubova, 318.

485 "Today is Carnival Sunday": Gilliard, 256.

CHAPTER 33 GOOD RUSSIAN MEN

487 "From there . . . via Japan": Kerensky, *Murder*, 118.

487 The family not be separated: Gilliard, 256.

487 Mysterious visitors with fine-combed beards: Botkina, 45; Bykov, 47.

488 Margaret Khitrivo: Kerensky, *Murder*, 138–9; Bulygin, 195–6.

488 "My lord, you bear the name of St. Hermogen": Bykov, 48.

488 Benckendorff's efforts: Pares, 486. Soloviev's leadership; *ibid.*, 486.

488 Who was Soloviev?: Bulygin, 197; Bykov, 50–1; Pares, 486.

489 "I went to Anya's house last night": Bulygin, 198.

489 "Gregory's family and his friends are active": Bulygin, 198. "The

489 Brotherhood of St. John of Tobolsk": *ibid.*, 199. "Three hundred faithful officers": Bykov, 57.

490–1 Soloviev in Tyumen: Bulygin, 199–201. Soloviev arrested by the Bolsheviks, *ibid.*, 211. Siberia to Berlin: *ibid.*, 211, 216. Petrograd banker: *ibid.*, 216. Romanova marries a Bolshevik: *ibid.*, 215. A German agent?: *ibid.*, 217. Released: *ibid.*, 207.

491 "The royalists were captained by the traitor Soloviev": Kerensky, *Murder*, 27. Agreement that Soloviev was a Bolshevik agent and possibly also a German agent: Wilton, 131–3.

492 Alexandra dreamed of English gardens: Vyrubova, 340. "God will not leave it like this": *ibid.*, 336.

492 The wooden sled on the stairs: Botkina, 56. Worst since Spala: Gilliard, 258–9. "He is frightfully thin and yellow": Vyrubova, 338. "Yesterday, for the first time . . .": *ibid.*, 339.

493 "The atmosphere is . . . electrified": *ibid.*, 341.

493 Loss of territory at Brest-Litovsk: Fischer, 287. One Russian general shot himself: Botkin, 172.

494 "Suicide," "a disgrace for Russia": Gilliard, 257. "To think that they called Her Majesty a traitor": Bulygin, 202. "I should never have thought the Emperor William . . .": Gilliard, 257.

494 "After what they have done to the Tsar": *ibid.*, 257.

494 The Red Urals: Bykov, 61. Bring the family to Ekaterinburg, *ibid.*, 62–3.

495 The Omsk detachment: Bulygin, 203. "Good Russian Men": *ibid.*, 201, 203, 205; Bykov, 58. "His Majesty tells me": Gilliard, 258.

495 Zaslavsky: Kobylinsky, 202.

495 Yakovlev: *ibid.*, 202; Bulygin, 206–8. Had tea with the Tsar: Gilliard, 259.

496 "Your Majesty" and "*Bonjour, Monsieur*": Bulygin, 208. "Everyone is restless and distraught": Gilliard, 259.

496 "The first document was addressed to me": Kobylinsky, 203. Yakovlev visits the Tsarvich: *ibid.*, 204; Gilliard, 259. "We feel we are forgotten by everyone": Gilliard, 260.

496–7 "I have received an order": Kobylinsky, 205. "After lunch at two o'clock": *ibid.*, 205. "I refuse to go": Bulygin, 208.

497 "They want to force me to sign": Kobylinsky, 206; Bulygin, 209, 222. "I shall also go": Kobylinsky, 206. "The commissar says that no harm will come": Gilliard, 260.

497–8 "But Mother, if Father has to go": *ibid.*, 261.

498 "Doctors demand immediate departure": Bulygin, 221; Bykov, 67. "Unfortunately we have no data": Bulygin, 221; Bykov, 67; Benckendorff, 135. "Had to submit": Bulygin, 221.

498 Yakovlev nervous: Koblinsky, 207. "It makes no difference to me": Bulygin, 209.

498–9 "Mama, Mama!": Gibbs, in Wilton, 249. "I am convinced the river will overflow": Bykov, 68.

499 The last evening in Tobolsk: Gibbs, in Wilton, 250. "This splendid serenity": Gilliard, 262.

499 The *tarantasses:* Gilliard, 262; Gilliard's deposition in Wilton, 234. The Empress sends Gilliard to Alexis: Gilliard, 263. Yakovlev's courtesy: Kobylinsky, 209; Bulygin, 209.

500 The girls sobbing: Gilliard, 263.

500 The journey to Tyumen: *ibid.*, 263; Bykov, 68–9; Pares, 490. Waving white handkerchiefs: Bykov, 69. The sign of the Cross: Kobylinsky, 209; Bulygin, 212.

500 Red cavalry: Bulygin, 212. "Proceeding safely": Kobylinsky, 210.

501 Yakovlev leaves in the wrong direction: Pares, 490.

501 "A traitor to the revolution," "To all, to all, to all": Bykov, 70.

501 Kulomzino: Gibbs, in Wilton, 235; Pares, 490. Telephone conversation with Sverdlov: Bykov, 71; Bulygin, 225.

501 "I have orders to take you to Ekaterinburg": Kobylinsky, 210.
501 "Judging from the local papers": Bykov, 72.
502 Yakovlev a monarchist agent: Bykov, 69. Pares believes that Yakovlev was trying to save the Imperial family from falling into the clutches of the Ekaterinburg Soviet and that he may possibly have been trying to rescue them completely: Pares, 491.
502 German domination of Russia: Bulygin, 223.
503 "Be calm": *ibid.*, 202, 219. The Kaiser's personal responsibility: *ibid.*, 220–1. Restoration of the Tsar: *ibid.*, 223.
503 Mirbach's game: Wilton, 151. Sverdlov's game: Gilliard, 282–3; Bulygin, 224–5.
504 Yakovlev deserted to Kolchak: Bykov, 73; Pares, 491.
504 Mirbach outwitted: Bulygin, 226.
504 Yussoupov and the German envoy: Yussoupov, 268.
504–5 "The fate of the Russian Emperor": Bulygin, 227. "The dictatorship of Mirbach": Bruce Lockhart, 296–7.

CHAPTER 34 EKATERINBURG

506 Ekaterinburg and the Ipatiev house: Wilton, 19; Bykov, 72.
506 "Show us the Romanovs": Bykov, 72.
506 Nicholas steps out, carrying his own bags: Bulygin, 230–1; Benckendorff, 136.
507 "Citizen Romanov, you may enter": Bulygin, 231.
507 "So far, we have had polite treatment": Kobylinsky, 216.
507 The swastika: Gilliard, 274; Kobylinsky, 239.
507 Telegram to Kobylinsky: Gilliard, 264.
507 "Dispose of the medicines": Bulygin, 232; Wilton, 74.
507 Tatiana supervised the children: Kobylinsky, 220.
507–8 Rodionov: Bulygin, 228–30; Gilliard, 264. "Nobody is permitted to look at the windows": Botkin, 208. "The child is ill": Bulygin, 230; Gilliard, 265. Fourth-class carriage: Bulygin, 233.
508 "Several carriages were drawn up": Gilliard, 269.
508–9 The suite divided: *ibid.*, 270. Gilliard rescued: *ibid.*, 273.
509 Living arrangements in the Ipatiev house: Medvedev, in Wilton, 287; Gilliard, 283. The guards: Bulygin, 231–2; Gilliard, 282. Avadeyev: Yakimov, in Wilton, 261–2.
509 Avadeyev's drinking and pilfering: Bulygin, 232; Yakimov, in Wilton, 267.
510 "Let them go to hell": Yakimov, in Wilton, 273.
510 The daily schedule: Bykov, 74; Benckendorff, 137; Yakimov, in Wilton, 271; Proskuriakov, in Wilton, 299; Gilliard, 284.
510 "You've had enough, you idle rich": Bulygin, 232.
510 Nagorny's defense of Alexis: Gibbs, in Wilton, 252–3; Gilliard, 272.

510–11 "Nagorny was going to the carriage": Gilliard, 272. In the cell with Prince Lvov: Gibbs, in Wilton, 252–3.

511 "I have still an impression of them": Yakimov, in Wilton, 274–5.

512 "We spent long hours discussing ways and means": Vorres, 243.

512 "Half-crazy ladies, countesses and baronesses": Bykov, 76.

512 "The hour of liberation is approaching": *ibid.*, 78. An assessment of the rescue plots in Ekaterinburg: Pares, 493–4.

512 "With God's help and your prudence": quoted by Bykov, 78.

513 "The second window from the corner": quoted by Bykov, 79.

513 "We spent an anxious night": *Krasny Arkhiv*, 1928, Vol XXVII, p. 136, quoted by Bykov.

513 The "Letts": Bulygin, 235; Wilton, 82–3; Yakimov, in Wilton, 268. Yurovsky: Wilton, 29, 81.

514 "This specimen we like least of all": Pares, 495.

514 "Anxiety unnecessary": Gilliard, 286; Bulygin, 235, 242.

514 Goloshchekin and Sverdlov: Bulygin, 243; Wilton, 27–8, 75; Pares, 495. Public trial with Trotsky as prosecutor: Bykov, 75.

514 The Czechs: Pares, 485.

515 The decision to shoot the Romanovs: Wilton, 127, 139; Bykov, 80.

515 The "Four Brothers": Bulygin, 248. Gasoline and acid: *ibid.*, 249, Wilton, 101.

515 Yurovsky had no strong feelings: Yakimov, in Wilton, 277. His conversation with Alexis: Bulygin, 237; Gilliard, 286.

516 Father Storozhov: Bulygin, 236. "At Rest with the Saints": Pares, 496.

516 Nicholas carried Alexis: Medvedev, in Wilton, 289. Anastasia and Jimmy: Wilton, 95. The basement room: Wilton, 88.

516 The Tsar and his daughters went for a walk: Yakimov, in Wilton, 277. "Tonight, we will shoot the whole family": Bulygin, 237; Medvedev, in Wilton, 288.

517 The murder: Bulygin, 237–8; Gilliard, 287–8; Pares, 497. Demidova pierced thirty times: Yakimov, in Wilton, 281. Jimmy killed: Wilton, 95. Anastasia: Gilliard, 288.

EPILOGUE

518 Destruction of the bodies: Bulygin, 249–50; Wilton 101–2; Gilliard, 290. "The world will never know what we did with them": Pares, 498. Voikov becomes Soviet ambassador: Pares, 496.

518 Ekaterinburg falls to the Whites: Wilton, 104. "Joy" found in the courtyard: Buxhoeveden, *Left Behind*, 154. Appearance of the murder room: Gilliard, 274.

519 "But the children—": Gilliard, 277. Sokolov: Bulygin, 248; Wilton, 15.

519 Evidence found in the mine: Gilliard, 293–4; Wilton, 116–17; Gibbs, in Wilton, 254; Bulygin, 252. Jimmy's body: Wilton, 95.

520 "Comrade Sverdlov wants to make a statement": Bykov, 82.

520 "Tell Sverdlov that the whole family met the same fate": Bulygin, 244.

520–1 Text of the death announcements: Gilliard, 292; Wilton, 14.

521 Bolsheviks arrest 28 Social Revolutionaries: Wilton, 21, 103.

522 "Oh, yes, and where is the Tsar?": *Trotsky's Diary in Exile, 1935* (Cambridge, Harvard University Press, 1953), p. 81.

522–3 Wilson at Lane's dinner party: Walworth, II, 171. Death of Grand Duke Michael: Wilton, 121; Pares, 493. Death of Grand Duchess Elizabeth: Wilton, 124; Benckendorff, 140–2; Bulygin, 256; Pares, 498–9. Death of the four Grand Dukes: Wilton, 127. "The Revolution does not need historians": Vyrubova, 294.

523 Was Lenin murdered by Stalin? In two recent biographies of Lenin, both excellent, the two biographers disagree. Louis Fischer doubts that Stalin had a hand in Lenin's death; Robert Payne is certain that Stalin had Lenin poisoned.

523 Yalta Conference in Livadia Palace: Winston Churchill, *Triumph and Tragedy* (Boston: Houghton Mifflin, 1953), 346, 349, and Robert E. Sherwood, *Roosevelt and Hopkins* (New York, Harper, 1948), 850–1.

523 Sverdlov's death: Wilton (p. 161) declares that although Sverdlov was said to have died naturally, he was in fact "knocked on the head" by a Moscow workman.

524 American correspondents visit Sverdlovsk: Harrison Salisbury, *New York Times,* Aug. 1, 1959.

524 The account of Empress Marie's last years is taken from Vorres (the memoirs of her daughter Grand Duchess Olga). Marie leaves Russia: Vorres, 163. Refuses to believe Nicholas is dead: *ibid.*, 171. Argues with King Christian over the light bill: *ibid.*, 169. A pension from King George V: *ibid.*, 170. Her death: *ibid.*, 181.

525 Grand Duchess Olga. Moves to Toronto: *ibid.*, 192. Invited to lunch by Queen Elizabeth: *ibid.*, 213. Dies in an apartment over a barbershop: *ibid.*, 221.

525 Grand Duke Cyril. Nicholas's heir: Vyrubova, 207; Vorres, 236. "The day of glory is near": Cyril's obituary in *New York Times,* Oct. 13, 1938. Vladimir Cyrilovich: Kschessinska, 252; Vorres, 236.

525 Grand Duke Nicholas: Pares, 501.

526 Grand Duke Dmitry: *Time,* March 16, 1941; Kschessinska, 159–60, 248.

526 The fate of the suite: Pares, 499.

526 The ministers: Pares, 500. Prince Lvov: Kokovtsov, 545.

526 Alexeiev and Kornilov: Pares, 500. Brusilov and Polivanov, *ibid.*, 501.

526 "The Poles are besieging Russian fortresses": Vorres, 232.

526 Sukhomlinov: Escaped in a sailboat: Kokovtsov, 526. Dedicated his memoirs to the Kaiser: Tuchman, 63. Wife married a Georgian officer and was killed: Vyrubova, 191.

527 Buchanan: Buchanan, II, 93, 261.

527 Benckendorff: Benckendorff, vii, 166. Fredericks: Botkin, 40

527 Vyrubova, *Polar Star:* Vyrubova, 276–7. Gorky: *ibid.*, 292–4.

527 Gilliard: from his obituary, *Gazette de Lausanne,* June 8, 1962.

528 Iliodor: New York *Herald Tribune,* July 5, 1933. *Time,* Feb. 11, 1952.

528 Maria Rasputin: *Time,* Dec. 4, 1939. In November, 1966, a circus poster advertising Mlle. Rasputin was on display in a collection of circus posters at the Lincoln Center Museum in New York City.

528 Kschessinska instructed Margot Fonteyn: Kschessinska, 237. Danced at Covent Garden, 238.

528 Yussoupov: The author attended the 1965 trial in its entirety.

529 Hemophilia. Alfonso and Gonzalo; McKusick, 94. The possibility that hemophilia will recur in this family is remote: Armand J. Quick, M.D. "International Forum on Hemophilia," *Spectrum,* Vol. 10, No. 2, (March–April, 1962).

529–30 The legend of the Romanov gold. All Imperial properties taken: Benckendorff, 125–6. Nicholas's capital on abdication: Benckendorff, 89. The relics buried near Paris: Vorres, 171. Marie's jewels valued at $2 million: *ibid.*, 183. Many appeared in Queen Mary's possession: *ibid.*, 184. Funds in Berlin: *ibid.*, 179. Valued at $1,500: New York *Herald Tribune,* Nov. 18, 1965.

530 English deposits brought back to Russia: Vorres, 179.

530 "I see Buchanan tomorrow": AF to N, 123, 125.

530 Sir Edward Peacock. Instructed by King George V: Vorres, 183. "I am pretty sure there never was any money": *ibid.*, 246.

531 The Tsar in London: Benckendorff, 146. In Rome: *ibid.*, 147. Family on a ship in the White Sea: Bulygin, 272. Dozens of claimants: *ibid.*, 271, 276–7.

531 Numerous Anastasias: Vorres, 201, 202. Mrs. Anderson and Grand Duchess Olga: *ibid.*, 175–6. "Dear Aunt Olga": *ibid.*, 200. "My telling the truth does not help": from a letter published in *Life,* Dec. 30, 1963, written by Ian Vorres.

Bibliography

PRIMARY SOURCES

Nicholas II, *Journal Intime.* Translated by A. Pierre. Paris, Payot, 1925. (Cited in Notes as N's Diary.)

The Letters of the Tsar to the Tsaritsa 1914–1917. London, Bodley Head; New York, Dodd, Mead, 1929. (Cited in Notes as N to AF.)

Letters of the Tsaritsa to the Tsar 1914–1916. Introduction by Sir Bernard Pares. London, Duckworth, 1923. (Cited in Notes as AF to N.)

The Secret Letters of the Last Tsar: The Confidential Correspondence Between Nicholas II and His Mother, Dowager Empress Marie Feodorovna. Edited by Edward J. Bing. New York, Longmans, Green, 1938. (Cited in Notes as N to MF or MF to N.)

Alexander, Grand Duke of Russia, *Once a Grand Duke.* New York, Garden City, 1932.

Benckendorff, Count Paul, *Last Days at Tsarskoe Selo.* London, Heinemann, 1927.

Botkin, Gleb, *The Real Romanovs.* New York, Revell, 1931.

Botkina, Tatiana Melnik, *Vospominanya o Tsarskoy Sem'ye.* Belgrade, Stefanonivich, 1921.

Bovey, Kate Koon, *Russian Coronation 1896.* Minneapolis, privately printed, 1942.

Bruce Lockhart, R. H., *British Agent.* New York and London, Putnam, 1933.

Buchanan, Sir George, *My Mission to Russia.* 2 vols. London and New York, Cassell, 1923. (Cited in Notes as Buchanan.)

Buchanan, Meriel, *The Dissolution of an Empire.* London, Murray, 1932.

Bulygin, Paul, and Alexander Kerensky, *The Murder of the Romanovs.* Introduction by Sir Bernard Pares. London, Hutchinson, 1935.

Buxhoeveden, Baroness Sophie, *Left Behind: Fourteen Months in Siberia*

During the Revolution. New York and London, Longmans, Green, 1929.

——, *The Life and Tragedy of Alexandra Feodorovna, Empress of Russia.* New York and London, Longmans, Green, 1928. (Cited in Notes as Buxhoeveden.)

Bykov, P. M., *The Last Days of Tsardom.* London, Martin Lawrence [1934].

Dehn, Lili, *The Real Tsaritsa.* London, Thornton Butterworth, 1922.

Gilliard, Pierre, *Thirteen Years at the Russian Court.* New York, Doran, 1921.

Golovine, Lieutenant General Nicholas, *The Russian Army in the World War.* Yale and Oxford University Presses, 1931.

Hanbury-Williams, Major-General Sir John, *The Emperor Nicholas as I Knew Him.* London, Arthur L. Humphreys, 1922.

(Iliodor) Trufanoff, Sergei, *The Mad Monk of Russia.* New York, Century, 1918.

(Izvolsky) Iswolsky, Alexander, *Memoirs.* Edited and translated by Charles L. Seeger. London, Hutchinson, 1920.

Kerensky, Alexander, *The Catastrophe.* New York, Appleton, 1927.

——, *The Crucifixion of Liberty.* New York, Day, 1934.

——, *Russia and History's Turning Point.* New York, Duell, Sloan and Pearce, 1965.

——, and Paul Bulygin, *The Murder of the Romanovs.* Introduction by Sir Bernard Pares. London, Hutchinson, 1935.

Knox, Major-General Sir Alfred, *With the Russian Army, 1914–1917.* New York, Dutton, 1921.

Kobylinsky, Colonel Eugene, Deposition in Robert Wilton, *The Last Days of the Romanovs.* London, Thornton Butterworth, 1920.

Kokovtsov, Count Vladimir N., *Out of My Past: The Memoirs of Count Kokovtsov.* Stanford University Press, 1935.

Kschessinska, Mathilde, *Dancing in Petersburg.* Translated by Arnold Haskell. Garden City, Doubleday, 1961.

Lloyd George, David, *War Memoirs: 1916–17.* Boston, Little, Brown, 1934.

Marye, George Thomas, *Nearing the End in Imperial Russia, 1914–1916.* Philadelphia, Dorance, 1929.

(Mosolov) Mossolov, A. A., *At the Court of the Last Tsar.* London, Methuen, 1935.

Narishkin-Kurakin, Elizabeth, *Under Three Tsars.* New York, Dutton, 1931.

Novikoff-Priboy, A., *Tsushima.* New York, Knopf, 1937.

Obolensky, Serge, *One Man in His Time.* New York, McDowell Obolensky, 1958.

Oukhtomsky, E. E., *Voyage en Orient, 1890–1891, de Son Altesse Imperiale le Tsarevitch.* Paris, Delegrave, 1893.

Paléologue, Maurice, *An Ambassador's Memoirs.* 3 vols. Translated by F. A. Holt. New York, Doran, 1925.

Pobedonostsev, Konstantin P., *Reflections of a Russian Statesman.* Ann Arbor Paperbacks, University of Michigan Press, 1965.
(Purishkevich) Pourichkevitch, Vladimir, *Comme j'ai tué Raspoutine.* Paris, Povolozky, 1923.
Rasputin, Maria, *My Father.* London, Cassell, 1934.
Red Archives [*Krasny Arkhiv*]. Edited by C. E. Vulliamy, translated by A. L. Hynes. London, Bles, 1929.
Reed, John, *Ten Days That Shook the World.* New York, Modern Library, 1935.
Rodzianko, M. V., *The Reign of Rasputin.* London, Philpot, 1927.
Sazonov, Serge, *Fateful Years.* New York, Stokes, 1928.
Spiridovitch, General Alexandre, *Les Dernières Années de la Cour de Tsarkoie-Selo.* 2 vols. Paris, Payot, 1928.
Trotsky, Leon, *The History of the Russian Revolution.* 3 vols. Translated by Max Eastman. New York, Simon and Schuster, 1932.
Vorres, Ian, *Last Grand Duchess: The Memoirs of Grand Duchess Olga Alexandrovna.* London, Hutchinson, 1964. New York, Scribner, 1965.
(Vyrubova) Viroubova, Anna, *Memories of the Russian Court.* New York, Macmillan, 1923.
The Willy-Nicky Correspondence. Edited by Herman Bernstein. New York, Knopf, 1918.
Wilton, Robert, *The Last Days of the Romanovs* (including Depositions of Colonel Kobylinsky, Pierre Gilliard, Sidney Gibbs, Anatoly Yakimov, Pavel Medvedev, Philip Proskuriakov). London, Thornton Butterworth, 1920.
Windsor, Edward, Duke of, *A King's Story.* New York, Putnam, 1947.
Witte, Count Sergius. *Memoirs.* Translated and edited by Abraham Yarmolinsky. New York, Doubleday, Page, 1921.
(Yussoupov) Youssoupoff, Prince Felix, *Lost Splendor.* London, Cape, 1953. (Cited in Notes as Yussoupov.)
——, *Rasputin.* New York, Dial, 1927.

GENERAL SOURCES

Almedingen, E. M. *The Empress Alexandra.* London, Hutchinson, 1961.
Bainbridge, Henry Charles, *Peter Carl Fabergé: An Illustrated Record and Review of His Life and Work.* London, Batsford, 1949.
Balfour, Michael, *The Kaiser and His Times.* Boston, Houghton Mifflin, 1964.
Billington, James H., *The Icon and the Axe.* New York, Knopf, 1966.
Chamberlin, William Henry, *The Russian Revolution 1917–1921.* 2 vols. New York, Macmillan, 1935.

Charques, Richard, *The Twilight of Imperial Russia.* Fair Lawn, N.J., Essential Books, 1959.

Cherniavsky, Michael, *Tsar and People.* Yale University Press, 1961.

Churchill, Winston S., *The World Crisis: The Aftermath.* London, Thornton Butterworth, 1929.

——, *The World Crisis.* New York, Scribner, 1931.

Cowles, Virginia, *The Kaiser.* New York, Harper and Row, 1963.

Dennis, Jessie McNab, "Fabergé's Objects of Fantasy," *Bulletin, Metropolitan Museum of Art,* Vol. 23, No. 7: 229–242 (March, 1965).

Fennell, J. L. I., editor and translator, *The Correspondence Between Prince A. M. Kurbsky and Tsar Ivan IV of Russia, 1564–1569.* Cambridge University Press, 1963.

Fischer, Louis. *The Life of Lenin.* New York, Harper Colophon Books, 1965.

Florinsky, Michael T., *The End of the Russian Empire.* New York, Collier Books, 1961.

——, *Russia: A History and an Interpretation.* 2 vols. New York, Macmillan, 1964. (Cited in Notes as Florinsky.)

Frankland, Noble, *Imperial Tragedy.* New York, Coward-McCann, 1961.

Fülöp-Miller, René, *Rasputin: The Holy Devil.* New York, Garden City, 1928.

Gorer, Geoffrey, and John Rickman, *The People of Great Russia: A Psychological Study.* New York, Norton, 1962.

Harcave, Sidney, *First Blood: The Russian Revolution of 1905.* New York, Macmillan, 1964.

Heckstall-Smith, Anthony. *Sacred Cowes.* London, Anthony Blond, 1965.

Kaun, Alexander, "The Twilight of the Romanov Dynasty," *American Review,* Vol. 3: 129-142 (1925).

Kennan, George, *Russia Leaves the War.* Princeton University Press, 1956.

Klyuchevsky, Vassily O., *Peter the Great.* New York, Dutton, 1963.

Laue, T. H. von, "Count Witte and the Russian Revolution of 1905," *The American Slavic and East European Review,* Vol. 17, No. 1 (February, 1958).

Leroy-Beaulieu, Anatole, *The Empire of the Tsars.* Translated by Z. Ragozin. 2 vols. New York, Putnam, 1898.

Longford, Elizabeth, *Queen Victoria: Born to Succeed.* New York, Harper and Row, 1964.

Magnus, Philip, *King Edward the Seventh.* New York, Dutton, 1964.

Mahan, Rear Admiral Alfred T., *On Naval Warfare.* Edited by Allan Westcott. Boston, Little, Brown, 1942.

Mansergh, Nicholas, *The Coming of the First World War.* New York, Longmans, Green, 1949.

Mazour, Anatole G., *Rise and Fall of the Romanovs.* Princeton, Van Nostrand, 1960.

——, *Russia Past and Present.* New York, Van Nostrand, 1951.

Moorehead, Alan, *The Russian Revolution.* New York, Harper, 1958.
Nicolson, Harold. *King George the Fifth.* London, Constable, 1952.
Pares, Bernard, *The Fall of the Russian Monarchy.* New York, Vintage Books, 1961. (Cited in Notes as Pares.)
—, *A History of Russia.* New York, Knopf, 1960 edition.
Payne, Robert, *The Life and Death of Lenin.* New York, Simon and Schuster, 1964.
Pope-Hennessy, James, *Queen Mary.* New York, Knopf, 1960.
Pridham, Francis, *Close of a Dynasty.* London, Wingate, 1956.
Radziwill, Catherine, *Nicholas II: The Last of the Tsars.* London, Cassell, 1931.
Riasanovsky, Nicholas V., *A History of Russia.* Oxford University Press, 1963.
Sacher, Howard M., *The Course of Modern Jewish History.* Cleveland, World, 1958.
Taper, Bernard, *Balanchine.* New York, Harper & Row, 1960.
Tuchman, Barbara, *The Guns of August.* New York, Macmillan, 1962. (Cited in Notes as Tuchman.)
——, *The Proud Tower.* New York, Macmillan, 1966.
Tupper, Harmon, *To the Great Ocean.* Boston, Little, Brown, 1965.
Walworth, Arthur, *Woodrow Wilson.* Boston, Houghton Mifflin, 1965.
Wheeler-Bennett, John, *King George VI.* New York, St. Martin's, 1958.
Wilson, Colin, *Rasputin and the Fall of the Romanovs.* New York, Farrar, Straus, 1964.
Wolfe, Bertram, *Three Who Made a Revolution.* 2 vols. New York, Time Inc., 1964.

MEDICAL SOURCES

Agle, David P., "Psychiatric Studies of Patients with Hemophilia and Related States," *Archives of Internal Medicine,* Vol. 114: 76–82 (July, 1964).
Brinkhous, Kenneth M., editor, *Hemophilia and Hemophiloid Diseases.* University of North Carolina Press, 1957.
Gun, W. T. J., "Hemophilia in the Royal Caste," *The Eugenics Review,* Vol. 29, No. 4: 245–246 (January, 1938).
Haldane, J. B. S., *Heredity and Politics.* New York, Norton, 1938.
——, "Sang Royal, Etude de l'Hémophilie dans les familles royales d'Europe," *La Pensée: Revue de rationalisme moderne,* Vol. 1, No. 1: 39–51 (Paris, 1939).
Iltis, Hugo, "Hemophilia: 'The Royal Disease' and the British Royal Family," *The Journal of Heredity,* Vol. 39, No. 4: 113–116 (April, 1948).

Lucas, Oscar, A. Finkelman and L. M. Tocantins, "Management of Tooth Extractions in Hemophiliacs by the Combined Use of Hypnotic Suggestion, Protective Splints and Packing of Sockets," *Journal of Oral Surgery, Anesthesia and Hospital Dental Service*, Vol. 20: 34/489–46/500 (November, 1962).

Massie, Robert K., "They Live on Borrowed Blood," *Saturday Evening Post*, Vol. 236, No. 7: 32–34 (May 4, 1963).

Mattsson, Ake, and Samuel Gross, "Adaptational and Defensive Behavior in Young Hemophiliacs and Their Parents" and "Social and Behavioral Studies on Hemophilic Children and Their Families" (Unpublished papers delivered at the American Psychiatric Association Meetings, New York, N.Y., May 3–8, 1965).

McKusick, Victor A., "The Royal Hemophilia," *Scientific American*, Vol. 213, No. 2: 88–95 (August, 1965).

REFERENCE WORKS

Almanach de Gotha, 1914 edition.

Chujoy, Anatole, *The Dance Encyclopedia*. New York, A. S. Barnes, 1949.

Duncan, David Douglas, *The Kremlin*. New York, Graphic Society, 1960.

Gosling, Nigel, *Leningrad*. New York, Dutton, 1965.

McGraw-Hill Encyclopedia of Russia and the Soviet Union. New York, McGraw-Hill, 1961.

Universal Jewish Encyclopedia, Vol. 9. New York, Universal Jewish Encyclopedia Inc., 1949.

Index

Robert K. Massie

Robert K. Massie was born in Lexington, Kentucky, in 1929. He studied American history at Yale University, from which he was graduated in 1950, and modern European history at Oxford University, which he attended as a Rhodes Scholar. As a writer and editor for *Collier's*, *Newsweek*, *USA-1* and *The Saturday Evening Post*, Mr. Massie has written numerous articles covering national politics, foreign affairs, medicine, the press and religion. His writing also has appeared in *The Reporter*, *Saturday Review*, *The New York Times Magazine* and *The New York Times Book Review*. Mr. Massie lives in Irvington, New York, with his wife and three children.

ATLANTIC OCEAN
LONDON
PARIS
NORTH SEA
COPENHAGEN
BALTIC SEA
MURMANSK
BARENTS SEA
KARA SEA
BERLIN
TANNENBURG
PRAGUE
WARSAW
SPALA
VIENNA
PRZEMYSL
BIALOWIEZA
BREST-LITOVSK
RIGA
REVAL
VYBORG
ST. PETERSBURG
MALAYA VISHERA
PSKOV
BARANOVICHI
MOGILEV
SARAJEVO
ROME
BUDAPEST
LEMBERG
CARPATHIAN MTS.
BELGRADE
ODESSA
KIEV
DNIEPER R.
KHARKOV
KOSTROMA
VOLGA R.
MOSCOW
R U S S I A
URAL MTS.
OB RIVER
KAZAN
PERM
TRANS-SIBERIAN RAILROAD
SIMBIRSK
EKATERINBURG
TOBOLSK
POKROVSKOE
TYUMEN
UFA
CHELYABINSK
OMSK
IRTYSH R.
TOBOL
SARATOV
DON RIVER
VOLGA
TSARITSYN
SEVASTOPOL
YALTA
BLACK SEA
CONSTANTINOPLE
MEDITERRANEAN SEA
CAUCASUS MTS.
CASPIAN SEA
ARAL SEA
BOKHARA
RED SEA
I N D I A N
MILES
0
500
1,000